Blackwell Handbook of Infant Development

Blackwell Handbooks of Developmental Psychology

This outstanding series of handbooks provides a cutting-edge overview of classic research, current research, and future trends in developmental psychology.

Each handbook draws together 25–30 newly commissioned chapters to provide a comprehensive overview of a sub-discipline of developmental psychology. The international team of contributors to each handbook has been specially chosen for their expertise and knowledge of each field. Each handbook is introduced and contextualized by leading figures in the field, lending coherence and authority to each volume.

The *Blackwell Handbooks of Developmental Psychology* will provide an invaluable overview for advanced students of developmental psychology and for researchers an authoritative definition of their chosen field.

Blackwell Handbook of Infant Development
Edited by Gavin Bremner and Alan Fogel

Blackwell Handbook of Childhood Cognitive Development
Edited by Usha Goswami

Blackwell Handbook of Childhood Social Development
Edited by Peter K. Smith and Craig H. Hart

Blackwell Handbook of Adolescent Development
Edited by Gerald Adams and Michael Berzonsky

Blackwell Handbook of Infant Development

Edited by

Gavin Bremner and Alan Fogel

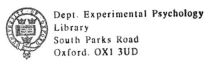

Dept. Experimental Psychology
Library
South Parks Road
Oxford. OX1 3UD

Copyright © Blackwell Publishers Ltd 2001

First published 2001

2 4 6 8 10 9 7 5 3 1

Blackwell Publishers Ltd
108 Cowley Road
Oxford OX4 1JF
UK

Blackwell Publishers Inc.
350 Main Street
Malden, Massachusetts 02148
USA

British Library Cataloguing in Publication Data

A CIP catalogue record for this book is available from the British Library.

Library of Congress Cataloging-in-Publication Data

Blackwell handbook of infant development / edited by Gavin Bremner and Alan Fogel.
    p. cm.
   Includes bibliographical references and index.
   ISBN 0-631-21234-5 (alk. paper)
   1. Infants – Development – Handbooks, manuals, etc.   2. Infants – Health and hygiene – Handbooks, manuals, etc.   I. Bremner, J. Gavin, 1949–   II.   Fogel, Alan.

RJ131 .B475 2001
305.231 – dc21   2001025582

Typeset in 10.5 on 12.5 pt Adobe Garamond
by Best-set Typesetter Ltd., Hong Kong
Printed in Great Britain by TJ International, Padstow, Cornwall

This book is printed on acid-free paper

Contents

Contributors

Rachel Barr, Rutgers University.

Marguerite Barratt, Michigan State University.

John E. Bates, Indiana University.

Marc H. Bornstein, National Institute of Child Health and Human Development, Bethesda, Maryland.

J. Gavin Bremner, Lancaster University.

George Butterworth (deceased), University of Sussex, Brighton.

Luigia Camaioni, Università degli Studi di Roma.

Joseph J. Campos, University of California, Berkeley.

Carol O. Eckerman, Duke University.

Anne Fernald, Stanford University.

William P. Fifer, New York State Psychiatric Institute and Departments of Psychiatry and Pediatrics, Columbia University, New York.

Alan Fogel, University of Utah.

Sarah L. Friedman, National Institute of Child Health & Human Development, Bethesda, Maryland.

Donna M. Gelfand, University of Utah.

Jill Grose-Fifer, Department of Psychology, City College of New York.

Matthew J. Hertenstein, University of California, Berkeley.

Mark H. Johnson, Birkbeck College, London.

Jeanne Thibo Karns, University of Akron, Ohio.

Anita Kochanoff, Research Triangle Institute, Rockville, Maryland.

Andrew Lock, Massey University, New Zealand.

Catherine E. Monk, Departments of Psychiatry and Behavioral Medicine, Columbia University, New York.

Sally Ozonoff, University of Utah.

Karen Peterman, Duke University.

Douglas R. Powell, Purdue University.

Gunilla Preisler, Stockholm University.

Suzanne Randolph, University of Maryland at College Park.

Vasudevi Reddy, University of Portsmouth.

Philippe Rochat, Emory University, Atlanta.

Carolyn Rovee-Collier, Rutgers University.

Alan Slater, University of Exeter.

Ad W. Smitsman, University of Nijmegen.

Mikle South, University of Utah.

Dale M. Stack, Concordia University and the Centre for Research in Human Development, the Montreal Children's Hospital, Quebec.

Catherine S. Tamis-LeMonda, New York University.

Dymphna van den Boom, University of Amsterdam.

Theodore D. Wachs, Purdue University.

David C. Witherington, University of Virginia.

Introduction

Over the last few decades, the field of infancy research has grown exponentially, and as we enter the new millennium we have more information on infant abilities – perceptual, cognitive, and social – than would have been dreamed of 30 or 40 years ago. There is good reason for this growth. For developmental psychologists, there exist vital questions regarding the origins and early manifestation of human abilities that can only be answered by investigating the abilities of infants, sometimes very young infants at that. In addition to questions about the perceptual, cognitive, and social capacities of the newborn, important questions exist regarding the processes underlying the exciting developments in motor skill, memory capacity, and perceptual, emotional, social, and cognitive ability that we see in infancy. The beginnings of communication and language are also detected in infancy. All these developments are of interest in their own right, but are also significant for what they may tell us about the origins and nature of later ability. Additionally, from an applied standpoint, there is growing emphasis on early detection of developmental problems and interventions that may alleviate or even prevent their emergence. These questions and concerns are not new, but their solutions require adequate techniques for studying infant ability.

One thing that makes the field of infancy so exciting today is the fact that investigative techniques are becoming so sophisticated that it sometimes appears that there is now no limit to the questions that can be answered about infant ability, even newborn ability. Additionally, particularly as ultrasound scanning techniques have developed, impressive evidence has been obtained indicating prenatal learning, so that older assumptions about birth as the starting point for psychological development have had to be revised. And the frequent outcome of studies of young infants is that their perceptual and cognitive abilities appear more sophisticated than we ever suspected. However, these findings bring with them a whole new set of questions. For instance, we are faced with why, if 3-month-olds know a great deal about physical reality, they fail to reveal this knowledge in their manual and locomotor actions until they are into their second year. In the last decade, there has been a growing backlash against "rich interpretations" of young infants' ability, with various counter-explanations emerging that treat the young infant's performance as based on relatively low-level perceptual capacities.

One possibility is that these ingenious techniques provide circumstances that amplify infant ability so that it appears more fully formed than it really is. An important advance in social development concerned the proposition that infants' abilities are initially highly fragile and only appear in situations in which adults provide the necessary support for their emergence. Although this sort of interpretation has mainly been applied to infant social development and social influences on infant cognitive development, the conclusions drawn can be similarly applied to the highly structured experimental settings used to investigate early perception and cognition. Thinking here is in its early stages, but it appears that there is a much more exciting alternative to reinterpreting the results of studies of young infants' perceptual and cognitive abilities as revealing only fairly dull low-level perceptual functioning. More probably, these early capacities, though relatively low level, are the developmental precursors of the more fully formed abilities we see later in infancy. These early capacities are initially revealed only in physical and/or social settings that support their appearance. Thus, young infants will walk with the support of a treadmill, reveal sophisticated knowledge of objects in structured experimental settings, and show social competence in interaction with an adult. But it will be many months before these capacities are transformed into abilities that exist independent of the supportive context provided by adults and investigators.

One fascinating challenge for theory-builders is to map out the developmental processes that lead from knowledge that is implicit in the relationship between young infants and the experimental or social setting, to knowledge that can guide the infant's intentional behavior in less structured or supportive settings. In many respects, very young infants appear to be well aware of their physical and social world and, in contrast to earlier theories such as Piaget's, their task is not to construct awareness of the world but to construct means of acting appropriately on the basis of this awareness. Although part of this process may occur as the infant investigates the world for him or herself, there is mounting evidence to indicate that infants gain much from parents in their task of interpreting their awareness. This largely unwitting help from parents appears to include structuring the infant's world of objects, and guiding their actions and emotional responses to objects. Through the process of *social referencing*, infants learn from their parents how to act and how to feel regarding their physical world.

Here we have only had space to select one or two of the exciting issues in infancy research that we now seem well equipped to investigate further. In this book you will find many other examples of progress being made on important developmental questions, and thus our aim here has been simply to whet the reader's appetite. The handbook contains 26 chapters by leading researchers whose brief was to write an up-to-date advanced-level review of theory and findings in their area of expertise. Chapter topics and authors were selected so as to provide comprehensive coverage of research areas that are currently of central importance in the field, in terms of basic research, applied research, and policy. Our primary criterion in selecting our authors was that they should all be leaders in their fields. In addition, in order to produce a truly international perspective, we sought our experts in a wide range of countries. We believe that the result is a stimulating balance between North American and European perspectives.

The book is organized in four main sections: Part I, Perception and Cognition; Part II, Social, Emotional, and Communicative Development; Part III, Risk Factors in Development; and Part IV, Contexts and Policy Issues. The sections adhere to conventional subdivisions of the discipline. However, both in the chapters themselves and in our editorial introductions to each section, the reader's notice will be brought to examples of the way these subdivisions are being progressively broken down, as accounts are developed that question the distinction between perception and cognition, provide links between social and cognitive development, and indicate the applied implications of basic empirical research.

Our aim has been to make the book accessible to a wide audience. Even though each chapter addresses current issues in a scientifically advanced way, we and the authors have worked hard to achieve a writing style in each chapter that does not depend upon prior knowledge of the field. Given the relatively high level at which chapters are pitched, we anticipate that the handbook will provide a thorough overview of the field that will be particularly attractive to graduate students, to advanced undergraduates, and to university teaching staff who teach infancy research but who either do not research the field or who are confident only in a limited area. We hope it will also be attractive to academics who are looking for a high-level treatment of the field that reviews central theoretical and practical issues and cutting-edge research.

J. Gavin Bremner
Alan Fogel

Part I

Perception and Cognition

Introduction

This section provides detailed coverage of current research on infants' ability to perceive and remember information in their world, and to act on the basis of this information. Knowledge of infants' perceptual and memory capacities, and at a higher level, their knowledge and understanding of the physical and social world they inhabit, is vital in itself and also for what it may imply about their social behavior and emotional responses. For instance, an ability to perceive parents and to discriminate them from other adults is an important precondition for the formation of attachment relationships, and the ability to perceive and discriminate sounds is likewise a necessary condition for the receptive side of verbal communication.

As indicated in the general introduction, there has been a revolution in what we know about young infants' perceptual abilities. In general, the current view is that young infants and even newborns have well-established perceptual capacities. In chapter 1, Slater reviews evidence on visual perception, concluding that even newborns perceive an objective world. This might lead one to conclude that there is no perceptual development during infancy, but current evidence suggests that phenomena such as object unity, in which we as adults "fill in" occluded parts of objects, are not present at birth and develop during the first four months or so. Phenomena such as these provide an indication that it is no longer easy to provide a straightforward distinction between perception and cognition, because the ability to complete the hidden parts of an object can be considered as either a high-level perceptual capacity, based on Gestalt principles, or a cognitive ability akin to knowledge of the permanence of hidden objects. One of the challenges for future work is to establish which of these conceptualizations is most appropriate. Slater also reviews current evidence on a key aspect of social perception: face perception. Again there is evidence that newborns have at least basic processes in place for perception of and discrimination between faces, abilities that become more refined as the infant gets older.

There is a tendency to concentrate investigation on infant visual perception at the expense of the other senses. However, social stimuli in particular have important auditory properties; information about people is contained as much in the auditory as the visual modality. In chapter 2, Fernald explains the techniques for measuring infants' auditory abilities and reviews the resulting evidence. Like the case of visual perception, young infants have impressive auditory abilities that develop further with age. Additionally, there is evidence for auditory learning and discrimination even before birth. The later sections of the chapter focus on infants' ability to perceive speech. Young infants show impressive abilities to discriminate speech sounds and are particularly attentive to the particular intonation patterns that adults use in their infant-directed speech. Clearly, these abilities are critical for the later development of language comprehension and production (see chapter 15).

Any account would be incomplete without a treatment of the development of action. Until relatively recently, accounts of motor development were offered according to which cortical developments led to motor activities coming progressively under purposive control. In chapter 3, Smitsman dispels the notion that the development of action can be explained purely in terms of changes in the brain, pointing out that development occurs through a dynamic process of self-organization in which brain, biomechanics, and environment interact. Dynamical systems theory has successfully modeled some of the changes that take place, and one benefit of this approach is that it can incorporate links between perception and action. Using reaching and grasping as an example, Smitsman indicates the need for an approach that takes account of a wide range of bodily and environmental factors. Postural control is required to support successful reaching, and thus motor subsystems must interact to produce the action. Also, it is evident that infants take account of environmental structure with growing precision in action guidance. Thus, to present a full account of the development of action it is necessary not just to model the relationship between different motor components, but to include in the model the relationship between these organism properties and the structure of the environment.

Although young infants have quite advanced perceptual capacities, it appears they have to develop the ability to use perceptual information to guide action. In chapter 4, Bremner reviews evidence for advanced awareness of objects in early infancy, but contrasts this literature with the wealth of evidence showing that it may be many months before individuals are able to use this information to guide their actions. Late emergence of knowledge-guided action cannot be put down to motor immaturity, and Bremner suggests that an important aspect of infant development concerns the discovery and construction of relationships between perception and action. One of the controversies in this area concerns the nature of early competence. Some researchers claim innate knowledge and the ability to reason about events, others that competence is based on lower-level perceptual principles. Bremner suggests that although the latter interpretation may be more appropriate, the capacities revealed in early infancy are vital precursors of cognitive abilities that emerge later in infancy.

None of the above abilities is possible without at least some rudimentary form of memory. Not so long ago, it was suspected that memory was quite severely limited in early infancy. In chapter 5, Rovee-Collier and Barr provide a thorough review of the methods used to investigate infant memory and learning, methods that range from simple habituation as evidence for recognition memory, to deferred imitation as evidence for recall of an action sequence. The evidence indicates that even in early infancy, memory is a good deal more long-lived and specific than was once thought. Additionally, the duration of memory can be dramatically increased by the use of simple brief reminders of the task and setting. Rovee-Collier and Barr conclude that although memory is somewhat limited in terms of duration and speed of retrieval, infant memory systems show all the same properties as adult systems, permitting them to retain a great deal of detailed information about the world over long periods.

Although various authors touch on the relationship between brain development and the phenomena with which they are dealing, these relationships deserve a thorough treatment in themselves. In chapter 6, Johnson argues for the need to take a multidisciplinary approach to developmental questions that takes account of what we know of the brain's development as well as the development of behavior. Additionally, he argues against the older notions that psychological developments can be put down simply to brain maturation, indicating that complex two-way processes are involved through which the development of the brain actually results from exercise of the behaviors that it controls. The reader will find many of the topics treated in earlier chapters revisited within this framework. These include face recognition (chapter 1), visually guided action (chapter 2), object permanence (chapter 4), and memory (chapter 5). The primary emphasis in every case is what can be gained from an approach that interprets development in terms of the dynamic relationship between development of brain and behavior, and Johnson makes a convincing case for the merits of this approach.

With the exception of material on face and voice perception, the first six chapters in this section focus on literature concerning infants' perception and knowledge of the physical world. The final three chapters change the focus to perception and understanding of self and others – abilities that are necessary components of infants' functioning as social beings. In chapter 7, Rochat presents evidence of infants' ability to detect disparities between proprioceptive information about limb movements and asynchronous visual information about their limb movements fed back to them experimentally. The conclusion is that intermodal information about limb position and movement, along with "double touch" information that arises when the infant touches a part of self, provides early perceptual specification of self. This implicit perception arises from exploration and exists long before explicit self-recognition. Rochat also claims social origins of self-knowledge, arguing that in imitation and emotional matching, young infants match their actions and emotions to those of others, and so develop an implicit sense of interpersonal self.

The final two chapters relate closely, but take rather different perspectives. In chapter 8, Butterworth takes a comparative perspective on joint visual attention in human infants. Interpretation of the locus of another's gaze or point is a complex spatial skill, and Butterworth presents evidence that infants are initially capable of identifying locus of attention only within the range of space in which viewer and target are simultaneously visible, later extending this to wider space. Additionally, younger infants tend to use head orientation rather than eye orientation to infer locus of attention, and even adults do not apply a precise geometric vector solution. Interestingly, infant abilities in these tasks are matched or exceeded by adult chimpanzees. Pointing, in principle, is a simpler spatial skill, but important questions arise as to how human infants and apes use it. Although apes do point, they do not appear to use pointing as a declarative gesture. In contrast, infants' pointing appears to be declarative from its emergence, indicating clear differences between humans and apes.

In chapter 9, addressing some of the same topics, Reddy focuses on what infants' actions tell us about early knowledge of the mind. Specifically, she looks at infants' knowledge of attention and intention by others. Knowledge of attention is revealed both in infants' subtle responses to the attentional acts of others, and in their attempts to direct the attention of others. Less is known about understanding of intentionality but there is evidence for its roots in early infancy. For instance, 4-month-old infants respond appropriately to playful intentions of others. Later, 9-month-olds show the beginnings of ability to read the intentions of others in their acts. Around the same time, infants begin to respond to parental commands and occasionally to show playful noncompliance, cases of teasing that Reddy interprets as implying growing awareness of others' intentions and how these can be disrupted. Abilities of this sort are identified as evidence for an implicit theory of mind, a capacity that is essential for the development of later social competence.

Chapter One

Visual Perception

Alan Slater

Introduction

The major characteristic of perception, which applies to all the sensory modalities, is that it is organized. With respect to visual perception, the world that we experience is immensely complex, consisting of many entities whose surfaces are a potentially bewildering array of overlapping textures, colors, contrasts, and contours, undergoing constant change as their position relative to the observer changes. However, we do not perceive a world of fleeting, unconnected retinal images; rather, we perceive objects, events, and people that move and change in an organized and coherent manner.

For hundreds of years there has been speculation about the development of the visual system and of perception of an organized world; however, answers to the many questions awaited the development of procedures and methodologies to test infants' perceptual abilities. Many such procedures are now available and, since the 1960s, many relevant infant studies have been reported. The findings from many of these studies are described in this chapter. The chapter is in four main sections. In the first section, "Theoretical Overview," an account is given of the theories of visual development that have helped shape our understanding of the infant's perceived world. In order to begin the business of making sense of the visual world, it has to be seen, and considerable research has been carried out to describe the sensory capacities of the young infant. An account of some of this research is given in the section headed "Sensory and Perceptual Functioning." In the next section, "Visual Organization at and Near Birth," research is described that has investigated the intrinsic organization of the visual world. Several lines of evidence converge to suggest that infants

*The author's research described in this chapter has been supported by research grants RC00232466 and R000235288/237709 from the Economic and Social Research Council. Earlier versions of some of the material contained in this chapter have appeared in Bremner, Slater, and Butterworth (1997), Vital-Durand, Atkinson, and Braddick (1996), and Slater (1998).

are born with some representation of the human face, and it has become apparent that infants rapidly learn about their visually perceived world. These themes are discussed under the headings "Is there an Innate Representation of the Human Face?" and "Early Experience and Learning." In the final section, emerging questions, paradigms, and issues are discussed.

Theoretical Overview

Until recent times the majority of theories of visual perception emphasized the extreme perceptual limitations of the newborn and young infant. For example, the "father of modern psychology" William James claimed (1890, Vol. 1, p. 488), in one of the most memorable phrases in developmental psychology, that "the baby, assailed by eyes, ears, nose, skin and entrails at once, feels it all as one great blooming, buzzing confusion." Hebb (1949), and Piaget (1953, 1954) argued that visual perception is exceptionally impoverished at birth and suggested that its development is a consequence of intensive learning in the months and years from birth. Hebb (1949, pp. 32–33) concluded that "The course of perceptual learning in man is gradual, proceeding from a dominance of colour, through a period of separate attention to each part of a figure, to a gradually arrived at identification of the whole as a whole: an apparently simultaneous instead of a serial apprehension," and he suggested that, "it is possible then that the normal human infant goes through the same process, and that we are able to see a square as such in a single glance only as the result of complex learning." Piaget (1953, p. 62) said of the young infant's vision: "Perception of light exists from birth and consequently the reflexes which insure the adaptation of this perception (the pupillary and palpebral reflexes, both to light). All the rest (perception of forms, sizes, positions, distances, prominence, etc.) is acquired through the combination of reflex activity with higher activities." Piaget did not discuss visual development in any detail. However, his constructionist approach suggested that perception becomes structured, in a sequence of stages as infancy progresses, as the infant becomes able to coordinate more and more complex patterns of activity. Thus, many perceptual abilities, such as intersensory coordination, size and shape constancy, an understanding that hidden objects continue to exist, and understanding of space and objects, develop relatively late in infancy.

The obvious alternative to learning or constructionist accounts of visual development is to adopt a nativist view that the ability to perceive a stable, organized visual world is an innate or inherent property of the visual system. A coherent and influential Gestalt theory of perception was developed by three psychologists, Max Wertheimer (1890–1943), Kurt Koffka (1886–1941), and Wolfgang Kohler (1887–1967). The Gestalt psychologists listed rules of perceptual organization that describe how groups of stimuli spontaneously organize themselves into meaningful patterns (research by Quinn and his colleagues into the Gestalt organizational principles of similarity, good continuation, and closure is described later). The Gestalt psychologists believed that the organization of visual perception is the result of neural activity in the brain which, in turn, depends on electrochemical processes. These physical processes obey the laws of physics, and are a fundamental characteristic of the human brain. It therefore follows that visual organization is a natural characteristic of the human species and is therefore innately provided.

The distinguished American psychologist J. J. Gibson (1904–1979) was for many years a leading critic of the empiricist or constructivist position. Gibson (1950, 1966, 1979) argued that the senses, or "perceptual systems," have evolved over evolutionary time to detect perceptual invariants directly, and without the need for additional supplementation by experience. Invariants are higher-order variables of perception that enable observers to perceive the world effectively, without the need for additional, constructive processes. Such invariants specify constancy of shape and size of objects, the permanence and properties of objects, the three-dimensional world of space, and so on: "Perception is not a matter of constructing a three-dimensional reality from the retinal image, either in development or in the perceptual acts of adults. The structure of the environment is 'out there' to be picked up, and perception is a matter of picking up invariant properties of space and objects" (Bremner, 1994, p. 118). Gibson was not a nativist. The invariances that infants detect cannot be easily specified, and perceptual development depends on the distinctive features that are detected at different ages, an empirical matter that cannot be easily resolved theoretically. However, when researchers began to discover perceptual abilities in young infants that could not be explained by recourse to empiricist, learning, and constructivist views, it was appealing to interpret findings in terms of Gibson's views: since perception is direct and does not need to be enhanced by experience, then Gibson's theory was the only "grand theory" able to accommodate the findings.

In recent years it has become apparent that Piaget's and Gibson's views both have much to offer: Piaget because he emphasized the role of action in sensorimotor development, and Gibson because his theory allows for the possibility of innate perceptual organization. These points will be touched on later in the chapter. No one would doubt that considerable learning about the visual world has to take place. However, as soon as research into infant perceptual abilities began in earnest, from the early 1960s, it became apparent that extreme empiricist views were untenable. As early as 1966 Bower concluded that "infants can in fact register most of the information an adult can register but can handle less of the information than adults can register" (p. 92). Research over the last 40 years has given rise to conceptions of the "competent infant," who enters the world with an intrinsically organized visual world that is adapted to the need to impose structure and meaning on the people, objects, and events that are encountered. This research has given rise to a number of theoretical views, concerned with specific aspects of visual development. Some of these views are described in the chapter, and an overview of some recent approaches is given in the final section.

Sensory and Perceptual Functioning

Unlike the other senses, there is no opportunity for visual experience prior to birth. It is therefore not surprising to find that the visual world of the newborn infant is quite different from that of the adult. Figure 1.1 shows schematic horizontal sections through the (left) eyes of the adult and the neonate to illustrate differences in overall size, in the shape of the lens, and in the depth of the anterior chamber. At birth the eye, like the brain, is relatively well developed, and both increase in volume about three or four times compared with the rest of the body, which increases about 21 times to reach adult size. Clearly,

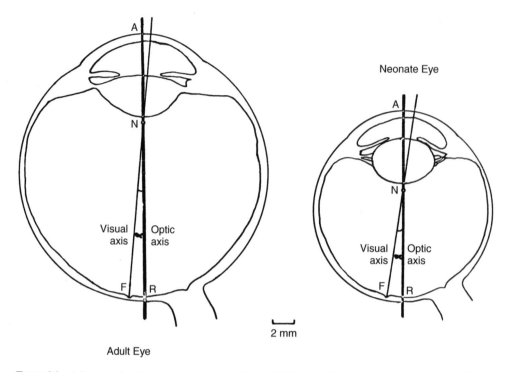

Figure 1.1 Schematic horizontal sections through the (left) eyes of the adult and neonate (to scale), to illustrate differences in gross size, in the shape of the lens, and in the depth of the anterior chamber. F, fovea; R, retina.

the eye and brain are relatively well developed at birth. At the time of normal birth (i.e., term) the peripheral retina of the eye is quite well developed, but the central retina (the macular region and the fovea) is poorly developed and undergoes considerable post-term changes (a detailed account of this development is given in Hainline, 1998). In order to perceive the visual world the perceiver needs a reasonable level of visual acuity (the ability to resolve detail), and the ability to distinguish the boundaries, colors, luminance levels, and textures of surrounding surfaces. The ability to track moving objects in the environment and to fixate (foveate) objects of interest is important, and depth perception is necessary to discriminate surfaces against the background. Excellent recent accounts of the development of infant vision are to be found in Atkinson (2000), Hainline (1998), and in various chapters in Vital-Durand, Atkinson, and Braddick (1996). A brief account of the development of visual functions is given here.

Contrast Sensitivity, Visual Acuity, Accommodation, and Color Vision

It is not surprising to find that the visual information detected by the newborn infant is impoverished when compared with that detected by the adult. Sensitivity to contrast differences is poor. A black and white pattern gives a contrast approaching 100 percent, and under good viewing conditions adults can discriminate between shades of gray giving contrast values of less than 1 percent; a contrast value of 30–40 percent is close to the newborn's threshold of detectability. Visual acuity is also poor. The most commonly used procedure to measure visual acuity is the visual preference method, often called preferential looking, or PL. In this procedure black and white stripes or gratings are shown to the infant at a distance of some 20 to 40 cm from the eyes, each stripe pattern paired with a gray patch of equal overall luminance. Infants tend preferentially to fixate the member of a stimulus pair they find more salient or interesting, and stripes are more interesting than a gray field, so if the stripes can be resolved, the infants more often look to that side than the other. If the stripe width is too small, however, the detail will not be visible, and no preference is observed. The infant's looking to each side is recorded by an observer, watching through a peephole or on a video monitor, and the smallest stripe width that is reliably preferred to the gray is taken as the estimate of acuity.

An alternative method for assessing visual acuity, and other visual functions, is measurement of visually evoked potentials (VEP). This consists of recording activity in the visual cortex (at the back of the skull) via electrodes placed on the scalp. When a stimulus such as a grating or checkerboard is presented, it is repeatedly phase-reversed (i.e., its dark elements switch to light as its light elements switch to dark). If the stimulus is registered by the visual system, the evoked potential signal should have a frequency component that matches the frequency of phase reversal.

Preferential looking studies suggest that neonate visual acuity is poor, about 1 to 2 cycles per degree, which is around 20/600 Snellen (Banks & Dannemiller, 1987; Brown, Dobson, & Maier, 1987; von Noorden, 1988; see also Hainline, 1998). (Adult visual acuity is typically around 30 cycles per degree, or 20/20 vision.) Thus, a neonate could resolve black and white stripes about one-eighth of an inch wide at a distance of 30 cm. Use of the visually evoked potential gives a more optimistic estimate (Hamer, Norcia, Tyler, & Hsu-Winges, 1989; Marg, Freeman, Peltzman, & Goldstein, 1976; Sokol, 1978). Acuity improves rapidly. The evoked potential technique suggests acuity is nearly adultlike by 6 months of age, but the preferential looking method indicates that more development in acuity occurs after this time (Banks & Dannemiller, 1987). The reasons for the discrepancy between the two procedures remain unclear (Banks & Dannemiller, 1987). As a rough guide, Figure 1.2 gives an indication of how the mother's face might look to a newborn infant, and how she might look to us: while the image is degraded and unfocused for the newborn, enough information is potentially available for the infant to learn to recognize the mother's face.

Accommodation refers to changes in the shape of the lens to focus on objects at different distances. Accommodation is initially poor, but since acuity is poor at birth it is likely that the "fine-tuning" afforded by accommodative changes makes little difference to the clarity of the perceived image. Accommodation responses improve along with changes in acuity, so that from 2 months, or earlier, all normal infants alter their accommodation in the appropriate direction as the distance of a visual target changes (Hainline, 1998; Howland, Dobson, & Sayles, 1987).

Figure 1.2   A face as it might appear to a newborn (left) and to us.

Newborn infants have been found to be limited in their abilities to detect color. A common misperception is that neonates are "color-blind," but this is not true. Hainline (1998, p. 27) summarizes research on infant color vision as follows: "It is difficult to know for certain, but it is probably safe to say that even young infants have a form of colour vision and it is probably like that of adults, (although) colours probably appear less intense than the same colours would to an older infant or adult."

Eye Movements, Scanning, and Fixations

Foveation consists of directing one's gaze to items of interest in the visual array. Foveation is most readily accomplished in humans via eye movements, although head and body movements also contribute. Even newborn infants foveate small objects, if they are motivated and the object is not too difficult to see (i.e., if it can be distinguished against the background and is close to the eyes). However, there are limitations in very young infants' abilities successfully to produce certain eye movements. For example, until 8 to 10 weeks of age, infants rarely engage in smooth pursuit, or the tracking of a slowly moving small target (Aslin, 1981). Saccadic eye movements are rapid movements which point the fovea at targets of interest: when reading a book such eye movements quickly direct the eye along the line of print. It has been observed that when one target disappears and another reappears young infants will often "approach" the new stimulus with a series of saccades rather than just one (Aslin & Salapatek, 1975). These are called "step-like" saccades. However, not all studies have found this apparent immaturity (Hainline & Abramov, 1985). Hainline (1998) points out that adults will occasionally produce step-like saccades when they are tired or inattentive, and suggests that perhaps the frequency of such saccades in infants might also be caused by lack of attention to the stimuli that are shown them in laboratory tests. She says that "We do not regularly observe step-saccades when infants look at natural scenes, so they may be an artifact of the laboratory," and concludes

"In general, the saccadic system seems quite mature and ready to function to reorient the fovea at high speeds, even early in life" (p. 36).

In summary, neonates seem to be limited in visual scanning skills, although attempts at foveation are readily observed. All types of eye movements are observed in young infants, and the eye movement and fixation system is mature by around 4 months (Hainline, 1998).

Depth Perception

> For those of a creationist bent, one could note that God must have loved depth cues, for He made so many of them. (Yonas & Granrud, 1985, p. 45)

By being physically separated in space the two eyes provide slightly different images of the perceived world. Detection of these small differences, or disparities, provides the basis for an important binocular cue to depth, stereopsis, in which the disparities are interpreted by the visual system as actual depth differences, and so gain three-dimensionality. The presence of stereopsis has been tested in infants by presenting them with two stimuli, one to each eye, the two images being slightly disparate: the infant wears goggles which allow the presentation of different images to the two eyes. If the infant has stereopsis, and fuses the images, a figure or shape is seen, and this is looked at in preference to a stimulus which does not produce a stereoscopic shape. Several researchers have reported that stereopsis appears around the end of the fourth month from birth (Braddick & Atkinson, 1983; Held, 1985; Teller, 1983). In adults very fine disparities can be detected and give rise to depth information. This fineness of stereopsis, called stereoacuity, improves rapidly from the onset of stereopsis and approaches adult levels within a few weeks (Held, 1985).

There are many other depth cues. Motion-carried, or kinetic depth cues are responded to at an early age. Newborn infants will selectively fixate a three-dimensional stimulus in preference to a photograph of the same stimulus, even when they are restricted to monocular viewing and the major depth cue is motion parallax (Slater, Rose, & Morison, 1984). Infants as young as 8 weeks perceive three-dimensional object shape when shown kinetic random-dot displays (Arterberry & Yonas, 2000). Appreciation of pictorial depth cues – those monocular cues to depth that are found in static scenes such as might be found in photographs – has been found from about 5 months. In an early experiment Yonas, Cleaves, and Pettersen (1978) used the "Ames window," a trapezoidal window rotated around its vertical axis. When adults view the two-dimensional Ames window monocularly a powerful illusion is perceived of a slanted window with one side (the larger) closer than the other. Yonas et al. reported that 6-month-olds are twice as likely to reach for the larger side of the distorted window than for the smaller side, suggesting that this depth cue is detected by this age. Sen, Yonas, and Knill (2001) have described a recently discovered static monocular cue to depth. This illusion is shown in Figure 1.3. In their experiment Sen et al. found that 7-month-olds, but not 5- or 5.5-month-olds, when tested monocularly, reached for the apparently closer end of the fronto-parallel cylinder. This finding gives further support to their suggestion that sensitivity to static monocular depth cues first appears around 6 months from birth.

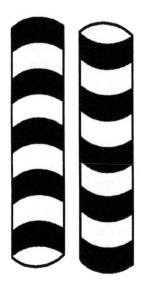

Figure 1.3   A 2D version of the 3D illusion used by Sen et al. (2001).

Overview

Some common myths about early vision can be dispelled. It is certainly not the case that babies are born blind, neither is it true that their vision is "locked on" at a particular distance from the eyes. The immediate input to the visual system is the image that falls on the two-dimensional retinae of the eyes. Although in no sense do we (or infants) ever "see" this retinal image, a commonly expressed view is that, since this image is upside down and reversed from right to left, at birth infants see the world similarly distorted. The simplest experiment convinces us that babies see the world the "right way round": if a light is shone to the left, or right (or up or down) of the baby's looking position the baby will turn its eyes in the correct direction. Of course, if the visual world were inverted or reversed the babies would look in the opposite direction, which they don't! Newborn infants also display some degree of color vision.

Clearly, the young infant's world is impoverished compared with that of the adult, but many visual functions approach adult standards three or four months from birth. Even the poor vision of very young infants does not hamper their development: there is "little indication that young infants are handicapped by their purported primitive visual abilities" (Hainline, 1998, p. 5). Young infants do not need to scrutinize the fine print in a contract, or to see things clearly at a distance. The most important visual stimuli are to be found in close proximity, and better acuity, which might allow infants to focus on distant objects that are of no relevance to their development, might well hinder, rather than promote, their development. Hainline (1998, p. 9) summarizes it rather nicely: "visually normal infants have the level of visual functioning that is required for the things that infants need to do."

Visual Organization at and Near Birth

We have seen that scanning abilities, acuity, contrast sensitivity, and color discrimination seem to be limited in neonates. However, despite these limitations the visual system is functioning at birth, and in this section several types of visual organization that are found in early infancy are discussed. Many parts of the brain, both subcortical and cortical, are involved in vision, but it is reasonable to claim that visual perception, in any meaningful sense, would not be possible without a functioning visual cortex, and this is discussed in the next section.

Cortical Functioning at Birth

The cortex is responsible for humans' memory, reasoning, planning, and many visual skills. The ability to foveate and to discriminate detail is also mediated by the visual cortex, and we presented evidence above which suggests that newborns can foveate stimuli. However, it has been proposed (Bronson, 1974) that the visual cortex is not functional at birth, and that the visual behaviors of infants for around the first two months from birth are mediated by subcortical structures such as the superior colliculus, which is particularly involved in the control of eye movements. Other researchers have also claimed that there is a shift from subcortical to cortical functioning around two months from birth (e.g., Atkinson, 1984; Johnson, 1990; Johnson & Morton, 1991; Pascalis, de Schonen, Morton, Deruelle, & Fabre-Grenet, 1995).

A critical test of cortical functioning is discrimination of orientation. In primates, orientation discrimination is not found in subcortical neurons, but it is a common property of cortical cells, and orientation selectivity is therefore an indicator of cortical functioning. Two studies tested for orientation discrimination in newborns (Atkinson, Hood, Wattam-Bell, Anker, & Trickelbank, 1988; Slater, Morison, & Somers, 1988). In these, newborn infants were habituated to a black and white stripes pattern (grating), presented in an oblique orientation, and on subsequent test trials they clearly gave a preference for the same grating in a novel orientation (the mirror-image oblique of the familiarized stimulus).

This finding is an unambiguous demonstration that at least some parts of the visual cortex are functioning at birth. The presence of visually evoked potentials (referred to earlier in the section on visual acuity) also implies cortical functioning. Several accounts have attempted to describe which parts of the visual cortex may be more functional than others (e.g., Atkinson, 1984, 2000; Johnson, 1990). However, even if the visual cortex is immature, it is difficult to know in what ways this imposes limitations on visual perception. As Atkinson and Braddick (1989, p. 19) have put it, "we do not really have any idea how little or how much function we should expect from the structural immaturity of new-born visual cortex." Certainly, as will be described in the next sections, it has become clear that the newborn infant is possessed of many ways in which to begin to make sense of the visual world.

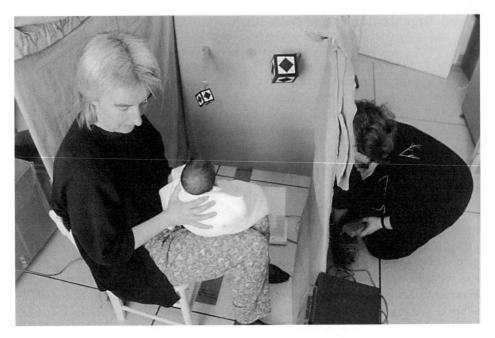

Figure 1.4   A newborn infant being tested in a size constancy experiment.

Shape and Size Constancy

As objects move, they change in orientation, or slant, and perhaps also their distance, relative to an observer, causing constant changes to the image of the objects on the retina. However, and as indicated in the Introduction, we do not experience a world of fleeting, unconnected retinal images, but a world of objects that move and change in a coherent manner. Such stability, across the constant retinal changes, is called perceptual constancy. Perception of an object's real shape regardless of changes to its orientation is called shape constancy, and size constancy refers to the fact that we see an object as the same size regardless of its distance from us. If these constancies were not present in infant perception, the visual world would be extremely confusing, perhaps approaching James's "blooming, buzzing confusion," and they are a necessary prerequisite for many other types of perceptual organization. However, recent experiments have given clear evidence that these constancies are present at birth, and these are discussed next.

In a study of size constancy, Slater, Mattock, and Brown (1990) used preferential looking (PL) and familiarization procedures. A newborn infant being tested in a size constancy experiment is shown in Figure 1.4. In the PL experiment they presented pairs of cubes of different sizes at different distances, and it was found that newborns preferred to look at the cube which gave the largest retinal size, regardless of its distance or its real size. These findings are convincing evidence that newborns can base their responding on retinal size alone. However, in the second experiment each infant viewed either a small cube or a large cube during familiarization trials: each infant was exposed to the same-

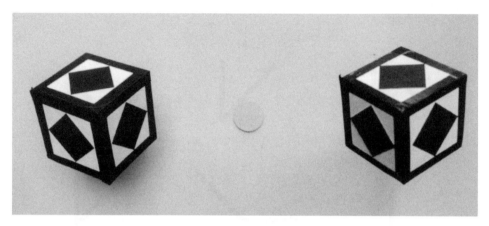

Figure 1.5 The stimuli shown to the infants on the post-familiarization test trials. This photograph, taken from the babies' viewing position, shows the small cube on the left at a distance of 30.5 cm, and the large cube on the right at a distance of 61 cm.

sized object shown at different distances on each trial. After familiarization, the infants were shown both cubes side by side, the small cube nearer and the large cube farther, such that their retinal images were the same size (Figure 1.5). The infants looked longer at the cube they were not familiarized with (consistent with the novelty preferences commonly observed in habituation studies). This indicates that the neonates differentiated the two cube sizes despite the similarities of the retinal sizes, and abstracted the familiar cube's real size over changes in distance.

Slater and Morison (1985) described experiments on shape constancy and slant perception and obtained convincing evidence both that newborn infants detect, and respond systematically to, changes in objects' slants, and also that they could respond to an object's real shape, regardless of its slant. Their results demonstrate that newborn babies have the ability to extract the constant, real shape of an object that is rotated in the third dimension: that is, they have shape constancy.

The findings of these studies demonstrate that shape and size constancy are organizing features of perception that are present at birth. E. J. Gibson (1969, p. 366) seemed to anticipate these findings:

> I think, as is the case with perceived shape, that an object tends to be perceived in its true size very early in development, not because the organism has learned to correct for distance, but because he sees the object as such, not its projected size or its distance abstracted from it.

Form Perception

The terms "figure," "shape," "pattern," and "form" are often used interchangeably, and as long ago as 1970 Zusne (p. 1) commented that "Form, like love, is a many-splendored thing . . . there is no agreement on what is meant by form, in spite of the tacit agreement

Habituation   Test

A   B

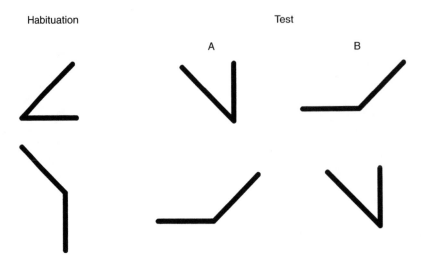

Figure 1.6 Habituation and test stimuli used in experiments on form perception by Cohen and Younger (1984) and Slater, Mattock, Brown, and Bremner (1991). Half the infants were habituated to the acute angle (upper left), half to the obtuse angle.

that there is." However, the most often used stimuli in studies of form perception are static, achromatic, two- or three-dimensional figures with easily detectable contours that can stand as figures in a figure–ground relationship, and it is primarily with reference to these that most theories of form perception have been concerned.

One of the most intractable issues in the study of form perception in early infancy is whether or not such figures or patterns are innately perceived as parts or as wholes. This can be illustrated with respect to the newborn infant's perception of simple geometric shapes. We know that newborns discriminate easily between the outline shapes of simple geometric forms such as a square, circle, triangle, and cross, but the basis of the discrimination is unclear since these shapes differ in a number of ways, such as the number and orientation of their component lines, and, as was mentioned earlier, newborns can discriminate on the basis of orientation alone.

One experiment which suggests that there is a change in the way form is perceived in early infancy was by Cohen and Younger (1984). They tested 6- and 14-week-old infants with simple stimuli, each consisting of two connected lines which made either an acute (45°) or an obtuse (135°) angle, similar to those shown in Figure 1.6. Following habituation they found that the 6-week-olds responded to a change in the orientation of the lines (where the angle remained unchanged, test stimulus A in Figure 1.6), but not to a change in angle alone (test stimulus B), while the 14-week-olds did the opposite in that they recovered attention to a change in angle, but not to a change in orientation. These findings suggest that 4-month-olds are able to perceive angular relationships, and hence have some degree of form perception, but suggest that form perception in infants 6 weeks and younger may be dominated by attention to lower-order variables such as orientation. However, an experiment by Slater, Mattock, Brown, and Bremner (1991, Experiment 2) used these stimuli and found that, with different conditions of testing, newborn infants can process the relationship between two line segments, that is, the angle, independently of its orientation. In this experiment each infant was shown either an obtuse or an acute angle, but the angle changed its orientation on each of six familiarization trials. After this familiarization period the infants were given test trials with the two angles, with each in a different orientation than any shown earlier, and they reliably looked longer at the novel angle. One interpretation of these findings is that newborn infants are able to respond both to low-order variables of stimulation, such as orientation, and also to higher-order variables, such as form (i.e., angles), and that the variable to which they respond depends on the experimental manipulation (but see Cohen, in Slater, Mattock, Brown, and Bremner, 1991, p. 405, for a different interpretation).

All visual stimuli are stimulus compounds in that they contain separate features that occur at the same spatial location, and which the mature perceiver "binds together" as a whole. With such an ability we see, for example, a green circle and a red triangle, while without it we would see greenness, redness, circularity, and triangularity as separate stimulus elements. Evidence suggests that newborn infants perceive stimulus compounds. In an experiment by Slater, Mattock, Brown, Burnham, & Young (1991) newborns were familiarized, on successive trials, to two separate stimuli. For half the infants these were a green vertical stripe and a red diagonal stripe; the other babies were familiarized to green diagonal and red vertical stripes. In the former case there are two novel combinations, these being green diagonal and red vertical, and on post-familiarization test trials the babies were shown one of the familiar compounds paired with one of the novel ones, and they showed strong novelty preferences. Note that the novel compounds consisted of stimulus elements that the babies had seen before (green, red, diagonal, vertical), and the novelty preferences are therefore clear evidence that the babies had processed and remembered the color/form compounds shown on the familiarization trials.

Subjective Contours and Gestalt Organizational Principles

Many organizational principles contribute to the perceived coherence and stability of the visual world. As discussed above, shape and size constancy are present at birth, as is some degree of form perception. Other types of visual organization have been found in young infants, and by way of illustration two of these are discussed here: subjective contours and Gestalt principles.

Subjective contours are contours that are perceived "in the absence of any physical gradient of change in the display" (Ghim, 1990). Such contours were described in detail by Kanizsa (1979) and the Kanizsa square is shown in Figure 1.7: the adult perceiver usually "completes" the contours of the figures, despite the fact that the contours are physically absent. Convincing evidence that 3- and 4-month-old infants perceive subjective contours was provided by Ghim (1990), who described a series of experiments leading to the conclusion that the infants perceived the complete form when viewing the subjective contour patterns.

One of the main contributions of the Gestalt psychologists was to describe a number of ways in which visual perception is organized. Quinn, Burke, and Rush (1993) reported evidence that 3-month-old infants group patterns according to the principle of similarity, or proximity. Two of the stimuli they used are shown in Figure 1.8. Adults reliably group

A   B

Figure 1.7   Pattern A (a Kanizsa square) produces subjective contours and is seen as a square. Pattern B contains the same four elements but does not produce subjective contours.

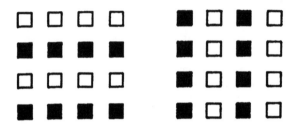

Figure 1.8   Stimuli used by Quinn et al. (1993) with 3-month-olds and by Farroni et al. (2000) with newborns. Infants, like adults, group by similarity and perceive the pattern on the left as rows, and that on the right as columns.

the elements of such stimuli on the basis of lightness (or brightness) similarity and represent the figure on the right as a set of columns, and the other as a set of rows. Three-month-olds do the same, in that those habituated to the columns pattern generalize to vertical lines and prefer (perceive as novel) horizontal lines, while those habituated to the rows prefer the novel vertical lines. In recent experiments, using similar stimuli, Farroni, Valenza, Simion, and Umilta (2000) found that newborn infants also group by similarity.

Quinn, Brown, and Streppa (1997) describe experiments using an habituation – novelty testing procedure, to determine if 3- and 4-month-old infants can organize visual patterns according to the Gestalt principles of good continuation and closure. The stimuli they used are shown in Figure 1.9. Following familiarization to pattern (a) in Figure 1.9, tests revealed that the infants parsed the pattern into a square and teardrop (b) rather than into the "less-good" patterns shown in (c): that is, they had parsed the familiarized figure into the two separate shapes of a square and a teardrop in the same way that adults do.

Overview

The above is just a sample of the many studies which demonstrate that young infants organize the visually perceived world in a similar manner to that of adult perceivers. But

Stimulus   Possible organizations

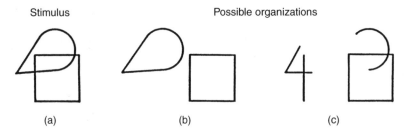

(a)   (b)   (c)

Figure 1.9 Patterns used by Quinn et al. (1997).

the newborn and young infant's world is very different from ours: "It must certainly lack associations, meaning and familiarity" (Gordon, 1997, p. 82). In the next two sections the possibility of innate (or prefunctional) representations that might guide early learning, and some of the ways in which perception is affected and changed by experience and learning in infancy, are discussed.

Is there an Innate Representation of the Human Face?[1]

Several lines of evidence converge to suggest that newborn infants come into the world with some representation of faces. Goren, Sarty, and Wu (1975) and Johnson and Morton (1991) present evidence that newborn infants are more likely to track (follow with their eyes) face-like patterns than non-face-like patterns. Johnson and Morton argue for the existence of an innate face-detecting device they call "Conspec" (short for conspecifics), which "perhaps comprises just three dark patches in a triangle, corresponding to eyes and mouth" (Pascalis et al., 1995, p. 80), and which serves to direct the newborn infant's visual attention to faces.

Imitation

Other evidence suggests that the newborn infant's hypothesized facial representation might be more detailed than simply a template that matches three dots. In particular it has been demonstrated that newborn (and older) infants will imitate a variety of facial gestures they see an adult model performing. One of the first published reports of imitation by newborn and older infants was by Meltzoff and Moore (1977), and there are now many reports of such imitation (e.g., Field, Woodson, Greenberg, & Cohen, 1982; Meltzoff & Moore, 1984, 1992, 1994, 1997; Reissland, 1988). Meltzoff (1995) suggests that "newborns begin life with some grasp of people" (p. 43) and that their ability to recognize when their facial behavior is being copied implies that "there is some representation of their own bodies" (p. 53). Infants can see the adult's face, but of course they cannot see their own. This means that in some way they have to match their own, unseen but felt, facial movements with the seen, but unfelt, facial movements of the adult. Meltzoff and Moore (1997, 2000) propose that they do this by a process of "active intermodal matching" (AIM).

A fundamental question is, "What is the motive for imitation in the newborn?" No man, and no baby, is an island, and one suggestion is that babies are born with a deep-seated need to communicate (Kokkinaki & Kugiumutzakis, 2000; Kugiumutzakis, 1993). A complementary interpretation is offered by Meltzoff and Moore (1992, 1994), who claim that imitation is an act of social cognition which serves to help the infant identify, understand, and recognize people: "infants use the non-verbal behavior of people as an identifier of who they (the people) are and use imitation as a means of verifying this identity" (1992, p. 479).

Infants Prefer Attractive Faces

Several experimenters have found that infants prefer to look at attractive faces when these are shown paired with faces judged by adults to be less attractive (e.g., Langlois, Ritter, Roggman, & Vaughn, 1991; Langlois et al., 1987; Samuels, Butterworth, Roberts, & Graupner, 1994; Samuels and Ewy, 1985). The "attractiveness effect" seems to be robust in that it is found for stimulus faces that are infant, adult, male, female, and of two ethnic groups (African American and Caucasian), and babies also preferred attractive to symmetrical faces when these two dimensions were varied independently. The effect has recently been found with newborn infants, who averaged less than three days from birth at the time of testing (Slater, Bremner, et al., 2000; Slater, Quinn, Hayes, & Brown, 2000; Slater et al., 1998).

A frequently expressed interpretation of the attractiveness effect is in terms of proto-type formation and a cognitive averaging process. The origins of this interpretation can be traced back to more than a hundred years ago. In the nineteenth century Charles Darwin received a letter from Mr. A. L. Austin of New Zealand (Galton, 1907, p. 227). The letter read:

> Although a perfect stranger to you, and living on the reverse side of the globe, I have taken the liberty of writing to you on a small discovery I have made in binocular vision in the stereoscope. I find by taking two ordinary *carte-de-visite* photos of two different persons' faces, the portraits being about the same sizes, and looking about the same direction, and placing them in a stereoscope, the faces blend into one in a most remarkable manner, producing in the case of some ladies' portraits, in every instance, a decided improvement in beauty.

Darwin passed the discovery to his half cousin, Francis Galton, who confirmed the effect. Galton went further and was the first scientist to average faces, which he did photographically by underexposing each individual picture. In recent times such averaging can be done by computer, and the resulting "average" or prototypical face is typically seen as more attractive than the individual faces that combine to produce it. For this reason, averageness has been claimed to be an important ingredient of attractiveness (Langlois & Roggman, 1990). According to this interpretation, therefore, attractive faces are seen as more "face-like" because they match more closely the prototype that infants have formed from their experience of seeing faces: thus, "Infants may prefer attractive or prototypical faces because prototypes are easier to classify as a face" (Langlois & Roggman, 1990, p. 119). It is possible that newborn infants' preferences for attractive faces result from an innate representation of faces that infants bring into the world with them: Langlois and Roggman (1990) discuss the possibility of an innate account for attractiveness preferences. Alternately, it is possible that even the newborn's preference for attractive faces is a preference for an image similar to a composite of the faces they have seen in the few hours from birth prior to testing. An evolutionary account of attractiveness preferences is offered by Etcoff (2000).

Overview

It seems now to be reasonably well agreed that "there does seem to be some representational bias . . . that the neonate brings to the learning situation for faces" (Karmiloff-Smith, 1996, p. 10). This representational bias is likely to be something more elaborate than simply a tendency to attend to stimuli that possess three blobs in the location of eyes and mouth ("Conspec"). This possibility is suggested by newborn infants' ability to imitate the facial gestures produced by the first face they have ever seen (Reissland, 1988), and also, perhaps, by newborn infants' preferences for attractive faces. It is perhaps likely that experiences *in utero* (for example, proprioceptive feedback from facial movements) contribute to the newborn infant's representation of faces, which might therefore result from innate evolutionary biases, in interaction with prenatal experiences. Meltzoff and Moore (1998, p. 229) offer the premise that "evolution has . . . bequeathed human infants . . . with initial mental structures that serve as 'discovery procedures' for developing more comprehensive and flexible concepts."

Early Experience and Learning

Infants learn rapidly about their visually encountered world: as Karmiloff-Smith (1996, p. 10) has put it, "At birth visual processing starts with a vengeance." This rapid learning is apparent in the ease with which even newborn infants will habituate to visual stimuli and subsequently recover attention to novelty. In this section some clear examples of early visual learning in infancy are discussed, under the headings of face perception, intermodal perception, and perception of object segregation, and unity.

Face Perception

This representational bias for faces discussed in the previous section ensures that newborn infants have a predisposition to attend to faces, and it is clear that soon after birth they learn to distinguish between individual faces, form prototypes of faces they have seen only briefly, and recognize faces across various transformations (such transformations as size changes and a change from facing straight ahead to half profile) (Bushnell, Sai, & Mullin,

1989; Field, Cohen, Garcia, & Greenberg, 1984; Walton, Armstrong, & Bower, 1997, 1998; Walton, Bower, & Bower, 1992). Apparently, this recognition is not dependent solely on facial features. The effect disappears if the women's hairlines are covered with a scarf (Pascalis et al., 1995). Thus, attention to outer contours seems to contribute to neonates' face-recognition abilities.

Such remarkable early learning might result from an innately endowed face-specific learning mechanism (e.g., Farah, Rabinowitz, Quinn, & Liu, 2000; Nelson, 2001), or it might be a product of a more general pattern-processing system that assists the infant in learning about complex visual stimuli.

Intermodal Perception

Most of the objects and events that we experience are intermodal in that they provide information to more than one sensory modality. Such intermodal information can be broadly categorized into two types of relation, amodal and arbitrary. Amodal perception is where two (or more) senses provide information that is equivalent in one or more respects, and many types of amodal perception have been demonstrated in early infancy. Newborn infants reliably turn their heads and eyes in the direction of a sound source, indicating that spatial location is given by both visual and auditory information (Butterworth, 1983; Muir & Clifton, 1985; Wertheimer, 1961). One-month-olds demonstrate cross-modal matching by recognizing a visual shape (a pacifier) that had previously been experienced tactually by sucking, indicating that the shape is coded both tactually and visually (Meltzoff & Borton, 1979). By four months infants are sensitive to temporal synchrony specified intermodally in that they detect the common rhythm and duration of tones and flashing lights (Lewkowicz, 1986). Four-month-olds also detect and match appropriately the sounds made either by a single unitary element or by a cluster of smaller elements (Bahrick, 1987, 1988). Thus, there is evidence that infants, from birth, perceive a wide range of invariant amodal relations.

Many intermodal events give both amodal and arbitrary information. For instance, when a person speaks the synchrony of voice and mouth provides amodal information, whereas the pairing of the face and the sound of the voice is arbitrary (in the sense that there is nothing in the face that specifies tone of voice, etc.). In several publications Bahrick (e.g., 1987, 1988, 1992, 2000; Bahrick & Pickens, 1994) has provided strong evidence that learning about arbitrary intermodal relations is greatly assisted if there is accompanying amodal information: "detection of amodal invariants precedes and guides learning about arbitrary object–sound relations by directing infants' attention to appropriate object–sound pairings and then promoting sustained attention and further differentiation" (Bahrick & Pickens, 1994, p. 226).

There is evidence that newborn babies are easily able to learn arbitrary intermodal relations, but only if the intermodal stimuli are accompanied by amodal information which specifies that they "go together." Such amodal information can include spatial co-location (sight and sound are found at the same place), temporal synchrony (lips and voice are synchronized), temporal microstructure (a single object striking a surface produces a single impact sound, but a compound object, consisting of several elements, will produce a more complex, prolonged sound). Morrongiello, Fenwick, and Chance (1998) found that newborn infants learned toy–sound pairs when the two stimuli were spatially co-located, but not when they were presented in different locations. Slater, Quinn, Brown, and Hayes (1999) tested newborn infants in two conditions. In their *auditory-contingent* condition 2-day-old infants were familiarized to two alternating visual stimuli (differing in color and orientation), each accompanied by its "own" sound. The spatially located sound was presented only when the infant looked at the visual stimulus – when the infant looked away the sound stopped. Thus, presentation of the sound was contingent upon the infant looking. In their *auditory-noncontingent* condition the sound was continuously presented, independently of whether the infant looked at the visual stimulus. They found that their newborn infants learned the arbitrary auditory–visual associations when the amodal *contingent* information was present, but not when it was absent. These findings give strong support to Bahrick's views, mentioned earlier. It is clear that rapid learning about intermodal events occurs from birth, and that the presence or absence of amodal information acts both as a powerful facilitator and a constraint on learning. It is of interest to note that when the mother speaks to her infant the amodal information of temporal synchrony of voice and lips is quite likely to facilitate learning to associate her face and voice, and it seems likely that this learning occurs very soon after birth.

Perception of Object Segregation, and Unity

The visual world that we experience is complex, and one problem confronting the young infant is knowing how to segregate objects, and knowing when one object ends and another begins. Sometimes changes to color, contour, contrast, etc., are found within a single object. For example, many animals have stripes, spots, changes to coloring, etc.; people wear different-colored clothing, and there are natural color and contrast changes, perhaps from hair to forehead, from eyes to face, and so on, but these changes of course are all part of the same person.

Sometimes, similar appearance is found for different objects, as when two or more similar objects are perceived. Thus, there is no simple rule that specifies that an abrupt or gradual change in appearance indicates one or more objects. This means that the segregation of surfaces into objects is an important problem confronting the infant, and many of the rules that specify object composition and segregation have to be learned from experience. Object *segregation* is when the perceptual information indicates that two or more objects are present, and object *unity* is where we appreciate that there is only one object, despite breaks in the perceptual display: an example of the latter is where parts of an object are partly occluded by (a) nearer object(s).

A clear difference has been found in infants' perception of *object unity* in the age range birth to 4 months. In a series of experiments on infants' understanding of partly occluded objects Kellman and his colleagues (Kellman & Spelke, 1983; Kellman, Spelke, & Short, 1986) habituated 4-month-olds to a stimulus (usually a rod) that moved back and forth behind a central occluder, so that only the top and bottom parts of the rod were visible (as in the upper part of Figure 1.10). On the post-habituation test trials the infants recovered attention to two rod pieces, but not to the complete rod (shown in the lower part

Habituation display

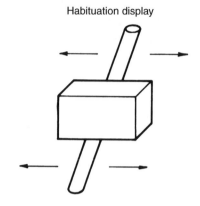

Test displays

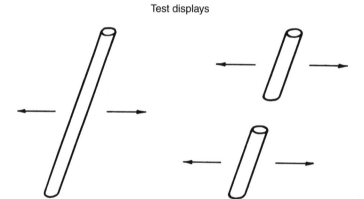

Figure 1.10   Habituation and test displays shown to infants to test perception of object unity. During habituation the rod, and during test trials the rod and rod parts, moved back and forth undergoing common motion.

of Figure 1.10), suggesting that they had been perceiving a complete rod during habituation and that the rod pieces were novel. However, when newborn babies have been tested with similar displays they look longer on the test trials at the complete rod (Slater, Johnson, Brown, & Badenoch, 1996; Slater, Johnson, Kellman, & Spelke, 1994; Slater, Morison, et al., 1990). Thus, neonates appear not to perceive partly occluded objects as consisting of both visible and nonvisible portions. Rather, they seem to respond only to what they see directly.

The difference in the response patterns of newborn and 4-month-old infants suggests that some period of development is necessary for perception of object unity to emerge in infants. Johnson and his colleagues (Johnson & Aslin, 1995; Johnson & Nanez, 1995) presented two-dimensional (computer-generated) rod-and-occluder displays, similar to the habituation display shown in Figure 1.10, to 2-month-olds. Johnson and Nanez (1995) found that, following habituation, the infants did not show a preference for either of the test stimuli, suggesting that they were perhaps not fully capable of perceiving object unity. Johnson and Aslin (1995) tested the hypothesis that "with additional visual information, infants at this young age would be more likely to perceive the unity of the rod parts" (Johnson, 1997, p. 10). They did this by testing their infants in three conditions, in each of which more of the rod was shown behind the occluder. In one of these conditions the occluder was simply made smaller in height; in another, a vertical gap was placed in the box; in the third, the occluder contained gaps. In all of these conditions the 2-month-olds now responded like 4-month-olds – that is, they showed preferences for the broken rod on the test trials, thereby indicating early perception of object unity. Thus, it appears that an understanding of the completeness, or unity, of partly occluded objects begins around two months from birth.

The young infant's limitations have been confirmed by others, in studies of *object segregation*. Spelke and her colleagues (e.g., Kestenbaum, Termine, & Spelke, 1987; Spelke, Breinlinger, Jacobson, & Phillips, 1993) have found that 3-month-olds interpret displays in which two objects are adjacent and touching as being a single unit, even though the objects may be very different in their features. Needham and Baillargeon (1998) showed 4-month-olds a stationary display consisting of a yellow cylinder lying next to, and touching, a blue box, and presented them with two test displays. In both events a gloved hand came into view, grasped the cylinder, and moved it to one side, but in one, the move apart condition, the box remained where it was, while in the other, the move together condition, the box moved with the cylinder. On these test trials the 4-month-olds looked about equally at the two test events, suggesting that they were uncertain whether the cylinder and box were one or two separate units. Needham and Baillargeon found that if the infants saw either the box or the cylinder alone for as little as 5 or 15 seconds, these brief exposures were sufficient to indicate to the infants that the cylinder-and-box display consisted of two objects.

Needham and Baillargeon (1997) investigated conditions under which 8-month-olds detect objects as separate or interconnected. They found that when the infants saw two identical yellow octagons standing side by side they expected them to be connected: on test trials the infants appeared surprised (as measured by increased looking) when the octagons moved apart, but not when they moved together. Needham and Baillargeon found that this expectation could be readily changed by experience: a nice additional finding was that a prior demonstration that a thin blade could be passed between the identical octagons at the point of contact led the infants to expect them to be two objects. When the objects shown the infants were a yellow cylinder and a blue box the infants appeared surprised when the objects moved *together*, but not when they moved apart. These findings are a clear demonstration that when the touching objects were identical 8-month-olds expected them to be one object, but when they were different in shape and color they expected them to be two objects.

The developmental story seems to be as follows. In the first two months from birth infants gradually learn about the continued existence of the unseen parts of partly occluded objects, and also come to understand the continued existence of unseen objects (Baillargeon, 1987). In terms of object segregation the young infant applies the rule "adjacency (touching) = a single unit/object"; by 4 months infants are uncertain, and experience plays a critical role in assisting them to parse the events they encounter. By 8 or 10 months the rule "different features = different objects" seems to be applied consistently, and has presumably been learned, or acquired, as a result of experience. One emerging theme from the literature is that very brief experiences can change infants' understanding of particular displays.

Emerging Questions, Paradigms, Issues

As research into infant visual perception has progressed there has become less of a reliance on the "grand theories" that were dominant in the early part of the twentieth century. Many theoretical views have emerged which deal with specific areas of development, and these views have often given rise to lively debates and have inspired critical experiments. The aim in this section is briefly to discuss three such areas that are highly interrelated: the relationship between neural structures and visual development; the role of action in visual development; early representation and thinking.

The Relationship between Neural Structures and Visual Development

Many different neural pathways are developing in the first year from birth (and later!), and it is a truism to state that perceptual and conceptual development are constrained and facilitated by their development. There are now many theoretical views which attempt to understand the relationship between neural, perceptual, and cognitive growth. Some of the issues debated include: the role of subcortical and cortical mechanisms in early visual development; hemispheric specialization and its role in face perception; the development of a ventral "what" pathway and its role in object identification and visual recognition, and a dorsal "where" or "how" pathway involved in visually guided action and spatial location (e.g., Farah et al., 2000; Milner & Goodale, 1995; Nelson, 2001); the development of the frontal cortex and its role in problem solving. Space does not permit discussion of these and other issues. An excellent introduction to the recent subdiscipline of developmental cognitive neuroscience is given by Johnson (1997).

The Role of Action in Visual Development

All spatially coordinated behaviors, such as visual tracking, visually locating an auditory source, reaching, sitting, crawling, walking, require that action and perceptual information are coordinated. In an excellent review of this topic Bertenthal (1996) quotes J. J. Gibson: "We must perceive in order to move, but we must also move in order to perceive." It has become clear that newborn infants perform many actions that are regulated by perceptual information. These include visual tracking, orienting to sounds, and hand to mouth coordination. However, while perception and action appear coordinated from birth these systems clearly develop as infancy progresses, and new couplings appear. For example, Campos, Bertenthal, and Kermoian (1992) reported that prelocomotor infants show no fear, or wariness, of heights, whereas age-matched crawling infants of the same age showed a significant amount of fear. It seems that experience with crawling changes infants' sensitivity to depth, objects, and surfaces: a detailed account and synthesis of the role of locomotor experiences in changing infants' perceptual, social, and cognitive development is given by Campos et al. (2000). Several researchers have speculated on the relation between perception and action. Bremner (1997) suggests that "development in infancy is very much to do with the formation of links between pre-existing objective perception and emerging action, so that knowledge of the world implicit in perception eventually becomes explicit knowledge in the sense that it can be used to guide action."

Several researchers have found evidence of precocious perceptual abilities in young infants. For example, newborn infants have size and shape constancy; infants as young as 3 months can represent the continued existence of invisible objects, and appear to know that solid objects should not pass through each other; 2–4-month-old infants perceive object unity in that they are aware that a partly occluded object is connected or complete behind the occluder. These findings appear to be in contradiction to Piaget's view, which is that these abilities develop only gradually over infancy, after extensive experience of observing and manipulating objects. For example, he described several observations showing how his own children appeared to acquire concepts of size and shape constancy by observing the effects of objects being moved towards and away from them (Piaget, 1954, Observations 86–91). There are at least three possible resolutions to these contradictory claims, all of which appear in the literature. One is simply to argue that Piaget was wrong. A second is to follow Bremner and make the distinction between implicit (perceptual) and explicit (in action) knowledge. A third, conceptually related, argument is to suggest that in the perception experiments the infant is a "couch potato" and that "the methods used for studying young infants are inadequate for revealing all of the knowledge and mental processes that are necessary for problem solving." In addition to perceptual abilities, "Problem solving also involves coordinating, guiding, monitoring, and evaluating a sequence of goal-directed actions" (Willatts, 1997, pp. 112, 113).

Early Representation and Thinking

Several researchers have argued that infants, from a very early age, possess a core of physical knowledge, and they also make use of active representations to reason with this knowledge. For example, newborn infants' ability to imitate facial gestures suggests that they have some innately specified representation of faces. With respect to the physical world, young infants appear to have knowledge about basic principles such as solidity, causality, trajectory, number, gravity, support, and so on. Research that demonstrates this understanding typically presents infants with "possible" and "impossible" events, where the latter violate one or other physical principle. When the infants look longer at the "impossible" event this is interpreted in terms of the infant *representing* the characteristics (or, e.g., continued existence) of the object(s), *reasoning* about the physical world, *understanding* the physical principle being tested, and being *surprised* at the violation. All the italicized words are characteristics of a conceptual system, and suggest that infants possess considerable physical knowledge from a very early age. Currently, however, these claims are highly controversial (see chapter 4). Bogartz, Shinskey, and Speaker (1997), Haith (1998), and Rivera, Wakeley, and Langer (1999) are among those who argue that these sorts of interpretations are too rich, and imbue young infants with too much conceptual ability. Haith argues that "Almost without fail we can account for infants' longer looking at an inconsistent or impossible event . . . in terms of well-established perceptual principles – novelty, familiarity, salience, and discrepancy" (p. 173). These conclusions and reinterpretations, of course, have been challenged (e.g., Spelke, 1998), and Meltzoff & Moore (1998, p. 201) "hypothesize that a capacity for representation is the starting point for infant development, not its culmination."

Conclusions

In the first section of this chapter evidence was presented suggesting that scanning abilities, acuity, contrast sensitivity, and color discrimination are limited in neonates. However, as Hainline and Abramov (1992, pp. 40–41) put it, "While infants may not, indeed, see as well as adults do, they normally see well enough to function effectively in their roles as infants." Thus, despite their sensory limitations, it is clear that newborn infants have several means with which to begin to make sense of the visual world. The visual cortex, while immature, is functioning at birth, and it seems to be the case that newborn infants possess at least rudimentary form perception. Newborn infants can clearly remember what they see, and they demonstrate rapid learning about their perceived world.

One prerequisite for object knowledge is distinguishing proximal from distal stimuli. The proximal stimulus is the sensory stimulation – in this case, the pattern of light falling on the retina. The distal stimulus consists of what is represented by the pattern of stimulation – the object itself. Neonates distinguish proximal from distal stimuli when they demonstrate size and shape constancy: the object is perceived accurately, despite changes to its retinal image. The picture of visual perception in early infancy that is emerging is complex: some aspects of visual perception are very immature, whereas others appear to be remarkably advanced at birth. Several lines of evidence converge to suggest that infants are born with an innate preference for, and representation of, the human face. It is clear that the young infant's visual world is, to a large extent, structured and coherent as a result of the intrinsic organization of the visual system.

However well organized the visual world of the young infant may be, it lacks the familiarity, meaning, and associations that characterize the world of the mature perceiver. Inevitably, some types of visual organization take time to develop. An appreciation of the underlying unity, coherence, and persistence of occluded objects is not present at birth, and a proper understanding of the physical properties of objects emerges only slowly as infancy progresses. As development proceeds, the innate and developing organizational mechanisms are added to by experience, which assists the infant in making sense of the perceived world.

Note

1   The term "innate" refers to behaviors and abilities that are inherited and not appreciably affected by experience. Thus, visual abilities that are present in the newborn infant are likely to be innate. In the case of face perception it is possible that proprioceptive feedback from its own facial and body movements *in utero* contributes to the newborn infant's facial representation. An alternative term, prefunctional, avoids the potential pitfalls of calling something "innate," but for present purposes the term innate is used without any assumption that we know how the ability(ies) originated.

Related Topics and Further Reading

Research into visual perception is carried out by many thousands of researchers, and in this chapter it is only possible to give a brief outline of its development in infancy. Topics that have either not been covered, or have not been discussed in any depth, include motion perception, neural development, abnormalities of development, intersensory perception, categorization, and perception of causality. Additional readings which deal with these and other topics in more detail are:

Atkinson, J. (2000). *The developing visual brain.* Oxford: Oxford University Press.

Kellman, P. J., & Arterberry, M. E. (1998). *The cradle of knowledge: Development of perception in infancy.* Cambridge, MA and London: MIT Press.

Lewkowicz, D. J. & Lickliter, R. (1994). *The development of intersensory perception: Comparative perspectives.* Hillsdale, NJ: Lawrence Erlbaum Associates.

Simion, F. & Butterworth, G. (Eds.). (1998). *The development of sensory, motor and cognitive capacities in early infancy.* Hove: Psychology Press.

Slater, A. (Ed.). (1998). *Perceptual development: Visual, auditory and speech perception in infancy.* Hove: Psychology Press.

Vital-Durand, F., Atkinson, J., & Braddick, O. J. (Eds.). (1996). *Infant vision.* Oxford, New York, and Tokyo: Oxford University Press.

References

Arterberry, M. E., & Yonas, A. (2000). Perception of three-dimensional shape specified by optic flow by 8-week-old infants. *Perception and Psychophysics, 62,* 550–556.

Aslin, R. N. (1981). Development of smooth pursuit in human infants. In D. F. Fisher, R. A. Monty, & J. W. Senders (Eds.), *Eye movements: Cognition and visual perception* (pp. 31–51). Hillsdale, NJ: Erlbaum.

Aslin, R. N., & Salapatek, P. (1975). Saccadic localization of visual targets by the very young human infant. *Perception and Psychophysics, 17,* 293–302.

Atkinson, J. (1984). Human visual development over the first six months of life: A review and a hypothesis. *Human Neurobiology, 3,* 61–74.

Atkinson, J. (2000). *The developing visual brain.* Oxford: Oxford University Press.

Atkinson, J., & Braddick, O. (1989). Development of basic visual functions. In A. Slater & G. Bremner (Eds.), *Infant development* (pp. 7–41). Hove and Hillsdale, NJ: Erlbaum.

Atkinson, J., Hood, B. M., Wattam-Bell, J., Anker, S., & Trickelbank, J. (1988). Development of orientation discrimination in infancy. *Perception, 17,* 587–595.

Bahrick, L. E. (1987). Infants' intermodal perception of two levels of temporal structure in natural events. *Infant Behavior and Development, 10,* 387–416.

Bahrick, L. E. (1988). Intermodal learning in infancy: Learning on the basis of two kinds of invariant relations in audible and visible events. *Child Development, 59,* 197–209.

Bahrick, L. E. (1992). Infants' perceptual differentiation of amodal and modality-specific audiovisual relations. *Journal of Experimental Child Psychology, 53,* 197–209.

Bahrick, L. E. (2000). Increasing specificity in the development of intermodal perception. In D. Muir & A. Slater (Eds.), *Infant development: The essential readings* (pp. 119–136). Oxford and Cambridge, MA: Blackwell.

Bahrick, L. E., & Pickens, J. N. (1994). Amodal relations: The basis for intermodal perception and learning in infancy. In D. J. Lewkowicz & R. Lickliter (Eds.), *The development of intersensory perception: Comparative perspectives* (pp. 205–233). Hillsdale, NJ: Erlbaum.

Baillargeon, R. (1987). Object permanence in 3.5- and 4.5-month-old infants. *Developmental Psychology, 23,* 655–664.

Banks, M. S., & Dannemiller, J. L. (1987). Infant visual psychophysics. In P. Salapatek & L. Cohen (Eds.), *Handbook of infant perception: Vol. 1. From sensation to perception* (pp. 115–184). London: Academic Press.

Bertenthal, B. I. (1996). Origins and early development of perception, action, and representation. *Annual Review of Psychology, 47,* 431–459.

Bogartz, R. S., Shinskey, J. L., & Speaker, C. (1997). Interpreting infant looking. *Developmental Psychology, 33,* 408–422.

Bower, T. G. R. (1966). The visual world of infants. *Scientific American, 215*(6), 80–92.

Braddick, O. J., & Atkinson, J. (1983). Some recent findings on the development of human binocularity: A review. *Behavioural Brain Research, 10,* 71–80.

Bremner, J. G. (1994). *Infancy.* Oxford: Blackwell.

Bremner, J. G. (1997). From perception to cognition. In G. Bremner, A. Slater, & G. Butterworth (Eds.), *Infant perception: Recent advances* (pp. 55–74). Hove: Psychology Press.

Bremner, G., Slater, A., & Butterworth, G. (Eds.) (1997). *Infant perception: Recent advances.* Hove: Psychology Press.

Bronson, G. W. (1974). The postnatal growth of visual capacity. *Child Development, 45,* 873–890.

Brown, A. M., Dobson, V., & Maier, J. (1987). Visual acuity of human infants at scotopic, mesopic and photopic luminances. *Vision Research, 27,* 1845–1858.

Bushnell, I. W. R., Sai, F., & Mullin, J. T. (1989). Neonatal recognition of the mother's face. *British Journal of Developmental Psychology, 7,* 3–15.

Butterworth, G. E. (1983). Structure of the mind in human infancy. In L. P. Lipsitt & C. K. Rovee-Collier (Eds.), *Advances in infancy research* (pp. 1–29). Norwood, NJ: Ablex.

Campos, J. J., Anderson, D. I., Barbu-Roth, M. A., Hubbard, E. M., Hertenstein, M. J., & Witherington, D. (2000). Travel broadens the mind. *Infancy, 1,* 149–219.

Campos, J. J., Bertenthal, B. I., & Kermoian, R. (1992). Early experience and emotional development: The emergence of wariness of heights. *Psychological Science, 3,* 61–64.

Cohen, L. B., & Younger, B. A. (1984). Infant perception of angular relations. *Infant Behavior and Development, 7,* 37–47.

Etcoff, N. (2000). *Survival of the prettiest: The science of beauty.* New York: Doubleday.

Farah, M. J., Rabinowitz, C., Quinn, G. E., & Liu, G. T. (2000). Early commitment of neural substrates for face recognition. *Cognitive Neuropsychology, 17,* 117–123.

Farroni, T., Valenza, E., Simion, F., & Umilta, C. (2000). Configural processing at birth: Evidence for perceptual organisation. *Perception, 29,* 355–372.

Field, T. M., Cohen, D., Garcia, R., & Greenberg, R. (1984). Mother–stranger face discrimination by the newborn. *Infant Behavior and Development, 7,* 19–25.

Field, T. M., Woodson, R., Greenberg, R., & Cohen, D. (1982). Discrimination and imitation of facial expressions by neonates. *Science, 218,* 179–181.

Galton, F. (1907). *Inquiries in human faculty and its development.* London: J. M. Dent & Sons.

Ghim, H.-R. (1990). Evidence for perceptual organization in infants: Perception of subjective contours by young infants. *Infant Behavior and Development, 13,* 221–248.

Gibson, E. J. (1969). *Principles of perceptual learning and development.* New York: Appleton-Century-Crofts.

Gibson, J. J. (1950). *The perception of the visual world.* Boston: Houghton Mifflin.

Gibson, J. J. (1966). *The senses considered as perceptual systems.* Boston: Houghton Mifflin.

Gibson, J. J. (1979). *The ecological approach to visual perception.* Boston: Houghton Mifflin.

Gordon, I. E. (1997). *Theories of visual perception* (2nd edn.). New York: Wiley.

Goren, C. C., Sarty, M., & Wu, P. Y. K. (1975). Visual following and pattern discrimination of face-like stimuli by newborn infants. *Pediatrics, 56,* 544–549.

Hainline, L. (1998). The development of basic visual abilities. In A. Slater (Ed.), *Perceptual development: Visual, auditory and speech perception in infancy* (pp. 37–44). Hove: Psychology Press.

Hainline, L., & Abramov, I. (1985). Saccades and small-field optokinetic nystagmus in infants. *Journal of the American Optometric Association, 56,* 620–626.

Hainline, L., & Abramov, I. (1992). Assessing visual development: Is infant vision good enough? In C. Rovee-Collier & L. P. Lipsitt (Eds.), *Advances in infancy research* (Vol. 7, pp. 1–43). Norwood, NJ: Ablex.

Haith, M. M. (1998). Who put the cog in infant cognition? Is rich interpretation too costly? *Infant Behavior and Development, 21,* 167–179.

Hamer, R. D., Norcia, A. M., Tyler, C. W., & Hsu-Winges, C. (1989). The development of monocular and binocular VEP acuity. *Vision Research, 29,* 397–408.

Hebb, D. O. (1949). *The organization of behavior.* New York: Wiley.

Held, R. (1985). Binocular vision: Behavioral and neuronal development. In J. Mehler & R. Fox (Eds.), *Neonate cognition: Beyond the blooming, buzzing confusion.* Hillsdale, NJ: Lawrence Erlbaum Associates.

Howland, H. C., Dobson, V., & Sayles, N. (1987). Accommodation in infants as measured by photorefraction. *Vision Research, 27,* 2141–2152.

James, W. (1890). *Principles of psychology.* New York: Henry Holt.

Johnson, M. H. (1990). Cortical maturation and the development of visual attention in early infancy. *Journal of Cognitive Neuroscience, 2,* 81–95.

Johnson, M. H. (1997). *Developmental cognitive neuroscience.* Oxford and Cambridge, MA: Blackwell.

Johnson, M. H., & Morton, J. (1991). *Biology and cognitive development: The case for face recognition.* Oxford: Blackwell.

Johnson, S. P. (1997). Young infants' perception of object unity: Implications for development of attentional and cognitive skills. *Current Directions in Psychological Science, 6,* 5–11.

Johnson, S. P., & Aslin, R. N. (1995). Perception of object unity in 2-month-old infants. *Developmental Psychology, 31,* 739–745.

Johnson, S. P., & Nanez, J. E. (1995). Young infants' perception of object unity in two-dimensional displays. *Infant Behavior and Development, 18,* 133–143.

Kanizsa, G. (1979). *Organization in vision: Essays on Gestalt perception.* New York: Praeger.

Karmiloff-Smith, A. (1996, Fall). The connectionist infant: Would Piaget turn in his grave? *SRCD Newsletter,* 1–3, 10.

Kellman, P. J., & Spelke, E. S. (1983). Perception of partly occluded objects in infancy. *Cognitive Psychology, 15,* 483–524.

Kellman, P. J., Spelke, E. S., & Short, K. R. (1986). Infant perception of object unity from translatory motion in depth and vertical translation. *Child Development, 57,* 72–86.

Kestenbaum, R., Termine, N., & Spelke, E. S. (1987). Perception of objects and object boundaries by 3-month-olds. *British Journal of Developmental Psychology, 5*, 367–383.

Kokkinaki, T., & Kugiumutzakis, G. (2000). Basic aspects of vocal imitation in infant–parent interaction during the first 6 months. *Journal of Reproductive and Infant Psychology, 18*, 173–187.

Kugiumutzakis, G. (1993). Intersubjective vocal imitation in early mother–infant interaction. In J. Nadel & L. Camioni (Eds.), *New perspectives in early communicative development* (pp. 23–47). London and New York: Routledge.

Langlois, J. H., Ritter, J. M., Roggman, L. A., & Vaughn, L. S. (1991). Facial diversity and infant preferences for attractive faces. *Developmental Psychology, 27*, 79–84.

Langlois, J., & Roggman, L. A. (1990). Attractive faces are only average. *Psychological Science, 1*, 115–121.

Langlois, J. H., Roggman, L. A., Casey, R. J., Ritter, J. M., Rieser-Danner, L. A., & Jenkins, V. Y. (1987). Infant preferences for attractive faces: Rudiments of a stereoptype? *Developmental Psychology, 23*, 363–369.

Lewkowicz, D. J. (1986). Developmental changes in infants' bisensory response to synchronous durations. *Infant Behavior and Development, 9*, 335–353.

Marg, E., Freeman, D. N., Peltzman, P., & Goldstein, P. J. (1976). Visual acuity development in human infants: Evoked potential measurements. *Investigative Ophthalmology and Visual Science, 15*, 150–153.

Meltzoff, A. N. (1995). Infants' understanding of people and things: From body imitation to folk psychology. In J. L. Bermudez, A. Marcel, & N. Eilan (Eds.), *The body and the self* (pp. 43–69). Cambridge, MA, and London: MIT Press.

Meltzoff, A. N., & Borton, R. W. (1979). Intermodal matching by human neonates. *Nature, 282*, 403–404.

Meltzoff, A. N., & Moore, M. K. (1977). Imitation of facial and manual gestures by human neonates. *Science, 198*, 75–78.

Meltzoff, A. N., & Moore, M. K. (1984). Newborn infants imitate adult gestures. *Child Development, 54*, 702–709.

Meltzoff, A. N., & Moore, M. K. (1992). Early imitation within a functional framework: The importance of person identity, movement, and development. *Infant Behavior and Development, 15*, 479–505.

Meltzoff, A. N., & Moore, M. K. (1994). Imitation, memory, and the representation of persons. *Infant Behavior and Development, 17*, 83–99.

Meltzoff, A. N., & Moore, M. K. (1997). Explaining facial imitation: A theoretical model. *Early Development and Parenting, 6*, 179–192.

Meltzoff, A. N., & Moore, M. K. (1998). Object representation, identity, and the paradox of early permanence: Steps toward a new framework. *Infant Behavior and Development, 21*, 201–235.

Meltzoff, A. N. & Moore, M. K. (2000). Resolving the debate about early imitation. In D. Muir & A. Slater (Eds.), *Infant development: The essential readings* (pp. 176–181). Oxford and Cambridge, MA: Blackwell.

Milner, A. D., & Goodale, M. A. (1995). *The visual brain in action.* Oxford: Oxford University Press.

Morrongiello, B. A., Fenwick, K. D., & Chance, G. (1998). Crossmodal learning in newborn infants: Inferences about properties of auditory–visual events. *Infant Behavior and Development, 21*, 543–553.

Muir, D. W., & Clifton, R. (1985). Infants' orientation to the location of sound sources. In G. Gottlieb & N. Krasnegor (Eds.), *The measurement of audition and vision during the first year of life: A methodological overview* (pp. 171–194). Norwood, NJ: Ablex.

Needham, A., & Baillargeon, R. (1997). Object segregation in 8-month-old infants. *Cognition, 62*, 121–149.

Needham, A., & Baillargeon, R. (1998). Effects of prior experience on 4.5-month-old infants' object segregation. *Infant Behavior and Development, 21*, 1–24.

Nelson, C. A. (2001). The development and neural bases of face recognition. *Infant and Child Development, 10*, 3–18.

Pascalis, O., de Schonen, S., Morton, J., Deruelle, C., & Fabre-Grenet, M. (1995). Mother's face recognition by neonates: A replication and an extension. *Infant Behavior and Development, 18*, 79–85.

Piaget, J. (1952). *The origins of intelligence in children.* New York: International University Press.

Piaget, J. (1953). *The origins of intelligence in the child.* London: Routledge & Kegan Paul.

Piaget, J. (1954). *The construction of reality in the child.* New York: Basic Books.

Quinn, P. C., Brown, C. R., & Streppa, M. L. (1997). Perceptual organization of complex visual configurations by young infants. *Infant Behavior and Development, 20*, 35–46.

Quinn, P. C., Burke, S., & Rush, A. (1993). Part–whole perception in early infancy: Evidence for perceptual grouping produced by lightness similarity. *Infant Behavior and Development, 16*, 19–42.

Reissland, N. (1988). Neonatal imitation in the first hour of life: Observations in Rural Nepal. *Developmental Psychology, 24*, 464–469.

Rivera, S. M., Wakeley, A., & Langer, J. (1999). The drawbridge phenomenon: Representational reasoning or perceptual preference? *Developmental Psychology, 35*, 427–435.

Samuels, C. A., Butterworth, G., Roberts, T., & Graupner, L. (1994). Babies prefer attractiveness to symmetry. *Perception, 23*, 823–831.

Samuels, C. A., & Ewy, R. (1985). Aesthetic perception of faces during infancy. *British Journal of Developmental Psychology, 3*, 221–228.

Sen, M. G., Yonas, A., & Knill, D. (2001). Development of infants' sensitivity to surface contour information for spatial layout. *Perception, 30*, 167–176.

Slater, A. (Ed.). (1998). *Perceptual development: Visual, auditory and speech perception in infancy.* Hove: Psychology Press.

Slater, A., Bremner, J. G., Johnson, S. P., Sherwood, P., Hayes, R., & Brown, E. (2000). Newborn infants' preference for attractive faces: The role of internal and external facial features. *Infancy, 1*, 265–274.

Slater, A., Johnson, S. P., Brown, E., & Badenoch, M. (1996). The roles of texture and occluder size on newborn infants' perception of partly occluded objects. *Infant Behavior and Development, 19*, 145–148.

Slater, A., Johnson, S. P., Kellman, P. J., & Spelke, E. S. (1994). The role of three-dimensional depth cues in infants' perception of partly occluded objects. *Early Development and Parenting, 3*, 187–191.

Slater, A., Mattock, A., & Brown, E. (1990). Size constancy at birth: Newborn infants' responses to retinal and real size. *Journal of Experimental Child Psychology, 49*, 314–322.

Slater, A., Mattock, A., Brown, E., & Bremner, J. G. (1991). Form perception at birth: Cohen and Younger revisited. *Journal of Experimental Child Psychology, 51*, 395–405.

Slater, A., Mattock, A., Brown, E., Burnham, D., & Young, A. W. (1991). Visual processing of stimulus compounds in newborn infants. *Perception, 20*, 29–33.

Slater, A., & Morison, V. (1985). Shape constancy and slant perception at birth. *Perception, 14*, 337–344.

Slater, A., Morison, V., & Somers, M. (1988). Orientation discrimination and cortical function in the human newborn. *Perception, 17*, 597–602.

Slater, A., Morison, V., Somers, M., Mattock, A., Brown, E., & Taylor, D. (1990). Newborn and older infants' perception of partly occluded objects. *Infant Behavior and Development, 13*, 33–49.

Slater, A., Quinn, P., Hayes, R., & Brown, E. (2000). The role of facial orientation in newborn infants' preference for attractive faces. *Developmental Science, 3,* 181–185.

Slater, A., Quinn, P., Brown, E., & Hayes, R. (1999). Intermodal perception at birth: Intersensory redundancy guides newborn infants' learning of arbitrary auditory–visual pairings. *Developmental Science, 2,* 333–338.

Slater, A., Rose, D., & Morison, V. (1984). Newborn infants' perception of similarities and differences between two- and three-dimensional stimuli. *British Journal of Developmental Psychology, 2,* 287–294.

Slater, A., von der Schulenburg, C., Brown, E., Badenoch, M., Butterworth, G., Parsons, S., & Samuels, C. (1998). Newborn infants prefer attractive faces. *Infant Behavior and Development, 21,* 345–354.

Sokol, S. (1978). Measurement of infant acuity from pattern reversal evoked potentials. *Vision Research, 18,* 33–40.

Spelke, E. S. (1998). Nativism, empiricism, and the origins of knowledge. *Infant Behavior and Development, 21,* 181–200.

Spelke, E., Breinlinger, K., Jacobson, K., & Phillips, A. (1993). Gestalt relations and object perception: A developmental study. *Perception, 22,* 1483–1501.

Teller, D. Y. (1983). Scotopic vision, color vision, and stereopsis in infants. *Current Eye Research, 2,* 199–210.

Vital-Durand, F., Atkinson, J., & Braddick, O. (Eds.). (1996). *Infant vision.* Oxford: Oxford University Press.

von Noorden, G. K. (1988). A reassessment of infantile esotropia. XLIV Edward Jackson Memorial Lecture. *American Journal of Ophthalmology, 105,* 1–10.

Walton, G. E., Armstrong, E. S., & Bower, T. G. R. (1997). Faces as forms in the world of the newborn. *Infant Behavior and Development, 20,* 537–543.

Walton, G. E., Armstrong, E. S., & Bower, T. G. R. (1998). Newborns learn to identify a face in eight/tenths of a second? *Developmental Science, 1,* 79–84.

Walton, G. E., Bower, N. J. A., & Bower, T. G. R. (1992). Recognition of familiar faces by newborns. *Infant Behavior and Development, 15,* 265–269.

Wertheimer, M. (1961). Psychomotor coordination of auditory and visual space at birth. *Science, 134,* 1692.

Willatts, P. (1997). Beyond the "couch potato" infant: How infants use their knowledge to regulate action, solve problems, and achieve goals. In G. Bremner, A. Slater, & G. Butterworth (Eds.), *Infant perception: Recent advances* (pp. 109–135). Hove: Psychology Press.

Yonas, A., Cleaves, N., & Pettersen, L. (1978). Development of sensitivity to pictorial depth. *Science, 200,* 77–79.

Yonas, A., & Granrud, C. E. (1985). Development of visual space perception in young infants. In J. Mehler & R. Fox (Eds.), *Neonate cognition: Beyond the blooming, buzzing confusion.* Hillsdale, NJ: Lawrence Erlbaum Associates.

Zuckerman, C. B., & Rock, I. (1957). A reappraisal of the roles of past experience and innate organizing processes in visual perception. *Psychological Bulletin, 54,* 269–296.

Zusne, L. (1970). *Visual perception of form.* New York: Academic Press.

Chapter Two

Hearing, Listening, and Understanding: Auditory Development in Infancy

Anne Fernald

Introduction

Infants now beam from the covers of popular magazines featuring articles on "how a child's brain develops" (*Time*, 1997) and "how learning begins" (*Newsweek*, 2000). This growing interest in the capabilities of infants has roots in ancient philosophical questions about the origins of human knowledge. However, the contemporary view of "the scientist in the crib" has been shaped most directly by recent advances in experimental research on development in infancy (Gopnik, Meltzoff, & Kuhl, 1999). Only 50 years ago, the assumption that human newborns were effectively deaf and blind was still entrenched in medical textbooks. This view only gradually receded with the refinement of new methods sensitive enough to reveal sensory and cognitive abilities far more acute and sophisticated than anyone had imagined. Much of the pioneering research on infant cognition that began in the 1960s focused on the early development of visual and auditory perception. Studies showing that newborns can indeed see and hear were newsworthy because of their obvious clinical relevance, since the ability to make accurate assessments of early sensory functioning enabled the design of effective and timely interventions. But beyond the important practical implications, research on visual and auditory development led to new theories about how infants use what they see and hear to make sense of their limited experience. Research on infants has now begun to illuminate those enduring questions about the human mind first posed by philosophers: How do children come to understand the world through their senses? And how is the child's interpretation of sensory information guided by inborn perceptual biases as well as by knowledge gained through experience?

This chapter reviews research on auditory development in infancy in relation to larger questions about the functions of hearing in the early acquisition of knowledge. The first section compares audition and vision and examines the historical argument that vision is the primary sensory modality in humans. The second section provides a brief overview of the physical and psychological dimensions of sound, the mechanics of hearing and the early maturation of the auditory system. The third section describes experimental methods used to assess auditory capabilities in infants, while the fourth section focuses on basic research on infant hearing and hearing disorders. The fifth section distinguishes listening from hearing, reviewing research on how infants use auditory information to discern socially and linguistically relevant information in the sounds of human voices, how they listen for patterns in speech long before they produce their first words, and how the language they hear shapes their strategies for listening and understanding.

Audition and Vision Compared

The idea of assessing visual and auditory capabilities in children may bring to mind standing in line in the school corridor, waiting to be asked to identify tiny letters on a wall chart or to respond to faint sounds presented through headphones. Performance on such tests determines whether certain aspects of visual and auditory function are "within the normal range" for an individual. However, the normal development of visual and auditory competence obviously involves much more than achieving 20/20 acuity and being able to detect low-intensity sounds. While establishing sensory thresholds at different ages provides valuable normative information, it is just the beginning of an account of how infants gain knowledge about things, people, and events in the world through what they see and what they hear.

Vision is often referred to as the primary sensory modality for vertebrates, because most depend crucially on vision for orientation, locomotion, and action in a three-dimensional world. Through evolution visual systems have undergone adaptation appropriate to the ecology of the species. Nocturnal predators such as owls have more rod photoreceptors sensitive to low illumination, while hawks have a higher concentration of cone photoreceptors which enable high acuity at a distance in bright illumination. In mammalian species, predators such as lions have eyes oriented forward, enhancing binocular vision and depth perception, while the ungulates they hunt have eyes positioned to enhance vision to the side and rear. These visual specializations enable detection and localization of other creatures and coordination of movement toward or away, abilities crucial to survival. Although many mammals use audition to some extent in responding to predators and prey, and a few species such as bats rely extensively on auditory signals, the generalization that vision is relatively more important than audition for spatial orientation, locomotion, and object identification seems reasonable, particularly for humans.

But visual and auditory experience yield fundamentally different kinds of knowledge. In comparing their functions, it is useful to consider the sources and nature of stimulation in these two modalities. The primary stimulus for vision is natural or artificial light reflected from surfaces. In rare instances, light is emitted (e.g., phosphorescence), but mostly it is reflected light which stimulates the photoreceptors and enables us to know about the location, shape, color, motion, and other aspects of objects and creatures nearby and at a considerable distance. While touch can also provide information about the identity and location of stationary things nearby, only through vision is it possible to have direct experience of stationary objects at a distance as well as knowledge of their location relative to other objects and to the observer.

The primary stimulus for audition is the movement of air molecules, caused most often by objects and living things in motion. Flowing water or vibrations in the vocal tract of a barking dog agitate adjacent air molecules, which in turn set the eardrum into motion and trigger the chain of mechanical and neural events in the auditory system which result in the perception of sound. For most vertebrates, attention to sounds caused by the movement of inanimate things such as fire can alert them to danger and thus is important for survival. But of much greater importance is attention to sounds reflecting the movements of conspecifics and other animals nearby whose actions have relevance for the listener. We can hear a multitude of acoustic stimuli at any moment but are typically most attentive to those sounds emitted by animals or people, or which result from their actions on inanimate things in the environment. Such actions would include stepping on a branch and also running a machine. Of course, sounds caused by objects in motion when no animate agent is involved are often informative; e.g., trees moving in the wind are salient to the hiker if a storm is gathering. But environmental noise is most often the background against which the less predictable sounds of an unseen bird, an approaching train, or the speech of a companion are more closely monitored. The important point is that sounds can only occur when someone or something is in motion within a limited distance from the listener. Since things which move spontaneously or which cause other things to move are likely to be alive, audition is especially informative about events involving people and other living creatures.

While vision may be primary in enabling infants to learn about the physical world, audition plays a powerful role in initiating infants into a social world. In reviewing research on the early development of hearing and listening, it is essential to keep this point in mind. Many studies have investigated how infants process particular dimensions of sound such as frequency or intensity, using stimuli which are carefully controlled but which never actually occur in the natural environment. Such basic research provides a foundation for understanding the processing of complex acoustic stimuli. However, auditory systems have not evolved to respond to isolated features of sound, but rather to give organisms access to dynamic events, where knowledge of these events is important for survival. For humans in general and for infants in particular, the most important sources of auditory stimulation are the sounds produced by other people.

The Auditory System

Whatever their cause, sounds have the same basic properties. The movement of leaves and the vibration of vocal cords agitate surrounding air particles, which in turn set other air particles into motion. The resulting series of pressure variations emanating outward from the vibrating sound source constitute the stimulus for hearing. When these sound waves reach the ear, they initiate mechanical and electrical changes which ultimately trigger neural responses in the brain. This neural activity is analyzed and interpreted in particular regions of the central nervous system which leads to the experience of hearing.

Physical and Psychological Dimensions of Sound

The amplitude and frequency of sound waves, which are physical dimensions of all acoustic stimuli, are related to the psychological qualities perceived as loudness and pitch. Amplitude refers to the intensity of pressure each air particle exerts on the next, typically measured at the crest of the waveform, while frequency refers to the number of crests per second in the waveform. Although many factors influence the relation between these physical features of sound and the psychological qualities of loudness and pitch, a sound will generally be heard as louder when intensity increases and as higher in pitch when frequency increases.

The frequency of a sound is measured in hertz (Hz), or cycles per second. Sounds produced by striking the 88 keys on a grand piano span the range from 27 Hz for the lowest note to 4186 Hz for the highest note. The range of human song is in between, with the bottom note of a bass voice around 80 Hz and the top note of a soprano voice around 1100 Hz. These values refer to the fundamental frequencies of notes produced by pianos and voices, which usually correspond to their perceived pitch. However, natural sounds are almost always complex waveforms which also comprise many frequencies higher than the fundamental. A human vocalization with an average fundamental frequency around 200 Hz may also contain energy at frequencies as high as 20,000 Hz. Young adults can hear sounds ranging from 20 Hz to 20,000 Hz, which means they can hear all the frequencies used in speech production, but cannot hear all the frequencies in sounds produced by birds and insects, which may exceed 100,000 Hz.

The amplitude of a sound is quantified in terms of decibels (dB), a relative measure of intensity level. The conventional zero-point of the decibel scale is the sound pressure of a 1000 Hz tone at threshold, i.e., the intensity at which a young adult with normal hearing can just barely detect a 1000 Hz tone. Typical sound pressure levels (SPL) for speech are 20 dB SPL for whispering, 60 dB SPL for conversational speech, and 100 dB SPL for shouting. Extremely intense sounds such as the takeoff of a jet engine can exceed the threshold of pain around 140 dB SPL.

Mechanisms of Hearing

For hearing to occur, the auditory system must accomplish three basic tasks: first, the acoustic stimulus must be gathered and directed to the auditory receptors; second, the sound wave must be converted from pressure variations into electrical signals; and third, these electrical signals must be processed in the brain so as to convey reliable information about the sound source.

Because in mammals the auditory receptors are located deep within the ear, acoustic stimuli must travel a complicated path through the outer ear and middle ear to reach the

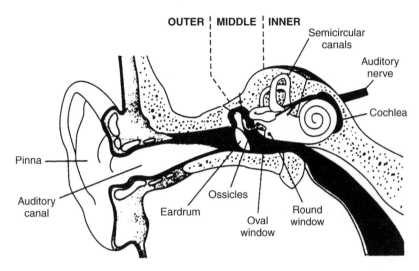

OUTER ¦ MIDDLE ¦ INNER

Semicircular
canals

Auditory
nerve

Cochlea

Pinna

Auditory
canal

Ossicles

Eardrum

Oval
window

Round
window

Figure 2.1   Diagram of the ear, showing its three subdivisions – outer, middle, and inner (adapted from Goldstein, 1999).

cochlea in the inner ear (see Figure 2.1). The outer ear consists of the pinna and the ear canal, which terminate in the eardrum. Sound waves collected in the outer ear cause the eardrum to vibrate. The movement of the eardrum acts on three tiny bones in the middle ear called maleus, the incus, and the stapes (referred to collectively as the auditory ossicles), which amplify the signal and convey it to the oval window. Amplification of the vibration through mechanical action of the ossicles serves a crucial function in delivering the signal to the auditory receptors (Handel, 1989). Less force is required to set air into motion than to set water into motion. Because the inner ear is filled with cochlear fluid, there is an impedance mismatch between the air at the eardrum and the fluid at the oval window. If the vibration of air molecules were to hit the cochlea directly, most of the sound pressure would be dissipated. Without amplification of the air vibration, only 1/1000th of the power would be effective in setting the fluid in the inner ear into motion. As a solution to this problem, the ossicles work as levers to increase the intensity of the signal, efficiently transferring the air vibration from the outer ear into fluid vibration in the cochlea of the inner ear.

The transduction of mechanical energy into electrical energy occurs in the cochlea, a bony snail-shaped structure which contains the basilar membrane. The actual auditory receptors are the hair cells lodged between the basilar membrane and other membranes in the cochlea. When sounds of different frequency and intensity pass through the outer and middle ear, they result in pressure changes in the cochlear fluid of the inner ear, which then create distinctive patterns of movement along the basilar membrane. These vibrations of the basilar membrane cause the hair cells to bend, generating an electrical signal which is transmitted to fibers in the eighth auditory nerve. Electrical signals triggered by bending of the hair cells then travel as neural impulses through the auditory pathways in the brain. The auditory nerve fibers originating in the cochlea first synapse in the cochlear nucleus, then synapse again in the brainstem, the midbrain, and the thalamus before connecting with neurons in the auditory cortex.

It is simple to say that neural impulses in the auditory pathways result in the experience of hearing, but very difficult to understand how this happens. One way in which hearing and seeing are fundamentally different is that visual perception is necessarily focused at one spatial location, while auditory perception is open to stimulation by sounds coming from all sides. At any moment, the pattern of light stimulating photoreceptors on the retina represents the spatial configuration of a particular scene at a particular place. At the very same moment, sound waves emanating from multiple sources at different distances in different directions all arrive simultaneously at the outer ear and combine into one complex pattern of vibration of the eardrum. After this complex pattern is transformed from mechanical to neural energy in the peripheral auditory system, it must then be sorted out centrally so that the listener experiences qualitatively different sounds coming from different sources. Bregman (1990) and Handel (1989) discuss the difficulty of this problem and review what is known about peripheral and central auditory processes involved in reconstructing reliable information about auditory sources from pressure variations in the air. For example, the role of the basilar membrane in coding information about frequency and intensity has been extensively studied, as have the mechanisms for integrating binaural input in sound localization. Less well understood are neural processes at higher levels of the auditory system involved in interpreting complex acoustic stimuli such as those characteristic of speech and music. This is an area of considerable interest, with new research showing that some cortical neurons respond specifically to particular dimensions of complex natural sounds (see Ribaupierre, 1997; Rouiller, 1997).

When Hearing Begins

The onset and development of auditory information processing clearly depend on the maturation of the auditory system at every level, from the opening of the auditory canal and mechanical efficiency of the middle ear to the developing sensitivity of the cochlear membranes and level of function of the auditory pathways in the brain. When early investigations of auditory development led to the conclusion that infants had very poor hearing, this apparent lack of sensitivity was attributed to maturational limitations such as rigidity of the eardrum and immobility of the auditory ossicles (Pratt, 1933). Research since that time has shown that in many respects the anatomy and physiology of the auditory system are in fact well developed by the time of birth and that infants begin to hear while still *in utero* (see chapter 18).

Werner and Marean (1996) review research on anatomical and physiological factors which could influence infants' responsiveness to sound both pre- and postnatally. The outer ear, auditory canal, eardrum, and middle ear cavity, as well as the eustachian tube connecting the chamber of the middle ear to the throat, all begin to form early in prenatal development and continue to change in shape and size throughout childhood. Although relating these anatomical changes to functional changes is not straightforward, they could be expected to have an influence on auditory sensitivity throughout this period. In contrast, the auditory ossicles grow extremely rapidly, attaining their adult size by around 15 weeks gestational age, with bone formation complete by 25 weeks. The cochlea also reaches its final size by 25 weeks, with patterns of sensory cells similar to those in the adult cochlea evident by 32 weeks. By the time of birth, both the anatomy and innervation of the organs in the cochlea are complete (Bredberg, 1985). Although the prenatal development of the peripheral auditory system is now fairly well documented, developmental changes in the neural pathways of the central auditory system are extremely complex and implications for the emergence of functional competence are not well understood. However, research using animal models has made progress in elucidating brain mechanisms underlying particular auditory functions such as auditory localization (see Rubel, Popper, & Fay, 1998).

Anatomical and electrophysiological evidence that the organs of the inner ear begin to function around the sixth month of fetal life is consistent with behavioral evidence for the onset of hearing around this time. Not surprisingly, pregnant women were aware that hearing begins prenatally long before scientists could be convinced. However, anecdotal reports of fetal movement following a loud sound (e.g., Forbes & Forbes, 1927) were regarded with skepticism, and the first scientific studies to explore this phenomenon (e.g., Sontag & Wallace, 1935) had methodological shortcomings. Reviewing early research on prenatal hearing, Aslin, Pisoni, and Jusczyk (1983) point out that because extremely loud sounds were used as stimuli, any fetal movement following the sound could have been triggered by the mother's startle response rather than by the sound itself. It was also not clear whether the fetal movement reflected an auditory response or a tactile response to the vibrations in the stimulus.

In recent years, however, several carefully controlled studies have provided more convincing evidence that the auditory system is functional to some extent by the sixth month of fetal life. Using ultrasound images to monitor fetal response to a vibroacoustic noise source, occasional blink-startle reactions were observed beginning around 25 weeks gestational age, and by 28 weeks these responses occurred consistently (Birnholz & Benacerraf, 1983). Other studies have shown reliable changes in fetal heart rate in response to sound beginning around the seventh month of gestation (e.g., Kisilevsky, Muir, & Low, 1992). As shown in Figure 2.2, fetuses from 23 to 28 weeks gestational age were unresponsive to acoustic stimuli, but by 32 weeks they responded consistently with an increase in heart rate (HR). By the end of pregnancy, fetuses are also able to discriminate between sounds coming from the external environment, responding with a change in heart rate when one low-pitched piano note is switched to another (Lecanuet, Graniere-Deferre, Jacquet, & DeCasper, 2000). Further evidence for the prenatal onset of auditory function comes from electrophysiological research with premature infants, showing that preterms born 30–35 weeks after conception are able to discriminate among vowel sounds which they hear postnatally (Cheour-Luhtanen et al., 1996).

If the fetus responds to sound several months before birth and attends to qualitative differences among sounds by the end of the prenatal period, what kinds of natural sounds are transmitted in the uterine environment? The stimuli used in research on fetal hearing have typically been high-intensity noises applied directly to the mother's abdomen. Are more natural sounds such as voices also perceptible within the uterus? Intrauterine recordings reveal that the prenatal environment is rich with both internal noise and externally generated sounds. The level of ambient noise from the mother's heartbeat, digestion,

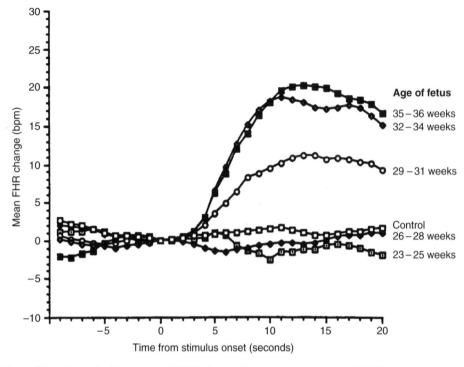

Figure 2.2   Mean fetal heart rate (FHR) change (in beats per minute – BPM) in response to a vibroacoustic stimulus applied to mother's abdomen. FHR change is shown as a function of time from onset of stimulus at 0 sec for fetuses in four age groups between 23 and 36 weeks post-conception. Control responding represents mean FHR change during a no-stimulus control trial averaged across all gestational ages (adapted from Kisilevsky et al., 1992).

and other physiological processes is around 85 dB SPL (Walker, Grimwade, & Wood, 1971), which means that less intense sounds from the external environment would be masked by the intrauterine background noise. Although the higher frequencies in sounds coming from outside the uterus are reduced in intensity, frequencies below 1000 Hz are transmitted with minimal attenuation (Armitage, Baldwin, & Vince, 1980). One study investigated the degree to which male and female voices and the mother's own voice are attenuated as they pass into the uterus (Richards, Frentzen, Gerhardt, McCann, & Abrams, 1992). Intrauterine sound levels of the mother's voice were enhanced by about 5 dB, while other voices were somewhat attenuated. Consistent with earlier findings, the higher frequencies in these voices were attenuated much more than the lower fundamental frequency. Thus the pitch and intonation of the voice, which are associated with the fundamental frequency, are potentially audible to the fetus. However, the acoustic information identifying many consonants and vowels, which is conveyed by frequencies higher than 1000 Hz, is relatively less intense within the uterus. Because speech intonation patterns are characteristic of particular languages and are also informative about the identity and emotional state of the speaker, prenatal auditory experience potentially gives the fetus access to linguistic and affective dimensions of human vocalizations.

Summary

Acoustic stimuli consisting of pressure variations in the air come from many sources and from all directions, converging simultaneously in the outer ear. Following an elaborate path through the middle and inner ear, this complex pattern of vibrations is translated into electrical energy in the auditory pathways of the brain. The anatomical structures and physiological processes essential for hearing begin to function in a rudimentary way during the prenatal period. By the sixth month of gestation, the fetus responds to loud sounds from the extrauterine environment, and by the ninth month discriminates among sounds differing in frequency. (See also chapter 18 for an account of auditory development *in utero*.) Because frequencies in the range of speech intonation are transmitted to the intrauterine environment, evidence for fetal sensitivity to sound has implications for understanding the role of prenatal exposure to human voices in early social and linguistic development.

Methods for Assessing Auditory Function in Infants

A review of research on auditory development in the 1954 edition of Carmichael's *Manual of Child Psychology* concluded that "there is no indubitable evidence that infants possess either differential responses to varying frequencies of vibration or the possibility of acquiring them during the neonatal period" (Pratt, 1954, p. 235). The contrast between this earlier view of the infant and the musically minded fetus described in recent research (Lecanuet et al., 2000) reflects a dramatic change. If the sensitivity of infants hasn't changed in the intervening years, the sensitivity of scientific methods used to study them certainly has. Studying audition in infants presents challenges not encountered when testing adults. Adults can follow instructions in experimental tasks, use language to convey their judgments, and remain attentive and motivated to give their best performance. Infants, in contrast, can neither follow verbal instructions nor give a verbal response, and they fluctuate widely in attention and motivation. Working within these limitations, developmental researchers have devised several effective methods for eliciting consistent responses from infants which can be used to make plausible inferences about infants' inner states. The most widely used methods are based on four general classes of response measures which give insight into some aspects of early auditory function: (1) spontaneous motor and psychophysiological responses; (2) electrophysiological responses; (3) operantly conditioned behavioral responses; and (4) eye movement responses.

Spontaneous Motor and Psychophysiological Responses

Although seeing requires moving the eyes toward a visual stimulus, there is no particular motor behavior essential for hearing. However, infants as well as adults tend to move spontaneously when hearing loud and unexpected sounds, which elicit blinks and startles even in the fetus (Birnholz & Benacerraf, 1983). Because such reactions are elicited by high-intensity sounds, this type of measure is not effective in detecting infants' sensitivity to softer sounds closer to the threshold of hearing. Thus gross motor responses have been used to determine whether the auditory system is functional at all, but not to assess responsiveness to different frequencies. Another spontaneous motor reaction to sound is the tendency to orient in the direction of an interesting sound. Spontaneous headturns toward suprathreshold sounds presented from the side have served as a useful measure of auditory localization abilities in newborns (e.g., Morrongiello, Fenwick, Hillier, & Chance, 1994), although without reinforcement this response can be unreliable (see Gravel, 1989). Changes in heart rate also occur naturally in response to both auditory and visual stimuli and were used extensively in studies of infant auditory function in the 1960s and 1970s (e.g., Bartoshuk, 1964; Moffitt, 1973). However, procedures using cardiac and other psychophysiological responses to sound are impractical in many ways (see Aslin et al., 1983) and they have been superseded by more effective neuropsychological and operant conditioning methods.

Electrophysiological Responses

Measures of neural responses to acoustic stimuli are now used widely with infants both in clinical tests of auditory function and in basic research on early perception of speech (e.g., Dehaene-Lambertz & Dehaene, 1994; Mills, Coffey-Corina, & Neville, 1997). Evoked response potentials (ERP) are obtained by attaching gross electrodes to the scalp or using a multichannel geodesic electrode net worn as a cap by the infant. Electrical activity across various regions of the brain is recorded in response to repeated time-locked stimuli. The resulting waveform, which represents an average across multiple stimulus repetitions, has several characteristic negative and positive peaks in amplitude which occur within 300 msec of stimulus onset. In infants as well as adults, the pattern and magnitude of these peaks are systematically related to particular aspects of the auditory signal, and reflect neural activity in particular loci in the auditory pathways. With development, the complexity of the waveform increases, new components occur, and ERP latencies become progressively shorter (see Thomas & Crow, 1994). These changes are thought to result from maturation of the auditory system at several levels, including increased efficiency in neural conductivity due to myelination in the brainstem and auditory nerve, and an increase in synaptic density in the auditory cortex.

The very early components in the first 10 msec of the ERP waveform are correlated with neural activity in subcortical regions of the auditory system (Hecox & Galambos, 1974). This short latency waveform, known as the auditory brainstem response (ABR), is now used extensively in screening newborns for hearing deficits (e.g., Sininger et al., 2000). Another ERP component which is proving to be extremely valuable in recent research on auditory development is the mismatched negativity (MMN) response. The MMN is elicited by any discriminable change in some repetitive aspect of auditory stimulation. That is, the MMN cannot be elicited by a single sound on its own or by repetitions of identical sounds, but only by an acoustically "deviant" stimulus which occurs in a sequence of homogeneous repeated "standard" stimuli. For example, within a stream of standard tones all at the same frequency, a tone of a different frequency presented occasionally would constitute the deviant stimulus. If the listener detects the difference between the deviant and standard tones, the MMN component will be evident in the ERP recording. Because the MMN is elicited by a stimulus change, it is considered to be the outcome of a comparison process involving memory traces in the auditory cortex, and may also reflect frontal lobe activity associated with shifts in attention to novel sounds (Cheour, Leppanen, & Kraus, 2000). Over the past decade, this method has been used to study an impressive range of questions related to auditory perception in infants, children, and adults (see Naatanen & Escera, 2000). The MMN response has great potential for furthering understanding of how young infants process complex auditory stimuli because it provides a reliable measure of central auditory processing which is unaffected by fluctuations in infant attention.

Conditioned Behavioral Responses

The most diverse and widely used class of procedures for investigating early auditory perception consists of methods in which infants are presented with sounds from two categories which differ in some interesting way, and then are rewarded for a learned behavior associated with attention to the sounds. The three major subgroups of methods involving operant conditioning are habituation procedures, auditory preference procedures, and visually reinforced headturn procedures.

Habituation procedures are used to test infants' ability to discriminate between sounds from two categories. In a typical habituation experiment, sound presentation is made contingent upon a particular behavior; e.g., auditory stimuli are played only when the infant sucks at high intensity or looks continuously at a visual target. As long as the infant continues to perform the behavior, stimuli from category A are repeatedly presented. Habituation occurs as the infant eventually tires of hearing sounds from category A and performs the required behavior less frequently. When the rate of sucking or looking drops below a criterion level, the stimulus is switched to a sound from category B. If the infant detects the change from A to B, the expectation is that the rate of sucking or looking will increase because the infant is motivated to hear the new sound. If the infant cannot discriminate A from B, dishabituation should not occur and the low rate of sucking or looking remains the same. In these procedures the sound stimuli serve as conjugate reinforcers. That is, the auditory stimulus itself becomes the reward when a spontaneous behavior such as sucking or looking (which is naturally associated with heightened attention) is brought under stimulus control by making sound presentation contingent on the behavior. The habituation procedures which have been most widely used in studies of infant speech perception are the high-amplitude-sucking (HAS) procedure (see Jusczyk, 1985) and variations of the visual fixation procedure originally developed by Boyd (1975).

In auditory preference procedures, the presentation of sounds from two categories is also contingent on a learned behavior such as sustained looking at a central or lateral target near the speaker from which the sound is played (see Kemler Nelson et al., 1995; Pinto, Fernald, McRoberts, & Cole, 1998). And as in habituation procedures, the sound stimuli serve as conjugate reinforcers. When the infant looks away from the target, the sound is stopped. However, in habituation studies there is typically only one switch from category A to category B, while in preference studies sounds from both categories are repeatedly interspersed over 15 to 30 trials. Habituation to both A and B sounds occurs over the course of the experiment but is not a factor influencing the outcome. Looking/ listening times are averaged for each trial type, and the mean looking/listening times for category A and B sounds are compared across subjects. In a variant of this procedure, infants are familiarized with sounds from one category before testing, to determine whether familiarization influences the subsequent listening preference (Jusczyk & Aslin, 1995). In some cases infants listen longer to familiar stimuli and in other cases prefer novel stimuli, depending on several factors such as age and length of exposure to sounds from each category. Preferential listening procedures provide a powerful and flexible method for exploring the early perception of linguistic structure in speech (see Jusczyk, 1997), as well as perception of music (Krumhansl & Jusczyk, 1990) and vocal affect (see Fernald, 1993), and have been used effectively with infants ranging in age from the newborn period to the end of the second year.

The third class of operant technique used to study auditory development are visually reinforced conditioned headturn procedures, in which infants learn to make headturns in response to sound and are rewarded for correct performance by an external reinforcer such as a moving toy display (Moore & Wilson, 1978). In one version referred to as visual reinforcement audiometry (VRA), infants learn to turn their head toward the reinforcer when they hear an acoustic stimulus over headphones. The initial training stimuli might be suprathreshold pure tones easily detected by a child with normal hearing. Then during testing, stimuli are gradually decreased in intensity until they are imperceptible, at which point the child is no longer able to make headturns at the appropriate time. The VRA method has become an invaluable clinical tool for measuring auditory thresholds in infants as young as 5 months of age. A variant of this procedure known as the observer- based psychoacoustic procedure (OPP; Olsho, Koch, Halpin, & Carter, 1987) can be used with younger infants too immature to learn to make conditioned headturns reliably. In studies using OPP, the infant hears a signal over headphones on some trials and not on others. The observer, who is blind to stimulus type, watches the infant's behavior and judges whether a signal or no-signal trial has occurred. The only information available to the observer is the initially spontaneous reaction of the infant to the sound stimulus, which sometimes includes a headturn but more often consists of occasional eye widen- ing and behavioral inhibition. Whenever the observer correctly identifies a signal trial based on these subtle changes in the infant's behavior, the infant is reinforced by activa- tion of the toy; thus the infant is rewarded for responding behaviorally in some fashion when hearing a sound. Although many infants cannot be trained to respond differentially in this way, the OPP has been used to gather data on auditory thresholds in infants as young as 3 months (e.g., Olsho, Koch, Carter, Halpin, & Spetner, 1988). A third version of the conditioned headturn technique (CHT) is used in research on speech perception (see Kuhl, 1985). The infant listens to a train of background stimuli such as the vowel /a/ repeated over and over. When the background vowel /a/ switches to a different vowel such as /i/, the infant is trained to make a headturn toward the reinforcer, which is activated as a reward. Thus the child's ability to discriminate /a/ from /i/ is revealed through a pattern of correct headturns. As in the VRA and OPP versions of this procedure, "catch trials" are also included to control for random headturns and false alarms. Unlike habituation and preference procedures, which only yield group comparisons about average responses to sounds in different categories, these conditioning techniques can provide detailed data about each individual subject and thus are used extensively in clinical applications.

Eye Movement Responses

When infants in the second year begin to understand word meanings, they will look quickly at an object as they hear it named with a familiar word. This rapid and reliable response to spoken words is used increasingly in studies of early comprehension. In the auditory-visual matching procedure originally developed by Golinkoff, Hirsh-Pasek, Cauley, & Gordon (1987), infants look at pairs of colorful pictures of objects while listening to speech naming one of the objects. The question of interest is whether infants look longer at the target picture after it has been named than at the equally interesting distracter picture which is not named (see Hollich, Hirsh-Pasek, & Golinkoff, 2000). Recent modifications of this procedure use frame-by-frame analyses of the infant's eye movements in response to the target word, yielding a precise record of the time course of spoken word recognition (see Swingley, Pinto, & Fernald, 1998). Such analyses provide detailed temporal information about age-related changes in the speed and accuracy of infants' response to familiar words (e.g., Fernald, Pinto, Swingley, Weinberg, & McRoberts, 1998).

Summary

Measuring auditory responsiveness in infants is methodologically challenging for many reasons. Over the past 30 years, developmental researchers have devised several effective methods for testing infant hearing, procedures which rely either on involuntary physiological and neuropsychological responses to sound, or on conditioning techniques which motivate the infant to respond to sound with an observable behavior. Some of the new methods described here have only recently become possible through technological developments, especially those measuring infants' brain activity during auditory processing. Others have resulted from intuitions about the minds of infants which were radical at the time but now seem completely obvious, such as the fact that infants will repeat a behavior over and over in order to hear a sound. These techniques have been used extensively in basic research investigating the emergence of auditory capabilities, as well as in clinical research evaluating auditory function in individual infants.

Hearing in Infancy

The Early Development of Basic Auditory Capacities

The mature auditory system is extraordinarily sensitive, able to detect pressure changes so small that they cause the eardrum to move less than the diameter of a hydrogen atom. In the most sensitive range of hearing, air pressure at the sensory threshold is only 10–15 dB above the air pressure variation caused by the random movements of air molecules (Goldstein, 1999). However, the threshold for detecting a sound depends both on its frequency and its intensity. For example, a pure tone at 200 Hz must have an intensity around 20 dB SPL to be audible to a young adult with normal hearing, although a 100 Hz tone presented at the same sound pressure level cannot be heard. Because adults are less sensitive at 100 Hz than at 200 Hz, more stimulus intensity is required to detect the lower-frequency tone. Sensitivity is greatest to frequencies between 2000 and 4000 Hz, with higher thresholds for frequencies below and above this range. Most of the important acoustic stimuli in the infant's natural environment are complex sounds made up of many different frequencies at different intensities which are changing continually. However, partly in order to maximize experimental control, responses to simpler sounds are used to characterize basic dimensions of auditory sensitivity such as absolute thresholds and discrimination of sounds differing in frequency, intensity, and duration.

The thresholds at which infants detect simple sounds such as pure tones have been measured using ABR (e.g., Hecox, 1975), VRA (e.g., Sinnott, Pisoni, & Aslin, 1983), and OPP procedures (e.g., Olsho et al., 1988). Although estimates of absolute thresholds vary somewhat across studies due to methodological differences (see Aslin, 2001), three general conclusions can be drawn from this research: First, the audibility curves for infants and adults are more or less parallel, as shown in Figure 2.3. Like adults, infants are also relatively more sensitive to frequencies between 2000 and 4000 Hz, a range which includes acoustic information especially important for identifying speech sounds. Second, sound thresholds for young infants are higher than those for adults at all frequencies. Results from the OPP study by Olsho et al. (1988) show that thresholds in 3-month-old infants are 15–30 dB higher than in adults, although by 6 months the difference is only 10–20 dB. Third, absolute thresholds continue to improve during the first two years. However, the extent and rate of improvement over this period is still unclear. For reasons mentioned earlier, it cannot be assumed that any measure of infant auditory sensitivity reflects optimal performance, given the many differences involved in conducting hearing tests with infants and adults. Thus it is difficult to determine the extent to which developmental differences in audibility curves are related to the maturation of peripheral or central auditory functions, and to what extent they may also reflect attentional and motivational factors limiting performance during testing.

Sounds in the environment often occur simultaneously, and one acoustic stimulus can interfere with the perception of another. When sounds close to threshold are presented in background noise, auditory sensitivity may be reduced through masking, in which case

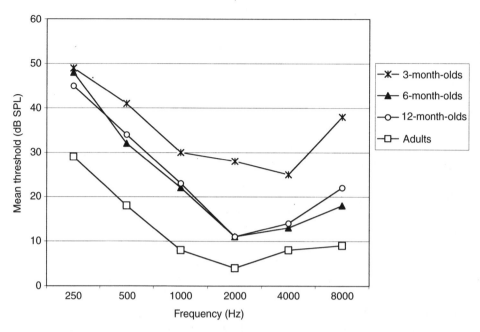

Figure 2.3 Mean thresholds for detecting pure-tone stimuli at different frequencies for 3-, 6-, and 12-month-old infants and for adults (adapted from Olsho et al., 1988).

the intensity of the signal has to be increased by a certain amount in order to make the signal audible. Because the particular frequency components and bandwidth of the noise affect the listener's ability to detect the signal, masking studies with infants provide another source of information about sensitivity to different frequencies in the developing auditory system. If infants are more adversely affected by masking than adults, this might indicate that infants are less able to resolve individual frequency components in a complex auditory stimulus. Several studies have investigated the increase in infant thresholds when sounds are presented in masking noise (e.g., Abdala & Folsom, 1995; Nozza & Wilson, 1984). In this situation infants show elevated thresholds as compared to adults. However, the level of signal intensity required by infants to hear the signal in noise is proportional to their higher absolute thresholds. In other words, although infants are less sensitive than adults overall, both infants and adults can detect a signal embedded in noise if it is intensified by the same relative amount. These findings suggest that the same mechanisms underlie masking in infants and adults when masker and signal occur simultaneously in time, and also that frequency resolution approaches adult levels by 6 months of age. In acoustical events such as speech and music, masking can also occur when one sound follows another. Sequential masking effects have not yet been studied extensively in infants, but a recent study by Werner (1999) suggests that forward masking, which occurs when the masker precedes the signal, also approaches adult levels by 6 months of age.

Being able to detect small changes in frequency, intensity, and duration is another important aspect of auditory processing. Although these abilities are typically studied using simple stimuli in which a single acoustic component is varied, in the natural environment they are crucial for analyzing and interpreting complex sounds in which such changes continually occur. For example, sensitivity to shifts in frequency, intensity, and temporal structure from one syllable to the next is essential for discriminating English words with different stress patterns. By 6 months of age, infants can detect an increment or decrement in frequency of about 2 percent, an improvement over the 3 percent threshold at 3 months but still higher than adult thresholds of 1 percent (Olsho, Koch, & Halpin, 1987). The ability to detect changes in intensity also improves over the first year, with a threshold shift from 6 dB to 4 dB between 6 and 12 months (Schneider, Bull, & Trehub, 1988; Sinnott & Aslin, 1985). Intensity discrimination continues to improve beyond infancy and in the preschool years is still approaching the adult threshold of 1 dB (Jensen & Neff, 1993).

Another aspect of basic auditory processing which is crucial for the perception of complex sounds is the ability to distinguish among acoustic stimuli which are brief and rapidly changing. For example, discriminating the syllables /ba/ and /pa/ requires detecting a very brief initial timing difference, while discriminating /ba/ and /da/ requires detecting rapid initial frequency changes; in both cases the critical acoustic differences are in the range of tens of milliseconds. Temporal resolution in infants has been studied using sequences of stimuli in which either the duration of the sounds or the duration of the silent gap between sounds is varied. In both duration discrimination and gap detection tasks, thresholds at 6 months are only about twice as long as adult thresholds (e.g., Trehub, Schneider, & Henderson, 1995; Werner, Marean, Halpin, Spetner, & Gillenwater, 1992), with continued improvement through early childhood. At 6 months, the ability to discriminate rising and falling tones from continuous tones is also good, although thresholds are higher for very rapid frequency sweeps (Aslin, 1989). It is increasingly clear that these findings are relevant to the development of speech processing. Tallal and colleagues have found that an inability to process rapidly changing acoustic stimuli underlies certain language-learning impairments (see Tallal, Miller, & Fitch, 1993), and several recent studies show that this temporal processing deficit can be ameliorated by training. When language-learning impaired children practiced discriminating rapidly sequenced acoustic stimuli for several weeks, and listened to temporally modified speech in which the rates of change in the consonants were synthetically extended, their performance on speech discrimination and language comprehension tasks improved significantly (Merzenich et al., 1996; Tallal et al., 1996).

Sound Localization by Infants

The ability to identify accurately where a sound is coming from is another dimension of basic auditory competence. Spatial localization in the horizontal plane using auditory information involves a binaural comparison of sound waves emanating from the same source. Because the ears are located symmetrically on opposite sides of the head, a sound coming from the midline reaches both ears at the same time; however, a sound coming from one side arrives slightly sooner at the ipsilateral ear than at the contralateral ear. Such interaural differences in the arrival time of a signal are systematically related both to the direction of the sound source and to the size of the head. For a human adult with an average head size, the interaural timing difference is approximately 700 microsec for a sound coming from a source located 90 degrees to one side. The corresponding interaural time difference for an infant would be less because the head size is smaller. A standard measure of the degree of precision in localizing a sound source is the minimal audible angle (MAA), which is the smallest shift in sound location a listener can reliably detect. The MAA for adults is 1–2 degrees, which requires sensitivity to interaural timing differences as brief as 10–20 microsec (see Yost & Gourevitch, 1987).

Early observers of auditory development reported that infants are unable to orient reliably to sound until 3–4 months of age (Chrisman, 1892). However, when tested in procedures which accommodate their motoric and cognitive limitations, newborns readily turn their heads toward off-center sounds (e.g., Muir & Field, 1979). The tendency to make directional headturns, which is evident at birth, then declines over several weeks before emerging again around the age of 4 months. Although neonates turn correctly to the side of the sound source, they show only limited ability to localize sounds precisely within the left and right hemifields (Morrongiello et al., 1994). By 4 months of age, infants can discriminate a change of about 22 degrees in the location of a sound source, and the MAA decreases steadily to around 9 degrees by 11 months. Thus there is substantial improvement in the spatial resolution of the auditory system over the first year of life.

What developmental factors could account for the temporary decline in orientation responses after the newborn period, followed by rapid improvement in the accuracy of sound localization? One general hypothesis is that the U-shaped function in infants' tendency to turn toward sound stimuli reflects cortical maturation over the first few months of life (Muir, Clifton, & Clarkson, 1989). According to this explanation, the crude orientation responses of newborns to sound do not exploit timing information and are mediated by subcortical brain structures functional at birth. In contrast, accurate localization of sounds relies on the processing of interaural timing differences, a cortically mediated ability which develops more slowly. A more specific and more readily testable hypothesis is that infants' competence in sound localization is constrained by limitations in the resolution of interaural timing differences. Infants may only gradually develop the sensitivity of adults, whose ability to localize off-center sounds in the horizontal plane requires resolution of timing differences ranging from 10 to 700 microsec. However, research by Ashmead, Davis, Whalen, and Odom (1991) shows that interaural time discrimination is not the limiting factor in the development of sound localization. When infants from 4 to 7 months were tested in a timing discrimination task that did not involve sound localization, their thresholds were in the range of 50 to 75 microsec with no apparent age differences. Although infants are less sensitive than adults, these thresholds are still much better than would be predicted from the measurements of infants' MAA at these ages in a sound localization task. In other words, the ability to discriminate a 75 microsec interaural timing difference could in principle enable infants to localize sounds much more precisely than they actually do. Ashmead et al. point out that sound localization depends not only on interaural time differences but also on intensity differences and other auditory cues. Moreover, accurate localization of sound sources requires the precise calibration of directional correlates to specific cue values, which change as the head grows larger.

Thus early development in the accuracy of sound localization reflects increasing integration across multiple auditory cues, as well as continual recalibration of the mapping between directional correlates and interaural timing differences which change rapidly over the first year of life.

Hearing Impairment in Infancy

These research findings on infants' responsiveness to different spectral and temporal properties of acoustic stimuli, and on their use of auditory cues to localize sound sources, show that the early development of hearing involves much more than changes in infants' ability to detect sound. However, the ability to detect sound cannot be taken for granted, and a brief discussion of the causes and consequences of hearing impairment in infancy is relevant here (see also chapter 22 on sensory deficits). Given the elaborate pathway from airborne vibrations in the outer ear to neural activation in the auditory cortex, the experience of hearing can be disrupted by problems at any stage of the process. Causes of hearing impairment are grouped in three general categories, related to the level of the auditory system affected. First, conductive hearing losses result from problems in the outer or middle ear which interfere with the transmission of sound vibrations to the receptors in the inner ear. For example, if there is blockage in the ear canal, an injury to the eardrum or the ossicles, or infection in the middle ear, acoustic signals will not be conducted properly and amplified sufficiently to reach the cochlea. Second, sensorineural hearing losses result from damage to the hair cells in the inner ear. When the auditory receptors in the cochlea are impaired, they fail to generate the electrical signals necessary to stimulate the auditory nerve. Third, central hearing losses result from problems in neural transmission in the brainstem or auditory cortex.

Deafness is among the most common disabilities present at birth; approximately one of every 1000 infants is born with severe hearing impairment. Many more are born with less severe hearing loss, and others develop hearing impairment during infancy or early childhood. Because reduced auditory sensitivity in the early years of life can interfere with normal development in many domains, it is important that the condition be identified as soon as possible. However, the average age at which hearing impairment is identified in US children is 3 years, by which time the child who is not learning a sign language has already been substantially deprived of linguistic, cognitive, and social stimulation during a crucial period of development. Early identification enables intervention which can take advantage of the plasticity of the developing brain and enhance the child's ability to adapt to life either in the hearing or the deaf community.

In 1993, the National Institutes of Health (NIH) issued a consensus report addressing critical questions related to the early identification of hearing impairment in infants and young children. This report considered the costs and benefits of screening, the issue of which infants should be tested and when, and the relative advantages of current screening methods (NIH, 1993). Over the past 30 years, numerous techniques have been explored for screening infant hearing at birth, with auditory brainstem response (ABR) audiometry emerging as the method of choice. However, a new method based on the measurement of evoked otoacoustic emissions (OAE) has recently proved to be reliable, as well as faster, less expensive, and easier to use. Otoacoustic emissions are sounds produced in response to acoustic stimulation in individuals with functional auditory systems, as a by-product of the activity of the outer hair cells in the cochlea. OAEs are measured by presenting a series of clicks to the ear thorough a probe inserted in the ear canal. The probe contains a loudspeaker to generate the clicks as well as a microphone to measure the resulting OAEs, which are produced in the cochlea and then reflected back through the middle ear into the outer ear canal. Because OAEs are not evoked if there is damage to the hair cells, this assessment method provides information about cochlear activity but not about brainstem activity. The NIH report recommended a two-stage screening process, in which all infants (not just those in a high-risk category) are routinely assessed for auditory function at birth using OAE audiometry, with further ABR screening for those who fail the OAE test.

To investigate the correlation among these neonatal measures and their predictive validity in relation to behavioral measures of hearing ability later in infancy, a longitudinal study was conducted in which almost 5000 infants were assessed with both OAE and ABR in the newborn period, and were then tested again using visually reinforced audiometry (VRA) between 8 and 12 months (see Norton et al., 2000). The results of this complex study document the advantages of both OAE and ABR as early assessment methods and reinforce the importance of universal screening of newborns for hearing impairment. Research on long-term developmental outcomes in relation to age of diagnosis shows that children whose hearing losses are identified by 6 months of age make significantly greater progress in language acquisition than children with equivalent degrees of hearing loss identified after 6 months of age (Yoshinaga-Itano, Secdey, Coulter, & Mehl, 1998).

Children born with normal auditory function may develop severe and permanent hearing loss later in infancy or early childhood following diseases such as meningitis and cytomegalovirus infection. Much more common are the temporary periods of mild hearing impairment associated with middle ear infections which cause the eustachian tubes to fill with fluid, a condition known as otitis media. Typically, 75 percent of children experience at least one episode of otitis media by their third birthday, and almost half have multiple episodes in the first three years. Following a bout of otitis media with effusion (OME), fluid may remain trapped in the middle ear for a period of several months, interfering to some degree with the transmission of sound to the cochlea. Gravel and Wallace (2000) found that children who had repeatedly experienced bilateral OME during their first three years had significantly poorer hearing than children with no history of OME. The difference was not extreme, however, with average thresholds for the OME children elevated by 5–10 dB relative to the control group. Because of clinical concern that recurrent hearing loss, however mild, could interfere with the normal development of auditory function and language development, numerous studies have investigated the short- and long-term effects of OME (see Roberts, Wallace, & Henderson, 1997). Short-term effects in infancy include poorer performance in localizing sounds (Morrongiello, 1989) and discriminating consonants (Clarkson, Eimas, & Cameron-Marean, 1989). However, it has been a matter of debate whether these negative effects of OME have a long-term cumulative impact on the development of language and communication skills. Some researchers have claimed that children experiencing prolonged periods of OME

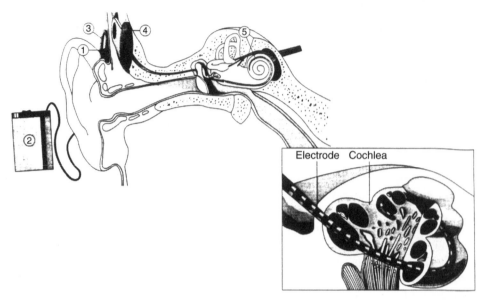

Figure 2.4   Cochlear implant device consisting of: (1) microphone; (2) speech processor; (3) transmitter; (4) receiver; (5) electrodes implanted inside the cochlea (adapted from Goldstein, 1999).

have lower scores on standardized language tests at age 3 (e.g., Teele, Klein, & Rosner, 1984), although more recent studies which control for other relevant environmental factors have found only weak and inconsistent long-term effects (e.g., Paradise et al., 2000; Roberts et al., 2000).

Although mild and intermittent hearing impairment may have minimal negative effects on language development, children born severely deaf or who become deaf before the age of 3 fall significantly behind their normal-hearing peers in mastering a spoken language (e.g., Levitt, McGarr, & Geffner, 1987; Moeller, Osberger, & Eccarius, 1986). The question of how children with severe hearing impairment should be raised and educated arouses deep philosophical differences between those who believe deaf children should attempt to learn a spoken language and be integrated into a hearing society, and those who believe they should learn a signed language and be integrated into a Deaf community (where use of a capital letter refers to the Deaf World culture rather than to hearing impairment – see Lane, 1992). With the recent development of cochlear implants for infants and children, this debate has become more intense. While hearing aids function by amplifying sound, cochlear implants are designed to bypass the hair cells, compensating for inner ear damage by directly stimulating the auditory nerve to produce a perception of hearing. The device has five basic components (see Figure 2.4): The microphone (1) worn behind the ear receives speech sounds, sending them as electrical signals to the speech processor (2), which shapes the signals to emphasize acoustic information necessary for perception of speech. These signals, now split into frequency bands, are sent from the processor to the transmitter (3) behind the ear, which transmits the coded signals through the skin to the receiver (4). The receiver, surgically mounted on the mastoid bone beneath the skin, converts the code into signals which are sent to electrodes (5) implanted inside the cochlea.

Although hearing through an implant is a very different experience from normal hearing, this technology has been effective in enabling recovery of speech perception by individuals who become deaf through disease or injury in adulthood and who can use information from the implant in conjunction with their knowledge of spoken language. However, it has been a controversial question whether cochlear implants are an effective intervention with children who become deaf prelingually. Several studies demonstrate that performance of profoundly deaf children on various speech recognition tasks is better for those who received an implant before the age of 5 than for those implanted at a later age (e.g., Fryauf-Bertschy, Tyler, Kelsay, Gantz, & Woodworth, 1997; Waltzman & Cohen, 1998). However, opponents argue that implanting a prelingually deafened child prevents the child from becoming integrated into the Deaf culture, without providing enough hearing to enable the child to function successfully in hearing society. Advocates of pediatric intervention argue that the technology of cochlear implants is rapidly improving and that profoundly deaf children who receive implants early in life are able to learn a spoken language more effectively than deaf children without implants. A recent study by Svirsky et al. (2000) concluded that the mean rate of oral language development in deaf children after implantation was close to that of children with normal hearing. These findings do not address the ethical concerns of those who argue for teaching signed languages and integrating children with profound hearing loss into the Deaf culture, but they do suggest that cochlear implants are becoming more effective as a means of restoring some forms of auditory function to congenitally deaf children.

Summary

In normal-hearing infants, absolute thresholds as well as sensitivity to fundamental properties of sound such as frequency, intensity, and temporal structure are close to adult thresholds by the age of 6 months. The ability to localize sound sources also improves substantially over the first year. Because the technology for assessing auditory function in newborns is now reliable, practical, and cost-effective, universal screening is recommended to identify potential hearing impairment at birth. For children who become deaf prelingually, cochlear implants provide an increasingly effective intervention for restoring some access to auditory stimuli. However, there is continued scientific and philosophical debate about the developmental consequences of early implantation and the advantages and disadvantages for profoundly deaf children of learning first a signed or an oral language.

Listening and Understanding in Infancy

Infants' competencies in hearing and discriminating distinct dimensions of acoustic stimuli and localizing sources of sound are put to use in the service of listening. In distinguishing listening from hearing, the intent is to emphasize that listening is a dynamic process in several respects. First, listening involves comparing and integrating multiple sources of auditory information simultaneously to identify, monitor, and gain knowledge about events in the world. Second, listening involves hearing in a particular context, where many different kinds of factors influence how auditory information is perceived and interpreted. Such factors range, for example, from the immediate emotional state of the listener to the widespread cultural norms for vocal expression which can also influence perception, and include both short-term experience in a particular social and linguistic context as well as long-term experience hearing and speaking a particular language. Listening is also dynamic in the sense that enduring strategies for organizing and interpreting auditory information emerge through learning guided by inborn perceptual biases.

Listening to Voices

The sound of a human voice reveals many kinds of information. After hearing a voice for only a few seconds, listeners make immediate and automatic judgments about whether the speaker is familiar or unfamiliar, female or male, old or young. Listening briefly to a voice may also trigger irresistible impressions that the speaker is angry or joyful, tired or energetic, healthy or ill. Even when the linguistic message cannot be understood, listening to the voice leads to rapid appraisal of numerous characteristics of the speaker which are socially relevant. When adults make judgments about identity, gender, age, and emotional state based on voice quality and prosody, their attributions are influenced by long experience in associating acoustic features of vocalizations with information from other sources of knowledge. However, research with infants shows that even listeners with minimal experience encode characteristics of vocal signals along multiple dimensions.

In a classic experiment, DeCasper and Fifer (1980) asked whether newborn infants show signs of recognizing their mother's voice. Infants only a few hours old were given the choice of listening to recorded samples of their own mother's voice or the voice of another woman. When tested in a conditioning procedure where they learned to adjust their sucking response in different ways to produce the different voices, newborns chose more often to listen to the recording of their own mother. These results indicated that they could discriminate a familiar from an unfamiliar voice, and also that the mother's voice was more effective as a reinforcer. Since the newborns had had almost no post-natal experience hearing the mother speak, and no opportunity to associate her voice with pleasurable experiences such as nursing or soothing, it appeared that the listening preference for the familiar voice was based on prenatal experience. This interpretation is quite plausible, given that at least the lower frequencies of the mother's voice are transmitted *in utero*, as described earlier. The father's voice, however, is less available to the fetus during the prenatal period, because he is not always present, and also because the intensity of his voice is attenuated compared to the mother's voice. In a subsequent study, DeCasper and colleagues found that newborns showed no listening preference for the father's voice.

Do these findings demonstrate that newborns can recognize the mother through her voice? Certainly not in the sense that an adult can recognize a voice on the phone and identify the speaker, nor even in the sense that a 6-month-old hearing the mother's voice shows recognition by smiling and turning in anticipation of her appearance. In both of these examples, recognition implies that the voice is part of a complex and multidimensional schema based on experience with and knowledge about the individual. For the newborn, in contrast, the mother's voice is an acoustic stimulus which is familiar in some respects but is not yet associated with any other aspects of her identity in postnatal experience. But even if this study demonstrated recognition in only a limited sense, the DeCasper and Fifer (1980) findings were exciting because they were the first to show that prenatal auditory experience could influence the listening preferences of the infant after birth. Moreover, these results indicated that the fetus had some kind of abstract memory for the constellation of features that distinguished the mother's voice from other similar voices. Because the fetus had presumably never heard the mother speak exactly the same words used in the experiment and because her voice *in utero* was strongly filtered, the recording the newborn listened to after birth was acoustically very different from anything heard previously in the womb. Nevertheless, something about the recorded voice was familiar and rewarding to listen to, suggesting that what the fetus had stored in memory were general characteristics of the mother's voice rather than an exact copy of the acoustic stimulus experienced prenatally.

The ability of the adult listener to identify multiple characteristics of the speaker in an instant is only possible by extracting features of the vocal signal along multiple dimensions at the same time, simultaneously processing acoustic information relevant to gender, age, mood, and other attributes. Although the competence of the newborn may seem limited in comparison, the fetus is also able to analyze speech along various dimensions, not only encoding auditory information which identifies the mother as an individual but also attending to acoustic patterns related to linguistic structure. For example, newborns can discriminate between two verses spoken in the same voice, one a verse read aloud by the mother several times toward the end of pregnancy and the other a similar verse never heard before by the fetus (DeCasper & Spence, 1986). Given this choice, newborns preferred to listen to the passage which they had heard while *in utero*. Since the mother was the speaker in both cases, the two verses could not be distinguished on the basis of acoustic characteristics unique to her voice, but only on the basis of rhythmic and other prosodic differences peculiar to each. Newborns can also distinguish one language from another, preferring to listen to the language they have been hearing prenatally (Mehler et al., 1988; Moon, Cooper, & Fifer, 1993). Although there is no evidence that such early listening preferences have lasting consequences, these findings reveal that infants pay attention to voices even before birth, and that as newborns they are already capable of extracting information from voices along multiple dimensions which will be socially and linguistically relevant in postnatal life.

After birth, the infant begins to experience voices as part of a life now rich in many forms of social stimulation. In many cultures and across quite different languages, the speech addressed to infants is more lively and musical than the speech typical of adult conversation. Infant-directed (ID) speech is typically higher in pitch with more exaggerated intonation contours than adult-directed (AD) speech (Fernald et al., 1989). This special speech form becomes associated with playful interaction, comforting, feeding, and many other pleasurable aspects of parent–infant interaction. In preferential listening experiments, infants show more interest in listening to ID speech than to AD speech (Cooper & Aslin, 1990; Fernald, 1985). They also respond with more positive emotion to ID speech (Fernald, 1993; Werker & McLeod, 1990). ID speech is engaging to infants for many reasons – because of its dynamic acoustic properties, because of its associations with other forms of stimulation in social interactions, and because of its effectiveness in conveying and eliciting emotion (Fernald, 1992). Moreover, although parents do not typically view interactions with the infant as language lessons, there are many features of ID speech that may help the inexperienced listener to identify linguistic units in continuous speech (Fernald, 2000).

Listening to Speech

From the very beginning infants find voices especially interesting, although it will be months before they listen for linguistic meaning in the sounds of speech. But long before they can appreciate speech as language, infants are attentive to regularities in the patterns of sound created by people talking. Even the fetus takes advantage of limited prenatal access to language, learning something about the prosodic regularities of the language spoken outside the womb through the muffled voices transmitted inside the womb (Mehler et al., 1988; Moon et al., 1993). After birth, the fine structure of speech can be heard more clearly, and already in the first months of postnatal life the infant's perception of spoken language is organized in ways that provide a foundation for eventual understanding.

One perceptual challenge facing the infant is how to partition the stream of speech into the critical units of language. To fluent language users speech sounds such as /ba/ and /pa/ seem clearly distinct, so it is difficult to appreciate how formidable this task could be. In fact, the consonants in these two syllables are acoustically very similar to each other. Moreover, they vary acoustically when they appear with different vowels or in different positions in a word and when spoken by different people. These are some of the reasons why computer scientists have found it difficult to develop reliable automatic speech recognition routines successful in identifying a /b/ as a /b/ across different speakers and different contexts. Infants, however, have no problem in this situation. Eimas et al. (1971) used the HAS procedure to show that even very young infants could distinguish /ba/ from /pa/, although they did not distinguish variations of /ba/ which were also acoustically different yet were members of the same phonetic category. Many other studies have also shown that young infants are able to discriminate phonetic units before they have much listening experience (see Jusczyk, 1997). Infants can also appreciate the fact that vowel tokens which are acoustically dissimilar may still be equivalent in terms of their phonetic identity. Using the CHT procedure, Kuhl (1979) found that 5-month-old infants readily discriminated /a/ from /i/ spoken with the same intonation by the same female speaker. However, they grouped together several different tokens of /a/ which were acoustically variable, spoken by male and female speakers using both rising and falling pitch contours. Of course, in other situations the difference between male and female voices and rising and falling intonation contours may be socially very relevant, and infants are certainly able to make these distinctions. What these findings show is that infants are capable of attending to the acoustic variability relevant to the phonetic identity of speech sounds while ignoring acoustic variability which is linguistically irrelevant.

Although infants are clearly born with perceptual abilities and biases that equip them for organizing speech sounds into linguistically relevant categories, these perceptual grouping strategies are neither unique to humans nor unique to speech sounds. Other primates organize human speech sounds categorically, and some other kinds of acoustic stimuli are perceived in a similar fashion (see Kuhl, 2000). What is presumably unique to humans is the perceptual learning that occurs over the first few months of life as a result of hearing a particular language. Adults often find it difficult or even impossible to distinguish certain speech sounds in an unfamiliar language. For example, the consonants /Ta/ and /ta/ are easily discriminated by native speakers of Hindi, but to monolingual English-speaking adults they sound like indistinguishable tokens from the English category /t/. However, 6-month-old infants raised in English-speaking families can effortlessly discriminate the Hindi contrast /Ta/-/ta/ (Werker & Tees, 1984). Research on the perception of speech sounds shows that adults have become specialists, attentive to phonetic distinctions relevant in the languages they have learned but less acute in making other distinctions; however, infants begin life with the potential to make a wide range of distinctions. When does this process of perceptual specialization begin? Werker and Tees used the CHT procedure to test English-learning infants at three ages between 6 and 12 months, to investigate whether they retained their ability to discriminate non-native speech contrasts across the first year. Infants at each age listened either to the Hindi consonants /Ta/-/ta/ or to consonants from the Nthlakampz language, /k'i/-/q'i/, which are also very difficult for English-speaking adults to discriminate. Almost all of the infants at 6–8 months could discriminate both non-English contrasts, although very few of the infants at 10–12 months were able to distinguish either pair (see Figure 2.5).

Further evidence for the influence of the ambient language on infants' emerging phonetic categories comes from research by Kuhl et al. (1992), who showed that 6-month-old infants hearing only Swedish or English already grouped vowels perceptually in categories appropriate to the language they were learning. Recent studies measuring brain activity in response to speech are generally consistent with the behavioral findings showing increasing specialization for familiar speech sounds over the first year. At 6 months of age, infants show a mismatched negativity (MMN) response to changes in both native and non-native speech contrasts, but by 12 months the MMN response is elicited only by changes in speech sounds native to the language the child has been hearing (Cheour-Luhtanen, 1995). These results indicate that auditory experience over the first year results in neural commitment to a particular perceptual organization of speech sounds appropriate to the ambient language.

This process of specialization in speech perception over the first year of life is sometimes loosely compared to the "critical period" effects found in research on visual development in animals, in which selective rearing conditions early in life can result in permanent loss of visual sensitivity (e.g., Hubel, Wiesel, & Levay, 1977). But it is important to remember that early visual deprivation is an abnormal occurrence and that the

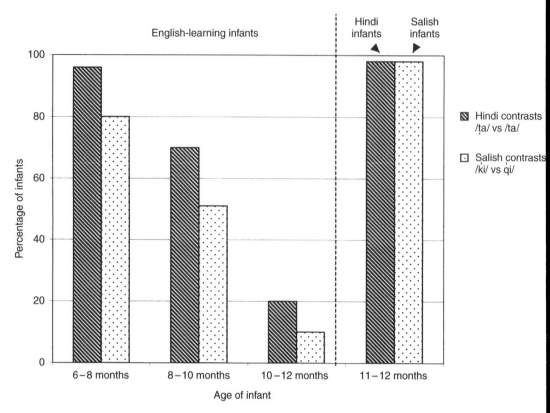

Figure 2.5   Percentage of English-learning infants at three ages reaching criterion in test of discrimination of Hindi and Nthlakampx (Salish) consonant contrasts. A small number of Hindi- and Salish-learning infants were also tested at 11–12 months as a control (adapted from Werker & Tees, 1984).

resulting sensory deficits are often irreversible. The situation is quite different in speech perception. An infant raised in a monolingual English-speaking family is indeed effectively "deprived" of the opportunity to hear speech sounds unique to Hindi, and no longer attends to Hindi speech contrasts after a year of hearing only English. However, while this acquired perceptual bias may be reflected in patterns of selective responsiveness at the cortical level, it does not indicate an irreversible neural commitment at all comparable to the negative effects of visual deprivation on cortical organization; otherwise by their first birthday infants would have lost the ability to distinguish speech sounds in any language different from the one to which they were initially exposed. In fact, there is considerable plasticity in the perceptual and cognitive systems underlying speech processing, and a new language encountered at any age during childhood can typically be readily learned. Although recent behavioral and neuropsychological studies of early speech processing have produced intriguing results about the effects of early exposure to a particular language, there is still much to discover about the nature and limits of plasticity in the development of auditory perception and language.

Finding the Words in Spoken Language

Although perceiving individual speech sounds and recognizing their perceptual equivalence across extensive acoustic variation are essential for spoken language comprehension, many other levels of organization in language must be appreciated as well. Understanding speech also requires knowledge of rules governing phonology, morphology, syntax, and semantics, as well as acquisition of word meanings. There is still much to be learned about how children construct these multiple levels of representation in acquiring linguistic competence. However, it is increasingly clear from developmental research that infants are born with complex and sophisticated learning strategies which interact with inborn biases for processing auditory information. For example, Saffran, Aslin, and Newport (1996) found that 6-month-old infants could recognize recurrent patterns of syllables after very brief exposure to an artificial language. The infants first listened to a meaningless string of speech sounds with monotone intonation and no breaks between syllables, e.g., *ba wo ti go su ba wo su go ti. . . .* Note that in this short example, *ba* is consistently followed by *wo*, while *wo* is followed by *ti* at one point in the sequence and by *su* at another. After a few minutes of familiarization with the string of syllables, the infants were then given the choice of listening either to familiar "words" such as *bawo*, consisting of familiar syllables in a familiar order, or to novel "words" such as *bati*, consisting of familiar syllables but in an unfamiliar order. In this situation, infants listened significantly longer to the novel words, indicating that they had paid attention to the repeated co-occurrence of particular syllables in what they heard previously. These findings show that very young infants are sensitive to statistical probabilities in strings of speech sounds. When listening to musical tones rather than syllables, infants performed the same kind of distributional analysis, indicating that this information-processing strategy is used for organizing auditory stimuli in general (Saffran et al., 1999). Although this ability to recognize recurrent sound sequences is not specific to language processing, it provides the infant with a powerful resource for identifying regular patterns in speech which are related to linguistic structure.

When listening for meaning in spoken language, infants must be able to identify individual words in the stream of speech. This too is a perceptual task more challenging than it may seem. Adults face the same segmentation problem when trying to find word boundaries in a completely unfamiliar language, when at first it is quite difficult to know what groups of sounds constitute words and where words begin and end. The finding that 5-month-olds prefer to listen to their own name (Mandel, Jusczyk, & Pisoni, 1995) shows that infants at this age already know something about word forms. However, because they have often heard their name spoken on its own, not surrounded by other words, the segmentation problem is less than it would be for words embedded in continuous speech. But by the age of 8 months, infants can also recognize words embedded in the middle of sentences. Jusczyk and Aslin (1995) played recorded passages to infants containing words like *cup* or *bike* in fluent speech, then later tested them in an auditory preference procedure. Infants preferred to listen to the familiar words, indicating that they had encoded these words even in a perceptually difficult context. This ability too is shaped by the infant's experience of listening to a particular language. For example, English-learning infants are used to hearing the strong-weak stress pattern typical of English nouns (as in *father* and *mountain*) and they seem to use this stress pattern to guide their search for the boundaries of unfamiliar words (see Jusczyk, 1997).

Although infants can recognize words as recurrent sound patterns by the age of 8 months, they are not yet able to associate words with conventional meanings. By the end of the first year, the experience of hearing these familiar sound patterns evokes associations in the infant's mind and words begin to serve a referential function. Comprehending words in fluent speech requires extremely rapid auditory and cognitive processing. Adults must process up to 20 phonemes each second in order to follow a conversation (Cole, 1980), and they can identify a familiar word after hearing only a few hundred milliseconds. Although infants in the second year may speak only a few words, they begin to make rapid gains in the speed and efficiency of understanding. By measuring gaze patterns as infants looked at pictures of objects and listened to words naming one of the objects, Fernald et al. (1998) found that 15-month-olds oriented to the matching picture after the end of the spoken word. However, 24-month-olds responded 400 msec more quickly, after hearing only the first part of the word (Swingley, Pinto, & Fernald, 1999). Indeed, by the age of 18 months, infants can recognize familiar words using only partial phonetic information, turning to the matching picture when they hear only the first syllable of the word (Fernald, Swingley, & Pinto, in press). These findings show that infants are becoming quick and efficient in processing spoken language even at the earliest stages of building a lexicon.

Summary

While the auditory systems of humans and other animals share common mechanisms and work in similar ways for functions such as frequency resolution and sound localization, humans are unique in using auditory information for understanding language. Some of the most surprising and theoretically provocative findings in the field of developmental psychology in recent years have emerged from research on how infants listen to voices. Infants are born with inborn perceptual biases and with learning strategies that enable them to detect regularities in patterns of speech sounds that will eventually give them access to linguistic structure. Even *in utero*, the fetus is attentive to sound patterns that will be crucial for learning to communicate in postnatal life. The experience of hearing a language over the first year shapes the early organization of auditory experience, preparing the infant's mind for language understanding.

Conclusions

Helen Keller reportedly remarked that being deaf was more difficult for her than being blind, because although blindness isolated her from things, deafness isolated her from people (Goldstein, 1999). Hearing and vision are both important in human

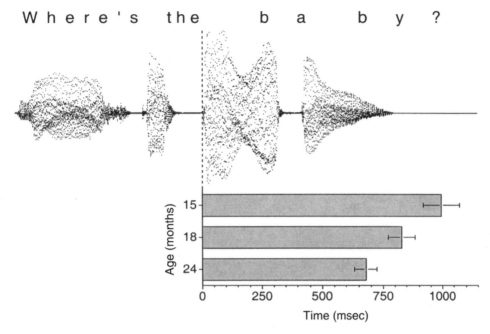

Figure 2.6 Mean reaction time to initiate a shift in gaze from the distractor picture to the target picture, measured from the beginning of the spoken target word, for 15-, 18-, and 24-month-old infants. The graph is aligned with an amplitude waveform of one of the stimulus sentences (from Fernald, Pinto, Swingley, Weinberg, & McRoberts, 1998, reprinted with permission from the American Psychological Society).

communication, but sound plays a special role because of its intrinsic association with movement. All sounds originate in movement, and the movements most crucial for us to detect, to monitor, and to interpret originate in the actions of other living beings, most notably the vocalizations of other people. For the hearing infant, the ability to detect and monitor sound is already active to some extent prenatally. After birth, the sounds of human voices move the infant emotionally and begin to convey fundamental information relevant to language. Infants are attentive to this information months before the dawning of language comprehension, learning about the rhythms and segmental structure of the sounds involved in speech. Music is another complex form of auditory stimulation associated with human movement. Although this important domain of auditory development was not covered in this brief overview, infants are also drawn to music and adept at discerning aspects of musical structure (e.g., Trehub, Schellenberg, & Hill, 1997). Like speech, music originates in human gestures produced and perceived sequentially over time.

Given the temporal structure of auditory stimulation, the ability to make sense of the complex streams of sounds in speech and music requires continuously "listening ahead," anticipating what will come next based on experience with what has come before.

Because speech consists of strings of sounds which are constantly changing, the listener must be able to process multiple phonemes every second in ordinary conversation. Yet this acoustic variability is always constrained; the sounds to be monitored in any auditory event represent small subsets of possible sounds associated with particular sources (see Bregman, 1990). The listener must also appreciate these commonalities in order to identify and follow speech by a particular speaker in a particular language, or music on a particular instrument in a particular key. In the earliest months of life, infants use innately guided listening strategies to recognize what is familiar and to appreciate what is changing in the sound sequences they hear. From the voices speaking to them and around them, they begin to discern the patterns of acoustic regularities associated with linguistic structure on many levels. By the end of the first year, as the child learns to interpret speech sounds as symbols in a language code, hearing and listening lead increasingly to understanding. A vocal gesture moves the air, which moves the eardrum of the young listener, and through these vibrations the child now has access to the meanings conveyed by language.

Further Reading

1   In *Listening: An introduction to the perception of auditory events*, Handel (1989) provides an in-depth yet accessible overview of research on human audition. Although the focus is on research with adults, this monograph provides valuable technical and theoretical background for understanding research in developmental psychoacoustics.

2   For a comprehensive review of research on infant auditory development and speech perception through 1982, see the chapter by Aslin, Pisoni, & Jusczyk (1983) in the 4th edition of the *Handbook of child psychology*. The same authors also review more recent research on infant speech perception in the 5th edition of the *Handbook of child psychology* (Aslin, Jusczyk, & Pisoni, 1998).

3   The *Handbook of developmental cognitive neuroscience* (Nelson & Luciana, 2001) includes a chapter by Aslin and Hunt on plasticity and learning in early auditory development, and a chapter by Werker and Vouloumanos on the influence of experience on infant speech processing.

4   *The discovery of spoken language* by Jusczyk (1997) provides an extensive review of research and theory in the area of infant speech perception.

5   The edited volume *Perception and cognition of music* (DeLiege & Sloboda, 1997) includes a review of the early development of music perception, an important domain of auditory competence not covered here, as well as a chapter on the sound environment *in utero*.

References

Abdala, C., & Folsom, R. (1995). Frequency contribution to the click-evoked ABR in human adults and infants. *Journal of the Acoustical Society of America, 97*, 2394–2404.

Armitage, S. E., Baldwin, B. A., & Vince, M. A. (1980). The fetal sound environment of sheep. *Science, 208*, 1173–1174.

Ashmead, D. H., Davis, D. L., Whalen, T., & Odom, R. D. (1991). Sound localization and sensitivity to interaural time differences in human infants. *Child Development, 62*, 1211–1226.

Aslin, R. N. (1989). Discrimination of frequency transition by human infants. *Journal of the Acoustical Society of America, 86*, 582–590.

Aslin, R. N., & Hunt, R. H. (2001). Development, plasticity, and learning in the auditory system. In C. A. Nelson & M. Luciana (Eds.), *Handbook of developmental cognitive neuroscience* (pp. 205–220). Cambridge, MA: MIT Press.

Aslin, R. N., Jusczyk, P. W., & Pisoni, D. B. (1998). Speech and auditory processing during infancy: Constraints on and precursors to language. In D. Kuhn & R. Siegler (Eds.), *Cognition, perception, and language* (Vol. 2, pp. 147–198). W. Damon (Ed.), *Handbook of child psychology* (5th ed.). New York: Wiley.

Aslin, R. N., Pisoni, D. B., & Jusczyk, P. W. (1983). Auditory development and speech perception in infancy. In M. M. Haith & J. J. Campos (Eds.), *Infancy and the biology of development* (Vol. 2, pp. 573–687). P. Mussen (Ed.). *Handbook of child psychology* (4th ed.). New York: Wiley.

Bartoshuk, A. K. (1964). Human neonatal cardiac responses to sound: A power function. *Psychonomic Science, 1*, 151–152.

Birnholz, J. C., & Benacerraf, B. R. (1983). The development of human fetal hearing. *Science, 222*, 516–518.

Boyd, E. F. (1975). Visual fixation and voice discrimination in 2-month-old infants. In F. D. Horowitz (Ed.), *Visual attention, auditory stimulation, and language discrimination in young infants.* Monographs of the Society for Research in Child Development (Serial No. 158, Vol. 39, No. 5–6).

Bredberg, G. (1985). The anatomy of the developing ear. In S. E. Trehub & B. Schneider (Eds.), *Auditory development in infancy* (pp. 3–20). New York: Plenum Press.

Bregman, A. S. (1990). *Auditory scene analysis: The perceptual organization of sound.* Cambridge, MA: MIT Press.

Cheour, M., Leppanen, P. H. T., & Kraus, N. (2000). Mismatch negativity (MMN) as a tool for investigating auditory discrimination and sensory memory in infants and children. *Clinical Neurophysiology, 111*, 4–16.

Cheour-Luhtanen, M., Alho, K., Kujala, T., Sainio, K., Reinikainen, M., Renlund, M., Aaltonen, O., Eerola, O., & Naatanen, R. (1995). Mismatch negativity indicates vowel discrimination in newborns. *Hearing Research, 82*, 53–58.

Cheour-Luhtanen, M., Alho, K., Sainio, K., Rinne, T., Reinikainen, K., Pohjavuori, M., Renlund, M., Aaltonen, O., Eerola, O., & Naatanen, R. (1996). The ontogenetically earliest discriminative response of the human brain. *Psychophysiology, 33*, 478–481.

Chrisman, O. (1892). The hearing of children. *Pedagogical Seminary, 2*, 397–404.

Clarkson, R. L., Eimas, P. D., & Cameron-Marean, G. (1989). Speech perception in children with histories of recurrent otitis media. *Journal of the Acoustical Society of America, 85*, 962–933.

Cole, R. A. (1980). *Perception and production of fluent speech.* Hillsdale, NJ: Erlbaum.

Cooper, R. P., & Aslin, R. N. (1990). Preferences for infant-directed speech in the first month after birth. *Child Development, 61*, 1584–1595.

DeCasper, A. J., & Fifer, W. P. (1980). Of human bonding: Newborns prefer their mothers' voices. *Science, 208*, 1174–1176.

DeCasper, A. J., & Spence, M. J. (1986). Prenatal maternal speech influences newborns' perception of speech sounds. *Infant Behavior and Development, 9*, 133–150.

Dehaene-Lambertz, G., & Dehaene, S. (1994). Speed and cerebral correlates of syllable discrimination in infants. *Nature, 370*, 292–295.

DeLiege, I., & Sloboda, J. (Eds.). (1997). *Perception and cognition of music.* Hove: Psychology Press.

Eimas, P. D., Siqueland, E. R., Jusczyk, P. W., & Vigorito, J. (1971). Speech perception in infants. *Science, 171,* 303–306.

Fernald, A. (1985). Four-month-old infants prefer to listen to motherese. *Infant Behavior and Development, 8,* 181–195.

Fernald, A. (1992). Maternal vocalisations to infants as biologically relevant signals: An evolutionary perspective. In J. H. Barkow, L. Cosmides, & J. Tooby (Eds.), *The adapted mind: Evolutionary psychology and the generation of culture* (pp. 391–428). Oxford: Oxford University Press.

Fernald, A. (1993). Approval and disapproval: Infant responsiveness to vocal affect in familiar and unfamiliar languages. *Child Development, 64,* 657–667.

Fernald, A. (2000). Speech to infants as hyperspeech. *Phonetica, 57,* 234–254.

Fernald, A., Pinto, J. P., Swingley, D., Weinberg, A., & McRoberts, G. W. (1998). Rapid gains in speed of verbal processing by infants in the second year. *Psychological Science, 9,* 72–75.

Fernald, A., Swingley, D., & Pinto, J. P. (in press). When half a word is enough: Infants can recognize spoken words using partial phonetic information. *Child Development.*

Fernald, A., Taeschner, T., Dunn, J., Papoušek, M., Boysson-Bardies, B., & Fukui, I. (1989). A cross-language study of prosodic modifications in mothers' and fathers' speech to preverbal infants. *Journal of Child Language, 16,* 477–501.

Forbes, H. S., & Forbes, H. B. (1927). Fetal sense reaction: Hearing. *Journal of Comparative Psychology, 7,* 353–355.

Fryauf-Bertschy, H., Tyler, R. S., Kelsay, D. M. R., Gantz, B. J., & Woodworth, G. G. (1997). Cochlear implant use by prelingually deafened children: The influences of age at implant and length of device. *Journal of Speech, Language, and Hearing Research, 40,* 183–199.

Goldstein, E. B. (1999). *Sensation and perception* (5th edition). Pacific Grove, CA: Brooks/Cole Publishing.

Golinkoff, R. M., Hirsh-Pasek, K., Cauley, K. M., & Gordon, L. (1987). The eyes have it: Lexical and syntactic comprehension in a new paradigm. *Journal of Child Language, 14,* 23–45.

Gopnik, A., Meltzoff, A. N., & Kuhl, P. K. (1999). *The scientist in the crib: Minds, brains, and how children learn.* New York: William Morrow & Co.

Gravel, J. S. (1989). Behavioral assessment of auditory function: Assessing auditory system integrity in high-risk infants and young children. *Seminars in Hearing, 10,* 216–227.

Gravel, J. S., & Wallace, I. F. (2000). Effects of otitis media with effusion on hearing in the first 3 years of life. *Journal of Speech, Language and Hearing Research, 43,* 631–644.

Handel, S. (1989). *Listening: An introduction to the perception of auditory events.* Cambridge, MA: MIT Press.

Hecox, K. (1975). Auditory psychophysics. In P. Salapatek & L. B. Cohen (Eds.), *Infant perception: From sensation to cognition* (Vol. 2). New York: Academic Press.

Hecox, K., & Galambos, R. (1974). Brainstem auditory evoked responses in human infants and adults. *Archives of Otolaryngology, 99,* 30–33.

Hollich, G. J., Hirsh-Pasek, K., & Golinkoff, G. M. (2000). *Breaking the language barrier: An emergentist coalition model of the origins of word learning.* Monographs of the Society for Research in Child Development (Serial No. 265, Vol. 65, No. 3).

Hubel, D. H., Wiesel, T. N., & Levay, S. (1977). Plasticity of ocular dominance columns in monkey striate cortex. *Philosophical Transactions of the Royal Society of London, B 278,* 307–409.

Jensen, J. K., & Neff, D. L. (1993). Development of basic auditory discrimination in preschool children. *Psychological Science, 4,* 104–107.

Jusczyk, P. W. (1985). The high amplitude sucking procedure as a methodological tool in speech perception research. In G. Gottlieb and N. A. Krasnegor (Eds.), *Measurement of audition and vision in the first year of postnatal life: A methodological overview* (pp. 195–222). Norwood, NJ: Ablex.

Jusczyk, P. W. (1997). *The discovery of spoken language.* Cambridge, MA: MIT Press.

Jusczyk, P. W., & Aslin, R. N. (1995). Infants' detection of the sound patterns of words in fluent speech. *Cognitive Psychology, 29,* 1–23.

Kemler Nelson, D. G., Jusczyk, P. W., Mandel, D. R., Myers, J., Turk, A., & Gerken, L. A. (1995). The headturn preference procedure for testing auditory perception. *Infant Behavior and Development, 18,* 111–116.

Kisilevsky, B. S., Muir, D. W., & Low, J. A. (1992). Maturation of human fetal responses to vibro-acoustic stimulation. *Child Development, 63,* 1497–1508.

Krumhansl, C. L., & Jusczyk, P. W. (1990). Infants' perception of phrase structure in music. *Psychological Science, 1,* 70–73.

Kuhl, P. K. (1979). Speech perception in early infancy: Perceptual constancy for spectrally dissimilar vowel categories. *Journal of the Acoustical Society of America, 66,* 1168–1179.

Kuhl, P. K. (1985). Methods in the study of infant speech perception. In G. Gottlieb and N. A. Krasnegor (Eds.), *Measurement of audition and vision in the first year of postnatal life: A methodological overview* (pp. 223–251). Norwood, NJ: Ablex.

Kuhl, P. K. (2000). A new view of language acquisition. *Proceedings of the National Academy of Science USA, 97,* 11850–11857.

Kuhl, P. K., Williams, K. A., Lacerda, F., Stevens, K. N., & Lindblom, B. (1992). Linguistic experience alters phonetic perception in infants by 6 months of age. *Science, 255,* 606–608.

Lane, H. L. (1992). *The mask of benevolence: Disabling the deaf community.* New York: Knopf.

Lecanuet, J. P., Graniere-Deferre, C., Jacquet, A. Y., & DeCasper, A. J. (2000). Fetal discrimination of low-pitched musical notes. *Developmental Psychobiology, 36,* 29–39.

Levitt, H., McGarr, N., & Geffner, D. (1987). Development of language and communication skills in hearing impaired children: Introduction. *ASHA Monographs, 26,* 1–8.

Mandel, D. R., Jusczyk, P. W., & Pisoni, D. B. (1995). Infants' recognition of the sound patterns of their own names. *Psychological Science, 6,* 315–318.

Mehler, J., Jusczyk, P. W., Lambertz, G., Halsted, N., Bertoncini, J., & Amiel-Tison, C. (1988). A precursor of language acquisition in young infants. *Cognition, 29,* 144–178.

Merzenich, M. M., Jenkins, W. M., Johnston, P., Schreiner, C., Miller, S., & Tallal, P. (1996). Temporal processing deficits of language-learning impaired children ameliorated by training. *Science, 271,* 77–81.

Mills, D. L., Coffey-Corina, S., & Neville, H. J. (1997). Language comprehension and cerebral specialization from 13 to 20 months. *Developmental Neuropsychology, 13,* 397–445.

Moeller, M. P., Osberger, M. J., & Eccarius, M. (1986). Language and learning skills of hearing-impaired students: Receptive language skills. *ASHA Monographs, 23,* 41–53.

Moffitt, A. R. (1973). Intensity discrimination and cardiac reaction in young infants. *Developmental Psychology, 8,* 357–359.

Moon, C., Cooper, R. P., & Fifer, W. P. (1993). Two-day-old infants prefer their native language. *Infant Behavior and Development, 16,* 495–500.

Moore, J. M., & Wilson, W. R. (1978). Visual reinforcement audiometry (VRA) with infants. In S. E. Gerber & G. T. Mencher (Eds.), *Early diagnosis of hearing loss* (pp. 72–95). New York: Grune & Stratton.

Morrongiello, B. A. (1989). Infants' monaural localization of sounds: Effects of unilateral ear infection. *Journal of the Acoustical Society of America, 86,* 597–602.

Morrongiello, B. A., Fenwick, K. D., Hillier, L., & Chance, G. (1994). Sound localization in newborn human infants. *Developmental Psychobiology, 27,* 519–538.

Muir, D. W., Clifton, R. K., & Clarkson, M. G. (1989). The development of a human auditory localization response: A U-shaped function. *Canadian Journal of Psychology, 43*, 199–216.

Muir, D. W., & Field, J. (1979). Newborn infants orient to sounds. *Child Development, 50*, 431–436.

Naatanen, R., & Escera, C. (2000). Mismatch negativity: Clinical and other applications. *Audiology and Neuro Otology, 5*, 105–110.

National Institutes of Health (NIH) (March 1–3, 1993). Early identification of hearing impairment in infants. *NIH Consensus Statement, 11*, 1–24.

Nelson, C. A., & Luciana, M. (Eds.). (2001). *Handbook of developmental cognitive neuroscience.* Cambridge, MA: MIT Press.

Newsweek. (2000, Fall/Winter). How learning begins. Special 2000 edition.

Norton, S. J., Gorga, M. P., Widen, J. E., Folsom, R. C., Sininger, Y., Cone-Wesson, B., Vohr, B. R., Mascher, K., & Fletcher, K. (2000). Identification of neonatal hearing impairment: Evaluation of transient evoked otoacoustic emission, distortion product otoacoustic emission, and auditory brain stem response test performance. *Ear and Hearing, 21*, 508–528.

Nozza, R. J., & Wilson, W. R. (1984). Masked and unmasked pure tone thresholds of infants and adults: Development of auditory frequency selectivity and sensitivity. *Journal of Speech and Hearing Research, 27*, 613–622.

Olsho, L. W., Koch, E. G., Carter, E. A., Halpin, C. F., & Spetner, N. B. (1988). Pure-tone sensitivity of human infants. *Journal of the Acoustical Society of America, 84*, 1316–1324.

Olsho, L. W., Koch, E. G., & Halpin, C. F. (1987). Level and age effects in infant frequency discrimination. *Journal of the Acoustical Society of America, 82*, 454–464.

Olsho, L. W., Koch, E. G., Halpin, C. F., & Carter, E. A. (1987). An observer-based psychoacoustic procedure for use with young infants. *Developmental Psychology, 23*, 627–640.

Paradise, J. L, Dollaghan, C. A., Campbell, T. F., Feldman, H. M., Bernard, B. S., Colborn, K., Rockette, H. E., Janosky, J. E., Pitcairn, D. L., Sabo, D. L., Kurs-Lasky, M., & Smith, C. G. (2000). Language, speech sound production, and cognition in three-year-old children in relation to otitis media in their first three years of life. *Pediatrics, 105*, 1119–1130.

Pinto, J. P., Fernald, A., McRoberts, G. W., & Cole, S. (1998). Reliability and validity in infant auditory preference procedures. In C. Rovee-Collier, L. Lipsitt, & H. Hayne (Eds.), *Advances in infancy research* (Vol. 12, pp. 278–290). London: Ablex.

Pratt, K. C. (1933). The neonate. In C. Murchison (Ed.), *A handbook of child psychology* (2nd ed.). Worcester, MA: Clark University Press.

Pratt, K. C. (1954). The neonate. In L. Carmichael (Ed.), *Manual of child psychology* (2nd ed.). New York: John Wiley & Sons.

Ribaupierre, F. de (1997). Acoustic information processing in the auditory thalamus and cerebral cortex. In G. Ehret & R. Romand (Eds.), *The central auditory system* (pp. 317–398). New York: Oxford University Press.

Richards, D. S., Frentzen, B., Gerhardt, K. J., McCann, M. E., & Abrams, R. M. (1992). Sound levels in the human uterus. *Obstetrics and Gynecology, 80*, 186–190.

Roberts, J. E., Burchinal, M. R., Jackson, S. C., Hooper, S. R., Roush, J., Mundy, M., Neebe, E. C., & Zeisel, S. A. (2000). Otitis media in early childhood in relation to preschool language and school readiness skills among black children. *Pediatrics, 106*, 725–735.

Roberts, J. E., Wallace, I. F., & Henderson, F. W. (1997). *Otitis media in young children.* Baltimore, MD: Brookes Publishing.

Rouiller, E. M. (1997). Functional organization of the auditory pathways. In G. Ehret & R. Romand (Eds.), *The central auditory system* (pp. 3–96). New York: Oxford University Press.

Rubel, E. W., Popper, A. N., & Fay, R. R. (Eds.). (1998). *Development of the auditory system.* New York: Springer Verlag.

Saffran, J. R., Aslin, R. N., & Newport, E. L. (1996). Statistical learning by 8-month-old infants. *Science, 274,* 1926–1928.

Saffran, J. R., Johnson, E. K., Aslin, R. N., & Newport, E. L. (1999). Statistical learning of tone sequences by adults and infants. *Cognition, 70,* 27–52.

Schneider, B. A., Bull, D., & Trehub, S. E. (1988). Binaural unmasking in infants. *Journal of the Acoustical Society of America, 83,* 1124–1132.

Sininger, Y. S., Cone-Wesson, B., Folsom, R. C., Gorga, M. P., Vohr, B. R., Widen, J. E., Ekelid, M., & Norton, S. J. (2000). Identification of neonatal hearing impairment: Auditory brainstem responses in the perinatal period. *Ear and Hearing, 21,* 383–399.

Sinnott, J. M., & Aslin, R. N. (1985). Frequency and intensity discrimination in human infants and adults. *Journal of the Acoustical Society of America, 78,* 1986–1992.

Sinnott, J. M., Pisoni, D. B., & Aslin, R. N. (1983). A comparison of pure tone auditory thresholds in human infants and adults. *Infant Behavior and Development, 6,* 3–17.

Sontag, L. W., & Wallace, R. F. (1935). The movement response of the human fetus to sound stimuli. *Child Development, 6,* 253–258.

Svirsky, M. A., Robbins, A. M., Kirk, K. I., Pisoni, D. B., & Miyamoto, R. T. (2000). Language development in profoundly deaf children with cochlear implants. *Psychological Science, 21,* 153–158.

Swingley, D., Pinto, J. P., & Fernald, A. (1998). Assessing the speed and accuracy of word recognition in infants. In C. Rovee-Collier, L. Lipsitt, & H. Hayne (Eds.), *Advances in infancy research* (Vol. 12, pp. 257–277). Ablex: London.

Swingley, D., Pinto, J. P., & Fernald, A. (1999). Continuous processing in word recognition at 24 months. *Cognition, 71,* 73–108.

Tallal, P., Miller, S., Bedie, G., Byma, G., Wang, X., Nagarajan, S. S., Schreiner, C., Jenkins, W., & Merzenich, M. (1996, January 5). Language comprehension in language-learning impaired children improved with acoustically modified speech. *Science, 271,* 81–84.

Tallal, P., Miller, S., & Fitch, R. (1993). Neurobiological basis of speech: A case for the pre-eminence of temporal processing. In P. Tallal, A. M. Galaburda, R. R. Llinas, & C. von Euler (Eds.), Temporal information processing in the nervous system: Special reference to dyslexia and dysphasia (pp. 27–47). *Annals of the New York Academy of Sciences, 682.*

Teele, D. W., Klein, J. O., & Rosner, B. A. (1984). Otitis media with effusion during the first three years of life and development of speech and language. *Pediatrics, 74,* 282–287.

Thomas, D. G., & Crow, C. D. (1994). Development of evoked electrical brain activity in infancy. In G. Dawson & K. W. Fischer (Eds.), *Human behavior and the developing brain* (pp. 207–231). New York: Guilford Press.

Time. (1997, February 3). How a child's brain develops, 48–58.

Trehub, S., Schellenberg, E., & Hill, D. (1997). The origins of music perception and cognition: A developmental perspective. In I. DeLiege & J. Sloboda (Eds.), *Perception and cognition of music.* Hove: Psychology Press.

Trehub, S. E., Schneider, B. A., & Henderson, J. L. (1995). Gap detection in infants, children, and adults. *Journal of the Acoustical Society of America, 98,* 2532–2541.

Walker, D. W., Grimwade, J. C., & Wood, C. (1971). Intrauterine noise: A component of the fetal environment. *American Journal of Obstetrics and Gynecology, 109,* 91–95.

Waltzman, S. B., & Cohen, N. L. (1998). Cochlear implantation in children younger than 2 years old. *American Journal of Otology, 19,* 158–162.

Werker, J. F., & McLeod, P. J. (1990). Infant preference for both male and female infant-directed-talk: A developmental study of attentional and affective responsiveness. *Canadian Journal of Psychology, 43,* 230–246.

Werker, J. F., & Tees, R. C. (1984). Cross-language speech perception: Evidence for perceptual reorganization during the first year of life. *Infant Behavior and Development, 7,* 49–63.

Werner, L. A. (1999). Forward masking among infant and adult listeners. *Journal of the Acoustical Society of America, 105,* 2445–2453.

Werner, L. A., & Marean, G. C. (1996). *Human auditory development.* Boulder, CO: Westview Press.

Werner, L. A., Marean, G. C., Halpin, C. F., Spetner, N. B., & Gillenwater, J. M. (1992). Infant auditory temporal acuity: Gap detection. *Child Development, 63,* 260–272.

Yoshinaga-Itano, C., Secdey, A. L., Coulter, D. K., & Mehl, A. L. (1998). Language of early- and later-identified children with hearing loss. *Pediatrics, 102,* 1161–1171.

Yost, W. A., & Gourevitch, G. (1987). *Directional hearing.* New York: Springer Verlag.

Chapter Three

Action in Infancy – Perspectives, Concepts, and Challenges: The Development of Reaching and Grasping

Ad W. Smitsman

Introduction

Action is of central significance to humans and other species. Its significance derives from the fact that all living organisms persist and maintain their autonomy due to this capacity. Therefore, the capacity for action must not only be present in adults, but also in neonates, and even before birth. Moreover, in order to persist, human beings as well as other organisms must be able to modify their way of acting because circumstances change during the lifetime. Part of human beings' persistence depends on the development of new ways of acting and finding new goals to achieve, when circumstances urge them do so. Therefore, to understand how infants persist and develop, we need to investigate what their capacity for action entails, but also how it expands and is modified after birth.

Action is characteristic of living organisms in all forms and stages. Being alive means being active for any organism, including a human newborn. To get a sense of what action entails for an organism, one may compare living organisms with machines. Machines can act too. Moreover, their actions are coordinated and well controlled, to mention two important characteristics of action. Their actions are certainly better controlled and coordinated than those of human neonates. Are human infants just incomplete, badly equipped machines that first begin to act after their behavior has become more smooth and efficient? The answer can hardly be affirmative. There is a fundamental difference between the activities of machines and those of living organisms, such as human infants. According to Eleanor Gibson (1994) and Ed Reed (1996), this difference concerns the property of agency, the kernel of being animate. Agency also forms the kernel of an agent's autonomy. It involves the capacity to live, grow, and develop by acting. Reed (1996) defines the term "animate" after James Gibson (1979) as an organism's "ability to regulate its relationship with its surrounding so as to take advantage of available resources" (p. 17). These resources are what James Gibson has labeled *affordances*, the environmental components to sustain action. Therefore, agency entails the ability to take advantage of what the environment affords for action, to select new affordances when the capacity for action changes, and new behavioral organizations for new affordances that are discovered. For a human infant, agency includes the ability to take advantage of the solidity, boundedness, and geometrical shape of surrounding objects for reaching and grasping. It entails also the ability to exploit the surface and substance of the ground for keeping postural balance during exploration when looking, listening, and tasting, and activities such as reaching, grasping, sitting, or locomotion. Finally, it involves being able to take advantage of postural and vocal gestures and bodily movements of conspecifics when socially interacting.

Because infants are agents, animate instead of inanimate beings, the capacity to regulate the relationship with their surroundings must be present in infants' actions from birth and even before. Another conclusion is that properties such as autonomy and identity are of significance not only later on when infants develop. They must also form the kernel of an infant's activities at and even before birth, of behavior that looks less smooth and efficient from the outside than it will be later. Autonomy and identity are expressed in such concrete actions as eating and drinking, reaching and locomotion, and social interaction. Finally, the infant's autonomy and identity depend on the affordances that are furnished by the animate and inanimate environment and the infant's bodily postures and movements to take advantage of those affordances (E. J. Gibson, 1988, 1994; Heft, 1989). These capacities are grounded in the infant's biological resources, such as limbs, muscles, sensory systems, and neural organizations, that are available at birth and become available over time when the infant grows up (Goldfield, 1995), and imply for their realization environmental resources called affordances.

The chapter starts with a short historical overview of the issues that have dominated the field in the past. It subsequently addresses the question of agency, focusing on issues such as why regulation is needed, what needs to be regulated, and what are the basic characteristics that need to be present for an organism in order to function as an agent. In addition, the discussion delineates how agency becomes realized in the way action is organized over time and directed at environmental affordances. The chapter then focuses on the organization of action into different action systems, specific to the goals that need to be achieved and the key issues of coordination and control of action. Finally, the chapter ends with an overview of research on an important action system that infants develop, namely reaching, grasping, and manipulation. This overview closes with a brief discussion of how these and other accomplishments during the first year of life set the stage for tool use, which forms the core of the action skills that develop afterwards. Following this is a brief synopsis of central issues in studying the development of action, in particular the issue of development.

Historical Overview and Issues

When psychologists started studying infants systematically, action became a topic of central interest. This interest waned during the 1950s and 1960s, but revived in the late

1970s (cf. Bertenthal & Clifton, 1998). Although detailed observations were made of infants' developing sensorimotor skills (e.g., Gesell and Amatruda, 1945; McGraw, 1935), the most central problems of action remained beyond the scope of research, leading to a reduced interest in action itself. This situation continued until new, refreshing theoretical and empirical insights, mainly stemming from Bernstein's work on action and James Gibson's ecological theory of perception, showed which issues needed to be addressed in the first place. The key issues with action, namely, the infant's agency and need to act, the coordination and control of activities, and the goals that are served by action, were still waiting to be solved. Acknowledgment of the significance of these issues led to an increasing number of studies by the end of the 1980s, continuing through the 1990s. These studies were inspired not only by new insights, but also by new techniques for direct measurement and modeling of the kinematic and dynamic properties of action.

What were these new insights, and in what respect did they differ from the more traditional insight that stemmed in particular from the works of Piaget (1954), Gesell and Amatruda (1945), and McGraw (1935)? Briefly, the study of action, or sensorimotor behavior, as it was labeled at that time, suffered from unwanted and untenable dichotomies. In addition, it suffered from overemphasis on the significance of the brain in the coordination and control of action, a misappraisal of the role of the body, and a misunderstanding of what it involves to be a living organism. Nevertheless, an interest in the meaning of being an organism cannot be denied, especially to Piaget, whose work explicitly rested on the organism metaphor (Sameroff, 1983). Interest in regulatory processes such as accommodation and assimilation, supposed to regulate an organism's relationship with its surrounding, formed a basic motivation for Piaget in his study of development. Problematic for Piaget's view of regulation, however, was the prevalent mind–body dualism that characterized his as well as Gesell's theorizing, and the mainstream of developmental psychology. As a consequence, the main interest in action in infancy was in its supposed relationship to the mind. Hence, action would be needed in the process of development of the mind instead of the regulation of an agent's relationship with its surroundings. This dualism led psychologists to conceive of the brain as the main resource for adaptation and the body as mechanistic and inflexible, unless controlled by the brain. Consequently, and also supported by the ideas of Sherrington (1906/1947) about the reflex arc and the related distinction of central and peripheral control (see Reed, 1982, for relevant critics), newborns' motor and sensory activities were conceived as rigid and reflexive. This rigid state would continue until later-developing cognitive structures, called schemes, would enable the infant to control his or her activities centrally. The mind–body dualism was complemented by an organism–environment dualism. Because sensory systems would give the infant only an impoverished description of his or her surroundings, action had to be guided by information about a mentally constructed reality rather than by information distributed over the body and brain and emerging over time by the organism's active engagement with the environment.

Bernstein's (1967) elaborate and elegant studies of human action showed that for two reasons the brain could not possibly control action fully. The first reason has been labeled the *degrees of freedom problem*, which concerns the immense task of controlling the incredible number of skeletal and neuromuscular components (joints, tendons, muscles, etc.), called degrees of freedom, involved in action. Even the coordination and control of a simple action such as extending an arm or leg involves innumerable degrees of freedom that span most of the body, a question that will be addressed in more detail later on. Bernstein proposed a simpler solution, by suggesting that the nonlinear interactions of these components over time would transform the movement apparatus into a controllable system, or synergy, with a considerably lower number of degrees of freedom to regulate. Tuller, Turvey, and Fitch (1982) described such synergies as coordinative structures, and modern dynamic systems theory as dynamic systems (see Goldfield, 1995; Thelen & Smith, 1994). A currently well-known example of a coordinative structure described by Tuller et al., among others, is a mass spring device, which models how spring-like properties of muscles and masses of limbs may cooperate in the movement of those limbs. In studying reaching in infants, Thelen and her colleagues found support for such a model (Thelen et al., 1993).

The second problem for central control of action is the *context-conditioned variability* of movements (Bernstein, 1984). Movements of limbs, such as the arms or legs, are undetermined for anatomical, mechanical, and physiological reasons. For example, the same pattern of muscle activation will lead to different movement consequences depending on the mechanical characteristics of the arm and its position in the gravity field. To get a limb moving, muscle activity is needed, but on moving, passive forces are generated that combine to affect the movement of the limb. Passive forces vary depending on how forcefully a body segment is set into motion and on its orientation to the gravity field. Passive forces are also modified on a longer time scale due to rapid growth of muscles and bones, and instantaneously due to tasks such as carrying an object or holding a tool (Smitsman, 1997; Smitsman & Bongers, in press). Objects the infant grasps and manipulates vary in size, shape, and mass. To coordinate and control activities in performing a task, infants have to be sensitive to the variations in passive forces that occur for reasons just mentioned. To regulate the movement of a limb such as the arm, they need to adapt muscle activity to the changed passive forces on the limb. Bernstein supposed that the above sources of variability are not dysfunctional but instead functional. They allow the infant to adapt action to varying circumstances. During development, infants explore and discover how to take advantage of the variability of forces acting on the body and how to exploit such forces in controlling movements of limbs and postures. Spontaneous activity may be conceived as highly significant in this respect (Goldfield, 1995), allowing the infant to explore and discover the relevant variables to adapt the action to varying circumstances, an issue that will be discussed in more detail later.

During the last two decades an increasing number of studies used these perspectives to study a variety of infants' actions (see Bertenthal & Clifton, 1998, and Goldfield, 1995, for overviews of the field). The focus has changed from an interest in motor development or sensorimotor development to the study of "perception and action" or action systems, after Reed's work (1982, 1996). The focus on perception *and* action highlights the interconnectedness or mutual dependency of perception and action, the active character of perceiving, and the perceiving character of acting. The perceiving character of action makes action proactive instead of reactive. This means that activities are goal-directed: they anticipate what will happen. When these characteristics are present even in neonates, action is intentional right from the start. To assess the goal-directedness of action, it is of more importance to focus on questions of coordination and control of infants' activities, and the mutual relation between environmental resources and the infant's growing biological resources, than to address only infants' performance, which is jerky at birth. Furthermore, besides the important issues of coordination and control, there is a more fundamental question that we are now beginning to face concerning the regulatory function of action itself. Why is regulation needed in the first place, and what needs to be regulated by an infant's activities? Furthermore, how are the goals the infant selects derived from what he or she needs to regulate, and how do these goals evolve from the way he or she solves problems of coordination and control? Finally, how do the answers to these questions relate to biological resources that become available in the growth of the infant's body and brain and the environmental challenges he or she meets?

Regulation of the Relationship with the Environment: Self-organization

Why does an infant need to regulate the relationship with the surroundings in order to guarantee his or her autonomy? Superficially, the question may even sound rather strange because it is a common conviction that caretakers ought to be the persons who regulate the infant's autonomy and persistence. To understand why regulation is needed, we should first realize that action does not just take place inside the infant, but that he or she is surrounded by animate and inanimate objects, substances, and surfaces as well as events, which include the activities of other agents. These environmental entities provide affordances for the infant's actions. Even when in supine or inclined posture, the surface upon which the infant lies or against which the infant leans forms an integral part of his or her posture and leg and arm movements. Reaction forces emerging from the surface and the gravity field that surround the infant's body provide for postural stability in combination with muscle forces that complement the surrounding forces. In fact, the stability of the infant's posture and movements forms the infant's self or autonomy at that moment in time (Fogel, 1993; Neisser, 1993; Rochat, 1995). Consequently, the infant's autonomy depends on how the infant can regulate muscle forces in relation to the surface and the gravity field. Of course, a caretaker may co-regulate the infant's posture and movements. Fogel (1993, pp. 18, 19) provides a challenging example of a caretaker who pulls the infant into a sitting position. Some caretakers may allow the infant to co-regulate the pull by complementing the infant's muscle force with their pulling force over time, whereas others may completely ignore the infant's efforts. According to Fogel (1993), the latter caretakers violate the infant's autonomy by ignoring the infant's activities.

The fact that the stability of an infant's movements and postures or "self" depends on how his or her activities negotiate environmental forces essentially means that behavior or self and environment form a unified system. Another way of phrasing this is by saying that the infant's behavior forms an open system with respect to the surrounding (Sameroff, 1983; Valsiner, 1987). Such a systems perspective on behavior allows us to describe its organization as a relationship between variables (Butterworth, 1990). In open systems, the variables that form the system belong to the environment as well as to the organism. Behavioral organizations are not only open to the surrounding; they are also essentially dynamic and nonlinear. They are dynamic because their state, a particular body posture, or topology of limb movements may change over time and are maintained by activity, which also varies over time. Nonlinearity means that the state alters abruptly on changes in one of the variables (e.g., the pattern of forces) at a critical level. Finally, such dynamic nonlinear dynamic systems show the capacity to self-organize. Self-organization entails the spontaneous formation of patterned behavior at a higher or macroscopic level under conditions of disequilibrium (Goldfield, 1995; Kelso, 1995; Prigogine & Stengers, 1984; Thelen & Smith, 1994). Patterns arise by the confluence and nonlinear interactions of many variables at a lower or microscopic level (Bernstein's degrees of freedom problem). For behavior, the heterogeneous components at the lower microscopic level include muscular, vascular, segmental, neuronal, and environmental components. The patterns that arise at the macroscopic level are patterns of behavior of the form of postures and movements. New patterns arise when changes in these lower-level components reach a critical value. An appealing, although distant, example of dynamic systems and self-organization is windsurfing. Here, self-organizing processes create air pressure systems around the sail, acting as a pulling force on sail and board, which creates a streaming pattern of water under the board, propelling the board over the waves and providing it with stability and the property to surf. The energetic systems that make windsurfing possible not only self-organize, but are also nonlinear. Nonlinearity can be seen by changes in such variables as wind direction and wave patterns. At a critical level, a slight change in wave patterns or direction of wind to sail will perturb the systems and properties as stability and speed are lost. The surfer cannot compose the energetic systems that are needed for windsurfing, but can only regulate their emergence and persistence by postures and movements that keep the sail at a proper angle to the wind. The energetic systems self-organize due to the confluence of the properties of sail and wind, board and water regulated by the surfer's posture and movements. Moreover, postural stability depends on the emergence of those aerodynamic and hydrodynamic systems. Therefore, postures and movement form an intrinsic component of the energetic systems that underlie the exchange with the aerial and watery environment.

Although windsurfing is not an activity that infants undertake, similar processes underlie the exchange with their animate and inanimate surroundings in daily activities such as eating, gesturing, and sitting. The energetic systems that constitute the relationship may differ and the components involved in regulating the systems may be different, but the way those systems arise, that is, by self-organization, and their manner of regulation are similar. When infants are agents surrounded by a structured animate and inanimate environment, they must regulate the exchange with this environment as the surfer regulates his or her relationship with the watery and aerial surroundings. In regulating the exchange, organization *per se* cannot be the problem for the infant, as the principle of self-organization indicates. Instead, regulation of order that furnishes controllable energetic systems is the action problem that the infant needs to solve.

We have seen that for an agent, the relationship with the surroundings depends on dynamic nonlinear organizations, energetic systems, which arise over time through action. What fundamental capacities need to be present for an agent whose persistence depends on what happens over time? To answer this question, we should realize that an infant's activities need to *make* things happen, using what has become available over time during the past, such as limbs, neuromuscular organizations, and environmental affordances. More generally, activities have to be *proactive* rather than *reactive*. They need to ensure that a wanted future state arises and unwanted future states are prevented, or, minimally, they must allow exploration and generation of information about what these future states might be. Proactivity may involve concrete goals, such as getting an attractive object, but also bodily states such as stability of gaze needed for visual exploration of the intended object. In any case, the child intends a stable relationship with the surroundings during action, a relationship he or she can regulate. Perhaps concrete goals follow from regions for which stable postures and movements of the body exist, as the affordance concept suggests. What ensures that the child can make his or her persistence dependent on structures that arise over time, given circumstances that vary over time? According to Eleanor Gibson (1994) and Ed Reed (1996), prospection, retrospection, and behavioral variability are the primary requirements of agency. Prospection entails the ability to apprehend what *will* happen on action. Retrospection involves the ability to look backwards, to ensure that action is adapted in the light of past encounters. Retrospection ensures continuity with the past. It is needed to apprehend what happens in the present and regulate what will happen in the future. However, circumstances vary all the time. Therefore, flexibility is also needed to harness an intended state against perturbations from the inside and the outside. To conclude, when we conceive prospection, retrospection, and flexibility or behavioral variability as the primary manifestations of agency and infants as agents, these capacities cannot be obtained later on when infants become more skillful. They must form prerequisites for infants to exist, develop, and become skillful. Therefore, to study infants' actions as the activities of agents instead of reactive machines, we have to address how prospection, retrospection, and flexibility are realized in infants' postures and movements.

The Organization of Action

Postures and movements form the variable means of regulating the relationship with the environment. But, as illustrated earlier by the example of windsurfing, the relationship depends on dynamic organizations that emerge over time from the interaction between environmental, biological, and task components (Newell, 1986, 1996). These components form what Thelen and Smith (1994) have called the underlying dynamics of the action system. As we will see, the underlying dynamics consist of flows of forces and flows of information that arise in the course of the exchange process regulated by postures and movements.

To understand what all this means for the infant, let us now take a closer look at an infant's activities. When we observe, for instance, a newborn's activities we often see the whole body involved. An exciting scenario may not only lead to gazing but also to mouthing, protrusion of the tongue, kicking, and extension of both arms. The problem faced by the infant is regulating the flow of energy through the body such that his or her excitement does not perturb the postural stability of the head and trunk needed for gazing and reaching (Bertenthal & Von Hofsten, 1998). From the background of ongoing activity, stable organizations have to arise regulated by the infant's postures and movements of limbs. Before going into more detail about action, remarks are needed about what is meant by postures and movements. Both take place at the same time. They imply one another. For instance, in walking, an upright posture is maintained by leg movements. On the other hand, postural stability is needed to guarantee unimpeded movements of the legs.

What does regulation of the relationship involve for the organization of action? Regulation requires in the first place flexibility, but of an organized sort, which involves solution of the problems of coordination and control. Second, the infant has to discover the important parameters to change, for instance, a state of sitting and kicking into a state of reaching or crawling. The infant does not change from inactive to active and vice versa, but from active in one way to active in another way. Third, information has to be continuously available about the ongoing state of the infant's activities. In the following sections each of these issues will be discussed in more detail.

Coordination and Control

To simplify matters, discussion of the problem of coordination and control will be confined to the skeleton. Of course other subsystems are involved as well, but that does not change the problem greatly. The skeleton forms a structure of different segments connected to one another by joints at which the segments may rotate over one or more axes. As a consequence, movement of one segment will affect other segments. If we consider the axes over which the different segments may rotate, the skeleton contains about 100 degrees of freedom. Assuming that each of these may vary in position and velocity gives 200 dimensions to define the state of the system (Bernstein's degrees of freedom problem). How are particular organizations selected from this enormous number of possibilities? To take reaching as an example, we easily see that the different ways of organizing a reach are not equally preferable. Only a few provide stable solutions to the task. An awkward way of organizing the different degrees of freedom would be to first lean forward by the hips or ankles, lift the upper arm by the shoulder, and then extend the underarm by the elbow. Postural stability will become easily perturbed when the reach is performed this way. For the skeleton, the problem of coordination essentially entails the exploration and selection of spatial temporal organizations of body segments or body topologies that provide stable solutions to the task at hand.

The problem of control is related to the problem of coordination. In fact, control depends on how the infant solves the coordination problem. Control essentially entails the problem of maintaining a topology, while flexibly adapting it to varying task demands. This will be more easily achieved depending on how the system is coordinated. To solve the control problem, the infant has to explore the flexible ways or parameters and their ranges according to which a system can vary while its basic topology is preserved. For instance, the topology of the step cycle in upright locomotion can be preserved over a large range of variations in speed, stride length, and environmental layout. The topology is maintained when, for instance, an increase in speed pushes the system from walking into running (Clark, Truly, & Phillips, 1990).

To understand in further detail how the problems of coordination and control are solved, we need to realize that each body segment functions as a lever. Motion of a segment is induced by torque at the joint at which the segment rotates. However, torque at a joint generates passive forces such as inertia not only on the segment itself, but also on the segments to which it is connected. Hence, smooth movements of a limb such as a leg or arm require muscle activity to get the intended segment moving, but also to compensate for the passive forces that are generated on the segment and the segments that are connected to it. In fact, in reaching, the muscles that span the arm, shoulder, neck, and trunk have to operate as a synergy to generate and preserve the stable topology of the reach. In controlling the reach toward an object, the infant has to discover how to secure the posture of trunk and head from destabilizing effects of the arm, as well as how to counterbalance unwanted flapping of the arm by stiffening particular muscles (Thelen et al., 1993).

Dynamic Systems

Dynamic systems theory provides challenging metaphors and models to describe the ways in which the problems of coordination and control can be solved (for tutorials see Goldfield, 1995; Hopkins & Butterworth, 1997; Savelsbergh, Wimmers, van der Kamp, & Davids, 1999; Thelen & Smith, 1994). Briefly, a dynamic system is a system that changes its state over time. Earlier, the example of windsurfing highlighted how dynamic systems or macroscopic low-dimensional organizations self-organize over time from the interaction of more microscopic multidimensional elements such as neuromuscular and environmental factors. Dynamic systems theory allows us to describe formally the states that evolve over time as time-dependent collective organizations. Stable organizations that arise over time are also called attractors, because they seek stability within a certain region of their state space. For instance, for the step cycle stable topologies will only be found for particular values of stride length and leg speed. To define the system we need to find a collective variable that specifies the macroscopic order, for instance a topology such as the step cycle. To further specify the behavior and stability of the system we have to find the underlying dynamics (e.g., the pattern of forces and the information) and control parameters (that provide for flexibility) on which the system's behavior depends. Changes in these control parameters perturb the system's behavior at critical values and lead to new forms of order. By studying changes in the collective variables we are able to determine whether new forms of behavior emerge. Investigation of the underlying dynamics enables us to unravel the control parameters (the control system) the infant needs to regulate in order to stabilize his or her postures and movements. Earlier we saw some examples of dynamic systems in the mass spring device and in windsurfing. Other examples of dynamic systems involve the oscillatory motion of a swinging pendulum. Rhythmic movement patterns like the step cycle in walking and running can be modeled as an analog to the oscillatory motion of two coupled pendulums (see, e.g., Clark, Truly & Phillips, 1990; Clark & Phillips, 1993). Instant velocity at each point of the pendulum's trajectory specifies the collective variable of a broad class of oscillatory motions. These include the cyclic sway of legs in walking. To further specify the flexibility and stability of the system, we need an equation of motion that describes the class of movements for which the system shows stable behavior, and the relevant parameters on which the stability depends. Mass, length, gravity, and stiffness form important parameters for such oscillatory motions. The parameters allow the system to behave flexibly within certain regions of scale. Changes in parameter values beyond that region will destabilize the system and lead to a transition to new patterns of behavior. To solve the control problem, that is, find and maintain stability for the system, an infant has to explore the regions and parameters for which the system is stable. To become proficient in actions such as reaching, crawling, and walking, infants have to explore, for example, the stiffness and compliance of muscles of the different segments involved and their concerted effect on the stability of the movements and postures intended.

Of course, stiffness and muscle force cannot be regulated independently of the spatial layout of the surrounding in which action takes place. Stability depends on how environmental factors and the organism combine. Discovery of what the environment affords for action also entails anticipation of how variation in spatial layout will affect the stability of a system.

Perception and Action

To be able to solve the problem of coordination and control, the infant has to be sensitive to what happens to his or her relationship with the environment when acting. The earlier discussed flow of energy and the macroscopic order which arise over time enable the active infant to regulate the relationship because they also contain information to guide action. Perception is tightly connected to action. The developmental significance of such a connection is underscored by several studies (Bertenthal & Clifton, 1998; Schmuckler, 1993).

James Gibson's (1966, 1979) ecological theory of perception offers challenging insights and concepts for the problem of unraveling the relation between perception and action and explaining how an agent can regulate the relationship with the environment due to this relation. The theory rests on two fundamental concepts: the concept of *information* and the concept of *affordance*. Both concepts unify the organism and the environment and connect perception and action, or sensory organizations and motor organizations. Because the concept of affordance rests on the concept of information, the latter concept will be discussed first.

Gibson's concept of information rests on the assumption that sensory systems have evolved in animals in relationship to motor systems, and that the evolution of motor systems would have been impossible without the co-evolution of sensory systems. Sensory systems evolved to take advantage of energy such as light and sound reflected on surrounding surfaces and those that belong to the organism's own body to guide action. The important insight is that events, substances, and surfaces of the environment as well as those of the acting organism structure this energy in ways specific to the action that is performed and the environment that surrounds the action. If we accept this position, it is not the static image of the environment at a receptor surface that is important, but the flow of energy that arises at the receptor fields during action. Only the flow is structured by what happens over time. For example, every movement of the head generates a flow-field of visual stimulation on the retina. In stretching the hand toward an object, a flow of tactile energy arises on the skin and sensory organs in muscles and tendons of the arm and shoulders. When at the same time hand and target are observed, the flow-field on the retina is modified by light reflected from the hand and target concurrent with the flow for the haptic system. Optically, the movement of the hand is projected at the target when its trajectory is toward the target. An infant that is able to pick up such patterns of structured energy can be aware of what happens to the relationship of arm and target. Moreover, the infant can regulate the relationship in the way the selection of, for instance, a reach away, toward, or to the side of the target will modify the emerging sensory structure accordingly. Of course, regulation is possible if and only if the patterns at the receptor surfaces are lawfully related to the important parameters of the action system (i.e., in the example, the distance, speed, and direction to reach). In developing laws of control, Kugler and Turvey (1987, 1988) have elaborated this line of thought in an attempt to clarify how the forces needed to act are lawfully related to flows of energy on sensory surfaces.

Before leaving this brief discussion of the concept of information, a few comments are appropriate. First, according to this view information is not similar to knowledge. It is not stored somewhere and, in fact, cannot be stored anywhere. It is an emergent structure that specifies an agent's relationship with the environment. Knowledge about the "self" as an agent and the environment results from the information that becomes available to the agent in action. Second, the information allows for co-perception of the "self" as an agent and the environment as a place to act. This means that awareness of the environment and the "self" as an agent form emergent properties of action. Third, because information emerges in relation to action, other information will be obtained about the "self" as an agent and affordances the environment furnishes when action evolves.

The concept of affordance follows from the concept of information and complements it. The essential point is that the environment is perceived as opportunities to express one's agency and the "self" as endowed with capacities to take advantage of those opportunities. Affordances form the environmental part of the underlying dynamics of the action system. Postures and movements the infant can realize and bodily components involved form the infant's part. Realization of a stable relationship depends on the fit between both. Therefore, to regulate the relationship, the infant's sensory systems need to be tuned to environmental entities that provide a fit for postures and movements the infant can realize, such as a place to sit or walk, or an object at a reachable distance when sitting or walking. More generally, in perceiving an affordance, the surrounding emerges to the infant as an opportunity to express the "self" and the "self" emerges as endowed with potentialities to take advantage of those opportunities. Neisser (1993) and others have called this "self" the ecological self to distinguish it from a more reflective "self," which would develop later on. In terms of the affordance concept, the environment forms a spatial layout within which to orient the gaze, to reach, to eat and drink, to locomote, or to socially interact. Each of these actions requires the spatial layout to be arranged in particular ways suited to the particular action and the action organized in a way suited to the layout of the surroundings. For instance, social interaction requires other agents, capable of perceiving and acting. Interaction with another child at home requires postures and movements from the infant that differ from those for interactions with a doll. In perceiving an affordance, the infant perceives what the particular spatial layout means for action. Consequently, perception of an affordance entails discovery of a goal to be realized, and the self as the agent to realize that goal. Conceived in this way, perceiving an affordance provides a future for the infant. When this future cannot be immediately realized because the behavioral means fail, discovery of an affordance may provide a direction for development of those means (Heft, 1989).

Educated in Cartesian dualism and Newtonian physics, it is tempting to consider the environment as composed of bounded elements such as objects and affordances as a particular kind of those elements. However, affordances are not isolated particles. They denote relationships to an agent's actions, and postures and movements to perform the actions. The stability of the postures and movements depends on the presence of those affordances. As opportunities for action affordances also entail goals for development to the child, because they specify regions for which stable behavioral forms can be obtained. The specific forms of behavior the child uses to take advantage of those affordances may change depending on the bodily resources that become available over time. Long before an infant takes her first walking steps, she may perceive whether a surface affords locomotion. She may explore this opportunity by belly crawling as soon as she is able, laying on her belly to lift her head and shoulders from the ground. Later on, when her hands and knees can support her body, she may explore the opportunity by crawling, and still later, when standing upon both feet becomes possible, by walking and running. Perceiving an opportunity for action that a surface provides encourages the child to explore the surface and postures and movements that can take advantage of what it affords (E. J. Gibson, 1988). If affordances are goals for development, an important issue that faces us concerns the differentiation of the relationship with the environmental layout, consonant with the growing action repertoire and the perception of the "self" as an agent. Discrimination of affordances is likely to entail a perceptual differentiation process of the sort earlier described by Eleanor Gibson (1969, 1988). A level at which to discriminate affordances would be that of the goals of action, such as locomotion or reaching. In the case of locomotion, a more differentiated perception would concern the particular postures and movements the spatial layout affords to realize action such as crawling, walking, running, or hopping. Presumably, infants begin to differentiate the environment at the level of goals such as locomotion, reaching, eating and drinking, or socially interacting, and explore and adapt their limited capacities distinctively according to those goals. Because in newborns these limited capacities are confined to particular organs or subsystems, such as the mouth, the infant will explore those subsystems for a variety of purposes later on, served by other more slowly developing organs, such as the hands. Research indeed indicates that oral activities are used for a variety of purposes other than gestation, such as exploration of objects and social interaction. Lying supine, kicking is even used for purposes such as activating mobiles when the legs are connected to those mobiles via a wire (Rovee-Collier, 1996). Investigations show that these activities are not performed indifferently but flexibly adapted to the task at hand (see Bertenthal & Clifton, 1998), indicating that activities are indeed directed to take advantage of affordances. When other subsystems become available, exploration of relationships affordances entail may become more differentiated, fitting the growing behavioral repertoire. Consonant with such a development, differentiation may also involve consequences of the spatial layout for the specific postures and movements that compose the action. Adolph's (1997) recent study of crawling and upright locomotion on flat rigid surfaces of varying slopes supports such a developmental process. She studied infants' behavior longitudinally from the period they crawled until the onset of upright locomotion. Results showed that in advance infants underestimated the steepness of downward slopes for keeping postural balance, first when they began to crawl and later on when they began to walk. Moreover, results also indicated that infants perceived this property in relation to the manner of locomotion and not as a property solely of the slope, which makes sense because of the different consequences steepness has for these behavioral organizations. The center of mass of the body is displaced differently for crawling and upright locomotion. After infants discovered over several weeks of crawling the critical slope level for maintaining stability in downward crawling, they started all over again in taking to difficult slopes when they began to walk.

Action Systems

When we look at the way action is organized we can distinguish several levels and time scales at which bodily and environmental components interact. In the case of skilled actions, such as running or tennis playing, we can register smoothly coordinated co-activity of skeletal, muscular, neuronal, and vascular components adapted to environmental and task components. At the higher level and longer time scale are the goals that are regulated by the activities. At the intermediate level are the postures and movements adapted to the goals that need to be fulfilled and sustained by the co-activity of bodily components at the lower level. Postures and movements in turn consist of precise topological relations of body segments the agent maintains over time and space. For instance, in walking and running, the knee, ankle, and hip bend and straighten in a precise spatial–temporal synergy to one another (cf. Bertenthal & Clifton, 1998). How can we sensibly distinguish the different actions from one another, taking into account the heterogeneous components involved and their manner of cooperation?

A more traditional way to categorize actions would be to look at the anatomical components or motor systems involved and to categorize actions according to those components and systems. On the other hand, because postures and movements of body segments composing an action follow from the goals that need to be realized, and the action problem that needs to be solved to obtain these goals, Reed (1982, 1996) categorizes actions according to those goals. He labels such broad categories of actions as action systems. Several arguments favor Reed's functional definition of action. The most important one is that although the anatomical components, such as the feet or hands, constrain the way action is performed, they do not determine its organization. For instance, behavioral organizations that involve the hands may be flexibly adapted for several goals, such as reaching and manipulation, gesturing, but also locomotion. To take an extreme example, if one were to try to walk upon the hands instead of the feet, displacement of the center of mass over the limbs that support the body would still be the action problem to solve. The solution will generate a step cycle in both cases, characteristic for upright locomotion, although anatomical components to solve the problem differ. The phenomenon that one may use different anatomical components for similar goals is called *motor equivalence* (Turvey, 1990).

Reed (1996) distinguishes seven broad categories of goals that, according to him, have to be fulfilled for any complex multicellular organism: (1) basic orientation, (2) perceptual exploration, (3) locomotion, (4) manipulation, (5) ingestion, (6) interaction with other individuals, and (7) play. The most fundamental goal is basic orientation. It is a prerequisite for any other goal and involves active maintenance of the body posture or that of body segments, such as the head and torso relative to gravity and surfaces and objects that surround the body. Postural control is needed for any other activity, such as exploration, locomotion, or interacting. For instance, in the case of visual exploration, the infant has to stabilize the gaze by controlling the posture of the head and torso to fixate moving and nonmoving objects. It is not only the basic orienting system that is involved in the activities of other systems; in many actions different systems cooperate. For instance, eating and drinking involves exploration, locomotion, grasping, and sometimes interaction as well.

Reed's definition of action systems, taking into account the existence of motor equivalence, enables us to look for flexibility in infants' behavior that otherwise might have been ignored. Bodily components mature at a different pace in infants. However, the existence of motor equivalence indicates that infants do not have to defer fulfillment of goals until development of more suitable bodily components takes place. There is an action problem that needs to be solved. The infant may use whatever means are available at a time to solve the problem. For instance, although young infants cannot move independently from one place to another or grasp objects manually in the first months, by vocal and facial gestures they can alert caretakers to assist them. As discussed before, the mouth, face, and eyes are organs the infant can articulate quite well in the first weeks of life, unlike the hands and legs. Research on, for instance, oral activity in neonates indicates that oral activity does serve several functions in addition to drinking and eating, such as exploration (Rochat, 1995) and interaction (Meltzoff & Moore, 1995; see also Fogel, 1993), and perhaps even grasping (see Goldfield, 1995, chap. 9 for an overview). Goldfield suggests that the early presence of the ability to modulate the underlying dynamical characteristics of the oral subsystem allows the infant to achieve the different functions.

In the following section we will briefly review the research on reaching and grasping to highlight the concepts outlined above. More elaborate reviews are presented by Berthental and Clifton (1998) and Goldfield (1995) for other systems as well.

Development of Reaching and Grasping

Reaching, grasping, and manipulation form important functions of the hand. However, the human hand is very flexible and may also serve several other functions that include pointing, pounding, tactile exploration, and even symbolic functions such as gesturing and counting. The task facing the infant is discovery of how to regulate the modifiable underlying dynamics of the system such that stable synergies emerge from this substrate for functions as diverse as those just mentioned. For the neonate, manual activity is embedded in behavioral configurations that involve the whole body. The problem for the neonate is not that behavior is uncoordinated at birth. In fact, it is highly coordinated. Movements of the head and trunk as well as interesting sights and the excitement that may result from these sights may elicit different types of activity of the arm and hand. For instance, mouthing may elicit flexion of the arm and movement of the hand into the direction of the mouth in neonates. Head turning may elicit extension of the ipsilateral hand into the direction the infant gazes via the atonic neck reflex (ATNR) (cf. Goldfield, 1995). What enables the infant to evolve goal-directed actions from this substrate of early coordinations?

A major problem for the infant involves activating the reach such that the posture of head and trunk form stable platforms to guarantee an unimpeded reach and grasp. In fact, extension of the arm displaces the center of mass outward and movements of the torso may aggravate this effect. Postural stability for the head as well as for the trunk are particularly important to compensate for such effects. Stability of the head is also needed to keep the gaze focused on targets to reach for. In the following sections these and other related issues will be addressed.

Pre-reaching

After birth, a period of pre-reaching precedes goal-directed reaching that develops at about 4 months of age. Arm extensions toward an object during this period are considered as pre-reaches because one may question whether the movements are guided by the object that is seen, or elicited by other activities such as gazing at the object or head turning. Although not goal-directed, manual activities are organized. They are coordinated to activities of the eyes and head. Von Hofsten (1982) therefore considered such manual activities as a form of orienting instead of reaching. Von Hofsten based his conclusion on the finding that arm extensions of 5- to 9-day-old infants toward an object were more in the vicinity of an object when the object was fixated. Moreover, well-aimed arm movements tended to slow down in the vicinity of the object that was fixated, suggesting some anticipation of an encounter with the object.

During the first four months of life important changes take place in the organization of the manual and visual activities of infants and in the muscular synergies that underlie such activities. These changes set the stage for the development of goal-directed reaching. For infants positioned in front of an object, reaching attempts decrease in the period from 1 to 7 weeks and the number of fixations of the object increases (Von Hofsten, 1984). In studying pre-reaching during the first 19 weeks of life, Von Hofsten (1984) also discovered a change in the coordination of activity of the hand and arm. In the period from 1 to 7 weeks the hands became fisted during approach, whereas they were opened again in the period of 9–17 weeks. A similar phenomenon was observed earlier by White, Castle, and Held (1964). Presumably, the synergy of muscles of head, shoulders, arm, and hand to perform a reach changes during the first 7 weeks, freeing the infant from behavioral configurations such as the ATNR response that are present at birth (cf.

Goldfield, 1995). The change enables infants to visually and haptically explore the freed degrees of freedom for extending the arms. White et al.'s (1964) study supports such a hypothesis. In studying infants' reaching behavior longitudinally from 1 through 5 months, White et al. discovered a dropping out of the behavioral asymmetry due to the ATNR response at the end of the first 2 months of age. After freeing the arms from the earlier asymmetry, unilateral movements were replaced by bilateral movements. At 4 months of age unilateral reaches reappeared, followed by interchanging periods of bilateral and unilateral reaches until the end of the first year (Corbetta & Thelen, 1996). During the period of bilateral movements in pre-reaching, there was increased haptic and later also visual exploration of both hands at midline.

More recent studies support the hypothesis that the transition of pre-reaching to goal-directed reaching is accompanied by a change in muscle synergies (Thelen & Spencer, 1998; Van der Fits & Hadders-Algra, 1998). Thelen and Spencer (1998) further reported variability during the transition from pre-reaching to goal-directed reaching, in combinations of muscles that were active.

Goal-directed Reaching

Goal-directed reaching requires the infant to configure dynamic organizations for the arms, head, and trunk that can be tuned to the shape and size of a target and its direction, distance, and orientation in space. The task that faces the infant is to regulate the exchange of energy on reaching between muscles, limbs, and surroundings such that one or both hands approach the target smoothly and can touch and grasp it. The range of reaching in space can be expanded by rotation of the trunk or leaning forward or to the sides. However, both leaning and rotation shift the center of mass of the body. Shifts of the center of mass easily lead to postural imbalance and consequently perturbation of the movement of the hand unless the infant can compensate in time for such a disturbance. How does the infant solve such action problems?

Von Hofsten and his colleagues (Von Hofsten, 1979, 1991; Von Hofsten and Ronnquist, 1993) studied infants' reaching longitudinally over the period from 15 until 42 weeks. By analyzing the velocity profile of the movement of the arm, they discovered that the reach is organized into smaller units, whereby each unit is characterized by an acceleration and a deceleration phase. With age the number of units decreases and the trajectory becomes smoother, a change that could largely be attributed to the lengthening of one unit, which they considered the transport unit. The longest unit was mostly the first unit.

Several studies addressed the issue of movement units. A first hypothesis, consistent with Piaget's (1952) hypothesis that eye–hand coordination is a prerequisite for reaching to develop, maintains that infants need to monitor the trajectory. Monitoring may become more efficient with age. A smart way of testing this hypothesis is by studying infants' reaching in the dark. When 6- to 25-week-old infants were shown glowing objects in the dark, results showed that they did not need to see the hand to touch the object (Clifton, Muir, Ashmead, & Clarkson, 1993). Of course infants have to see the target, but they do not need to see the hand to regulate its trajectory toward the target. Further evidence for such a conclusion comes from a study in which in darkness a lighted target was suddenly displaced during the reach by switching the light toward an adjacently placed toy (Ashmead, McCarty, Lucas, & Belvedere, 1993). At the age of 5 months infants did not adapt the reach toward the new position of the target. Adaptation first occurred in 9-month-old infants in the approach phase of the reach, and only when infants were wearing a visible marker on their hands.

A second hypothesis for the existence of movement units maintains that the smoother trajectories of older infants result from their improved ability to plan the reach (Von Hofsten, 1989, 1997). Although on first sight such a hypothesis is appealing, it may be questioned whether the planning of the reach is the sole cause of the units and the irregularity of the trajectory. Movement units may also arise in neonates, at an age when arm extensions presumably are not planned at all but are elicited, as Von Hofsten and Ronnquist (1993) showed. Moreover, an elegant modeling study by Out, Savelsbergh, Van Soest, and Hopkins (1997) of reaching in 12- to 20-week-old infants indicated that movement units may arise at the low level of the biomechanics of the system instead of being the result of the higher abstract level of planning. This later finding is consistent with dynamic systems theory. According to this view, smooth trajectories and consequently adequate planning may result from the ability to regulate the modifiable dynamical characteristics of arms and shoulders such as muscle stiffness in relation to muscle activation. Besides, planning would be of little help to the infant without the ability to regulate those characteristics. In a longitudinal investigation of the hypothesis derived from dynamic systems theory, Thelen et al. (1993) used what they call a multilevel approach. They studied reaching in infants from 3 to 52 weeks of age. Their approach consists of measuring the space–time characteristics of the movement, such as its trajectory in space, velocity, and change in velocity, in relation to the underlying muscle activation patterns used by infants to generate and control the movement, which they also call the intrinsic dynamics. Their study involved four infants. Consistent with the dynamic systems view, and in particular conceiving the arm as a mass spring device, smoother trajectories resulted from an improved ability of older infants to regulate the underlying dynamics of the system. Interestingly, infants differed in the strategy they followed to solve the action problem. Two infants used too much muscle force to set the arm into motion at the onset of reaching and relatively too little muscle stiffness to damp oscillatory flapping motions of the arm toward the target. For the other two infants, trajectories looked much smoother and better controlled than those of the first two infants at the onset of reaching. However, smoothness was the result of a lower energy level used to activate the system instead of better control. In the case of less muscle activation, compliance of muscles will be less likely to lead to flapping movements and irregular trajectories. But activation may then be too low to reach the target when lifting the arm against gravity. Such was indeed the case for the two infants who used this strategy. In sum, although infants differed in the strategy they used to solve the action problem, their solutions were similar: regulation of muscle activation relative to muscle stiffness by muscle co-activation. Stiffness and activation are two important parameters of dynamic systems such as a mass spring device.

When young infants' arms are very active before the reach starts and muscles are highly activated, high movement speed may be the result. Movement speed in turn may perturb the infant's ability to properly regulate forces to stabilize reaching. To obtain insight into this parameter, Thelen, Corbetta, and Spencer (1996) further analyzed the reaches of the infants studied by Thelen et al. (1993) in terms of movement speed. Analyses showed that irregularity of the reach was related to a high movement speed. The relationship existed for reaches and spontaneous nonreaching movements, and was most clearly shown in an active period that occurred before infants were able to control the reach adequately. After the onset of goal-directed reaching, all infants passed through such an active period in which they, according to Thelen et al. (1996), seemingly explored how to fine-tune the system after they had discovered how to configure the reach. The timing and length of the active period varied among infants. Control considerably improved for all infants after this active period between 30 and 36 weeks of age. Interestingly, it is in this period that infants begin to sit independently (Rochat, 1992) and to crawl (Goldfield, 1993). Moreover, at about 10 months infants perceive that they can reach further by extending the arm and leaning forward, whereas at 8 months they perceive the reaching distance only for the extended arm, not for the arm and trunk. At 12 months they begin to perceive that the reaching distance can also be extended by using an implement such as a spoon (McKenzie, Skouteris, Day, Hartman, & Yonas, 1993). Improved postural stability due to the discovery of new synergies for the trunk, arms, and shoulders may underlie the development of each of these skills.

A related issue of importance to the development of reaching and grasping concerns the cooperation between both hands. For most infants, arms move together synchronously until late in the first year. This happens for spontaneous manual activities as well as for reaching. In bimanual reaching, one hand touches the object, but both arms extend symmetrically along the midline toward the object. The precise patterning may change between 7 and 11 months (Goldfield & Michel, 1986). In adults both hands cooperate when tasks require such a division of labor. For instance, in tasks such as manufacturing, one hand may be used to hold an object in position and the other to work on it. Bimanual reaching is only needed for objects that are too large for one hand to seize. In infants, bimanual activity that is scaled to the size of the object first develops in the beginning of the second year (Fagard & Jacquet, 1996).

Why does it take so long for infants to adapt bimanual activity to the task at hand? According to Corbetta and Thelen (1996), we have to realize that new patterns such as unimanual or bimanual reaches always emerge from a substrate of existing forms of coordination. We have seen that in neonates, unimanual arm movements occurred by exploiting the ATNR response when this was prevalent. Symmetrical bilateral movements first occurred after the original substrate of asymmetrical configurations disappeared. To obtain insight into the underlying behavioral configurations for reaching over the first year of life, Corbetta and Thelen (1996) analyzed patterns of interlimb coordination for reaching and nonreaching arm movements, using data from the infants earlier studied by Thelen et al. (1993). Periods of bimanual and unimanual reaching appeared to interchange over the whole first year of life, but at a time scale that differed between infants. As expected, during periods of bimanual reaching, synchronous spontaneous bimanual activity was found for reaching and nonreaching arm movements. However, during periods of unilateral reaches such a synchronous movement was not found. Reaching apparently exploited patterns of interlimb coordination that were prevalent at a time.

What are the causes of the changing prevalence of patterns of interlimb coordination? Corbetta and Thelen mention several factors that may operate at different time scales in different infants. One factor is the energetic state of the infant. When young babies get excited for some reason, all their limbs are activated and it may be difficult to channel energy such that the whole shoulder girdle is not involved, and only one hand extends and the other is kept still. Other factors include developing skills such as the ability to sit independently and bimanual skills that infants acquire at the end of the first year of life, attention to new affordances relevant to those skills, and finally, task constraints such as the shape and size of objects that are presented. Consistent with the above suggestions, a study by Rochat (1992) indeed showed that infants differ in their manner of reaching, depending on whether they are able to sit independently. Independent sitters more frequently reached with one hand than nonsitters. Also, the acquisition of bimanual skills is important for a change in the manner of reaching. Fagard and Pezé (1997) showed that an increase in bimanual reaching by the end of the first year of life coincided with success in bimanual tasks, such as taking a toy out of a container while lifting the lid with the other hand. Moreover, unilateral reaches were especially prevalent in the period before first successes in the bimanual task, which took place between 8 and 10 months of age. In sum, bimanual reaching may have different origins at 6 months of age when it is prevalent and at 11 and 12 months of age when it becomes prevalent again (Fagard & Pezé, 1997). For reasons mentioned earlier, 6-month-old infants may be unable to uncouple both hands or to couple them more adequately according to the task that needs to be fulfilled. By the end of the first year of life, infants may be able to accomplish a division of labor between both hands. Anticipation of such division of labor for manipulating objects may lead to bimanual reaching. Finally, task demands may determine the manner of reaching. Newell, Scully, McDonald, and Baillargeon (1990) found a differentiation in bimanual and unimanual grasping in infants of 4 through 8 months of age according to the shape and size of the object. In their study small toy cups in diameters of 1.25, 3.5, and 8.5 cm were presented with the cup opening facing either downwards or upwards. When a cup was not only touched but also grasped, which occurred in 71 percent of cases in 4-month-olds and in 90 percent of cases over all ages, one hand was mainly used for the smaller cups. For the largest cup one hand was used only when the cup opening was facing upwards. When the latter cup was facing downwards two hands were used to grasp the cup.

Grasping

Grasping and manipulation of objects are important goals of reaching. Other goals include exploration of surfaces, beating, and finding a base of support in leaning and crawling (see Goldfield, 1993). The transition of pre-reaching to goal-directed reaching is accompanied by a short period between about 15 and 18 weeks when infants only touch objects after completion of a reach (Von Hofsten & Lindhagen,1979; Wimmers, Savelsbergh, Beek, & Hopkins 1998). Wimmers et al. (1998), using catastrophe theory, demonstrated that the transition of reaching to reaching followed by grasping indeed involves a qualitative shift in behavior of the infant. A reason why infants only touch objects instead of grasping them at the onset of goal-directed reaching might be the difficulty of adjusting the hand to a target during approach. Such adjustments are difficult to achieve when trajectory control still forms a problem. Grasping of objects requires timed adjustments of the hand and grip configuration to the shape, size, and orientation in space of an object, especially when an infant has to catch a moving object. In addition, contrary to what is the case for trajectory control, visual guidance is of importance to adjust the hand and grip to the target.

To study hand adjustments for grasping, Lockman, Ashmead, and Bushnell (1984) presented 5- and 9-month-old infants vertically and horizontally oriented dowels. Results showed that 9-month-olds, but not 5-month-olds, adjusted the hand to the orientation of the dowel before touching. Contrary to Lockman et al.'s (1984) findings, Von Hofsten and Fazel-Zandy (1984) discovered that even 18-week-old infants adjusted the hand to vertically or horizontally positioned rods. In a subsequent study, Von Hofsten and Ronnquist (1988) discovered that 5-month-old infants started to close the hand around the object just before the hand encountered the object. For 9- and 13-month-old infants, closing started earlier during approach. In addition, the span of the hand became adjusted to the target size at these older ages, whereas it was not in the youngest age group. Finally, Savelsbergh, Von Hofsten, and Jonsson (1997) showed preparation of the grasp during reaching in 9-month-old infants. To experimentally investigate whether grasps are prepared during the reach, they suddenly displaced a target to the side during the reach. In designing their study, they reasoned that a sudden change of target position would perturb a reach that anticipates the grasp, but not a reach that does not prepare to encounter the object. In the latter case, grasping starts first after the reach is ended. Longer times to execute a reach and more errors in touching an object for perturbed reaches confirmed the hypothesis that reaches prepared the grasp. Their finding that infants needed to finish the reach and start a new reach of a similar temporal structure to grasp the object further supported the latter hypothesis.

For grasping, the hand has to be adjusted to the orientation of an object in space and the configuration of fingers and thumb to the shape and size of the object. Newell and his colleagues (Newell, McDonald, & Baillargeon, 1993; Newell et al., 1990) showed that grip patterns of infants of 4 to 8 months of age varied systematically with object size in grasping cups of different sizes. About five patterns were found out of a considerably larger number of possible combinations for the ten digits of both hands. The combinations differed in the number of fingers used to touch the object along with the thumb, involving more digits for larger objects. To compare critical object sizes at which grip patterns change for infants and adults, Newell et al. (1993) measured the ratio of object size to hand size. Relating this ratio to the five grip configurations that were found revealed that infants and adults shift to another grip pattern at about the same ratio. Finally, results revealed that at the age of 4 months grip differentiation was mainly haptically guided. It occurred on touching the object. At the age of 8 months of age it occurred mainly before touching the object and was visually guided. Newell and his colleagues conceive object sizes as task constraints. Their results show that those task constraints affect the selection of a grip in a way that is similar for infants and adults. Taken together, these findings show that orientation of the hand and preparation of the grip guided by visual information becomes part of the reach at about the onset of goal-directed reaching. Improvement of the preparation of the grip takes place in the months that follow the onset of goal-directed reaching. Part of this improvement may result from the progressively better control infants obtain over the trajectory of the hand in exercising reaching and grasping. Adjustments are more easily achieved when the hand follows a smooth trajectory instead of oscillating on its approach toward the target. Another part may result from an improved ability to pick up visual information to guide the approach toward an object. Control of movement of the hand and stabilization of the head and torso for reaching will make it easier for them to pick up such information to guide adjustments for grasping (Bertenthal & Von Hofsten, 1998).

In most tasks used to study reaching and grasping, infants can move the hand freely in space. There are no obstacles to avoid or narrow openings to orient and pass through before the hand can grasp an object. Moreover, when the object has been grasped it can be retrieved freely without the need to avoid obstacles in its path. Activities become more complexly nested when adjustments of the hand and digits not only involve grasping but also approaching and retrieving a target with obstacles to avoid and openings to pass through. Such a task requires the infant to shift hand orientation over time and to pick up visual information to guide the hand. Moreover, when retrieval also involves avoidance of obstacles, regulation includes the orientation of the object that is held with respect to these obstacles. Robinson, McKenzie, and Day (1996) used such tasks to study hand adjustments infants make for grasping. Results showed that, in contrast to adults, 10-month-old infants did not adjust the hand to a narrow elongated aperture behind which an elongated object was placed in an orientation that differed from the aperture. However, adjustments to the aperture were made when they were only needed for passing through, but not for grasping or grasping and retrieving. This occurred when behind the aperture an object was presented that could only be touched because of its large size in relation to the aperture and hand size. Apparently, infants perceived what the task afforded them to do. This was also the case when adjustments were needed to a handle placed on the top of an object too large to grasp by one hand. These results show that at the age of 10 months, regulation of hand orientation may concern different goals and entities for infants: objects, openings, and handles. However, when hand orientation has to shift over time and serves different goals, one goal (passing through an obstacle) embedded in another goal (grasping an object), the task becomes too complicated for infants of this age.

Tool Use

By the end of the first year of life the human infant has attained important milestones in reaching, grasping, and manipulation of objects. Improved postural balance and flexibility in sitting by that time greatly enhance these skills (Bertenthal & Von Hofsten, 1998; Thelen & Spencer, 1998). The ability to lean forward and to the sides without losing balance also expands the reaching space (Rochat & Goubet, 1995). The space is further enhanced by upright bipedal locomotion that occurs also by the end of the first year and the beginning of the second year of life. The significance of such accomplishments extends far beyond the immediate goals they serve, such as getting and manipulating objects and exploring surfaces haptically. These accomplishments set the stage for the development of new skills that rest on tool use. Tool use plays a central role in children's developing action repertoire after the first year of life. It underlies the expansion of the capacity to act that takes place after the first year of life. In expanding this capacity, it enables children to partake in the cultural heritage of the society within which they grow up. The dynamic systems view sheds new light on how expansion of the capacity to act may take place (Smitsman, 1997; Smitsman & Bongers, in press). It rests, for instance, on the way hand-held tools modify the geometrical and dynamical properties of the action system. Such modifications set the stage for configuring new forms of behavior, obtaining new goals, and performing new tasks. For example, as a device to reach, the arm extends further in space when the hand holds a stick. As a consequence, surfaces that previously could not be touched because they were too far away or might have hurt the skin can now be touched safely. Of course, new opportunities arise given that the infant is able to take advantage of the changed metrics and dynamics of the action system that now includes the stick. Holding a stick also means that forces exerted on surrounding surfaces will change depending on the length, shape, and center of mass of the object. Forces also change for the arm that holds the stick and the rest of the body that ensures a stable posture. A child, who can take advantage of these changes, has new resources for engaging in new relationships with the environment and discovering new affordances. Environmental properties, before with no meaning for action, become affordances and existing affordances lose their meaning depending on how the action system is modified and the behavioral patterns the infant configures due to these modifications. In earlier sections, we saw flexibility in the way bodily components can be assembled for a task and in the way modifiable dynamical characteristics such as muscle stiffness can be regulated. Tool use highlights a new kind of flexibility, namely, the possibility of instantaneously and temporarily modifying the components themselves of the action system for a task. In a sense, in tool use the child becomes the creator of himself or herself, of course aided by the diversity of implements that are available for action in the social environment within which he or she grows up. Tool use means that the capacity to act is no longer solely distributed over the body but also over the environment from which elements can be taken to enhance the capacity for a task.

Some Future Goals of Action Research

The dynamic systems view discussed in this chapter addresses postures and movements to perform a task and their kinematics as emergent properties of underlying dynamic systems or regimes. An infant selects and regulates such regimes in coupling the multiple components of his or her action system over time. Therefore, a key question in studying an infant's actions and the way these develop consists of unraveling the dynamic organizations that underlie action and the sensory information that becomes available as part of the activities to guide performance of a task. This question includes the different components of action systems. Their dynamic, geometric, and information-gathering properties in relation to affordances that fit those components form the basis for establishing a particular regime. Changes in components throughout life affect the underlying dynamics of action systems, perturbing prevailing behavioral organizations. But these changes also provide new dynamic regimes for selection, given the affordances the environment provides for those regimes. In that case they challenge engagement of new relationships with the animate and inanimate environment. This occurs when an infant's body grows rapidly and new affordances become available for action, but also as a result of growing action skills. A consequence of such skills is that they allow the infant instantaneously and temporarily to vary the characteristics of an action system. As we have seen, the growing ability to manipulate objects at the end of the first year of life enables the child to use objects he or she manipulates as tools. By modifying the dynamic, geometric, and information-gathering characteristics of an action system, control problems caused by limitations of the system can be solved and relationships with the surrounding that otherwise would be impossible can be engaged. Humans have exploited this opportunity the environment provides to great length as long as they have existed. In every society, all kinds of artifacts and practices challenge the child to modify his or her action systems, constrain the relationships she or he engages, and the action skills, knowledge, and insights he or she develops (Smitsman & Bongers, in press). In sum, the core developmental issue for understanding infants' actions involves unraveling the dynamic regimes an infant explores and selects as a function of changes in dynamical, geometrical, and information-gathering characteristics of a system's components. Studying such questions will also deepen our insight into what agency entails, a term used at the beginning of this chapter to describe infants' behavior. Agency is expressed in an individual's exploration and selection of existing means and new means as they become available, and in the construction of other means when existing ones fail. This capacity enables infants to develop when bodily and environmental components change as a result of growth, or otherwise. It enables toddlers and older individuals to regulate such changes in tools they select to overcome limitations for action and development. From this perspective, tool use could be a fruitful field in which to study development and agency, because it allows us to vary the underlying dynamics of an action system more systematically. Its study may also deepen our insight into how culture contributes to development.

Further Reading

Bertenthal, B. I., & Clifton, R. K. (1998). Perception and action. In W. Damon, D. Kuhn, & R. S. Siegler (Eds.), *Handbook of child psychology: Vol. 2. Cognition, perception, and language* (pp. 51–102). New York: Wiley. An invaluable overview of the theoretical insights, issues, methods, and results that guided research of the last two decades on the development of action in the first years of life. Overview focuses on basic orientation, manipulation, and locomotion.

Goldfield, E. C. (1995). *Emergent forms: Origins and early development of human action and perception.* New York and Oxford: Oxford University Press. This book is written for a broad readership. Interdisciplinary in its scope, it integrates insights from different disciplines and perspectives. These include James Gibson's ecological psychology of perception and action, biomechanics, the dynamic systems approach, in particular the principle of self-organization, and biological principles of morphogenesis and selection. Combining these insights provides a fresh and intriguing, broad and in-depth view on the emergence of new patterns of behavior in normal and physically handicapped children during the first years of life.

Hopkins, B., & Butterworth, G. (1997). Dynamical systems approaches to the development of action. In J. G. Bremner, A. Slater, & G. Butterworth (Eds.), *Infant development: Recent advances* (pp. 75–100). Hove: Psychology Press. This book provides a readable synopsis of the major concepts of dynamic systems theory and their application to the study of action and its development.

Reed, E. S. (1996). *Encountering the world: Toward an ecological psychology.* New York: Oxford University Press. Elaborating from James Gibson's ecological-psychological perspective and evolutionary perspective, this book presents a fascinating in-depth view of the significance of the concept of agency and action systems for understanding the evolution and onto-genesis of living organisms, including human beings, in their animate and inanimate surroundings.

Thelen, E., & Smith, L. B. (1994). *A dynamic systems approach to the development of cognition and action.* Cambridge, MA: MIT Press. This book provides a readable, provocative, and insightful view of the dynamic systems approach and its significance for the study of development in general, and action in particular, as contrasted to more traditional approaches. The book reviews research performed by Thelen and her colleagues and that of others to highlight the power of the dynamic systems perspective for answering (traditional) developmental questions.

References

Adolph, K. A. (1997). Learning in the development of infant locomotion. *Monographs of the Society for Research in Child Development, 62,* 1–140.

Ashmead, D. H., McCarty, M. E., Lucas, L. S., & Belvedere, M. C. (1993). Visual guidance in infants' reaching toward suddenly displaced targets. *Child Development, 64,* 1111–1127.

Bernstein, N. (1967). *The coordination and regulation of movements.* Oxford: Pergamon.

Bernstein, N. (1984). Biodynamics of locomotion. In H. T. A. Whiting (Ed.), *Human motor actions: Bernstein reassessed* (pp. 171–222). Amsterdam: North Holland.

Bertenthal, B. I., & Clifton, R. K. (1998). Perception and action. In W. Damon, D. Kuhn, & R. S. Siegler (Eds.), *Handbook of child psychology: Vol. 2. Cognition, perception, and language* (pp. 51–102). New York: Wiley.

Bertenthal, B. I., & Von Hofsten, C. (1998). Eye, head and trunk control: The foundation for manual development. *Neuroscience and Biobehavioral Reviews, 22,* 515–520.

Butterworth, G. (1990). On reconceptualising sensori-motor development in dynamic systems terms. In H. Bloch & B. I. Bertenthal (Eds.), *Sensory-motor organizations and development in infancy and early childhood* (pp. 57–73). Dordrecht: Kluwer.

Clark, J. E., & Phillips, S. J. (1993). A longitudinal study of intralimb coordination in the first year of independent walking: A dynamical systems analysis. *Child Development, 64,* 1143–1157.

Clark, J. E., Truly, T. L., & Phillips, S. J. (1990). A dynamical systems approach to understanding the development of lower limb coordination in locomotion. In H. Bloch & B. I. Bertenthal (Eds.), *Sensory-motor organizations and development in infancy and early childhood* (pp. 363–378). Dordrecht: Kluwer.

Clifton, R. K., Muir, D. W., Ashmead, D. H., & Clarkson, M. G. (1993). Is visually guided reaching in early infancy a myth? *Child Development, 64,* 1099–1110.

Corbetta, D., & Thelen, E. (1996). The developmental origins of bimanual coordination: A dynamic perspective. *Journal of Experimental Psychology: Human Perception and Performance, 22*, 502–522.

Fagard, J., & Jacquet, A. Y. (1996). Changes in reaching and grasping objects of different size between 7 and 13 months of age. *British Journal of Developmental Psychology, 14*, 65–78.

Fagard, J., & Pezé, A. (1997). Age changes in interlimb coupling and the development of bimanual coordination. *Journal of Motor Behavior, 29*, 199–208.

Fogel, A. (1993). *Developing through relationships: Origins of communication, self, and culture.* New York: Harvester Wheatsheaf.

Gesell, A., & Amatruda, C. S. (1945). *The embryology of behavior.* New York: Harper.

Gibson, E. J. (1969). *The principles of perceptual learning and development.* New York: Prentice-Hall.

Gibson, E. J. (1988). Exploratory behavior in the development of perceiving and acting, and the acquiring of knowledge. *Annual Review of Psychology, 39*, 1–41.

Gibson, E. J. (1994). Has psychology a future? *Psychological Science, 5*, 69–76.

Gibson, E. J. (1997). An ecological psychologist's prolegomena for perceptual development: A functional approach. In C. Dent-Read & P. Zukow-Goldring (Eds.), *Evolving explanations of development: Ecological approaches to organism–environment systems* (pp. 413–443). Washington, DC: American Psychological Association.

Gibson, J. J. (1966). *The senses considered as perceptual systems.* Boston: Houghton Mifflin.

Gibson, J. J. (1979). *The ecological approach to visual perception.* Boston: Houghton Mifflin.

Goldfield, E. C., & Michel, G. F. (1986). Spatiotemporal linkage in infant interlimb coordination. *Developmental Psychobiology, 19*, 259–264.

Goldfield, E. C. (1993). Dynamic systems in development: Action systems. In L. B. Smith & E. Thelen (Eds.), *A dynamic systems approach to development: Applications* (pp. 51–71). Cambridge, MA: MIT Press.

Goldfield, E. C. (1995). *Emergent forms: Origins and early development of human action and perception.* New York and Oxford: Oxford University Press.

Goubet, N., & Clifton, R. K. (1998). Object and event representation in 6-month-old infants. *Developmental Psychology, 34*, 63–76.

Heft, H. (1989). Affordances and the body: An intentional analysis of Gibson's ecological approach to visual perception. *Journal for the Theory of Social Behaviour, 19*, 1–30.

Hopkins, B., & Butterworth, G. (1997). Dynamical systems approaches to the development of action. In J. G. Bremner, A. Slater, & G. Butterworth (Eds.), *Infant development: Recent advances* (pp. 75–100). Hove: Psychology Press.

Kelso, J. A. S. (1995). *The self-organization of brain and behavior.* Cambridge, MA: MIT Press.

Kugler, P. N., & Turvey, M. T. (1987). *Information, natural law, and the self-assembly of rhythmic movement.* Hillsdale, NJ: Erlbaum.

Kugler, P. N., & Turvey, M. T. (1988). Self-organization, flow fields, and information. *Human Movement Science, 7*, 97–129.

Lockman, J. J., Ashmead, D. H., & Bushnell, E. W. (1984). The development of anticipatory hand orientation during infancy. *Journal of Experimental Child Psychology, 37*, 176–186.

McGraw, M. B. (1935). *Growth: A study of Johnny and Jimmy.* New York: Appleton-Century-Crofts.

McKenzie, B. E., Skouteris, H., Day, R. H., Hartman, B., & Yonas, A. (1993). Effective action by infants to contact objects by reaching and leaning. *Child Development, 64*, 415–429.

Meltzoff, A. N., & Moore, M. K. (1995). A theory of the role of imitation in the emergence of self. In P. Rochat (Ed.), *The self in infancy: Theory and research* (pp. 73–93). Amsterdam: Elsevier.

Neisser, U. (1993). The self perceived. In U. Neisser (Ed.), *The perceived self: Ecological and inter-personal sources of self-knowledge* (pp. 3–21). Cambridge: Cambridge University Press.

Newell, K. M. (1986). Constraints on the development of coordination. In M. G. Wade & H. T. A. Whiting (Eds.), *Motor development in children: Aspects of coordination and control* (pp. 341–360). Dordrecht: Nijhoff.

Newell, K. M. (1996). Change in movement and skill: Learning, retention, and transfer. In M. L. Latash & M. T. Turvey (Eds.), *Dexterity and its development* (pp. 393–429). Mahwah, NJ: Erlbaum.

Newell, K. M., McDonald, P. V., & Baillargeon, R. (1993). Body scale and infant grip configurations. *Developmental Psychobiology, 26,* 195–205.

Newell, K. M., Scully, D. M., McDonald, P. V., & Baillargeon, R. (1990). Task constraints and infant grip configurations. *Developmental Psychobiology, 22,* 817–832.

Out, L., Savelsbergh, G. J. P., Van Soest, A. J., & Hopkins, B. (1997). Influence of mechanical factors on movement units in infant reaching. *Human Movement Science, 16,* 733–748.

Piaget, J. (1952). *The origins of intelligence in children.* New York: International Universities Press.

Piaget, J. (1954). *The construction of reality in the child.* New York: Basic Books.

Prigogine, I., & Stengers, I. (1984). *Order out of chaos: Man's new dialogue with nature.* New York: Bantam.

Reed, E. S. (1982). An outline of a theory of action systems. *Journal of Motor Behavior, 14,* 98–134.

Reed, E. S. (1996). *Encountering the world: Toward an ecological psychology.* New York: Oxford University Press.

Robinson, J. A., McKenzie, B. E., & Day, R. H. (1996). Anticipatory reaching by infants and adults: The effect of object features and apertures in opaque and transparent screens. *Child Development, 67,* 2641–2657.

Rochat, P. (1992). Self-sitting and reaching in 5- to 8-month-old infants: The impact of posture and its development on early eye–hand coordination. *Journal of Motor Behavior, 24,* 210–220.

Rochat, P. (1995). Early objectification of the self. In P. Rochat (Ed.), *Advances in psychology 112. The self in infancy: Theory and research* (pp. 73–93). Amsterdam: Elsevier.

Rochat, P., & Goubet, N. (1995). Development of sitting and reaching in 5- to 6-month-old infants. *Infant Behavior and Development, 18,* 53–68.

Rovee-Collier, C. (1996). Shifting focus from what to why. *Infant Behavior and Development, 19,* 385–400.

Sameroff, A. J. (1983). Developmental systems: Contexts and evolution. In W. Kessen (Ed.), *Handbook of child psychology: Vol. 1. History, theory, and methods* (pp. 237–294). New York: Wiley.

Savelsbergh, G. J. P., Von Hofsten, C., & Jonsson, B. (1997). The coupling of head, reach and grasp movement in nine-months-old infant prehension. *Scandinavian Journal of Psychology, 38,* 325–333.

Savelsbergh, G., Wimmers, R., van der Kamp, J., & Davids, K. (1999). The development of movement control and coordination: An introduction to direct perception, natural physical and the dynamic systems perspective. In A. F. Kalverboer, M. L. Genta, & B. Hopkins (Eds.), *Current issues in developmental neuropsychology* (pp. 107–136). Dordrecht: Kluwer.

Schmuckler, K. M. (1993). Perception–action coupling in infancy. In G. J. P. Savelsbergh (Ed.), *Advances in psychology 97: The development of coordination in infancy.* Amsterdam: Elsevier.

Sherrington, C. S. (1947). *The integrative action of the nervous system.* New Haven, CT: Yale University Press. (Original work published 1906)

Smitsman, A. W. (1997). The development of tool use: Changing boundaries between organism and environment. In C. Dent-Read & P. Zukow-Goldring (Eds.), *Evolving explanations of development: Ecological approaches to organism–environment systems* (pp. 301–329). Washington, DC: American Psychological Association.

Smitsman, A. W., & Bongers, R. M. (in press). Tool use and tool making: A dynamical developmental perspective. In J. Valsiner & K. J. Connolly (Eds.), *Handbook of developmental psychology.* London: Sage.

Thelen, E., Corbetta, D., Kamm, K., Spencer, J. P., Schneider, K., & Zernicke, R. F. (1993). The transition to reaching: Mapping intention and intrinsic dynamics. *Child Development, 64,* 1058–1098.

Thelen, E., Corbetta, D., & Spencer, J. P. (1996). Development of reaching during the first year: Role of movement speed. *Journal of Experimental Psychology: Human Perception and Performance, 22*(5), 1059–1076.

Thelen, E., & Smith, L. B. (1994). *A dynamic systems approach to the development of cognition and action.* Cambridge, MA: MIT Press.

Thelen, E., & Spencer, J. (1998). Postural control during reaching in young infants: A dynamic systems approach. *Neuroscience and Biobehavioral Reviews, 22*(4), 507–514.

Thelen, E., & Ulrich, B. D. (1991). Hidden skills. *Monographs of the Society for Research in Child Development, 56,* 1–106.

Tuller, B., Turvey, M. T., & Fitch, H. (1982). The Bernstein perspective: 2. The concept of muscle linkage or coordinative structure. In J. S. A. Kelso (Ed.), *Human motor behavior: An introduction* (pp. 253–270). Hillsdale, NJ: Erlbaum.

Turvey, M. T. (1990). Coordination. *American Psychologist, 45,* 938–953.

Valsiner, J. (1987). *Culture and the development of children's action.* Chichester: Wiley.

Van der Fits, I. B. M., & Hadders-Algra, M. (1998). The development of postural response patterns during reaching in healthy infants. *Neuroscience and Biobehavioral Reviews, 22,* 521–526.

Von Hofsten, C. (1979). Development of visually directed reaching: The approach phase. *Journal of Human Movement Studies, 5,* 160–178.

Von Hofsten, C. (1980). Predictive reaching for moving objects by human infants. *Journal of Experimental Child Psychology, 30,* 369–382.

Von Hofsten, C. (1982). Eye–hand coordination in the newborn. *Developmental Psychology, 18,* 450–461.

Von Hofsten, C. (1984). Developmental changes in the organization of prereaching movements. *Developmental Psychology, 20,* 378–388.

Von Hofsten, C. (1989). Motor development and the development of systems: Comments on the special section. *Developmental Psychology, 25,* 950–953.

Von Hofsten, C. (1991). Structuring of early reaching movements: A longitudinal study. *Journal of Motor Behavior, 23,* 280–292.

Von Hofsten, C. (1997). On the early development of predictive abilities. In C. Dent-Read & P. Zukow-Goldring (Eds.), *Evolving explanations of development: Ecological approaches to organism–environment systems* (pp. 163–195). Washington, DC: American Psychological Association.

Von Hofsten, C., & Fazel-Zandy, S. (1984). Development of visually guided hand orientation in reaching. *Journal of Experimental Child Psychology, 38,* 208–219.

Von Hofsten, C., & Lindhagen, K. (1979). Observations on the development of reaching for moving objects. *Journal of Experimental Child Psychology, 28,* 158–173.

Von Hofsten, C., & Ronnquist, L. (1988). Preparation for grasping an object: A developmental study. *Journal of Experimental Psychology: Human Perception and Performance, 14,* 610–621.

Von Hofsten, C., & Ronnquist, L. (1993). The structuring of neonatal arm movements. *Child Development, 64,* 1046–1057.

White, B. L., Castle, P., & Held, R. (1964). Observations on the development of visually directed reaching. *Child Development, 35,* 349–364.

Wimmers, R. H., Savelsbergh, G. J. P., Beek, P. J., & Hopkins, B. (1998). Evidence for a phase transition in the early development of prehension. *Developmental Psychobiology, 32*(3), 235–248.

Chapter Four

Cognitive Development: Knowledge of the Physical World

J. Gavin Bremner

Theoretical Overview

The term *cognition* is generally used to describe psychological processes that in some way go beyond straightforward perception. Conventionally, there are two respects in which cognition has been identified as vital for a full awareness of the world. First, it has been claimed that cognitive processes are required to interpret and organize perception: although perception may provide rich information about the physical world, at least until recently the notion has been that meaning and other types of high-level structuring can only be attached to perceptual experience through the functioning of cognitive interpretative processes. Second, there is the argument that cognition involves the process of *mental representation*, a process that supports mental activity in the absence of relevant perceptual input. Thus, cognitive processes are seen as structuring and interpreting perception, and function both in the presence and absence of perceptual subject matter.

Piaget's (1936/1954) account of the development of *sensorimotor intelligence* in infancy is based on the principle that cognitive development occurs through a process of construction in which individuals develop progressively more complex knowledge of the world through their actions in it. The crowning achievement of sensorimotor intelligence is the emergence of mental representation, making possible the awareness that objects remain permanent even when out of sight, and although from the middle of the period onwards evidence for representational ability begins to emerge, it is only at the end of the period that representational processes become truly independent of perception and action.

In recent years, there have been a growing number of challenges to *constructionist* accounts of this sort. These have been based on growing evidence for sophisticated awareness of the world in very young infants, and have been in two quite distinct forms. First, based on Gibsonian theory of *direct perception* (J. J. Gibson, 1979), investigators have argued that perception of environmental structures and even their meanings is objective: the structure is out there and can be directly perceived in relation to the individual's acts (E. J. Gibson, 1977). As we shall see, this account leaves no place for representation in everyday awareness of the world: perception *is* knowing, and there is no need to invoke representational processes to explain development during infancy. In contrast, *nativist* theorists see cognitive processes as central, but rather than see them as constructed from scratch, postulate innate mental structures and processes which they believe are necessary to explain the impressive abilities of young infants (Baillargeon, 1993; Spelke, Breinlinger, Macomber, & Jacobson, 1992).

In the following sections, compelling evidence that young infants respond to high-level properties of perceptual input will be reviewed. Most of the evidence pointing to psychological precocity arises from versions of habituation–novelty tasks (see chapter 2). In what are often called *violation of expectancy* tasks, this technique has been extended to investigate infants' knowledge of the world by familiarizing them to lawful events and then presenting test events, one of which violates certain physical rules of object movement, stability, etc. Longer looking at the violation event is interpreted as indication that the infant has noted the violation and is thus aware of the principle in question. Recently, however, there has been a serious challenge to cognitive interpretations of this sort, it being argued that positive results from violation of expectation studies can actually be interpreted in terms of low-level properties of attention and perceptual memory (Bogartz, Shinskey, & Speaker, 1997; Haith, 1998; Willatts & Fabricius, 1999). Given the crucial importance of establishing an appropriate level of interpretation of these data, this controversy will be a major focus in the sections that follow.

A further important objective in relation to claims about early cognitive competence is to explain why early awareness of properties like object permanence and causality is not revealed in the infant's actions until much later. Although Piaget's constructivist theory has suffered growing criticism, the data on which he based it, revealing limitations in infants' actions toward objects, replicate readily. For instance, we are left to explain why, if young infants understand the continuing existence of hidden objects (object permanence), they do not reveal this understanding in their manual search for hidden objects until the age of 9 months or later. Recently, there has been a renewed focus on deficits in search by infants around 9 months of age and older, and various accounts have emerged to explain why these errors exist. In one way or another, all these accounts lay stress on the developing relationship between perception and action, and here a recent theoretical orientation has gained popularity. According to *dynamic systems theory*, psychological development is the outcome of self-organization; complex systems progress naturally through states of instability followed by new, relatively stable states, and very subtle and often simple factors are capable of triggering highly complex changes (see chapter 3). In many respects, this approach to development is similar to Piaget's constructionism. But in replacing construction with self-organization, it shifts the emphasis away from mentalistic theorizing toward theorizing about organization that is distributed across the system rather than situated in hypothetical mental structures.

However, there are other viable candidate accounts of errors in action. Diamond (1985; Diamond & Goldman-Rakic, 1989) suggests that immaturity of frontal cortex leads to inability to both represent hidden objects and inhibit past actions. This account is a good example of a cognitive science approach to developmental questions, with its interdisciplinary emphasis on coordinating evidence about development of brain and behavior. A related approach is neural network and connectionist modeling, in which the primary base for model-building is computer modeling of hypothetical neural systems connecting perception and action. Munakata, McClelland, Johnson, and Siegler (1997) have developed a neural network model that explains object search errors in terms of relative strengths of active memory for the object and latent memory based on past experiences.

As we shall see, to a greater or lesser extent each of the above models manages to explain search errors without being challenged by the evidence of earlier object knowledge revealed by habituation–novelty tasks. However, there remains considerable doubt as to which of these accounts is more appropriate, and the problem of interpreting both the habituation–novelty evidence and the object search evidence persists. The following sections of this chapter will review research evidence on these topics, and the final section will revisit the theoretical issues outlined here and propose a developmental account that integrates both the evidence for early competence and later emerging skill in self-guided action.

Development of Object Knowledge

Historical Background

Until the 1960s, the dominant account of the development of object knowledge stemmed from Piaget's theory of sensorimotor development. According to him, infants are born without knowledge as such but are equipped with particular ways of functioning in their environment which ensure construction of progressively comprehensive knowledge of the properties of the world. As new objects or events are perceived and acted on they are incorporated (assimilated) within existing sensorimotor knowledge structures, and as a consequence, these structures are modified (accommodated) in order to incorporate the new information contained in these objects or events. During infancy, knowledge is in the form of structures coordinating perception and action (hence sensorimotor), and it is only toward the end of the sensorimotor period that infants develop mental structures based on representations of reality. Thus, development of mental representation is the key achievement of the infancy period. As a result, there is little surprise that Piaget placed so much stress on the development of object permanence (the knowledge that objects have continuity of existence even when out of sight), because according to him this property of objects can only be appreciated through mental representation.

According to this account, object permanence begins to emerge around 8 or 9 months, as evidenced by the emergence of search for hidden objects. However, this was an elementary form of awareness, and it is only by the end of the sensorimotor period that object representation loses its dependence on perception and action. In a later section, the evidence on search errors on which Piaget based his claims, and the body of work which continues to develop around these phenomena, will be reviewed. However, the most striking challenge to constructionist accounts has come from work, commencing in the 1960s and continuing today, suggesting that very young infants have sophisticated awareness of the physical world well before they are able to search for objects.

Work carried out in the 1960s by T. G. R. Bower and his associates had a strong influence on thinking about young infants' abilities. A major limitation of object search tasks as measures of object knowledge is that infants only begin to search for hidden objects sometime around 8 months of age, and Bower recognized that other means were needed to investigate object knowledge in very young infants. He developed a family of ingenious techniques, mainly based on measuring infants' response to events that violated physical principles, the rationale behind these being that if infants registered surprise at a violation event, we could conclude that they had knowledge of the physical principle being violated. Thus, for instance, he presented infants with an object which was gradually occluded by a moving screen. After this event, the screen's movement was reversed, either to reveal the object as before or to reveal an empty location (Bower, 1966). Using heart-rate change as a measure of surprise, Bower measured greater surprise at nonreappearance by infants as young as 20 days. With these very young infants, this effect disappeared for longer occlusion times, indicating that it was based on fairly fragile and transient awareness. In contrast, older infants tolerated longer occlusion times. Bower's conclusion was that even in the first month of life, infants understand object permanence, knowing that an object that had disappeared through an occlusion event should reappear when the occluder was removed.

Bower and his colleagues carried out similar studies involving objects that moved behind occluders, violation trials involving reemergence too soon for the rate of movement at disappearance, or emergence of a new object on the same trajectory (Bower, Broughton, & Moore, 1971). Results revealed that very young infants note trajectory violations but only after 6 months note changes in object form, and Bower developed an account according to which infants, despite precocious knowledge of object permanence, fail to identify moving and stationary object as the same entity. However, there were a number of criticisms of Bower's conclusions (Goldberg, 1976; Moore, Borton, & Darby, 1978) and failures of replication (Meicler & Gratch, 1980; Muller & Aslin, 1978), and it was about a decade before other investigators developed techniques that appeared to be able to tackle the same questions with fewer attendant interpretative problems.

Research on Young Infants' Object Knowledge

Perception of object unity

Some of the evidence relating to object knowledge and permanence arises from habituation–novelty studies of infant perception (see chapter 1), specifically, perception of object unity. The initial study on which much recent work has been based was by Kellman and Spelke (1983). Four-month-old infants were habituated to a rod that moved back and

Habituation display

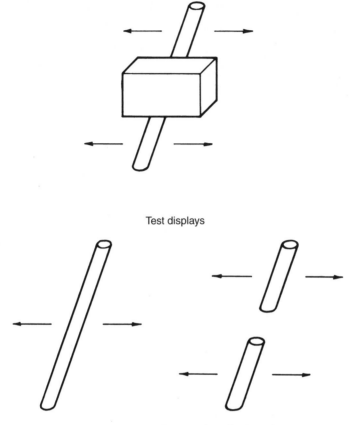

Test displays

Figure 4.1 A subset of the stimuli used by Kellman and Spelke (1983) to investigate young infants' perception of object unity. (Reprinted with permission from Academic Press)

forth behind a box, and were then tested for novelty preference on two displays in which the box was absent: (a) the two rod parts (what they had literally seen of the rod during habituation) and (b) a complete rod (Figure 4.1). Infants showed a novelty preference for the two rod parts, indicating that, during habituation, they had perceived a complete rod moving behind the box. This phenomenon, in which infants are apparently "filling in" the absent part of the rod, may be compared to object permanence, in which the infant represents the whole absent object. This work has been extended to show that infants rely on a variety of perceptual information to segregate surfaces and perceive object unity (Johnson & Aslin, 1996; Johnson & Náñez, 1995). For instance, depth information provided by a background texture is necessary if 4-month-olds are to detect object unity in computer-generated versions of the rod and box display.

These effects are only obtained if the occluded object is in motion, pointing to the possibility that common motion is an important factor in perception of unity. But it appears that common motion is not a sufficient factor for detection of object unity.

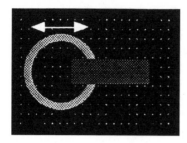 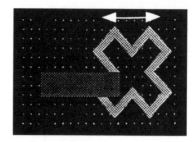

Figure 4.2   Habituation stimuli used by Johnson et al. (2000). After habituation to either the circle or cross display, infants are presented with test displays with the occluding bar removed, consisting of either a complete cross or circle, or the same with the previously occluded part omitted. (Reprinted with permission from Academic Press)

Johnson and Aslin (1996) showed that 4-month-olds did not perceive object unity in displays in which the rod was a dog-leg form with unaligned, differently oriented visible parts or if the visible parts, although parallel, were out of alignment. Thus, alignment of parts as well as common motion appears to be important. However, other higher-level stimulus properties appear to be important, too. Johnson, Bremner, Slater, and Mason (2000) showed that 4-month-olds perceived object unity in displays in which the occluded object was a circle or a cross (see Figure 4.2). In both cases, although there was no alignment of figure elements immediately either side of the occluding box, infants were apparently using the principle of overall figural "goodness" to perceive object unity.

Interestingly, perception of object unity in these displays appears to develop between birth and 2 months. When newborns were tested on the Kellman and Spelke display, they showed a preference for the complete rod (Slater, Johnson, Brown, & Badenoch, 1996), indicating that during habituation they perceived what was visible, the two rod parts, treating the complete rod as novel. However, by 2 months, infants have been found to perceive object unity, provided the occluding box is narrow (Johnson & Aslin, 1995).

Strangely, these effects do not appear to apply to all forms of object movement. Although positive results are also obtained for vertical translations and movements in depth (Kellman, Spelke, & Short, 1986), negative results are obtained at 4 months for rotational movements (Eizenman & Bertenthal, 1998). There is a developmental progression here, however, because Eizenman and Bertenthal showed that 6-month-olds perceived object unity in both the rotating and translating rod tasks. Interestingly, the way in which relative motion is generated between occluded object and its occluder also determines perception of unity, because Kellman, Gleitman, and Spelke (1987) found that relative motion generated by movement of the infant rather than by movement of the occluded object did not lead to perception of unity.

In summary, although perception of object unity appears to imply something about the permanence of the hidden parts of an object, the processes leading to it may have more to do with Gestalt-like perceptual processes than with awareness of object permanence. The likelihood remains, however, that there is a developmental link between perception of unity and object permanence.

Habituation

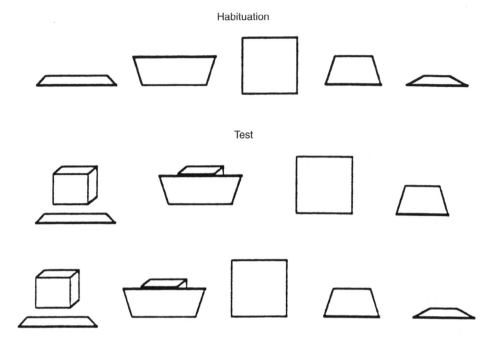

Test

Figure 4.3 The infant's view of the possible and impossible events in Baillargeon et al. (1985). (Reprinted from *Cognition, 20,* Baillargeon et al., "Object permanence in five-month-old infants," 191–208, copyright © 1985, with permission from Elsevier Science)

Violation of expectancy as a measure of infant knowledge

The technique used in many recent studies of object knowledge involves familiarizing infants with an event sequence and then presenting them with test events which either do or do not violate the physical principle under test. The procedure here is similar to habituation studies of perception, with an important difference. It is assumed that infants will look longer at events that violate physical principles rather than events that are simply perceptually novel. So increased looking at a new event sequence indicates more than surface discrimination: it indicates not just that something is different but that something is wrong with the new event. If this interpretation is appropriate it is possible to diagnose the level of infants' awareness of object permanence or the rules by which one object moves relative to another, because if they note a violation they must be aware of the principle that has been violated. One of the first studies to use this technique was carried out by Baillargeon, Spelke, and Wasserman (1985). In what is often called the *drawbridge task*, 5-month-old infants were familiarized with a repeated event in which a flap rotated from flat on the table through 180 degrees. From the infant's perspective, this would look like the raising of a drawbridge, except that the rotation went through a full 180 degrees. After familiarization, two types of test event were presented, in both of which a cube was placed in the path of the flap (Figure 4.3). In a "possible" test event, the flap rotated but came to a stop on making contact with the cube, whereas in an "impossible" test event, it rotated through 180 degrees as usual, appearing to annihilate the cube in the process.

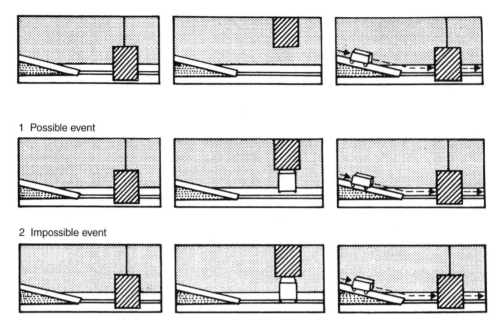

1 Possible event

2 Impossible event

Figure 4.4   The procedure used by Baillargeon (1986) to investigate young infants' object knowledge. The familiarization event is at the top and the two test events are shown below. (Reprinted from *Cognition*, *23*, Baillargeon, "Representing the existence and the location of hidden objects: Object permanence in 6- and 8-month-old infants," 21–41, copyright © 1986, with permission from Elsevier Science)

Note that this comparison nicely creates an opposition between surface event similarity, in which the impossible event (full 180-degree rotation) is more similar to the familiarization event than is the possible event (less than 180-degree rotation), and event lawfulness, in which only the impossible event presents a violation of physical reality. Thus, if infants were simply dishabituating on the basis of perceptual dissimilarity, we would expect more looking at the possible event where there is both a new object (the block) and a different rotation. However, they actually looked more at the impossible event. The conclusion was that infants of this age both understand object permanence and know that one object cannot move through another.

This initial finding was later replicated with infants as young as 3.5 months old (Baillargeon, 1987a). Additionally, Baillargeon (1987b) used the same technique to investigate the accuracy with which older infants could anticipate events of this sort. She found that 7-month-olds had quite precise expectations about such collisions, expecting that the screen would stop rotating sooner if the cube was larger or closer to the screen, but expecting it to stop later if the object in its path was compressible.

Figure 4.4 illustrates another application of this approach (Baillargeon, 1986). Infants were familiarized with an event sequence in which a toy truck rolled down a ramp and passed behind a screen (prior to each trial the screen was raised, revealing nothing behind it, and lowered again). After familiarization, infants saw one of two test events. In the possible event, a block was placed behind the screen, but behind the track so that it did

Habituation events

Short-carrot event

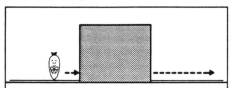

Tall-carrot event

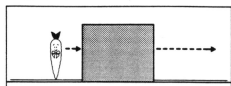

Test events

Possible event

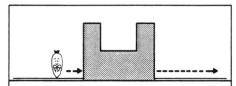

Impossible event

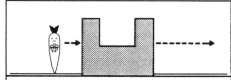

Figure 4.5 The stimuli used by Baillargeon and DeVos (1991) to investigate how infants' knowledge of how the size of an object affects its visibility. (Reprinted with permission)

not obstruct the path of the truck. In the impossible event, the block was placed behind the screen on the track, so that it presented an obstruction. In both cases, the screen was raised to reveal the block and lowered again, whereupon the truck rolled down the track and reemerged from behind the screen as usual. Baillargeon found that 6- to 8-month-olds looked longer at the impossible event, a finding replicated by Baillargeon and DeVos (1991). Apparently, infants not only appreciate the continued existence of the block but can use precise memory for its position to reach a conclusion about whether or not the truck event is possible.

Spelke et al. (1992) used modified versions of this task to test even younger infants. In one case, they familiarized 2.5-month-olds to an event in which a ball rolled behind a screen, whereupon the screen was lifted to show that the ball had come to rest against an end wall. On test trials, a box was placed in the path of the ball so that when the screen was lowered only the top part of the box was visible. Two events followed, a possible event, in which removal of the screen revealed the ball resting against the box having collided with it, and an impossible event in which the object was revealed resting against the end wall, having apparently passed through the box to come to rest in its usual place. Infants looked longer at the impossible event, suggesting that 2.5-month-olds can detect the position of the whole box from perception of a visible part, and understand that one object cannot move through another in its path.

This approach can be used to investigate infants' understanding of a wide range of object properties. For instance, Baillargeon and DeVos (1991) investigated infants' awareness of how the dimensions of an object affect its visibility as it passes behind a screen. They used the arrangement shown in Figure 4.5, first to familiarize infants with an event

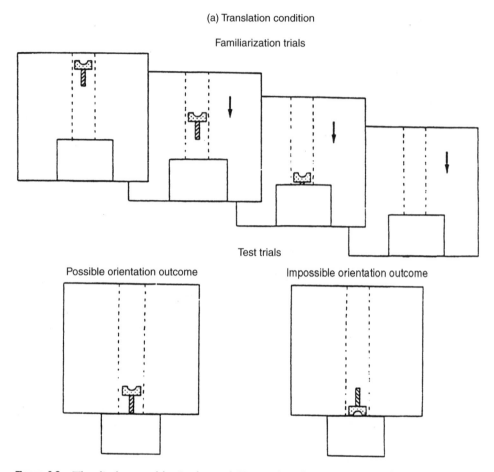

Figure 4.6   The displays used by Rochat and Hespos (1996) to investigate infants' awareness of how the trajectory of an object affects its final orientation. (Reprinted from *Cognitive Development, 11*, Rochat & Hespos, "Tracking and anticipation of invisible spatial transformations by 4- to 8-month-old infants," 3–17, copyright © 1996, with permission from Elsevier Science)

in which either a tall or a short carrot moved behind a screen, to reemerge at the opposite side. Test trials were followed with a new screen with a window cut in it. The size of the window was such that the small carrot would not appear there, whereas the top of the large carrot would appear. But neither the small or the large carrot appeared at the window on these test trials, making the small-carrot event sequence lawful and the large-carrot event sequence unlawful. Three-and-a-half-month-old infants looked more at the unlawful test event, leading to the conclusion that they have a good awareness of the conditions under which one object will occlude another.

Another study investigated infants' understanding of how an object's trajectory affects its final orientation. Rochat and Hespos (1996) exposed 4- to 8-month-olds to an object moving either on a linear vertical trajectory or a rotating circular trajectory (see Figure 4.6). In each case, the object ended its movement behind a screen, which was then lifted

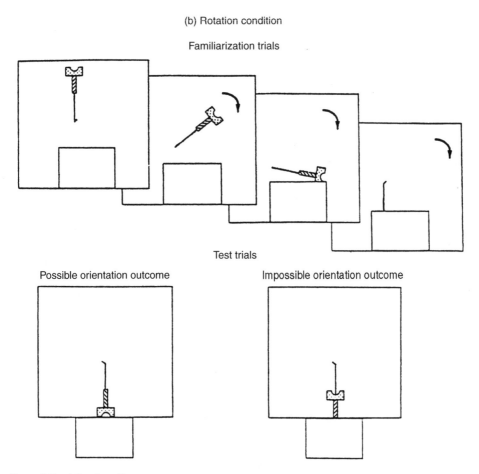

(b) Rotation condition

Familiarization trials

Test trials

Possible orientation outcome   Impossible orientation outcome

Figure 4.6 (*Continued*)

to reveal it either in its original orientation (correct for the linear trajectory), or inverted (correct for the rotational trajectory). In the linear trajectory condition, 4-month-olds and older looked longer at the inverted object, whereas in the rotational trajectory condition, they looked longer at the object in its original orientation. In other words, they looked longer at the impossible outcome in each case. Further evidence indicated that these looking tendencies depended on perception of the movement information prior to object disappearance, and Rochat and Hespos interpret this as evidence that infants are able to predict object orientation on the basis of trajectory information.

Needham and Baillargeon (1993) investigated infants' knowledge of the conditions under which one object provides support for another by presenting events in which an object moved along a support to a point at which it either remained supported or should fall off. Their finding was that infants of 4.5 months appear to treat contact as sufficient for support, failing to identify the degree of support necessary. Baillargeon, Needham, and DeVos (1992) showed that, in contrast, 6.5-month-olds had developed a more sophisticated understanding, recognizing when contact was insufficient to provide support.

Two studies (Spelke et al., 1992) indicate that young infants have general problems in understanding movement under gravitational force. In the first, 4-month-old infants were habituated to a sequence in which an object fell behind a screen, which was subsequently lifted to reveal it at rest on a surface (see Figure 4.7a). On test trials, a higher shelf was introduced (still behind the screen when it was down), the object was dropped, and infants either saw an end result of the object resting on the shelf, or the object resting on the original (lower) surface. Infants looked longer at the latter (impossible) outcome, suggesting that they understood movement under gravity and the solidity constraint of the interposed shelf. However, this conclusion is shown to be premature by the results of a follow-up study in which the same 4-month-olds were presented with, effectively, the initial study in reverse. Infants were habituated to events in which an object fell behind a screen, on removal of which it was revealed at rest on a raised shelf (Figure 4.7b). Test trials were done with the shelf removed. Again the ball fell behind the screen and the screen was lifted to reveal it either at rest on the lower surface or suspended in mid-air just where the shelf had previously supported it. Under these conditions, 4-month-olds looked longer at the first outcome, despite the fact that this was the appropriate end point of a movement under gravity. Spelke et al. (1992) conclude that young infants do not understand *inertia* (that objects do not change direction or rate of movement suddenly or without the operation of some external force) or *gravity* (that objects move downwards in the absence of support).

Object segregation, numerical identity, and numerical knowledge

OBJECT SEGREGATION

Piaget (1936/1954) noted that infants had difficulty segregating objects placed in contact, and Kestenbaum, Termine, and Spelke (1987) showed that 3-month-olds segregated objects that were separated in depth but not objects that were adjacent in depth. Needham and Baillargeon (1997) investigated conditions under which infants detect objects as separate or interconnected. Their finding was that when two objects are in contact, infants of 8 months generally treat them as interconnected and so expect them to move together. However, a nice additional finding was that a prior demonstration that a blade could be passed between the objects at the point of contact led infants to expect them to move separately. Additionally, they showed that prior experience, in the form of previously seeing two objects singly, led 4-month-olds to segregate them when they were presented in contact (Needham & Baillargeon, 1998). Furthermore, Needham (1998) showed that 4-month-olds could use featural information to segregate objects in simple arrays, and that 7-month-olds could do so in the case of arrays that were in principle harder to segregate. There is a natural link here to numerical knowledge, because segregation of the world into separate units is a precondition for enumerating them.

NUMERICAL IDENTITY

Several studies have investigated knowledge of number in an indirect way which ties in directly with work on object identity. For instance, Xu and Carey (1996) investigated

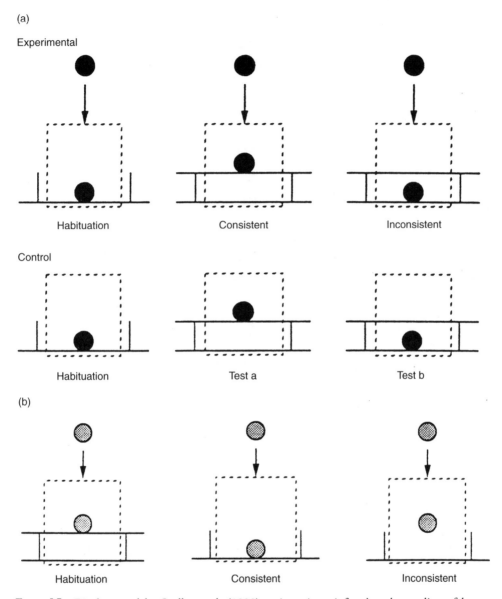

Figure 4.7 Displays used by Spelke et al. (1992) to investigate infants' understanding of how objects move under the effect of gravity. (Copyright © 1992 by the American Psychological Association. Reprinted with permission)

10- to 12-month-olds' use of featural versus spatiotemporal knowledge to decide whether one or more than one object was involved in the tested events. In a *discontinuous* condition, infants were shown events in which one object was seen to emerge and then disappear behind one screen, followed by emergence of an identical object from a second screen, whereas in a continuous condition, the events were the same except that a single

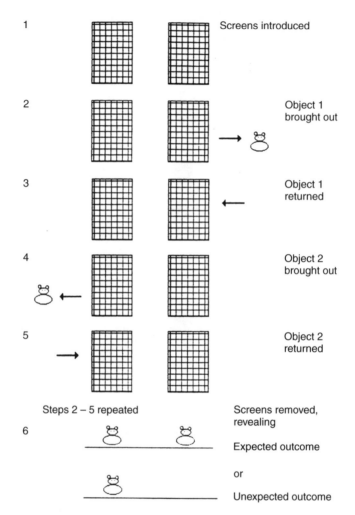

Figure 4.8   The discontinuous movement event used by Xu and Carey (1996) to investigate infants' knowledge of numerical identity. After familiarization with the event sequence, the screens are removed to reveal either one or two objects. The continuous event sequence differs only in the respect that a single object is involved which thus appears between the screens as well as to left and right. (Reprinted with permission from Academic Press)

object contributed to the event, traveling between the screens. After repetitions of these events, the screens were lowered to reveal either one or two objects (see Figure 4.8). Infants in the *discontinuous* condition looked significantly longer at the one-object outcome, whereas those in the *continuous* condition looked marginally significantly longer at the two-object display. These results were taken as evidence that infants use continuity/discontinuity of movement as a means of estimating the number of objects involved: when the screens were removed infants in the discontinuous condition expected two objects and those in the continuous condition expected one object. However, in a similar study with a single screen and distinct objects, infants showed no evidence of expecting to see two objects when the screen was removed. Xu and Carey therefore proposed that 10-month-olds do not use featural information to individuate objects.

Working with much younger infants, Spelke, Kestenbaum, Simons, and Wein (1995) obtained rather similar results to those of Xu and Carey in their first experiment. Following a two-screen task, 3- and 4-month-olds showed different looking preferences for one or two objects dependent on whether they had seen no object between screens or a continuous movement past both screens. However, when two screens were replaced by one, and events corresponded to a single object moving back and forth on a constant trajectory, 3- to 4-month-olds provided no evidence of using this constant trajectory information (what Spelke et al. called smoothness of motion) to determine that only one object was involved. This may not be so surprising, because the events in question could be produced by one or two objects. However, in a subsequent experiment, Spelke et al. (1995) found that infants showed no evidence of using violation of trajectory (early or instantaneous reemergence) to conclude that two objects were involved.

Wilcox and Baillargeon (1998) suggest that tasks of this sort may underestimate young infants' ability because of their complexity. They draw a distinction between "event-mapping" tasks, in which infants make a judgment about an end event in terms of earlier events, and "event-monitoring" tasks, in which all the information is based in the event itself, and claim that the former are in principle more complex than the latter. In support of this claim, they replicated Xu and Carey's results in a similar event-mapping task, but obtained positive results with infants as young as 7 months in an event-monitoring task. This task was ingeniously designed to investigate infants' inferences about the number of objects involved in the event. Infants saw one object move behind a screen and a distinct one reemerge at the other side under two conditions. In a wide-screen condition, the screen was large enough to hide both objects, whereas in a narrow-screen condition, it could hide only one object. Infants of 7 to 9 months looked longer at the narrow-screen event, suggesting that they knew that the change in object form indicated a different object and that this was an impossible sequence only when the screen was too narrow to hide both. It is possible, however, that the difference in screen width might explain this effect. Wilcox and Baillargeon controlled for this by testing infants again with the narrow screen, using smaller objects both of which could be concealed behind it, and finding that infants treated this event in the same way as the wide-screen event with larger objects.

NUMERICAL KNOWLEDGE

Earlier work established evidence that quite young infants were capable of discriminating small numbers. Starkey and Cooper (1980) habituated 4- to 7-month-old infants to patterns of a particular number of dots (two or three) and tested for dishabituation to the other number (three or two). They also included a large number condition in which there were either four or six dots. Infants dishabituated to number change in the small-number but not in the large-number condition. This supported their supposition that infants' number discrimination was based on *subitizing*, an ability to enumerate number perceptually which is limited to small numbers. Additionally, the negative result with larger numbers serves to make unlikely discrimination on the basis of lower-level stimulus properties such as contour density or brightness differences, because these differences were actually greater in the large number arrays. Starkey, Spelke, and Gelman (1990) reduced further the possibility that discrimination between arrays could be based on lower-order perceptual properties by habituating infants to pictures of sets of different objects in different spatial arrangements which were always in groups of the same number, testing them on sets of novel objects in novel arrangements that were either the same or different in number. Despite the fact that all test arrays contained novel objects in novel arrangements, 6- to 9-month-olds looked longer at arrays containing a novel number of objects. In addition to confirming the earlier work, this result suggests that infants' discrimination of number is not limited to comparisons between sets of identical objects, a limitation that had at one time been assumed to apply to young children's enumeration of sets. And results of this sort are not limited to infants of 4 months and over, because Antell and Keating (1983) replicated Starkey and Cooper's results with newborn infants.

There is also evidence that 6-month-olds are capable of discriminating large number arrays, such as 8 versus 16 (Xu & Spelke, 2000). However, discriminations of this sort are conditional on the ratio being large. That is, infants discriminate between 8 and 16, but not between 8 and 12. Thus, Xu and Spelke conclude that what is being uncovered here is an ability to represent approximate numerosity, probably subserved by the different system from the one supporting small-number discrimination.

Perception of number does not appear to be limited to the visual modality, or indeed to one modality. Starkey et al. (1990) also showed that infants were capable of detecting the numerical equivalence between sets of objects and groups of sounds. Six- to 8-month-olds were presented with pairs of visual arrays, one containing two and the other three objects, while a drumbeat pattern of either two or three beats was presented. They found that infants looked longer at stimuli containing the same number of objects as the number of drumbeats presented.

These are striking results, particularly because the abilities attributed to infants are greater than have so far been shown in preschool children. However, they have not gone unquestioned. For instance, Moore, Benenson, Reznick, Peterson, and Kagan (1987) and Mix, Levine, and Huttenlocher (1997) obtained the opposite auditory–visual matching result, finding that infants looked longer at the display that was not numerically equivalent to the sound pattern. This in itself is not a fatal problem, because the opposite effect still implies detection of a consistent relationship between auditory and visual numerosity. And there is no reason to assume that infants should look at the pattern with the same number rather than the pattern with a different number. However, the inconsistency of results raises concern about the reliability of the techniques used. In addition, Mix et al. (1997) point out that the auditory–visual correspondence could be based on an imprecise match in quantity between visual array and sound. Furthermore, in previous work, auditory numerosity was always confounded with either pattern frequency or pattern duration, and when Mix et al. (1997) randomized these variables within the task, they found no significant preference for either the corresponding or different number visual array. However, randomly altering these variables may add an attention-getting factor to the task that distracts infants from the numerical correspondence. So it may be that this test is too strong. The positive results, despite their inconsistency, suggest that

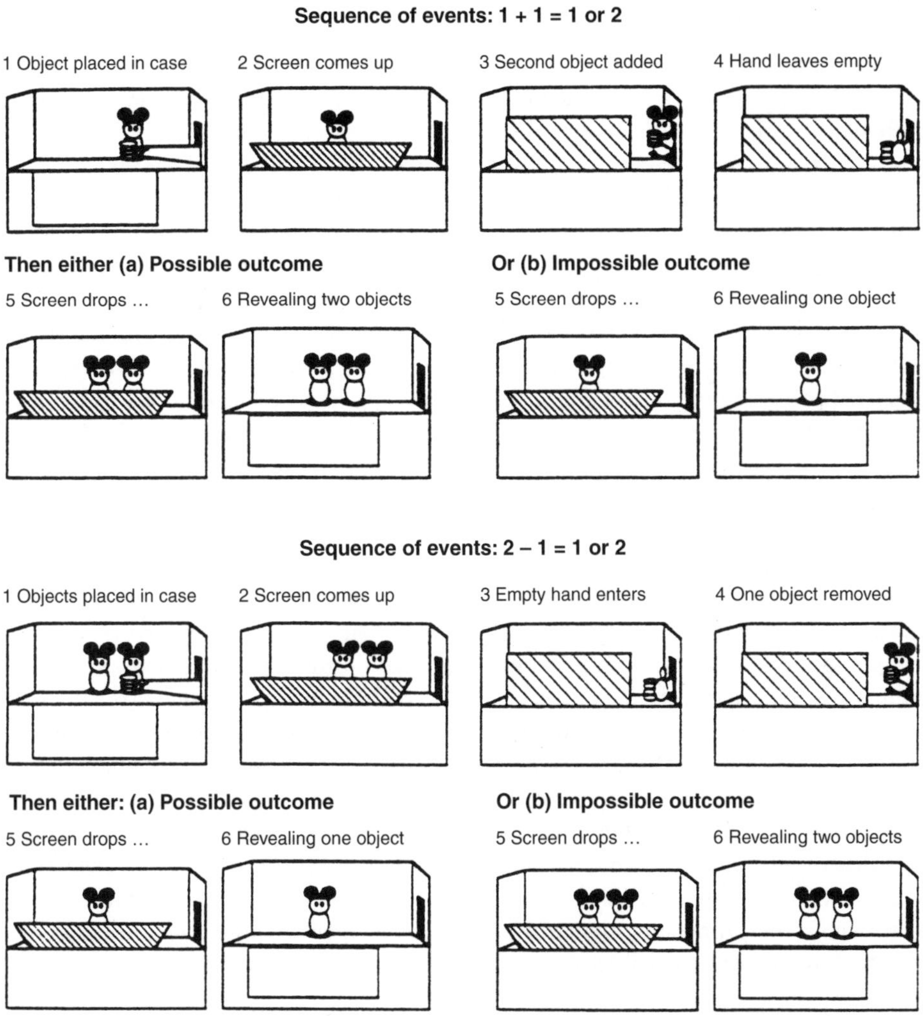

Sequence of events: 1 + 1 = 1 or 2

1 Object placed in case   2 Screen comes up   3 Second object added   4 Hand leaves empty

Then either (a) Possible outcome

5 Screen drops ...   6 Revealing two objects

Or (b) Impossible outcome

5 Screen drops ...   6 Revealing one object

Sequence of events: 2 – 1 = 1 or 2

1 Objects placed in case   2 Screen comes up   3 Empty hand enters   4 One object removed

Then either: (a) Possible outcome

5 Screen drops ...   6 Revealing one object

Or (b) Impossible outcome

5 Screen drops ...   6 Revealing two objects

Figure 4.9 Displays used by Wynn (1992) to investigate infants' knowledge of addition and subtraction. The addition event sequence is above and the subtraction event sequence below.

at least some rather global notion of quantity is present in the first year of life. If it does not constitute numerical competence, it is probably one of its important developmental precursors.

Wynn (1992, 1995) carried out a number of ingenious studies designed to go beyond research on numerical correspondence, to establish whether infants possess a number system as such, that is, whether they understand numerical operations such as addition and subtraction. Her basic method is illustrated in Figure 4.9. In the addition task, infants are presented with a single object, a screen is raised to hide it, whereupon a hand appears with a second object and places it behind the screen (the addition operation). The screen is then lowered for the test trial to reveal either one object (original array but impossible given addition of the second object) or two objects (novel array but correct given addition). In the subtraction task, two objects are presented initially, and the hand removes one once they are screened. Thus in this case on the test trial the single-object outcome is correct and the two-object outcome is incorrect. Four- and 5-month-olds performed differently on the test trials, looking longer at the single object in the addition case and longer at the double object in the subtraction case. Wynn concluded that infants have an understanding of addition and subtraction, but recognized that this could be a very approximate system in which any larger or smaller number would be accepted as the result of addition and subtraction respectively. Thus she conducted a further study in which 4-month-olds were exposed to the 1 + 1 addition task and on test trials were presented with either two or three objects. Infants looked longer at the three-object outcome, and Wynn concluded that their knowledge of addition was quite precise, to the extent that they expected precisely two objects and just not more objects to result from a 1 + 1 operation. To explain these abilities, she proposes an accumulator mechanism (originally developed by Meck & Church, 1983, to account for discrimination of number by rats) through which discrete pulses for each object "counted" are passed into an accumulator, and relative numerosity judgments are then based on the fullness of the accumulator between the two sets of objects "counted."

In conclusion, there is fairly good evidence that young infants can discriminate small numbers, both within and across modalities, and that they are aware of the outcome of simple addition and subtraction operations. Additionally, they appear to predict the number of objects involved in certain events. All this evidence relates to very small numbers of objects, and it appears likely that perceptual processes such as subitizing support this early ability. Despite the negative results with larger numbers of objects, there is evidence that infants respond to the perceptual correlates of number in larger number arrays. Tan and Bryant (2000) have shown that 6-month-olds respond to changes in density and (under certain conditions) changes in length accompanying changes in number in arrays of four to six objects. Although we cannot conclude from this evidence that infants are enumerating the arrays, by 6 months they are responding to perceptual variables that typically signal changes in number.

Interpreting the Evidence: Must We Assume Innate Cognitive Structures?

Object identity

Taken alone, the results of some of the earlier studies by Baillargeon and Spelke suggest that very young infants have an awareness of the world which virtually matches that of adults. However, the results of these investigations of support and connectedness indicate a qualification to such a conclusion. Although young infants do appear to possess a good basic understanding of physical principles, this becomes more sophisticated as they get older, and both Baillargeon et al. (1992) and Spelke et al. (1992) argue that initial core knowledge becomes elaborated through experience. As Baillargeon et al. (1992) put it: "in their first pass at understanding physical events, infants construct all-or-none representations that capture the essence of the events but few of the details. With further experience, these initial, core representations are progressively elaborated."

The picture emerging from this literature is radically different from the conventional Piagetian constructionism. It is argued that infants are endowed with innate knowledge and psychological processes. They possess core knowledge concerning fundamental physical principles of *continuity* (that objects move on continuous paths) and *solidity* (that objects occupy space and no two objects can occupy the same space simultaneously). Early knowledge, however, is limited, as indicated by the evidence that young infants do not understand principles of gravity or inertia, and development of further knowledge is based on experience.

To summarize, young infants possess innate core knowledge of physical principles on the basis of which they form active representations about events which allow them to reason about outcomes that are not directly perceived. However, their initial core knowledge accords to certain general truths about physical reality (continuity, solidity) but not to others (inertia, gravity, smoothness of motion), and experience leads to elaboration of knowledge around a constant preexisting core.

Other accounts rely on at least the notion that young infants form mental representations of objects. For instance, as a first stage in their account of the development of object permanence, Meltzoff and Moore (1998) argue that young infants form representations of objects that serve to specify their continued existence over breaks in sensory contact. There are, however, growing criticisms of all these approaches. First, it is not clear whether the data demand interpretation in terms of cognitive processes, in particular the notion of infant reasoning. The only factor in moving object studies that appears to demand interpretation in terms of reasoning, or indeed representation, is the presence of a screen concealing part of the object's trajectory. Supposedly, to produce positive results, the infant must have represented the continuing existence of the screened object and reasoned about its continued history on the basis of knowledge of physical reality. However, alternative conceptualizations exist. In particular, one of the principles of the ecological approach to perception (J. J. Gibson, 1979) is that perceptual input is dynamic and continuous over time. The movement of an individual through the world generates a continuous flow of information which specifies the relationship between objects in the world and their changing relationship to the individual. True, there are gaps in perception as one object is temporarily occluded by another. But the information flow before and after occlusion serves to specify the object continuously over this gap: perceptual information specifies the occlusion of a further object by a near one, not its annihilation, and the same applies on its reappearance. Thus, according to ecological theorists, detection of an object's spatiotemporal history arises directly from perpetual information and does not require representational processes or reasoning. In other words, perceptual extrapolation fills breaks in sensory contact, and there is no need to invoke representational processes. It may be that there is a parallel here with the work on object unity as well as Bower's (1966) early work with a screened stationary object. In object unity studies, it is deduced that there is persistence of perception across a spatial gap. Similarly, in the case of a stationary object temporarily hidden from view, there may be persistence of perception across a temporal gap. And in the case of an object that moves behind a screen, persistence takes place across a spatiotemporal gap.

Another form of criticism of nativist interpretation gets more to the roots of the tasks themselves. Investigators such as Bogartz et al. (1997) and Haith (1998) argue that it is at least premature to apply interpretations of these recent data, it being possible to explain much of the evidence in terms of much more basic properties of perception and memory. One of the puzzles regarding recent studies is why there is a need for initial familiarization trials prior to test trials. After all, if we are tapping into innate knowledge and reasoning processes, violation test trials should be detected as discrepant without prior familiarization. And yet, it is apparent that positive results depend on prior familiarization. Possibly, this is because early knowledge is sufficiently weak to require prior repeated experience of an event to bolster judgment. Alternatively, infants' responses in these tasks may reflect detection of a departure from an expectation built up over the series of familiarization trials rather than violation of a core principle of physical reality.

Bogartz et al. (1997) point out how the detection of disparity between familiarization and test event can be at quite a low level, tapping into basic attentional or perceptual processes. As already noted, Baillargeon and DeVos habituated infants either to a short or a tall carrot passing behind a screen, and test trials were identical except that a gap was cut in the top of the screen which should reveal the tall but not the short carrot. But in neither test trial did a carrot appear in the gap. Their interpretation is that infants can reason about visibility on the basis of the height of the carrot. In contrast, Bogartz et al. (1997) suggest that in the short-carrot display, infants' attention is attracted to the carrot's face and they scan across the screen at that height. Thus they do not notice the change in the top of the screen. Infants in the tall-carrot condition, however, scan at the higher level of the carrot's face, and note the gap on test trials. Thus, increased looking is due solely to the change in the screen, and whether or not this change is detected is determined by the attentional focus built up during familiarization. They press home this point by performing an extended version of Baillargeon and DeVos's study, using a complex balanced design in which infants are habituated to either lawful or unlawful events and are tested on the remaining two events. The outcome was that patterns of increased looking could be accounted for in terms of perceptual mismatches between habituation and test events, and that there was no evidence that increased looking was guided by impossibility of the carrot not appearing at the window.

Other studies also appear to be open to alternative interpretations. For instance, investigating the drawbridge task (Baillargeon et al., 1985), Rivera, Wakeley, and Langer (1999) suggest that infants' longer looking at the impossible event in which the drawbridge rotates apparently through the position of the block may be due to a simple preference for a longer rotation, involving as it does greater perceptual change. Baillargeon (1987a) dismisses such an interpretation because she found no preference for 112-degree rotation over 180-degree rotation in a control task in which no block is placed in the path of the drawbridge. However, these test trials followed normal habituation trials with the 180-degree rotation, and as Rivera et al. point out, under these circumstances one would expect a novelty preference for the 112-degree rotation. They hypothesize that infants actually have a preference for the larger rotation which is lost due to exposure to this event during habituation, and test this possibility by replicating the Baillargeon technique omitting prior habituation trials. Under these circumstances, infants show a preference for the 180-degree rotation, the strength of which is unaffected by whether there is a block in the path of the drawbridge or not.

It does appear that the incomplete designs used in much of this work limit the conclusions that can be drawn. However, it is not yet clear to what extent this yields interpretative problems across the board. Also, it is true that some of the findings are open to alternative interpretations that rely on quite simple processes. Typically, however, each of the findings requires a different low-level interpretation, which leads to the question of whether such interpretations are really more parsimonious or plausible. Additionally, it is very hard to explain some findings in these terms, in particular, the effect obtained by Baillargeon (1986: see Figure 4.4), in which the difference between possible and impossible test events lay in whether the block lay on or behind the track of the toy truck. It seems inescapable that, at some level, perceptual or cognitive, infants registered whether the block obstructed the track or not, and that looking duration was determined by a combination of this information and the fixed outcome of object reemergence.

Numerical knowledge

It should be noted that, despite the apparently high levels of control in studies of number discrimination, some workers question whether discrimination of number is really at the root of the findings. For instance, Clearfield and Mix (1999) point out that number was often confounded with total contour (three objects have more total contour than two objects of the same size). In a study investigating this, they found that infants dishabituated to changes in contour but not to changes in small number (2 vs. 3) with contour held constant. Thus they conclude that when the appropriate controls are applied, evidence for number discrimination disappears. In contrast, however, Xu and Spelke (2000) obtained positive results for large numbers with total contour controlled. The problem is that certain ways of applying controls may actually suppress an ability that is really there. Clearfield and Mix presented a block of test trials, each one of which involved either a change in total contour or a change in number. The change in contour that they used looks to adult eyes more striking than the change in number, and this may have led infants to operate at the level of contour rather than number. In contrast, Xu and Spelke varied contour during habituation trials, holding number constant, a technique that is more likely to lead infants to focus on number as the constant variable during habituation.

Haith (1998) criticizes the conclusions that Wynn draws from her work, on the basis that her results can be interpreted at a simple perceptual level. He bases his argument on a "thought experiment" in which Wynn's procedures are carried out exactly the same way but with the screen absent. In this scenario, impossible outcomes are manifested in the sudden appearance or disappearance of an object seen to have been removed or added. His claim is that if one assumes a lingering (though decaying) sensory trace, the two situations become comparable, and all that infants are responding to is something strange in the outcome. There is, however, reason to be doubtful about this argument. In the subtraction conditions in Wynn's studies, infants do not see the object move from its original resting place: they only see it once it emerges from the screen at some distance from this point, so in some way they have to detect that the object revealed is one of the two originally seen, inferring rather than directly perceiving that one of them has been removed. Indeed, the infant has no way of knowing which object has been removed or even (without knowledge of object identity) whether the one removed is actually one of them. And in the addition case, they do not see where the added object is put, so they have no evidence on which to detect a violation, other than on the basis that the number of objects is wrong. True, they may detect that something is wrong in the end display (that being the assumption on which this technique relies), but it is only wrong on the basis of the number of objects present.

Willatts and Fabricius (1999) present an alternative interpretation based on the notion that infants only form a representation on the basis of half of the display. Take the case of subtraction. Half the infants base their representation on the left-hand object, and because this object is present in both the "expected" and "unexpected" outcome, they show no preference between the two. The other half focus on the right-hand object, see it removed, and look longer at the unexpected outcome of its continued presence. The overall outcome (50 percent no preference plus 50 percent preference for the one-object display) leads to an overall preference for the "unexpected" outcome. The same logic can be applied to the case of addition. Half the infants focus their representation on the one object present before the screen is raised, and show no preference between "expected" and "unexpected" outcomes because it is present in both. The other half form their representation on the basis of the added object, and show longer looking if it is not present in the test display. This account initially looks plausible, and could be tested by investigating the distribution of preference scores, which should be bimodally distributed about no preference versus a strong preference for the "expected" display. But it appears to make some assumptions that may be unwarranted. Presumably even if infants base their representation on only one object, all note the addition or removal of an object. The account is based on the assumption that half the infants treat this event as involving "their" object and half not. But taking subtraction, would one not assume that an infant forming a representation of only one object would assume that the object removed was theirs, and thus expect no objects as outcome? And in the case of addition, the infants who focus on the added object (a) do not know where it ends up behind the screen, and (b) have no representation of the preexisting object, and so should show no preference for either display. And this interpretation is made further unlikely by the fact that Koechlin (1994) replicated Wynn's work using an array that rotated constantly. This result rules out the possibility that positive results were based on presence or absence of an object at a particular location.

Summary

Research based on violation of expectancy tasks has yielded a wealth of evidence regarding young infants' reactions to a variety of events embodying different physical principles governing the persistence and movement of objects. However, there is a healthy controversy over the interpretation of these results, nativists arguing that they reveal innate core knowledge and the ability to reason about physical reality, and direct perception theorists arguing that the phenomena can be explained on the basis of simpler perceptual principles through which the structure of events is picked up directly and without the need for mediating cognitive processes. Other workers even question whether the phenomena relate to awareness of the assumed physical principles, suggesting that the results are effectively artifacts that can be explained in terms of underlying preferences for particular events or attentional biases to certain parts of displays. It appears, however, that these latter accounts struggle to explain the breadth of evidence. My current view is that many of these studies reveal important information about infants' early awareness of physical reality. And if they do not reveal innate knowledge structures, they are almost inevitably the developmental precursors of the knowledge individuals use to guide action later in infancy.

Object Search and Object Knowledge

Whatever the final interpretation of the body of work focusing on knowledge of the world in early infancy, we are left with the problem of explaining the negative evidence regarding rather older infants' knowledge of objects which is revealed in tasks in which infants have to search for hidden objects. If the evidence from early infancy does indicate innate knowledge, there is a real problem to be faced in explaining why this knowledge is not revealed in action, even several months later. If, on the other hand, the evidence from early infancy reveals some lower-level developmental precursor of mature object knowledge, there is less of a problem in reconciling this evidence with the object search phenomena, but it is still vital to provide a developmental model that integrates the two bodies of evidence, showing how early awareness develops into a form of knowledge that can be used to guide action. In order to link these two bodies of research, it is important to look closely at the object search phenomena and the various interpretations that have been offered.

Piaget's account

Piaget's view was that it was only through developing and coordinating sensorimotor schemes that infants began to construct a representation of hidden objects. Initially, there is no objective awareness of a separate world of objects, and infants treat objects as sensations arising from their own actions. As they construct more complex sensorimotor schemes, infants begin to build the precursors of mental representation, the beginnings of which can be seen at around 8 months when infants begin to search for hidden objects. Search requires the coordination of separate schemes directed to occluder and object, and it is in coordinating these that infants construct the spatial relationship between object and occluder and hence begin to represent the hidden object. Even at this point, however, object representation is not fully independent of action, and it is only by the end of the sensorimotor period that infants have a well-developed representational ability that is independent of action.

Two of Piaget's findings provide persistent problems for accounts that portray the young infant as aware of object permanence. First, infants fail to search for hidden objects until they are about 8 months old. Second, once they begin to search for objects they make systematic errors in search. If the object is first hidden in one place and then another, they retrieve it successfully from the first place but continue to search there when it is hidden in the new place.

Search failure

One obvious possibility is that infants below 8 months fail to search for a hidden object because they are unable to organize the response required to retrieve it. In effect, this was a central point in Piaget's sensorimotor theory; it is only through coordinating action schemes directed to cover an object in the correct sequence that infants construct the relationship between them and thus come to represent the invisible object. However, it is possible that they understand permanence but cannot organize the necessary actions for retrieval. Rader, Spiro, and Firestone (1979) found that infants were more likely to search if the cover was easily manipulable. However, this result may have been artifactual, because the more manipulable cover was also more likely to be dislodged by swiping movements. Bower and Wishart (1972) showed that although 6-month-old infants would not lift an opaque upturned cup to retrieve a hidden object, they retrieved the object successfully if it was placed under a transparent cup, a result recently replicated by Shinskey, Bogartz, and Poirier (2000) for the case of an object hidden behind a vertical curtain. Thus it is clear that infants are capable of the necessary actions, and that invisibility of the object is the key feature determining search failure. It may be, however, that limitations in infants' understanding or perception of the specific occluder–object relationship may be part of the reason for their difficulty. Neilson (1977) showed that the presence of a clear separation in depth between object and occluder as it went out of sight enhanced search. Six-month-olds failed to search when an object disappeared immediately behind a screen, but searched successfully when there was a clear separation in depth at the point of disappearance. It is interesting to speculate on the possibility that this effect may be related closely to object segregation phenomena discussed earlier.

The A not B search error

The A not B or stage IV search error is a tantalizing phenomenon that to date has eluded convincing explanation. The fascination of this phenomenon is that it is so unexpected. An attentive 9-month-old infant searches accurately at the first place (A) and will do so almost without error over a series of trials. When the object is then hidden at the new position (B) the infant, without hesitation, searches again at position A. And in strong examples of the error, no attempt at correction occurs and errors of a similar sort recur over a series of further hidings at B. Not all infants show such a convincing pattern, possibly because in any cross-sectional sample infants are bound to be at different developmental levels, but the convincing cases make the phenomenon a real explanatory puzzle.

Piaget's explanation of this phenomenon was that infants had only a limited awareness of the hidden object's continued existence. They were beginning to represent the absent object, but they could only do this in a limited way, imagining it to be present in the hiding place where it had previously been found. Thus a move to a new hiding location led to error. Not all investigators accepted this interpretation, however, and in the

1970s and 1980s a substantial body of work accumulated investigating possible explanations of the phenomenon.

THE ROLE OF ACTION

According to Piaget, the infant's ability to represent the object was dependent on action: the error involved repeating the action that had been successful in the past. However, it turned out that action was not necessary for error: infants who had simply seen the object hidden and revealed at the first location made errors when permitted to search on B trials (Butterworth, 1974; Evans, 1973; Landers, 1971). These data also appear to rule out a simpler account of the error, namely, that it is no more than response perseveration.

MEMORY INTERFERENCE?

At first sight, it is tempting to guess that the error is due to forgetting the location of the object. However, the phenomenon cannot be due to global forgetting, because infants are highly successful from the first A trial. The problem is why they should encode the object's location accurately on A trials but fail to do so on B trials. Harris (1973) suggested that this arose through memory interference: when the object is hidden at A, search is successful, but when the new location is used, interference takes place between memory for the past location and memory for the present location, such that infants often search back at the old location. In support of this account, Harris found that errors were infrequent when infants were allowed to search immediately on B trials. Gratch, Appel, Evans, LeCompte, and Wright (1974) found that a delay of only a second was sufficient to produce errors at the normal rate, but that delays above one second did nothing to increase error, so if interference is at the root of things, it has its effect very quickly. Gratch et al. (1974) interpret their results differently, suggesting that the lack of error with delays less than a second is due to the maintenance of a postural orientation (and possibly a partial reach) toward the correct location. Infants are fortuitously correct because they simply continue an act that began when the object was in view.

Bjork and Cummings (1984) provide a different memory account, suggesting that infants make a rather imprecise coding of the object's position on B trials, so that they often make errors. Their evidence for this was that if infants were provided with more than two potential hiding places, errors on B trials were rarely to the original location, being more often directed to positions close to the B location.

There is, however, a major problem for all memory accounts. Piaget noted that the error still occurred when the object was visible at the new location. This finding has been replicated by Butterworth (1977) and Harris (1974) in versions of the task using transparent covers, and by Bremner and Knowles (1984), who did not even cover the object on B trials. It is not clear how memory accounts can explain this, since there should be no need to hold the visible object in memory. Additionally, there is now clear evidence that search failure and errors are not due to a simple lack of awareness of where the object has gone. Wilcox, Nadel, and Rosser (1996) presented infants of between 2.5 and 6.5 months with event sequences in which an object disappeared at one of two locations and after a delay either reappeared at the opposite location (impossible event) or in the same location (possible event). All age groups looked reliably longer at the impossible event, suggesting that they were capable of holding the location of the hidden object in memory, and noting a violation when it reappeared in the wrong place. If such young infants have well-developed location memory, it seems unlikely that this would be a major aspect of the problem six or seven months later. This is confirmed by Ahmed and Ruffman (1998), who made a direct comparison between 8- to 12-month-olds' performance on an A not B search task and a comparable violation of expectation task in which after concealment and reappearance at A an object was hidden at B and revealed either at B (possible) or at A (impossible). Infants who made search errors nevertheless anticipated reemergence at B, even after delays of 15 seconds. Additionally, Hofstadter and Reznick (1996) found that infants were more likely to make manual search errors than looking errors in an A not B task, again suggesting that infants have a better memory of object position than their search suggests.

SPATIAL ANALYSES

One possible explanation of the error is that infants have difficulty updating the spatial location of the object when it is moved from A to B. A number of workers have investigated the spatial demands of the stage IV task. Harris (1973), and later Butterworth (1975), pointed out that when the object is moved from the A location to the B location, both its absolute position in space changes and its relative position changes, that is, it goes from, say, the left-hand to the right-hand container. By changing the position of the containers between A and B trials Butterworth made it possible to hide the object either in the same relative location but a different absolute position, or in the same absolute position but a different relative location. The finding was that a change in location according to either of these spatial reference systems led to error at about the same rate as if object location changed relative to both reference systems at once. So apparently infants use both ways of coding the position of the hidden object and have difficulty if its position changes relative to either.

Bremner and Bryant (1977) pointed out that because infants remained stationary throughout the task, it was impossible to tell if they were coding the object's position in absolute terms, or through self-reference, in relation to their own body. However, the confound between these two types of coding is removed if the infant is moved to the opposite side of the table. Bremner and Bryant found that on B trials following such a movement, infants searched at the same position relative to self as before, and hence at a different absolute position. This happened despite the fact that the two locations lay on clearly different backgrounds. However, Bremner (1978) found that if differently colored covers were used, the effect was reversed: infants now searched at the same absolute location after movement, and hence at a different self-referent location. Thus it appears that absolute position coding is possible if the alternative locations are clearly distinguished.

It may well be that these studies, whilst telling us a good deal about how infants code spatial locations, tell us little about the reasons for the A not B error. Bremner (1985) has suggested that these manipulations do not reduce the error but rather affect the way infants define the single place to which they direct their search efforts. However, Butterworth, Jarrett, and Hicks (1982) did find that differentiating the covers reduced errors in a standard A not B task, and claim that knowledge of object identity is intimately linked to keeping track of the spatial history of the object. It is only through linking the successive positions of an object that infants perceive its identity over the move, and it is because infants encounter difficulties in doing this that search errors occur.

LOCATIONS AS PLACES OF CONCEALMENT

Two things happen when an object is hidden: it disappears and a place takes on the function of container or place of concealment. Most previous accounts have assumed that object search phenomena tell us about object permanence. It is possible, however, to develop an account based on knowledge of places as containers (Bremner, 1985). During the early years infants spend a good deal of time removing objects from containers (for instance taking toys from toy boxes), but they very rarely put them back: as Piaget noted, the act of putting one object inside another is a relatively late development. It is thus plausible that they have semi-magical notions about containers as sources of objects, notions which are based more on finding objects there than on seeing them go there. Admittedly, seeing an object disappear at a place must be a sufficient cue to lead to search at that place, otherwise infants would never search for an object on the first trial. And even the perceptual features of the container may cue its function. But Bremner's hypothesis was that object retrieval or revelation is a much more potent cue to a place as a container. Thus, once an object has been retrieved (or has been revealed) at A, that place is firmly established as a container where an object will be found. When the object is hidden at B, there is a conflict between object disappearance at B and the newly established function of A as a container, and the greater salience of the latter normally wins that day. This account does not make assumptions about limited object representation as the basis of error, an advantage given the evidence that some form of object knowledge is well developed in the early months.

ACTION HISTORY

Despite earlier dismissals of the action perseveration explanation, Smith, Thelen, McLin, and Titzer (1999) revisit the notion that the error is due to motor history of reaching to A. They obtained evidence that infants made search errors even when no objects were hidden. Instead of hiding an object at A and later at B, they simply attracted infants' attention to A (by waving and tapping the container lid) and later to B in the same way. They found that infants made "search" errors with the same incidence as in the standard task, and concluded that the phenomenon was due to establishment of a reaching habit and nothing to do with memory or representation of the object at A.

Although this is a plausible possibility, it encounters the same difficulty as previous action perseveration accounts. As already mentioned, infants make search errors even if they have only seen the object hidden and revealed at the A location. Smith et al. (1999) rightly point out that most procedures involve warm-up trials in which the infant is encouraged to retrieve a partially hidden object from A prior to full hiding there. And such a procedure prior to observational A trials could be enough to establish the reaching habit. However, Butterworth (1974) took care to avoid such a problem by giving warm-up trials at the midline. Thus, on commencement of B trials infants had no prior experience of reaching to A, but erred nonetheless. Additionally, the account contains a logical difficulty. If similar "errors" occur when no object is hidden, it does not follow that the hiding of the object in the standard A not B task is irrelevant; superficially similar behaviors can have quite different bases. In short, their research does not provide conditions in which different performance is predicted dependent on whether or not an object is hidden, whereas experimental logic depends on showing significant effects of different manipulations. Additionally there is evidence that the presence of an object does affect behavior. Munakata (1997) compared infants' reaching in two tasks, one of which replicated that of Smith et al. (1999) in which no object was hidden on A or B trials, and another in which no object was hidden on A trials, but an object was hidden on B trials. In the replication condition, just as Smith et al. (1999) found, infants made errors, but on the version in which the object was introduced and hidden on B trials, they made few errors, despite the fact that up to that point the motor history of both groups was identical. The object had no prior history at A, and they searched correctly when it was hidden for the first time at B. Munakata concludes that the hiding of an object has an effect and so is an important factor in the standard task. And other work confirms this conclusion. A. J. Bremner and Bryant (in press) showed that cover differentiation had opposite effects on error rate depending on whether an object was hidden or not. When an object was hidden, cover differentiation led to a reduction in error, the same result as obtained by Butterworth et al. (1982). In contrast, when no object was hidden, cover differentiation increased error rate. It seems likely that when no object is hidden, cover differentiation simply helps infants to individuate the cover that becomes the focus of action during A trials, and there is no real reason to change this focus when the experimenter turns their attention to the new location. However, when an object is hidden, the hidden object is the focus of action, and cover differentiation helps infants to identify its new location on B trials.

A NEUROPHYSIOLOGICAL ACCOUNT

Diamond (1988) has suggested that the error can be explained by the fact that the frontal cortex becomes fully functional only rather late in infancy, an account that is based in part on the finding that rhesus monkeys with lesions of frontal cortex perform poorly on the stage IV task (Diamond, 1990). She proposes that a primary function of frontal cortex is to support two capacities, the maintenance of an object representation in memory and inhibition of incorrect responses, and her claim is that although infants are capable of these singly, the load becomes too great when they have to do both. There is some evidence that there is a link between error and frontal cortex development. For instance, Bell and Fox (1992) showed that infants who did not make the stage IV error showed more developed frontal EEG patterns than those who erred. We must note, however, that this is correlational evidence which does not allow us to assume a direct causal link.

A key aspect of Diamond's evidence is that there is a clear relationship between delay between hiding and search and error. Errors are more likely after longer delays, and older children tolerate longer delays without error than younger ones. This certainly suggests a memory factor. However, this evidence is rather different from the result obtained by Gratch et al. (1974), namely, that the increase in error occurred entirely between zero and one second delay. There are two reasons why Diamond's results may be different. First, she employed a distraction procedure in which the infant's attention was drawn from the correct location after the object had been hidden. This procedure is unnecessary, because infants make errors even when fully attentive, but any distraction is likely to increase or introduce memory load. Second, she adopts a multitrial reversal procedure in which the B location becomes the A location for the next test. Under such circumstances, once some way into a test session, infants have a complex and probably confusing past search history. Thus again the task may become more about the real problem of simply remembering the last location acted on than understanding the sequence of hidings as an integrated whole. There is thus reason to question whether Diamond's task taps into the same factors as a more conventional A not B task.

Despite these question marks, by presenting a multifactor explanation, Diamond's account is an advance over previous accounts that have tried to explain the error in terms of a single factor. However, there is reason to doubt the detail of the argument. It does not appear that failure to inhibit a previous response can explain the error, either alone or in conjunction with a memory factor. Remember that early studies (Butterworth, 1974; Evans, 1973; Landers, 1971) obtained errors after observational trials. In this case, no prior response had been established. And the problem for the memory component of her account is that although she recognizes that errors sometimes occur when the object is visible, the prediction is that these should be very occasional. However, using transparent covers, Butterworth (1977) obtained errors at much the same rate as when using opaque covers, and a similar rate of error occurred when the object was not even covered on B trials (Bremner & Knowles, 1984). There is no evidence from these sources that errors were significantly reduced by object visibility.

A CONNECTIONIST MODEL OF SEARCH ERRORS

Munakata has developed a connectionist model to account for the data regarding the stage IV error (Munakata, 1998a; Munakata et al., 1997). This is based on the notion that infants' search is determined by the interaction of two factors, "latent" and "active" memory traces. Latent traces are reflected in the experience-based strengthening of connections between units in the system, leading to certain responses being likely in the presence of certain inputs (comparable to long-term memory), and active traces are reflected in the level of ongoing activity maintained within the system (comparable to working memory). Thus, when faced with concealment of the object at B, infants' responses are determined by the relative dominance of latent traces specifying place A and active traces specifying place B. Working from these basic assumptions, Munakata develops a sophisticated model which accounts for much of the data on infant search and makes new predictions, such as the counterintuitive one that, during development, errors should increase gradually before decreasing again.

This is an important approach, because it allows precise specification of predicted effects on search of different factors such as delay, number, and distinctiveness of locations. However, models of this sort run into difficulties over some of the more subtle aspects of the error. In particular, errors are significantly reduced if differently colored covers are used (Butterworth et al., 1982), whereas they are not significantly reduced when the object is visible at B. One would have thought that a visible object would serve to differentiate locations in a most salient way, yet it does not have the effect that cover differentiation has. Munakata (1998b) claims that errors with the object visible are occasional random errors, citing evidence from a study by Sophian and Yengo (1985), which suggested that errors with a visible object at B were due to lapses of attention rather than real problems locating the object. However, in contrast to Butterworth (1977) and Bremner and Knowles (1984), Sophian and Yengo obtained very few errors when the object was visible. And Bremner and Knowles's data provide no support for the notion that these errors are random, because they obtained errors under very precise conditions, when the object was uncovered at B but the A location was covered. Virtually no errors were obtained when there was no covered location, and when the object was uncovered at A but the B location was covered. In this study it was clear that the presence of a covered location at A was as strong a determinant of search as the visible presence of the object at B. Such a finding fits with Bremner's account of the stage IV error in terms of place knowledge and calls for the need to consider the infant's notions about locations as hiding places as well as their notions about hidden objects.

PROBLEM-SOLVING ANALYSES

Baillargeon, Graber, DeVos, and Black (1990) argue that by their fifth month infants are both able to represent hidden objects and to identify the actions necessary to recover them. Evidence for the second claim comes from ingenious experiments in which infants watch possible and impossible object-retrieval events; as in other work of this nature, infants look longer at the impossible sequences. Baillargeon et al. (1990) thus conclude that the infant's difficulty lies in certain aspects of problem solving. Failure to search can be explained by inability to plan means–ends sequences, and even once infants are capable of this, the stage IV error arises due to a tendency to repeat old means–ends solutions. In addition to explaining manual search failure and later errors in the face of apparently contrary evidence revealed in violation of expectation tasks, this sort of analysis can also explain superior object localization reflected in looking (Hofstadter & Reznick, 1996). Looking does not involve problem solving in the way that manual search does. This, however, is only one possible analysis in terms of problem solving. Willatts (1997) questions whether the evidence presented by Baillargeon et al. (1990) really indicates that infants can identify the necessary retrieval actions, pointing out that recognition of possible versus impossible retrievals does not imply awareness of how to execute retrieval. Again, we are back to the point that studies based on violation of expectation cannot really tell us about the infant's ability to construct solutions in action. Willatts also questions whether early examples of search really involve means–ends problem solving, suggesting instead that success initially arises from trial and error. Thus, although bearing a number of similarities to the account presented by Baillargeon et al. (1990), Willatts's account presents the infant as more fundamentally lacking in problem-solving skills. It alerts us to the fact that there is more to correct object search than simply having a sufficiently strong representation of the object, and he cites evidence from other problem-solving tasks involving retrieval of visible but inaccessible objects through use of supports to show that infants' difficulties have a generality that extends beyond hidden-object problems.

It is interesting to note a parallel between the literatures on object knowledge and problem solving. Just as there is evidence for early knowledge of objects which cannot immediately be used to guide action, there is evidence that quite young infants detect causality in event sequences (Cohen & Amsel, 1998; Cohen & Oakes, 1993; Leslie & Keeble, 1987) quite some time before they are able to understand causality in their own acts. This looks like another example of early knowledge only becoming reflected in action later in development.

CONCLUSION

These recent accounts of search failure and search errors have made considerable progress in identifying factors that influence search and in modeling possible underlying processes. More than ever, it becomes clear that several factors underlie behavior, including memory arising from past history of events at A and active memory of the most recent event. Furthermore, there is value in attempts to localize the neural substrate supporting different functions as well as modeling the processes involved. There is a good deal in common between Diamond's account and Munakata's model, and much may be gained by incorporating aspects of both. However, probably something has to be added as well. Just as the model developed by Smith et al. (1999) may be accused of laying too much stress on action and action history, the other accounts may be criticized for relying too much on relatively simple memory processes. Arguably as a result, every account has difficulty in accounting for all the phenomena, and it may be that further progress will only result from recognizing that infants are in the process of making sense of the world, not just acting on it and forming memories about it. Sure enough, during infancy making sense of the world is probably inseparable from action, but it involves more than strengthening simple connections and forming memories. This is where models of the infant as an active problem solver become valuable, and where it becomes difficult to proceed without recognizing the presence of active mental representations. One model that goes some way toward reconciling all three of the above accounts, and which also treats the infant as possessing knowledge of the world, is the *competing systems* account (Marcovitch & Zelazo, in press; Zelazo, Reznick, & Spinazzola, 1998). According to this account, two potentially separate systems determine search in the A not B task, a response-based system the activity of which is determined by past motor history, and a representational system linked to the infant's conscious representation of the location of the hidden object. The more searches that have been directed to A, the stronger the effect of the response-based system in directing search back to location A on B trials. Support from this aspect of the model comes from a meta-analysis of A not B results indicating that the number of A trials is a determinant of error on B trials. However, this aspect of the model is also its weakness, because it fails to explain errors following observational A trials, and it may be necessary to add other components to the representational side of such a model, including infants' representations of places as containers, and also to extend the model to recognize the infant as an active problem solver.

Challenges for Future Work

The evidence reviewed in the early sections of this chapter indicates that, by the middle of their first year, infants have a fairly sophisticated basic awareness of the world, including object permanence and the physical rules governing object motion and stability. However, it would appear that they are not initially able to use this information to guide action. It may well be that the awareness involved in violation of expectation tasks is very much more basic than is required to guide action, involving simple recognition of when an outcome is or is not appropriate. Guidance of action may require a self-maintained active representation of the hidden object which may be beyond the infant's capabilities, and beyond that, the ability to plan means–ends solutions. Given this state of affairs, infants have to use other means to guide action, which are liable to relate to visible objects in the scene and what they offer for action. Thus, initial search and retrieval at A may be, as Willatts suggests, the result of accident or trial and error, but it leads to knowledge of place A as a container of things, knowledge which may subsequently guide action even in the visible presence of the object at another location. In this sense, infants are detecting affordances of objects for the actions involved in the task. Problem-solving analyses tie in closely with notions about the development of executive functions (Hughes, 1998; Russell, 1996), and it may be argued that a large part of what is happening while infants develop the ability to use object knowledge to guide action has to do with the development of basic executive functions.

In the sense that infants possess awareness of the world but are unable to use it to guide action, we may consider early perceptual capacities *implicit knowledge*, because although they involve detection of information vital for action guidance they do not yet qualify as *explicit knowledge* at the most basic level of "knowing how." And one suggestion (Ahmed & Ruffman, 1998; Bremner, 1997, 1998) is that a vital developmental process in early infancy involves the transformation of knowledge implicit in perception into explicit knowledge that can be used to guide action.

Some investigators apply this distinction to knowledge revealed through action versus knowledge revealed through language. For instance, J. J. Gibson (1979, p. 260) defines explicit knowledge as information that can be linguistically expressed. Karmiloff-Smith (1992) defines implicit knowledge more generally as a form of representation not available to guide the mental activities of the individual, and proposes that this is transformed into explicit knowledge through a process of representational redescription. There is also a tendency to relate the distinction to conscious versus unconscious processes, with implicit learning conceptualized as the result of unconscious processing (Cleeremans, 1993) and *tacit knowledge* the outcome of such learning (Reber, 1993). However, the present definition need not be at variance with other uses of the distinction provided we define the level of psychological activity to which we are applying it. Thus, it becomes acceptable for a form of knowledge to be explicit with respect to manual activity, while at the same time being implicit (procedural) knowledge with respect to linguistic activity. The key assumption is that there is a set of levels (principally perceptual, procedural, and declarative) at which knowledge becomes available to guide the activities of the individual, and this progression may be repeated during development on successively higher levels of psychological activity.

One clear advantage of interpreting infant development in terms of this implicit–explicit conceptualization is that, rather than portraying infants as progressing from a state of no or little knowledge to a state of mature knowledge, they are conceptualized as in a sense knowing the world from the start, and development is treated as a set of changes in the way in which this knowledge or information is utilized as perception and action are progressively coupled.

Links Between Theories and Pointers to Developmental Processes

The implicit–explicit distinction is descriptive because, in itself, it does not illuminate the processes underlying development. However, we may look to other theories to identify some possible developmental processes. Gibsonian theory generates some straightforward predictions and dynamic systems analysis (see chapter 3 in this volume) may in time provide a detailed account of some of the processes involved. In particular, important predictions emerge in relation to the concept of affordances. As Adolph, Eppler, and Gibson (1993) state, "An affordance is the fit between an animal's capabilities and the environmental supports that enable a given action to be performed." And a given feature of the environment will hold one type of affordance for one species and a different one for another. This has the important developmental parallel that the affordances detected will depend on the infant's ability to act. To say that a particular object affords grasping or that a particular surface affords crawling only makes sense in relation to infants who can grasp and crawl, respectively. Thus as new motor achievements come on the scene, new affordances emerge. Since these affordances are essentially relationships between environmental structure and the structure of action, it is here that dynamic systems theory may help us to understand the process by which new affordances are developed, through the meshing of the organism and environmental components of the system. And the current thrust of this approach is to describe the emergence of new affordances as taking place in an automatic manner through the natural functioning of the infant in his or her environment. Before the emergence of a new affordance, the relevant environmental feature was available to perception. Thus, the environmental information specifying the affordance was implicit in perception. But it is not until this information is meshed in as part of a system including both perception and the appropriate action that we can say that the affordance has been detected. And because an affordance is a relationship between perception and action which in itself may be sufficient to guide action, it is appropriately labeled explicit knowledge.

The claim of the dynamic systems approach is that there is no need to go beyond consideration of the environmental, mechanical, and biological constraints in the system in order to reach an adequate developmental explanation. On the one hand, through its denial of the need to rely on mentalistic concepts, this approach has some clear advantages: reliance on mentalistic terminology (such as knowledge, understanding, and reasoning) in explanations of infants' ability often seems inherently inappropriate. However, it seems evident that there is more to infant development than the natural emergence of functions that link behavior to the environment. Although in time the dynamic systems approach may help to explain many of the basic activities of infants, activities which both emerge and are exercised at a relatively automatic unconscious level, this approach will have greater difficulties in dealing with the infant as an active problem solver engaged in means–ends analysis (Willatts, 1997).

This distinction between automatic behaviors and the purposive ones seen in problem solving seems crucial. Both forms are self-guided, but the latter are purposive in the sense that they involve deliberate manipulation and variation by the individual. It seems likely that this is not a rigid subdivision, because development may be partly a matter of behaviors becoming automatic after a period of achievement as a result of active problem solving. Thus, for instance, locomotion may become automatic, although its initial achievement may have been partly based on the infant trying out motor and postural variations. However, at a given point in development, there are some behaviors that appear automatic, while there are others that appear to involve problem solving under the control of a component of the system which we may want to call the mind, brain, or executive control system. It thus appears likely that affordances are acquired in some cases as a result of purposive problem solving rather than just through automatic functioning. Any new motor achievement such as further manual skill or locomotion permits further environmental exploration, but at the same time new problems are encountered, the solutions to which constitute new knowledge.

We can describe the outcomes of development through these processes in terms of different forms of implicit-to-explicit shift. As already mentioned, detection of perceptual variables specifying an affordance makes that affordance implicit in perception, but this cannot be called explicit knowledge until the infant can use it to guide action. In relation to object search, it seems likely that this transformation occurs largely through the infant's efforts as a purposive problem solver, discovering through this activity certain ways in which perception and action fit together. And it should be noted that this shift from implicit to explicit involves more than a formation of a simple connection between implicit knowledge to the action system. Problem-solving analyses demonstrate that the connections between perception and action are liable to be quite complex, including processes connected with both knowledge of objects and causality. The task of future research is to identify both the form of these connections and the processes leading to their formation. It is here that both dynamic systems analysis and connectionist modeling are liable to have important roles in providing precise specifications of the conditions for development. Additionally, this endeavor is liable to be informed by neuropsychological analyses (see chapter 9 in this volume). Some quite detailed analyses of frontal cortex function already exist that are highly relevant to developmental questions, specifically development of links between perception and action. For instance, Thatcher (1992) identifies a parallel between functioning of the lateral and medial frontal cortex and Piagetian concepts of assimilation and accommodation, and Goldberg (1985) identifies another region of frontal cortex, the *supplementary motor area*, as having an important role in control of intentional action. Thus, rather than limiting the analysis to the role of frontal cortex in inhibition of past responses (Diamond, 1985), it should be possible to broaden the analysis to identify this brain region as intimately involved in the control of executive functions. In this respect, there may be close links between the development of frontal cortex and the development of explicit knowledge for the guidance of intentional action.

Related Topics and Further Reading

Infant perception

Much of the literature on perception in early infancy is relevant to issues discussed in this chapter, in particular because much of the work points toward objective perception of the world by very young infants. This work is well reviewed in:

Slater, A. (1998). The competent infant: Innate organization and early learning in infant visual perception. In A. Slater (Ed.), *Perceptual development: Visual, auditory, and speech perception in infancy* (pp. 105–130). Hove: Psychology Press.

Causality and problem solving

The development of perception of causality and investigation of possible links between this and infant problem solving deserve a fuller treatment than could be included here because of space constraints. A thorough review of the work on perception of causality is contained in:

Oakes, L. M., & Cohen, L. B. (1994). Infant causal perception. In C. Rovee-Collier & L. P. Lipsitt (Eds.), *Advances in infancy research* (Vol. 9, pp. 1–54). Norwood, NJ: Ablex.

and fuller detail of problem-solving research is contained in:

Willatts, P. (1997). Beyond the "couch potato" infant: How infants use their knowledge to regulate action, solve problems, and achieve goals. In G. Bremner, A. Slater, & G. Butterworth (Eds.), *Infant development: Recent advances* (pp. 109–135). Hove: Psychology Press.

Categorization

Categorization in infancy is another area in which there is evidence for early perceptual categorization as a precursor of conceptual categories, with the argument that only the latter constitute true knowledge (Mandler, 1997). This appears to be another area in which there is scope for application of the implicit–explicit developmental shift. Detailed reviews of this literature are contained in:

Mandler, J. M. (1997). Development of categorization: Perceptual and conceptual categories. In G. Bremner, A. Slater, & G. Butterworth (Eds.), *Infant development: Recent advances* (pp. 163–191). Hove: Psychology Press.
Quinn, P. C. (1998). Object and spatial categorization in young infants: "What" and "where" in early visual perception. In A. Slater (Ed.), *Perceptual development: Visual, auditory, and speech perception in infancy* (pp. 131–165). Hove: Psychology Press.

References

Adolph, K. E., Eppler, M. A., & Gibson, E. J. (1993). Development of perception of affordances. In C. Rovee-Collier & L. P. Lipsitt (Eds.), *Advances in infancy research* (Vol. 8, pp. 51–98). Norwood, NJ: Ablex.
Ahmed, A., & Ruffman, T. (1998). Why do infants make A not B errors in a search task, yet show memory for the location of hidden objects in a nonsearch task? *Developmental Psychology, 34,* 441–453.
Antell, S. E., & Keating, D. P. (1983). Perception of numerical invariance in neonates. *Child Development, 54,* 695–701.
Baillargeon, R. (1986). Representing the existence and the location of hidden objects: Object permanence in 6- and 8-month-old infants. *Cognition, 23,* 21–41.

Baillargeon, R. (1987a). Object permanence in 3.5- and 4.5-month-old infants. *Developmental Psychology, 23,* 655–664.

Baillargeon, R. (1987b). Young infants' reasoning about the physical and spatial properties of a hidden object. *Cognitive Development, 2,* 179–200.

Baillargeon, R. (1993). The object concept revisited: New directions in the investigation of infants' physical knowledge. In C. E. Granrud (Ed.), *Visual perception and cognition in infancy* (pp. 265–316). Hillsdale, NJ: Erlbaum.

Baillargeon, R., & DeVos, J. (1991). Object permanence in young infants: Further evidence. *Child Development, 62,* 1227–1246.

Baillargeon, R., Graber, M., DeVos, J., & Black, J. (1990). Why do young infants fail to search for hidden objects? *Cognition, 36,* 255–284.

Baillargeon, R., Needham, A., & DeVos, J. (1992). The development of young infants' intuitions about support. *Early Development and Parenting, 1,* 69–78.

Baillargeon, R., Spelke, E. S., & Wasserman, S. (1985). Object permanence in five-month-old infants. *Cognition, 20,* 191–208.

Bell, M. A., & Fox, N. A. (1992). The relations between frontal brain electrical activity and cognitive development during infancy. *Child Development, 63,* 1142–1163.

Bjork, E. L., & Cummings, E. M. (1984). Infant search error: Stage of concept development or stage of memory development. *Memory and Cognition, 12,* 1–19.

Bogartz, R. S., Shinskey, J. L., & Speaker, C. (1997). Interpreting infant looking. *Developmental Psychology, 33,* 408–422.

Bower, T. G. R. (1966). The visual world of infants. *Scientific American, 215,* 80–92.

Bower, T. G. R., Broughton, J. M., & Moore, M. K. (1971). The development of the object concept as manifested by changes in the tracking behavior of infants between seven and 20 weeks of age. *Journal of Experimental Child Psychology, 11,* 182–193.

Bower, T. G. R., & Wishart, J. G. (1972). The effects of motor skill on object permanence. *Cognition, 1,* 165–172.

Bremner, A. J., & Bryant, P. E. (in press). The effect of spatial cues on infants' responses in the AB task, with and without a hidden object. *Developmental Science.*

Bremner, J. G. (1978). Spatial errors made by infants: Inadequate spatial cues or evidence for egocentrism? *British Journal of Psychology, 69,* 77–84.

Bremner, J. G. (1985). Object tracking and search in infancy: A review of data and a theoretical evaluation. *Developmental Review, 5,* 371–396.

Bremner, J. G. (1997). From perception to cognition. In G. Bremner, A. Slater, & G. Butterworth (Eds.), *Infant development: Recent advances* (pp. 55–74). Hove: Psychology Press.

Bremner, J. G. (1998). From perception to action: The early development of knowledge. In F. Simion & G. Butterworth (Eds.), *Perceptual, motor and cognitive abilities in early infancy* (pp. 239–255). Hove: Psychology Press.

Bremner, J. G., & Bryant, P. E. (1977). Place versus response as the basis of spatial errors made by young infants. *Journal of Experimental Child Psychology, 23,* 162–171.

Bremner, J. G., & Knowles, L. S. (1984). Piagetian stage IV errors with an object that is directly accessible both visually and manually. *Perception, 13,* 307–314.

Butterworth, G. (1974). *The development of the object concept in human infants.* Unpublished D.Phil. thesis, University of Oxford.

Butterworth, G. (1975). Object identity in infancy: The interaction of spatial location codes in determining search errors. *Child Development, 46,* 866–870.

Butterworth, G. (1977). Object disappearance and error in Piaget's stage IV task. *Journal of Experimental Child Psychology, 23,* 391–401.

Butterworth, G., Jarrett, N., & Hicks, L. (1982). Spatio-temporal identity in infancy: Perceptual competence or conceptual deficit. *Developmental Psychology, 18,* 435–449.

Campos, J. J., & Bertenthal, B. I. (1988). Locomotion and psychological development. In F. Morrison, K. Lord, & D. Keating (Eds.), *Applied developmental psychology* (pp. 176–198). New York: Academic Press.

Clearfield, M. W., & Mix, K. S. (1999). Number versus contour length in infants' discrimination of small visual sets. *Psychological Science, 10,* 408–411.

Cleeremans, A. (1993). *Mechanisms of implicit learning: Connectionist models of sequence processing.* Cambridge, MA: MIT Press.

Cohen, L. B., & Amsel, G. (1998). Precursors of infants' perception of the causality of a simple event. *Infant Behavior and Development, 21,* 713–732.

Cohen, L. B., & Oakes, L. M. (1993). How infants perceive simple causality. *Developmental Psychology, 29,* 421–433.

Diamond, A. (1985). Development of the ability to use recall to guide action, as indicated by infants' performance on A not B. *Child Development, 56,* 868–883.

Diamond, A. (1988). Abilities and neural mechanisms underlying A performance. *Child Development, 59,* 523–527.

Diamond, A. (1990). The development and neural bases of memory functions as indexed by the A and delayed response tasks in human infants and infant monkeys. In A. Diamond (Ed.), *The development and neural bases of higher cognitive functions* (pp. 267–317). New York: New York Academy of Sciences Press.

Diamond, A., & Goldman-Rakic, P. S. (1989). Comparison of human infants and rhesus monkeys on Piaget's A task: Evidence for dependence on dorsolateral prefrontal cortex. *Experimental Brain Research, 74,* 24–40.

Eizenman, D. R., & Bertenthal, B. I. (1998). Infants' perception of object unity in translating and rotating displays. *Developmental Psychology, 34,* 426–434.

Evans, W. F. (1973). *The stage IV error in Piaget's theory of object concept development.* Unpublished dissertation, University of Houston.

Gibson, E. J. (1977). How perception really develops: A view from outside the network. In D. LaBerge & S. J. Samuels (Eds.), *Basic processes in reading: Perception and comprehension* (pp. 155–173). Hillsdale, NJ: Erlbaum.

Gibson, J. J. (1979). *The ecological approach to visual perception.* Boston: Houghton Mifflin.

Goldberg, G. (1985). Supplementary motor area structure and function: Review and hypotheses. *Behavioral and Brain Sciences, 8,* 567–616.

Goldberg, S. (1976). Visual tracking and existence constancy in five-month-old infants. *Journal of Experimental Child Psychology, 22,* 478–491.

Gratch, G., Appel, K. J., Evans, W. F., LeCompte, G. K., & Wright, N. A. (1974). Piaget's stage IV object concept error: Evidence of forgetting or object conception. *Child Development, 45,* 71–77.

Haith, M. M. (1998). Who put the cog in cognition? Is rich interpretation too costly? *Infant Behavior and Development, 21,* 167–179.

Harris, P. L. (1973). Perseverative errors in search by young infants. *Child Development, 44,* 28–33.

Harris, P. L. (1974). Perseverative search at a visibly empty place by young infants. *Journal of Experimental Child Psychology, 18,* 535–542.

Hofstadter, M., & Reznick, J. S. (1996). Response modality affects human infant delayed-response performance. *Child Development, 67,* 646–658.

Hughes, C. (1998). Executive function in preschoolers: Links with theory of mind and verbal ability. *British Journal of Developmental Psychology, 16,* 233–253.

Johnson, S. P. (in press). The development of visual surface perception: Insights into the ontogeny of knowledge. In C. Rovee-Collier & L. Lipsitt (Eds.), *Advances in infancy research* (Vol. 13). Norwood, NJ: Ablex.

Johnson, S. P., & Aslin, R. N. (1995). Perception of object unity in 2-month-old infants. *Developmental Psychology, 31,* 739–745.

Johnson, S. P., & Aslin, R. N. (1996). Perception of object unity in young infants: The roles of motion, depth, and orientation. *Cognitive Development, 11,* 161–180.

Johnson, S. P., & Náñez, J. E. (1995). Young infants' perception of object unity in two-dimensional displays. *Infant Behavior and Development, 18,* 133–143.

Johnson, S. P., Bremner, J. G., Slater, A. M., & Mason, U. C. (2000). The role of good form in infants' perception of partly occluded objects. *Journal of Experimental Child Psychology, 76,* 1–25.

Karmiloff-Smith, A. (1992). *Beyond modularity: A developmental perspective on cognitive science.* Cambridge, MA: MIT Press.

Kellman, P. J., & Spelke, E. R. (1983). Perception of partly occluded objects in infancy. *Cognitive Psychology, 15,* 483–524.

Kellman, P. J., Gleitman, H., & Spelke, E. (1987). Object and observer motion in the perception of objects by infants. *Journal of Experimental Psychology: Human Perception and Performance, 13,* 586–593.

Kellman, P. J., Spelke, E., & Short, K. R. (1986). Infant perception of object unity from translatory motion in depth and vertical translation. *Child Development, 57,* 72–76.

Kestenbaum, R., Termine, N., & Spelke, E. S. (1987). Perception of objects and object boundaries by three-month-old infants. *British Journal of Developmental Psychology, 5,* 367–383.

Koechlin, E. (1994). Paper presented at the International Interdisciplinary Workshop on Mathematical Cognition, Trieste.

Landers, W. F. (1971). The effect of differential experience on infants' performance in a Piagetian stage IV object concept task. *Developmental Psychology, 5,* 48–54.

Leslie, A. M., & Keeble, S. (1987). Do six-month-old infants perceive causality? *Cognition, 25,* 265–288.

Mandler, J. M. (1997). Development of categorization: Perceptual and conceptual categories. In G. Bremner, A. Slater, & G. Butterworth (Eds.), *Infant development: Recent advances* (pp. 163–191). Hove: Psychology Press.

Marcovitch, S., & Zelazo, P. D. (in press). The A-not-B error: Results from a logistic meta-analysis. *Child Development.*

Meck, W. H., & Church, R. M. (1983). A mode control model of counting and timing processes. *Journal of Experimental Psychology: Animal Behavior Processes, 9,* 320–334.

Meicler, M., & Gratch, G. (1980). Do five-month-olds show object conception in Piaget's sense? *Infant Behavior and Development, 3,* 265–282.

Meltzoff, A. N., & Moore, M. K. (1998). Object representation, identity, and the paradox of early permanence: Steps toward a new framework. *Infant Behavior and Development, 21,* 201–235.

Mix, K. S., Levine, S. C., & Huttenlocher, J. (1997). Numerical abstraction in infants: Another look. *Developmental Psychology, 33,* 423–428.

Moore, D., Benenson, J., Reznick, J. S., Peterson, M., & Kagan, J. (1987). Effect of auditory numerical information on infants' looking behavior: Contradictory evidence. *Developmental Psychology, 23,* 655–670.

Moore, M. K., Borton, R., & Darby, B. L. (1978). Visual tracking in infants: Evidence for object identity or object permanence? *Journal of Experimental Child Psychology, 25,* 183–198.

Muller, A. A., & Aslin, R. N. (1978). Visual tracking as an index of the object concept. *Infant Behavior and Development, 1,* 309–319.

Munakata, Y. (1997). Perseverative reaching in infancy: The roles of hidden toys and motor history in the A not B task. *Infant Behavior and Development, 20,* 405–416.

Munakata, Y. (1998a). Infant perseveration and implications for object permanence theories: A PDP model of the AB task. *Developmental Science, 1,* 161–184.

Munakata, Y. (1998b). Infant perseveration, rethinking data, theory, and the role of modelling. *Developmental Science, 1,* 205–211.

Munakata, Y., McClelland, J. L., Johnson, M. J., & Siegler, R. S. (1997). Rethinking infant knowledge: Toward an adaptive process account of successes and failures in object permanence tasks. *Psychological Review, 104,* 686–713.

Needham, A. (1998). Infants' use of featural information in the segregation of stationary objects. *Infant Behavior and Development, 21,* 47–76.

Needham, A., & Baillargeon, R. (1993). Intuitions about support in 4.5-month-old infants. *Cognition, 47,* 121–148.

Needham, A., & Baillargeon, R. (1997). Object segregation in 8-month-old infants. *Cognition, 62,* 121–149.

Needham, A., & Baillargeon, R. (1998). Effects of prior experience on 4.5-month-old infants' object segregation. *Infant Behavior and Development, 21,* 1–24.

Neilson, I. (1977). *A reinterpretation of the development of the object concept in infancy.* Unpublished Ph.D. thesis, University of Edinburgh.

Piaget, J. (1954). *The construction of reality in the child* (Trans. M. Cook). New York: Basic Books. (Original work published in French 1936)

Rader, N., Spiro, D. J., & Firestone, P. B. (1979). Performance on a stage IV object-permanence task with standard and nonstandard covers. *Child Development, 50,* 908–910.

Reber, A. S. (1993). *Implicit learning and tacit knowledge: An essay on the cognitive unconscious.* Oxford: Oxford University Press.

Rivera, S. M., Wakeley, A., & Langer, J. (1999). The drawbridge phenomenon: Representational reasoning or perceptual preference? *Developmental Psychology, 35,* 427–435.

Rochat, P., & Hespos, S. J. (1996). Tracking and anticipation of invisible spatial transformations by 4- to 8-month-old infants. *Cognitive Development, 11,* 3–17.

Russell, J. (1996). *Agency: Its role in mental development.* Hove: Erlbaum/Taylor & Francis.

Shinskey, J. L., Bogartz, R. S., & Poirier, C. R. (2000). The effects of graded occlusion on manual search and visual attention in 5- to 8-month-old infants. *Infancy, 1,* 323–346.

Slater, A., Johnson, S. P., Brown, E., & Badenoch, M. (1996). Newborn infants' perception of partly occluded objects. *Infant Behavior and Development, 19,* 145–148.

Smith, L. B., Thelen, E., McLin, D., & Titzer, R. (1999). Knowing in the context of acting: The task dynamics of the A-not-B error. *Psychological Review, 106,* 235–260.

Sophian, C., & Yengo, L. (1985). Infants' search for visible objects: Implications for the interpretation of early search errors. *Journal of Experimental Child Psychology, 40,* 260–278.

Spelke, E. (1994). Initial knowledge: Six suggestions. *Cognition, 50,* 431–445.

Spelke, E. R., Breinlinger, K., Macomber, J., & Jacobson, K. (1992). Origins of knowledge. *Psychological Review, 99,* 605–632.

Spelke, E. S., Katz, G., Purcell, S. E., Ehrlich, S. M., & Breinlinger, K. (1994). Early knowledge of object motion: Continuity and inertia. *Cognition, 51,* 131–176.

Spelke, E. S., Kestenbaum, R., Simons, D. J., & Wein, D. (1995). Spatiotemporal continuity, smoothness of motion and object identity in infancy. *British Journal of Developmental Psychology, 13,* 113–142.

Starkey, P., & Cooper, R. G. (1980). Perception of number by human infants. *Science, 210,* 1033–1035.

Starkey, P., Spelke, E. S., & Gelman, R. (1990). Numerical abstraction by human infants. *Cognition, 36,* 97–128.

Tan, L. S. C., & Bryant, P. E. (2000). The cues that infants use to distinguish discontinuous quantities: Evidence using a shift-rate recovery paradigm. *Child Development, 71,* 1162–1178.

Thatcher, R. W. (1992). Cyclic cortical reorganization during early childhood. *Brain and Cognition, 20,* 24–50.

Wilcox, T., & Baillargeon, R. (1998). Object individuation in infancy: The use of featural information in reasoning about occlusion events. *Cognitive Psychology, 37,* 97–155.

Wilcox, T., Nadel, L., & Rosser, R. (1996). Location memory in healthy preterm and full-term infants. *Infant Behavior and Development, 19,* 309–324.

Willatts, P. (1997). Beyond the "couch potato" infant: How infants use their knowledge to regulate action, solve problems, and achieve goals. In G. Bremner, A. Slater, & G. Butterworth (Eds.), *Infant development: Recent advances* (pp. 109–135). Hove: Psychology Press.

Willatts, P., & Fabricius, W. (1999, April). *Don't think twice it's all right: Getting by on half a representation in looking paradigm studies of infant cognition.* Poster presented to the biennial conference of the Society for Research in Child Development, Albuquerque, NM.

Wynn, K. (1992). Addition and subtraction by human infants. *Nature, 358,* 749–750.

Wynn, K. (1995). Origins of numerical knowledge. *Mathematical Cognition, 1,* 35–60.

Xu, F., & Carey, S. (1996). Infants' metaphysics: The case of numerical identity. *Cognitive Psychology, 30,* 111–153.

Xu, F., & Spelke, E. S. (2000). Large number discrimination in 6-month-old infants. *Cognition, 74,* BI–Bll.

Zelazo, P. D., Reznick, J. S., & Spinazzola, J. (1998). Representational flexibility and response control in a multistep multilocation search task. *Developmental Psychology, 34,* 203–214.

Chapter Five

Infant Learning and Memory

Carolyn Rovee-Collier and Rachel Barr

Introduction

Since Freud first proposed that adult behavior is rooted in the infancy period, the experiences of infants have been viewed as the cornerstone of behavioral and cognitive development. Most psychologists assume that the effects of early experiences gradually accrue, producing an individual who is increasingly complex. Implicit in this assumption, however, is a capacity for long-term memory – some means by which a relatively enduring record of those early experiences is preserved. Paradoxically, this is a capacity that infants are thought to lack – a belief that also originated with Freud (1935), who thought that early memories are forced into an unconscious state where they motivate subsequent behavior but cannot be recalled. The phenomenon of infantile amnesia – that we usually cannot remember what occurred before the age of 2 or 3 – supports Freud's view.

What young infants remember about their prior experiences is, however, difficult to study. Not only can they not verbalize what they remember, but also younger infants lack the motoric competence to perform most of the nonverbal tasks that have been used to study memory with older infants and children. In addition, factors such as the presence or absence of the caregiver, the familiarity or novelty of the setting, and the infant's momentary state of arousal radically affect memory performance and do so differently at different ages. In describing the major experimental procedures that have been applied to the study of memory development, this chapter will reveal how some of the problems associated with conducting research with human infants have been overcome. In the first section, we consider what infants can learn, how long they can remember it, and how reminder procedures affect their memories. In the second section, we consider some current issues in infant memory research, including the development of multiple memory systems, infantile amnesia, and memory distortions.

Research on Infant Learning and Memory

Over the course of ontogeny, infants' learning ability is thought to progress along an evolutionary continuum extending from the simplest nonassociative learning exhibited by
single-celled organisms to the most complex conceptual learning exhibited by adult primates. Traditionally, habituation anchored one end of this continuum, and imitation (a
form of observational learning) anchored the other (Buss, 1973). Today, however, the
entire continuum has been documented in infants 6 months and younger, challenging
the old adage that ontogeny recapitulates phylogeny – a challenge also raised by Steven
Jay Gould (1998), the noted evolutionary biologist.

In what follows, we present a "broad brush" picture of what infants can learn and
remember. Because most systematic research on infant memory has used habituation,
conditioning, and imitation procedures, we focus on that work.

Habituation

Habituation occurs at all phyletic levels – from protozoa to humans – and is thought to
play a central role in an individual's adaptive capacity as the means of eliminating
nonessential responses to biologically irrelevant stimuli. It is defined as a stimulus-
specific response decrement that results from repeated exposure to a stimulus that causes
the individual to orient either toward or away from it (Wyers, Peeke, & Herz, 1973).
Note that the individual's response must be an active one. If this condition is not met,
as occurs when an infant is swaddled or placed in bright illumination or under a heat
lamp, the resulting response decrement is called *acclimatization*. Likewise, the term
"repeated" implies that a single stimulus presentation followed by a test is not an
habituation procedure; in habituation, at least two presentations must precede the test.
Thompson and Spencer (1966) set forth these defining characteristics of habituation
(examples are in italics):

1   Repeated stimulus presentations result in decreased response (habituation) that
    usually is a negative exponential function of the number of presentations. Eventually
    this response reaches asymptote or zero response level (i.e., it habituates). *A new object
    is revealed when a cloth over it is removed. The infant stares at the object until the cover
    is replaced. This sequence is repeated again and again. Over successive repetitions, the
    infant looks at the object less and less; eventually, the infant stops orienting to it altogether.*
2   If the stimulus is withheld, responding tends to recover over time. This is called spon-
    taneous recovery. *If the object remains covered for a period of time before the cover is
    removed again, the infant will reorient to the object again.*
3   If repeated series of habituation training and spontaneous recovery trials are given,
    habituation becomes progressively more rapid. *Imagine that the object is repeatedly pre-
    sented until orienting ceases, it remains covered for a period of time, the cover is then*

removed again, the infant reorients, and this entire sequence is repeated over and over. On each occasion, the infant ceases orienting (i.e., habituation) and, after a period of time, reorients again (i.e., spontaneous recovery). Each time this sequence is repeated, the infant renews orienting toward the object for a shorter period of time until, at some point, the infant ignores it altogether.

4   Other things being equal, the more rapid the frequency of stimulation, the more rapid and/or pronounced is habituation. *The shorter the time between successive exposures, the faster the infant will stop looking at the object.*

5   The weaker the stimulus, the more rapid and/or pronounced is habituation. *The simpler the object is, the faster the infant will stop looking at it.*

6   Habituation can continue below the observable baseline or sub-zero level. When this occurs, the level of spontaneous recovery will be less than had habituation proceeded only until responding had initially ceased. *If the object continues to be exposed despite the fact that the infant seemingly pays no attention to it, then responding to it will spontaneously recover to a lower level than would have been expected had its exposure ceased when the infant had ceased looking at it.*

7   Habituation of response to one stimulus generalizes to other stimuli to the extent that the habituating and new stimuli share common elements. (This is the basis of all discrimination tests with similar stimuli after infants met an initial habituation criterion. The extent to which infants do not generalize to the test stimulus defines the extent to which infants perceive the habituating and the test stimulus as different.) *If the infant was habituated to a green triangle, for example, then he or she would look less if tested with a green square than with a red square.*

8   Presentation of another (usually strong) stimulus results in recovery of the previously habituated response to the original habituating stimulus (dishabituation). Dishabituation presumably results from the superimposition of a sensitization (excitatory) process on the ongoing habituation (inhibitory) process and that the observed level of responding reflects their sum. Presumably, a strong distractor disrupts the active inhibitory process, allowing the response to be expressed at a higher level. By this account, habituation does not permanently eliminate a response but only temporarily suppresses it. *If a very loud noise is sounded in the middle of a series of habituation trials with a particular object, then the infant will look at the object longer on the next trial than on the trial before the noise was sounded.* "Dishabituation" has been widely misapplied to describe the infant's increased response to a new test stimulus instead of the increase in responding to the prior habituation stimulus (Clifton & Nelson, 1976; Jeffrey & Cohen, 1971).

9   With repeated presentations of the dishabituating stimulus, the amount of dishabituation habituates; that is, the sensitization response also habituates. *If the loud noise is repeatedly sounded, the infant will ultimately habituate to it. As a result, its excitatory effect on looking will progressively diminish, and the infant will look progressively less at the original object during its subsequent exposures.*

The preceding characteristics exclude response decrements associated with fatigue, sensory adaptation, circadian rhythms, and physiological processes. In addition, it is important to distinguish habituation from *familiarization* – a term that has often been used interchangeably with it. Whereas habituation specifically refers to a short-term, discrete-trial procedure in which the decrease in response is measured over successive trials, familiarization is synonymous with "exposure learning" (Kling & Riggs, 1971) or "perceptual learning" (Gibson, 1963). It refers to any procedure during which the individual is preexposed to the test stimulus, and this preexposure results in a relatively permanent change in behavior as reflected, for example, on a discrimination task (Weizmann, Cohen, & Pratt, 1971). Unlike habituation, familiarization can be short term or long term and can occur in discrete trials or in one continuous exposure. Also, responding during familiarization may or may not be measured.

Before Sokolov (1963) published his model of habituation of the orienting reflex during conditioning, studies of habituation with infants were rare. Afterward, however, numerous researchers exploited habituation as a means of revealing infants' perceptual and cognitive abilities. In Sokolov's model, an internal representation or engram of a stimulus is formed each time it is encountered, and the extent to which the external stimulus matches that representation determines how long subjects look at it on succeeding encounters: As the representation becomes progressively fleshed out by new information that subjects notice, they attend to the external stimulus progressively less; once their representation is complete (i.e., no new information remains to be added to it), then subjects no longer look at it. As the representation decays over time (i.e., forgetting), however, subjects renew looking to the extent that the internal representation and the external stimulus no longer match. Once the delay is so long that subjects look at the stimulus for as long as they did on trial 1, when the stimulus was novel, then forgetting is said to be "complete."

Fantz (1964) obtained habituation to a repeated visual stimulus with infants between 2 and 6 months of age but not younger, and the rate of habituation was faster among the older infants – a relation that has since been reported by many others (e.g., Lewis & Goldberg, 1969). Graham, Leavitt, Strock, and Brown's (1978) subsequent finding that an anencephalic infant habituated to an auditory stimulus that produced no habituation in normal infants revealed that habituation is controlled at multiple levels of the central nervous system, with the functions of newly developing structures being superimposed on more primitive ones. This ontogenetic pattern parallels the evolutionary development of the brain (MacLean, 1967).

Using an habituation procedure, Stinson (1971, cited in Werner & Perlmutter, 1979) obtained the first forgetting function with preverbal infants (4-month-olds). In his study, each high-amplitude suck on a nonnutritive nipple briefly illuminated a visual stimulus on a front screen (see Figure 5.1). After an infant's sucking had fallen to a fraction of its original level (habituation), he interposed a delay of 0, 15, 30, or 75 sec for independent groups of infants before they were allowed to suck for the stimulus again. As expected, the greater the delay, the greater the responding after the delay, indicating that infants again treated the habituation stimulus as novel. After delays longer than 15 sec, infants' sucking had returned to its original, prehabituation level, indicating that they had forgotten seeing the visual stimulus and perceived it as novel. Since then, other researchers have consistently found that forgetting is complete after 15 sec in infants of a variety of ages across the first year of life, suggesting that the duration of retention in single-session

Figure 5.1   A 4-month-old infant producing illumination of a visual target by means of high-amplitude sucks. (Photograph courtesy of Dr. E. R. Siqueland)

habituation studies is age-invariant. This result probably reflects the upper limit of short-term memory.

Classical Conditioning

Classical conditioning, like habituation, occurs at all phyletic levels and involves repeated stimulus presentations. In habituation studies, however, the correlation between the repeated stimulus and a subsequent environmental event is zero, and subjects stop attending to it. By contrast, in classical conditioning studies, the correlation between the repeated stimulus and a subsequent environmental event is 1.00, and subjects not only continue to attend to it but also come to anticipate the event it predicts. Because many events in nature occur in an orderly fashion, classical conditioning permits organisms to exploit this orderliness and anticipate potentially significant events instead of simply reacting to them, as in habituation. The classical conditioning procedure initially requires two basic components – an unconditional stimulus (US) that reliably elicits a reflex (the unconditional response, or UR), and a stimulus (the eventual conditional stimulus, or CS) that does not initially elicit the same reflex as the US. After repeated pairings of the CS and US in close temporal contiguity, the CS comes to elicit a response (the conditional response, or CR) that is similar to the UR, either before the US is actually presented or on trials when it is omitted. In essence, in classical conditioning, subjects do not learn a new response but a new occasion for the old response.

The timing of the appearance of the first conditional reflexes was of particular concern to early Soviet researchers. Pavlov thought that unconditioned reflexes were exclusively subcortical and that conditioned reflexes were exclusively cortical. As a result, Soviet psychologists viewed classical conditioning as a means by which to study the functional development of the cortex. One of Pavlov's students, Krasnogorskii (1913, cited in Elkonin, 1957), concluded that the cortex of infants younger than 6 months was insufficiently innervated to permit the formation of cortical connections, as required in classical conditioning. Subsequently, however, Koltsova (1949) reported conditioned sucking reactions at the breast during the third postnatal week, and Irzhanskaia and Felberbaum (1954) reported conditioned eyeblink reflexes by 1.5-month-olds who were 2.5 months premature.

Most of the early studies of classical conditioning were single-subject studies that traced an individual's conditioning performance over a substantial period of time. As such, they also provided evidence of long-term memory. The most famous of these early classical conditioning studies was conducted by Watson and Rayner (1920) with an 11-month-old named Albert. In this study, they sounded a loud gong (the US) which produced crying and withdrawal (the UR) each time Albert touched a white rat (the CS). One week later, when Albert was merely shown the rat, he withdrew his hand (the CR). Later in that same session, he received five more CS–US pairings. Five days afterward, Albert not only exhibited CRs at the sight of the rat, but he also generalized these conditioned emotional reactions to previously neutral stimuli that resembled the rat in some way, including a rabbit, a dog, a fur coat, a Santa Claus mask, and a swatch of cotton wool. He did not, however, produce the CR to wooden blocks, which differed perceptually from the rat. Ten days later, his CR to the rat had become muted and was "freshened" with another CS–US presentation (a reinstatement procedure; see "Reminder procedures," below). At this time, the US was also explicitly paired once with the rabbit and once with a dog. One month after the reinstatement – almost two months after his initial conditioning experience – Albert still exhibited strong CRs to the rat, the dog, the mask, and the fur coat. This study demonstrated not only that infants can be classically conditioned during their first year but also that conditioned emotional reactions are established rapidly, can be maintained over a substantial period by occasional repetition, and generalize readily to stimuli that bear a physical resemblance to the original CS. In a single-subject study that was explicitly designed to measure the retention of classical conditioning, Jones (1930) repeatedly presented a 7-month-old with a tapping sound (CS) followed by an electrotactual stimulus (US) for five consecutive days, after which the infant received no more CS–US pairings. Even without them, the infant still exhibited the CR seven weeks later!

Despite the fact that many successful classical conditioning studies were conducted with newborns from the late 1950s through the 1970s (for review, see Siqueland, 1970), critics continued to challenge evidence that newborns could be classically conditioned (Sameroff, 1971). Finally, in 1984, Blass, Ganchrow, and Steiner laid these challenges to rest once and for all, unequivocally demonstrating that even newborns as young as 2 hours could be classically conditioned. Conditioning sessions took place 2 hours after a scheduled feeding and lasted 45–50 min. The experimental group received forehead stroking (the CS) immediately followed by the delivery of sucrose (the US) through a glass pipette, while an explicitly paired control group received the same number of CS–US trials, but the sucrose was received after a longer and variable delay. A second control group, included to test for the possible effects of sensitization (a lowered response threshold induced by repeated presentations of the US), received the US only, with no exposure to the CS prior to the extinction phase. During acquisition, both the experimental and the explicitly paired control groups exhibited the same incidence of head-orienting responses, but those of the experimental group were confined to the CS portion of the trial whereas those of the control group were not. Moreover, the experimental group exhibited a high level of pucker-sucks during the CS and a classic extinction function once the US was withheld, with the sharpest decline in conditioned responding occurring between the first and second trials.

Of particular interest were other behavioral changes exhibited by the experimental group during extinction: "After 1 or 2 extinction trials, the infant's expression appeared to be that of surprise, which gave way to a frowning or angry face, to be followed by crying or whimpering. Crying was short-lived; and at its termination, the infants generally slept" (Blass et al., 1984, p. 230). Their crying was not elicited by withdrawing the sucrose: Only one of 16 infants in the two control groups cried during the extinction phase, yet all had received sucrose during training. Rather, infants in the experimental group had learned the predictive relation between stroking and sucrose delivery and, apparently, cried because their expectancy was violated. This same phenomenon was described in one of the earliest conditioning studies of infant feeding (Marquis, 1941), underscoring the fact that responding during US-omission trials – either interspersed during the conditioning trials or during the extinction phase – can be particularly revealing of whether infants have learned the contingency.

Furthermore, in heart-rate conditioning studies with newborns and decerebrate infants, responding during the specified CS–US interval is often impossible for the infant. In these cases, interspersing US-omission trials among CS–US training trials is a particularly effective way of determining whether a conditioned association has formed between the two stimuli. If a heart-rate change is seen when the predicted US does not occur, then a conditioned association has formed (Berntson, Tuber, Ronca, & Bachman, 1983; Clifton, 1974; Tuber, Berntson, Bachman, & Allen, 1980). Interestingly, the direction of infants' heart-rate change usually reflects the quality of the omitted US. When an aversive US (e.g., a very loud noise) is omitted, *heart-rate acceleration* occurs; when an appetitive US (e.g., sucrose) is omitted, *heart-rate deceleration* occurs. These changes in heart rate are thought to reflect a defensive (protective) response and an orienting (what-is-it?) response, respectively. There is an important exception to this rule: Premature and decerebrate infants usually exhibit heart-rate acceleration to all US omissions.

Little, Lipsitt, and Rovee-Collier (1984) demonstrated both single-session eyeblink conditioning (the CR) and long-term retention with 10-, 20-, and 30-day-olds using a CS–US (tone–air puff) interval of 1500 msec. A control group that received the same CS–US pairings with a 500-msec interstimulus interval exhibited no conditioning whatsoever. Because 500 msec is the optimal interval in conditioning studies with adults, it is likely that many of the early failures to find classical conditioning with immature subjects resulted from the use of an interstimulus interval that was appropriate for adults but not for infants. As in the Blass et al. (1984) study, a greater percentage of CRs occurred on US-omission trials that were interspersed among the CS–US conditioning trials than during the CS–US interval *per se*, although both measures indicated that learning had occurred. During the retention session, both the 20- and 30-day-olds exhibited significant savings 10 days later, and the 20-day-olds outperformed 30-day-olds who were being trained for the first time.

Operant Conditioning

Unlike classically conditioned responses, which are reflexive, operant responses are emitted. This means that subjects must spontaneously perform the response or some component of it at a low or moderate rate before it is ever reinforced (e.g., rewarded) in the first place. Also, there is no essential biological relation between the type of reinforcer and the response it influences. Infants increase their rate of sucking, for example, as readily when their sucks are followed by their mother's voice (DeCasper & Fifer, 1980), a computer-generated speech sound (Eimas, Siqueland, Jusczyk, & Vigorito, 1971), or a colored slide of geometric shapes (Milewski & Siqueland, 1975) as when their sucks are followed by a squirt of sugar water (Siqueland & Lipsitt, 1966) or milk (Sameroff, 1968). Most of the early studies of operant conditioning with infants were criticized for either failing to obtain an adequate sample of the infant's operant level or failing to demonstrate operant control. Operant control refers to the requirement that the response must be solely attributable to the contingency; it cannot be elicited by the reinforcer or otherwise result from behavioral arousal. This turned out to be a major problem in early studies of "social reinforcers" (i.e., auditory and visual stimulation provided by adults). Although social reinforcers appeared to be particularly effective, they elicited reciprocal social or affective behavior that either competed with or mimicked conditioning (Bloom, 1984).

In one of the earliest studies of infant social conditioning, Brackbill (1958) explored whether smiling behavior of 3- and 4-month-olds was sensitive to the schedule of reinforcement. Their operant (baseline) level of smiling was determined while the experimenter stood motionless and expressionless above each infant. Then, during the acquisition phase, infants in the *continuous-reinforcement* group were smiled at, picked up, held, jostled, patted, and talked to by the experimenter for 30 sec following each and every smile. Infants in the *intermittent-reinforcement* group initially received the same treatment except that over the course of acquisition, the number of smiles they were required to emit before each reinforcement was administered was gradually increased.

Although the response rates of the two groups did not differ during either baseline or the initial common treatment phase, the response rate of the intermittent-reinforcement group increased thereafter as the reinforcement schedule became progressively higher. In extinction, Brackbill also obtained the classic result – the intermittent-reinforcement group exhibited a higher response rate and more total responses than the continuous-reinforcement group. Notably, in the latter group, smiling was completely replaced by gaze aversion and crying when the experimenter's face became motionless and expressionless during extinction – a result like that found by Blass et al. (1984) during extinction of anticipatory (classically conditioned) mouthing responses. Brackbill's study was subsequently criticized because it did not include noncontingent-reinforcement controls and because the continuous-reinforcement group received a greater total amount of stimulation during acquisition than the intermittent-reinforcement group. The accumulated evidence on the role of social reinforcers in infant operant conditioning since that time, however, has confirmed her original conclusions.

With the exception of studies using social reinforcers and studies of sucking and head-turning with newborns (Papoušek, 1959; Siqueland & Lipsitt, 1966), most attempts to operantly condition young infants in the 1950s and 1960s were plagued by the use of discrete reinforcers that were ineffective over sustained periods. Most studies, therefore, used sessions lasting only a few minutes. Since it was not known whether infants could be operantly conditioned in the first place, such short sessions obviously worked against obtaining a positive answer. As a result, many critics claimed that infants could not learn operant contingencies until they were substantially older – a claim firmly rooted in Piagetian theory as well (Piaget, 1952). These claims were finally laid to rest, however, with the introduction of the mobile conjugate reinforcement procedure (Rovee & Rovee, 1969). This procedure promoted rapid learning and sustained responding over repeated sessions lasting as long as 45–55 minutes in infants as young as 8–10 weeks. In the mobile procedure, infants' kicks move a crib mobile via a ribbon strung from one ankle to the mobile suspension hook (see Figure 5.2a). Infants learn rapidly and usually double or triple their rate of kicking within just a few minutes.

Ironically, Piaget had recorded in his diary that his own 3-month-old increased the sweeping movements of his hand after it hit and moved an object that was suspended over the bassinet. He had attributed this to an "elicited joy reaction," arguing that infants could not initiate "interesting spectacles" themselves until they were several months older. Rovee and Rovee demonstrated, however, that infants' increased kicking did not merely reflect an increase in excitement that was elicited by the moving mobile. Infants in arousal control groups who saw the mobile moving noncontingently (i.e., whether they had kicked or not) never increased their rate of kicking, even though the mobile moved at exactly the same rate that infants in the experimental group had moved it by kicking.

More recently, the mobile procedure has been used with infants between 2 and 6 months of age to assess their capacity for long-term memory. In these studies, the to-be-remembered information is displayed either directly on the mobile objects or on a cloth context draped over the sides of the crib or playpen, and infants are trained in two sessions 24 hours apart. In session 1, the ribbon and mobile are connected to different hooks so that infants' kicks cannot move the mobile, and their level of unlearned activity is recorded (the *baseline phase*). Thereafter, the ribbon is moved to the same hook as the mobile, and kicks move the mobile in a graded manner that is commensurate with their rate and vigor ("conjugate reinforcement"). At the end of each session, the baseline conditions are reinstated. This nonreinforcement phase at the end of session 2 (*the immediate retention test*) allows a measure of the infant's final level of learning and retention after zero delay. During the *delayed recognition test*, which occurs at some later time, infants are merely shown either the original mobile or one that differs in some way (see Figure 5.2b). This is a "yes/no" recognition test. They kick robustly ("yes") if they recognize the test mobile; otherwise, they kick at baseline ("no"). Because the mobile and ankle ribbon are attached to different

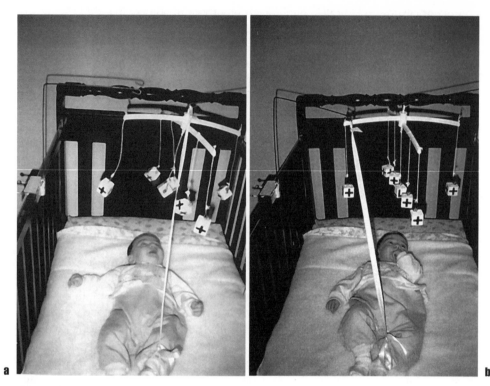

Figure 5.2   The experimental arrangement used with 2- to 6-month-olds in the mobile conjugate reinforcement task, shown here with a 3-month-old. (a) *Acquisition phase*: The ribbon and mobile are attached to the same overhead hook so that kicks move the mobile. (b) *The delayed recognition test*: The ribbon and mobile are attached to different hooks so that kicks cannot move the mobile.

hooks during testing, infants' kicks cannot move the mobile; as a result, their responding reflects only what they actually bring into the test session and not new learning or savings at the time of testing. Rovee and Fagen (1976), for example, trained 3-month-olds with one mobile for 9 min per day for 3 days and then tested them 24 hours later with either the same mobile or a different one. During testing, infants recognized only the original mobile – a finding subsequently replicated with 8-week-olds. They did not kick above baseline level when they were tested with the different mobile. Besides demonstrating 24-hour retention, this study showed that even the youngest infants can detect whether a mobile differs from one they had last seen 24 hours earlier!

The preceding data contradicted the widely accepted conclusion that longterm memory does not emerge until 8 to 9 months of age (Kagan & Hamburg, 1981). This conclusion was based on the observation that for the first time at 8 to 9 months, infants become distressed when a stranger enters the room after their mother has left it. Presumably, the discrepancy between the characteristics of the *physically present* stranger and the *remembered* characteristics of the mother makes them cry (i.e., stranger anxiety). Stranger anxiety was not thought to appear before that age because younger infants could not hold

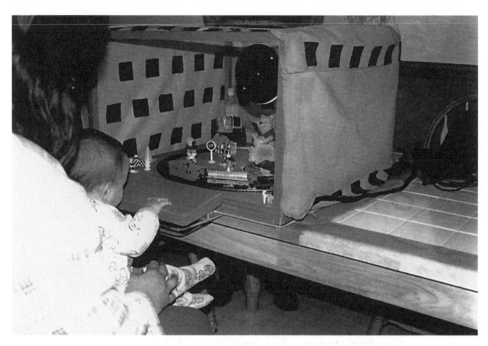

Figure 5.3   The experimental arrangement used with 6- to 18-month-olds in the train task, shown here with a 6-month-old. During baseline and the delayed retention test, the lever is deactivated so that presses cannot move the train. Note the complex array of toys in the train box.

a representation of their mother "on the stage of memory" for even a few minutes. However, if 8-week-olds could remember the appearance of a fiveobject mobile that they had previously seen for a total of less than an hour and had not seen since the day before, then even 8-week-olds can obviously remember what their own mother looks like after she has been out of sight for more than a few minutes!

Because infants older than 7 months rapidly lose interest in the mobile task, another task is used with older infants. Here, each lever press briefly moves a miniature train around a circular track set in a complex array of toys (see Figure 5.3). During baseline and all retention tests, the lever is deactivated so that infants can see the train but cannot move it by lever-pressing. The train task is an upward extension of the mobile task: At 6 months, infants' learning and memory performance in the two tasks is identical (Hartshorn & Rovee-Collier, 1997). Combining data from the two tasks reveals that the duration of retention increases linearly between 2 and 18 months of age (see Figure 5.4; Hartshorn et al., 1998b). This increase is not due to age differences in either original learning or motoric competence. Infants of all ages learn the two tasks equally rapidly, and their baseline response rates are the same at all ages, irrespective of task. This standardized retention function is a reference function against which retention obtained from infants tested in different tasks and with different task parameters can be meaningfully compared. Although some researchers have used different parameters of encoding (e.g., the duration, number, and distribution of training sessions, the attention-getting

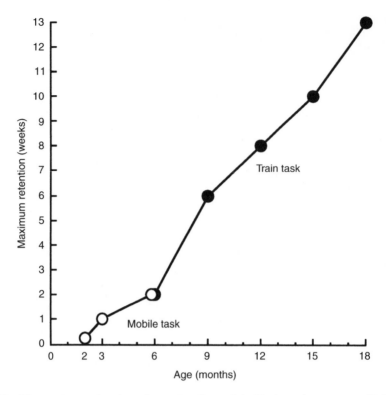

Figure 5.4   The maximum duration of retention (in weeks) of independent groups of infants over the first 18 months of life in studies using one of two operant tasks. Six-month-olds were trained and tested in both the mobile and the train tasks.

properties of the training stimuli) than those used by Hartshorn et al. (1998b), the pattern of retention that they obtain at different ages should be the same. In addition, this function provides a standard against which diagnosticians can evaluate both the results of tests that screen the learning and memory abilities of compromised infants and the effectiveness of the intervention procedures that are used with such infants.

In the Hartshorn et al. (1998b) study, the experimental conditions at the time of training and testing were identical. In fact, a general law of memory is that retention is best when the conditions of encoding (training) and retrieval (testing) most closely match. In everyday life, however, the likelihood that these conditions will remain the same decreases as the retention interval becomes longer. An important developmental question, then, is how differences between the conditions of training and testing affect long-term memory over the infancy period.

To answer this, Hartshorn et al. (1998a) trained infants between 3 and 12 months of age in either the mobile or train task and tested them with different cues (mobiles or trains) or in different contexts after delays that spanned the entire forgetting function of each age. Between 3 and 6 months of age, infants who were tested with a different cue in the original context exhibited no retention after any delay. Moreover, their memories were highly specific. Three-month-olds, for example, failed to recognize a test mobile composed of small pink blocks, for example, if the +s that had been displayed on its sides one day earlier (see Figure 5.2a) were just 25 percent smaller or larger than the +s on their test mobile. At 9 and 12 months of age, however, infants' memory performance was very different: They *discriminated* (i.e., did not respond to) a novel test cue from their original training cue *only* after relatively long test delays and *generalized* (i.e., responded) to a novel test cue *only* after shorter delays. This result was counterintuitive. After all, the details of a cue are usually remembered best – and discriminated – after short delays, and generalization is usually seen after longer delays, when the details have been forgotten. This pattern occurs because we usually remember the specific details of an event (e.g., who said what to whom in a movie) best immediately it happens; as time passes, we gradually forget its specific details, and eventually, we remember only its gist (e.g., what the movie was generally about). Moreover, the fact that infants discriminated the very same novel test cue after long delays meant that they could surely discriminate that it was different from their training cue after short delays as well! This raised an interesting question: Why did the older infants *disregard* the perceptible difference between the training and test cues after delays so short (i.e., one day–two weeks) that they could easily remember the details of the original cue? Apparently, by 9 months of age, infants have begun to "test the waters" to determine if other objects that they encounter in a particular context are *functionally equivalent* to objects that they previously encountered in that same, distinctive context. That is, the older infants checked whether the discriminably different new objects "worked" in the same way as the old ones. After longer delays when retrieval was more difficult, the cues presented at the time of testing had to match those that were present at the time of encoding (training) in order for the memory to be retrieved.

Infants who were tested with the original cue in a *different context* exhibited a different developmental pattern. After all test delays except the very longest, infants at all ages except 6 months recognized the training cue even though the context in which they were tested was different. At 6 months – the age just before infants are able to crawl from one place to another, the opposite pattern was seen. In essence, infants readily generalized what they had learned from one place to another except after the longest delays, when retrieval was much more difficult. As was the case with the test cue, a more complete set of retrieval cues was required in order for the memory to be successfully retrieved at this point. As a result, the test context had to match the context in which encoding had occurred after long retention intervals. This finding reveals that information about the place where something happened is represented in the infant's memory but is unimportant for retrieval of that event except after very long delays. Parents should be comforted to know that their infants can show what they learned at the day-care center or at grandma's house once they get home – a different context – if given an opportunity to do so before too much time has passed!

Deferred Imitation

Memory for an event can also be measured by an infant's ability to reproduce a behavior that was previously modeled by another individual after a delay – a paradigm called deferred imitation. This paradigm provides a measure of cued-recall. Deferred imitation was originally described by Piaget (1962) from observations of his own children. He

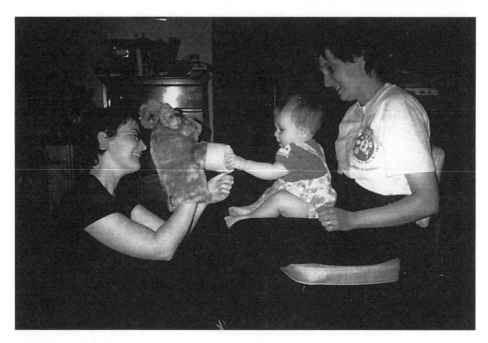

Figure 5.5 The experimental arrangement used with 6- to 24-month-old infants in the deferred imitation paradigm. Shown here is a 6-month-old removing a mitten from the puppet's hand – an action modeled by the experimenter 24 hours earlier.

described how his daughter (Jacqueline) precisely imitated a peer's temper tantrum that she had seen 24 hours earlier. According to Piaget, Jacqueline watched as a peer tried to get out of his playpen. The boy screamed, moved the playpen backwards, and stamped his feet. The following day when Jacqueline was placed in her playpen, she imitated the same series of actions even though the boy was not there. To be consistent with Piaget's original conception of deferred imitation, a "true" deferred imitation paradigm requires that infants do not practice the target behavior(s) prior to the long-term test so that their memory performance can be based only on a representation of the originally modeled event and not on a memory of their own prior actions (Meltzoff, 1990).

Piaget (1962) claimed that deferred imitation did not emerge until infants were 18 to 24 months of age. Although some studies have supported Piaget's developmental timetable (Abravanel, Levan-Goldschmidt, & Stevenson, 1976; McCall, Parke, & Kavanaugh, 1977), others have lacked essential control groups, making conclusions regarding the earliest appearance of deferred imitation tenuous at best. Meltzoff (1990) challenged Piaget's fundamental assumptions. Examining deferred imitation under highly controlled experimental conditions, he demonstrated that 14-month-olds exhibited deferred imitation after a 4-month delay (Meltzoff, 1995) and 9-month-olds did so after a 24-hour delay (Meltzoff, 1988a). Subsequently, Barr, Dowden, and Hayne (1996) found that infants as young as 6 months of age also exhibited deferred imitation after a 24-hour delay. In their study, an experimenter modeled a sequence of three specific actions with a puppet. The sequence was removing a mitten from a puppet's hand, shaking the mitten to ring a bell that was attached inside the mitten, and replacing the mitten on the puppet's hand (see Figure 5.5). These target actions were modeled either three times for a total of 30 sec or six times for a total of 60 sec, and deferred imitation was assessed 24 hours later during a time-limited response period. If allowed sufficient exposure to the modeling, 6-month-olds exhibited deferred imitation of the puppet task, responding successfully if the demonstration lasted 60 sec but not if it lasted only 30 sec. These results challenge previous claims that deferred imitation is not possible before 9 months of age because the prefrontal cortex or the limbic system is too immature before then (Bachevalier & Mishkin, 1984; Diamond, 1990), and they add to prior evidence, gathered in operant conditioning studies, that long-term memory emerges well before 8 to 9 months of age.

To examine 6-month-old infants' ability to imitate multiple actions, Collie and Hayne (1999) constructed infant activity or "busy" boards that resemble those that are commercially available. During the demonstration session, the experimenter modeled the target actions on half of the objects that were arranged on either a 6-object or 12-object board, while the other half of the objects on each board served as distractors and were never touched by the experimenter during the demonstration. Each target action was modeled six times. To succeed on the test, infants had to locate the target objects amongst the distractors and then remember what to do with them. Despite the increased difficulty of the task, 6-month-olds successfully imitated the modeled actions during the response period 24 hours later. Taken together, these studies suggest that failures to document deferred imitation by young infants are more likely to reflect the choice of an inappropriate task or task parameters as to reflect infants' fundamental inability to imitate what they saw an adult doing earlier.

As in the studies with mobiles and trains (see preceding section), older infants generalize imitative responding to novel test cues only after relatively short delays, when they can clearly distinguish that the test cues are different. After longer delays, they will not imitate actions if presented with test objects that differ in some way from the object on which the actions were originally modeled. At 12–14 months of age, for example, infants in deferred imitation studies generalize to an object that differs in color but not in form after 10 min (Barnat, Klein, & Meltzoff, 1996; Hayne, MacDonald, & Barr, 1997) but not after one day; by 18 months of age, however, they generalize to an object that differs in color after one day; and by 21 months of age, they generalize to a cue that differs in both color and form after one day (Hayne et al., 1997). Likewise, 12- to 14-month-olds readily imitate a simpler task (one that they remember for as long as four months) in contexts different from where they had originally seen the actions modeled after delays as long as 28 days (Hanna & Meltzoff, 1993; Klein & Meltzoff, 1999).

Developmental increases in generalized responding may also explain recent reports of changes in infants' ability to imitate actions seen on television. In general, infants' ability to imitate a televised demonstration lags well behind their ability to imitate a live demonstration. When the demonstration is live, for example, 6-month-olds imitate an adult's actions on objects after a 24-hour delay (Barr et al., 1996), but when the same demonstration is televised, infants do not imitate the same multistep actions before they are 18 months old (Barr & Hayne, 1999). Between 14–15 months, however, infants can imitate some televised actions (Barr & Hayne, 1999; Meltzoff, 1988b). One potential explanation for these findings is that the physical attributes of the three-dimensional object seen at the time of testing and the two-dimensional image seen during the original demonstration may not overlap sufficiently to permit retrieval of the original memory representation at younger ages.

In the past, the fundamental barrier to systematic research on memory development during the infancy period was the lack of tasks that were appropriate for infants of different ages, whose motor abilities and interest vary dramatically. As shown in Figure 5.4, development of the train task as an upward extension of the mobile task finally enabled age-related changes in long-term retention to be documented across a wide age range. Another problem has plagued studies using deferred imitation procedures. In the past, the lack of proper controls for potential age-related changes in the spontaneous production of target behaviors compromised conclusions about age-related changes in deferred imitation (i.e., retention). Studies using the puppet task (described above), however, have included age-matched control groups and have found that infants' spontaneous production of target behaviors is consistently low between 6 and 24 months of age. This finding enabled the assessment of developmental differences in deferred imitation across a wide age range. To examine potential age-related differences in retention, Barr and Hayne (2000) compared the imitation performance of 6-, 12-, and 18-month-olds who were tested either immediately or after delays ranging from 1 to 42 days. They found that long-term retention increased linearly across this age range, following the same pattern depicted in Figure 5.4: 6-month-olds exhibited retention after 1 but not 7 days, 12-month-olds exhibited retention after 7 but not 14 days, and 18-month-olds exhibited retention after 28 but not 42 days.

In a variation of the deferred imitation procedure ("elicited imitation"), infants are given an opportunity to practice the target behaviors prior to the retention interval (e.g., Bauer, Hertsgaard, & Dow, 1994). Unfortunately, task parameters have varied not only from study to study but also within studies. In one study, for example, infants manipulated the objects until they began to mouth them or throw them on the floor. As a result, the duration of their baseline and test phases ranged from 20 sec to 145 sec for different infants within the same experiment (Bauer & Hertsgaard, 1993). Yet, a mere 30 sec is the difference in whether or not a 6-month-old can exhibit deferred imitation one day later (Barr et al., 1996)! As a result, conclusions about age-related changes in imitation that are based on data from studies using this procedure are difficult to evaluate. Nonetheless, 1- to 2-year-olds were reported to exhibit retention after six weeks (Bauer & Shore, 1987), and limited evidence of retention at this age was reported after eight months (Bauer et al., 1994). Furthermore, retention was consistently influenced by the structure of the target event (Bauer & Mandler, 1989; Bauer & Shore, 1987). Without exception, infants recalled a series of actions that could only be performed in a specific order ("enabling" or "causal" events, such as making a rattle by placing a ball in a container, putting a lid on it, and shaking it) better than actions that could be performed in any order ("arbitrary" events, such as dressing a teddy bear by putting a ring on its finger, a scarf around its neck, and a cap on its head). The result was found even when the enabling and arbitrary events were matched on the basis of target actions and event goals (Barr & Hayne, 1996) and was obtained with older children (Fivush, Kuebli, & Clubb, 1992) and adults (Ratner, Smith, & Dion, 1986) as well.

At any given age, the particular behaviors that infants can imitate after a delay depend on task difficulty and complexity (Barr & Hayne, 1999, 2000). With increasing age, the range of behaviors that infants can imitate expands from facial and body movements (Meltzoff & Moore, 1994), to specific actions on a specific object and then on similar objects (Barr et al., 1996; Hayne et al., 1997), to intended actions and social goals (Meltzoff, 1995). This gradual developmental progression is thought to reflect developmental increases in infants' motor competence and cognitive abilities as well as age changes in their social niche. The ability to defer imitation *per se*, however, may be present much earlier.

Reminder Procedures

Many prominent theories of human development assume that the increasing number and complexity of behaviors that appear over the course of infancy and early childhood are constructed from and shaped by infants' prior experiences, which gradually and progressively accrue. This account requires that young infants maintain a relatively enduring record of their experiences sufficiently long that their subsequent experiences can, in fact, accumulate with them. Some psychologists, however, have argued that the young infant's brain is too immature before the end of the first year to encode and maintain memories over the long term (Kagan & Hamburg, 1981; C. Nelson, 1995; Schacter & Moscovitch, 1984), and others have argued that until children are verbal and can rehearse events by periodically talking about them, it is not possible for them to retain a memory over a long period of time (K. Nelson, 1990). Assertions such as these have cast serious doubt on the reputed importance of early experiences. Reminders, however, can dramatically protract infants' memories. Two reminder paradigms that are increasingly used in memory studies with infants and young children are reinstatement and reactivation. Whereas reactivation has primarily been used with infants between 2 and 18 months of age, reinstatement has primarily been used with preschool- and school-aged children. Both types of reminder protract retention so that it is exhibited after delays not otherwise possible, and many developmental psychologists use the terms "reinstatement" and "reactivation" interchangeably, but they are very different both procedurally and functionally.

Reinstatement

The reinstatement procedure was introduced by Campbell and Jaynes (1966), who proposed that it was a mechanism by which early memories could be maintained over significant periods of development. They defined reinstatement as a small amount of periodic practice or repetition of an original experience throughout a retention interval. As evidence for their proposal, they gave rat pups 30 shocks on the black side of a shuttlebox in a fear-conditioning procedure. Thereafter, pups received a single shock 7, 14, and 21 days later and a retention test for conditioned fear 28 days later – one week after their last reinstatement. A forgetting control group was trained and tested 28 days later without any interpolated shocks, and a reinstatement control group received the weekly shocks and the retention test but was not originally trained. During the test, only rats who were both trained and reminded exhibited retention of conditioned fear. Presumably, the periodic reminders *forestalled* forgetting in a fashion akin to throwing a new log on a dying fire. Other researchers (e.g., Campbell & Randall, 1976; Riccio & Haroutunian, 1979) have studied the efficacy of presenting other fractional components of the original training situation (CS+, CS−, apparatus cues, context) as reinstatements. However, none maintained retention as effectively as a partial training trial.

Hartshorn (1998) was the first to test the reinstatement hypothesis with human infants. After learning the train task at 6 months of age, infants received a brief reinstatement at 7, 8, 9, and 12 months of age and were tested at 18 months of age. The reinstatements involved a small amount of repeated practice with the train – a 2 min period during which lever presses made the train move. Although 6-month-olds otherwise forget after two weeks, after receiving periodic reinstatements, they exhibited significant retention during the 18-month test – one year after training was over. Immediately after the 18-month test, infants received a fifth reinstatement. When retested at 2 years of age, five of six infants still exhibited excellent retention despite having received only a single reinstatement in the preceding year (at 18 months of age). Controls who received the same reinstatement regimen without prior training exhibited no retention after any delay.

Hartshorn also found that infants may not express a memory that has been maintained over a long period in the same form as they originally encoded it. Recall that 6-month-olds typically exhibit excellent retention if tested in the original training context but none whatsoever if tested in a context different from where they were trained – a room in the infant's home (Hartshorn & Rovee-Collier, 1997). In contrast, 8-month-olds typically respond in different test contexts for as long as 5–6 weeks. Hartshorn (1998) trained infants at 6 months of age, gave them a 2-min reinstatement in the original training context four weeks later, and then tested their retention four weeks later, at 8 months of age. During the test, infants exhibited excellent retention whether tested in the original context or in a different one. Apparently, the context-dependent memory that infants had encoded as 6-month-olds was converted when it was retrieved two months later and expressed in the form characteristic of 8-month-olds – as a context-independent memory (see Tulving, 1983, for a discussion of conversion). Thus, old memories can still be retrieved and used when infants are older, but they may not be recognizable if they are expressed differently than when they were originally established.

Reactivation

The reactivation procedure was introduced by Spear and Parsons (1976). Instead of distributing reminders throughout the retention interval, as in the reinstatement procedure, they gave weanling rats a single (shock) reminder 27 days after fear conditioning was over and tested them one day later. Surprisingly, the weanlings' retention was as good as that of rat pups who were exposed to periodic shocks throughout the retention interval. Weanlings who were trained but not reminded and weanlings who were reminded but not trained exhibited no evidence of retention during the long-term test. Spear and Parsons described their alleviated forgetting procedure as "reactivation" in order to distinguish it from reinstatement, which presumably allows no forgetting in the first place.

Unlike reinstatement, in which subjects are exposed to multiple reminders throughout the retention interval, during reactivation, subjects are exposed to a single memory prime, or reminder, at the *end* of the retention interval, after forgetting is complete but in advance of the long-term retention test. Also unlike reinstatement, in which subjects receive a partial training trial with the full complement of original training cues, during reactivation, subjects are exposed to only an isolated component of the original training situation, such as the original cue or context.

In addition to differing procedurally, reinstatement and reactivation also differ functionally, but most developmental psychologists have not distinguished between them. In fact, Howe, Courage, and Bryant-Brown (1993) wrote that "the distinction between reinstatement and reactivation is . . . artificial in that both . . . have similar (if not the same) memory-preserving effects" (p. 855). Reinstatement, however, is most effective when the memory is active (i.e., is remembered), whereas reactivation is most effective after the memory has been forgotten. When 3-month-olds were given either a single, 3-min reactivation treatment or a single 3-min reinstatement three days after training, when their memory was still active, they remembered the training event for one week after reactivation but for two weeks after reinstatement (Adler, Wilk, & Rovee-Collier, 2000). On the other hand, when infants were given the same reminders 20 days after training, when the memory was forgotten, they again remembered the training event one day after reactivation (Hayne, 1990) but not after reinstatement (Galluccio & Rovee-Collier, 1999). Just as researchers have attempted – with little success – to use fractional components of the training situation as reinstatements, they have also attempted to use multiple reactivations to protract retention even longer. These subsequent reactivations were effective only if the memory had been reforgotten by the time of reminding (Hayne, 1990).

In the first test of reactivation with human infants, 3-month-olds were trained in the mobile task, exposed to a prime either 13 or 27 days later, and tested one day afterward (Rovee-Collier, Sullivan, Enright, Lucas, & Fagen, 1980). During the reactivation procedure, infants were in a sling-seat in their cribs to minimize kicking; also, the ribbon was not attached to infants' ankle but was held by the experimenter, who pulled it to move the mobile at the same rate each infant had moved it by kicking during the final minutes of acquisition. Although 3-month-olds otherwise forget the mobile task within a week, a single reactivation completely restored their retention during both the 2- and 4-week tests, and a second reactivation extended it for another two weeks (Hayne, 1990). Controls who were primed without being trained exhibited no retention. In subsequent studies of reactivation using the train task, infants sit on their mother's lap in front of the train set as they did during original training, but the lever is deactivated, and the train is computer-programmed to move as it had during an infant's final minutes of acquisition. The effectiveness of reminder procedures with infants is not limited to studies using operant conditioning tasks. The memories of 14- to 18-month-olds who participated in observational learning procedures are also protracted by exposure to a reactivation reminder (Barr & Hayne, 2000; Sheffield & Hudson, 1994).

Particularly important is the finding that reactivated memories are not transient but remain accessible to shape future behavior. Between 3 and 12 months of age, infants forget reactivated memories at approximately the same rate that they forgot the original memory, even though their duration of retention increases over this period. Thus, just a single reactivation treatment, if administered one week after infants last remembered the task, essentially doubles the period over which a memory can be retrieved over the first year of life (Hildreth, Wawrzyniak, Barr, & Rovee-Collier, 1999).

At 3 months of age, Fagen and Rovee-Collier (1983) found that a prime took 24 hours to recover the forgotten memory, and the memory was not fully recovered for three days. Recently, Hildreth and Rovee-Collier (1999) have found that the latency of response to priming increases linearly over the first year of life. Because the memory prime was presented one week after infants of a given age last remembered the task, the absolute delay between training and priming also increased with age because the older infants took longer to forget. Nonetheless, at 6 months, infants again recognized the test cue within 1 hour of being exposed to a prime; at 9 months, they recognized it within 1 min; and by 12 months, they recognized it instantaneously. The increased speed of priming with age is consistent with evidence from visual habituation studies that the speed of information processing increases with age (Colombo & Mitchell, 1990). Even at 3 months of age, however, a prime recovers information that has been forgotten instantaneously if it is administered only 24 hours after training is over (Gulya, Rovee-Collier, Galluccio, & Wilk, 1998). Moreover, Hayne, Gross, Hildreth, and Rovee-Collier (2000) found that reactivating (priming) 3-month-olds' memory two times decreased the latency of response from 24 hours (after one prime) to only 1 hour (after two primes). Taken together, these findings indicate that developmental differences in the speed of priming are not caused solely by maturational changes in the neural mechanisms that mediate it. Obviously, priming reflects a complex interaction between maturational processes and experiential factors. The particular neurobiological processes that underlie the effectiveness of priming (reactivation), however, have yet to be elucidated.

Issues in Infant Memory

In the final section of this chapter, we consider (1) the development of multiple memory systems in infancy, (2) recent evidence pertaining to the phenomenon of infantile amnesia, and (3) memory distortions in infancy – a ubiquitous phenomenon with practical implications for eyewitness testimony by children and adults.

Ontogeny of Multiple Memory Systems

Until recently, memories of older infants and adults were thought to be mediated by a fundamentally different system than memories of younger infants (McKee & Squire, 1993; Schacter & Moscovitch, 1984). Implicit (procedural) memory was viewed as a primitive system, functional shortly after birth, that processes information automatically, whereas explicit (declarative) memory was viewed as a late-maturing system that became functional late in the first year. This notion was based on the Jacksonian principle, which states that the last sensory and motor functions to appear during development are the first to disappear when the organism undergoes demise. Because performance on implicit memory tasks (e.g., priming and perceptual identification) is spared in aging amnesics, but performance on explicit memory tasks (e.g., recall and recognition) is impaired in amnesics, psychologists were quick to conclude that implicit memory develops early in development and that explicit memory develops much later. Ironically, this hypothesized developmental hierarchy was never directly tested in studies with infants; instead, it was only inferred from the memory dissociations of amnesics on priming and recognition tasks (McKee & Squire, 1993). Normal adults also display the same dissociations on tasks commonly used to distinguish implicit from explicit memory when instructed to respond, for example, with "the first word that comes to mind" on a priming task or by "circling the word you studied on the list a few minutes ago" on a recognition task (Tulving & Schachter, 1990).

Recently, Rovee-Collier (1997) cited evidence from studies using a variety of procedures that the same independent variables that produce memory dissociations in adults on priming and recognition tests produce exactly the same memory dissociations in 2- to 6-month-olds on the same types of tests. Given that memory dissociations are considered a diagnostic for two memory systems in adults, the fact that very young infants also exhibit them suggests that they possess two memory systems as well. After all, it is illogical to use memory dissociations as the basis for positing two memory systems in adults but only a single memory system in young infants! Moreover, the finding that even 6-month-olds exhibit 24-hour deferred imitation (Barr et al., 1996), which is an explicit memory task that amnesics cannot perform (McDonough, Mandler, McKee, & Squire, 1995), raises serious questions about the meaningfulness of arguing that young infants possess only a primitive (implicit) memory system (Schacter & Moscovitch, 1984; Tulving & Schacter, 1990). If indeed there are two memory systems, then they do not mature at different rates but develop simultaneously and in parallel throughout the infancy period.

Infantile Amnesia

Although some adults can remember one or two events that occurred when they were 2 years old (Usher & Neisser, 1993), most do not remember what occurred before the age of 3 or 4 (Dudycha & Dudycha, 1933). This phenomenon, infantile amnesia, is usually attributed to the functional immaturity of the neurological mechanisms responsible for maintaining memories over the long term (C. Nelson, 1995) and to the inability of preverbal infants to remember a prior event before they can rehearse it by talking about it (K. Nelson, 1990). Recently, however, even very young preverbal infants have been shown to remember a prior event after very long delays if they were periodically exposed to multiple, *nonverbal* reminders (Rovee-Collier, 1999).

In one study, 8-week-olds learned the mobile task (Rovee-Collier, Hartshorn, & DiRubbo, 1999) and then received periodic reminders every three weeks thereafter through 26 weeks of age (six reminders altogether). Immediately before each reminder, infants received a preliminary retention test to determine whether the memory was active or not at the time of reminding. Infants who exhibited retention during the preliminary test received a reinstatement reminder (active memory). Infants who did not exhibit reten-

tion received a reactivation reminder (inactive memory). All infants received a final retention test at 29 weeks of age, when the experiment had to be terminated because infants
outgrew the task. Although 8-week-olds otherwise forget the mobile task after only 1–2
days, they still exhibited significant retention 4.5 months later after being exposed to periodic reminders, and four of the six infants still remembered 5.25 months later when the
experiment had to be terminated. Had it been possible to continue the study, some of
these infants undoubtedly would have remembered even longer. Yoked reminder controls
who were not originally trained but received the same reminders as their experimental
counterparts exhibited no retention after any delay.

Recall also that Hartshorn (1998) had maintained a memory of the train task
(described earlier) that had been established at 6 months of age for 1.5 years, through
2 years of age, after exposing infants to only five, periodic reinstatements. Taken together,
these studies provide unequivocal support for the hypothesis that periodic reminding can
maintain early memories over a significant period of development. Moreover, because
periodic nonverbal reminders maintained the memories of *two comparable events* (the
mobile task and the train task) over an overlapping period between 2 months and 2 years
of age, it is highly likely that appropriate periodic nonverbal reminders could also
maintain the memory of *a single event* from 2 months through 2 years of age, if not
longer. This time encompasses the entire span of the developmental period thought to
be characterized by infantile amnesia (Fivush & Hamond, 1990; Usher & Neisser, 1993).
These findings will necessitate a second look at the various accounts of infantile amnesia.
Clearly, both of the current accounts – brain immaturity and the inability to verbalize –
are incomplete.

What might be some alternative explanations of infantile amnesia? First, because the
memory attributes that represent contextual information (i.e., when and where an event
happened) are relatively fragile, and this kind of information is lost over repeated
reminders (Hitchcock & Rovee-Collier, 1996; see below), older children and adults may
actually remember early-life events but be unable to pinpoint their origins. Second,
because memories encoded early in life have probably been modified or updated many
times, their original source may be impossible to identify. And, third, because memories
are converted at the time of retrieval and expressed in an age-appropriate manner, they
may simply not be recognized as having originated at a much earlier time.

Memory Distortions

Memory distortions speak to the issue of the accuracy of memory and are as ubiquitous
among infants as they are among older children and adults. It is important to distinguish
between accuracy and completeness. A memory can be accurate but incomplete, but it is
neither accurate nor complete if it is distorted. The accuracy of infants' memories depends
largely on the delay after which the memory is retrieved, how many times the memory
was previously retrieved, and whether potentially interfering information was encountered between the original event and its retrieval.

Very young infants' memories are surprisingly accurate for the details of an event and,
like the memories of adults, become increasingly fuzzy as time passes. Eventually, they

forget the specific details of the event even though they still remember its general features or gist (Rovee-Collier & Sullivan, 1980). Hitchcock and Rovee-Collier (1996) also found that specific information about the place where an event occurred and the details of the event itself eventually become "lost" from the infant's memory over the course of repeated reactivations, even if the repeated reminders are always in the original context with the original cue. After several reactivations over a long period of time, infants subsequently recover only a highly generalized memory. Moreover, the details of the context in which the event originally occurred are lost before the details of the event itself. These results were anticipated by Furlong (1951, cited in Tulving, 1983), who hypothesized that "retrospective" memory becomes nonretrospective memory *as the context fades.* The fact that the first information to be lost from infants' memory is contextual may also contribute to the phenomenon of infantile amnesia (see above).

Despite their accuracy, however, infants' memories are highly susceptible to modification – sometimes thought of as "updating" – by information that they subsequently encounter. This modification occurs in the same way that memories of children and adults are distorted in studies of eyewitness testimony (Rovee-Collier, Borza, Adler, & Boller, 1993). In all instances, new information that subjects merely witness after an event is over affects their subsequent memory of that event. This modification can take two forms – retention of the original event is impaired, and/or the new information is incorporated into the original memory. Not surprisingly, memories are more easily modified when they are weaker – the longer the delay between the original event and the new information, the stronger the effect. Moreover, if the delay is sufficiently long that the details of the original cue or context have been forgotten at the time when the new information is encountered, then the details of the most recent cue or context are actually substituted for the original details, producing a relatively permanent memory distortion (Boller, Rovee-Collier, Gulya, & Prete, 1996; Rovee-Collier, Adler, & Borza, 1994). Exactly this same process is thought to underlie the memory distortions of children and adults (Neisser, 1997). Memory distortions are, however, more amenable to experimental investigation in infants than in adults for two primary reasons. First, infants' memories are less enduring, making it possible to study the effect on memory of introducing new information at different points along the individual's entire forgetting function. Second, the source of new information can more rigorously be controlled in infants.

The ubiquity of memory distortions, however, suggests that what we, as adults, view as an anomaly of memory may actually be adaptive. After all, it may be more efficient to simply update an old memory to reflect current circumstances than to encode and store an altogether new memory along with an old one that is no longer predictive. One would expect this to be particularly true for less mature organisms who undergo periods of rapid change.

Conclusions

Irrespective of the paradigms that have been used to assess infant memory, the mechanisms that mediate memory processing appear to be fundamentally the same in infants and adults: Memories are forgotten gradually, are recovered by reminders, and are modified by new information that overlaps with old. In addition, infants' early memories are highly specific and include information about the setting where events take place. As in children and adults, however, their memories are readily updated by new information that substitutes for information in the original memory once its details are forgotten. Even though memory processing does not change *qualitatively* over the course of development, it does change *quantitatively*. The temporal parameters of memory processing, for example, change with age: Both the duration of retention and the speed of retrieval increase dramatically with age, although the absolute values of each depend on the parameters of original training at all ages.

Recent evidence of the sophistication, longevity, and specificity of infants' early memories, gathered from different paradigms, directly contradicts older views that young infants' memories are primitive, short-lived, diffuse, and devoid of place information. In short, infants pick up a lot of information both about their environments and the relationships in it, and they remember that information for long periods – especially in relation to the brief period of time they have lived! After a single reminder of an event in which they participated, infants can remember twice as long as they did originally, and after multiple reminders, they can remember for longer than a year. If individuals periodically encounter appropriate nonverbal reminders of an event that occurred during early infancy, they could theoretically remember that event forever!

Further Reading

The following list expands upon the topics reviewed in the present chapter. The list includes seminal papers on habituation, operant conditioning, deferred imitation, and reminder procedures. The Rovee-Collier (1997) article provides a comprehensive review of data and theory pertaining to the development of memory systems.

Barr, R., Dowden, A., & Hayne, H. (1996). Developmental changes in deferred imitation by 6- to 24-month-old infants. *Infant Behavior and Development, 19,* 159–170. This is the first report of deferred imitation in infants as young as 6 months and also of developmental changes in deferred imitation across a wide age range using the same task.

Barr, R., & Hayne, H. (2000). Age-related changes in imitation: Implications for memory development. In C. Rovee-Collier, L. P. Lipsitt, & H. Hayne (Eds.), *Progress in infancy research* (Vol. 1, pp. 21–67). Mahwah, NJ: Erlbaum. This chapter summarizes recent work on age-related changes in deferred imitation expanding upon the present discussion.

DeCasper, A. J., & Fifer, W. P. (1980). Of human bonding: Newborns prefer their mothers' voices. *Science, 208,* 1174–1176. This paper reports that infants within a day or so of birth will learn an operant response that gives them selective access to the voice that they had heard in the womb.

Fantz, R. L. (1964). Visual experience in infants: Decreased attention to familiar patterns relative to novel ones. *Science, 46,* 668–670. This classic study showed that infant attention habituates during repeated exposures to the same pattern but is maintained at a high level during repeated exposures to changing patterns.

Galluccio, L., & Rovee-Collier, C. (1999). Reinstatement effects on retention at 3 months of age. *Learning and Motivation.* This study with 3-month-olds directly compares reinstatement and reactivation procedures administered along the same general timeline but when the memory is active or inactive, respectively.

Meltzoff, A. N., & Moore, M. K. (1977). Imitation of facial and manual gestures by human neonates. *Science, 198,* 75–78. This important report of imitation by infants only hours old initiated a storm of controversy over the imitative capacity of young infants.

Rovee, C. K., & Rovee, D. T. (1969). Conjugate reinforcement of infant exploratory behavior. *Journal of Experimental Child Psychology, 8,* 33–39. This was the first report of free operant conditioning with very young infants. It is notable for the unusual character of the reinforcer, its long sessions, and its arousal controls.

Rovee-Collier, C. (1997). Dissociations in infant memory: Rethinking the development of implicit and explicit memory. *Psychological Review, 104,* 467–498. This article reviews numerous parallels between memory data from infants, who are thought to be capable of implicit memory only, and adults, who are thought to be capable of explicit memory as well. It concludes that infants and adults possess the same memory systems.

References

Abravanel, E., Levan-Goldschmidt, E., & Stevenson, M. B. (1976). Action imitation: The early phase of infancy. *Child Development, 47,* 1032–1044.

Adler, S. A., Wilk, A., & Rovee-Collier, C. (2000). Differential effects of reinstatement and reactivation on an active memory in infants. *Journal of Experimental Child Psychology, 75,* 93–115.

Bachevalier, J., & Mishkin, M. (1984). An early and a late developing system for learning and retention in infant monkeys. *Behavioral Neuroscience, 98,* 770–778.

Barnat, S. A., Klein, P. J., & Meltzoff, A. N. (1996). Deferred imitation across changes in context and object: Memory and generalization in 14-month-old infants. *Infant Behavior and Development, 19,* 241–251.

Barr, R., Dowden, A., & Hayne, H. (1996). Developmental changes in deferred imitation by 6- to 24-month-old infants. *Infant Behavior and Development, 19,* 159–170.

Barr, R., & Hayne, H. (1996). The effect of event structure on imitation in infancy: Practice makes perfect? *Infant Behavior and Development, 19,* 253–257.

Barr, R., & Hayne, H. (1999). Developmental changes in imitation from television during infancy. *Child Development, 70,* 1067–1081.

Barr, R., & Hayne, H. (2000). Age-related changes in imitation: Implications for memory development. In C. Rovee-Collier, L. P. Lipsitt, & H. Hayne (Eds.), *Progress in infancy research* (Vol. 1, pp. 21–67). Mahwah, NJ: Erlbaum.

Bauer, P. J., & Hertsgaard, L. A. (1993). Increasing steps in recall of events: Factors facilitating immediate and long-term memory in 13.5- and 16.5-month-old children. *Child Development, 64,* 1204–1223.

Bauer, P. J., Hertsgaard, L. A., & Dow, G. A. (1994). After 8 months have passed: Long-term recall of events by 1- to 2-year-old children. *Memory, 2,* 353–382.

Bauer, P. J., & Mandler, J. M. (1989). One thing follows another: Effects of temporal structure on 1- to 2-year-olds' recall of events. *Developmental Psychology, 25,* 197–206.

Bauer, P. J., & Shore, C. M. (1987). Making a memorable event: Effects of familiarity and organization on young children's recall of action sequences. *Cognitive Development, 2,* 327–338.

Berntson, C. G., Tuber, D. S., Ronca, A. E., & Bachman, D. S. (1983). The decerebrate human: Associative learning. *Experimental Neurology, 81*, 77–88.

Blass, E. M., Ganchrow, J. R., & Steiner, J. E. (1984). Classical conditioning in newborn humans 2–48 hours of age. *Infant Behavior and Development, 7*, 223–235.

Bloom, K. (1984). Distinguishing between social reinforcement and social elicitation. *Journal of Experimental Child Psychology, 38*, 93–102.

Boller, K., Rovee-Collier, C., Gulya, M., & Prete, K. (1996). Infants' memory for context: Timing effects of postevent information. *Journal of Experimental Child Psychology, 63*, 583–602.

Brackbill, Y. (1958). Extinction of the smiling response in infants as a function of reinforcement schedule. *Child Development, 29*, 115–124.

Buss, A. (1973). *Psychology: Man in perspective.* New York: Wiley.

Campbell, B. A., & Jaynes, J. (1966). Reinstatement. *Psychological Review, 73*, 478–480.

Campbell, B. A., & Randall, P. K. (1976). The effect of reinstatement stimulus conditions on the maintenance of long-term memory. *Developmental Psychobiology, 9*, 325–333.

Clifton, R. K. (1974). Heart rate conditioning in the newborn infant. *Journal of Experimental Child Psychology, 18*, 9–21.

Clifton, R. K., & Nelson, M. N. (1976). Developmental study of habituation in infants: The importance of paradigm, response system, and state. In T. J. Tighe & R. N. Leaton (Eds.), *Habituation* (pp. 159–205). Hillsdale, NJ: Erlbaum.

Collie, R., & Hayne, H. (1999). Deferred imitation by 6- and 9-month-old infants: More evidence for declarative memory. *Developmental Psychobiology, 35*, 83–90.

Colombo, J., & Mitchell, D. W. (1990). Individual differences in early visual attention: Fixation time and information processing. In J. Colombo & J. W. Fagen (Eds.), *Individual differences in infancy* (pp. 193–227). Hillsdale, NJ: Erlbaum.

DeCasper, A. J., & Fifer, W. P. (1980). Of human bonding: Newborns prefer their mothers' voices. *Science, 208*, 1174–1176.

Diamond, A. (1990). The development and neural basis of memory functions as indexed by the AB and delayed response tasks in human infants and infant monkeys. In A. Diamond (Ed.), *Annals of the New York Academy of Sciences* (Vol. 608). *The development and neural bases of higher cognitive functions* (pp. 267–317). New York: New York Academy of Sciences.

Dudycha, G. J., & Dudycha, M. M. (1933). Some factors and characteristics of childhood memories. *Child Development, 4*, 265–278.

Eimas, P., Siqueland, E., Jusczyk, P., & Vigorito, J. (1971). Speech perception in infants. *Science, 171*, 303–306.

Elkonin, D. B. (1957). The physiology of higher nervous activity and child psychology. In B. Simon (Ed.), *Psychology in the Soviet Union* (pp. 47–68). London: Routledge & Kegan Paul.

Fagen, J. W., & Rovee-Collier, C. (1983). Memory retrieval: A time-locked process in infancy. *Science, 222*, 1349–1351.

Fantz, R. L. (1964). Visual experience in infants: Decreased attention to familiar patterns relative to novel ones. *Science, 46*, 668–670.

Fivush, R., & Hamond, N. R. (1990). Autobiographical memory across the preschool years: Toward reconceptualizing childhood amnesia. In R. Fivush & J. A. Hudson (Eds.), *Knowing and remembering in young children* (pp. 223–248). Cambridge: Cambridge University Press.

Fivush, R., Kuebli, J., & Clubb, P. A. (1992). The structure of events and event representation: A developmental analysis. *Child Development, 63*, 188–201.

Freud, S. (1935). *A general introduction to psychoanalysis.* New York: Clarion Books.

Galluccio, L., & Rovee-Collier, C. (1999). Reinstatement effects on retention at 3 months of age. *Learning and Motivation, 30*, 296–316.

Gibson, E. J. (1963). Perceptual learning. *Annual Review of Psychology, 14*, 29–56.

Gould, S. J. (1998, April). *Ontogeny and phylogeny revisited, or why the child is not the evolution-ary father to the man.* Invited address presented at the International Conference on Infant Studies, Atlanta, GA.

Graham, F. K., Leavitt, L., Strock, B., & Brown, H. (1978). Precocious cardiac orienting in a human anencephalic infant. *Science, 199*, 322–324.

Gulya, M., Rovee-Collier, C., Galluccio, L., & Wilk, A. (1998). Memory processing of a serial list by very young infants. *Psychological Science, 9*, 303–307.

Hanna, E., & Meltzoff, A. N. (1993). Peer imitation by toddlers in laboratory, home, and day-care contexts: Implications for social learning and memory. *Developmental Psychology, 29*, 701–710.

Hartshorn, K. (1998, October). *The effect of reinstatement on infant long-term retention.* Unpub-lished doctoral dissertation, Rutgers University, New Brunswick, NJ.

Hartshorn, K., & Rovee-Collier, C. (1997). Infant learning and long-term memory at 6 months: A confirming analysis. *Developmental Psychobiology, 30*, 71–85.

Hartshorn, K., Rovee-Collier, C., Gerhardstein, P., Bhatt, R. S., Klein, P. J., Aaron, F., Wondoloski, T. L., & Wurtzel, N. (1998a). Developmental changes in the specificity of memory over the first year of life. *Developmental Psychobiology, 33*, 61–78.

Hartshorn, K., Rovee-Collier, C., Gerhardstein, P., Bhatt, R. S., Wondoloski, T. L., Klein, P., Gilch, J., Wurtzel, N., & Campos-de-Carvalho, M. (1998b). The ontogeny of long-term memory over the first year-and-a-half of life. *Developmental Psychobiology, 32*, 1–31.

Hayne, H. (1990). The effect of multiple reminders on long-term retention in human infants. *Developmental Psychobiology, 23*, 453–477.

Hayne, H. (1996, April). *A developmental analysis of memory retrieval.* Paper presented at the Inter-national Conference on Infant Studies, Providence, RI.

Hayne, H., Gross, J., Hildreth, K., & Rovee-Collier, C. (2000). Repeated reminders increase the speed of memory retrieval by 3-month-old infants. *Developmental Science, 3*, 312–318.

Hayne, H., MacDonald, S., & Barr, R. (1997). Developmental changes in the specificity of memory over the second year of life. *Infant Behavior and Development, 20*, 233–245.

Hildreth, K., & Rovee-Collier, C. (1999). Decreases in response latency to priming over the first year of life. *Developmental Psychobiology, 35*, 276–290.

Hildreth, K., Wawrzyniak, K., Barr, R., & Rovee-Collier, C. (1999, April). *The reforgetting of reac-tivated memories between 6 and 12 months of age.* Paper presented at the meeting of the Eastern Psychological Association, Providence, RI.

Hitchcock, D. F. A., & Rovee-Collier, C. (1996). The effect of repeated reactivations on memory specificity in infants. *Journal of Experimental Child Psychology, 62*, 378–400.

Howe, M. L., Courage, M. L., & Bryant-Brown, L. (1993). Reinstating preschoolers' memories. *Developmental Psychology, 29*, 854–869.

Irzhanskaia, K. N., & Felberbaum, R. A. (1954). Nekotorye dannye ob uslovnoreflektornoi deiatelnosti nedonoshennykh detei. (Conditioned reflex activity in premature children.) *Fizio-logicheskii Zhurnal SSSR, 40*, 668–672. [Translated and reprinted in Y. Brackbill & G. T. Thompson (Eds.) (1967), *Behavior in infancy and early childhood* (pp. 246–249). New York: Free Press.]

Jeffrey, W. E., & Cohen, L. B. (1971). Habituation in the human infant. In H. W. Reese (Ed.), *Advances in child development and behavior* (Vol. 6, pp. 63–97). New York: Academic Press.

Jones, H. E. (1930). The retention of conditioned emotional reactions in infancy. *Journal of Genetic Psychology, 37*, 485–498.

Kagan, J., & Hamburg, M. (1981). The enhancement of memory in the first year. *Journal of Genetic Psychology, 138*, 3–14.

Klein, P. J., & Meltzoff, A. N. (1999). Long-term memory, forgetting, and deferred imitation in 12-month-old infants. *Developmental Science, 2*, 102–113.

Kling, J. W., & Riggs, L. A. (1971). *Woodworth & Schlosberg's experimental psychology: Vol. 2. Learning, motivation, and memory* (3rd ed.). New York: Holt, Rinehart, & Winston.

Koltsova, M. M. (1949). On the rise and development of the second signal system in the child. *Research of the Laboratory of I. P. Pavlov, 4*, 49–102.

Lewis, M., & Goldberg, S. (1969). Perceptual-cognitive development in infancy: A generalized expectancy model as a function of the mother and infant interaction. *Merrill-Palmer Quarterly, 15*, 81–100.

Little, A. H., Lipsitt, L. P., & Rovee-Collier, C. (1984). Classical conditioning and retention of the infant's eyelid response: Effects of age and interstimulus interval. *Journal of Experimental Child Psychology, 37*, 512–524.

MacLean, P. D. (1967). The brain in relation to empathy and medical education. *Journal of Nervous and Mental Disease, 144*, 374–382.

Marquis, D. P. (1941). Learning in the neonate: The modification of behavior under three feeding schedules. *Journal of Experimental Psychology, 29*, 263–282.

McCall, R. B., Parke, R. D., & Kavanaugh, R. D. (1977). Imitation of live and televised models by children one to three years of age. *Monographs of the Society for Research in Child Development, 42* (5, Serial No. 173).

McDonough, L., Mandler, J. M., McKee, R. D., & Squire, L. R. (1995). The deferred imitation task as a nonverbal measure of declarative memory. *Proceedings of the National Academy of Sciences, 92*, 7580–7584.

McKee, R. D., & Squire, L. R. (1993). On the development of declarative memory. *Journal of Experimental Psychology: Learning, Memory, and Cognition, 19*, 397–404.

Meltzoff, A. N. (1988a). Infant imitation and memory: Nine-month-olds in immediate and deferred tests. *Child Development, 59*, 217–225.

Meltzoff, A. N. (1988b). Imitation of televised models by infants. *Child Development, 59*, 1221–1229.

Meltzoff, A. N. (1990). Towards a developmental cognitive science: The implications of cross-modal matching and imitation for the development of representation and memory in infancy. In A. Diamond (Ed.), *Annals of the New York Academy of Sciences* (Vol. 608). *The development and neural bases of higher cognitive functions* (pp. 1–37). New York: New York Academy of Sciences.

Meltzoff, A. N. (1995). Understanding the intentions of others: Re-enactment of intended acts by 18-month-old children. *Developmental Psychology, 31*, 838–850.

Meltzoff, A. N., & Moore, M. K. (1994). Imitation, memory, and the representation of persons. *Infant Behavior and Development, 17*, 83–89.

Milewski, A. E., & Siqueland, E. R. (1975). Discrimination of color and pattern novelty in one-month human infants. *Journal of Experimental Child Psychology, 19*, 122–136.

Neisser, U. (1997, November). *Enabling conditions for false memories.* Colloquium presented to the Department of Psychology, Rutgers University, New Brunswick, NJ.

Nelson, C. A. (1995). The ontogeny of human memory: A cognitive neuroscience perspective. *Developmental Psychology, 31*, 723–738.

Nelson, K. (1990). Remembering, forgetting, and childhood amnesia. In R. Fivush & J. A. Hudson (Eds.), *Knowing and remembering in young children* (pp. 301–316). Cambridge: Cambridge University Press.

Papoušek, H. (1959). A method of studying conditioned food reflexes in young children up to the age of six months. *Pavlov Journal of Higher Nervous Activity, 9*, 136–140.

Piaget, J. (1952). *Origins of intelligence in children.* New York: International Universities Press.

Piaget, J. (1962). *Play, dreams and imitation in childhood* (Trans. C. Gattegno & F. M. Hodgson). New York: Norton.

Ratner, H., Smith, B., & Dion, S. (1986). Development of memory for events. *Journal of Experimental Child Psychology, 41*, 411–428.

Riccio, D. C., & Haroutunian, V. (1979). Some approaches to the alleviation of ontogenetic memory deficits. In N. E. Spear & B. A. Campbell (Eds.), *Ontogeny of learning and memory* (pp. 289–309). Hillsdale, NJ: Erlbaum.

Rovee, C., & Fagen, J. W. (1976). Extended conditioning and 24-hour retention in infants. *Journal of Experimental Child Psychology, 21*, 1–11.

Rovee, C. K., & Rovee, D. T. (1969). Conjugate reinforcement of infant exploratory behavior. *Journal of Experimental Child Psychology, 8*, 33–39.

Rovee-Collier, C. (1997). Dissociations in infant memory: Rethinking the development of implicit and explicit memory. *Psychological Review, 104*, 467–498.

Rovee-Collier, C. (1999). The development of infant memory. *Current Directions in Psychological Science, 8*, 80–85.

Rovee-Collier, C., Adler, S. A., & Borza, M. A. (1994). Substituting new details for old? Effects of delaying postevent information on infant memory. *Memory and Cognition, 22*, 644–656.

Rovee-Collier, C., Borza, M. A., Adler, S. A., & Boller, K. (1993). Infants' eyewitness testimony: Integrating postevent information with a prior memory representation. *Memory and Cognition, 21*, 267–279.

Rovee-Collier, C., Hartshorn, K., & DiRubbo, M. (1999). Long-term maintenance of infant memory. *Developmental Psychobiology, 35*, 91–102.

Rovee-Collier, C., & Sullivan, M. W. (1980). Organization of infant memory. *Journal of Experimental Psychology: Human Learning and Memory, 6*, 798–807.

Rovee-Collier, C., Sullivan, M. W., Enright, M. E., Lucas, D., & Fagen, J. W. (1980). Reactivation of infant memory. *Science, 208*, 1159–1161.

Sameroff, A. J. (1968). The components of sucking in the human newborn. *Journal of Experimental Child Psychology, 6*, 607–623.

Sameroff, A. J. (1971). Can conditioned responses be established in the newborn infant: 1971? *Developmental Psychology, 5*, 1–12.

Schacter, D. L., & Moscovitch, M. (1984). Infants, amnesics, and dissociable memory systems. In M. Moscovitch (Ed.), *Advances in the study of communication and affect: Vol. 9. Infant memory* (pp. 173–216). New York: Plenum.

Sheffield, E. G., & Hudson, J. A. (1994). Reactivation of toddlers' event memory. *Memory, 2*, 447–465.

Siqueland, E. R. (1970). Basic learning processes. I. Classical conditioning. In H. W. Reese & L. P. Lipsitt (Eds.), *Experimental child psychology* (pp. 65–95). New York: Academic Press.

Siqueland, E. R., & Lipsitt, L. P. (1966). Conditioned headturning in human newborns. *Journal of Experimental Child Psychology, 3*, 356–376.

Sokolov, E. N. (1963). Higher nervous functions: The orienting reflex. *Annual Review of Physiology, 25*, 545–580.

Spear, N. E., & Parsons, P. J. (1976). Analysis of a reactivation treatment: Ontogenetic determinants of alleviated forgetting. In D. L. Medin, W. A. Roberts, & R. T. Davis (Eds.), *Processes of animal memory* (pp. 135–165). Hillsdale, NJ: Erlbaum.

Thompson, R. F., & Spencer, W. A. (1966). A model phenomenon for the study of neuronal substrates of behavior. *Psychological Review, 73*, 16–43.

Tuber, D. S., Berntson, G. G., Bachman, D. S., & Allen, J. N. (1980). Associative learning in premature hydraencephalic and normal twins. *Science, 210*, 1035–1037.

Tulving, E. (1983). *Elements of episodic memory*. Oxford: Clarendon Press.

Tulving, E., & Schacter, D. L. (1990). Priming and human memory systems. *Science, 247*, 301–306.

Usher, J. A., & Neisser, U. (1993). Childhood amnesia and the beginnings of memory for four early life events. *Journal of Experimental Psychology: General, 122*, 155–165.

Watson, J. B., & Rayner, R. R. (1920). Conditioned emotional reactions. *Journal of Experimental Child Psychology, 3*, 1–14.

Weizmann, F., Cohen, L. B., & Pratt, R. J. (1971). Novelty, familiarity, and the development of infant attention. *Developmental Psychology, 4*, 149–154.

Werner, J. S., & Perlmutter, M. (1979). Development of visual memory in infants. In H. W. Reese & L. P. Lipsitt (Eds.), *Advances in child development and behavior* (Vol. 14, pp. 1–56). New York: Academic Press.

Wyers, E. J., Peeke, H. V. S., & Herz, M. J. (1973). Behavioral habituation in invertebrates. In H. V. S. Peeke & M. J. Herz (Eds.), *Habituation I* (pp. 1–57). New York: Academic Press.

Chapter Six

Functional Brain Development During Infancy

Mark H. Johnson

Theoretical Overview

What is development? Many introductory biology textbooks define development in terms of an "increasing restriction of fate." What this means is that as the biological development of an individual (ontogeny) proceeds, the range of options for further specification or specialization available to the organism at that stage decreases. Structural or functional specialization is an end state in which there are few or no options left to the organism. By this view, plasticity can be defined as a developmental stage in which there are still options available for alternative developmental pathways. Another dimension of ontogenetic development is that it involves the construction of increasingly complex levels of biological organization, including the brain and the cognitive processes it supports. As we will see later in this chapter, organizational processes at one level, such as cellular interactions, can establish new functions at a higher level, such as that associated with overall brain structure. This characteristic of ontogeny means that a full picture of developmental change requires different levels of analysis to be investigated simultaneously. The developmentalist, I suggest, needs to go beyond statements such as a psychological change being due to "maturation," and actually provide an account of the processes causing the change at cellular and molecular levels. Thus, as distinct from most other areas of psychology, a complete account of developmental change specifically requires an interdisciplinary approach. Some of the dimensions of ontogenetic development discussed above are summarized in Figure 6.1. This

Sections of text in this chapter are adapted from Johnson (1997a,b; Johnson & de Haan, in press), and I am grateful to my various colleagues and collaborators who commented on those works for their indirect contribution to the present chapter. The preparation of this chapter was funded by Medical Research Council grant G97 155 87, and EC Biomed 2 grant BMH4-CT97-2032.

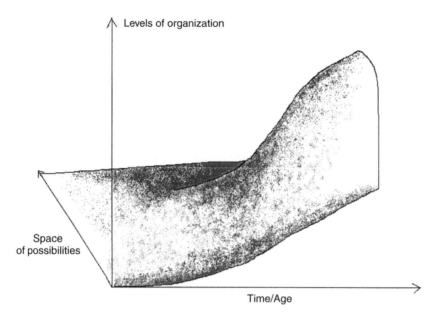

Figure 6.1   An abstract representation of some changes that occur during development.

figure illustrates three dimensions of change in development, with the space of possible outcomes becoming narrowed while the levels of organization present (molecular, cellular, organismal) increase.

Despite the above considerations, it is only in the past decade that there has been renewed interest in examining relations between brain and cognitive development (e.g., Diamond, 1991; Johnson, 1993; Nelson & Bloom, 1997). Biological approaches to human behavioral development fell out of favor for a variety of reasons, including the widely held belief among cognitive psychologists in the 1970s and 1980s that the "software" of the mind is best studied without reference to the "hardware" of the brain. However, the recent explosion of basic knowledge on mammalian brain development makes the task of relating brain to behavioral changes considerably more viable than previously. In parallel, new molecular and cellular methods, along with theories of self-organizing dynamic networks (see chapter 3 in this volume), have led to great advances in our understanding of how vertebrate brains are constructed during ontogeny. These advances, along with those in functional neuroimaging, have led to the recent emergence of the interdisciplinary science of developmental cognitive neuroscience (see Johnson, 1997a,b).

There are a number of assumptions commonly made about the relation between brain development and behavioral change which stem from the adoption of a "predetermined epigenesis" view of development. Epigenesis refers to the process through which genes interact with their environment (at various levels, inside and outside the organism) to produce new structures. Gottlieb (1992) has distinguished between *predetermined epigenesis* and *probabilistic epigenesis.* Predetermined epigenesis is the view that there is a one-way causal pathway from genes to proteins to brain to cognition. In other words, there is a "genetic blueprint" which imposes itself on the developing organism in a direct way. In contrast, probabilistic epigenesis is the view that there are two-way interactions through all levels of organization. While most people would acknowledge that there are complex interactions between genes and environment and back at the molecular, genetic, and cellular level involved in development, the predetermined epigenesis view still tends to dominate assumptions about the relation between brain development and cognition. Specifically, it is often assumed that brain development involves a process of unfolding of a genetic plan, and that "maturation" in particular regions of the brain causes or allows specific advances in cognitive, perceptual, or motor abilities in the infant or child. This overly static view of brain development fails to capture the importance of two-way interactions between brain and behavior, and the importance of activity-dependent processes in neural development. Brain development is not just a genetic process, but is an epigenetic one crucially dependent on complex interactions at the molecular, cellular, and behavioral levels. Indeed, later I will argue that attentional biases in human infants contribute to their subsequent patterns of brain specialization.

Another contentious topic in brain and behavioral development concerns the nature of plasticity. When brain development is commonly viewed simply as the unfolding of a genetic blueprint, recovery of function after early brain damage is then attributed to specialized mechanisms of plasticity which are only activated in such cases. In fact, plasticity is probably better viewed as an inherent property of development. As mentioned earlier, and like any aspect of biological development, brain growth involves a process of increasing specialization (restriction of fate) in the sense that tissue or cells become more specialized in their morphology and functioning during the process. Plasticity simply represents the state of not yet having achieved specialization at some level. For example, a piece of tissue from the cerebral cortex may not yet have developed specialization for processing a certain category of information when a neighboring region is damaged. The same developmental mechanisms that would have ensured specialization for one type of processing may now bias the tissue toward the type of processing normally subserved by its unfortunate neighbor. Thus, in many instances abnormal patterns of brain specialization in developmental disorders may reflect the action of normal developmental processes following some earlier perturbation from the normal pathway. Identifying and understanding the mechanisms underlying specialization, particularly in postnatal life, remains one of the major challenges for developmental cognitive neuroscience.

Methods

Part of the reason for the recently renewed interest in relating brain development to cognitive change comes from advances in methodology which allow hypotheses to be generated and tested more readily than previously (see also Nelson & Bloom, 1997). One set of tools relates to brain imaging – the generation of "functional" maps of brain activity based on either changes in cerebral metabolism, blood flow, or electrical activity. Some of these imaging methods, such as positron emission tomography (PET), are of limited utility for studying transitions in behavioral development in normal infants and children due to their invasive nature (requiring the intravenous injection of radioactively labeled substances) and their relatively coarse temporal resolution (of the order of minutes). Two brain-imaging techniques are currently being applied to development in normal children – event-related potentials (ERPs) and functional magnetic resonance imaging (fMRI).

ERPs involve using sensitive electrodes on the scalp surface to measure the electrical activity of the brain generated as groups of neurons fire synchronously. These recordings can either be of the spontaneous natural rhythms of the brain (EEG), or the electrical activity induced by the presentation of a stimulus (ERP). Normally the ERP from many trials is averaged, resulting in the spontaneous natural rhythms of the brain that are unrelated to the stimulus presentation averaging to zero. With a high density of electrodes on the scalp, algorithms can be employed which infer the position of the brain sources of electrical activity (dipoles) for the particular pattern of scalp surface electrical activity. Recent developments of the ERP method allow relatively quick installation of a large number of sensors, thus opening new possibilities in the investigation of infant brain function.

Functional MRI allows the noninvasive measurement of cerebral blood flow (Kwong et al., 1992), with the prospect of millimeter spatial resolution and temporal resolution on the order of seconds. Although this technique has been applied to children (Casey et al., 1997), the distracting noise and vibration, and the presently unknown possible effects of high magnetic fields on the developing brain, make its usefulness for healthy children under 4 or 5 years of age unclear. However, there has been at least one fMRI study of infants initially scanned for clinical reasons (Tzourio et al., 1992), and the advent of "open" scanners in which the mother can hold the infant may increase possibilities further.

Another useful approach for linking brain development to behavior is the "marker task." This method involves the use of specific behavioral tasks which have been linked to a brain region or pathway in adult primates and humans by neurophysiological, neuropsychological, or brain-imaging studies. By testing infants or children with versions of such a task at different ages, the researcher can use the success or otherwise of individuals as indicating the functional development of the relevant regions of the brain. Later in this chapter, several lines of inquiry which illustrate the marker-task approach are discussed.

Finally, the recent emergence of connectionist neural network models offers the possibility of assessing the information-processing consequences of developmental changes in the neuroanatomy and neurochemistry of the brain. For example, O'Reilly and Johnson (1994) demonstrated how the microcircuitry of a region of vertebrate forebrain could lead to certain self-terminating sensitive period effects. Such models promise to provide a bridge between our observations of development at the neural level and behavioral change in childhood.

Postnatal Brain Development: The First Two Years

While some developmental processes can be traced from pre- to postnatal life, in post-natal development there is obviously more scope for influence from the world outside the infant. This need not be a passive process, but rather may reflect the actions of the infant within his or her environment. A striking feature of human brain development is the comparatively long phase of postnatal development, and therefore the increased extent to which the later stages of brain development can be influenced by the environment of the child.

A number of lines of evidence indicate that there are substantive changes during post-natal development of the human brain. At the most gross level of analysis, the volume of the brain quadruples between birth and adulthood. This increase comes from a number of sources such as more extensive fiber bundles, and nerve fibers becoming covered in a fatty myelin sheath which helps to conduct electrical signals. But perhaps the most obvious manifestation of postnatal neural development as viewed through a standard microscope is the increase in size and complexity of the dendritic tree of many neurons. The extent and reach of a cell's dendritic tree may increase dramatically, and it often becomes more specific and specialized. Less apparent through standard microscopes, but more evident with electron microscopy, is a corresponding increase in density of func-tional contacts between neurons, synapses.

Huttenlocher (1990) and colleagues have reported a steady increase in the density of synapses in several regions of the human cerebral cortex. For example, in parts of the visual cortex, the generation of synapses (synaptogenesis) begins around the time of birth and reaches a peak around 150 percent of adult levels toward the end of the first year. In the frontal cortex (the anterior portion of cortex, considered by most investigators to be critical for many higher cognitive abilities), the peak of synaptic density occurs later, at around 24 months of age (but see Goldman-Rakic, Bourgeois, & Rakic, 1997). Although there is variation in the timetable, in all regions of cortex studied so far, synaptogenesis begins around the time of birth and increases to a peak level well above that observed in adults.

Somewhat surprisingly, regressive events are commonly observed during the develop-ment of nerve cells and their connections in the brain. For example, in the primary visual cortex the mean density of synapses per neuron starts to decrease at the end of the first year of life (e.g., Huttenlocher, 1990). In humans, most cortical regions and pathways appear to undergo this "rise and fall" in synaptic density, with the density stabilizing to adult levels at different ages during later childhood. The postnatal rise and fall develop-mental sequence can also be seen in other measures of brain physiology and anatomy. For example, PET studies of children can measure the glucose uptake of regions of the brain. Glucose uptake is necessary in regions of the brain that are active, and because it is trans-ported by the blood is also a measure of blood flow. Using this method, Chugani, Phelps, and Mazziotta (1987) observed an adult-like distribution of resting brain activity within and across brain regions by the end of the first year. However, the overall level of glucose uptake reaches a peak during early childhood which is much higher than that observed in adults. The rates return to adult levels after about 9 years of age for some cortical regions. The extent to which these changes relate to those in synaptic density is currently the topic of further investigation.

A controversial issue in developmental neuroscience concerns the extent to which the differentiation of the cerebral cortex into areas or regions with particular cognitive, perceptual, or motor functions can be shaped by postnatal interactions with the external world. This issue reflects the debate in cognitive development about whether infants are born with domain-specific "modules" for particular cognitive functions such as language, or whether the formation of such modules is an activity-dependent process (see Elman et al. 1996; Karmiloff-Smith, 1992). Brodmann (1912) was one of the first to propose a scheme for the division of cortex into structural areas assumed to have differing functional properties. A century of neuropsychology has taught us that the majority of normal adults tend to have similar functions within approximately the same regions of cortex. However, we cannot necessarily infer from this that this pattern of differentiation is intrinsically prespecified (the product of genetic and molecular interactions), because most humans share very similar pre- and postnatal environments. In developmental neurobiology this issue has emerged as a debate about the relative importance of neural activity for cortical differentiation, as opposed to intrinsic molecular and genetic specification of cortical areas. Supporting the importance of the latter processes, Rakic (1988) proposed that the differentiation of the cortex into areas is due to a protomap. The hypothesized protomap either involves prespecification of the tissue that gives rise to the cortex during prenatal life or the presence of intrinsic molecular markers specific to particular areas of cortex. An alternative viewpoint, advanced by O'Leary (1989) among others, is that genetic and molecular factors build an initially undifferentiated "protocortex," and that this is subsequently divided into specialized areas as a result of neural activity. This activity within neural circuits need not necessarily be the result of input from the external world, but may result from intrinsic, spontaneous patterns of firing within sensory organs or subcortical structures that feed into cortex, or from activity within the cortex itself (e.g., Katz & Shatz, 1996).

Although the neurobiological evidence is complex, and probably differs between species and regions of cortex, overall it tends to support the importance of neural activity-dependent processes (see Elman et al., 1996; Johnson, 1997a,b for reviews). With several exceptions, it seems likely that activity-dependent processes contribute to the differentiation of functional areas of the cortex, especially those involved in higher cognitive functions in humans. During prenatal life, this neural activity may be largely a spontaneous intrinsic process, while in postnatal life it is likely also to be influenced by sensory and motor experience. However, it is unlikely that the transition from spontaneous intrinsic activity to that influenced by sensory experience is a sudden occurrence at birth, for in the womb the infant can process sounds and generate movement, and in postnatal life the brain maintains spontaneously generated intrinsic electrical rhythms (EEG).

As just one of many examples of the effect of experience on cortical specialization, PET studies of word recognition in adults have identified a localized region of the left visual cortex as being involved in English word recognition, while not responding to other stimuli such as random letter strings (Petersen, Fox, Posner, Mintun, & Raichle, 1988). It seems implausible to suggest that we are born with a region of cortex prespecified for English word recognition, so we are forced to conclude that at least some cortical functional specialization is experience-dependent. Other lines of evidence also support this conclusion. For example, studies of scalp-recorded event-related potentials in congenitally deaf subjects show that regions of the temporal lobe which are normally auditory, or multimodal, become dominated by visual input (Neville, 1991). Despite these examples it is clear that there are also limits on the plasticity of cortex. Analyzing normal and abnormal processes of postnatal cortical specialization will be one of the major challenges for developmental cognitive neuroscience over the next decade.

Postnatal Brain Development and Behavioral Change

Much of the theorizing about relations between brain development and behavioral change has centered on the notion of increasing influence of parts of the cerebral cortex over more primitive subcortical circuits, or the influence of "higher" parts of cortex (such as the frontal lobes) over other regions of cortex. There is, thus, the notion of an increasing hierarchy of control over behavior. The reader will recognize that, cast in these terms, this is very much an implicit causal epigenesis viewpoint with the development of certain structures "enabling" new levels of control. Later in this chapter I will suggest these transitions can also be viewed from a probabilistic epigenesis framework. One of the main domains in which increasing levels of brain control have been studied concerns visual orienting and other simple visually guided actions.

Visually Guided Action and Orienting

In one of the first attempts to relate changes in behavior to brain development in infants, Bronson (1974, 1982) argued that visually guided action in the newborn human infant is controlled primarily by the subcortical retino-collicular visual pathway, and that it is only by around 3 months of age that the control over visually guided behavior switches to cortical pathways. Bronson reviewed a variety of neuroanatomical, electrophysiological, and lesion evidence which indicated that structures on the subcortical visual pathway are developmentally in advance of those on the cortical visual pathway in early infancy, and used this evidence to account for differences between visually guided behavior in the newborn infant as compared to that of the 3- or 4-month-old infant. More recently, however, it has become apparent that there is probably some, albeit limited, cortical activity in newborns, and that the onset of cortical control is gradual rather than a sudden transition. In 1990, I proposed a cognitive neuroscience model of the emerging levels of control for visually guided movements, and especially eye movements (Johnson, 1990), which was based on brain circuits for oculomotor control in the primate brain (Schiller, 1985) (see Figure 6.2). The neural pathways illustrated in this figure have been identified with particular functions associated with eye-movement control and shifts of attention. For brevity, only three of these pathways will be discussed here: (1) the pathway

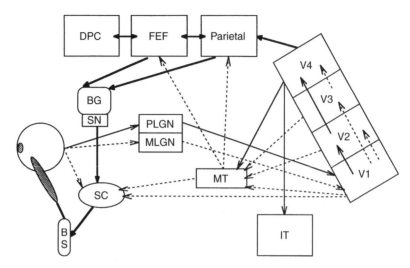

Figure 6.2 A diagram representing some of the main neural pathways and structures involved in visual orienting and attention. The solid lines indicate primarily parvocellular input, while the dashed arrows represent magnocellular. V1–V4 = visual cortex, FEF = frontal eye fields, DPC = dorsolateral prefrontal cortex, BG = basal ganglia, SN = substantia nigra, LGN = lateral geniculate (magno and parvo portions), MT = middle temporal area, IT = inferotemporal cortex, SC = superior colliculus, BS = brain stem.

from the eye to the superior colliculus (this subcortical pathway has heavy input from the temporal visual field and is thought to be important for rapid reflexive eye movements to easily discriminable stimuli); (2) a pathway from the primary visual cortex (V1) projecting to temporal lobe areas, such as the medial temporal area (MT) (believed to play an important role in the detection of motion and in the smooth tracking of moving targets); and (3) a pathway from V1 to other visual cortical regions, and then on to the parietal cortex and the frontal eye fields (FEF). Structures on this third pathway are thought to be involved in more complex aspects of eye-movement planning and attention, such as "anticipatory" saccades (which predict the location of a visual target) and learning sequences of scanning patterns.

I proposed that the characteristics of visually guided behavior of the infant at particular ages is determined by which of the pathways (shown in Figure 6.2) is functional. Which of these pathways is functional is, in turn, determined by whether or not they are receiving structured input from the primary visual cortex at that stage. The primary visual cortex is the major gateway to most of the cortical pathways involved in oculomotor control (Schiller, 1985), and, I argued, two factors determine which oculomotor pathways have access to information from this structure at particular points in development. The first factor is that there is a specific pattern of inputs and outputs from different layers of the primary visual cortex (e.g., Rockland & Pandya, 1979). The second factor is that the primary visual cortex, like other cortical regions, shows a postnatal continuation of the prenatal "inside-out" pattern of growth with the deeper layers (5 and 6) showing greater dendritic branching, length and extent of myelinization than more super-ficial layers (2 and 3) around the time of birth. By combining these observations with information about the developmental neuroanatomy of the primary visual cortex, I hypothesized a particular sequence of postnatal development of the pathways underlying oculomotor control, with pathways which receive input from the deeper layers of the primary visual cortex being functional before those which depend on the upper layers for input. Evidence was then collected from various behavioral "markers" of performance to see if this corresponded with the predictions.

The model predicted that the locus of control in the newborn involved the subcorti-cal pathway from the eye directly to the superior colliculus, and possibly also some cor-tical projections from the deeper layers of V1 to superior colliculus. Due to the limitations of this pathway visually guided movements at this age can be characterized as exogenously driven. For example, the visual tracking of a moving stimulus is saccadic rather than smooth, and these eye movements lag behind the movement of the stimulus, rather than predicting its trajectory (Aslin, 1981). One important question that remained is whether the subcortical visual pathway, in isolation of the cortical pathways, can drive saccades on its own in infants. Braddick et al. (1992) studied two infants who had undergone complete hemispherectomy (removal of the cortex on one side) to alleviate severe epilepsy. They established that these infants were indeed able to make directed eye movements to targets that appeared in their "cortically blind" visual field, indicating that the subcorti-cal (collicular) pathway is capable of supporting saccades in human infants in the absence of the cortex.

By around 2 months of age further development of middle layers in V1 would allow output to the pathway involving MT (sometimes known as V5). In accord with this pre-diction, at this age infants begin to show periods of smooth visual tracking, and become sensitive to coherent motion in visual input (Johnson, 1990; Wattam-Bell, 1991). Further growth of dendrites within the upper layers of the primary visual cortex could strengthen projections to other cortical areas around 3 months of age, thus allowing pathways to the frontal eye fields to become functional. This neuroanatomical development may allow infants to make anticipatory eye movements and learn sequences of looking patterns, both functions associated with the frontal eye fields. With regard to the visual tracking of a moving object, at 3 months infants not only show smooth tracking, but their eye move-ments often predict the movement of the stimulus in an anticipatory manner.

Consistent with the predictions from the model, behavioral marker tasks for the pari-etal cortex, frontal eye fields (FEF), and dorsolateral prefrontal cortex (DLPC) all show rapid development of abilities between 2 and 6 months of age. These behavioral marker tasks are versions of tasks known to engage particular neural circuits or structures in adults from neuropsychology and/or functional neuroimaging. A number of these tasks are sum-marized in Table 6.1.

The approach discussed so far involves trying to test a neurodevelopmental model by looking at behavioral markers for different neural pathways and systems. While this approach often provides a good start in investigating brain–behavior relations during infants' development, it is desirable to use more direct methods. Two such methods that have been applied to the development of visual orienting and attention are the investiga-tion of performance in infants who unfortunately suffered early perinatal brain damage,

Table 6.1   Marker tasks for the development of visual orienting and attention

Brain region	Marker task	Studies
Superior colliculus	Inhibition of return; Vector summation saccades	Clohessy et al. (1991); Simion et al. (1995); Johnson, Gilmore, Tucker, & Minister (1995)
MT	Coherent motion detection; Structure from motion; Smooth tracking	Wattam-Bell (1991); Aslin (1981)
Parietal cortex	Spatial cueing task	Hood & Atkinson (1991); Hood (1993); Johnson & Tucker (1993); Johnson (1994)
	Eye-centered saccade planning	Gilmore & Johnson (1997)
Frontal eye fields	Inhibition of automatic saccades; Anticipatory saccades	Johnson (1995); Haith et al. (1988)
Dorsolateral PFC	Oculomotor delayed response task	Gilmore & Johnson (1995)

and the use of event-related potentials (ERPs). An example of the former approach is a recent study in which infants who had suffered focal cortical damage in one or more of four quadrants of the cortex (anterior, posterior; left, right) were administered a behavioral marker test for the parietal cortex, the "spatial cueing" paradigm (Johnson, Tucker, Stiles, & Trauner, 1998). The parietal cortex is thought to play an important role in so-called "covert" shifts of attention. That is, shifts of spatial attention that take place without head or eye movements. The spatial cueing paradigm is an experimental procedure in which attention is cued to particular spatial locations. Based on the assumptions of the model and the marker-task approach, we predicted that the infants with posterior damage would show a deficit. In fact, to our surprise it was infants with anterior damage, and particularly left anterior quadrant damage, who showed the deficit. Further support for this surprising result came from a high-density ERP study with infants (Csibra, Tucker, & Johnson, 1998). In this study we examined the electrical potentials associated with planning eye movements in infants. Here we also found evidence that level frontal activity was important, specifically in maintaining fixation and facilitating saccades to a peripheral target. These findings may require some changes in the Johnson (1990) model, since circuits involving the frontal lobe were hypothesized to be the last to develop. Smith and Canfield (1998) have proposed an elaboration of this original model in which a pathway to the frontal eye fields is functional earlier than was previously supposed. Such an elaborated model may contribute to explaining the precocial involvement of frontal regions in eye-movement control. Later in this chapter I discuss evidence from other domains indicating that the frontal lobes may be active earlier then was supposed.

A number of conclusions can be drawn from studies reviewed in this section, and suggest that we should be cautious about making simple assumptions about brain–

behavior relations during infant development. The first is that even a form of action as apparently simple as shifting the eyes involves multiple cortical and subcortical pathways. Further, multiple neural pathways and structures are probably engaged by any behavioral task, making simple one-to-one mappings between tasks and regions difficult to make. Nevertheless, there has been progress in generating and testing specific models that relate aspects of developmental neuroanatomy to changes in visually guided behavior.

The Development of Face Recognition

While cortical regions involved in visually guided behaviors such as those described in the last section are part of the so-called dorsal pathway (or "how" pathway due to its involvement in visually guided actions) for visual processing, another pathway, the ventral pathway, extends from visual cortex to regions of the temporal lobe and is sometimes termed the "what" pathway (see Milner & Goodale, 1995). One of the functions of this pathway is the processing of faces. Johnson and Morton (1991; Morton & Johnson, 1991) reviewed much of the existing behavioral literature on face recognition in infants and found two apparently contradictory bodies of evidence: while most of the evidence supported the view that it takes the infant two or three months of experience to learn about the arrangement of features that compose a face (for reviews see Maurer, 1985; Nelson & Ludemann, 1989), one team of researchers (Goren, Sarty, & Wu, 1975) suggested that even newborns would track, by means of head and eye movements, a face-like pattern further than various "scrambled" face patterns. This latter study has now been replicated several times (Johnson, Dziurawiec, Ellis, & Morton, 1991; Maurer & Young, 1983).

The apparent conflict between the results of the newborn studies and those with older infants raised a problem for existing theories of the development of face recognition that involved only one process. Johnson and Morton (1991) proposed a two-process theory of infant face preferences that, to some extent, was built on contemporary theories of the development of visually guided behavior discussed in the last section (a closely related account was provided by de Schonen & Mathivet, 1989). They argued that the first system is accessed via the subcortical visuo-motor pathway (but likely also involves some cortical structures) and controls the preferential orienting to faces in newborns. However, the influence of this system over behavior declines (possibly due to inhibition by later developing cortical systems) during the second month of life. The second process depends upon cortical functioning, and exposure to faces over the first month or so, and begins to influence infant orienting preferences from around 2 months of age. The newborn preferential orienting system biases the input to circuitry on the ventral cortical pathway which is still specializing. This circuitry is configured through processing face input, before it comes to control the infant's actions around the second month. At this point the cortical system is sufficiently specialized for faces to ensure that it continues to acquire further information about this class of stimulus. Thus, a specific, early-developing brain circuit acts in concert with the species-typical environment to bias the input to later-developing brain circuitry. In this sense, the young infant actively selects appropriate inputs for his or her own further brain specialization.

Turning to the second (cortical ventral pathway) system, we can use evidence from adult neuroimaging and neuropsychological studies to ask the question, when do infants show the same pattern of cortical specialization for face processing as adults? PET, fMRI, ERP, and cellular recording experiments have all implicated regions of the inferior temporal cortex as being important for face processing. For example, Bentin et al. (1996) identified a component of the scalp-recorded ERP which occurs around 180 msec after the presentation of a face, and which is localizable to parts of the inferior temporal cortex. In many, but not all, adults the specificity of this region for face processing tends to be lateralized with the right side being more face specific than the left. Again, this finding confirms reports with other brain-imaging methods (Kanwisher, McDermott, & Chun, 1997). Using a high-density ERP recording system, de Haan, Oliver, and Johnson (1998) replicated this finding for adults, and gave the same task to 6-month-old infants. The results for infants were both similar and different to those obtained with adults. They were similar in that there was a face-selective effect observed in the ERP. They were different in that this effect occurred at a much longer latency than in adults, the processing appeared to be less localized than in adults, and the face response was less selective to human faces (for details see Johnson & de Haan, in press). These results were consistent with the view that 6-month-olds show partial specialization for face processing on their ventral visual pathway. Studying older infants in the same paradigm will allow us to trace the emergence of the adult level of neural specialization with more accuracy.

While the above studies were largely concerned with the discrimination and processing of faces as compared to other stimuli, there has also been extensive behavioral work on the development of the recognition of individual faces. These studies have shown that even infants a day or two old are capable of some rudimentary recognition of faces, such as that of their own mother. Johnson and Morton's (1991) theory argued that this ability was due to a third, visual pattern-learning, system. Johnson and de Haan (in press) have used evidence on the neurodevelopment of memory systems (described further in the next section) to propose that while the ventral cortical pathway is unspecialized in newborns, it is capable of limited processing of visual information and of interacting with the hippocampus to construct a memory representation. The memory representations constructed in this way, however, do not use the same cues and processing as individual face recognition in adults. Only when the ventral cortical pathway becomes specialized through experience of faces do the memory representations stored in interaction with the hippocampus become like those utilized by adults for individual recognition. One of the predictions of this revised model is that infants will go through a dip in their ability to recognize individual faces when their initial processing of faces changes around 2 months of age. Preliminary evidence for such a dip has already been observed (de Schonen, Mancini, & Liegeois, 1998).

Memory

Learning is clearly important in psychological development. However, it is sometimes difficult to tease apart the development of specific memory processes from general developmental plasticity. One of the first specific hypotheses advanced about the neurodevelopment of memory was that the brain mechanisms necessary for the long-term storage of information, most probably in the limbic system, are not functional for the first year or two of life (Bachevalier & Mishkin, 1984; Schacter & Moscovitch, 1984). These authors pointed to similarities between the amnesic syndrome (in which limbic system damage in adults results in deficits in recognition memory but relative sparing of learning stimulus–response "habits") and the behavioral profile of memory abilities in infants, and argued that the profile of infant memory abilities reflected the relatively delayed postnatal maturation of limbic circuitry. However, recent evidence from both cognitive and neuroscience studies has cast some doubt on this view. The cognitive evidence comes from studies indicating that human infants can recall experiences from the first year of life several years later (Rovee-Collier, 1993), suggesting some continuity of memory mechanisms from early infancy to later life, and no marked transition from one form of memory to another during development. The neuroscience evidence is that lesions to the limbic system impair recognition memory abilities in infant monkeys in the first month of life (Bachevalier, Brickson, & Hagger, 1993), indicating that even from this early age the limbic system plays some role in memory processes.

Nelson (1995) proposed that there are several types of memory system that develop from infancy: explicit, pre-explicit, working memory, and habit memory. While they have overlapping developmental timetables, pre-explicit and habit memory are present from birth, while explicit and working memory start to emerge after about 8 months. Specifically, he suggests that between 8 and 18 months of age infants become able to perform certain tasks (such as "delayed nonmatch to sample" – identifying the novel object of a pair) that depend on explicit or cognitive memory. This form of memory requires adequate development of the hippocampus, but also related cortical areas within the temporal lobe. However, apparently successful performance can be elicited from infants younger than 8 months in tasks that depend solely on them showing a novelty preference, and which do not require them to determine how often events were presented or do not involve a delay before the response is required. Nelson (1995) hypothesizes that this form of "pre-explicit" memory requires only the functioning of the hippocampus, and not the related temporal cortex structures. Around 8 months of age in the human infant, the development of temporal cortical areas, or their integration with the hippocampus, correlates with a transition from pre-explicit to explicit memory.

Another memory system develops around the same age but shows more protracted development, working memory. Like others, Nelson (1995) suggests that the dorsolateral prefrontal cortex is a critical component of the neural substrate for this form of memory. Nelson's proposal corresponds with the observation that 6-month-olds can successfully perform a marker task for the dorsolateral prefrontal cortex, the oculomotor delayed response task (Gilmore & Johnson, 1995). Automatic "habit" memory is present from birth, and shows a less protracted development than the other types. It is manifest in tasks such as leg-kick conditioning (Rovee-Collier, 1993), eyeblink conditioning, and simple visual discriminations. Some of these types of procedural learning probably involve the cerebellum.

From the evidence discussed in this section it is evident that most memory tasks probably engage multiple memory systems, in a similar way to the partially independent brain pathways that are engaged in eye-movement control and attention shifts. Thus, a lack of maturity in one or other pathway may be masked in some tasks due to compensatory activity in other pathways. Possibly it is the extent of integration between different memory pathways that is the most significant change with postnatal development. If this is the case it is not until we have a more integrative account of the relations between different brain memory pathways that we will be able to make sense of the developmental data.

Frontal Cortex Development, Object Permanence, and Planning

The region of the frontal lobe anterior to the primary motor and premotor cortex, the prefrontal cortex, accounts for almost one-third of the total cortical surface in humans (Brodmann, 1909) and is considered by most investigators to be critical for many higher cognitive abilities (Fuster, 1989; Goldman-Rakic, 1987; Milner, 1982). In adults, types of cognitive processing that have been associated with frontal cortex concern the planning and execution of sequences of action, the maintenance of information "on-line" during short temporal delays (working memory), and the ability to inhibit a set of responses that are appropriate in one context but not another. The frontal cortex shows the most prolonged period of postnatal development of any region of the human brain, with changes in synaptic density detectable even into the teenage years (Huttenlocher, 1990), and for this reason it has been the part of the brain most frequently associated with cognitive development.

Two alternative approaches to the relation between frontal cortex structural development and advances in cognitive ability in childhood have been taken. One of these is the attempt to relate structural developments in the frontal cortex at a particular age to changes in certain cognitive abilities. A refinement of this approach is that the frontal lobes are composed of a number of regions which subserve different functions and show a different timetable of maturation (e.g., Diamond, 1991). The alternative approach is based on the assumption that the frontal cortex is involved in acquisition of new skills and knowledge from very early in life, and that it may also play a key role in organizing other parts of cortex (e.g., Thatcher, 1992). According to this latter view, regions of frontal cortex are important in many cognitive transitions primarily because of the regions' involvement in the acquisition of any new skill or knowledge. A corollary of this is that frontal cortex involvement in a particular task or situation may decrease with increased experience or skill in the domain. There is currently evidence consistent with both of these approaches.

One of the most comprehensive attempts to relate a cognitive change to underlying brain developments has concerned marked behavioral changes around 8 to 10 months of age. In particular, Diamond, Goldman-Rakic, and colleagues (Diamond & Goldman-Rakic, 1986, 1989; Goldman-Rakic, 1987) argued that the maturation of prefrontal cortex during the last half of the human infant's first year of life accounts for a number of transitions observed in the behavior of infants in object permanence and object retrieval tasks. One of the behavioral tasks they have used to support this argument comes from Piaget (1954), who observed that infants younger than 8 months often fail to accurately retrieve a hidden object after a short delay period if the object's location is changed from one where it was previously successfully retrieved. Infants often made a particular preservative error in which they reach to the hiding location where the object was found on the immediately preceding trial. This characteristic pattern of error was cited by Piaget (1954) as evidence for the failure to understand that objects retain their existence or permanence when moved from view. By around 9 months, infants begin to succeed in the task at successively longer delays of 1–5 sec (Diamond, 1985), although their performance remains unreliable up to about 12 months if the delay between hiding and retrieval is incremented as the infants age (Diamond, 1985) (but see chapter 4 in this volume for criticisms of this work).

Diamond and Goldman-Rakic (1989) tested monkeys in a modification of the above object permanence task. Consistent with the observations on human infants, infant monkeys failed to retrieve the hidden object. Further, adult monkeys with lesions to the dorsolateral region of the prefrontal cortex (DLPC) were also impaired in this task. Lesions to some other parts of the brain (parietal cortex, or the hippocampal formation) did not significantly impair performance, suggesting that the DLPC plays a central role in tasks which require the maintenance of spatial or object information over temporal delays.

Further evidence linking success in the object permanence task to frontal cortex maturation in the human infant comes from two sources. The first of these is a series of EEG studies with normal human infants (Bell, 1992a,b; Bell & Fox, 1992; Fox & Bell, 1990), in which increases in frontal EEG responses correlate with the ability to respond successfully over longer delays in delayed response tasks. The second source is work on cognitive deficits in children with a neurochemical deficit in the prefrontal cortex resulting from phenylketonuria (PKU). Even when treated, this inborn error of metabolism can have the specific consequence of reducing the levels of a neurotransmitter, dopamine, in the dorsolateral prefrontal cortex. These reductions in dopamine levels in the dorsolateral prefrontal cortex result in these infants and children being impaired on tasks thought to involve parts of the prefrontal cortex such as the object permanence task and object retrieval tasks, and being relatively normal in tasks thought to depend on other regions of cortex such as the DNMS (delayed nonmatch to sample) task mentioned earlier (Diamond et al., 1997; Welsh, Pennington, Ozonoff, Rouse, & McCabe, 1990).

Having established a link between prefrontal cortex maturation and behavioral change in a number of tasks, Diamond (1991) has speculated on the computational consequence of this aspect of postnatal brain development. Specifically, she suggested that the DLPC (dorsolateral prefrontal cortex) is critical for performance when (1) information has to be retained or related over time or space, and (2) a prepotent response has to be inhibited. Only tasks that require both of these aspects of neural computation are likely to engage the DLPC. In the case of the object permanence task, a spatial location has to be retained over time and the prepotent previously rewarded response inhibited. A recent experiment suggests that the prefrontal cortex maturation hypothesis is not the whole story, however, and that some modification or elaboration of the original account will be required. Gilmore and Johnson (1995) observed that infants succeed on a task that requires temporal spatial integration over a delay at a much younger age than is indicated by the object permanence tasks. Specifically, they devised an infant version of the oculomotor delayed response task, a task in which participants have to wait for several seconds before making an eye movement toward a previously cued target location. Several neurophysiological and neuroimaging studies in adult humans and monkeys had linked this task to the DLPC. Gilmore and Johnson (1995) found that 6-month-olds were able to perform successfully in this task, suggesting that their DLPC was functioning, at least to some extent.

In addition, studies by Baillargeon (1987, 1993) and others entailing infants viewing "possible" and "impossible" events involving occluded objects have found that infants as young as 3.5 months look longer at impossible events, indicating that they have an internal representation of the occluded object. While this evidence does not directly contradict Diamond's hypothesis, it would have to be taken into account in a fuller explanation of the development of responses to occluded objects. In order to account for the apparent discrepancy between these results and those with the reaching measures, some have provided "means–ends" explanations, arguing that infants are unable to coordinate the necessary sequence of motor behaviors to retrieve a hidden object (Baillargeon, 1993; Diamond, 1991). To test this hypothesis, Munakata, McClelland, Johnson, and Siegler (1997) trained 7-month-olds to retrieve objects placed at a distance from them by means of pulling on a towel or pressing a button. Infants retrieved the objects when a transparent screen was interposed between them and the toy, but not if the screen was sufficiently opaque to make the object invisible. Since the same means–ends planning is required whether the screen is transparent or opaque, it was concluded that "means–ends" explanations cannot account for the discrepancy between the looking and the reaching tasks. Munakata et al. (1994) proposed an alternative "graded" view of the discrepancy implemented as a connectionist model. This model was trained on a series of inputs representing objects moving behind occluders. After a period of training, the patterns of links between nodes within the model adjusted their strengths such that some nodes developed representations of objects which persisted for a while even when the object was occluded. Initially, during the early phases of training (taken to correspond to the young infant), the object representations are weak and do not linger for long after occlusion. Under these circumstances the representation (pattern of activation) can be just about strong enough to guide the model's "looking" response, but not strong enough to guide its "reaching." With further training, the strength of the representation after object occlusion is sufficient to drive both reaching and looking responses.

An alternative approach to understanding the role of the prefrontal cortex in cognitive development has been advanced by several authors who have suggested that the region plays a critical role in the acquisition of new information and tasks. By this account the prefrontal cortex involvement in the object retrieval tasks is only one of many manifestations of prefrontal cortex involvement in cognitive change. A concomitant of this general view is that the cortical regions crucial for a particular task will change with the stage of acquisition. Two recent lines of evidence are consistent with the view that regions of frontal cortex are not only active in early infancy, but that the frontal lobes may in fact play a greater role during the acquisition of new skills during infancy. Johnson et al. (1998) studied infants with perinatal focal lesions to parts of cortex in a visual attention task. Damage to parietal cortical regions would be expected to produce deficits in this task in adults, but only infants with perinatal lesions to the anterior (frontal) regions

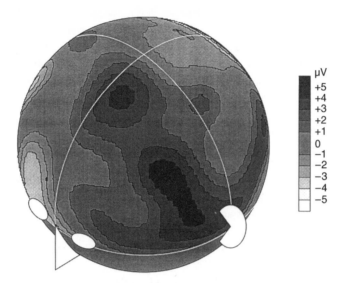

Figure 6.3   A diagram illustrating activation over frontal cortical regions during a visual fixation and orienting task with 6-month-old infants (from Csibra et al., 1998).

of cortex were impaired, suggesting that these regions were involved to a greater extent in the task in infants than in adults. Similarly, a recent high-density ERP study involving visual attention and eye-movement planning in infants showed suggestive evidence of frontal cortex involvement in infants (Csibra et al., 1998; see Figure 6.3). The same effect was not observed in adults, although they did show frontal cortex involvement in other aspects of the task. These two lines of evidence are at least suggestive of early frontal cortical activity that may occur in at least some situations where it is not observed in adults.

Emerging Issues

The lines of research reviewed in this chapter illustrate the potential of the new interdisciplinary field of developmental cognitive neuroscience. While this field is still young, there are already a number of themes emerging across different domains. One of these concerns the importance of activity-dependent processes at a number of levels in both prenatal and postnatal life. It is apparent that at least some aspects of specialization of the cerebral cortex are due to intrinsic activity-dependent processes. This is continued into postnatal life with the primitive biases of the newborn (such as its tendency to look toward faces) serving to bias the input to later-developing circuits. In this sense infants can be said to be actively contributing to the later stages of their own brain specialization. It is also possible that parts of the frontal cortex contribute to the specialization of other parts of the cortex. Later in infancy, social experience and interaction with caregivers may contribute further to the specialization of late-developing parts of the cerebral cortex. Much of later postnatal brain development, therefore, can be viewed as an active process to which both the child and its caregivers contribute. Thus, studying the postnatal emergence of cortical specialization for different cognitive functions offers the possibility of new perspectives not only on the study of perceptual and cognitive development in healthy human infants, but also for social development, education, and atypical developmental pathways.

With regard to atypical development, the perspective outlined above suggests that an early abnormality in brain function, or in environmental factors, could be greatly compounded by subsequent interactions with the environment which are abnormal. Thus, a slight deviation from the normal developmental trajectory early on could become more severe with subsequent development (see Karmiloff-Smith, 1998). However, the positive side of this approach to understanding developmental disorders is that it suggests hope for early remediative strategies. Indeed, there are already some, albeit limited, examples of how early alterations of environmental input may help to alleviate subsequent abnormalities (Tallal et al., 1996).

Some domains of cognition, such as language, appear plastic in the sense that regions of cortex are not exclusively dedicated to them from birth, while other domains, such as face processing, may have fewer options. Less extensive plasticity does not necessarily imply strict genetic determinism, however, because functions more closely tied to sensory input or motor output are likely to be more restricted to the cortical regions that have the appropriate information in their input. For example, face recognition is necessarily restricted to structures on the visual "what" (ventral) pathway because it requires both visual analysis and encoding of particular items within a category. Language may be less constrained in the sense that it is less restricted to particular information-processing routes within the cortex. Thus, a key point about the emergence of localization of functions within the cortex is that the restrictions on localization may be more related to which cortical routes of information processing are viable for supporting the functions, rather than being due to pre-wired intrinsic circuitry within regions of cortex.

The study of functional brain development in infancy is still just beginning. However, the insights into this process gained so far suggest that further study of this topic will be rewarded with a deeper understanding of how the specificity of function observed in adults' cognitive abilities is attained. The next few decades promise some exciting breakthroughs.

Further Reading

Elman, J., Bates, E., Johnson, M. H., Karmiloff-Smith, A., Parisi, D., & Plunkett, K. (1996). *Rethinking innateness: A connectionist perspective on development.* Cambridge, MA: MIT Press. This book explores relations between connectionist (neural network) modeling, brain development, and cognitive development, and argues for a synthesis between the three.

Johnson, M. H. (1997a). *Developmental cognitive neuroscience: An introduction.* Oxford: Blackwell. An introductory survey of facts and theories about the relation between brain development and the emergence of cognitive abilities in humans.

Johnson, M. H., Gilmore, R. O., & Munakata, Y. (in press). *Brain development and cognition: A reader* (2nd ed.). Oxford: Blackwell. Contains a number of "classic" and new readings by various authors on the relation between brain development and cognition.

Krasnegor, N. A., Lyon, G. R., & Goldman-Rakic, P. S. (1997). *Development of the prefrontal cortex: Evolution, neurobiology and behavior.* Baltimore, MD: Paul H. Brookes.

References

Aslin, R. N. (1981). Development of smooth pursuit in human infants. In D. F. Fisher, R. A. Monty, & J. W. Senders (Eds.), *Eye movements: Cognition and visual perception* (pp. 31–51). Hillsdale, NJ: Erlbaum.

Bachevalier, J., Brickson, M., & Hagger, C. (1993). Limbic-dependent recognition memory in monkeys develops early in infancy. *NeuroReport, 4*, 77–80.

Bachevalier, J., & Mishkin, M. (1984). An early and a late developing system for learning and retention in infant monkeys. *Behavioral Neuroscience, 98*, 770–778.

Baillargeon, R. (1987). Object permanence in very young infants. *Cognition, 20*, 191–208.

Baillargeon, R. (1993). The object concept revisited: New directions in the investigation of infants' physical knowledge. In C. E. Granrud (Ed.), *Visual perception and cognition in infancy* (pp. 265–315). Hillsdale, NJ: Lawrence Erlbaum Associates.

Bell, M. A. (1992a). Electrophysiological correlates of object search performance during infancy. *Infant Behavior and Development, 15*, Special International Conference on Infant Studies issue, 3.

Bell, M. A. (1992b). A not B task performance is related to frontal EEG asymmetry regardless of locomotor experience. *Infant Behavior and Development, 15*, Special International Conference on Infant Studies issue, 307.

Bell, M. A., & Fox, N. A. (1992). The relations between frontal brain electrical activity and cognitive development during infancy. *Child Development, 63*, 1142–1163.

Bentin, S., Allison, T., Puce, A., Perez, E., & McCarthy, G. (1996). Electrophysiological studies of face perception in humans. *Journal of Cognitive Neuroscience, 8*(6), 551–565.

Braddick, O. J., Atkinson, J., Hood, B., Harkness, W., Jackson, G., & Vargha-Khadem, F. (1992). Possible blindsight in infants lacking one cerebral hemisphere. *Nature, 360*, 461–463.

Brodmann, K. (1909). *Vergleichende Lokalisationslehre der Grosshirnrinde in ihren Prinzipien dargestellt auf Grund des Zellenbaues.* Leipzig: Barth.

Brodmann, K. (1912). Neue Ergebnisse über die vergleichende histologische Lokalisation der Grosshirnrinde mit besonderer Berücksichtigung des Stirnhirns. *Anatomischer Anzeiger (Suppl.), 41*, 157–216.

Bronson, G. W. (1974). The postnatal growth of visual capacity. *Child Development, 45*, 873–890.

Bronson, G. W. (1982). *The scanning patterns of human infants: Implications for visual learning.* Norwood, NJ: Ablex.

Casey, B. J., Trainor, R. J., Orendi, J. L., Schubert, A. B., Nystrom, L. E., Giedd, J. N., & Xavier Castellanos, J. L. (1997). A developmental functional MRI study of prefrontal activation during performance of a go-no-go task. *Journal of Cognitive Neuroscience, 9*(6), 835–847.

Chugani, H. T., Phelps, M. E., & Mazziotta, J. C. (1987). Positron emission tomography study of human brain functional development. *Annals of Neurology, 22*, 487–497.

Conel, J. L. (1939–1967). *The postnatal development of the human cerebral cortex* (Vols. 1–6). Cambridge, MA: Harvard University Press.

Csibra, G., Tucker, L. A., & Johnson, M. H. (1998). Neural correlates of saccade planning in infants: A high-density ERP study. *International Journal of Psychophysiology, 29*, 201–215.

De Haan, M., Oliver, A., & Johnson, M. H. (1998). Electrophysiological correlates of face processing by adults and 6-month-old infants. *Journal of Cognitive Neuroscience Annual Meeting Supplement, 36.*

De Schonen, S., & Mathivet, H. (1989). First come, first served: A scenario about the development of hemispheric specialization in face recognition during infancy. *European Bulletin of Cognitive Psychology, 9*, 3–44.

De Schonen, S., Mancini, J., & Liegeois, F. (1998). About functional cortical specialization: The development of face recognition. In F. Simion & G. Butterworth (Eds.), *The development of sensory, motor and cognitive capacities in early infancy* (pp. 103–120). Hove: Psychology Press.

Diamond, A. (1985). Development of the ability to use recall to guide action, as indicated by infants' performance on AB. *Child Development, 56*, 868–883.

Diamond, A. (1991). Neuropsychological insights into the meaning of object concept development. In S. Carey & R. Gelman (Eds.), *The epigenesis of mind: Essays on biology and cognition* (pp. 67–110). Hillsdale, NJ: Lawrence Erlbaum Associates.

Diamond, A., & Goldman-Rakic, P. S. (1986). Comparative development of human infants and infant rhesus monkeys of cognitive functions that depend on prefrontal cortex. *Neuroscience Abstracts, 12*, 274.

Diamond, A., & Goldman-Rakic, P. S. (1989). Comparison of human infants and infant rhesus monkeys on Piaget's AB task: Evidence for dependence on dorsolateral prefrontal cortex. *Experimental Brain Research, 74*, 24–40.

Diamond, A., Hurwitz, W., Lee, E. Y., Bockes, T., Grover, W., & Minarcik, C. (1997). Cognitive deficits on frontal cortex tasks in children with early-treated PKU: Results of two years of longitudinal study. *Monographs of the Society for Research in Child Development, 252*(4), 1–207.

Elman, J., Bates, E., Johnson, M. H., Karmiloff-Smith, A., Parisi, D., & Plunkett, K. (1996). *Rethinking innateness: A connectionist perspective on development.* Cambridge, MA: MIT Press.

Fox, N. A., & Bell, M. A. (1990). Electrophysiological indices of frontal lobe development. In A. Diamond (Ed.), *The development and neural bases of higher cognitive functions* (pp. 677–698). New York: New York Academy of Sciences.

Fuster, J. M. (1989). *The prefrontal cortex.* New York: Raven Press.

Gilmore, R. O., & Johnson, M. H. (1995). Working memory in infancy: Six-month-olds' performance on two versions of the oculomotor delayed response task. *Journal of Experimental Child Psychology, 59*, 397–418.

Goldman-Rakic, P. S. (1987). Development of cortical circuitry and cognitive function. *Child Development, 58*, 601–622.

Goldman-Rakic, P. S., Bourgeois, J.-P., & Rakic, P. (1997). Synaptic substrate of cognitive development: Life-span analysis of synaptogenesis in the prefrontal cortex of the nonhuman primate. In N. A. Krasnegor, G. R. Lyon, & P. S. Goldman-Rakic (Eds.), *Development of the prefrontal cortex: Evolution, neurobiology, and behavior* (pp. 27–48). Baltimore, MD: Paul H. Brookes.

Goren, C. C., Sarty, M., & Wu, P. Y. K. (1975). Visual following and pattern discrimination of face-like stimuli by newborn infants. *Pediatrics, 56*, 544–549.

Gottlieb, G. (1992). *Individual development and evolution.* New York: Oxford University Press.

Huttenlocher, P. R. (1990). Morphometric study of human cerebral cortex development. *Neuropsychologia, 28*, 517–527.

Johnson, M. H. (1990). Cortical maturation and the development of visual attention in early infancy. *Journal of Cognitive Neuroscience, 2*(2), 81–95.

Johnson, M. H. (1993). Constraints on cortical plasticity. In M. H. Johnson (Ed.), *Brain development and cognition: A reader* (pp. 703–721). Oxford: Blackwell.

Johnson, M. H. (1997a). *Developmental cognitive neuroscience: An introduction.* Oxford: Blackwell.

Johnson, M. H. (1997b). The neural basis of cognitive development. In W. Damon (Ed.), *Handbook of child psychology* (Vol. 2, pp. 1–49). New York: John Wiley.

Johnson, M. H., & de Haan, M. (in press). Developing cortical specialisation for visual-cognitive function: The case of face recognition. In J. L. McClelland & R. S. Seigler (Eds.), *Mechanisms of cognitive development: Behavioural and neural perspectives.* Hillsdale, NJ: Lawrence Erlbaum Associates.

Johnson, M. H., Dziurawiec, S., Ellis, H. D., & Morton, J. (1991). Newborns' preferential tracking of face-like stimuli and its subsequent decline. *Cognition, 40,* 1–19.

Johnson, M. H., & Morton, J. (1991). *Biology and cognitive development: The case of face recognition.* Oxford: Blackwell.

Johnson, M. H., Tucker, L. A., Stiles, J., & Trauner, D. (1998). Visual attention in infants with perinatal brain damage: Evidence of the importance of anterior lesions. *Developmental Science, 1,* 53–58.

Kanwisher, N., McDermott, J., & Chun, M. M. (1997). The fusiform face area: A module in human extrastriate cortex specialized for face perception. *Journal of Neuroscience, 17*(11), 4302–4311.

Karmiloff-Smith, A. (1992). *Beyond modularity: A developmental perspective on cognitive science.* Cambridge, MA: MIT Press/Bradford Books.

Karmiloff-Smith, A. (1998). Development itself is the key to understanding developmental disorders. *Trends in Cognitive Science, 2*(10), 389–398.

Katz, L. C., & Shatz, C. J. (1996). Synaptic activity and the construction of cortical circuits. *Science, 274,* 1133.

Kwong, K. E., Belliveau, J. W., Chesler, D. A., Goldberg, I. E., Weisskoff, R. M., Poncelet, B. P., Kennedy, D. N., Hoppel, B. E., Cohen, M. S., Turner, R., Cheng, H. M., Brady, T. J., & Rosen, B. R. (1992). Dynamic magnetic resonance imaging of human brain activity during primary sensory stimulation. *Proceedings of the National Academy of Sciences, 89,* 5675–5679.

Maurer, D. (1985). Infants' perception of facedness. In T. N. Field & N. Fox (Eds.), *Social perception in infants* (pp. 73–100). Norwood, NJ: Ablex.

Maurer, D., & Young, R. E. (1983). Newborns' following of natural and distorted arrangements of facial features. *Infant Behavior and Development, 6,* 127–131.

Milner, A. D., & Goodale, M. A. (1995). *The visual brain in action.* Oxford: Oxford University Press.

Milner, B. (1982). Some cognitive effects of frontal-lobe lesions in man. *Philosophical Transactions of the Royal Society of London, 298,* 211–226.

Morton, J., & Johnson, M. H. (1991). CONSPEC and CONLERN: A two-process theory of infant face recognition. *Psychological Review, 98*(2), 164–181.

Munakata, Y., McClelland, J. L., et al. (1994). *Now you see it, now you don't: A gradualistic framework for understanding infants' successes and failures in object permanence tasks.* Carnegie Mellon University. Technical Report PDP.CNS.94.2.

Munakata, Y., McClelland, J. L., Johnson, M. H., & Siegler, R. S. (1997). Rethinking infant knowledge: Toward an adaptive process account of successes and failures in object permanence tasks. *Psychological Review, 104*(4), 686–713.

Nelson, C. A. (1995). The ontogeny of human memory: A cognitive neuroscience perspective. *Developmental Psychology, 31*(5), 723–738.

Nelson, C. A., & Bloom, F. E. (1997). Child development and neuroscience. *Child Development, 68*(5), 970–987.

Nelson, C. A., & Ludemann, P. M. (1989). Past, current and future trends in infant face perception research. *Canadian Journal of Psychology, 43,* 183–198.

Neville, H. J. (1991). Neurobiology of cognitive and language processing: Effects of early experience. In K. R. Gibson & A. C. Petersen (Eds.), *Brain maturation and cognitive development: Comparative and cross-cultural perspectives* (pp. 355–380). New York: Aldine de Gruyter.

O'Leary, D. D. M. (1989). Do cortical areas emerge from a protocortex? *Trends in Neuroscience, 12*, 400–406.

O'Reilly, R., & Johnson, M. H. (1994). Object recognition and sensitive periods: A computational analysis of visual imprinting. *Neural Computation 6*, 357–390.

Petersen, S. E., Fox, P., Posner, M., Mintun, M., & Raichle, M. (1988). Positron emission tomographic studies of the cortical anatomy of single-word processing. *Nature, 331*, 585–589.

Piaget, J. (1954). *The construction of reality in the child.* New York: Basic Books.

Rakic, P. (1987). Intrinsic and extrinsic determinants of neocortical parcellation: A radial unit model. In P. Rakic & W. Singer (Eds.), *Neurobiology of neocortex* (pp. 5–27). Chichester: John Wiley.

Rakic, P. (1988). Specification of cerebral cortical areas. *Science, 241*, 170–176.

Rockland, K. S., & Pandya, D. N. (1979). Laminar origins and terminations of cortical connections of the occipital lobe in the rhesus monkey. *Brain Research, 179*, 3–20.

Rovee-Collier, C. K. (1993). The capacity for long-term memory in infancy. *Current Directions in Psychological Science, 2*(4), 130–135.

Schacter, D., & Moscovitch, M. (1984). Infants' amnesia and dissociable memory systems. In M. Moscovitch (Ed.), *Infant memory* (pp. 173–216). New York: Plenum Press.

Schiller, P. H. (1985). A model for the generation of visually guided saccadic eye movements. In D. Rose & V. G. Dobson (Eds.), *Models of the visual cortex* (pp. 62–70). Chichester: John Wiley.

Smith, E. G., & Canfield, R. L. (1998, April). *Two-month-olds make predictive saccades: Evidence for early frontal lobe function.* Poster presentation at the International Conference of Infant Studies, Atlanta, GA.

Tallal, P., Miller, S. L., Bedi, G., Byma, G., Wang, X., Nagarajan, S. J., Srikantan, S., Schreiner, C., Jenkins, W. M., & Merzenich, M. M. (1996). Language comprehension in language-learning impaired children improved with acoustically modified speech. *Science, 271*, 81–84.

Thatcher, R. W. (1992). Cyclic cortical reorganization during early childhood. Special issue: The role of frontal lobe maturation in cognitive and social development. *Brain and Cognition 20*(1), 24–50.

Tzourio, N., de Schonen, S., Mazoyer, B., Bore, A., Pietrzyk, U., Bruck, B., Aujard, Y., & Deruelle, C. (1992). Regional cerebral blood flow in two-month-old alert infants. *Society for Neuroscience Abstracts, 18*(2), 1121.

Wattam-Bell, J. (1991). Development of motion-specific cortical responses in infants. *Vision Research, 31*, 287–297.

Welsh, M. C., Pennington, B. F., Ozonoff, S., Rouse, B., & McCabe, E. R. B. (1990). Neuropsychology of early-treated phenylketonuria: Specific executive function deficits. *Child Development, 61*, 1697–1713.

Chapter Seven

Origins of Self-concept

Philippe Rochat

Introduction

Questions regarding the origins and nature of self-knowledge are arguably the most fundamental in psychology. What is knowledge about oneself made of and where does it come
from? The aim of this chapter is to discuss recent progress in infancy research that sheds new
light on these questions. The issue of whether self-knowledge finds its root in language
development is first considered. On the basis of recent empirical evidence, I will then assert
that self-knowledge does not depend exclusively on language development. Infancy research
demonstrates that self-knowledge is expressed at an *implicit* level long before children
become symbolic and competent talkers. The main idea running through the chapter is that
at the origin of explicit and conceptual self-knowledge (i.e., self-concept) is an implicit
knowledge about the self developing in the preverbal child. The focus here is on the nature
of early implicit self-knowledge and its link to later-emerging explicit self-knowledge.

In general, the chapter will try to show that infants from birth, and particularly from
2 months of age, develop two types of implicit self-knowledge. On one hand, infants
develop implicit knowledge about their own body via self-exploration and self-produced
action on objects. On the other, they develop specific knowledge about their own
affective dispositions via interaction and reciprocation with others. The origins of these
two types of implicit self-knowledge are, respectively, *perceptual* and *social*.

But prior to this presentation, the origins of self-knowledge in relation to language
and the emergence of symbolic functioning by the second year of life should briefly be
situated.

Thank you to Tricia Striano for her helpful comments on the first version of the manuscript. While
writing this chapter, the author was supported by a grant no. SBR-9507773 from the National Science
Foundation.

Self and Language

We all have some notions of who we are and what distinguishes us from others. We know what we look like, have some sense of our relative power, as well as the personality we project to the outside world. We have a sense of what belongs to us and what doesn't, the things we excel in and those we don't. In short, we all have some explicit conception of ourselves, a so-called explicit *self-concept*. The explicit self-concept of adults is to a large extent articulated in words as we frequently engage in talking about ourselves, perform silent monologues, and display a universal compulsion for internal speech, adopting the self as audience and as sole witness of . . . ourselves.

An explicit, hence reflective, conception of the self is already apparent at the early stage of language acquisition. As argued by Bates (1990), "the acquisition of any natural language requires a preexisting theory of self – a theory of the self as distinct from other people, and a theory of the self from the point of view of one's conversational partners" (p. 165). By 18 months, infants start to mark contrasts between themselves and other people in their verbal production. They express semantic roles that can be taken either by themselves or by others (Bates, 1990). Does that mean, however, that the nature of self-concept is primarily linguistic? In other words, does it imply that the roots of an explicit sense of self are to be found in language and its development?

It is feasible that self-concept emerges under the pressure of growing linguistic competence, essentially a linguistic epiphenomenon. With language would come self-marking and labeling, with children somehow compelled to become explicit about who they are in terms of their own desires (e.g., "Candy!"), beliefs (e.g., "Katy nice!"), feelings (e.g., "Happy!"), and other states of mind (e.g., the unfortunately too typical "Mine!"). Communicating verbally does indeed require much explicit reference to the self as the subject of action, intentions, and beliefs.

The idea that the emergence of self-concept is linked to the development of language is corroborated by the roughly synchronous developmental timing of mirror self-recognition in the young child. By the time children start to utter their first conventional words, using arbitrary sounds that are acknowledged by their community as standing for things in the world, they also start to show clear signs of self-recognition in mirrors. It is also by the middle of the second year, around the time children typically start to speak, that they also start to show self-referencing (e.g., pointing to themselves) and self-conscious emotions (e.g., embarrassment) in front of mirrors (Lewis & Brooks-Gunn, 1979). In the context of the famous mirror "rouge task," this is evident when children perceive their own reflection, noticing that a stain of rouge has been surreptitiously smeared over their face (as an illustration, see Figure 7.1).

From the perspective of evolution, formal and generative language is what differentiates humans from other animal species. Interestingly, self-concept is also a trademark of humans, including a few of our close primate relatives who demonstrate mirror self-recognition in the context of the "rouge" task (i.e., orangutans and chimpanzees; see the thorough review by Tomasello & Call, 1997). Thus, if language and self-concept are connected in child development, they also appear to be linked as major cognitive trademarks in primate evolution (Gallup, 1982; Povinelli, 1993).

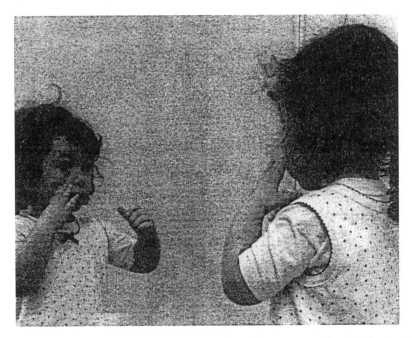

Figure 7.1   Self-referencing and embarrassment manifested by an 18-month-old infant in front of a mirror during the rouge test. (Photo Pascale L. R.)

In child development, although language and explicit self-concept appear connected in the timing of their emergence, it does not mean that they are mutually dependent. On one hand, there is much ground to assume that language acquisition and the learning of word meanings rest on an understanding of self as intentional. When children hear a new word and learn that *this* particular word stands for *that* specific object or event in the world, they connect the intention of others with their own to communicate about objects and events in the environment (Tomasello & Akhtar, 1995). The child clearly shows the distinct notion of others and of him or herself as intentional communicators (Tomasello, 1995). On the other hand, children do not wait until they are symbolically competent to express some *implicit* or *preconceptual* self-knowledge. As proposed by William James over a century ago, it is necessary to distinguish implicit and explicit levels of self-knowledge.

Self-knowledge Without Language

In his seminal writing on the self, James (1890) distinguishes the "Me" and the "I" as two basic aspects of the self. The "Me" corresponds to the self that is identified, recalled, and talked about. It is the conceptual self that emerges with language and which entails explicit re-cognition or re-presentation. It is beyond the grasp of infants, who by definition are preverbal, not yet expressing themselves within the conventions of a shared symbol system. On the other hand, there is the self that is basically implicit, not depending on any conscious identification or recognition. The "I" is also referred to as the *existential self* (Lewis & Brooks-Gunn, 1979) or the *implicit self* (Case, 1991). It is, for example, the sense of their own body expressed by young infants when they start to reach and grasp objects around them. Infants implicitly express a sense of themselves as agent (reachers) as well as a sense of their own physical situation in the environment (objects around them are perceived by the infant as reachable and graspable depending on size and distance; see Rochat, 1997). Infancy research shows that the "I" is expressed long before any signs of a conceptual (explicit) sense of self (the "Me").

If we accept James's distinction, the question is what kind of relation these two fundamental aspects of the self entertain, and in particular, how do they relate in their development? One possibility is that they are developing independently of each other and that somehow their functioning is parallel and unrelated. Another possibility, proposed here and supported by infancy research, is that the development of the conceptual self emerging by the second year is *rooted in* and *prepared by* an implicit sense of self already present at birth and developing from the outset (the early sense of an existential self or "I" following James's distinction).

In the tradition set by James but expanding his work, Neisser (1991) further distinguishes two kinds of *implicit self* or "*Is*" manifested in early infancy, long before the developmental emergence of a conceptual self. Neisser proposes that from the outset of development, infants have two kinds of selves within either the social or physical domain. Each domain provides the infant with specific perceptual information specifying different aspects of the self: the *interpersonal* in the social domain, and the *ecological* self in the physical domain.

The interpersonal self grows out of the infant's transactions with others, in particular the developing sense of shared experience and reciprocity. In the physical domain, infants develop a sense of their own body in relation to other objects, what Neisser labels "the ecological self." The ecological self is the sense infants develop of their own physical body as a differentiated, situated agent in relation to other objects furnishing the environment. The ecological self develops as infants interact with physical objects and also as they perceive their own body directly via self-exploration (see below, Rochat, 1998; Rochat & Morgan, 1995).

Neisser's conceptualization of the self in infancy is justified based on a growing body of observations provided by current infancy research (see Butterworth, 1995). We will see next that this research demonstrates that at the origin of development, infants manifest a sense of the ecological as well as the interpersonal self.

The Self in Infancy

Infants from a very early age differentiate perceptually between self- and non-self-stimulation, namely, between themselves and other entities in the environment. Early on, for example, infants differentiate between their own movements in the environment, whether passively or actively produced, and the independent movements of objects observed from a stationary point in space (Kellman, Gleitman, & Spelke, 1987). Young infants and even newborns respond with markedly different postural adjustments (e.g., straightening of the trunk or head movements) when they are surreptitiously set in motion, or if their surrounding is set in motion with them maintained stationary (Bertenthal & Rose, 1995; Jouen & Gapenne, 1995).

Aside from being situated in the environment, infants also manifest an implicit sense of their own effectivity in the world. From birth, infants learn to be effective in relation to objects and events. For example, within hours after birth, neonates are capable of learning to suck in certain ways and apply specific pressures on a dummy pacifier to hear their mother's voice or see their mother's face (DeCasper & Fifer, 1980; Walton, Bower, & Bower, 1992). This remarkable instrumental learning capacity testifies to the fact that early on infants manifest a sense of themselves as an *agent* in the environment, an important aspect of the (implicit) ecological self (Neisser, 1995; Rochat, 1997).

As we will see, in the social domain there is also good evidence of implicit self-knowledge. From at least 2 months of age infants start to reciprocate with others, smiling, gazing, and cooing in face-to-face exchanges with a social partner. They show some signs of what Trevarthen (1979) coined "primary intersubjectivity," the sense of shared experience infants manifest in dyadic face-to-face interactions. When social partners adopt a sudden still-face, staring at the infant with a neutral, frozen facial expression, infants from 2 months of age react with strong negative facial expressions: they gaze away, smile markedly less, and even cry (Toda & Fogel, 1993; Tronick, Als, Adamson, Wise, & Brazelton, 1978). This robust phenomenon suggests that infants already have an implicit sense of others, as well as of themselves, as reciprocating (social) agents. They expect social partners to reciprocate in certain ways to their *own* emotional displays. If they smile, they expect others to reciprocate with analogous emotional expressions.

Early on, others are social mirrors in which infants contemplate and learn about themselves via imitation (Meltzoff & Moore, 1995) and the behavioral mirroring provided by caretakers who tend to feed back to the infant what they just did. Adult mirroring of the infant contains rich information about the self, characterized by systematic exaggeration of infants' emotions and precise marking of such mimicking by the adult (Gergely & Watson, 1999). In short, there is now good evidence as well as solid ground for the early development of an implicit sense of self as *social agent*, reciprocating with people in systematic ways and developing social expectations (Rochat, Querido & Striano, 1999; Rochat & Striano, 1999a).

The abundance of findings supporting the existence of both an ecological and interpersonal self at the origin of development contrasts sharply with the theoretical assertions that have been traditionally put forth by developmentalists. Current research has radically changed the traditional view of an originally confused infant devoid of any implicit sense of self. Infants do not appear to start off in a state of fusion and confusion in regard to their situation in the environment. James's (1890) famous account of the world of newborns as a "blooming, buzzing confusion" does not fare well with current infancy research.

In general, the view of an initial state of undifferentiation between the infant and the environment (e.g., Mahler, Pine, & Bergman, 1975; Piaget, 1952; Wallon, 1942/1970) needs to be revised in light of evidence of remarkable abilities in newborns for instrumental learning, social attunement, as well as differential responding to self- and non-self-stimulation (DeCasper & Fifer, 1980; Rochat & Hespos, 1997; Walton, Bower, & Bower, 1992). What remains unclear, however, is how various kinds of implicit sense of self might develop to become explicit beyond infancy, when for example infants start explicitly to label and to recognize themselves in mirrors. If we accept Neisser's assertion of an implicit sense of the ecological and interpersonal self that would develop prior to language, questions remain as to how they develop and relate to each other. Do they develop independently? Does one precede the other? Do they need to be integrated for infants eventually to become explicit about themselves, such as through self-recognition in mirrors or starting to label themselves as *persons?*

Different Views on the Origins of Self-knowledge

For some infancy researchers like Fogel (1993, 1995) or Lewis (1999), the implicit sense of self in infancy develops primarily through *relationships with others*. An implicit sense of the interpersonal self is viewed as central to infant psychological development and as having some developmental precedence over others. In the tradition of George Herbert Mead (1934), the emphasis is on an early sense of self molded into the adult state via social interaction (see also Meltzoff & Moore, 1995, regarding early imitation and the origin of self).

Although focusing on the interpersonal world of infants, Stern (1985) proposes that infants in the first two months of their life develop an implicit sense of themselves that is somehow presocial, not yet based on a reciprocation with others *per se*. For Stern, during the first two months of life, infants develop an implicit sense of what he calls the *emergent self*. The emergent self precedes the development of the *core self*, which corresponds to Neisser's interpersonal self (Neisser, 1991, 1995). In Stern's view, during the first two months, infants primarily experience their own behavioral organization in terms of fluctuating states, growing sensorimotor organization, and in terms of learning about the relations between various sensory experiences: simultaneous sounds and sights, smells and touch stimulation, proprioceptive and visual sensations. The sense of an emergent self would correspond to both a sense of the process and of the product of growing intermodal and sensorimotor integration (Stern, 1985, p. 45). As a by-product of early sensorimotor learning and experience, the sense of an emergent self would be primary, developing in relative independence of social interactions.

Between 2 and 6 months, when infants start to reciprocate with people and view others as differentiated entities with distinct histories, Stern proposes that infants then develop the sense of a *core self* that is interpersonal, based on the relationship with others emphasized by Fogel (1993). Once again, in Stern's view, there is a developmental precedence of a sense of self as a functioning entity that feels, acts, and develops, over a sense of self (the core or interpersonal self) that is revealed to infants exclusively in social interactions.

Other infancy researchers emphasize the importance of an implicit sense of the self infants develop by interacting with their environment, without putting a particular emphasis on either physical or social objects (people). Eleanor J. Gibson (1988, 1995) construes self-knowledge within the general context of infants learning about what the physical and social objects afford for action, so-called *affordances* (J. J. Gibson, 1979).

In the process of exploring and detecting affordances, E. J. Gibson suggests that infants learn first about their own *effectivities* as perceiver and actors in a meaningful environment. For example, by detecting mouthable objects, sucking on them and eventually extracting food from them, infants come to grasp their own capacities for perception and action. This is, according to Gibson, a primary sense of self developing from birth, long before children can start to talk about or recognize themselves in mirrors.

In summary, to account for the implicit sense of self infants appear to manifest from the outset of development, infancy researchers distinguish different kinds of preconceptual knowledge pertaining to the self: knowledge infants develop in the physical domain (e.g., the ecological self) and social domain (e.g., the interpersonal self). Different theories are proposed as to how these kinds of selves might relate in development, some emphasizing the primacy of the interpersonal self (e.g., Fogel, 1993; Meltzoff & Moore, 1995), and others considering them as emerging in succession (Stern, 1985; but also Neisser, 1991), or on a more equal footing (E. J. Gibson, 1995). The problem of their integration and the extent to which this integration might contribute to the development of the conceptual self emerging by the second year remains an open question. What research shows, however, is that both perceptual and social factors need to be considered in trying to capture the developmental origins of self-concept. These two factors are reviewed next.

Perceptual Origins of Self-knowledge

The body is a primary object of perceptual exploration in infancy. As infants move and act, they perceive their own body moving and acting, hence detect its own organization, its physical characteristics, as well as its own vitality. As proposed by J. J. Gibson (1979), perceiving and acting always entail co-perceiving oneself, perception and action being inseparable. When, for example, we perceive and act on objects, we situate ourselves in relation to these objects, co-perceiving ourselves as perceivers and actors. In an analogous way, when newborns move about, kick, cry, suck, or systematically bring their hand to the mouth (Butterworth & Hopkins, 1988; Rochat, Blass, & Hoffmeyer, 1988), they pick up perceptual information that *specifies their own body as a unique entity in the environment* (e.g., double-touch information in the case of hand–mouth contacts, Rochat, 1995; see below).

Self-produced action comes with the experience of uniquely contingent and analog perception across modalities. This is an important feature of what infants gain from engaging in self-exploration. This experience specifies the body as differentiated from other objects in the environment. When my hand crosses my visual field, for example, I perceive that it is my hand and not someone else's, because I see it as well as I feel it proprioceptively moving at exactly the same time and by a commensurate amount. The experience of the body entails proprioception with contingent and analog inputs from other sense modalities.

The robust propensity of infants from birth, and even prenatally, to bring their hand in contact with the mouth and face provides a perceptual experience that specifies the body in a unique way. This experience, in addition to proprioception, entails a "double touch," a specific self-experience. When the hand of infants touches their face or mouth, the tactile sensation goes both ways in reference to their own body: the hand feels the face and at the same time, the face feels the hand. Again, this double-touch experience uniquely specifies their own body as opposed to other objects in the environment.

Rochat and Hespos (1997) tested newborn infants within 24 hours of their birth to see whether they would manifest a discrimination between double-touch stimulation specifying themselves, and external (one-way) tactile stimulation specifying non-self objects. For testing, we used the robust rooting response all healthy infants manifest from birth and by which tactile stimulation at the corner of the mouth is followed by the infant's headturn with mouth opening toward the stimulation. Following a simple procedure, we recorded the frequency of rooting in response to either external tactile stimulation, the experimenter stroking the infant's cheek, or in response to tactile self-stimulation when infants spontaneously brought one of their hands in contact with their cheek. We found that newborns tended to manifest rooting responses almost three times more often in response to external compared to self-stimulation. These observations suggest that already at birth, infants pick up the intermodal invariants (single touch or double touch combined with proprioception) that specify self- versus external stimulation, showing evidence of an early sense of their own body, hence an early perceptually based sense of themselves.

The early sense of the body developed by infants from birth does not only pertain to the physical body, but also to the dynamics of their own affectivity. The intermodal experience of the body is inseparable from feelings about their own vitality (Stern, 1985, 1999). Suppose that an infant engages in exploring her own hands by raising and moving them in front of her eyes. Suppose now that in a sudden burst of excitement, she claps them together. Aside from the intermodal perception of joint touch and proprioception, as well as the double-touch experience we discussed above, the infant perceives the dynamic of her own vitality: from calm to being excited, then calm again. This dynamic is perceived both privately and publicly. It is privately experienced because the infant feels from within a state change, from being calm to being excited with specific waxing and waning of tensions. It is publicly experienced because the hands move accordingly in front of the infant's eyes. In a way, the movement of the hands is a choreography of what the infant feels from within. Self-exploratory activity thus provides infants with an opportunity to objectify the feelings of their own vitality via perceived self-produced action of the body (Rochat, 1995).

By at least 3 months of age and as a result of self-produced action and perception, infants manifest an intermodal calibration of their own body. Recent evidence shows that young infants develop a sense of perfect contingency and invariant co-variations across modalities that specify the body as a dynamic entity with particular characteristics. This calibration is necessary not only to provide the perceptual foundations of self-knowledge, but also for infants to use their body in order to act on objects in the environment.

Daniel Stern (1985) reports some striking observations made with "Siamese twins" or physically conjoint twins. These infants were congenitally attached on the ventral surface, facing one another. They shared no organs and were surgically separated at 4 months. Stern and colleagues noticed that often they would suck one another's fingers. A week before separation, Stern and his colleagues conducted a series of tests to assess the extent to which these infants, despite their odd situation of forced binding, differentiated what was part of their own body and what belonged to the attached sibling. In one of the tests, they compared each infant's reactions to the gentle removal from their mouth of either their own fingers they were sucking, or the fingers of their sibling. They found that the twins responded differentially depending whether it was theirs or the other's hand that was removed.

These observations corroborate our own with healthy newborns who showed differential rooting responses to their own hand touching their face compared to the finger of an experimenter (Rochat & Hespos, 1997). In these observations, infants show that they differentiate between two basic categories of perceptual information, one category pertaining to their own body, the other to surrounding entities. This information is intermodal and in most instances involves a sense of self-produced action via proprioception.

If young infants appear capable of perceiving their own body as a differentiated entity, the question is what exactly do they perceive of their own bodies as physical and acting entities. We performed research demonstrating that infants from at least 3 months of age are aware of complex aspects of their own body as a dynamic and organized entity with particular featural characteristics (Morgan & Rochat, 1998; Rochat, 1998; Rochat & Morgan, 1995). We measured 3- to 5-month-old infants' preferential looking to different views of their own body. For example, facing two television screens, infants saw on each of them their own body videotaped from the waist down. Both views were on-line, thus perfectly contingent. When infants moved their legs, they saw them moving simultaneously on either of the screens (see Figure 7.2).

Within this experimental setup, we measured infants' preferential looking for either view. One of the views presented their own legs as they would be specified via direct visual-proprioceptive feedback, for example by bringing them in the field of view while laying supine in their crib. The other view provided an experimentally modified on-line view of their own legs.

In general, what we found is that from 3 months of age, infants tend to look significantly longer at the view of the legs that is unfamiliar, namely that violates the visual-proprioceptive calibration of the body in terms of general movement directionality, relative movement of the limbs, as well as overall leg configuration in relation to the rest of the body (Rochat, 1998). In particular, infants are shown to look significantly longer as well as to move their legs more, while looking at a view of their legs that reverses by 180° the seen and felt directionality of movement, or that reverses the way legs move in relation to each other. In all, this research suggests that by moving and acting, infants from at least 3 months of age manifest an intermodal calibration of their own body, developing an intermodal body schema. This body schema is an implicit, perceptually based "protorepresentation" of the body as specified by the intermodal redundancy accompanying perception and action. The intermodal redundancy specifying the body is experi-

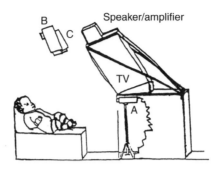

Figure 7.2(a) Apparatus and experimental setup of the infant wearing black and white socks while reclined in front of the large TV monitor projecting an on-line view of the legs from the waist down. Camera A provided a close-up of the infant's face for the analysis of gazing at the display as cameras B and C each provided a particular view of the legs (i.e., ego vs. reversed ego view).

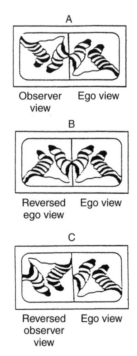

Figure 7.2(b) The two views of their own legs as seen by the infant on the TV in the three experimental conditions studied in Rochat and Morgan (1995): (A) observer view vs. ego view (Experiment 1); (B) reversed ego view vs. ego view (Experiment 2); (C) reversed observer view vs. ego view (Experiment 3).

enced and explored by infants from birth. Considering the rich behavioral repertoire of fetuses 20 weeks and older, it may also be experienced in the confines of pregnancy (e.g., Prechtl, 1984).

In summary, from the earliest age, perception and action specify the body as a differentiated entity among other entities in the environment. Early on, infants appear to calibrate their own body based on intermodal (i.e., perceptual) invariants that specify the sense of their own ecological self: a sense of their *own bodily self* that is differentiated, situated, and acts as an agent in the physical environment (Neisser, 1991; Rochat, 1997). This may form the perceptual origins of what will eventually develop as an explicit or conceptual sense of self by the second year of life.

Social Origins of Self-knowledge

If infants learn about themselves by being actors in the physical world, another major source of self-knowledge comes from social interactions. Not unlike adults, very early on children objectify themselves in others, searching for social approval and learning about themselves as differentiated, unique entities. As adults, we use others to reveal who we are, as a sort of social mirror. Much of how we perceive ourselves is measured against how we think others perceive us. Self-perception is inseparable from our perception of others as *on-lookers of us.* This is what being "self-conscious" means and it is close to impossible to escape the so-called "audience effect." People are undoubtedly the main source of feedback by which we objectify ourselves. This process is also evident from the outset of development.

As mentioned above, the first words of children are mainly oriented toward attracting attention of others to objects, but also mainly to themselves. When children keep calling parents to watch them doing what they view as challenging feats, such as jumping off a diving board or riding their bicycle with no training wheels, they seek confirmation of who they think they are: courageous, outrageous, funny, or smart, aside from attempting to impress an audience. The perception of themselves becomes essentially social. They project and recognize themselves in others. In this process, self- and social knowledge are inseparable. But what about infants, prior to any explicit expression of such process via language? Infancy research points to the fact that from a very early age infants learn about themselves by monitoring others and the way they respond to their own behavior.

The most common way parents interact with their young baby is by reciprocating and *mirroring* their emotions. There is much parental imitation of their infant in early face-to-face interaction. In this process the emotions displayed by infants are fed back to them, amplified, and clearly demarcated with exaggerated gestures and intonations (Gergely & Watson, 1999). This emotional mirroring is certainly a source of self-knowledge for the infant as it provides them with a perceptual scaffolding for the objectification of their own affects: what they feel from within, project to the outside and are externalized as they are reflected back to them by the social partner. In this process, infants are exposed to an explicit, analyzable form of what they feel privately at an implicit level (Rochat, 1995).

As adults, we are strongly compelled to empathize with babies. When for example they start to show signs of distress and start to cry, we typically comfort them by providing physical proximity, stroking their back while adopting a sad voice with lowered brows and inverted U shaped mouth. In doing so, we actually provide infants with an emotional *simulation* of what they are supposed to feel, a simulation of their subjective life.

When infants monitor people's faces and begin to reciprocate in face-to-face interaction, they lay down the foundations of both social and self-awareness. Because of the strong propensity of adults to engage in mirroring and affective attunement, they also learn about themselves being somehow simulated or *reenacted*. From the earliest age, caretakers present infants with a social mirror that reflects back to them their own vitality and affective life, in some sort of a running commentary they are compelled to produce as in the case of sportcasters verbalizing and mimicking actions back to an audience. Aside from the sense of the ecological self infants develop by acting and perceiving the physical environment, this emotional simulation by caretakers is probably also at the origin of explicit *self-consciousness*, clearly manifested by infants once they pass the symbolic gateway marking the end of infancy, referring to themselves verbally and identifying themselves in mirrors.

Prior to the symbolic gateway, the idea of an implicit self-knowledge gained by young infants in their interaction with others is supported by numerous studies demonstrating sophisticated social attunement of the infant from birth, in particular their propensity to pay special attention to faces (see Butterworth, chapter 8 in this volume), and to imitate social partners.

Over the last 20 years, many studies have reported cases of imitative responses in very young infants. In well-controlled laboratory conditions, neonates only a few hours old are shown to reproduce a remarkably wide range of gestural acts modeled by an experimenter, such as tongue protrusion, lip pursing, and head and finger movements (Meltzoff & Moore, 1977, 1995). If such precocious imitative ability has been replicated in various laboratories around the world, the interpretation of the phenomenon continues to cause much controversy. For some "leaner" interpreters of neonatal imitation, it is essentially a fleeting phenomenon, limited to one gesture (i.e., tongue protrusion) and determined by low-level processes such as automatic release mechanisms (Anisfeld, 1991) or rigidly triggered oral exploration (Jones, 1996). On the contrary, for Meltzoff and Moore neonatal imitation is the expression of a much richer ability, the expression of an active cross-modal matching between vision and proprioception (Meltzoff & Moore, 1997). In particular, in the case of facial imitation, the infant sees the model and reproduces motorically a corresponding gesture *without* any possibility of a visual–visual comparison between model and imitative response. Thus, if one accepts the view that infants are actually engaged in an attempt to match their own motoric response to the specific behavior displayed by the adult, neonatal imitation does entail an *active* intermodal matching process of self to others. More importantly, it also entails that infants from birth do not behave in a social vacuum, but rather are actively linking their own behavior to the behavior of others.

Other research demonstrates that the behavioral matching effort displayed by young infants is not merely reduced to the reproduction of body part movements in another person, but also to an *affective* matching of others. Social mirroring appears to be a two-way phenomenon from the very beginning of life. If caretakers have the proclivity to reproduce infants' actions and affects in scaffolding face-to-face interactions, infants from birth are also inclined to do the same. Field, Woodson, Greenberg, & Cohen (1982) observed that newborn infants tend to reproduce facial expressions of happiness, sadness, or surprise. In their study newborns were observed while facing the experimenter, who displayed in successive episodes such well-contrasted emotions. They showed a significant widening of the lips when attending to the happy expression of the experimenter, increased protrusion of lower lips during the sad expression episode, and increased opening of the eyes and mouth during the surprise episode. Via early imitation of facial expressions, infants do not only match the surface characteristics of others with their own, but also others' feelings, in particular their dispositional characteristics in relation to their own (happy, sad, or surprised). Early facial imitation allows infants from birth to establish intersubjectivity with others and specify their own dispositional (affective) qualities by matching those of others.

The early propensity to imitate is probably a major mechanism by which infants start objectifying their own actions and affective dispositions. In matching the behavior of others, they also simulate themselves. Infants from birth do acquire knowledge about themselves via their inclination to reproduce the action and emotion of others.

The combination of adults' systematic scaffolding of face-to-face exchanges and young infants' early proclivity to imitate others is an important aspect of what constitutes the developmental origins of self-knowledge. In the context of protoconversations and play games typically initiated by caretakers (e.g., peek-a-boo games, see below), infants specify themselves as a function of how others respond to them, in particular how contingent and attuned they are to their *own* behavior (Trevarthen, 1979).

By imitating each other, the infant–adult pair engages primarily in reciprocating affects and feelings. Such reciprocation is at the origin of intersubjectivity, itself foundation of early social cognition and, I propose, an important source of implicit self-knowledge, in particular of the self as a *communicative agent* (the interpersonal self according to Neisser, 1991). Via mutual imitation adults and infants can probe the degree to which they communicate with one another.

Evidence of a developing interpersonal self in early infancy is now numerous. By the second month, when starting to reciprocate by smiling and engaging in long bouts of gazing toward others (Wolff, 1987), infants are shown to become increasingly sensitive to specific timing in social interaction and develop expectations regarding the behavior of others in relation to the self (Rochat & Striano, 1999a). Such timing indexes the quality of communicative flow, and in particular the level of relative matching between their own dispositions and those displayed by the social partner. The social expectations developing by the second month are inseparable from the developing sense of the interpersonal self or social self of infants.

As an illustration, we recently explored the sensitivity of 2- to 6-month-old infants to the relative structure of the interactive frame offered by an adult stranger (Rochat et al., 1999). The rationale for this study was to capture how infants from 2 months on refine their ability to detect regularities in ongoing social interaction and develop specific expectations based on a sensitivity to the structure of the interaction. We hypothesized that between 2 and 6 months infants develop specific expectations in the dyadic context based on cues specifying the *quality* of response of a social partner to their own behavior, in other words, *the relative attunement of the social partner to the self*.

We videotaped 2-, 4-, and 6-month-old infants interacting with a female stranger in a face-to-face situation that did not include any touching. Aside from baseline periods, in two different experimental conditions, the experimenter introduced the infant to a peek-a-boo routine that was either structured or unstructured. In the structured condition, the peek-a-boo routine was strictly organized into three phases articulating a total of eight subroutines. In the unstructured condition, the experimenter was wearing an earpiece connected to a tape recorder playing instructions of subroutines to be performed in a random, disorganized way. In other words, in the unstructured condition, the experimenter engaged in a *scrambled* peek-a-boo game, with unrelated subroutines that did not coalesce to form a compelling, socially attuned script.

The scoring of infants' smiling and gazing at the experimenter revealed that 2-month-olds looked toward the experimenter and smiled equally in both the structured and unstructured peek-a-boo conditions. In contrast, 4- and 6-month-olds looked significantly more toward the experimenter and smiled markedly less in the unstructured compared to the structured peek-a-boo condition.

In all, these results illustrate how from a diffuse sense of others' attunement to the self, by 4 months infants begin to monitor social partners in the way they relate to them. Based on such monitoring, infants develop an implicit sense of an interpersonal or social self, expecting not only that others pay attention and smile at them, but also that they relate to them in ways that are attuned or contingent with their own behavior (Murray & Trevarthen, 1985; Stern, 1985).

Origins of Self-recognition

From an implicit sense of their own physical, behaving body and an implicit sense of themselves as social entities, how do infants develop an *explicit sense of themselves* as indexed by mirror self-recognition? What are the origins of the conceptual self manifested by children when they start to speak and pass the symbolic threshold that separates infancy from childhood? In this last section, we can speculate that mirror self-recognition is one of the first signs of explicit self-concept that originates from the fusion of implicit self-knowledge developed in the physical and social domains over the first months of life. The rationale for such discussion is that, although mirror self-recognition is limited to one particular experience (i.e., the specular or mirror image of the self), it informs us about what it takes for infants to become explicit about themselves, hence to have a conceptual sense of self as "Me" in addition to the existential sense of self as "I."

Three-month-old infants placed in front of mirrors spend much time exploring their reflection, staring at themselves in the eyes and moving their limbs often with smiles and cooing (Amsterdam, 1972). They are attracted by their specular image but that does not mean that they yet *recognize* themselves in it. They are using the opportunity offered by the mirror to experience and explore the perfect contingency and spatial calibration between proprioception and vision. This opportunity is unique and possibly particularly attractive to infants because it also offers the visual-proprioceptive experience of larger portions of the body, much larger than the hands and feet perceivable directly in certain postures. As adults, we also use the optical affordance of mirrors to work on our appearance, except that the behavior of fixing hair and making up is an explicit expression that we know it is us in the mirror.

Clearly, the behavior of young infants in front of mirrors does not imply the same level of awareness of either adults applying lipstick or toddlers showing embarrassment and manual contact with the face because they discover some rouge has surreptitiously stained their nose, as in the classic rouge task already mentioned at the beginning of this chapter (Gallup, 1982; Lewis & Brooks-Gunn, 1979).

Bahrick, Moss, & Fadil (1996) reported that infants as young as 3 months do show some discrimination between viewing a frontal prerecorded view of themselves or viewing an analogous view of another infant wearing the same bib. Infants were carefully matched for age and gender. In general, infants are reported to spend significantly more time looking at the image of the other child compared to their own. The question is whether this apparent visual discrimination actually means that they *re-cognize* themselves on the TV. In other words, does this discrimination entail some rudiments of self-concept? It is certainly not a direct demonstration of self-concept. This discrimination, although remarkable, probably means that from an early age, infants are familiarized with their own featural (i.e., facial) characteristics and vitality based on previous mirror experiences. In the context of the Bahrick et al. experiment, the feature characteristics of the other child are newer, therefore more interesting to the infant, so explaining their visual preference. The observations reported by Bahrick and her collaborators are no evidence that infants as young as 3 months "know" it is them on the TV.

So, from the early sensitivity to intermodal contingency (Amsterdam, 1972), the early intermodal calibration of the body (Rochat, 1998), and early perceptual learning (Bahrick et al., 1996), how do infants develop the ability to eventually recognize and identify themselves in mirrors?

First, it should be pointed out that, although telling something about self-recognition, the mirror test should be considered with caution to account for the origins of self-concept. Mirrors are unusual objects in the environment, carrying with them the experience of a fundamental paradox: the "*self–other paradox.*" As mentioned above, when you look at your own mirror reflection, you perceive aspects of your body that you cannot experience directly, in particular a full view of your face. Considering that eye contact in social exchanges is an important determinant of social interaction from the outset of development, the specular image of a full face with eyes gazing toward the self specifies what is normally experienced with others, not in relation to the self. Therefore, self-recognition in a mirror requires the *suspension* of the normal social experience of others facing you with eye contacts. Mirror reflection of the self is paradoxical in the sense that what is seen in the mirror is the self as another person: it is you in what is normally perceived of another person. As the self in disguise of the other, the specular image reflects what can be called the fundamental *you but not you,* or *self–other paradox.* On one hand, the specular image reflects the self via perfect contingency and spatial analog of visual-proprioceptive information (i.e., the ecological self). On the other hand, it does reflect another (non-self) person as specified by past experience (en-face view with potential eye contact).

The self reflected by mirrors does not match the embodied self infants experience directly from birth, namely, the self situated in the body. Rather, it reflects back to the infant the implicit sense of an *interpersonal or social self* (i.e., themselves interacting with what appears to be someone else).

To some extent, inspecting oneself in a mirror and recognizing that it is "Me" out there on this reflecting surface is very much an "out of the body experience." What mirror self-recognition and other video and picture self-recognition tasks measure is primarily the ability of individuals to suspend what they normally experience of themselves, step back and literally reflect on the new, out of the body aspects the mirror reveals of themselves. Mirror images are indeed physical reflections of the body on a polished surface that call for mental reflection to be *re-cognized*, hence *conceptualized*. This conceptualization requires the suspension of perceptual experiences typically specifying self *or* others, not self as others.

Observations made by anthropologists introducing reflecting devices to adult individuals who presumably never experienced their own mirror reflection are particularly telling of the fundamental paradox attached to the experience of self in mirrors. Edmund Carpenter (1975) introduced mirrors to members of an isolated tribe (the Biami) living in the Papuan plateau where neither slate or metallic surfaces exist, and where rivers are murky, not providing clear reflections. Recording the initial reaction of adults confronted for the very first time with a large mirror reflection of themselves, Carpenter reports:

> They were paralyzed: after their first startled response – covering their mouths and ducking their heads – they stood transfixed, staring at their images, only their stomach muscles betraying great tension. Like Narcissus, they were left numb, totally fascinated by their own reflections: indeed, the myth of Narcissus may refer to this phenomenon. (Carpenter, 1975, pp. 452–453)

We might add that Narcissus, aside from falling in love with himself, probably got first fascinated with the existential experience of the "self–other" paradox that reflecting surfaces offer.

Despite the intrinsic paradox attached to mirrors, mirror self-recognition tests remain a valid instrument to assess self-knowledge at a conceptual and re-cognitory level. It is particularly valid to assess the ability of children to *objectify* themselves and eventually get over the "self–other" paradox. This requires stepping back and reflectiveness in the sense of mental reflection, beyond direct perception and action.

There are two questions that are of interest from a developmental perspective. The first is, when do infants start to become contemplative in the exploration of themselves, not merely experiencing their embodied self via direct perception and action? The second is, what might be the process enabling infants to adopt a contemplative, reflective stance when exploring themselves? These are important "how" and "why" questions regarding the origins of self-concept. These questions are still wide open for speculation. Nevertheless, in light of recent progress in infancy research, it is possible to speculate (i.e., "reflect") on the developmental origins of self-recognition, hence self-concept.

Conclusion: Developing Objectification of the Self in Infancy

We have seen that infants appear to be born with an ability to pick up perceptual information that specifies themselves as differentiated from other physical and social entities in the environment. The development of self-knowledge does not start from an initial state of confusion. Infants are born with the perceptual means to discriminate themselves from other objects and people. Early on, they express an implicit sense of themselves as embodied, differentiated, situated, and effective in the physical and social environment. This sense of self corresponds to the ecological and interpersonal selves of infants described by Neisser (1991, 1995).

These implicit kinds of selves are determined by direct perception and action, not mental reflection or conception. The early propensity of infants to engage in self-exploration when, for example, watching their own legs moving on a TV screen (Rochat, 1998) does not entail any awareness that it is their own legs on the screen. If, as some studies show, infants prefer to look at the view displaying the legs of another baby rather than an on-line view of their own (see, for example, Bahrick & Watson, 1985; Schmuckler, 1995), it is because the visual perception of these legs does not correspond to the proprioceptive perception of their own legs moving. It is not because they recognize that it is another infant kicking on the TV. For infants to recognize that it is their own legs or, on the contrary, that they are the legs of someone else, it would take an additional reflective step, namely, the step toward an *objectification of the self.* Such a process would entail the ability to integrate the sense of the embodied (ecological) self, and the representation of the disembodied "Me" projected on the TV screen.

The question, of course, is how such an integration might come about. To conclude, I will propose that an important determinant of this development might be young infants' propensity to explore their own actions and their consequences via repetition or so-called "circular reactions" (Baldwin, 1884/1925; Piaget, 1952).

By the second month, infants become inquisitive and start reciprocating with others as indexed by the emergence of smiling and eye contact (Wolff, 1987; Rochat & Striano, 1999a). They also become playful in relation to themselves. They start to spend a lot of time self-entertaining, exploring their own body by repeating visually controlled actions either on themselves or on objects. They grab their hands and feet, bringing them in the field of view for long bouts of inspection. They seize any opportunity to reproduce actions that are accompanied by interesting consequences. In addition to perceiving and acting in the context of highly organized action systems (e.g., sucking, rooting, tracking), 2-month-olds compared to newborns express behavioral novelty by engaging in the *contemplation of their own effectivity* based on a sense of the own body (i.e., proprioception) that can be linked to perceived events: the auditory event of self-activating the vocal system, the proprioceptive-visual event of moving a hand in the visual field, of kicking a mobile (Rochat & Striano, 1999b).

In this new process, infants manifest much repetition of actions for the apparent sake of exploring how they feel in their execution and how they are linked to particular perceptual consequences.

This active contemplation of self-produced perceptual consequences (e.g., self-produced sounds or object motion) is probably an important factor in the progressive objectification of the self. Infants need to break away from the direct perception of the embodied self as specified by intermodal invariants and the contingency of others' behavior in order to start *re-presenting* or conceptualizing themselves as object of reflection. That does not mean that the implicit sense of the embodied ecological and social self vanish to be replaced by a conceptual self. Rather, the sense of the ecological and social self, bearing no traces of anything that looks like conscious or intentional processes, is complemented with a new stance on self-perception that allows for explicit re-presentation, as evidenced by mirror self-recognition.

There is certainly an important development, yet largely unspecified, occurring from the time infants seem to show the first signs of breaking away from the direct perception of the embodied self, to explicit self-recognition. The original process that might trigger this development is the propensity of infants by 2 months to engage and start paying particular attention to the result of their own playful and repetitive actions. With such engagement, they start to probe their own vitality, systematically reproducing certain effects, and discovering themselves as a dynamic system with means to achieve goals (Baldwin, 1884/1925). This process determines a new sense of self as *intentional* or planful, in parallel to the direct sense of the embodied self (ecological self) and social self they develop early on in their interaction with objects and people. By intentional (a semantically loaded term), what is meant here is a sense of self as a planning entity that can anticipate future events and relate to past ones, whether physical or social. It is a sense of self which, in contrast to the embodied ecological and interpersonal selves, is not linked to the immediacy or "here and now" aspect of direct perception and action in physical or social contexts. It is actually a sense of self that cuts across the ecological and interpersonal self, transcending them and resting on their integration as suggested by mirror self-recognition.

In conclusion, at the origin of an explicit sense of self, there might be the early ability to contemplate and repeat actions in order to explore their consequences, beyond the immediate, embodied sense of self infants experience from birth in their interaction with physical objects and people. This process, I propose, contributes to an early objectification of the self which eventually develops into an explicit self-concept by the middle of the second year. Aside from this general process, questions remain regarding the factors that lead infants toward self-conceptualization and what the actual content of self-concept is when emerging by the second year of life.

Related Issues

Some theories emphasize the role of social frames from which infants develop a sense of self that is primarily interpersonal (Fogel, 1993; Kaye, 1982). Other theories emphasize the role of active interaction between infants and their environment, whether physical or social (Baldwin, 1884/1925; Piaget, 1952, 1954). Furthermore, some theorists suggest that infants develop first a sense of the core (intermodal) self that eventually grows into an interpersonal and conceptual self (Stern, 1985). On the contrary, other theories state that the concept of self is inseparable from social relationships and the relational narratives infants create in interaction with people (Fogel, 1995).

The debate is still very much open and it is only with more empirical data that we will make progress in approximating what counts in the early development of self-concept, namely, the development of the self recognized in a mirror or objectified in the action on physical objects, but also the self that is conceptualized and develops in relation to others. The question of the origins of self-concept is indeed inseparable from issues regarding the origins of physical knowledge, as well as the origins of social knowledge (Rochat, 1999), emotional development (Lewis, 1992), and theories of mind (Hala, 1997).

Further Reading

Fogel, A. (1993). *Developing through relationships: Origins of communication, self and culture.* Hemel Hempstead: Harvester Press. A theoretical view on the essentially social nature of self-knowledge, developing from the outset in relation to others.

Lewis, M. (1992). *Shame: The exposed self.* New York: The Free Press. An account of self-development in infancy and early chidhood as it relates to emotional development, in particular the emergence by the second year of life of secondary (self-conscious) emotions such as embarrassment, guilt, and shame.

Rochat, P. (Ed.). (1995). *The self in infancy: Theory and research.* Amsterdam: North-Holland/Elsevier. An edited volume assembling chapters by major infancy researchers and theorists on the issue of developing self-knowledge in the first year of life.

Rochat, P. (Ed.). (1999). *Early social cognition: Understanding others in the first months of life.* Mahwah, NJ: Lawrence Erlbaum Associates. An edited volume assembling chapters on the issue of understanding others, but also indirectly on the issue of developing an understanding of the self in interaction with others during the first year of life.

References

Amsterdam, B. (1972). Mirror self-image reactions before age two. *Developmental Psycholobiology, 5,* 297–305.

Anisfeld, M. (1991). Neonatal imitation. *Developmental Review, 11,* 60–97.

Bahrick, L., Moss, L., & Fadil, C. (1996). Development of visual self-recognition in infancy. *Ecological Psychology, 8*(3), 189–208.

Bahrick, L. E., & Watson, J. S. (1985). Detection of intermodal proprioceptive-visual contingency as a potential basis of self-perception in infancy. *Developmental Psychology, 21*(6), 963–973.

Baldwin, J. M. (1925). *Mental development of the child and the race: Methods and processes.* London: Macmillan. (Original work published 1884)

Bates, E. (1990). Language about me and you: Pronominal reference and the emerging concept of self. In D. Cicchetti & M. Beeghly (Eds.), *The self in transition: Infancy to childhood* (pp. 165–182). Chicago: University of Chicago Press.

Bertenthal, B. I., & Rose, J. L. (1995). Two modes of perceiving the self. In P. Rochat (Ed.), *The self in infancy: Theory and research* (pp. 303–326). Amsterdam: North-Holland/Elsevier.

Butterworth, G. E. (1992). Origins of self-perception in infancy. *Psychological Inquiry, 3*(2), 103–111.

Butterworth, G. E. (1995). The self as an object of consciousness in infancy. In P. Rochat (Ed.), *The self in infancy: Theory and research* (pp. 35–52). Amsterdam: North-Holland/Elsevier.

Butterworth, G., & Hopkins, B. (1988). Hand–mouth coordination in the new-born baby. *British Journal of Developmental Psychology, 6,* 303–314.

Carpenter, E. (1975). The tribal terror of self-awareness. In P. Hikins (Ed.), *Principles of visual anthropology* (pp. 56–78). The Hague: Mouton.

Case, R. (1991). Stages in the development of the young child's first sense of self. *Developmental Review, 11,* 210–230.

DeCasper, A. J., & Fifer, W. P. (1980). Of human bonding: Newborns prefer their mother's voices. *Science, 208,* 1174–1176.

Field, T. M., Woodson, R., Greenberg, R., & Cohen, D. (1982). Discrimination and imitation of facial expressions by neonates. *Science, 218,* 179–181.

Fogel, A. (1993). *Developing through relationships: Origins of communication, self and culture.* Hemel Hempstead: Harvester Press.

Fogel, A. (1995). Relational narratives of the prelinguistic self. In P. Rochat (Ed.), *The self in infancy: Theory and research* (pp. 117–140). Amsterdam: North-Holland/Elsevier.

Gallup, G. G. (1982). Self-awareness and the emergence of mind in primates. *American Journal of Primatology, 2,* 237–248.

Gergely, G., & Watson, J. S. (1999). Early social-emotional development: Contingency perception and the social-biofeedback model. In P. Rochat (Ed.), *Early social cognition: Understanding others in the first months of life* (pp. 101–136). Mahwah, NJ: Lawrence Erlbaum Associates.

Gibson, E. J. (1988). Exploratory behavior in the development of perceiving, acting, and the acquiring of knowledge. *Annual Review of Psychology, 39,* 1–41.

Gibson, E. J. (1995). Are we automata? In P. Rochat (Ed.), *The self in infancy: Theory and research* (pp. 3–16). Amsterdam: North-Holland/Elsevier.

Gibson, J. J. (1979). *The ecological approach to visual perception.* Boston: Houghton Mifflin.

Hala, S. (Ed.). (1997). *The development of social cognition.* Hove: Psychology Press.

James, W. (1890). *The principles of psychology.* Henry Holt & Co.

Jones, S. (1996). Imitation or exploration? Young infants' matching of adults' oral gestures. *Child Development, 67,* 1952–1969.

Jouen, F., & Gapenne, O. (1995). Interactions between the vestibular and visual systems in the neonate. In P. Rochat (Ed.), *The self in infancy: Theory and research* (pp. 277–302). Amsterdam: North-Holland/Elsevier.

Kalnins, I. V., & Bruner, J. S. (1973). The coordination of visual observation and instrumental behavior in early infancy. *Perception, 2,* 307–314.

Kaye, K. (1982). *The mental and social life of babies.* Chicago: Chicago University Press.

Kellman, P. J., Gleitman, H., & Spelke, E. S. (1987). Object and observer motion in the perception of objects by infants. *Journal of Experimental Psychology: Human Perception and Performance, 13,* 586–593.

Lewis, M. (1992). *Shame: The exposed self.* New York: The Free Press.

Lewis, M. (1995). Aspects of the self: From systems to ideas. In P. Rochat (Ed.), *The self in infancy: Theory and research* (pp. 95–116). Amsterdam: North-Holland/Elsevier.

Lewis, M. (1999). Social cognition and the self. In P. Rochat (Ed.), *Early social cognition: Understanding others in the first months of life* (pp. 81–100). Mahwah, NJ: Lawrence Erlbaum Associates.

Lewis, M., & Brooks-Gunn, J. (1979). *Social cognition and the acquisition of self.* New York: Plenum Press.

Mahler, M. S., Pine, F., & Bergman, A. (1975). *The psychological birth of the human infant: Symbiosis and individuation.* New York: Basic Books.

Mead, G. H. (1934). *Mind, self and society.* Chicago: University of Chicago Press.

Meltzoff, A. N., & Moore, M. K. (1977). Imitation of facial and manual gestures by human neonates. *Science, 198,* 75–78.

Meltzoff, A. N., & Moore, M. K. (1994). Imitation, memory, and the representation of persons. *Infant Behavior and Development, 17,* 83–99.

Meltzoff, A. N., & Moore, M. K. (1995). A theory of the role of imitation in the emergence of self. In P. Rochat (Ed.), *The self in infancy: Theory and research* (pp. 73–94). Amsterdam: North-Holland/Elsevier.

Meltzoff, A. N., & Moore, M. K. (1997). Explaining facial imitation: A theoretical model. *Early Development and Parenting, 6,* 3–4, 179–192.

Morgan, R., & Rochat, P. (1998). Two functional orientations of self-exploration in infancy. *British Journal of Developmental Psychology, 16,* 139–154.

Muir, D. W., & Hains, S. M. (1993). Infant sensitivity to perturbations in adult facial, vocal, tactile, and contingent stimulation during face-to-face interactions. In B. de Boysson-Bardies (Ed.), *Developmental neurocognition: Speech and face processing in the first year of life* (pp. 171–183). Amsterdam: Elsevier.

Murray, L., & Trevarthen, C. (1985). Emotional regulation of interactions between two-month-olds and their mothers. In T. M. Field & N. A. Fox (Eds.), *Social perception in infants* (pp. 177–197). Norwood, NJ: Ablex.

Neisser, U. (1991). Two perceptually given aspects of the self and their development. *Developmental Review, 11,* 197–209.

Neisser, U. (1995). Criteria for an ecological self. In P. Rochat (Ed.), *The self in infancy: Theory and research* (pp. 17–34). Amsterdam: North-Holland/Elsevier.

Piaget, J. (1952). *The origins of intelligence in children.* New York: International Universities Press.

Piaget, J. (1954). *The child's construction of reality.* New York: International Universities Press.

Povinelli, D. J. (1993). Reconstructing the evolution of mind. *American Psychologist, 48,* 493–509.

Prechtl, H. F. R. (Ed.). (1984). *Continuity of neural functions from prenatal to postnatal life.* Oxford: Blackwell.

Rochat, P. (1995). Early objectification of the self. In P. Rochat (Ed.), *The self in infancy: Theory and research* (pp. 53–71). Amsterdam: North-Holland/Elsevier.

Rochat, P. (1997). Early development of the ecological self. In C. Dent-Read & P. Zukow-Goldring (Eds.), *Evolving explanations of development* (pp. 91–122). Washington, DC: American Psychological Association.

Rochat, P. (1998). Self-perception and action in infancy. *Experimental Brain Research, 123,* 102–109.

Rochat, P. (Ed.). (1999). *Early social cognition: Understanding others in the first months of life.* Mahwah, NJ: Lawrence Erlbaum Associates.

Rochat, P., Blass, E. M., & Hoffmeyer, L. B. (1988). Oropharyngeal control of hand–mouth coordination in newborn infants. *Developmental Psychology, 24,* 459–463.

Rochat, P., & Hespos, S. J. (1997). Differential rooting response by neonates: Evidence for an early sense of self. *Early Development and Parenting, 6*(2), 150.1–8.

Rochat, P., & Morgan, R. (1995). Spatial determinants in the perception of self-produced leg movements by 3–5 month old infants. *Developmental Psychology, 31,* 626–636.

Rochat, P., Neisser, U., & Marian, V. (1998). Are young infants sensitive to interpersonal contingency? *Infant Behavior and Development, 21*(2), 355–366.

Rochat, P., Querido, J. G., & Striano, T. (1999). Emerging sensitivity to the timing and structure of protoconversation in early infancy. *Developmental Psychology, 35*(4), 950–957.

Rochat, P., & Striano, T. (1999a). Social cognitive development in the first year. In P. Rochat (Ed.), *Early social cognition: Understanding others in the first months of life* (pp. 3–34). Mahwah, NJ: Lawrence Erlbaum Associates.

Rochat, P., & Striano, T. (1999b). Emerging self-exploration by 2-month-olds. *Developmental Science, 2,* 206–218.

Schmuckler, M. A. (1995). Self-knowledge of body position: Integration of perceptual and action system information. In P. Rochat (Ed.), *The self in infancy: Theory and research* (pp. 221–242). Amsterdam: North-Holland/Elsevier.

Stern, D. (1985). *The interpersonal world of the infant.* New York: Basic Books.

Stern, D. (1999). Vitality contours: The temporal contour of feelings as a basic unit for constructing the infant's social experience. In P. Rochat (Ed.), *Early social cognition: Understanding others in the first months of life* (pp. 67–80). Mahwah, NJ: Lawrence Erlbaum Associates.

Toda, S., & Fogel, A. (1993). Infant response to the still-face situation at 3 and 6 months. *Developmental Psychology, 29,* 532–538.

Tomasello, M. (1995). Joint attention as social cognition. In C. Moore & P. Dunham (Eds.), *Joint attention: Its origins and role in development* (pp. 103–130). Hillsdale, NJ: Erlbaum.

Tomasello, M., & Akhtar, N. (1995). Two-year-olds use pragmatic use to differentiate reference to objects and actions. *Cognitive Development, 10,* 201–224.

Tomasello, M., & Call, J. (1997). *Primate cognition.* New York: Oxford University Press.

Trevarthen, C. (1979). Communication and cooperation in early infancy: A description of primary intersubjectivity. In M. M. Bullowa (Ed.), *Before speech: The beginning of interpersonal communication* (pp. 321–347). New York: Cambridge University Press.

Tronick, E. Z., Als, H., Adamson, L., Wise, S., & Brazelton, T. B. (1978). The infant's response to entrapment between contradictory messages in face-to-face interaction. *Journal of the American Academy of Child Psychiatry, 17,* 1–13.

Wallon, H. (1970). *De l'acte à la pensée: Essai de psychologie comparée.* Paris: Collection Champs Flammarion. (Original work published 1942)

Walton, G. E., Bower, N. J. A., & Bower, T. G. R. (1992). Recognition of familiar faces by newborns. *Infant Behavior and Development, 15,* 265–269.

Wolff, P. (1987). *The development of behavioral states and the expression of emotions in early infancy.* Chicago: University of Chicago Press.

Chapter Eight

Joint Visual Attention in Infancy

George Butterworth[†]

Introduction: Defining Joint Visual Attention

It is relatively easy to understand what is entailed in joint visual attention by defining it operationally as "looking where someone else is looking." Such a definition has the advantage that it is straightforward to establish whether and when babies can locate objects on the basis of a change in the direction of gaze of their partner. Put slightly more subtly, joint visual attention (henceforth JVA) may be defined as following the direction of attention of another person to the object of their attention (Emery, Lorincz, Perret, Oram, & Baker, 1997). As Bruner (1995) points out, however, there is much more to JVA than the mere coincidence of separate lines of gaze. Joint attention in infancy forms a bedrock for shared social realities, a precondition for the acquisition and use of language, and, in its deepest sense, for the formation and maintenance of culture: it also depends on sharing the focus, context, and presuppositions about objects that guide attention. For attention to be joint, separate individuals may have common knowledge of the focus of each other's attention and the focus of attention of one partner may be regulated by that of the other person. In some cases, the orienting behavior of one partner may have the effect of redirecting the focal attention of the other partner, to bring into the foreground what was

I am grateful to the Economic and Social Research Council of Great Britain, who funded many of my own studies reviewed here. I should like to acknowledge the generous assistance of Alan Fogel in helping me trace the antecedents of pointing. I have had helpful discussions with Shoji Itakura, David Leavens, Kim Bard, Daniel Povinelli, Michael Tomasello, Tetsuro Matsuzawa, and Mark Krause in introducing me to the flourishing world of research on chimpanzee joint attention. Thanks also to the Japanese Society for the Promotion of Science for a research fellowship held while this chapter was written, and to the University of Sussex for sabbatical leave.
[†] George Butterworth died in February 2000, shortly after completing this chapter. The chapter was revised by his wife, Margaret Harris.

previously in the background of awareness (Campbell, 2000). Joint attention emerges when both participants engage focally with the same object.

Adamson and MacArthur (1995) list the constituent components for episodes of joint attention in infancy as: the developing infant, the caregiver, objects explicitly present in the immediate vicinity and the symbolic elements, implicitly present within culturally conventional codes of speech. The order in which these various components of joint attention first emerge in development has been the subject of some controversy, not least because the very idea that infants can share points of view with adults was not accepted in traditional theories that presupposed infant egocentrism (e.g., Piaget, 1954). Clearly, one would not wish to ascribe a capacity for shared attention to the infant if sharing depends solely on the adult monitoring the focus of the infant's gaze. Any sharing in such a circumstance would be entirely one-sided and not mutual.

The beginning of a more fully articulated definition of JVA rests on the idea that shared attention depends on deixis: a word derived from the Greek *deiknunai* meaning "to show" (Collins Softback English dictionary, 1991). In deictic gaze and in deictic gestures, such as pointing, there is reciprocity between the participants based on the complementarity of their separate perspectives. One member in the interaction takes the change of gaze, or the direction of the pointing hand, as a signal which "shows" the location of something of mutual interest. Showing, however, admits of various degrees of precision, ranging from drawing attention to whole scenes to individuating a particular object or part of an object. Different cues for joint attention vary in their effectiveness, both at different times in development, between species and in their precision of reference. The precision with which a referent is singled out in episodes of JVA is important because it relates to the question of ambiguity of reference, that is, how we can know precisely what someone is referring to.

The deictic definition of joint attention, which includes mutuality as a defining condition, may be teased apart even further. The earliest form of reciprocity may refer to shared experiences which do not actually involve inanimate objects as third parties. Infant and adult are mutually attentive in face-to-face interaction and each is the object of the other's attention. Trevarthen (1979) described such basic mutuality as "primary intersubjectivity," which he defines as a capacity for perceiving others as intentional agents with feelings. Primary intersubjectivity is especially evident in the emotional attunement of mother and her 3-month infant in dyadic interaction. The infant looks attentively at the mother's face, reacts with smiles, makes lip and tongue movements resembling speech and gestures with the hands in a finely attuned, rhythmic, and reciprocal turn-taking (see also Trevarthen, 1993). Mutual gaze and gaze avoidance play an important part in regulating these early interactions, which are especially evident in the first 3 months, before babies become engrossed with handling physical objects.

Triangular interpersonal relations, as for example between mother, father, and the 3-month infant, are of particular interest. Fivaz-Depeursinge and Corboz-Warnery (1999) described such triangular sharing of attention in 3-month-olds. While the baby is interacting actively with one parent, she may nevertheless orient frequently to the other parent, not only looking but also smiling, transferring affect from one parent to the other as if intent on maintaining the experience of three people together. The authors suggest that such "social triangulation" may be a developmental precursor of the triadic referential

Table 8.1 Phases in the development of joint attention during human infancy

Developmental phase	Age of onset
Shared attentiveness (Primary intersubjectivity)	From birth
Interpersonal engagement	6–8 weeks
Triangular relations	
Fragile triadic JVA	3–4 months
Object involvement	5–6 months
Robust triadic JVA (Secondary intersubjectivity)	9–15 months
Canonical pointing	11 months
Emergence of symbols	18 months

Source: Adapted from Adamson & MacArthur (1995)

relations that incorporate inanimate objects and which are typically observed later in the first year. Stern (1999) has described the experience of feelings in realtime by young infants as being modulated by "vitality contours." Vitality contours are a reflection of the manner in which actions are carried out; they are captured by such terms as surging, fading away, fleeting, explosive, or tentative which describe the dynamic flow of action and interaction. Of particular relevance to triangular relations is the way in which vitality contours give rise to attunement of affect, in which the parents amodally match the vitality contour of the baby's action, as a message indicating that they have shared the emotional experience (e.g., of joy or sorrow). Later in development, vitality contours carry information in the context of social referencing, as the baby seeks reassurance about how to act and feel with strange, perhaps frightening objects (Campos et al., 1983).

Incorporating an external referent is evidence for a developmental change toward communication around a topic – what Trevarthen (1979) calls "secondary intersubjectivity" – and this marks an important progression in the infant's capacity for JVA. However, we should not forget that this progression builds upon earlier aspects of mutuality, shared attention and shared emotions.

The scope of contemporary studies of JVA has in recent years been extended to take into account comparative evidence from monkeys and apes (Itakura, 1996; Povinelli & Eddy, 1996a,b,c). The way in which jointly shared attention maps into language acquisition in toddlers has also been studied (Baldwin, 1993; Bloom, 2000). Links with developmental psychopathology have also been suggested, such that deficits in JVA may be among the primary causes of childhood autism (Baron-Cohen, Leslie, & Frith, 1985).

Table 8.1 helps to bring some order to the contemporary evidence in this complex field. It is a modified version of a table by Adamson and MacArthur (1995), which describes phases in the development of joint attention. Put very simply, Adamson and MacArthur (1995) suggest that, in the first 9 months, it is mainly mothers who adjust their gaze to the interests of the infant rather than vice versa. From 9 months onward the infant initiates more and the dyadic interaction becomes capable of incorporating "third-party" objects, with each participant contributing to the sharing of attention. The phases before and after 9 months have been respectively characterized as "supported" and "coordinated" JVA (Bakeman & Adamson, 1984). From about 13 months the conventional codes of the culture, including language, begin to emerge within episodes of joint engagement. This broad framework offers a useful timetable for the emergence of robust forms of JVA and for its potential links with language. However, recent research suggests that coordinated JVA, in which the baby follows the adult's change of gaze, can be observed long before the 9-month watershed if the testing conditions are right. Adamson and MacArthur's taxonomy needs to be modified to allow a capacity for "fragile" JVA at least as early as 3 months and an early capacity for triangular relations. Issues about the origins of JVA are important because they help to determine whether the capacity is acquired through social interaction (e.g., Vygotsky, 1962) or operant conditioning (e.g., Corkum & Moore, 1995) or whether it is itself constitutive of social experience and social learning as Bruner (1995) maintains.

The Phylogeny of Joint Visual Attention

Coordinated visual attention is widespread in the animal kingdom. It is not a specifically human behavior and has been observed among birds (Ristau, 1991), monkeys, and apes (Itakura & Tanaka, 1998). However, a variety of mechanisms might explain visual co-orientation in animals and it is not necessarily the case that complex cognitive abilities involving mental state attribution are implicated. For example, it is sufficient for one monkey simply to be in the proximity of food to attract another monkey to that place, an effect known as local enhancement, without any more specifically localised visual signal serving as a cue. It is only recently that the gaze cues (defined as coupled head and eye movement) to which monkeys and apes respond have been systematically studied. Itakura and Tanaka (1998) found that two 21-year-old chimpanzees (*Pan troglodytes*) and a 5-year-old orangutan (*Pongo pygmaeus*) could, after training, find hidden food when given cues by a human who either tapped on the correct container, gazed and pointed at the container, gazed with head movement close up to or further away from the correct container, or signaled with eye movements alone. The primates' performance was accurate and comparable to that of children aged 2.5 years. Capuchin monkeys can also be trained to use gaze cues but they failed, even with extensive training over 120 trials, to make use of eye movements alone to find hidden food (Itakura & Anderson, 1996). These results suggest that physical proximity to an object may be a sufficient signal for many species and that head movements, but not necessarily eye movements, serve as cues for attention among primates.

Tomasello and Call (1997), in a review of gaze following in nonhuman primates, note that most studies confound bodily orientation with gaze direction. This has also been true for most studies of human infant gaze following, an issue which will be considered later. Very few studies control for the different components of the signal, with the notable exception of Povinelli and Eddy (1996a) with 7-year-old chimpanzees. In one condition, the human experimenter moved eyes and head, while in another only eye movements served as the cue. Chimpanzees looked to where the human was looking at above baseline levels in both conditions. Furthermore, chimpanzees would follow gaze into the visual space behind them, something achieved by human infants at about 18 months (Butterworth & Jarrett, 1991). If the experimenter's line of gaze was impeded by an opaque barrier, they attended to the barrier, as if they knew that it blocked the line of sight. This comparative study suggests that chimpanzees share or even exceed some of the capacities for JVA in babies. However, these experiments need not imply that chimpanzees (or babies) understand seeing as a mentalistic construct. In fact, Povinelli and Eddy (1996b) went on to show that chimpanzees mainly use forward-facing head orientation as a cue for attention, without any mentalistic understanding of seeing. Chimpanzees failed to identify the knowledgeable member of a pair of experimenters, when one had eyes open and one had eyes closed during food baiting of the rewarded location, so long as both persons faced forward. Similarly, when one of the forward-facing humans had a bandage over the eyes, or even when one of a forward-facing pair of experimenters wore a bucket over the head, chimpanzees failed to take into account that that individual could not have seen where the reward had been hidden. This argues rather strongly against mental-state attribution as the basis for JVA in higher primates and for body posture and facial orientation as the important signals on which shared attention is based.

Tomasello, Call, and Hare (1998) showed that individuals in five primate species (chimpanzees, sooty mangabeys, rhesus macaques, stump-tail macaques, and pigtail macaques) would follow the gaze of conspecifics to locate food on over 80 percent of occasions within 1 second of when the change of gaze occurred. They suggest that gaze following is common both in monkeys and apes. Perret and colleagues have discussed a possible neurophysiological base for joint visual attention in monkeys (Lorincz, Baker, & Perret, 1999). They suggest that cells in the superior temporal sulcus of macaque monkeys may code attention direction. Some cells code for whether the monkey is being looked at or not, while other cells code for attention to locations in extrapersonal space. For the latter populations of cells, different types of posture information are coded in a hierarchical, coordinated fashion. For example, if a particular cell codes for gazing to the right, the same cell will respond even if the eyes are not visible but there is a right-facing profile. Even if the head happens to be occluded the same cell will respond to a right-facing body profile. Priority is given to certain cues: In some cells, eye direction takes priority in combining cues, whereas in other cells there is no priority. In macaques, visual cues from head posture proved to be more important than those from body posture. A change in eye direction with constant head direction increased the probability of following eye direction in static displays, even though macaques will normally follow changes in head direction in preference to changes in eye direction. Thus, at the neurophysiological level (if not always at the behavioral level), macaques use orientation of trunk and eyes to identify the locus of visual attention of other macaques.

In summary, visual co-orientation is readily observed in nature with examples documented in birds, monkeys, and apes. There is evidence that higher primates are similar to human infants in actually monitoring gaze (i.e., head and eye movements) for joint attention. To the extent that joint visual attention occurs, cues for spatial orientation from head, eyes, and trunk are implicated, perhaps in a hierarchical fashion. Joint visual attention need not imply that an organism understands seeing as a mental state since the bodily orientation of the conspecific carries sufficient information for JVA to occur. Thus, joint attention in its most elementary form may be considered as a form of selective orienting based on postural cues of the social partner which serve as signals for potentially interesting objects in the environment.

The Emergence of Joint Attention

The major theoretical impact of Scaife and Bruner's (1975) pioneering study was on received theories of infant egocentrism (Butterworth, 1987). Scaife and Bruner (1975) showed that infants as young as 2 months followed a change in the orientation of gaze of an adult. Their observation was initially met with some skepticism since JVA in infancy is not possible in traditional theories, such as Piaget's (1952, 1954); and Collis (1977) was unable to replicate the results with such young babies. In Scaife and Bruner's (1975) original study, babies followed the adult's direction of gaze, to left or right, into an empty visual field and the absence of objects may have made the effect particularly fragile. Many subsequent studies, which have incorporated objects, have placed the onset of JVA very much later, usually after 9 months (Carpenter, Nagel, & Tomasello, 1998; Corkum & Moore, 1995; Moore & Corkum, 1994; Morissette, Ricard, & Gouin-Decarie, 1995).

One reason why the age of emergence of JVA has been so much later in replication studies than in Scaife and Bruner's original observation is that conservative diagnostic criteria have often been adopted. The spatial conditions of testing may have placed great demands on babies' ability to integrate the change in the adult's focus of attention with the target. In Carpenter et al.'s (1998) study babies had to accurately localize targets placed at approximately 45 or 80 degrees to the right or left of the midline. Babies were not credited with JVA unless they could accurately localize all the targets (Carpenter et al., 1998, Figure 1). Similarly, Corkum and Moore (1995) applied a stringent criterion that infants should show spontaneous gaze following and also produce five consecutive correct responses in order to be credited with the capacity of JVA. Morissette et al. (1995) also used large spatial separations of the targets and stringent scoring criteria which showed JVA to be coincident with comprehension of pointing at 12–15 months. Stringent performance criteria and demanding spatial conditions will certainly show when a *robust* ability for JVA is available (see Table 8.1), but these criteria do not allow for early-appearing JVA.

Other studies, using less stringent criteria for JVA, have consistently claimed that joint visual attention can be observed at least as early as 3 months, as Scaife and Bruner (1975) claimed. For example, Butterworth and Cochran (1980) and Butterworth and Jarrett (1991) showed JVA in a simple, uncluttered laboratory environment in 6-month-old babies. More recently, D'Entremont, Hains, and Muir (1998) showed JVA in 4-month-old babies using targets that were placed each side of the baby's midline and in the periphery of vision. There was no requirement to single out a particular target among many potential targets and joint attention was inferred from the fact that the response terminated at the target located on the appropriate side. Thus, in the D'Entremont et al. study, the infant could succeed by simply encoding the direction of the adult's gaze (left or right), following which the specific referent would single itself out as it came into the periphery of vision. This interpretation is consistent with the finding of Hood, Willens, and Driver (1998) that babies of 4 months would look in a particular direction when cued by the orientation of the eyes on a face presented as a computer display.

In adults, the eye movements in computer displays take precedence in allocating attention, even when their direction does not predict the location of a subsequent event, a phenomenon which has been described as "reflexive social orienting" (Friesen & Kingstone, 1998, p. 494). Furthermore, adults are significantly faster in responding to a display comprising head and eyes when both are oriented in the same direction than when eyes and head are oriented in opposite directions (Langton, 1999). This suggests that, for adults, a directional decision may be based on the orientation of both the head and eyes, or possibly that incongruous signals, where eyes face one way and head the other, confound interpersonal and extrapersonal attention mechanisms (see discussion below of Butterworth & Itakura, 1999).

Clearly, the recent data from babies suggest that some components of joint visual attention must already be in place by 4 months, albeit in fragile form, based on monitoring head orientation, eye movements, or both. Controlled comparisons at different ages are needed to establish what is changing with development of JVA. Butterworth and Cochran (1980) and Butterworth and Jarrett (1991) carried out such studies with participants as young as 6 months, in a homogeneous laboratory environment where the walls were screened by curtains to form a neutral background. Identical targets were systematically, symmetrically located, relatively close to the experimenter and infant (minimum and maximum distances in the infant's visual field were approximately 1 m at 60 degrees from the midline and 2.60 m at 30 degrees from the midline). Adults and infant were seated "en face," at the same height as the targets. The adult changed her focus of attention to one of the targets by reorienting head, eyes, and trunk, holding her posture for approximately 5 seconds. The aim was to establish the spatial conditions under which 6-month-old babies could "follow into" a change in the adult's direction of gaze. Babies at 6 months showed significantly more responses to targets on the correct side and were clearly capable of triadic attention (Butterworth & Jarrett, 1991). Further studies showed that babies of this age could accurately locate the correct target either if it was stationary and first along the baby's scan path into the periphery of vision, or if both targets were simultaneously in motion and the correct target was the more peripheral of the two (Grover, 1988). That is, attention-worthy attributes of objects in the periphery of vision may assist the young baby to identify a common focus for joint attention.

There appear to be important developments in the extent of the visual field that a baby will scan in looking for an object. Butterworth and Cochran (1980) used the adult orientation procedure with an empty visual field. Babies at 12 months searched through about 40 degrees from their own midline following an adult orientation and then gave up. If the adult gazed at a target located in the space behind the baby, the infant at 12 months still turned only through 40 degrees and then gave up. This implies that, at 12 months, the infant takes the adult's gaze to refer to a potential object that is somewhere within a shared visual space. If the baby's own change in the focus of attention fails to locate an object (because the shared visual field is empty) the process of shifting attention terminates (see also Caron, Krakoswki, Liu, & Brooks, 1996). However, Butterworth and Jarrett (1991) showed that by 18 months babies did search behind them when the visual field in front was empty, which suggests that they are now aware of a surrounding space. Therefore, once the competing evidence is carefully analyzed, it is clear that triadic JVA is possible, under appropriate conditions, before the 9–12-month watershed (Butterworth & Grover, 1988, 1989; Butterworth & Jarrett, 1991). With development, new abilities to attend to targets at greater and greater angular distances from the baby progressively supplement a basic "ecological" mechanism.

Butterworth and Jarrett (1991) suggested that three successive mechanisms of joint visual attention can be discerned in the age range between 6 and 18 months. At 6 months, babies look to the correct side of the room, as if to see what the adult is looking at, but they cannot tell which of the two identical targets on the same side of the room is correct, unless it happens to move or in some way be the more salient. Joint visual attention depends on the differentiated structure of the natural environment so that what initially attracts the adult's attention and leads her to turn (thus providing the baby with information about *spatial direction* through the change in her postural orientation) is also likely to capture the attention of the infant (thus providing information about *spatial location* through the object's intrinsic properties). This ecological mechanism enables a "meeting of minds" in the self-same object.

Between 12 and 18 months the infant begins to localize the target correctly, even when it is further into the periphery than an identical distracter target (Butterworth & Jarrett, 1991). This new mechanism was called "geometric" because it appeared to require extrapolation of a vector between the mother's head orientation and the referent of her gaze. Butterworth and Itakura (1999) investigated the hypothesis that babies become capable of "geometric" vector extrapolation but it emerged that neither babies, children, nor adults used such a precise mechanism to locate the referent of another's gaze. Instead, it turned out that the onset of robust JVA is marked by a progressive increase in the ability to localize targets that are further into the periphery than a distracter target – thus, at this age, the attention-capturing properties of objects themselves become less important. However, JVA continues to be limited by the boundaries of the babies' visual space until 18 months of age when babies become capable of searching the space behind them.

Why does robust joint visual attention take so long to develop? Among the most important constraints on joint attention in early infancy is the capacity to integrate actions and events across gaps in space and time. Millar and Schaffer (1972, 1973) showed that babies of 6 months readily learned to bang on a canister for contingent light reinforcement, which occurred at the same place where they were banging (i.e., under conditions of complete contiguity between stimulus and response). They also learned such a response when the location of the light reinforcement did not occur in the same location as the response, providing that there was a spatial cue within their visual field to draw attention to the light. However, when there was no visible cue to the reinforcement light, babies failed to learn the response. Millar and Schaffer conclude that, before 9 months, dividing attention between an action and its consequences presents major difficulties for the infant because attention must be coordinated between separate foci. Evidence is widespread that a rapid stage-like change occurs between 9 and 12 months in the ability to bridge such gaps. This change may be linked with maturation of frontal lobe functions, which allow infants to make rapid progress in solving delayed response tasks (Diamond, 1991: see chapter 6).

However, frontal lobe maturation may not be the whole story because, as was said earlier, babies of 3–4 months engage in triangular relations with adults across spatial separations which are much greater than those which they fail to encompass in triadic JVA (Fivaz-Depeursinge & Corboz-Warnery, 1999). It seems possible that the underlying change is from direct triangulation within social relationships, observed at least as early as 3–4 months, to referential triangulation (i.e., triadic JVA), in which the preexisting ability for social triangulation is now used to single out (refer to) inanimate objects. Careful experiments are needed to establish exactly how such a transition might occur, since factors such as the size, visibility, animacy, and distance of the people and objects involved in triangular vs. triadic relations have not so far been systematically controlled.

In summary, the ability to integrate information across spatiotemporal gaps may be one of the basic underlying processes that allows the transition to robust JVA. The increasing distance of targets that are accessible with age may simply reflect changes in the ability to integrate attention to events at differently spaced foci. Other cognitive changes may contribute, however, particularly the ability to search for hidden objects on the basis of minimal cues. Robust JVA may mark a transition from communication primarily within directly perceived, effectively based human relationships to referential communication incorporating objects.

Pointing and Joint Visual Attention

The characteristics of the signal that indicate a change in direction of gaze (change in head orientation with eye movements or eye movements alone) influence the incidence and accuracy of infant responses. It is relatively difficult to find evidence for eye movements alone being effective in joint attention in large-scale spaces before about 18 months (Butterworth & Jarrett, 1991; Corkum & Moore, 1995). Studies of older children and adults also suggest that eyes alone are not a good cue to gaze direction. Contrary to what one might have expected, Butterworth and Itakura (1999) found that adult observers were more accurate in locating a target when the experimenter was wearing sunglasses than when the eyes were visible; and children aged 4.5 years were more accurate in locating the target when the experimenter had his eyes closed rather than open. Findings such as these suggest that the eyes are not necessarily the primary source of information for singling out the object in triadic JVA. However, there is another cue that does appear to be uniquely important in determining the object of JVA – pointing.

The second major phase shown in Table 8.1, which we have characterized as robust JVA, is marked by the onset of pointing. Index finger pointing is a means of making definite reference that is intimately linked to gesture and speech. Here we will examine evidence for its species-specificity to humans and will offer some evidence for the universality of the gesture. First, it is necessary to describe the typical posture of the hand in pointing to avoid confusion with other indicative gestures. In pointing, the index finger and arm are extended in the direction of the interesting object, while the remaining fingers are curled under the hand, with the thumb held down and to the side. The orientation of the hand, either palm downward or rotated so the palm is vertical with respect to the body midline, may also be significant in further differentiating subtypes of indexical pointing. Pointing is a deictic gesture which is used to reorient the attention of another person so that an object becomes the shared focus for attention. Rolfe (1996) offers three criteria for deictic pointing: (1) it is dialogic in that it requires an audience and is for someone else's benefit; (2) the gesture serves to single something out which the addressee comprehends to be the referent; (3) the direction of what is being pointed at is seen as away from the pointing hand. These three characteristics constitute the contextual and cognitive requirements for the comprehension and production of pointing. We will begin by considering some comparative studies to evaluate the claim that pointing is species-specific to humans.

Comparative Evidence on the Species-Specificity of Pointing

The precise definition of the pointing gesture is rather important in evaluating comparative evidence. For example, the pointer dog, according to Hewes (1981), has been associated with humans in hunting for at least two and a half thousand years. The dog aligns its whole body with the target, from tip of nose to extended tail, sometimes with a front paw raised, in a manner partly analogous to human deictic behavior. The orientation of the dog indicates the general direction of fallen wildfowl, which assists the hunter locate the prey. However, it is not the case that the dog engages in a dialogue with the hunter and, furthermore, whole-body orienting differs in other important ways from indexical pointing. For example, the dog does not see itself orienting toward the prey, whereas sight of the hand and the object in the visual field may be integral to the production and comprehension of pointing in humans.

Chimpanzees (*Pan troglodytes*) and orangutans (*Pongo pygmaeus*) are capable of signaling with manual indicative gestures, in which the arm, open hand, and extended fingers are oriented in the direction of an interesting sight. The behavior is usually made by captive, trained chimpanzees to their human trainers and it is rarely seen between conspecifics. Higher primates generally give no prominence to the index finger in making indicative gestures (Blaschke & Ettlinger, 1987; Call & Tomasello, 1994; Menzel, 1974). Hewes (1981) describes an observational study of a pair of captive bonobos (*Pan paniscus*) in which only 21 indicative gestures were observed in 600 hours of filming. These were made by the male and served to indicate to the female that she should move to another part of the enclosure. The question is whether such open-handed, indicative gestures in chimpanzees should be considered equivalent to human pointing. Some authors have argued that they are equivalent and that the *function* of indicating is more important than the *form* of the gesture (Krause & Fouts, 1997). One factor that may limit index finger pointing in apes is the anatomy of the hand. An intriguing observation by Povinelli and Davis (1994) points to subtle differences in the anatomy of the human and chimpanzee hand: they noted that the resting posture of the index finger in anaesthetized humans is slightly proud of the remaining fingers, whereas in chimpanzees all the fingers remain aligned when at rest.

However, this need not mean that indexical pointing is impossible for chimpanzees. It has recently been shown that chimpanzees (*Pan troglodytes*) can signal with an index finger (Leavens, Hopkins, & Bard, 1996). The clearest evidence came from a chimpanzee named Clint, aged 14 years, who extended the index finger through the cage mesh (with left and right hand) apparently as a request to the experimenter for food which had fallen on the ground. Index finger extension was less frequent (38 instances) than whole-hand indicative gestures (102 instances). Indicative gestures were used by Clint as an imperative for food items (i.e., give me that food) and it is possible that his index finger extensions may have been learned as a particular consequence of social contact with humans since he was never observed to use index finger pointing with conspecifics. Nevertheless, some of his index finger extensions were accompanied by checking where the experimenter was looking – suggesting that the gesture required an audience – and he only made the gesture when the experimenter was facing him. Leavens and Hopkins (1998), in a study of 115 chimpanzees aged from 3 to 56 years, found that 47 animals made whole-hand indicative gestures and six animals used indexical points with arm extended to single out the location of food. Of 78 chimpanzees who made gestures of any kind, 35 percent of the gestures were accompanied by vocalization, a figure rather lower than usually found with babies. High levels of gaze alternation (checking) were observed, however (80 percent of animals showed checking from 8 years), which is typical of humans too.

Krause (1998) has reported human-like indexical pointing, with arm extension, in a 21-year-old captive chimpanzee who was trained to indicate to a naive experimenter which of four possible places contained a hidden object. These conditions required greater precision than is usually demanded of chimpanzees in such tasks, which may have influenced selection of the gesture. However, it is possible that the gesture was learned from human caretakers, since the chimpanzee was sign language-trained. Furthermore, it was made with scant regard to hand orientation, so that pointing was sometimes observed with the upside-down hand (M. A. Krause, personal communication, 1998). G. E. Butterworth (personal observation, 1998) found that 19 out of 20 examples of pointing in ten babies occurred with the palm downward, and one with the palm sideways. That is, upside-down pointing never occurred, which suggests that Krause's chimpanzee may have been trained to point by molding the begging gesture.

As has already been noted, feral chimpanzees have not been observed to point indexically and, indeed, whole-body orienting may be sufficiently communicative for the chimpanzee's purposes in the wild (Menzel, 1974). Povinelli, Bering, and Giambrone (2000) note that neither of the two long-term studies of chimpanzees in the wild which extend over 40 years have ever reported pointing in chimpanzees. Furthermore, even if pointing in chimpanzees is morphologically similar to that in humans (and there is very little evidence for this), this would not necessarily imply that pointing is understood in the same way by chimpanzees and humans. Povinelli, Reaux, Bierschwale, Allain, and Simon (1997) showed that, whereas 2-year-old children had no difficulty finding hidden objects on the basis of a manual pointing cue (i.e., independent of gaze or distance cues), adolescent chimpanzees responded in terms of the distance between the pointing hand and the target, choosing whichever target happened to be the nearer to the hand. This suggests they do not comprehend the pointing gesture as referential. When the experimenter pointed across the body to a distant box, but his body was actually closer to the incorrect box, chimpanzees reliably chose the incorrect box. In contrast, a study by Lee, Eskritt, Symons, and Muir (1998) showed that 3-year-old children consistently responded to the pointing cue when they saw a videotaped event in which an actor pointed toward one object but looked at another. Furthermore, Couillard and Woodward (1999) showed that 3- to 4.5-year-old children could easily ignore a misleading cue about the location of a reward if it was a simple marker placed at the incorrect location of two. However, they were unable to ignore a misleading point, which suggests that the communicative functions of pointing tend to preclude it being interpreted as a deceptive cue until quite late into childhood.

The contrast in prevalence and comprehension of pointing in humans as compared with chimpanzees is graphically illustrated in a study of congenitally deaf infants by Goldin-Meadow and Feldman (1977). They found that 51 percent of as many as 5000 gestures produced by toddlers aged 17 to 47 months were indexical points at things, people, or places (cited in Hewes, 1981). Franco and Butterworth (1996) also found that pointing comprised more than 55 percent of the gestures of babies aged 14 months, whereas other indicative gestures involving the whole hand, or extended arm and closed fist, or isolated index finger extension, accounted for only 18 percent of gestures in total. Furthermore, whole-hand indicative gestures and index finger pointing were uncorrelated in development, with indicative gestures remaining at a low constant level between 12 and 18 months, whereas pointing increased exponentially. A similar low correlation between pointing and other indicative gestures was found by Lock, Young, Service, and Chandler (1990). All this evidence suggests that open-hand indicative gestures and pointing are unrelated and therefore may serve different purposes in communication. For babies indexical pointing is the preferred means of sharing attention, whereas for chimpanzees production of indexical behavior is at best very rare and may, in any case, serve primarily as a request (protoimperative) rather than to share attention (protodeclarative).

The recent upsurge of research on pointing in chimpanzees suggests that it is not possible to maintain an absolute divide between humans and other higher primate species with respect to open-handed indicative gestures. Thus, some aspects of the capacity for sharing attention by indicating may be shared with other primates. This makes explaining indexical pointing all the more interesting since, unlike the case for JVA, there are many strong contrasts between humans and chimpanzees. These include the incidence of the gesture, its precise form, and the preference for pointing in babies over other means of indicating. In particular, canonical index finger pointing in humans is done for conspecifics – whereas it has never been observed to occur between chimpanzees – and it is declarative (it serves to redirect attention toward an object), whereas in chimpanzees almost all examples are imperative (it usually serves as a request). On the evidence to date, by these broader deictic criteria, declarative indexical pointing is probably species-specific to humans, unlike gaze cues, which widely serve joint visual attention in nature.

Pointing Comprehension in Humans

We will first discuss pointing comprehension, which begins around 11 months, before going on to factors involved in pointing production. Many studies agree that the comprehension of pointing slightly precedes its production, but this may simply reflect relative lack of knowledge about the precursors (Franco & Butterworth, 1996; Leung & Rheingold, 1981; Messer, 1994). There is evidence that the spatial conditions of testing influence whether infants comprehend pointing or not. An early study by Lempers (1976) found that babies of 9 months comprehend pointing to nearby targets and by 12 months they comprehend pointing to more distant targets. Morissette et al. (1995) in a longitudinal study also found that comprehension of manual pointing to relatively distant targets begins at about 12 months. The most frequent error of babies was to look at the pointing hand rather than at the designated target. Murphy and Messer (1977) found that pointing comprehension was earlier (9 months) for targets on the same side of the room as the pointing hand than when the point was into the contralateral half of the infant's visual space, across the body midline of the adult seated en face (12 months). Butterworth and Grover (1989) showed that pointing was understood by 12 months in that pointing produced head turning in the direction indicated by the pointing hand. By contrast, infants at 6 or 9 months were as likely to fixate the pointing hand as the designated target. Morissette et al. (1995) and Carpenter et al. (1998) found that pointing comprehension occurred earlier for nearby than for more distant targets and the angle subtended by the targets, relative to the baby, influenced the probability of pointing comprehension. Others have also found similar effects (Lempers, 1976; Murphy & Messer, 1977). Carpenter et al. (1998) noted that babies comprehended pointing to targets to their right two months before targets to their left, a phenomenon also reported by Butterworth and Itakura in a symmetrical environment (1999). These observations on asymmetries favoring the right side of space in JVA are very recent and they require further validation. In the Butterworth and Itakura (1999) study, the asymmetry in babies' attention was only apparent for gaze plus pointing which took attention further into the right visual periphery than the left. The asymmetry was not apparent for gaze cues alone, which took attention a lesser distance equally into the left or right periphery. Asymmetries in attention allocation to the right visual field, possibly mediated by left hemisphere brain functions, could be very important in linking the pointing gesture in development with species-typical brain mechanisms for speech.

Detailed longitudinal studies are needed to establish exactly how babies begin to understand pointing. Mothers go to a great deal of trouble, with exaggerated hand movements, to lead the young infant's gaze from the hand onto the target (Murphy & Messer, 1977). Grover (1988) showed that the infant's latency to fixate the correct target significantly decreased between 9 and 12 months, which suggests that the gesture rapidly acquired the status of a signal. Babies at 12 months were significantly more likely to respond to a change of gaze plus point than to gaze alone, and they fixated a target further into the periphery of vision for pointing than for gaze alone. When the salience of the targets was experimentally manipulated by setting them into motion, the infant's response to pointing increased to ceiling level. Target motion was sufficient to eliminate hand fixation in 9-month infants, although babies then went on to fixate only the first target along their scan path from the adult's hand. By 15 months, however, babies did alight on the second, more peripheral target, in a sequence of fixations. Thus, infants are not merely fixating the first object they encounter when they fully comprehend pointing. However, when babies first begin to understand pointing the attention-worthy object may first "pluck" the child's attention from the pointing hand.

Butterworth and Itakura (1999) tested infants at 6 months, 12 months, and 15 months for the accuracy with which they could locate one of two identical targets at angular separations ranging from 25 degrees to 55 degrees. Mother and baby sat "en face" and one target was always at 10 degrees to the left of the baby's midline (the first target along their scan path from the mother), and the second was at a more peripheral leftward position. The mother either looked at the target (with head and eye movements) or looked and pointed at the target. For all three age groups there was little evidence that babies could accurately select the more peripheral of the pair just on the basis of head and eye movements. However, from 12 months, manual pointing had a significant effect on the accuracy of the response to the more peripheral target and, by 15 months, there was a clear advantage to pointing in localizing the more peripheral target at all angular distances. Infants' success following the pointing cue, despite the narrow angular separation between the 10- and 25-degree targets, suggested that they might be solving the problem by extrapolating a linear vector along the pointing arm to intersect with the object.

In further experiments with 4.5-year-old children and adults Butterworth and Itakura (1999) tested the vector extrapolation hypothesis by presenting targets three at a time on each side of the visual field. The angular separations between targets varied from 4 to 45 degrees for adults and it was held constant at 10 degrees for children, again at 2.7 m (as for the babies). The task required the participant, who sat next to the experimenter, simply to state the color of the target that was being singled out by a pointing gesture or by combinations of head and eye movements. Children were accurate following pointing but they were not accurate for head and eye movements. Pointing allowed accuracy only to the periphery of each visual hemifield and children were inaccurate to the intermediate targets. Adults were generally as accurate following head and eye movements as following pointing to the targets at separations of 15 degrees or greater (i.e., about 70 cm separation between target centers). However, they were inaccurate for the intermediate target positions at separations of 15 degrees or less. That is, the pointing gesture successfully drew attention to the peripheral boundaries of vision both for children and adults, but precise linear vector extrapolation was not used to follow pointing since there is no reason why a linear vector should be less accurate for intermediate than peripheral positions.

Butterworth and Itakura (1999) explain the effect on accuracy of manual pointing to peripheral target locations in terms of the movement of the "lever" formed by the arm. For any given spatial separation between a pair of targets, the horizontal excursion of a long lever, like the arm, will be greater than that of a shorter lever, like the head and nose, or very short levers, like the eyes. Each component of the orienting system may serve to specify different regions of space. The eyes are most effective just each side of the midline and they serve as a particularly useful cue as to whether one is being looked at. Head orientation takes attention further away from the midline and pointing takes attention to the periphery of vision. Thus, one part of the body, the arm and pointing hand may have become specialized for referential communication in humans because it is particularly useful in taking attention to the extreme periphery of vision (Butterworth, 1997). The results of the Butterworth and Itakura study show that, even for adults, following pointing is not a completely precise method of achieving JVA. The process of achieving JVA does not operate by extrapolation of linear vectors and, in a cluttered environment, accuracy also requires attention-worthy cues from the object to help single it out.

The conclusion from these studies is that babies, children, and adults are partially dependent on target qualities to identify the specific referent of the gaze or pointing signal. That is, JVA is a two-part process, one part being specified by change in gaze or postural orientation which define the broad zones of visual space likely to be of mutual interest, and the other part depending on the object to single itself out in a crowded environment. Thus, what attracts the adult's attention and leads her to turn eventually also captures the infant's attention and enables a meeting of minds at the location of the object. Head and eye movements, which are perceived as referential actions from early in development, come to be supplemented by the pointing gesture, which carries attention further into the periphery once the infant can integrate experience across the greater distances involved.

The Production of Pointing

A number of studies now agree on the emergence of canonical pointing (as defined by the precise hand posture above) at an average age of 11 months, although babies as young as 8.5 months have been observed to point (Butterworth & Morissette, 1996; Schaffer, 1984). Approximately 33 percent of parents of 8-month-old babies in the United States report that their babies already point (Fenson et al., 1994). Carpenter et al. (1998), in a longitudinal study of 24 babies, also in the United States, found that pointing to nearby objects occurred at 11 months, two months before more distal pointing. Butterworth and Morissette (1996), in a similar longitudinal study of 27 babies in England, also found the average age for pointing onset to be in the eleventh month (11.2 months for females and 11.7 months for males). Ohama (1984) in a longitudinal study in Japan reported that five out of nine of her sample pointed by 11 months and eight out of nine by 13 months. By 12 months pointing comprises more than 60 percent of all gestures made by the infant (Lock et al, 1990). Pointing typically emerges suddenly (Lock et al., 1990), as if after a stage transition. Pointing is accompanied by checking with the adult (3.4 percent of points at 12 months, according to Lock et al., and about 20 percent at 18 months in Franco & Butterworth, 1996). Pointing is also accompanied by vocalization (50 percent of pointing gestures, according to Lock et al., 1990, 76 percent in Franco & Butterworth, 1996, 87 percent in Leung & Rheingold, 1981 – all at 12 months). L. Fenson (personal communication, 1997) found an accelerated pointing onset for female babies until 12 months, when the number of males who are said to point catches up. Sex differences in pointing onset could have important implications for understanding female advantage in aspects of language acquisition, further strengthening the link between JVA and communication development.

It was once widely believed that pointing emerges by the differentiation of index finger extension from a more primitive open-handed "waving" posture, after the seventh month (e.g., Leung & Rheingold, 1981; Murphy & Messer, 1977). Although the canonical form of pointing emerges toward the end of the first year, there is evidence that antecedents of pointing, in particular the independent extension of the index finger, can be observed much earlier than was traditionally believed. Isolated extension of the index finger, with the other fingers curled inwards in the pointing posture, has been observed in the 3-month-old baby, in close association with "speech-like" sounds, when the infant is engaged in social interaction (Fogel & Hannan, 1985; Hannan 1987; Masataka, 1995). In a longitudinal single-case study Hannan and Fogel (1987) observed pointing movements, predominantly of the right hand, from 18 days. "Pointing" was accompanied by movements of the eyes and mouth which occurred as a cluster of orienting behaviors. The pointing movements occurred when the babies were engaged in social interaction and they continued until the age of 6 months (Fogel, 1981). These microanalytic studies of babies reveal that "embryonic" forms of the pointing gesture are already in the repertoire even though mothers are not typically aware that their babies are pointing. Thus, the typical pointing posture of the hand does not emerge from a less differentiated form but shows the typical hand shape from soon after birth.

There are isolated reports that babies can sometimes be observed making pointing movements for themselves before they engage in pointing for others. Tran-Duc Thao (1984) described such behavior as reinforcing for oneself the "sense certainty" of the object, and Lempert and Kinsbourne (1985) relate it to involuntary orienting movements, or expressions of interest, which are perhaps similar to the transitional phenomena observed by Franco and Butterworth (1996). These authors found that at 10 months babies sometimes point at an object, then turn to the mother as if to check with her, whereupon they point at the mother. This phenomenon was also noted by Masur (1983) when the mother was holding the object. It is as if visual checking and manual pointing are coming together in a new coordinated structure comprising pointing and checking, which is not yet appropriately sequentially organized across the spatial gap. Checking has been taken as strong evidence of communicative intent since the audience is being "interrogated" for comprehension. Lempert and Kinsbourne (1985) also suggest that such "dual directional signaling" is evidence for communicative intent. However, this does not mean that pointing that is not accompanied by checking is necessarily egocentric. An alternative hypothesis is that pointing is an aspect of a communication production system, whereas checking is a complementary aspect of the system seeking confirmation of comprehension. This requires further research. In general, the evidence on the antecedents of pointing takes the form of the gesture into very early human development, again suggesting it is of biological origin.

The social conditions necessary for pointing in babies were investigated by Franco and Butterworth (1990), who tested babies alone or when with adults who actively pointed or remained still. Pointing occurred only under conditions where a social partner was available for communication and babies did not point when alone with attractive objects. When reunited with the mother this often released a flood of pointing to the targets. Furthermore, pointing by the baby did not require that the adult also point, nor was the rate of infant pointing a function of the adult rate. That is, infant pointing implies an audience, even if the partner is another baby, and it is not a function of the adult also pointing (Franco, Perruchino, & Butterworth, 1992).

Butterworth, Franco, McKenzie, Graupner, and Todd (1998) carried out a series of experiments designed to test the "spotlight" metaphor of focal attention in pointing. Remotely controlled targets, comprising six doll figures that could move their arms and legs, were set in motion both focally and at different positions in the periphery from

50 degrees left to 50 degrees right of the midline. Each trial began with the baby fixating at the midline and then the dolls were set in motion, either singly or in combinations of pairs. When targets were activated singly, all positions were equally likely to elicit pointing, despite large differences in the distance from the initial fixation point, which suggests that stimulus factors eliciting pointing may operate in parallel and do not favor the initial focal position. When targets were activated in pairs, babies were more likely to point at the target on the right side of visual space than to the target on the left, which suggests that the conflict is resolved by attending preferentially to the right side of visual space. The primary effect of target position was to determine which hand does the pointing, with the right hand chosen most often. In subsequent experiments the dolls were modified so that sound was added to their repertoire. Babies could hear a voice saying "hello baby" on trials in which sound was combined with doll movement, and this was compared with trials in which babies heard sound alone (without movement) or movement (without sound). The bimodal condition proved to elicit significantly more pointing overall, and females produced significantly more right-handed pointing than males. Under unimodal visual conditions, the hand chosen tended to be ipsilateral to the side of target movement. In bimodal conditions, the right hand was favored among females even for targets to the left of the body midline (babies were aged 13.6 months). In another study, which involved a toy clown moving across the visual field, latency of pointing was shown to be a function of event complexity. Pointing to a simple translation of motion was significantly faster than if the clown moved or vanished during translation. Complex events of this nature actually tend to suppress pointing. Pointing was again mainly right-handed, despite the translation of the clown across the field of vision in both directions.

Thus, once pointing develops in babies, it meets Rolfe's (1996) criteria for deictic reference: it requires an audience, refers away from the hand, and has a dialogic character. Although pointing may terminate in focal attention, targets at widely spaced positions relative to the observer are equally likely to elicit the gesture. The right hand and the right side of visual space are privileged in eliciting pointing, but it occurs with either hand. When events differing in complexity are used to elicit pointing, there is a tendency for more complex event structures to suppress the gesture, as if the capacity for attention allocation is in danger of being exceeded.

Pointing and Prehension

Traditional views of the origins of pointing are of two types, which stress either that pointing develops out of prehension (e.g., Vygotsky, 1988) or that it is a communicative gesture from the outset. Within the latter type of theory it is often assumed that pointing is initially performed for the self and becomes ritualized through social interaction until it serves purposes of social communication (e.g., Werner & Kaplan, 1963). Vygotsky believed that pointing derives from unsuccessful grasping movements, which are interpreted by the mother as a request. In coming to her infant's aid, the mother converts the movement into a gesture for others and it acquires an imperative character. No explanation for the specific hand posture is offered except that it is considered somehow transitional with grasping.

Franco and Butterworth (1996) tested both these types of theory in a study which compared the incidence of pointing and reaching gestures in 10–14-month-old babies in declarative and imperative communicative contexts. Babies had the opportunity to point at or make grasping gestures to interesting objects that were both in and out of reach. From the onset pointing was never confused with reaching gestures. It occurred primarily to distal targets (2.7 m away) and was accompanied by vocalization and checking with the partner. Both these accompanying behaviors increased exponentially with age. Reaching gestures were not strongly correlated with checking and they remained at a low level. These findings run against the view of the origins of pointing as theorized by Vygotsky (1988), since pointing was not tied in any way to failed grasping and there was no evidence that the imperative use of the gesture had primacy. Carpenter et al. (1998) in their longitudinal study also found no evidence that the imperative use of pointing emerges before the declarative. That is, on the detailed empirical evidence to date, the pointing gesture in humans initially serves a protodeclarative purpose (i.e., look at that) rather than a protoimperative purpose (i.e., give me that).

In a reinterpretation of the literature on early communicative development Camaioni (1993; see also chapter 15 in this volume) has argued that imperative and declarative pointing gestures may differ in their cognitive complexity. The former implies an understanding of others as "agents of action," whereas the latter implies an understanding of others as "agents of contemplation." Exercising a causal effect on the world through physical contact with a person is said to be intellectually less demanding than understanding that interactions can be causally influenced by distal means. Rather than the declarative function of pointing being derived from the imperative function, she suggests that they may be independent. This distinction may partly explain the use of indicative gestures in chimpanzees, where almost all the evidence shows they are used imperatively and not declaratively.

That is not to say that pointing has nothing at all to do with prehension in humans. A clue to the reasons for the morphology of the human pointing gesture comes from the specific adaptations of the hand. The human hand is highly flexible, with a very great capability for precision based on the fully opposable index finger and thumb – a factor considered to be one of the key features differentiating humans from other primates. Based on rather minimal evidence from two 2-year-old chimpanzees clutching a grape, Napier (1960) argued that only humans are capable of the pincer grip. The relative size and position of finger and thumb (the opposability index) sets limits on the extent to which the base of the thumb can be abducted against the tip of the index finger. He gave values for the opposability index of 0.65 for humans and 0.43 for chimpanzees, a difference due mainly to the relatively short thumb of the chimpanzee, which is positioned low down the wrist.

Two studies have recently reported that the pincer grip is in fact in the repertoire of the chimpanzee. In one experiment, 80 captive chimpanzees (*Pan troglodytes*) aged from 1 to 25 years were observed picking up raisins measuring 1.0 to 1.5 cm from the cage floor. A human-like pattern of pincer grip was observed at 2 years, which reached a peak of 10 percent of all responses at 6 years, (Tonooka and Matsuzawa 1995). The same study showed that males were more likely than females to use the pincer grip once they were over ten years old. A second study of 13 captive chimpanzees (*Pan troglodytes*) aged from 2 to 5 years showed that precision grips involving the thumb and index finger at or below the first, distal joint occurred on 25 percent of trials (Jones-Engel & Bard, 1996). The human-like pincer grip with thumb pad to finger pad abduction occurred on 2 percent of trials.

These studies suggest that chimpanzees are capable of a degree of precision but they do not establish how precision grips develop. In human infants the pincer grip and imprecise opposition of the index finger and thumb above the first distal joint (the inferior forefinger grip typically adopted by chimpanzees) can already be observed at 8 months. The pincer grip is systematically selected by 15 months to grip cubes of 0.5 cm. Power grips, where the object is held between flexed fingers and palm, without thumb opposition, are rarely used by human infants older than 15 months with objects of these sizes (Butterworth, Verweij, & Hopkins, 1997). To obtain more detailed comparative evidence, Butterworth and Itakura (1998) studied 11 captive chimpanzees (*Pan troglodytes*) aged from 4 to 20 years who were video-recorded grasping cubes of apple measuring 0.5, 1.0, and 2.0 cm. This study confirmed that chimpanzees do have precision grips in their repertoire, at least from the age of 2 years, where the object is held between thumb tip and at or below the first joint of the index finger. Precision grips increase in frequency slowly, until chimpanzees are adult, and they are not systematically selected on the basis of object size at any age. Chimpanzees also use a species-typical precision grip, from about 8 years, in which they hold a small object between the index and middle fingers (the so-called "cigarette" grip). Power grips are commonly selected in chimpanzees to the age of 8 years, even when grasping small objects. This new developmental evidence shows that chimpanzees, by comparison with human infants, lack strongly systematic selection of precise grips for small objects. Their relative lack of precision extends across the age range from 2 years to full adulthood. Although a human-like pincer grip is in their repertoire, generally the whole index finger is selected and the exact position of opposition of the thumb is relatively uninfluenced by object size.

Once again, the contrast with human infants is revealing since the chimpanzee makes a developmental transition from predominance of power to precision grips very much later than is observed in babies. In human infants, there is a transition (between 8 and 15 months) when power grips which do not involve the thumb are eliminated and the pincer grip is systematically selected by object size (Butterworth et al., 1997). In human infants, the pincer grip develops earlier in females than in males (Butterworth et al., 1997). Thus, just as for pointing and indicative gestures, the repertoire of precise grips in chimpanzees overlaps that of humans, but the rapid rate of development in humans, especially females, ensures that precision grips and pointing will be used consistently even in infancy. By contrast, precise grips are infrequent, not consistently selected, and more typical of adult male chimpanzees.

The theory to be proposed here is that pointing and the pincer grip are co-evolved but are different aspects of hand function that are specialized respectively for precise instrumental action and for precise communication (see Butterworth, 1997, 1998). The characteristic hand posture observed in human pointing may be related to the pincer grip but as its "antithesis." Darwin (1904) first proposed the principle of antithesis to explain how animal communication often exploits visual signals to convey information. For example, an animal may signal readiness to attack by making "intention movements" which are preparatory to fighting. After a fight, the subdued posture of the defeated dog signals submission because the muscles are activated in the opposite configuration, or antithesis, to those involved in aggression (Marler, 1959).

In the case of pointing the opposition of the tip of the index finger and thumb in the pincer grip is postulated to have pointing as its postural antithesis. This also involves a change in the focus of visual attention. In precise manual activities with tools, focal attention is on the hand, the tool and the object in the service of precise control of manipulation. In pointing, by contrast, attention is outer-directed and serves rather precisely to reorient the attention of another person so that an object at some distance can become a focus for shared experience. On this theory, the emergence of pointing should be related to the development of other precise uses of the hand, and this indeed is what Butterworth and Morissette (1996) established. The pincer grip was invariably in the infant's repertoire and it was systematically selected by infants approximately one month before pointing onset, females earlier than males. Exploration of objects with the tip of the index finger (tipping) has also been linked to the onset of pointing (Shinn, 1900). Butterworth et al. (1997) showed that "tipping" and the pincer grip are closely related in development, with the incidence of tipping declining as the pincer grip becomes established.

In summary, the theory that pointing is the antithesis of the pincer grip links precise, instrumental, manual action, pointing onset, and species-specific aspects of hand anatomy and function to the underlying processes governing focused attention. On this argument, precise tool use and precise manual communication through the pointing gesture are co-evolved human abilities. Not only do we share some aspects of hand function with other primates, but also there are human species-typical aspects of hand function that harness the human capacity for precision both in tool use and social communication. Both the pincer grip and the pointing gesture require focal attention, but each is a specialized adaptation: respectively for precise instrumental action for the self in near space and for precise communication for others in more distal space (see Butterworth, 1997, 1998).

Pointing and the Transition to Language

A variety of studies have linked preverbal referential communication with language acquisition. Baldwin (1995) points out that the baby, by monitoring the adult's attentional focus, should be able to link the adult's utterances with the correct referent and thus avoid mapping errors in speech acquisition. Baldwin (1991, 1993) tested the theory by labeling one object when 18-month-old babies were focusing on a different object. Babies turned to check the adult's referent and thus avoided mapping errors in speech comprehension. It seems very likely that it is the identity of experience of the object in JVA which authorizes the sound stream to be treated as an aspect of the jointly attended object. In speech production there is evidence that the amount of pointing at 12 months predicts speech production rates at 24 months (Camaioni, Castelli, Longobardi, & Volterra, 1991). Links between pointing onset and comprehension of object names have also been established, with infants understanding their first object name in the same week as they point (Harris, Barlow-Brown, & Chasin, 1995). Carpenter et al.'s (1998) study showed that maternal language following into the infant's focus of attention is the most important predictor of the infant's subsequent speech comprehension and production. For maternal following in to be effective, the JVA system must already be operating reciprocally between mother and baby. The duration of joint engagement around 14 months was particularly important for predicting subsequent speech production, which may link up with research by Butterworth and Morissette (1996), who found that changes in lateralization at this age, favoring right-handedness particularly among females, may contribute to rapid acquisition of speech.

Butterworth and Morissette (1996) studied the relation between age of pointing onset and the subsequent comprehension and production of speech and gestures. A longitudinal study was carried out linking pointing, handedness, and onset of the pincer grip to early verbal and gestural communication as measured by the MacArthur infant language inventory (Fenson et al., 1994). The earlier the onset of pointing, the greater was the number of different gestures produced and the greater the number of animal sounds comprehended at 14.4 months. That is, age of pointing onset appears to be related both to a gesture and an auditory-vocal developmental pathway. The relative balance of use between left and right hands in unimanual tasks predicted MacArthur speech production and comprehension scores at 14.4 months. Girls showed more right-handed pointing than boys. The amount of right-handed pointing, and the relative balance of pincer grips between the left and right hands (a measure of lateralized fine motor control), predicted speech comprehension and production at 14.4 months. Bimanual use of the hands, terminating in right-handed object retrieval, was significantly correlated with MacArthur speech production at 14.4 months. At this age boys had relatively few words in production (about three), whereas girls had on average 12 words. There is evidence from the MacArthur norms that by 16 months the sex difference in rate of speech production is marked. At that age females have 95 words in production, males 25 words, a difference which begins to even out by 20 months (Fenson et al., 1994).

Thus, earlier onset of pointing, earlier and more frequent right-handed pointing, and more rapid development of speech in girls may suggest that there is a link between pointing, cerebral lateralization, gender, and the development of language.

Pointing, Theory of Mind, and Childhood Autism

In recent years the capacity for JVA has been linked to the acquisition of a theory of mind and to developmental psychopathology, particularly in the case of childhood autism. JVA has been proposed as a precursor for the later-developing ability to attribute to others mentalistic concepts, such as desires and beliefs. Baron-Cohen and Swettenham (1996), following a modular theory of brain organization, have suggested that humans are normally born with a shared attention module (SAM). According to Baron-Cohen (1996), SAM could develop in either of two ways: it either metamorphoses to become a theory of mind module (TOMM) or it activates an innate TOMM, much as a key opens a lock.

The special purpose of SAM is to produce triadic representations from dyadic interactions such as may be expressed as "I see Mummy sees the cup is on the table." This theory needs to be modified to take into account the recent evidence on triangular and triadic relations in early infancy. Even so, Baron-Cohen et al. (1994) found that deficits in joint attention and pointing were diagnostic of autism. They screened 16,000 children aged 18 months in the south of England with a checklist that included declarative pointing, gaze monitoring, and pretend play. Ten out of the 12 children who failed this test were subsequently diagnosed as autistic, which suggests that pointing and JVA deficits may indeed be diagnostic indicators for autism.

The question is whether failures in JVA and the development of pointing are necessary and sufficient for autism. Boucher (1996) suggests that a single critical deficit in a shared attention module (SAM) may not be a sufficient explanation for autism, since the DSM III criteria by which it is diagnosed include variants, such as children with Aspergers syndrome, who do not show theory of mind deficits. Hobson (1991) has also been critical of a purely attentional approach to autism, emphasizing instead the importance of emotional relatedness and the attendant social-affective deficits typical of the disorder. Taking these criticisms into account suggests that there may indeed be an attentional deficit particularly evident in failures of declarative pointing, but other factors need to be considered.

Manual pointing is not observed in the congenitally blind, yet these individuals are not normally autistic (Fraiberg, 1977; Hewes, 1981). Pointing is present in the congenitally deaf, which suggests that auditory experience is not necessary for its development. Autistic children, in contrast, have particular problems with language and symbolic processes (Feldman, Goldin-Meadow, & Gleitman, 1978). The evidence already reviewed suggests that the age of pointing in normal babies predicts speech onset and that pointing has precursors in systems for monitoring gaze and the orientation of body posture. This may mean that the developmental link between JVA deficits and autism might be through deficits in orienting responses. We may think of the signals provided by a change in gaze, eye movements, or in the orientation of the trunk as the external manifestation of attention processes which reposition the body for optimal perception. Deficits in production of such signals may be accompanied by parallel problems in reading the same signals in the bodily reorientation of others. That brainstem-mediated deficits in orienting may be characteristic of autism is shown by recent research implicating damage to the motor cranial nerve nuclei, occurring between days 20 and 24 of gestation, at a time when the brainstem is being formed (Rodier, Ingram, Tisdale, Nelson, & Romano, 1996; Stromland, Nordin, Miller, Akerstrom, & Gillberg, 1994). This primary deficit may have developmental consequences for the subsequent growth of the limbic system (and emotion regulation) and for the cerebellum (and postural control).

If autism is fundamentally a social affective disorder, then links with JVA may arise through an inability to share affective experiences in triadic relations. Mundy, Kasari, and Sigman (1992) found that normal babies display significantly more positive affect when establishing joint attention through pointing, or making eye contact, than when pointing or eye contact merely served as requests for an object. Positive affect accompanied joint attention for between 56 percent and 70 percent, whereas the range for requests was from 18 percent to 36 percent. Thus, sharing experience, the hallmark of JVA, is normally accompanied by sharing positive affect and autistic children may have deficiencies in both these areas. Further research on the affective aspects of JVA may be useful in reconciling the cognitive approach to autism typified by Baron-Cohen and Swettenham's (1996) model with Hobson's (1991) socio-affective theory. In such a reconciliation joint visual attention may serve as the common denominator between cognitive and emotional approaches to the origins of language and the mind.

Conclusion

Joint visual attention in infants has been extensively studied over the last 25 years. This chapter has shown that gaze and whole-body orientation serve widely as signals in the animal kingdom. Comparisons with primates show that species differences emerge strongly only when manual pointing is separated out from the complex of bodily orienting movements that serve as signals for JVA. Even though chimpanzees can produce gestures that are morphologically similar to those of humans, they do not appear to interpret pointing as referential and actually seem to prefer gaze and trunk cues as signals rather than the pointing hand. Pointing in humans is intimately connected with species-typical handedness, with the precision grip, and with the acquisition of language. It is one of a set of indicative gestures, some of which overlap with those of the higher primates, but on the evidence to date, only humans use the pointing gesture declaratively to share attention with conspecifics. Pointing serves to refer as precisely as possible to objects in the periphery of vision for joint attention, cases for which eye and head movements do not provide accurate information about location. The relative precision of pointing may arise because it makes use of the same anatomical adaptations and attention mechanisms that serve precise tool use. Pointing serves not only to individuate an object but also to authorize the link between the object and speech from the baby's perspective. Finally, deficits in JVA and in pointing may be diagnostic of other problems in social relatedness which are especially apparent in autism. However, mechanisms for joint visual attention need to be linked with those responsible for emotional sharing and for postural reorienting to more fully explain developmental psychopathology.

References

Adamson, L., & MacArthur, D. (1995). Joint attention, affect and culture. In C. Moore & P. Dunham (Eds.), *Joint attention: Its origins and role in development* (pp. 189–204). Hillsdale, NJ: Erlbaum.

Bakeman, R., & Adamson, L. (1984). Coordinating attention to people and objects in mother–infant and peer–infant interaction. *Child Development, 55,* 1278–1289.

Baldwin, D. (1991). Infants' contribution to the achievement of joint reference. *Child Development, 62,* 875–890.

Baldwin, D. (1993). Early referential understanding: Infants' ability to recognise referential acts for what they are. *Developmental Psychology, 29,* 832–843.

Baldwin, D. A. (1995). Understanding the link between joint attention and language. In C. Moore & P. J. Dunham (Eds.), *Joint attention: Its origins and role in development* (pp. 131–158). Hillsdale, NJ: Erlbaum.

Baron-Cohen, S., Cox, A., Baird, G., Swettenham, J., Drew, A., & Charman, T. (1994). *Psychological markers in the detection of autism in infancy, in a large population.* Unpublished manuscript, cited in Baron-Cohen & Swettenham (1996).

Baron-Cohen, S., Leslie, A., & Frith, U. (1985). Does the autistic child have a theory of mind? *Cognition, 21,* 37–46.

Baron-Cohen, S., & Swettenham, J. (1996). The relationship between SAMM and TOMM: Two hypotheses. In P. Carruthers & P. K. Smith (Eds.), *Theories of theories of mind* (pp. 158–168). Cambridge: Cambridge University Press.

Blaschke, M., & Ettlinger, G. (1987). Pointing as an act of social communication by monkeys. *Animal Behaviour, 35,* 1520–1525.

Bloom, P. (2000). *How children learn the meanings of words.* Cambridge, MA: MIT Press.

Boucher, J. (1996). What could possibly explain autism? In P. Carruthers & P. K. Smith (Eds.), *Theories of theories of mind* (pp. 223–241). Cambridge: Cambridge University Press.

Bruner, J. S. (1995). From joint attention to the meeting of minds. In C. Moore & P. Dunham (Eds.), *Joint attention: Its origins and role in development* (pp. 1–14). Hillsdale, NJ: Erlbaum.

Butterworth, G. E. (1987). Some benefits of egocentrism. In J. S. Bruner & H. Weinreich-Haste (Eds.), *Making sense of the world: The child's construction of reality* (pp. 62–80). London: Methuen.

Butterworth, G. E. (1991). The ontogeny and phylogeny of joint visual attention. In A. Whiten (Ed.), *Natural theories of mind* (pp. 223–232). Oxford: Blackwell.

Butterworth, G. E. (1997). Starting point. *Natural History 106*(4), 14–16.

Butterworth, G. E. (1998). What is special about pointing? In F. Simion & G. E. Butterworth (Eds.), *The development of sensory motor and cognitive capacities in early infancy: From perception to cognition* (pp. 171–187). Hove: Psychology Press.

Butterworth, G. E., & Cochran, E. (1980). Towards a mechanism of joint visual attention in human infancy. *International Journal of Behavioural Development, 3,* 253–272.

Butterworth, G. E., Franco, F., McKenzie, B., Graupner, L., & Todd, B. (1998). *Dynamic aspects of event perception and the production of pointing by human infants.* Unpublished manuscript, University of Sussex.

Butterworth, G. E., & Grover, L. (1988). The origins of referential communication in human infancy. In L. Weiskrantz (Ed.), *Thought without language* (pp. 5–25). Oxford: Oxford University Press.

Butterworth, G. E., & Grover, L. (1989). Joint visual attention, manual pointing and preverbal communication in human infancy. In M. Jeannerod (Ed.), *Attention and performance XII* (pp. 605–624). Hillsdale, NJ: Erlbaum.

Butterworth, G. E., & Itakura, S. (1998). Development of precision grips in chimpanzees. *Developmental Science, 1,* 39–43.

Butterworth, G. E., & Itakura, S. (1999). How the head, eyes and hands serve definite reference. *British Journal of Developmental Psychology.*

Butterworth, G. E., & Jarrett, N. L. M. (1991). What minds have in common is space: Spatial mechanisms for perspective taking in infancy. *British Journal of Developmental Psychology, 9,* 55–72.

Butterworth, G. E., & Morissette, P. (1996). Onset of pointing and the acquisition of language in infancy. *Journal of Reproductive and Infant Psychology, 14,* 219–231.

Butterworth, G. E., Verweij, E., & Hopkins, B. (1997). The development of prehension in infants. Halverson revisited. *British Journal of Developmental Psychology, 15,* 223–236.

Call, J., & Tomasello, M. (1994). The production and comprehension of referential pointing by orang-utans (*Pongo pygmeaus*). *Journal of Comparative Psychology, 108*, 307–317.

Camaioni, L. (1993). The development of intentional communication: A re-analysis. In J. Nadel & L. Camaioni (Eds.), *New perspectives in early communicative development* (pp. 82–96). London: Routledge.

Camaioni, L., Castelli, M. C., Longobardi, E., & Volterra, V. (1991). A parent report instrument for early language assessment. *First Language, 11*, 345–360.

Campbell, J. (2000). Two conceptions of joint attention. In N. Eilan, C. Hoerl, T. McCormack, & J. Roessler (Eds.), *Joint attention: Communication and other minds*. Oxford: Oxford University Press.

Campos, J. J., Barrett, K. C., Lamb, M. E., Hill, H., Goldsmith, H., & Stenberg, C. (1983). Socio-emotional development. In P. Mussen (Ed.), *Handbook of child psychology* (Vol. 2, pp. 783–917). New York: Wiley.

Caron, A., Krakowski, O., Liu, A., & Brooks, R. (1996, April). *Infant joint attention: Cued orienting or implicit theory of mind?* Paper presented at the International Conference on Infant Studies, Providence, RI.

Carpenter, M., Nagel, K., & Tomasello, M. (1998). Social cognition, joint attention and communicative competence from 9 to 15 months of age. *Monographs of the Society for Research in Child Development*.

Collis, G. (1977). Visual co-orientation and maternal speech. In H. R. Schaffer (Ed.), *Studies in mother–infant interaction* (pp. 325–354). New York: Academic Press.

Corkum, V., & Moore, C. (1995). The origins of joint visual attention. In C. Moore & P. Dunham (Eds.), *Joint attention: Its origins and role in development* (pp. 61–83). Hillsdale, NJ: Erlbaum.

Couillard, N. L., & Woodward, A. L. (1999). Children's comprehension of deceptive points. *British Journal of Developmental Psychology*.

Darwin, C. (1904). *The expression of the emotions in men and animals*. London: John Murray.

D'Entremont, B., Hains, S. M. J., & Muir, D. W. (1998). A demonstration of gaze following in 3 to 6 month olds. *Infant Behavior and Development, 20*, 569–572.

Diamond, A. (1991). Frontal lobe involvement in cognitive changes during the first year of life. In K. R. Gibson & A. C. Petersen (Eds.), *Brain maturation and cognitive development: Comparative and cross-cultural perspectives* (pp. 127–180). New York: Aldine de Gruyter.

Emery, N. J., Lorincz, E. N., Perret, D. I., Oram, M. W., & Baker, C. I. (1997). Gaze following and joint attention in rhesus monkeys (Macaca mulatta). *Journal of Comparative Psychology, 111*, 1–8.

Feldman, M., Goldin-Meadow, S., & Gleitman, L. (1978). Beyond Herodotus: The creation of language by linguistically deprived deaf children. In A. Lock (Ed.), *Action, gesture and symbol: The emergence of language* (pp. 351–414). London: Academic Press.

Fenson, L., Dale, P. S., Reznick, L., Bates, E., Thail, D., & Pethick, S. J. (1994). Variability in early communicative development. *Monographs of the Society for Research in Child Development, 59*(5).

Fivaz-Depeursinge, E., & Corboz-Warnery, A. (1999). *The primary triangle*. New York: Basic Books.

Fogel, A. (1981). The ontogeny of gestural communication: The first six months. In R. E. Stark (Ed.), *Language behaviour in infancy and early childhood* (pp. 17–44). Amsterdam: Elsevier.

Fogel, A., & Hannan, T. E. (1985). Manual actions of nine to fifteen week old human infants during face to face interaction with their mothers. *Child Development, 56*, 1271–1279.

Fraiberg, S. (1977). *Insights from the blind*. New York: Basic Books.

Franco, F., & Butterworth, G. E. (1990, August). *Effects of social variables on the production of infant pointing*. Poster presented at the 4th European Conference on Developmental Psychology, University of Stirling, Scotland.

Franco, F., & Butterworth, G. E. (1996). Pointing and social awareness: Declaring and requesting in the second year of life. *Journal of Child Language*, 307–336.

Franco, F., Perruchino, P., & Butterworth, G. (1992, September). *Pointing for an age mate in 1 to 2 year olds*. Paper presented at the 6th European Conference on Developmental Psychology, Seville, Spain.

Friesen, C. K., & Kingstone, A. (1998). The eyes have it: Reflexive orienting is triggered by non-predictive gaze. *Psychonomic Bulletin and Review*, *53*, 490–495.

Goldin-Meadow, S., & Feldman, H. (1977). The development of language-like communication without a language model. *Science*, *197*, 401–403.

Grover, L. (1988). *Comprehension of the pointing gesture in human infants*. Unpublished Ph.D. thesis, University of Southampton, England.

Hannan, T. E. (1987). A cross-sequential assessment of the occurrence of pointing in 3 to 12 month old human infants. *Infant Behavior and Development*, *10*, 11–22.

Hannan, T. E., & Fogel, A. (1987). A case study assessment of pointing during the first three months of life. *Perceptual and Motor Skills*, *65*, 187–194.

Harris, M., Barlow-Brown, F., & Chasin, J. (1995). Early referential understanding: Pointing and the comprehension of object names. *First Language*, *15*, 19–34.

Hewes, G. W. (1981). Pointing and language. In T. Myers, J. Laver, & J. Anderson (Eds.), *The cognitive representation of speech* (pp. 263–269). Amsterdam: North-Holland.

Hobson, P. (1991). Against the theory of theory of mind. *British Journal of Developmental Psychology*, *9*, 33–51.

Hood, B., Willens, J. D., & Driver. (1998). Adult's eyes trigger shifts of visual attention in human infants. *Psychological Science*, *9*, 131–134.

Itakura, S. (1996). An exploratory study of gaze-monitoring in nonhuman primates. *Japanese Psychological Research*, *38*, 174–180.

Itakura, S., & Anderson, J. R. (1996). Learning to use experimenter given cues during an object choice task by a capuchin monkey. *Current Psychology of Cognition*, *15*, 103–112.

Itakura, S., & Tanaka, M. (1998). Use of experimenter-given cues during object-choice tasks by chimpanzees (*Pan troglodytes*), an orangutan (*Pongo pygmaeus*) and human infants (*Homo sapiens*). *Journal of Comparative Psychology*, *112*, 119–126.

Jones-Engel, L. E., & Bard, K. A. (1996). Precision grips in young chimpanzees. *American Journal of Primatology*, *39*, 1–15.

Krause, M. A. (1998, April). *Comparative perspectives on joint attention in children and apes: Development, functions and the effects of rearing history*. Paper presented at the 11th Biennial Conference on Infant Studies, Atlanta, GA.

Krause, M. A., & Fouts, R. S. (1997). Chimpanzee (*Pan troglodytes*) pointing: hand shapes, accuracy and the role of eye gaze. *Journal of Comparative Psychology*, *111*, 330–336.

Langton, S. R. H. (1999). The mutual influence of gaze and head orientation in the analysis of social attention direction. *Quarterly Journal of Experimental Psychology*.

Leavens, D. A., & Hopkins, W. D. (1998). Intentional communication by chimpanzees: A cross-sectional study of the use of referential gestures. *Developmental Psychology*, *34*, 813–822.

Leavens, D. A., Hopkins, W. D., & Bard, K. A. (1996). Indexical and referential pointing in chimpanzees (*Pan troglodytes*). *Journal of Comparative Psychology*, *110*, 346–353.

Lee, K., Eskritt, M., Symons, L. A., & Muir, D. (1998). Children's use of triadic eye gaze information for "mind reading." *Developmental Psychology*, *34*, 525–539.

Lempers, J. D. (1976). *Production of pointing, comprehension of pointing and understanding of looking behavior in young children*. Unpublished doctoral dissertation, University of Minnesota.

Lempert, H., & Kinsbourne, M. (1985). Possible origin of speech in selective orienting. *Psychological Bulletin*, *97*, 62–73.

Leung, E. H. L., & Rheingold, H. L. (1981). Development of pointing as a social gesture. *Developmental Psychology, 17*, 215–220.

Lock, A., Young, A., Service, V., & Chandler, P. (1990). Some observations on the origins of the pointing gesture. In V. Volterra & C. J. Erting (Eds.), *From gesture to language in hearing and deaf children* (pp. 42–55). Berlin: Springer Verlag.

Lorincz, E. N., Baker, C. I., & Perret, D. I. (1999). Visual cues for attention following in rhesus monkeys. *Cahiers de Psychologie Cognitive.*

Marler, P. (1959). Developments in the study of animal communication. In P. R. Bell (Ed.), *Darwin's biological work.* Cambridge: Cambridge University Press.

Masataka, N. (1995). The relation between index-finger extension and the acoustic quality of cooing in three month old infants. *Journal of Child Language, 22*, 247–257.

Masur, E. F. (1983). Gestural development, dual directional signalling, and the transition to words. *Journal of Psycholinguistic Research, 12*, 93–109.

Menzel, E. W., Jr. (1974). A group of young chimpanzees in a one acre field. In A. Schrier & F. Stollnitz (Eds.), *Behaviour of non-human primates: Modern research trends.* San Diego, CA: Academic Press.

Messer, D. J. (1994). *The development of communication: From social interaction to language.* Chichester: Wiley.

Millar, W. S., & Schaffer, H. R. (1972). The influence of spatially displaced visual feedback on infant operant conditioning. *Journal of Experimental Child Psychology, 14*, 442–452.

Millar, W. S., & Schaffer, H. R. (1973). Visual manipulative response strategies in infant operant conditioning with spatially displaced feedback. *British Journal of Psychology, 64*, 545–552.

Moore, C., & Corkum, V. (1994). Social understanding at the end of the first year of life. *Developmental Review, 14*, 349–372.

Morissette, P., Ricard, M., & Gouin-Decarie, T. (1995). Joint visual attention and pointing in infancy: A longitudinal study of comprehension. *British Journal of Developmental Psychology, 13*, 163–177.

Mundy, P., Kasari, C., & Sigman, M. (1992). Non-verbal communication, affective sharing and intersubjectivity. *Infant Behavior and Development, 15*, 377–381.

Murphy, C. M. (1978). Pointing in the context of shared activity. *Child Development, 49*, 371–380.

Murphy, C. M., & Messer, D. J. (1977). Mothers, infants and pointing: A study of gesture. In H. R. Schaffer (Ed.), *Studies of mother–infant interaction* (pp. 325–354). London: Academic Press.

Napier, J. (1960). Studies of the hands of living primates. *Proceedings of the Zoological Society of London, 134*, 647–657.

Ohama, K. (1984). Development of pointing behavior in infants and mother's responsive behavior: Longitudinal study of infants from 9 to 30 months. In M. Ogino, K. Ohama, K. Saito, S. Takei, & T. Tatsuno (Eds.), *The development of verbal behavior VI.* Bulletin of the Faculty of Education, University of Tokyo.

Piaget, J. (1952). *The origins of intelligence in children.* New York: Norton.

Piaget, J. (1954). *The construction of reality in the child.* New York: Basic Books.

Povinelli, D., Bering, J. M., & Giambrone, S. (2000). Chimpanzee pointing: Another error of the argument by analogy. In S. Kita (Ed.), *Pointing: Where language, culture and cognition meet.* Cambridge: Cambridge University Press.

Povinelli, D. J., & Davis, D. R. (1994). Differences between chimpanzees (*Pan troglodytes*) and humans (*Homo sapiens*) in the resting state of the index finger. *Journal of Comparative Psychology, 108*, 134–139.

Povinelli, D. J., & Eddy, T. J. (1996a). Factors influencing young chimpanzees' (*Pan troglodytes'*) recognition of attention. *Journal of Comparative Psychology, 110*, 336–345.

Povinelli, D. J., & Eddy, T. J. (1996b). What young chimpanzees know about seeing. *Monographs of the Society for Research in Child Development, 61,* 247.

Povinelli, D. J., & Eddy, T. J. (1996c). Chimpanzees: Joint visual attention. *Psychological Science, 7,* 129–135.

Povinelli, D. J., Reaux, J. E., Bierschwale, D. T., Allain, A. D., & Simon, B. B. (1997). Exploitation of pointing as a visual gesture in young children but not adolescent chimpanzees. *Cognitive Development, 12,* 423–461.

Ristau, C. (1991). Attention, purposes and deception in birds. In A. Whiten (Ed.), *Natural theories of mind* (pp. 209–233). Oxford: Blackwell.

Rodier, P. M., Ingram, J. L., Tisdale, B., Nelson, S., & Romano, J. (1996). Embryological origin for autism: Developmental anomalies of the cranial nerve motor nuclei. *Journal of Comparative Neurology, 370,* 247–261.

Rolfe, L. (1996). Theoretical stages in the prehistory of grammar. In A. Lock & C. R. Peters (Eds.), *Handbook of human symbolic evolution* (pp. 776–792). Oxford: Oxford University Press.

Scaife, M., & Bruner, J. S. (1975). The capacity for joint attention in the infant. *Nature, 253,* 265–266.

Schaffer, H. R. (1984). *The child's entry into a social world.* New York: Academic Press.

Shinn, M. (1900). *The biography of a baby.* Boston: Houghton Mifflin.

Stern, D. (1999). Vitality contours: The temporal contour of feelings as a basic unit for constructing the infant's social experience. In P. Rochat (Ed.), *Early social cognition: Understanding others in the first months of life* (pp. 67–80). Hillsdale, NJ: Lawrence Erlbaum Associates.

Stromland, K., Nordin, V., Miller, M., Akerstrom, B., & Gillberg, C. (1994). Autism in thalidomide embryopathy: A population study. *Developmental Medicine and Child Neurology, 36,* 351–356.

Tomasello, M., & Call, J. (1997). *Primate cognition.* Oxford: Oxford University Press.

Tomasello, M., Call, J., & Hare, B. (1998). Five primate species follow the visual gaze of conspecifics. *Animal Behaviour, 55.*

Tonooka, R., & Matsuzawa, T. (1995). Hand preferences of captive chimpanzees (*Pan troglodytes*) in simple reaching for food. *International Journal of Primatology, 16,* 17–23.

Tran-Duc Thao (1984). *Investigations into the origins of language and consciousness* (Trans. D. J. Herman & R. L. Armstrong). Dordrecht: Reidel.

Trevarthen, C. (1979). Communication and cooperation in early infancy: A description of primary intersubjectivity. In M. Bullowa (Ed.), *Before speech: The beginning of human communication* (pp. 321–347). Cambridge: Cambridge University Press.

Trevarthen, C. (1993). The functions of emotions in early infant communication and development. In J. Nadel & L. Camioni (Eds.), *New perspectives in early communicative development* (pp. 48–81). London: Routledge.

Vygotsky, L. S. (1962). *Thought and language.* New York: Wiley.

Vygotsky, L. S. (1988). Development of the higher mental functions. In K. Richardson & S. Sheldon (Eds.), *Cognitive development to adolescence* (pp. 61–80). Hove: Lawrence Erlbaum.

Werner, H., & Kaplan, B. (1963). *Symbol formation: An organismic-developmental approach to language and the expression of thought.* New York: Wiley.

Chapter Nine

Mind Knowledge in the First Year: Understanding Attention and Intention

Vasudevi Reddy

Introduction

In 1979, in an early book on infant social cognition, Michael Lewis and Jeanne Brooks-Gunn criticized psychology for focusing too much on the infant's knowledge of the physical properties of the world and too little on knowledge of people. Twenty years later in a book devoted to early social cognition, the editor observed that developmental research on social cognition has focused mainly on changes occurring after the end of the first year (Rochat, 1999, p. viii); we are still hesitant to use the terms social cognition or mind knowledge to refer to infants in their first year, although we know a lot more today about social interactions in the early months.

The primary reason for this lack of knowledge and for this reluctance stems from the way we conceive of mind. Western psychology generally assumes a mind–*behavior* dualism in which minds are seen as internal, invisible, nonmaterial entities which guide and influence outward behavior and can only be inferred, never directly known. Inevitably, since inferring the existence of a mind "behind" mere behavior must be a difficult mental achievement, such a skill has generally been reserved for humans and only after the end of infancy (Perner, 1991; Piaget, 1926; Wellman, 1990). However, there are several reasons to object to such an approach to mind. It is premised upon a mind–*body* dualism which psychology has long been uncomfortable with; it adopts a dual process theory of intelligent action (first a mental plan, then the physical behavior) which is not defensible, even in adult humans (Costall & Still, 1987; Coulter, 1979; Ryle, 1949); it reduces people to minds and bodies where they are better understood as persons (Hobson, 1991); and, taken to its logical conclusion, implies a developmental starting position of "mind-blindness" such as is attributed to children with autism (Baron-Cohen, 1997). Assuming mind–*behavior* dualism leads to the prediction of a sharp developmental discontinuity in the understanding of other minds (infants perceive mere behavior while children infer minds) and of a discontinuity in action (once children can infer minds, but not before, they can act on that knowledge to manipulate, inform, or deceive minds). However, developmental evidence does not support such discontinuities and often argues for the contrary (see, for instance, debates about the development of deception; Newton, Reddy, & Bull, 2000; Sodian, 1994).

Alternative approaches argue for the analysis of mind *in* rather than *behind* action, with mind seen as an adverb – the *way* in which actions are conducted – rather than as a separate entity – their hidden cause (Asch, 1952; Coulter, 1979; Jopling, 1993; Ryle, 1949). If mind is visible in action it can be perceived rather than necessarily inferred, and the extent to which it is perceived can be read, similarly, in *actions* with others' mindful behavior. This assumption of the observability and knowability of mind allows us to take seriously infants' psychological engagement with others and to understand the attunement and sharing *between* minds (whether emotional, intentional, or perceptual) as being primary and not derivative. The more widespread assumption (that infants can only perceive and interact with others' behavior, and not their minds) imposes a ban on the consideration of early interactions as aspects of mind knowledge. Actions which, in children and adults, would be taken as evidence of mind knowledge are neglected in infancy because of this theoretical assumption and a (methodological) double standard. This chapter thus focuses on infant actions with minds as both evidence of, and the basis for, mind knowledge.

A focus on infant action with other mindful persons allows us to describe the limits, constraints, and developments in psychological engagement. Infants do not develop social understanding through social voyeurism (Rochat & Striano, 1999, p. 4), and the process of engagement (between infant and adult or between adults) is a continuously creative process in which each partner monitors and jointly regulates the other's acts (Fogel, 1993). Understanding mind, then, is not simply a process of perceiving it in others; it must be simultaneously a question of creating it. The necessary presence of a reciprocating other for the realization, instantiation, and development of psychological processes has been demonstrated in the realm of intentions (Habermas, 1970), language and meaning (Halliday, 1975), and affective and communicative processes (Field et al., 1988). Infants learn about minds and psychological processes through the engagements they co-create.

This chapter attempts to describe what infants do with two fundamental aspects of mentality in others: their attention and their intentions. It could be argued that there is a third aspect to be discussed – affect – which is, if anything, more fundamental than either attention or intention; however, affect is not included here as a separate topic. Although *all* aspects of people are inseparably involved in action and separating them is an artificial device of the scientist to simplify matters, affect is the most inextricable of all such aspects. It is present, as Stern (1985, 1999) argues, in every act and glance and thought. It makes as little sense to disengage affect from attention and intention as it does to separate the mind from the body, except in pathological conditions where it may be precisely this separation of the act from the attitude that is the source of psychological problems (Hobson, 1999).

Within each section the research evidence is organized in subsections, starting from the infant's *direct engagement with others*, proceeding to *engagement with others through acts by the self*, and then to *engagement with others through others' acts on external targets*, dealing first with infant *responses to* such engagement, then with infant *attempts to direct* it. This developmental scheme extrapolates from current theories about the intersubjective origins of mind knowledge (Adamson & Russell, 1999; Hobson, 1991; Rochat & Striano, 1999; Trevarthen, 1977) as well as from older non-developmental views about the primacy of the I–Thou relation over the I–It (Buber, 1937). The presumption is that understanding begins in simple dyadic mutuality, i.e., in the infant's direct relation with each aspect, and then develops into triadic and referential engagement that includes aspects of the world and other people.

Understanding Attention

You cannot engage with psychological states or processes unless you perceive first of all (sometimes wrongly) that the entity you are dealing with can attend to you. The most pervasive feature of attention is the orientation of the body, often involving a breaking of posture, a stilling of body movements, cardiac deceleration, and a turning of the eyes, head, and body toward a target. To detect such attention clearly has survival value for the organism. It is useful to know when someone is looking at oneself as well as when someone is looking at another interesting, desirable, or threatening target (Baron-Cohen, 1995). This section will review evidence about visual attention because this is the only aspect of attention that has been well researched; however, this emphasis on vision must be kept in mind as it can mislead us into particular theoretical distortions (e.g., thinking about targets of attention in spatial rather than temporal terms, or overemphasizing infant gaze to the other's face and eyes and neglecting infant awareness of the other's body, orientation and actions), and may underestimate the infant's abilities, for example, in the understanding of touching.

The transition to what is normally called joint attention, at the end of the first year, is usually seen as the most, or even the first, significant development in the understanding of attention, involving a triangulation or coordination of attention between infant, other, and object, and as critical to the development of referential communication, language, and symbolization (Bakeman & Adamson, 1984; Camaioni, 1993; Mundy & Sigman, 1989; Werner & Kaplan, 1963). The very problem of reference and how it develops can be restated according to Bruner, as the problem of how people manage and direct each others' attention (Bruner, 1983). However, there are still debates and uncertainties about the age at which an understanding of attention develops, about continuities in its development, and about the "causes" of its emergence (Camaioni, 1993). Perner (1991) suggests that it cannot be present until 18 months, when the infant becomes capable of multiply representing not just a seen reality (the other's behavior) but also an imagined one (i.e., the attentional state of the other); and that earlier attentional engagement involves no understanding of attention as mental – merely of the other's behavior. Others suggest that attention is understood as a mental process from around 9 to 12 months of age, emerging from an implicit conceptual discovery of some kind (Bretherton, 1991; Bretherton, McNew, & Beeghly-Smith, 1981; Tomasello, 1999). Yet others suggest that attention is perceived as a psychological event even earlier, from at least 2 months of age, through an innate capacity for primary intersubjectivity (Trevarthen, 1977), and that what develops by the end of the first year is an expansion of the targets it relates to (Reddy, Hay, Murray, & Trevarthen, 1997). An alternative early mind knowledge theory suggests that an innate and early mechanism called the eye direction detector (EDD) allows the simple perception of attentional and intentional links between eyes and targets (Baron-Cohen, 1995, 1997), and much later allows triadic engagement through the importing of a new clause into the dyadic relation (Baron-Cohen, 1995, 1997). Related to this, a second theoretical issue in this area concerns the existence and nature of infant under-standing of attention in the first half of the first year. While the dominant view is cur-rently that triadic attentional relations cannot be perceived early in life but emerge from the dyadic, there are some suggestions that a perception of triadic relations, i.e., between others' eyes, external targets, and the self, are already evident before 6 months of age and develop simultaneously with dyadic understanding (Fivaz-Depeursinge & Corboz-Warnery, 1999; Muir & Hains, 1999).

Responding to Attention Directed to the Self

Human neonates are known to be very interested in faces (Goren, Sarty, & Wu, 1975; Johnson & Morton, 1991); however, when does the infant realize that the faces are, at least in a global sense, directing attention to him or her? The eyes themselves are not the main focus of neonatal attention to faces until after the first 2 months. How-ever, are young infants even sensitive to the directionality and orientation of the head? And what does it mean to infants to have a head turned toward rather than away from them?

Evidence of orientation discrimination at 6 weeks has led to the suggestion that some form of orientationally tuned detectors are present even at birth (Atkinson, Hood, Wattam-Bell, & Anker, 1988). Several studies have shown that 3-month-olds can detect head orientation, responding with less gaze and smiling to adults with averted heads (Caron, Caron, Mustelin, & Roberts, 1992). Reading eye direction *per se* may be diffi-cult for young infants, but differential responses have been shown in 3-month-olds to shut eyes (Caron et al., 1992), in 4-month-olds to averted versus frontal gaze in line draw-ings of faces (Vecera & Johnson, 1995), and in 5-month-olds to averted gaze (Laskey & Klein, 1979). More naturalistically, Wolff (1987) showed that making and breaking eye contact affected infants even from 8 weeks of age. Three-month-olds smile less when adults look away from them, with a 20-degree deflection of the eyes (Muir & Hains, 1999, p. 175), or even a 5-degree horizontal deflection (i.e., to the ears rather than the eyes), but not to a 5-degree vertical deflection (i.e., to the forehead or chin; Symons, Hains, & Muir, 2000).

Adult attention does not merely act as a cue to the infant to interact but allows subtle engagement and the organized play of many "prespeech" behaviors in addition to gaze and smiling (Trevarthen, 1977), and leads to complex affective responses. Reddy (2000) described shy or coy smiles (consisting of smiling with gaze and head aversion and curving arm movements in front of the face) in 2- and 3-month-olds in response to attentional contact with adults, and especially following the renewed onset of mutual attention. There is anecdotal evidence of even 2-month-olds using unemotional head and gaze aversion to avoid mutual gaze with adults when the adult repeatedly tries to gain eye contact, and of negative responses to mutual gaze when the infant cannot disengage, perhaps for reasons of neurological immaturity (Brazelton, 1986). For infants as for adults, the attention of others is arousing and inducing of multiple emotional reactions (i.e., positive, negative, neutral, and ambivalent).

Studies comparing infant responses to people and to things suggest that 5- to 8-week-olds selectively imitate people but not objects (Legerstee, 1991), 2- to 3-month-olds show different configurations of hand movement and affect to persons than to animated dolls (D'Entremont, Hains, & Muir, 1997; Legerstee, Corter & Kienapple, 1990), and 4-month-olds also differentiate between familiar and novel persons (but not objects) in their interactive behavior (Legerstee, 1994). However, by 12 months, even animated robots with faces can induce gaze following and smiling (Johnson, Slaughter, Collins, Tyan, & Carey, 1996). Clearly, these studies manipulate more than orientation of head, body, and eyes but suggest an early detection of a global animateness in engagement.

Evidence of infant responses to attention comes also from studies which create inappropriate attention, showing that by 2 months of age infants are sensitive not just to the presence of attention but also to the quality of attentive behavior. When adults change from interactive attention to still-faced attention even 6-week-olds become distressed (Cohn & Tronick, 1989; Murray, 1980), showing either a sensitivity to the abnormal quality of attention in the still-face condition or to the change from a dynamic to a static display. In a ground-breaking study Murray and Trevarthen (1985) showed that even watching video-replays of their mothers in which the mothers were expressing positive and interactive behaviors led to 2-month-old infants becoming perturbed, alternating between attempts to reengage interactive attention and gaze aversion and frowning. This finding was replicated with 9-week-olds by Nadel and Tremblay-Leveau (1999), who also showed that during a second live condition to control for fatigue effects, infants showed a clear recovery with a significant increase in gaze to the mother, as if in scrutiny. This is strong evidence for concluding that 2-month-olds not only detect attention and inattention, but detect and respond appropriately to the appropriateness of the attention they receive. Similarly, it is not just the presence of attention or the withdrawal of positive attention that is responsible for infant distress. When adults withdrew positive attention from the infants to talk to the experimenter who had just entered the room, infants showed no distress or attempts to reengage the mother, but maintained a relaxed expression, watching both adults (Murray & Trevarthen, 1985).

Nonetheless, however complex and appropriate the infant's reactions to others' attention and inattention or inappropriate attention when directed to the self, this evidence is still limited in connection with understanding that others are actually thinking about the thing they are looking at. In other words, emotional reactions to attention are clearly only one part of the understanding of attentiveness. For this, the traditional test has been to ask whether the infant or other organism can understand the relevance of others' attention when directed to an external target. This is important for establishing one of the most central developments in communication and social understanding – that of having a shared focus of attention and of understanding that attention in others (and in the self) can have a focus at all, that it can be "about" something.

Responding to Attention Directed to an External Target

Scaife and Bruner (1975) first suggested that infants of 2 months could follow others' gaze to an external target and that this was dramatic evidence of infant ability to understand the mental significance of others' gaze. However, such early gaze monitoring appears to be hard to demonstrate and subsequent studies have established its presence more clearly by 6 months of age (for a review see Butterworth, 1995, and Moore, 1999). Butterworth suggests that three successive mechanisms are involved in the development of joint visual reference: an early "ecological" mechanism allows the identification of the general direction of an adult's head and eyeturn by 6 months of age, but is limited by the attention-capturing features of the target itself (Grover, 1988, cited in Butterworth, 1995) and does not occur until about 10 months if there is no target at all (Corkum & Moore, 1994). It is not until 12 months of age that infants can use adult gaze for precise location of a target in the right direction, demonstrating an ability to extrapolate precise angles of orientation of the head and eyes and showing what Butterworth calls a "geometric" mechanism. Interestingly, joint visual reference appears to be limited by the boundaries of the infant's visual space – it is not until 18 months of age that infants turn their heads to search in space that is behind them, and then only if the current visual field is empty of targets. Infants appear to perceive their own visual space to be held in common with others and it is only after 18 months that the primacy of their visual field may be overcome by a mechanism allowing access to "representational" space (Butterworth & Jarrett, 1991). Evidence of accurate gaze-following abilities in the first year has also been found by Morissette, Ricard, and Gouin-Decarie (1995), showing correct headturns above chance in some 6- and 9-month-olds, and by Morales, Mundy, and Rojas (1997), who also showed that this ability in 6-month-olds related to later-developing receptive and expressive language abilities. Infants can also be conditioned to follow adult head turning, both when the head is turned toward, and when it is turned away from, a target (Corkum & Moore, 1998). Moore (1999) suggests that early gaze following is an exogenously controlled reflexive shift in visual orienting to the same direction as the adult's headturn, implying no awareness of the others' object of regard, or indeed even of the other's regard. From this view, for establishing the infant's understanding of the psychological significance of orienting to another target, evidence is needed of either further response complexity in young infants or of discriminatory responses to gaze in the absence of a target.

Willen, Hood, and Driver (1997), in a study which manipulated eye direction independent of head turning, showed that infants as young as 10 weeks could process changes in gaze alone. When the pupils of the eyes in an animated face shifted to the periphery of the field and were followed by a target at that side, infants turned to look at the target significantly more often than if the peripheral target were not preceded by shifting gaze. While it is not yet clear whether the shifting of any stimulus might have the same effect on infant gaze, it is evident that even before 3 months infants can be sensitive to shifts in gaze direction. D'Entremont et al. (1997) investigated infant eye-turning behavior when an adult with whom they were interacting turned to look at one of two puppets on either side of her. They found that even at 3 months, infants spontaneously turned their eyes to look at the correct puppet (significantly more often than at the incorrect puppet), with no age differences in accuracy between 3-, 5-, and 6-month-olds. Interestingly, this adult distraction (turning four times in 4 minutes to talk to one of the puppets for 10 seconds) had an overall distracting effect on the infants, with infant gaze frequently alternating between the adult and the puppet. Infant headturns to the correct object had a surprisingly long latency of 2 seconds, suggesting that the turn is not simply an automated tracking but possibly the result of some consideration about the fact of the adult's turn, as well as a recognition of its direction.

Bakeman and Adamson (1984) identified a category of infant–person–object engagement which they called passive joint attention, involving attention to the object of the other's current attention (indicated not by gaze alone but by action, vocalization, and whole-body engagement), without any alternation of gaze between the object and the other's face, or any specific following of the other's gaze to the target. This type of engagement is likely to be a very common feature of infant–parent interaction during the middle months of the first year, with parents often highlighting objects to regain infant attention, or engaging in games and songs involving the infant's body (Stern, 1985; Trevarthen, 1977). Bakeman and Adamson (1984) found that such passive joint attention accounted for about a fifth of interaction time between 6 and 18 months of age and, like later-developing coordinated joint attention, was often preceded and followed by engagement with objects. Passive joint attention was likely to be closely tied to parental actions, with adults providing an implicit context for referential communication.

Directing Attention to the Self

Infants of 2 and 3 months are clearly capable of responding with appropriate affect and reciprocity when they are already the targets of others' attention. However, can infants *seek* such attention? Studies using still-face or video-replay disruptions in the adult's communicative behavior show that when deprived of adult responsiveness, even 6-week-old infants attempt a series of other-directed acts including vocalizations and arm movements with gaze to the other's face. These have been interpreted as attempts to regain adult attention to the self (Cohn & Tronick, 1989; Murray, 1980) and are at the very least attempts to reengage interaction. Further, in the presence of an inadequately responsive adult, infants can increase the intensity of their normal vocal and facial expressions (Reddy et al., 1997; Trevarthen, 1990). There is some evidence that after about 3 or 4 months of age infants take on a more active initiating role in interaction. This could imply a growing confidence in adult responsiveness in the context of dyadic interactions, as well as a developing ability to engage in varied vocalizations and facial expressions. Although there is some anecdotal suggestion that infants at this age develop different kinds of shrill, "calling" vocalizations when adults are absent or naturally inattentive (Reddy et al., 1997), there is as yet no definite evidence of such abilities until the second half of the first year.

Directing Attention to Acts by the Self

Within naturalistic interactions infants from around 7 months of age engage in attention-seeking behaviors that go beyond simply trying to regain the other's attention to the self. Infants now seek to gain it for acts by the self. They start to do things for effect, which at the simplest level involves a breaking of the flow of the interaction in some way, and at more complex levels involves a repetition of acts that have previously received adult attention (Bates, 1976). Such acts show an awareness not just of simple attentiveness, but that attention in others can relate to specific aspects of, or events involving, the self.

Infants from this age produce two different kinds of attention-directing acts – "showing off" and "clowning" (Bates, 1976; Reddy, 1991; Trevarthen & Hubley, 1978), showing a developing awareness of being an actor (Reddy et al., 1997). Both involve the repetition of acts for re-eliciting responses from the other; showing off can involve "clever" acts for praise or "silly" acts for attention, and clowning involves exaggerated or rule-violating acts for laughter. The commonest forms of clowning at 8 months involve repetitive movements of particular parts of the body, such as shaking the head vigorously, making odd facial expressions, odd movements of the body, putting odd things such as pyjamas on the head, and blowing raspberries. Clowning and showing off through the performance of silly acts are reported by parents to be common at 8 months. While the prevalence of silly acts for attention is not reported to change with age (some children do it and some don't), the prevalence of clowning and showing off through the repetition of clever acts (such as clapping or waving or saying a word) does increase with age. It is not until after 11 months that 50 percent of children engage in clever showing off (Reddy & Williams, in preparation).

Directing Attention to External Targets

There are a variety of ways in which infants take a more active role in triadic engagements involving not just their own acts but also external targets. They begin to develop their own "primitive marking system for singling out the noteworthy" (Bruner, 1983, p. 77), which includes vocalizations, gestures, and even making contact with an object a potential partner is manipulating (Adamson & Bakeman, 1991). And even 9-month-old infants can use communicative signals that make reference to the toy and to the adult when the adult suddenly misses a turn in a game (Ross & Lollis, 1987). Bates (1976) found that the first signs of the "protodeclarative" (early, nonverbal forms of telling someone something) involve the directing of attention to an external target and were seen in giving/showing an object – at around 10 months of age. Research in this area has focused primarily on protodeclarative pointing, which emerges on average between 12 and 14 months of age (Franco & Butterworth, 1988; Perucchini & Camaioni, 1993).

There is an old debate about the ontogeny of pointing, with the Vygotskyan view suggesting that pointing emerges from the parents' attribution of intentional reference to acts of simple reaching (Vygotsky, 1926/1962). However, recent evidence suggests that pointing is rarely confused with reaching (Franco & Butterworth, 1991, cited in Butterworth, 1995) and that pointing is not dependent on the adult's social scaffolding, emerging simultaneously with adults and with peers (Franco, Perucchini, & Butterworth, 1992). Some suggest that protodeclarative pointing may be merely a conditioned response or experimental test of others' reactions (Perner, 1991), but this is not consistent with evidence about the social significance of pointing (Franco & Butterworth, 1988) and of the communicative purposes of early pointing. In one study the purposes of protodeclaratives in a 14-month-old infant varied from reference to affectively charged targets (such as horses and tractors), reference to novel events or objects, reference to just perceived persons, events, or objects, routine reference to specific objects around the house such as photographs, and sober-faced reference to any nearby object in almost ritualistic greetings to strangers. The majority of protodeclaratives occurred immediately following the infant's perceptual onset of the target, suggesting that it was interest in the target rather than *just* in the other's response that led to early protodeclaratives (Reddy, 1992).

The infant's alternation of gaze between the adult's face and the target of attention (to which either the infant is directing adult attention or to which the adult is looking or pointing) has generally been taken as evidence for joint attention and for establishing the infant's grasp of attention in the other (for an exception, see Perner, 1991), and as a necessary criterion for protodeclarative pointing (Perucchini & Camaioni, 1993). However, adults do not always look at the recipient's face during communication, sometimes assuming attention from other cues. Similarly, gaze to the adult's face is not common during infant pointing in picture-book reading (Cox, 1986), nor during infant pointing when the adult is carrying, or in physical contact with, the infant (Reddy, 1992), and tends to increase with distance between the infant and the recipient (Reddy & Simone, 1995, in preparation). Franco and Butterworth (1988) showed that while gaze alternating during pointing occurs on average from 14 months, gaze to the other's face *before* pointing does not begin until 15 months. Descrochers, Morissette, and Ricard (1995) showed that only pointing *with* gaze to face (typically occurring after 15 months) related to later language development, suggesting that at least in the early phases pointing without gaze to face may not be a communicative act. It is likely that since proximity often accompanies joint body orientation and prior joint attention to targets in the same region of space, young infants may be engaging in acts of attention directing with a less differentiated assumption of attentiveness on the other's part (judged from proximity and body orientation), an assumption which becomes elaborated during the second year to exclude certain externally directed inattentive behaviors.

Thus far we have seen that responding to the visual attention of others is a complex and coordinated process even in the first few months of life. Evidence of appropriate emotional responses to attention, inattention, and inappropriate attention to the self is present from around 2 months of age. There is controversial evidence suggesting that from as early as 3 months of age we may see the beginnings of appropriate responses to attention directed to external targets, a skill normally evident from the middle of the first year. The ability to direct the attention of others appears to begin from around 3 months of age. The targets to which others' attention can be directed by the infant change with age. The initial target of the global self (at around 3 months) differentiates into different aspects of the self's acts (from around 7 or 8 months) to targets distant from the self (from 11 months). To some extent the significance of an act of attention, especially its referential significance, involves an understanding of the intentionality of the attentional act. This aspect of attending has received much recent attention from psychological research on infants' understanding of intentions, which we will now consider.

Understanding Intentions

We know less about infant understanding of intentionality in others than we do about their understanding of attentionality. However, the apparent developmental schedule of this understanding and issues about its development share common features. There are a number of advantages to being able to read intentions in others: it is useful for anticipating and responding to particular actions, for distinguishing between intentional and accidental communicative actions in order to ignore the latter, for differentiating between playful and serious intentions and responding to each appropriately, for understanding others' intentions for one's own actions and complying with (or defying) them, for controlling others' intentions for their own actions, for identifying the intentional directedness of actions and utterances in order to detect communicative referents, and for understanding intentional relations between significant others.

In the understanding of intentions as in the understanding of attention, it is the developments around the end of the first year, of an interest in others' intentional and motivational states for their own sake (Bretherton et al., 1981; Trevarthen & Hubley, 1978), or what Stern calls "inter-intentionality" (Stern, 1985), that have been identified as important milestones. Here, too, events before this period are less clearly understood but are vital for theorizing. Two key debates are worth mentioning in this area. One concerns the question of whether intentions need inferential understanding or whether they can be directly perceived. This is not simply a question of distinguishing between those intentions which may be said to be visible in action and those which are not (Searle, 1983): some would argue that even when intentions may be detectable in action, to read the cues for intention and to understand the behavior as intentional needs an inferential or interpretative process on the part of the infant (Baldwin & Baird, 1999; Gergely, Nadasdy, Csibra, & Biro, 1995), while others have argued that intentions can be perceived in action without inference (Asch, 1952). More extreme positions have posited that intention is a mental state equivalent to belief and cannot genuinely be understood without a theory of mind at around 3 or 4 years of age (Astington, 1991). The second and related debate concerns the question of whether an understanding of intention begins with an understanding of intentionality in general that allows the infant to understand different kinds of specific intentions, or whether the developmental process starts from an understanding of particular specific intentions and then proceeds to a more general understanding of intentionality. Some theorists argue for a "hard-wired" ability that allows the interpretation of all self-propelled movement as intentional (especially if vigorous and persistent beyond a baseline; Premack, 1990; Premack & Premack, 1995), or an innate module called the ID (intentionality detector), present possibly from birth, which performs a similar reading of self-propelled movement (Baron-Cohen, 1997). These, along with some "theory of mind" theories, imply an abstract origin to the understanding of intention. Others (e.g., Woodward, in press), show that this is not supported by experimental evidence: infants do not read all self-propelled movement as intentional, only particular actions. This could either imply that intentions are understood only in context – i.e., only if they are familiar – or that they are understood in an even more generalized way than suggested by Premack and Baron-Cohen, through the ability to read muscle tension and other subtle intention cues rather than just self-propelled movement.

Responding to Intentions Directed to the Self

There is little direct evidence about very early understanding of the intentionality of actions. Some indirect evidence comes from infant responses to adult attempts to pick them up. Infants from about 4 months of age are reported to accommodate their bodies to the reaching movement of others' arms and hands, a reaction which children with autism are reported not to show (Lord, 1994).

Possibly relevant is infant response to a third perturbation condition in the Murray and Trevarthen (1985) study reported earlier: when the mother interrupted interaction with the infant to talk to another adult the infants were quiet and appeared to wait for the mother's attention to return. This could simply imply that in this condition the mother's attention was completely withdrawn, or it could be that the mother's suspension of interaction was detected as not intentionally directed to the infant, but further research needs to test these possibilities.

Infants respond to the playful intentions of others from at least around 4 months of age, as evidenced by their laughter and participation in games, especially those involving potentially threatening acts by others such as tickling, chasing, and looming. There is little evidence as yet of early discrimination between playful and serious intentions in different contexts. One study explored infant reactions to mothers' playful "threats" with a mask in a free-play context and showed that 9-month-old infants reacted with laughter to this action, while 18-month-olds reacted with anxiety (Nakano, 1994). Different interpretations are possible of this intriguing developmental shift; Nakano suggests that playful intentions are perceivable as such and do not need a knowledge of meta-intentions in order for the infant to distinguish them from serious acts, as suggested by Bateson (1973).

Responding to Intentions for Actions by the Self

Trevarthen and Hubley (1978) report a dramatic shift after 9 months of age in infant coordination of object and person attention, involving an understanding of the other person's motivational and intentional states. The clearest context for understanding of others' intentions appears to be an understanding of the other's instructions for the infant's own actions. This can be seen in episodes where the mother provides incomplete demonstrations of actions which she wants the infant to complete – such as showing the place where the doll is to be placed. Rather than copy the exact demonstration (which, being incomplete, would have been inappropriate), infants displayed an understanding of the intent by obeying the instruction. Using such evidence Bretherton argues that infants of 9 months of age show the first signs of an implicit theory of mind (Bretherton, 1991; Bretherton et al., 1981).

Tomasello, Kruger and Ratner (1993) make a similar point from studies of imitation and modeling, arguing that from around the end of the first year infants are capable of reading others' intentions in their acts. Rather than engage in exact "mimicking" of irrelevant aspects of modeled acts, infants from this age engage in genuine imitation in which the goal of the action is sought even if through a slightly different set of acts.

It is also in the last quarter of the first year that parents begin to give commands to their infants and that infants begin to comply with instructions (Stayton, Hogan, & Ainsworth, 1971). It is likely that the onset of parental commands at this age is partly the result of their sensing that their infants are capable of responding to such directive intentions. From around 7 or 8 months of age infants become capable of responding with some compliance to positive directives such as "Put the dolly there," "Wave bye-bye," "Clap hands," "Come to Mummy," and "Give me the biscuit." All of these directives are usually delivered through partial demonstrations, open-palm invitations, and so on. Infants also start responding (not necessarily with compliance) to prohibitions concerning their actions and incomplete intentions in ways that suggest that they are detecting both the presence of others' intentions for infant action as well as the level of seriousness of the intentions.

In a longitudinal analysis of parental reports about infant compliance we found (Reddy, 1998) that some sensitivity to prohibitions (other than simply being startled by them) was present in 50 percent of 8-month-olds; occasional compliance to verbal prohibitions was present in less than a third of the children at this age, but in over two-thirds of the children by 11 months and in all children by 14 months. There were some instances of apparent regression between 8 and 11 months, where infants who had previously shown sensitivity and even compliance to verbal commands started to ignore them either with laughter or with sober-faced unresponsiveness. Provocative noncompliance (i.e., noncompliance for its effect on the other rather than just from desire for the prohibited goal) was rare at 8 months, but present in 50 percent of the infants by 11 months. Infants distinguished between serious and nonserious issues, probably through tone of voice and other signs of playfulness in the parents, and early provocative noncompliance was limited primarily to nonserious issues.

Other forms of teasing were more prevalent at 8 and 11 months, involving playful offer and withdrawal of objects and playful disruption of others' acts. Such disruption usually involved acts that were directed to the infant rather than acts that were dyadic between the other and an external target. For instance, one infant at 11 months showed several instances of false requests, repeatedly asking for a drink and then refusing it until his mother realized that he was teasing her. Similarly, another infant at 11 months developed a game where he refused his mother's kiss until she was nearly out of the door. There were a few instances of teasing that involved a disruption of the other's acts toward another target, such as tipping the toy box out as soon as his sibling had tidied it up, or throwing the cushions down on the floor while the mother was tidying up preparatory to vacuuming the floor (Reddy, 1991). These reflect some understanding of the other's goal-directed actions toward external targets.

Responding to Intentions Directed Toward External Targets

When do infants detect the intentionality of others' actions directed toward external targets? Tomasello and Barton (1994) showed that when 24-month-olds heard an adult model a novel verb, they learned the verb only when it preceded an intentional action, not an accidental action. Using a discrepant labeling paradigm (i.e., with an adult speaker labeling and looking at an object while the addressee, the infant, is looking at a different object), Baldwin showed that infants of 18 months (Baldwin, 1991, 1993) and even infants as young as 12 months (Baldwin, Bill, & Ontai, 1996) are capable of actively seeking out clues such as gaze direction to the speaker's intended referent, and of using such cues to inform their language learning. Baldwin suggests that infants by around 12 months of age already engage in genuine intentional inference, analyzing even novel and complex actions in terms of underlying intentions (Baldwin & Baird, 1999). She suggests that action analysis is a necessary first step in development but it is soon superseded by intentional inference. Meltzoff (1995) showed that 18-month-olds who were shown models of an adult unsuccessfully trying to perform actions reenacted what the adult intended to do, not what the adult had actually done. This did not hold for infants watching a non-humanoid mechanical device's intended but unsuccessful action. Meltzoff suggests that before 18 months infants have already adopted a folk psychology in which persons but not things are understood within a framework involving goals and intentions. Similarly, Carpenter, Akhtar, and Tomasello (1998) showed that 14- to 18-month-olds imitated more intentional actions upon objects (followed by a verbal "There!") than accidental actions (followed by a "Whoops!") when adults modeled both types of acts in the infants' presence and explicitly asked the infant to have a go. The success of even 14-month-olds suggests that the ability to "screen out" others' unintentional, meaningless actions, which is so important in the acquisition of culture and language, is present by the end of the first year.

Premack predicted that infants can interpret some kinds of goal-directed actions in others, including the behavior of two objects toward each other. The adult ability to perceive chasing, escaping, hiding, and so on in the lawful movements and interactions of blobs on a screen (Heider & Simmel, 1944) has recently been investigated in infants by Gergely and colleagues (Csibra & Gergely, 1996, cited in Baldwin & Baird, 1999; Gergely et al., 1995), who have shown that 10- to 15-month-old infants interpret actions of balls on a screen in an intentional way. Following habituation to displays of a ball jumping over a barrier to reach another ball, infants dishabituated more to intentionally odd but spatially similar movements (jumping even when there was no barrier) than to spatially novel but intentionally sensible movements (taking a new but more direct path), and showed sensitivity to different kinds of path taken by a ball depending on the space available for the passage. One-year-olds thus appear to be adopting the intentional stance in relation to objects that do not involve them.

Woodward (in press) showed that even 5-month-old infants (although not as strongly as 9-month-olds) differentiated between a behavior that seemed to be goal-directed (grasping an object) and one that seemed unintentional (dropping the back of the hand in front of an object). Following habituation to a grasp, infants dishabituated more to the grasp of a new object than to a different path to the same object, but following habituation to the unintentional movement, they did not differentiate between a change of object and change of path. Showing that this difference was not attributable to differential interest in the grasping hand as opposed to the limp hand, Woodward argues that these findings challenge the view that infants are innately predisposed to perceive all action as intentional provided that they are self-propelled (Baron-Cohen, 1997; Gergely et al., 1995; Premack, 1990). Woodward suggests that the recognition of the unintentionality of the back of hand movement could be due either to the specific unfamiliarity to the infant of the act itself, or to the absence of intentionality cues such as muscle tension and palm orientation. Woodward and Somerville (in press) also showed that 12-month-olds understood the relevance of the sequentiality of actions to the presence of overarching goals. They construed ambiguous actions (such as an adult's hand touching the lid of a box) as relevant to the overall goal only if the subsequent action was causally related to it (i.e., removing the lid and grasping the toy inside the box) and not if the action was temporally but not causally linked to it (i.e., removing the lid but grasping the toy that was outside the box).

Sodian and Thoermer (1998) suggest that at 12 months infants do not yet infer the goal of an action from the actor's gaze direction alone (even with a facial expression of desire and interest). Showing that infants only reacted appropriately to gaze direction in certain conditions, they suggest that 12- and even 15-month-olds are more influenced by the effects such as novelty than by the relation between gaze direction and gaze-related action. Brooks, Caron, and Butler (1998) showed, on the contrary, that 14- and 18-month-olds did in fact use gaze direction as a cue to the relevance of the thing looked at. Using a violation of expectancy procedure, they found that infants looked longer at a new object that appeared on the same side as the adult had looked at previously than at the old object on a different side. This effect was present only if the adult who did the looking had her eyes open. Interestingly, in the eyes closed condition the opposite effect prevailed. The lack of difference between 14- and 18-month-olds in this study suggests that infants come to understand the intentional and referential function of looking before 14 months of age.

Directing Intentions Toward the Self

There is very little evidence about infant attempts to direct others' actions toward themselves. Early anticipatory responses to others' actions (such as arching the back toward another's reach) may develop into acts that are performed as an expression of need (i.e., arching the back in order to be picked up). While such acts occur in the first 6 months, it is not until about 9 months that they are used with any degree of specificity for others' intentions (see Service, 1984, for a discussion of developments in the hands-raised, pick-me-up gesture). Other actions such as crying and calling could also be argued to develop from simple expressions of internal states which just happen to elicit intentional actions in others, to attempts to seek intentional actions towards the self. Further research is needed, however, for understanding how such intentional engagements develop. Clearly though, in the early months, such attempts seek intentional actions toward the self as a global entity, not toward specific actions or aspects of the self, nor toward any external targets.

Directing Intentions Toward Actions by the Self

Once again, direct evidence on this topic is sparse. However, there is reason to believe, as with attention, that initial attempts to direct others' mentality (whether their attention or their intentions) toward the self as a global entity change first to directing them toward specific actions by the self, before directing them toward external targets. The holding out of objects to show/give them to others is one of the first signs of person–person–object interactions (Bates et al, 1979) in which the infant is actually directing the other's actions to adjust to an action by the self. Infants may start holding out objects to others from around 8 months, with signs of communication including gaze to the others' face and vocalizations, but not be able to successfully release them until several weeks later. This often leads to genuine uncertainty about whether they are intending to give or to show or some intermediate state (Reddy, 1998). Two aspects of such interactions are of importance here. One, that what is being sought by the infant is an intentional action by the other toward the act of holding out the object (rather than toward the object itself, or toward the self globally). Second, that infants often spontaneously offer and then playfully withdraw objects (especially interesting when these actions occur after infants are capable of releasing objects, and when they are not simple changes of mind but are marked by half-smiles and cheeky expressions). Both these actions are active attempts by infants from 8 months on to elicit intentional actions toward actions by the self.

Directing Intentions Toward External Targets

Toward the end of the first year, at around the same time as infants are able to comply with others' intentions for acts by the self, infants also demonstrate an ability to direct others' intentions for acts on external targets for the infant's benefit. There is some debate about whether this ability develops prior to or at the same time as the ability to direct others' attention to external targets. A Piagetian analysis of protoimperatives (early, non-verbal forms of commands) sees them as developmentally equivalent to protodeclaratives, with both emerging at the same time and from the same underlying cognitive advance – an understanding of means–ends relations and tool use (Bates, Benigni, Bretherton, Camaioni, & Volterra, 1979). However, protoimperative pointing may in fact predate protodeclarative pointing by about two months (Perucchini & Camaioni, 1993) and may be the result of a simpler instrumental perception of others' actions than the understanding of attentionality implied in protodeclaratives (Camaioni, 1993). The mere presence of protoimperatives need imply no understanding of others' intentionality, as has been shown in a subtle analysis of the development of a protoimperative act in a gorilla

(Gomez, 1991). In order to obtain its own goal, the gorilla first used the human as an object, then as a tool, then as an agent, and finally as an intentional being. The latter was observed through an indicative rather than forceful expression of an intention for the human's act, and through the presence of eye contact following this. In human infants, imperative pointing (i.e., indicative rather than forceful directives) is evident by 11 months (Perucchini & Camaioni, 1993), with gaze to the face at some point during the act. Even earlier than this, human infants appear to indicate a need through, for example, reaching for an object and waiting for adults to come to their help (Bates et al., 1979).

Thus far we have seen that the playfulness and global infant-directedness of others' intentional acts may be detected and appropriately responded to by around 3 or 4 months of age. Beginning at around 7 or 8 months, infants become responsive to others' intentions for directing the infants' own actions and show a sensitivity to the seriousness of these directive intentions by differential noncompliance. By the end of the first year provocative noncompliance and other forms of teasing that manipulate others' intentions and expectations are clearly established. Some intriguing evidence suggests that even 5-month-olds may be able to detect intentional actions directed to external targets, although most evidence suggests that this is clear after about 12 months. Infants' ability to direct intentions in simple global ways or in relation to their own acts is little understood. By the end of the first year, however, they succeed in clear ways in directing others' intentional acts toward external targets.

Early Mind Knowledge: Key Issues

This section raises three related issues for the reader to consider in relation to the understanding of attention and intention in the first year, given what we now know about infant engagement with these aspects of others. First, is there really a 9-month revolution allowing the possibility of mind knowledge? Or is there evidence for continuities in mind knowledge before this? Second, is early mind knowledge necessarily an inferential process? Third, is there evidence to suggest that mutual engagement between minds is the basis of all subsequent mind knowledge?

Have we simply replaced the excitement of discovering the 4-year false belief watershed (believed to signal the child's acquisition of a "theory of mind"; e.g., Perner, 1991) and the 18-month metarepresentational mechanism (believed to signal the capacity for pretense; e.g., Leslie, 1987) with the 9-month intentional revolution (believed to signal the onset of mind knowledge; e.g., Tomasello, 1999)? Recent developmental research has clearly moved away from postulations of a conceptual primacy in the understanding of minds and has reported skills of engagement with minds earlier and earlier in infancy. However, we appear to have widened the goal posts rather than changed the game. A surprising number of skills seem to emerge at 9 months, leading theorists to argue for a revolution in understanding others as intentional agents at this age (Tomasello, 1995, 1999). However, this confluence of developments could be an artifact of our continuing attachment to stage theoretical explanations of change, rather than reflecting genuine synchronicity. There are two reasons to suspect theoretical sleight of hand in our portrayal of these developments: (1) the advances do not all happen at 9 months, ranging in fact from 8 months to 14 months; and (2) events before 9 months also seem closely linked to events after.

Reported average ages for the various skills identified as part of the 9-month revolution range over a 6-month period (which is a very large slice of the infant's life at this age): social referencing happens from about 8 months, and is even prefigured at 5 months (Fivaz-Depeursinge & Corboz-Warnery, 1999), as are positive affect sharing and passive joint attention; imitative learning is shown at about 9 months, the ability to give objects at 10 months, protoimperatives at about 11 months, protodeclaratives at about 12 to 14 months, gaze following in various ways between 6 and 18 months, and so on. Within individual infants the development of some of these skills may span 4 months (Tomasello, 1999). These developments also appear to be preceded by a series of prior abilities, such as the ability to coordinate and respond appropriately to mutual attention and its perturbations at 2 months, or the ability to discriminate others' intentions even when directed to external targets at 5 months, which have been argued here to be of direct relevance to the developments after 9 months.

Tomasello (1999) argues that it is the discovery of the similarity of others to oneself that is the catalyst for these changes at 9 months and for the realization that others are intentional beings. Given the evident continuities in developments from early on in the first year, an alternative explanation may be possible. There may be no discovery of mindedness at 9 months or, indeed, at any single period of time. Mindedness may be something the infant can always perceive, but with increasing elaborations over the course of development which involve increasing skill with contexts and targets as well as linguistic/conceptual skills. Discontinuous portrayals of development are dangerous (although they are common to theories of very different persuasions) – they encourage us to ignore developmental data between the "steps," treating them instead as irrelevant behavioral noise. We need process-based theories for a full understanding of the development of mind knowledge (Fogel, 1993), but are still far from achieving them.

Related to this is the question of inference versus perception in early mind knowledge. Inference has been argued as a necessary step for understanding attention as well as intention. Most current views maintain that such understanding occurs before a conceptual or causal grasp is achieved. The inferential process in early understanding is believed to involve the mental positing of an unperceivable entity in the interpretation of a perceived act. Baldwin argues, for example, that action analysis is only a first step in the understanding of intentions, and that by 12 months of age infants are inferring goals and interpreting perceived actions in this manner. The interpretations appear to be attributed to human actions as well as to animated blobs on a screen. Similarly in the understanding of attention, 12-month-old infants are argued to infer the presence of an attentional state in the other in order to seek to share targets with them. As has been shown, debates abound around these issues, with counterarguments positing, plausibly, that most of these cases of apparent infant inference of mentality could be explained by the infant's perception of observable differences in others' actions and either a reflexive or a complex associationist reaction to them (see, e.g., Perner, 1991, on explanations of social referencing and protodeclarative pointing, and Gomez, 1993, on the representational similarity of protodeclaratives and protoimperatives). Infants may indeed be perceiving the object directedness rather than inferring the goal of the adult's actions (see Vedeler, 1991, for a discussion of this distinction in infant intentionality following Merleau-Ponty). Similarly, they can indeed be anticipating and responding to perceived adult actions to targets of attention rather than inferring mental states. However, an opposition between the perception of behavior and the attribution of mental states is only necessary if we assume a mind–behavior dualism, and if we assume that the developmental goal is the inference of mind alone, not the perception of mind–behavior. Infants are not dualists, they perceive mentality in action; arguably, even adults are not dualists, except when they have a problem to solve. To insist on purely inferential understanding for mentality in infancy is to set up a false goal that rules out most of the infant's rich understanding of minds.

Does mind knowledge emerge from mutual engagement and intersubjectivity? Is it the case that we understand others only to the extent that we have previously engaged with them? Buber argued for the primacy of relation; for the primacy of experiences in which we engage directly with an entity (treat it as a Thou) before we see it in detachment (as an It). Do we then understand others' mentality when it is directed to us before we understand it when it is directed elsewhere? Werner and Kaplan's theory of the origins of the symbol within the primordial sharing situation suggests that interpersonal relationships provide both the motive and the skill for the emergence of social cognition (Werner & Kaplan, 1963). Naturalistic descriptions of developmental phenomena show that dyadic interpersonal engagement precedes and supports the expansion of the infant's actions and understanding into activities involving ever more distal targets. However, there are some problems with this simple schematization. First, the apparent primacy of dyadic competence may be an artifact of the scientific neglect of triadic interpersonal engagement (mother, father, and infant) which is clear and coordinated even in 3-month-olds (Fivaz-Depeursinge & Corboz-Warnery, 1999). Further, both in the sphere of understanding attention and understanding intention, recent experimental evidence shows surprisingly early skills – even in the first 6 months – in which infants appear able to understand others' attentional and intentional directedness to external targets when they themselves are not directly engaged with the adult. This could suggest either that both dyadic and triadic understanding is developing simultaneously, or that a sequential process (from the dyadic to the triadic) is happening earlier than we suspected. However, even early triadic interactions may involve the infant's active engagement with both the others in the triad. Buber's I and Thou may be expanded to include two Thous without triads necessarily becoming I–It relations – mutuality and engagement may still be the key.

References

Adamson, L. B., & Bakeman, R. (1991). The development of shared attention during infancy. In R. Vasta (Ed.), *Annals of child development* (Vol. 8, pp. 1–41). London: Jessica Kingsley.

Adamson, L. B., & Russell, C. L. (1999). Emotion regulation and the emergence of joint attention. In P. Rochat (Ed.), *Early social cognition: Understanding others in the first months of life* (pp. 281–92?). Mahwah, NJ: Lawrence Erlbaum Associates.

Asch, S. (1952). *Social psychology*. Englewood Cliffs, NJ: Prentice-Hall.

Astington, J. (1991). Intention in the child's theory of mind. In D. Frye & C. Moore (Eds.), *Children's theories of mind* (pp. 157–172). Hillsdale, NJ: Lawrence Erlbaum Associates.

Atkinson, J., Hood, B., Wattam-Bell, J., & Anker, S. (1988). Development of orientation discrimination in infancy. *Perception, 17*(5), 587–595.

Bakeman, R., & Adamson, L. B. (1984). Co-ordinating attention to people and objects in mother–infant and peer–infant interaction. *Child Development, 55,* 1278–1289.

Baldwin, D. (1991). Infants' contribution to the achievement of joint reference. *Child Development, 62,* 875–890.

Baldwin, D. (1993). Early referential understanding: Infants' ability to recognise referential acts for what they are. *Developmental Psychology, 29,* 832–843.

Baldwin, D., & Baird, J. A. (1999). Action analysis: A gateway to intentional inference. In P. Rochat (Ed.), *Early social cognition: Understanding others in the first months of life* (pp. 215–240). Mahwah, NJ: Lawrence Erlbaum Associates.

Baldwin, D., Bill, B., & Ontai, L. L. (1996, April). *Infants' tendency to monitor others' gaze: Is it rooted in intentional understanding or a result of simple orienting?* Paper presented at the International Conference on Infant Studies, Providence, RI.

Baron-Cohen, S. (1995). The eye direction detector (EDD) and the shared attention mechanism (SAM): Two cases for evolutionary psychology. In C. Moore & P. Dunham (Eds.), *Joint attention: Its origins and role in development* (pp. 41–59). Hillsdale, NJ: Lawrence Erlbaum Associates.

Baron-Cohen, S. (1997). *Mindblindness: An essay on autism and theory of mind.* Cambridge, MA: MIT Press.

Barresi, J., & Moore, C. (1996). Intentional relations and social understanding. *Behavioral and Brain Sciences, 19,* 107–154.

Bates, E. (1976). *Language and context: The acquisition of pragmatics.* New York: Academic Press.

Bates, E., Benigni, L., Bretherton, I., Camaioni, L., & Volterra, V. (1979). Cognition and communication from 9–13 months: correlational findings. In E. Bates (Ed.), *The Emergence of Symbols: Cognition and Communication in Infancy.* New York: Academic Press.

Bateson, G. (1973). *Steps to an ecology of mind.* London: Paladin Books.

Brazelton, T. B. (1986). The development of newborn behavior. In F. Faulkner & J. M. Tanner (Eds.) *Human Growth: A comprehensive Treatise*, Vol. 2 (pp. 519–540). New York: Plenum Press.

Bretherton, I. (1991). Intentional communication and the development of an understanding of mind. In D. Frye & C. Moore (Eds.), *Children's theories of mind* (pp. 49–75). Hillsdale, NJ: Lawrence Erlbaum Associates.

Bretherton, I., McNew, S., & Beeghly-Smith, M. (1981). Early person knowledge as expressed in gestural and verbal communication: When do infants acquire a "theory of mind"? In M. E. Lamb & L. R. Sherrod (Eds.), *Infant social cognition* (pp. 333–373). Hillsdale, NJ: Lawrence Erlbaum Associates.

Brooks, R., Caron, A. J., & Butler, S. C. (1998, April). *Infant comprehension of looking as intentional behavior.* Poster presented at the International Conference on Infant Studies, Atlanta, GA.

Bruner, J. (1983). *Child's talk: Learning to use language.* New York: Norton.

Bruner, J. (1995). From joint attention to the meeting of minds: An introduction. In C. Moore & P. Dunham (Eds.), *Joint attention: Its origins and role in development* (pp. 1–14). Hillsdale, NJ: Lawrence Erlbaum Associates.

Buber, M. (1937). *I and Thou.* Edinburgh: T & T Clark.

Butterworth, G. (1995). Origins of mind in perception and action. In C. Moore & P. Dunham (Eds.), *Joint attention: Its origins and role in development* (pp. 29–40). Hillsdale, NJ: Lawrence Erlbaum Associates.

Butterworth, G., & Grover, L. (1990). Joint visual attention, manual pointing, and preverbal communication in human infancy. In M. Jeannerod (Ed.), *Attention and performance XIII* (pp. 605–624). Hillsdale, NJ: Lawrence Erlbaum Associates.

Butterworth, G., & Jarrett, N. L. M. (1991). What minds have in common is space: Spatial mechanisms serving joint visual attention in infancy. *British Journal of Developmental Psychology, 9,* 55–72.

Camaioni, L. (1993). The development of intentional communication: A re-analysis. In J. Nadel & L. Camaioni (Eds.), *New perspectives in early communicative development* (pp. 82–96). London: Routledge.

Caron, A., Caron, R., Mustelin, C., & Roberts, J. (1992). Infant responding to aberrant social stimuli. *Infant Behavior and Development, 19,* 335.

Carpenter, M., Akhtar, N., & Tomasello, M. (1998). Fourteen- through eighteen-month-olds differentially imitate intentional and accidental actions. *Infant Behavior and Development, 21,* 315–330.

Cohn, J. F., & Tronick, E. Z. (1989). Specificity of infants' response to mothers' affective behavior. *Journal of the American Academy of Child and Adolescent Psychiatry, 28,* 242–248.

Corkum, V., & Moore, C. (1994). Development of joint visual attention in infants. In C. Moore & P. Dunham (Eds.), *Joint attention: Its origins and role in development* (pp. 61–83). Hillsdale, NJ: Lawrence Erlbaum Associates.

Corkum, V., & Moore, C. (1998). The origin of joint visual attention in infants. *Developmental Psychology, 34,* 28–38.

Costall, A., & Still, A. (1987). *Cognitive psychology in question.* New York: St. Martin's Press.

Coulter, J. (1979). *The social construction of mind.* London: Macmillan.

Cox, M. (1986). *The child's point of view.* New York: St. Martin's Press.

D'Entremont, B., Hains, S. M. J., & Muir, D. (1997). A demonstration of gaze following in 3- to 6-month-olds. *Infant Behavior and Development, 20,* 569–572.

Desrochers, S., Morisette, P. & Ricard, M. (1995). Two perspectives on pointing in infancy. In C. Moore & P. Dunham (Eds.), *Joint attention: Its origins and role in development* (pp. 85–101). Hillsdale, NJ: Lawrence Erlbaum Associates.

Field, T. N., Healy, B., Goldstein, S., Perry, S., Bendell, D., Schanberg, S., Zimmermann, E. A., & Kuhn, C. (1988). Infants of depressed mothers show "depressed" behavior even with non-depressed adults. *Child Development, 59,* 1569–1579.

Fivaz-Depeursinge, E., & Corboz-Warnery, A. (1999). *The primary triangle.* New York: Basic Books.

Fogel, A. (1993). *Developing through relationships: Origins of communication, self and culture.* New York: Harvester Wheatsheaf.

Franco, F., & Butterworth, G. (1988). *The social origins of pointing in human infancy.* Paper presented at the Annual Conference of the Developmental Section of the British Psychological Society, Colleg Harlech, Wales.

Franco, F., Perucchini, P., & Butterworth, G. (1992). *Referential communication between babies.* Paper presented at the 5th European Conference on Developmental Psychology, Seville, Spain.

Gergely, G., Nadasdy, Z., Csibra, G., & Biro, S. (1995). Taking the intentional stance at 12 months of age. *Cognition, 56,* 165–193.

Gibson, J. J., & Pick, A. D. (1963). Perception of another person's looking behavior. *American Journal of Psychology, 76,* 386–394.

Golinkoff, R. M. (1993). When is communication a "meeting of minds"? *Journal of Child Language, 20,* 199–207.

Gomez, J. C. (1991). Visual behaviour as a window for reading the minds of others in primates. In A. Whiten (Ed.), *Natural Theories of mind: Evolution, development and simulation of everyday mindreading* (pp. 195–207). Oxford: Basil Blackwell.

Gomez, J. C. (1993). The comparative study of early communication and theories of mind: Ontogeny, phylogeny and pathology. In S. Baron-Cohen, H. Tager-Flusberg, & D. Cohen (Eds.), *Understanding other minds: Perspectives from autism* (pp. 397–426). New York: Oxford University Press.

Goren, C. G., Sarty, M., & Wu, P. Y. K. (1975). Visual following and pattern discrimination of face-like stimuli by newborn infants. *Paediatrics, 56,* 544–549.

Habermas, J. (1970). Towards a theory of communicative competence. In H. P. Dreitzel (Ed.), *Recent sociology* (Vol. 12, pp. 115–148). London: Macmillan.

Hains, S., & Muir, D. W. (1996). Infant sensitivity to adult eye direction. *Child Development, 67,* 1940–1951.

Halliday, M. A. K. (1975). *Learning how to mean: Explorations in the development of language.* London: Edward Arnold.

Heider, F., & Simmel, M. (1944). An experimental study of apparent behavior. *American Journal of Psychology, 57,* 243–259.

Hobson, R. P. (1991). Against the theory of "theory of mind." *British Journal of Developmental Psychology, 9,* 33–51.

Hobson, R. P. (1999, June 11–13). *Intersubjective foundations for joint attention: Co-ordinating attitudes (rather than actions).* Paper presented at the workshop on Joint Attention, University of Warwick, England.

Johnson, M. H., & Morton, J. (1991). *Biology and cognitive development: The case of face recognition.* Oxford: Blackwell.

Johnson, S. C., Slaughter, V., Collins, K., Tyan, J., & Carey, S. (1996, April). *Whose gaze will infants follow: Features that elicit gaze following in 12-month-olds.* Paper presented at the International Conference on Infant Studies, Providence, RI.

Jopling, D. (1993). Cognitive science, other minds and the philosophy of dialogue. In U. Neisser (Ed.), *The perceived self: Ecological and interpersonal sources of self knowledge* (pp. 290–309). New York: Cambridge University Press.

Laskey, R. E., & Klein, R. E. (1979). The reactions of five-month-old infants to eye contact of the mother and a stranger. *Merill Palmer Quarterly, 25,* 163–170.

Legerstee, M. (1991). The role of person and object in eliciting early imitation. *Journal of Experimental Child Psychology, 51,* 423–433.

Legerstee, M. (1994). Patterns of 4-month-old infant responses to hidden silent and sounding people and objects. *Early Development and Parenting, 2,* 51–61.

Legerstee, M., Corter, C., & Kienapple, K. (1990). Hand, arm and facial actions of young infants to a social and non-social stimulus. *Child Development, 61,* 774–784.

Leslie, A. (1987). Pretense and representation: The origins of "theory of mind." *Psychological Review, 94,* 412–426.

Lord, C. (1994). The complexity of social behaviour in autism. In S. Baron-Cohen & H. Tager-Flusberg (Eds.), *Understanding other minds: Perspectives from autism* (pp. 292–316). New York: Oxford University Press.

Meltzoff, A. (1995). Understanding the intentions of others: Re-enactment of intended acts by 18-month-old children. *Developmental Psychology, 31*(5), 838–850.

Moore, C. (1999). Gaze following and the control of attention. In P. Rochat (Ed.), *Early social cognition: Understanding others in the first months of life* (pp. 241–256). Mahwah, NJ: Lawrence Erlbaum Associates.

Morales, M., Mundy, P., & Rojas, J. (1997). Gaze following and language development in 6- and 8-month-olds. *Infant Behavior and Development, 21,* 349–372.

Morissette, P., Ricard, M., & Gouin-Decarie, T. (1995). Joint visual attention and pointing in infancy: A longitudinal study of comprehension. *British Journal of Developmental Psychology, 13,* 163–177.

Muir, D., & Hains, S. (1999). Young infants' perception of adult intentionality. In P. Rochat (Ed.), *Early social cognition: Understanding others in the first months of life* (pp. 155–188). Mahwah, NJ: Lawrence Erlbaum Associates.

Mundy, P., & Sigman, S. (1989). The theoretical implications of joint-attention deficits in autism. *Development and Psychopathology, 1,* 173–183.

Murray, L. (1980). *The sensitivities and expressive capacities of young infants in communication with their mothers.* Unpublished Ph.D. thesis, University of Edinburgh.

Murray, L., & Trevarthen, C. (1985). Emotional regulation of interactions between two-month-old infants and their mothers. In T. Field & N. Fox (Eds.), *Social perception in infancy* (pp. 177–197). Norwood, NJ: Ablex.

Nadel, J., & Tremblay-Leveau, H. (1999). Early perception of social contingencies and interpersonal intentionality: Dyadic and triadic paradigms. In P. Rochat (Ed.), *Early social cognition: Understanding others in the first months of life* (pp. 189–212). Mahwah, NJ: Lawrence Erlbaum Associates.

Nakano, S. (1994). *Developmental changes in young children's understanding of their mothers' play intentions during playful teasing.* Paper presented at The 13th Biennial Meeting of the ISSBD, Amsterdam, The Netherlands.

Newton, P., Reddy, V., & Bull, R. (2000). Early deception and performance on false-belief tasks. *British Journal of Developmental Psychology. 18,* 297–317.

Newtson, D. (1993). The dynamics of action and interaction. In L. B. Smith & E. Thelen (Eds.), *A dynamic systems approach to development: Applications* (pp. 241–264). Cambridge, MA: Bradford Books/MIT Press.

Perner, J. (1991). *Understanding the representational mind.* Cambridge, MA: MIT Press.

Perucchini, P., & Camaioni, L. (1993). *Proto-declarative and proto-imperative pointing.* Poster presented at the Annual Conference of the Developmental Section of the British Psychological Society, Birmingham, England.

Piaget, J. (1926). *The language and thought of the child.* London: Routledge.

Premack, D. (1990). The infant's theory of self-propelled objects. *Cognition, 36,* 1–16.

Premack, D., & Premack, A. J. (1995). Intention as psychological cause. In *Causal cognition* (6th Symposia of the Fyssen Foundation, pp. 185–199). Oxford: Oxford University Press.

Reddy, V. (1991). Playing with others' expectations: Teasing and mucking about in the first year. In A. Whiten (Ed.), *Natural theories of mind* (pp. 143–158). Oxford: Blackwell.

Reddy, V. (1992, September). *Proto-declarative pointing: Gaze control or shared attention?* Paper presented at the Annual Conference of the Developmental Section of the British Psychological Society, Edinburgh, Scotland.

Reddy, V. (1998). *Person-directed play: Humour and teasing in infants and young children.* Research report to the Economic and Social Research Council.

Reddy, V. (2000). Coyness in early infancy. *Developmental Science, 3*(2), 186–192.

Reddy, V., Hay, D., Murray, L., & Trevarthen, C. (1997). Communication in infancy: Mutual regulation of affect and attention. In G. J. Bremner, A. Slater, & G. Butterworth (Eds.), *Infant development: Recent advances* (pp. 247–273). Hove: Psychology Press.

Reddy, V., & Simone, L. (1995). *Acting on attention: Towards an understanding of knowing in infancy.* Paper presented at the Annual Conference of the Developmental Section of the British Psychological Society, Strathclyde, Scotland.

Reddy, V., & Simone, L. (in preparation). Eighteen-month-olds' sensitivity to knowledge and igno-rance: Co-ordinating others' knowledge through proto-declaratives.

Reddy, V., & Williams, E. (in preparation). Precursors to joint attention in infancy.

Rochat, P. (Ed.). (1999). *Early social cognition: Understanding others in the first months of life*. Mahwah, NJ: Lawrence Erlbaum Associates.

Rochat, P., & Striano, T. (1999). Social cognitive development in the first year. In P. Rochat (Ed.), *Early social cognition: Understanding others in the first months of life* (pp. 3–34). Mahwah, NJ: Lawrence Erlbaum Associates.

Ross, H. S., & Lollis, S. P. (1987). Communication within infant social games. *Developmental Psychology, 23*, 241–248.

Ryle, G. (1949). *The concept of mind*. Harmondsworth: Penguin.

Scaife, M., & Bruner, J. (1975). The capacity for joint visual attention in the human infant. *Nature, 253*, 265–266.

Searle, J. (1983). *Intentionality*. Cambridge: Cambridge University Press.

Service, V. (1984). Maternal styles and communicative development. In A. Lock & E. Fisher (Eds.), *Language development* (pp. 132–140). London: Croom Helm.

Sodian, B. (1994). Early deception and the conceptual continuity claim. In C. Lewis & P. Mitchell (Eds.), *Children's early understanding of mind* (pp. 385–401). Hove: Lawrence Erlbaum Associates.

Sodian, B., & Thoermer, C. (1998, April). *Do one-year-olds represent human actions as guided by perception?* Paper presented at the International Conference on Infant Studies, Atlanta, GA.

Stayton, D. J., Hogan, R., & Ainsworth, M. (1971). Infant obedience and maternal behavior: The origins of socialisation reconsidered. *Child Development, 42*, 1057–1070.

Stern, D. (1985). *The interpersonal world of the infant*. New York: Basic Books.

Stern, D. (1999). Vitality contours: The temporal contour of feelings as a basic unit for constructing the infant's social experience. In P. Rochat (Ed.), *Early social cognition: Understanding others in the first months of life*. (pp. 67–80). Mahwah, NJ: Lawrence Erlbaum Associates.

Symons, L. A., Hains, S. M. J., & Muir, D. W. (in press). Look at me: 5-month-olds' sensitivity to very small deviations in eye-gaze during social interactions. *Infant Behavior and Development*.

Tomasello, M. (1995). Joint attention as social cognition. In C. Moore & P. Dunham (Eds.), *Joint attention: Its origins and role in development* (pp. 103–130). Hillsdale, NJ: Lawrence Erlbaum Associates.

Tomasello, M. (1999). Social cognition before the revolution. In P. Rochat (Ed.), *Early social cognition: Understanding others in the first months of life* (pp. 301–314). Mahwah, NJ: Lawrence Erlbaum Associates.

Tomasello, M., & Barton, M. (1994). Learning words in non-ostensive contexts. *Developmental Psychology, 30*, 639–650.

Trevarthen, C. (1977). Descriptive analyses of infant communication behavior. In H. R. Schaffer (Ed.), *Studies in mother–infant interaction: The Loch Lomond symposium* (pp. 227–270). London: Academic Press.

Trevarthen, C. (1987). Sharing makes sense: Intersubjectivity and the making of an infant's meaning. In R. Steele & T. Threadgold (Eds.), *Language topics: Essays in honour of Michael Halliday* (pp. 177–199). Amsterdam & Philadelphia: John Benjamins.

Trevarthen, C. (1990). Signs before speech. In T. A. Sebeok & J. Umiker-Sebeok (Eds.), *The semiotic web* (pp. 689–755). Berlin: Mouton de Gruyter.

Trevarthen, C., & Hubley, P. (1978). Secondary intersubjectivity: Confidence, confiding and acts of meaning in the first year. In A. Lock (Ed.), *Action, gesture and symbol* (pp. 183–229). London: Academic Press.

Vecera, S. P., & Johnson, M. H. (1995). Gaze detection and the cortical processing of faces: Evidence from infants and adults. *Visual Cognition, 2,* 59–87.

Vedeler, D. (1991). Infant intentionality as object directedness: An alternative to representationalism. *Journal for the Theory of Social Behavior, 21*(4), 431–448.

Vygotsky, L. (1962). *Thought and language.* Cambridge, MA: MIT Press. (Original work published 1926)

Wellman, H. M. (1990). *The child's theory of mind.* Cambridge, MA: MIT Press.

Werner, J., & Kaplan, B. (1963). *Symbol formation.* New York: Wiley.

Willen, J. D., Hood, B. M., & Driver, J. R. (1997). An eye direction detector triggers shifts of visual attention in human infants. *Investigative Ophthalmology and Visual Science, 38,* 313.

Wolff, P. H. (1987). *The development of behavioral states and the expression of emotions in early infancy: New proposals for investigation.* Chicago: University of Chicago Press.

Woodward, A. L. (in press). Infants' ability to distinguish between purposeful and non-purposeful behaviors. *Infant Behavior and Development.*

Woodward, A. L., & Somerville, J. A. (2000). Twelve-month-olds interpret action in context. *Psychological Science, 11*(1), 73–77.

Part II

Social, Emotional, and Communicative Development

Introduction

Part II covers the basic features of social development in infancy. During the first three years of life, growth in social and emotional abilities is rapid. By the end of the second year, children have the rudiments of language, a fully developed repertoire of emotional expressions and feelings, and they understand to a limited extent that other people have different points of view than themselves. How do infants develop these abilities to engage with other people and to understand themselves? The chapters in this section address these issues.

The first chapter in this section, by Bornstein and Tamis-LeMonda, reviews the research on motherhood and the mother–infant interaction. They address issues such as the function of mother–infant interaction for infant development and research methods that have been used to study mother–infant relationships. In addition, this chapter puts the mother–infant relationship into its larger context of infant and mother psychological functioning, social networks, demographic patterns, and cultural differences. They call for a multidimensional and dynamic approach to the mother–infant relationship, in the sense that the effectiveness of mothers for their infants depends upon the circumstances in which they live and on the aspect of maternal behavior that is being assessed. Family, friends, and cultural beliefs all contribute, facilitating or hampering the mother's ability to parent.

Following in a similar vein, the chapter by van den Boom covers the development of attachments between infants and adults. The chapter takes a detailed look at the theories used to explain the development of attachment and individual differences. Why and how do attachments form during infancy? What are the factors that promote healthy attachments? What are the species similarities and cultural differences in patterns of attachment? How does the parent–infant attachment affect later relationships? Attachment security is one of the best predictors of social behavior in early childhood in North American society where the tests for attachment were developed. The definition of a healthy attachment may vary between cultures, however. In any case, the attachment relationship between infants and their parents is crucial for the maintenance of normal developmental progress. The chapter concludes with some speculations about the future of attachment theory and research.

The chapter by Eckerman and Peterman takes up the question of how children develop the social skills to establish coordinated interactions with their peers. They ask about the types of skills needed for young children to begin to play games, resolve conflicts, and have conversations with each other. Peer relationships play a unique role in infancy, distinct from relationships with adults. Peers, for example, form primarily egalitarian relationships compared to the differences in size and status between parents and infants. With peers, children can explore the roles of leader and follower, and discover the meaning of friendship. The authors review the types of peer communication observed in infants of different ages. The chapter also considers the ways in which infants are exposed to peers in daycare settings and the importance of the "peer culture."

Stack's chapter examines the particular role of touch in infant development. Touch, though relatively neglected in infancy research, is of essential importance for infants given that the skin is the largest sensory organ in the body. It helps to establish the first attachments between parents and infants and helps infants with emotional regulation. Touch has been shown to benefit premature infants by increasing weight gain and enhancing physiological functioning. Touch augments communication in infants with sensory impairments. Touch between parents and infants occurs in all cultural groups, but some cultures emphasize touch more than others.

The chapter by Lock considers other aspects of nonverbal communication in infancy, those not necessarily related to touch. The chapter is organized with respect to the major developmental transitions in nonverbal communication during infancy: at 2, 5, and 9 months. At 2 months, infants begin to smile and gaze at adults' faces, creating opportunities for extended bouts of face-to-face play. At 5 months, infants begin to incorporate objects into their interactions with adults. By 9 months there is a profound shift toward the awareness of being an intentional communicator, deliberately seeking information and support from adults, and recognizing adults as separate intentional beings. Each of these transitions leads to increasingly complex social skills such as turn-taking and joint attention with adults. The chapter concludes by considering theoretical perspectives on how nonverbal communication during the first year is the prelude to linguistic communication in the second year.

This topic is taken up in the chapter by Camaioni, who shows that linguistic communication is founded upon the patterns of nonverbal communication observed during the first year. Language does not suddenly emerge in the second year but arises out of a developmental history of shared understandings between infant and parent. This chapter traces the development of vocabulary, the emergence of word combinations and sentences, and the growing ability of infants to use language to reference internal states and desires. The chapter considers the role of maternal speech in individual differences in language acquisition and cultural differences in this process. A child-centered speech style, which follows the child's speech as a starting point, is found in parents who are educated and middle class across a variety of cultures. On the other hand, working-class families and families from rural and traditional cultures are more likely to use a directive style of speech. These studies show that children can acquire language under a wide variety of rearing conditions.

Witherington, Campos, and Hertenstein review the processes of emotional development in infancy. They consider questions such as what emotions are and how they develop. They take a functionalist perspective on emotion, such that emotions are the processes by which an individual attempts to establish, maintain, or change relationships with the environment on matters of significance to the person. Emotions are not identified with particular feelings but rather with the behaviors that serve the person in their relationship with the world (such as approaching or avoiding another person or object). Infants become increasingly sophisticated in the experience and regulation of emotions. Infants do not feel anger until 6 months, they do not feel fear until 10 months, and they do not feel pride or shame until at least the age of 2 years. The authors suggest that emotion is a multidimensional and dynamic process, involving interactions between perception, action, and cognition.

The final chapter in this section, by Wachs and Bates, reviews the research on whether there are persistent patterns of individual differences between infants, the topic of temperament. They consider the research and theoretical issues related to how temperament is defined and measured. Next, they discuss the developmental origins of temperamental differences and the relative roles of biological predispositions and environmental factors. Even biological characteristics such as prematurity, Down's syndrome, gender, genetic influences, and malnutrition do not predict temperament in the absence of parent–child relationships and other environmental factors. The authors present research on the long-term consequences of infant temperamental differences. While temperament seems to have important consequences for later adjustment, more research is needed, particularly on children in clinical and educational settings.

Chapter Ten

Mother–Infant Interaction

Marc H. Bornstein and Catherine S. Tamis-LeMonda

> There is no such thing as an infant.
>
> D. W. Winnicott (1965, p. 39)

Introduction

Each day nearly one-half million women in the world experience the happiness and heartache of becoming mother to a newborn infant. Meaningful mothering begins even before a baby's birth and continues in some form throughout the life of the mother and child – as we all acknowledge, *once a mother, always a mother*. Nonetheless, mothering responsibilities are arguably greatest during infancy, when human beings are most dependent on caregiving and their ability to cope alone is minimal. It has also been contended on evolutionary reasoning that the extended duration of human infancy allows for enhanced parental influence and prolonged learning (Bjorklund & Pelligrini, 2000). Thus, infancy is normatively a period of great investment; the birth of a child rivets a mother's attention and stirs her emotions; and infants alter everything about their mothers, beginning with who they are and how they define themselves. Reciprocally, infants profit from maternal care: Infancy is the phase of the human life cycle when caregiving is thought to exert significant and salient influences. The sheer amount of interaction between mother and infant is great, infants may be particularly susceptible and responsive to mother-provided experiences, and mother–infant interaction has long been thought to be a critical determinant in the development of the individual. Mother–infant interactions are the subject of historical and continuing interest (Bornstein & Lamb, 1992; Bremner, 1994; Fogel, 1991; Hrdy, 1999).

This chapter summarizes selected aspects of our own and others' research, and portions of the text have appeared in previous scientific publications cited in the references. We thank E. Hunter, M. Voigt, and B. Wright for assistance.

This chapter surveys basic mother and infant behaviors, their characteristics, their interrelations, and the contexts in which their interactions are embedded. We begin with a discussion of some of the key functions of mother–infant interactions for the infant's emerging social-emotional and cognitive development. We next review methodological approaches to the study of mother–infant interactions and describe behaviors of mothers, infants, and the dyad that have been considered meaningful indicators of the mother–infant relationship. We then discuss the nature of associations between mothering and infant development – that is, relations as specific or general and the patterning of relations over time. Finally, we consider the mother–infant relationship in its larger context by examining factors that moderate or mediate the nature and consequences of mother–infant interactions, including characteristics of infants, mothers' psychological functioning, social networks, sociodemographic factors, and culture.

Functions of Mother–Infant Interactions

Universally, mothers establish (or are expected to establish) with their infants successful routine interactions, clear patterns of communication, dependable emotional attachments, and to guide their infants through all of the important "firsts" of life. Human infants do not and cannot grow up as solitary individuals; mothering constitutes an initial and all-encompassing ecology of infant development. Infants and mothers constantly engage in *dyadic interactions* – to which both contribute, through which each alters the other, and by which both are changed – so that infant, mother, and dyad each has its own character. What essential functions, aside from the basic needs of protection and survival, do mother–infant interactions serve for the developing infant? Four significant functions, among many, are noteworthy: promotion of social understanding, development of attachment, acquisition of language, and emotional regulation. We highlight each briefly.

Mother–infant interactions have been referred to as the "cradle of social understanding" (Rochat & Striano, 1999). From birth, babies appear both ready and motivated (albeit in rudimentary form) to communicate and share meaning with others. By 2 months of age, infants engage in complex, highly responsive interactions with their mothers (termed "protoconversations"; Bateson, 1979). These interactions are characterized by mutual give-and-take exchanges in the form of coos, gazes, smiles, grunts, and sucks (Beebe, Jaffe, Feldstein, Mays, & Alson, 1985; Messinger & Fogel, 1998; Murray & Trevarthen, 1985). Through reciprocal engagements with others, especially mother, infants come to develop a sense of shared experience (termed "intersubjectivity"; Trevarthen, 1993) that over time evolves to a greater level of social and cognitive understanding, including the development of social anticipations and expectations about others' behaviors in relation to self (Rochat & Striano, 1999). During the first 6 months, infants develop a growing sensitivity to the invariant characteristics of their social partners, as they begin to extract information about patterns and routines in face-to-face and other dyadic interactions. These early interactions lay the foundation for further developments in social cognition, including the understanding of self and others as intentional agents. By 9 months, infants demonstrate "secondary intersubjectivity" as they monitor and coordinate their own perspectives and attention with the perspectives and attention of others (Baldwin & Baird, 1999; Trevarthen, 1979).

A second and related function of mother–infant interaction is its role in the development of secure infant attachment. According to an evolutionary perspective, the development of attachment in human infants reflects natural selection – infants who sought to maintain proximity to their primary caregivers were more likely to be cared for and protected from potential predators and to survive. Consequently, the proclivity toward attachment became integral to the infant's repertoire of behaviors (Bowlby, 1973). The development of "secure" infant attachment appears to depend on the quality of mother–infant interactions over the course of the first years of life (Ainsworth, 1973). Mothers who are attuned to their infants' behavioral and emotional cues and needs are more likely to rear secure infants than are mothers who are less sensitive; in turn, secure infants are more likely to develop into prosocial and competent toddlers and children (Belsky, 1999).

A third function of mother–infant interactions, mediated by the infant's growing intersubjectivity, is the infant's continuous progress toward more mature forms of communication and language (Bloom, 1993; Bornstein, 2000). Mothers foster their infants' acquisition of language and communicative skills. For example, mothers use sound play with 2-month-olds to selectively reinforce babbling that will foretell speech (Kugiumutzakis, 1998). Eventually, shared expressions of affect and shared experiences lead to infants and mothers sharing experience in speech (Fogel, Messinger, Dickson, & Hsu, 1999). Episodes of "joint attention" provide a prominent framework for the acquisition of language (Moore & Dunham, 1995).

Finally, mother–infant interactions play a prominent role in infants' emotional development – by both heightening emotions in infants as well as helping babies regulate their emotions. From the first days of life, mothers support babies' experience of joy through their facial expressions, vocalizations, and touch, and evoking gazing, smiling, and laughing from their infants (Papoušek & Papoušek, 1995). The progressive escalation of excitement inherent in mother–infant games boosts infants to higher levels of joy than they achieve on their own (Stern, 1993). In typical theme-and-variation play, caregivers build predictable sequences of behavior and repeat or vary them based on the infant's response, for example slowly creeping their fingers up the infant's stomach, waiting for the infant's expectant gaze or smile, and then tickling or giving a loud raspberry. It is the infant's growing awareness of contingency in these elementary interactions that adds to feelings of pleasure, in addition to enabling greater tolerance for higher arousal states (Roggman, 1991). Beyond affect, mothers play an important role in regulating their infant's distress and physiological arousal. Infant emotion regulation is conceptualized as developing within the context of parent–child relationships (Grolnick, McMenamy, & Kurowski, 1999; Tronick, 1989). Because very young infants vary arousal by shifting visual control (Tronick & Weinberg, 1990), the mother's use of visual distractions, as one example, may operate to soothe overly excited infants (Bornstein, Tamis-LeMonda et al., 1992; Thompson, 1994). During later infancy, mother–infant play involves teasing games and rituals that help the infant practice negotiation skills that in turn build more intricate intersubjective understanding (Trevarthen, 1993).

In overview, mother–infant interactions serve multiple cognitive and linguistic, social and emotional functions for the developing infant. Infants acquire social understanding and a sense of intersubjectivity through ongoing, mutually reciprocal interactions with their mothers. Sensitive mother–infant interactions also pave the way to secure attachment relationships, thereby providing a foundation for healthy social and emotional development. In turn, the infant's developing sense of intersubjectivity and attachment serve as the foundation and motivation for exploring and learning about the world, communicating with others, understanding self and others, and developing positive social relationships.

Methodological Approaches to Studying Mother–Infant Interactions

To find out about mother–infant interactions scientifically entails numerous decisions about the behaviors and beliefs to assess, how to measure them, and the sorts of analyses that are most suitable to the questions being posed. How are meaningful behaviors in mothers, infants, and dyads described, characterized, and quantified?

Behaviors and Beliefs in Mothers

The complex of everyday maternal behaviors with infants is analyzable into a number of domains, and patterns among those behaviors constitute associated styles. Which behaviors in the ongoing stream of gestures, vocalizations, and facial expressions mothers display are most crucial to assess, how are they best evaluated, and in what situations?

Two distinct approaches have been taken to classifying maternal–infant interactions. The first emphasizes the content of maternal behaviors specifically by focusing on domains of engagement. The second emphasizes the quality of maternal engagements, for example, the extent to which maternal behaviors are sensitive to infants' abilities or needs. With respect to *content*, one useful approach has been to classify behaviors into categories of mothering (which for the infant are experiences). Bornstein (1989a, 1995) described one such system that includes nurturant, social, didactic, and material caregiving. *Nurturant caregiving* meets the biological, physical, and health requirements of the infant, as when mothers provide sustenance, grooming, protection, supervision, and the like. *Social caregiving* encompasses visual, affective, and physical behaviors mothers employ to engage infants in interpersonal exchanges, impart trust and love, help the infant to regulate affect and emotions, and manage and monitor the infant's other social relationships. *Didactic caregiving* is deployed when stimulating the infant to engage and understand the environment outside the dyad, and includes focusing the infant's attention on properties, objects, or events in the immediate surround, introducing, mediating, and interpreting the external world, describing and demonstrating, and provoking or providing opportunities to observe, imitate, learn, and the like. *Material caregiving* consists of how mothers provision and organize the infant's physical world in terms of inanimate objects, levels of ambient stimulation, physical safety, and so forth.

Together these categories encompass virtually all of mothers' important activities with infants. That is, human infants universally are reared in, influenced by, and adapt to social and physical environments that are characterized by the elements in this taxonomy. Taken as a totality, however, this taxonomy constitutes a varied and demanding set of caregiving tasks. Each element of the taxonomy of mothering is conceptually and operationally distinct, although in practice of course mother–infant interaction is intricate, meshed, and multidimensional, and mothers regularly engage in combinations of these categories; that is, these different categories of engagement can be expected to overlap. Furthermore, nurturant caregiving seems more fixed and compulsory, to the extent that infant survival depends on the essential activities that comprise this domain; in contrast, social, didactic, and material sorts of caregiving may be more flexible and discretionary – mothers vary among themselves in the extent to which they engage in these domains of interaction as well as in the ways they express such behaviors. This taxonomy also incorporates stimulation (that is, types of caregiving that normally serve to promote infant well-being and development) as well as compensation (that is, types of caregiving that, for whatever antecedent cause, attempt to return an infant to accepted states of well-being or development). Of course, these categories of caregiving apply to normal mothering of normal infants, and their instantiation or emphasis can be expected to vary with child age and contextual or cultural setting.

Beyond the contents of these domains of interaction lies the *quality* of maternal engagements, sometimes referred to as patterns or styles. Perhaps the best known system of parenting styles classifies mothers into three main types: authoritative, authoritarian, and indulgent-permissive (Baumrind, 1991; Maccoby & Martin, 1983). Permissive parents tend to make fewer demands on their children in comparison to other parents, thus allowing their children to regulate their own activities as much as possible. Authoritarian parents tend to be directive with children and value unquestioning obedience in their exercise of authority. Authoritarian parents are detached and less warm, discourage verbal give-and-take, and favor punitive measures to maintain or control their children's behavior. By contrast, authoritative parents provide clear and firm direction for their children and exercise disciplinary clarity through warmth, reason, flexibility, and verbal give-and-take. These styles in turn vary along more global dimensions of parental warmth and control, and different parenting styles reflect combinations of high or low levels of these dimensions. Research on these full-blown styles of interaction has been conducted mainly with parents of older children. Maternal "warmth" and "sensitivity" reflect the extent to which mother is positively and appropriately responsive to her infant's needs and abilities, and this dimension is marked by wide individual differences. Maternal responsiveness *per se* encompasses the contingent, prompt, and appropriate reactions mothers display to infant activities (Bornstein, 1989b). Maternal responsiveness has attracted attention from infancy researchers for two principal reasons. First, it reflects faithfully a recurring and significant three-term event sequence in everyday exchanges between infant and mother that involves child act, parent reaction, and effect on child. Second, specific kinds of maternal responsiveness have been found to exert meaningful predictive effects over a range of domains of infant development, from imbuing effectance and a sense of self to security of attachment to fostering the growth of verbal and cognitive competencies. Infants appear to be especially sensitive to contingencies between their own actions and the reactions of others, and such contingencies are the hallmark of responsive parenting (Gergely & Watson, 1999). Empirically, infants who experience contingent responding are more likely to pause after an adult response, engage more regularly in turn-taking, and express more speech-like sounds than infants who experience random stimulation (Bloom, 1999). On these accounts, developmentalists since Bowlby (1973) and Ainsworth (1973) have tended to regard positive maternal responsiveness to infants – wherever it occurs – as a good thing.

With respect to "control," mothers may support their infants' autonomy or interfere, inhibit, or intrude on their infants' interests. Infants of overstimulating or intrusive mothers tend to be classified as avoidantly attached, perhaps in an effort to control their level of arousal or in angry response to their mothers' inappropriate interactions (Belsky, Rovine, & Taylor, 1984; Isabella & Belsky, 1991; Pederson et al., 1990). Depressed mothers, for example, demonstrate a style of interaction marked by intrusiveness, anger, irritation, and rough handling of their infants, a style of engagement that is often received with gaze aversion and avoidance by infants (Field, 1995). Maternal intrusiveness is also associated with elevated catecholamine and cortisol levels in infants, a finding that is consistent with the notion that infants of intrusive mothers experience more stress and anger (Jones et al., 1997). Moreover, mothers who behave in a controlling manner, either by using inappropriate strategies to control their infants' emotions or by not allowing their infants the opportunity to practice self-regulation, may undermine infants' developing capacity for autonomous self-regulation (Grolnick, McMenamy, & Kurowski, 1999).

A domain of interaction that cuts across both content and quality concerns mothers' speech to infants. *Language* directed to infants is perhaps the most common feature of mothering, and language serves numerous functions for the infant. Language helps to establish emotional ties between mother and infant, to transmit knowledge and promote learning in the infant, and to socialize the infant into a culture. Notably, mothers modulate their vocal pitch in interaction with young infants, and prosodic contours of so-called "child-directed" speech are thought to provoke or potentiate infant attention and thereby promote infant learning (Papoušek, Papoušek, & Bornstein, 1985).

Mothers shape most, if not all, of their infants' experiences and directly influence infant development by the behaviors they exhibit as well as by the beliefs they hold. Parenting beliefs include, for example, perceptions about, attitudes toward, and knowledge of parenting and childhood. So, how mothers see themselves *vis-à-vis* infants generally can lead to their expressing one or another kind of affect, thinking, or behavior in childrearing. How mothers construe infancy functions in the same way: Mothers who believe that they can or cannot affect infant personality or intelligence modify their parenting accordingly. How mothers see their own infants has its specific consequences too: Mothers who regard their infants as being difficult are less likely to pay attention or respond to their infants' overtures, and their inattentiveness and nonresponsiveness can then foster temperamental difficulties and cognitive shortcomings.

Beliefs are displayed as everyday customs with regard to babies and provide important contexts for understanding the nature of infancy. Beliefs thus represent a key aspect of the context of childrearing (Bornstein, 1991; Darling & Steinberg, 1993; Goodnow & Collins, 1990; Miller, 1988). Beliefs themselves develop within particular ecologies of class and culture, and ethnotheorists focus on how beliefs are manifested in particular childrearing practices (McGillicuddy-De Lisi & Sigel, 1995; Harkness & Super, 1995).

Behaviors in Infants

Infant behaviors in mother–infant interactions are also understood in terms of their content and quality. For example, it is possible to distinguish between infant dyadic versus extradyadic engagements: Dyadic engagements on the part of infants consist of behaviors focused on interpersonal interactions – smiles, coos, and face-to-face interactions with mothers – whereas extradyadic engagements concern babies' focus on objects, events, and activities outside the dyad. In this regard, the distinction between primary and secondary intersubjectivity is especially relevant, in that early mother–infant interactions often focus within the dyad, whereas later interactions entail co-communications about objects and events outside the dyad (Bornstein, Tal et al., 1992; Bornstein & Tamis-LeMonda, 1990).

With respect to *quality*, infants' behaviors are responsive to and synchronized with those of their mothers. Infants appear to be attuned to their mothers from the first weeks of life (Bateson, 1975, 1979; Stern, 1974): They engage in miming of conversation, are emotionally reactive, and play an active role in regulating the ebb and flow of interactions (Beebe et al., 1985; Trevarthen, 1993). Nonetheless, substantial variation exists among infants in terms of their own responsiveness to maternal solicitations and abilities at maintaining synchronous interactions. Some infants appear better able to regulate their attention and emotions than others and so engage in more rewarding bouts of joint attention with their caregivers (Raver, 1996). As a specific example, preterm infants often have difficulty regulating engagements with caregivers, as evidenced in increased gaze aversion, decreased joint play, and lower levels of joint attention (Landry, 1995). Some infants exhibit clear, consistent, and responsive cues to changes in their mothers' actions, whereas others do not; these early patterns of infant responsiveness set the stage for productive or problematic engagements over the next months and years of life (Kochanska, Forman, & Coy, 1999).

Behaviors of the Dyad

Although mother and infant behaviors can be considered separately, the dyad of mother *and* infant may be the central and most meaningful unit of analysis: The essence of the mother–child relationship is captured by synchronies that distinguish the two interacting partners (Fogel & Lyra, 1997). Trevarthen (1993, p. 139) compared mother–infant dyadic communications to a musical duet – the "two performers seek harmony and counterpoint on one beat to create together a melody that becomes a coherent and satisfying narrative of feelings in a time structure that they share completely. In a good performance by two or more musicians each partakes of, or identifies with, the expression of the whole piece, the ensemble." As such, patterned sequences of engagements, comprised of cyclical turn-taking in both mother and infant behaviors, become the focus of investigation.

Logistics of Studying Mother–Infant Interactions

Once meaningful forms of behavior have been identified in mothers, infants, and the dyad, an appropriate coding strategy for quantifying interactions must be determined. Three general approaches are noteworthy; each has inherent strengths and limitations: comprehensive coding, sampling, and rating.

Data collection built around comprehensive observational procedures is rigorous and powerful and provides precise measures of both behavioral frequency and duration on the basis of their occurrence in the noninterrupted, natural time flow. Computer-video-linked application programs are utilized in such "real-time" coding schemes. As the coder observes the ongoing interaction (typically on prerecorded videotape), the onset and offset of every instance of each target event is noted. Such data from real-time recording enable the researcher to obtain a rich and highly detailed record of the interaction. From a running record of interactions, it is also possible to evaluate the temporal sequencing of events relative to one another, thereby permitting the examination of conditional probabilities among events of interest. The co-dependencies between behavioral events can be assessed within and between mothers and infants, and changing patterns of co-dependencies can be evaluated across developmental time. For example, Messinger, Fogel, and Dickson (1999) assessed changes to the temporal phases of infant smiles between 1 and 6 months of age, based on 5 minutes of face-to-face mother–infant interactions. Their fine-grained analysis of infant smile types, durations of smiles, and temporal relations between smiles enabled theorizing about the developmental processes underlying infant emotional functioning and how such processes might differ from adult emotionality. Messinger and Fogel (1998) similarly assessed development in infants' nonverbal communications (e.g., gestures, vocalizations, and gazes) between 9 and 15 months during play with mothers. By assessing which actions preceded (and/or occurred concomitantly with) others (within infants and between mothers and infants), they were able to illustrate week-to-week changes in the form and function of infant communicative initiatives. Some disadvantages to such microanalytic approaches stem from the very time-consuming nature of the coding; depending on the number of events in the coding scheme and the nature of those events, it can take many hours to code only a few minutes of mother–infant interaction.

As an alternative to comprehensive coding, behavior may be sampled (Suen & Ary, 1989). In time- or event-sampling, the observational period is divided into a number of briefer intervals (e.g., 10 seconds), and the presence or absence of the target behavior in mother, infant, and/or the dyad is noted during each interval. Benefits to this approach are its low cost and simplicity; coders typically find it easier to note whether or not something has occurred than to determine when exactly the event began and ended in the stream of ongoing behaviors. Limitations, however, include not being able to extract exact measures of frequency or duration and the potential distortion of information with overly long sampling intervals (Smith & Connolly, 1972; Suen & Ary, 1989). In event coding, the unit that is recorded is the event, rather than the interval.

Using a third approach of rating, the coder observes an interaction in whole or in part and, rather than coding specific events or intervals, rates the molar impression of mother, infant, or dyad on quantitative or qualitative dimensions (e.g., persistence on a task, responsiveness) on a scale. This approach to quantifying dyadic interactions is cost-effective and most appropriate when the goal is to evaluate mothers and/or infants in terms of global dispositions (such as sensitivity) or the aim is to assess interactions in very large samples (such as those obtained in large, multisite studies [e.g., NICHD Early Child Care Research Network, 1994]). Rating scales have been used, for example, to investigate infant–mother attachment, in which the goal is to describe relations between maternal sensitivity and infant attachment status (e.g., Egeland & Farber, 1984; Seifer, Schiller, Sameroff, Resnick, & Riordan, 1996; Susman-Stillman, Kalkoske, Egeland, & Waldman, 1996). The rating scales used in many contemporary studies of mother–infant interaction build on Ainsworth's (1973) conceptualization of sensitivity, which included awareness of and appropriate responsiveness to infant signals. However, researchers who aim to describe the exact nature of mother–infant interactions, contingencies among mother and infant behaviors, and changes to mother–infant interactions over time may be better served by microanalytic approaches.

In overview, discrete and observable maternal, infant, and dyadic behaviors can be studied in quantitative and qualitative terms. These behaviors have been approached using a variety of strategies, including comprehensive coding, sampling, and rating.

The Nature of Mother–Infant Interactions

In infancy – that is, before children are old enough to enter formal social learning situations, like school, or even informal ones, like play groups – most of children's experiences stem directly from interactions within the family. Ecology, class, and culture certainly influence individual development from infancy (Bornstein, 1991; Super & Harkness, 1986), but parents normally are the "final common pathway" to infant oversight and caregiving, development and stature (Bornstein, 1995). As a consequence, many social theorists have posited that the mother–infant relationship constructs the crucible for the early and eventual development of individuals in our species. Starting with the premise that mothers meaningfully affect the development of infants, two questions regarding the nature of their associations warrant discussion: To what extent are relations between parenting and child development general or specific? How are the influences of mothers on infants, and infants on mothers, modeled within and across time?

Generality Versus Specificity

Classical authorities, including notably psychoanalysts, ethologists, and behavior geneticists, have tended to conceptualize maternal behavior as more or less monolithic in nature – as "good," "sensitive," "warm," or "adequate" – despite the wide range of activities mothers naturally engage in with infants (e.g., Ainsworth, Blehar, Waters, & Wall, 1978; Mahler, Pine, & Bergman, 1975; Rohner, 1985; Scarr, 1992; Winnicott, 1965). This view assumes in part that parenting reflects personality traits, and that mothers therefore behave in consistent ways toward babies across domains of interaction, time, and context (Holden & Miller, 1999). Alternatively, maternal activities need not be linked to one another; rather, mothers might vary in the constellation and patterns of their activities (Bornstein, 1989a, 1995). Mothers engage their infants in diverse activities, as we have learned, and mothers do not necessarily behave in uniform or consistent ways across domains of interaction. Mothers who nurture infants more, for example, do not necessarily or automatically engage in more didactics (whether they are US Americans, English, French, Israeli, or Japanese; Bornstein, Azuma, Tamis-LeMonda, & Ogino, 1990; Bornstein & Tamis-LeMonda, 1990; Bornstein, Tamis-LeMonda, Pêcheux, & Rahn, 1991; Bornstein, Toda, Azuma, Tamis-LeMonda, & Ogino, 1990; Dunn, 1977). That is, generally speaking mothers' activities do not covary with one another (nor, it turns out, do those of infants).

An assumption often associated with the monistic view of mothering is that the overall level of parental stimulation affects the child's overall level of development (see Maccoby & Martin, 1983). In contrast, the *specificity principle* states that specific experiences mothers provide infants at specific times in development exert specific effects over specific aspects of development in specific ways (Bornstein, 1995). Contemporary cross-cultural analyses support such a multivariate view of specificity in mother–infant interactions (Bornstein et al., in preparation). Some specific mother and infant activities correspond to one another, of course, and mothers and infants influence one another over time in specific ways. As partners, mothers and infants are open to one another's influence from an early period in the infant's life. Indeed, the character and quality of their individual behaviors indicate that mothers and their babies are to a certain degree flexible, plastic, and adaptable. But, mothers and infants specialize, and their specializations match; that is, mother–infant interactions can be described as (for the most part) mutually corresponding. So, for example, mothers' responses to their infants' communicative overtures might be central to children's early acquisition of language, but exert less influence on the growth of play, motor abilities, or cognition broadly conceived (Tamis-LeMonda & Bornstein, 1994).

In order to adequately test models of mother–infant specificity, it is important to examine multiple behavioral predictors in mothers and multiple criteria in infants. Consider a short-term longitudinal study in which prominent domains of mother–infant engagement were assessed and then mutually analyzed when babies were 2 and 5 months of age (Bornstein & Tamis-LeMonda, 1990). During two home visits, the frequencies of social and didactic forms of mother–infant interaction were evaluated, as were mothers' and babies' verbal/vocal exchanges. The frequencies of mothers' social, didactic, and verbal interactions tended to be unrelated, reinforcing the idea that mothers are "specialists" rather than "generalists." Mothers who more often encouraged their infants to look at them in interactions did not necessarily encourage their infants to attend to the extradyadic environment; similarly, for infants, looking more at mothers was not associated with more environmental exploration. Significantly, relations between mothers' and infants' activities were highly specific at each age and across these first months of life: Mothers who were more social in engaging their infants had infants who more often attended to their mothers, and mothers who were more didactic in their interactions had infants who attended to the environment and manipulated objects more. In addition, mothers' child-directed speech related to their babies' developing nondistress vocalizations.

Similar principles obtain in the infant's second year. The second year is a time of momentous mental transition (e.g., McCall, Eichorn, & Hogarty, 1977), as reflected in the emergence of language (Bates, Bretherton, & Snyder, 1988) and first expressions of pretense in play (Belsky & Most, 1981). In sequential longitudinal studies, mothers and infants were videotaped during free-play interactions at the start (13–14 months) and near the end (20–21 months) of the second year. For each contingent response on the part of mothers, the target of the response (i.e., what the mother responded to – e.g., a vocalization or play act on the part of the infant) and the content of the response (i.e., how the mother responded – e.g., by imitating her infant's vocalization, prompting her infant to engage in a specific play activity) were assessed. In children, two specific outcomes were evaluated – abilities in productive and receptive language and sophistication of play (Tamis-LeMonda & Bornstein, 1994; Tamis-LeMonda, Bornstein, Baumwell, & Damast, 1996). Maternal responsiveness was domain-specific: Responsiveness in the language domain did not relate to responsiveness in the play domain, suggesting that mothers key into different aspects of their infants' abilities. Moreover, responsiveness to infants' vocalizations (responses that imitated/expanded on children's vocalizations) uniquely predicted children's language, and responsiveness to children's play (responses that prompted further play engagements) uniquely predicted children's play both when they played alone and when children played with mothers.

The Temporal Patterning of Associations

What patterns of associations obtain between mother and infant behaviors in infancy? The question of generality versus specificity is distinct from that of timing. Several models of mutual effects have been identified in infancy research (see Bornstein, 1989a, 1989b; Bradley, Caldwell, & Rock, 1988). These models address the extent to which early and/or later experiences uniquely predict children's current or later development. Three define unique effects of one member of the dyad on the other, and one emphasizes their transactional nature. An "early experience" model posits that infants' first experiences *uniquely* affect later child development; that is, experiences vital to development are early occurring and determinative of later development. In this model, the activity of mother uniquely affects the infant at an early time point, and the consequent change in the infant thenceforward endures, independent of later interactions between the mother and infant and independent of whatever individual differences the infant carries into the future. Theoreticians and researchers have long supposed that the child's earliest experiences affect the course of later development (Plato, *ca.* 355 BC/1970), and data derived from ethology, psychoanalysis, behaviorism, and neuropsychology (like sensitive periods; Bornstein, 1989c) support this model. Empirically, mothers encouraging their 2-month-olds to attend to properties, objects, and events in the environment uniquely predicts infants' tactual exploration of objects at 5 months; that is, over and above stability in infant tactual exploration and any contemporaneous 5-month maternal stimulation (Bornstein &

Tamis-LeMonda, 1990). Similarly, mothers who attune to changes in their 9-month-old infants' emotional expressions by matching the gradient dimensions of their infants' expressions have toddlers who achieve key developmental milestones in language development sooner, over and above mothers' later attunements (Nicely, Tamis-LeMonda, & Bornstein, 1999).

A second model focuses on the role of the "contemporary environment"; that is, later experiences can uniquely affect development, overriding the effects of earlier experiences. In this view, mothers exert unique influences over their infants only at later points in development and independent of whatever individual differences infants carry forward into their own future. Empirical support for this model typically consists of recovery of functioning from early deprivation (including studies in which malnourished or disadvantaged infants are adopted into advantaged homes), failure of early intervention studies to show long-term effects, and the like (Clarke & Clarke, 1976; Lewis, 1997; Rutter and the English and Romanian Adoptees Study Team, 1998). Empirically, mothers' didactic encouragement at 5 months uniquely predicts infants' visual exploration of the environment at 5 months, and does so more so than mothers' didactic encouragement at 2 months (Bornstein & Tamis-LeMonda, 1990).

A third model combines the first two into a "cumulative/additive/stable environment" view. Cumulative effects presumably emerge from consistent environmental influences. Empirically, maternal didactic stimulation at 2 and at 5 months has been shown to aggregate to predict unique variance in infant nondistress vocalization at 5 months (Bornstein & Tamis-LeMonda, 1990). Olson, Bates, and Bayles (1984) likewise found that environmental contributions to 24-month toddler development depended on stability in the environment between 6 and 24 months. Although longitudinal data in the first 6 months provide evidence for unique early, unique later, and combined early and late experiential effects between mothers and infants, for the most part it is typical for children to be reared in stable environments (Holden & Miller, 1999), so that cumulative experiences are very likely (Collins, Maccoby, Steinberg, Hetherington, & Bornstein, 2000).

These models of parenting effects notwithstanding, the *transaction principle* asserts that experiences shape the characteristics of an individual through time just as, reciprocally, the characteristics of an individual shape his or her experiences. Thus, the importance and pervasiveness of "infant effects" on mothers are well recognized (e.g., Bell & Harper, 1977). In some degree, infants influence which experiences they will be exposed to, as well as how they absorb and interpret those experiences, and, so, how those experiences might ultimately affect them. Infant and mother bring distinctive characteristics to, and infant and mother alike change in distinctive ways as a result of, their mutual interactions; both mother and infant then enter future interactions as "different" individuals. Maternal sensitivity does not exert a direct and singular effect on infant attachment security; rather, infant temperament and maternal sensitivity operate in tandem to affect one another and the attachment status of babies (Seifer et al., 1996). In essence, transactional, goodness-of-fit models best explain the development of attachment relationships (Cassidy, 1994) and much else in infant development.

In overview, the nature of mother–infant interactions appears to be specific rather than general, and different patterns of association between the two ensue over time. Monolithic conceptualizations of parenting fail to acknowledge the range and diversity in mothering content and style, and hence overlook the possibility that different mothers emphasize or encourage different modes of engagement and different developmental outcomes in their infants. Even in a particular form of parenting (e.g., contingent responsiveness), mothers differ substantially in the ways they express themselves behaviorally: Different mothers can be equally "responsive" overall, but still differ in the sorts of activities to which they respond and in the contents of their responsiveness. Different theoretical models define the temporal patterning of mother–infant associations, and it is probable that each model accurately portrays some aspects of mother–infant interactions for some domains of infant development. Whether or not early or later interactions exert unique, combined, or transactional effects depends on the developmental achievement being investigated and the window of time within which that achievement is assessed.

The Ecological Context of Mother–Infant Interaction

Mothers are the persons primarily responsible for infant rearing (Barnard & Martell, 1995; Bianchi, 2000); moreover, although infants do influence mothers, in the balance of mutual influence maternal effects outweigh infant effects in terms of the variety, complexity, and consistency of influence. In assessing the framework of mother–infant interactions, therefore, we focus principally on mothers.

Our best understanding of mother–infant interaction is informed by an ecological view in which multiple factors – some distal, others proximal to mother and infant – are conceived to contribute to the emergence, ontogenetic course, and eventual character of mother and infant activities with each other. Furthermore, a multivariate systems approach allows us to parse the independent and interdependent roles of these different sources of influence on mother–infant interaction. The origins of variation in maternal behaviors are extremely complex, but certain factors seem of paramount importance, including characteristics in infants, biological determinants and psychological functioning in mothers themselves, and contextual influences, such as family situation and support, socioeconomic status, and cultural ideology (Belsky, 1984; Bornstein, 1988, 1995). For example, the accumulation of risk or protective factors in the ecological context determines the extent to which competent mothering is or is not supported (Sameroff, Seifer, Barocas, Zax, & Greenspan, 1987).

Infant Effects

By virtue of their helplessness and "babyish" characteristics, which are structural and universal, infants appear to elicit heightened attention and nurturance from their mothers (Lorenz, 1935/1970). The nature of infancy is change, and normative developments in infancy, even such elementary ones as gaining the ability to stand upright and walk, also influence the nature and quality of parenting (e.g., Biringen, Emde, Campos, & Appelbaum, 1995). During infancy, the child transforms from an immature being unable to move his or her limbs in a coordinated manner to a more mature one who controls complicated sequences of muscle contractions and flections in order to walk, reach, or grasp; and from one who can only cry or babble to one who makes his or her needs and desires clear with remarkably articulate language. These ontogenetic changes no doubt alter the experiences of infants. Every infant also develops at his or her own rate, and the ages at which individual infants achieve developmental milestones vary enormously, just as infants of a given age vary among themselves on nearly every index of development. Infants differ amongst themselves in temperament, emotional regulation, and social style. These individual differences characteristic of early personality influence parenting and thereby exert both direct and indirect influences on the infant's development. For example, mothers of irritable infants show them less visual and physical contact and less responsiveness and less involvement over time when compared to mothers of nonirritable babies (van den Boom & Hoeksma, 1994). Both normative change and individual differences in infants can in these ways affect the job parents do. Certainly, dynamic developmental change in the context of individual variation among infants challenge and shape parenting in every domain of interaction.

Maternal Biology and Psychological Functioning

Basic physiology is mobilized to support parenting, and several aspects of mothering are believed initially to arise out of biological processes associated with pregnancy and parturition. For example, pregnancy causes the release of hormones thought to be involved in the development of protective, nurturant, and responsive feelings toward offspring (Rosenblatt, 1995). Prenatal biological characteristics – age, diet, and stress level – affect postnatal parenting as well as infant development (Heinicke, 1995). In addition, human beings appear to possess some intuitive knowledge about parenting; that is, some characteristics of parenting may be "wired" into the biological makeup of the species (Papoušek & Papoušek, 1995). For example, mothers speak to babies, even though they know that babies cannot understand language and will not reply, and mothers even do so in a special vocal register of "child-directed speech."

Mothering equally draws upon transient as well as enduring personality characteristics, including intelligence and personality as well as attitudes toward the parenting role, motivation to become involved with children, and childcare and childrearing knowledge and skills. Some personality characteristics that favor good mothering include well-being, empathic awareness, predictability, responsiveness, and emotional availability. Psychological status can support or inhibit felicitous mother–infant interactions. Mothers who feel efficacious and competent in their role as parents are more responsive (Parks & Smeriglio, 1986; Schellenbach, Whitman, & Borkowski, 1992), more empathic, less punitive, and more appropriate in their developmental expectations (East & Felice, 1996). Perceived self-efficacy is likely to affect parenting positively because mothers who feel effective *vis-à-vis* their infants are motivated to engage in further interactions which in turn provide mothers with additional opportunities to understand and interact positively and appropriately with their infants (Teti, O'Connell, & Reiner, 1996). Mothering is also marked by challenging demands, changing and ambiguous criteria, and frequent evaluations, and the demands of mothering may become overwhelming in the presence of a mother's compromised psychological functioning. For example, depression adversely affects a mother's ability to parent competently (Bowlby, 1973; Downey & Coyne, 1990; Field, 1995). Depressed mothers are generally less responsive and communicative with their infants (Cohn, Campbell, Matias, & Hopkins, 1990) and are more likely to yell at or physically punish their children (Dumas & Wekerle, 1995; Jackson, 1993). Depressed mothers are more inconsistent and less likely to provide discipline, structure, or rule enforcement when compared to nondepressed mothers (Goodman & Brumley, 1990). Unsurprisingly, maternal depression adversely affects the synchrony of mother–infant interactions (Field, 1995). Self-efficacy appears to mediate the effects of certain risk factors on maternal sensitivity, including maternal depression and parenting a child with special needs (e.g., premature and medically ill infants; Teti et al., 1996).

Reciprocally, becoming a mother can enhance a woman's psychological development, self-confidence, and sense of well-being. Mothering can augment self-esteem and fulfillment and provide ample occasion to test and display diverse competencies. Mothers often find interest and derive pleasure in their relationships and activities with their infants. Furthermore, mothering translates into a constellation of new trusts and often affords a unique perspective on the "larger picture" of life.

Social Support

Mother–infant interactions are embedded in a nexus of multiple contexts and environments that contribute in critical ways to promote and support infancy (Bronfenbrenner, 1979). Of particular relevance to the mother–infant relationship is a mother's support network. Social support consists of the people that mother considers important in her life, including her spouse or significant other, relatives, friends, and neighbors (Jennings, Stagg, & Connors, 1991). These networks may provide a coping resource to mothers by offering emotional support, advice, guidance, and practical help (Vaux & Harrison, 1985). Mothers with more supportive networks are better able to meet their own needs, and consequently better able to meet the needs of their children (Cochran & Niego, 1995). Social support can improve parenting satisfaction, affecting the availability of mothers to their infants as well as the quality of mother–infant interactions (Bradley & Whiteside-Mansell, 1997). Social support networks of mothers in part determine the quality of parenting, and therefore influence child development indirectly (Belsky, 1984; Crnic & Greenberg, 1987; Hall, Gurley, Sachs, & Kryscio, 1991; McLloyd, 1990).

In many families, support from husbands has been found to have the most general positive consequences for maternal competence, family dynamics, and infant outcomes. In nuclear families, in which mother and father are both present in the infant's life, parents influence their infants by virtue of their influence on each other. Such indirect effects on infant development are more subtle and less noticeable than direct maternal effects, but perhaps no less meaningful. The ways in which spouses provide support and show respect in parenting, how they work together as a co-parenting team, may have far-reaching consequences for infants and children (Fincham, 1998). For example, the quality of mother–child and father–child relationships and child outcomes are all affected by marital quality and father involvement (Gable, Crnic, & Belsky, 1994; Tamis-LeMonda & Cabrera, 1999). The presence of a supportive partner in the home is associated with consistency in discipline, more patience, and less exhaustion in mothers (Furstenberg, Brooks-Gunn, & Chase-Lansdale, 1989; Lamb, Sternberg, & Thompson, 1997; Marsiglio, 1995) and moderates the effects of infant difficulty on maternal depression (Cutrona & Troutman, 1986) and sensitivity (Crnic & Greenberg, 1987).

Maternal support networks are especially crucial to woman and children living in at-risk circumstances such as poverty. Often, poorer mothers exist in inadequate support networks (McLoyd, 1990); nearly 70 percent of women on welfare are unmarried when they have their first child (Tamis-LeMonda & Cabrera, 1999). Empirically, social support moderates relations between poverty and maternal punitiveness, sensitivity, satisfaction, and life stress (Crnic, Greenberg, Robinson, Ragozin, & Basham, 1983; Hashima & Amato, 1994; Miller-Loncar, Erwin, Landry, Smith, & Swank, 1998).

Socioeconomic Status

At a more distal level, socioeconomic status (SES) affects the mother–infant relationship. Mothers in different SES groups behave similarly in certain parenting domains, however SES – perhaps through differential provisions in the environment and education of mothers – also orders home circumstances and other attitudes and actions of mothers toward infants. In many cases, low SES is considered a risk factor in children's development on account of its detrimental effect on the quality of mother–infant interaction (Dodge, Pettit, & Bates, 1994). The numerous negative circumstances associated with poverty are thought to compromise a mother's ability to engage in sensitive, consistent, and involved parenting (McLoyd, 1990). Low SES adversely affects mothers' psychological functioning and promotes harsh or inconsistent disciplinary practices (Conger, McMarty, Yang, Lahey, & Kropp, 1984; McLoyd & Wilson, 1990; Simons, Whitbeck, Conger, & Wu, 1991). Relations between social class and mothers' language (e.g., Hoff-Ginsberg & Tardif, 1995), specific parenting practices (e.g., Garbarino & Kostelny, 1993; Hart & Risley, 1992), and developmental expectations, theories, and values (e.g., Sameroff & Feil, 1985) have been identified. In general, the challenges to rearing an infant are exacerbated by sociodemographic risk. More generally, a fruitful way of examining social-class differences in early development has been advanced by Kohn (1987), who suggested that, both within and across cultures, parents try to inculcate values that will maximize their children's chances of success in the social station in which the children are likely to find themselves as mature adults.

Cultural Ideology

Cross-cultural investigation shows that virtually all aspects of mothering infants – beliefs and behaviors – are shaped by culture. Interwoven in all contents and styles of mother-

ing are the values, beliefs, and customs of the larger culture in which mother–infant interactions take place (Bornstein et al., in preparation). For example, the extent to
which mothers "play" with their infants as well as their goals in play vary with culture;
thus, even the elementary act of a mother demonstrating how a toy works to her infant
carries with it cultural meaning (e.g., Bornstein, Haynes, Pascual, Painter, & Galperín,
1999). Mothers not only communicate information to their infants about the features
of the specific toy, but also convey information about the role of toys and how social partners in a society co-construct knowledge. Göncü and Mosier (1991) studied mothers'
views about the importance of play in children's early development across various cultures
and also assessed the extent to which mothers actually engaged in play with their young
children. Middle-class US and Turkish parents think of themselves as play partners for
their children and, consistent with such views, participated in frequent pretend play with
their children. In contrast, Mayan Indians think of play as exclusively a child's
activity, and in line with this belief Mayan mothers engaged in little or no pretense with
their children.

Culture influences mothering practices and patterns (and, in turn, infant development)
from a very early age in terms of when and how mothers care for their infants and
which behaviors mothers appreciate and emphasize. Reciprocally, infants begin to build
their initial knowledge of the world, of persons, and of events during those self-
same social exchanges with their mothers. Even with generally similar ultimate goals of
successful childrearing, cultures often contrast in terms of the types of competencies
mothers promote in infants, the paths mothers follow to instill in infants the desire to
achieve those goals, and the developmental timetables mothers wish their infants to
meet. Thus, the most basic and concrete features of infant development are affected
by culture, as are the most subtle and abstract. Rebelsky (1967, 1972) found that
Dutch infants, who are physically stimulated by their mothers less than US American
infants, scored lower than US Americans on scales of psychomotor ability; by contrast, Super (1976) found advanced sitting, standing, and walking among Kenyan
Kipsigis babies, where Kipsigis mothers deliberately taught their infants to sit, stand,
and walk. (Super, 1976, also found that Kipsigis infants reared in the manner of
European babies lose the advantage of their traditionally reared, genetically similar
compatriots.)

Central to a concept of culture is the expectation that different peoples possess different ideas as well as behave in different ways with respect to childrearing. To the extent
that internalized constructs are shaped by culture, parenting views reflect cultural ideologies that parents uphold and transmit to their children. In other words, parents' cognitions implicitly guide parenting interactions which in turn affect infant development
(Bornstein, 1991; Bornstein et al., 1996; Goodnow, 1995; Goodnow & Collins, 1990;
McGillicuddy-De Lisi & Sigel, 1995; Toda, Fogel, & Kawai, 1990). The general view is
that culture informs ideas that in turn generate behaviors or mediate their effectiveness.
Thus, culture helps to organize the world of parenting because cultural ideas affect
parents' sense of self and competence in their role and shape their priorities; in a larger
sense, cultural ideas contribute to the "continuity of culture" by helping to define culture
and the transmission of cultural information across generations. Goodnow (1995)
observed that parents encounter the prevailing views of their social group both before and

after they become parents and often appropriate those views ready-made from the culture at large. Views about activities that are central to children's development, and the ways that parents foster development in their children, are, to some extent, therefore culturally determined. Moreover, LeVine (1988) contended that parenting beliefs might be especially conservative cultural constructs. That said, most cross-cultural studies of mothering have focused on parenting behaviors rather than on cognitions that might guide those behaviors (e.g., Cote & Bornstein, 2000; Franco, Fogel, Messinger, & Frazier, 1996). However, understanding human behavior advances when the meanings that actors assign behaviors are better understood.

In research with Latino and European American families in the United States, Harwood, Miller, and Irizarry (1995) found that, over and above socioeconomic factors, European American mothers underscored the importance of values such as independence, assertiveness, and creativity when asked to describe an ideal child. Latina mothers, in contrast, underscored the importance of obedience and respect for others. In line with these values, US mothers were observed to foster independence in infants in a variety of ways; for example, during naturalistic mother–infant interactions during feeding, US mothers encouraged their infants to feed themselves at 8 months of age, sometimes leaving them in a highchair with food and utensils. In contrast, Latina mothers held their infants closely on their laps during mealtime and took control of feeding them meals from start to finish.

Cross-cultural investigations between Japan and the United States illustrate the ways that mother–infant interactions support larger cultural goals (Bornstein, Azuma et al., 1990; Bornstein, Toda et al., 1990). US mothers encourage and respond more to infant object orientation, and the content of mothers' responses is more often didactic. That is, when infants in the United States look at or explore objects in their surrounds, mothers support those explorations and attempt to maintain the infant's interest on the objects they explore by showing infants how objects work or what can be done with them. In contrast, Japanese mothers respond more to their infants' social bids, and their responses tend to be oriented around the dyad. That is, Japanese mothers more often encourage face-to-face social exchanges with their infants. Sequential analysis of mother–infant exchanges showed that Japanese mothers tended to encourage their infants to attend to them even when their infants were actively engaged in exploring objects of the environment (Bornstein, Azuma et al., 1990; Bornstein, Toda et al., 1990). A comparison of the base-rate frequencies with which infants vocalized, looked at their mothers, and looked at and/or touched objects in the two cultures showed that infants behaved similarly, providing mothers with equivalent starting points. Thus, the contrasting emphases by mothers in the two cultures, on object versus social engagements, did not simply spring from differences in infant behaviors, but were consonant with larger cultural goals.

In overview, mother–infant interactions do not unfold in a vacuum. Divergent styles of mothering can best be understood in an ecological framework that takes into account infant effects, the mother's own biology and psychological functioning, social supports, social class, and cultural ideology. To interpret meaning in patterns of mother–infant interaction, it is critical to discover why parents parent the way they do and to elucidate the values they find to be important.

Conclusions

Parenting is central to childhood, to child development, and to society's long-term investment in children. For new mothers, the first years with an infant constitute a period of adjustment and transformation; for infants, interactions with mothers constitute critical experiences in development. Moreover, certain enduring psychological characteristics of the individual are believed to arise early in life, and the nature of mother–infant interaction is thought to contribute at least one important source of their development. As a result, mother–infant interactions have often been looked to in attempts to address fundamental questions about human origins and development. A better understanding of the nature of the human being is afforded by examining mother–infant interaction and its consequences in the period of the dyad's initial accommodation – the unique and specific influences of mother on infant and of infant on mother.

Mother–infant interactions command attention for several reasons. First, they are significant in themselves because infancy is a critical period in the life cycle, characterized by noteworthy developments in emotional, social, communicative, and cognitive competencies. Mother–infant interactions serve as the prime context for these early achievements. Second, who infants are and what they do influence their social interactions with mothers, and in indirect ways infants affect their own development. Third, the experiences of infancy (separate from continuing post-infancy experiences) are principally provided by mothers and may endure, influencing the rate, course, and perhaps eventual resting level of subsequent development. Focus on mother–infant interaction is also portentous for practical reasons. Appreciating factors that affect infant development (as well as those that do not) promises to inform efforts at intervention and remediation. Infancy is a time of vulnerability; it is formative in habit development; and it may be foundational for decision making for the balance of the life course.

As Winnicott (1965) keenly observed, infants cannot exist alone. Rather, infants can exist only with their mothers (or other caregivers). In turn, infants and mothers do not exist alone, but are embedded in larger social contexts that include family members, communities, social class, and culture. Moreover, mothers change in their persons and positions, and infants constantly develop, and each influences the other so that elements of who infants were yesterday, who they are today, and who they will be tomorrow are in constant transformation. To fathom the nature of mothering and mother–infant relationships within families therefore calls for a multivariate and dynamic stance. Only multiple levels of analysis can adequately capture the individual, dyadic, and family-unit forces on development and reflect the embeddedness of mother and infant within all relevant extrafamilial systems. The dynamic aspect involves the many different developmental trajectories of mother and infant that unfold through time.

References

Ainsworth, M. D. S. (1973). The development of infant–mother attachment. In B. M. Caldwell & H. N. Riciutti (Eds.), *Review of child development research* (Vol. 3, pp. 1–94). Chicago: University of Chicago Press.

Ainsworth, M. D. S., Blehar, M. C., Waters, E., & Wall, S. (1978). *Patterns of attachment: A psychological study of the Strange Situation.* Hillsdale, NJ: Erlbaum.

Baldwin, D. A., & Baird, J. A. (1999). Early perception of social contingencies and interpersonal intentional inference. In P. Rochat (Ed.), *Early social cognition: Understanding others in the first months of life* (pp. 189–214). Mahwah, NJ: Lawrence Erlbaum Associates.

Barnard, K. E., & Martell, L. K. (1995). Mothering. In M. H. Bornstein (Ed.), *Handbook of parenting* (Vol. 3, pp. 3–26). Mahwah, NJ: Lawrence Erlbaum Associates.

Bates, E., Bretherton, I., & Snyder, L. (1988). *From first words to grammar: Individual differences and dissociable mechanisms.* Cambridge: Cambridge University Press.

Bateson, M. C. (1975). Mother–infant exchanges: The epigenesis of conversational interaction. In D. Aronson & R. W. Rieber (Eds.), *Annals of the New York Academy of Sciences* (Vol. 263). *Developmental psycholinguistics and communication disorders* (pp. 101–113). New York: New York Academy of Sciences.

Bateson, M. C. (1979). "The epigenesis of conversational interaction": A personal account of research development. In M. Bullowa (Ed.), *Before speech: The beginning of human communication* (pp. 63–77). New York: Cambridge University Press.

Baumrind, D. (1991). Effective parenting during the early adolescent transition. In P. A. Cowan, E. M. Hetherington, et al. (Eds.), *Family transitions. Advances in family research series* (pp. 111–163). Hillsdale, NJ: Lawrence Erlbaum Associates.

Beebe, B., Jaffe, J., Feldstein, S., Mays, K., & Alson, D. (1985). Interpersonal timing: The application of an adult dialogue model to mother–infant vocal and kinesic interactions. In T. M. Field & N. Fox (Eds.), *Social perception in infants* (pp. 217–247). Norwood, NJ: Ablex.

Bell, R. Q., & Harper, L. (1977). *Child effects on adults.* Hillsdale, NJ: Lawrence Erlbaum Associates.

Belsky, J. (1984). The determinants of parenting: A process model. *Child Development, 55,* 83–96.

Belsky, J. (1999). Infant–parent attachment. In L. Balter & C. S. Tamis-LeMonda (Eds.), *Child psychology: A handbook of contemporary issues* (pp. 45–63). Philadelphia, PA: Psychology Press.

Belsky, J., & Most, R. K. (1981). From exploration to play: A cross-sectional study of infant free-play behavior. *Developmental Psychology, 17,* 630–639.

Belsky, J., Rovine, M., & Taylor, D. G. (1984). The Pennsylvania infant and family development project III: The origins of individual differences in infant–mother attachment: Maternal and infant contributions. *Child Development, 55,* 718–728.

Bianchi, S. M. (2000, March 24). *Maternal employment and time with children: Dramatic change or surprising continuity?* 2000 Presidential Address delivered to the Population Association of America. Westin Bonaventure Hotel, Los Angeles, CA.

Biringen, Z., Emde, R. N., Campos, J. J., & Appelbaum, M. I. (1995). Affective reorganization in the infant, the mother, and the dyad: The role of upright locomotion and its timing. *Child Development, 66,* 499–514.

Bjorklund, D. F., & Pelligrini, A. (2000). Child development and evolutionary psychology. *Child Development, 72,* 1687–1708.

Bloom, L. (1993). *The transition from infancy to language.* New York: Cambridge University Press.

Bloom, L. (1999). Language acquisition in its developmental context. In W. Damon (Series Ed.) & D. Kuhn & R. S. Siegler (Vol. Eds.), *Handbook of child psychology: Vol. 2. Cognition, perception, and language* (5th ed., pp. 309–370). New York: John Wiley.

Bornstein, M. H. (1988). Mothers, infants, and the development of cognitive competence. In H. E. Fitzgerald, B. M. Lester, & M. W. Yogman (Eds.), *Theory and research in behavioral pediatrics* (Vol. 4, pp. 67–99). New York: Plenum.

Bornstein, M. H. (1989a). Between caretakers and their young: Two modes of interaction and their consequences for cognitive growth. In M. H. Bornstein & J. S. Bruner (Eds.), *Interaction in human development* (pp. 197–214). Hillsdale, NJ: Lawrence Erlbaum Associates.

Bornstein, M. H. (Ed.). (1989b). *Maternal responsiveness: Characteristics and consequences.* San Francisco: Jossey-Bass.

Bornstein, M. H. (1989c). Sensitive periods in development: Structural characteristics and causal interpretations. *Psychological Bulletin, 105,* 179–197.

Bornstein, M. H. (Ed.). (1991). *Cultural approaches to parenting.* Hillsdale, NJ: Lawrence Erlbaum Associates.

Bornstein, M. H. (1995). Parenting infants. In M. H. Bornstein (Ed.), *Handbook of parenting* (Vol. 1, pp. 3–39). Mahwah, NJ: Lawrence Erlbaum Associates.

Bornstein, M. H. (2000). Infant into conversant: Language and nonlanguage processes in developing early communication. In N. Budwig, I. Č. Užgiris, & J. V. Wertsch (Eds.), *Communication: An arena of development* (pp. 109–129). Stamford, CT: Ablex.

Bornstein, M. H. et al. (in preparation). *Infancy, parenting, and culture.* Manuscript in preparation, National Institute of Child Health and Human Development.

Bornstein, M. H., Azuma, H., Tamis-LeMonda, C. S., & Ogino, M. (1990). Mother and infant mother activity and interaction in Japan and in the United States: I. A comparative macroanalysis of naturalistic exchanges. *International Journal of Behavioral Development, 13,* 267–287.

Bornstein, M. H., Haynes, O. M., Pascual, L., Painter, K. M., & Galperín, C. (1999). Play in two societies: Pervasiveness of process, specificity of structure. *Child Development, 70,* 317–331.

Bornstein, M. H., & Lamb, M. E. (1992). *Development in infancy: An introduction* (3rd ed.). New York: McGraw-Hill.

Bornstein, M. H., Tal, J., Rahn, C., Galperín, C. Z., Pêcheux, M.-G., Lamour, M., Toda, S., Azuma, H., Ogino, M., & Tamis-LeMonda, C. S. (1992). Functional analysis of the contents of maternal speech to infants of 5 and 13 months in four cultures: Argentina, France, Japan, and the United States. *Developmental Psychology, 28,* 593–603.

Bornstein, M. H., & Tamis-LeMonda, C. S. (1990). Activities and interactions of mothers and their firstborn infants in the first six months of life: Covariation, stability, continuity, correspondence, and prediction. *Child Development, 61,* 1206–1217.

Bornstein, M. H., Tamis-LeMonda, C. S., Pascual, L., Haynes, M. O., Painter, K. M., Galperin, C. Z., & Pêcheux, M.-G. (1996). Ideas about parenting in Argentina, France, and the United States. *International Journal of Behavioral Development, 19,* 347–367.

Bornstein, M. H., Tamis-LeMonda, C. S., Pêcheux, M.-G., & Rahn, C. (1991). Infant and mother activity and interaction in France and in the United States: A comparative study. *International Journal of Behavioral Development, 14,* 21–43.

Bornstein, M. H., Tamis-LeMonda, C. S., Tal, J., Ludemann, P., Toda, S., Rahn, C. W., Pêcheux, M.-G., Azuma, H., & Vardi, D. (1992). Maternal responsiveness to infants in three societies: The United States, France, and Japan. *Child Development, 63,* 808–821.

Bornstein, M. H., Toda, S., Azuma, H., Tamis-LeMonda, C. S., & Ogino, M. (1990). Mothers and infant activity and interaction in Japan and in the United States: II. A comparative microanalysis of naturalistic interactions focused on the organization of infant attention. *International Journal of Behavioural Development, 13,* 289–308.

Bowlby, J. (1973). *Attachment and loss: Vol. 2. Separation: Anxiety and anger.* New York: Basic Books.

Bradley, R. H., Caldwell, B. M., & Rock, S. L. (1988). Home environment and school performance: A ten-year follow-up and examination of three models of environmental action. *Child Development, 59,* 852–867.

Bradley, R. H., & Whiteside-Mansell, L. (1997). Children in poverty. In R. T. Ammerman & M. Hersen (Eds.), *Handbook of prevention and treatment with children and adolescents* (pp. 13–58). New York: Wiley.

Bremner, J. G. (1994). *Infancy* (2nd ed.). Malden, MA: Blackwell.

Bronfenbrenner, U. (1979). *The ecology of human development.* Cambridge, MA: Harvard University Press.

Cassidy, J. (1994). Emotional regulation: Influences of attachment relationships. In N. A. Fox (Ed.), The development of emotion regulation: Biological and behavioral considerations (pp. 228–249). *Monographs of the Society for Research in Child Development, 59* (Serial No. 240).

Clarke, A. M., & Clarke, A. D. B. (Eds.). (1976). *Early experience: Myth and evidence.* New York: Free Press.

Cochran, M., & Niego, S. (1995). Parenting and social networks. In M. H. Bornstein (Ed.), *Handbook of parenting* (Vol. 3, pp. 393–418). Mahwah, NJ: Lawrence Erlbaum Associates.

Cohn, J. F., Campbell, S. B., Matias, R., & Hopkins, J. (1990). Face-to-face interactions of post-partum depressed and nondepressed mother–infant pairs at 2 months. *Developmental Psychology, 26,* 15–23.

Collins, W. A., Maccoby, E. E., Steinberg, L., Hetherington, E. M., & Bornstein, M. H. (2000). Contemporary research on parenting: The case for nature *and* nurture. *American Psychologist, 55,* 218–232.

Conger, R. D., McMarty, J., Yang, R., Lahey, B., & Kropp, J. (1984). Perception of child, child rearing values, and emotional distress as mediating links between environmental stressors and observed maternal behavior. *Child Development, 55,* 2234–2247.

Cote, L. R., & Bornstein, M. H. (2000). Social and didactic parenting behaviors and beliefs among Japanese American and South American-U.S. mothers and infants. *Infancy, 1,* 363–374.

Crnic, K. A., & Greenberg, M. T. (1987). Maternal stress, social support, and coping: Influences on the early mother–infant relationship. In C. Boukydis (Ed.), *Research on support for parents and infants in the postnatal period* (pp. 25–40). Norwood, NJ: Ablex.

Crnic, K. A., Greenberg, M. T., Robinson, N. M., Ragozin, A. S., & Basham, R. B. (1983). Effects of stress and social support on mothers and premature and full-term infants. *Child Development, 54,* 209–217.

Cutrona, C. E., & Troutman, B. R. (1986). Social support, infant temperament, and parenting self-efficacy: A mediational model of postpartum depression. *Child Development, 57,* 1507–1518.

Darling, N., & Steinberg, L. D. (1993). Parenting style as context: An integrative model. *Psychological Bulletin, 113,* 487–496.

Dodge, K. A., Pettit, G. S., & Bates, J. E. (1994). Socializing mediators of the relation between socioeconomic status and child conduct problems. *Child Development, 65,* 649–665.

Downey, G., & Coyne, J. C. (1990). Children of depressed parents: An integrative review. *Psychological Bulletin, 108,* 50–76.

Dumas, J. E., & Wekerle, C. (1995). Maternal reports of child behaviors and personal distress as predictors of dysfunctional parenting. *Development and Psychopathology, 7,* 465–479.

Dunn, J. B. (1977). Patterns of early interaction: Continuities and consequences. In H. R. Schaffer (Ed.), *Studies in mother–infant interaction* (pp. 438–456). London: Academic Press.

East, P. L., & Felice, M. E. (1996). *Adolescent pregnancy and parenting: Findings from a racially diverse sample.* Mahwah, NJ: Erlbaum.

Egeland, B., & Farber, E. A. (1984). Infant–mother attachment: Factors related to its development and changes over time. *Child Development, 55,* 753–771.

Field, T. (1995). Psychologically depressed parents. In M. H. Bornstein (Ed.), *Handbook of parenting* (Vol. 4, pp. 85–99). Mahwah, NJ: Lawrence Erlbaum Associates.

Fincham, F. D. (1998). Child development and marital relations. *Child Development, 69,* 543–574.

Fogel, A. (1991). *Infancy: Infant, family, and society* (2nd ed.). St. Paul, MN: West Publishing.

Fogel, A., & Lyra, M. C. D. P. (1997). Dynamics of development in relationships. In F. Masterpasqua & P. A. Perna (Eds.), *The psychological meaning of chaos: Translating theory into practice* (pp. 75–94). Washington, DC: American Psychological Association.

Fogel, A., Messinger, D. S., Dickson, K. L., & Hsu, H.-C. (1999). Posture and gaze in early mother–infant communication: Synchronization of developmental trajectories. *Developmental Science, 2,* 325–332.

Franco, F., Fogel, A., Messinger, D. S., & Frazier, C. A. (1996). Cultural differences in physical contact between Hispanic and Anglo mother–infant dyads living in the United States. *Early Development and Parenting, 5,* 119–127.

Furstenberg, F. F., Brooks-Gunn, J., & Chase-Lansdale, P. L. (1989). Teenaged pregnancy and childbearing. *American Psychologist, 44,* 313–320.

Gable, S., Crnic, K., & Belsky, J. (1994). Coparenting within the family system: Influences on children's development. *Family Relations, 43,* 380–386.

Garbarino, J., & Kostelny, K. (1993). Neighborhood and community influences on parenting. In T. Luster & L. Okagaki (Eds.), *Parenting: An ecological perspective* (pp. 203–236). Hillsdale, NJ: Erlbaum.

Gergely, G., & Watson, J. S. (1999). Early socio-emotional development: Contingency perception and the social-biofeedback model. In P. Rochat (Ed.), *Early social cognition: Understanding others in the first months of life* (pp. 101–136). Mahwah, NJ: Erlbaum.

Göncü, A., & Mosier, C. (1991). *Cultural variation in the play of toddlers.* Paper presented at the Biennial Meetings of the Society for Research in Child Development, Seattle, WA.

Goodman, S., & Brumley, E. (1990). Schizophrenic and depressed women: Relational deficits in parenting. *Developmental Psychology* [Special Issue], *26,* 31–39.

Goodnow, J. J. (1995). Parents' knowledge and expectations. In M. H. Bornstein (Ed.), *Handbook of parenting* (Vol. 3, pp. 305–332). Mahwah, NJ: Lawrence Erlbaum Associates.

Goodnow, J. J., & Collins, W. A. (1990). *Development according to parents: The nature, sources, and consequences of parents' ideas.* Hillsdale, NJ: Lawrence Erlbaum Associates.

Grolnick, W. S., McMenamy, J. M., & Kurowski, C. O. (1999). Emotional self-regulation in infancy and toddlerhood. In L. Balter &C. S. Tamis-LeMonda (Eds.), *Child psychology: A handbook of contemporary issues* (pp. 3–22). Philadelphia, PA: Psychology Press.

Hall, L. A., Gurley, D. N., Sachs, B., & Kryscio, R. J. (1991). Psychosocial predictors of maternal depressive symptoms, parenting attitudes and child behavior in single-parent families. *Nursing Research, 40,* 214–220.

Hart, B., & Risley, T. R. (1992). American parenting of language-learning children: Persisting differences in family–child interactions observed in natural home environments. *Developmental Psychology, 28,* 1096–1105.

Harkness, S., & Super, C. M. (1995). Culture and parenting. In M. H. Bornstein (Ed.), *Handbook of parenting* (Vol. 2, pp. 211–234). Mahwah, NJ: Lawrence Erlbaum Associates.

Harwood, R. L., Miller, J. G., & Irizarry, N. L. (1995). *Culture and attachment: Perceptions of the child in context.* New York: Guilford Press.

Hashima, P. Y., & Amato, P. R. (1994). Poverty, social support, and parental behavior. *Child Development, 65,* 394–403.

Heinicke, C. M. (1995). Determinants of transition to parenting. In M. H. Bornstein (Ed.), *Handbook of parenting* (Vol. 3, pp. 277–303). Mahwah, NJ: Lawrence Erlbaum Associates.

Hoff-Ginsberg, E., & Tardif, T. (1995). Socioeconomic status and parenting. In M. H. Bornstein (Ed.), *Handbook of parenting* (Vol. 2, pp. 161–188). Mahwah, NJ: Lawrence Erlbaum Associates.

Holden, G. W., & Miller, P. C. (1999). Enduring and different: A meta-analysis of the similarity in parents' child rearing. *Psychological Bulletin, 125,* 223–254.

Hrdy, S. B. (1999). *Mother nature: A history of mothers, infants, and natural selection.* New York: Pantheon.

Isabella, R. A., & Belsky, J. (1991). Interactional synchrony and the origins of infant–mother attachment: A replication study. *Child Development, 62,* 373–384.

Jackson, A. (1993). Black, single, working mothers in poverty: Preferences for employment, well-being, and perceptions of preschool-age children. *Social Work, 38,* 26–34.

Jennings, K. D., Stagg, V., & Connors, R. E. (1991). Social networks and mothers' interactions with their preschool children. *Child Development, 62,* 966–978.

Jones, N. A., Field, T., Fox, N. A., Davalos, M., Malphurs, J., Carraway, K., Schanberg, S., & Kuhn, C. (1997). Infants of intrusive and withdrawn mothers. *Infant Behavior and Development, 20,* 175–186.

Kochanska, G., Forman, D. R., & Coy, K. C. (1999). Implications of the mother–child relationship in infancy for socialization in the second year of life. *Infant Behavior and Development, 22,* 249–265.

Kohn, M. L. (1987). Cross national research as an analytic strategy. *American Sociological Review, 52,* 713–731.

Kugiumutzakis, G. (1998). Neonatal imitation in the intersubjective companion space. In S. Braten (Ed.), *Intersubjective communication and emotion in early ontogeny. Studies in emotion and social interaction* (pp. 63–88). New York: Cambridge University Press.

Lamb, M., Sternberg, K., & Thompson, R. (1997). The effects of divorce and custody arrangements on children's behavior, development, and adjustment. *Family and Conciliation Courts Review, 35,* 393–404.

Landry, S. H. (1995). The development of joint attention in premature low birthweight infants. Effects of early medial complications and maternal attention-directing behaviors. In C. Moore & P. J. Dunham (Eds.), *Joint attention: Its origins and role in development* (pp. 223–250). Hillsdale, NJ: Lawrence Erlbaum Associates.

LeVine, R. A. (1988). Human parental care: Universal goals, cultural strategies, individual behavior. In R. A. LeVine, P. M. Miller, & M. M. West (Eds.), *Parental behavior in diverse societies* (pp. 3–12). San Francisco: Jossey-Bass.

Lewis, M. (1997). *Altering fate: Why the past does not predict the future.* New York: Guilford Press.

Lorenz, K. (1970). *Studies in animal and human behavior* (Trans. R. Martin). London: Methuen. (Original work published 1935)

Maccoby, E. E., & Martin, J. A. (1983). Socialization in the context of the family: Parent–child interaction. In M. Hetherington (Ed.), *Handbook of child psychology* (Vol. 10, pp. 1–103). New York: Wiley.

Mahler, M., Pine, A., & Bergman, F. (1975). *The psychological birth of the human infant.* New York: Basic Books.

Marsiglio, W. (1995). Young nonresidential biological fathers. *Marriage and Family Review, 20,* 325–348.

McCall, R. B., Eichorn, D. H., & Hogarty, P. S. (1977). Transitions in early mental development. *Monographs of the Society for Research in Child Development, 42* (Serial No. 171), 1–93.

McGillicuddy-De Lisi, A. V., & Sigel, I. E. (1995). Parental beliefs. In M. H. Bornstein (Ed.), *Handbook of parenting* (Vol. 3, pp. 333–358). Mahwah, NJ: Lawrence Erlbaum Associates.

McLoyd, V. C. (1990). The impact of economic hardship on black families and children: Psychological distress, parenting, and socioemotional development. *Child Development, 61,* 311–346.

McLoyd, V. C., & Wilson, L. (1990). Maternal behavior, social support, and economic conditions as predictors of distress in children. *New Directions in Child Development, 46,* 49–70.

Messinger, D. S., & Fogel, A. (1998). Give and take: The development of conventional infant gestures. *Merrill-Palmer Quarterly, 44,* 566–590.

Messinger, D. S., Fogel, A., & Dickson, K. L. (1999). What's in a smile? *Developmental Psychology, 35,* 701–708.

Miller, S. A. (1988). Parents beliefs about their children's cognitive development. *Child Development, 59,* 259–285.

Miller-Loncar, C. L., Erwin, L. J., Landry, S. H., Smith, K. E., & Swank, P. R. (1998). Characteristics of social support networks of low socioeconomic status African American, Anglo American, and Mexican American mothers of full-term and pre-term infants. *Journal of Community Psychology, 26,* 131–143.

Moore, C., & Dunham, P. J. (Eds.). (1995). *Joint attention: Its origins and role in development* (pp. 223–250). Hillsdale, NJ: Lawrence Erlbaum.

Murray, L., & Trevarthen, C. (1985). Emotional regulation of interactions between two-month-olds and their mothers. In T. M. Field & N. A. Fox (Eds.), *Social perception in infants* (pp. 177–197). Norwood, NJ: Ablex.

Nicely, P., Tamis-LeMonda, C. S., & Bornstein, M. H. (1999). Mothers' attuned responses to infant affect expressivity promote earlier achievement of language milestones. *Infant Behavior and Development, 22,* 557–568.

NICHD Early Child Care Research Network. (1994). Child care and child development: The NICHD study of early child care. In S. Friedman & H. Haywood (Eds.), *Developmental follow up: Concepts, domains and methods* (pp. 377–396). New York: Academic Press.

Olson, S. L., Bates, J. E., & Bayles, K. (1984). Mother–infant interaction and the development of individual differences in children's cognitive competence. *Developmental Psychology, 20,* 166–179.

Papoušek, H., & Papoušek, M. (1995). Intuitive parenting. In M. H. Bornstein (Ed.), *Handbook of parenting* (Vol. 2, pp. 117–136). Mahwah, NJ: Lawrence Erlbaum Associates.

Papoušek, H., Papoušek, M., & Bornstein, M. (1985). The naturalistic vocal environment of young infants: On the significance of homogeneity and variability in parental speech. In T. Fields & N. Fox (Eds.), *Social perception in infants* (pp. 269–298). Norwood, NJ: Ablex.

Parks, P. L., & Smeriglio, V. L. (1986). Relationships among parenting knowledge, quality of stimulation in the home and infant development. *Family Relations, 35,* 411–416.

Pederson, D. R., Moran, G., Sitko, C., Campbell, K., Ghesquire, K., & Acton, H. (1990). Maternal sensitivity and the security of infant–mother attachment: A Q-sort study. *Child Development, 58,* 1974–1983.

Plato. (*ca.* 355 BC/1970). [*The laws*] (Trans. T. J. Saunders). Harmondsworth: Penguin.

Raver, C. C. (1996). Success at catching and keeping toddlers' attention: An examination of joint attention among low-income mothers and their 2-year olds. *Early Development and Parenting, 5,* 225–236.

Rebelsky, F. G. (1967). Infancy in two cultures. *Nederlands Tijdschrift voor de Psychologie, 22,* 379–385.

Rebelsky, F. G. (1972). First discussant's comments: Cross-cultural studies of mother–infant interaction. *Human Development, 15,* 128–130.

Rochat, P., & Striano, T. (1999). Social-cognitive development in the first year. In P. Rochat (Ed.), *Early social cognition: Understanding others in the first months of life* (pp. 3–34). Mahwah, NJ: Lawrence Erlbaum Associates.

Roggman, L. A. (1991). Assessing social interactions of mothers and infants through play. In C. E. Schaefer, K. Gitlin, & A. Sandgrund (Eds.), *Play diagnosis and assessment* (pp. 427–462). New York: John Wiley.

Rohner, R. (1985). *The warmth dimension.* Beverly Hills, CA: Sage Publications.

Rosenblatt, J. S. (1995). Hormonal basis of parenting in mammals. In M. H. Bornstein (Ed.), *Handbook of parenting* (Vol. 2, pp. 3–25). Mahwah, NJ: Lawrence Erlbaum Associates.

Rutter, M., & the English and Romanian Adoptees Study Team. (1998). Developmental catch-up and delay, following adoption after severe global early privation. *Journal of Child Psychology and Psychiatry, 39*, 465–476.

Sameroff, A. J., & Feil, L. A. (1985). Parental concepts of development. In I. E. Sigel (Ed.), *Parent belief systems: The psychological consequences for children* (pp. 83–105). Hillsdale, NJ: Erlbaum.

Sameroff, A. J., Seifer, R., Barocas, R., Zax, M., & Greenspan, S. (1987). Intelligence quotient scores of 4-year-old children: Social-environmental risk factors. *Pediatrics, 79*, 342–350.

Scarr, S. (1992). Developmental theories for the 1990s: Development and individual differences. *Child Development, 63*, 1–19.

Schellenbach, C. J., Whitman, T. L., & Borkowski, J. G. (1992). Toward an integrative model of adolescent parenting. *Human Development, 35*, 81–99.

Seifer, R., Schiller, M., Sameroff, A. J., Resnick, S., & Riordan, K. (1996). Attachment, maternal sensitivity, and infant temperament during the first year of life. *Developmental Psychology, 32*, 12–25.

Simons, R. L., Whitbeck, L. B., Conger, R. D., & Wu, C.-I. (1991). Intergenerational transmission of harsh parenting. *Developmental Psychology, 27*, 159–171.

Smith, P. K., & Connolly, K. (1972). Patterns of play and social interaction in preschool children. In N. Blurton-Jones (Ed.), *Ethological studies of child behaviour* (pp. 65–95). London: Cambridge University Press.

Stern, D. N. (1974). Mother and infant at play: The dyadic interaction involving facial, vocal, & gaze behaviors. In M. Lewis & L. Rosenblum (Eds.), *The effect of the infant on its caregiver* (pp. 187–211). New York: Wiley.

Stern, D. N. (1993). The role of feelings for an interpersonal self. In U. Neisser (Ed.), *The perceived self: Ecological and interpersonal sources of self-knowledge* (pp. 205–215). Cambridge: Cambridge University Press.

Suen, H. K., & Ary, D. (1989). *Analyzing quantitative behavioral observation data.* Hillsdale, NJ: Lawrence Erlbaum Associates.

Super, C. M. (1976). Environmental effects on motor development: The case of "African infant precocity." *Developmental Medicine and Child Neurology, 18*, 561–567.

Super, C. M., & Harkness, S. (1986). The developmental niche: A conceptualization at the interface of child and culture. *International Journal of Behavioral Development, 9*, 545–569.

Susman-Stillman, A., Kalkoske, M., Egeland, B., & Waldman, I. (1996). Infant temperament and maternal sensitivity as predictors of attachment security. *Infant Behavior and Development, 19*, 33–47.

Tamis-LeMonda, C. S., & Bornstein, M. H. (1994). Specificity in mother–toddler language-play relations across the second year. *Developmental Psychology, 30*, 283–292.

Tamis-LeMonda, C. S., Bornstein, M. H., Baumwell, L., & Damast, A. M. (1996). Sensitivity in parenting interactions across the first two years: Influences on children's language and play. In C. S. Tamis-LeMonda (Guest Ed.), Parenting sensitivity: Individual, contextual and cultural factors in recent conceptualizations. *Early Development and Parenting, 5* [Thematic Issue], 173–183.

Tamis-LeMonda, C. S., & Cabrera, N. (1999). Perspectives on father involvement: Research and policy. *Social Policy Report, Society for Research in Child Development, 13*, 1–25.

Teti, D. M., O'Connell, M. A., & Reiner, C. D. (1996). Parenting sensitivity, parental depression and child health: The mediational role of parental self-efficacy. *Early Development and Parenting, 5*, 237–250.

Thompson, R. A. (1994). Emotional regulation: A theme in search of definition. In N. A. Fox (Ed.), The development of emotion regulation: Biological and behavioral aspects (pp. 25–52). *Monographs of the Society for Research in Child Development, 59* (2–3, Serial No. 240).

Toda, S., Fogel, A., & Kawai, M. (1990). Maternal speech to three-month-old infants in the United States and Japan. *Journal of Child Language, 17,* 279–294.

Trevarthen, C. (1979). Communication and cooperation in early infancy: A description of primary intersubjectivity. In M. M. Bullowa (Ed.), *Before speech: The beginning of interpersonal communication* (pp. 321–347). New York: Cambridge University Press.

Trevarthen, C. (1993). The self born in intersubjectivity: The psychology of an infant communicating. In U. Neisser (Ed.), *The perceived self* (pp. 121–173). New York: Cambridge University Press.

Tronick, E. Z. (1989). Emotions and emotional communication in infants. *American Psychologist, 44,* 112–119.

Tronick, E. Z., & Weinberg, M. K. (1990, April). *The stability of regulation behaviors.* Paper presented at the Biennial Meeting of the International Conference on Infant Studies, Montreal, Quebec, Canada.

Van den Boom, D., & Hoeksma, J. (1994). The effect of infant irritability on mother–infant interaction: A growth curve analysis. *Developmental Psychology, 30,* 581–590.

Vaux, A., & Harrison, D. (1985). Social network characteristics associated with support satisfaction and perceived support. *American Journal of Community Psychology, 13,* 245–268.

Winnicott, D. W. (1965). *The maturational processes and the facilitating environment: Studies in the theory of emotional development.* New York: International Universities Press.

Chapter Eleven

First Attachments: Theory and Research

Dymphna van den Boom

Introduction

Despite a long history of scholarly interest in mother–infant attachment (Adams, 1886), it is only in the twentieth and twenty-first centuries that the ability to form relationships has been scientized. Work on the child's first relationship in particular has become an important growth area in the past few decades.

Within developmental psychology attachment theory and research are most concerned with the evolutionary heritage that human beings bring to the early mother–infant relationship. It also considers the first period of childhood as most relevant for adult personality formation, without suggesting that childhood experiences leave indelible marks that later experiences cannot correct or obviate. If so, then the individuals with the largest potential impact on children would arguably be the parents. These are the basic data from which much of attachment theory and research proceed.

This chapter reviews theory and research on the development of children's attachment relationships, focusing especially on infancy. The principal approach to explain this development – ethological attachment theory – is described first and compared to new viewpoints from psychobiology and evolutionary ecology. Reviews of each theory summarize key constructs and evidence, recent advances, and strengths and limitations. A sampling of studies that were conducted during the most recent generation of attachment research is organized and reviewed in relation to two kinds of research objectives: (1) assessment and origins of attachment, and (2) precursors of internal working models. The chapter then concludes with some guesses about the future of the field.

Explanations of Attachment

Attachment conveys the idea that an infant has acquired a special emotional relationship with those who care for him or her, and experiences pleasure or security in their presence, but anxiety and distress when they are gone. Attachments are established through interaction with caregiving adults and they vary in quality depending upon the nature of the interaction. Although the physical presence of the mother is ameliorative, her psychological availability is even more so (Sroufe & Waters, 1977).

Attachment theory is based in part on biological considerations concerned with the selective forces that probably acted in our environment of evolutionary adaptedness (Bowlby, 1969). For instance, in our evolutionary past, the so-called irrational fears of childhood must have been adaptive for an infant. Nowadays, human development occurs in diverse cultural environments. Modern ecological niches may or may not be within the range of our environments of evolutionary adaptedness. And behavior that was once biologically adaptive may be so no longer (Hinde & Stevenson-Hinde, 1990).

While considerations of biological adaptation throw considerable light on the nature of human behavior, cultural considerations have taken on increasing importance. Cultural values may have a profound effect on the relationship between the child and his or her caregiver, too. These cultural imperatives may coincide with, or run counter to, biological ones (Hinde & Stevenson-Hinde, 1990). Culture, however, is not to be seen as something imposed on individuals. Rather, the propensities that give rise to culture must themselves be seen as products of natural selection. Individuals, shaped by an interplay between biological and environmental factors, themselves play a part in determining the nature of the cultural climate in which they live. Human culture is not at all easily separable from human biology. In humans the two are inextricably entangled (Richerson, 1997).

In the lively debate about the evolutionary reasons for attachment there have been two major explanations – besides Bowlby's ethological theory – that have predominated: psychoanalysis, by suggesting that infants become attached to the people who satisfy their need for food, and secondary drive models, by suggesting that infants become attached to people who satisfy their drive for hunger. It was believed that as a result of the repeated association between the gratification of hunger and the presence of the mother the child would be classically conditioned to view the mother in positive terms and to seek to interact with her even when she was not providing nourishment. Since discussion of these two perspectives has been dealt with most in the past, they will not be taken as the point of departure in the present chapter. See, however, Westen (1998) and Steele and Steele (1998) for recent revivals of psychoanalytic accounts of attachment phenomena. Instead we will focus on approaches that served as cornerstones of Bowlby's (1969) attachment theory, but that need some rethinking because of the updating of psychobiology and evolutionary ecological theory. These perspectives may contribute valuable new insights into the development and functioning of attachment. First, we will recapitulate the basic tenets of ethological attachment theory.

Ethological Attachment Theory

Based on his clinical experience (Bowlby, 1944) and observations of the effect of the forced institutionalization of many children caused by the two world wars in Europe (Bowlby, 1951), Bowlby became convinced that early family relationships shape personality development. His attachment theory, which is concerned with the broad principles of the mother–child relationship, is based on concepts derived from a number of sources such as psychoanalysis, cybernetics and information theory, but above all by ethology, with its emphasis on the evolutionary origins and biological functions of behavior (Bowlby, 1969, 1973, 1980).

By virtue of its genetic endowment the young child develops attachments to its caretakers, according to Bowlby. The function of this behavior can only be understood in relation to the environment of evolutionary adaptedness. The general assumption is that many aspects of the behavior of infants and mothers have been shaped by natural selection. Within such an adaptationist perspective, attachment behaviors are viewed as having evolved as a response to particular environmental stresses. Though such behavior may seem to be irrational today, in our evolutionary past, anxiety over actual or threatened separation from the mother and security in maintaining proximity with her must have been crucial for survival for an infant and thus adaptive (Hinde & Stevenson-Hinde, 1990). Of course, such behavior will only be effective if the parent reciprocates the child's behavior. Therefore, natural selection acted to elaborate attachment behavior systems in complementary fashion in both parent and infant.

The various types of attachment behavior are seen as integrated by an attachment behavior system. A behavior system is a software description of the relations between behavior and its initiating and terminating conditions. It is seen as the immediate cause of behavior. The attachment behavior system is distinct from, but interacting with, other systems such as affiliation, exploration, and fear (Bowlby, 1969; Gubler & Bischof, 1990). Bowlby also emphasized the importance of cognitive, affective, perceptual, and motor systems for attachment. Attachment is viewed as a goal-corrected system that becomes increasingly flexible with age. Rather than characterizing attachment as a rigid, instinctive, and stereotyped behavior system, it is seen as the result of a complex interplay of behavioral systems that is able to provide a graded response to environmental events (Hinde, 1982).

For the cognitive side of attachment Bowlby draws extensively on control systems theory to describe the dynamics of the attachment relationship. The degree to which infants attempt to attain proximity with their attachment figure depends on a variety of internal and external circumstances. For example, if there is a stranger present or the child is in unfamiliar surroundings, there will be increasing attempts to maintain contact. Or if the child is tired and irritable it may be more likely to be distressed by the absence of its mother. The child behaves as if there is a set point, such that if the caretaker goes beyond it or if the set point itself is altered by the presence of strangers or unfamiliar surroundings, then the attachment behaviors of the child are triggered. Hence, attachment is a highly flexible response to changing environmental conditions.

In the course of the first two years in particular attachments go through some marked developmental changes. Bowlby identified four stages for viewing these changes. Initially, infants display a range of diverse attachment behaviors, which are purely indiscriminative. In this phase of social orientation lasting from birth to 8–12 weeks all behaviors serve to promote proximity to a protective caretaker. In due course infants come to distinguish their regular caretakers from other people. In this period of discriminating sociability (to about 6–8 months) familiar people will elicit attachment responses more readily and more intensely than strangers will. It is not till the third quarter of the first year that unequivocal indications of full-blown attachments appear. The diverse attachment behaviors now become focused on specific individuals only, while unfamiliar people are likely to be greeted with wariness or even fear. Separation upset appears at this age. Once attachment relationships have emerged they undergo further change, which takes place largely in tandem with cognitive developments. Children become increasingly sophisticated in their ability to behave intentionally, plan their actions in the light of goals, and take into account the feelings and goals of the other person. Beginning during the third or fourth year children now form what Bowlby referred to as a goal-corrected partnership.

One further development that has received increasing attention in recent research concerns internal working models. As children become capable of representing the world to themselves in symbolic form, they form models of themselves, of significant others, and of the relationship they have with others. Such models, which enable the child to anticipate the other person's behavior and plan an appropriate line of response, are increasingly used to guide the child's actions. Internal working models are built up on the basis of experience with particular attachment figures and reflect the quality of the relationship with that figure. A parent who consistently pushes the positive buttons is likely to have a child who develops a scheme of its caretaker as sensitive, responsive, and a source of security and support. As a result the child will expect the mother to be predictably available as a haven of safety and develop positive emotions toward her. This cognitive prototype is then carried forward and affects the child's expectations and likely responses of other people. Once formed, therefore, the model is imposed like a template onto new interactions. However, if experience repeatedly disconfirms the child's expectations the model will need to be adapted and reformed. Internal working models are constructed of all-important aspects of the world, but none are as important as those involving the child's interpersonal relationships. This is especially so because the child's model of the self is built up through such relationships. A punitive, rejecting mother will leave the child with a sense of failure and lack of worth. If the self is not acceptable in the eyes of the attachment figure the experience will have negative impact on the way in which the child construes its own image. Thus the working models of self and attachment figures develop in complementary fashion, and the attachment relationship consequently has psychological implications well beyond the relationship itself.

If one is concerned, as Bowlby was, with the broad principles of mother–infant interaction, his evolutionary scenario is a reasonable one. However, since we are now concerned with the nature of individual differences between mother–infant relationships, it is necessary to be increasingly sophisticated in our biological theorizing. After a descrip-

tion of the assessment of attachment we will turn to such a more sophisticated psychobiological view on attachment.

Assessing attachment: Individual differences

The development of the Strange Situation (Ainsworth & Wittig, 1969) was a major step
forward in the study of attachment relationships. It was based on Ainsworth's recognition that the security or insecurity of attachment constituted a crucial aspect of individual differences in such relationships. In brief, it comprises a series of episodes in which
the infant can explore or interact with an unfamiliar adult in the presence or absence of
the mother. Ainsworth described three patterns of the infant's response to reunion
episodes with the mother. Children who showed mild protest following the departure of
the mother, seek the mother upon her return, and are easily placated by her are regarded
as securely attached (type B). Infants who do not protest maternal departure, and who
do not approach the mother when she returns, are labeled insecure-avoidant (type A).
Finally, children who become seriously upset by the departure, and who, though seeking
contact with the mother, resist her attempts to soothe them, are regarded as insecure-
resistant (type C). The original threefold typology has been amended somewhat, first by
introducing subdivisions into the existing categories and then by adding a fourth, completely new category, referring to insecure-disorganized (type D) infants (Main &
Solomon, 1986, 1990). Disorganized infants appear to lack a coherent strategy for managing exploration and attachment. In addition they engage in odd behaviors (e.g., covering face with hands, freezing, turning in circles), which are only explicable in the context
of fear or confusion in the presence of the mother. Recently, new procedures have been
developed for use post-infancy (see Thompson, 1998, for a review).

The Strange Situation has become a standard form of measurement in attachment
research allowing an analytical empirical approach of Bowlby's theorizing. This procedure
has provided extensive data about the balance between attachment and exploratory behavior and about the eliciting and terminating conditions for attachment behavior. It furthered international communication and exchange of empirical data across studies and
countries. Despite these manifest strengths, however, some reservations have been articulated concerning this measure (Lamb, Thompson, Gardner, & Charnov, 1985; Lamb,
Thompson, Gardner, Charnov, & Estes, 1984). To begin with, it is very dependent on
brief separations and reunions having the same meaning for all children. This may be a
constraint when applying the procedure in cultures where childrearing practices differ
from those in the United States, for example, in Japan (Miyake, Chen, & Campos, 1985),
or in Israel (Sagi et al., 1985). Questions have also been raised about whether independent behavior is mistakenly judged to be evidence of avoidance, especially in cases of
routine nonmaternal care (Clarke-Stewart, 1989). A further reservation concerns the possible role of the child's temperament on attachment classification. Despite the fact that
the question that the vulnerability to stress might account for observed differences in
the Strange Situation rather than qualitative variations in attachment security has been
much debated (e.g., Belsky & Rovine, 1987; Kagan, 1984), the issue remains unsettled.
Although it is unthinkable that an individual attribute as general as temperament would
not affect behavior in any situation, it may be no more than one influence among several

(Schaffer, 1996). Unfortunately, as a matter of convenience, the Strange Situation seems to have become *the* attachment situation that can be used for all kinds of attachments from mothers to infants (Ainsworth, Blehar, Waters, & Wall, 1978), from infants to inanimate objects (Passman, 1987), and even from owners to dogs (Topál, Miklósi, Csányi, & Dóka, 1998). Moreover, it has served as a substitute for rather than an adjunct to field observation (Waters, 1981).

The stability of attachment classification has been investigated both over time and with the same person, but also between different individuals at the same point in time. The first series of inquiries elucidated considerable stability in attachment classification in stable, relatively stress-free family situations (Waters, 1978). More recent research demonstrates a variety of stability estimates both in middle-class and lower-income samples (see Thompson, 1998, for a review of these studies). Although stability was initially equated with reliability, it remains unclear why that should be the case. First, both outside events and developmental changes may alter the nature of the parent's interaction with the child. Second, why should one expect temporal stability in a theory that is concerned with the *development* of attachment? Stability of attachment across persons need not be expected either, in so far as attachment classifications are supposed to reflect something about the *relationship*. And indeed, a meta-analysis by van IJzendoorn and de Wolff (1997) uncovered a modest similarity of infant attachments to mother and to father, that is, infant attachment security did not appear to generalize substantially across relationships within the family. Also in Schneider Rosen and Burke's study (1999), the stability coefficient achieved conventional levels of significance, but there remained noteworthy instability. Infants seem to develop qualitatively different attachment relationships with mothers and fathers (Cox, Owen, Henderson, & Margand, 1992; Volling & Belsky, 1992). There is also no guarantee that a given child's attachments are all of the same quality, as is shown in studies with caregivers outside the home. Their security is generally independent of the security of the attachment relationship with the parent (e.g., Goossens & van IJzendoorn, 1990; Howes & Hamilton, 1992a,b; Howes, Rodning, Galluzzo, & Myers, 1988; Sagi et al., 1985; van IJzendoorn, Sagi, & Lambermon, 1992). Furthermore, attachments with extrafamilial caregivers appear to have unique psychosocial correlates that are independent of, or interact with, the effects of mother–infant attachment security (Howes et al., 1988; Oppenheim, Sagi, & Lamb, 1988; van Ijzendoorn, Sagi, et al., 1992). In sum, concordance of attachment type across different relationships is not a necessary condition, because whatever is measured in the Strange Situation is specific to particular relationships and reflects the nature and history of that relationship.

Psychobiological Attachment Theory

Psychobiological perspectives on attachment (e.g., Hofer, 1994a; Kraemer, 1992; Polan & Hofer, 1999) focus primarily on its neurobiological basis. They provide a new view of how the infant's tie to the mother first develops. In addition, separation from the mother is put into a new perspective. Although psychobiological processes underlying the parent–infant relationship have been examined mainly in other species, they provide a comparative perspective and suggest how attachment in humans evolved.

Bowlby hypothesized that the formation of attachment in infants is an imprinting-like process comparable to bond-formation in birds. However, in his theory the actual processes involved in the acquisition of behaviors that keep infants close to their mothers remained unknown. In the psychobiological approach psychological and biological processes are assumed to merge into each other within the mother–infant interaction, that is, both the infant's behavior and physiology are regulated by the caregiver (Hofer, 1987). Different components of the interaction (e.g., warmth, nutrients, olfactory or tactile stimulation) regulate different behavioral and/or physiological systems, independently of each other. The fact that infant and mother stay close and interact intensely with each other creates the setting in which these so-called "hidden" regulators can develop (Hofer, 1994b).

Although since Harlow (1958) the role of feeding and nursing in attachment has generally been downplayed, the feeding context provides a compelling example of the linkage of the homeostatic systems of mother and infant into a superordinate organization. On the one hand, the regulation of the infant's physiology is being partially delegated to processes within the relationship with its mother. The mother, in turn, is dependent on the infant's behavior for her to be able to carry on her role as a supplier of milk. In a strict sense, the secondary-drive theory of attachment – which postulates that attachment owes its origination *solely* to association of the mother with milk reward – is wrong. But in a deeper sense, all the interactions with the mother that normally lead to suckling, acting in concert with milk reward, provide the momentum that drives the formation of the infant's attachment (Kraemer, 1992).

Behavioral systems that maintain an infant in close proximity to the mother do not fulfill the criteria for a fully developed attachment system. Another essential component is a particular set of responses to maternal separation. Bowlby proposed that when an attachment system is sufficiently developed, the infant perceives separation from the mother as a signal of danger. The affect of security, established during the previous close interactions with the mother, is now replaced by the affect of fear and the behaviors and physiological changes that express this state. Separation anxiety, Bowlby reasoned, is activated when attachment behaviors are elicited but fail to result in the infant's reaching the appropriate terminating stimuli for it. Thus the explanation of the separation response afforded by attachment theory depends not only on the development of an attachment system, but also upon an infant that is capable of perceiving the danger signal of separation and of responding affectively to it. The behavioral and physiological changes induced by separation are viewed as parts of an integrated psychophysiological response, as is commonly understood to occur in emotional responses to stress.

Psychobiologists provide a different explanation for the early responses of infants to separation – one based upon loss, rather than upon a response to a signal of danger inherent in the event of separation, or a response to disruption of an affective bond. Central to this new understanding is the idea described above that certain components of the mother–infant interaction regulate the infant's behavior and physiological systems. The loss of these "hidden" regulators in maternal separation can produce behavioral and physiological changes in the infant resulting in the patterns of changes known as the "protest" and "despair" phases of separation. Release from regulatory controls within the mother–infant relationship provides a way of understanding the response to separation independent of recognition of a danger signal or disruption of an inferred affective bond (Polan & Hofer, 1999).

Studies with human infants confirm the propositions put forward. Davidson and Fox (1989) found that those infants who show right-sided frontal activation in the brain (measured by EEG) are more likely to cry upon maternal separation. Reactivity of the hypothalamic-pituitary-adrenocortical system, commonly measured by salivary cortisol, was used as an indicator of the psychophysiological response to stress by Nachmias, Gunnar, Mangelsdorf, Parritz, and Buss (1996). These investigators found that 18-month-olds who were both insecurely attached to their mothers and behaviorally inhibited to novelty showed increases in cortisol in response to novelty and a Strange Situation session. Spangler and Grossmann (1993) reported higher cortisol levels for insecurely compared to securely attached infants. Furthermore, infants in the disorganized classification had the highest mean cortisol levels, and, compared to the securely attached infants, the type D infants exhibited greater increases in cortisol over baseline. These findings were replicated by Hertsgaard, Gunnar, Erickson, and Nachmias (1995) in a sample at risk for type D attachments. In a longitudinal study, spanning from 2 months to 18 years, a relation was found between caretaking histories and cortisol regulation. Children who were exposed to severe caretaking problems during infancy frequently exhibited either unusually low basal cortisol levels with occasional high spikes, or chronically high cortisol levels that were associated later with antisocial behavior and anxiety, respectively (Flinn & England, 1995).

In sum, the discovery of regulatory interactions within the mother–infant relationship avoids the circularity of the traditional attachment model, in which the response to separation is attributed to the disruption of the social bond, the existence of which is inferred from the presence of that same separation response. Early proximity maintenance behaviors are much more flexible and complex than Bowlby envisaged, and later they continue to play important roles in other functions within the relationship rather than becoming focused entirely on maintaining the "set goals" of an attachment system. Events that were thought to be central to attachment have been found to be produced by other, independent mechanisms, for example, the response to separation. Instead of a hierarchical goal-corrected control system, a self-organizing regulatory system consisting of mother and infant as a unit is used as a model in the psychobiological perspective in which a great deal more is regulated than the proximity of the infant to the mother alone (Polan & Hofer, 1999).

Life History Approach to Attachment

Bowlby's theory of attachment is heavily dependent on evolutionary theory. It has an exclusive focus on the differential *survival* of individuals. Modern evolutionary theory, however, predicts that parents will care for their children because children share their parents' genes and are their parents' means of propagating their genes to the next generation. Therefore, life history theory's focus is on differential *reproduction*.

The answer to the question of how to explain the course of human development can be phrased in different ways. One answer would be in terms of *proximate* (or immediate) causes, which is predominant in attachment theory with its primary focus on individual differences in behaviors that are related to that person's earlier attachment history (e.g., Cassidy & Berlin, 1994; Main, 1991). The other is to resort to *ultimate* (or remote) causes more common in evolutionary theories which examine the way in which particular response patterns have come into being in the course of the millions of years that constitute the history of the species. The basic principle, as originally put forward by Darwin (1859), to account for this process was that of *natural selection*. This is the notion that members of a species differ from one another in their genetic endowments. Those variants that equip an organism particularly well to cope with the exigencies of the environment will be the most likely to be preserved in the struggle for existence and so become the prevailing type. Genetic variability within each species makes it possible for characteristics advantageous for survival to be perpetuated. Individuals possessing them are most likely to succeed in reaching maturity and reproduction. In so far as such characteristics are inherited they can be passed on to offspring, who in turn will have a competitive advantage. Over generations, therefore, species will gradually become better adapted to the environment in which they live (Schaffer, 1996).

Although a flood of evolutionary theories ensued in the 1970s, life history theory has been the driving force behind recent research on the way different patterns of attachment witnessed in children may affect social and personality development, culminating in different reproductive strategies in adulthood. Reproduction can take different forms. The production of offspring through mating to increase their quantity is one possible type. Another one is producing relatively few offspring with a high investment in parenting.

To leave descendents, across the life span individuals must solve problems related to survival, growth, development, and reproduction with the help of outside factors (resources). Resources can be physical (e.g., food, shelter), social (e.g., caretakers, peers), and informational (e.g., novel or familiar stimulation from objects, contexts, or persons). During development, individuals should invest different amounts of time, energy, and resources at different rates of expenditure into growth and development versus mating and parenting, depending on prevailing environmental conditions. Dictated by the nature of the local environment, "optimal" solutions to problems at earlier stages of development (e.g., survival given a specific pattern of attachment) should affect later stages of development (e.g., mating and parenting). For that matter the control of resources is of fundamental importance (Charlesworth, 1988). Natural selection will tend to favor mechanisms that achieve the optimal allocation of limited resources, but what is optimal may differ between environments (Chisholm, 1996). For example, in risky or uncertain environments a short-term reproductive strategy of maximizing number of offspring in the current generation may be the optimal strategy. Maximizing the probability of having at least some offspring who manage to survive and reproduce minimizes the probability of having one's own genes vanish from the gene pool. On the other hand, in environments that are safe and predictable the long-term strategy of consistently producing fewer offspring with a high parental investment over many generations may be optimal (Chisholm, 1996).

In humans it seems unlikely that natural selection would lead directly to one optimal outcome (e.g., secure attachment). Individuals differ and society is complex, and mothers and babies will be programmed not simply to form one sort of relationship but a range of possible relationships according to circumstances. In humans natural selection must surely have operated to produce *conditional* maternal and child strategies (Hinde, 1982). Consequently, there is no *a priori* "normal" pattern of attachment. Both secure and insecure attachments evolve contingent on ecological and caregiving conditions (Belsky, 1999; Belsky, Steinberg, & Draper, 1991; Blurton Jones, 1993; Chisholm, 1996; Hinde & Stevenson-Hinde, 1990).

An implication of life history theory is that there should be a relation between early attachment and later reproductive behavior (i.e., mating, parenting) (Belsky, 1999). Empirical evidence is scarce because it can only be gained from studies of lives over time. Although there are few such studies available on attachment, there is some speculative evidence. Under conditions of low environmental risk and uncertainty, the optimal reproductive strategy will be the high-parenting effort strategy of maximizing future reproduction by investing heavily in relatively few high-quality offspring (secure attachment). Empirical findings indicate that in secure individuals there is a high investment in parenting and stable and satisfying relationships in adulthood (Belsky, 1999). Avoidant attachment represents a facultative adaptation to parental unwillingness (not necessarily conscious) to invest. Maternal rejection which is characteristic of the parenting behavior of avoidant mothers may, in terms of ultimate causation, have been a reliable indicator of the mother's relative unwillingness to invest. Her optimal reproductive strategy is to allocate resources to already existing children with greater reproductive value, or to the production of additional offspring. There are some data that show that avoidant individuals show a higher investment in mating than in parenting, that is, they engage in sex in the absence of strong feelings of love, have sex outside established relationships, and have more than one partner. The quality of parenting with their preschool children is low, that is, cold, remote, and controlling (Belsky, 1999). Ambivalent attachment represents a facultative adaptation to parental inability to invest. The inconsistency inherent in the parenting behavior of ambivalent mothers may, in terms of ultimate causation, have been a reliable indicator of a mother's relative inability to invest because of her own inadequate or unpredictable resources. Research findings suggest that resistant individuals invest in indirect reproduction, that is, mothering sibs and/or cousins. The quality of interaction with their offspring is characterized by promoting dependency and fostering child anxiety (Belsky, 1999).

Another important implication that follows from life history theory is that broader contextual features of the environment are as influential in the formation of attachment patterns as is maternal sensitivity (Isabella, 1998; Thompson, 1998). Belsky (1997a,b) has pointed out repeatedly that attachment needs to be studied in context, not for the purpose of discovering which contextual factors are most or least important, but for the purpose of chronicling the cumulative impact of multiple determinants. And indeed, there is an abundance of evidence showing that both maternal psychological attributes (personality, psychological health) as well as social-contextual sources of stress and support (i.e., marital relationship, nonspousal social support) are related to attachment security (for a review of literature, see Belsky, 1997b).

Cultural Perspectives on Attachment

One of the central themes of Bowlby's ethological theory is that biologically based affective interactions facilitate a variety of behaviors in children. During human evolutionary history warm parent–child interactions were most adaptive because they reliably resulted in children acquiring the cultural beliefs of their parents. There is every reason to suppose that transmission of cultural values to children is one of the most important tasks of parents, because cultural practices are often a vital component of biological fitness in human societies. Failure to adopt the social and religious ideology of the society or failure to learn the technology available to the society could result in decreases in reproductive capability (MacDonald, 1988).

However, the environment can rapidly change, so that a mechanism that is adaptive in Bowlby's environment of evolutionary adaptedness may not be adaptive in highly altered circumstances. One of the difficulties faced by an evolutionary ecological account of human behavior has been the difficulty of providing a meaningful conceptualization of adaptation in contemporary industrial societies. Nowadays behavior may be aimed toward goals other than the maximization of inclusive fitness, i.e., the total of individuals' reproductive success through their offspring plus that of their relatives. These goals are determined in large part by the cultural norms and values of the society in which individuals live. These cultural values may have a profound effect on the relationship between the child and his or her caregiver (Hinde & Stevenson-Hinde, 1990).

The first cross-cultural and cross-national studies on attachment sought to answer the question of cultural (in)consistency of the relative distribution of attachment classifications. In a meta-analysis of the Strange Situation van IJzendoorn and Kroonenberg (1988) found evidence indicating that cultural values are labile, differing not only between cultures but also within cultures. Although several reasons have been hypothesized for this diversity, ecological influences accounting for rearing practices have figured most prominently. Japanese and Israeli samples show an overrepresentation of the resistant classification. The high resistance in Japan was attributed to a rearing practice consisting of physical closeness for most of the day, where child distress rarely mounts to intense levels and is relieved quickly when it does (Miyake et al., 1985; Takahashi, 1986). For the Japanese infant separation from the mother turned out to be a much more stressful event than for children from the North German city of Bielefeld (Grossmann & Escher-Graub, 1984; Grossmann, Grossmann, Huber, & Wartner, 1981; Grossmann, Grossmann, Spangler, Suess, & Unzner, 1985), where emotional independence is fostered at an early age, resulting in a high proportion of avoidant classifications. Among Israeli kibbutz-reared infants the heightened rate of insecure resistance is ascribed to the stresses of repeated encounters with a stranger, probably being too challenging for infants raised in a small, closely knit kibbutz community (Sagi et al., 1985; Sagi & Lewkowicz, 1987). The proportion of securely attached children in a sample from Indonesia (Zevalkink, Riksen-Walraven, & van Lieshout, 1999) was comparable to that found in other countries, but the proportion of avoidance versus resistance differed, with avoidance being relatively rare. Inconsistency in the level of maternal support, which was high at home but low during structured interactions in a strange environment, accounted for this finding.

However, in Japan, Israel, and Germany findings to the contrary have been reported. The heightened resistance, for instance, was not observed when the sample studied by Takahashi (1990) was observed nine months later, nor in an independent sample of infants from another city in Japan (Durrett, Otaki, & Richards, 1984). Resistance was also high in a comparison sample of city-dwelling infants from day-care centers in Israel. A replication with another sample in Regensburg, South Germany, yielded a distribution with a high percentage of securely attached infants (in Sagi & Lewkowicz, 1987). Within the United States variations in patterns of attachment have been shown to be related to economic stress, which undermines the quality of care (McLoyd, 1990). Other studies show variations in attachment classifications based on ethnic or subcultural childrearing norms (Fracasso, Busch-Rossnagel, & Fisher, 1993; Lieberman, Weston, & Pawl, 1991; Li-Repac, 1982). Although previous research demonstrated variations in attachment patterns in normative (Belsky & Rovine, 1988; Clarke-Stewart, 1989) and nonnormative (Carlson, Cicchetti, Barnett, & Braunwald, 1989) variations in early child care, such results did not appear in the National Institute of Child Health and Human Development (NICHD) study of Early Child Care (NICHD Early Child Care Research Network, 1997, 1998), which revealed no significant differences in attachment security related to child-care participation after selection effects, child effects (i.e., temperament, sex), and mother effects (i.e., sensitivity, psychological adjustment) were taken into account. These latter findings were confirmed in a Canadian sample (McKim, Cramer, Stuart, & O'Connor, 1999). These studies clearly demonstrated the lability of cultural norms, which seem to differ between and within cultures, but also with time in any one culture.

The challenges faced in future cultural-ecological studies of attachment are manifold. First, if alterations in rearing environments occur so quickly, a unitary concept of attachment could turn out to be less useful than a set of related concepts specifying the nature of the interactions that produce the emotional bond (Kagan, 1984). It is conceivable, for instance, that two children growing up in different cultural settings, though raised very differently, both become securely attached, while other qualities of their attachment may differ. Unraveling the components of the global concept of attachment may be necessary to be able to address the issue of lability of (sub)cultural values. The meaning of a particular classification depends on childrearing goals and values and cultural belief systems (Harwood, 1992; Harwood, Miller, & Irizarry, 1995). Second, if cultural change in modern societies occurs at a very fast pace, the idea that warm parent–child interactions are most adaptive may need reevaluation. Initiating or participating in novel ideas and practices may be more adaptive in a rapidly changing society where innovation is highly prized. Third, an ecological approach to the study of attachment demands adequate attention to a proper conceptualization of the environment. In the past, environment has been investigated often as a very large context for behavior. In much research environment is dealt with in ways that have been assumed to require virtually no measurement, such as social class or (sub)culture. These broad contexts are assumed to organize a set of stable and predictable conditions and experiences that impinge similarly on all children within them. While this approach is informative about average group differences, issues of process cannot be clarified. There is no way of knowing which conditions or subsets of variables within the classifying concepts are responsible for any behavioral differences that are found, leaving room for speculative interpretation. In one exemplary study

(Zevalkink et al., 1999), contextual characteristics were extensively measured. Insecure-disorganized children compared to resistant infants more often lived in an extended household with mothers who were active in preventive health care. Mothers of avoidant children were less inclined to engage in child-centered festivities than mothers of non-avoidant children.

Most scenarios of human evolution emphasize how our young ancestors' helplessness led to selection for increased parental investment (e.g., Lancaster & Lancaster, 1987; Lovejoy, 1981). Thus, emotional attachments in infancy allow the organism to survive during a time when its ability to transact with the environment is extremely limited. The child's acquisition of the cultural skills, another important part of human adaptation, has hardly been a focus of interest in attachment research. Emotional and motivational mechanisms are not only an essential part of attachment processes (Jones, 1985), but also of cultural learning (Tomasello, Kruger, & Ratner, 1993) and cognitive development (Flavell, 1999). Not only will certain kinds of emotional relationships set the stage for the acquisition of the cultural skills, but in some cases the understanding of emotions turns out to be a very important part of the learning process itself (Tomasello & Barton, 1994). The relevant emotional and motivational mechanisms evolved to serve different functions at different developmental periods. An important aspect of cognitive development, the capacity for intersubjectivity as the core of internal working models, depends on and builds on the prior sharing of emotional states between infants and caregivers. Cultural learning may thus be an important process toward the development of internal working models. The developmental course of this process will be outlined in the section on attachment representations.

Attachment Antecedents: The Sensitivity Hypothesis

It is generally assumed that the main reason for qualitative differences in children's attachments lies in the mother's sensitive responsiveness in interacting with the infant during the first year of life. The first data on this topic were generated in an intensively investigated sample of 26 middle-class Baltimore mother–child dyads (Ainsworth et al., 1978). Since then numerous studies have been conducted to replicate the proposed link between early maternal behavior and subsequent child attachment security (the "sensitivity hypothesis"). In 1987 Goldsmith and Alansky conducted a meta-analysis on 12 inquiries and concluded that there is a weak association between mothering and attachment. A decade later de Wolff and van IJzendoorn (1997) conducted a 66-study meta-analysis, arriving at the conclusion that maternal sensitivity appears to be an important, though not exclusive, condition for the development of attachment security. Hence, the sensitivity hypothesis has received some, but by no means unanimous, support from other studies. Besides correlational, there is experimental evidence which van IJzendoorn, Juffer, and Duyvesteyn (1995) have subjected to meta-analytic evaluation. The results pointed to a reliable effect of mothering on attachment security. A meta-analysis evaluating inquiries on disorganized attachment in early childhood (van IJzendoorn, Schuengel, & Bakermans-Kranenburg, 1999) identified frightening or frightened and dissociated parental behavior as an antecedent to disorganization. However, this did not seem to be the only factor involved. Disorganized attachment does not just accrue from parental insensitivity. Other precursors proposed are maltreatment and unresolved loss in the parent. Further validational research is clearly necessary. Despite this endless stream of studies on the sensitivity hypothesis, a puzzling degree of inconsistency throws doubt over the hypothesized sensitivity–security link.

There may be several reasons for this inconsistency. For one thing, it is highly likely that attachment security is not just determined by parental behavior but that other factors also play a part. Second, maternal sensitivity is not a stable trait and if it changes from one age to another it is hardly likely to provide a satisfactory explanation for infants' attachment security (Isabella, 1993), at least if it is not examined in a dynamic way. For example, several studies both support and fail to support the sensitivity–security linkage depending on the time of assessment (e.g., Belsky, Rovine, & Taylor, 1984; Egeland & Farber, 1984; Miyake et al., 1985). Such findings may indicate either that this relation is significant for only part of the range, or could be due to attempts to impose an analysis of linear trends on nonlinear relations (van den Boom, 1997). Third, sensitivity is basically a statement about the interaction and, hence, is meaningless without reference to both partners. This makes the study of *infant* antecedents to attachment equally important, though such inquiries are rare (Hoeksma, van den Boom, Koomen, & Koops, 1997). Fourth, it is much more likely that a number of factors need to be considered in conjunction and that their joint effect predicts the formation of attachments rather than the effect of each on its own. This is well illustrated by Belsky, Rosenberger, and Crnic (1995), who found that the consequences of sensitive behavior on the part of the mothers could only be understood in the context of other important variables.

Child contributions

If attachment security is not just determined by parental behavior but also by other factors, a likely other influence is the child's individuality.

In initial discussions on the relation between temperament and attachment, temperament was regarded as a stable individual feature, while attachment was considered to be relational in nature, creating some reluctance of integrating the two (Rothbart & Bates, 1998). Although numerous studies have been conducted to examine the link between temperament and attachment, the matter is still unsettled. Inquiries directly linking parent-report measures of infant temperament with attachment classifications in the Strange Situation have generally yielded nonsignificant results (Thompson, 1998). Evidence on a link between resistant attachment and neonatal irritability is found by some (Goldsmith & Alansky, 1987), yet not by others (van den Boom, 1994). There is some evidence indicating that parental reports of temperamental difficulty distinguish B3/B4/C infants from infants in the A/B1/B2 classifications (Belsky & Rovine, 1987), although other studies could not replicate this finding (Mangelsdorf, Gunnar, Kestenbaum, Lang, & Andreas, 1990; Seifer, Schiller, Sameroff, Resnick, & Riordan, 1996). It has been suggested that temperament does not so much determine type of attachment classification as the way in which security or insecurity is expressed (Belsky & Rovine, 1987).

When attachment is measured with the Attachment Q-sort (AQS) (Waters & Deane, 1985), on the contrary, results are more consistent. Security scores and temperament reports of negative emotionality are negatively associated (Seifer et al., 1996; Vaughn et al., 1992; Wachs & Desai, 1993). It remains to be seen, however, whether the traditional Strange Situation attachment classifications and the AQS security scores measure the same aspects of attachment.

It is unthinkable that an individual attribute as general as temperament would not affect behavior in any situation (Schaffer, 1996). Why then is it so difficult to find a clear and consistent link with attachment? Several reasons come to mind. First, several indices of temperament have been used. Temperament has been measured through direct behavioral observations and questionnaires. However, the correlations between direct observations of children and adult descriptions of what appear to be the very same behaviors are low (Kagan, 1994). It seems to be necessary to appreciate that the theoretical meaning of any temperamental construct when observed behavior is the source of evidence may not be the same as the meaning when adult descriptions are the source of evidence. Seifer et al. (1996), using both parent-report and observational temperament measures, did find a significant relation between temperament and AQS security scores, although the manner whereby they operate is complex. Second, given the interweaving of temperamental with social interactive forces, it is increasingly recognized that the expression of temperament changes throughout development (Rothbart & Bates, 1998). This may also influence the findings obtained. Most likely, though, it will be when taken in conjunction with other, experiential factors that temperamental characteristics can be seen to influence the developmental course. The idea that one factor can be expected to provide an infallible pointer to the future has been abandoned by most.

High-risk infants are of particular interest, for their behavior is at first more disorganized and less predictable and will thus place a much greater burden on a mother's capacity for sensitivity. Here, too, the findings are mixed with some studies reporting high rates of insecure attachment in a variety of clinical samples (Goldberg, 1990), and others not accounting for marked deviations in the relative rates of secure and insecure classifications (van IJzendoorn, Goldberg, Kroonenberg, & Frenkel, 1992). Taken in conjunction with the previously mentioned findings about temperament, one must conclude that the question of antecedents of attachment quality cannot be answered by looking at child effects alone, any more than by looking at maternal caregiving alone (Schneider Rosen & Rothbaum, 1993).

Attachment Representations in Infancy

Lately, attachment research has moved into the realm of internal working models. As earlier summarized, working models are gradually built up from the child's specific experiences with attachment figures and come to represent the pertinent attributes of each and the kind of relationship that has developed with that individual. These mental representations include emotional as well as cognitive components. Once formed they exist outside consciousness and tend to be stable, but are by no means impervious to the influence of further relationship experiences (Bowlby, 1969, 1973, 1980).

Attachment researchers have directed most of their efforts at elucidating *adult* representational processes, mostly by means of the Adult Attachment Interview (George,

Kaplan, & Main, 1985; Main & Goldwyn, 1994) to examine the existence of intergenerational continuity. They try to provide an answer to the question whether people parent their children the way they were parented. Since the focus of this chapter is on infancy, the interested reader is referred to van IJzendoorn (1995) for a review of studies on the issue of intergenerational continuity.

Although, thanks to Bretherton's work (1991, 1993), there is general recognition that internal working models gradually emerge from shared communications in infancy, attachment research on the early precursors of these mental representations is relatively rare. A few assessment procedures were developed to examine attachment-related representations at an early age, for example by means of doll-play stories, drawings, and responses to family photographs. The notion of internal working models, however, requires greater clarity to increase its testable explanatory power. A prospective instead of a retrospective approach seems to be more fruitful to get a grip on the construction of working models from infancy onward. The fact that interpersonal relatedness within the family is not only dyadic but also triadic in nature is an issue that deserves more attention (Harris, 1997). The development of social cognition seems to be a likely candidate for further scrutiny.

Attachment theory assumes that infants and young children interpret and predict other people's actions. Research on the young child's theory of mind and social referencing is centrally concerned with such interpretive and predictive skills (Harris, 1997). It has been found that by 18 months infants give an experimenter food she reacts to with apparent happiness rather than disgust, even when they themselves prefer the latter food (Repacholi & Gopnik, 1997). This appears to be the first empirical evidence that infants have at least some limited ability to reason nonegocentrically about people's desires. Infants also learn the names for things by noting what object the adult appears to be attending to when the adult says the label (Baldwin & Moses, 1994; Tomasello, 1995; Woodward & Markman, 1998). They seem to recognize that it is the adult's attentional focus rather than their own that gives clues as to the adult's referential intent. By 12 months infants seek or use information about objects' positive or negative qualities conveyed by adults' emotional reactions to these objects, called social referencing (Baldwin & Moses, 1994; Mumme, Won, & Fernald, 1994). Older infants sometimes appear to be trying to manipulate other people's emotional responses rather than, as in social referencing, just reading these. Toddlers, for instance, begin to comfort younger siblings in distress by patting, hugging, or kissing them and they may even bring a security blanket to an adult in pain (Zahn-Waxler, Radke-Yarrow, Wagner, & Chapman, 1992). On the negative side, they sometimes tease or otherwise annoy siblings, as though hoping to frustrate or anger them (Dunn, 1988). These findings suggest that young children are beginning to identify the conditions that elicit or change emotions or behaviors. Generalizing across these studies, it seems that infants show a number of behaviors that seem relevant to the development of knowledge about people.

Attachment researchers entertain the idea that children's initial awareness is of undifferentiated relationships that give rise to the first internal working models. Even so, the two cannot be understood without reference to each other, for they represent obverse aspects of the same relationship. Research on social cognition is beginning to show that cognitive differentiation of self and other may appear relatively early. Children start using some desire terms appropriately by age 1.5 to 2 years (Bartsch & Wellman, 1995), and tend to grasp simple causal relations among desires, outcome, emotions, and actions. The use of emotion-descriptive language begins late in the second year and increases rapidly during the third year (Bretherton & Beeghly, 1982; Wellman, Harris, Banerjee, & Sinclair, 1995). In subsequent years children come to understand subtler and more complex things about emotions, for instance, that people do not always really feel what they appear to feel (Flavell & Miller, 1998). By age 3, children may have some ability to distinguish intended actions from nonintentional behaviors such as reflexes and mistakes (Shultz, 1991; Schultz & Wellman, 1997). Children also come to appreciate psychological causes of behavior other than intentions: emotions, motives, abilities, percepts, knowledge, beliefs, and personality traits. This fundamental insight of realizing that many emotional reactions depend on the fulfillment or frustration of particular plans or goals is likely to have important implications for the child's working model of his or her relation to a caretaker. Attachment theory assumes that the child takes note of recurrent emotional relations between self and key attachment figures and uses these to forecast the course of future encounters. The above findings suggest that, at least by the age of 3, children recognize that other people feel emotion relative to their own goals rather than those of the child.

The above findings appear to indicate early signs of mental state attributions. Throughout virtually the entire body of research on social cognition in infancy it has been found that children make little differentiation between different people (Harris, 1997). However, the notion of a working model suggests that the child is able to do so. In attachment theory, it is assumed that the child arrives at a generalization that is highly charged with emotion because the ultimate conclusion concerns a feeling of security. In the area of social cognition the generalizations are free of affective valence and more of a cognitive enterprise. Attachment theorists assume that people will often not succeed in articulating explicitly their working models, not even in adulthood. It is inferred from their discourse during the Adult Attachment Interview. Research on social cognition suggests, on the contrary, that children will increasingly talk explicitly about people's desires and beliefs (Harris, 1997). The above findings suggest that combining cognitively oriented research on social cognition and socioemotionally oriented research on attachment might be a fruitful enterprise.

Only very recently the extent to which interpersonal experiences can aid the child's development has been examined. Representational skills appear to develop faster in a context of multiple relationships. Preschoolers who have more siblings to interact with perform better on false-belief tasks than those who have fewer or none (Jenkins & Astington, 1996; Perner, Ruffman, & Leekam, 1994). Both conflict and support in sibling interactions have been linked to children's skills such as affective perspective-taking and consideration of other people's feelings and beliefs (Brown & Dunn, 1992; Dunn, Brown, & Beardsall, 1991; Howe, 1991; Howe & Ross, 1990; Youngblade & Dunn, 1995). A family environment that provides for certain types of linguistic encounters (especially about mental experience) appears to accelerate performance on theory of mind tasks (Dunn, Brown, Slomkowski, Tesla, & Youngblade, 1991). In addition, children who engage in more pretense perform better on theory of mind tasks (Astington & Jenkins, 1995; Taylor & Carlson, 1997; Youngblade, 1993). Multiple relationships within the family apparently enhance the child's understanding of the goals of the other person. Once that skill has developed it may be expected that children will systematically pursue to effect the emotional reactions of the caretaker instead of merely accepting recurrent emotional responses of the parent in the interest of his or her feelings of security. Social-cognitive research suggests that even in infancy the child may play an active role in regulating what the caretaker will do.

If children develop the ability to take the emotions and goals of other people into account from early on and separate those from their own, the possibility that children can conceptualize a triadic relationship can be seriously entertained. In one of the few studies conducted, it was found that from the age of 3, third parties are particularly influential in the case of dyadic conflict (Vuchinich, Emery, & Cassidy, 1988). Additional family members frequently joined dyadic family conflicts, they were about equally likely to attempt to end or to continue the conflict, they formed alliances about half of the time, and their intervention strategies were related to the outcome of the conflict as well as its patterning. Such findings suggest that conflict and support may not simply be the opposite ends of a continuum, but can coexist and give children a variety of experiences in learning to deal with others. Apparently, a balance of support and conflict in family relationships may exert a positive effect on promoting social competence and its concomitant expectations regarding social relationships. Such a balance can provide a unique opportunity for children to develop social-cognitive and behavioral competencies and expectations that are linked to managing conflict and anger on the one hand, while providing support and nurturance on the other. Hence, already in infancy one relationship can affect another relationship. And early attachment and later behaviors not all have to be viewed as a persistence of attachment qualities. There is a need both to consider dyadic relationships in terms that go beyond attachment concepts, and to consider social systems that extend beyond dyads (Hinde & Stevenson-Hinde, 1988).

The initial emergence of expectations regarding other persons is a complex process consisting of many constituents. Findings on social cognition seem to suggest that internal working models are built up gradually during infancy, take different forms at different ages, and are influenced by relationships with key attachment figures as well as by siblings and triadic interactions. The combination of social-cognition and attachment research will lead to a more realistic and balanced account of the way internal working models gradually emerge from infancy.

Perspective

We have learned a great deal about the development of children's first relationships, especially due to Mary Ainsworth's development of the Strange Situation, whereby attachment security could be assessed and empirically investigated. We learned about the origins, stability, and representations of individual differences in attachment security in infancy. Nevertheless, inconsistencies and unpredictabilities in developmental paths keep challenging attachment theory and research. There has been no shortage of psychological research on attachment. But psychological research is not the only source of information on attachment. How might the biological and evolutionary perspectives on attachment contribute to a further understanding of the attachment process?

Attachment and Brain Function

Psychobiological perspectives on attachment provide opportunities for enhancing the depth and scope of ethological attachment theory. General agreement exists on the fact that affect constitutes the core of attachment processes (e.g., Sroufe & Waters, 1977; Waters & Deane, 1982). Emotions, however, are not only psychological but they are physiological processes as well. Therefore, information about the representation of emotion in the brain may also shed light on the nature of emotional processes such as interpersonal attachments (LeDoux, 1995).

Recent findings suggest that there is an actual physiological-anatomical component to emotional reactions (Post et al., 1998). Environmental experience of a specific quantity or quality, particularly when it occurs in crucial phases of development, may be capable of exerting profound effects on the organization and anatomy of the central nervous system (Cicchetti & Tucker, 1994; Nelson & Bloom, 1997). Ethological attachment theory does not address the topic of the regulation of the infant's physiology but assumes it to be a product of genetic endowment. Although the primary structure of the neuronal pathways is determined genetically, its functional microstructure may be determined in large measure by the environment. Ultimately, only those pathways are preserved that are actually used. But at some point the functional characteristics of processes that can be modified by environmental stimuli must be "locked." Thereafter sensorimotor systems cannot be tuned to the environment the way they would have been at an earlier developmental stage (Kraemer, 1992). Apparently, early childhood experiences exert a powerful lasting influence on the central nervous system.

In studies using electrical brain stimulation to probe emotion it has been demonstrated that in contrast to cognitive neural pathways, the affective neural pathway operates without even a pretense of objectivity. For example, a cool stimulus applied to the skin can be pleasant if one is overheated and unpleasant if one is hypothermic, indicating that the affective value of a stimulus depends in part on the prevailing physiological and ecological conditions (Shizgal, 1999). In light of these findings one can imagine a strikingly different impact of similar types of experience at different stages of an infant's psychological and physiological development. For instance, deprivation related to neglect and the converse (that related to abuse) in early childhood may affect the basic organization of the central nervous system by early life experience differently. Also, if the basic wiring of the central nervous system has been impacted in early childhood by deprivational experiences, children will develop a different comparison standard than children not having such negative experiences. The basic wiring will set the stage for future evaluations of emotional experiences in attachment relationships. Given the relativity of emotion the results of the evaluations can be vastly different depending on the standard of comparison that has been developed (Post et al., 1998). Much work remains to delineate the critical periods for such impact and windows of opportunity for ameliorative manipulations. Of similar interest would be the question of what stimulation is most pertinent to developing a long-term resetting of neural pathways that is of potential clinical and bio-logical relevance. Hence, physiological investigations not only delineate underlying mech-anisms but also contribute to better psychological theories by inspiring what is possible and by placing constraints on what is plausible.

In sum, findings about the neural basis of attachment might suggest new insights into the functional organization of attachment that were not apparent from psychological find-ings alone. After all, Bowlby saw the attachment system as having the qualities of a phys-iological homeostatic system.

Attachment and Ecology

Empirical tests of attachment theory's account of mechanism have been relatively rare. Evolutionary ecological theory has an explicit focus on mechanisms in trying to uncover *why* sensitivity would foster a particular attachment relationship in functional evolution-ary terms. The answer to that question may differ depending on the particular ecological niche the infant is raised in. The interrelatedness between individuals and context may have profound effects on the patterns of developmental change in attachment processes. Research has shown that the idea that securely attached babies are the norm, for which overwhelming evidence exists in the United States of America, is untenable in light of other findings indicating that the securely attached category is much less common in other cultural groups, i.e., West Germany, Israel. In addition, ecological contexts are complex and diverse. Relationships are affected by the presence of other individuals, the mother's relationship with the father, infant characteristics, and so on. Consequently, it is difficult to ascertain what the best mothering style would be, for different styles may be better in different circumstances. Natural selection would act to favor individuals with a range of potential styles from which they select appropriately (Hinde, 1982). The issue is further complicated by the importance of norms, indicating that what is best can only be assessed against the whole complex of family, social group, and cultural beliefs in which mother and child are embedded. What a proper preparation for life is, may differ between cultures. The ecological context, therefore, needs to be taken into account in order to arrive at a proper account of attachment processes.

Some contextual events also seem to be more salient than others. There is, for instance, evidence for a negativity bias in the affect system. A wide range of evidence shows that negative events in a context evoke stronger and more rapid physiological, cognitive, emo-tional, and social responses than neutral or positive events (Taylor, 1991; Westerman, Spies, Stahl, & Hesse, 1996). Exploratory behavior can provide useful information about an infant's environment, but exploration can also place an infant in proximity to hostile stimuli. Because it is more difficult to reverse the consequences of an injurious or fatal assault than those of an opportunity unpursued, the process of natural selection may also have resulted in the propensity to react more strongly to negative than to positive stimuli (e.g., Cacioppo & Berntson, 1994). A relatively positive versus a negative rearing context may, thus, set the tone for vastly different interpersonal relationships.

Another contextual feature is the question of multiple attachments, which has hardly been dealt with as of yet (Hinde & Stevenson-Hinde, 1988). How does the child deal with multiple relationships, and how are discrepant relationships dealt with? Is it the case that one relationship dominates, or is there a balance between differing relationships? Does one secure relationship compensate for insecurities in others? As of yet no satisfactory explanations have been found and tested. Although internal working models have been posited as the mechanisms that carry relationships forward, so far they have failed to give any increased precision to our understanding of the processes involved.

A Developmental Account of Attachment

Despite the fact that in the domain of attachment many longitudinal studies have been conducted, nondevelopmental concepts and the statistical procedures associated with them still dominate the field. However, Roberts (1986; Roberts & Strayer, 1987) pointed at the existence of a threshold effect in parental warmth, that is, very low levels of parental warmth are associated with a deficit in child competence. Crossing the threshold results in a rapid rise in levels of competence, which is followed by a plateau in which further increases in parental warmth have little effect on child competence. Hence, in the case of parental warmth an almost exclusive reliance upon linear relations does not seem to be justified. The few studies that document curvilinear relations between indices of the parent–child relationship and child development suggest that there may be a point of diminishing returns (van den Boom, 1997).

Although the relevance of nonlinear models for longitudinal research has often been preached, it has been put into practice only rarely. Notable exceptions are the studies by Olthof, Kunnen, and Boom (2000) and van der Maas and Raijmakers (2000). In order to become truly developmental, the field of attachment needs a move in the direction of greater complexity both in concept and in method (Fogel, 1993, 1997; Kunnen, Olthof, & Boom, 2000; van den Boom & Hoeksma, 1994, 1997). Such a developmental orientation would make the field more person- instead of variable-oriented, that is, insight would be gained in intraindividual patterns of change. And it may turn out to be very well the case that there are different routes that lead to broadly similar outcomes. Such a focus on developmental change not only leads to a better understanding of the nature of the parent–child relationship, but may also yield valuable information for practical efforts made to bring about improvements in that relationship. Finally, a developmental orientation on attachment could change our view of the sources of individual differences. Variability in outcome measures is well documented, but variability in process is less well understood. It means that children may reach similar outcomes by different pathways. The detection of such diverging or converging pathways promises to be a major challenge in the years to come.

References

Adams, F. (1886). *The genuine works of Hippocrates* (Vol. 1). New York: William Wood & Co.

Ainsworth, M. D. S., Blehar, M. C., Waters, E., & Wall, S. (1978). *Patterns of attachment.* Hillsdale, NJ: Erlbaum.

Ainsworth, M. D. S., & Wittig, B. A. (1969). Attachment and exploratory behavior of one-year-olds in a Strange Situation. In B. M. Foss (Ed.), *Determinants of infant behavior* (Vol. 4, pp. 111–136). London: Methuen.

Astington, J. W. (1993). *The child's discovery of the mind.* Cambridge, MA: Harvard University Press.

Astington, J. W., & Jenkins, J. M. (1995). Theory of mind development and social understanding. *Cognition and Emotion, 9,* 151–165.

Baldwin, D. A., & Moses, L. J. (1994). Early understanding of referential intent and attentional focus: Evidence from language and emotion. In C. Lewis & P. Mitchell (Eds.), *Children's early understanding of mind: Origins and development* (pp. 133–156). Hillsdale, NJ: Erlbaum.

Bartsch, K., & Wellman, H. M. (1995). *Children talk about the mind.* New York: Oxford University Press.

Belsky, J. (1997a). Theory testing, effect-size evaluation, and differential susceptibility to rearing influence: The case of mothering and attachment. *Child Development, 68,* 598–600.

Belsky, J. (1997b). Classical and contextual determinants of attachment security. In W. Koops, J. B. Hoeksma, & D. C. van den Boom (Eds.), *Development of interaction and attachment: Traditional and non-traditional approaches* (pp. 39–58). Amsterdam: North-Holland/Elsevier.

Belsky, J. (1999). Patterns of attachment in modern evolutionary perspective. In J. Cassidy & P. Shaver (Eds.), *Handbook of attachment theory and research.* New York: Guilford Press.

Belsky, J., & Cassidy, J. (1994). Attachment: Theory and evidence. In M. Rutter, D. Hay, & S. Baron-Cohen (Eds.), *Developmental principles and clinical issues in psychology and psychiatry* (pp. 373–402). Oxford: Blackwell.

Belsky, J., Rosenberger, K., & Crnic, K. (1995). Maternal personality, marital quality, social support and infant temperament: Their significance for infant–mother attachment in human families. In C. Pryce, R. Martin, & D. Skuse (Eds.), *Motherhood in human and nonhuman primates: Prosocial determinants* (pp. 115–124). Basel: Karger.

Belsky, J., & Rovine, M. (1987). Temperament and attachment security in the Strange Situation: An empirical rapprochement. *Child Development, 58,* 787–795.

Belsky, J., & Rovine, M. (1988). Nonmaternal care in the first year of life and the security of infant–parent attachment. *Child Development, 59,* 157–167.

Belsky, J., Rovine, M., & Taylor, D. G. (1984). The Pennsylvania infant and family development project, III: The origins of individual differences in infant–mother attachment: Maternal and infant contributions. *Child Development, 55,* 718–728.

Belsky, J., Steinberg, L., & Draper, P. (1991). Childhood experience, interpersonal development and reproductive strategy: An evolutionary theory of socialization. *Child Development, 62,* 647–670.

Blurton Jones, N. (1993). The lives of hunter–gatherer children: Effects of parental behavior and parental reproductive strategy. In M. Pereira & L. Fairbanks (Eds.), *Juvenile primates: Life history, development and behavior* (pp. 309–326). New York: Oxford University Press.

Bowlby, J. (1944). Forty-four juvenile thieves: Their characters and home life. *International Journal of Psychoanalysis, 25,* 19–128.

Bowlby, J. (1951). *Maternal care and mental health.* Geneva: World Health Organization.

Bowlby, J. (1969). *Attachment and loss: Vol. 1. Attachment.* New York: Basic Books.

Bowlby, J. (1973). *Attachment and loss: Vol. 2. Separation: Anxiety and anger.* New York: Basic Books.

Bowlby, J. (1980). *Attachment and loss: Vol. 3. Loss: Sadness and depression.* New York: Basic Books.

Bretherton, I. (1991). Pouring new wine into old bottles: The social self as internal working model. In M. R. Gunnar & L. A. Sroufe (Eds.), Self processes and development. *Minnesota Symposia on Child Psychology* (Vol. 23, pp. 1–41). Hillsdale, NJ: Erlbaum.

Bretherton, I. (1993). From dialogue to internal working models: The co-construction of self in relationships. In C. A. Nelson (Ed.), Memory and affect in development. *Minnesota Symposia on Child Psychology* (Vol. 26, pp. 237–263). Hillsdale, NJ: Erlbaum.

Bretherton, L., & Beeghly, M. (1982). Talking about internal states: The acquisition of an explicit theory of mind. *Developmental Psychology, 18*, 906–921.

Brown, J. R., & Dunn, J. (1992). Talk with your mother or your sibling? Developmental changes in early family conversations about feelings. *Child Development, 63*, 336–349.

Cacioppo, J. T., & Berntson, G. G. (1994). Relationship between attitudes and evaluative space: A critical review, with emphasis on the separability of positive and negative substrates. *Psychological Bulletin, 115*, 401–423.

Carlson, V., Cicchetti, D., Barnett, D., & Braunwald, K. G. (1989). Finding order in disorganization: Lessons from research on maltreated infants' attachment to their caregivers. In D. Cicchetti & V. Carlson (Eds.), *Child maltreatment* (pp. 494–528). Cambridge: Cambridge University Press.

Cassidy, J., & Berlin, L. J. (1994). The insecure/ambivalent pattern of attachment: Theory and research. *Child Development, 65*, 971–991.

Charlesworth, W. (1988). Resources and resource acquisition during ontogeny. In K. MacDonald (Ed.), *Sociobiological perspectives on human development* (pp. 42–117). New York: Springer.

Chisholm, J. S. (1996). The evolutionary ecology of attachment organization. *Human Nature, 7*, 1–37.

Cicchetti, D., & Tucker, D. (1994). Development and self-regulatory structures of the mind. *Development and Psychopathology, 6*, 533–549.

Clarke-Stewart, K. A. (1989). Infant day-care: Maligned or malignant? *American Psychologist, 44*, 266–273.

Cox, M. J., Owen, M. T., Henderson, V. K., & Margand, N. A. (1992). Prediction of infant–father and infant–mother attachment. *Developmental Psychology, 28*, 474–483.

Darwin, C. (1859). *On the origin of species*. London: John Murray.

Davidson, R. J., & Fox, N. A. (1989). Frontal brain asymmetry predicts infants' response to maternal separation. *Journal of Abnormal Psychology, 98*, 127–131.

De Wolff, M. S., & van IJzendoorn, M. H. (1997). Sensitivity and attachment: A meta-analysis on parental antecedents of infant attachment. *Child Development, 68*, 571–591.

Dunn, J. (1988). *The beginnings of social understanding*. Oxford: Blackwell.

Dunn, J., Brown, J., & Beardsall, L. (1991). Family talk about feeling states and children's later understanding of others' emotions. *Developmental Psychology, 27*, 448–455.

Dunn, J., Brown, J., Slomkowski, C., Tesla, C., & Youngblade, L. (1991). Young children's understanding of other people's feelings and beliefs: Individual differences and their antecedents. *Child Development, 62*, 1352–1366.

Durrett, M. E., Otaki, M., & Richards, P. (1984). Attachment and the mother's perception of support from the father. *International Journal of Behavioral Development, 7*, 167–176.

Egeland, B., & Farber, E. A. (1984). Infant–mother attachment: Factors related to its development and changes over time. *Child Development, 55*, 753–771.

Flavell, J. H. (1999). Cognitive development: Children's knowledge about the mind. *Annual Review of Psychology, 50*, 21–45.

Flavell, J. H., & Miller, P. H. (1998). Social cognition. In W. Damon (Series Ed.) & D. Kuhn & R. S. Siegler (Vol. Eds.), *Handbook of child psychology: Vol. 2. Cognition, perception, and language* (pp. 851–898). New York: Wiley.

Flinn, M. V., & England, B. G. (1995). Childhood stress and family environment. *Current Anthropology, 36*, 854–866.

Fracasso, M. P., Busch-Rossnagel, N. A., & Fisher, C. B. (1993). The relationship of maternal behavior and acculturation to the quality of attachment in Hispanic infants living in New York City. *Hispanic Journal of Behavioral Sciences, 16,* 143–154.

Fogel, A. (1993). *Developing through relationships.* Chicago: University of Chicago Press.

Fogel, A. (1997). A relational perspective on attachment. In W. Koops, J. B. Hoeksma, & D. C. van den Boom (Eds.), *Development of interaction and attachment: Traditional and non-traditional approaches* (pp. 219–232). Amsterdam: North-Holland/Elsevier.

George, C., Kaplan, N., & Main, M. (1985). *Adult Attachment Interview.* Unpublished manuscript, University of California, Berkeley.

Goldberg, S. (1990). Attachment in infants at risk: Theory, research, and practice. *Infants and Young Children, 2,* 11–20.

Goldsmith, H. H., & Alansky, J. A. (1987). Maternal and infant temperamental predictors of attachment: A meta-analytic review. *Journal of Consulting and Clinical Psychology, 55,* 805–816.

Goossens, F. A., & van IJzendoorn, M. H. (1990). Quality of infants' attachment to professional caregivers: Relation to infant–parent attachment and day-care characteristics. *Child Development, 61,* 832–837.

Grossmann, K. E., & Escher-Graub, D. (1984, April). The status of Ainsworth's Strange Situation in North and South German attachment research. In A. Sagi (Chair), *The Strange Situation procedure: Insights from an international perspective.* Symposium conducted at the Biennial Meeting of the International Conference on Infant Studies, New York.

Grossmann, K. E., Grossmann, K., Huber, F., & Wartner, U. (1981). German children's behavior towards their mothers at 12 months and their fathers at 18 months in Ainsworth's Strange Situation. *International Journal of Behavioral Development, 4,* 157–181.

Grossmann, K., Grossmann, K. E., Spangler, G., Suess, G., & Unzner, L. (1985). Maternal sensitivity and newborns' orientation responses as related to quality of attachment in Northern Germany. In I. Bretherton & E. Waters (Eds.), Growing points of attachment theory and research (pp. 233–256). *Monographs of the Society for Research in Child Development, 50* (1–2, Serial No. 209).

Gubler, H., & Bischof, N. (1990). A systems' perspective on infant development. In M. Lamb & H. Keller (Eds.), *Infant development: Perspectives from German-speaking countries* (pp. 1–37). Hillsdale, NJ: Erlbaum.

Harris, P. L. (1997). Between strange situations and false beliefs: Working models and theories of mind. In W. Koops, J. B. Hoeksma, & D. C. van den Boom (Eds.), *Development of interaction and attachment: Traditional and non-traditional approaches* (pp. 187–199). Amsterdam: North-Holland/Elsevier.

Harlow, J. F. (1958). The nature of love. *American Psychologist, 13,* 673–685.

Harwood, J. F., Miller, J. G., & Irizarry, N. L. (1995). *Culture and attachment.* New York: Guilford Press.

Harwood, R. L. (1992). The influence of culturally derived values on Anglo and Puerto Rican mothers' perceptions of attachment behavior. *Child Development, 63,* 822–839.

Hertsgaard, L., Gunnar, M., Erickson, M. F., & Nachmias, M. (1995). Adrenocortical response to the Strange Situation in infants with disorganized/disoriented attachment relationships. *Child Development, 66,* 1100–1106.

Hinde, R. A. (1982). Attachment: Some conceptual and biological issues. In C. Parkes & J. Stevenson-Hinde (Eds.), *The place of attachment in human behavior* (pp. 60–76). New York: Basic Books.

Hinde, R. A., & Stevenson-Hinde, J. (1988). *Relationships within families: Mutual influences.* Oxford: Clarendon Press.

Hinde, R. A., & Stevenson-Hinde, J. (1990). Attachment: Biological, cultural and individual desiderata. *Human Development, 33,* 62–72.

Hoeksma, J. B., van den Boom, D. C., Koomen, H. M. Y., & Koops, W. (1997). Modeling the sensitivity-attachment hypothesis. In W. Koops, J. B. Hoeksma, & D. C. van den Boom (Eds.), *Development of interaction and attachment: Traditional and non-traditional approaches* (pp. 157–168). Amsterdam: North-Holland/Elsevier.

Hofer, M. A. (1987). Early social relationships: A psychobiologists' view. *Child Development, 58,* 633–647.

Hofer, M. A. (1994a). Early relationships as regulators of infant physiology and behavior. *Acta Paediatrica Supplement, 397,* 9–18.

Hofer, M. A. (1994b). Hidden regulators in attachment, separation, and loss. In N. A. Fox (Ed.), The development of emotion regulation: Biological and behavioral considerations (pp. 192–207). *Monographs of the Society for Research in Child Development, 59* (2–3, Serial No. 240).

Howe, N. (1991). Sibling-directed internal state language, perspective-taking, and affective behavior. *Child Development, 62,* 1503–1512.

Howe, N., & Ross, H. (1990). Socialization, perspective-taking, and the sibling relationship. *Developmental Psychology, 26,* 160–165.

Howes, C., & Hamilton, C. E. (1992a). Children's relationships with child care teachers: Stability and concordance with parental attachments. *Child Development, 63,* 867–878.

Howes, C., & Hamilton, C. E. (1992b). Children's relationships with caregivers: Mothers and child care teachers. *Child Development, 63,* 859–866.

Howes, C., Rodning, C., Galluzzo, D. C., & Myers, L. (1988). Attachment and child care: Relationships with mother and caregiver. *Early Childhood Research Quarterly, 3,* 403–416.

Isabella, R. A. (1993). Origins of infant–mother attachment: Maternal interactive behavior across the first year. *Child Development, 64,* 605–621.

Isabella, R. A. (1998). Origins of attachment: The role of context, duration, frequency of observation, and infant age in measuring maternal behavior. *Journal of Social and Personality Relationships, 15,* 538–554.

Jenkins, J. M., & Astington, J. W. (1996). Cognitive factors and family structure associated with theory of mind development in young children. *Developmental Psychology, 32,* 70–78.

Jones, S. S. (1985). On the motivational bases for attachment behavior. *Developmental Psychology, 21,* 848–857.

Kagan, J. (1984). *The nature of the child.* New York: Basic Books.

Kagan, J. (1994). *Galen's prophecy.* New York: Basic Books.

Kraemer, G. W. (1992). A psychobiological theory of attachment. *Behavioral and Brain Sciences, 15,* 493–541.

Kunnen, S. E., Olthof, T., & Boom, J. (2000). Theory and mathematics in building dynamic systems models: What prevails? A reply to van der Maas and Raijmakers. *Infant and Child Development, 9,* 85–89.

Lamb, M. R., Thompson, R., Gardner, W., & Charnov, E. (1985). *Infant–mother attachment: The origins and developmental significance of individual differences in strange situation behavior.* Hillsdale, NJ: Erlbaum.

Lamb, M. R., Thompson, R., Gardner, W., Charnov, E., & Estes, D. (1984). Security of infantile attachment as assessed in the "Strange Situation": Its study and biological interpretations. *Behavioral and Brain Sciences, 7,* 127–147.

Lancaster, J. B., & Lancaster, C. S. (1987). The watershed: Change in parental investment and family formation strategies in the course of human evolution. In J. Altman, A. Rossi, & L. Sherrod (Eds.), *Parenting across the life span: Biosocial dimensions* (pp. 87–205). New York: Aldine de Gruyter.

LeDoux, J. E. (1995). Emotion: Clues from the brain. *Annual Review of Psychology, 46,* 209–235.

Lieberman, A. F., Weston, D. R., & Pawl, J. H. (1991). Preventive intervention and outcome with anxiously attached dyads. *Child Development, 62,* 199–209.

Li-Repac, D. C. (1982). *The impact of acculturation on the child rearing attitudes and practices of Chinese-American families: Consequences for the attachment process.* Unpublished doctoral dissertation, University of California, Berkeley.

Lovejoy, C. O. (1981). The origin of man. *Science, 211,* 341–350.

MacDonald, K. B. (1988). *Social and personality development: An evolutionary synthesis.* New York: Plenum Press.

Main, M. (1991). Metacognitive knowledge, metacognitive monitoring and singular (coherent) versus multiple (incoherent) models of attachment; Findings and directions for future research. In C. M. Parkes, J. Stevenson-Hinde & P. Marris (Eds.), *Attachment across the life cycle* (pp. 127–159). New York: Routledge.

Main, M., & Goldwyn, R. (1994). *Adult attachment classification system.* Unpublished manuscript, University of California, Berkeley.

Main, M., & Solomon, J. (1986). Discovery of an insecure-disorganized/disoriented attachment pattern. In T. B. Brazelton & M. W. Yogman (Eds.), *Affective development in infancy* (pp. 95–124). Norwood, NJ: Ablex.

Main, M., & Solomon, J. (1990). Procedures for identifying infants as disorganized/disoriented during the Ainsworth Strange Situation. In M. T. Greenberg, D. Cicchetti, & E. M. Cummings (Eds.), *Attachment in the preschool years* (pp. 121–160). Chicago: University of Chicago Press.

Mangelsdorf, S., Gunnar, M., Kestenbaum, R., Lang, S., & Andreas, D. (1990). Infant proneness-to-distress temperament, maternal personality, and mother–infant attachment: Associations and goodness of fit. *Child Development, 61,* 820–831.

McKim, M. K., Cramer, K. M., Stuart, B., & O'Connor, D. L. (1999). Infant care decisions and attachment security: The Canadian *Transition to Child Care Study. Canadian Journal of Behavioural Science, 31,* 92–106.

McLoyd, V. C. (1990). The impact of economic hardship on black families and children: Psychological distress, parenting, and socioemotional development. *Child Development, 61,* 311–436.

Miyake, K., Chen, S. J., & Campos, J. J. (1985). Infant temperament, mothers' mode of interaction, and attachment in Japan: An interim report. In I. Bretherton & E. Waters (Eds.), Growing points of attachment theory and research (pp. 276–297). *Monographs of the Society for Research in Child Development, 50* (1–2, Serial No. 209).

Mumme, D. L., Won, D., & Fernald, A. (1994). *Do one-year-old infants show referent specific responding to emotional signals?* Paper presented at the Meeting of the International Conference on Infant Studies, Paris.

Nachmias, M., Gunnar, M., Mangelsdorf, S., Parritz, R. H., & Buss, K. (1996). Behavioral inhibition and stress reactivity: The moderating role of attachment security. *Child Development, 67,* 508–522.

Nelson, C., & Bloom, F. (1997). Child development and neuroscience. *Child Development, 68,* 670–687.

NICHD Early Child Care Research Network. (1997). The effects of infant child care on mother–infant attachment security: Results of the NICHD study of early child care. *Child Development, 68,* 860–879.

NICHD Early Child Care Research Network. (1998). Early child care and self-control, compliance, and problem behavior at twenty-four and thirty-six months. *Child Development, 69,* 1145–1170.

Olthof, T., Kunnen, E. S., & Boom, J. (2000). Simulating mother–child interaction: Exploring two varieties of a non-linear dynamic systems approach. *Infant and Child Development*, *9*, 33–60.

Oppenheim, D., Sagi, A., & Lamb, M. E. (1988). Infant–adult attachments on the kibbutz and their relation to socioemotional development 4 years later. *Developmental Psychology*, *24*, 427–433.

Passman, R. H. (1987). Attachment to inanimate objects: Are children who have security blankets insecure? *Journal of Consulting and Clinical Psychology*, *55*, 825–830.

Perner, J., Ruffman, T., & Leekam, S. R. (1994). Theory of mind is contagious: You catch it from your sibs. *Child Development*, *65*, 1228–1238.

Polan, H. J., & Hofer, M. A. (1999). Psychobiological origins of infant attachment and separation responses. In J. Cassidy & P. Shaver (Eds.), *Handbook of attachment theory and research* (pp. 162–180). New York: Guilford Press.

Post, R. M., Weiss, S. R. B., Li, H., Smith, M. A., Zhang, L. X., Xing, G., Osuch, E. A., & McCan, U. D. (1998). Neural plasticity and emotional memory. *Development and Psychopathology*, *10*, 829–855.

Repacholi, B. M., & Gopnik, A. (1997). Early reasoning about desires: Evidence from 14- and 18-month-olds. *Developmental Psychology*, *33*, 12–21.

Richerson, P. J. (1997, March). Culture and human "nature." *Politics and the Life Sciences*, 40–42.

Roberts, W. L. (1986). Nonlinear models of development: An example from the socialization of competence. *Child Development*, *57*, 1166–1178.

Roberts, W. L., & Strayer, J. (1987). Parents' responses to the emotional distress of their children: Relations with children's competence. *Developmental Psychology*, *23*, 415–422.

Rothbart, M. K., & Bates, J. E. (1998). Temperament. In W. Damon (Series Ed.) & N. Eisenberg (Vol. Ed.), *Handbook of child psychology: Vol. 3. Social, emotional and personality development* (pp. 105–176). New York: Wiley.

Sagi, A., Lamb, M. E., Lewkowicz, K. S., Shoham, R., Dvir, R., & Estes, D. (1985). Security of infant–mother, –father, and –metapelet attachments among kibbutz-reared Israeli children. In I. Bretherton & E. Waters (Eds.), Growing points of attachment theory and research (pp. 257–275). *Monographs of the Society for Research in Child Development, 50* (1–2, Serial No. 209).

Sagi, A., & Lewkowicz, K. S. (1987). A cross-cultural evaluation of attachment research. In L. W. C. Tavvecchio & M. H. van IJzendoorn (Eds.), *Attachment in social networks* (pp. 427–459). Amsterdam: Elsevier.

Schaffer, R. H. (1996). *Social development*. Oxford: Blackwell.

Schneider Rosen, K., & Burke, P. B. (1999). Multiple attachment relationships within families: Mothers and fathers with two young children. *Developmental Psychology*, *35*, 436–444.

Schneider Rosen, K., & Rothbaum, F. (1993). Quality of parental caregiving and security of attachment. *Developmental Psychology*, *29*, 358–367.

Schultz, C. A., & Wellman, H. M. (1997). Explaining human movements and actions: Children's understanding of the limits of psychological explanation. *Cognition*, *62*, 291–324.

Seifer, R., Schiller, M., Sameroff, A. J., Resnick, S., & Riordan, K. (1996). Attachment, maternal sensitivity, and temperament during the first year of life. *Developmental Psychology*, *32*, 3–11.

Shizgal, P. (1999). On the neural computation of utility: Implications from studies of brain stimulation reward. In D. Kahneman, E. Diener, & N. Schwartz (Eds.), *Well-being: The foundations of hedonic psychology*. New York: Russell Sage Foundation.

Shultz, T. R. (1991). From agency to intention: A rule-based, computational approach. In A. Whiten (Ed.), *Natural theories of mind: Evolution, development, and simulation of everyday mindreading*. Oxford: Blackwell.

Spangler, G., & Grossmann, K. E. (1993). Biobehavioral organization in securely and insecurely attached infants. *Child Development, 64,* 1439–1450.

Sroufe, L. A., & Waters, E. (1977). Attachment as an organizational construct. *Child Development, 48,* 1184–1199.

Steele, H., & Steele, M. (1998). Attachment and psychoanalysis: Time for a reunion. *Social Development, 7,* 92–126.

Takahashi, K. (1986). Examining the Strange Situation procedure with Japanese mothers and 12-month-old infants. *Developmental Psychology, 22,* 265–270.

Takahashi, K. (1990). Are the key assumptions of the "Strange Situation" procedure universal? A view from Japanese research. *Human Development, 33,* 23–30.

Taylor, M., & Carlson, S. M. (1997). The relation between individual differences in fantasy and theory of mind. *Child Development, 68,* 436–455.

Taylor, S. E. (1991). Asymmetrical effects of positive and negative events: The mobilization-minimization hypothesis. *Psychological Bulletin, 110,* 67–85.

Thompson, R. A. (1998). Early sociopersonality development. In W. Damon (Series Ed.) & N. Eisenberg (Vol. Ed.), *Handbook of child psychology: Vol. 3. Social, emotional and personality development.* New York: Wiley.

Tomasello, M. (1995). Joint attention as social cognition. In C. Moore & P. Dunham (Eds.), *Joint attention: Its origins and role in development* (pp. 103–130). Hillsdale, NJ: Erlbaum.

Tomasello, M., & Barton, M. (1994). Learning words in nonostensive contexts. *Developmental Psychology, 30,* 639–650.

Tomasello, M., Kruger, A. C., & Ratner, H. H. (1993). Cultural learning. *Behavioral and Brain Sciences, 16,* 495–552.

Topál, J., Miklósi, A., Csányi, V., & Dóka, A. (1998). Attachment behavior in dogs (*Canis familiaris*): A new application of Ainsworth's (1969) Strange Situation test. *Journal of Comparative Psychology, 112,* 219–229.

Van den Boom, D. C. (1994). The influence of temperament and mothering on attachment and exploration: An experimental manipulation of sensitive responsiveness among lower-class mothers with irritable infants. *Child Development, 65,* 1457–1477.

Van den Boom, D. C. (1997). Sensitivity and attachment: Next steps for developmentalists. *Child Development, 68,* 592–594.

Van den Boom, D. C., & Hoeksma, J. B. (1994). The effect of infant irritability on mother–infant interaction: A growth-curve analysis. *Developmental Psychology, 30,* 581–590.

Van den Boom, D. C., & Hoeksma, J. B. (1997). How is development conceptualized in mother–child interaction research? In W. Koops, J. B. Hoeksma, & D. C. van den Boom (Eds.), *Development of interaction and attachment: Traditional and non-traditional approaches* (pp. 141–156). Amsterdam: North-Holland/Elsevier.

Van der Maas, H. L. J., & Raijmakers, M. E. J. (2000). A phase transition model for mother–child interaction: Comment on Olthof et al., 2000. *Infant and Child Development, 9,* 75–83.

Van IJzendoorn, M. H. (1995). The association between adult attachment representations and infant attachment, parental responsiveness, and clinical status: A meta-analysis on the predictive validity of the Adult Attachment Interview. *Psychological Bulletin, 113,* 404–410.

Van IJzendoorn, M. H., & de Wolff, M. S. (1997). In search of the absent father – Meta-analyses of infant–father attachment: A rejoinder to our discussants. *Child Development, 68,* 604–609.

Van IJzendoorn, M. H., Goldberg, S., Kroonenberg, P. M., & Frenkel, O. J. (1992). The relative effects of maternal and child problems on the quality of attachment: A meta-analysis of attachment in clinical samples. *Child Development, 63,* 840–858.

Van IJzendoorn, M. H., Juffer, F., & Duyvesteyn, M. G. C. (1995). Breaking the intergenerational cycle of insecure attachment: A review of the effects of attachment-based interventions on maternal sensitivity and infant security. *Journal of Child Psychology and Psychiatry, 36,* 225–248.

Van IJzendoorn, M. H., & Kroonenberg, P. M. (1988). Cross-cultural patterns of attachment: A meta-analysis of the Strange Situation. *Child Development, 59,* 147–156.

Van IJzendoorn, M. H., Sagi, A., & Lambermon, M. W. E. (1992). The multiple caretaker paradox: Data from Holland and Israel. In R. C. Pianti (Ed.), *Beyond the parent: The role of other adults in children's lives* (New Directions for Child Development Series, No. 57, pp. 5–24). San Francisco: Jossey-Bass.

Van IJzendoorn, M. H., Schuengel, C., & Bakermans-Kranenburg, M. J. (1999). Disorganized attachment in early childhood: Meta-analysis of precursors, concomitants, and sequelae. *Development and Psychopathology, 11,* 225–249.

Vaughn, B. E., Stevenson-Hinde, J., Waters, E., Kotsaftis, A., Lefever, G. B., Shouldice, A., Trudel, M., & Belsky, J. (1992). Attachment security and temperament in infancy and early childhood: Some conceptual clarifications. *Developmental Psychology, 28,* 463–473.

Volling, B. L., & Belsky, J. (1992). Infant, father, and marital antecedents of infant–father attachment security in dual-earner and single-earner families. *International Journal of Behavioral Development, 15,* 83–100.

Vuchinich, S., Emery, R. E., & Cassidy, J. (1988). Family members as third parties in dyadic family conflict: Strategies, alliances, and outcomes. *Child Development, 59,* 1293–1302.

Wachs, T. D., & Desai, S. (1993). Parent-report measures of toddler temperament and attachment: Their relation to each other and to the social microenvironment. *Infant Behavior and Development, 16,* 391–396.

Waters, E. (1978). The reliability and stability of individual differences in infant–mother attachment. *Child Development, 49,* 483–494.

Waters, E. (1981). Traits, behavioral systems, and relationships: Three models of infant–adult attachment. In K. Immelman, G. Barlow, L. Petrinovich, & M. Main (Eds.), *Behavioral development* (pp. 621–650). Cambridge: Cambridge University Press.

Waters, E., & Deane, K. E. (1982). Infant–mother attachment: Theories, models, recent data, and some tasks for comparative developmental analysis. In L. Hoffman & R. Gandelman (Eds.), *Parental behavior: Causes and consequences* (pp. 19–53). Hillsdale, NJ: Erlbaum.

Waters, E., & Deane, K. E. (1985). Defining and assessing individual differences in infant attachment relationships: Q-methodology and the organization of behavior. In I. Bretherton & E. Waters (Eds.), Growing points of attachment theory and research (pp. 41–65). *Monographs of the Society for Research in Child Development, 50* (Serial No. 209).

Wellman, H. M., Harris, P. L., Banerjee, M., & Sinclair, A. (1995). Early understanding of emotion: Evidence from natural language. *Cognition and Emotion, 9,* 117–149.

Westen, D. (1998). The scientific legacy of Sigmund Freud: Toward a psychodynamically informed psychological science. *Psychological Bulletin, 124,* 333–371.

Westerman, R., Spies, K., Stahl, G., & Hesse, F. W. (1996). Relative effectiveness and validity of mood induction procedures: A meta-analysis. *European Journal of Social Psychology, 26,* 557–580.

Woodward, A. L., & Markman, E. M. (1998). Early word learning. In W. Damon (Series Ed.) & D. Kuhn & R. S. Siegler (Vol. Eds.), *Handbook of child psychology: Vol. 2. Cognition, perception, and language* (pp. 371–420). New York: Wiley.

Youngblade, L. (1993, April). *Individual differences in young children's pretend play with mother and sibling: Links to relationship quality and understanding of other people's feelings and beliefs.* Paper presented at the Society for Research in Child Development.

Youngblade, L., & Dunn, J. (1995). Individual differences in young children's pretend play with mother and sibling: Links to relationships and understanding of other people's feelings and beliefs. *Child Development, 66,* 1472–1492.

Zahn-Waxler, C., Radke-Yarrow, M., Wagner, E., & Chapman, M. (1992). Development of concern for others. *Developmental Psychology, 28,* 126–136.

Zevalkink, J., Riksen-Walraven, J. M. A., & van Lieshout, C. F. M. (1999). Attachment in the Indonesian caregiving context. *Social Development, 8,* 21–40.

Chapter Twelve

Peers and Infant Social/Communicative Development

Carol O. Eckerman and Karen Peterman

Introduction

During their first three years of life children master the basic skills enabling them to generate with one another such coordinated interactions as games, verbal conversations, collaborative problem solving, and the resolution of conflicts. The goal of this chapter is to understand the developmental pathway to this mastery. What social, communication, and cognitive skills enable coordinated interactions and how do they develop? Are the coordinated interactions found among peers in day-care centers similar to or different from those of less familiar peers? Are peer conflicts related to cooperative coordinated action? We evaluate today's answers to these questions and comment on the distinctive roles peer interactions may play in infant social/communicative development. First, however, we present a brief history of studies of infant peers and the changing questions that have guided them. The answers to these earlier questions are the foundation for the present attempt to trace the developmental pathway to coordinated action between infant peers.

A Brief History: Changing Questions About Infant Peers

The modern empirical study of infant peers began in the mid-1970s, building upon a few studies during the 1930s of institutionalized infants (e.g., Bridges, 1933; Buhler, 1930; Maudry & Nekula, 1939). The first studies in the 1970s were exploratory and descriptive. At the time, the study of infant social development was focused upon infants' relationships with their mothers – both mother–infant attachment (e.g., Ainsworth, Blehar, Waters, & Wall, 1977; Bowlby, 1969) and the details of the moment-by-moment flow of *en-face* interaction between mothers and their young infants (e.g., Brazelton,

Koslowski, & Main, 1974; Stern, 1974). If thought was given to infant peers at all, the expectation was that either little would happen or they would fight over objects given their interest in the same toys. The first studies sought to discover what, if anything, did happen when family-reared infant peers met.

The findings were clear. A great deal happened, much of which could be described as infants behaving sociably toward one another (see reviews by Eckerman & Didow, 1988; Mueller & Vandell, 1979). By "sociable" we mean behaving in ways that bring about or sustain friendly interpersonal contact. When pairs of unfamiliar peers met in a free-play setting with their mothers, whether at 10–12, 16–18, or 22–24 months, the infants spent much of their time looking at one another, being close together in space, and contacting the same play material (Eckerman, Whatley, & Kutz, 1975). Further, they directed smiles, vocalizations, and gestures to one another and touched or patted one another – behaviors that when directed toward mothers were called "sociable." They also took toys from one another, struggled over toys, and hit each other, but these behaviors were much less frequent than those customarily called "sociable." Similar findings were obtained for pairs of 9-month-olds as they became acquainted over 16 near-daily meetings (Becker, 1977) and for very familiar peers in group settings (e.g., Roopnarine & Field, 1983; Vincze, 1971). Even unfamiliar infant peers as young as 6 months of age directed a variety of behaviors at one another, the most frequent of which were vocalizations, smiles, and touches and the least frequent of which were hits or pushes (Vandell, Wilson, & Buchanan, 1980). Thus, infants quite often were sociable with one another – both in novel and familiar play settings, with an unfamiliar peer and those quite familiar, at the start of an acquaintanceship and after many encounters, and in dyads and in groups.

Finding sociable behavior between such young peers was so unexpected that some sought to reinterpret the behaviors seen as nonsocial. Could behaviors described as directed toward the peer be instead reactions to the inanimate spectacles peers create through their actions on toys? A child thought to be smiling at a peer might really be responding happily to the intriguing sights and sounds of toys produced by the peer. A variation on this theme was the claim that infants' interest in one another grew out of their interest in similar play material; as a result of their attraction to the same toys, infants found themselves together and in a position to notice and react to each other's actions upon the toys. In this view, truly sociable behavior grew out of a developmentally prior interest in the inanimate play material (e.g., Mueller & Brenner, 1977; Mueller & Lucas, 1975). Thus, the question became whether the behaviors between infant peers that some called sociable were really social at all.

To address this question, at least four studies contrasted peer encounters in the presence versus absence of toys (Eckerman & Whatley, 1977; Hay, Pedersen, & Nash, 1982; Ramey, Finkelstein, & O'Brien, 1976; Vandell et al., 1980). Again, the findings were very clear. In each study, more of the behaviors called sociable occurred when the infant peers met in the absence of toys. This was as evident for 6-month-olds as for 2-year-olds. Clearly, many of their gazes, smiles, vocalizations, approaches, and touches were directed toward one another and in that sense social or sociable.

Now that infants were acknowledged to be sociable with one another, the question became one of whether young peers really interacted or communicated with one another.

The temporal flow of what transpired between infant peers was examined for evidence that they were interacting (mutually influencing one another) or communicating (sharing some understanding of what they were doing together). Two research strategies emerged: a sequential chain approach and a social phenomenon approach. The sequential chain approach looked for sequences of peer-directed smiles, sounds, touches, and gestures alternating between two children. For example, in a playgroup of familiar peers (Mueller & Brenner, 1977) sequences at least three acts long (child A, child B, child A, . . .) increased from an average of 0.4 times in 15 minutes at 12 months of age to 3.1 times at 23 months. The social phenomenon approach, in contrast, focused upon defining a social phenomenon that by its very existence implied mutual influence and some shared understanding. For example, Ross (1982) defined a game as a sequence of at least four alternating peer-directed behaviors (two for each infant) with a common play theme such as follow-the-leader or chase; such games occurred on average less than once in 24 minutes for unfamiliar 15-month-olds and increased to 1.42 times for 24-month-olds.

Both approaches provided some evidence of interaction and communication between infant peers, but they also highlighted how difficult it was for infant peers to generate these forms of social interaction and the prolonged developmental courses involved. As a result, some suggested that peer interactions played only a most limited constructive role in early development (e.g., Bronson, 1981), but others suggested that the potential for early peer interaction and communication should be examined in other ways. Implicit in the sequential chain approach was an adult-like model of communication that emphasized turn-alternation and the directing of distal social signals to one another (smiles, sounds, gestures). This may not be the primary form early peer interaction and communication takes. Although the social phenomenon approach allowed many more infant actions to be viewed as communicative, its focus upon fully formed phenomena might preclude an awareness of less well-formed interactions and communications.

These latter considerations have led to the focal question of this chapter: By what developmental pathway do infant peers come to generate cooperative coordinated action with one another? Implicit in this question is (1) an openness to look for forms of communication, social influence, and coordinated action among young peers unlike those stressed for infant–parent encounters or even older peer encounters, and (2) a wish to understand how earlier forms of coordinated action develop into more mature forms.

The Development of Cooperative Coordinated Action Between Peers

Table 12.1 presents an example of interaction between two 32-month-olds. Observers of this interaction readily infer that each child's actions are being influenced both in form and timing by those of the other; there is mutual social influence. Further, both children's actions seem to contribute to a common theme; their actions are thematically (semantically) related to one another. Further still, the children are using integrated verbal and nonverbal means of communication. Nonverbal imitative acts form much of the substance of their coordinated action, and their verbalizations both highlight the nonverbal actions (e.g., "I get it") and communicate further how these nonverbal acts are to be done (e.g., "Watch"). The evidence of mutual social influence and joint action on a common

Table 12.1 An example of cooperative coordinated action between two 32-month-olds. Each child's actions are listed in sequential order with verbalizations in quotation marks

Child A	Child B
Joins peer at playhouse	
	Sits on floor of playhouse
Sits beside peer	
	Throws ball out window + "I want to throw, okay?"
"Okay"	
Throws ball out window	
	Retrieves ball + "I better get some"
Retrieves ball + "I get this"	
	Enters house + "I go back in"
Enters house + "I go back in"	
Sits down	
	Sits down + "You next to me"
	Holds ball up to throw + ". . . throw this ball"
Holds ball up to throw	
Throws ball out window	
	Throws ball out door + "Watch"
	Retrieves ball + ". . . I get it"
Retrieves ball + "I got it"	
	Enters house + "I got it, I go back in"
Enters house + ". . . back in"	
	Sits down
Sits down	

theme leads us to call this an episode of cooperative coordinated action. The integrated use of both nonverbal and verbal means of communication suggests it is a relatively mature form of coordinated action.

To understand the development of cooperative coordinated action, we will examine each of these three key ingredients – social influence, joint action on a common theme, and integrated nonverbal and verbal means of communication. First, we examine forms of social influence between young peers that occur long before there is much coordinated action. Second, we ask how young peers begin to engage in joint action on a common theme and what behavioral and cognitive skills seem to be involved. Third, we ask about the emergence of verbal means of facilitating coordinated action among young peers and their integration with nonverbal means.

Discovering New Forms of Social Influence

Although coordinated action seldom occurs among prelocomotor infants, social influence can be found. Pairs of 6-month-olds showed little evidence of immediate responses to each other's fusses/cries or physical contacts (Hay et al., 1982). Nevertheless, systematic relationships were discovered between the two infants' behaviors. Infants were more likely to respond with fussing/crying to a peer's distress as the length of time the peer was fussing/crying increased. Or, if one infant responded to the other infant's touch with a reci-procal touch, then the first infant was more likely to continue touching. Despite such hints of intriguing forms of social influence, there has been little research on social influence between such young peers. Much more has been done with older infants and toddlers.

With locomoting infants, peer interactions increasingly involve inanimate play materials. This is true, too, of mother–infant interactions and has led to the stress upon understanding how the mother–infant dyad negotiates social interactions that involve toys (e.g., the coordinated joint engagement of Bakeman & Adamson, 1984; the joint atten-tion of Tomasello & Farrar, 1986). If we ask how infant peers come to jointly attend to a common object about which they then may interact, we find a pervasive way infants influ-ence one another – they approach and manipulate the same play material as their peer. Clear documentation of this form of influence came from a study of dyads of unfamiliar 18- or 24-month-olds (Eckerman & Stein, 1982). Each time one child made contact with an object not already contacted by the peer, the time elapsing before the second child contacted this same object or its duplicate was recorded. At both ages, the toddlers contacted the same object often and rapidly, and significantly more often than predicted by chance probabilities. For example, over 40 percent of the time, 24-month-olds contacted the same toy within 20 seconds. Frequent and rapid touch-ing of the same object also has been found among triads of very familiar 3-year-olds (Nadel-Brulfert & Baudonniere, 1982); 62 percent of the time at least one child picked up the same toy as a peer within 10 seconds. Thus, a peer's contacts with play material are very salient to toddlers, and toddlers show a pervasive response of going to and contacting the same play material. A similar responsiveness has been documented for even younger chil-dren (12-month-olds) with an unfamiliar adult playmate (Eckerman, Whatley, & McGehee, 1979), and hence may characterize the interactions of even younger peers.

Achieving Joint Action on a Common Theme

Although going to and contacting the same play material as one's peer brings about joint attention to objects, we still are a long way from understanding how young peers come to act upon an object of joint attention in ways that are thematically and cooperatively related to one another. Unfamiliar 16-month-old peers join each other readily and manipu-late the same play material, but seldom do we find any more meaningful connection between their actions (Eckerman, Davis, & Didow, 1989). One child rolls a ball down a slide and the peer may quickly act upon the same ball by throwing or squeezing it. How do they proceed from ready engagement of the same toys to generating cooperative co-ordinated action (e.g., taking turns rolling the ball down the slide or throwing the ball to one another)?

One answer is that toddlers begin to readily imitate each other's play actions. Imitat-ing another's actions seems an excellent strategy for forming a thematically related response to another's action and one that may be especially well suited to the actions of young peer partners. Relatively few of a toddler's play actions specify, even for a skillful adult partner, a specific appropriate response. Yet imitation can be used for virtually any action. Further, with imitative acts, the thematic connection between one toddler's actions and another's seems especially perceptually salient in that there is a clear similarity in the form of overt action. Thus, this deceptively simple way of behaving – doing what another has just done – may have great power and effectiveness (cf. Nadel, 1986; Nadel-Brulfert & Baudonniere, 1982; Uzgiris, 1991).

Although the prevalence of imitative acts in early peer encounters has often been noted (e.g., Grusec & Abramovitch, 1982; Nadel, 1986; Ross, 1982), its role in enabling toddlers to generate cooperative coordinated action was highlighted in a longitudinal study of pairs of unfamiliar peers who met at 16, 20, 24, 28, and 32 months of age (Eckerman et al., 1989). Each child's actions with objects, movements in space, vocalizations, and gestures were coded independently from videotaped records and subsequently integrated along a common timeline. Then, all instances of coordinated acts were identified, that is, acts that were cooperatively and thematically related to the ongoing or immediately prior actions of the peer. These could be imitative acts, complementary role acts (e.g., "finding" a "hiding" peer), complementary verbal or gestural directives (e.g., saying "jump" as the peer stood poised to jump, or handing a ball to the peer who had just previously rolled the ball down a slide), or appropriate responses to verbal or gestural directives. An imitative act reproduced at least one central feature of the peer's action (other features could be omitted or new ones added) and the action reproduced had to be a distinctive play action rather than such routine actions as picking up a toy or walking from one location to another.

Coordinated acts were infrequent at 16 months of age but increased markedly over the next 12 months, and almost all the increase came from nonverbal imitative acts. Imitative acts came to occur as frequently as once every 11 seconds when the peers were engaged with the same play material! The only other form of coordinated act that increased significantly was complementary verbal directives, but these remained infrequent even at 32 months of age (less than once in 3 minutes). For individual dyads, the increase in imitative acts occurred relatively suddenly at a median age of 20–24 months; at earlier ages, the peers seldom imitated each other and then four months later they imitated each other much more frequently and maintained this increased rate at subsequent ages.

Toddlers' ready imitation of a peer's nonverbal play actions enables not only many more instances of coordinated responses but also the generation of sustained bouts of coordinated action – games. Games consisted of at least two turns of action by each child where the actions of the two children formed a common theme such as chase, follow-the-leader, or reciprocal imitation and the actions of each were agreeable to the other. Such games showed a sudden, marked increase in frequency at the same point in development as the sudden increase in nonverbal imitative acts.

Imitative acts seem to solve a major task for toddlers – that of reaching agreement on a topic for coordinated action when specific rituals of interaction cannot be relied on and they do not yet have the verbal skills to negotiate what they want to do together. With their parents, infants and toddlers first become full participants in generating sustained coordinated action in such well-practiced rituals as "peek-a-boo," give-and-take, and picture-book "reading" (e.g., Adamson, 1996; Bruner, 1983; Schaffer, 1984). The topics of rituals become understood by the infant as a result of repeated experience with the ritual. To engage in a ritual initiated by someone else, the infant only has to recognize the familiar play actions and respond appropriately. To initiate the ritual, the infant only has to perform one of its distinctive actions and his or her intent is likely to be understood by the partner with whom this ritual has so often been enacted. Outside of these rituals, however, specifying a topic for coordinated action is a difficult task for toddlers. Imitating one of a partner's actions upon an object of joint attention seems an excellent nonverbal way of highlighting one action of the many possible and suggesting it as a topic for interaction. It may communicate something like "Let's do this together" or "I like this" (cf. Uzgiris, 1991).

What evidence supports this claim that imitating a peer's actions helps establish a topic for sustained coordinated action? First, imitative acts tend to beget further imitative acts, thus establishing a common topic – the act itself. An adult's imitation of 24-month-old toddlers' play actions (versus performing an unrelated act with the same toy) led to toddlers more often continuing to act on that toy. Further, given that they continued, they were over twice as likely to perform the same play action again and hence imitate the adult (Eckerman & Stein, 1990). Similarly, in the longitudinal peer study from 16 to 32 months of age, toddlers markedly increased their reciprocating imitative acts at the same time as they increased their initiating imitative acts – that is, they responded to being imitated by performing the same action again and thus engaging in reciprocal imitation (Eckerman, 1993b). Once a reciprocating imitative act occurred, there was a high probability (.52) that it would lead to a subsequent reciprocating imitative act and hence the generation of a game composed of both children alternating in performing similar actions.

Further evidence comes from the games actually generated by the toddler peers. Imitative acts formed the content of the game role for one or both children in 85 percent of the games. Reciprocal imitation games were the most frequent form (57 percent of the games); both toddlers took turns repeating similar play actions. But imitative acts enabled other forms of games, too, the most frequent of which (40 percent) were generated by one child performing different play actions across successive turns and the other child imitating each in turn, either "follow-the-leader" games composed of distinctive play actions involving body parts or objects or "lead-follow" games composed of playful movements to different points in a room. Imitative acts also enabled a few games with an even more complex structure, games in which a follow-the-leader sequence formed the content of a game turn and that sequence was repeated in similar form over subsequent turns, as in Table 12.1 (Eckerman, 1993a). The reciprocal imitation games, too, were quite creative affairs, described better as variations on a theme than repetitive duplication of the same action. The understanding that "we are imitating each other" seemed to enable the toddlers to vary their play actions across turns, adding more and more elements at times, or deleting some and adding others, while still smoothly maintaining their reciprocal imitation game. If we put these three findings together (the tendency for imitative acts to beget reciprocating imitative acts, follow-the-leader sequences, and variation in the form of the imitative act by adding and/or omitting elements), it is possible for toddlers to generate a nearly inexhaustible variety of new forms of cooperative coordinated action.

During the same developmental period in which ready imitation of a peer's nonverbal play actions emerges, other nonverbal ways of behaving that facilitate cooperative coordinated action also appear. Musatti and Mueller (1985) assessed changes in the ability to sequence a variety of signals directed toward a peer with an act suggesting a theme for their play. For toddlers meeting daily in a playgroup, social planning, turn-taking, and playfulness expressions increased markedly around 18 months of age, as did the number of these expressions that were combined during a single performance of a play theme. Social planning expressions occurred 1–3 seconds prior to the play theme act and included looking intently at or gesturing, vocalizing, or smiling to the peer. Turn-taking expressions occurred at least 1 second after the performance of the play theme and included new looks to the peer, sustained intense gaze at the peer, or pointing to an object important to the theme. Finally, playfulness expressions occurred either during or after the theme expression and included exaggerated forms of affective expressions (laughter, screeches, playful exaggeration of action). Musatti and Mueller considered these expressions evidence of representational growth and reasoned that representational growth (or planning to share a theme with a peer) contributed importantly to toddlers' abilities to generate interactions with shared meaning. Whether these expressions and their combinations begin to increase in frequency at the same time as toddlers' imitation of one another, earlier, or later remains unknown.

While Musatti and Mueller examined changes in "invitations to play," Ross and Lollis (1987) examined changes from 9 to 18 months of age in signals for a partner to reengage in a game. An adult established a game with the child and then failed to take her turn for 15 seconds. Seven potentially communicative acts occurred more often during these interruptions than when the game was proceeding smoothly – vocalizations to the adult, alternating gaze between the adult's face and the object involved in the game, pointing to or touching the adult, offering or giving the toy to the adult, showing the toy to the adult, repeating the child's turn, and taking the adult's turn. Four of these increased significantly with age – vocalizing, showing the toy, offering the toy, and taking the adult's turn – as did the number of different communicative acts emitted during an interruption and the frequency with which the children combined communicative acts into a "message" that included reference to the adult as the play partner, the object involved in the game, and the actions constituting the game. Although these findings come from games with an adult who presumably had helped the child to understand what they were doing together, they suggest important changes that may come into play in toddlers' games together once they have been established by other means.

A final example concerns toddlers' changing abilities to solve a problem requiring them to assume complementary roles in a temporally coordinated way (Brownell & Carriger, 1990, 1991). This appears a more difficult task than generating games by means of imitative acts. One child had to manipulate a handle on one side of an apparatus in order to provide access in another location to an attractive toy, while the other child had to be in the appropriate location to get the toy when a barrier was removed as a result of the first child's action. Solutions did not occur until 18 months of age, and even at this age the toddlers' "cooperation" appeared serendipitous. One child seemed to note the effects of the other child's manipulation and take advantage of them opportunistically. At 24 and 30 months of age, however, the toddlers solved the problem multiple times and more quickly each time, suggesting purposeful, jointly regulated coordination of their behavior. They more often followed manipulation of the handle with a pause that gave time for their peer to respond, gave vocal and gestural directives, and moved to the appropriate positions opposite one another.

Cognitive Developments and the Development of Cooperative Coordinated Action

Numerous changes in toddlers' cognitions occur during the general developmental period in which their ready imitation of one another, sustained coordinated action, and collaborative problem solving emerge. There are changes in combinatorial abilities (Brownell, 1986, 1988; O'Connell & Gerard, 1985), negotiation strategies (Klimes-Dougan, 1993), volitional behavior (Bullock & Lutkenhaus, 1988), abilities to generate new means to achieve a goal (Frye, 1991), and understandings of self and others (Asendorpf, Warkenton, & Baudonniere, 1996; Brownell & Carriger, 1990, 1991; Meltzoff, 1995; Pipp, Fisher, & Jennings, 1987). Changes in toddlers' understandings of themselves and others seem most pertinent for understanding developmental changes in cooperative coordinated action. To maturely cooperate with others would seem to demand an understanding of both self and others as active independent agents, an understanding of both one's own and another's goals, an ability to negotiate to arrive at a common goal, an ability to monitor another's actions in relation to one's own actions, and an ability to monitor one's own and the partner's actions with respect to a joint goal in order to make corrections, to develop new means, and so on.

Despite the intuitive appeal of such ideas, little research has been done relating independently assessed cognitive skills to toddlers' coordinated action. Only a few hints of relationships exist. One study (Asendorpf & Baudonniere, 1993) demonstrated that more holding or manipulating of the same play material occurred in dyads of 19-month-olds when both showed self-awareness (assessed by a mirror-recognition task) than when one or both failed to show self-awareness. A subsequent study (Asendorpf et al., 1996) found that much longer bouts of imitation of an adult's different play actions occurred for 18-month-olds who showed self-awareness. The researchers argued that the capacity for self-awareness relied upon the same capacity to form secondary representations that was necessary to take the perspective of a social partner, and that an understanding of another's intentions or plans was a necessary prerequisite for coordinated action. Another study (Brownell & Carriger, 1990, 1991) related toddlers' success in solving a problem requiring cooperation in performing complementary acts to toddlers' understanding of others as active independent agents (assessed through elicited imitation of pretend sequences with dolls). It was not until 24 months of age that truly cooperative problem solving began to be seen, and 24.6 months was the average age at which the toddlers seemed to recognize others as active independent agents. Finally, there is the provocative demonstration by Meltzoff (1995) that 18-month-olds seem to process another's actions in terms of his or her intentions and choose to imitate the "intended" action rather than the actions actually performed by the other. Although we are unaware of any attempt to relate this achievement to the generation of coordinated action, such a study would be most interesting.

Beyond the important issue of reaching agreement on how to assess the cognitive and social achievements that we wish to relate to one another lies the thorny problem of how to reason about the meaning of any correlations obtained. Recent research related to toddlers' coordinated action is still seeking correlations between cognitive and social achievements; the difficult task of determining whether any causal relationships exist remains.

Integrating Verbal and Nonverbal Means of Generating Coordinated Action

The generation of sustained nonverbal forms of cooperative coordinated action is not the end of our developmental story for toddlers. After the emergence of these nonverbal forms, toddlers increasingly integrate their burgeoning language production abilities into their nonverbal coordinated action. They accompany their nonverbal imitative acts with words describing these acts, use words to direct each other in their nonverbal coordinated action, and respond verbally in a topically connected way to each other's verbalizations (Eckerman, 1993a; Eckerman & Didow, 1989, 1996).

The bouts of nonverbal coordinated action appear to facilitate toddlers' development of verbal means of achieving coordinated action. Further analyses of the peer dyads observed from 16 to 32 months of age revealed that regulatory speech (using words to direct a peer's actions) only began to increase during the four months *after* the emergence of ready nonverbal imitation (Eckerman & Didow, 1996). Regulatory speech that negotiated the roles to be played by the two children (e.g., "Play ball" or "Jump") increased first, followed later by regulatory speech that addressed such details as the timing of the acts (e.g., "Wait") or a partner's attention (e.g., "Watch"). Also, verbal descriptions of one's own nonverbal action (e.g., "I get it") began to increase eight months after ready imitation emerged. Further, answering the peer's verbal utterances in a thematically well-connected way (that is, rudimentary verbal conversations) began to increase, too, only when the peers began to readily imitate each other's nonverbal actions. Finally, both regulatory speech and thematically related verbal responses occurred much more often during the games formed of nonverbal imitative acts than during the times the two children were engaging the same play material in a non-conflictual, less-coordinated way.

We propose that as toddlers generate games by means of nonverbal imitation, they are generating joint understandings of what they are doing together. These joint understandings then aid them in talking about their activities and understanding and meaningfully answering each other's speech. Thus, through their nonverbal imitative acts, toddlers *themselves* appear to scaffold their own efforts at verbal communication with one another.

A Proposed Developmental Pathway to Cooperative Coordinated Action

A developmental sequence for how toddler peers come to generate cooperative coordinated action can be gleaned from the research reviewed so far (see Table 12.2). At 16 months of age, toddlers' skillful participation in cooperative coordinated action is restricted largely to such well-practiced rituals of interaction with adults and older chil-

Table 12.2   A proposed developmental progression in toddlers' generation of cooperative coordinated action

16 months	*Participation in ritualized coordinated action.* Toddlers' participation in coordinated action is largely restricted to well-practiced rituals of interaction, usually with familiar older partners. Sociability and social influence characterize peer interaction but little sustained coordinated action occurs.
20–24 months	*Emergence of ready imitation and non-ritualized coordinated action with peers.* Toddlers now readily imitate the nonverbal actions of others in social encounters and respond to others' imitation of them with reciprocating imitative acts. Through these nonverbal imitative acts, they now generate sustained non-ritualized forms of coordinated action (e.g., reciprocal imitation and follow-the-leader games), even with unfamiliar partners and those no more skillful than themselves (i.e., peers). New social-cognitive skills, representational skills, and ways of responding to game interruptions are seen.
28–32 months	*Integrated verbal and nonverbal means of achieving coordinated action.* Words are increasingly integrated into toddlers' nonverbal coordinated action with peers (e.g., verbal imitation, regulatory speech, topically well-connected verbal responses and verbal descriptions). Rudimentary verbal conversations between peers occur embedded in bouts of nonverbal coordinated action.

dren as peek-a-boo, stack-and-topple, give-and-take, and playing ball. However, there is much sociable behavior directed toward peers and a variety of forms of social influence that may aid infants in developing the skills required for cooperative coordinated action. Going to and acting upon the same objects as one another, for example, solves the task of achieving joint attention to an object and would seem to place young peers in a position to learn much about one another.

Ready imitation of peers' play actions emerges toward the end of the second year of life and brings a major advance in toddlers' ability to generate coordinated action. The tendencies to (1) reciprocate imitative acts, (2) perform imitative acts as variations on a theme, and (3) generate follow-the-leader sequences of imitative acts enable toddlers to generate a seemingly infinite variety of non-ritualized forms of sustained cooperative coordinated action. Such cognitive skills as viewing others as active intentional agents and inferring the goals/intentions of others may be integrally involved with these behavioral developments, as well as with the new advances found in social planning, turn-taking, and playfulness signals, and signals to a partner to resume a role during game interruptions.

In the next step, toddlers integrate verbal means of communication into their non-verbal coordinated action. In generating nonverbal coordinated action, toddlers generate joint understandings of what they are doing together that aid them in talking to each other and answering each other's talk about their joint activity. They come to verbally direct each other in this activity, describe their nonverbal actions, and generate verbal conversations embedded within their nonverbal coordinated action.

We can add that, still later, children become capable of generating the games or conversations composed solely of verbal turns so aptly described for preschoolers by Garvey (1974). Later, too, we suspect that imitative acts come to play a less important role in the generation of cooperative coordinated action as the children's verbal skills increase (e.g., Baudonniere, 1988; Grusec & Abramovitch, 1982; Nadel & Fontaine, 1989).

Three further points about the proposed pathway require stressing. First, it is derived largely from the study of unfamiliar US peers. A study among the Seltaman people of Papua New Guinea (Eckerman & Whitehead, 1999), however, found some key similarities in a markedly different cultural context. Ready imitation of one another emerged among the Seltaman toddlers during the same developmental period as for the US toddlers and functioned similarly to enable them to generate sustained cooperative coordinated action – a wide variety of reciprocal imitation games. The behavioral content of the games differed from that of the US toddlers, however, in ways predictable from the different socialization orientations of the two cultures. Still, in different cultural settings and/or with more familiar peers, we might find other pathways to cooperative coordinated action, differences in the timing of this pathway, or the need to elaborate the pathway further.

A second point is that the ages given are rough guidelines. They are the median ages for unfamiliar US peers observed at four-month intervals (Eckerman et al., 1989). Even within this study, there were marked individual differences. Although ready imitation of a peer's play actions occurred at a median age of 20–24 months, two dyads already showed this phenomenon at 16 months and one failed to show it even at 32 months.

The final point is that an emphasis on the role of imitative acts in enabling toddlers to generate non-ritualized forms of cooperative coordinated action is not necessarily in conflict with earlier suggestions that games composed of complementary roles or reciprocal roles (reversing complementary roles) are the more mature forms of coordinated action seen among toddlers (e.g., Howes & Matheson, 1992; Mueller & Lucas, 1975; Ross, 1982). Imitative acts can be central players in the generation of games with complementary roles (e.g., follow-the-leader and lead-follow games). There also are complementary features to many of the games called reciprocal imitation games. When two peers take turns hitting their ball against the peer's ball, one child takes the role of holding his or her own ball to be hit and the other child takes the complementary role of hitting the ball, and then these complementary roles are reversed. All turn-taking games in fact have a complementary feature and role reversals – one child waits while the other child takes a turn and then these complementary roles are reversed.

Peer Interactions in Day-care Contexts

We turn now to attempts to understand the emergence of cooperative coordinated action among infants who meet near-daily in a group context. Research here is more difficult since these group contexts exist for reasons other than research. Children enter and leave the groups according to their families' needs and the availability of space within the group, and adult caregivers may change as well as philosophies about how to structure the physical environment and manage young children in groups. These changes pose substantial problems for attempts to trace the development of infants' skills in interacting and communicating with one another; and they make it difficult to compare across group settings. Children, too, are not randomly assigned to different care settings; parents with different characteristics may choose different group settings. The research of Howes and her colleagues in a variety of day-care settings (e.g., Howes & Stewart, 1987) illustrates well the multiplicity of factors to consider in interpreting observations in such settings.

As a result, our understanding of the developmental course of coordinated action in day-care contexts has lagged behind that provided by the more laboratory-based research. Still, day-care settings provide such rich and extensive early exposure to peers that, in other ways, they are an ideal setting for research. Further, they are a prime context in which children in many cultures are today interacting with peers and they form an extensive part of the social experience of many infants. Hence, they warrant study in their own right. Although it is beyond the scope of this chapter to explore the multiplicity of factors that influence early peer interactions in day-care settings, we will summarize what can be gleaned about the general developmental course of coordinated action over the first two years of life.

Howes and her colleagues have sought evidence in day-care settings for a hypothesized developmental sequence of the complexity of peer play (the Howes Peer Play Scale; see Howes, 1980, 1988; Howes & Matheson, 1992). In its 1992 form, the proposed sequence begins with *parallel play* (peers are close together and engaging in the same activity but they do not acknowledge one another) and progresses sequentially to *simple social play* (peers engage in similar activity and in some further social interaction such as smiling, talking, or offering/taking toys), *complementary and reversible game roles* (peers enact complementary and reversible game roles in such games as run-and-chase or peek-a-boo), *cooperative social pretend play* (peers enact complementary roles within social pretend play), and *complex social pretend play* (social pretend play accompanied by some form of metacommunication such as naming the roles, assigning roles, or prompting one's partner).

In a longitudinal test of this sequence, 48 children in a variety of US day-care settings were observed six times, starting when they were between 13 and 24 months of age and then at successive six-month intervals (Howes & Matheson, 1992). The highest level of play complexity did indeed increase as expected with age. Complementary and reciprocal play was the highest level for the majority of children during their second year, whereas cooperative social pretend play was the highest level during the third year. These findings led to the claim that attaining complementary and reciprocal play was the central achievement of the second year of life – a conclusion that could be at odds with our emphasis on the role of imitative acts in generating games.

Several problems, however, arise in trying to relate these findings to those leading to the developmental progression of Table 12.2. Reciprocal imitation games are not explicitly mentioned in the Howes Peer Play Scale; hence we do not know how they were coded. More generally, the absence of descriptive information about the reciprocal and complementary play observed in the day-care centers means we cannot determine to what extent imitative acts occurred within these games. Remember that the games generated through imitative acts often had complementary role features to them as well as the reversal of roles. The focus in the day-care study, too, was upon determining the highest level of play achieved by a child at a given age, whereas the focus of the studies emphasizing imitative acts was more on how cooperative coordinated action was customarily generated. No distinction was made between rituals/routines and non-ritualized games in the day-care setting, whereas the developmental sequence of Table 12.2 emphasizes the role of imitative acts in enabling non-ritualized games. Finally, given the availability of peers of several different ages in the day-care context, we do not know whether the level of play seen for a child reflects the skills of that child versus the skills of an older child who scaffolded the younger child's activities. Scaffolding by an older child is plausible given that younger toddlers "prefer" interaction with older toddlers in day-care settings (e.g., Rothstein-Fisch & Howes, 1988) and that dyads composed of a younger and older toddler show some forms of interaction more characteristic of the older toddler (e.g., Brownell, 1990). Thus, it remains unclear from the studies of Howes and her colleagues whether toddlers in day-care settings show more coordinated action with only complementary roles or whether they, too, construct most of their cooperative coordinated action (games) using imitative acts. Although Camaioni, Baumgartner, and Perucchini (1991) explicitly sought to examine the developmental course of complementary versus imitative interactions within one Italian day-care center, their definitions of complementary and imitative interactions differed markedly from those of the studies already reviewed and hence cannot resolve this issue.

Fortunately, other research provides detailed descriptions of some of the phenomena found among young peers in day-care settings. Although this research does not document the developmental course of coordinated activity, it provides useful hints about development. For example, Verba and her colleagues (e.g., Stambak & Verba, 1986; Verba, 1994; Verba, Stambak, & Sinclair, 1982) observed small groups of familiar children (13- to 17-month-olds, 1.5- to 2-year-olds, and 2- to 4-year-olds) within day-care centers and preschools in France. Three different "modes of collaboration" were described as occurring within all three age groups (Verba, 1994). The *observation-elaboration* mode occurs when one child's activity triggers activity in another and serves as a model for the other child's activity. The second child either reproduces the same activity or elaborates/extends the activity. There is little further direct social exchange. The *co-construction* mode involves children putting their activities together to achieve a shared goal that either has been predefined or develops during the course of interaction. The activities of the children may be either similar or different. Negotiation occurs between the partners to establish joint understandings and the participants share management of the activity. Finally, in the *guided action* mode one child manages the interaction by guiding the activities of another child (e.g., through prompting or demonstration or affective signals) in relation to an explicit or inferred goal.

The examples detailed for each of these modes of collaboration during the first two years of life all include imitative acts as central features. Further, when the collaborations are extended ones, the descriptions are similar in flavor to the games described for toddlers brought together for research purposes. In one sequence between two 14-month-olds, for example, the two children first take turns licking a piece of paper, with some offering of the paper to each other. The sequence then evolves into exchanges of the paper without licking, and later into a short sequence of taking turns in both offering and licking the paper. These examples, too, illustrate the intermixing of imitative and complementary features in toddlers' cooperative coordinated action.

Beyond these similarities, the studies of Verba and her colleagues introduce two new elements. First, the conceptualization of the three modes of collaboration provides a useful tool for future studies of the developmental course of cooperative coordinated action. Second, examples of sustained cooperative coordinated action are provided for the youngest group observed (13- to 17-month-olds), suggesting that familiar peers in day-care contexts may generate sustained coordinated action at even younger ages than customarily observed for less familiar peers.

Another new element highlighted by studies in day-care contexts is the occurrence of routines, or well-practiced rituals of interaction, among young peers. Corsaro and Molinari (1990) analyzed three routines occurring within an Italian *asilo nido* (a day-care setting for children from about 6 months to 3 years of age). In one routine ("little chairs"), the children pushed several little chairs into the middle of the room, arranged them with other pieces of furniture into a path, and then walked on top of the chairs and furniture and jumped off with great noise and excitement. Again, the examples provided reveal features already emphasized in the laboratory-based research – a predominance of doing the same actions together or in turn (imitative acts), embellishments or slight alterations of the activities imitated (variations upon a theme), the intermixing of complementary features (e.g., putting a chair where a peer has pointed) with imitative action, and the use of verbalizations to regulate the largely nonverbal activity.

Such routines, while influenced by the physical characteristics of the day-care setting and perhaps by the activities adults structure for the children, nevertheless appear to be independent peer productions and core elements of what we might call the peer culture. Descriptions of routinized patterns of cooperative coordinated action also appear for peers meeting repeatedly in a playgroup (e.g., curtain-running; Brenner & Mueller, 1982), as well as in others' descriptions of toddlers' interactions in day-care centers (e.g., Lokken, 1996; Musatti & Panni, 1981). It remains to study how these routines get started and develop across time, determine the role of imitative acts in their formation, and determine how early in development they are seen and whether their frequency and/or form changes with the developmental status of the participants.

A phenomenon of "group glee" also has been detailed for toddlers in day-care settings, a phenomenon that seems at times a routine of interaction, and at other times a new construction. In her study of Norwegian toddlers in two day-care centers, Lokken (1996, personal communication) detailed episodes she called "group glee" after Sherman's (1975) description of these episodes among nursery school groups as "joyful screaming, laughing and intense physical acts which occurred in a simultaneous burst or which spread in a contagious fashion from one child to another." In 12 hours of videotaping there were at least 13 eruptions of group glee. The longest eruption lasted for 11 minutes and was described as a series of group glee "bubbles" successively rising to the water surface. Each bubble consisted of as many as six toddlers engaging together in such acts as banging on a table with laughter, shouts, and smiles. In some instances of group glee, fragments of activities engaged in with adult caregivers occurred (e.g., up to five well-known songs were recognizable). Other instances of group glee seemed to start out as fortuitous occurrences (e.g., hand clapping and thumping a table at the end of a meal), but then became ritualized to become a persistent part of ending the meal. Lokken suggested that participating in group glee furthered the feeling of being related to the group; thus, it too may be a component of the peer culture.

What, then, have we gleaned about the developmental course of coordinated peer action from studies of young peers in day-care settings? First, importantly, we find many parallels to the phenomena described for less familiar peers meeting in research settings (e.g., sustained episodes of cooperative coordinated action in which imitative acts play central roles, repeated changes in the elements added to or omitted from imitative acts that result in coordinations best described as variations on a theme, the intermixing of imitative and complementary features, and the use of words and conventional gestures to direct the largely nonverbal coordinated action). Second, sustained episodes of cooperative coordinated action may be seen at earlier ages in day-care contexts, although the reasons for this are not yet clear (e.g., the greater familiarity with specific peers, the greater experience in peer interaction, the presence of older toddlers who scaffold the efforts of younger ones, or greater ease in achieving jointly understood topics as a result of routines or rituals). Third, we find descriptions of specific routines of cooperative coordinated action in day-care settings that appear to be independent constructions of the children, rather than generalizations to peers of rituals engaged in with adults. It remains unclear, however, how these rituals emerge and change across time, the extent to which they are built upon fragments of activities with adults, whether such rituals are even earlier-emerging forms of cooperative coordinated action with peers than those forms that appear to be newly constructed on-the-spot, whether rituals are more characteristic of peer interactions in the day-care context than non-ritualized cooperative coordinated action, and what role imitative acts play in the generation of these rituals. Finally, these rituals as well as the phenomenon of group glee raise the possibility that coordinated activity among peers both generates and reflects a "peer culture" that develops within each day-care setting.

We can use these gleanings to speculate about how the developmental progression suggested earlier may need to be modified as we learn more about the interactions of toddlers in day-care contexts (see Table 12.3). First, rituals of cooperative coordinated action may develop among peers in familiar group contexts earlier than the non-ritualized forms that emerge among less familiar peers toward the end of the second year of life. With their parents, infants first become skillful partners in generating coordinated action within well-practiced rituals and only later become skillful in non-ritualized and non-scaffolded interactions. We may find a similar progression for peer interactions within day-care settings. Second, we may find that the three modes of collaboration distinguished by Verba and her colleagues form a developmental progression within rituals and/or non-ritualized forms of cooperative coordinated action. Young peers may first construct cooperative coordinated action in the observation-elaboration mode and only later in the co-construction and guided action modes. Third, we may find that the developmental

Table 12.3 Potential modifications to the developmental pathway of Table 12.2 suggested by studies of (1) coordinated action among toddlers in day-care settings and (2) peer conflicts

16 months and younger	*Conflicts and routines of cooperative coordinated action.* Conflictual coordinated action occurs as well as rituals or routines of cooperative coordinated action with peers (especially among toddlers meeting near-daily in group care settings). Both may contribute to the social and cognitive skills that later enable peers to generate non-ritualized forms of cooperative coordinated action.
20–24 months	*Modes of structuring cooperative coordinated action.* As non-ritualized forms of cooperative coordinated action appear among peers, a developmental progression may be found in how they are structured (e.g., from an observation-elaboration mode to co-construction and guided action modes). As the later modes emerge, truly collaborative problem solving with complementary roles becomes possible.
Throughout	*Variations in developmental pace and new group phenomena.* The typical ages for the emergence of new forms of coordinated action may differ for children in group day-care settings versus children with less exposure to peers and/or peers in a group context. Also, new phenomena of coordinated action may be found in day-care settings that reflect group processes and contribute to a peer culture.

pathway is sped up for familiar peers observed in day-care contexts. Finally, we may discover still further forms of coordinated action among peers in day-care contexts, and especially forms that appear the result of group processes.

Are Peer Conflicts Episodes of Coordinated Action?

Conflictual interactions also may inform us about the development of coordinated action. A conflictual act occurs when one participant opposes, actively resists, or interferes with the actions of another. For some researchers (e.g., Hay & Ross, 1982), a conflict begins with the first conflictual act and continues until there are no conflictual actions for at least 30 seconds. Others require that both participants engage in conflictual actions before a conflict is said to exist (e.g., Brenner & Mueller, 1982; Shantz, 1987); a conflictual act has to be met with an answering conflictual act. Note that both ways of defining a conflict demand less sustained coordinated action between peers (that is, acting on the same theme) than does the customary definition of a game, which requires at least two thematically related acts by each participant. Still, the second definition seems to possess the same two characteristics stressed for cooperative coordinated action; there is mutual social influence and the actions of the participants are thematically related.

In contrast to cooperative coordinated action, there is little evidence of developmental change in conflicts during the second year of life – in their frequency, duration, or topic (see review by Hay, 1984). While conflicts occur often when toddlers meet, they typically are quite brief and account for only a small proportion of their time together. Most conflicts involve struggles over play material, although sometimes toddlers protest behaviors not related to object possession (e.g., a hug or touch, or when a peer begins to act). Conflicts do become more verbal over the first three years of life, but descriptions of prolonged verbal conflicts only appear for preschoolers (e.g., Eisenberg & Garvey, 1981).

More informative for our purposes are studies detailing how children communicate and influence one another during conflicts. Hay and Ross (1982) have highlighted the social nature of conflicts over objects. The same pairs of initially unfamiliar 21-month-old toddlers were observed over three play sessions; and then for the fourth session, half the toddlers met again with the same peer and half met with a new peer. Several findings suggested that their conflicts were quite social affairs. First, conventional communicative gestures (e.g., gestures to go away or shaking the head "no") and words (e.g., "no," "mine," or "my ball") often occurred during the conflicts – behaviors that depend upon effective communication with another for their presumed desired effect. Second, there was a patterned structure to the conflict; different types of acts tended to occur at the beginning, middle, and end of conflicts. Third, the outcome of a prior conflict affected the next conflict; the child who lost the prior conflict was more likely to initiate the next one. Fourth, experience with a particular peer altered the toddlers' behavior during conflict; how ready a toddler was to yield during the fourth session could be predicted from the toddler's experience during the first three sessions, but only for those toddlers who met with the same peer rather than a new peer. Finally, there were indicators that power over the peer's actions might be a salient factor in these object-centered conflicts. The toddlers often dropped the toy they had just successfully wrested from or defended against the peer; or they showed no interest in the toy beside them until the peer reached for it.

Other analyses of conflicts also have highlighted their potential for communication and mutual influence. Bronson (1981) in longitudinal observations of familiar children in a group noted that the longest sequences of alternating peer-directed behaviors throughout the first two years of life were conflicts. Brenner and Mueller (1982), when looking for evidence of "shared meaning" in the interactions among peers in a playgroup, found that conflicts over objects provided one of the earliest forms of shared meaning. Only later did the children seem to share meanings in more cooperative interactions. Finally, Didow and Eckerman (1991) compared toddlers' use of speech with one another during conflicts and cooperative games; both contexts facilitated toddlers' use of speech. They argued that both games and conflicts readily led to joint understandings of what the two children were doing together and hence increased their use of speech.

We suggest that infants have relatively little trouble negotiating a common conflictual topic. Infants readily go to the play material another is manipulating and attempt to manipulate it also. Often these attempts interfere with another child's activities. Thus, a conflictual act occurs; and another's conflictual act, since it opposes, resists, or interferes with one's own action, has both a demand quality and an immediately clear, understandable relation to one's own actions – it interferes with it. The infant only has to attempt to continue in his or her own action to respond in a thematically related way, in this case with an answering conflictual act, and a conflict is established.

Realizing the different demands placed upon the infant to generate conflicts versus cooperative coordinated action helps explain why conflicts occur earlier in development. This realization also raises the provocative possibility that infants' experiences in conflicts may facilitate their development of the skills required for cooperative co-ordinated action. Could experience in peer conflicts aid toddlers in coming to understand distinctions between themselves and others and in viewing others as similar to themselves in being autonomous, intentional agents of action? Or, could experience in using words in conflicts aid toddlers in learning effective ways of using words to affect a peer? Viewing both conflicts and games as patterned interactions where acts are thematically related to one another and meaningful communication occurs, and realizing that young peers experience many conflicts before they start to generate sustained cooperative co-ordinated action together raise just such questions. Hopefully, they will prod further research.

Concluding Comments

It remains to ask what our understanding of the development of coordinated action between young peers suggests about the roles of peers in infant social/communicative development. Four points will be briefly mentioned. First, the study of what transpires between young peers has opened our eyes to the substantial demands placed upon a young child to generate cooperative coordinated action with another outside of well-practiced rituals of interaction and outside of scaffolded interactions with more skillful partners. The developmental pathway toward generating cooperative coordinated action with peers is a long and demanding one. By analyzing these demands and the skills required, studies of early peer interaction have highlighted questions about infants' social, communicative, and cognitive skills whose answers promise to greatly enrich our understanding of infant social/communicative development.

Second, the fact that peers are near equals in social/communicative skill means that when they do generate non-ritualized coordinated action with one another, they are more likely to be equal partners in both generating and maintaining the coordinated action than in interactions with their parents, other adults, or siblings. During play times with adults, toddlers often determine the topic for play depending upon what objects they engage and what they do with them; adults, then, build upon the toddlers' activities, actively adjusting their actions to those of the toddler to structure their time together and create alternating action on a common theme. With older siblings, toddlers less often even determine the topic of play; older siblings often direct toddlers' activities, telling them what to do and what to touch, performing antics with toys to engage the toddler's interest, and at times generally bossing them about (e.g., Dunn & Kendrick, 1982). Thus, in their interactions with peers, infants and toddlers often face more and harder task demands to make interpersonal things happen; and these task demands as well as infants' experiences upon successfully meeting them may well contribute distinctively to their social/communicative development.

Third, the coordinated action generated by peers provides distinctive experiences with others that may facilitate toddlers' development of social-cognitive skills. Reciprocal imitation games, for example, would seem a prime context for toddlers' experiencing both their separateness and similarity to one another as well as experiencing success in inferring another's goals/intentions. Separateness would seem facilitated by the turn-alternation structure of such games and variations in the imitative acts, while similarity would seem to be especially perceptually salient given that the two children are doing very similar actions. Further, success in inferring the goals/intentions of another would seem facilitated, given that the goal of the other is the same or similar to one's own – doing similar things together. Perhaps much of the excitement and attraction of extended bouts of doing similar things together results from these experiences. Even though adults and older children imitate toddlers' actions on occasion, they seldom do so for many routine play actions of toddlers (e.g., running, jumping, throwing objects, spitting) or the prolonged periods of time often involved in peer interactions. Similarly, conflicts during play likely occur more frequently among peers than with adults; and these too may provide distinctive opportunities for learning new social and cognitive skills.

Finally, among young peers who meet near-daily in group contexts, we may continue to find phenomena of coordinated action quite unlike those stressed with parents or siblings. Group glee and rituals that appear independent productions of the children have been mentioned so far, but we may discover many more such phenomena. These group phenomena, together with our understanding of how they originate/develop and of the functions they play in the "peer culture," also promise to greatly enhance our understanding of infants' social/communicative development.

Further Reading

Corsaro, W. A., & Molinari, L. (1990). From seggiolini to discussione: The generation and extension of peer culture among Italian preschool children. *Qualitative Studies in Education,* *3*(3), 213–230. This article provides ethnographic descriptions of young children's interactions in an *asilo nido* (6 months to 3 years) and *scuola materna* (3 to 6 years of age) in Bologna, Italy – group day-care contexts for preschool children. It discusses the methodology of participant observation and ethnographic description and presents detailed descriptions of three primarily nonverbal play routines that were produced consistently over the course of the school year by the younger peers. The routines of the younger children are compared to those of older children. The authors conclude that peer culture can emerge during the first two years of life and that this culture shares continuities with the peer culture of older preschool children.

Eckerman, C. O., Davis, C. C., & Didow, S. M. (1989). Toddlers' emerging ways of achieving social coordinations with a peer. *Child Development, 60,* 440–453. Fourteen pairs of initially unfamiliar, same-aged children were observed interacting in a laboratory playroom designed to facilitate cooperative coordinated action at four-month intervals – at 16, 20, 24, 28, and 32 months of age, using the type of detailed observational methodology and quantitative analysis of data favored by ethologists. This is the study that first highlighted the pivotal role of non-verbal imitation of each other's play actions in enabling young toddlers to form coordinated responses to each other's actions and sustained bouts of cooperative coordinated action (games) when specific rituals of interaction could not be depended upon. Its findings provide the basis for much of the developmental progression presented in Table 12.2.

Hay, D. F., & Ross, H. S. (1982). The social nature of early conflict. *Child Development, 53,* 105–113. Twenty-four pairs of initially unfamiliar 21-month-olds were observed in a laboratory free-play setting and all their conflicts involving objects were examined in fine detail. Each child was observed with the same partner on three consecutive days; and then on the fourth day, half the children met with the same partner while the other half met with a new partner. This study provided a conceptualization of conflict that has been very influential and a variety of findings that suggested that these conflicts involving objects were quite social affairs. There was patterned interaction, explicit communicative intent, and social influence both within a meeting and across successive meetings.

Ross, H. S. (1982). Establishment of social games among toddlers. *Developmental Psychology, 18*(4), 509–518. Pairs of 15-, 18-, 21-, and 24-month-olds were observed in a laboratory play setting. Some pairs at each age received prior training with an adult play partner in specific games that could be played with the toys that were available; the children of the remaining pairs played independently with these same toys. This experimental manipulation was an attempt to provide common experiences in how to play together with the toys (a short-term experience with the same rituals or routines of play), thinking that such experiences might aid especially the younger toddlers in generating cooperative coordinated action together. The overwhelming finding, however, was that the toddlers used new play actions to invite the peer to play, to respond to play invitations, and to play games. Games became more frequent at older ages, and much descriptive detail is provided about the structural complexity of the games generated.

Verba, M. (1994). The beginnings of collaboration in peer interaction. *Human Development, 37,* 125–139. Three groups of young peers (13- to 17-month-olds, 1.5- to 2-year-olds, and 2- to 4-year-olds) were videotaped in their day-care centers and preschools in France while engaged in spontaneous activities with objects. Each episode of shared activity with the objects was analyzed qualitatively, resulting in a conceptualization of three basic modes of co-elaboration that were observed in all three groups. These three modes were an observation-elaboration mode in which one child's activity seemed to trigger the related activity of another without any further direct social exchange, a co-construction mode in which two children put their ideas/actions together to achieve a shared goal, and guided activity in which the related activity of one child is carried out through the help/guidance of the other child. Detailed descriptions illustrating these modes are presented for the youngest group of peers, and the similarity between the modes of collaboration across age groups leads to the claim for a functional continuity in social-cognitive processes from infancy to the preschool period.

References

Adamson, L. B. (1996). *Communication development during infancy.* Madison, WI: Brown & Benchmark.

Ainsworth, M. D. S., Blehar, M. C., Waters, E., & Wall, S. (1977). *Patterns of attachment.* Hillsdale, NJ: Erlbaum.

Asendorpf, J. B., & Baudonniere, P. (1993). Self-awareness and other-awareness: Mirror self-recognition and synchronic imitation among unfamiliar peers. *Developmental Psychology, 29*, 88–95.

Asendorpf, J. B., Warkenton, V., & Baudonniere, P. (1996). Self-awareness and other-awareness II: Mirror self-recognition, social contingency awareness, and synchronic imitation. *Developmental Psychology, 32*(2), 313–321.

Bakeman, R., & Adamson, L. B. (1984). Coordinating attention to people and objects in mother–infant and peer–infant interaction. *Child Development, 55*, 1278–1289.

Baudonniere, P. (1988). Evolution in mode of social exchange in 2, 3 and 4 year old peers. *European Bulletin of Cognitive Psychology, 8*(3), 241–263.

Becker, J. M. (1977). A learning analysis of the development of peer-oriented behavior in nine-month-old infants. *Developmental Psychology, 13*, 481–491.

Bowlby, J. (1969). *Attachment and loss: Vol. 1. Attachment.* London: Hogarth Press.

Brazelton, T. B., Koslowski, B., & Main, M. (1974). The origins of reciprocity: The early mother–infant interaction. In M. Lewis & L. A. Rosenblum (Eds.), *The effect of the infant on its caregiver* (pp. 49–76). New York: Wiley.

Brenner, J., & Mueller, E. (1982). Shared meaning in boy toddlers' peer relations. *Child Development, 53*, 380–391.

Bridges, K. M. B. (1933). A study of social development in early infancy. *Child Development, 4*, 36–49.

Bronson, W. C. (1981). *Toddlers' behaviors with agemates: Issues of interaction, cognition, and affect.* Norwood, NJ: Ablex.

Brownell, C. A. (1986). Convergent developments: Cognitive-developmental correlates of growth in infant/toddler peer skills. *Child Development, 57*, 275–286.

Brownell, C. A. (1988). Combinational skills: Converging developments over the second year. *Child Development, 59*, 675–685.

Brownell, C. A. (1990). Peer social skills in toddlers: Competencies and constraints illustrated by same-age and mixed-age interaction. *Child Development, 61*, 838–848.

Brownell, C. A., & Carriger, M. S. (1990). Changes in cooperation and self–other differentiation during the second year. *Child Development, 61*, 1164–1174.

Brownell, C. A., & Carriger, M. S. (1991). Collaborations among toddler peers: Individual contributions to social contexts. In L. B. Resnick, J. M. Levine, & S. D. Teasley (Eds.), *Perspectives on socially shared cognition* (pp. 365–383). Washington, DC: American Psychological Association.

Bruner, J. (1983). *Child's talk: Learning to use language.* New York: W. W. Norton.

Buhler, C. (1930). *From birth to maturity: An outline of the psychological development of the child.* London: Routledge & Kegan Paul.

Bullock, M., & Lutkenhaus, P. (1988). The development of volitional behavior in the toddler years. *Child Development, 59*, 664–674.

Camaioni, L., Baumgartner, E., & Perucchini, P. (1991). Content and structure in toddlers' social competence with peers from 12 to 36 months of age. *Early Child Development and Care, 67*, 17–27.

Corsaro, W. A., & Molinari, L. (1990). From seggiolini to discussione: The generation and extension of peer culture among Italian preschool children. *Qualitative Studies in Education, 3*(3), 213–230.

Didow, S. M., & Eckerman, C. O. (April, 1991). *Developments in toddlers' talk with unfamiliar peers.* Poster presented at the Biennial Meeting of the Society for Research in Child Development, Seattle, WA.

Dunn, J., & Kendrick, C. (1982). *Siblings: Love, envy, and understanding.* Cambridge, MA: Harvard University Press.

Eckerman, C. O. (1993a). Toddlers' achievement of coordinated action with conspecifics: A dynamic systems perspective. In L. B. Smith & E. Thelen (Eds.), *A dynamic systems approach to development* (pp. 333–357). Cambridge, MA: MIT Press.

Eckerman, C. O. (1993b). Imitation and toddlers' achievement of co-ordinated action with others. In J. Nadel & L. Camaioni (Eds.), *New perspectives in early communicative development* (pp. 116–156). London: Routledge.

Eckerman, C. O., Davis, C. C., & Didow, S. M. (1989). Toddlers' emerging ways of achieving social coordinations with a peer. *Child Development, 60,* 440–453.

Eckerman, C. O., & Didow, S. M. (1988). Lessons drawn from observing young peers together. *Acta Paediatrica Scandinavica, 77,* 55–70.

Eckerman, C. O., & Didow, S. M. (1989). Toddlers' social coordinations: Changing responses to another's invitation to play. *Developmental Psychology, 25*(5), 794–804.

Eckerman, C. O., & Didow, S. M. (1996). Nonverbal imitation and toddlers' mastery of verbal means of achieving coordinated action. *Developmental Psychology, 32*(1), 141–152.

Eckerman, C. O., & Stein, M. R. (1982). The toddler's emerging interactive skills. In K. H. Rubin & H. S. Ross (Eds.), *Peer relationships and social skills in childhood* (pp. 41–71). New York: Springer Verlag.

Eckerman, C. O., & Stein, M. R. (1990). How imitation begets imitation and toddlers' generation of games. *Developmental Psychology, 26,* 370–378.

Eckerman, C. O., & Whatley, J. L. (1977). Toys and social interaction between infant peers. *Child Development, 48,* 1645–1656.

Eckerman, C. O., Whatley, J. L., & Kutz, S. L. (1975). Growth of social play with peers during the second year of life. *Developmental Psychology, 11*(1), 42–49.

Eckerman, C. O., Whatley, J. L., & McGehee, L. J. (1979). Approaching and contracting the object another manipulates: A social skill of the 1-year-old. *Developmental Psychology, 15,* 585–593.

Eckerman, C. O., & Whitehead, H. (1999). How toddler peers generate coordinated action: A cross cultural exploration. *Early Education and Development, 10,* 241–266.

Eisenberg, A., & Garvey, C. (1981). Children's use of verbal strategies in resolving conflicts. *Discourse Processes, 4,* 149–170.

Frye, D. (1991). The origins of intention in infancy. In D. Frye & C. Moore (Eds.), *Children's theories of mind. Mental states and social understanding* (pp. 15–38). Hillsdale, NJ: Lawrence Erlbaum Associates.

Garvey, C. (1974). Some properties of social play. *Merrill-Palmer Quarterly, 20,* 163–180.

Grusec, J. E., & Abramovitch, R. (1982). Imitation of peers and adults in a natural setting: A functional analysis. *Child Development, 53,* 636–642.

Hay, D. F. (1984). Social conflict in early childhood. *Annals of Child Development, 1,* 1–44.

Hay, D. F., Pedersen, J., & Nash, A. (1982). Dyadic interaction in the first year of life. In K. H. Rubin & H. S. Ross (Eds.), *Peer relationships and social skills in childhood* (pp. 11–39). New York: Springer Verlag.

Hay, D. F., & Ross, H. S. (1982). The social nature of early conflict. *Child Development, 53,* 105–113.

Howes, C. (1980). Peer play scale as an index of complexity of peer interaction. *Developmental Psychology, 16,* 371–372.

Howes, C. (1988). Peer interaction of young children. *Monographs of the Society for Research in Child Development, 53*(1), 1–78.

Howes, C., & Matheson, C. C. (1992). Sequences in the development of competent play with peers: Social and social pretend play. *Developmental Psychology, 28*(5), 961–974.

Howes, C., & Stewart, P. (1987). Child's play with adults, toys and peers: An examination of family and child-care influences. *Developmental Psychology, 23*(3), 423–430.

Klimes-Dougan, B. (1993, April). *The emergence of negotiation.* Poster presented at the Biennial Meeting of the Society for Research in Child Development, New Orleans, LA.

Lokken, G. (1996). *Nar sma barn motes* (When early toddlers meet). Oslo: Cappelen Akademisk Forlag.

Maudry, M., & Nekula, M. (1939). Social relationships between children of the same age during the first two years of life. *Journal of Genetic Psychology, 54*, 193–215.

Meltzoff, A. N. (1995). Understanding the intentions of others: Re-enactment of intended acts by 18-month-old children. *Developmental Psychology, 31*(5), 838–850.

Mueller, E., & Brenner, J. (1977). The origins of social skills and interaction among playgroup toddlers. *Child Development, 48*, 854–861.

Mueller, E., & Lucas, T. A. (1975). A developmental analysis of peer interaction among toddlers. In M. Lewis & L. A. Rosenblum (Eds.), *Friendship and peer relations* (pp. 223–258). New York: Wiley.

Mueller, E., & Vandell, D. (1979). Infant–infant interaction. In J. D. Osofsky (Ed.), *Handbook of infant development* (pp. 591–622). New York: Wiley Interscience.

Musatti, T., & Mueller, E. (1985). Expressions of representational growth in toddlers' peer communication. *Social Cognition, 3*(4), 383–399.

Musatti, T., & Panni, S. (1981). Social behavior and interaction among day care center toddlers. *Early Child Development and Care, 7*, 5–27.

Nadel, J. (1986). *Imitation and communication between young children* (Vol. 5). Paris: Presses Universitaires de France.

Nadel, J., & Fontaine, A. (1989). Communicating by imitation: A developmental and comparative approach to transitory social competence. In B. H. Schneider, G. Attili, J. Nadel, & R. P. Weissberg (Eds.), *Social competence in developmental perspective* (pp. 131–144). London: Kluwer Academic Publishers.

Nadel-Brulfert, J., & Baudonniere, P. M. (1982). The social function of reciprocal imitation in 2-year-old peers. *International Journal of Behavioral Development, 5*, 95–109.

O'Connell, B. G., & Gerard, A. B. (1985). Scripts and scraps: The development of sequential understanding. *Child Development, 56*, 671–681.

Pipp, S., Fisher, K. W., & Jennings, S. (1987). Acquisition of self- and mother-knowledge in infancy. *Developmental Psychology, 23*, 86–96.

Ramey, C. T., Finkelstein, N. W., & O'Brien, C. (1976). Toys and infant behavior in the first year of life. *Journal of Genetic Psychology, 129*, 341–342.

Roopnarine, J. L., & Field, T. M. (1983). Peer-directed behaviors of infants and toddlers during nursery school play. *Infant Behavior and Development, 6*, 133–138.

Ross, H. S. (1982). Establishment of social games among toddlers. *Developmental Psychology, 18*(4), 509–518.

Ross, H. S., & Lollis, S. P. (1987). Communication within infant social games. *Developmental Psychology, 23*(2), 241–248.

Rothstein-Fisch, C., & Howes, C. (1988). Toddler peer interaction in mixed-aged groups. *Journal of Applied Developmental Psychology, 9*, 211–218.

Schaffer, R. (1984). *The child's entry into a social world.* London: Academic Press.

Shantz, C. U. (1987). Conflicts between children. *Child Development, 58*, 283–305.

Sherman, L. W. (1975). An ecological study of glee in small groups of preschool children. *Child Development, 46*, 53–61.

Stambak, M., & Verba, M. (1986). Organization of social play among toddlers: An ecological approach. In E. Mueller & C. R. DeLooper (Eds.), *Process and outcome in peer relationships* (pp. 229–247). New York: Academic Press.

Stern, D. N. (1974). Mother and infant at play: The dyadic interaction involving facial, vocal and gaze behaviour. In M. Lewis & L. A. Rosenblum (Eds.), *The effect of the infant on its caregiver* (pp. 187–214). New York: Wiley.

Tomasello, M., & Farrar, M. J. (1986). Joint attention and early language. *Child Development, 57,* 1454–1463.

Uzgiris, I. C. (1991). The social context of infant imitation. In M. Lewis & S. Feinman (Eds.), *Social influences and socialization in infancy* (pp. 215–251). New York: Plenum Press.

Vandell, D. L., Wilson, K. S., & Buchanan, N. R. (1980). Peer interaction in the first year of life: An examination of its structure, content and sensitivity to toys. *Child Development, 51,* 481–488.

Verba, M. (1994). The beginnings of collaboration in peer interaction. *Human Development, 37,* 125–139.

Verba, M., Stambak, M., & Sinclair, H. (1982). Physical knowledge and social interaction in children from 18 to 24 months of age. In G. Forman (Ed.), *Action and thought: From sensorimotor schemes to symbolic operations* (pp. 267–296). New York: Academic Press.

Vincze, M. (1971). The social contacts of infants and young children reared together. *Early Child Development and Care, 1,* 99–109.

Chapter Thirteen

The Salience of Touch and Physical Contact During Infancy: Unraveling Some of the Mysteries of the Somesthetic Sense

Dale M. Stack

It has always fascinated me that two of the earliest sensory experiences in fetal development, touch and pain, are also the experiences that help us stay in contact with life until life ends.

Fanslow (1984, p. 183)

Overview

The primary objective of this chapter is to provide a detailed overview of the research regarding touch and development. Given that the chapter is placed in the social, emotional, and communicative part of the handbook, and due to recent directions in the field, the emphasis will be on touch as it occurs in a social context, between an infant and another person, usually its caregiver. One objective of the present chapter is to highlight the importance of parental (especially maternal) touch in early social and emotional development, specifically focusing on its role(s) in social contexts and communication. The goal is to provide evidence for the contributions of parental and adult touch to early interactions and the developing relationship. Although it is important to note that these contributions extend into cognition and perception by providing the context within which to practice and learn new skills, a discussion of these domains is beyond the scope of the chapter. A second objective is to draw together diverse lines of research on touch

This chapter was written with the support of Conseil Québécois de la Recherche Sociale (CQRS) and Fonds pour la Formation de Chercheurs et l'Aide à la Recherche (FCAR). The author expresses her gratitude to Yves Beaulieu and Diane Poulin-Dubois for their detailed comments on an earlier version of this chapter, and to Alan Fogel for his thorough review. Thanks are also extended to Marie-Hélène Brody, Nadine Girouard, and Barbara Welburn for their help with literature searches, library work, and preparation of the final version of the chapter.

and physical contact and integrate these findings into an emerging body of literature which both underscores the importance of touch and physical contact and at the same time points to new directions of investigation.

Introduction

The somesthetic system (kinesthetic and cutaneous processes) is the earliest sensory system to develop in the human embryo (Maurer & Maurer, 1988; Montagu, 1971), followed by the vestibular, auditory, and visual systems (Gottlieb, 1983). Given that the skin is the largest sensory system in the body, the fact that its capacities are among the most basic, and the fact that this system matures early, it seems reasonable to expect that the somesthetic system plays a fundamental role in development. Somesthesis collectively includes kinesthetic sensitivity, referring to spatial position and movement information derived from mechanical stimulation of the muscles and joints, and cutaneous sensitivity, referring to the sensitivity of the skin to touch, pressure, temperature, or pain (Klatzky & Lederman, 1987; Schiffman, 1982). For purposes of the present chapter, the emphasis is on cutaneous sensitivity, specifically the infant's sensitivity and responsivity to human touching. However, because it is difficult to separate the tactile from the kinesthetic component, the use of the term "touch" refers to both components. Although the size of the system and its early development suggest a system of fundamental importance, the volume of research specifically associated with the tactile modality is scant and diverse. Yet along with its early developmental timing, it is known that fetuses respond to vibroacoustic stimulation while developing in the womb (e.g., Kisilevsky & Low, 1998; Kisilevsky, Muir, & Low, 1992; Lecanuet, Fifer, Krasnegor, & Smotherman, 1995; Lecanuet, Granier-Deferre, & Bushnel, 1989), and that touch/pressure is one of the first sensations newborns experience (e.g., Maurer & Maurer, 1988; Schiffman, 1982).

Importance of Touch for Nonhuman Species

Evidence for the importance of tactile stimulation for normal development of nonhuman species is well established. Examples include the survival functions of maternal washing of the young (Montagu, 1971) and the specific beneficial effects of handling on survival (Hamnett, 1921, 1922), growth, development, and resistance to disease (Denenberg, 1968), as well as increased exploratory behavior (Denenberg, 1969). Harlow's (1959) classic work with rhesus monkeys substantiated the importance of tactile stimulation by demonstrating that contact was more important than reducing the feeding drive for the development of social attachment.

Research with rat pups has shown that a mother's licking and grooming of her pup regulates its growth (Kuhn & Schanberg, 1998; Schanberg & Field, 1987). This important regulatory function, which is only served by the mother, has been investigated by Hofer (1993) in his work on separation and its effects. Among other things, he demonstrated that the mother regulates her infant rat pup's physiology and behavior, and that there is a sensory foundation to the mother–infant bond. Stern (1989, 1990, 1996, 1997) contends that rat pups impel their mothers to nurture them, largely in the form of tactile stimulation. Relatedly, Schanberg and colleagues (e.g., Kuhn & Schanberg, 1998) have shown that maternal separation, even for just one hour, produces a decrease in the enzyme, ornithine decarboxylase, an enzyme necessary for growth. They have also shown that this change is directly related to the lack of a specific form of tactile stimulation enacted on the pup by the mother, namely, maternal licking (Schanberg & Field, 1987).

Suomi (1997) has described nonverbal communication in nonhuman primates such as the rhesus monkey, and argues that tactile stimulation is at the root of such activities as grooming, play, and sexual and aggressive episodes, and it continues in the form of rough-and-tumble play. Additional data from primate and rodent models have implicated physical contact and touch (tactile stimulation) as significant concomitants of the infant's ability to regulate its own responses to stress (Levine, 1956, 1960; Levine & Stanton, 1990).

Importance of Touch for Human Infants

The importance of touch for human infants has not gone unnoticed. Classic observations on maternal deprivation of humans and the lack of tactile stimulation underscored the potential value of tactile contact (Provence & Lipton, 1962; Spitz & Wolf, 1946). There were reports of catastrophic effects on infants who were deprived of mothering for lengthy periods of time and institutionalized infants who were given only the essential care with no extra attention from staff (Provence & Lipton, 1962; Spitz & Wolf, 1946). This work, at least in part, led to more systematic work on maternal attachment, bonding, and deprivation. According to Casler (1961, 1968), the crucial factors contributing to the development and behavior of institutionalized infants are the degree of sensory stimulation and the range of experiences. In contrast, Ainsworth (1962) argued that the lack of intimate relationships is the factor responsible for institutionalized children's problems. Unfortunately, the maternal deprivation literature is replete with methodological problems, permitting only cautious interpretations. Owing to these limitations, the results from past studies cannot answer the question of the necessity of touch for optimal development of the human organism.

Despite advances and the acknowledged importance of tactile stimulation, the specific contribution of tactile stimulation to early development (e.g., first year of life) remains relatively undefined. There is evidence to suggest that touch regulates physiological and behavioral reactions (e.g., Brazelton, 1990; Montagu, 1986) during early infant development. That is, touch can aid in controlling the state of arousal (behavioral state, i.e., maintaining alertness, reducing drowsiness, etc.), where state is considered to be an organized pattern of responding, at the physical and physiological levels, which is related to the activation of the infant (Fogel, 1997). Touch is also an effective stimulus for soothing neonates (Birns, Blank, & Bridger, 1966; Korner & Thoman, 1972). In a study conducted by Korner and Thoman (1972), the magnitude of success in reducing crying was greatest when contact had vestibular-proprioceptive stimulation. Nonetheless, contact alone was effective. In the natural environment, tactile contact and vestibular-proprioceptive stimulation are often paired to soothe the baby. In addition, rocking on the shoulder in the upright position, which includes contact, has been demonstrated to be effective in quieting distressed newborns of 24–72 hours (Byrne & Horowitz, 1981), relative to infants merely held at the shoulder or given no intervention at all.

The effects of touch/contact are also seen in studies where touch is used to induce or change behavioral state. That is, in many studies touch or tactile-kinesthetic stimulation is used between intervals of a study to maintain alert state in babies, to calm them, or as an attention-getting stimulus (e.g., Barrera & Maurer, 1981; Muir & Field, 1979). In the neonate, touch can reduce stimulation, acting like a control system to maintain state. According to Brazelton (1984), touch can also stimulate the infant, illustrating how touch can both instigate and maintain communication. Research with humans has also suggested that nonverbal maternal behaviors provide a means of modulating the overall level of stimulation to which the infant is exposed, potentially facilitating regulation of its own state and level of arousal (e.g., Koester, Papoušek, & Papoušek, 1989).

Studies of tactile stimulation have focused, to a large extent, on its potential for aiding the physical or perceptual development of high-risk infants. For example, tactile-kinesthetic stimulation (often in the form of stroking and flexion and extension, but in some cases verbal information and encouragement of tactile stimulation) has been shown to increase weight gain and caloric intake in premature infants (e.g., Helders, Cats, & Debast, 1989; Scafidi et al., 1990; Watt, 1990). As a result of this focus on physical and sensory development, less attention has been devoted to touch as it relates to infants' social and emotional development. Moreover, there has been a general lack of research on the tactile modality until recently, evidenced by an apparent relative neglect of tactile over auditory and visual modalities in perceptual research and over facial and vocal channels in social-emotional research. If touch is so fundamental, the question can be raised as to whether it is a communication channel and, if so, what is communicated. This issue will figure more prominently later in the chapter. In the proceeding sections the available literature relevant to touch, its effects, and its role(s) during the period of infancy, particularly as they pertain to social-emotional development, will be covered. Special emphasis will be given to the first year of life, because it is the most researched period to date. As well, in most of the literature reviewed it is the mother who is the participant; there are fewer studies conducted with fathers to date.

Physical Contact Between Parent and Newborn: The Benefits of Touch

Physical contact between parent(s) and their newborn, immediately following the birth as well as several months later, has received some research attention. For example, specific forms of maternal contact of their young are displayed by various species. As described earlier, immediate maternal licking of the newborn of several species (e.g., rat pups) serves a cutaneous function necessary for survival (Montagu, 1971, 1986). Other forms of contact continue after birth. For example, primates exhibit varying amounts and patterns of holding, carrying, touching, and grooming. On the basis of his and other similar observations, Montagu suggests an evolutionary progression from licking to tooth combing to finger grooming to hand stroking or caressing (seen in humans). Schiefen-hövel (1997) contends that social grooming (grooming that takes place by one or more individuals [groomers] toward one individual [groomee]) is a "phylogenetically rooted, culturally repressed behavior" (p. 70). That is, while still occurring in humans of industrialized countries, Scheifenhövel argues that grooming is much reduced, and often activities considered social grooming are professionalized (e.g., hair stylist, dermatologist, manicurist, pedicurist, etc.). However, social types of grooming behaviors occur between parents and their children, even in industrialized societies. Social grooming is also common among mammals, occurs in diverse species of birds and even among insects. It is also seen in traditional societies (e.g., Eipo of Western New Guinea, Trobriand Islanders of Eastern New Guinea, Bayaka Oygmies, etc.; Schiefenhövel, 1997), and includes, among other activities, cleaning the body surface of the newborn, removing skin scales, and gentle massage. What is notable about social-grooming activities for purposes of this chapter is that they typically involve touching.

The socialization of human newborns and their parents, that first relationship, begins early, even in the womb. Beyond its survival value, contact and affection between mother/father and infant are likely to serve the infant's developing social and emotional needs. One aspect of research on the role of maternal contact with her newborn has examined whether there are commonalities in how mothers touch their newborns (e.g., Carlsson et al., 1978; de Chateau, 1976; Klaus, Kennell, Plumb, & Zuelke, 1970; Rubin, 1963; Trevathan, 1981). For example, Rubin (1963) reported that mothers follow a specific pattern of touching when first handling their newborns, beginning by using their fingertips then full palms to examine first the infant's extremities, and then the trunk. Klaus et al. (1970) not only confirmed Rubin's findings but also found that mothers of preterm infants follow the same pattern, but at a slower rate. This pattern has also been displayed by fathers (Yogman, 1982), although they take longer to show the progression. In contrast, Trevathan (1981) disputes the argument favoring a species-typical pattern of touching, as he found no evidence of an invariant pattern of maternal tactile behavior. Consistent with Trevathan, Tulman (1985) compared mothers and unfamiliar nursing students' initial handling of newborns; she found differences between the groups but it was the students rather than the mothers who followed the typical pattern reported in the literature.

Kaitz and colleagues (Kaitz, Lapidot, Bronner, & Eidelman, 1992; Kaitz, Meirov, Landman, & Eidelman, 1993) demonstrated that mothers are uniquely sensitive to their newborns through the tactile sense. Using an innovative design and procedure, they were able to show that mothers could recognize their own baby 5–79 hours after delivery by stroking the dorsal surface of their infant's hand, and this was without the added benefit of visual, auditory, and olfactory cues. That is, mothers were blindfolded and their noses were covered with a scarf. On the basis of their findings, they argued that mothers learn the special tactile characteristics of their infant during the course of routine contact and interaction.

Studies have also been conducted on maternal contact with newborn infants and its effects. Often this body of work is subsumed under what is known as "bonding." Bonding is viewed differently than attachment because it is considered a unidirectional affectional tie from the parent to the infant, and it is believed to form rapidly during the first hours and days following birth (Campbell & Taylor, 1980; Toney, 1983). Physical contact is thought to enhance the effects, and some believed that the bonding that occurred had lasting effects on subsequent development and the parent–child relationship. Lamb and Hwang (1982) in their evaluation of the literature cautiously claimed that early contact may have immediate positive effects but that long-term effects occur less reliably because replications of findings have been rare, and where there is some degree of replication other methodological problems plague the research. Nonetheless, observations of parents' first contacts with their newborns reveal the use of touch as integral and seemingly central to those first communications.

In a study investigating the effects of maternal contact, Carlsson et al. (1978) found that extended body contact between mother and newborn immediately after delivery was related to an increase in what the authors refer to as affective components of maternal nursing behavior observed 2 to 4 days later; that is, increased contact behaviors such as rubbing, rocking, touching, and holding were shown during nursing and there were fewer non-contact behaviors. The authors substantiated the claim of Klaus et al. (1972) that events occurring immediately after birth influence subsequent maternal behavior. Along similar lines, de Chateau (1976) examined the influence of a close, natural contact between mothers and their newborns after delivery who were given 10–15 min of extra contact during the first post-partum hour on later behavior at 3 days and 3 months. Mothers with extra contact experience showed more holding, encompassing, looking "en face," and less cleaning behaviors at 36 hours than mothers provided with only routine care. Infants with extra contact smiled more and cried less at the 3-month observation. While cautioning that such a brief period of contact cannot explain all the differences, de Chateau (1976) concluded that neonatal care influences maternal behavior, noting that brief initial contact has an effect.

Incorporating a different means to capture the early touching behaviors occurring between mothers and their newborns, Robin (1982) analyzed videotapes of maternal tactile contacts in the days following birth, looking at both fullterm and premature neonate–mother dyads. Findings indicated that utilitarian contacts (e.g., wiping the infant's mouth, cleaning, patting for a burp, etc.). were the most frequent in an 8-min observation period which included a feeding, followed closely by face and hand contacts. Neither birth order, term, or infant age seemed to distinguish the frequency of these contacts; however, a greater frequency of maternal tactile contacts were shown with female infants.

Beyond contact at birth, infants' responses to the complexity of naturally occurring patterns of touch provided to them by adults are also reflected in the descriptions of infant massage. According to Field (1998), touch therapies, and particularly massage therapy, were primary forms of medicine before the advent of the pharmaceutical age and they date back to at least 1800 BC. Leboyer (1976) graphically illustrates an East Indian body massage lasting 30 min completed daily on infants up to 6 months of age. Leboyer's premise is that infants' bodies crave touch. Although his work was descriptive with no experimental manipulations undertaken, the technique of body massage is designed to relieve tension and anxiety, facilitate relaxation, and in infant massage, transmit love from the caregiver to the infant. Reissland and Burghart (1987) discuss the importance of massage in Mithila (South Asia), where women are expected to massage their infants daily.

Some of the assumed benefits include hardening bone structure, enhancing movement and coordination, and even instilling fearlessness.

As part of the Sunraysia Australia Intervention Project, Samuels, Scholz, and Edmundson (1992) found positive effects of baby relaxation baths and massage. Families in the treatment group were shown (and fathers practiced) the baby bath and massage techniques at the 4-week visit, while comparison families were not. On the basis of time diaries completed daily between the 4- and 12-week visits, fathers in the treatment group bathed and massaged their infants more relative to the comparison group. This was an important goal of their intervention project (Scholz & Samuels, 1992). In addition, higher degrees of marital satisfaction and self-esteem were shown, as well as lower levels of post-partum depression at the 12-week visit. However, their study sample consisted of only 32 couples and it is likely that other factors may also have played a role.

It is not clear from these studies what beneficial effects these handling and massage practices have on socioemotional development and on the parent–infant relationship. However, what is clear is that it is a daily routine where parent and infant spend circumscribed amounts of time together. While there are limitations, it appears from these studies that positive effects may be observed on the whole family system, rather than solely impacting on the infant.

What is also clear from the preceding discussion is that there are diverse roles for touching in the newborn period. Beyond the significance it holds for nonhuman species, the role for touch in human development has been demonstrated. From its importance in growth and development, to early contact and touching behaviors, to massage, to mothers being able to recognize their own newborn through touch, it is apparent that the sense of touch holds meaning for both parent and infant.

Beyond the Newborn Period: Adult–Infant Touching in Social Contexts

It is only recently that researchers have begun to explore the role of touch in early interactions. In the past the focus was on the more distal behavioral indices of gaze and affect to the relative exclusion of touch and gesture. Yet touch is commonly employed by mothers, along with their vocal and visual expressions, during face-to-face interactions and during play. For example, during face-to-face interactions, the infant and adult (primarily the mother) are seated at eye-level to each other during a series of brief interaction periods. Caregivers interact spontaneously, using their facial, vocal, and tactile expressions, while infants themselves respond to and even initiate interactions. Face-to-face interactions have been one of the primary means used to study the infant's social communication (Kaye & Fogel, 1980), emotional expressions and responses to stressful episodes (Field, Vega-Lahr, Scafidi, & Goldstein, 1986), and the development of social expectations (Cohn & Tronick, 1983). However, typically, researchers have analyzed maternal and infant facial and vocal behavior, but not touch, although incidental reports reveal that maternal touch occurs during 33 percent to 61 percent of brief interaction periods (e.g., Field, 1984; Kaye & Fogel, 1980; Symons & Moran, 1987). Recently, other measures such as posture (Fogel, Dedo, & McEwen, 1992), manual hand actions (Toda & Fogel, 1993), and gesture (Stack & Arnold, 1998) have been documented. Contextual features such as location during play, position, inclination of position, proximity of contact, etc., are other examples of what appear to be important factors in influencing the infant's engagement during face-to-face play (e.g., Lavelli & Fogel, 1998; Stack, Arnold, Girouard, & Welburn, 1999).

Still-Face Studies

The still-face (SF) procedure (Tronick, Als, Adamson, Wise, & Brazelton, 1978), a modification of the face-to-face procedure, has proven to be a valuable tool to examine the role of touching. The mother–infant interaction is divided into three brief periods (90–120 sec). In period 1, mothers interact normally, using facial expression, voice, and touch (Normal), in period 2 they assume a neutral, non-responsive still face and provide neither vocal nor tactile stimulation (SF), and in period 3 they resume Normal interaction. During the SF compared to Normal periods, infants typically decrease gazing and smiling at mothers (Gusella, Muir, & Tronick, 1988; Lamb, Morrison, & Malkin, 1987; Mayes & Carter, 1990), increase neutral to negative affect, and increase vocalizing (Ellsworth, Muir, & Hains, 1993; Stack & Muir, 1990).

Gusella et al. (1988) compared the responses during SF periods between groups of infants where some infants received maternal touch in the preceding Normal period, and others received only maternal face and voice. They found that 3-month-olds smiled and gazed less at mothers during the SF than during the Normal period (compared to a no-change control group who received three Normal periods), but their behavior was significantly different from the control group only when maternal touch was permitted during the Normal period preceding the SF. That is, 3-month-olds exhibited the SF effect only when maternal touching was part of the prior Normal periods and their attention declined over time without the tactile stimulation. This suggests, according to Gusella et al., that maternal touch during the Normal periods facilitated the maintenance of attention in these very young infants.

Indirect evidence to support the importance of touch in early interactions is derived from a study by Field et al. (1986). They compared responses of 4-month-olds to a SF episode with those to a separation sequence and reported that the infants found the SF sequence more stressful. For example, infants demonstrated more motor activity, gaze aversion, distress brow, and crying, and less smiling. More maternal tactile-kinesthetic behavior was shown following the SF period. That is, maternal proximal and comforting behaviors were potentiated. These findings support the view that infants are sensitive to maternal cues, and suggest both the soothing role and communicative nature of touching.

Studies examining infants' responsiveness to their mother's touch and their sensitivity to touch when other forms of stimulation are absent provide important insight into why mothers use touch during the first 6 months of life. A number of studies have helped to elucidate these important issues. By comparing a standard SF with one where mothers could touch during the SF period (SF with touch), Stack and Muir (1990) showed that by adding touch infants were not distressed, they showed increased smiling, and they maintained the high levels of gaze that are typical in Normal interactions. This new role for touch in moderating the SF effect has been replicated a number of times (e.g., Peláez-Nogueras, Field, et al., 1996; Stack & LePage, 1996; Stack & Muir, 1992). Infants' sensitivity to changes in their mothers' touch has also been demonstrated through the SF procedure by providing mothers with different verbal instructions (Stack & LePage, 1996; Stack & Muir, 1990, 1992). For example, it has been shown that mothers can use touch to elicit specific behaviors from their infants (e.g., maximize their infants' smiling; Stack & LePage, 1996; shift infants' attention to their mothers' hands; Stack & Muir, 1992). Using a still-face with touch procedure and making comparisons to a no-change control group, Stack and Arnold (1998) examined *how* touch and gesture alone are used to obtain specific infant responses. They found that infants are sensitive to changes in maternal touch and hand gestures and that when instructed, mothers appear successful in eliciting specific behaviors from their infants using only nonverbal channels of communication. For example, maternal touch and hand gestures attracted infants' attention to their mothers' faces even when the face was still and expressionless.

Using a modification of the SF with touch procedure, LePage (1998; LePage & Stack, 1997) investigated infants' abilities to perceive a tactile contingency (or the lack of contingency) during social interactions. Infants in the contingent condition were reinforced for gazing at the experimenter's neutral face with standardized tactile stimulation (still-face interaction with touch as the reinforcer). Infants in the non-contingent condition received the same tactile stimulation as their matched counterparts regardless of their behaviors. All infants in the contingent condition learned the contingency; for example, their level of gazing at the experimenter's face was higher, and gazing away was lower, relative to infants in the non-contingent condition. LePage thus demonstrated that 4- and 7-month-olds could perceive and learn a contingent relationship presented through the tactile modality during social adult–infant interactions, underscoring that infants of this age are both sensitive to and reinforced by touch.

Multiple Modalities and Non-Still-Face Studies

While the still-face with touch studies were essential to isolating the contribution of touch to mother–infant interchange, information is typically multimodally specified for the developing infant. Several studies have addressed touch (directly or indirectly) through procedures that either do not use the SF or that attempt to bring together multiple behavioral actions in some unified way.

For example, in one of the few attempts to systematically separate the social components of maternal behavior, Roedell and Slaby (1977) explored 24-week-old infants' preferences for three adults who interacted in different ways. One adult (distal) smiled, talked, sang, and made facial expressions; another (proximal) carried, rocked, bounced, patted, and stroked the infant but remained silent with a neutral face; and a third (neutral) was silent, unresponsive, and made no eye contact. Over a three-week period, infants increased their time spent near the distal adult while no changes were made to the proximal and neutral adults, and infants chose to look more at the distal than at the proximal adult.

Unfortunately, there were no measures of affect, the adult was not permitted to maintain eye contact in the proximal condition, and the infant did not need to establish eye contact with the proximal adult to receive stimulation. This lack of natural social interaction may have contributed to the poor responses elicited by the proximal adult, and may have driven the infants to look away (Stack & Muir, 1990).

It has also been shown that rhythmic is preferred over non-rhythmic touch in dyads (Peláez-Nogueras, 1995), and infants are more responsive when touch is added to face and voice (Peláez-Nogueras, Gewirtz, et al., 1996). To reinforce the position that touch can elicit specific responses, Wolff (1963) studied the development of smiling and found that, between the fourth and sixth week of life, pat-a-cake becomes an efficient stimulus for smiling. In order to ensure that it was the proprioceptive-tactile stimuli rather than extraneous stimulation that elicited the smile, Wolff played the game in such a way that the infant could not see or hear the person during the test. The smiles evoked in this way were described as broad, the intensity of smiling was high, and it was difficult to habituate the response with repeated stimulation. Pat-a-cake is not the only game to elicit such positive responses from infants. There are other parent–infant games that also involve much touching and physical contact, e.g., lap games, tickle games, I'm-gonna-get-you games, finger-walking games (e.g., Stern, 1985), even bouncing games and "horsey" games.

As a final example, the earlier contention by Gusella et al. (1988) that touch may have served to maintain attention during a SF procedure is consistent with observations by Roggman and Woodson (1989). While not a SF study, they compared two 3-min play sessions where mothers refrained from touching their 3–4-month-olds' in one period and not in the other. They reported that maternal touch facilitated attention during face-to-face interactions. However, it is important to note that in both the Roggman and Woodson (1989) and the Gusella et al. (1988) studies, touch was confounded with concurrent stimulation from both visual and auditory modalities.

The importance of multiple measures and the examination of patterns of responses from mothers and infants have been underscored in recent research. Previously, emphasis was placed on facial expressions with the result that attention to touch, gestures, postural changes, vocalizations, and the relations between measures has been inadequate (Tronick, 1989). According to functionalist theories of emotion, reliance solely on facial expression as indications of affect and arousal is insufficient. Emotional signals are context-specific and shaped by the immediate goals of organism–environment relationships (Campos, Mumme, Kermoian, & Campos, 1994; Thompson, 1993). The implications are threefold: (1) inclusion of multiple measures; (2) importance of context; (3) inclusion of approaches that address discrete measures, relations between measures, and the interaction itself (e.g., patterns, sequencing). According to Toda and Fogel (1993), "emotional" responses in young infants cannot be judged entirely from the face but must involve the whole body and the patterns of temporally organized action in a context (Fogel et al., 1992). Weinberg and Tronick (1994) provide some support for these contentions. In their study examining mothers and their 6-month-old infants, they examined multiple modalities including the infants' gaze, vocalizations, gestures, facial expressions, self-regulatory, and withdrawal behaviors. They found evidence for behavioral clusters or "affective configurations" that they argued conveyed information about the infant's state and intentions. Increased emphasis on coding and integrating touch and gesture is warranted in order to better understand their roles in communication.

Summary

Taken together, interaction studies have provided important insights and have advanced what we know about the young infant's sensitivity to manipulations in facial, vocal, and now tactile expressions, underscoring the complexity and sophistication of mother–infant dyadic interactions and the importance of including measures of touch. Moreover, through these studies, an abundance of new findings have been revealed. For example, mothers frequently use touch during normal face-to-face interactions with their infants (65 percent of the time; Stack & Muir, 1990; Symons & Moran, 1987). Touch alone can maintain infant attention and elicit positive affect at least as well as vocal and facial expression, for brief periods of time (LePage & Stack, 1992). Third, infants are sensitive to subtle changes in maternal touch (e.g., Stack & Arnold, 1998; Stack & LePage, 1996) and prefer stimulus compounds that include touch (Peláez-Nogueras, Gewirtz, et al., 1996). Results from these studies have also enlightened us about infants' sensitivity to maternal behavior, in particular their sensitivity to their mothers' touch. Most importantly, these studies have provided evidence for a functional context for touch that is not limited to the regulation of distress.

Patterns of Touching During Social Interactions

While the importance of the above-mentioned studies is not in question, past findings are limited in at least two ways. First, the functions and adaptability of touch have largely been inferred based on evidence taken from infant responses to their caregivers, rather than direct measures of caregiver touch. Second, even in those studies where touch has been directly assessed, the measures have largely been the duration of all touching (e.g., Gusella et al., 1988) or they have been intensity levels (e.g., Stack & Muir, 1990). Despite the fact that overall levels of touching are important, they do not inform us about qualitative aspects of touching or how particular types of touch may be used more or less often under specific circumstances. It makes a difference, for example, whether one strokes, caresses, pats, or pokes. All touch may not be used or interpreted similarly; different types of touch and the way touch is applied may have different meanings.

To illustrate, Stack, LePage, Hains, and Muir (2001) developed the Caregiver–Infant Touch Scale (CITS) to measure types of touch and associated quantitative characteristics (e.g., intensity, speed) in social contexts such as mother–infant play, and to examine changes across age. The CITS is a scale designed to code touch second-by-second from videotapes of play and interactions. After assessing its psychometric properties, Stack et al. applied the CITS in an experimental paradigm (a modified face-to-face "still-face" procedure) that was known to produce reliable shifts in infants' social responses. This application was designed to test not only the scale's sensitivity in describing differential maternal tactile stimulation, but also to determine whether mothers used different types of touch as a function of different perturbation periods. Following a period of natural face-to-face interaction mothers and their 5.5-month-old infants participated in three SF with touch periods. The SF with touch perturbation periods included (1) normal touch, (2) touch to maximize infant smiling, and (3) touch restricted to one area of the body. There was a baseline comparison group also included who received four periods of natural face-to-face interaction.

Analyses indicated a number of important findings. First, the natural and *all* SF (touch-alone) periods were significantly different, and there were clear differences between each SF period. Specific patterns or profiles of touching were shown across perturbation period. For example, when asked to maximize infant smiling, mothers used more active types of touch (lifting, tickling), used more surface area, and greater intensity and speed. During the SF period where mothers were asked to touch their babies in only one area, there was increased stroking and far less shaking. Touching was also less intense, and most types of touch during this period were judged to be executed more slowly. Thus, the more tactilely active profile was revealed during the period where smiling was maximized. This finding supports the notion of heightened activity during playful interactions. From these results it is clear that mothers' profiles of touching change during brief interactions as a function of experimenter instruction, suggesting that what was being communicated through the touch was different.

These findings suggest that simple touch duration is not a sufficient index to characterize adult behavior – qualitative and quantitative variations in touching occur for a variety of reasons and are important to measure and describe. What is also clear is that mothers use different patterns of touching for different functions (Stack, LePage, Hains, & Muir, 1996; Stack et al., 2001).

Touch and Attachment: Contact Behaviors As They Relate to Emotion and Emotional Communication

Emotions may be communicated through touch and at the very least communication occurs. That is, touch conveys meaning (soothe calm/active happy). Although there are few to no systematic studies to support such claims, touch appears to convey emotion very directly and the type of touch conveys particular emotions. Emotions (feeling states or messages) that might be communicated through touch include: love and caring, sympathy, empathy, anger, and sense of security. According to Montagu (1986), for example, through "feeling" we frequently refer to emotional states, such as happiness, joy, sadness, melancholy, and depression, and by the term often imply a reference to touching. According to Virel (anthropologist and neurologist), the skin may be seen as a mirror of the organism's functioning: "its color, texture, moistness, dryness, and every one of its other aspects, reflect our own state of being, psychological as well as physical. We blanch with fear and turn red with embarrassment. Our skin tingles with excitement and feels numb with shock; it is a mirror of our passions and emotions."

It seems clear that touching as a sensory system and as a means of communication is important to that first relationship, that between parent and infant, as well as important to the infant him or herself. Touching seems to communicate, to bring out meaning. "Although touch is not itself an emotion, its sensory elements induce those neural, glandular, muscular, and mental changes which in combination we call an emotion" (Montagu, 1986, p. 128). Touch is also involved in attachment and the affectional systems. In effect we see abundant examples of how touch is related to tender, loving care, from the beginnings of life at the breast, to being held and cuddled, rocked to sleep, stroked and swayed to reduce distress, and hugged for affection and comfort; it is even important at the end of life.

The interaction studies previously described highlighted the importance of mothers' and infants' sensitivity to each other's behavior, and the role of touch in behavioral regulation. Sensitivity and responsiveness have direct links to attachment, relationship quality, and future interactions. Moreover, the amount and quality of physical contact (touching; proximity) are important to the mother–infant relationship (Montagu, 1986; Stack & Muir, 1992). Contact behaviors have been found to be integral features of emotional communication between mothers and infants, and higher levels of touch are related to secure positive attachment (Ainsworth, Blehar, Waters, & Wall, 1978; Bowlby, 1969). Key components of current theories of attachment include physical proximity and proximity-seeking measures. Landau (1989), in her examination of the relationship between kissing, hugging, patting, and attachment behavior in infancy, argued that there is an intricate relationship between infant affectionate behavior and attachment. More studies are warranted in order to relate specific types of touch to attachment constructs, such as proximity.

Maternal sensitivity, considered a key contributor to synchronous and mutually reciprocal interactions, has been recently related to optimal patterns of attachment (Isabella, Belsky, & von Eye, 1989). The characteristics of maternal sensitivity and responsiveness often involve physical closeness and physical touching behaviors. In addition, the frequency and duration of touch are considered by some researchers to be an index of mothers' attachment (Anisfeld & Lipper, 1983; Grossman, Thane, & Grossman, 1981; Schaller, Carlsson, & Larson, 1979).

Tracy and Ainsworth (1981) conducted a study designed to examine the role of maternal affectionate behavior in the definition of maternal patterns of care. They were especially interested in the expression of affection from mothers of anxious-avoidant infants. Twenty-six babies were studied in naturalistic home observations at three-week intervals across the first year of life. Twenty-three of the 26 were assessed in the Strange Situation when they were 12-month-olds. No differences were found between the three groups of anxious-avoidant (A), secure (B), and anxious-resistant (C) in terms of overall frequency of affectionate acts. However, mothers of Type A babies emphasized kissing over hugging and cuddling, which the authors argued is consistent with their aversion to close bodily contact. While aware that the behaviors they studied are only *assumed* to reflect affectionate feelings and warmth to another, Tracy and Ainsworth contended that were they able to directly measure affectionate feelings from the mother, they would correlate with the frequency of affectionate acts. Interestingly, MacDonald (1992), in an evolutionary analysis of warmth as a developmental construct, argues that warmth must be separated from security of attachment and that the relationship between warmth and attachment classification is a complex one.

In an experimental study of the effects of physical contact on the development of mother–infant attachment in a low-income, inner-city sample, Anisfeld, Casper, Nozyce, and Cunningham (1990) assigned soft baby carriers to the experimental mothers (identified as involving increased physical contact) and infant seats to the control group mothers. They found that there was greater maternal contingent responsiveness and more secure attachment with increased physical contact.

Beyond physical contact, attachment, and the early relationship, there are also relationships that have been posited between touch and emotion and regulation. However, few studies in the infant social interaction literature have been specifically designed to explore these relationships systematically. The soothing function of touch directly links touching to emotional regulation, and it is already known that emotions play a critical part in infants' evaluation of their goals (Tronick, 1989). It has also been proposed that touch is a mode of communication (e.g., Fisher, Rytting, & Heslin, 1976). However, within the large literature on emotional communication it is striking that touch has received little attention (Beyette, Atkinson, & Kendall, 1989).

Touch and the At-Risk Infant

Evidence from those few studies that have directly examined touch in early development supports the claim that touch is important to the quality of the parent–child relationship and to the overall development of the infant. This is also revealed in studies with at-risk infants. For example, Polan and Ward (1994) found some support that physical affection and physical interaction were reduced in mothers of failure to thrive. Similarly, positive touch stimulation has been shown to enhance positive affect and attention in infants of depressed mothers (Peláez-Nogueras, Field, et al., 1996; Peláez-Nogueras, Gewirtz, et al., 1996). Paradoxically, in their study of parenting stress, depression, and anxiety and its relationship to behavior during interactions, Fergus, Schmidt, and Pickens (1998) found that it was those mothers who reported more symptoms of depression who touched their infants more relative to non-depressed mothers. However, the pattern of interaction was more intrusive and overstimulatory in nature. As they reported, more poking and tickling were used and these symptomatic mothers (mild to moderate levels of depressive symptoms) attempted more attention-getting strategies such as finger snapping. Similarly, Cohn and Tronick (1989) described depressed mothers as using more poking and jabbing with their infants; these touching behaviors were associated with negative affect and gaze aversion on the part of infants. Combined, these studies point to the importance of types of touch and converge to suggest that touch might be an important parenting measure.

Infants who are sensory impaired reveal yet another way that touch is used as an important communicative channel. In these cases, whether visually or hearing impaired, the tacto-gestural modality might be seen as assuming some of the roles that vision or audition might have otherwise subsumed. Both the visual and tactile channels are of significance to the deaf infant (Koester, 1992). Yet according to Meadow-Orlans and Steinberg (1993), compared to mothers of 18-month-old hearing infants, mothers of deaf infants used less frequent and positive touch, and were less sensitive and more intrusive. Nonetheless, as Koester, Papoušek, and Brooks (1995) pointed out, when deaf mothers use these more intrusive touch behaviors with their infants, it forms a style of communication that the infants respond to. MacTurk, Meadow-Orlans, Koester, and Spencer (1993) also found that maternal visual-tactile responsiveness was lower in mothers of deaf infants at 9 months, however visual-tactile responsiveness contributed to positive interactions at 18 months.

Bentley (1997) examined the relationship between maternal risk status and mother–child touch behavior in an intergenerational sample of mothers with a history of childhood aggression and social withdrawal as part of the Concordia Longitudinal Risk Project. Although mothers' childhood levels of aggression and/or social withdrawal did not significantly predict total positive touch behavior and little negative touch was observed, her findings did reveal that the age of the child was associated with the frequency that mothers touched. That is, mothers of younger children engaged in more touching behaviors than did mothers of older children, underscoring its role in early development.

Currently, there is some support for massage and tactile stimulation as having positive effects and being successful in facilitating growth in the newborn, particularly with the preterm infant (e.g., Rose, Schmidt, Riese, & Bridger, 1980; Scafidi et al., 1986; Solkoff, Yaffe, Weintraub, & Blase, 1969). For example, weight gain and caloric intake in premature infants have been shown to increase with tactile stimulation (e.g., Helders et al., 1989; Phillips & Moses, 1996; Scafidi et al, 1990; Watt, 1990; White & Labarba, 1976). In addition to a 47 percent greater weight gain for preterm infants given tactile stimulation, Scafidi et al. (1986) demonstrated that treated infants spent more time in awake and active states, showed more mature behaviors on the Brazelton scale, and were discharged from hospital six days earlier. In Phillips and Moses's (1996) study, massaged infants maintained a calmer state and were less irritable.

In a review of 24 studies on the effects of supplemental stimulation on premature infants, Harrison (1985) found evidence to support the positive effects of extra tactile stimulation as well as extra auditory, gustatory, and visual stimulation. Beneficial effects included those mentioned above, as well as decreased irritability, and more advanced social and neurological development. However, she also noted a number of limitations to the studies (e.g., small samples, wide variation in samples). In their program of supplemental tactile stimulation, Róiste and Bushnell (1996) found that treated infants were quicker to feed, discharged from hospital earlier, and appeared to show more advanced cognitive development at 15 months. However, the advanced cognitive development outcome should be considered with caution as it may have been due to other causes.

Kangaroo care or skin-to-skin holding, where the preterm infant is held on the parent's chest under the clothing, was introduced to American NICUs in the late 1980s (Gale, 1998). The practice originated in Bogota, Colombia in the 1970s. Its positive effects seem to be primarily in the physiologic domain (heart rate, respiration rate, oxygen saturation, thermoregulation; e.g., Anderson, 1995); however, there is some recent evidence for improved development (Ludington-Hoe & Swinth, 1996). Controversies still appear to surround this technique, particularly its practice with very small babies, thus more research is warranted to determine its efficacy and with whom it is both effective and appropriate.

Whether specific regimens of tactile stimulation or massage have beneficial effects on the fullterm neonate is not clear. According to Field (1998), massage therapists suggest that there are beneficial effects (e.g., reducing stress responses, reducing pain, helping to induce sleep); however, there are no data to support these claims. Koniak-Griffin and Ludington-Hoe (1987) found paradoxical effects in their examination of the effects of unimodal and multimodal stimulation. Unimodal stimulation was offered in the form of a skin-to-skin stroking procedure, and multimodal through use of a multi-sensory hammock during sleep. The hammock offered tactile stimulation in the form of a sheepskin base and terrycloth fabric, and auditory and vestibular stimulation via a battery-operated heart located at the head of the hammock. After one month, treated infants showed less mature behavior on the Neonatal Behavioral Assessment Scale (NBAS; Brazelton, 1973), and weight gain was not enhanced. However, a positive relationship was found between quantity of multimodal stimulation and positive maternal perception of infant behavior scored on the Neonatal Perception Inventory (Broussard & Hartner, 1970).

Based on their findings, Koniak-Griffin and Ludington-Hoe (1987) recommended that programs of sensory enrichment that model intervention programs for premature infants be applied cautiously to normal healthy newborns. Critics of applying these models to the healthy-term newborn argue that additional stimulation is unnecessary and that detrimental effects can occur if parents pay more attention to protocol than inter-action with their babies (Klaus & Kennell, 1983).

Touch and Culture

To this point touch has been surveyed as it relates to parent–infant and parent–child inter-actions, as well as hospital regimens for tactile stimulation with risk infants. Observing variations and similarities in touching across different cultures is yet another important avenue to explore. Studying parenting-in-culture is important to developmental investi-gations (Bornstein, 1991). Parents across the world have ways with which they have both learned and developed to rear their children and to teach them to become a part of the culture. There also seem to be both culture-specific and culture-universal parenting activ-ities. It is not surprising, then, that ways of touching and the amount of physical contact between parent and child can be different across culture, as well as levels of affection and how affection is expressed.

It has been demonstrated that different cultural groups engage in different *styles* of touching (Fogel, Toda, & Kawai, 1988; Franco, Fogel, Messinger, & Frazier, 1996). For example, differences in the type and timing of Japanese mothers' behavior toward their infants were reflected in a higher probability of facial expressions and vocalizations being interspersed with touches and looming upper-body movements (Fogel et al., 1988). In addition, when infants shifted their gaze from away to toward the mother, Japanese mothers were more likely to respond with increased touch. American mothers provided largely facial and vocal displays to their infants and placed their faces closer to the infants', in effect leaning toward their infants. Few hand displays were shown, in contrast to the

Japanese mothers, who used these several times during a session. Interestingly, there were no differences in amount of touching – mothers from both cultures touched their infants about 50 percent of the time. However, in a longitudinal study of American and Japanese dyads over the first year of life, Kawakami, Takai-Kawakami, and Kanaya (1994) found that American dyads engaged in interactions more often and American mothers touched their infants more. In a comparison of Hispanic and Anglo mothers living in the United States (Franco et al., 1996), mothers from both groups reported touching their infants daily. However, the Hispanic mothers reported higher frequencies of touching, affection, and skin-to-skin contact. Coding of videotaped observations of free play (15 min) revealed that Hispanic mothers showed more close touch (e.g., resting against mother, body contact, tight hugs) as well as more close and affectionate touch, relative to Anglo mothers, who showed more distal touch (e.g., playing at a distance, extended arms, etc.). No overall differences in amount of mother–infant touch were observed during the interactions. The fact that Franco et al.'s results revealed no differences in overall touching between mothers and their infants implies in their view that touch is an integral component of early interactions, even in cultures who have different attitudes about affection and touching.

Ritualized behaviors form part of the developing relationship between parent and infant (Casati, 1991). Childcare routines also differ across cultures and social groups. Whether and for how long a relationship is tactile differs as a function of culture and such factors as age of the child. Sigman and Wachs (1991) studied families in Kenya and in Egypt. They found that amount of physical contact declined from 18 to 27 months and then increased from 27 to 29 months. In another culture, Konner (1976) showed that !Kung infants were in physical bodily contact with someone 75 percent of the time during their first 3–6 months of life.

Caregiving practices may also benefit the infant in critical ways. Tronick, Thomas, and Daltabuit (1994) describe the manta pouch used by Quechua mothers (located in a high-altitude desert of Peru) to buffer their infants against high altitude. In this case, the infant is tightly swaddled and enclosed in cloths and blankets. As the infant ages, the pouch is modified to permit entry of increasing levels of the external environment.

While the majority of studies conducted to date, especially those which address touch, have involved mothers or female adults, there is an accumulating literature on fathers. It is known that fathers engage in more vigorous, physically stimulating play with their infants (e.g., Arco, 1983; Hewlett, 1987; Parke & O'Leary, 1976; Yogman, 1982), and it is believed by some that their style of play serves to create a critical means for the development of attachment (e.g., Lamb, 1981). There have also been a few studies of fathers' touching with their infants in different cultures. For example, Hewlett (1987) observed the Aka pygmies of the tropical forest region of southern Central African Republic. While fathers held their infants substantially less than mothers, several patterns emerged. Fathers' holding was often context-specific (e.g., leisure time). Interestingly, however, it was the Aka fathers who were more likely to engage in minor physical play such as tickling and bouncing with their infants. Aka fathers did not engage in the vigorous type of play characteristic of American fathers.

In their observations of Italian fathers, New and Benigni (1987) described fathers' interactions with their infants as more distal rather than proximal, involving more looking and talking. Fathers' touches were described as awkward and brief, and holding by the father was often limited to times when the mother was preparing the feeding. Their physical contact typically included tickling and poking.

The characteristics of holding and play in different cultures can also be a revealing means of examining some aspects of physical touch and affection during parent–infant interchange. In a study describing Indian (New Delhi) mothers and fathers' holding patterns, Roopnarine, Talukder, Jain, Joshi, and Srivastav (1990) found that mothers held their babies more than fathers, were also more likely to pick them up, to feed and comfort them while holding, and to display affection while holding. However, the overall durations of holding were less than what is typically reported for the North American family. This could be explained by the fact that many other family members and friends hold the Indian baby in a day. When fathers were holding their infants, typically affection was displayed. Tickling and lap bouncing were rare occurrences between Indian parents and their infants. However, peek-a-boo play was more common between mothers and infants. Finally, the infants themselves were more likely to vocalize, to smile at and follow their mothers compared to fathers, but there was no difference in the amount of touch or approach behaviors to mothers and fathers. More research with fathers is warranted, particularly pertaining to fathers' use and styles of touching during interactions.

Taken together, the findings from this brief overview of some of the cross-cultural findings have shown that touch is important and even intrinsic to other cultures. It can also be used differently in some contexts (e.g., holding patterns, pouches, swaddling) or be more frequent. The results converge to suggest that touching is used to bring people together, for closeness and intimacy, proximity and play, as well as for survival purposes in environments that require it.

Conclusions

One of the most significant themes to surface from this review of the literature is that while facial and vocal expressions are important, they are only two of many behaviors that are used to express and communicate. Although accumulating, far less data exist on "tactile expressiveness" and communication through touch. Thus, it is clear that continued examination of this modality is warranted. Touch is emerging as a diverse and adaptable modality, a modality which, while often used alone, also accompanies other modalities and channels of communication. Touch is used frequently in the first year of life and it serves a multitude of purposes, ranging from maintaining infant's state, to increasing weight gain and caloric intake in preterm infants, to providing comfort and warmth, to providing a means of social communication, to adjusting posture, to serving an important means of developing the early parent–infant relationship, among other roles.

The findings described underscore the point that the tactile modality provides an important means for parents and infants to maintain a connection with each other (as well as to the environment and to the self). It illustrates the flexibility and adaptability of touch but as well, the adaptability of the communication system – both partners modify their behavior, to adjust and compensate for the situation. Both are responsive to each other. It is also clear that touch is used across a variety of cultures and that patterns of touching may be different.

Yet while facial, vocal, and tactile components are frequently used during interactions, less is known about how they are used in combination, how they are used to achieve goals, and, if they do convey messages, how this is accomplished. Moreover, how touching is integrated with the other communication channels that are available to parents warrants examination (e.g., Arnold, Brouillette, & Stack, 1996). Although understanding each component's discrete and independent roles is important, the context within which much of early development occurs is social and multimodal. Consequently, how the modalities are used in combination, and whether message salience is increased by using multiple modalities as a result of the increased redundancy in the message, become important questions (i.e., do combinations of modalities communicate more clearly?). Whether there are intentional messages embedded in touch at all is yet another issue.

Beyond the aforementioned, several additional questions and pivotal issues are prominent and have emerged from the existing literature. First, what is being communicated through touch? Second, assuming that communication is occurring (based on the evidence to date), and that touch is serving a multitude of important roles and functions, the next question becomes determining how to measure this process. Measurement issues remain a challenge. This is the case in at least two ways: (1) how to systematically measure touch, and (2) whether to use discrete or relational measures. Touch is inherently relational. The act of tickling is a good example. Tickling is interesting because it is not possible to tickle oneself – that is, respond with laughter to the tickling. The laughter evoked by tickling appears to depend entirely upon the social situation. The act of stroking and the strokability of the infant (allowing someone to touch him or her) are inherent in touch and are also relational measures. Similarly, to experience hugging demands a partner (Stern, 1985). Each of these examples makes clear the relational aspect, but an important challenge is to determine a systematic means of measuring the touching that occurs and beyond this, to ascertain its meaning.

Third, addressing the quantitative and qualitative characteristics (patterns) and their salience over age, as well as what changes occur in infants' and caregivers' communicative behaviors (e.g., affective, gaze, and touching behaviors) over time, are essential. A more dynamic perspective would view the dyad as developing together, thus making it irrelevant, and even inappropriate, to attempt to divide the communicative process into the sender and receiver of the message. Process is primordial and the history of the dyad is an important consideration. This issue is related to what was discussed above concerning how touch is inherently relational and requires measurement that takes this into consideration.

Fourth, throughout the first few years of life, the infant (and its parents) are developing, changing, and adjusting. It is important to pursue and be aware of how development itself plays a role in the changes we see related to touch, physical contact, and affection (e.g., locomotor ability, language, referential communication, etc.; also, fine motor abilities and haptic exploration).

In closing, one important direction is to bring together the literature and research findings into a clear and cohesive developmental picture. In attempting to achieve success with such a goal, however, one is faced with changing contexts, procedures/paradigms, individual differences, and varied response measures as infants develop physically, cognitively, socially, and emotionally. As Kisilevsky, Stack, and Muir (1991) once argued, the challenge remains to develop studies that determine whether the role of touch changes across development and how it changes, or whether changes merely reflect the fact that procedures, contexts, and responses vary across ages. Remembering that we have in the human infant an intelligent organism that is responsive to tactile stimulation from late gestation to infancy, one of our greatest challenges is to determine parallel measures, paradigms, and procedures so that functional and relational development can be clearly described.

The future is an exciting one. While there are many unresolved questions and issues to pursue, at the same time, the research is at a point where cutting-edge issues are surfacing, studies are accumulating, and findings are converging. There is much to discover, reveal, and integrate into existing research and theory. Indeed, touch offers us a rich world to discover, and one which has implications for a variety of fields of inquiry. It is also a privileged field for promising interactions and convergence across a number of disciplines.

Related Topics

1   The role and use of gestures/manual hand movements in interaction and communication.
2   Haptic and tactile information processing.
3   Holding patterns.
4   The role of touch in the development of self-exploration.
5   The infants' use of touch (less known) and the development of affection and affectionate behaviors during infancy.
6   Tactile exploration in the blind infant or sensory impaired infant.
7   Touch across the life span (its role in labor, pain, with the elderly, the acutely ill, therapeutic touch).
8   Touch and affection in group care settings (e.g., day care, preschool, school).

Further Reading

Barnard, K. E., & Brazelton, T. B. (Eds.). (1990). *Touch: The foundation of experience.* Connecticut: International Universities Press.

Kaitz, M., Lapidot, P., Bronner, R., & Eidelman, A. I. (1992). Parturient women can recognize their infant by touch. *Developmental Psychology, 28,* 35–39.

Kuhn, C. M., & Schanberg, S. M. (1998). Responses to maternal separation: Mechanisms and mediators. *International Journal of Developmental Neuroscience, 16,* 261–270.

Montagu, A. (1986). *Touching: The human significance of the skin* (3rd ed.). New York: Harper & Row.

Peláez-Nogueras, M., Gewirtz, J. L., Field, T., Cigales, M., Malphurs, J., Clasky, S., & Sanchez, A. (1996). Infants' preference for touch stimulation in face-to-face interactions. *Journal of Applied Developmental Psychology, 17,* 199–213.

Schanberg, S. M., & Field, T. M. (1987). Sensory deprivation stress and supplemental stimulation in the rat pup and preterm human. *Child Development, 58,* 1431–1447.

Stack, D. M., & Arnold, S. L. (1998). Changes in mothers' touch and hand gestures influence infant behavior during face-to-face interchanges. *Infant Behavior and Development, 21,* 451–468.

Stack, D. M., & LePage, D. E. (1996). Infants' sensitivity to manipulations of maternal touch during face-to-face interactions. *Social Development, 5,* 41–55.

Stack, D. M., & Muir, D. W. (1992). Adult tactile stimulation during face-to-face interactions modulates 5-month-olds' affect and attention. *Child Development, 63,* 1509–1525.

References

Ainsworth, M. D. S. (1962). The effects of maternal deprivation: A review of findings and controversy in the context of research strategy. *Deprivation of maternal care: A reassessment of its effects.* Geneva: World Health Organization.

Ainsworth, M. D. S., Blehar, M. C., Waters, E., & Wall, S. (1978). *Patterns of attachment: A psychological study of the Strange Situation.* Hillsdale, NJ: Erlbaum.

Anderson, G. C. (1995). Touch and the kangaroo care methods. In T. M. Field (Ed.), *Touch in early development* (pp. 35–51). Mahwah, NJ: Lawrence Erlbaum Associates.

Anisfeld, E., Casper, V., Nozyce, M., & Cunningham, N. (1990). Does infant carrying promote attachment? An experimental study of the effects of increased physical contact on the development of attachment. *Child Development, 61,* 1617–1627.

Anisfeld, E., & Lipper, E. (1983). Early contact, social support and mother–infant bonding. *Pediatrics, 72,* 79–83.

Arco, C. M. (1983). Infant reactions to natural and manipulated temporal patterns of paternal communication. *Infant Behavior and Development, 6,* 391–399.

Arnold, S. L., Brouillette, J., & Stack, D. M. (1996, August). *Changes in maternal and infant behavior as a function of instructional manipulations during unimodal and multimodal interactions.* Poster session presented at the Biennial Meeting of the International Society for the Study of Behavioral Development, Quebec City, Quebec, Canada.

Barrera, M. E., & Maurer, D. (1981). The perception of facial expressions by the three-month-old. *Child Development, 52,* 203–206.

Bentley, V. M. (1997). *Maternal childhood risk status as a predictor of emotional availability and physical contact in mother–child interactions: An intergenerational study.* Unpublished master's thesis, Concordia University, Montreal, Quebec, Canada.

Beyette, M. E., Atkinson, M. L., & Kendall, S. (1989, June). *Emotional communication by touch.* Poster presented at the Canadian Psychological Association Annual Convention, Halifax, Nova Scotia, Canada.

Birns, B., Blank, M., & Bridger, W. H. (1966). The effectiveness of various soothing techniques on human neonates. *Psychosomatic Medicine, 28,* 316–322.

Bornstein, M. H. (1991). Approaches to parenting in culture. In M. H. Bornstein (Ed.), *Cultural approaches to parenting* (pp. 3–19). Hillsdale, NJ: Lawrence Erlbaum Associates.

Bowlby, J. (1969). *Attachment and loss: Vol. 1. Attachment.* New York: Basic Books.

Brazelton, T. B. (1973). *Neonatal Behavioral Assessment Scale.* Philadelphia: Lippincott.

Brazelton, T. B. (1984). Introduction. In C. C. Brown (Ed.), *The many facets of touch* (pp. xv–xviii). Skillman, NJ: Johnson & Johnson Baby Products Co. Pediatric Round Table Series, 10.

Brazelton, T. B. (1990). Touch as a touchstone: Summary of the round table. In K. E. Barnard & T. B. Brazelton (Eds.), *Touch: The foundation of experience* (Clinical Infant Reports, No. 4, pp. 561–566). Madison, WI: International Universities Press.

Broussard, E. R., & Hartner, S. S. (1970). Maternal perceptions of the neonate as related to development. *Child Psychiatry and Human Development, 1*, 432–499.

Byrne, J. M., & Horowitz, F. D. (1981). Rocking as a soothing intervention: The influence of direction and type of movement. *Infant Behavior and Development, 4*, 207–218.

Campbell, S. B. G., & Taylor, P. M. (1980). Bonding and attachment: Theoretical issues. In P. M. Taylor (Ed.), *Parent–infant relationships* (pp. 3–23). New York: Grune & Stratton.

Campos, J. J., Mumme, D. L., Kermoian, R., & Campos, R. G. (1994). A functionalist perspective on the nature of emotion. *Monographs of the Society for Research in Child Development, 59*, 284–303.

Carlsson, S. G., Fagerberg, H., Horneman, G., Hwang, C.-P., Larsson, K., Rodholm, M., Schaller, J., Danielsson, B., & Gunderwall, C. (1978). Effects of amount of contact between mother and child on the mother's nursing behavior. *Developmental Psychobiology, 11*, 143–150.

Casati, I. (1991). Hugging and embracing; kisses given, kisses received. Preludes to tenderness between infant and adult. *Early Child Development and Care, 67*, 1–15.

Casler, C. R. (1961). Maternal deprivation: A critical review of the literature. *Monographs of the Society for Research in Child Development, 26*(2).

Casler, C. R. (1968). Perceptual deprivation in institutional settings. In G. Newton & S. Levine (Eds.), *Early experience and behavior.* New York: Springer.

Cohn, J. F., & Tronick, E. Z. (1983). Three-month-old infants' reaction to simulated maternal depression. *Child Development, 54*, 185–193.

Cohn, J. F., & Tronick, E. Z. (1989). Specificity of infants' response to mothers' affective behavior. *Journal of the American Academy of Child and Adolescent Psychiatry, 28*, 242–248.

De Chateau, P. (1976). The influence of early contact on maternal and infant behavior on primiparae. *Birth and the Family Journal, 3*, 149–155.

Denenberg, V. H. (1968). A consideration of the usefulness of the critical period hypothesis as applied to the stimulation of rodents in infancy. In G. Newton & S. Levine (Eds.), *Early experience and behavior* (pp. 142–167). Springfield, IL: Charles C. Thomas.

Denenberg, V. H. (1969). The effects of early experience. In E. S. E. Hafez (Ed.), *The behavior of domestic animals* (2nd ed.). London: Baillure, Tindall, & Cox.

Ellsworth, C. P., Muir, D. W., & Hains, S. M. H. (1993). Social competence and person–object differentiation: An analysis of the still-face effect. *Developmental Psychology, 29*, 63–73.

Fanslow, C. (1984). Touch and the elderly. In C. C. Brown (Ed.), *The many facets of touch* (pp. 183–189). Skillman, NJ: Johnson & Johnson Baby Products Co. Pediatric Round Table Series, 10.

Fergus, E. L., Schmidt, J., & Pickens, J. (1998, April). *Touch during mother–infant interactions: The effects of parenting stress, depression and anxiety.* Poster session presented at the Biennial Meeting of the International Society of Infant Studies, Atlanta, GA.

Field, T. M. (1984). Early interactions between infants and their postpartum depressed mothers. *Infant Behavior and Development, 7*, 517–522.

Field, T. M. (1998). Touch therapy effects on development. *International Journal of Behavioral Development, 22*, 779–797.

Field, T. M., Vega-Lahr, N., Scafidi, F., & Goldstein, S. (1986). Effects of maternal unavailability on mother–infant interactions. *Infant Behavior and Development, 9*, 473–478.

Fisher, J. D., Rytting, M., & Heslin, R. (1976). Hands touching hands: Affective and evaluative effects of an interpersonal touch. *Sociometry, 39*, 416–421.

Fogel, A. (1997). *Infancy: Infant, family, and society.* St. Paul, MN: West Publishing.

Fogel, A., Dedo, J., & McEwen, I. (1992). Effect of postural position and reaching on gaze during mother–infant face-to-face interaction. *Infant Behavior and Development, 15,* 231–244.

Fogel, A., Toda, S., & Kawai, M. (1988). Mother–infant face-to-face interaction in Japan and the United States: A laboratory comparison using 3-month-old infants. *Developmental Psychology, 24,* 398–406.

Franco, F., Fogel, A., Messinger, D. S., & Frazier, C. A. (1996). Cultural differences in physical contact between Hispanic and Anglo mother–infant dyads living in the United States. *Early Development and Parenting, 5,* 119–127.

Gale, G. (1998). Kangaroo care. *Neonatal Network, 17,* 69–71.

Gottlieb, G. (1983). The psychobiological approach to developmental issues. In M. M. Haith & J. J. Campos (Eds.), *Infancy and developmental psychobiology* (pp. 1–26). In P. H. Mussen (Ed.), *Handbook of child psychology* (4th ed., Vol. 2). New York: John Wiley.

Grossman, K., Thane, K., & Grossman, K. E. (1981). Maternal tactual contact of the newborn after various conditions of mother–infant contact. *Developmental Psychology, 17,* 158–169.

Gusella, J. L., Muir, D. W., & Tronick, E. Z. (1988). The effect of manipulating maternal behavior during an interaction of 3- and 6-month-olds' affect and attention. *Child Development, 59,* 1111–1124.

Hamnett, F. S. (1921). Studies in the thyroid apparatus. *American Journal of Physiology, 56,* 196–204.

Hamnett, F. S. (1922). Studies of the thyroid apparatus. *Endocrinology, 6,* 221–229.

Harlow, H. F. (1959). Love in infant monkeys. *Scientific American, 200,* 68.

Harrison, L. (1985). Effects of early supplemental stimulation programs for premature infants: Review of the literature. *Maternal Child Nursing Journal, 14,* 69–90.

Helders, P. J. M., Cats, B. P., & Debast, S. (1989). Effect of a tactile stimulation/range-finding programme on the development of VLBW-neonates during the first year of life. *Child Care, Health and Development, 15,* 369–380.

Hewlett, B. S. (1987). Intimate fathers: Patterns of paternal holding among Aka pygmies. In M. E. Lamb (Ed.), *The father's role: Cross-cultural perspectives* (pp. 295–330). Hillsdale, NJ: Lawrence Erlbaum Associates.

Hofer, M. (1993). Developmental roles of timing in the mother–infant interaction. In G. Turkewitz & D. A. Devenny (Eds.), *Developmental time and timing* (pp. 211–231). Hillsdale, NJ: Lawrence Erlbaum Associates.

Isabella, R. A., Belsky, J., & von Eye, A. (1989). Origins of infant–mother attachment: An examination of interactional synchrony during the infant's first year. *Developmental Psychology, 25,* 12–21.

Kaitz, M., Lapidot, P., Bronner, R., & Eidelman, A. I. (1992). Parturient women can recognize their infant by touch. *Developmental Psychology, 28,* 35–39.

Kaitz, M., Meirov, H., Landman, I., & Eidelman, A. I. (1993). Infant recognition by tactile cues. *Infant Behavior and Development, 16,* 333–341.

Kawakami, K., Takai-Kawakami, K., & Kanaya, Y. (1994). A longitudinal study of Japanese and American mother–infant interactions. *Psychologia: An International Journal of Psychology in the Orient, 37,* 18–29.

Kaye, K., & Fogel, A. (1980). The temporal structure of face-to-face communication between mothers and infants. *Developmental Psychology, 16,* 454–464.

Kisilevsky, B. S., & Low, J. A. (1998). Human fetal behavior: 100 years of study. *Developmental Review, 18,* 1–29.

Kisilevsky, B. S., Muir, D. W., & Low, J. A. (1992). Maturation of human fetal responses to vibro-acoustic stimulation. *Child Development, 63,* 1497–1508.

Kisilevsky, B. S., Stack, D. M., & Muir, D. W. (1991). Fetal and infant response to tactile stimulation. In M. Salomon Weiss & P. R. Zelazo (Eds.), *Newborn attention: Biological constraints and the influence of experience* (pp. 63–98). Norwood, NJ: Ablex.

Klatzky, R. L., & Lederman, S. (1987). The intelligent hand. In G. H. Bower (Ed.), *The psychology of learning and motivation* (Vol. 21, pp. 121–151). San Diego, CA: Academic Press.

Klaus, M., Jerauld, R., Kreger, N., McAlpine, W., Steffa, M., & Kennell, J. (1972). Maternal attachment: Importance of the first post-partum days. *New England Journal of Medicine, 286,* 460.

Klaus, M. H., & Kennell, J. H. (1983). An evaluation in the premature nursery. In J. Davis, M. Richards, & N. Robertson (Eds.), *Parent–baby attachment in premature infants* (pp. 86–99). New York: St. Martin's Press.

Klaus, M. H., Kennell, J. H., Plumb, N., & Zuelke, S. (1970). Human maternal behavior at the first contact with her young. *Pediatrics, 46,* 187–192.

Koester, L. S. (1992, May). *Effects of maternal or infant deafness on early interaction patterns.* Paper presented at the Biennial Meeting of the International Conference on Infant Studies, Miami, FL.

Koester, L. S., Papoušek, H., & Brooks, L. (1995, March). *The role of tactile contact in deaf and hearing mother–infant dyads.* Poster session presented at the Biennial Meeting of the Society for Research in Child Development, Indianapolis, IN.

Koester, L. S., Papoušek, H., & Papoušek, M. (1989). Patterns of rhythmic stimulation by mothers with three-month-olds: A cross-modal comparison. *International Journal of Behavioral Development, 12,* 143–154.

Koniak-Griffin, D., & Ludington-Hoe, S. (1987). Paradoxical effects of stimulation on normal neonates. *Infant Behavior and Development, 10,* 261–277.

Konner, M. J. (1976). Maternal care, infant behavior and development among the !Kung. In R. B. Lee & I. DeVore (Eds.), *Kalahari hunter–gatherers: Studies of the !Kung San and their neighbors* (pp. 218–245). Cambridge, MA: Harvard University Press.

Korner, A. F., & Thoman, E. B. (1972). The relative efficacy of contact and vestibular-proprioceptive stimulation in soothing neonates. *Child Development, 43,* 443–453.

Kuhn, C. M., & Schanberg, S. M. (1998). Responses to maternal separation: Mechanisms and mediators. *International Journal of Developmental Neuroscience, 16,* 261–270.

Lamb, M. E. (1981). *The role of the father in child development* (Rev. ed.). New York: Wiley.

Lamb, M. E., & Hwang, C.-P. (1982). Maternal attachment and mother–neonate bonding: A critical review. In M. E. Lamb & A. L. Brown (Eds.), *Advances in developmental psychology* (Vol. 2, pp. 1–39). Hillsdale, NJ: Lawrence Erlbaum.

Lamb, M. E., Morrison, D. C., & Malkin, C. M. (1987). The development of infant social expectations in face-to-face interaction: A longitudinal study. *Merrill-Palmer Quarterly, 33,* 241–254.

Landau, R. (1989). Affect and attachment: Kissing, hugging, and patting as attachment behaviors. *Infant Mental Health Journal, 10,* 50–69.

Lavelli, M., & Fogel, A. (1998, April). *Developmental changes in early mother–infant face-to-face communication.* Poster session presented at the Biennial Meeting of the International Conference on Infant Studies, Atlanta, GA.

Leboyer, F. (1976). *Loving hands.* New York: Alfred A. Knopf.

Lecanuet, J.-P., Fifer, W. P., Krasnegor, N. A., & Smotherman, W. P. (1995). *Fetal development: A psychobiological perspective.* Hillsdale, NJ: Lawrence Erlbaum.

Lecanuet, J.-P., Granier-Deferre, C., & Bushnel, M. C. (1989). Differential fetal auditory reactiveness as a function of stimulus characteristics and states. *Seminars in Perinatology, 13,* 421–429.

LePage, D. E. (1998). *Four-and 7-month-old infants' sensitivities to contingency during face-to-face social interactions.* Unpublished doctoral dissertation, Concordia University, Montreal, Quebec, Canada.

LePage, D. E., & Stack, D. M. (1992, June). *Do manipulations of maternal face, voice and touch differentially effect infant responses?* Poster session presented at the Canadian Psychological Association, Quebec City, Quebec, Canada. Abstract published in *Canadian Psychology, 32,* 351.

LePage, D. E., & Stack, D. M. (1997, April). *Four- and 7-month-old infants' abilities to detect tactile contingencies in a face-to-face context.* Poster session presented at the Biennial Meeting of the Society for Research in Child Development, Washington, DC.

Levine, S. (1956). A further study of infantile handling and adult avoidance learning. *Journal of Personality, 25,* 70–80.

Levine, S. (1960). Stimulation in infancy. *Scientific American, 202,* 80.

Levine, S., & Stanton, M. E. (1990). The hormonal consequences of mother–infant contact. In K. E. Barnard & T. B. Brazelton (Eds.), *Touch: The foundation of experience* (Clinical Infant Reports, No. 4, pp. 165–194). Madison, WI: International University Press.

Ludington-Hoe, S. M., & Swinth, J. Y. (1996). Developmental aspects of kangaroo care. *Journal of Obstetric, Gynecologic, and Neonatal Nursing, 25,* 691–703.

MacDonald, K. (1992). Warmth as a developmental construct: An evolutionary analysis. *Child Development, 63,* 753–773.

MacTurk, R. H., Meadow-Orlans, K. P., Koester, L. S., & Spencer, P. E. (1993). Social support, motivation, language, and interaction: A longitudinal study of mothers and deaf infants. *American Annals of the Deaf, 138,* 19–25.

Maurer, D., & Maurer, C. (1988). *The world of the newborn.* New York: Basic Books.

Mayes, L. C., & Carter, A. S. (1990). Emerging social regulatory capacities as seen in the still-face situation. *Child Development, 61,* 754–763.

Meadow-Orlans, K. P., & Steinberg, A. G. (1993). Effects of infant hearing loss and maternal support on mother–infant interactions at 18 months. *Journal of Applied Developmental Psychology, 14,* 407–426.

Montagu, A. (1971). *Touching: The human significance of the skin.* New York: Columbia University Press.

Montagu, A. (1986). *Touching: The human significance of the skin* (3rd ed.). New York: Harper & Row.

Muir, D., & Field, J. (1979). Newborn infants orient to sounds. *Child Development, 50,* 431–436.

New, R. S., & Benigni, L. (1987). Italian fathers and infants: Cultural constraints on paternal behavior. In M. E. Lamb (Ed.), *The father's role: Cross-cultural perspectives* (pp. 139–167). Hillsdale, NJ: Lawrence Erlbaum Associates.

Parke, R. D., & O'Leary, S. (1976). Family interaction in the newborn period: Some findings, some observations and some unresolved issues. In K. Riegan & J. Meacham (Eds.), *The developing individual in a changing world* (pp. 653–663). The Hague: Mouton.

Peláez-Nogueras, M. (1995, March). *Rhythmic and nonrhythmic touch during mother–infant interactions.* Poster session presented at the Biennial Meeting of the Society for Research in Child Development, Indianapolis, IN.

Peláez-Nogueras, M., Field, T. M., Hossain, Z., & Pickens, J. (1996). Depressed mothers' touching increases infants' positive affect and attention in still-face interactions. *Child Development, 67,* 1780–1792.

Peláez-Nogueras, M., Gewirtz, J. L., Field, T., Cigales, M., Malphurs, J., Clasky, S., & Sanchez, A. (1996). Infants' preference for touch stimulation in face-to-face interactions. *Journal of Applied Developmental Psychology, 17,* 199–213.

376 Dale M. Stack

Phillips, R. B., & Moses, H. A. (1996). Skin hunger effects on preterm neonates. *The Transdisciplinary Journal, 6*, 39–49.

Polan, H. J., & Ward, M. J. (1994). Role of the mother's touch in failure to thrive: A preliminary investigation. *Journal of the American Child and Adolescent Psychiatry, 33*, 1098–1105.

Provence, S., & Lipton, R. C. (1962). *Infants in institutions.* New York: International Universities Press.

Reissland, N., & Burghart, R. (1987). The role of massage in South Asia: Child health and development. *Social Science and Medicine, 25*, 231–239.

Robin, M. (1982). Neonate–mother interaction: Tactile contacts in the days following birth. *Early Child Development and Care, 9*, 221–236.

Roedell, W. C., & Slaby, R. G. (1977). The role of distal and proximal interaction in infant social preference formation. *Developmental Psychology, 13*, 266–273.

Roggman, L. A., & Woodson, R. (1989, April). *Touch and gaze in parent–infant play.* Poster presented at the Society for Research in Child Development Conference, Kansas City, KS.

Róiste, A., & Bushnell, I. W. R. (1996). Tactile stimulation: Short- and long-term benefits for preterm infants. *British Journal of Developmental Psychology, 14*, 41–53.

Roopnarine, J. L., Talukder, E., Jain, D., Joshi, P., & Srivastav, P. (1990). Characteristics of holding, patterns of play, and social behaviors between parents and infants in New Delhi, India. *Developmental Psychology, 26*, 667–673.

Rose, S. A., Schmidt, K., Riese, M. L., & Bridger, W. H. (1980). Effects of prematurity and early intervention on responsivity to tactual stimuli: A comparison of preterm and full-term infants. *Child Development, 51*, 416–425.

Rubin, R. (1963). Maternal touch. *Nursing Outlook, 11*, 328–331.

Samuels, C. A., Scholz, K., & Edmundson, S. (1992). The effects of baby bath and massage by fathers on the family system: The Sunraysia Australia Intervention Project. *Early Development and Parenting, 1*, 39–49.

Scafidi, F. A., Field, T. M., Schanberg, S. M., Bauer, C. R., Tucci, K., Roberts, J., Morrow, C., & Kuhn, C. M. (1990). Massage stimulates growth in preterm infants: A replication. *Infant Behavior and Development, 13*, 167–188.

Scafidi, F. A., Field, T. M., Schanberg, S. M., Bauer, C. R., Vega-Lahr, N., Garcia, R., Poirier, J., Nystrom, G., & Kuhn, C. M. (1986). Effects of tactile/kinesthetic stimulation on the clinical course and sleep/wake behavior of preterm neonates. *Infant Behavior and Development, 9*, 91–105.

Schaller, J., Carlsson, S. G., & Larson, K. (1979). Effects of extended post-partum mother–child contact on the mother's behavior during nursing. *Infant Behavior and Development, 2*, 319–324.

Schanberg, S. M., & Field, T. M. (1987). Sensory deprivation stress and supplemental stimulation in the rat pup and preterm human. *Child Development, 58*, 1431–1447.

Schiefenhövel, W. (1997). Universals in interpersonal interactions. In U. Segerstråle & P. Molnár (Eds.), *Nonverbal communication: Where nature meets culture* (pp. 61–79). Mahwah, NJ: Lawrence Erlbaum Associates.

Schiffman, H. R. (1982). *Sensation and perception* (2nd ed.). New York: John Wiley.

Scholz, K., & Samuels, C. A. (1992). Neonatal bathing and massage intervention with fathers, behavioral effects 12 weeks after birth of the first baby: The Sunraysia Australia Intervention Project. *International Journal of Behavioral Development, 15*, 67–81.

Sigman, M., & Wachs, T. D. (1991). Structure, continuity, and nutritional correlates of caregiver behavior patterns in Kenya and Egypt. In M. H. Bornstein (Ed.), *Cultural approaches to parenting* (pp. 123–137). Hillsdale, NJ: Lawrence Erlbaum Associates.

Solkoff, N., Yaffe, S., Weintraub, D., & Blase, B. (1969). Effects of handling on the subsequent developments of premature infants. *Developmental Psychology, 1*, 765–768.

Spitz, R. A., & Wolf, K. M. (1946). Anaclitic depression: An inquiry into the genesis of psychiatric conditions in early childhood. *The Psychoanalytic Study of the Child, 2,* 313–342.

Stack, D. M., & Arnold, S. L. (1998). Changes in mothers' touch and hand gestures influence infant behavior during face-to-face interchanges. *Infant Behavior and Development, 21,* 451–468.

Stack, D. M., Arnold, S. L., Girouard, N., & Welburn, B. (1999, April). *Infants' reactions to maternal unavailability in very low birth weight preterm and fullterm infants.* Paper presented at the Biennial Meeting of the Society for Research in Child Development, Albuquerque, NM.

Stack, D. M., & LePage, D. E. (1996). Infants' sensitivity to manipulations of maternal touch during face-to-face interactions. *Social Development, 5,* 41–55.

Stack, D. M., LePage, D. E., Hains, S. M., & Muir, D. W. (1996). Qualitative changes in maternal touch as a function of instructional condition during face-to-face social interactions. *Infant Behavior and Development, 19,* 761.

Stack, D. M., LePage, D. L., Hains, S., & Muir, D. W. (2001). *Differential touch as a function of instruction during mother–infant interactions: Application of the Caregiver–Infant Touch Scale (CITS).* Manuscript under revision.

Stack, D. M., & Muir, D. W. (1990). Tactile stimulation as a component of social interchange: New interpretations for the still-face effect. *British Journal of Developmental Psychology, 8,* 131–145.

Stack, D. M., & Muir, D. W. (1992). Adult tactile stimulation during face-to-face interactions modulates 5-month-olds' affect and attention. *Child Development, 63,* 1509–1525.

Stern, D. N. (1985). *The interpersonal world of the infant: A view from psychoanalysis and developmental psychology.* New York: Basic Books.

Stern, J. M. (1989). Maternal behavior: Sensory, hormonal, and neural determinants. In F. R. Brush & S. Levine (Eds.), *Psychoendocrinology* (pp. 105–226). New York: Academic Press.

Stern, J. M. (1990). Multisensory regulation of maternal behavior and masculine sexual behavior: A revised view. *Neuroscience and Biobehavioral Reviews, 14,* 183–200.

Stern, J. M. (1996). Somatosensation and maternal care in Norway rats. In J. S. Rosenblatt & C. T. Snowden (Eds.), *Evolution, mechanisms, and adaptive significance of parental care. Advances in the study of behavior.* (Vol. 25, pp. 243–294). New York: Academic Press.

Stern, J. M. (1997). Offspring-induced nurturance: Animal–human parallels. *Developmental Psychobiology, 31,* 19–37.

Suomi, S. (1997). Nonverbal communication in nonhuman primates: Implications for the emergence of culture. In U. Segerstråle & P. Molnár (Eds.), *Nonverbal communication: Where nature meets culture* (pp. 131–146). Mahwah, NJ: Lawrence Erlbaum Associates.

Symons, D. K., & Moran, G. (1987). The behavioral dynamics of mutual responsiveness in early face-to-face mother–infant interactions. *Child Development, 58,* 1488–1495.

Thompson, R. A. (1993). Socioemotional development: Enduring issues and new challenges. *Developmental Review, 13,* 372–402.

Toda, S., & Fogel, A. (1993). Infant response to the still-face situation at 3 and 6 months. *Developmental Psychology, 29,* 532–538.

Toney, L. (1983). The effects of holding the newborn at delivery on paternal bonding. *Nursing Research, 32,* 16–19.

Tracy, R. L., & Ainsworth, M. D. S. (1981). Maternal affectionate behavior and infant–mother attachment patterns. *Child Development, 52,* 1341–1343.

Trevathan, W. R. (1981). Maternal touch at 1st contact with the newborn infant. *Developmental Psychobiology, 14,* 549–558.

Tronick, E. Z. (1989). Emotions and emotional communication in infants. *American Psychologist, 44,* 112–119.

Tronick, E. Z., Als, H., Adamson, L., Wise, S., & Brazelton, T. B. (1978). The infant's response to entrapment between contradictory messages in face-to-face interactions. *Journal of the American Academy of Child Psychiatry, 17*, 1–13.

Tronick, E. Z., Thomas, R. B., & Daltabuit, M. (1994). The Quechua manta pouch: A caretaking practice for buffering the Peruvian infant against the multiple stressors of high altitude. *Child Development, 65*, 1005–1013.

Tulman, L. J. (1985). Mother's and unrelated persons' initial handling of newborn infants. *Nursing Research, 34*, 205–210.

Watt, J. (1990). Interaction, intervention, and development in small-for-gestational-age infants. *Infant Behavior and Development, 13*, 273–286.

Weinberg, M. K., & Tronick, E. Z. (1994). Beyond the face: An empirical study of infant affective configurations of facial, vocal, gestural, and regulatory behaviors. *Child Development, 65*, 1503–1515.

White, J. L., & Labarba, R. C. (1976). The effects of tactile and kinesthetic stimulation on neonatal development in the premature infant. *Developmental Psychobiology, 9*, 569–577.

Wolff, P. H. (1963). Observations on the early development of smiling. In B. M. Foss (Ed.), *Determinants of infant behavior II* (pp. 113–138). London: Methuen.

Yogman, M. W. (1982). Development of the father–infant relationship. In H. F. Fitzgerald, B. M. Lester, & M. W. Yogman (Eds.), *Theory and research in behavioral pediatrics* (Vol. 1, pp. 221–279). New York: Plenum Press.

Chapter Fourteen

Preverbal Communication

Andrew Lock

Introduction

This would have been a short chapter 25 years ago. It would have said something about how the early and classic studies of infancy by, for example, Tiedemann (1787; see Murchison and Langer, 1927) and Darwin (1877) noted that infants were able to communicate by cries and gestures before they could talk. There would have been mention of McCarthy's classic review of language development in the first edition of *Carmichael's Manual of Child Psychology*, where she noted that:

> It is quite generally agreed that the child understands gestures before he understands words and, in fact, that he uses gestures himself long before he uses language proper. . . . It has been claimed that words constitute substitutes for actual gross motor activity. (McCarthy, 1954, p. 521)

There may have been some mention of both the Gesell (1945) and Bayley (1969) developmental scales containing some items related to communication in infancy. And there might have been a note to the effect that Spitz (e.g., 1957) had contributed some interesting notes from a psychoanalytic perspective on how infants managed to convey "yes" and "no" through smiles and head shaking. And that would have been about the sum of it.

Today, it is difficult to know quite how best to review the field in the space available here. The research literature is now massive, both at an empirical and theoretical level, and its sophistication is such that a number of projects exploring the robotic modeling of "embodied cognition" are able to actively pursue the construction of machines that can build their own preverbal abilities for recognizing and reproducing the gestural actions of others, and to coordinate their attention onto objects so as to "learn" about communication and "how to learn" (e.g., Bonasso, Huber, & Kortenkamp, 1995; Ferrell & Scassellati, 1998; Kahn & Swain, 1995; Kozima & Ito, 1998).

Technological advances in other areas have themselves been central to the growth of this research topic in general. Video is the primary example, in that it has allowed us to capture and replay events unfolding in real-time and "real" environments. We now take video replays for granted, particularly of sporting events on television, along with instant statistics relating to the course of a game as it progresses. This familiarity tends to make us forget that quasi-portable video equipment only became available 25 years or so ago, and the ability to link video to on-line computer analysis is itself more recent still. Similarly, we tend to forget that theoretical and conceptual issues that are now taken for granted as legitimate and central to the questions current in the field – such as regarding infants as developing the ability to intentionally communicate – have a chequered history, and that the mere claim a quarter-century ago by an emerging generation of postgraduate students that they were concerned to discover how infants could "learn how to mean" could send their professors into fits of apoplexy.

This chapter cannot be a comprehensive review. Instead, it focuses on age-related changes during the preverbal period; empirical areas of research – for example, turn-taking, joint attention, and gestures (particularly the pointing gesture); and two theoretical issues: the "nature" of preverbal communication and the social construction of early abilities through adult–infant interaction.

Overview

The course of preverbal communicative development is punctuated by three major transitions during the first year of life. The *first* of these occurs at around 2 months of age, when infants begin to engage communicatively with adults. This change is sudden – "almost as clear a boundary as birth itself" (Stern, 1985, p. 37) – and is correlated with changes in other areas of the infant's abilities (see Emde & Robinson, 1979). The *second* transition occurs late in the fifth month of age, when infants, again quite suddenly, appear to lose their interest in face-to-face interactions with adults and become engrossed by objects that they can manipulate (Lamb, Morrison, & Malkin, 1987; Messer & Vietze, 1984). The *third* transition is less clear cut, but occurs around 9 to 10 months of age and involves the connecting up of infants' interest in objects with their emerging grasp of the agentive abilities of other people. We begin to see "real" communication emerging at this time, with infants starting to use their partners in order to achieve their goals. This third transition is associated with a number of newly emerging abilities (see Trevarthen & Hubley, 1978, pp. 221–222) that appear to have a common developmental basis – a "grasp" of their own and others' agency – and the course that any particular infant now takes in moving forward to verbal communication will vary as the different areas of this grasp and his or her emerging representational abilities are elaborated and feed back into the construction of specific skills. It is perhaps this increasing multideterminedness of development from this time on that leads to this transitional point being a little less clear cut than the two previous ones. In all cases, however, changes in cognitive abilities as new biologically determined "bits of kit" come on-line suggest that maturational factors and the general course of growth are major underwriters of the changes we see in infant communicative behaviors and actions.

The most unclear temporal point for this entire topic of "preverbal communication" is the time at which it might be said to end. There are two issues involved here. First, the individual differences between infants as to when they begin to "talk" are large, such that any time during the second year of life could be regarded as "normal." But second, when does a communicative episode or item stop being "preverbal" and become "verbal"? How one answers this question is very important. On the one hand, a clear, operational definition could be regarded as an important topic to settle, for if the "data" being studied are ill-defined, then the first stage of a scientific investigation is stymied. Yet on the other hand, clear definitions can create artifactual developmental Rubicons that then obscure the very processes of change that scientific investigations are seeking to understand. These are problems that will be returned to later in this chapter. What needs to be borne in mind until then, however, is that all of the phenomena being dealt with here are at root *transitional* rather than *categorical* ones. At the outset, infants are "without speech"; by the age of 2 years, small increments in the different strands of their development have fed back and forth amongst themselves to endow them with the qualitatively different ability of being able to "talk."

From Birth to 2 Months

This first period of an infant's life is a very difficult one to get a scientific handle on. This is not to say that a large body of reliable findings has not been established as to the major features of this time, for it has. But three difficulties have to be faced. First, as will be obvious when dealing with the development of communication, at least two partners have to be involved in the process. Thus, it is not immediately apparent what the most appropriate "unit of analysis" is: individuals or the dyads they constitute. Second, "communication" is a quite variable phenomenon. Some aspects of communication can be handled by a purely objective approach, and we can talk sensibly, for example, of communicative *signals* produced by individual animals that have become chained together to produce patterns of behaviors in which each stimulates the other to produce the stimulus for the next act, and so on (see, for example, almost any ethological study of animal courtship behaviors). Communication, at this level, is just the coordination of the activities of two individuals, and the question "what does animal A *mean* when it does X?" is not one that need be asked. This is not the case, though, with respect to linguistic communication, which, at least, has intentional and meaningful aspects that go beyond a purely objective level of description and explanation. Which is the most appropriate strategy with respect to early human infant communication – dealing with infant "behaviors" or "communicated meanings"?

Third, and related to this dilemma, is the question of subjectivity and intersubjectivity. Consider eye contact. Do we, as adults, look at each others' eyes because we find them interesting objects, either in their own right or as sources of useful information, such as what the other person is looking at? Or do we see them as "animated," and part of a channel of "communion" as opposed to "information"? This is a difficult issue if one approaches the study of eye contact from the perspective of a detached, objective observer. It is a very different issue if one acts in the role of a participant, interactive observer. The situation is similar if one is interacting with an infant. Mutual eye contact is one of the most emotionally charged and satisfying forms of interchange adults participate in with their young offspring. But what do infants make of it? Is it also a satisfying sharing or communion of being for them, or are adult eyes just very interesting things to look *at*, rather than *into*? These issues will be left for a later section. Here, the general course of communicative development will be sketched.

A major achievement by the end of this period is that adults and infants come to share increasing amounts of time "staring at each other." There appear to be a number of developmental strands that contribute to this achievement. To begin with, newborn infants periodically, but briefly, show a transitory state of quiet or inactive alertness, which is a "fragile and easily disrupted condition" (Wolff, 1987, p. 66). Infants have been reported to spend about 10 percent of their waking time in this state during their first week of life (Berg, Adkinson, & Strock, 1973), and these periods increase in both frequency and length until they occupy around half of daylight waking hours in the third month (Wolff, 1987). This state is increasingly induced when distressed infants are soothed by physical contact with others (Korner & Grobstein, 1966; Korner & Thoman, 1970). Being able to maintain this state is clearly crucial to the infant and adult subsequently sharing and modulating mutual attention to each other.

Second, an increasing "control" by the infant over the "components" of his or her states of arousal becomes apparent. Crying by newborns, for example, is not just a vocal activity but a whole package of facial distortions, limb movements, changes in skin coloration and muscle tone, breathing patterns and hand clenching (Wolff, 1987; Papoušek & Papoušek, 1977). The activity appears to be a species-specific response to distress, and the amplitude of crying conveys information about the infant's level of distress rather than any more specific information as to what the nature of that distress is. Anything more specific about what a cry might mean is a construction on the part of the adult (see, e.g., Frodi, 1985; Gustafson & Harris, 1990; Murray, 1985; Zeskind, 1985; Zeskind & Marshall, 1988). The early developmental course of crying follows what Barr (1990) has termed a *normal cry curve*: its frequency rises from birth to a peak during the second month, and then declines to a low level around 4 months of age. This turns out to be true even in cultures where, because of differences in care in comparison to those Western societies from which most of the data come, infants cry much more rarely. Konner (1976) reported that in !Kung San hunter–gatherer societies, where infants are held for 80 percent of the day and fed on average four times an hour, crying was quite a rare and brief event, and infant distress was detected by their parent more by movement than crying. Infants came to use cries just in "real" emergencies. Nonetheless, a reanalysis of the original data by Barr, Konner, Bakeman, and Adamson (1991) found the same crying curve as in other studies. Thus, while it is clear that it is infants who are doing the crying, and that there is something endogenous to infants that determines their crying behavior, the realization of this underlying developmental pattern is influenced by the social context within which it unfolds.

A similar pattern holds true for sleep–wake cycles. Neonates appear to have particular endogenous sleeping rhythms, for example, but even as early as the second week of life these are beginning to alter so as to come more in line with the diurnal patterns of their caretakers. At a subdiurnal level, periods of infant alertness come to overlap more and more with the adult routines of holding and talking to them (Chappell & Sander, 1979; Sander, 1977; Sander, Stechler, Burns, & Julia, 1970). Sander (1977, p. 147) comments that it is through these early interactions that "unique and idiosyncratic characteristics of exchange" develop that increasingly regulate the interactions of individual adult–infant dyads: endogenous rhythms become restructured around social ones, providing a patterned framework within which development proceeds.

Third, other aspects of infant emotional expression are also initially under more endogenous than exogenous control (Emde, Gaensbauer, & Harmon, 1976). Very young infants produce the whole gamut of adult facial expressions (Oster & Ekman, 1978), sometimes on appropriate occasions, such as when they taste sweet or bitter solutions (Rosenstein & Oster, 1988), but generally they do so out of any appropriate situational context. These expressions give no evidence that they are intended as communicative, but are just spontaneously produced. Infant vocalizations at this time appear to be only accompaniments to other activities rather than being under voluntary control. Major anatomical and neurological developments (both central and peripheral) are needed before sound production can be controlled. For example, as Kent (1981) has noted, the substrate required to control the 100+ facial muscles needed to modulate speech sounds is not in place until around 5 months of age. Similarly, the upper respiratory anatomy of the young infant has a typically mammalian pattern in which the larynx is placed high in the neck, enabling the air and food tracts to function independently and simultaneously (which reduces the chances of the suckling infant choking as a result of milk going into its trachea rather than its oesophagus). The typical adult human anatomy, where the larynx is descended in relation to the oesophageal opening and the air and food tracts are shared for a short distance in the throat, is not attained until the end of the first year of life (Laitman & Reidenberg, 1993).

Fourth, neonates can be described as being variously "preadapted" to having their attention drawn to different components of the communicative systems they are immersed in. Emerging perceptual systems are *selectively tuned* (to use Richards's, 1974, phrase) to dimensions that form the characteristic constellations of objects and events in their social worlds. Stern (1977, p. 37) has termed this "innateness once removed." Thus, for example, infants may not initially be specifically attracted to human faces *per se*, but adult human faces presented to them in the real time of everyday life may be sites that condense the varied perceptual dimensions that are individually attractive to infants: contrast, organization, movement, and multimodality. In addition, as with other mammals, infant auditory systems function categorically from the outset, making them well attuned to the distinctions that structure the speech sounds they are immersed in (e.g., Kuhl, 1987). In addition, the way that adults modify their social actions toward infants tends to be in ways that exaggerate those dimensions that infants already find attractive, thus making them even more attractive to infants (e.g., Fernald, 1991, for the characteristics of speech directed to infants; and Stern, 1977, for facial expression and its rhythmic integration with sound and touch).

Fifth, and unlike older infants who are most attracted to novelty, young infants are most attracted to familiar events: 2-week-old breastfed infants prefer the smell of their own mothers; within two days of birth neonates prefer their mothers' faces to those of other adults (Field, Cohen, Garcia, & Greenberg, 1984; Walton, Bower, & Bower, 1992); and because of what they will have heard most often in the womb before birth, they prefer the characteristic sounds and tempos of their mother's voice from the outset (DeCasper & Spence, 1986). Note, though, that these kinds of familiar events are always varying in their specific occurrences and manifestations. If they did not, then infants would habituate to them rather than find them so attractive.

From 3 to 6 Months

Infants change quite dramatically at the end of their second month: they begin to become intensely interested in people, and they become very rewarding "human" partners in the eyes of those who care for them (see, for details, Emde et al., 1976; Fischer & Hogan, 1989). While this change is most likely rooted in maturational factors, it has a qualitative rather than purely quantitative flavor: infants present a different interactive "feel" to adults who engage with them. This "presence" arises quickly. The objectifiable changes that accompany it fall into four areas: alertness, gaze control, smiling, and cooing. Infants are now in a state of alert awareness for around 80 percent of their waking time (Wolff, 1987) and give the impression of being able to both select objects in their environment to attend to, as well as initiate interpersonal actions, rather than merely have their attention captured by external events. Eye movements are under better control (e.g., Aslin, 1987); the caretaker's eyes can be focused on so that periods of sustained mutual regard become possible; and the distance over which coordinated interchanges can occur extends continuously outward, no longer occurring only while infants are held (Papoušek & Papoušek, 1977).

Facial expressions become more animated, and their timing synchronizes with the shared properties of the visual and physical interactions infants are engaged in, so as to leave the adult participant in no doubt that these expressions are part of their interaction with a human partner, rather than being merely random activities on the infant's part. Smiling, in particular, shifts from what has been termed endogenous to exogenous control, and is often directed to the adult with whom mutual gaze is being sustained (Emde et al., 1976; Wolff, 1987). Trevarthen (1979) has called attention to the increasing movements of the tongue and lips of the infant during interactions, terming it *prespeech*, and Fogel and Hannan (1985) have noted how such prespeech can be accompanied by hand movements that adults also read as having an expressive content. In addition, the infant's repertoire of vocal productions expands, particularly the "coos and goos" that are taken as characteristic features of infancy.

Overall, infants of this age become much more attuned to the finer details of the adult's vocal and facial expressions, and especially so to the temporal patterning of these. It is these tempos that increasingly moderate the interpersonal meshing of affect for both partners, and these properties of their interaction begin to be clearly exploited by adults so as to maintain mutually enjoyable interactions with infants. "Baby talk," exaggerated facial expressions, and the captivating of the infant's attention by exaggerating the temporal characteristics of "conversation" are prime aspects of the flowering of what Papoušek and Papoušek (1987) term "intuitive parenting." At the same time, infants become increasingly active participants in determining the course of interactions, such that the patterning of social interchanges results from the moment-to-moment responsiveness of each partner to the other, rather than being imposed by one or the other. The basics of human communicative "dancing" are in place by about 6 months of age. And then infants head off on a new tack: they become dominated by an interest in "things" rather than people.

From 6 to 9 Months

Piaget (e.g., 1936/1963) was one of the first investigators to emphasize the importance of this three-month period in an infant's life. At the beginning of this time, what he calls "secondary schemes" – aimed at objects rather than the infant's body itself (primary schemes) – make their first appearance, and these become coordinated around three months later to produce what he considered as the first truly intelligent and intentional behaviors: infants begin to act in ways that strongly suggest they are doing one thing *in order* that a particular end might be achieved. What Piaget did not emphasize in his classic account was the impact this interest in objects has for the development of communication. This shift to objects initially ruptures the episodes of mutual regard (Kaye & Fogel, 1980; Trevarthen & Hubley, 1978), but it simultaneously presents adults and infants with a new and crucially important problem – how to incorporate each other's attention into ongoing activities so as to share this emerging interest in objects, or, more generally, the world that exists beyond the boundaries of the infant's previous absorption in the microcosm of faces and voices. Where the ability to jointly focus on each other has already been achieved, the new challenges facing the infant are to coordinate these separate attentions on an extraneous feature of the world; to be able to initiate these coordinations; and to be able to tell when these have not been achieved.

From a communicative perspective, these are very important challenges, for mastering them must in some way underpin the eventual move to achieving *reference*, to be able to talk *about* a common world, which is a primary characteristic of human language. At the root of these challenges is a complicated problem of imaginative interpersonal geometry: to come to understand, for example, that another's emotional expression can be a comment about something that is happening outside of the expression itself; to be able to "read" where another is looking so as to be able to locate and share in the event they are talking about, rather than to be clueless as to what is going on; to grasp that actions of self and other can "point to" something beyond themselves, such that one doesn't look *at* another's fingers and hands when they point with them, but needs to look *in the direction* they are indicating to share in what they are pointing out. These are not easy problems to solve, and human infants are almost the only organisms known to be able to master them (see below). This mastery is very much a joint achievement rather than an individual one, with adults providing a framework for it. Adults provide a "scaffolding context" (Bruner, 1975; Wood, Bruner, & Ross, 1976) whereby they engage and sustain their involvement with infants-and-objects before infants can do this for themselves.

What infants can actually do at this point in their lives is currently unclear. Butterworth (e.g., Butterworth & Cochran, 1980; Butterworth & Jarrett, 1991; see also Scaife & Bruner, 1975), for example, argues that there is evidence that 6–9-month-olds act on the assumption that their own visual space is held in common with those they are interacting with, in that they can use the visual information of where adults are looking to guide their own looking, but what in particular they are meant to look at when they turn to follow another's gaze is not something they can work out from just observing the adult. Rather, they end up looking at something that "stands out" as worth looking at in that direction when they orient that way, it being the "ecological" features of the environment that act to complete the message that the adult is signaling. By contrast, Corkum and Moore (1995) find no evidence that infants of this age can follow another's line of regard, and that while this ability begins to come in around 12 months of age, it is still rudimentary and not fully formed until at least 15 months.

While it is important to gather more data on what infants can actually do in this period, I want to suggest that at this age it is the actions of the *adult* that are of the prime developmental significance. What I mean is this: if we take the central point from Piaget that infants learn through their actions on the world, then how the world they are learning about is structured becomes of major significance as to what they learn. There are some very important maturational changes going on with respect to infants' psychological makeup at this time, such that a number of new capabilities come "on-line" in the last quarter of the first year of their lives (see below). How these abilities are structured as they emerge, and what it is that they are put to work on, is crucially dependent on the raw material they both work on and are forged through. That is, it is not just the case that infants act on the world, but that the world itself is *transacted* to them in the way another presents it.

Consider how an adult can interact with an infant whose interests are focused on object manipulation when the objects are part of a formboard into which the pieces can be fitted. If the pieces are in their places, then they can be difficult for a 7-month-old to extract. But the infant's hands and grip can be physically assisted by the adult's actions, enabling her to achieve her aim. If the pieces are not in their places, then getting them there is even more difficult (shapes have to be oriented and matched to places, for example). Putting pieces in places is not a goal these infants can likely even formulate. But they can achieve it if the adult places the piece in such a way that it is likely to fall into its place just by touch. There are numerous reports in the literature that draw attention to the ways adults, often seamlessly, structure the opportunities infants have for attending to and manipulating their environments (e.g., Adamson & Bakeman, 1984; Bruner, 1983; Trevarthen & Hubley, 1978). In addition, it is important to remember that the actions of adults are themselves not just opportunistically forged in the changing possibilities their infants offer as they act on objects that afford different canonical actions, either (balls are for rolling and blocks are for stacking – not just sucking, for example). Rather, the momentary possibilities for where-to-go-next are themselves embedded in the form-conserving practices, techniques, and formats of the cultural sphere within which adults structure their own plans and intentions:

> the very essence of cultural development is in the collision of mature cultural forms of behaviour with the primitive forms that characterize the child's behaviour. (Vygotsky, 1981, p. 151)

While Vygotsky's point applies equally to earlier periods, its importance is more apparent and critical as infants of this age begin to act with objects.

Toward the end of this period, we begin to see glimpses of infants being able to show the first stirrings of a coordination between their previous person-oriented communication skills and at least their "reactions" with respect to objects and events. For example, Trevarthen and Hubley (1978, p. 200) report for an infant called Tracey that, at 38 weeks,

> Tracey and her mother banged hands on the table in alternation and Tracey, while looking at her mother, grinned at the effect they produced.

But to begin with, as these hints of an emerging awareness of the agency of others become apparent, there are few indications that infants can properly integrate action on objects into their communicative interactions with adults. Tomasello (1995, pp. 107–108) interprets the situation to this point thus:

> prior to 9 months of age adult–infant simultaneous looking is either fortuitous, a case of onlooking [see Bakeman & Adamson, 1984], a case of alternating attention, or results from infant gaze following as a learned response in which an adult head turn is used as a discriminative cue that an interesting sight is to be found in a particular direction. There is no joint attention or any other indication that infants at this age understand others as intentional agents.

From 9 to 12 Months

> At 40 weeks, Tracey's mother became an acknowledged participant in actions. Tracey repeatedly looked up at her mother's face when receiving an object, pausing as if to acknowledge receipt. She also looked up to her mother at breaks in her play, giving an indication of willingness to share experiences as she had never done before. (Trevarthen & Hubley, 1978, p. 200)

Nine- to 12-month-old infants also seem to be in a transitional phase. Beginning around this time, their actions on the world, and the staged integration of these into their social interactions with their culture that intrude on their otherwise individual "obsessions," start to bear fruit, enabling an active integration of infant, adult, object, and intention into more deliberate actions. There is a lot going on during this period, and the changes that are reported in infants' abilities are important in that, *first*, they evidence a qualitative shift in the character of their performance; and *second*, these changes in a number of abilities – for example, imitation (Meltzoff, 1988); conventionalized gesturing (Bates, Benigni, Bretherton, Camaioni, & Volterra, 1979); social referencing (e.g., contributors to Feinman, 1992); giving and taking objects (Clark, 1978; Griffiths, 1954) – either severally contribute to infants coming to understand that others are separate beings with intentions and attentions that may differ from their own and that need to be brought into line with their goals if they are to accomplish their own intentions, or are themselves consequent upon that emerging understanding. Interactions become increasingly coordinated (Adamson & Bakeman, 1985), such that, by the end of their first year, infants undergo "a revolution in their understanding of persons . . . that is just as coherent and dramatic as the one they undergo at around their fourth birthday" (Tomasello, 1995, p. 104; see also Bates, O'Connell, & Shore, 1987; Bretherton, 1992; Tomasello, Kruger, & Ratner, 1993).

The general course of development at this time is now quite well established in the literature. Around 9 months of age, infants begin to change their pattern of attention when interacting with objects and people simultaneously. Prior to this time, infants will focus their attention exclusively on an object that they either want or have. In the first case, infants give the appearance of being "frustrated" at their lack of success in reaching for an object, for example, and express that frustration while continuing to look at the object. The participating adult may act to give the object to the infant. But at around 9 months, infants begin to break their gaze in such situations away from the object to look back and forth between it and the adult: assistance in the pursuit of intentions is recruited rather than fortuitously received (Bates et al., 1979; Bates, Camaioni, & Volterra, 1975; Lock, 1978, 1980). Similarly, actions in pursuit of direct goals start to become stylized and aimed at the goal of getting the adult to act on the infant's behalf. Desired objects can be "requested," and interesting sights can be "pointed" to so as to establish joint attention on them, and infants develop a number of, often idiosyncratic, gestures that can convey their desires (*protoimperatives*) and interests (*protodeclaratives*) (Bates, 1976).

Requests and "referential" gestures appear to have separate roots. Requests develop first and are usually styled, or iconized, from direct actions: a stylized reach or upturned palm in the recruitment of assistance in obtaining an object (e.g., Bruner, Roy, & Ratner, 1982; Clark, 1978), or raising both arms so as to be picked up (Service, 1984), for example. To begin with, these gestures are tied very closely to their immediate context of occurrence and only later extend beyond this as the infant's abilities to predict events increases. Thus, for example, a 9-month-old might arm-raise when confronted with indications that she is about to be picked up; whereas a 13-month-old might anticipate being picked up because a meal is imminent and so indicate by arm-raising to a nearby adult in anticipation of needing to be moved to his chair. Similarly, the distance over which objects can be requested also increases (Bruner et al., 1982; Werner & Kaplan, 1963), as can the specificity of what is being requested by an increasing repertoire of stylized actions that can be recruited for the purpose of communicating particular intentions (for example, using a twisting motion of the wrist and hand to specify "open this jar for me").

Pointing becomes productive later than requests, at around 12 months. Despite an increasing number of studies of this gesture, its actual developmental origins are still unclear. Some have argued (e.g., Vygotsky, 1966; Werner & Kaplan, 1963) that it is an abbreviated reach. Others (e.g., Bates, 1976; Leung & Rheingold, 1981) have claimed that it is originally an action for the self, enabling an infant to better keep his or her own attention on an object, and that this only later becomes imported into directing the attention of others. Still others contend that its origins are to be found in direct object exploration using the index finger, and all that happens developmentally is that this exploratory action is called into play with respect to objects that are just out of reach, and so it socially functions by default to direct another's attention, later becoming controlled by the infant for this purpose. Yet others have argued that the gesture is likely innate, since it has been regarded as a species-specific characteristic of humans alone (e.g., Butterworth, 1995); while further, some have claimed it is learned by imitation. There is now some evidence that it is a gesture that is used by chimpanzees, especially those with a deal of experience with human social interaction, and so it is not truly a unique species characteristic of humans (Leavens & Hopkins, 1998; Leavens, Hopkins, & Bard, 1996).

The fact, however, that this has taken so long to be reported after countless hours have been put into studying primates in the past 30 years – studies that have clearly demonstrated "request" gestures of various sorts – suggests that pointing does not come easily to nonhuman primates, and that divorcing "desires" from objects into just wanting to "say something" about an object, event, or where one is looking is that much more difficult to achieve than requesting. (Note also that humans are additionally adapted to be "attention-directing organisms" by the coloration of their eyes – unique amongst primates in having "whites" to them which might well function to increase the detectability of another's gaze.) We might also infer this from the fact that a number of breeds of domestic dog are very good at incorporating gaze checking into ongoing object games with their owners – looking from ball to owner to ball – and can use objects as props to specify their desires – bringing leads to go for a walk or dishes to get fed – but do not "point" so as to direct attention to interesting events, nor comprehend pointing gestures either (rather, they look at or sniff one's fingers). Pointing does appear to have a separate origin from request gestures and is most likely rooted in attention directing rather than trying to gain contact with objects, with other factors fitting into providing the foundations for the mature performance of the act (for example, the anatomical configuration of the human hand predisposes the use of the index rather than any other finger for the actual performance of a point – see, e.g., Lock, Young, Service, & Chandler, 1990; Povinelli & Davis, 1994).

Developments during this time have been theorized as arising in different ways. Cognitive explanations have tended to be either inspired by the Piagetian notion of a fundamental reconfiguration of cognition that informs action in many different spheres (e.g., Adamson, Bakeman, & Smith, 1990; Fischer & Farrar, 1988), or by developments occurring separately in different domains that in concert establish a base for a new emergent ability which capitalizes on the achievements in the developmental strands that enable it. Bates and her colleagues (e.g., 1979) found that measures of an infant's abilities with respect to conventionalized communicative skills, imitation, tool use (an index of the infant's understanding of means–end relations), object permanence, and spatial relations were independent of each other at any particular age for infants in their study, but that the measures for the first three at the earlier ages were predictive of the time of emergence of productive symbolic communicative acts at a later age. This makes intuitive sense in that to use a conventional "word" requires one to know how to communicate, know how to reproduce (imitate) a conventional sound, and to have abstracted that sound out of the flow of speech one is immersed in (abstraction being integral to the mastery of means–end relations).

By contrast, Trevarthen (1988) argues for a genetic base to the emergence of intentional communication, taking the view that there is a real difference in the nature of understanding the causal world of objects and the intentional nature of people, and that the basis for this latter understanding is built into the design of the developing human brain, which is anatomically partitioned from the outset into three modes:

> These modes are probably three real systems of the brain that achieve functional differentiation by interaction with each other and with the environment. Forms of action and perceptual processing appropriate for (1) knowing and using objects (praxic mode), for (2) communicating with the human world (communicative mode), and for (3) acting in a self-directed or thoughtful manner (reflective mode) appear as distinct rudiments in the newborn. (Trevarthen & Hubley, 1978, p. 213)

It is the maturation of these systems, and the consequent possibilities for the integration of the developing "contents," that accounts for the timing of the emergence of new levels of communicative competence. The evidence consistent with this claim is that there are detectable changes in cortical functioning that correlate with the timing of the changes noted thus far in the first year of life (e.g., Thatcher, Walker, & Giudice, 1987); cortical maturation correlates with the onset of new, apparently modular, abilities (e.g., Baron-Cohen, 1995); the universality of the timing of these shifts cross-culturally (e.g., Bakeman, Adamson, Konner, & Barr, 1990; Trevarthen, 1988); and Bruner's trenchant question (1995, p. 2):

> could any infant, or anybody for that matter, ever learn from scratch, from experience alone, that somebody was looking at something, and it was the same thing the infant was looking at? You would somehow have to know a priori that somebody was looking at something before it would occur to you to figure out what they were looking at.

Thus, Trevarthen and Hubley (1978, p. 213) posit an innate *intersubjectivity*:

> This function identifies persons, regulates motivation and intention toward them, and simultaneously forms rudimentary acts of speech and gesture in patterned combinations and sequences. It also provides internal images of face and hand movements for the identification and imitation of the expressions of others.

It would seem most likely that both cognitive achievements and maturation are integral to these changes in infant abilities, and that the course of development in any particular child is determined by the unique constellation of events that child's maturing "wetware" has available to it in the course of its structural – and hence functional – differentiation. One such account is the *dynamic systems perspective* (e.g., Fogel, 1990; Thelen, 1989; Thelen & Smith, 1994; van Geert, 1991). Clearly, one thing that we do know beyond doubt from the intensive work on infancy in the past 40 years is that single-factor explanations are wide of the required mark. This realization enriches our conception of these early developmental processes, but at the same time makes the "telling of a normative tale" as to the actual course of development that much more difficult, for there is no one way in which infants might go on to "crack the symbolic code." Rather, there are lots of individual trajectories that can be traversed to reach a successful outcome (Nelson, 1996).

That said, however, we can expect, at the end of this period – that is, around the infant's first birthday – to find ourselves confronted by a sophisticated communicator who as yet cannot use language but who can, amongst other things,

- execute intentions alone and in harness with others;
- coordinate objects and people together in pursuit of these intentions;
- use gestures to partly specify these intentions (see below);
- subordinate his or her own actions to the regulatory control of a limited number of another's words;
- voluntarily give, take, and request objects in interaction with others, and who has "fined down" some control of his or her own repertoire of sound production.

By this age, the infant is on the verge of the symbolic realm, being able, for example, to use objects inventively to "stand for" other objects in pretend play and to reproduce others' actions over long time delays (deferred imitation).

Developments in the Second Year

Consider the episodes captured in Figures 14.1 and 14.2, which portray a 12-month infant deploying all the skills she has amassed during her first year of life so as to very clearly convey to another what she wants: in one case an apple, in the other "more to drink." How does she go from here into "language"? On the one hand, the apparently simple task of offering a description of the schedule of changes that we can expect to occur has proved more difficult to arrive at than might be expected. On the other hand, the much more difficult task of explaining how language is arrived at has proved to be just that: much more difficult.

The Schedule of Events

> "In the beginning was the word" is exactly wrong; in the beginning was the utterance. (McShane, 1980, p. 1)

Water-tight definitions of what words and reference are have proved to be elusive. This makes simple story, such as the following, at once useful and inadequate. Infants begin to use single words around the start of their second year of life (citing references here would be superfluous). Their vocabularies increase slowly at first, with only a few items

Figure 14.1   Unable to reach the apple (1), the child turns to attract the adult's attention by vocalizing (2). Having established eye contact with the adult (3), the child uses a pointing gesture to direct the adult's attention to the apple (4), thereby identifying the object implied as being wanted by the tonality of the vocalization (from Lock, 1980, p. 98).

added each month. Gestures tend to co-occur with utterances at this time, and seem to act in concert with what is spoken (Zinober & Martlew, 1986: a point, for example, serves to identify the object that is simultaneously named). Gestures tend to outnumber words in the first part of the second year, but after that vocal signs become more dominant (Iverson, Capirici, & Caselli, 1994). The shift from gesture to words probably results from the verbal envelope of everyday social life that infant development is immersed in, there being little evidence that infants are predisposed to favor vocal over manual production, or vice versa (Bates et al., 1979). Somewhere toward the middle of the second year, a rapid increase in the rate of development sets in (e.g., Halliday, 1975; Nelson, 1973). A number of the early investigators (e.g., Moore, 1896; Stern & Stern, 1907), as well as more recent ones (e.g., McShane, 1980), argue that it is at this point that infants gain the *insight* that words name or refer to things, and that armed with this principle they can learn new words more rapidly than by building up more laborious individual sound–object associations. Gestures now seem to accompany utterances as complements to "words": that is, a point may single out an object that something can then be said about (Zinober & Martlew, 1986). By the end of their second year, children (they are not infants anymore) are combining words together in predictable and regular ways, and these regularities can be captured in simple rule systems. Whether these rule systems are productive or descriptive of the child's output is not settled at this point, and neither is

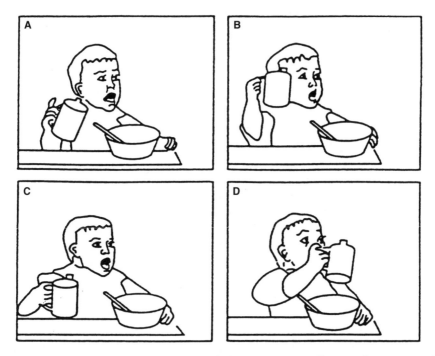

Figure 14.2   Incorporating an object into preverbal communication (from Lock, 1980, p. 98).

the question of whether the regularities found in child speech at this age are generated by the same mechanisms that have been claimed to later underwrite "true" grammar.[1] Gestures become much less frequent in the language activities of hearing children from the age of 2, and the burden of "making meaning" falls on words, their ordering, their intonation, and their emphases.

Most researchers would probably accept this story as a reasonable generalization, and there are both studies with large numbers of subjects (e.g., Bates, Bretherton, & Snyder, 1988; Caselli et al., 1995), and also compilations across studies of the period (e.g., McCarthy, 1954; Reich, 1986) that do suggest a set of "average milestones." But the problem with it is not just that we need to add provisos as to individual differences amongst infants – as to how this sequence is actually played out developmentally (e.g., Nelson, 1973, has characterized two broad styles of early language development, referential and expressive: referential infants tend to show a vocabulary spurt as described above; expressive children do not). Rather, and in contradiction to the claim that the above is a reasonable generalization, there is in fact quite a lack of agreement amongst different researchers as to the nature of early speech: for example, Dale (1980) finds naming to be the earliest-appearing form of speech; whereas Halliday (1975) finds no evidence of naming at all for the child he studied during the same period. There are a number of reasons why this could be the case. First, there are marked individual differences amongst the children whose language development has been studied. From these differences we need to note that:

1   The view that there is a universal sequence of stages is a myth. Elucidating the way in which this myth has been constructed and interwoven with theoretical claims as to the innate bases of language in humans – claims which have then become categories that mold the data to fit them – would make for a paradigmatic case study in the history of science; and

2   It is more likely that language emerges from a system of underlying competencies (e.g., van Geert, 1991; cf. above on dynamic systems approaches), and that any biological imperatives are of a general nature that make "language" of salience to infants (Bates & Carnavale, 1993), rather than depending on a single module or suite of modules.

Second, different researchers use both different coding schemes and different theoretical perspectives, and these can make comparisons between studies and the drawing of generalizations from them very difficult. Third, and perhaps the major problem, is that there is no clear definition of the boundaries of what constitutes meaningful and conventional language. This last problem is crucial. It might reasonably be thought that little progress can be made without clearly defined operational categories. However, such categories, in setting up Rubicons that must be traversed, can fundamentally obscure the nature of development in this period: and theoretical convenience should not act so as to mask the nature of developmental processes of change over time. It is unlikely that there exists in the infant at any point in time a definable cognitive system for us to discover. We should not ask, for example, "what does the infant mean when he or she says 'doggie'?" with the hope of uncovering the semantic features of this word that are represented in the infant's mind. Rather, we should be asking questions such as: "What might the infant be on the way to meaning when saying such a thing? What might the infant be taken to be meaning by an adult in saying this, and how is the 'acting out' of this interpretation 'responded to' by the infant?" We need a more adequate framework within which to locate our understanding of changes during this period.

Toward a More Adequate Theorization of Early Communicative Development

What might we need by way of a theory to deal with these changes in infancy? This is dangerous speculative territory, but I offer the following suggestions nonetheless. For a number of reasons, the fact that all our psychological abilities work in concert to provide us with an *experience* of being-in-the-world has been underemphasized in contemporary psychological science, to the point where we tend to forget that this is the case. We have been committed to a rigid division of the objective from the subjective through adopting the methodologies of sciences that study *the* environment from the position of a detached, disembodied observer whose senses are augmented by prosthetic devices (Bruner, 1966; La Barre, 1954) that allow us to sense worlds otherwise hidden from us. We have forgotten that *the* environment is different from *our* environment. I suggest that there are a number of strands of work that provide the outlines of a potential framework that allow us to get back to where we really belong.

(1) Katherine Nelson (1996, p. 10) has recognized one of the steps we need to make:

> it is necessary for psychologists to understand the nature of the child's experience at different points in development. This requires in part the specification of the environment, as in ethological and ecological studies; it requires as well, and specifically, an effort to understand the perspective of the experiencing individual.

However, while endorsing this stance on Nelson's part, I am leaving aside the particular framework within which she goes on to develop her discussion once she has made this shift: that is, as a framework within which to better elucidate the ways in which a child comes to *represent* the world. My reasons for this caveat are that there are real concerns as to the continuing usefulness of the entire representational cognitive paradigm when it comes to dealing with "experience," irrespective of how useful this view might continue to be in explaining how "information is shunted around and processed" by the underlying physiological systems that act to create that experience. A self-contained, discretely representative knowledge system seems an increasingly unlikely candidate as an explanatory device now that other alternatives have come to challenge its hegemony over our ways of dealing with the issues. There are now clear alternatives that need to be weighed against each other.

(2) Of these, the framework of "embodied cognition" that has emerged in current artificial intelligence and robotic science provides a second strand, more suited to dealing with "experience" in that it allows us to get away from the problems inherent in disembodying knowledge as symbolic representational mental systems, and reunites "mind and body, world and action" (for a review, see Clark, 1996). What we find here is a framework that enables us to "dump" a great deal of the information required for the control of ongoing action back into *the* environment, in a sense using the objects in the world as the best representations of themselves, as a scaffold for *our* own effective, behavioral environments.

(3) Once we have distributed "intelligence" back into the mutually supportive and constitutive relationship between form and environment, then we can pick up on two related concepts separately stated by Macmurray (1961) and Vygotsky (1966). First, Macmurray's view is that the human infant:

> is not an independent individual. He lives a common life as one term in a personal relationship. Only in the process of development does he learn to achieve a relative independence, and that only by appropriating the techniques of a rational social tradition. . . . The unit of the personal is not the "I," but the "You and I." (1961, pp. 50, 61)

Vygotsky's take on this is his insight that:

> Any function in the child's cultural development appears on the stage twice, on two planes, first on the social plane and then on the psychological, first among people as an intermental category and then within the child as an intermental category. (1966, p. 44)

Figure 14.3 A "hidden figure" that, once seen, continues to be seen on subsequent reviewings (from Lindsay & Norman, 1972, p. 146).

Putting these points together enables us to grasp how the "sense" that infants come to find in the events that make up their perceptual world is structured not just by their own actions, but by those of others. In this sense, "making sense" of the world is accomplished communicatively, and objects and events come to be known on their reappearance in the infant's perceptual field for what they can do: properties are constituted as intrinsic to objects and events through their social nature as "props" in the interactive acting out of intentions.

As an analogy for this suggested "way of looking" at the problem, consider the random dots in Figure 14.3. Unlike the famous reversing figure–ground images beloved by Gestalt psychologists, once one has "seen" the Dalmatian dog in the pattern one cannot go back to seeing it as a random collection. This, I suggest, is what happens to objects and events the infant encounters: these come to present themselves differently to the infant's immediate perception of them as they come to have more and more "affordances" structured into them.

A more precise way of dealing with these changes, particularly from the point of understanding the course of communicative development, is to theorize infants as involved in uncovering the implicit properties of their actions in the world (e.g., Lock, 1980, 1997). These implicit properties have been made explicit by previous generations and are part and parcel of the cultural system infants grow up in. One cultural rendering we could give to Figure 14.1 is that the infant means "I want you to give me that apple." The infant controls this implication in her actions. She began by gaining control of lower-level implications: knowing what she needs, she will reach for an object; but only post-9 months of age will she come to control the implication that "if I want that, and can't reach it, then you must give it to me," and we start to see her "appealing" to adults for assistance. And only very late in the play will she bring out for herself an explicit marking of her implied existence: post the attainment of symbols and propositions, she will "assume" her self, a self that has been there as an object of others' acts to and with her, but not constructed as something that can be talked about until language is in place.

Preverbal communication can thus be seen as a period in which infants are coming to control the implications of their situation in the world. Their developing biological and psychological "mechanisms" are simultaneously structured by the perceptual environment they constitute as infants' emerging experience or *Umwelt*. As new bits of "kit" come on-line, infants are thereby enabled to grasp, in an ordered fashion, the implications of their situation. The nature of communicative development is best captured by (1) describing it as the "coming to control" the implications of being an infant; and (2) explaining it as an interplay between emerging "wetware" and the socially mediated experiential world that this wetware underwrites.

Note

1   On this latter point, for example, it is now clear that under particular circumstances both species of *Pan* can use words in as complicated ways as human 2-year-olds. It is less certain that *Pan* individuals go beyond this level. It could be that species other than humans lack a set of organizing resources for language that "come on-line" in humans around the age of 2, and that these early word combinations have nothing truly linguistic about them in their structural aspects at all. On the other hand, it could be that a linguistic organizer comes in quite early for human infants, and our two-word utterances are not homologously generated as compared to those of other species.

Further Reading

1   Romanes, G. (1897). Origins of human faculty. In C. L. Morgan (Ed.), *Essays by George John Romanes* (pp. 86–112). London: Longman, Green. [Reprinted 1984 in A. Lock & E. Fisher (Eds.), *Language development* (pp. 25–38). London: Croom Helm.] This is a wonderful descriptive paper. Romanes shows himself to be a "systems thinker" of the first order in setting out, in the metaphors of his day, how a language system might put itself together in the first place. Romanes's concern is to state *what* has to be done and hint at *how* it might be done. His statements may now appear a little quaint, but he does set out a famework within which our own thoughts about the current database can be ordered. His paper thus still provides a clear introduction to what infants are doing, and allows us to formulate questions about how they do it.
2   Bullowa, M. (1979). *Before speech*. Cambridge: Cambridge University Press; Golinkoff, R. (1983). *The transition from prelinguistic to linguistic communication*. Hillsdale, NJ: Erlbaum; Lock, A. J. (Ed.). (1978). *Action, gesture, and symbol: The emergence of language*. London: Academic Press; Schaffer, R. (1977). *Studies in mother–infant interaction*. London: Academic Press. This group of "early modern" edited volumes between them set the agenda for the field as it is today. They contain a number of "data-rich" papers, as well as conceptual ones on concepts such as "intersubjectivity," "joint attention and action," and "prelinguistic communication."

3   Adamson, L. B. (1995). *Communication development during infancy*. Boulder, CO: Westview Press. Adamson's book is a thorough and very readable introduction to the field as it had developed up until the mid-1990s. It is both accessible by undergraduates by virtue of the clarity of its explanation of central concepts, and detailed enough to serve as a reference source for researchers.

References

Adamson, L. B., & Bakeman, R. (1984). Mothers' communicative acts: Changes during infancy. *Infant Behavior and Development, 7*, 467–478.

Adamson, L. B., & Bakeman, R. (1985), Affect and attention: Infants observed with mothers and peers. *Child Development, 56*, 582–593.

Adamson, L. B., Bakeman, R., & Smith, C. B. (1990). Gestures, words, and early object sharing. In V. Volterra & C. Erting (Eds.), *From gesture to language in hearing and deaf children* (pp. 31–41). New York: Springer Verlag.

Aslin, R. N. (1987). Visual and auditory development in infancy. In J. D. Osofsky (Ed.), *Handbook of infant development* (2nd ed., pp. 5–97). New York: Wiley.

Bakeman, R., & Adamson, L. B. (1984). Coordinating attention to people and objects in mother–infant and peer–peer interaction. *Child Development, 55*, 1278–1289.

Bakeman, R., Adamson, L. B., Konner, M., & Barr, R. G. (1990). !Kung infancy: The social context of object exploration. *Child Development, 61*, 794–809.

Baron-Cohen, S. (1995). The eye direction detector (EDD) and the shared attention mechanism (SAM): Two cases for evolutionary psychology. In C. Moore & P. J. Dunham (Eds.), *Joint attention: Its origins and role in development* (pp. 41–59). Hillsdale, NJ: Erlbaum.

Barr, R. G. (1990). The normal crying curve: What do we really know? *Developmental Medicine and Child Neurology, 32*, 369–374.

Barr, R. G., Konner, M., Bakeman, R., & Adamson, L. B. (1991). Crying in !Kung San infants: A test of the cultural specificity model. *Developmental Medicine and Child Neurology, 33*, 601–611.

Bates, E. (1976). *Language and context: The acquisition of pragmatics.* New York: Academic Press.

Bates, E., Benigni, L., Bretherton, I., Camaioni, L., & Volterra, V. (1979). *The emergence of symbols: Cognition and communication in infancy.* New York: Academic Press.

Bates, E., Bretherton, I., & Snyder, L. (1988). *From first words to grammar: Individual differences and dissociable mechanisms.* Cambridge: Cambridge University Press.

Bates, E., Camaioni, L., & Volterra, V. (1975). The acquisition of performatives prior to speech. *Merrill-Palmer Quarterly, 21*, 205–226.

Bates, E., & Carnavale, G. F. (1993). New directions in research on language development. *Developmental Review, 13*, 436–470.

Bates, E., O'Connell, B., & Shore, C. (1987). Language and communication in infancy. In J. D. Osofsky (Ed.), *Handbook of infant development* (2nd ed., pp. 149–203). New York: Wiley.

Bayley, N. (1969). *Bayley scales of infant development.* Cleveland, OH: Psychological Corporation.

Berg, W. K., Adkinson, C. D. P., & Strock, B. D. (1973). Duration and frequency of periods of alertness in neonates. *Developmental Psychology, 9*, 434.

Bonasso, R. P., Huber, E., & Kortenkamp, D. (1995, Fall). *Recognizing and interpreting gestures within the context of an intelligent robot control architecture.* American Association for Artificial Intelligence (AAAI) Symposium on *Embodied Language and Action.*

Bretherton, I. (1992). Social referencing, intentional communication, and the interfacing of minds in infancy. In S. Feinman (Ed.), *Social referencing and the social construction of reality in infancy* (pp. 57–77). New York: Plenum Press.

Bruner, J. S. (1966). On cognitive growth. In J. S. Bruner, P. Greenfield, & R. Olver (Eds.), *Studies in cognitive growth* (pp. 1–29). Cambridge, MA: Harvard University Press.

Bruner, J. S. (1975). From communication to language: A psychological perspective. *Cognition, 3,* 255–287.

Bruner, J. S. (1983). *Child's talk: Learning to use language.* New York: Norton.

Bruner, J. S. (1995). From joint attention to the meeting of minds: An introduction. In C. Moore & P. J. Dunham (Eds.), *Joint attention: Its origins and role in development* (pp. 1–14). Hillsdale, NJ: Erlbaum.

Bruner, J. S., Roy, C., & Ratner, N. (1982). The beginnings of request. In K. E. Nelson (Ed.), *Children's language* (Vol. 3, pp. 91–138). Hillsdale, NJ: Erlbaum.

Butterworth, G. E. (1995). Origins of mind in perception and action. In C. Moore & P. J. Dunham (Eds.), *Joint attention: Its origins and role in development* (pp. 29–40). Hillsdale, NJ: Erlbaum.

Butterworth, G. E., & Cochran, E. (1980). Towards a mechanism of joint visual attention in human infancy. *International Journal of Behavioural Development, 3,* 253–272.

Butterworth, G. E., & Jarrett, N. L. M. (1991). What minds have in common is space: Spatial mechanisms for perspective taking in infancy. *British Journal of Developmental Psychology, 9,* 55–72.

Caselli, M. C., Bates, E., Casadio, P., Fenson, L., Sanderl, L., & Weir, J. (1995). A cross-linguistic study of early lexical development. *Cognitive Development, 10,* 159–200.

Chappell, P. F., & Sander, L. W. (1979). Mutual regulation of the neonatal–maternal interactive process: Context for the origins of communication. In M. Bullowa (Ed.), *Before speech: The beginning of interpersonal communication* (pp. 89–109). Cambridge: Cambridge University Press.

Clark, A. (1996). *Being there: Putting brain, body, and world together again.* Cambridge, MA: MIT Press.

Clark, R. A. (1978). The transition from action to gesture. In A. J. Lock (Ed.), *Action, gesture, and symbol: The emergence of language* (pp. 231–257). London: Academic Press.

Corkum, V., & Moore, C. (1995). The origins of joint visual attention. In C. Moore & P. Dunham (Eds.), *Joint attention: Its origins and role in development* (pp. 61–83). Hillsdale, NJ: Erlbaum.

Dale, P. S. (1980). Is early pragmatic development measurable? *Journal of Child Language, 7,* 1–12.

Darwin, C. (1877). A biographical sketch of an infant. *Mind, 2,* 285–294.

DeCasper, A. J., & Spence, M. J. (1986). Prenatal maternal speech influences newborns' perception of speech sounds. *Infant Behavior and Development, 9,* 133–150.

Emde, R. N., Gaensbauer, T. J., & Harmon, R. J. (1976). Emotional expression in infancy: A biobehavioral study. *Psychological Issues* (Monograph No. 37). New York: International Universities Press.

Emde, R. N., & Robinson, J. (1979). The first two months: Recent research in developmental psychobiology and the changing view of the newborn. In J. Noshpitz (Ed.), *Basic handbook of child psychiatry* (pp. 72–105). New York: Basic Books.

Feinman, S. (Ed.). (1992). *Social referencing and the social construction of reality in infancy.* New York: Plenum Press.

Fernald, A. (1991). Prosody in speech to children: Prelinguistic and linguistic functions. In R. Vasta (Ed.), *Annals of child development* (Vol. 8, pp. 43–80). London: Jessica Kingsley.

Ferrell, C., & Scassellati, B. (1998). *Infant-like social interactions between a robot and a human caretaker.* Paper submitted to Special Issue of *Adaptive Behavior* on Simulation Models of Social Agents, Guest Ed. Kerstin Dautenhahn.

Field, T. M., Cohen, D., Garcia, R., & Greenberg, R. (1984). Mother–stranger face discrimination by the newborn. *Infant Behavior and Development, 7,* 19–25.

Fischer, K. W., & Farrar, M. J. (1988). Generalizations about generalizations: How a theory of skill development explains generality and specificity. In A. Demetriou (Ed.), *The neo-Piagetian theories of cognitive development: Toward an integration* (pp. 137–171). Amsterdam: Elsevier.

Fischer, K. W., & Hogan, A. E. (1989). The big picture for infant development: Levels and variations. In J. J. Lockman & N. L. Hazen (Eds.), *Action in social context: Perspectives on early development* (pp. 275–305). New York: Plenum Press.

Fogel, A. (1990). The process of developmental change in infant communicative action: Using dynamic systems theory to study individual ontogenies. In J. Colombo & J. Fagen (Eds.), *Individual differences in infancy: Reliability, stability, prediction* (pp. 341–358). Hillsdale, NJ: Erlbaum.

Fogel, A., & Hannan, T. E. (1985). Manual actions of nine- and fifteen-week-old human infants during face-to-face interaction with their mothers. *Child Development, 56,* 1271–1279.

Frodi, A. M. (1985). When empathy fails: Aversive infant crying and child abuse. In B. M. Lester & C. F. Z. Boukydis (Eds.), *Infant crying: Theoretical and research perspectives* (pp. 217–277). New York: Plenum Press.

Gesell, A. (1945). *The embryology of behavior: The beginnings of the human mind.* New York: Harper Brothers.

Griffiths, R. (1954). *The abilities of babies.* London: London University Press.

Gustafson, G. E., & Harris, K. L. (1990). Women's responses to young infants' cries. *Developmental Psychology, 26,* 144–152.

Halliday, M. A. K. (1975). *Learning how to mean.* London: Arnold.

Iverson, J. M., Capirici, O., & Caselli, M. C. (1994). From communication to language in two modalities. *Cognitive Development, 9,* 23–44.

Kahn, R. E., & Swain, M. J. (1995, November). *Understanding people pointing: The Perseus system.* International Symposium on Computer Vision.

Kaye, K., & Fogel, A. (1980). The temporal structure of face-to-face communication between mothers and infants. *Developmental Psychology, 16,* 454–464.

Kent, R. D. (1981). Sensorimotor aspects of speech development. In R. N. Aslin, J. R. Alberts, & M. R. Petersen (Eds.), *Development and perception: Psychobiological perspectives* (Vol. 1, pp. 161–189). New York: Academic Press.

Konner, M. J. (1976). Maternal care, infant behavior and development among the !Kung. In R. B. Lee & I. DeVore (Eds.), *Kalahari hunter–gatherers: Studies of the !Kung San and their neighbors* (pp. 218–245). Cambridge, MA: Harvard University Press.

Korner, A. F., & Grobstein, R. (1966). Visual alertness as related to soothing in neonates: Implications for maternal stimulation and early deprivation. *Child Development, 37,* 867–876.

Korner, A. F., & Thoman, E. B. (1970). Visual alertness in neonates as evoked by maternal care. *Journal of Experimental Child Psychology, 10,* 67–78.

Kozima, H., & Ito, A. (1998). Towards language acquisition by an attention-sharing robot. International Conference on *Computational Natural Language Learning (CoNLL-98, Australia),* 245–246.

Kuhl, P. K. (1987). Perception of speech and sound in early infancy. In P. Salapatek & L. Cohen (Eds.), *Handbook of infant perception* (Vol. 2, pp. 275–382). Orlando, FL: Academic Press.

La Barre, W. (1954). *The human animal.* Chicago: University of Chicago Press.

Laitman, J. T., & Reidenberg, J. S. (1993). Comparative and developmental anatomy of human laryngeal position. In B. Bailey (Ed.), *Head and neck surgery: Otolaryngology* (Vol. 1, pp. 36–43). Philadelphia: Lippincott.

Lamb, M. E., Morrison, D. C., & Malkin, C. M. (1987). The development of infant social expectations in face-to-face interaction. A longitudinal study. *Merrill-Palmer Quarterly, 33,* 241–254.

Leavens, D. A., & Hopkins, W. D. (1998). Intentional communication by chimpanzees: A cross-sectional study of the use of referential gestures. *Developmental Psychology, 34,* 813–822.

Leavens, D. A., Hopkins, W. D., & Bard, K. A. (1996). Indexical and referential pointing in chimpanzees (*Pan troglodytes*). *Journal of Comparative Psychology, 110,* 346–353.

Leung, E. H. L., & Rheingold, H. L. (1981). Development of pointing as a social gesture. *Developmental Psychology, 17,* 215–220.

Lindsay, P. H., & Norman, D. A. (1972). *Human information processing: An introduction to psychology.* New York: Academic Press.

Lock, A. (Ed.). (1978). *Action, gesture, and symbol: The emergence of language.* London: Academic Press.

Lock, A. (1980). *The guided reinvention of language.* London: Academic Press.

Lock, A. (1997). The role of gesture in the establishment of symbolic abilities: Continuities and discontinuities in early language development. *Evolution of Communication, 1,* 159–192.

Lock, A., Young, A. W., Service, V., & Chandler, P. (1990). The origins of infant pointing gestures. In V. Volterra & C. Erting (Eds.), *From gesture to language in hearing and deaf children* (pp. 42–55). New York: Springer Verlag.

Macmurray, J. (1961). *Persons in relation.* London: Faber & Faber.

McCarthy, D. (1954). Language development in children. In L. Carmichael (Ed.), *Manual of child psychology* (2nd ed., pp. 492–630). New York: Wiley.

McShane, J. (1980). *Learning to talk.* Cambridge: Cambridge University Press.

Meltzoff, A. N. (1988). Infant imitation and memory: Nine-month-olds in immediate and deferred tests. *Child Development, 59,* 217–225.

Messer, D. J., & Vietze, P. M. (1984). Timing and transitions in mother–infant gaze. *Infant Behavior and Development, 7,* 167–181.

Moore, K. (1896). The mental development of a child. *Psychological Review, Monograph Supplements, 1,* 115–145.

Murchison, C., & Langer, S. K. (1927). Tiedemann's observations on the development of the mental faculties of children. *The Pedagogical Seminary and Journal of Genetic Psychology, 34,* 205–230.

Murray, A. D. (1985). Aversiveness is in the mind of the beholder: Perception of infant crying by adults. In B. M. Lester & C. F. Z. Boukydis (Eds.), *Infant crying: Theoretical and research perspectives* (pp. 217–239). New York: Plenum Press.

Nelson, K. (1973). Structure and strategy in learning to talk. *Monographs of the Society for Research in Child Development, 38* (1–2, Serial No. 149).

Nelson, K. (1996). *Language in cognitive development.* Cambridge: Cambridge University Press.

Oster, H., & Ekman, P. (1978). Facial behavior in child development. In W. A. Collins (Ed.), *Minnesota symposium on child psychology* (Vol. 11, pp. 231–279). Hillsdale, NJ: Erlbaum.

Papoušek, H., & Papoušek, M. (1977). Mothering and the cognitive headstart: Psychobiological considerations. In H. R. Scaffer (Ed.), *Studies in mother–infant interaction* (pp. 63–88). London: Academic Press.

Papoušek, H., & Papoušek, M. (1987). Intuitive parenting: A dialectic counterpart to the infant's integrative competence. In J. D. Osofsky (Ed.), *Handbook of infant development* (2nd ed., pp. 669–720). New York: Wiley.

Piaget, J. (1963). *The origins of intelligence in children.* New York: Norton. (Original work published 1936)

Povinelli, D. J., & Davis, D. R. (1994). Differences between chimpanzees (*Pan troglodytes*) and humans (*Homo sapiens*) in the resting state of the index finger: Implications for pointing. *Journal of Comparative Psychology, 108*, 134–139.

Reich, P. (1986). *Language development.* Englewood Cliffs, NJ: Prentice-Hall.

Richards, M. P. M. (1974). First steps in becoming social. In M. P. M. Richards (Ed.), *The integration of a child into a social world* (pp. 83–97). Cambridge: Cambridge University Press.

Rosenstein, D., & Oster, H. (1988). Differential facial responses to four basic tastes in newborns. *Child Development, 59*, 1555–1568.

Sander, L. W. (1977). The regulation of exchange in the infant–caretaker system and some aspects of the context–content relationship. In M. Lewis & L. A. Rosenblum (Eds.), *Interaction, conversation, and the development of language* (pp. 133–156). New York: Wiley.

Sander, L. W., Stechler, G., Burns, P., & Julia, H. (1970). Early mother–infant interaction and 24-hour patterns of activity and sleep. *Journal of the American Academy of Child Psychiatry, 9*, 103–123.

Scaife, M., & Bruner, J. S. (1975). The capacity for joint visual attention in the infant. *Nature, 253*, 265–266.

Service, V. (1984). Maternal styles and communicative development. In A. Lock & E. Fisher (Eds.), *Language development* (pp. 132–140). London: Croom Helm/Routledge.

Spitz, R. A. (1957). *No and yes: On the beginnings of human communication.* New York: International Universities Press.

Stern, D. N. (1977). *The first relationship: Infant and mother.* Cambridge, MA: Harvard University Press.

Stern, D. N. (1985). *The interpersonal world of the infant: A view from psychoanalysis and developmental psychology.* New York: Basic Books.

Stern, W., & Stern, C. (1907). *Die Kindersprache.* Leipzig: Barth.

Thatcher, R. W., Walker, R. A., & Giudice, S. (1987). Human cerebral hemispheres develop at different rates. *Science, 236*, 1110–1113.

Thelen, E. (1989). Self-organization in developmental processes: Can systems approaches work? In M. R. Gunnar & E. Thelen (Eds.), *Systems and development* (Vol. 22, pp. 77–117). Hillsdale, NJ: Erlbaum.

Thelen, E., & Smith, L. (1994). *A dynamic systems approach to the development of cognition and action.* Cambridge, MA: MIT Press.

Tiedemann, D. (1787). *Über die Entwickelung der Seelenfahigkeiten bei Kinden* (Trans. and reprinted by Murchison & Langer, 1927).

Tomasello, M. (1995). Joint attention as social cognition. In C. Moore & P. J. Dunham (Eds.), *Joint attention: Its origins and role in development* (pp. 103–130). Hillsdale, NJ: Erlbaum.

Tomasello, M., Kruger, A. C., & Ratner, H. H. (1993). Cultural learning. *Behavioral and Brain Sciences, 16*, 495–552.

Trevarthen, C. (1979). Communication and cooperation in early infancy: A description of primary intersubjectivity. In M. Bullowa (Ed.), *Before speech: The beginning of interpersonal communication* (pp. 321–347). New York: Cambridge University Press.

Trevarthen, C. (1988). Universal cooperative motives: How infants begin to know the language and culture of their parents. In G. Jahoda & I. M. Lewis (Eds.), *Acquiring culture: Cross cultural studies in child development* (pp. 37–90). London: Croom Helm.

Trevarthen, C., & Hubley, P. (1978). Secondary intersubjectivity: Confidence, confiding and acts of meaning in the first year. In A. Lock (Ed.), *Action, gesture and symbol: The emergence of language* (pp. 183–229). London: Academic Press.

Van Geert, P. (1991). A dynamic systems model of cognitive and language growth. *Psychological Review, 98*, 3–53.

look like parallel views on the same phenomenon. However, the frequently drawn contrast between the "social" theorist Vygotsky (1978) and the "individual" theorist Piaget (1945) is partly misleading. Piaget and Vygotsky share a continuity-based approach to language acquisition, meaning that there is a developmental link between language and earlier nonlinguistic cognition and communication. Both Vygotsky's insistence upon the primacy of meaning as a socially shared construction and Piaget's commitment to the developmental continuity linking language to representation and symbolic thought are important assumptions, and they stand in contrast to the discontinuity approach of generativist theories (e.g., Chomsky).

Another developmental model for explaining the child's transition to language was proposed by Werner and Kaplan in their seminal book on *Symbol Formation* (1963). Adopting the Gestalt concepts of gradual emergence of figure within ground and distancing of the figure from the ground, Werner and Kaplan argued that symbols arise when what they call the "primordial sharing situation" becomes gradually differentiated in its components (basically, the self, the object, and the other person) and gives rise to a new form. Initially nonrepresentational acts of reference – for example, exchanging things and looking at them with another person – are transformed so that a symbol can represent the referent. In such a view, social-affective as well as sensorimotor actions are seen as the developmental source of symbols.

From these classical theories we derive both a constructivist perspective and a continuity view on the transition from prelinguistic communication to language. Acquiring language is an active process in which infants build their knowledge and construct shared meanings on the basis of experiences with objects and interactions with people. Also, as we shall examine in the next section, there is a very gradual transition from communicating through sounds and gestures to producing and understanding words as symbols that represent objects and events. Thus, communication and language development can be conceptualized as a three-stage continuous process involving, first, a transition from preintentional to intentional communication and, second, a transition from conventional to symbolic communication or from conventional to symbolic modes of reference.

The present chapter focuses on the second transition. However, in the next section I shall start by outlining the entire developmental course of what we call the "ontogenesis of reference," from the onset grounded on joint attention and interpersonal sharing until the endpoint, in which symbols are used to communicate about shared meanings. Following that, the emergence of first words, their nature and function, the gradual or sudden growth in vocabulary that occurs around the middle of the second year, and finally, the passage from single words to multiword combinations will be considered in the third section. The last section highlights the role of individual differences both in the way children acquire their mother tongue, and in the linguistic input addressed to them by caregivers living in different cultures and speaking different languages.

From Attentional to Conventional to Symbolic Reference

In the view I propose here, to refer basically implies to pick out some aspect of the world, so that the figured aspect becomes a topic of shared attention. This picking out of aspects

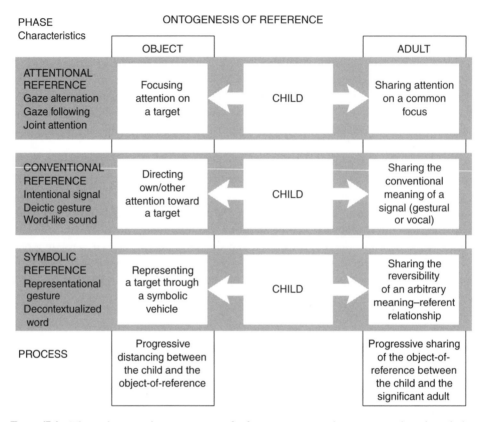

Figure 15.1 Three phases in the ontogenesis of reference: attentional, conventional, and symbolic.

of the world may be analyzed as a Gestalt process of gradual emergence of figure within ground and distancing of the figure from the ground. Instrumental actions originally adequate for achieving the child's goals and desires mechanically (e.g., reaching, grasping, approaching) are gradually separated from the concrete attempt to reach objects and become communicative acts, appropriate for communicating the child's goals to another person rather than for fulfilling these goals directly.

At the same time, in picking out aspects of the world I refer to something for you and what is referred to is the world that I share with you. The intersubjective experience of sharing may be conceptualized as a dyadic relational "frame" which evolves from sharing attention on a common focus to sharing the conventional meaning of signals to sharing the reversibility and arbitrariness of meaning–referent relationships.

The ontogenesis of reference is a complex transactional process in which both child–object relations and child–other person relations evolve according to a three-stage model (see Figure 15.1).

Around the middle of their first year of life infants begin to alternate their gaze back and forth between an object/event of interest and another person. In "social referencing"

(Klinnert, Campos, Sorce, Emde, & Svejda, 1983) for example, babies regulate their reaction to a novel object or event (approaching/avoiding, manipulating/not manipulating) on the basis of appreciating their mothers' emotional reaction to the same object/event.

Soon thereafter, infants become able to coordinate attention toward an object/event and another person in one and the same episode ("coordinated person–object orientation"; Sugarman, 1978), and to engage in relatively extended episodes of joint attention with a social partner (Bakeman & Adamson, 1984). Also at this time infants begin to follow another person's direction of gaze to outside entities (Corkum & Moore, 1995).

These triadic interactions in which infants actively coordinate their visual attention to person and object, for example, by following the adult gaze or by looking to an adult periodically as they play together with a toy, identify the first phase in the ontogenesis of reference, i.e., the construction of an *attentional referent*.

In the last months (9–12) of the first year of life infants begin to use gestures to actively direct adult attention to external entities inside the previously established triadic interactions (Bates et al., 1975; Masur, 1983; Sugarman, 1978). Gestures such as pointing, showing, offering, giving, and ritualized requests (i.e., extending the arm with hand open, palm up or down) are called *deictic* since they are used to refer to external objects/events and express *only* the child's communicative intent. Differently from the instrumental actions of reaching and grasping, these gestures are inadequate for achieving the child's intended goal mechanically; they are, however, perfectly adequate for conveying this goal to another person communicatively. Usually they do not involve any contact with the recipient, with respect to the gesture or the goal (although some of them require that the object be located in the infant's hand; see Masur, 1983). In most cases they are accompanied by the infant's looking at the partner, either solely or in alternation with looks to the object. The ability to alternate gaze between the object and the partner indicates that the child is aware of the effects his or her signals will have on the recipient, i.e., the signal is used intentionally (Bates, Benigni, Bretherton, Camaioni, & Volterra, 1979).

Three features of deictic gestures – pointed out by Tomasello and Camaioni (1997) – are worthy of note here: (1) they are *distal* signals, adequate for influencing an agent perceived as capable of self-initiated action in fulfilling goals; (2) they are *triadic* in the sense that they attempt to direct another person to some outside entity; and (3) they are accompanied by *eye contact* with the partner, or by *gaze alternation* between the partner and the target, as a way of checking the signal's efficacy on the partner's impending action or attention.

In the same age period, children acquire a repertoire of word-like sounds to express their communicative intentions. These sounds are used alone or accompanied by gestures: for example, a child points and vocalizes "da" to direct the mother's attention to an interesting object, and another child uses a two-syllable "na-na" in any request situation, from wanting an object to calling an adult from another room (Bates et al., 1975).

In terms of the ontogenesis of reference, deictic gestures and word-like sounds, used as intentional signals for communicative purposes, characterize a new phase in which the *referent* becomes *conventional*. At first, children use gestures as instrumental actions, as means for reaching goals. They are then gradually ritualized and performed in a stylized manner, with less and less resemblance to the original action from which they emerged. The same process of ritualization applies to early vocalizations, which gradually become vocal signals.

Soon after children's use of deictic gestures, they begin using a new type of gesture, called *representational*. Differently from deictic gestures, whose referent can only be interpreted by looking at the extralinguistic context, these new gestures represent a specific referent and thus their meaning does not change with context. For example, the child raises her palms, meaning "all gone," when she finishes drinking her milk or juice. Around the middle of their second year of life infants use representational gestures both to regulate social interaction – for example, waving for "bye-bye," head shaking for "no," raising the palms for "all gone" – and to label specific objects or actions – for example, opening/closing the mouth for "fish," driving motions for "car," blowing for "hot things," flapping the hands for "birdie". Some of these gestures seem culturally universal, whereas some are culturally specific (Acredolo & Goodwyn, 1988; Iverson, Capirci, & Caselli, 1994).

The representational gestures first appear in imitation games between infant and mother, or within social routines and pretend-play episodes repeatedly produced in the context of infant–parent interaction (Caselli, 1983). They seem learned mainly via imitation, as there are no spontaneous child behaviors that could be ritualized in this manner. According to Acredolo and Goodwyn (1990), the mean number of different types of representational gestures in the repertoires of the infants they examined range between 0 and 16, with a mean of 3.9.

From my perspective, the acquisition of these gestures provides a bridge toward symbolic communication and helps the child through the distancing process, i.e., in moving from object-related and contextualized gestures to more abstract and arbitrary relationships between referent and meaning.

Initial "first words" acquisition has also been described as context- or event-bound, in that words are typically produced in highly specific contexts rather than used to refer to absent events or mental contents (Barrett, 1986). For example, the child waves and says "bye-bye" only when closing a book, or utters "mama" when crying in anger. During the one-word stage children learn to gradually decontextualize words, hearing the same word in different contexts as well as hearing different words in similar contexts (Bloom, 1973).

In summary, the decontextualized use of first words and representational gestures corresponds to the last phase in our three-stage model of the ontogenesis of reference, i.e., *symbolic reference*. The capacity to use words and gestures as symbols marks the maximum of "distancing" between the child and the object-of-reference, since the child has to fully realize that the symbol is not the same thing as its referent. At the same time, this capacity marks the maximum of sharing between the child and the other person since such an arbitrary, culturally defined, meaning–referent relationship could only be co-constructed and mutually coordinated in the context of child–caregiver interaction. In the next section, the development of speech is reviewed from the emergence of first words until the transition to multiword combinations.

First Words

Between babbles and early words, most infants produce idiosyncratic sounds whose meaning is understood only by the infant's intimate partners, usually the parents. Differently from words, these protowords (Halliday, 1975), also called "phonetically consistent forms" (Dore, Franklin, Miller, & Ramer, 1976), are attached to a specific context through an iconic or figurative relationship, for example, in the context of an action format (e.g., making a sound "vroom" when pushing a toy car and "bam" when knocking down a tower) or the context of an emotional state (e.g., producing "ha-ha-ha" when hugging a doll). Protowords are clearly transitional forms that announce the future appearance of words.

When is a word a word? In order to decide whether a spoken sound is a word, Vihman and McCune (1994) propose two major criteria: (1) a phonetic form that approximates an adult word, and (2) situational consistency in use. Thus a word is a phonetically consistent form used to refer to a specific object/event or to a class of objects/events.

What are the child's first words? Three categories of early word have been proposed in the literature over the past two decades. The first and most prominent category is early names for objects (e.g., *car, shoes, teddy, bottle*; see Nelson, 1974). The second category is words used to regulate social interaction like *hello, no, yes, bye-bye*, first noted by Bloom (1973), who found that these social words occur more frequently than names although there are fewer of them. Other investigators (see Gopnik, 1988) have identified a third category of cognitive-relational words encoding concepts such as failure, disappearance, recurrence, and location (e.g., *no, gone, more, there*).

There is evidence that disappearance words (*gone*) emerge in conjunction with the ability to solve tasks involving invisible displacements of objects (i.e., looking for a previously visible object which is placed out of sight; see Gopnik, 1984), while words for success and failure are concomitant with the development of problem-solving abilities (Gopnik & Meltzoff, 1984). English-speaking children typically use "uh-oh" and "oh dear" to express failure and words such as "there" and "good" to express success. Some words may be used in a social-routine context at the beginning and then be extended to new contexts. The word *more*, for example, initially used only to request actions or objects, is subsequently used to comment on the recurrence of actions or objects.

What do early words mean? Typically, infants assign meaning to their early words using some kind of implicit rule such as noting similarities, perceptual or functional, among objects and events. For example, objects may share a perceptual property such as size, shape, or sound; in other cases different objects may share a similar function. Thus all objects that a child puts on her head are called *hat*, regardless of their shape or size. Another child may use the word *ball* to label a red balloon as well as an Easter egg and a round canister lid. These overextensions of words are the most frequent in early vocabularies, but children also underextend some words, for example, *duck* used only to name toy ducks or *animal* applied only to mammals (not to birds, fish, and insects). As a consequence, the range of application of some early words needs to be expanded in later lexical development, whereas the meaning of other words has to be narrowed.

Interestingly, some overextensions might represent the earliest sign of metaphoric use in children's speech, since the power of a metaphor lies in drawing attention to an unexpected dimension of similarity between objects, while overlooking a number of dissimilarities (de Villiers & de Villiers, 1979). For example, the de Villiers' son Nicholas, having learned to call the hairy family dog by her name *Nunu*, overextended the word to black olives the first time he saw them topping a salad. According to his parents, Nicholas's use of *Nunu* for olives may have meant "like *Nunu.*" In his desire to communicate or draw the adult's attention to a new object, the child will use the word in his limited vocabulary that best fits that object, even though he knows it is not quite right.

Do early words lack the symbolic status of true words, i.e., the *symbolic autonomy* "which allows them to be drawn into ongoing communicative exchanges but to remain relatively independent from a specific event" (Adamson, 1996, p. 168)? Some words seem very context-bound and consequently are used in the same way as pro-towards, i.e., only within specific routines or events. Other words, however, are used across a range of contexts and for different communicative functions. Considering the ten-word productive vocabulary as a landmark, it is worth noting that these early vocabularies contain at least a few decontextualized words that can function flexibly across contexts (Barrett, 1989). So it seems that different representations of word meaning coexist as complementary forms of knowledge in the one-word stage and that children rely on both event and categorical representations when they produce words (Dromi, 1987). When a word is learned in a context that enhances categorization, it shows adult-like standard meaning from the outset; in other cases the child uses the word as a cover term for the whole unanalyzed situation while relying on the schematic representation of that situation.

Some authors point to a moment within the one-word stage when children seem to discover that things have names and that there is an arbitrary relationship between names and their referents. This *naming insight* (Dore, 1985; McShane, 1980) reflects the child's new conceptual grasp of naming. Whereas early words tend to be acquired very slowly (about one to three words a month), the naming insight signals a marked increase in vocabulary growth and children suddenly produce a large number of new words.

The Vocabulary Spurt

After the naming insight, at around 18 months, a child's vocabulary explodes, expanding at a rate of more than five words a week. This "naming explosion" or "vocabulary spurt" is a quite specific phenomenon. First, the increase in vocabulary consists mostly of object names (Goldfield & Reznick, 1990). Second, children show a near obsession with naming in this period (Gopnik & Meltzoff, 1997).

For example, children may repeatedly produce an expression such as "What-da?" to request names for objects and may also point to every object they see, asking for a name or giving it a name. The increased capacity to learn new names seems to reflect a new insight; children understand not only that things can be labeled, but also that there is a word for every object kind. The child uses also a kind of "mutual exclusivity" principle (Carey, 1978; Mervis & Bertrand, 1994) which allows him or her to map a novel word to a category for which he or she does not yet have a name. Given a familiar named object (a hammer), an unfamiliar object (a wrench), and a new unfamiliar name (*wrench*), the child immediately realizes that this name refers to the new object category and learns the new name.

The naming spurt is a striking linguistic phenomenon interestingly related to new conceptual insights in the cognitive domain. Gopnik and Meltzoff (1987, 1992) have found that children develop a naming spurt within a few weeks of the time they demonstrate "exhaustive sorting" abilities (i.e., sorting objects so that all objects of one kind are in one location and all objects of another kind are in another location). The naming spurt has also been associated with "fast-mapping" abilities (Mervis & Bertrand, 1994) and with the development of "specific constructions" (i.e., placing objects in order to use their particular properties in relation to one another, such as feeding a doll with a spoon; Bloom, Lifter, & Broughton, 1985).

In sum, when children at about 18–19 months of age learn new names, they not only associate the word with some well-known object property, but they assume instead that every kind of object or event will have a distinctive name and that this name will apply to other instances as well.

The typical 18-month-old understands far more of the speech she hears than her one-word utterances would lead one to expect. It is well known that comprehension of words and utterances precedes the spontaneous use of them. This happens also because in comprehension the child has available more information than the speech alone. The child may use her knowledge of events and objects being mentioned, which usually are not only familiar to her but also present in the context of the verbal exchange.

Early Word Combinations

At 20 months of age children have, on average, 150 different words in their productive vocabulary (see Bates et al., 1988; Camaioni, Caselli, Longobardi, & Volterra, 1991; Camaioni, Caselli, Volterra, & Luchenti, 1992). By 24 months they are expected to produce about 300 words. In spite of their rapidly expanding vocabularies, in the single-word period children utter only one word at a time (Bloom, 1973).

It has been shown that a single word often conveys a sentence's meaning ("holophrase") and therefore the semantics expressed by single-word utterances might be quite complex (see Greenfield & Smith, 1976). However, a major question in child language research has been why it takes children so long to be capable of producing two words within one utterance, an argument frequently used to support the hypothesis that syntax and semantics have independent developmental courses.

The emergence of first-word combinations at about 20 months of age becomes less mysterious when we consider that this major accomplishment is reached through a series of gradual and more manageable steps. The various transitional forms identified so far characterize what Dore and colleagues (1976) called "something more than one word and something less than syntax."

First, children combine single-word utterances with a gesture, either deictic (e.g., a point) or representational (e.g., waving bye-bye), thus expressing a complex relationship. For example, a child might point to a book and say *mommy*, meaning "this is mommy's book." Second, children start to produce so-called "vertical constructions" or "successive single-word utterances," i.e., two words that are semantically related but uttered in different turns (e.g., *Cup. Hot*; Scollon, 1976).

Third, children produce two successive words with an interword pause but a single intonation contour in the period just before they begin to use multiword utterances (Branigan, 1979). Fourth, children may add an invented sound or "dummy form" (e.g., *wida*) to their single-word utterances, as if to reserve a place for a word they do not possess yet (Dore et al., 1976). In this way they learn and exercise how to string two words together without being concerned with meaning. Finally, children often produce sentences borrowed entirely from the speech of others without being composed or analyzed that have been called "formulas" or "amalgamas" (Hickey, 1993; Pine & Lieven, 1993). Examples of these rote-learned phrases are *what's that, what's this, howdoyoudo*, and *matteroffact*, a very unusual formula produced by a linguist's young son!

In light of all these observations, the emergence of word combinations "is no longer a mountain to be scaled, but a slope which the child can roll down gently" (Snow & Gilbreath, 1983, p. 285).

When children start to combine words in sentences, usually between 18 months and 2 years, they relate words to other words according to the rules they select from the linguistic input. Children learning different languages seem to express the same range of meanings in their first sentences; particularly frequent are relationships of possession (*My teddy*), location (*Car garage*), nonexistence (*No more soup*), and recurrence (*Tickle again*). Also, they talk a lot about actions (*Me fall, Car go*) and less frequently about experiences (*See that, Listen clock*) and states (*Daddy happy*).

In attempting to learn the regularities of their mother tongue, children use a variety of strategies that make easier the task of acquiring syntax. Slobin (1973) has suggested several of these strategies, such as "pay attention to the ends of words" or "avoid exceptions." This last strategy may account for the overgeneralization of some forms, such as the plural *-s* and the past tense *-ed*. For example, children acquiring English typically replace irregular past tenses like *broke* (for break) by an overgeneralization of the regular *-ed* ending, *breaked*. Adam (one of the three children intensively studied by Roger Brown) produced errors such as *holded, falled, foots*, and *sheeps*.

On the other hand, if children use the strategy "pay attention to the ends of words," they should learn suffixes before prefixes and, in fact, this is the case. In an experimental study (Kuczaj, 1979), preschool children were taught novel suffixes and prefixes. For example, some of them heard "the boy drove the *ip*-car," while others heard "the boy drove the car-*ip*." They were more likely to learn the suffix form than the prefix form; also, children were more likely to imitate sentences correctly when *ip* was a suffix than when it was a prefix.

Another common strategy we find in early grammar is that general rules are typically learned before rules for special cases. So many children in a certain stage interpret any noun–verb–noun sequence as expressing agent–action–object relationships. This is appropriate for the simple active sentences that the child frequently hears, whereas for the more rare passive sentences just the opposite interpretation is correct; the object comes first and the agent is last. As a consequence, young children easily misunderstand passive sentences whose meaning may not be derived from context, which is also the case for the so-called reversible passive sentences in which both events are equally likely. These sentences contain, in fact, no clues to meaning other than the order of words and the presence of *by*.

For example, even young children easily understand "The candy is eaten by the girl," since there is only one plausible interpretation of this sentence. However, on hearing "The cow is kicked by the horse," a 3-year-old treats the sentence as if it means "The cow kicked the horse," therefore assuming that the first noun is the agent, which is true for the more common active sentences. In testing one girl, de Villiers and de Villiers (1979) presented her with the passive sentence "The truck is bumped by the car" and she took the truck and bumped the car. When they told her "Now make the truck bump the car," she said "Again?" with a withering glance at them.

Early References to Internal States

When do children begin to label states of *perception* (e.g., see, hear, smell, cold, hot), *physiology* (e.g., hungry, thirsty, sleep, tired), *emotion* (e.g., happy, sad, mad, smile, cry), *volition/desire* (e.g., want, wish, need), and *cognition* (e.g., know, think, remember, forget, pretend, dream) explicitly? We know that during the first two years of life infants come to recognize that others are persons who perceive, feel, intend, and know in much the same way as the infants themselves. This discovery makes it possible to use language in order (1) to refer to self and other by personal names as well as to master personal pronouns; (2) to verbally express internal states imputed to self and other.

In a seminal study, Bretherton, McNew, and Beeghly-Smith (1981) have shown that internal-state language emerges late in the second year of life and burgeons in the third. Mothers of thirty 20-month-old children were asked to report child utterances containing six categories of internal-state words: perception, physiology, affect, volition/ability, cognition, and moral judgment/obligation. Words referring to perception, volition, and physiological states were more common in the vocabulary of these children than words referring to affect and moral obligation. Cognition words were least common. Interestingly, use of each of these terms applied to the self was more common than the use of these terms applied to the other. At 13 months of age, most of the children had begun to produce the labels Mommy or Daddy, whereas only 10 percent of them could say a version of their own name on request or in response to seeing their image in a mirror. By 20 months, 60 percent of the children could say their names and 75 percent had mastered at least one first-person pronoun.

In a case study, Shatz, Wellman, and Silber (1983) analyzed the frequency and function of verbs of mental reference in the speech of one child from 2 to 4 years of age, as well as in 30 two-year-olds over a six-month period. First attempts at mental reference begin to appear in some children's speech in the second half of the third year. *Know* and *think* were the most frequent verbs, comprising 48 percent and 27 percent, respectively, of all mental verbs used. Other verbs appeared only sporadically (e.g., *figure, understand*), whereas others appeared rarely at first and then more consistently (e.g., *bet, dream*). However, the earliest uses of mental reference are for conversational functions rather than for mental reference and may involve rote-learned expressions (such as "Know what?" or "I don't know!").

The most comprehensive account so far is a longitudinal study of the spontaneous conversation of ten English-speaking children from 2 to 5 years of age (Bartsch & Wellman, 1995). The authors found that genuine psychological reference to desires via the verb "want" is well established before the second birthday, whereas reference to beliefs via the verbs "think" and "know" begins much later, just before the third birthday. Talk about thoughts and beliefs becomes as frequent as talk about desires only around the fifth birthday. This result could be interpreted as corroborating Wellman's (1991) hypothesis that young children understand desires more easily than beliefs and consequently they start as desire psychologists rather than belief-desire psychologists.

A different explanation for the lag between desire and belief talk is offered by Paul Harris (1996). Initially young children conceive of other people primarily as "agents with goals" (i.e., agents who act to satisfy their desires and wishes), but around 3 years of age they start to construe people as "epistemic subjects," capable of exchanging information for the formation and updating of beliefs. Hence they shift from a desire psychology to a belief-desire psychology. In this shift conversation plays a central role; the child's participation in the exchange of information through conversation is a critical precondition for understanding beliefs but not desires.

Harris's account considers language as an appropriate medium for accurately assessing mental-state understanding, in contrast to the idea that early psychological understanding may be misconstrued – either overestimated or underestimated – because of the child's linguistic immaturity (see Shatz et al., 1983). Harris's view also proposes that language is the medium through which the child learns more directly about the content of other people's thoughts, beliefs, and intentions, the congruence of these thoughts/beliefs and intentions with his or her own, and their congruence with reality.

In a study based on naturalistic speech samples from 21 Italian-speaking children, we investigated not only which internal-state references children used at 20 months of age, but also how these references are used and what they may tell us about children's early psychological understanding (Camaioni & Longobardi, 1997). First, instances of genuine psychological reference were distinguished from other uses, such as conversational uses, idioms, or requests (e.g., "Know what?," or "Want!" simply to request a toy). Conversational uses were clearly derived from the semantic properties of the verbs in question, yet they were not intended to make specific reference to the listener's or speaker's internal state. Second, we asked whether children were able to use the internal-state terms to refer to nonpresent experiences (past, future, and hypothetical situations, refusals and denials), and whether the internal vocabulary was applied to self *and* other rather than used only for self *or* other.

Use of an internal-state word for only self (56 percent) was almost as frequent as use for only other persons (44 percent); even more important, 52 percent of the sample (11 children) were able to impute the same term to both self and other, showing a decontextualized and flexible use of a psychological reference. Almost all internal-state words referred to present experiences, but they were produced in real as well as in pretend situations (e.g., pretend play, story telling, talking about past or future experience). Finally, the great majority of all references were produced as comments, whereas only 14 percent on average were expressed in a request format. This finding confirms that, even at this early age, we are really evaluating genuine psychological reference. In conclusion, the type of psychological reference and how it is used in spontaneous speech could be interpreted as an indicator of the child's explicit understanding of his or her own and others' mind, i.e., as a first step in the construction of a "theory of mind." In the next section, individual differences in patterns of language acquisition are discussed.

Individual Differences in Language Acquisition

Some children may be "bold" or "rash" learners in language speaking; they start at a very early age and generalize quickly, thus making initially more errors than those who go slowly and cautiously until they are sure of what they are saying. There is no single route for all children to follow, but rather a range of possible routes. So it is important to look both at what children do in common as they acquire their mother tongue and at what they do differently.

Historically, individual differences in learning language have been considered mainly with respect to sex, speed of acquisition, and variation in vocabulary size (for a review, see Horgan, 1981; Macaulay, 1978). It was widely accepted that children vary dramatically in the age of onset of speech and that girls and firstborns are linguistically more advanced than boys and laterborns, respectively. Some of these findings were not confirmed later on. The systematic study by Bates and colleagues (1988) on a sample of 27 children found no effects of IQ, sex, or birth order on rate of language development. Interindividual variation in vocabulary size, especially in the early stages of acquisition, is, however, very well documented in the literature and applies to children learning a variety of languages (see Table 15.1).

During the 1970s a new approach concerned with individual differences of a more qualitative kind identified two general strategies or styles in learning language, called *referential* vs. *expressive* by Nelson (1973). A similar pattern of individual differences was discovered by Bloom, who called it *nominal* vs. *pronominal* (Bloom, Lightbown, & Hood, 1975). Nelson found that the majority of the 18 children she studied were referential. They filled their 50-word vocabularies with names for objects. On the other hand, a minority of children were more expressive. They produced a low proportion of nouns together with a considerable number of social-interactional words (e.g., *bye, thank you*) and multiword formulas (*stop it, don't want it*). Bloom and her colleagues examined four English-speaking children and found that two of them produced a telegraphic speech, with minimal use of grammatical function words. They also avoided first- and second-person pronouns, referring to themselves and to the listener by name, leading Bloom to characterize their approach to acquiring language and grammar as nominal. The other two children used pronouns from the beginning of multiword speech, together with a variety of function words and inflections, so that their approach could be characterized as a pronominal style.

Table 15.1   Variation in vocabulary size at 20 months in children acquiring different languages

	Sample	Language	Socioeconomic status	Sex	Mean vocabulary	Range	Total vocabulary
LARGE-SCALE STUDIES							
Bates et al. (1988)	27	English	middle	13 F 14 M	142	1–404	
Camaioni et al. (1992)	50	Italian	middle	25 F 25 M	147	5–628	
Dale et al. (1989)	161	English	middle-low	81 F 80 M	168	22–415	
SINGLE-CASE STUDIES							
Dromi (1987)	1	Hebrew	middle-upper	F			337
Gillis (1987)	1	Dutch	middle-upper	M			451
Mervis (1987)	1	English	middle-upper	F			600

Children with a referential-nominal style show a predominance of common nouns in their early vocabularies and a rapid vocabulary growth; they tend to speak slowly and with good articulation, and to be relatively fast language learners. The expressive-pronominal style, on the other hand, includes a predominance of pronouns rather than nouns, slower vocabulary growth, a tendency to employ formulas in constructions, poor articulation, and slower language development (Bates et al., 1988; Bloom et al., 1975; Dore, 1974; Lieven, 1978; Nelson, 1973; Peters, 1977). However, as Pine and Lieven (1990) have suggested, the possibility of a confound between developmental variance and measures of style poses a serious challenge to these findings. When vocabulary levels are controlled, the often-cited association between referential style and linguistic precocity or faster rates of development disappears (Bates et al., 1994). Although relatively advanced referential learners do exist, so do relatively advanced expressive learners; in sum, the expressive style is not necessarily poor or "bad" for children.

It is important to note that the referential–expressive dimension is not a dichotomy but rather a continuum along which children may vary, with most of them showing a rather balanced distribution of referential and expressive items, and only a few children exhibiting a clear preference, which could be defined as a distinct style. Whereas in Nelson's original study ten out of 18 children evidenced a clear predominance of nominals in their lexicon and were therefore coded as referential, more recent studies (Goldfield, 1987; Hampson & Nelson, 1993) based on samples of comparable size found fewer referential children than had been expected. Five out of 12 children in Goldfield's study fit the criterion of 50 percent or more nominals for a referential style, while six out of 45 children (only 13.3 percent of the sample) in Hampson and Nelson's study were categorized as referential. In a study that examined 15 Italian-speaking children with vocabularies ranging from 30 to 100 word-types (mean: 51 words), only one child was categorized as referential and one as expressive (Camaioni & Longobardi, 1995). Therefore the great majority of these children are acquiring language with a relative balance of referential and expressive items in their early vocabulary.

On the basis of these findings, the appropriateness of categorizing an infant as either referential or expressive seems quite doubtful. Peters (1977), among others, noted that individual children can vary their strategy along the referential–expressive continuum as a function of the particular context of communication. A nice example of this is given by the acquisition of English as first language and Italian as second language by Elizabeth Bates's daughter Julia. Julia was a highly referential learner in her acquisition of English, but when learning Italian in the context of large family lunchtimes she had a more expressive approach. Based on this example and other data, it is reasonable to conclude that style categories "may not be characteristic of individual children at all but of the same children at different times and in different contexts" (Nelson, 1981, p. 176).

Such a conclusion urged researchers to search for factors that influence children to concentrate on one dimension of language over another. Both internal and external factors have been proposed. Internal or child-based factors include differential maturation of the brain, birth order, and different cognitive styles. External or contextual factors are concerned primarily with the style and content of parental speech to language-learning infants, an issue that will be addressed in the following section.

Maternal Speech and Child Language Acquisition

Several studies have analyzed mothers' speech to their children in terms of its effects on individual differences in language acquisition rate (e.g., vocabulary growth) and style (e.g., referential vs. expressive style). Della Corte, Benedict, and Klein (1983) found that mothers' directives (normally imperatives, e.g., "Sing a song!" or "Turn it!") in addressing their children were negatively associated with early lexical development. They also noted that mothers of referential children talked more during caretaking activities and used more descriptions, compared to mothers of expressive children. These latter talked much less during caretaking activities and used more directives. In the same line of research, Jones and Adamson (1987) have documented that speech used to regulate social interaction by the mothers is negatively related to the child's lexical growth, whereas the use of utterances that focus on language itself by mothers is positively related. Examples of this so-called metalingual speech are "say 'hello'!" or "Can you say 'flower'?"

McDonald and Pien (1982) characterized the mothers of children in their third year of life as either attempting to control their children's actions or to elicit their conversational participation. Tomasello and colleagues (Tomasello & Farrar, 1986; Tomasello & Todd, 1983) investigated attention-regulation strategies adopted by mothers, establishing that there is a positive association between child's vocabulary size and the amount of time mother and child spent attending to the same object/event. In particular, maternal object references following into child attentional focus facilitate lexical development, whereas their object references while directing or redirecting child attention do not.

Another line of research analyzed maternal utterances to children learning to talk in order to throw into relief peculiar features than can facilitate language acquisition. For example, expansions of the child's previous speech supplied by the mother positively affect both vocabulary (cf. Cross, 1978) and syntax (cf. Nelson, Carskaddon, & Bonvillian, 1973). The following are some examples of expansions: Child: "Boy dog," Mother: "Yes, that's the boy's dog"; Child: "That Clancy brush," Mother: "That is Clancy's brush. Do you want to brush him?" These examples show that the adult not only repeats, in whole or in part, the child's previous utterance to provide a valuable kind of feedback, but she also builds up that utterance by adding syntactic and semantic units.

A suitable nonverbal context associated with the utterance (e.g., accompanying the word or sentence with a pointing gesture) helps the child to understand the linguistic message and encourages the acquisition process by speeding it up (Harris, Jones, Brookes, & Grant, 1986). Examining maternal speech to 13-month-old children, Hampson and Nelson (1993) pointed out that it is above all the use of descriptions (utterances that refer to aspects of the communication context, e.g., "That's a cow" or "See the dog") and referential repetitions (e.g., "That's a dog. That's a big dog") that distinguishes the mothers of linguistically precocious children from those of children with slower language development.

In sum, the ways in which mothers use language may affect their infants' language acquisition. However, also the child's own speech influences parental speech (cf. Cross, 1977); accordingly, parents adjust their speech as the child's linguistic ability changes and matures. In addition, it is possible that children who are linguistically more advanced would affect their mother's speech at Time 1; this could result in a spurious correlation betwen maternal speech at Time 1 and children's speech at Time 2 (cf. Messer, 1994). In general, we may not assume that the effects of maternal speech are similar at all ages and levels of linguistic development, since children acquire language at widely varying rates and mothers are sensitive to such a variation.

Besides these methodological issues, a major limitation of all these studies is that they concern the acquisition of English by children from middle- or upper-class environments in the United States and in the UK. Such claims have a limited scope, however, unless they are tested against studies based in cultural settings other than those of Western industrialized societies and for languages other than English (Lieven, 1994). These latter studies are important since they may document how wide is the range of environments in which children learn to talk, and whether and how parents from different cultures adjust their speech to children. For example, in nonindustrialized cultures such as Samoa and Papua New Guinea, little or no speech is addressed to infants until they themselves start to talk. This of course presents a challenge to the idea that "child-directed" speech is universal and therefore necessary to children's learning language.

In Samoa, during the first 6 months of age infants are not treated as conversational partners but are usually "spoken to" in songs; adults do not simplify their speech toward infants, who are considered low-ranking individuals and are expected to adapt to the needs of high-ranking individuals (Ochs & Schieffelin, 1984). In Papua New Guinea, Kaluli people still live a traditional life, depending on agriculture for subsistence. In such a small-scale, nonliterate society, mothers and other caregivers use no "baby-talk" lexicon with children since they think it is not a good idea to teach children childish forms. In African rural societies such as Senegal, mothers believe that one should not communicate with an infant as one does with an adult; the child who has not yet learned to walk and especially to talk is only a "potential" human being. These traditional societies are characterized by childrearing practices based on an authoritarian–submissive relationship; consonant with such views, African mothers use a higher percentage of imperatives when speaking to their children and control infant state and posture more directly, compared to French mothers (Rabain-Jamin & Sabeau-Jouannet, 1997).

Considering different subcultures (rural vs. urban) within the same nation (Italy), we found that Italian mothers talk to their language-acquiring children in very different ways, reflecting the ideologies of childrearing characteristic of their particular culture (Camaioni, Longobardi, Venuti, & Bornstein, 1998). Urban mothers adopt the typical child-centered style, which emphasizes the expansion of utterances and the reformulation of intentions that originate with the child and which involves a sort of "putting the child first." On the other hand, rural mothers do not try so much to treat their children as conversational partners and make fewer speech adjustments when talking to them, compared to urban mothers.

In general, the use of a "child-centered" speech style – which takes the child's initiatives as a starting point and expands them in a conversation-like exchange – has been found to characterize parents from academic and middle-class backgrounds in a variety of cultures, including Japanese, Korean, Italian, and Israeli. In contrast, a more "directive" speech style is frequently adopted by parents from working-class families in Western societies as well as by caregivers in rural, economically traditional societies (Hoff-Ginsberg & Tardif, 1995). In the next section, I will consider a factor that appears to influence the language-acquisition process, i.e., the specific language children hear as mother tongue and the sociocultural environment in which child–caregiver exchanges take place.

Noun vs. Verb Emphasis in Child and Mother Speech

In the child language literature there was until recently a widespread consensus on a phenomenon called *noun bias*; it was assumed that nouns are always learned before verbs and represent the predominant category in children's early lexicon.

Several studies, based on either maternal checklists or diaries, have documented how children acquire more nouns than verbs in their early vocabularies in languages such as English (Goldfield, 1993), Italian (Caselli et al., 1995), and Hebrew (Dromi, 1987). According to Gentner (1982), the noun-first predisposition is universal in language learning and must be explained by underlying perceptual and cognitive factors that predispose children to learn nouns. Recently, however, evidence has begun to accumulate which challenges the universality of this noun-bias pattern.

Data from Mandarin (Tardif, 1996) and Korean (Choi & Gopnik, 1995) have indicated that children learning these languages use more verbs or action words than nouns or object labels in their early spontaneous speech. In a study based on nine Korean-speaking children, Choi and Gopnik found that the majority of these children have a period of rapid vocabulary growth that could be best classified as a *verbing spurt* rather than a naming spurt. For those children who show both a verb spurt and a noun spurt, the rapid increase in verbs precedes the rapid increase in nouns. According to Tardif, the greater use of verbs by the Mandarin-speaking children she studied is tied neither to repetitive uses of a small number of verbs nor to a particular level of vocabulary development.

These data suggest that the predominance of nouns, or verbs, cannot be explained solely in terms of universal cognitive predispositions toward learning a particular vocabulary type and lead to a reexamination of the role of the language spoken in the child's community (linguistic input).

In fact, the hypothesis that input factors may be important determinants for the presence of a noun bias in children's early vocabularies in some languages as well as for its absence in others was partly confirmed. Tardif, Shatz, and Naigles (1997) found that speech of English-speaking caregivers emphasizes nouns over verbs, whereas that of Mandarin-speaking caregivers emphasizes verbs over nouns. Specifically, English adult-to-child speech tends to emphasize nouns by placing them in utterance-final position and asking questions about objects, whereas Mandarin tends to emphasize verbs by producing them more frequently than nouns, and placing verbs in the utterance-final position.

Gopnik and colleagues (1996) compared English and Korean mothers in the same setting and with the same play materials, encouraging similar activities with their children ("book reading" and "toy play"). If differences still emerge, it is reasonable to conclude that such differences are not simply cultural differences in the kinds of activities the mothers engage in spontaneously. The results show how Korean-speaking mothers consistently emphasize actions and verbs; on the other hand, English-speaking mothers center their conversation with infants around objects and names. Interestingly, Korean (like Japanese) is a verb-final language, which has a very rich verb morphology and depends on verb endings to make a variety of semantic distinctions. In informal conversation, Korean allows massive noun deletion; consequently, parental speech in this language often consists of highly inflected verbs with very few nouns.

Examining the child-directed speech produced by 15 Italian middle-class mothers, we found that these mothers consistently produced verbs more frequently than nouns, and placed verbs more frequently than nouns in salient utterance position (Camaioni & Longobardi, in press). Such emphasis on verbs is consistent with the fact that Italian, like Mandarin, is a language in which sentence subjects are often optional and consequently omitted, so putting verbs more likely in salient sentence-initial position.

In conclusion, these differences in linguistic input may be responsible for the children's different patterns of language learning, as well as for further variation in their cognitive development. There is evidence suggesting that both the emergence of a naming explosion and the development of categorization abilities are delayed in Korean-speaking children relative to children in a comparable English-speaking sample (Gopnik & Choi, 1995). In contrast, Korean-speaking children are significantly advanced in both problem-solving abilities and in using words for success and failure when compared to the same-aged English speakers.

Conclusion

The way in which the field of language acquisition has evolved in the past 20 years has added substantial knowledge to our understanding of the "miracle" of language and has highlighted key issues. Historically, the field of language acquisition may be understood by segmenting it into separate periods in which new ideas were proposed and considered worthy for study.

In the first period, Chomsky proposed an exclusively syntactic approach to language acquisition, but the early ambitious attempts to look for grammatical rules behind children's linguistic productions were mostly unsuccessful. In the second period, several scholars (e.g., Bloom, Slobin, Schlesinger) incorporated semantics into the study of language acquisition, and started to analyze not only the form but also the content of children's earliest utterances. These verbal productions were taken also to reflect considerable world knowledge; as a consequence, language acquisition was seen as prompted by prior cognitive development. In the third period, researchers discovered the child as a social being in a cultural context and theoretical concerns shifted toward pragmatics, or the functions of language during communication. In the fourth period, some researchers returned to studying the acquisition of syntax *per se*, although with a new emphasis on semantics derived from the second period. Other researchers preferred instead to maintain a social-functional approach to language acquisition and they put the child's environment (both linguistic and social) to the forefront in the study of language acquisition.

Having been present during almost all the periods illustrated so far, the author of this chapter is no longer a naive individual but instead is able to perceive our "naked state" in the face of the complexities of language acquisition (see Golinkoff & Gordon, 1993). Syntax, semantics, pragmatics, context, culture, meaning, lexicon, knowledge, cognition, intersubjectivity are issues introduced in different historical periods which continue to be considered and studied extensively. Nor do the concerns and ideas of the last period supersede earlier concerns. At the same time, explanations of language development that rely exclusively on either social, cognitive, or innate mechanisms fail to capture the strikingly rich and multifaceted process of language learning.

In sum, unlike the biblical creation of the world, the creation of the field of language acquisition is not complete; it has many chapters yet to be written, beside the present one.

Further Reading

Adamson, L. B. (1996). *Communication development during infancy.* Boulder, CO: Westview Press. This book traces children's developmental path from birth through the third year of life, drawing together the vast literature on infant's cognition, emotion, and social relationships as related to early communication and language. The author reviews four normative phases of communication between infants' first moments of interpersonal engagement and their language-filled dialogues about objects and events.

De Villiers, P. A., & de Villiers, J. G. (1979). *Early language.* Cambridge, MA: Harvard University Press. This short and readable book provides an entertaining account of the child's entrance into the world of language. According to the de Villiers' point of view, the key to understanding language acquisition lies in the child's linguistic inventions and systematic errors.

Gopnik, A., & Meltzoff, A. N. (1997). *Words, thoughts and theories.* Cambridge, MA: MIT Press. The authors show how children just beginning to talk are engaged in profound restructurings of several domains of knowledge. These restructurings influence children's early semantic development and stimulate theory changes similar to those occurring in science. The book defends a view of the relation between semantic and cognitive development according to which these two developments emerge simultaneously and neither type appears to precede the other.

Messer, D. J. (1994). *The development of communication. From social interaction to language.* Chichester: Wiley. The book highlights the importance of social processes in the development of communication while providing a meeting point for different theoretical perspectives on language acquisition. Some chapters consider the development of communciation and language in children with disabilities.

References

Acredolo, L., & Goodwyn, S. (1988). Symbolic gesturing in normal infants. *Child Development, 59*, 450–466.

Acredolo, L., & Goodwyn, S. (1990). Sign language in babies: The significance of symbolic gesturing for understanding language development. In R. Vasta (Ed.), *Annals of child development* (pp. 1–42). London: Jessica Kingsley.

Adamson, L. B. (1996). *Communication development during infancy.* Boulder, CO: Westview Press.

Adamson, L. B., & McArthur, D. (1995). Joint attention, affect, and culture. In C. Moore & P. Dunham (Eds.), *Joint attention: Its origins and role in development* (pp. 205–221). Hillsdale, NJ: Erlbaum.

Bakeman, R., & Adamson, L. B. (1984). Coordinating attention to people and objects in mother–infant and peer–infant interaction. *Child Development, 55*, 1278–1289.

Barrett, M. D. (1986). Early semantic representations and early word-usage. In S. A. Kuczaj & M. D. Barrett (Eds.), *The development of word meaning* (pp. 39–67). New York: Springer Verlag.

Barrett, M. D. (1989). Early language development. In A. Slater & J. G. Bremner (Eds.), *Infant development* (pp. 211–241). London: Erlbaum.

Bartsch, K., & Wellman, H. M. (1995). *Children talk about the mind.* New York: Oxford University Press.

Bates, E., Benigni, L., Bretherton, I., Camaioni, L., & Volterra, V. (1979). *The emergence of symbols: Cognition and communication in infancy.* New York: Academic Press.

Bates, E., Bretherton, I., & Snyder, L. (1988). *From first words to grammar: Individual differences and dissociable mechanisms.* Cambridge: Cambridge University Press.

Bates, E., Camaioni, L., & Volterra, V. (1975). The acquisition of performatives prior to speech. *Merrill-Palmer Quarterly, 21*, 205–226.

Bates, E., Marchman, V., Thal, D., Fenson, L., Dale, P., Reznick, J. S., Reilly, J., & Hartung, J. (1994). Developmental and stylistic variation in the composition of early vocabulary. *Journal of Child Language, 21*, 85–123.

Bloom, L. (1973). *One word at a time.* The Hague: Mouton.

Bloom, L., Lifter, K., & Broughton, J. (1985). The convergence of early cognition and language in the second year of life: Problems in conceptualization and measurement. In M. D. Barrett (Ed.), *Children's single-word speech* (pp. 149–180). New York: Wiley.

Bloom, L., Lightbown, P., & Hood, L. (1975). Structure and variation in child language. *Monographs of the Society for Research in Child Development, 40*(160).

Branigan, G. (1979). Some reasons why successive single word utterances are not. *Journal of Child Language, 6*, 411–421.

Bretherton, I., McNew, S., & Beeghly-Smith, M. (1981). Early person knowledge as expressed in gestural and verbal communication: When do infants acquire a "theory of mind"? In M. E.

Lamb & L. R. Sherrod (Eds.), *Infant social cognition: Empirical and theoretical considerations* (pp. 333–373). Hillsdale, NJ: Lawrence Erlbaum Associates.

Bruner, J. (1983). *Child's talk: Learning to use language.* New York: Norton.

Camaioni, L. (1993). The development of intentional communication. A re-analysis. In J. Nadel & L. Camaioni (Eds.), *New perspectives in early communicative development* (pp. 82–96). London: Routledge.

Camaioni, L., Caselli, M. C., Longobardi, E., & Volterra, V. (1991). A parent report instrument for early language assessment. *First Language, 11,* 345–359.

Camaioni, L., Caselli, M. C., Volterra, V., & Luchenti, S. (1992). *Questionario sullo sviluppo comunicativo e linguistico nel secondo anno di vita.* Florence: Organizzazioni Speciali.

Camaioni, L., & Longobardi, E. (1995). Nature and stability of individual differences in early lexical development of Italian-speaking children. *First Language, 15*(44), 203–218.

Camaioni, L., & Longobardi, E. (1997). Referenze a stati interni nella produzione linguistica spontanea a venti mesi. *Età Evolutiva, 56,* 16–25.

Camaioni, L., & Longobardi, E. (in press). Noun versus verb emphasis in Italian mother-to-child speech. *Journal of Child Language.*

Camaioni, L., Longobardi, E., Venuti, P., & Bornstein, M. H. (1998). Maternal speech to 1-year-old children in two Italian cultural contexts. *Early Development and Parenting, 7,* 9–17.

Carey, S. (1978). The child as word learner. In M. Halle, J. Bresnan, & G. A. Miller (Eds.), *Linguistic theory and psychological reality* (pp. 264–293). Cambridge, MA: MIT Press.

Caselli, M. C. (1983), Gesti comunicativi e prime parole (Communicative gestures and first words). *Età Evolutiva, 16,* 36–51.

Caselli, M. C., Bates, E., Casadio, P., Fenson, J., Fenson, L., Sanderl, L., & Weir, J. (1995). A cross-linguistic study of early lexical development. *Cognitive Development, 10,* 159–199.

Choi, S., & Gopnik, A. (1995). Early acquisition of verbs in Korean: A cross-linguistic study. *Journal of Child Language, 22,* 1–33.

Corkum, V., & Moore, C. (1995). The origins of joint visual attention. In C. Moore & P. Dunham (Eds.), *Joint attention: Its origins and role in development* (pp. 61–83). Hillsdale, NJ: Erlbaum.

Cross, T. (1977). Mother's speech adjustments: The contribution of selected child listener variables. In C. Snow & C. A. Ferguson (Eds.), *Talking to children* (pp. 151–188). Cambridge: Cambridge University Press.

Cross, T. (1978). Mother's speech and its association with rate of linguistic development in young children. In N. Waterson & C. Snow (Eds.), *The development of communication: Social and pragmatic factors in language acquisition* (pp. 199–216). London: Wiley.

Dale, P., Bates, E., Reznick, S., & Morisset, C. (1989). The validity of a parent report instrument of child language at 20 months. *Journal of Child Language, 16,* 239–249.

De Villiers, P. A., & de Villiers, J. G. (1979). *Early language.* Cambridge, MA: Harvard University Press.

Della Corte, M., Benedict, H., & Klein, D. (1983). The relationship of pragmatic dimensions of mother's speech to the referential–expressive distinction. *Journal of Child Language, 10,* 35–43.

Dore, J. (1974). A pragmatic description of early language development. *Journal of Psycholinguistical Research, 3,* 343–350.

Dore, J. (1985). Holophrases revisited: Their "logical" development from dialog. In M. D. Barrett (Ed.), *Children's single-word speech* (pp. 23–58). New York: Wiley.

Dore, J., Franklin, M. B., Miller, R. R., & Ramer, A. L. H. (1976). Transitional phenomena in early language acquisition. *Journal of Child Language, 3,* 13–28.

Dromi, E. (1987). *Early lexical development.* Cambridge: Cambridge University Press.

Gentner, D. (1982). Why nouns are learned before verbs: Linguistic relativity versus natural partitioning. In S. A. Kuczaj (Ed.), *Language development: Vol. 2. Language, thought and culture* (pp. 301–332). Hillsdale, NJ: Lawrence Erlbaum Associates.

Gillis, S. (1987). *Words and categories at the onset of language acquisition: Product versus process.* Unpublished manuscript, University of Antwerp.

Goldfield, B. (1987). The contributions of child and caregiver to referential and expressive language. *Applied Psycholinguistics, 8,* 267–280.

Goldfield, B. (1993). Noun bias in maternal speech to one-year-olds. *Journal of Child Language, 20,* 85–99.

Goldfield, B. A., & Reznick, J. S. (1990). Early lexical acquisition: Rate, content, and the vocabulary spurt. *Journal of Child Language, 17,* 171–183.

Golinkoff, R. M., & Gordon, L. (1983). In the beginning was the word: A history of the study of language acquisition. In R. M. Golinkoff (Ed.), *The transition from prelinguistic to linguistic communication* (pp. 1–25). Hillsdale, NJ: Lawrence Erlbaum.

Gopnik, A. (1984). The acquisition of "gone" and the development of the object concept. *Journal of Child Language, 11,* 273–292.

Gopnik, A. (1988). Three types of early word: The emergence of social words, names and cognitive-relational words in the one-word stage and their relation to cognitive development. *First Language, 8,* 49–70.

Gopnik, A., & Choi, S. (1995). Names, relational words, and cognitive development in English and Korean speakers: Nouns are not always learned before verbs. In M. Tomasello & W. E. Merriman (Eds.), *Beyond names for things: Young children's acquisition of verbs* (pp. 63–80). Hillsdale, NJ: Erlbaum.

Gopnik, A., Choi, S., & Baumberger, T. (1996). Cross-linguistic differences in early semantic and cognitive development. *Cognitive Development, 11,* 197–227.

Gopnik, A., & Meltzoff, A. N. (1984). Semantic and cognitive development in 15- to 21-month-old children. *Journal of Child Language, 11,* 495–513.

Gopnik, A., & Meltzoff, A. N. (1987). The development of categorization in the second year and its relation to other cognitive and linguistic developments. *Child Development, 58,* 1523–1531.

Gopnik, A., & Meltzoff, A. N. (1992). Categorization and naming: Basic-level sorting in eighteen-month-olds and its relation to language. *Child Development, 63,* 1091–1103.

Gopnik, A., & Meltzoff, A. N. (1997). *Words, thoughts and theories.* Cambridge, MA: MIT Press.

Greenfield, P. M., & Smith, J. H. (1976). *The structure of communication in early language development.* New York: Academic Press.

Halliday, M. A. K. (1975). *Learning how to mean: Exploration in the development of language.* London: Edward Arnold.

Hampson, J., & Nelson, K. (1993). The relation of maternal language to variation in rate and style of language acquisition. *Journal of Child Language, 2,* 313–342.

Harris, P. (1996). Desires, beliefs and language. In P. Carruthers & P. K. Smith (Eds.), *Theories of theories of mind* (pp. 200–220). Cambridge: Cambridge University Press.

Harris, M., Jones, D., Brookes, S., & Grant, J. (1986). Relations between the non-verbal context of maternal speech and rate of language development. *British Journal of Developmental Psychology, 4,* 261–268.

Hickey, T. (1993). Identifying formulas in first language acquisition. *Journal of Child Language, 20,* 27–41.

Hoff-Ginsberg, E., & Tardif, T. (1995). Socioeconomic status and parenting. In M. H. Bornstein (Ed.), *Handbook of parenting* (Vol. 2, pp. 161–188). Mahwah, NJ: Lawrence Erlbaum.

Horgan, D. (1981). Rate of language acquisition and noun emphasis. *Journal of Psycholinguistic Research, 10*(6), 629–640.

Iverson, J. M., Capirci, O., & Caselli, M. C. (1994). From communication to language in two modalities. *Cognitive Development, 9*, 23–43.

Jones, C. P., & Adamson, L. B. (1987). Language use in mother–infant and mother–child–sibling interactions. *Child Development, 58*, 356–366.

Klinnert, M. D., Campos, J. J., Sorce, J. F., Emde, R. N., & Svejda, M. (1983). Emotions as behavior regulators: Social referencing in infancy. In R. Plutchik & H. Kellerman (Eds.), *Emotion: Theory, research and experience: Vol. 2. Emotions in early development* (pp. 57–86). New York: Academic Press.

Kuczaj, S. (1979). Evidence for a language learning strategy. On the relative ease of acquisition of prefixes and suffixes. *Child Development, 50*, 1–13.

Lieven, E. (1978). Conversations between mothers and young children: Individual differences and their possible implications for the study of language learning. In N. Waterson & C. Snow (Eds.), *The development of communication* (pp. 173–187). New York: Wiley.

Lieven, E. M. V. (1994). Crosslinguistic and crosscultural aspects of language addressed to children. In C. Gallaway & B. Richards (Eds.), *Input and interaction in language acquisition* (pp. 56–73). Cambridge: Cambridge University Press.

Macaulay, R. K. S. (1978). The myth of female superiority in language. *Journal of Child language, 5*, 353–363.

Masur, E. F. (1983). Gestural development, dual-directional signaling, and the transition to words. *Journal of Psycholinguistic Research, 12*(2), 93–109.

McDonald, L., & Pien, D. (1982). Mother conversational behavior as a function of interactional intent. *Journal of Child Language, 9*, 337–358.

McShane, J. (1980). *Learning to talk.* Cambridge: Cambridge University Press.

Mervis, C. B. (1987). Child-basic object categories and early lexical development. In U. Neisser (Ed.), *Concepts and conceptual development: Ecological and intellectual factors in categorization* (pp. 201–233). Cambridge: Cambridge University Press.

Mervis, C., & Bertrand, J. (1994). Acquisition of the novel name–nameless category principle. *Child Development, 65*, 1646–1662.

Messer, D. J. (1994). *The development of communication. From social interaction to language.* Chichester: Wiley.

Nelson, K. E. (1973). Structure and strategy in learning to talk. *Monographs of the Society for Research in Child Development, 38*(149).

Nelson, K. E. (1974). Concept, word, and sentence: Interrelations in acquisition and development. *Psychological Review, 81*, 267–285.

Nelson, K. (1981). Individual differences in language development: Implications for development and language. *Developmental Psychology, 17*, 170–187.

Nelson, K. (1988). Constraints on word learning? *Cognitive Development, 3*, 221–246.

Nelson, K. E., Carskaddon, G., & Bonvillian, J. (1973). Syntax acquisition: Impact of experimental variation in adult verbal interaction with the child. *Child Development, 44*, 497–504.

Ochs, E., & Schieffelin, B. B. (1984). Language acquisition and socialization. In R. A. Schweder & R. A. Levine (Eds.), *Culture theory* (pp. 276–320). Cambridge: Cambridge University Press.

Peters, A. (1977). Language learning strategies: Does the whole equal the sum of the parts? *Language, 53*(3), 560–575.

Piaget, J. (1945). *La formation du symbole chez l'enfant.* Neuchatel: Delachaux et Niestlée.

Pine, J. M., & Lieven, E. V. M. (1990). Referential style at thirteen months: Why age-defined cross-sectional measures are inappropriate for the study of strategy differences in early language development. *Journal of Child Language, 17*, 625–631.

Pine, J. M., & Lieven, E. V. M. (1993). Reanalysing rote-learned phrases: Individual differences in the transition to multi-word speech. *Journal of Child Language, 20*, 551–571.

Rabain-Jamin, J., & Sabeau-Jouannet, E. (1997). Maternal speech to 4-months-old infants in two cultures: Wolf and French. *International Journal of Behavioral Development, 20*(3), 425–451.

Scollon, R. (1976). *Conversations with a one-year-old.* Honolulu, HI: University Press of Hawaii.

Shatz, M., Wellman, H., & Silber, S. (1983). The acquisition of mental verbs: A systematic investigation of the first reference to mental state. *Cognition, 14*, 301–321.

Slobin, D. I. (1973). Cognitive prerequisites for the development of grammar. In C. A. Ferguson & D. I. Slobin (Eds.), *Studies of child language development* (pp. 607–619). New York: Holt, Rinehart, & Winston.

Snow, C. E., & Gilbreath, B. J. (1983). Explaining transitions. In R. M. Golinkoff (Ed.), *The transition from prelinguistic to linguistic communication* (pp. 281–296). Hillsdale, NJ: Lawrence Erlbaum.

Sugarman, S. (1978). Some organizational aspects of preverbal communication. In I. Markova (Ed.), *The social context of language* (pp. 49–66). New York: Wiley.

Tardif, T. (1996). Nouns are not always learned before verbs: Evidence from Mandarin speakers' early vocabularies. *Developmental Psychology, 32*, 492–504.

Tardif, T., Shatz, M., & Naigles, L. (1997). Caregiver speech and children's use of nouns versus verbs: A comparison of English, Italian, and Mandarin. *Journal of Child Language, 24*, 535–565.

Tomasello, M., & Camaioni, L. (1997). A comparison of the gestural communication of apes and human infants. *Human Development, 40*, 7–24.

Tomasello, M., & Farrar, M. J. (1986). Joint attention and early language. *Child Development, 57*, 1454–1463.

Tomasello, M., & Todd, J. (1983). Joint attention and lexical acquisition. *First Language, 4*, 197–212.

Vihman, M. M., & McCune, L. (1994). When is a word a word? *Journal of Child Language, 21*, 517–542.

Vygotsky, L. S. (1978). *Mind in society: The development of higher psychological processes.* Cambridge, MA: Harvard University Press.

Wellman, H. M. (1991). From desires to beliefs: Acquisition of a theory of mind. In A. Whiten (Ed.), *Natural theories of minds* (pp. 19–38). Oxford: Blackwell.

Werner, H., & Kaplan, B. (1963). *Symbol formation.* New York: Wiley.

Chapter Sixteen

Principles of Emotion and its Development in Infancy

David C. Witherington, Joseph J. Campos, and Matthew J. Hertenstein

Overview

The field of emotional development has made considerable theoretical and empirical strides over the last 30 years. From these advances, we lay out some basic principles that characterize what is known about emotion and its development. Adopting a functionalist perspective, we review what emotions are and how they develop, highlighting many of the factors involved in their development and the processes by which this development occurs. The chapter is organized around the following five topics: (1) the nature of the emotion process and the properties that comprise it; (2) the role evolution may play in emotional development; (3) the developmental processes of differentiation and integration that organize some aspects of development; (4) the role of cognitive factors in emotional development; and (5) the importance of conceptualizing emotional development as a multicomponent process.

A Perspective on the Nature of Emotion

False Starts in the Study of Emotion

Select any treatment of emotion and chances are that it begins with an apology. Emotion, the readings will say, is difficult to define and to dissociate from other mental and behavioral phenomena, including cognition, motivation, and social interaction. Chances are, too, that the treatment will begin with citation from a dictionary. Typically, such cita-

Preparation of this chapter was supported by an NICHD postdoctoral training grant HD07323 to David C. Witherington, an NIH grant HD25066 to Joseph J. Campos, and an NRSA predoctoral fellowship MH12320 to Matthew J. Hertenstein.

tions beg the question of what emotion is ("an affective state of consciousness in which joy, sorrow, fear, hate, and the like are experienced as distinguished from cognition or volition"). They in turn rely on criteria not specific to emotion, such as increased heartbeat, respiration, muscular tension, and the like – states that are evident in exercise as well as emotion. Moreover, all too often they characterize emotion as a disruptive and disorganizing phenomenon.

To the extent that such dictionary definitions capture common usage, and to the extent that common usage dictates starting points for studying emotion, it is not surprising that the study of emotion and emotional development has had a fitful and contentious history. The problem in the study of emotion rests not with the concept of emotion, but with the conception of emotion implicit in definition by common usage. For us, emotion is *not* (or at least, not just) an intrapsychic state of consciousness; it is *not* something that can be defined by pointing to physiological, or for that matter, any other reaction; and it is *not* (or not necessarily) disruptive and disorganizing.

Emotion is not just a feeling state because it powerfully affects both one's own behavior and the behavior of others. In fact, we can have emotions without feelings (Lazarus, 1991), our feelings often follow an emotion episode (Frijda, 1986; James, 1892/1963), and feelings may play no causal role in emotion (Bowlby, 1973; Ryle, 1949). While feelings are a crucial facet of emotion, they are not its core; they are not what determines everything else about the emotion process.

Emotion is not physiological arousal because any physiological response can be shown to change in states in which there is no emotion (for example, even in meaningless motoric activity). After a century of searching, no one has yet convincingly demonstrated the existence of "autonomic signatures" of emotion – those physiological patterns that are found in one emotional state but not in another (see Cacioppo, Klein, Berntson, & Hatfield, 1993). Even those reactions that are occasionally reported across a variety of eliciting circumstances (e.g., Ekman, 1999a,b) tend to be related to discrete emotions weakly and inconsistently (Boiten, 1996; Ekman, Levenson, & Friesen, 1983; Levenson, 1992; Levenson, Ekman, Heider, & Friesen, 1992; Stemmler, 1989).

Facial or other expressions cannot serve as a criterion for emotion either. Although most textbooks tout the universality of facial expressions for emotions such as anger, fear, joy, sadness, surprise, and disgust, such impressive reports come from studies of *recognition* of facial expressions, not from studies of *production* of facial expressions, where the findings are rarely robust. The facial expressions of infants or adults undergoing emotions in real-life settings are not strongly related to the states that they are supposed to express; often, facial expressions are rarely or never seen when they should be. Such is the case for the facial expression of fear, which is seldom seen in situations that provoke intense fear states, including fear of heights, of looming objects, and of strangers (Campos, 1985; Camras et al., 1998; Hiatt, Campos, & Emde, 1979).

Finally, emotions need not disorganize, contrary to many theoreticians' proposals (e.g., Goleman, 1995; Hebb, 1949; Leeper, 1948; Mandler, 1975, 1979). By their very nature, emotions can be organizing and adaptive. They are designed to help the individual adapt to problems that emerge in his or her transactions with the world, and they organize both intrapersonal and social processes. Positive and negative emotions can help overcome problems, encourage engagement with the world, and structure one's perceptions and thoughts. Without properly sharing emotions with a caregiver, and without obtaining emotional security from that person, one could never arrive at the favorable and harmonious relationship called "secure attachment" (Sroufe & Waters, 1977). Furthermore, emotions presumed to be "disruptive," such as anger and fear, can motivate successful undertakings by overcoming inhibitions and bringing about successful coping. To define emotion by reference to presumably disruptive characteristics seems limiting, misleading, and inaccurate.

An Alternative Conceptualization of Emotion

How does one conceptualize emotion fruitfully? Our attempt will begin with a different starting point than that of common usage. We will delineate what we believe are the major features of emotions that differentiate them from the nonemotional, and also present a set of general criteria for differentiating one emotion from the other. In the process, we will set a frame for explaining major aspects of emotional development in infancy. The discussion of what follows draws heavily from prior writings by Campos, Barrett, Lamb, Goldsmith, and Stenberg (1983), Barrett and Campos (1987), Frijda (1986), and Lazarus (1991, in press). These writings constitute the basis for what is called the functionalist approach to emotion.

William James (1892/1963) began his famous chapter on emotion in his textbook, *Principles of Psychology*, by stating that emotions end at the periphery of the body and do not proceed beyond. In so doing, James, who was trying to explain the origin of feeling states, epitomized the approach to emotion that emphasizes its intrapersonal, intrapsychic, and self-centered bases. In contrast to James, we believe that emotions reach out to the social and physical world. We believe that emotions are *relational* – their origin results from the impact of events on what the person is trying to do. Emotions come about neither from the self nor from the environment but from the fusion of external event and internal intent. Far from ending at the periphery of the body, emotions broadcast to the outside world. They communicate (intentionally or otherwise) powerful messages and consequently regulate the behavior of others. Viewed in this light, emotions are not intrapsychic but transactional, integrating the real or imagined physical and social world to the person's strivings. Emotions are thus intimately tied to adaptation. When self and world clash, creating problems which require steps to address, negative emotions such as anger and fear occur. When self and world suddenly coordinate effectively, creating smooth progress to a goal, positive emotions, such as joy, relief, love, triumph, etc., are generated.

A working definition of emotion

In effect, *emotions are the processes by which an individual attempts to establish, change, or maintain his or her relation to the environment on matters of significance to the person.* The attempt can be overt, as when an individual actively engages in transactions with the world, or covert, as when the person is merely in a state of action readiness for dealing with the world (Campos & Barrett, 1984; Frijda, 1986). Emotions are thus not identified, as they are in dictionary definitions, with any particular feeling, nor with any individual facial or vocal or other expression, or even with any specific instrumental behavior. Emotions can best be identified by seeing the adaptive function that a particular behavior or set of behaviors appears to serve as the person deals with his or her relation to the world. Specific behaviors acquire their emotional meaning only in terms of the role they play in person–environment transactions. A smile, therefore, can serve many masters, as Kagan (1971) stated; in context, it can as readily be in the service of scorn as of joy.

What Makes Our Interaction with the World Emotional?

Emotion and significance

Not all attempts by a person to change his or her relation to the environment are emotional. Perhaps the most unambiguous feature distinguishing emotion from the non-emotional is *personal significance* – that is, the value, importance, or relevance of the transaction for the person. Transactions that have value are emotional; those without value are not. Put another way, what is potentially damaging or beneficial to oneself is emotional; what is routine is not.

The notion of significance is at the core of contemporary theories of emotion. Usually, for most of these theories, what makes an event significant, and hence emotional, is the relevance of the event for the attainment of one's goals. For Lazarus (1991), the generation of emotion begins with the issue of whether an event is congruent or incongruent with one's goals. As Frijda (1986) suggests, emotions "serve concern satisfaction; they do so by monitoring the relevance of events and by modulating or instigating action accordingly" (p. 475). Extrapolating from Lazarus and Frijda, we believe that emotions typically begin the moment that an event is related to one's goals, change when the goal is attained or is relinquished once and for all, and end when the significance of the transaction abates. When viewed in this light, emotions can be brief or enduring; unlike conceptualizations linking emotion to facial expressions, emotions are not necessarily succinct or micromomentary (as Ekman, 1999b, proposes).

The link between emotion and the goals (motivations, intentions, concerns) of an individual is thus an intimate one. However, there are other ways besides goal relevance by which events become significant. One of these is social signals. Such signals from others – their smiles, growls, coos, scowls, laughs, stares, sneers, etc. – have an impact on one's actions, and give those actions a value previously lacking. Social signals also can change the existing significance of an event or action, from aversive to engaging, or the reverse. As such, these signals communicate emotional significance in a process that pervades the entire life span.

The social signals of others can, under certain circumstances, generate a like emotional state in the perceiver of those signals, a process called affect contagion (Hatfield, Cacioppo, & Rapson, 1994). One form of affect contagion is present at birth: the empathic distress reaction of infants. Newborn infants cry in response to the cries of other newborns, but not in response to their own cry or to acoustically similar sounds of equal loudness and duration like white noise (Dondi, Simion, & Caltran, 1999; Martin & Clark, 1982; Sagi & Hoffman, 1976; Simner, 1971). By 10 weeks, affect contagion responses have broadened; at this age, infants may respond to positive emotions with positive reactions, to anger signals with anger-like expressions, and to sad displays somewhat more diffusely with mouthing and tonguing, when such signals are jointly conveyed through face and voice (Haviland & Lelwicka, 1987).

Emotional communication via social signaling may be a necessary component for the generation of somewhat later-appearing emotions such as shame, guilt, and pride (Barrett & Campos, 1987). Shame, for instance, requires that the shamed individual detect disappointment, anger, sadness, or otherwise disapproving emotional communication from a significant other. Pride, too, involves expected praise in the form of exuberant paralinguistic and gestural communications from another. Guilt requires the perception of the emotional signals of sadness, pain, fear, or suffering one's actions have caused in another. Whatever cognitive factors are involved in addition, emotional signals seem a prerequisite for generating these later-appearing emotions, sometimes called "self-conscious" emotions (Fischer & Tangney, 1995; M. Lewis, 1993), but which we believe are more appropriately called "other-conscious" emotions (after J. S. Watson, personal communication, 1999).

How Are Emotions Generated and Manifested?

The significance of one's transaction with the world assumes different forms depending on the nature of relation between person and event. Emotions like joy or relief arise from congruence between a person's strivings and events, resulting in active attempts to maintain such congruence. Emotions like anger and sadness arise when incongruence marks person–event relations. Both anger and sadness involve frustrating encounters with an obstacle to goal attainment, but in anger the possibility of overcoming the obstacle – and hence the incongruence – exists. When goal restoration is deemed unattainable, sadness ensues.

Some events go beyond simple goal congruence or incongruence. In fear, for example, the relation of an event to one's goals involves a particular goal – that of personal security; the event is a threat to one's safety, well-being, or status. In shame, on the other hand, the event involves the person behaving in the world under the watchful eye of a significant other and is related to concern that one's action will elicit rebuke from the other (Mead, 1934). In pride, a person not only solves a problem but also obtains the approval of others; joy at mastery transforms into something quite different by the meaning and desirability of the praise of others.

Whatever the specific nature of exchange between person and event, it is at the level of relation between the two that the emotion process resides (Frijda, 1986; Lazarus, 1991). Preciously few if any events have intrinsic capacity to generate emotion. Even social signals, which otherwise have such power to create like emotion in the perceiver, can produce very different effects depending on the context in which the perceiver is embedded. A cheery smile and enthusiastic pickup gesture, for example, can be unpleasant to a tired and overstimulated infant (Stern, 1971, 1977). The cry of a peer, potent for the newborn, rarely promotes empathic distress by 6 months of age (Hay, Nash, & Pedersen, 1981). At a minimum events must be considered in the context of a person's goals and strivings to understand the generation of emotion, for the same event can acquire a different emotional meaning the moment it is linked to a different goal.

The meaning of an event also depends on what a person can do, or thinks he or she can do, in relation to the event. As we have mentioned, having the means available to eliminate an obstacle can mean the difference between whether anger or sadness arises in the context of goal frustration. Thus, understanding the generation of emotion depends on a simultaneous integration of event, the person's goals and strivings, and the action repertoire available to the person for evaluating and regulating his or her relation to the event. Understanding the generation of emotion, in other words, depends on an assessment of *relational meaning*, between person and event (e.g., Frijda, 1986; Lazarus, 1991). The relational meaning of person–event transactions helps explain how the same event can hold different meaning for a person depending on his or her goals and strivings.

Relational meaning explains how different events can generate the same emotions. As Barrett (1998) has noted, fear of heights, fear that one's child is late in coming home, and fear of losing one's savings in a stock market crash differ in the physical characteristics of the antecedent event, yet we classify all as fear. We do so because all these event–person relations involve threat and some form of protective withdrawal. As an abstract principle, the concept of relational meaning reveals organization in the enormous variability that characterizes events of emotion generation.

Relational meaning and "action tendencies"

Relational meaning is also necessary to understand the organization of an individual's emotional *behavior*. In recent years, following Frijda (1986), it has become customary to refer to the "action tendency" of an emotion as the organization of such emotional behaviors. Morphologically rather different behaviors constitute manifestations of the *same* action tendency. For instance, in fear, there can be avoidance of threat by freezing or by running away. Indeed, in certain cases, avoidance can involve moving toward a threat (such as in fear-related attack). In shame, one can circumvent social contact by hiding in a corner; but one can also accomplish the same end in almost the opposite way – by directly confronting the potentially shaming person and engaging in social contact designed to distract that person from observing the offending act. Action tendencies are thus broad sets of behaviors unified into classes, and differentiated from one another, by *the function that those behaviors serve*. Action tendencies do not refer to specific behaviors, like "fear faces," or to "autonomic signatures." Rather, they are abstract and categorical, deriving their meaning, their common specification, not ostensively, by anything we can point to, but instead by the results that the behaviors seem aimed to accomplish. The same behavior can be in the service of many emotions, and different behaviors can serve the same emotion. It is only by reference to unifying functions that we can understand the extraordinary flexibility that characterizes emotions and emotional behavior.

Action tendencies are not strictly speaking end-states of a linear process that goes from affective stimulus to emotional state to emotional response. Rather, action tendencies enter directly into the evaluation of the generation of emotion itself. Counterintuitive as it may be, the end of the emotion process enters into its initiation. We do not fear what we can avoid; we do not get angered at obstacles that we can readily remove; we do not show sadness at losses if they are not irrevocable. Our action tendency potential helps regulate the impact of a stimulus on our strivings and goals. The emotion process is not a linear one but a complex loop that involves both feedback (the response mitigating the effect of a stimulus) and feedforward effects (the response creating a future state in which the stimulus has a different impact).

The specific emotional behavior that comprises action tendencies takes two forms. Note that both kinds of behavior are relational – serving to create, maintain, or change the relation of the person to the environment. Both are intrinsically functional. One kind of behavior is called by common usage "expressive." "Expressions" are designed to change the relation of the person to the environment, but not by affecting the environment directly. Rather, they do so by recruiting the intervention of another, such as by social signaling. Examples of expressions are smiles, scowls, frowns, and sneers in the facial realm; screams, groans, and squeals in the vocal domain; and cringing, cowering, snuggling, and puffing up in the gestural domain. None of these reactions will make a frightening encounter go away, or a frustrating one become less so. The relational impact of expressions is largely tied in with their potential to affect others. The smile may communicate to someone else "keep up what you are doing"; the cry can command "change my situation"; a grimace may imply "I am about to attack"; weeping may suggest "come provide succorance." Viewed in this way, the term "expressive" is not apt. The importance of expressive behaviors comes about not so much from their serving as readouts of internal states, as means of telling another what one's "feelings" are (Planalp, 1999), but from influencing how the other behaves, and forecasting what the "expressing" person will do next. Although we will continue to use the term "expression" because so much research uses that term, we much prefer avoiding the term, and using the more apt designation "social signal."

The second kind of emotional behavior is called "instrumental." In contrast to expressions, these actions affect the world directly. Instrumental behaviors are designed to remove us from a threat (e.g., by running away or freezing). They allow us to displace or eliminate obstacles (e.g., by attack or effortfully pushing the obstacle aside). And they help us avoid social contact when we have engaged in a disapproving act (e.g., by leaving the field, by avoiding social communication with the disapproving other, or by distracting the other from our transgression).

Emotion regulation

Heretofore, we have emphasized the role that emotions play in regulating the relation between the person and the environment. However, emotions are also *regulated*. That is, a given emotion is often attenuated, accentuated, or transformed into a completely different emotion (although the latter probably occurs only after the period of infancy). Research that deals with emotions as regulated falls under the rubric of emotion regulation.

Emotion regulation operates at several levels in the emotion process. Campos, Mumme, Kermoian, and Campos (1994) analyzed the various mechanisms of such regulation in terms of three processes: (1) the control of perceptual input; (2) changing the meaning of the person–environment relation; and (3) inhibiting or amplifying responses. An example of control over perceptual input is "niche-picking" – the selection of environments in which a problem is not likely to arise. Infants show such tendencies when they avoid social contact with others, when they retreat in private after an unannounced bowel movement, and when they show "avoidant-attachment" behavior to a caregiver whose interactions with the child have been insensitive. In contrast to the first process, little, if any, empirical evidence exists to indicate that infants are capable of changing the meaning of the person–environment relation. It is probably not until the preschool years that a child has the capacity to regulate his or her emotions using this process. Finally, infants develop the ability to inhibit and amplify their emotional displays. We see the latter when infants, for instance, cry louder than is typical to gain the attention of their caregiver in another distant room and smile broadly at important people in their environment. We see the former when infants inhibit their crying behavior to gain succor from mothers who are unlikely to pick up their infants during crying episodes.

Evolutionary Processes in Emotional Development

As we have discussed, emotions are processes that typically arise when an individual faces a problem, with the nature of the problem determining the quality of the emotion. Emotions are thus inseparable from attempts at adaptation; they are designed to help the person create a better fit with his or her environment. The term adaptation has two meanings. One refers to successful dealings with the environment in the here-and-now and is the cornerstone of the "functionalist" theory of emotions (Barrett & Campos, 1987; Campos & Barrett, 1984; Frijda, 1986; Lazarus, 1991). The second meaning refers to evolutionary value, to the fit of an individual in the past history of the species with the so-called "environment of evolutionary adaptedness," and is foundational to the "evolutionary psychology" of emotions (Cosmides & Toobey, 2000). Our approach in this chapter is a functionalist, not an evolutionary, one. We emphasize ontogeny, not phylogeny. Nevertheless, evolutionary factors may serve as primitives or starting points for an explanation of emotional development. So, a functionalist theory of emotion must make some educated guesses about the contribution of evolution in the human infant's emotional makeup.

It is very difficult to infer the operation of evolutionary factors in emotion (Haig & Durrant, 2000; Ketelaar & Ellis, 2000). In general, we can infer an evolutionary role in emotion when as many as possible of the following criteria are met: (1) universality of manifestation across cultures; (2) presence very early in ontogeny; (3) presence later in ontogeny in the absence of experience (e.g., the smile in blind infants); (4) evidence for underlying brain organization and circuitry that make possible a phenomenon when such brain circuits do not depend upon experience for their organization; and (5) apparent adaptive value in the sense that appropriate responding to certain situations results in the person surviving to pass along his or her genes. Using some of these criteria as a guide, and operating under the assumption that human evolution has been made possible largely by the development of flexibility rather than rigidity of responding, we will describe a number of ways in which we believe that evolutionary processes could play a role in explaining emotional development.

When we look at humans in their environments, certain relational commonalities emerge that universally capture emotional functioning. As we noted in the introduction, each emotion is marked by an abstract relational meaning structure: when we encounter an obstacle to our goals and have no means of overcoming the obstacle, sadness results, but when events match our goals, then we experience happiness. Such abstract patterns appear to be evident in all cultures (Kitayama & Markus, 1994; Mesquita & Frijda, 1992; Wallbott & Scherer, 1988), and such universality suggests the potential for an evolutionary origin to these patterns. The potential role of evolution in these patterns, however, does not likely extend to specific event–emotion linkages. For example, in some cultures eating insects is considered a delicacy; in others, it is repulsive. Although what is repulsive differs across cultures, disgust is nonetheless universal, so long as the event–person relation involves an appreciation of contamination and a rejection of oral incorporation (Rozin & Fallon, 1987).

Universality thus characterizes emotions at an abstract level of person–event transaction. However, specific events, actions, goals, and evaluations involved in the emotion process are flexible and intimately linked to culture and ontogenetic experience rather than to evolutionary factors *per se*. In this respect, the role of evolution in emotion is analogous to the role of evolution in language. No one will question that language has evolved and is adaptive. Yet no one will say that we have evolved to speak French, English, or Swahili. The words used for environmental referents and the specific pronunciation of those words are simply too different across cultures, and too malleable across historical time, to have evolved. Thus, we are evolutionarily capable of fear, and such fear emerges when we perceive threat; but there are not necessarily any specific events that constitute threat across all cultures, and there are not necessarily any specific behaviors humans employ to universally deal with threat.

Nonetheless, there are some specific aspects of the emotion process for which evolutionary factors seem to play a role. In what follows we will review evolutionary influence at the level of emotional responses, emotional evaluations of stimuli and events, and at the level of a fundamental process that helps humans early in development to attach specific emotional meaning to the world: motor mimicry.

Evolution and Emotional Response Patterns

Behavioral flexibility is not limitless. Even if one does not always or generally see an anger face when someone is expressing anger, it seems very likely that *elements* of such a facial display are *more likely* in a state of anger than elements of a facial display communicating sadness or joy. Such constraints on response were alluded to by Darwin (1872/1965) in his principle of serviceable associated habits. This principle states that we show certain facial movements and not others when in a given emotional state because such movements in the past served very specific adaptive functions. In anger, for instance, the narrowing of the eyes and elevation of the cheek served a protective function of minimizing the surface of the eye that could be injured in potential combat. The baring of teeth was adaptive as a preparation for biting in attack. The fixed stare was adaptive in keeping prey or adversaries in view for the purpose of monitoring their behavior. Over evolutionary time, as a function of their likely adaptive value, these responses gradually became readily shown in states of anger. Similar considerations apply to the serviceable habits in other emotions as well, including fear, disgust, and joy.

Evolutionary constraints thus may affect the relative place in a response hierarchy where a particular behavior is found – i.e., how easily the response is shown. What has evolved may be the constraints on behavior (and these constraints appear not to be very strong), but possibly not the patterned "emotional behaviors" themselves. We know of no evidence nor speculation as to why each individual "serviceable associated habit" has to be elicited in concert with every other such habit to make a patterned "fear face." Thus, we propose that evolutionary factors may organize parts of emotional displays, but probably not wholes.

Evolution and Biological Preparedness for Learning

Since events do not have intrinsic, biologically determined meaning structures of their own, we propose that experiential and learning factors must play a role in the capacity of a stimulus to generate emotion. However, we do believe that evolution can play a critical role in learning. There is now abundant evidence that evolutionary factors affect learning by influencing how quickly a stimulus is linked to emotion, how enduring the learning is, and how strong is the emotion that occurs following an encounter between a person and an event. The fact that some emotions can be learned more quickly and retained in more enduring fashion to certain stimuli but not others is called "biological preparedness for learning." We propose such preparedness as another way in which evolution plays a role in emotional development. It is a means of ensuring flexibility of behavior while simultaneously constraining flexibility to some degree.

In infancy, biological preparedness for learning was demonstrated as long ago as 1930 by C. W. Valentine. He presented his year-old offspring with stimuli that he reported differentially were conditioned to the sound of a loud whistle. One stimulus he presented, for instance, was a caterpillar – a wiggly and furry creature that initially elicited no aversion by the infant. However, as soon as the insect was shown to his daughter and then followed by a loud whistle, she began to tremble and to move away from it. By contrast, when Valentine showed the baby a pair of opera glasses followed by the same loud whistle, the baby startled to the whistle but did not avoid the glasses as she did the caterpillar. Valentine concluded that, while fear of the specific stimuli was not innate, the reaction to certain types of stimuli represented a fear "lurking to come out" with the proper experiential provocation.

More recently, and in much better-controlled studies, Cook and Mineka (1990; Mineka & Cook, 1993) demonstrated how laboratory-reared monkeys who had never been exposed to a snake or to a flower, and who initially showed no wariness to either stimulus, quickly learned lasting avoidance responses to the snake but not to the flower. Like Valentine, Cook and Mineka concluded that organisms are not innately afraid of stimuli, but are prepared to learn to be wary of stimuli likely to indicate dangerous properties in the environment of evolutionary adaptedness.

Lest it seem that biological preparedness for learning is limited to insects and snake-like stimuli, it should be noted that similar preparedness has been demonstrated for taste stimuli (when these are associated with subsequent nausea but not shock; Garcia & Koelling, 1966), for fear and joy faces (when used to signal electric shock, fear faces produce physiological responses much more resistant to extinction than do joy faces; Ohman, 1993), and for appetitive responses such as learning to suck for sugary substances (Lipsitt, 1986). Similarly, Walden and Passaretti (1996) reported that 18-month-old infants seem prepared to associate maternal messages specifying positive emotion and security to mechanical stimuli, but not to snake-like stimuli. In sum, preparedness for learning emotional meanings, although relatively underinvestigated, seems to be a robust finding. It clearly is a principle with vast implications for understanding emotional development and the role of the ecology within which the child is developing.

Evolution and Part–Whole Phenomena

A third way in which evolutionary factors may organize emotion in the infant and young child is through the close link between relatively simple *featural* parameters of stimulation and the generation of aspects of emotion. There has been a tendency in early ethological studies to draw too rich an interpretation of what elicits emotional behavior in animals and infants. The tendency is to attribute to a whole stimulus – to a pattern or Gestalt – effects that are in fact due to a stimulus feature or element embedded in the pattern. We propose instead that certain parameters of stimulation – certain stimulus features – have the capacity to elicit aspects of emotional response, and that such a capacity is the outcome of evolution. However, we are skeptical that evolution typically leaves behind sensitivity to more patterned and higher-order variables of stimulation.

Consider this classic study in ethology. Tinbergen (1948, 1951) studied the scurrying fear-like reactions of goslings when a particular display was presented to them. The display consisted of a long neck, an oval expansion that looks like the wings of a bird, then a short extension. The design is such that, if moved in one direction, the leading edge of the display had the long-necked shape of a goose. If moved in the opposite direction, the leading edge had the short-necked shape of a hawk. Tinbergen observed that the goslings scurried when exposed to the overhead movement of the hawk-like shape, and showed no such behavior when exposed to the overhead movement of the goose-like shape. He inferred that the hawk-like stimulus fit a biologically adapted template that facilitated avoidance, and hence survival.

Subsequent studies by several researchers (reviewed in Schneirla, 1965, and Gould, 1982) have confirmed the phenomenon Tinbergen described, but disconfirmed the interpretation. Instead of using the hawk–goose display, Goethe (cited in Schneirla, 1965) used a dark triangle, the base of which was presented vertically, such that when moved in one direction, the base of the triangle appeared first, and when moved in the opposite direction, the apex appeared first. Although this stimulus lacked any fit to an evolutionarily derived template of a potential predator, the base-appearing-first presentation led to scurrying in the goslings studied; but the apex-appearing-first display did not. Schneirla (1965) proposed that the scurrying-inducing element was the rate of change of stimulation, not the hawk or goose shape of the stimulus. When the rate of change is abrupt (as in the short-necked hawk stimulus or the base of the triangle), scurrying occurs. When the rate of change is gradual (as in the goose neck or the apex of the triangle), scurrying is lacking. Schneirla thus concluded that the goslings were sensitive to the relatively simple parameter of rate of change of stimulation, and not to the complex Gestalt of goose or hawk.

There are many instances of apparently preadapted reactions of human infants to relatively simple features of stimulation. At one time, it was thought that the heartbeat sound had an innate capacity to soothe infants because of the imprinting of heartbeat sounds to the infant while the infant was in the womb (Salk, 1962). In point of fact, heartbeat sounds do soothe infants, but not because they are heartbeat sounds. Brackbill, Adams, Crowell, and Gray (1966) showed that it was the rhythmicity of stimulation in the heartbeat sound that soothed, not the quality of the heartbeat itself. As with the hawk–goose phenomenon, a relation reliably demonstrated across studies has been shown to be the consequence of a feature embedded within a complex display, not the complex display itself. Such may also be the case for the empathic distress response of neonates to another neonate's cry; neonates may be sensitive to specific acoustic parameters of another's cry, but not to the cry as a whole.

At this writing, there is considerable interest in identifying whether the human being's reaction to music is innate, or acquired through acculturation and experience (Sloboda, 1986). Music is an excellent example of a complex event with features – especially rise time, loudness, tempo, and rising and falling acoustic contour patterns – that are likely to affect the arousal component of emotion. However, whether a complex organization of notes has the intrinsic capacity to go beyond arousal to elicit discrete emotions like fear, sadness, joy, etc., in the absence of experience or expectation, remains to be demonstrated (Meyer, 1957). One of the best studied of the features that can generate arousal is loudness. When presented with an acoustic stimulus of low intensity (e.g., less than 75 dB), infants characteristically show a heart-rate deceleration and the slowing of bodily activity characteristic of orienting. When the acoustic stimulus is of high intensity (e.g., 90 dB), the infant shows cardiac acceleration, jerky bodily movement, and other signs of a defensive response (Hatton, Berg, & Graham, 1970). Although less studied than loudness, intonational contours seem to have a bearing on emotion, with rising contours arousing, and descending contours soothing, the infant (Fernald, 1992). Studies of infants' emotional reactions to music similarly show clear reaction to tempo, loudness, and pitch; the reactions of infants to more complex aspects of musical composition remain to be demonstrated (Sullivan, Gentile, & Pick, 1998).

Co-evolution of Reception and Action

The vast majority of researchers, from Darwin (1872/1965) to the present, have focused the bulk of their theoretical and empirical attention on the role that evolution plays in organisms' emotional expressions, especially facial expressions (e.g., Ekman, 1972;

Tomkins, 1962, 1963; for an exception see Fridlund, 1997). However, if emotions are relational and if they have signal value for others, then the recipient is indispensable to the emotion process. Typically, emotional displays are only effective in a social context if they are perceived and acted upon by another (Fridlund, 1997). From this viewpoint, evolution must necessarily play a role not only in the production of expressions, but also in the reception of others' emotional displays. This issue raises the question of whether there is a process, or a set of processes, by which the expressive responses of the human and the perception of those responses when made by others can be unified. We believe that there is such a process, and propose that motor mimicry, and feedback to the brain from the motor behavior, is the best candidate for explaining the co-evolution of response and reception. Two lines of empirical work suggest that phylogeny may contribute to organisms' sensitivities to others' emotional displays and influence subsequent action in response to such displays. The first line of evidence comes from work on human infants and the second from rhesus monkeys.

Researchers have demonstrated that infants, in their first days and even first hours of life, can imitate certain facial displays such as tongue protrusions and pursed lips (e.g., Meltzoff & Moore, 1977, 1983), although not robustly and not always replicably (Anisfeld, 1991; Anisfeld et al., 2001). Over the first few months of life, imitation becomes increasingly prominent in the life of the infant (Uzgiris & Hunt, 1975). Many researchers have interpreted the existence of imitation as a "meeting of the minds" between modeler and caregiver (e.g., Gopnik & Meltzoff, 1997), such that the infant can feel what the modeler is feeling (e.g., joy when seeing a smile). From both an evolutionary and a functionalist perspective on emotions, what is important is not that the infant feels a like emotion, but that the infant can predict the future behavior of the emoting person (Fridlund, 1997). Regardless of which stance one takes on the issue of feeling, some (e.g., Hoffman, 2000) have pointed out that motor mimicry and imitation form the basis for empathy and ultimately prosocial and moral development. Taken from this perspective, neonatal imitation may be a phylogenetically mediated mechanism and precursor to forecasting others' behaviors that has ready adaptive value for the infant and that enables the human to be integrated into the social fabric of the group.

The mechanism of imitation has important implications for explaining what otherwise seems to be a contradiction in the proposal that evolution works by recruiting simple featural elements, and not complex patterns of perception. An important study has shown that rhesus monkeys less than 2 months of age respond appropriately to the social signals of conspecifics even when reared in the absence of social experience. For instance, infant rhesus monkeys show marked avoidance reactions to the presentation of a staring, immobile face; on the other hand, the same monkeys approach a figure engaging in lipsmacking behavior (Kenney, Mason, & Hill, 1979).

At first scrutiny, this study suggests that infant rhesus monkeys show innate reactions to complex social signals, with obvious evolutionary adaptive value by permitting the monkey to react appropriately to other monkeys almost from the beginning of life. However, we think that the evolutionarily based tendency toward motor mimicry may account for these findings, if a staring figure creates through response matching a momentary state of immobility and this immobility feeds information to the brain that is assimilated into representations of prior aggressive actions by the perceiver. Such feedback, then, would generate a "meaning" to the perception of a stare and lead to the assumption of avoidance responses. Similarly, perception of lipsmacking may result in reproduction in some way of lipsmacks by the perceiver monkey. If the feedback to the brain from such imitative lipsmacks is assimilated to actions such as feeding, the "meaning" of the lipsmack would then be positive and result in approach behaviors.

Motor mimicry is a fundamental axiom of behavior, evident in the human and non-human primate in very early life without social learning. Such mimicry is an important building block for generating complex emotional meanings, such as those so critically provided to conspecifics by social signals.

Differentiation and Integration Processes in Emotional Development

Evolution both prepares the infant for various organism–environment transactions that result in emotions and establishes very general constraints on the manifestation of emotions. However, evolutionary factors offer relatively limited insight into the actual changes that take place as emotion develops. As a result, the nature and course of emotional organization in infancy and beyond is specifically discovered through an examination of ontogenesis.

Infants' emotional lives change remarkably over the first 2 years of life. New emotions appear on the developmental landscape, and existing emotions undergo change in their own right. In the first few months, for example, the young infant shows neither shame nor pride, but by the end of the second year, these emotions are an active part of the infant's affective repertoire. Newborns do not smile in response to external events. By 2 months, however, infants not only smile to the outside world but do so especially to faces and voices of other human beings. Saying "no" to a 20-month-old may provoke a temper tantrum, but for a 6-month-old the word holds little meaning. When 4-month-olds are threatened by a looming stimulus, they will turn their heads away or raise their arms defensively; despite some reports to the contrary, newborns are not likely to do so.

What, then, are the starting points in the ontogenesis of emotion? One very widespread view, accepted by many cognitive and psychoanalytic theorists, is that the newborn is capable of manifesting only one emotion – a diffuse state of excitement, perhaps "tinged with unpleasure" (Bridges, 1932; Spitz, 1965). At about 4 weeks of age, the emotion of distress, characterized by a more clearly negative expressiveness, differentiates out of excitement. At 6 weeks, the emotion of joy branches off from excitement, characterized by the social smile directed principally to any face-like stimulus that consists of two adjacent eye-like dots, and a nodding oval contour. At 4 months, anger differentiates out of distress, at 6 months, disgust springs off from anger, and at 8 months, fear becomes evident. According to Bridges (1932) and others, this differentiation of discrete emotions from an originally diffuse arousal state constitutes a basic principle of emotional development.

Variants of Bridges's differentiation view persist to this day. Most recently, Camras (1992; see also Oster, Hegley, & Nagel, 1992) characterized certain facial and behavioral expressions of emotion as undifferentiated. Specifically, she reported that infant facial patterns of distress–pain, anger, and sadness – patterns often interpreted as reflecting discrete emotional states (e.g., Izard, 1991) – frequently co-occur under a variety of contexts designed to elicit only anger, only sadness, or only distress. Given these observations, Camras argued that anger and sadness expressions in the first year simply reflect intensity differences in a highly undifferentiated "unhappiness" or distress reaction that builds up over time in response to aversive events. "Anger" facial expressions thus correspond not to anger as a qualitatively distinct state but to intense distress, just as "sadness" facial expressions reflect mild distress. Going beyond Bridges, Camras (1992) has proposed that these emotional expressions remain relatively undifferentiated even into the second year of life.

Although differentiation as a process certainly characterizes many aspects of emotional development, emotional organization as a whole seems far more articulated than many differentiation accounts suggest. The work of Weinberg and Tronick (1994), for example, has revealed a number of distinct positive and negative affect patterns in the repertoire of 6-month-olds. Infants in their research were studied during an initial face-to-face play interaction with their mothers, followed by a period in which their mothers looked at but did not respond to their infants, and a subsequent "reunion" period in which mothers reestablished dyadic play interaction. Examining patterns of coherence across different modes of expressive and instrumental actions – such as facial displays, vocalizations, gestures, postural orientation, and gaze behavior – Weinberg and Tronick reported the presence of four distinct affect configurations, each specific to certain periods of the interaction context. A "Social Engagement" configuration, specific to the context of initial play interaction and the reunion, involved infant facial expressions of joy and positive vocalizations coupled with gazing at the mother and the mouthing of hands or feet. During the period of maternal unresponsiveness, infants exhibited an "Object Engagement" configuration, involving gazing at and the mouthing of objects, general scanning activity of the room, and facial expressions of interest. Infants also demonstrated during this period distinct organizations of "Passive Withdrawal" – involving fussy vocalizations, sad facial expressions, and indicators of stress such as hiccupping and spitting up – and "Active Protest" – involving angry expressions, scanning behavior, crying, attempts to escape, as well as fussy vocalizations and stress indicators – which carried over into the reunion period of interaction as well.

Each of the configurations Weinberg and Tronick (1994) identified serves a specific function with respect to the infant's relation to the world. As their labels suggest, Social Engagement functions to establish and maintain contact with social others, Object Engagement focuses the infant on object exploration, Passive Withdrawal serves to disengage or withdraw the infant from interaction, and Active Protest functions to engage the infant in efforts to eliminate an obstacle.

If we approach the study of younger infants from this functionalist standpoint, we see evidence not for an undifferentiated state of excitement or distress but for more specific emotion systems (Sroufe, 1979, 1996). Under conditions of loss of support, the neonate will typically startle and draw his or her arms around the chest in what functions as a protective embrace (Peiper, 1963). This pattern of response contrasts sharply with the head withdrawal, arm-flailing, and pushing behavior we see in neonates whose nostrils have been inadvertently occluded during breastfeeding; these infants do not clasp in protective fashion but instead implement actions that function, however crudely, as a defensive attack on the condition of respiratory occlusion (Gunther, 1961; Lipsitt, 1976). Yet another functionally distinct pattern of behavior surfaces when neonates encounter bitter-tasting substances; in this context, the infant retracts his or her lips and often extends his or her tongue in a facial action that functions to reject or orally discharge the offending substance (Steiner, 1979). In each of these cases, we see patterns of behavior that, when considered in relation to specific events, serve distinct functions of protection, obstacle removal, and rejection. Even the neonate, therefore, has an action repertoire sufficiently differentiated to deal with distinct forms of aversive stimulation.

Like Sroufe (1979, 1996), we argue for the presence of some distinct, precursor emotion organizations in the neonatal period, rather than for nothing but undifferenti-ated arousal. However, this in no way undermines the importance of a process like dif-ferentiation for the characterization of emotional development. Processes of differentiation transform aspects of the emotion process, such as facial expressions, instru-mental actions, and evaluations, from more global, homogeneous organizations to specific, increasingly heterogeneous ones, but they do so with respect to distinct, protoemotion systems (Sroufe, 1996). An example from Buhler (1930) aptly demon-strates the differentiation process with respect to the protoanger system evident in the neonate. Buhler observed that young infants, when having their noses wiped, responded with undirected, whole-body movement; their arms and legs would move wildly without necessarily contacting the hand of the individual wiping their noses. Later in develop-ment, infants increasingly coordinated their arm movements to push aside the hand and resist having their noses wiped. By 8 months, infants began to prepare for nose wiping by swiping at the hand before it could reach their noses. Thus, in this example, the rela-tional meaning of infants' action in the context of nose wiping – obstacle removal – pro-vides a continuity in the organization of infant–environment transactions, but the specific properties of infant action in relation to an obstacle undergo increasing differentiation with development.

Differentiation is itself part of a larger process. Each differentiation in a system is accom-panied by an integration or coordination of differentiated material. As differentiation serves to render systems less homogeneous and diffuse, integration establishes in differen-tiated systems new, more cohesive and stable organizations. These two processes routinely complement one another. Thus, the increasing specificity of infants' action in response to having their noses wiped constitutes both a differentiation from the more global whole-body reaction of the young infant and an integration/coordination of more specific action with specific targets of that action (i.e., the hand wiping the nose). Differentiation and inte-gration imply one another, and the combined process constitutes a fundamental means of characterizing much of the change that occurs in emotional development. In the next two segments, we highlight the differentiation/integration process as it applies to perceptual processes and action components of infant emotional development.

Perceptual Differentiation/Integration in Early Emotional Development

Recall that emotions do not involve stimuli or "emotion elicitors" at the input end – at the initiation of the emotional process. We prefer to use the term "engagement" to refer to the process whereby person and event are unified into an affectively meaningful unit. To engage in the world, the individual must have adequate sensory capacities. At birth, those capacities can be extraordinarily limited, thereby minimizing the likelihood of engagement and hence emotional responding.

Take the social smile, for instance. The social smile is a response the infant begins to show between 4 and 6 weeks of age, first to auditory stimuli and then to visual ones (Wolff, 1987). This event is powerful for parents and bystanders alike to witness, and devastating when it is manifested abnormally (as with Down's syndrome infants; see Emde, Katz, & Thorpe, 1978). What brings about the social smile?

In all likelihood, the social smile, at least when construed in terms of visual engagement, is the result of major perceptual differentiation processes occurring in the infant's visual system. Newborns have a strong tendency to scan contours. This tendency is so strong that when they scan a face, the scan typically does not reach the interior of the face; rather, it stops at the high-contrast hairline of the face or the edge of the head. At around 6 weeks of age, the infant, possibly as a result of habituation processes, reduces the tendency to scan exterior contours and begins to scan the inside of the face, especially the eyes (Haith, Bergman, & Moore, 1977). We know that the smile can be elicited "artificially" by a cardboard containing an oval, two dark dots, and a hairline, presented in nodding fashion to the infant at the age of onset of the social smile (Spitz, 1965). This display is the event that engages the infant, that is assimilated to the experiences of being held and fed by the mother, and that brings about the social smile. Any process that minimizes the chance of the newborn shifting from scanning exterior contours to interior ones will, we predict, slow down the manifestation of the social smile to faces. Any process that accelerates the shift will similarly accelerate the social smile. (Note the role of both experience and biological preparedness for learning in this interpretation of social smiling to faces.)

The process of perceptual differentiation does not end with the onset of social smiling. As discussed, 2-month-olds begin to scan the internal features of the face but focus primarily on the eyes, especially when they view a talking face (Haith et al., 1977). Consequently, infants at this age may not be as sensitive to emotional information conveyed through other features of the face, such as the mouth. Between 4 and 5 months, however, infants expand their scanning of the face to routinely include multiple features, such as mouth and nose as well as eyes (Caron, Caron, Caldwell, & Weiss, 1973). As infants begin to process more features of the face, they in turn begin to integrate those features to establish the prototypical facial Gestalts of emotional expressions that adults readily recognize (Nelson, 1987). By 7 months, infants distinguish between some facial displays of positive (e.g., happiness) and negative (e.g., anger) emotions as well as among some facial displays of the same valence, such as sadness vs. anger or happiness vs. surprise (Ludemann & Nelson, 1988; Nelson, 1987; Soken & Pick, 1999). Thus, through processes of differentiation and integration, infants gradually forge sensitivities to many different social signals conveyed as facial displays.

There are many other instances of perceptual differentiation related to emotion. Among these is the differentiation of mother from stranger through the use of vision. For the infant to engage with the mother visually, he or she must be able to see her relatively clearly, especially from a variety of distances. This process of seeing persons clearly from a distance develops remarkably slowly in the first 6 months of life (Banks & Salapatek, 1983; Kellman & Banks, 1998). The vision of the young child is extraordinarily smudgy and indistinct. Although there may be special orientations and distances under which infants in the first couple of months can see relatively clearly, and so can tell who is the mother and who is not, it is likely that such discriminations will be limited and context-bound. Not until the infant's visual resolution approaches more adult-like levels, beginning around 6 months (Banks & Salapatek, 1983), will the infant be able to identify the mother and establish an integrated, coherent scheme of her across a wide variety of situations. Consequently, the development of the child's attachment to the mother, especially either proximity-seeking or signaling to her across large distances (Bowlby, 1969), may need to await perceptual developments that do not become relatively well developed until 5 months or later. These considerations make it clear that differentiation and integration processes play an important role in emotional development.

Response Differentiation/Integration in Early Emotional Development

Differentiation/integration processes apply not just to the evaluation side of the emotion process but also to the "response" side. We have already cited evidence from Buhler (1930) for a progressive differentiation and coordination of instrumental responding to events of restraint. Work by Stenberg and Campos (1990) on the development of anger-*expressive* patterning in 1-, 4-, and 7-month-old infants further underscores the presence of differentiation/integration processes in emotional development. In their study, anger was generated by gently holding the infant's arms but preventing them from readily moving, and the infant's facial and vocal expressions, as well as their instrumental behaviors, were recorded. The study yielded three important findings.

First, infants showed intense negativity in emotional reaction at every age tested. Facially, their reactions became coordinated into an anger-like pattern between 1 and 4 months of age. More specifically, infants' facial displays showed few components related to fear, disgust, sadness, or other negative emotions. At 1 month, the components shown were mostly, though not exclusively, those associated with anger; the infants lowered their brows and drew them together and they elevated their cheeks. However, they also showed two facial components that indicated incomplete, partially diffuse organization of facial movements. In one, they closed their eyes rather than narrowed them (as would be expected in an anger encounter), displaying a more general distress pattern. In the second, they stuck their tongues out rather than pulling the corners of the mouth back. Although they also vocalized negatively, 1-month-olds did not specifically target their expressions at anything relevant in the environment, looking instead all over the room in a relatively diffuse manner.

Second, by 4 months, infants' facial actions were more organized, with the eyes showing the expectable narrowing (rather than closing), and the oral region the proto-typical pulled-back appearance. Moreover, the infants directed their facial movements toward the site of the frustration – the hands of the experimenter holding the infants' arms – suggesting that the emotional state had a target or an aim. The voice, too, showed greater coordination with the face. It was as if the facial movements were in the service of vocalizing, because in general the vocalizations that were observed followed rather than preceded the facial patterning.

Third, at 7 months, a major reorganization took place not in the face or the voice, but in the targeting component of the emotion. The infants directed their expressions both to the frustrating experimenter as well as to the mother (who was a bystander in the testing procedure). Indeed, they vocalized only when looking at the person frustrating their movements, or at their bystander mothers.

There have not been many other studies that complement the picture Stenberg and Campos (1990) provide for progressive response organization and integration. Nevertheless, there are analogs in the development of the smile in the first few weeks of life. Infants' endogenous smiles are low intensity and involve simply turning up the corners of the mouth (Emde & Koenig, 1969). Infants' first waking smiles are of a slightly larger magnitude but still only involve turning up of the mouth corners (Emde, Gaensbauer, & Harmon, 1976; Wolff, 1987). Both smiling forms are due to the contraction of a single muscle (Ekman & Oster, 1979). By the end of the third week, however, infants' smiles begin to recruit other muscles and increasingly involve a brightening and crinkling of the eyes in conjunction with the contraction of the mouth corners to produce a full "grin" (Wolff, 1987).

Infants' emotional expressions (including facial and vocal, and possibly gestural and tactile), as well as instrumental behaviors, thus become more differentiated and articulated in the course of development. Ultimately, infants' increasingly articulated expressive and instrumental responses allow them to better achieve their goals and strivings in the world. As general processes, differentiation and integration offer a systematic way of outlining the course of emotional development, both in infancy and later in life. We now turn to more specific elements of the emotion process that organize its development.

Cognitive Factors in Emotional Development

The study of emotion in the last 30 years has revolved to a large extent around the role that cognitive factors play in the generation of emotion (Lazarus, 1991). The role of cognition in emotion involves those aspects of emotion generation that are not immediately available in the stimulus array, in which processes such as memory, expectancy, belief, schemes, problem solving, and symbol systems structure a person's attempts to make sense of the world. Although cognition does not generate emotion by itself, without its linkage to something that makes it significant, it is nevertheless important to ask, "What role do cognitive factors play in the generation and development of infant emotion?"

Specific Cognitive Organizations and Emotional Development

Linking stages of sensorimotor intelligence to emotional development

Anyone who has observed infants will notice a major transition in the second half of their first year. At this time, infants begin to show wariness and distress both in the presence of strangers and in the absence of their primary caregivers. These robust phenomena are the starting points for many accounts which highlight the role of specific cognitive advances in the emergence of certain emotions. Some psychoanalytic theorists, for example, view stranger and separation distress as an outgrowth of the infant's emergent ability to mentally represent the mother – a representation that allows infants to notice discrepancies between mother and strangers and to keep the mother in mind even during her absence (Decarie, 1965; Spitz, 1965). Tests of this proposal have often relied on Piaget's (1954) developmental account of object permanence – the infant's understanding that people and objects exist independent of the infant's own perception and action. Specifically, the emergence of Stage 4 object permanence, in which infants begin to search for objects that are no longer visually present, occurs around the same time as stranger and separation distress appear in development. However, no evidence to date supports a relation between Stage 4 object permanence and either stranger or separation distress (Campos et al., 1983; Campos & Stenberg, 1981).

More empirically promising is the relation between development in self-awareness (an index of Stage 6 sensorimotor intelligence) and the emergence of embarrassment (M. Lewis, 1995). Between 15 and 18 months, infants whose noses have been marked with rouge demonstrate face and nose touching when they are placed in front of a mirror, indicative of mirror self-recognition. Prior to 15 months, infants in such a situation interact with the mirror itself but do not act as if they recognize themselves in it (M. Lewis & Brooks-Gunn, 1979). M. Lewis and his colleagues suggest that the emergence of mirror self-recognition indexes the acquisition of an objective self-awareness, in which infants begin to *consciously* reflect on themselves as individuals with a distinct identity. This acquisition must be in place, according to M. Lewis (1995), for infants to experience embarrassment. There is, in fact, a link between the development of objective self-awareness, indexed by mirror self-recognition, and the subsequent emergence of embarrassment (M. Lewis, Sullivan, Stanger, & Weiss, 1989).

Although evidence for links between specific sensorimotor intellectual advances and emotional development remains limited, no one can doubt the importance of cognitive organization in emotion. Clearly an understanding of absence plays a role in the developmental emergence of separation distress. We must keep in mind, however, the developmental nature of cognition in infancy. Piaget's object permanence involves six distinct stages of organization, each of which reflects the gradual consolidation of an understanding that self and other are distinct, integrated entities. Stage 4 object permanence elaborates on previous stages of object permanence; we cannot, as a result, isolate it as *the* point when infants begin to view their mothers as independent, integrated entities. Self-awareness, similarly, does not emerge fully formed with the arrival of mirror self-recognition but develops from previous forms.

If cognitive development is gradual and does not emerge fully formed, then it may be possible to observe less than fully formed manifestations of the emotion at earlier ages than the normative as well. That is precisely the case with separation distress, stranger distress, and embarrassment. Many mothers report a period of early stranger distress in infants between 3 and 6 months – a reaction that is not as strong, as consistent, or as independent of context as the reaction will be later. Similarly, some observers, such as Stayton, Ainsworth, and Main (1973), report a spurt in negative reactions to separation at 5 months of age, but these reactions are observed principally in the home setting. Finally, M. Lewis et al. (1989) report that a substantial minority of infants who do *not* yet show mirror self-recognition nevertheless react with embarrassment.

Cognition in context: The role of ecological factors in cognition–emotion relations

As we have noted, cognitive factors by themselves are not sufficient to generate emotion. Like shame, embarrassment involves not simply an objective self-awareness but a sense of being "under the watchful eye of the other" (Mead, 1934). The child in an embarrassing transaction must expect either a negative social signal for what he or she has done, or the absence of an expected positive signal. Most research on emotional development does not consider the importance of the child's embeddedness in a specific ecology that, when combined with minimal cognitive developments, results in emotion. Similar considerations apply to separation and stranger distress. Separation from the mother is rare for the Japanese infant; when it occurs, it results in a far more intense reaction in the Japanese infant than in German infants, whose parents frequently leave them alone (Grossmann, Grossmann, Huber, & Wartner, 1981; Miyake, Chen, & Campos, 1985). Sadness, another emotion linked to the development of representation and thought to "emerge" at 6 months or so (Spitz, 1965), can be observed at much earlier ages if the circumstances facilitate its manifestation (such as being reared in abusive and neglectful situations; Gaensbauer, 1980).

General Cognitive Processes and Emotional Development

Memory and discrepancy from the familiar in the first 6 months

More general cognitive processes such as memory and expectancy have also been implicated in emotional development. One such process involving memory development is the principle of discrepancy from the familiar (e.g., Hebb, 1946). Such discrepancy from the familiar is a crucial ingredient for all emotional processes as it signals noteworthy change in the person's relation to his or her environment. An infant's interest and arousal in the context of a novel event vary systematically with the degree of that event's discrepancy from the infant's past; this fundamental principle holds from the newborn period and beyond (Friedman, Bruno, & Vietze, 1974; McCall & Kagan, 1967). Repeated presentations of a stimulus (e.g., a vertical arrow) produce a waning of interest in infants – they habituate to the stimulus – and once familiarity is established, additional presentations will fail to reinvigorate infant attention. Presentation of a new stimulus (e.g., a diagonal arrow) will revive infant attention and arousal but only up to a point; with sufficient magnitudes of stimulus discrepancy (e.g., a horizontal arrow following familiarization with a vertical arrow), infant attention remains low.

The discrepancy principle has been extended beyond arousal to specific valenced emotions as well (Hebb, 1949; McCall & McGhee, 1977). Stimuli or events that moderately diverge from an infant's past experience, that require some degree of effort to incorporate into memory ("effortful assimilation"), but that nonetheless ultimately comply with memory, are said to result in positive emotion such as joy (Kagan, 1971). Events that actively conflict with infant memory – familiar in some respects but discrepant enough to prove incompatible with past experience – produce negative emotion such as fear, whereas highly familiar events that readily match memory provoke much less interest and even boredom from the infant (McCall & McGhee, 1977).

How does the discrepancy principle affect emotional *development?* In infancy, discrepancy from the familiar follows a two-step developmental sequence. In the infant's first 6 to 8 months, discrepancy takes the form of basic event recognition. Infants simply assess an event as matching or not matching their previous experience; in effect, their processing maps onto the question, "Have I encountered this event before or not?" (Schaffer, 1974). Instructive in this regard is work linking discrepancy to smiling via effortful assimilation. Seven-month-olds, who were habituated to a standard stimulus, smiled most and cried least when subsequently presented with a stimulus moderately discrepant from the standard (Hopkins, Zelazo, Jacobson, & Kagan, 1976). In work by Zelazo and Komer (1971), infants as young as 3 months smiled most midway through a series of repeated stimulus presentations, presumably at a point between initial unfamiliarity and well-established familiarity. The emergence of social smiling can thus be explained as evidence for infants' initial consolidation of memory for faces in general.

Similarly, the emergence of infant distress to an unresponsive, expressionless mother supports a discrepancy framework of explanation. Beginning around 3 months, infants cry and protest when their mothers simulate depression during face-to-face interaction (Cohn & Tronick, 1983). Around this time, infants begin to demonstrate marked sensitivity to routines and specific contingencies in dyadic interaction, suggesting that between 2 and 4 months infants establish expectations for how primary caretakers should interact with them (Rochat, Querido, & Striano, 1999). Thus, by 3 months of age, a stiff-faced, unresponsive mother conflicts with most infants' past experience, thereby generating negative affect.

Discrepancy from the familiar: The emergence of stranger anxiety

Between 7 and 9 months, infants move beyond mere recognition in memory to rudimentary levels of recall (Meltzoff, 1988; Schaffer, 1974). Infants' processing of discrepancy consequently assumes a new form and establishes the basis for stranger distress. We previously reported that infants as young as 3 months show a muted form of stranger distress; at this time, infants recognize strangers as unfamiliar (Bronson, 1972). Between 7 and 9 months, however, infants no longer rate a stranger as simply unfamiliar but as *different from* their mothers, in effect asking the question "How does this event compare or relate to my other experiences?" (Schaffer, 1974). Kagan (1974) calls this new process "activation of hypotheses," in which infants actively scan their memory for the purpose of relating multiple representations to discrepant events. In general, the transition in discrepancy processing from recognition of familiarity to active comparison of events with stored memories reflects a shift from sequential to simultaneous processing. In the first 6 months, infants process events in isolation of other events and never contrast the processing of a current event with other event representations in their memory store. But after 6 months, simultaneous processing becomes evident, in which infants compare/contrast discrepant events with stored representations of similar but different events (Schaffer, 1974).

Insufficiency of discrepancy in explaining emotional development

Discrepancy processes play a critical role in emotion for infants and adults alike. Mismatches between events and our expectations – derived from past experience – render us attentive, increase our arousal, and prime us for meaningful interaction with the world. Discrepancy processes, however, are insufficient for explaining either the generation of specific emotions or emotional development in general. For example, the same event for the same infant can generate markedly different emotions depending on various contextual factors. Ten-month-olds, when presented with their mothers wearing a mask, invariably smile and frequently laugh when the presentation occurs at home, but show much less positive affect to the same event conducted in the lab; similarly, a stranger's approach elicits greater heart-rate acceleration in the lab than in the infant's home (Sroufe, Waters, & Matas, 1974). These results and others like them suggest that the specific quality of an infant's emotion depends on much more than an event and its discrepancy from past experience. Discrepancy affects emotional arousal levels and consequently the intensity of emotional responses and experience, but something more is needed to account for specific, valenced emotions such as fear and joy (M. Lewis & Goldberg, 1969; Sroufe, Waters, & Matas, 1974; Stechler & Carpenter, 1967).

What is needed, in fact, is a way to turn "cold" cognitive processes – like discrepancy – and structures – like object permanence and objective self-awareness – into "hot" cognitions, cognitions that *evaluate* events and as a result render events significant and emotion-relevant (Campos & Barrett, 1984; Sroufe, 1996). One such candidate is the process of appraisal, to which we now turn.

Appraisal Processes and Emotional Development

Sroufe's emphasis on the context of events in generating emotion underscores the need to embed general cognitive processes such as discrepancy from the familiar in a larger organizational framework. With the notion of appraisal, researchers have specifically begun to view cognition's influence on emotion within a larger motivational context. Appraisal represents a special form of cognition that involves the infant's evaluation of an event in terms of its significance or relevance for his or her goals and concerns (Campos & Barrett, 1984). As such, appraisal is an integral part of the emotion process and is not considered a purely cognitive process but a cognitive-motivational process (Barrett & Campos, 1987; Mascolo & Fischer, 1995; Mascolo & Harkins, 1998).

The cognitive transition from sequential to simultaneous processing gains new meaning when we embed it in significant transactions between the infant and the world. Between 6 and 9 months, infants' affective exchanges with their caregivers extend beyond the realm of dyadic interaction to triadic interaction, a process termed "secondary intersubjectivity" (Trevarthen & Hubley, 1978). In effect, infants begin to share emotion with their caregivers *about* a third event – such as an object in the environment or another person – and to understand that others' emotional displays and gaze patterns can refer to people and events outside the caregiver–infant dyad (Bates, 1979). This shift in emotional communication relies on the emergence of simultaneous processing – infants must appreciate the emotion communicated by the caregiver in simultaneous relation to a distinct event or person – but is not reducible to purely cognitive processes, for secondary intersubjectivity is ultimately about a new form of affective sharing in infancy.

Social referencing: An example of appraisal in infancy

Social referencing, a fundamental appraisal process, is perhaps the emotional cornerstone of secondary intersubjectivity. Infants who social reference use the facial, vocal, and gestural affective displays of others to evaluate ambiguous events and to regulate subsequent action in relation to those events (Campos & Stenberg, 1981). This process relies on the infant's being able to relate the valenced meaning conveyed by a social other to an event whose meaning is not clear cut – such as the presence of a novel toy, the approach of a stranger, or the drop-off of a support surface on the visual cliff. Infants as young as 9 months do indeed relate the general positive or negative affective meaning conveyed by social others to ambiguous people/events and adjust their responses to the person/event accordingly. If, for example, a mother displays fear in relation to the drop-off edge of the visual cliff, infants rarely cross the cliff to their mothers, but in the context of a happy display from the mother, infants readily cross (Sorce, Emde, Campos, & Klinnert, 1985); similarly, infants respond much more positively to a stranger's approach or to a strange toy when their mothers react to the event with smiles and positive vocalizations (Boccia & Campos, 1989; Feinman & Lewis, 1983; Mumme, Fernald, & Herrera, 1996).

The process of social referencing tailors the cognitive emergence of simultaneous processing to the emotion system proper; it involves evaluations of situations that directly affect infants' goals and strivings and makes use of expressive behavior via the face, voice, and gesture. In investigations of the development of pride, shame, and guilt, Mascolo and Fischer (1995) also address cognitive factors from the standpoint of appraisal. Pride appraisals, for example, involve self-evaluations of *responsibility* for acting in ways that garner social approval (Mascolo & Harkins, 1998). Pride appraisals originate, according to Mascolo and his colleagues, in the infant's detection of contingencies between his or her action and its effects. Infants as young as 2 months smile when their actions affect outcomes in the world. At the end of the first year, infants begin to establish more complex action–effect contingencies by enjoying both the immediate effects of their action and the positive reactions from social others to their action. Toward the end of the second year, infants begin to reflect on their action as a product of their own agency (Mascolo & Fischer, 1995). Although this and other appraisal sequences for shame and guilt take root in general forms of infant cognitive development, the appraisal component itself involves specific forms of cognition, such as notions of responsibility and evaluations of social approval, that intimately relate to the strivings of the infant.

Stranger and separation reactions as disruptions of expectations about communication

Cognitive advances in object permanence and self-awareness as well as cognitive processes such as memory and expectancy have been theoretically and empirically linked to emotional development in infancy. But none of these factors holds inherent meaning for the emotional life of the infant; as a result, we must approach cognitive factors from the standpoint of relational meaning patterns in emotion and ultimately embed "cold" cognitions within a motivational context of the infant's goals and strivings. Such a consideration sheds new light on the very phenomena that have inspired traditional cognitive explanations in emotional development: stranger and separation distress. Factors such as memory and expectancy may indeed play a role in these developments, but to fully understand that role, we must reconceptualize these factors from the standpoint of significance in the infant's life.

To this end, separation and stranger distress may emerge as a consequence of specific expectations infants have for how social others should behave when communicating with them (Bower, 1977). With the emergence of primary intersubjectivity at 2 to 3 months, infants and their primary caregivers gradually co-construct unique modes of communicating and sharing emotion with one another, consisting of specific and routinized sequences of facial signaling, vocalizing, gesturing, body orientation, and tactile contact. These communication modes have powerful regulatory effects on infant arousal levels and emotional state (Tronick, 1989). Eventually, infants come to expect these specific forms of communication in the context of social interaction. Infants for whom these expectations are consolidated will encounter a rather dramatic violation of expectancy when a stranger interacts with them; similarly, when separated from the primary caregiver, these same infants will be without an important source of emotional regulation via the loss of a significant communicational partner. By couching the emergence of stranger and separation distress in the context of infant–caregiver communication patterns and their regulatory consequences, we can see why, for example, infants are most likely to react with distress when a stranger tries to interact with them but rarely ever show distress to the mere presence of a stranger (Schaffer, 1971).

Multiple Component Processes and Emotional Development

The Importance of Context in Emotion and Its Development

Appraisal processes in emotional development highlight the importance of embedding one component of the emotion process – cognition – within a context of other components – goals and strivings. Equally important is the consideration of *physical* and *social contexts* when studying the emotion process and its development. Context is crucial as a factor that affects the manifestation of emotion in a specific emotional transaction, and also as a catalyst that helps to organize the development of emotion. We will illustrate these points in this section of the chapter.

The word "context" is usually taken to mean the presence or absence of some environmental factor in relation to a person's behavior. For example, an infant's reaction to a stranger will be rather different depending upon whether the mother is or is not present in the testing room. The mother's presence is thus a contextual factor in stranger distress (see Sroufe et al., 1974). However, for us, context involves much more than just modulation of emotional responding. In a relational approach to emotion, context refers to the broad social, economic, and historical *ecology* within which the infant is developing, and it simultaneously refers to the *appropriateness of the fit* of the infant into that ecological niche. Viewed in this way, not only does the infant develop, but so too does the environment. The concepts of harmony, discord, and reciprocity between the infant's behavior and that of caregivers are thus crucial for understanding developmental transitions in emotion.

Examples of the role of context in real-time interaction

The work of Fogel and his colleagues illustrates the importance of one aspect of context – the type of behavior of the mother and the type of games she plays with her infant – for the organization of infant's expressive behavior during dyadic interaction. Fogel's work demonstrates how specific factors in the play of caregiver and infant shape the forms that infant smiling behavior assumes (Dickson, Walker, & Fogel, 1997). Twelve-month-olds' smiles in the play context of book reading typically consist only of lip-corner raises. During physical play, open-mouth smiling prevails, and when caregivers vocalize with their infants, infant smiling includes both lip-corner raises and contraction of the muscles surrounding the eyes. Fogel's work thus advances our understanding of the way that parents' behavior can help to organize infants' expressive behavior.

Context and the parent–child system

Context can have an impact broader than the organization of emotional expression (Sander, 1964). Emotional development does not take place in a social vacuum: the infant's development is indissociably tied in with developmental tasks the baby and the mother jointly face. How these developmental tasks are resolved can profoundly affect personality development.

Sander proposes five developmental tasks that mothers and infants jointly face in the first two years of life. One concerns coordination of patterns of feeding, quieting, sleep, and arousal regulation (birth to 3 months). A second deals with newly emerged smiling and vocalization patterns (4–6 months). A third revolves around the child's new initiative skills (7–9 months). A fourth involves issues relating to the establishment of the mother as the principal attachment figure (10–12 months). And the fifth centers on the emergence of the infant's self-assertion (15 to 20 months of age). Posing context as Sander does in terms of broad patterns in parent–child interactions is very valuable. For example, it shows how mothers can react very differently to the way a baby develops emotionally. A mother who is very happy dealing with a dependent and relatively helpless infant (Phases 1 and 2) may become saddened, upset, and less sensitive toward the infant when the infant becomes increasingly autonomous (Phase 3). If so, the mother may inadvertently create a context in which the child's *fit* with her behavior shifts from harmonious to disruptive. (The reverse can also be true, if the mother values the newfound autonomy of her baby and moves away from disliking the baby as helpless to seeing the baby as more grown up.) A similar consideration applies to the role of the father. A father who has enjoyed playing with his baby in Phase 3 may be disturbed when he sees the baby making the mother his or her first love in Phase 4. Sander has shown (1962, 1964) how interactional failures in the parents' and the child's navigation of these developmental tasks can result in personality disorders later on. In sum, one must take into account the context – the appropriateness of fit between baby and parents – to understand normal and deviant emotional development.

Context and Beyond: The Multicomponential Nature of Emotional Development

Recognizing the critical role context plays in the emotion process underscores the need to view emotional development as a multicomponent process, comprised of elements such as action and action tendency, goals and concerns, physiological, appraisal, and experiential feeling components, as well as social and physical context components. Just as no one component serves as criterion for emotion in its mature form, no one component of the emotion process serves as criterion for either a given developmental level of organization in emotion or a transition between levels of organization in development. Thus, characterizing the emotional life of a 4-month-old – as distinct from an 8-month-old – requires more than simply knowing the child's appraisal skills, because event appraisals necessarily depend on the actions available to the infant for engaging the event (Campos et al., 1994). We must also know the action repertoire available to the 4-month-old. But this is only half the picture, for we must also know about the world in which the 4-month-old resides, the social and physical contexts in which the infant is embedded. Our evaluations of and actions on the world are both an outgrowth and organizer of our transactions with the world.

If the emotion process consists of multiple, interrelated components, then emotional development stems from systematic changes in the interactions among these components (Fogel et al., 1992). Both individual developments of particular components themselves and interactions among components establish organizational changes in emotion; to understand emotional development, therefore, requires an assessment of how the components of emotion interact to produce behavior at different levels of developmental organization, from birth forward (M. D. Lewis, 2000; M. D. Lewis & Granic, 1999; Mascolo & Griffin, 1998).

Change in one component of emotion may destabilize the system, but establishment of a new developmental organization in emotion requires consideration of all its components in interaction with one another. As a result, physical and social contextual factors are as important as intrapersonal factors such as appraisal in conceptualizing emotion, both in its real-time unfolding and in its developmental organizations. As active, self-organizing processes, emotions take root directly in activity geared toward adaptation in the world. Emotions, in brief, develop through person–environment transactions (Campos et al., 1994; Griffin & Mascolo, 1998; Thompson, 1993). We now illustrate these fundamental principles by detailing how a major transition in person–environment relations – the onset of crawling – incites sweeping reorganization in emotion and how the actual process of reorganization derives from new interactions among various elements of the emotion system.

Locomotor experience and emotional development

Crawling and the experience it generates affect the emotional life of the infant in profound ways. With the onset of crawling, infants have at their disposal a new means of acting on the world and adapting to the world. In the literature on infant attachment, crawling has long been considered an important step for the emergence of specific attachments to caregivers; using the caregiver as a secure base from which to explore the world intimately depends on the availability of independent movement for the infant (Ainsworth, Blehar, Waters, & Wall, 1978; Bowlby, 1969). Through crawling and the newfound autonomy it provides, infants can not only entertain new goals but also more fully explore existing goals. The crawling infant furthermore affects the social system in which he or she is embedded. Caregivers must regulate the infant's newfound opportunities for exploration to ensure their infants' safety, which in turn impacts communication patterns between caregiver and infant.

Caregivers, in fact, report major increases in their infants' displays of anger and temper tantrums following crawling onset (Campos, Kermoian, & Zumbahlen, 1992). Once infants begin to crawl, caregivers themselves target more positive affect toward infant exploration and the discovery of new events and situations. At the same time, caregivers begin to assign a more sophisticated intentionality to their infants and treat them as more responsible for their actions. This change, coupled with the increased chance for a mobile infant to encounter dangerous situations, produces a substantial increase in parental targeting of fear and anger to their infants once crawling begins (Campos, Bertenthal, & Kermoian, 1992; Zumbahlen & Crawley, 1996).

In short, the onset of crawling, a basic action component of the process of relating to the world, prompts the need for fundamental reorganization in the infant's emotional life, both at the level of infant affectivity and at the level of the emotional climate in which the infant resides. Once infants begin to crawl, their goals, evaluations, expectations, and interactions with others undergo major transition in conjunction with the new adaptive demands they face. The organization of the infant's emotional life consequently assumes new forms as various components of the emotion process reestablish stable interaction with one another. One of these new forms is the emergence of wariness of heights. In what follows, we outline an account for this new form of fear in infancy that vividly instantiates the need to view emotional development as a self-organizing, multicomponent system. The account demonstrates how crawling experience prompts a reorganization in the way infants register self-motion by providing new opportunities for infants to relate what their eyes tell them is their motion with what their body feels is their motion. This reorganization, in turn, affects how infants control their posture and ultimately generates expectations about the information available for self-motion detection. It is under conditions which violate these expectations that fear is aroused.

The emergence of wariness of heights: An example

It is well established that experience with self-produced locomotion, either through crawling or through the use of a "walker," gives rise to wariness of heights (Campos, Bertenthal et al., 1992; Campos, Hiatt, Ramsay, Henderson, & Svejda, 1978). How crawling experience ultimately engenders fear of heights, however, remains open to speculation. We present here an account for wariness of heights that relies on work done with adults on height vertigo. Brandt and his colleagues have demonstrated that height vertigo derives from conflict in information available for determining self-motion (Brandt, Arnold, Bles, & Kapteyn, 1980; Brandt, Bles, Arnold, & Kapteyn, 1979). Extensive evidence suggests that as adults, we use both visual information and information derived from the vestibular system to judge our movement in the world and that we rely on what we see to maintain our posture and balance, as is evident when we shut our eyes while standing (e.g., Dichgans & Brandt, 1978; Lee & Lishman, 1975; Lishman & Lee, 1973). Brandt and his colleagues argue that adults implicitly expect what they see to correspond to their internally derived sensations of motion. Such a correspondence is violated under conditions likely to produce height vertigo. When we stand at the edge of a cliff, our normal body sway tells us, via the vestibular system, that we are moving, but our eyes tell us next to nothing about our body sway because normally available optical textures in our surround – such as the ground stretching out in front of us – are largely absent. They are too far away to be noticed or to be effective. To overcome the conflict, adults typically increase their postural sway to generate motion in their visual surround, but this ultimately results in greater postural instability and height vertigo.

We have extended this argument to the emergence of wariness of heights in infancy by suggesting that experience with crawling sets in motion processes that ultimately establish infant expectations of specific correspondence between visual and vestibular sources of self-motion information (e.g., Bertenthal & Campos, 1990; Campos, Kermoian, & Witherington, 1996). First, with experience in crawling, infants demonstrate a new sensitivity to certain forms of visual motion information for controlling their posture (Higgins, Campos, & Kermoian, 1996). Specifically, crawling infants begin to use patterned visual information available in their peripheral visual field to determine self-motion.

Second, crawling experience establishes specific correspondences between visual and vestibular information for self-motion. When infants are passively moved, nothing compels them to look in their direction of motion; as a result, they will not consistently generate the visual information in the peripheral visual field that accompanies forward motion. Crawling infants, on the other hand, typically look in their direction of motion and consequently experience specific, correlated information about their movement from both the visual and vestibular systems.

Third, crawling infants form expectations about this correlated input. In fact, crawling infants rely more than ever on information for self-motion because their newly established mobility carries with it increased encounters with postural instability. The specific expectations infants establish for correlated input are in the service of maintaining postural stability and are as a result imbued with affective significance for the infant. Loss of support and the vestibular input accompanying it are a significant source of negative emotion throughout development (Campos & Bertenthal, 1989; Jersild, 1946).

Thus, crawling experience lays the foundation for systematic changes in perception, action, and cognition which in turn organize a new form of fear in context: wariness of heights. We, in fact, have preliminary evidence to suggest that increases in infants' sensitivity to peripheral visual information for controlling body posture directly map onto demonstrations of wariness of heights (Witherington, Kermoian, & Campos, 2001). Such evidence underscores both the potential for this specific account and the need for accounts in general that treat emotion and its development as a complex, multicomponent process.

Conclusion

Emotions are multifaceted processes, and explaining their development requires a multifaceted approach. Emotion as a process is comprised of many components – both intra- and extraorganismic – all of which contribute to its organization at any given time and to transformations in its organization across development. Characterizing emotion in terms of its components and their interactions affords us insight into the nature of the developmental process itself. We fully capture emotional development, in turn, when we derive from this multicomponential analysis a synthetic rendering of person–environment relations across development. Such a synthesis as yet eludes the study of emotion in any period of development. Still, by treating emotion in relational terms, as the outgrowth of evaluations and actions in physical and social contexts, we know where to tap critical transition points in emotional development. It is at points in development when the person's relation to his or her environment is fundamentally altered that we know the person's emotional life will reorganize. For the infant, motoric changes should serve as major transition points in emotional development. We have already outlined the important emotional changes that arrive with crawling experience. Other motoric transitions, such as the emergence of smooth-pursuit eye tracking, visually guided reaching and grasping, independent sitting, standing and walking, all potentially mark major reorganizations in the infant's emotional stance toward the world. Notwithstanding work on infant crawling, relatively little research to date has mined the potential of these important developmental transitions (Biringen, Emde, Campos, & Appelbaum, 1995; M. D. Lewis, 1993; Witherington, 1999).

With each motoric transition, infants establish more effective means of meaningfully interacting with the social and physical world. New means of action fundamentally alter the manner in which infants implement their existing goals/strivings and establish for the infant new sets of goals, as well. In essence, emotional development in infancy revolves around systematic changes in the way infants *regulate* their goal-directed activity, their significant engagement with the people and things that surround them. At every point in development, then, emotion can be viewed from the standpoint of its regulatory effects on person–environment relations. Emotional development is *not* about trying to control our emotions *per se*, as the literature sometimes suggests. The emotion system is *inherently regulatory*, and to study it we must look at the functional relations between person and environment. We must establish what the person is trying to do to understand anything about his or her emotional stance toward the world. It is at this level – the level of infants regulating their relation to the world – that the fundamental and most significant properties of infant emotional development will be discovered.

References

Ainsworth, M., Blehar, M., Waters, E., & Wall, S. (1978). *Patterns of attachment: A psychological study of the Strange Situation*. Hillsdale, NJ: Erlbaum.

Anisfeld, M. (1991). Neonatal imitation. *Developmental Review, 11*, 60–97.

Anisfeld, M., Turkewitz, G., Rose, S. A., Rosenberg, F. R., Sheiber, F. J., Couturier-Fagan, D. A., Ger, J. S., & Sommer, I. (2001). No compelling evidence that newborns imitate oral gestures. *Infancy, 2*, 111–122.

Banks, M. S., & Salapatek, P. (1983). Infant visual perception. In P. H. Mussen (Series Ed.) & M. Haith & J. J. Campos (Vol. Eds.), *Handbook of child psychology: Vol. 2. Infancy and developmental psychobiology* (4th ed., pp. 435–571). New York: Wiley.

Barrett, K. C. (1998). A functionalist perspective to the development of emotions. In M. F. Mascolo & S. Griffin (Eds.), *What develops in emotional development?* (pp. 109–133). New York: Plenum Press.

Barrett, K. C., & Campos, J. J. (1987). Perspectives on emotional development: II. A functionalist approach to emotions. In J. D. Osofsky (Ed.), *Handbook of infant development* (2nd ed., pp. 555–578). New York: Wiley.

Bates, E. (1979). Intentions, conventions, and symbols. In E. Bates, L. Benigni, I. Bretherton, L. Camaioni, & V. Volterra (Eds.), *The emergence of symbols: Cognition and communication in infancy* (pp. 33–68). New York: Academic Press.

Bertenthal, B., & Campos, J. J. (1990). A systems approach to the organizing effects of self-produced locomotion during infancy. In C. Rovee-Collier & L. P. Lipsitt (Eds.), *Advances in infancy research* (Vol. 6, pp. 1–60). Norwood, NJ: Ablex.

Biringen, Z., Emde, R. N., Campos, J. J., & Appelbaum, M. I. (1995). Affective reorganization in the infant, the mother, and the dyad: The role of upright locomotion and its timing. *Child Development, 66*, 499–514.

Boccia, M., & Campos, J. J. (1989). Maternal emotional signals, social referencing, and infants' reactions to strangers. In N. Eisenberg (Ed.), *New directions for child development* (Vol. 44, pp. 25–49). San Francisco: Jossey-Bass.

Boiten, F. (1996). Autonomic response patterns during voluntary facial action. *Psychophysiology, 33*, 123–131.

Bower, T. G. R. (1977). *A primer of infant development*. San Francisco: W. H. Freeman.

Bowlby, J. (1969). *Attachment and loss: Vol. 1. Attachment*. New York: Basic Books.

Bowlby, J. (1973). *Attachment and loss: Vol. 2. Separation*. New York: Basic Books.

Brackbill, Y., Adams, G., Crowell, D., & Gray, M. (1966). Arousal level in neonates and preschool children under continuous auditory stimulation. *Journal of Experimental Child Psychology, 4*, 178–188.

Brandt, T., Arnold, F., Bles, W., & Kapteyn, T. S. (1980). The mechanism of physiological height vertigo I. Theoretical approach and psychophysics. *Acta Otolaryngologica, 89*, 513–523.

Brandt, T., Bles, W., Arnold, F., & Kapteyn, T. S. (1979). Height vertigo and human posture. *Advances in Oto-Rhino-Laryngology, 25*, 88–92.

Bridges, K. (1932). Emotional development in early infancy. *Child Development, 3*, 324–341.

Bronson, G. W. (1972). Infants' reactions to unfamiliar persons and novel objects. *Monographs of the Society for Research in Child Development, 37* (3, Serial No. 148).

Buhler, C. (1930). *The first year of life*. New York: Day Press.

Cacioppo, J. T., Klein, D. J., Berntson, G. G., & Hatfield, E. (1993). The psychophysiology of emotion. In M. Lewis & J. M. Haviland (Eds.), *Handbook of emotions* (pp. 119–142). New York: Guilford Press.

Campos, J. J. (1985, August). *Current issues in the study of emotion and emotional development.* Paper presented at a symposium on cognition–emotion relations at the meetings of the American Psychological Association, Los Angeles, CA.

Campos, J. J., & Barrett, K. C. (1984). Toward a new understanding of emotions and their development. In C. E. Izard, J. Kagan, & R. B. Zajonc (Eds.), *Emotions, cognition, and behavior* (pp. 229–263). Cambridge: Cambridge University Press.

Campos, J. J., Barrett, K. C., Lamb, M. E., Goldsmith, H. H., & Stenberg, C. (1983). Socioemotional development. In P. H. Mussen (Series Ed.) & M. Haith & J. J. Campos (Vol. Eds.), *Handbook of child psychology: Vol. 2. Infancy and developmental psychobiology* (4th ed., pp. 783–915). New York: Wiley.

Campos, J. J., & Bertenthal, B. I. (1989). Locomotion and psychological development in infancy. In F. Morrison, C. Lord, & D. Keating (Eds.), *Applied developmental psychology* (Vol. 3, pp. 229–258). New York: Academic Press.

Campos, J. J., Bertenthal, B. I., & Kermoian, R. (1992). Early experience and emotional development: The emergence of wariness of heights. *Psychological Science, 3,* 61–64.

Campos, J. J., Hiatt, S., Ramsay, D., Henderson, C., & Svejda, M. (1978). The emergence of fear on the visual cliff. In M. Lewis & L. Rosenblum (Eds.), *The development of affect* (pp. 149–182). New York: Plenum Press.

Campos, J. J., Kermoian, R., & Witherington, D. (1996). An epigenetic perspective on emotional development. In R. D. Kavanaugh, B. Zimmerberg, & S. Fein (Eds.), *Emotion: Interdisciplinary perspectives* (pp. 119–138). Mahwah, NJ: Erlbaum.

Campos, J. J., Kermoian, R., & Zumbahlen, M. (1992). Socioemotional transformations in the family system following infant crawling onset. In N. Eisenberg & R. A. Fabes (Eds.), *New directions for child development: Emotion and its regulation in early development* (Vol. 55, pp. 25–40). San Francisco: Jossey-Bass.

Campos, J. J., Mumme, D. L., Kermoian, R., & Campos, R. G. (1994). A functionalist perspective on the nature of emotion. In N. Fox (Ed.), The development of emotion regulation: Biological and behavioral considerations (pp. 284–303). *Monographs of the Society for Research in Child Development, 59* (2–3, Serial No. 240).

Campos, J. J., & Stenberg, C. R. (1981). Perception, appraisal, and emotion: The onset of social referencing. In M. E. Lamb & L. R. Sherrod (Eds.), *Infant social cognition: Empirical and theoretical considerations* (pp. 273–314). Hillsdale, NJ: Erlbaum.

Camras, L. A. (1992). Expressive development and basic emotions. *Cognition and Emotion, 6,* 269–283.

Camras, L. A., Oster, H., Campos, J., Campos, R., Ujiie, T., Miyake, K., Wang, L., & Meng, Z. (1998). Production of emotional facial expressions in European American, Japanese, and Chinese infants. *Developmental Psychology, 34,* 616–628.

Caron, A. J., Caron, R. F., Caldwell, R. C., & Weiss, S. J. (1973). Infant perception of the structural properties of the face. *Developmental Psychology, 9,* 385–399.

Cohn, J. F., & Tronick, E. Z. (1983). Three-month-old infants' reaction to simulated maternal depression. *Child Development, 54,* 185–193.

Cook, M., & Mineka, S. (1990). Selective associations in the observational conditioning of fear in rhesus monkeys. *Journal of Experimental Psychology: Animal Behavior Processes, 16,* 372–389.

Cosmides, L., & Toobey, J. (2000). Evolutionary psychology and the emotions. In M. Lewis & J. M. Haviland-Jones (Eds.), *Handbook of emotions* (2nd ed., pp. 91–115). New York: Guilford Press.

Darwin, C. (1965). *The expression of the emotions in man and animals.* Chicago: University of Chicago Press. (Original work published 1872)

Decarie, T. (1965). *Intelligence and affectivity in early childhood.* New York: International Universities Press.

Dichgans, J., & Brandt, T. (1978). Visual–vestibular interactions: Effects on self-motion and postural control. In R. Held, H. W. Leibowitz, & H. L. Teuber (Eds.), *Handbook of sensory physiology* (Vol. 8, pp. 755–804). Heidelberg: Springer.

Dickson, K. L., Walker, H., & Fogel, A. (1997). The relationship between smile type and play type during parent–infant play. *Developmental Psychology, 33,* 925–933.

Dondi, M., Simion, F., & Caltran, G. (1999). Can newborns discriminate between their own cry and the cry of another newborn infant? *Developmental Psychology, 35,* 418–426.

Ekman, P. (1972). Universals and cultural differences in facial expressions of emotion. In J. Cole (Ed.), *Nebraska symposium on motivation* (pp. 207–283). Lincoln, NE: University of Nebraska Press.

Ekman, P. (1999a). Basic emotions. In T. Dalgleish & M. Power (Eds.), *Handbook of cognition and emotion* (pp. 45–60). New York: Wiley.

Ekman, P. (1999b). Facial expressions. In T. Dalgleish & M. Power (Eds.), *Handbook of cognition and emotion* (pp. 301–320). New York: Wiley.

Ekman, P. W., Levenson, R. W., & Friesen, W. V. (1983). Autonomic nervous system activity distinguishes among emotions. *Science, 221,* 1208–1210.

Ekman, P., & Oster, H. (1979). Facial expressions of emotion. *Annual Review of Psychology, 30,* 527–554.

Emde, R. N., Gaensbauer, T., & Harmon, R. J. (1976). Emotional expression in infancy: A biobehavioral study. *Psychological Issues Monograph Series, 10*(37), 1–198.

Emde, R. N., Katz, E. L., & Thorpe, J. K. (1978). Emotional expression in infancy: II. Early deviations in Down's syndrome. In M. Lewis & L. A. Rosenblum (Eds.), *The development of affect* (pp. 351–360). New York: Plenum Press.

Emde, R. N., & Koenig, K. (1969). Neonatal smiling and rapid eye movement states. *Journal of American Academic Child Psychiatry, 8,* 57–67.

Feinman, S., & Lewis, M. (1983). Social referencing at ten months: A second-order effect on infants' responses to strangers. *Child Development, 54,* 878–887.

Fernald, A. (1992). Meaningful melodies in mothers' speech to infants. In H. Papoušek, U. Juergens, & M. Papoušek (Eds.), *Nonverbal vocal communication: Comparative and developmental approaches* (pp. 262–282). Cambridge: Cambridge University Press.

Fischer, K. W., & Tangney, J. P. (1995). Self-conscious emotions and the affect revolution: Framework and overview. In J. P. Tangney & K. W. Fischer (Eds.), *Self-conscious emotions: The psychology of shame, guilt, embarrassment, and pride* (pp. 3–22). New York: Guilford Press.

Fogel, A., Nwokah, E., Dedo, J. Y., Messinger, D., Dickson, K. L., Matusov, E., & Holt, S. A. (1992). Social process theory of emotion: A dynamic systems approach. *Social Development, 1,* 122–142.

Fridlund, A. J. (1997). The new ethology of human facial expressions. In J. A. Russell & J. M. Fernandez-Dols (Eds.), *The psychology of facial expression* (pp. 103–129). Cambridge: Cambridge University Press.

Friedman, S., Bruno, L. A., & Vietze, P. (1974). Newborn habituation to visual stimuli: A sex difference in novelty detection. *Journal of Experimental Child Psychology, 18,* 242–251.

Frijda, N. (1986). *The emotions.* Cambridge: Cambridge University Press.

Gaensbauer, T. J. (1980). Anaclitic depression in a three-and-one-half-month-old child. *American Journal of Psychiatry, 137,* 841–842.

Garcia, J., & Koelling, R. A. (1966). Relation of cue to consequence in avoidance learning. *Psychonomic Science, 4,* 123–124.

Goethe, F. (1940). Beobachtungen und Versuche uber angebornene Schreckreaktronen junger Auerhuhner (Tetrao u. urogallus L.). *Zeitschrift Tierpsychologie, 4*, 165–167.

Goleman, D. (1995). *Emotional intelligence.* New York: Bantam Books.

Gopnik, A., & Meltzoff, A. N. (1997). *Words, thoughts, and theories.* Cambridge, MA: MIT Press.

Gould, J. L. (1982). *Ethology: The mechanisms and evolution of behavior.* New York: W. W. Norton.

Griffin, S., & Mascolo, M. F. (1998). On the nature, development, and functions of emotions. In M. F. Mascolo & S. Griffin (Eds.), *What develops in emotional development?* (pp. 3–27). New York: Plenum Press.

Grossmann, K. E., Grossmann, K., Huber, F., & Wartner, U. (1981). German children's behavior towards their mothers at 12 months and their fathers at 18 months in Ainsworth's Strange Situation. *International Journal of Behavioral Development, 4*, 157–181.

Gunther, M. (1961). Infant behavior at the breast. In B. Foss (Ed.), *Determinants of infant behavior* (Vol. 1, pp. 37–44). London: Methuen.

Haig, B., & Durrant, R. (2000). Theory evaluation in evolutionary psychology. *Psychological Inquiry, 11*, 34–38.

Haith, M. M., Bergman, T., & Moore, M. J. (1977). Eye contact and face scanning in early infancy. *Science, 198*, 853–855.

Hatfield, E., Cacioppo, J., & Rapson, R. (1994). *Emotional contagion.* New York: Cambridge University Press.

Hatton, H. M., Berg, W. K., & Graham, F. K. (1970). Effects of acoustic rise time on heart rate response. *Psychonomic Science, 19*, 101–103.

Haviland, J. M., & Lelwicka, M. (1987). The induced affect response: 10-week-old infants' responses to three emotion expressions. *Developmental Psychology, 23*, 97–104.

Hay, D. F., Nash, A., & Pedersen, J. (1981). Responses of six-month-olds to the distress of their peers. *Child Development, 52*, 1071–1075.

Hebb, D. O. (1946). On the nature of fear. *Psychological Review, 53*, 88–106.

Hebb, D. O. (1949). *The organization of behavior: A neuropsychological theory.* New York: Wiley.

Hiatt, S. W., Campos, J. J., & Emde, R. N. (1979). Facial patterning and infant emotional expression: Happiness, surprise, and fear. *Child Development, 50*, 1020–1035.

Higgins, C. I., Campos, J. J., & Kermoian, R. (1996). Effect of self-produced locomotion on infant postural compensation to optic flow. *Developmental Psychology, 32*, 836–841.

Hoffman, M. L. (2000). *Empathy and moral development: Implications for caring and justice.* Cambridge: Cambridge University Press.

Hopkins, J. R., Zelazo, P. R., Jacobson, S. W., & Kagan, J. (1976). Infant reactivity to stimulus–schema discrepancy. *Genetic Psychology Monographs, 93*, 27–62.

Izard, C. E. (1991). *The psychology of emotions.* New York: Plenum Press.

James, W. (1963). *Psychology.* Greenwich, CT: Fawcett Publications. (Original work published 1892)

Jersild, A. T. (1946). Emotional development. In L. Carmichael (Ed.), *Manual of child psychology* (pp. 752–790). New York: Wiley.

Kagan, J. (1971). *Change and continuity in infancy.* New York: Wiley.

Kagan, J. (1974). Discrepancy, temperament, and infant distress. In M. Lewis & L. A. Rosenblum (Eds.), *The origins of fear* (pp. 229–248). New York: Wiley.

Kellman, P. J., & Banks, M. S. (1998). Infant visual perception. In W. Damon (Series Ed.) & D. Kuhn & R. S. Siegler (Vol. Eds.), *Handbook of child psychology: Vol. 2. Cognition, perception, and language* (5th ed., pp. 103–146). New York: Wiley.

Kenney, M., Mason, W., & Hill, S. (1979). Effects of age, objects, and visual experience on affective responses of rhesus monkeys to strangers. *Developmental Psychology, 15*, 176–184.

Ketelaar, T., & Ellis, B. J. (2000). Are evolutionary explanations unfalsifiable? Evolutionary psychology and the Lakatosian philosophy of science. *Psychological Inquiry, 11*, 1–21.

Kitayama, S., & Markus, H. R. (1994). *Emotion and culture.* Washington, DC: American Psychological Association.

Lazarus, R. S. (1991). *Emotion and adaptation.* New York: Oxford University Press.

Lazarus, R. S. (in press). Relational meaning and discrete emotions. In K. R. Scherer, A. Schorr, & T. Johnstone (Eds.), *Appraisal processes in emotion: Theory, methods, research.* Cambridge: Cambridge University Press.

Lee, D. N., & Lishman, J. R. (1975). Visual proprioceptive control of stance. *Journal of Human Movement Studies, 1*, 87–95.

Leeper, R. W. (1948). A motivational theory of emotion to replace "emotion as a disorganized response." *Psychological Review, 55*, 5–21.

Levenson, R. W. (1992). Autonomic nervous system differences among emotions. *Psychological Science, 3*, 23–27.

Levenson, R. W., Ekman, P., Heider, K., & Friesen, W. V. (1992). Emotion and autonomic nervous system activity in the Mingangkabau of West Sumatra. *Journal of Personality and Social Psychology, 62*, 972–988.

Lewis, M. (1993). The emergence of human emotions. In M. Lewis & J. M. Haviland (Eds.), *Handbook of emotions* (pp. 223–235). New York: Guilford Press.

Lewis, M. (1995). Embarrassment: The emotion of self-exposure and evaluation. In J. P. Tangney & K. W. Fischer (Eds.), *Self-conscious emotions: The psychology of shame, guilt, embarrassment, and pride* (pp. 198–218). New York: Guilford Press.

Lewis, M., & Brooks-Gunn, J. (1979). *Social cognition and the acquisition of self.* New York: Plenum Press.

Lewis, M., & Goldberg, S. (1969). The acquisition and violation of expectancy: An experimental paradigm. *Journal of Experimental Child Psychology, 7*, 70–80.

Lewis, M., Sullivan, M. W., Stanger, C., & Weiss, M. (1989). Self-development and self-conscious emotions. *Child Development, 60*, 146–156.

Lewis, M. D. (1993). Emotion–cognition interactions in early infant development. *Cognition and Emotion, 7*, 145–170.

Lewis, M. D. (2000). Emotional self-organization at three time scales. In M. D. Lewis & I. Granic (Eds.), *Emotion, development, and self-organization: Dynamic systems approaches to emotional development* (pp. 37–69). Cambridge: Cambridge University Press.

Lewis, M. D., & Granic, I. (1999). Self-organization of cognition–emotion interactions. In T. Dalgleish & M. Power (Eds.), *Handbook of cognition and emotion* (pp. 683–701). New York: Wiley.

Lipsitt, L. P. (1976). Developmental psychobiology comes of age: A discussion. In L. P. Lipsitt (Ed.), *Developmental psychobiology: The significance of infancy* (pp. 109–127). Hillsdale, NJ: Erlbaum.

Lipsitt, L. P. (1986). Toward understanding the hedonic nature of infancy. In L. P. Lipsitt & J. H. Cantor (Eds.), *Experimental child psychologist: Essays and experiments in honor of Charles C. Spiker* (pp. 97–109). Hillsdale, NJ: Erlbaum.

Lishman, J. R., & Lee, D. N. (1973). The autonomy of visual kinaesthesis. *Perception, 2*, 287–294.

Ludemann, P. M., & Nelson, C. A. (1988). Categorical representation of facial expressions by 7-month-old infants. *Developmental Psychology, 24*, 492–501.

Mandler, G. (1975). *Mind and emotion.* New York: Wiley.

Mandler, G. (1979). Emotion. In E. Hearst (Ed.), *The first century of experimental psychology* (pp. 275–322). Hillsdale, NJ: Erlbaum.

Martin, G. B., & Clark, R. D. (1982). Distress crying in neonates: Species and peer specificity. *Developmental Psychology, 18*, 3–9.

Mascolo, M. F., & Fischer, K. W. (1995). Developmental transformations in appraisals for pride, shame, and guilt. In J. P. Tangney & K. W. Fischer (Eds.), *Self-conscious emotions: The psychology of shame, guilt, embarrassment, and pride* (pp. 64–113). New York: Guilford Press.

Mascolo, M. F., & Griffin, S. (1998). Alternative trajectories in the development of anger-related appraisals. In M. F. Mascolo & S. Griffin (Eds.), *What develops in emotional development?* (pp. 219–249). New York: Plenum Press.

Mascolo, M. F., & Harkins, D. (1998). Toward a component systems approach to emotional development. In M. F. Mascolo & S. Griffin (Eds.), *What develops in emotional development?* (pp. 189–217). New York: Plenum Press.

McCall, R. B., & Kagan, J. (1967). Stimulus–schema discrepancy and attention in the infant. *Journal of Experimental Child Psychology, 5,* 381–390.

McCall, R. B., & McGhee, P. E. (1977). The discrepancy hypothesis of attention and affect in infants. In I. C. Uzgiris & F. Weizmann (Eds.), *The structuring of experience* (pp. 179–210). New York: Plenum Press.

Mead, G. (1934). *Mind, self, and society: From the standpoint of a social behaviorist.* Chicago: University of Chicago Press.

Meltzoff, A. N. (1988). Infant imitation and memory: Nine-month-olds in immediate and deferred tests. *Child Development, 59,* 217–225.

Meltzoff, A. N., & Moore, M. K. (1977). Imitation of facial and manual gestures by human neonates. *Science, 198,* 75–78.

Meltzoff, A. N., & Moore, M. K. (1983). Newborn infants imitate adult facial gestures. *Child Development, 54,* 702–709.

Mesquita, B., & Frijda, N. (1992). Cultural variations in emotions: A review. *Psychological Bulletin, 112,* 179–204.

Meyer, L. B. (1957). *Emotion and meaning in music.* Chicago: University of Chicago Press.

Mineka, S., & Cook, M. (1993). Mechanisms involved in the observational conditioning of fear. *Journal of Experimental Psychology: General, 122,* 23–38.

Miyake, K., Chen, S. J., & Campos, J. J. (1985). Infant temperament, mothers' mode of interaction, and attachment in Japan: An interim report. In I. Bretherton & E. Waters (Eds.), Growing points of attachment theory and research (pp. 276–297). *Monographs of the Society for Research in Child Development, 50* (1–2, Serial No. 209).

Mumme, D. L., Fernald, A., & Herrera, C. (1996). Infants' responses to facial and vocal emotional signals in a social referencing paradigm. *Child Development, 67,* 3219–3237.

Nelson, C. A. (1987). The recognition of facial expressions in the first two years of life: Mechanisms of development. *Child Development, 58,* 889–909.

Ohman, A. (1993). Stimulus prepotency and fear learning: Data and theory. In N. Birbaumer & A. Ohman (Eds.), *The structure of emotion: Psychophysiological, cognitive and clinical aspects* (pp. 218–239). Gottingen: Hogrefe & Huber.

Oster, H., Hegley, D., & Nagel, L. (1992). Adult judgments and fine-grained analysis of infant facial expressions. *Developmental Psychology, 28,* 1115–1131.

Peiper, A. (1963). *Cerebral function in infancy and childhood.* New York: Consultants Bureau.

Piaget, J. (1954). *The construction of reality in the child.* New York: Basic Books.

Planalp, S. (1999). *Communicating emotion: Social, moral, and cultural processes.* Cambridge: Cambridge University Press.

Rochat, P., Querido, J. G., & Striano, T. (1999). Emerging sensitivity to the timing and structure of protoconversation in early infancy. *Developmental Psychology, 35,* 950–957.

Rozin, P., & Fallon, A. E. (1987). A perspective on disgust. *Psychological Review, 94,* 23–41.

Ryle, G. (1949). *The concept of mind.* Harmondsworth: Penguin.

Sagi, A., & Hoffman, M. L. (1976). Empathic distress in the newborn. *Developmental Psychology, 12*, 175–176.

Salk, L. (1962). Mother's heartbeat as an imprinting stimulus. *Transactions of the New York Academy of Science, 24*, 753–763.

Sander, L. (1962). Issues in mother–child interaction. *Journal of the American Academy of Child Psychiatry, 1*, 141–166.

Sander, L. (1964). Adaptive relationships in early mother–child interaction. *Journal of the American Academy of Child Psychiatry, 3*, 231–264.

Schaffer, H. R. (1971). *The growth of sociability*. Baltimore: Penguin.

Schaffer, H. R. (1974). Cognitive components of the infant's response to strangers. In M. Lewis & L. A. Rosenblum (Eds.), *The origins of fear* (pp. 11–24). New York: Wiley.

Schneirla, T. C. (1965). Aspects of stimulation and organization in approach/withdrawal processes underlying vertebrate behavioral development. In D. S. Lehrman, R. A. Hinde, & E. Shaw (Eds.), *Advances in the study of behavior* (Vol. 1, pp. 1–74). New York: Academic Press.

Simner, M. L. (1971). Newborn's response to the cry of another infant. *Developmental Psychology, 5*, 136–150.

Sloboda, J. (1986). *The musical mind: The cognitive psychology of music*. Oxford: Clarendon Press.

Soken, N. H., & Pick, A. D. (1999). Infants' perception of dynamic affective expressions: Do infants distinguish specific expressions? *Child Development, 70*, 1275–1282.

Sorce, J. F., Emde, R. N., Campos, J. J., & Klinnert, M. D. (1985). Maternal emotional signaling: Its effect on the visual cliff behavior of 1-year-olds. *Developmental Psychology, 21*, 195–200.

Spitz, R. (1965). *The first year of life*. New York: International Universities Press.

Sroufe, L. A. (1979). Socioemotional development. In J. D. Osofsky (Ed.), *Handbook of infant development* (pp. 462–516). New York: Wiley.

Sroufe, L. A. (1996). *Emotional development: The organization of emotional life in the early years*. Cambridge: Cambridge University Press.

Sroufe, L. A., & Waters, E. (1977). Attachment as an organizational construct. *Child Development, 48*, 1184–1199.

Sroufe, L. A., Waters, E., & Matas, L. (1974). Contextual determinants of infant affective response. In M. Lewis & L. A. Rosenblum (Eds.), *The origins of fear* (pp. 49–72). New York: Wiley.

Stayton, D. J., Ainsworth, M. D. S., & Main, M. B. (1973). Development of separation behavior in the first year of life: Protest, following, and greeting. *Developmental Psychology, 9*, 213–225.

Stechler, G., & Carpenter, G. (1967). A viewpoint on early affective development. In J. Hellmuth (Ed.), *The exceptional infant* (Vol. 1, pp. 163–190). Seattle, WA: Special Child Publications.

Steiner, J. E. (1979). Human facial expressions in response to taste and smell stimulation. In H. W. Reese & L. P. Lipsitt (Eds.), *Advances in child development and behavior* (Vol. 13, pp. 257–295). New York: Academic Press.

Stemmler, G. (1989). The autonomic differentiation of emotions revisited: Convergent and discriminant validation. *Psychophysiology, 26*, 617–642.

Stenberg, C. R., & Campos, J. J. (1990). The development of anger expressions in infancy. In N. L. Stein, B. Leventhal, & T. Trabasso (Eds.), *Psychological and biological approaches to emotion* (pp. 297–310). Hillsdale, NJ: Erlbaum.

Stern, D. (1971). A microanalysis of mother–infant interaction: Behavior regulating social contact between a mother and her 3-and-a-half-month-old twins. *Journal of the American Academy of Child Psychiatry, 10*, 501–517.

Stern, D. (1977). *The first relationship: Infant and mother*. Cambridge, MA: Harvard University Press.

Sullivan, S. F., Gentile, D. A., & Pick, A. D. (1998, April). *The perception of emotion in music by eight-month-old infants.* Poster presented at the meetings of the International Conference on Infant Studies, Atlanta, GA.

Thompson, R. A. (1993). Socioemotional development: Enduring issues and new challenges. *Developmental Review, 13,* 372–402.

Tinbergen, N. (1948). Social releasers and the experimental method required for their study. *Wilson Bulletin, 60,* 6–52.

Tinbergen, N. (1951). *The study of instinct.* Oxford: Clarendon Press.

Tomkins, S. S. (1962). *Affect, imagery, consciousness: The positive affects.* New York: Springer Verlag.

Tomkins, S. S. (1963). *Affect, imagery, consciousness: The negative affects.* New York: Springer Verlag.

Trevarthen, C., & Hubley, P. (1978). Secondary intersubjectivity: Confidence, confiders, and acts of meaning in the first year of life. In A. Lock (Ed.), *Action, gesture, and symbol: The emergence of language* (pp. 183–229). New York: Academic Press.

Tronick, E. (1989). Emotions and emotional communication in infants. *American Psychologist, 44,* 112–119.

Uzgiris, I. C., & Hunt, J. McV. (1975). *Assessment in infancy: Ordinal scales of psychological development.* Urbana, IL: University of Illinois Press.

Valentine, C. W. (1930). The innate bases of fear. *Journal of Genetic Psychology, 37,* 394–420.

Walden, T., & Passaretti, C. (1996, April). *"I don't care what you say, I am not touching that snake": Biologically relevant fear and infant social referencing.* Paper presented at the meetings of the International Society for Infant Studies, Providence, RI.

Wallbott, H. G., & Scherer, K. R. (1988). How universal and specific is emotional experience? Evidence from 21 countries and five continents. In K. R. Scherer (Ed.), *Facets of emotion: Recent research* (pp. 31–56). Hillsdale, NJ: Erlbaum.

Weinberg, M. K., & Tronick, E. Z. (1994). Beyond the face: An empirical study of infant affective configurations of facial, vocal, gestural, and regulatory behaviors. *Child Development, 65,* 1503–1515.

Witherington, D. C. (1999). Visually-guided reaching and the development of anger in infancy (Doctoral dissertation, University of California, Berkeley, 1998). *Dissertation Abstracts International: Section B: The Sciences & Engineering, 59*(8–B), 4514.

Witherington, D. C., Kermoian, R., & Campos, J. J. (2001). *Visual proprioception and the developmental emergence of wariness of heights.* Manuscript submitted for publication.

Wolff, P. H. (1987). *The development of behavioral states and the expression of emotions in early infancy.* Chicago: University of Chicago Press.

Zelazo, P., & Komer, M. (1971). Infant smiling to non-social stimuli and the recognition hypothesis. *Child Development, 42,* 1327–1339.

Zumbahlen, M., & Crawley, A. (1996, April). *Infants' early referential behavior in prohibition contexts: The emergence of social referencing?* Paper presented at the meetings of the International Conference on Infant Studies, Providence, RI.

Chapter Seventeen

Temperament

Theodore D. Wachs and John E. Bates

Introduction

Temperament is a word that comes from Latin, referring to the mixing of ingredients, especially the four humors (or kinds of bodily moisture) that ancient Greek physicians described. The humors were formed eventually into the familiar fourfold typology (sanguine – for blood, phlegmatic – for phlegm, choleric – for yellow bile, and melancholic – for black bile) favored by Europeans of the Middle Ages (Rothbart, 1989). Although concepts of the physiological bases of temperament have greatly changed in modern times, the basic dimensions of personality that the four humors describe still have some validity. Temperament is a conceptual tool for describing and understanding early-appearing individual differences in behavior.

After many decades of absence as a focus of modern psychological studies of personality, the concept of temperament began returning to prominence by the early 1960s. Most notably for developmental and clinical psychology, the psychiatrists Thomas and Chess and their colleagues in the New York Longitudinal Study (Thomas, Chess, & Birch, 1968; Thomas, Chess, Birch, Hertzig, & Korn, 1963) provided a set of temperament concepts for describing behavioral characteristics from early infancy into childhood. Thomas and Chess provided such concepts at a time when the field had begun to realize that social development reflected more than just environmental influences. For example, as pointed out by Bell (1968), the dominant theories of unidirectional effects of parenting variations upon the social development of children were not supported by evidence or logic. Results indicating that parental hostility was associated with child misbehavior could reflect either the influence of the parent upon the child or the influence of the child's characteristics upon the parent–child system. In the writings of Thomas and Chess, temperament was viewed as a conceptual tool that could be used for describing characteristics children might bring to patterns of parent–child relationships. Thomas and Chess also were exemplary in their refusal to fall into an either-or trap. They recognized, especially in their concept of "goodness of fit" (Thomas et al., 1968), that the ultimate products of temperament were an interactive product of both the child's initial tendencies and environmental pressures. Whether a difficult temperament results in a high-strung but productive and well-socialized person or a hostile and destructive person depends on how agents of socialization deal with the child's temperament. A good fit would occur if parents are demanding of proper behavior in a supportive way, while a poor fit would occur if parents are hostile and emotionally disorganized in the face of the child's characteristics. The critical question for Thomas and Chess, as well as for later generations of temperament researchers, is how socialization and temperament concepts are to be integrated. Prior to addressing this question we will first deal with issues involving the nature, measurement, and sources of individual differences in temperament.

What is Temperament?

The Definition of Temperament

Currently there is not a universally agreed upon definition of temperament. This state of affairs may be surprising to some, given the increasing theoretical interest in temperament as a bio-behavioral phenomenon, and the increasing number of empirical studies on issues involving temperament. However, the lack of a precise definition is not unique to temperament. A similar lack of agreement on both definition and major domains is also seen in other major areas of psychological inquiry such as intelligence (Neisser et al., 1996). The fact that there are multiple definitions of a given construct is not necessarily a problem, as long as there is general consensus among researchers as to the major features that define a given construct and the nature of the domains that fit under this construct (McCall, 1986). Such a situation clearly exists for temperament. While there is disagreement about the details, a majority of researchers would accept the following as a "working definition" of temperament:

> biologically rooted individual differences in behavior tendencies that are present early in life and are relatively stable across various kinds of situations and over the course of time. (Bates, 1989a, p. 4)

While a working definition allows temperament researchers to go about their business of investigating the nature and consequences of individual differences in temperament, such definitions by their very nature have a certain level of ambiguity. For example, although "early appearing" is a central aspect of our working definition, there remains disagreement in the literature about how late in development a trait can appear and still be viewed as fitting the definition of temperament. Some temperament researchers argue that traits must appear in the first year of life to be defined as temperament (Buss, 1991). In contrast, other temperament researchers would argue that not all temperament traits need be evident in the earliest days of a child's life. In the case of negative emotionality, what is seen in the neonatal period is only a very weak forecaster of later emotionality (Bates, 1989b). Meaningful individual differences in fearful response to novelty depend on a level of cognitive development that typically occurs in the second half of the first year, and meaningful differences in attentional persistence or conscientiousness cannot appear until the third or fourth year, as the executive attentional control system is developed.

Along the same lines, the major features found in our consensus definition of temperament (early appearing, relatively stable, biologically rooted) also apply to behaviors that researchers in different domains would claim as examples of intelligence or motivation. For example, behavioral patterns involving selective attention, attention span, and goal-directed behavior are used to categorize a number of temperament domains including self-regulation (Rothbart, 1991), activity level (Strelau, 1989), and persistence (Caspi, 1998). However, these same behavioral patterns have also been claimed by theorists in both cognition (Borkowski & Dukewich, 1996; Kinchla, 1992) and motivation (Barrett & Morgan, 1995) as fundamental elements of their domains. Clearly, we cannot assume that just because a theorist or a researcher defines a given behavioral trait as an example of temperament, the trait, in fact, falls primarily within the domain of temperament.

The fact that similar behaviors can be viewed as simultaneously falling within the sphere of multiple psychological domains need not necessarily be a problem, if there are underlying mechanisms that are common to the multiple domains. For example, Steinmetz (1994) has illustrated how the same neural structures involved in temperament are also involved in learning and memory processes. The problem occurs when we do not have evidence for common underlying mechanisms and similar behaviors are viewed as simultaneously falling within the sphere of multiple different psychological domains.

Given the risk of imprecision inherent in consensus definitions of temperament, it may well be that, at present, temperament is best viewed as an example of a "fuzzy set" where the boundary conditions between different traits are not necessarily well defined (Masarro, 1987). Applying the fuzzy set concept to the domain of temperament, we would hypothesize that certain individual traits such as emotionality, reactivity, difficultness, and activity appear to fit primarily within the domain of temperament. For these traits there should be relatively little overlap in the boundaries between temperament and nontemperament domains. For other individual traits such as attention or task orientation, we would hypothesize that these traits may form a separate "hybrid class" sharing definitional criteria with both temperament and nontemperament domains (Wachs, 1999). For this latter class of traits there may well be a greater overlap between domain boundaries (e.g., the boundaries of attention as temperament may well overlap with the boundaries of attention as cognition).

Given that both researchers and theorists approach the study of temperament from a variety of different perspectives, it is not surprising to find healthy disagreement on the definition of temperament. In this sense a common working definition is a useful tool that brings some degree of order to what otherwise could devolve into chaos. However, we expect the working definition of temperament used in this chapter to evolve beyond its present form. If we are to generate more precise theories of temperament, it is important to emphasize that this working definition should be viewed as a work in progress.

Dimensions of Temperament

Historically, a number of behavioral dimensions have been described as fitting the criteria used to define temperament. These dimensions include: indices of negative emotionality such as fear or anger, ability to adapt to new situations or people (inhibition), characteristic level of motor activity, pleasure in social interactions (sociability), and complex multitrait dimensions such as difficultness (highly intense, easily evoked negative moods) (Bates, 1989a).

However, the contributions of temperament to individual behavioral variability go beyond the contributions of narrowly focused behavioral dimensions, as listed above. In part this is because temperament as a construct is multilevel, encompassing behavioral, neurological, and constitutional individuality (Bates, 1989a). As one further step toward the definition of temperament, the specific behavioral dimensions listed above are beginning to be understood in a broader conceptual bio-behavioral framework. Rothbart has argued that there are two, basic processes involved in the behaviors that make up the dimensions of temperament (see Rothbart & Bates, 1998). *Reactivity* refers to characteristic responses to stimulation, such as how quickly infants react to a noxious stimulus such as their arm being restrained, or whether an emotional response to a novel, manipulable object is positive or negative emotion. Reactivity also refers to how strong the response is. *Self-regulation* refers to the ways in which one internally controls emotional or motivational responses. For example, infants may differ on whether they regulate distress by directing attention away from objects producing frustration, by sucking their fingers and thereby reduce distress, or whether they maintain attention to the distressing stimulus and thereby increase distress.

What psychobiological systems might encompass the behavioral variations in reactivity and self-regulation that we typically think of as temperament? One psychobiological system that is especially used in temperament work is that of Gray (1991). Gray describes two major brain systems that support motivation. The first is a behavioral approach or activation system that responds to cues of potential reward or termination of punishment. The strength of an infant's joyful approach to an interesting object would depend on characteristics of this neural system. The second is a behavioral inhibition or anxiety system that responds to cues for punishment or nonreward. It is likely that a 9-month-old infant's freezing in the presence of a stranger represents the activation of this system. It is especially important to note here that, consistent with the separate neural systems for positive emotion or approach and fear or inhibition (Gray, 1991), there are relatively independent dimensions of behavioral differences on extraverted, approaching behavior and fearful, inhibited behavior. This means that a given infant could be both very attracted to social and other stimuli but also fearful of novelty, another might be high on one trait but low on the other, and a third infant might be low on both traits.

Another psychobiological system necessary to provide the underpinnings of the Rothbart approach to temperament processes includes those systems involved in the control of attention (Rothbart & Bates, 1998). As noted earlier, attentional mechanisms are most likely to be "hybrid" in nature, encompassing contributions from both temperament and cognitive processes. There appear to be two attentional systems that are involved in individual behavioral variability. First, there is an early-appearing attentional system, centered in posterior portions of the brain, that is involved in orienting toward novel stimuli. Infants who are more strongly interested in stimuli tend to be ones who show more positive emotion, and this may be a part of later tendencies to strongly approach when locomotor abilities develop. Second, there is a later-developing attentional system, centered in anterior portions of the brain, which is involved in executive control of attention. This latter system, which appears to begin developing after about 18 months, allows the child to purposefully control attention and dissociate attention to a stimulus from action on that stimulus, and to modulate emotional responses such as anger.

The Measurement of Temperament

Four approaches to assessing individual differences in early temperament have been developed: (1) structured or semi-structured clinical interview of parents; (2) parent or caregiver responses to questionnaires; (3) laboratory-based observation of infant behavior in structured situations; (4) direct observations of infant's unstructured behavior in naturalistic contexts. We will focus primarily on questionnaires and laboratory observations. While parent-interview procedures were the basis of the groundbreaking New York Longitudinal Study (NYLS; Chess & Thomas, 1984) and have occasionally been utilized in later studies (e.g., Worobey, 1986), for the most part interview procedures have been less often used in recent years. Likewise, although unstructured observational procedures have been used for assessing temperament in the neonatal period (e.g., Ricciuti & Breitmeyer, 1988) and with older infants and toddlers (e.g., Bates, 1979; Bornstein, Gaughran, & Segui, 1991; Rothbart, 1986; Seifer, Sameroff, Barrett, & Crafchuk, 1994), and mechanical devices such as actometers have been used to assess children's naturally occurring activity level (e.g., Eaton & Dureski, 1986), there has been relatively little systematic development of unstructured observational approaches.

The majority of parent report scales come from a clinical research perspective, particularly the NYLS; however, some instruments have a more psychobiological perspective (Windle, 1988). Examples of these two major classes of infant–toddler assessment instruments are shown in Table 17.1.

There are fewer available examples of laboratory-based observations of temperament. Some of the more well-known examples are also shown in Table 17.1. Typically, laboratory assessment of temperament is based on presenting a series of structured situations to infants or toddlers and videotaping and then coding their reactions to these situations. In addition to the laboratory procedures shown in Table 17.1, there have also been observations of infant temperament in structured testing situations using the Brazelton Scale in the neonatal period and the Bayley Infant Behavior Record for older infants and toddlers (Slabach, Morrow, & Wachs, 1991).

Table 17.1 Examples of temperament measures used during the infancy and toddler period

Type	Measure	Reference
I. Parent report questionnaires.		
A. Clinical research perspective instruments.	Revised Infant Temperament Questionnaire. Used during the first year of life and assesses the nine NYLS dimensions.	Carey & McDevitt (1978).
	Toddler Temperament Questionnaire. Follow-up scale to Revised Infant Temperament Questionnaire. Assesses same dimensions and used in the second and third years.	Fullard, McDevitt, & Carey (1984).
	Infant Characteristics Questionnaire. Focuses on indices of difficult temperament. Used in the first and second years.	Bates & Bayles (1984).
B. Psychobiological perspective instruments.	Infant Behavior Questionnaire. Used in the first and second years. Assesses five dimensions: activity, positive affect, fear, distress to limits, and soothability.	Rothbart (1986).
	Toddler Behavior Assessment Questionnaire. Follow-up to Infant Behavior Questionnaire. Used in the 18–36-month range. Assesses activity, positive affect, fearfulness, anger proneness, and interest persistence.	Goldsmith (1996).
II. Structured laboratory assessments.		
	Louisville Temperament Assessment Battery. Used in the 3–30-month range. Assesses emotional tone, activity, social orientation, attentiveness, and reaction to restraint.	Matheny (1991).
	Louisville Neonatal Assessment Battery. Downward extension of Louisville Temperament Assessment Battery to neonatal period. Assesses activity, emotionality, attention, and soothability.	Riese (1987).
	Lab-Tab. Used in the first two years of life. Assesses fear, anger, positive emotionality, persistence, and activity level.	Goldsmith & Rothbart (1991).
	Inhibition assessment procedures. Used over the first several years of life to assess infant and toddler inhibition to unfamiliar situations or persons.	Kagan et al. (1984).

While a variety of procedures exist for the assessment of early temperament, none has proven to be totally satisfactory. A listing of the major problems associated with parent report, unstructured observation, and laboratory assessment methods has been organized by Rothbart and Bates (1998) and is shown in Table 17.2. In addition to problems listed in Table 17.2, it is also important to recognize that laboratory-based coding approaches often lack needed data on the internal consistency and stability of the temperament dimensions being coded (Goldsmith & Reiser-Danner, 1990). It is also important to recognize that many of the problems associated with naturalistic observations, as shown in Table 17.2, can be minimized by the use of repeated observations. While repeated observations can serve to both decrease child and parent reactivity to the presence of an observer, and to increase the stability of observational data (Wachs, 1987), the use of repeated observations can be quite costly in terms of time demands. For example, Seifer et al. (1994) suggest that six to eight observational sessions may be needed to obtain stable measures of infant temperament, and even this degree of effort may not yield sufficient information to index temperament traits that are not frequently expressed in the observation situations (Rothbart & Bates, 1998). Further, while use of the same observer across multiple observations will reduce subject reactivity it can also increase the likelihood of observer halo effects. This could introduce the same potential measurement uncertainty that many worry about with parental reports of temperament.

Parent report questionnaire assessments have a number of positive features such as ease of administration and built-in aggregation, since caregivers usually base their ratings on experience with their child on repeated occasions and across different contexts. However, as also shown in Table 17.2, there are also a number of problems associated with use of parent report measures. Perhaps the most serious charge is that rather than assessing child characteristics, parent report measures actually are assessing parental emotional characteristics, such as anxiety and depression or parental expectancies about their child (Mebert, 1991; Sameroff, Seifer, & Elias, 1982; Seifer et al., 1994). While agreeing that parent report measures do have subjective components, defenders of this approach have presented data indicating that these measures also contain a substantial objective component that does accurately assess children's individual characteristics (Bates & Bayles, 1984; Rothbart & Bates, 1998). For example, evidence shows how parental reports of child temperament predict children's behavior in laboratory or testing situations where the parent's influence is minimal (Matheny, Wilson, & Thoben, 1987; Slabach et al., 1991). Such prediction would not be likely to occur if temperament questionnaires were assessing parental rather than child characteristics. Rather than simply throwing out the baby with the questionnaire, a more appropriate approach would be to attempt to apply correction procedures to minimize the potential influence of parent characteristics upon their response to temperament questionnaires (Bates, 1987). For example, to complement the recently developed Toddler Behavior Assessment Questionnaire, Goldsmith (1996) has developed a set of social desirability items that assess the degree to which parents bias their report to make their child seem more socially appropriate than the child may be in actuality.

While questions of bias on parent responding to questionnaires have received the most attention from temperament researchers, other important problems have been given far less emphasis. One such problem is the modest level of correlations reported between

Table 17.2 Potential sources of measurement error in three child temperament assessment methods

	A. Rater characteristics relatively independent of child behavior	B. Bias in assessment as a function of child behavior or rater–child interaction	C. Method factors relatively independent of both child and rater characteristics
I. Parent questionnaires	1. Comprehension of instructions, questions, and rating scales 2. Knowledge of child's behavior (and general impression rater has of the child) 3. Inaccurate memory: recency effects, selective recall 4. State when completing rating task, e.g., anxiety 5. Response sets, e.g., social desirability and acquiescence 6. For ratings, knowledge of implicit reference groups 7. Accuracy in detecting and coding rare but important events 8. Kind of impression (if any) rater (mother) wants child/self to make on researcher	1. Observed child behavior occurring in response to parental behavior 2. Parents' interpretations of observed behavior a function of parental characteristics	1. Need to inquire about rarely observed situations 2. Adequacy of item selection, wording, and response options

II. Home observation measures (*in vivo* coding)	1. Limited capacity of coder to process all relevant behavior 2. Coding of low-intensity ambiguous behaviors 3. State of coder during observation 4. Limits of precision of coding 5. For ratings, knowledge of implicit reference groups 6. Accuracy in detecting and coding of rare, but important events	1. Caregiver–child interaction moderating behavior coded 2. For ratings, halo effects	1. Change in child and caregiver behavior due to presence of coder (e.g., decreased conflict) 2. Difficulties of sensitively coding the context of behavior 3. Limitations of number of instances of behavior (esp. rare ones) that can be observed 4. Lack of normative date 5. Lack of stability in reasonable length time windows – limited sample of behavior
III. Laboratory measures (objective measures scored from videotape in episodes designed to elicit temperament-related reactions)	1. Scoring of low-intensity, ambiguous reactions 2. For ratings, knowledge of implicit reference groups 3. Limited capacity of coder to process all relevant behavior 4. State of coder during observation 5. Limits of precision of coding 6. Accuracy in detecting and coding of rare, but important events	1. Effects of uncontrolled caregiver behavior or other experience prior to/during testing 2. Selection of sample, including completion of testing on the basis of child reactions (e.g., distress-prone infants not completing procedures) 3. Subtle variations in experimenter reactions to different children (e.g., more soothing behavior directed toward distress-prone infant)	1. Lack of adequate normative data 2. Limitations of number of instances of behavior that can be recorded 3. Carryover effects in repeated testing 4. Constraints on range of behavioral options 5. Novelty of laboratory setting 6. Adequate identification of episodes appropriate to evoking temperamental reactions

Source: Rothbart & Bates (1998)

temperament ratings of mothers and fathers on their own children. While degree of parent agreement varies to some extent, depending on what temperament dimensions are being rated, for the most part interparent agreement correlations hover in the low–mid .4 range (Martin & Halverson, 1991; Slabach et al., 1991). It could be argued that lower levels of interparent agreement are restricted primarily to psychometrically weaker temperament scales or subscales. However, even when a carefully developed and well-validated instrument such as the Toddler Behavior Assessment Questionnaire is used, the average agreement between parents on the same temperament dimensions is $r = .41$ (range $r = .29$ to $r = .54$; Goldsmith, 1996). In general, low correlations between parents' and observers' ratings can be explained on the basis of parents having greater experience with their child's behavior, and thus basing their ratings on a more representative database (Carey, 1989). Similarly, the consistently low correlations between parent and teacher ratings can be explained on the basis that children may well be showing different facets of temperament in different contexts such as the home and day-care center (Goldsmith, 1996; Goldsmith, Rieser-Danner, & Briggs, 1991). There have been a variety of explanations on why relatively modest parent agreement correlations occur (e.g., children vary their behavior pattern for each parent; parents differ in degree of contact; or parents use different rating criteria). However, at present no satisfactory explanation is available (Slabach et al., 1991).

The fact that each approach to assessing temperament has specific measurement problems has led to an increasing emphasis by temperament researchers on the importance of aggregation: assessing common dimensions of temperament using different measurement approaches at the same point in time (Rothbart & Bates, 1998). For example, measurement of infant activity level can be based on a combination of parent report, coding of child activity in a structured laboratory situation, and actometer readings when the child is in day-care or at home. Assessments based on multiple measurements of the same construct strategies are more likely to give us an accurate and stable picture of a child's temperament than assessments that are based on only a single measurement approach. Although more costly, aggregated approaches to assessing temperament may well be the best way to avoid the measurement problems associated with each individual type of assessment strategy, and thus to maximize our ability to detect existing relations between temperament and other important aspects of development.

Sources of Individual Differences in Temperament

As noted above, biological roots are an essential definitional feature of temperament. Conceptually, the biological basis of temperament can occur in two ways (Bates, 1989a). First, there are patterns of "neurological individuality." Second, there are individual constitutional factors such as genetics, biomedical history, and nutritional status. In regard to neurological individuality there is a growing body of evidence that documents the role of specific central nervous system structures and neurotransmitter processes in the development and maintenance of individual differences in temperament (for a detailed review of this evidence, see Bates & Wachs, 1994). Much of this evidence is summarized in Table 17.3. As seen in Table 17.3, central nervous system structures such as the hippocampus, amygdala, and frontal cortex, as well as specific neural transmitters such as dopamine and serotonin, have all been implicated as mediating individual differences in temperament. Other aspects of neurological individuality that have been shown to be related to individual variation in temperament include autonomic nervous system function markers such as vagal tone, which has been shown to predict negative emotionality and soothability (Huffman et al., 1998), and variability in level of hormones such as prolactin, which is related to negative emotionality (Lozoff et al., 1995).

While characteristics of the central nervous system as well as peripheral nervous and hormonal systems are linked to individual differences in temperament, variability in these systems is the result of the operation of prior developmental influences (Wachs, 2000a). These prior influences and the role they play in individual variability in temperament are discussed below.

Biological Influences

Genetics

One critical source of variability in the neurological foundations of temperament involves individual differences in genetic makeup. Not surprisingly, there is a large and consistent literature showing genetic influences upon individual differences in infant and toddler activity, emotionality, inhibition, reactivity, persistence, and sociability (Braungart, Fulker, & Plomin, 1992; Buss & Plomin, 1986; Emde et al., 1992; Plomin et al., 1993; Robinson, Kagan, Reznick, & Corley, 1992; Saudino & Eaton, 1991; Saudino, Plomin, & DeFries, 1996). For the most part the heritability of temperament (percentage of variability in temperament accounted for by genetic influences) is in the moderate range (e.g., depending upon the age of assessment, the heritability of activity ranges from .20 to .28 while the heritability of affect ranges from .31 to .35; Saudino et al., 1996).

Although the genetic basis for individual differences in temperament seems well established, it is important to recognize that the nature and extent of genetic influences appear to depend on the temperamental dimension under consideration, the age of the individual, and the population under study. For example, there appears to be far less genetic influence on expressions of positive emotionality than upon expressions of negative emotionality (Emde et al., 1992; Goldsmith, 1996; Plomin et al., 1993). Evidence further indicates that genetic influences upon temperament appear to be far less during the first year of life than in later years (Riese, 1990; Wilson & Matheny, 1986). Further, heritability estimates of genetic influences tend to be higher in twins than in non-twin populations (Saudino, 1997; Saudino, McGuire, Reiss, & Hetherington, 1995), perhaps reflecting lower than expected correlations among dizygotic twins (DZ), which can inflate heritability estimates for twin populations (Spinath & Angleitner, 1998). One possible reason for lower than expected DZ correlations may be greater differences in the prenatal environment of DZ twins, leading to lower phenotypic resemblance among DZ twins after birth (Devlin, Daniels, & Roeder, 1997). The likelihood that the genetics of temperament depend on particular traits, developmental stages, and whether individuals

Table 17.3 Summary of biological roots of temperament

Temperament dimension/trait	System(s) cited	Relevant structures/neurochemicals	Researcher[a]
Positive/negative affect Approach/behavioral inhibition	Hemispheric activation	Frontal cortex (with amygdala perhaps underlying EEG asymmetries in infancy)	Calkins & Fox
Stress vulnerability	Hypothalmic-pituitary-adreno-cortical	System influenced by various structures including the amygdala and its projections to the motor system, cingulate and motor cortex and hypothalamus	Gunnar
Approach/positive affect Reactivity to novelty	Behavioral activation	Amygdala; temporal pole, orbitoprefrontal cortex; ventral striatum; ventral pallidum; motor cortices	Nelson
Withdrawal/negative affect Reactivity to novelty	Behavioral inhibition	Hippocampal formation and its surrounding structures (especially septal area, entorhinal area, dentate gyrus, hippocampus, subiculum, presubiculum); prefrontal cortex (including the orbitoprefrontal cortex); portions of the motor system	Nelson
Activity level	Genetic influence	Preliminary findings of marker for activity level in a gene for the enzyme tyrosinase, which is involved in tyrosine metabolism	Plomin & Saudino

Approach/positive affect	Behavioral activation Behavioral facilitation	Limbic system projections to the brain stem and their interaction with various dopaminergic systems	Rothbart, Derryberry, & Posner
Behavioral/inhibition, avoidance/fear, response to novel stimuli	Behavioral inhibition	Hippocampus and related structures, as well as neurochemical processes	Rothbart et al.
Irritability/anger	Fight–flight	Basolateral and centromedial nuclei of the amygdala, ventromedial nucleus of the hypothalamus, central gray region of the midbrain, somatic and motor effector nuclei of the lower brain stem	Rothbart et al.
Emotionality	Interaction of limbic system with ANS and effector systems, and with brain stem areas involved in arousal or vigilance	Includes septohippocampal system, limbic cortex, hypothalamus, amygdala. Example = basal ganglia Examples – raphe nuclei and locus coerulus	Steinmetz
Arousability (which may subsume several temperament and personality traits)	Brain stem reticular formation	Cortex, reticular formation, limbic system, ANS, neurotransmitters, enzymes, hormones	Strelau
Impulsive unsocialized sensation seeking	Neurochemical and hormonal	Dopamine (approach), serotonic (inhibition), norepinephrine (arousal; attention focusing)	Zuckerman

EEG = electroencephalographic; ANS = autonomic nervous system

[a] Researchers refer to chapters by these individuals contained in Bates & Wachs (1994)

Source: Wachs & King (1994)

are twins does not challenge our overall conclusion that genetic influences are important for temperament, but it does suggest the need for caution when discussing the extent and nature of these influences.

A need for caution is also suggested when we look at evidence on the role played by genetic influences on change in temperament. While the evidence is not totally consistent (e.g., Wilson & Matheny, 1986), for the most part available evidence indicates that genetic factors influence the stability of temperament across time and across contexts, whereas changes in individual temperament patterns across contexts or over time appear to be due to either environmental influences (Plomin et al., 1993; Saudino, 1997; Saudino et al., 1996) or to the joint operation of both genetic and environmental influences (Robinson et al., 1992). The relevance of environment as an influence upon individual variation in temperament will be discussed shortly. Prior to discussing environmental influences we will first look at the role played by biological influences other than genetic factors.

Nutritional influences

Those aspects of central nervous system (CNS) structure (e.g., the hippocampus) and neurotransmitter metabolism (e.g., serotonin) that have been shown to be influenced by variability in nutritional intake are, in many cases, the same CNS areas and metabolic processes that have been implicated in individual variability in temperament (Wachs, 2000b). Given this linkage we would expect to find relations between individual variability in temperament and individual variability in dietary intake patterns. Available evidence not only documents such relations but also indicates what aspects of diet may be most relevant for individual variability in temperament. Experimental infrahuman studies have reported that malnutrition is related to lower sociability, higher emotionality, lower approach, and higher inhibition (Barrett, 1984). Similarly, experimentally induced iron deficiency has been associated with greater emotional reactivity (Munro, 1987) and lower activity level in infrahuman species (Barzideh, Burright, & Dorovich, 1995). At the human level, infants who are severely malnourished, and then nutritionally rehabilitated, later in life show behavioral patterns characterized by greater distractibility and lower reactivity, emotional control and activity level (Grantham-McGregor, 1995; Simeon & Grantham-McGregor, 1990). Chronic undernutrition has been related to lower activity and reactivity in infancy and lower activity and sociability in childhood (Wachs, 2000b). Infants with iron-deficiency anemia show a behavioral pattern characterized by lower activity, lower reactivity, higher inhibition, and greater negative emotionality as compared to nonanemic infants (Lozoff, 1998; Walter, de Andraca, Chadud, & Perales, 1989). Evidence further suggests relatively permanent influences of iron-deficiency anemia upon those aspects of central nervous system development and neurotransmitter metabolism that may be related to variability in temperament (Lozoff, 1998).

Pre- and perinatal biomedical problems

Evidence on the relationship of prematurity and low birth weight to variability in temperament in the first year of life is not highly consistent. As compared to full-terms, preterm infants have been characterized as being less difficult, less sociable, less active–reactive, showing lower approach, having a lower threshold or having a more positive mood than full-terms (Garcia-Coll, Halpern, Vohr, Seifer, & Oh, 1992; Newman, O'Callaghan, et al., 1997; Prior, Sanson, & Oberklaid, 1989; Sajaniemi, Salokorpi & vonWendt, 1998). However, other studies report no relation between temperament and perinatal characteristics like low birth weight (Riese, 1994) or weight for gestational age (Robson & Cline, 1998). Part of the difference may reflect the fact that preterm infants, particularly if they are small for gestational age, appear to show lower stability in temperament over time than either full-term infants or preterm infants who have birth weights that are appropriate for their gestational age (Gennaro, Medoff, & Lotas, 1992; Riese, 1992).

Whether differences in temperament associated with preterm births or low birth weight are directly related to these birth problems or are an indirect consequence of such problems remains an open question. Maternal smoking has been associated both with an increased risk of preterm births (Christen & Christen, 1998) and with increased neonatal irritability (van den Boom & Gravenhorst, 1995). Similarly, factors that covary with preterm births such as an increased risk for intraventricular hemorrhage, longer hospitalization, and greater use of ventilation have also been associated with variability in temperament during the first year of life (Garcia-Coll et al., 1992).

Biomedical syndromes

A popular stereotype is that Down's syndrome children are more likely to have an easy temperament than are non-Down's children. However, the evidence supporting this stereotype is not particularly strong. While some studies do show that Down's children are overrepresented in the easy temperament category and underrepresented in the difficult temperament category (Ratekin, 1996), other studies report Down's syndrome children as being either more difficult (Goldberg & Marcovitch, 1989) or that there are no differences in temperament in Down's syndrome and normal children (Vaughn, Contreras, & Seifer, 1994). However, at least some support for this stereotype may be seen in evidence suggesting that the stability of difficult temperament in normal children is greater than the stability of difficult temperament for Down's syndrome children, who tend to show more easy temperament patterns as they grow older (Goldberg & Marcovitch, 1989; Vaughn et al., 1994).

Psychosocial Environmental Influences

While temperament is fundamentally a biologically rooted trait, even the most biologically based temperament theories allow a role for the environment (e.g., Buss & Plomin, 1984; Rothbart & Derryberry, 1981). In referring to the role of environmental influences on individual differences in temperament patterns we are not referring to cultural differences in the consequences of temperament, which will be discussed later in this chapter. Rather, we are referring to evidence indicating that the nature of children's temperament patterns can be changed by environmental factors, particularly when these factors operate cumulatively over time. In understanding environmental contributions to temperament, it would be easy to assume that the environment primarily influences the behavioral manifestations of individual variability in temperament. However, such an assumption may not be correct. Environmental characteristics have been shown to influence both central nervous system development (Greenough & Black, 1992) and the operation of neural-hormonal systems (Gunnar, 1994), both of which form the biological basis of temperament. Hence, environmental contributions to temperament may operate both at a behavioral and a biological level. Evidence for the role of environmental influences upon individual differences in temperament patterns comes from several sources.

Change in temperament

In studies that concurrently measure temperament and environment it is often difficult to distinguish whether it is the child's environment influencing his or her temperament or the child's temperament influencing the characteristics of his or her environment (Crockenberg, 1986). Longitudinal investigations in which environmental assessment precedes measurement of temperament, or in which change in temperament is the outcome variable, offer one way of dealing with this potential confound. Two domains of temperament that have been identified by longitudinal studies as being particularly sensitive to environmental influences are negative emotionality and inhibition. Increases in infant's negative emotionality have been associated with lower parental involvement (Belsky, Fish, & Isabella, 1991), a lack of parental responsivity to infant distress (Wachs et al., 1993), and living with parents who have high levels of marital problems (Belsky et al., 1991; Engfer, 1986). A reduction in infants' negative emotionality was related to more responsive, sensitive caregiving (Belsky et al., 1991) and living with mothers who had higher levels of social support (Fish, 1997). Evidence also indicates that children who are highly inhibited early in life became less inhibited over time if their parents were less "over-solicitous," setting firm age-appropriate behavioral limits, responding less to infant distress and more to infant positive affect, and being more intrusive in their children's lives (Arcus, 2001; Park, Belsky, Putnam, & Crnic, 1997). Similarly, toddlers who show stable patterns of behavioral inhibition across laboratory task situations have mothers who are over-solicitous and who keep their child from practicing appropriate coping skills (Rubin, Hastings, Stewart, Henderson, & Chen, 1997). One reason for this seemingly paradoxical finding of positive changes appearing to be related to what seems to be less sensitive parenting is that inhibited infants who are not overly protected may learn better coping strategies for dealing with minor stresses in the relatively familiar and safe environment of the home (Arcus, 2001).

The physical context

A second way of dealing with potential temperament–environment confounds is to look at environmental contexts that are potentially less sensitive to the influence of child temperament. One such context is the physical environment – the stage or setting upon which social transactions between child and caregiver take place (Wohlwill & Heft, 1987). One aspect of the physical environment that has been related to temperament is environmental chaos, which involves factors such as crowding and high levels of nonhuman noise in the home. Several studies have reported that higher levels of environmental noise, confusion, and crowding in the homes of toddlers in the second year of life are associated with less "tractability" and the child's having more intense negative moods (Matheny et al., 1987; Wachs, 1988).

Intervention studies

In intervention studies specific aspects of the child's environment are manipulated and the effect of this manipulation upon changes in temperament is described. Using a sample of highly irritable 6-month-old infants, van den Boom (1994) has reported that short-term training of mothers in a special program designed to increase maternal sensitivity and responsivity resulted in higher levels of infant sociability and self-regulation, and lower levels of negative emotionality, as compared to highly irritable infants whose mothers were not enrolled in this type of training program. However, such short-term interventions may have time-limited effects, at least for some temperament dimensions. Specifically, 27 months after the intervention had terminated, while infants whose mothers had received the intervention were independently coded as more cooperative, there were no group differences on measures of positive or negative emotionality (van den Boom, 1995). Time-limited intervention effects highlight the importance of continuing interventions, particularly for infants who may have temperament patterns that may place them at later developmental risk (see the section on temperament and child behavior problems later in this chapter).

Taken together, the evidence from these three lines of research converges on a conclusion that at least some aspects of temperament can be influenced by environmental factors. This evidence does not contradict conclusions about the essential biological nature of temperament, but does underline the fact that an understanding of individual variability in temperament requires us to go beyond pure biological influences.

Gender Differences

The role of gender in the etiology of temperament can be viewed as both a biological (chromosomal, hormonal) and environmental (differential treatment) set of influences. Overall, there is a good deal of inconsistency in the literature relating different dimensions of temperament to gender, particularly in the first year of life (Martin, Wisenbaker, Baker, & Huttenen, 1997). However, at least two sets of findings suggest an increasing relation between gender and temperament after 12 months of age. First, there is a consistent body of evidence showing that males have a higher activity level than females (Eaton & Enns, 1986; Prior et al., 1989), particularly after the first year of life (Martin et al., 1997). Second, males show higher levels of approach behavior than females (Prior et al., 1989; Rothbart, 1989), or alternatively, females are higher in inhibition than are males (Robinson et al., 1992). While these differences may reflect biological influences, evidence indicating that there are stronger correlations between maternal behavior and activity and shyness for females than for males suggests that not all of the gender differences can be clearly ascribed to biological influences (Stevenson-Hinde & Hinde, 1986).

Summary

What has been documented in this section is that while temperament consists of biologically rooted phenomena, its biological roots encompass many potential influences, including genetics, nutrition, and biomedical factors. Further, the multidetermined nature of individual differences in temperament is further documented by evidence suggesting that environmental influences also play a role in the etiology and the development of such individual differences.

Consequences of Individual Differences in Temperament

Temperament and Later Personality

In some theories, "early-emerging personality traits" are one of the definitional criteria for temperament (Buss & Plomin, 1984). Some personality theorists have argued that temperament is not the starting point for later personality, but rather that temperament and personality essentially reflect the same basic tendencies that are expressed differently at different ages (Costa & McCrae, 2001). Implicit in both points of view is the idea that there should be linkages between early temperament in the infancy and preschool period and later adult personality. Second-order factor analyses of multiple personality questionnaires often find similar structures of between three and five dimensions (Caspi, 1998; Digman, 1990; Goldberg, 1993; Zuckerman, 1991). The leading model at this time is the five-factor model, with the following dimensions: *Extraversion*, involves sociability, emotionally positive interest in novel objects, and active efforts to dominate the environment. *Agreeableness* concerns friendly, trusting, cooperative responses to others. *Conscientiousness* is characterized by attentiveness to task demands, reflection before action, and persistent efforts to meet others' expectations. *Neuroticism* refers to anxious, inhibited, tense behavior and proneness to distress. Finally, *openness*, sometimes called *intellect*, involves curious, intellectually explorative and creative traits.

Given both a starting point (infant temperament dimensions) and an end point (the Big 5 dimensions in adulthood), a number of conceptual schemes have been proposed that link infant temperament to the Big 5 (Ahadi & Rothbart, 1994; Hagekull, 1994). For example, early self-regulation and task persistence in infancy and the preschool period have been considered as the developmental antecedents of adult conscientiousness (Kohnstamm, Zhang, Slotboom, & Elphick, 1998), while early sociability has been conceptually linked to later adult agreeableness (Hagekull, 1994). Infants differ on how positively responsive they are to people and objects (conceptually relevant to extraversion). They also differ on how prone to distress and inhibition or how fearful they are in the presence of novelty (an early analog of neuroticism). Infants also differ on how they persist in attention (possibly an early analog of conscientiousness). Unfortunately, for the most part such theoretical speculation has far outrun the availability of data on this question (Caspi, 1998). There is evidence available linking infant temperament to childhood temperament and childhood temperament to adult personality, as well as evidence showing that dimensions of infant and childhood temperament can be classified using the Big 5 framework (for reviews of this evidence, see Caspi, 1998; Halverson, Kohnstamm, & Martin, 1994; Kohnstamm, Halverson, Mervielde, & Havill, 1998). However, overall there is little empirical evidence on the critical question of whether there are links between infant temperament and adult personality. Further, what little evidence is available on this question often cannot be encompassed easily within a Big 5 personality framework.

Three longitudinal data sets are of particular relevance in regard to the question of linkages between early temperament and later personality. The *Fels* study is based on repeated home observations assessing children's behavioral patterns over the first several years of life. Follow-up of infants in this sample into early adolescence (10–14 years) was based on use of personality tests and observation of behavior patterns in school; in adulthood follow-up interviews were used (Kagan & Moss, 1962). Data from the *Dunedin* study is based on behavior ratings of children when they were age 3, which were then used to form five clusters of children with different behavioral patterns: undercontrolled, inhibited, confident, reserved, and well adjusted. At age 18 personality questionnaires assessing constraint and positive and negative emotionality were utilized. In adulthood friends and family did behavioral ratings of individuals in this study using rating dimensions that were consistent with the five-factor model of personality (Caspi & Silva, 1995; Newman, Caspi, et al., 1997). In the *Bloomington* longitudinal study mothers reported on their infant's temperament using the Infant Characteristics Questionnaire, and both maternal and self-report on the Big 5 Personality Questionnaire were used to categorize the child's personality at 17 years of age (Bates & Bayles, 1984; Lanthier & Bates, 1995). Not all information from these three data sets is directly relevant to our question of linkages between early temperament and later personality, but those findings that are most relevant are summarized in Table 17.4. Where it seemed appropriate we have put in parentheses the dimensions of temperament or personality that appear to be tapped by the characteristics assessed in the original studies.

As can be seen from Table 17.4, there are a number of significant linkages in the expected direction between early temperament and later personality in each of the individual studies. These include a significant negative relation between early sociability and later introversion, between early inhibition and later sociability, and between early resistance to control and later agreeableness. Similarly, there are also positive relations between later neuroticism–maladjustment and prior undercontrol and unadaptability. However, this table also shows that many of the observed relations that might be expected from theory are nonsignificant or do not replicate across studies (e.g., infant difficultness and later agreeableness; infant sociability and adolescent or adult introversion–extraversion; early self-control and later neuroticism). Part of the nonsignificance or lack of replication may reflect methodological factors, such as a heavy reliance on adolescent or adult self-report data. However, it is of interest to note that there were no major long-term

Table 17.4   Linkages between temperament in the first 3 years of life and adolescent and adult personality

Study	Major findings
Fels	Early passivity (inhibition) unrelated to adult withdrawal from stressful situations. Early behavioral disorganization (negative emotionality) unrelated to adolescent negative emotionality, or to ease of adult anger arousal (reactivity); early disorganization is related to adult repression of angry thoughts (self-regulation) for males but not for females. Early social spontaneity is unrelated to adult social spontaneity but is related to adult social tension (introversion) for males, though not for females.
Dunedin adolescent sample	Early inhibition and reserve is significantly related to later constrained behavior in adolescence. Early undercontrol (low self-regulation) significantly related to lower constrained behavior and higher negative emotionality in adolescence. Early differences in positive emotionality unrelated to later behavioral patterns in adolescence.
Dunedin adult sample	Early inhibition related to lower communality (sociability), lower culture (openness to experience), and higher maladaptive behavior (neuroticism) in adulthood. Early undercontrol related to higher maladaptive behavior, lower culture, and lower conscientiousness in adulthood. Early reserved behavior unrelated to later adult personality.
Bloomington	Infant resistance to control negatively related to agreeableness at 17 years of age; infant difficultness negatively related to age 17 extraversion; low infant adaptability related to higher neuroticism at age 17; infant sociability related to lower neuroticism and greater openness to experience at age 17. Infant sociability unrelated to later extraversion; infant difficultness unrelated to later agreeableness; neuroticism at age 17 unrelated to earlier resistance to control or difficultness.

predictive differences in the Dunedin study for the three largest clusters of children whose early temperament characteristics defined them as confident, reserved, and well adjusted. Further, some of the significant relations that were found would not necessarily be predicted from current temperament or personality theory – e.g., the significant positive correlation between early negative emotionality and later indices of self-regulation in the Fels data.

Should we expect linkages between early temperament and later personality?

To the extent that temperament is either isomorphic with or the precursor of later personality dimensions we should expect linkages between early temperament and later personality. To the extent that there is a common genetic substrate underlying both temperament and personality dimensions we should also expect linkages (Wachs, 1994). Further, to the extent that individual differences in temperament influence both the types of reactions elicited from others and the types of environmental "niches" that individuals select into we should also expect temperament–personality continuity, since differential reactivity and niche selection act to stabilize temperament over time and temperament dimensions ultimately shade into characteristic adult personality dimensions (Caspi, 1998). For example, inhibited children having less experience with standard peer social interactions are less likely to respond appropriately to such interactions when they occur. Carried over time we would expect to see an increase in social isolation for children who are originally inhibited (Caspi, Elder, & Bem, 1988). Further, as adults, individuals who are initially inhibited would be more likely to marry other individuals with a similar personality pattern, thus further strengthening linkages from early temperament to later personality linkages (Caspi & Herbner, 1990).

Alternatively, looked at in a different light we should not necessarily expect such processes to automatically produce linkages between temperament and personality. One necessary requirement for expecting linkages between temperament and personality is that both phenomena are relatively stable. However, available evidence indicates only moderate degrees of stability for either temperament (Slabach et al., 1991) or personality (Alwin, 1995). In part, such modest stability may reflect different gene systems coming on-line at different time periods leading to discontinuity (Goldsmith, 1988), or to environmental influences acting to change individual developmental temperament patterns as discussed above. Further, it is unrealistic to expect individual differences in temperament to automatically elicit stable patterns of reactivity from others in the environment or to automatically promote stable patterns of niche selection by the individual. Evidence in regard to the former point will be discussed in the following section. In regard to niche selection acting as a stabilizing force, the child's ability to select stable environmental niches will vary as a function of the availability of niches for individuals with a given temperament living in a given culture during a given time period (Wachs, 1996). For example, Kerr (2001) has shown that the occupational niches available to males with inhibited temperaments are much more restricted in the United States than in a culture such as Sweden, where inhibited behavior is not looked upon as a disadvantageous trait.

An example illustrating the probabilistic nature of the processes governing linkages between temperament and personality is shown in Figure 17.1. As seen in this figure, even for two children at the same initial level of inhibited temperament there are a variety of potential intervening factors that can act to shape whether or not such an individual ends up with an adult personality characterized as extraverted or introverted. Besides the contextual factors shown in Figure 17.1, other individual characteristics can also act to moderate potential linkages between temperament and personality. For example, less intelligent inhibited children appear to have greater difficulty shifting toward an uninhibited behavioral pattern than do more intelligent inhibited children (Asendorpf, 1994). At present, both theory and the overall pattern of evidence suggest that we should not necessarily assume that temperament and personality are invariably or even logically linked together.

Initial temperamental trait: Child A & Child B equally Inhibited.	Child A	Child B
	Potential Environments	
Social microenvironment	Caregivers (parents) who are sensitive, but who do not reward their child's fearful behaviors and who place age-appropriate demands on their child	Caregivers who use inappropriate "low-level control" and attempt to force their child into new situations or who reinforce their child's fearful behaviors
Physical microenvironment	Presence of "stimulus shelters" or "defensible spaces," which the child can retreat to when there is too much stimulation	The child continually encounters noisy, chaotic environments that allow no escape from stimulation
Nonfamily: Peer groups	Peer groups have other inhibited children with common interests, so the child feels accepted	Peer groups consist of athletic extraverts, so the child feels rejected
Mesosystem: School environment	School is "undermanned," so children are more likely to be tolerated and feel they can make a contribution	School is "overmanned," so children are less likely to be tolerated and feel undervalued
Personality outcomes in adulthood	Child A closer to extraversion and emotional stability poles	Child B closer to introversion and neuroticism poles

Figure 17.1   Proposed transition paths between early temperament and later personality (adapted from Wachs, 1994).

Temperament and Child–Caregiver Relations

A fundamental assumption deriving both from the New York Longitudinal Study (Thomas et al., 1968) and from behavioral genetic research (Plomin, DeFries, & Loehlin, 1977) is that children with specific temperaments will elicit specific patterns of reactivity from their parents. For example, parents will likely react to highly intense difficult infants in ways that will lower the level of their child's behavior, but will attempt to raise the child's level of behavior if their child is overly passive (Bell & Chapman, 1986). However, it is essential to emphasize that relations between temperament and caregiver behavior patterns are probabilistic and not deterministic in nature. Having a specific temperament will increase the probability of eliciting certain reactions from caregivers but does not guarantee it. A variety of nontemperament factors can alter the degree to which variability in individual temperament is related to variability in caregiver reactions. For example, parents who are skilled in disciplinary techniques would not respond as emotionally to children with difficult temperaments. In addition, the consequences of a given temperament trait will depend upon the nature of other temperament traits possessed by the child (Rothbart & Bates, 1998). For example, caregiver reactions may be quite different for a highly irritable, highly soothable child, as compared to an equally highly irritable child who is not soothable.

Our assumption of the probabilistic nature of caregiver reactivity to infant temperamental characteristics is supported by evidence relating infant temperament to parent–child relationship patterns. Particularly during the first year of life evidence is clearly mixed. Some studies have reported differences in interaction patterns by caregivers of irritable versus caregivers of non-difficult temperament infants (Lounsbury & Bates, 1982; van den Boom & Hoeksma, 1994). However, other well-designed studies have reported few significant relations between early infant temperament and subsequent caregiver behavioral patterns (Pettit & Bates, 1984; Worobey & Blajda, 1989).

There have been a variety of attempts to explain such an inconsistent pattern of evidence. It has been suggested that the influence of infant temperament upon caregiver behavior patterns is most likely to be found for infants with extreme temperament traits (Clarke & Clarke, 1988). Alternatively, it has been argued that neurologically driven inconsistencies in the expression of infant temperament over the first year of life make it difficult for parents to detect a consistent behavioral pattern they can consistently react to (Wachs & King, 1994). Based upon measurement considerations discussed earlier in this chapter, it is possible that parents are adjusting to temperament characteristics of their infant, but that the pattern of parental adjustment is too subtle to be detected by short-term observations. At present there is little evidence available on any of these hypotheses.

What evidence is available on this question suggests the need to look longitudinally at moderation of parent reactivity to infants with different temperaments. Studies looking at trajectories of caregiver behavior over time suggest a pattern of declining involvement by parents toward fussy difficult infants (Maccoby, Snow, & Jacklin, 1984; van den Boom & Hoeksma, 1994). While studies of developmental trajectories suggest there is differential reactivity, depending upon the specific time point chosen one could see either differences or no differences in parent reaction to temperamentally difficult infants.

Alternatively, a second explanatory framework involves moderation of relations between infant temperament and caregiver behavior patterns as a function of specific infant and adult characteristics. Moderators of potential linkages between temperament and caregiver behavior patterns can include child characteristics such as age and gender, parental preference for certain types of child behavior patterns, child or parent nutritional status as well as higher-order contextual characteristics (Slabach et al., 1991; Wachs, 1992). Other potential moderators that have been identified include maternal substance abuse (Schuler, Black, & Starr, 1995) and maternal attitudes about how responsive they should be toward their infant (Crockenberg & McCluskey, 1986). Thus, within a probabilistic framework it is not surprising to find that experienced mothers or mothers who believe they have the capability to influence their infants' behavior reacted differently to their fussy difficult infants than did less experienced mothers or mothers who were unsure about their ability to cope (Cutrona & Troutman, 1986; Lounsbury & Bates, 1982).

What seems clear from the above evidence is that if we are to understand how and when infant temperament acts to influence caregiver behavior patterns, it is essential to go beyond just temperament and look at temperament as part of a larger system involving contributions from nontemperament child and adult characteristics. An essential part of such a system will be bidirectional influences between temperament and parent characteristics, with infant temperament acting to influence parent characteristics, which in turn influence the subsequent nature of infant temperament. Examples of such bidirectional influences are seen in a variety of studies (Crockenberg & McCluskey, 1986; Maccoby et al., 1984; Thoman, 1990). For example, Engfer (1986) has shown that while maternal sensitivity in the neonatal period relates to lower infant difficultness at 4 months of age, infant difficultness at 4 months predicts lower maternal sensitivity at 8 months, which in turn predicts level of child difficultness at 18 months of age. Rather than a main effect model of temperament → parental behavior, what the available evidence suggests is a more transactional framework. Within such a framework child temperament can act to influence caregiver behavioral patterns; these subsequent caregiver behavior patterns in turn can act to influence subsequent child temperament (temperament → environment → temperament).

Temperament and Abnormal Development

Can temperament traits of infants and toddlers forecast their risk for later development of adjustment problems? We use the term adjustment to describe not just the presence or absence of psychopathology, but also the presence or absence of positive traits such as prosocial orientation and creativity. This is a question of considerable interest, especially to clinically oriented developmental psychologists. In broadest overview, the literature does show linkages between children's temperament and their adjustment (Rothbart & Bates, 1998). The literature is too young for this conclusion to be beyond question, but it is relatively robust at this point. The literature on temperament–adjustment linkages can be divided into studies showing direct links and studies showing indirect links.

Direct links

First, we consider direct predictions from temperament to adjustment. Most relevant to this issue are several projects showing predictions from early temperament to adjustment in subsequent years. These projects include the *Bloomington Longitudinal Study* (Bates & Bayles, 1988; Bates, Bayles, Bennett, Ridge, & Brown, 1991; Bates, Maslin, & Frankel, 1985; Lee & Bates, 1985), the *Dunedin* study (Caspi & Silva, 1995; Caspi, Henry, McGee, Moffitt, & Silva, 1995), the *Australian Temperament Project* (Pedlow, Sanson, Prior, & Oberklaid, 1993; Sanson, Prior, & Kyrios, 1990), and the *Fullerton Longitudinal Project* (Guerin & Gottfried, 1986; Guerin, Gottfried, & Thomas, 1997), as well as individual studies by Hagekull (1994) and by Rothbart, Ahadi, and Hershey (1994). These studies provide support for what we have called "differential linkage" (Bates, 1989a,b; Bates, 1990; Rothbart & Bates, 1998). This term means that specific temperament constructs can be differentially linked to specific dimensions of adjustment in later years. As described earlier in this chapter, temperament can be measured as a set of relatively independent dimensions, and longitudinal studies of measures of temperament tend to find differential continuity within dimensions (Bates & Bayles, 1984). This continues into measures of adjustment outcomes: Early fearfulness is not always linked to later psychopathology, but when it is, it is typically more strongly linked to internalizing problems – such as anxiety or depression – than to externalizing problems – aggression and disinhibition. On the other hand, early unmanageability and unresponsiveness to caregiver controls are linked more strongly to later externalizing problems rather than to internalizing problems. Negative emotionality traits in infancy or early childhood are equally predictive of both kinds of adjustment problem. Given the negative emotions frequently observed in both internalizing and externalizing problems, this seems appropriate. The correlations that have been reported reflect small to moderate effect sizes, and the pattern is not always the same, but overall there does appear to be consistency in the findings. The pattern suggests continuity from early temperament into profiles of adjustment in childhood.

The meanings of the observed linkages between early temperament and later adjustment have been questioned on methodological grounds. It is sometimes argued (e.g., Belsky, Hsieh, & Crnic, 1998) that temperament–adjustment correlations are only found when both the temperament and adjustment measures are from parent report. To the extent this is correct, biased perceptions in the source of information about both the antecedent and outcome variables might be the explanation of the predictive relationship. For example, a parent who sees life in a more generally negative way is more likely to see the child's behavior in a negative way. However, there are at least two counterarguments: *First*, the differential linkage pattern just described suggests that if biased perception is operating it is certainly a more complex and differentiated perceptual bias than has been previously considered in research on personality questionnaires. The *second* counterargument is the fact that the relations are shown across sources. For example, Caspi et al. (1995) showed relations between experimenters' ratings of children's temperament and adjustment ratings by both parents and teachers, while Bates, Pettit, Dodge, and Ridge (1998) showed relations between early parent reports of temperament and later outcomes as reported by both parents and teachers. Likewise, Guerin et al. (1997) reported predictions from parent reports of temperament in infancy to teacher reports in middle childhood.

Another methodological issue that has been repeatedly discussed in the literature involves "contamination" of measures. Contamination is not simply a methodological issue, but also a conceptual issue, returning us to questions of how separate temperament should be from other psychological domains. The basic concern is that the questionnaires that measure temperament and adjustment have some overlap in item content so the temperament–adjustment linkage would be an artifact of measuring the same thing, especially for temperament and internalizing behavior problem scales (Sanson et al., 1990). Conceptually, there is no compelling reason why the temperament and adjustment domains should be completely nonoverlapping. Indeed, given that there are predictive, differentiated relations between various temperament dimensions and later adjustment, some of which are cross-informant, it seems likely that there are meaningful developmental linkages between the domains of temperament and adjustment. Sheeber (1995) has argued that if measures of temperament and behavior problems are assessing the same construct, then parent participation in an intervention program designed to deal with child behavioral problems should produce parallel changes in both parent behavior problem and temperament ratings. In fact, rating changes occurred only for behavior problem and not temperament ratings, which lends empirical support to the hypothesis that linkages between temperament and behavior problems are not simply an artifact of contaminated measures (Sheeber, 1995). Further support comes from Lengua, West, and Sandler (1998), who identified and removed items from temperament scales that had overlap with psychopathology symptoms. Lengua et al. found that children's temperament still correlated with their symptoms, in a differentiated pattern like the one we have described, even after the temperament scales were "decontaminated."

In brief, there are some replicated findings of early temperament directly predicting later adjustment in children in a conceptually coherent way. However, the amounts of variance accounted for in these findings have tended to be moderate, leaving considerable room for intervening processes to facilitate or impede any temperament–adjustment correlation, in addition to the usual limitations of accuracy of measurement. Apparently, what is seen in the infant or toddler's temperament does not necessarily become translated into comparable individual differences in later childhood. Such a conclusion is similar to what we pointed out previously in regard to the question of the continuity of temperament to personality. This brings us to a consideration of indirect links between temperament and adjustment.

Indirect links

While there are a number of possible indirect processes (Rothbart & Bates, 1998), the two we are especially interested in involve the interaction of one temperament trait with another and of a temperament trait with characteristics of caregiving. There are very few empirical examples of predictions from temperament to adjustment being moderated by another temperament variable. One of the few important examples we have is from Eisenberg, Fabes, and their colleagues (1995), who reported that children's negative emotionality predicted later behavior problems more strongly when the child's self-regulation was low or medium rather than when it was high.

The number of replicated findings of temperament–environment is still small relative to the number of direct, main-effect linkages between temperament and adjustment (Bates & McFadyen-Ketchum, in press). One such replicated finding has been documented by Kochanska (1991, 1995, 1997; also see Colder, Lochman, & Wells 1997). Children who were temperamentally fearful in a novel situation were likely to show, concurrently and in the future, more complete development of internalized self-control or conscience when their mothers were relatively gentle in their control of the child rather than harsh. On the other hand, relatively fearless children's development of conscience was essentially unrelated to the gentleness of maternal discipline. However, fearless children did show higher levels of conscience, such as cheerful compliance or resistance to temptation, when their mothers reported that they had a secure attachment relationship with the child. This finding is an example of how the adjustment implications of a parenting characteristic can be moderated by the temperament of the child. A second temperament–parenting interaction effect focuses upon the other vantage point – how implications of temperament are moderated by parenting. Bates et al. (1998) found, in two separate studies, and with both mother-reported and teacher-reported outcomes, that parent reports of temperamental resistance to control (unmanageability) measured in early childhood predicted later externalizing behavior problems more strongly in cases where the mothers had been observed to be low rather than high in frequency of controlling the child's behavior. Theoretically, this may partly reflect the high-control mother being more persistent in countering a high level of child resistance to control, and ultimately succeeding in getting such a child to be more responsive to social limits, as opposed to falling into coercion traps with the child or giving free rein to the child's temperamental unmanageability (Patterson, 1982).

In summary, temperament does show an interesting, conceptually coherent pattern of predictions to later behavioral adjustment. However, the effect sizes found for temperament as a predictor of adjustment are small enough to emphasize the need for further work on measurement of the temperament and adjustment constructs, as well as on the moderating effects of other temperament variables and environmental variables.

Practical Implications

A large part of the interest in temperament has stemmed from the hope that knowledge of a child's temperament will ultimately help in promoting optimal development (Bates, 1989b). Perhaps this already occurs, in relatively intuitive ways, as sensitive, accepting parents, teachers, and other caregivers work with their children. At the current time, we cannot say that there are empirically validated clinical assessments and treatments based on temperament. We have described elsewhere a number of ways in which more explicit applications of temperament concepts can be made (Bates, 1989b; Bates, Wachs, & Emde, 1994). Here we will give just a few examples.

In child psychiatry and clinical psychology, Chess and Thomas (1986) have provided parents and children guidance that frames adjustment problems in terms of conflicts between children's temperament characteristics and the expectations and responses of the environment. For example, a child who initially shrinks back from novel situations could come into conflict with parents who insensitively push and criticize the child and are critical of a lack of initiative; however, if the parents and child can appreciate the adjustment problem as a temperament–environment fit problem, they can take more adaptive steps to solve the problem. Such "re-framing" interventions are used by a number of other clinicians in treatment of behavior problems. For example, at the Indiana University clinic for treatment of Oppositional Defiant Disorder, we often frame children's dominating behaviors as partly rooted in a temperamental style that parents can appreciate but still shape into more acceptable behavioral expressions. Cameron and his colleagues (e.g., Cameron, Hansen, & Rosen, 1989) have found some value in giving anticipatory guidance to parents in a large health maintenance organization, sending written material that describes how a child of a given temperament profile may respond to imminent developmental challenges.

In the field of educational psychology there have been a number of studies of childhood temperament traits associated concurrently with school performance. Specifically, low activity level and higher attentional persistence are associated with higher levels of learning performance (Keogh, 1989; Martin, 1989). Along the same lines Matheny (1989b) has reported higher levels of cognitive performance by infants and children with more "tractable" temperaments, characterized by better adaptability, more positive mood, and more social orientation. It may be that less tractable children are more focused on negative contextual features in their surroundings and are thus less able to incorporate developmentally facilitative stimuli, as might occur in a preschool or school classroom. These findings clearly have implications for identifying children who may be at risk for school failure.

In pediatrics and pediatric psychology, there are also a number of practitioners using temperament ideas. Most notable are the continuing efforts by Carey to help practitioners distinguish between core temperamental characteristics of a child that may contribute to management problems and a meaningfully diagnosable disorder. Carey (1999) argued that much of the current diagnosis of Attention Deficit Hyperactivity Disorder fails to take into account normal variations in children's temperament. There are many other possible applications in this general area. For example, Matheny (1989a) has suggested that prevention of accidents in young children might be facilitated by assessment of children's temperament.

Given the cost and limited successfulness of treating many forms of adjustment problem, it is ultimately hoped that problems can be prevented. Perhaps when the processes involved in temperament–adjustment linkage are better understood, temperament assessed early in life can be a tool in helping caregivers provide more optimal environments, better suited to the particular needs of the child. For example, van den Boom (1994) found that infants who were extremely irritable in the neonatal period were at risk for receiving relatively unresponsive parenting and for forming insecure attachments by the end of the first year. However, if the mothers of such infants were given a moderate amount of special training in responsiveness, the infants grew to be better modulated and the attachment outcomes were more positive. Perhaps comparable effects might be found ultimately in interventions based on the temperament–parenting interaction effects that were reviewed in this chapter, providing caregivers precisely targeted management strategies for fearful versus fearless and resistant versus nonresistant toddlers.

References

Ahadi, S., & Rothbart, M. (1994). Temperament, development and the Big 5. In C. J. Halverson, G. A. Kohnstamm, & R. P. Martin (Eds.), *The developing structure of temperament and personality from infancy to adulthood* (pp. 189–208). Hillsdale, NJ: Erlbaum.

Alwin, D., 1995. Taking time seriously: Social change, social structure and human lives. In P. Moen, G. Elder, & K. Luscher (Eds.), *Examining lives in context* (pp. 211–263). Washington, DC: American Psychological Association.

Arcus, D. (2001). Inhibited and uninhibited children: Biology in the social context. In T. D. Wachs & D. Kohnstamm (Eds.), *Temperament in context* (pp. 43–60). Hillsdale, NJ: Erlbaum.

Asendorpf, J. (1994). The malleability of behavioral inhibition. *Developmental Psychology, 30,* 912–919.

Barrett, D. (1984). Conceptualization, assessment and illustrative results. In J. Brozek & B. Schurch (Eds.), *Malnutrition and behavior: Critical assessment of key issues* (pp. 280–306). Lausanne: Nestlé Foundation.

Barrett, K., & Morgan, G. (1995). Continuities and discontinuities in mastery motivation during infancy and toddlerhood. In R. MacTurk & G. Morgan (Eds.), *Mastery motivation: Origins, conceptualizations and applications* (pp. 57–94). Norwood, NJ: Ablex.

Barzideh, O., Burright, R., & Dorovich, P. (1995). Dietary iron and exposure to lead influence susceptibility to seizures. *Psychological Report, 76,* 971–976.

Bates, J. (1979). *Coding system for home observations of temperament.* Department of Psychology: Indiana University, Bloomington, IN.

Bates, J. (1987). Temperament in infancy. In J. Osofsky (Ed.), *Handbook of infant development* (2nd ed., pp. 1101–1149). New York: Wiley.

Bates, J. (1989a). Concepts and measures of temperament. In G. A. Kohnstamm, J. E. Bates, & M. K. Rothbart (Eds.), *Temperament in childhood* (pp. 3–26). New York: Wiley.

Bates, J. E. (1989b). Applications of temperament concepts. In G. A. Kohnstamm, J. E. Bates, & M. K. Rothbart (Eds.), *Temperament in childhood* (pp. 321–355). Chichester: Wiley.

Bates, J. E. (1990). Conceptual and empirical linkages between temperament and behavior problems: A commentary on the Sanson, Prior, and Kyrios study. *Merrill-Palmer Quarterly, 36,* 193–199.

Bates, J. E., & Bayles, K. (1984). Objective and subjective components in mothers' perceptions of their children from age 6 months to 3 years. *Merrill-Palmer Quarterly, 30,* 111–130.

Bates, J. E., & Bayles, K. (1988). Attachment and the development of behavior problems. In J. Belsky & T. Nezworski (Eds.), *Clinical implications of attachment* (pp. 253–299). Hillsdale, NJ: Erlbaum.

Bates, J. E., Bayles, K., Bennett, D. S., Ridge, B., & Brown, M. M. (1991). Origins of externalizing behavior problems at eight years of age. In D. Pepler & K. Rubin (Eds.), *Development and treatment of childhood aggression* (pp. 93–120). Hillsdale, NJ: Erlbaum.

Bates, J. E., Maslin, C. A., & Frankel, K. A. (1985). Attachment security, mother–child interaction, and temperament as predictors of behavior problem ratings at age three years. In I. Bretherton & E. Waters (Eds.), *Society for Research in Child Development Monographs: Growing points in attachment theory and research* (Serial No. 209).

Bates, J. E., & McFadyen-Ketchum, S. A. (in press). Temperament and parent–child relations as interacting factors in children's behavioral adjustment. In V. J. Molfese & D. Molfese (Eds.), *Temperament and personality development across the life span.* Hillsdale, NJ: Erlbaum.

Bates, J. E., Pettit, G. S., Dodge, K. A., & Ridge, B. (1998). The interaction of temperamental resistance to control and restrictive parenting in the development of externalizing behavior. *Developmental Psychology, 34,* 982–995.

Bates, J., & Wachs, T. D. (Eds.). (1994). *Temperament: Individual differences at the interface of biology and behavior.* Washington, DC: American Psychological Association.

Bates, J. E., Wachs, T. D., & Emde, R. N. (1994). Toward practical uses for biological concepts of temperament. In J. E. Bates & T. D. Wachs (Eds.), *Temperament: Individual differences at the interface of biology and behavior* (pp. 275–306). Washington, DC: American Psychological Association.

Bell, R. (1968). A reinterpretation of the direction of effects in studies of socialization. *Psychological Review, 75,* 81–95.

Bell, R., & Chapman, M. (1986). Child effects in studies using experimental or brief longitudinal approaches to socialization. *Developmental Psychology, 22*, 595–603.

Belsky, J., Fish, M., & Isabella, R. (1991). Continuity and discontinuity in infant negative and positive emotionality. *Developmental Psychology, 27*, 421–431.

Belsky, J., Hsieh, K., & Crnic, K. (1998). Mothering, fathering, and infant negativity as antecedents of boys' externalizing problems and inhibition at age 3 years: Differential susceptibility to rearing experience? *Development and Psychopathology, 10*, 301–319.

Borkowski, J., & Dukewich, T. (1996). Environment covariations and intelligence. In D. Detterman (Ed.), *Current topics in human intelligence: The environment* (Vol. 5, pp. 3–16). Norwood, NJ: Ablex.

Bornstein, M., Gaughran, J., & Segui, I. (1991). Multimethod assessment of infant temperament. *International Journal of Behavioral Development, 14*, 131–151.

Braungart, J., Fulker, D., & Plomin, R. (1992). Genetic mediation of the home environment during infancy. *Developmental Psychology, 28*, 1048–1055.

Buss, A. (1991). The EAS theory of temperament. In J. Strelau & A. Angleitner (Eds.), *Explorations in temperament: International perspectives on theory and measurement* (pp. 43–60). New York: Plenum Press.

Buss, A., & Plomin, R. (1984). *Temperament: Early developing personality traits.* Hillsdale, NJ: Erlbaum.

Buss, A., & Plomin, R. (1986). The EAS approach to temperament. In R. Plomin & J. Dunn (Eds.), *The study of temperament: Changes, continuities, and challenges* (pp. 67–80). Hillsdale, NJ: Erlbaum.

Cameron, J. R., Hansen, R., & Rosen, D. (1989). Preventing behavioral problems in infancy through temperamental assessment and parental support programs. In W. B. Carey & S. C. McDevitt (Eds.), *Clinical and educational applications of temperament research* (pp. 155–165). Berwyn, PA: Swets North America.

Carey, W. (1989). Clinical use of temperament data in pediatrics. In W. Carey & S. McDevitt (Eds.), *Clinical and educational applications of temperament research* (pp. 127–140). Amsterdam: Swets & Zeitlinger.

Carey, W., & McDevitt, S. (1978). Revision of the Infant Temperament Questionnaire. *Pediatrics, 61*, 735–739.

Carey, W. B. (1999). Problems in diagnosing attention and activity. *Pediatrics, 103*, 664–667.

Caspi, A. (1998). Personality development across the life course. In W. Damon (Series Ed.) & N. Eisenberg (Vol. Ed.), *Handbook of child psychology: Vol. 3. Social, emotional, and personality development* (pp. 311–388). New York: Wiley.

Caspi, A., Elder, G., & Bem, D. (1988). Moving away from the world: Life course patterns of shy children. *Developmental Psychology, 24*, 824–831.

Caspi, A., Henry, B., McGee, R. O., Moffitt, T. E., & Silva, P. A. (1995). Temperamental origins of child and adolescent behavior problems: From age three to age fifteen. *Child Development, 66*, 55–68.

Caspi, A., & Herbner, E. (1990). Continuity and change: Assortitive marriage and the consistency of personality in adulthood. *Journal of Personality and Social Psychology, 58*, 250–258.

Caspi, A., & Silva, P. (1995). Temperamental qualities at age three predict personality traits in young adulthood. *Child Development, 66*, 486–498.

Chess, S., & Thomas, A. (1984). *Origins and evolution of behavior disorders.* New York: Brunner-Mazel.

Chess, S., & Thomas, A. (1986). *Temperament in clinical practice.* New York: Guilford Press.

Christen, J., & Christen, A. (1998). *The female smoker: From addiction to recovery.* Indianapolis, IN: Indiana University Medical Educational Resources Program.

Clarke, A., & Clarke, A. (1988). The adult outcome of early behavioral abnormalities. *International Journal of Behavioral Development, 11,* 3–19.

Colder, C. R., Lochman, J. E., & Wells, K. C. (1997). The moderating effects of children's fear and activity level on relations between parenting practices and childhood symptomatology. *Journal of Abnormal Child Psychology, 25,* 251–263.

Costa, P., & McCrae, R. (2001). A theoretical context for adult temperament. In T. D. Wachs & G. Kohnstamm (Eds.), *Temperament in context* (pp. 1–22). Hillsdale, NJ: Erlbaum.

Crockenberg, S. (1986). Are temperamental differences in babies associated with predictable differences in caregivers? In J. Lerner & R. Lerner (Eds.), *Temperament and psychosocial interaction in children* (pp. 53–73). San Francisco: Jossey-Bass.

Crockenberg, S., & McCluskey, K. (1986). Change in maternal behavior during the baby's first year of life. *Child Development, 57,* 746–753.

Cutrona, C., & Troutman, B. (1986). Social support, infant temperament and parenting self-efficacy. *Child Development, 57,* 1507–1518.

Devlin, B., Daniels, M., & Roeder, K. (1997). The heritability of IQ. *Nature, 388,* 468–471.

Digman, J. (1990). Personality structure: Emergence of the 5 Factor Model. *Annual Review of Psychology, 41,* 417–440.

Eaton, W., & Dureski, C. (1986). Parent and actometer measures of motor activity level in the young infant. *Infant Behavior and Development, 9,* 383–393.

Eaton, W., & Enns, L. (1986). Sex differences in human motor activity level. *Psychological Bulletin, 100,* 19–28.

Eisenberg, N., Fabes, R. A., Murphy, M., Maszk, P., Smith, M., & Karbon, M. (1995). The role of emotionality and regulation in children's social functioning: A longitudinal study. *Child Development, 66,* 1360–1384.

Emde, R., Plomin, R., Robinson, J., Reznick, J., Campos, J., Corley, R., DeFries, J., Fulker, D., Kagan, J., & Zahn-Waxler, C. (1992). Temperament, emotion and cognition at 14 months. *Child Development, 63,* 1437–1455.

Engfer, A. (1986). Antecedents of perceived behavior problems in infancy. In G. Kohnstamm (Ed.), *Temperament discussed* (pp. 165–180). Lisse: Swets & Zeitlinger.

Fish, M. (1997, April). *Stability and change in infant temperament.* Paper presented to the Society for Research in Child Development, Washington, DC.

Fullard, W., McDevitt, S., & Carey, W. (1984). Assessing temperament in one- to three-year-old children. *Journal of Pediatric Psychology, 9,* 205–216.

Garcia-Coll, C., Halpern, L., Vohr, B., Seifer, R., & Oh, W. (1992). Stability and correlates of change of early temperament in preterm and full term infants. *Infant Behavior and Development, 15,* 137–153.

Gennaro, S., Medoff, B., & Lotas, M. (1992). Perinatal factors in infant temperament. *Nursing Research, 41,* 375–377.

Goldberg, L. R. (1993). The structure of phenotypic personality traits. *American Psychologist, 48,* 26–34.

Goldberg, S., & Marcovitch, S. (1989). Temperament in developmentally disabled children. In G. A. Kohnstamm, J. E. Bates, & M. K. Rothbart (Eds.), *Temperament in childhood* (pp. 387–404). New York: Wiley.

Goldsmith, H. (1988). Human developmental behavior genetics. *Annals of Child Development, 5,* 187–227.

Goldsmith, H. (1996). Studying temperament via construction of the Toddler Behavior Assessment Questionnaire. *Child Development, 67,* 218–235.

Goldsmith, H., & Reiser-Danner, L. (1990). Assessing early temperament. In C. Reynolds & R. Camphaus (Eds.), *Handbook of psychological and educational assessment of children: Vol. 2. Personality behavior and context* (pp. 345–378). New York: Guilford Press.

Goldsmith, H., Rieser-Danner, L., & Briggs, S. (1991). Evaluating convergent and discriminant validity of temperament questionnaires for preschoolers, toddlers and infants. *Developmental Psychology, 27,* 566–579.

Goldsmith, H., & Rothbart, M. (1991). Contemporary instruments for assessing early temperament by questionnaire and in the laboratory. In J. Strelau & A. Angleitner (Eds.), *Explorations in temperament: International perspectives on theory and measurement* (pp. 249–272). New York: Plenum Press.

Grantham-McGregor, S. (1995). A review of studies of the effect of severe malnutrition on mental development. *Journal of Nutrition – Supplement, 125,* 2233S–2238S.

Gray, J. A. (1991). The neuropsychology of temperament. In J. Strelau & A. Angleitner (Eds.), *Explorations in temperament: International perspectives on theory and measurement* (pp. 105–128). New York: Plenum Press.

Greenough, W., & Black, J. (1992). Induction of brain structure by experience. In M. Gunnar & C. Nelson (Eds.), *Developmental behavioral neuroscience* (pp. 153–232). Hillsdale, NJ: Erlbaum.

Guerin, D., & Gottfried, A. (1986, April). *Infant temperament as a predictor of preschool behavior problems.* Paper presented to the International Conference on Infant Studies, Los Angeles, CA.

Guerin, D. W., Gottfried, A. W., & Thomas, C. W. (1997). Difficult temperament and behaviour problems: A longitudinal study from 1.5 to 12 years. *International Journal of Behavioural Development, 21,* 71–90.

Gunnar, M. (1994). Psychoendocrine studies of temperament and stress in early childhood. In J. Bates & T. D. Wachs (Eds.), *Temperament: Individual difference at the interface of biology and behavior* (pp. 175–198). Washington, DC: American Psychological Association.

Hagekull, B. (1994). Infant temperament and early childhood functioning: Possible relations to the 5 Factor Model. In C. J. Halverson, G. A. Kohnstamm, & R. P. Martin (Eds.), *The developing structure of temperament and personality from infancy to adulthood* (pp. 227–240). Hillsdale, NJ: Erlbaum.

Halverson, C. J., Kohnstamm, D., & Martin, R. (1994). *The developing structure of temperament and personality from infancy to childhood.* Hillsdale, NJ: Erlbaum.

Huffman, L., Bryan, Y., del Carmen, R., Pedersen, F., Doussard, J., & Porges, S. (1998). Infant temperament and cardiac vagal tone: Assessments at 12 weeks of age. *Child Development, 69,* 624–635.

Kagan, J., & Moss, H. (1962). *Birth to maturity: A study in psychological development.* New York: Wiley.

Kagan, J., Reznick, J., Clarke, C., Snidman, N., & Garcia-Coll, C. (1984). Behavioral inhibition to the unfamiliar. *Child Development, 55,* 2212–2225.

Keogh, B. K. (1989). Applying temperament research to school. In G. A. Kohnstamm, J. E. Bates, & M. K. Rothbart (Eds.), *Temperament in childhood* (pp. 437–450). New York: Wiley.

Kerr, M. (2001). Culture as a context for temperament. In T. D. Wachs & G. Kohnstamm (Eds.), *Temperament in context* (pp. 139–152). Hillsdale, NJ: Erlbaum.

Kinchla, R. (1992). Attention. *Annual Review of Psychology, 43,* 711–742.

Kochanska, G. (1991). Socialization and temperament in the development of guilt and conscience. *Child Development, 62,* 1379–1392.

Kochanska, G. (1995). Children's temperament, mothers' discipline, and security of attachment: Multiple pathways to emerging internalization. *Child Development, 66,* 597–615.

Kochanska, G. (1997). Multiple pathways to conscience for children with different temperaments: From toddlerhood to age 5. *Developmental Psychology, 33,* 228–240.

Kohnstamm, G., Halverson, C., Mervielde, I., & Havill, V. (Eds.). (1998). *Parental descriptions of child personality.* Hillsdale, NJ: Erlbaum.

Kohnstamm, G., Zhang, Y., Slotboom, A., & Elphick, E. (1998). A developmental integration of conscientiousness from childhood to adulthood. In G. Kohnstamm, C. Halverson, I. Mervielde, & V. Havill (Eds.), *Parental descriptions of child personality* (pp. 65–84). Hillsdale, NJ: Erlbaum.

Lanthier, R., & Bates, J. (1995, May). *Infancy era predictors of the Big 5 personality dimensions in adolescence.* Paper presented to the Midwestern Psychological Association, Chicago, IL.

Lee, C. L., & Bates, J. E. (1985). Mother–child interaction at age two years and perceived difficult temperament. *Child Development, 56,* 1314–1325.

Lengua, L. J., West, S. G., & Sandler, I. N. (1998). Temperament as a predictor of symptomatology in children: Addressing contamination of measures. *Child Development, 69,* 164–181.

Lounsbury, M., & Bates, J. (1982). The cries of infants of differing levels of perceived temperamental difficultness. *Child Development, 53,* 677–686.

Lozoff, B. (1998). Exploratory mechanism for poorer development in iron-deficient anemic infants. In *Nutrition, health and child development. Pan American Health Organization Scientific Monograph Number 566* (pp. 162–178). Washington, DC: Pan American Health Organization.

Lozoff, B., Felt, B., Nelson, E., Wolf, A., Meltzer, H., & Jimenez, E. (1995). Serum prolactin levels and behavior in infants. *Biological Psychiatry, 37,* 4–12.

Maccoby, E., Snow, M., & Jacklin, C. (1984). Children's disposition and mother child interactions at 12 and 18 months. *Developmental Psychology, 20,* 459–472.

Martin, R., & Halverson, C. (1991). Mother–father agreement in temperament ratings: A preliminary investigation. In J. Strelau & A. Angleitner (Eds.), *Explorations in temperament: International perspectives on theory and measurement* (pp. 235–248). New York: Plenum Press.

Martin, R., Wisenbaker, J., Baker, J., & Huttenen, M. (1997). Gender differences in temperament at six months and five years. *Infant Behavior and Development, 20,* 339–347.

Martin, R. P. (1989). Activity level, distractibility, and persistence: Critical characteristics in early schooling. In G. A. Kohnstamm, J. E. Bates, & M. K. Rothbart (Eds.), *Temperament in childhood* (pp. 451–461). New York: Wiley.

Masarro, D. (1987). *Speech perception by ear and eye.* Hillsdale, NJ: Erlbaum.

Matheny, A. (1991). Play assessment of infant temperament. In C. Schaefer, K. Gitling, & A. Sandgrund (Eds.), *Play diagnosis and assessment* (pp. 39–63). New York:Wiley.

Matheny, A. P., Jr. (1989a). Injury prevention and temperament. In W. B. Carey & S. C. McDevitt (Eds.), *Clinical and educational applications of temperament research* (pp. 103–106). Berwyn, PA: Swets North America.

Matheny, A. P., Jr. (1989b). Temperament and cognition: Relations between temperament and mental test scores. In G. A. Kohnstamm, J. E. Bates, & M. K. Rothbart (Eds.), *Temperament in childhood* (pp. 263–282). New York: Wiley.

Matheny, A. P., Jr., Wilson, R. S., & Thoben, A. S. (1987). Home and mother: Relations with infant temperament. *Developmental Psychology, 23,* 323–331.

McCall, R. (1986). Issues of stability and continuity in temperament research. In R. Plomin & J. Dunn (Eds.), *The study of temperament: Changes, continuities, and challenges* (pp. 13–26). Hillsdale, NJ: Erlbaum.

Mebert, C. (1991). Dimensions of subjectivity in parents' ratings of infant temperament. *Child Development, 62,* 352–361.

Munro, N. (1987). A two year study of iron deficiency and behavior in rhesus monkeys. *International Journal of Biosocial Research, 9*, 35–62.

Neisser, U., Boodo, G., Bouchard, T., Boykin, A., Brody, N., Ceci, S., Halpern, D., Loehlin, J., Perloff, R., Sternberg, R., & Urbina, S. (1996). Intelligence: Knowns and unknowns. *American Psychologist, 51*, 77–101.

Newman, D., Caspi, A., Silva, P., & Moffitt, T. (1997). Antecedents of adult interpersonal functioning. *Developmental Psychology, 33*, 206–217.

Newman, D., O'Callaghan, M., Harvey, J., Tudehope, D., Gray, P., Burns, Y., & Mohay, H. (1997). Characteristics at four months follow-up of infants born small for gestational age. *Early Human Development, 49*, 169–181.

Park, S., Belsky, J., Putnam, S., & Crnic, K. (1997). Infant emotionality, parenting and 3 year inhibition. *Developmental Psychology, 33*, 218–227.

Patterson, G. (1982). *Coercive family process.* Eugene, OR: Castalia Press.

Pedlow, R., Sanson, A. V., Prior, M., & Oberklaid, F. (1993). The stability of temperament from infancy to eight years. *Developmental Psychology, 29*, 998–1007.

Pettit, G., & Bates, J. (1984). Continuity of individual differences in the mother infant relationship from 6 to 13 months. *Child Development, 55*, 729–739.

Plomin, R., DeFries, J., & Loehlin, J. (1977). Genotype environment interaction and correlation in the analysis of human development. *Psychological Bulletin, 84*, 309–322.

Plomin, R., Emde, R., Braungart, J., Campos, J., Corley, R., Fulker, D., Kagan, J., Reznick, J., Robinson, J., Zahn-Waxler, C., & DeFries, J. (1993). Genetic change in continuity from 14 to 20 months. *Child Development, 64*, 1354–1376.

Prior, M., Sanson, A., & Oberklaid, F. (1989). The Australian temperament project. In G. Kohnstamm, J. Bates, & M. Rothbart (Eds.), *Temperament in childhood* (pp. 537–556). New York: Wiley.

Ratekin, C. (1996). Temperament in children with Down's syndrome. *Developmental Disabilities Bulletin, 24*, 18–32.

Ricciuti, H., & Breitmeyer, B. (1988). Observational assessment of infant temperament in the natural setting of a newborn nursery. *Merrill-Palmer Quarterly, 34*, 281–299.

Riese, M. (1987). Longitudinal assessment of temperament from birth to two years. *Infant Behavior and Development, 10*, 347–363.

Riese, M. (1990). Neonatal temperament in monozygotic and dizygotic twin pairs. *Child Development, 61*, 1230–1237.

Riese, M. (1992). Temperament prediction for neonate twins: Relation to size for gestational age in same-sex pairs. *Acta Geneticae Medicae et Gemellologiae: Twin Research, 41*, 123–135.

Riese, M. (1994). Discordant twin pairs: The relation between gestational age and neonatal temperament differences in co-twins. *Acta Geneticae Medicae et Gemellologiae: Twin Research, 43*, 165–173.

Robinson, J., Kagan, J., Reznick, J., & Corley, R. (1992). The heritability of inhibited and uninhibited behavior. *Developmental Psychology, 28*, 1030–1037.

Robson, A., & Cline, B. (1998). Developmental consequences of intrauterine growth retardation. *Infant Behavior and Development, 21*, 331–344.

Rothbart, M. (1986). Longitudinal observations of infant temperament. *Developmental Psychology, 22*, 356–365.

Rothbart, M. K. (1989). Biological processes of temperament. In G. A. Kohnstamm, J. E. Bates, & M. K. Rothbart (Eds.), *Temperament in childhood* (pp. 77–110). New York: Wiley.

Rothbart, M. (1991). Temperament: A developmental framework. In J. Strelau & A. Angleitner (Eds.), *Explorations in temperament: International perspectives on theory and measurement* (pp. 61–74). New York: Plenum Press.

Rothbart, M. K., Ahadi, S. A., & Hershey, K. L. (1994). Temperament and social behavior in childhood. *Merrill-Palmer Quarterly, 40,* 21–39.

Rothbart, M. K., & Bates, J. E. (1998). Temperament. In W. Damon (Series Ed.) & N. Eisenberg (Vol. Ed.), *Handbook of child psychology: Vol. 3. Social, emotional, and personality development* (5th ed., pp. 105–176). New York: Wiley.

Rothbart, M., & Derryberry, D. (1981). Development of individual differences in temperament. In M. Lamb & A. Brown (Eds.), *Advances in developmental psychology* (Vol. 1, pp. 37–86). Hillsdale, NJ: Erlbaum.

Rubin, K., Hastings, P., Stewart, S., Henderson, H., & Chen, X. (1997). The consistency and concomitants of inhibition. *Child Development, 68,* 467–483.

Sajaniemi, N., Salokorpi, T., & vonWendt, L. (1998). Temperament profiles and their role in neurodevelopmental assessed pre-term children at two years of age. *European Child and Adolescent Psychiatry, 7,* 145–152.

Sameroff, A., Seifer, R., & Elias, P. (1982). Sociocultural variability in infant temperament ratings. *Child Development, 53,* 164–173.

Sanson, A. V., Prior, M., & Kyrios, M. (1990). Contamination of measures in temperament research. *Merrill-Palmer Quarterly, 36,* 179–192.

Saudino, K. (1997). Moving beyond the heritability question: New directions in behavioral genetics studies of personality. *Current Directions in Psychological Science, 6,* 86–90.

Saudino, K., & Eaton, W. (1991). Infant temperament and genetics. *Child Development, 62,* 1167–1174.

Saudino, K., McGuire, S., Reiss, D., & Hetherington, E. (1995). Parent ratings of EAS temperaments in twins, full siblings, half siblings, and step siblings. *Journal of Personality and Social Psychology, 68,* 723–733.

Saudino, K., Plomin, R., & DeFries, J. (1996). Tester rated temperament at 14, 20 and 24 months. *British Journal of Developmental Psychology, 14,* 129–144.

Schuler, M., Black, M., & Starr, R. (1995). Determinants of mother infant interaction. *Journal of Clinical Child Psychology, 24,* 397–405.

Seifer, R., Sameroff, A., Barrett, L., & Crafchuk, E. (1994). Infant temperament measured by multiple observations and mother report. *Child Development, 65,* 1478–1490.

Sheeber, L. (1995). Empirical dissociations between temperament and behavior problems. *Merrill-Palmer Quarterly, 41,* 554–561.

Simeon, D., & Grantham-McGregor, S. (1990). Nutritional deficiencies and children's behavior and mental development. *Nutrition Research Review, 3,* 1–24.

Slabach, E., Morrow, J., & Wachs, T. D. (1991). Questionnaire measurement of infant and child temperament: Current status and future directions. In J. Strelau & A. Angleitner (Eds.), *Explorations in temperament: International perspectives on theory and measurement* (pp. 205–234). New York: Plenum Press.

Spinath, F., & Angleitner, A. (1998). Contrast effects in Buss and Plomin's EAS Questionnaire. *Personality and Individual Differences, 25,* 947–963.

Steinmetz, J. (1994). Brain substrates of emotion and temperament. In J. Bates & T. D. Wachs (Eds.), *Temperament: Individual differences at the interface of biology and behavior* (pp. 17–46). Washington, DC: American Psychological Association.

Stevenson-Hinde, J., & Hinde, R. (1986). Changes in associations between characteristics and interactions. In R. Plomin & J. Dunn (Eds.), *The study of temperament: Changes, continuities, and challenges* (pp. 115–130). Hillsdale, NJ: Erlbaum.

Strelau, J. (1989). The regulative theory of temperament as a result of east–west influences. In G. A. Kohnstamm, J. E. Bates, & M. K. Rothbart (Eds.), *Temperament in childhood* (pp. 35–48). New York: Wiley.

Thoman, E. (1990). Sleeping and waking states of infants. *Neuroscience and Biobehavioral Reviews, 14,* 93–107.

Thomas, A., Chess, S., & Birch, H. (1968). *Temperament and behavior disorders in children.* New York: New York University Press.

Thomas, A., Chess, S., Birch, H. G., Hertzig, M. E., & Korn, S. (1963). *Behavioral individuality in early childhood.* New York: New York University Press.

Van den Boom, D. (1994). The influence of temperament and mothering on attachment and exploration: An experimental manipulation of sensitive responsiveness among lower-class mothers and irritable infants. *Child Development, 65,* 1457–1477.

Van den Boom, D. (1995). Do first year intervention effects endure: Follow-up during toddlerhood of a sample of Dutch irritable infants. *Child Development, 66,* 1798–1816.

Van den Boom, D., & Gravenhorst, J. (1995). Prenatal and perinatal correlates of neonatal irritability. *Infant Behavior and Development, 18,* 117–121.

Van den Boom, D., & Hoeksma, J. (1994). The effect of infant irritability on mother infant interaction. *Developmental Psychology, 30,* 581–590.

Vaughn, B., Contreras, J., & Seifer, R. (1994). Short term longitudinal study of maternal ratings of temperament in samples of children with Down's syndrome and children who are developing normally. *American Journal on Mental Retardation, 98,* 607–618.

Wachs, T. D. (1987). Short term stability of aggregated and nonaggregated measures of parent behavior. *Child Development, 58,* 796–797.

Wachs, T. D. (1988). Relevance of physical environment influences for toddler temperament. *Infant Behavior and Development, 11,* 431–445.

Wachs, T. D. (1992). *The nature of nurture.* Newbury Park, CA: Sage.

Wachs, T. D. (1994). Fit, context and the transition between temperament and personality. In C. J. Halverson, G. A. Kohnstamm, & R. P. Martin (Eds.), *The developing structure of temperament and personality from infancy to adulthood* (pp. 209–220). Hillsdale, NJ: Erlbaum.

Wachs, T. D. (1996). Known and potential processes underlying developmental trajectories in childhood and adolescence. *Developmental Psychology, 32,* 796–801.

Wachs, T. D. (1999). The what, why and how of temperament. In T. LeMonda & L. Balter (Eds.), *Child psychology: A handbook of contemporary issues* (pp. 23–44). New York: Garland.

Wachs, T. D. (2000a). *Necessary but not sufficient: Multiple influences on human development.* Washington, DC: American Psychological Association.

Wachs, T. D. (2000b). Linking nutrition and temperament. In D. Molfese & T. Molfese (Eds.), *Temperament and personality development across the life span* (pp. 57–84). Hillsdale, NJ: Erlbaum.

Wachs, T. D., Bishry, Z., Sobhy, A., McCabe, G., Shaheen, F., & Galal, O. (1993). Relation of rearing environment to adaptive behavior of Egyptian toddlers. *Child Development, 67,* 586–604.

Wachs, T. D., & King, B. (1994). Behavioral research in the brave new world of neuroscience and temperament: A guide to the biologically perplexed. In J. Bates & T. D. Wachs (Eds.), *Temperament: Individual differences at the interface of biology and behavior* (pp. 307–336). Washington, DC: American Psychological Association.

Wachs, T. D., & Plomin, R. (1991). *Conceptualization and measurement of organism environment interaction.* Washington, DC: American Psychological Association.

Walter, T., de Andraca, I., Chadud, P., & Perales, C. (1989). Iron deficiency anemia: Adverse affects on infant psychomotor development. *Pediatrics, 84,* 7–17.

Wilson, R., & Matheny, A. (1986). Behavior genetics research in infant temperament. In R. Plomin & J. Dunn (Eds.), *The study of temperament: Changes, continuities, and challenges* (pp. 81–97). Hillsdale, NJ: Erlbaum.

Windle, M. (1988). Psychometric strategies of measures of temperament: A methodological critique. *International Journal of Behavioral Development, 11*, 171–201.

Wohlwill, J., & Heft, H. (1987). The physical environment and the development of the child. In I. Altman & J. Stokols (Eds.), *Handbook of environmental psychology* (pp. 281–328). New York: Wiley.

Worobey, J. (1986). Convergence among assessments of temperament in the first month. *Child Development, 57*, 47–55.

Worobey, J., & Blajda, V. (1989). Temperament ratings at two weeks, two months and one year. *Developmental Psychology, 25*, 257–263.

Zuckerman, M. (1991). *Psychobiology of personality.* Cambridge: Cambridge University Press.

Part III

Risk Factors in Development

Introduction

This section covers some of the major risk factors in infancy, including prenatal risk, poverty, mental and adjustment disorders, and sensory deficits. Additional potential risk factors such as prematurity, maternal employment and day care, safety, and nutrition, are discussed in Part IV, Contexts and Policy Issues.

The chapter by Fifer, Monk, and Grose-Fifer gives a detailed portrait of development during the prenatal period. This chapter focuses on both physiological development (especially the neurophysiology) and on behavior. Due to advances in fetal monitoring, a great deal more is known about human fetal behavioral development than even a few years ago. The authors point out the complex linkages between the environment of the womb and the development of the fetus, revealing that fetal development is not entirely genetically controlled. These linkages become particularly salient when the fetus is exposed to toxins that result in higher risk for birth defects. The chapter also covers risk factors associated with genetic and chromosomal abnormalities.

Powell's chapter focuses on intervention programs for infants at risk due to factors in the family environment, particularly the effects of poverty. How is this risk to be alleviated? Despite the importance of this question, Powell's careful review of research shows that the answers are surprisingly unclear due to variability between programs, between communities, and between research methods used to evaluate the programs. One clear finding is that parent education alone is not likely to have a significant impact on family functioning. Parent education, when combined with early education and enrichment for infants, is more likely to effectively support the healthy development of families at risk.

The chapters by Ozonoff and South, and by Gelfand, deal with risk associated with infant mental health factors. Gelfand offers a comprehensive overview of the important social and policy issue of making mental health diagnoses for infants. She places the current concerns for infant mental health into a historical and research context that has gradually accepted the value of diagnosis and treatment of infant psychological disorders.

She gives a complete overview of the current categories of infant adjustment disorders found in the *Diagnostic and Statistical Manual of Mental Disorders*, 4th edition (DSM-IV) of the American Psychiatric Association, and the *International Classification of Diseases* (ICD-10) of the World Health Organization. One of those disorders, infantile autism, is the topic of the chapter by Ozonoff and South. They give a thorough review of the developmental deficits of autistic infants, the current theories that attempt to explain it, and the current state of the research on the early diagnosis of autism. Because autism is relatively rare, finding the early signs of it in the general population is difficult. On the other hand, if convincing factors that distinguish autistic infants from those who are not can be found during the first year, it may open new possibilities for treatment and prevention.

The final chapter in this section, by Preisler, focuses on the development of infants born deaf, blind, and deaf-blind. The parent–infant communication in these cases highlights both similarities and differences with normally developing infants. Preisler's review of research shows that the developmental course of the parent–infant relationship in sensory-deficit infants is similar to that of normally developing infants, especially if the parents have the skills to understand and to adapt to the child's sensory abilities, and allow the child to take an active part in the communication. Since parents often have little experience with sensory deficits, they need education to enhance their abilities. While the sensory worlds of these children are different from children without such impairments, they may be protected from consequent social and emotional difficulties under appropriate rearing conditions.

Chapter Eighteen

Prenatal Development and Risk

William P. Fifer, Catherine E. Monk, and Jill Grose-Fifer

Introduction

As is the case throughout infancy, normal fetal development demands constant and complex interactions between genes, environment, and the emerging organism. Although certain developmental pathways are more highly canalized than others, that is, resistant to perturbations, the opportunities for altering trajectories are infinite. Adverse effects range from abnormal morphological and physiological growth to risks for adult-onset disease. Maternal stress, nutrition, and exposure to toxins are some of the agents that can play a role in causing changes in fetal development, which have implications for long-term health and functioning.

Fuller appreciation now exists regarding the long-term implications of the prenatal laying down of brain–behavior relationships. Up until recently, much of the child development literature that has considered the fetal stage has primarily emphasized physical development and/or malformations, with a focus on teratological risk factors. However, the intensely dynamic nature of the developing, fetal brain–behavior relationships and the relevance of this process for future functioning are becoming more and more evident. These dynamic processes reflect continuous fetal adaptation to a changing uterine environment.

This perspective suggests a paradigm shift in the examination of influences on child development. Although it is common to consider the postnatal environment, from socioeconomic status to parenting characteristics, as greatly affecting the child's trajectory, fetal research points to the striking relevance of the prenatal environment for fetal as well as child development. The impact of the prenatal environment occurs on multiple levels, from biochemical factors influencing gene expression in the fetus's neuronal circuitry to characteristics of the mother's lifestyle affecting the fetal milieu.

More specifically, cells acquire identities, axons are guided from the periphery to target, synaptic connections are induced and reinforced, and other cells are programmed to die based on and shaped by exquisitely timed, complex interactions between the genes and environmental input. At another level, sensory development too is shaped by the prenatal environment. For example, what the mother ingests will affect not only the biochemical supply for fetal neuronal growth but the future child's eating habits as well. Flavors and smells, as well as protein and vitamins, are passed on to the fetus. Therefore, in addition to receiving the required nutrients, the future baby is learning food preferences too. Another way by which the maternal environment shapes the fetal environment is via maternal mood. For example, exposure to life stress affects maternal physiology and appears to be associated with long-term changes in their offsprings' future behavior and stress reactivity. These data suggest that mood-based alterations in maternal physiology amount to a changed environment affecting the fetus, although the precise mechanisms of such influence have yet to be established.

In what follows, we describe fetal neurobehavioral development throughout gestation and, in particular, focus on the role of the *in utero* environment in facilitating – and altering – fetal growth and behavior. Until recently, the richness and complexity of both fetal behavior and the *in utero* environment were inaccessible or largely ignored. The dynamic and complex nature of these fetal–environment interactions demands multiple perspectives as well as interdisciplinary research. Today, investigations from diverse disciplines such as epidemiology, obstetrics, neurobiology, genetics, neonatology, and psychobiology provide novel methods, perspectives, and results in the search for the fetal roots of human behavior.

The First Trimester

The Developing Embryo

The window of opportunity for environmental shaping of infant development actually opens prior to conception. For example, both male and female fertility is affected by nutrition and stress (Negro-Vilar, 1993; Wynn & Wynn, 1994), smoking (Adlerete, Eskenazi, & Sholtz, 1995; Fraga, Motchnik, Wyrobek, Rempel, & Ames, 1996) and alcohol consumption (Grodstein, Goldman, & Cramer, 1994). Once the sperm and egg unite, the genetic material from the mother and father combine to make a blueprint for infant development, but ample opportunity will arise for environmental input. Once the egg has been fertilized, it begins moving slowly through the fallopian tube to the uterus. The timing of its arrival is critical in order for the pregnancy to be sustained. The uterine lining is being made ready, under the influence of progesterone produced by the corpus luteum. It has been suggested that dieting can reduce the size of the corpus luteum, causing insufficient hormone levels to sustain pregnancy (Wynn & Wynn, 1994). Once the blastocyst reaches the uterus, it floats around for about three days, dividing continually. For conception to be successful, the ball of cells has now to implant in the wall of the uterus. Once the implantation has been successful, the embryo starts to secrete chemicals which enable signals eliciting a series of adaptations to the state of pregnancy. For example, the mucus in the cervix thickens to become a dense plug, which prevents any infection from entering the uterus and disrupting the pregnancy, and the immune system is modified so that the tiny embryo is not attacked (Roth et al., 1996). When the blastocyst implants in the uterine lining, the outer layer of cells, called the trophoblast, multiplies rapidly. These cells perform many important functions in forming various protective and support systems for the fetus. Some cells have already differentiated to form the amniotic sac, which will contain the amniotic fluid in which the fetus will develop, and the yolk sac, which is the early blood cell factory for the fetus. Some trophoblast cells fuse to form a protective cushion around the amniotic sac (the chorion), while others aggregate to form columns which stick to and then invade the uterine lining (chorionic villi). Recent research has shown that the formation of these columns is an essential part of first trimester placental growth, and that maternal smoking can actually decrease the number of columns that are formed (Genbacev, Bass, Joslin, & Fisher, 1995). Recreational exercise, on the other hand, is thought to have a beneficial effect and may even promote placental growth (Clapp & Rizk, 1992). Placental growth is largely dependent on the growth of these villi, which gradually lengthen and then the tiny blood vessels within them expand (Jackson, Mayhew, & Boyd, 1992).

The fetus is attached to the chorion via a short stem, which develops into the umbilical cord by 14 weeks of pregnancy. It is at the very tip of the thread-like capillaries within the chorionic villi that the exchange of oxygen and nutrients from the mother's blood vessels occurs. The blood of the fetus and mother do not intermingle (this is why mother and child can have different blood types): Instead, substances (both beneficial and harmful) diffuse through the thin membranes separating the maternal and fetal bloodstreams. Thus, the walls of the blood vessels act as a filter. The growth of the placenta is influenced both by hormonal control and by metabolism, and recent scientific evidence suggests that even some of the growth hormones may be under the influence of nutrients (Robinson et al., 1995). Not surprisingly, placental growth affects fetal growth and, as will be discussed later, research also suggests that babies who are disproportionately small at birth are at higher risk for coronary heart disease and hypertension in later life. It has been suggested that these diseases are "programmed" by inadequate nutrition to the developing fetus (Godfrey & Baker, 1995). (See subsequent section on Nutrition.)

Nervous System Development

During the first few months of gestation, a hierarchy of control systems emerges within the nervous system that largely determines what the fetus is doing and when. The hierarchical structure becomes more complex as the fetus develops. The more functions in the fetus's repertoire, the greater the need for organization by the nervous system. Initially, the fetus's behaviors are of a reflexive nature, and the circuitry controlling them may consist only of a few sensory cells directly connected to some motor cells, which may even be found in the spinal cord and work independently of the brain (Hofer, 1981). The spinal cord is made up of nerves that carry messages back and forth from the trunk and limbs to the brain. The types of behavior mediated by the spinal cord are likely to be the early movements seen starting around 7–8 weeks of the pregnancy.

The emergence of the senses follows a predetermined pattern of development that is similar in all mammals. The first sensory system to develop is touch. By about 9 weeks, if the area around the lips is touched, the fetus will respond by moving. By 12 weeks the fetus will begin to make grasping movements when the fingers are touched. The sense of taste and smell becomes functional next, then the vestibular system, which gives a sense of balance and position at 14 weeks. The auditory system begins to function at about 21 weeks, and finally vision at 26 weeks. It is fascinating that in the development of all of these senses, the systems work *in some basic way,* even before they are anatomically complete (Hofer, 1981). In terms of memory, language and thought, the control and integration of movement and the senses, the primary part of the brain responsible is the cerebral cortex, the outer crust of the hemispheres. For the first two or three months of pregnancy there is relatively little development in this "crust." It is not surprising, therefore, that behaviors emerging before this time, for example, early fetal movements, are largely reflexive and are controlled via simpler circuits that arise in the midbrain (Flower, 1985).

The cerebral hemispheres develop from the forebrain at about 9 weeks and rapidly increase in size, expanding to form different regions that will later become highly specialized. By mid-pregnancy, the cerebral hemispheres have expanded so much that they cover the rest of the brain. By the fourth month of pregnancy, the cells in the cerebral hemispheres begin to proliferate and migrate (Lou, 1982). As these higher centers of the brain develop, and more neural inputs become active, increasingly sophisticated messages can be sent from the brain. Particularly important at this time is that the process of inhibition becomes functional. This means when the fetus's brain sends a nerve impulse to the muscles, instead of only being able to cause movement, it can now begin to modify it. Consequently, this eventually leads to better control and refinement of movement. A by-product of this process is that at about 15 weeks there is a bit of a lull in activity. This is followed by a period of reorganization of behaviors: reflexive circuits are still in place, but these are now "controlled" by more sophisticated nerve cells in the new "higher" brain centers.

Emerging Behavioral Repertoire

One of the earliest movements the child will make is a startle, where the fetus's arms and legs shoot outwards in abrupt fashion. These occur at about 8 weeks of pregnancy. Within a week following this, the child will make graceful general movements of the head, trunk, and limbs. A stretch is usually seen for the first time at about 10 weeks: the fetus's head moves back, the trunk arches, and the arms are lifted into the air. Yawning usually begins a week later (DeVries, 1992).

Why does the fetus move so much? In a sense, it is because she is unable to stop. The neural circuits that control movement are very rudimentary at this time. Early in development, the circuit may be confined to the spinal cord, which is made up of nerve fibers carrying messages back and forth to the trunk and limbs. As the child develops, so these pathways become more sophisticated, and connect in the midbrain. This is the most significant center of neural activity in the brain up until mid-pregnancy

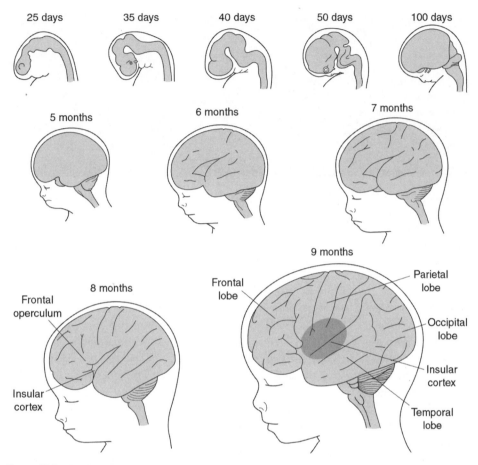

Figure 18.1 Brain centers.

(Flower, 1985). Once these early nerve cells start firing, the fetus starts moving. It is not until the birth of nerve cells which inhibit behavior and which can modify the action of these primitive circuits that the fetus has longer periods of rest (Hofer, 1981). Many more neurons than are needed develop between the limbs and the brain, and once the full range of co-coordinated movement is established in the fetus, some of these cells die off. It appears that fetal movement is necessary in order for the physical systems to develop normally and stimulates further development of muscles, tendons, and ligaments (DeVries, 1992). If muscles are immobilized during development, then joints can fuse and make future movement an impossibility (Pittman & Oppenheim, 1979). Additionally, frequent changes in position, head rotations followed by rump rotations, alternating extensions of the legs and bending the head backwards may promote better circulation and help to prevent skin from sticking together and forming adhesions (DeVries, 1992).

These motor behaviors result in the movement of amniotic fluid through the fetal body. Originally it was thought that a major role of this fluid was a protective one, since it cushions the fetus when the mother moves around. However, it now

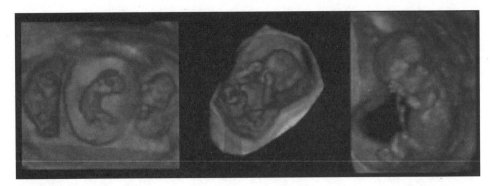

Figure 18.2   From left to right, photos are images of first trimester fetuses captured by noninvasive 3D ultrasound. Photo 1 is 11-week-old triplet fetuses, photo 2 is a 12-week-old fetus with arms brought to face, and photo 3 is a 13-week-old singleton fetus. (Photos courtesy of (1) Dr. Martin Metzenbauer, Austria; (2) Dr. Armin Breinl, Austria; (3) Dr. Leonardo Mandujano, Chile)

appears that the movement of amniotic fluid through the fetal body is extremely important for normal structural growth of the fetus, particularly in relation to lung and gut development (DeVries, 1992). It is likely that movement alone, when amniotic fluid passes through the fetal body, provides physical stimulation for the development of certain structures, such as the mouth, jaw, and palate. Jaw opening can be seen in the fetus toward the end of the first trimester. The emergence of sucking follows closely behind (DeVries, 1992). When the fetus sucks, her jaw opens and closes rhythmically at a rate of about once a second. When her mouth opens, her tongue is pushed against the roof of her mouth, creating suction and causing the amniotic fluid to move in and out. This pressure is probably responsible for the positional change of the bones in the palate at this time, and the prevention of cleft palate formation. It seems likely that early sucking could serve as "preparatory exercise" for nursing once the fetus is born (Prechtl, 1984). In addition to its later nutritive role, sucking may provide comfort to the newborn and perhaps even the fetus. Amniotic fluid surrounds the fetus and is contained within a membrane called the amniotic sac. This fluid is thought to be produced initially by the amniotic membrane itself. Later on, the fetus's lungs and kidneys are also important contributors to amniotic fluid. The vessels of the umbilical cord also may be involved in amniotic fluid production (Gebrane-Younes, Hoang, & Orcel, 1986). The exact composition of amniotic fluid varies throughout pregnancy, and a major constituent is fetal urine (Seeds, 1980). This fluid contains a high percentage of water, but its constituents are also thought to play a minor role in fetal nutrition. It has been suggested that amniotic fluid may provide 10 to 14 percent of the nutritional requirements of the fetus, but also contains some important growth-stimulating factors for the gastrointestinal tract (Mulvihill et al., 1985).

Once the child is born, breathing is of course necessary for the exchange of blood gases. In the fetus, breathing movements are thought to be vital for lung development, even though they do not cause any exchange of blood gases. These movements are usually seen for the first time around the end of the first trimester (DeVries, 1992). Sometimes just one breathing movement is made, often resembling a sigh, whereas at other times there may be short periods of regular or irregular breathing movements. Although fetal breathing does not cause amniotic fluid to move in and out of the lungs themselves, they do cause large changes in tracheal pressure and to-and-fro flow within the bronchial tree. The lungs are liquid-filled throughout fetal life. The lung liquid is produced by the lungs themselves and leaves by the trachea, where then it is either swallowed or exits the mouth into the amniotic fluid. This liquid keeps the lungs distended, which is necessary for them to develop properly. The volume of lung liquid is regulated by the resistance provided by the upper airways. During breathing movements, the larynx is dilated and resistance to the lung liquid is reduced; however, contractions of the diaphragm retard liquid loss during breathing movements (Hooper & Harding, 1995). Since neural control is operating at a very basic level at this stage in development, hiccups are seen more frequently than breathing movements, although both result in the movement of the diaphragm. This is probably because hiccups represent a reflexive type of behavior, whereas breathing reflects the development of more advanced motor patterns which currently are immature (Stark & Myers, 1995).

The Earliest Sensations

At the same time that the fetus is beginning to move, she is also developing a sense of touch. By about the ninth week of pregnancy, the fetus responds when her lips or the area around the mouth is touched. Initially the fetus moves her head and neck away from the source of touch, often with her mouth open: Later in pregnancy, the fetus will move toward the "touch." This is the precursor of the "rooting reflex," which helps the baby to find the nipple for nursing. Similarly, a little later in development, if the palm of the fetus's hand is stroked then her fingers will close for a moment and the toes curl if the sole of the foot is touched (Hepper, 1992). Once the fetus starts to move around she will be touching the uterine wall, the umbilical cord, and also herself. The fetus will touch her own face more frequently than any other body part. So the fetus is provided with a wide breadth of physical sensations which probably help to promote further development of the physical sensation of touch.

The Second Trimester

The Visual System

By the fourth month of pregnancy, the gross structures of the eyes are almost completely formed. The muscles of the eyes are not yet fully formed, but the eyes are already beginning to make movements. The fetus's eyes will sometimes make slow rolling movements, or faster movements that may be smooth or jerky in nature. These movements are probably important for further muscle development. Behind the lens, the neural part of the eye and its supportive network of tissues are developing. As yet, the light-sensitive cells – the rods and cones – are only present in the central area of the retina. However, the nerve cells that will connect with these light receptors have already grown long fibers or axons that have already reached the thalamus. This is considered to be the first relay station for visual information, which is then sent to higher centers of the brain. The lower visual pathways are now considered to be complete. In about the fifth month of pregnancy the cells within the thalamus become specialized to deal with various aspects of visual information, such as color, fine detail, and so on. Even though the connections may be present between the thalamus and the cortex, there is fairly little differentiation within the visual cortex at this stage in development.

The Chemosensory System

Chemosensory development encompasses both the gustatory and olfactory senses, but it is difficult to say exactly what the fetus can smell and taste. Both flavors and smells from the mother's diet can pass into her bloodstream and then into both the amniotic fluid and fetal blood. There are three possible sites where "chemosensation" can occur during development: the nose, the mouth, and via the bloodstream itself (Schaal, Orgeur, & Rognon, 1995). The fetus swallows amniotic fluid regularly throughout the day. This fluid passes into the stomach, where it will then be broken down further and sent to other organs, the brain, liver, and kidneys, before it is expelled from the bladder back into the amniotic fluid again. During the fourth month, the plugs of tissue that were previously blocking the nostrils have gone, and when the fetus "inhales," amniotic fluid also passes through the nose. The fetus actually inhales twice as much fluid as she swallows (Duenholter & Pritchard, 1976), so the sensory receptors within the nose are continuously being bathed in amniotic fluid. During the second half of pregnancy, the constitution of amniotic fluid becomes increasingly dependent on fetal urination. This may be particularly important for stimulation of the chemosensory system, since it contains large amounts of ammonia-smelling urea.

Flavors and smells from the food consumed will also pass into the bloodstream after digestion. These will then pass via the placenta into the fetal circulation blood. Unlike the amniotic fluid, the smells and tastes within the blood have not been broken down or metabolized and are relatively undiluted, and consequently more intense. The blood will flow in tiny capillaries through the fetal nose and mouth and therefore have ample opportunity to diffuse into the sensory apparatuses that detect smell and taste. It appears that nearly all babies show a preference for sweet substances over bitter. If the amniotic fluid tastes sweet then the fetus will swallow more regularly than if it contains bitter substances (Hepper, 1992). Not surprisingly, after a meal and when glucose levels rise within the maternal bloodstream and the amniotic fluid, there is more breathing and swallowing. The amniotic fluid probably tastes sweeter as a result of the additional glucose. Swallowing by the fetus will also regulate the volume of the amniotic fluid. While some of the fetus's ability to detect and prefer certain flavors over others may be genetically determined, other preferences may be learned *in utero*. Exposure to alcohol while in the womb has been shown to increase fetal swallowing and may cause preferences for alcohol later in life (Molina, Chotro, & Dominguez, 1995). It appears that preferences for smells may be more individually tailored for individual babies, depending on what flavors and smells they have been exposed to during life in the womb. Research with newborns has shown that babies can recognize the smell of their mother's breastmilk, and it has been suggested that this arises through the early learning about their mother's diet that took place in the womb. This has been particularly supported by studies that have shown that if a mother dramatically changes her diet after her pregnancy, her baby may have a more difficult time learning to suckle (Hepper, 1988).

The Vestibular System

As described above, the fetus does a lot of moving around *in utero*, constantly changing position within the warm amniotic fluid that cushions her from the outside world. Additionally, since the mother is moving about for much of the day, the fetus is also subjected to constant passive motion and will experience positional changes relative to gravity, depending on whether the mother is standing up, sitting, or lying down. This information is sensed by the vestibular apparatus consisting of three semicircular canals, set at right angles to each other within the fetus's inner ear. These canals are fluid-filled and when the fetus moves (or is moved) the fluid within at least one of the canals will move, stimulating tiny hairs within the canal lining. Depending on the direction and plane of movement, one semicircular canal may be stimulated more than another. This information is then sent to the brain to be processed and information about motion and position extracted.

Although it is difficult to elicit responses to vestibular stimulation in babies *in utero* (Hepper, 1992), this does not mean that this system is not functioning. By 25 weeks, the fetus will show a righting reflex (Hooker, 1952), and it is possible that the vestibular system is in some way responsible for most babies lying head down prior to delivery. We do not know exactly how much information about position and motion the fetus is actually processing at this time. We do know that the system is actively being stimulated, and that this stimulation is very important for many aspects of normal fetal growth and development. Vestibular stimulation plays an important role in changing arousal states, and this will become more apparent as time goes on. Initially, during the pregnancy, the fetus is often quiet when the mother is moving about a lot and causing a lot of vestibular stimulation. In contrast, when the mother is lying down at night, the fetus is receiving minimal vestibular stimulation and is often at her most active. Once the fetus is born, the parent will probably instinctively rock the fetus when she is fussy or to put her to sleep. Again, the vestibular system is being stimulated and may play a role in eliciting changes in the arousal state of the child. The level of vestibular stimulation received by the fetus during the pregnancy is particularly high. The activity alone provides a level of stimulation to the vestibular system that will probably not be matched until the baby starts to independently walk (Hofer, 1981). Studies of preterm infants (who are deprived of the vestibular stimulation that would have been provided by their mother's movement) have detected lags in neurobehavioral development which may in part be due to a lack of vestibular stimulation. Weight gain, visual responsiveness, and even later expressive language development have been shown to be improved if the incubator is gently rocked

(Masi, 1979). Along the same lines, if preterm babies are put on waterbeds instead of mattresses, the rocking movement of the water may compensate for the vestibular stimulation that they missed out on *in utero* and may result in better sleep organization (Korner, Schneider, & Forrest, 1983).

Brain Development

Month five is a time of considerable growth and reorganization within the fetus's brain. Much of the basic circuitry that controls reflexive acts is already in place in the spinal cord and the brain stem, the swelling at the top of the spinal cord. These areas of the brain will control many of the basic functions that the fetus will need to survive, such as breathing and temperature regulation. Other more sophisticated actions need more "processing" by the brain, and it is the cerebral cortex within the cerebral hemispheres that is responsible for this. This is a particularly important time for development within the cerebral hemispheres, which have now grown so much that they cover the rest of the brain (Cowan, 1979). They develop fairly late in relation to other brain structures and have a much longer developmental time course, not reaching full maturation until nearly adulthood. Maturation of the cerebral hemispheres is marked by three main events: First, the generation of nerve cells from the initially thin walls; second, the migration of cells to specific areas of the brain; and third, differentiation of the cells to become specialized to perform specific tasks (Kandel et al., 2000). Developmental neurobiologists have begun to discover the intricate intracellur processes, including complex gene–environment interactions, leading to cell birth, differentiation, and survival as well as the pathways by which axons reach their target neurons and how synapses are formed and elaborated.

Neural cells are rapidly generated in the walls of the cerebral hemispheres, starting around the third month of pregnancy. This process is still continuing at a rate of thousands of cells per second. Consequently, many more brain cells than ever will be needed by the fetus are created, and a normal part of further brain maturation is the pruning of some of these cells, often after the fetus is born. It may be that the excess of nerve cells is created as a safety measure. If some brain cells are nonfunctional or become damaged during development, others may be able to take over (Kandel, 2000).

As the cells are generated, so the process of migration begins. Each cerebral hemisphere is divided into four lobes, frontal, temporal, parietal, and occipital. Each of these lobes is thought to deal with specific functions. The frontal lobe is generally thought to be associated with movement. The parietal lobe is concerned with sensation of touch, pain, and limb position. The temporal lobe is important for hearing, memory, and a sense of self and time. The occipital lobe is the visual center of the brain. How do the newly generated brain cells know which area of the brain they have to migrate to, and how do they get there? It is likely that the actual vicinity where the brain cell was generated will in part determine its final location. However, there are probably other factors, such as the time or order in which the cells are programmed to migrate, that enter into the equation (Rakic, Stensas, Sayre, & Sidman, 1974; Sidman & Rakic, 1973). In addition to the nerve cells themselves, a network of supporting glial cells is growing; these provide support both structurally and functionally to the nerve cells. The glial cells form a supportive scaffolding for the nerve cells to migrate along to the surface of the cerebral hemispheres (Rakic et al., 1974). This migration causes the outer layer of the cerebral hemispheres to become densely packed with cells, and the outer surface takes on a grayish appearance, hence the name gray matter. Below this, many fibers from other deeper and earlier-formed nerve cells are invading the cerebral cortex, forming a whitish zone (white matter). Once formed, the nerve cells in the cerebral hemispheres will also send out nerve fibers to other nerve cells throughout the brain and the rest of the body. These too will pass through the white matter. Once the nerve cells have reached their target area in the cortex, they tend to form into distinctive layers.

It is likely that the generation of nerve cells has stopped in the cerebral cortex. However, the fetus's brain is continuing to grow in size and complexity. The bodies of the nerve cells themselves increase in size and, even more strikingly, the wiring between nerve cells has increased enormously. In order to contain all this nervous tissue within the relatively tight quarters of the fetus's skull, the brain surface begins to crumple up, forming grooves and humps (Cowan, 1979). The nerve cells themselves have to form many connections. This phase of neural development is progressing rapidly at this time. Messages from a nerve cell are sent via axonal processes. The axons usually travel long distances to connect with cells in specific areas of the brain or the rest of the body. For instance, a nerve cell in the motor cortex might have to make a connection with a muscle in the fetus's leg. A growth cone forms, which sends out tiny tubes that attach and then retract, pulling the growth cone forwards. It appears that the growth cone knows where it is going and with which structures it should make connections. The tube makes contact with many structures and "feels" the surface of the cell membranes, ensuring that connections only occur with those that are specific to the nerve cell and its axon (Lund, 1978).

In addition to brain development resulting from nerve–axon connections, nerve cells also make important links with other nerve cells via dendrites. When a nerve impulse travels along the axon and reaches the gap that separates it from the dendrites of the nerve cell, it causes the release of chemical substances into the gap which then act on the dendritic spine, causing the impulse to be transmitted to the connecting cell across the synapse. Cells that do not have many connections will be eliminated later in development. Connections are strengthened by experience; this is probably why fetal behavior and the *in utero* environmental factors that can impact on emerging fetal behavior are so important for normal development. A good example of this is seen with the fetus's early movements. Every time the fetus moves, nerve impulses are sent back and forth from the brain to the limbs, strengthening the connections between the synapses and ensuring that these movements continue to mature. It is known that early in development, one nerve cell may activate many muscle cells in a limb. However, as more nerve cells form connections, something closer to a 1 : 1 relationship develops between nerve cells and muscle cells, and the earlier connections from just one nerve cell become eliminated. This in turn allows for more sophisticated types of movement to develop (Hofer, 1981). Fetal breathing – which is dependent on nerve communication between the brain and abdomen, lungs, and thorax – is seen less frequently in fetuses of women who smoke and, as a consequence, these babies often have lung-related problems at birth (Milner, Marsh, Ingram, Fox, & Susiva, 1999).

In the sixth month of the pregnancy, axons begin to be myelinated. The myelin acts as an insulator for the nerves and prevents the leakage of the nerve impulses. This leads to an increase in speed in travel for the nerve impulses, which then results in a more fluent and rapidly responding system. Although myelination begins around the sixth month of pregnancy, this is really limited to the lower centers of the brain and by birth much of the baby's brain will still be unmyelinated. It is likely that the first area of cerebral cortex that undergoes myelination is the primary motor cortex, the area of the brain that controls the fetus's movements. The first nerve cells that become functional are those which control the trunk and arms, and these also become myelinated well before those governing leg movement. This is why babies will have relatively well coordinated arm and hand movements long before they begin to walk (Kolb & Wishaw, 1985). The primary sensory areas of the cortex concerned with processing information from the sense organs also mature after birth. Those fibers that are responsible for touch become myelinated first, followed by the primary visual system and then the auditory system. Among the last nerve fibers to become myelinated are those that belong to the corpus callosum, the bundle of fibers that connect one side of the brain to the other. Higher brain centers that integrate information are not completely myelinated until puberty. Although systems can still function in the absence of myelin, its formation leads to better neuronal stability and to a large increase in the speed at which messages between the nerves can travel (Hasegawa et al., 1992). It is estimated that the speed of transmission probably triples to over 60 ft per second once the nerves become myelinated (Purpura, 1975). The myelin coating is not of a uniform thickness, but becomes constricted at regular intervals. These constrictions in the myelin are called the Nodes of Ranvier, and the nerve impulses are thought to jump from node to node. The thickness of the myelin determines the speed of the transmission, and thickness continues to increase over a long period, for example, for about two years in the visual system (Magoon & Robb, 1981). The formation of myelin can be affected by multiple factors; prenatal exposure to lead may lead to problems with myelination, as can insufficient fat and fatty acids in the young infant's diet (Lampert & Schochet, 1968).

Expanding Behavioral Repertoire

Pregnant women may be just becoming aware of a faint fluttering sensation associated with fetal movements and a dramatic behavioral shift in activity reflecting major reorganizational changes within the brain. The neural circuits that can turn off or modify body movements (inhibitory pathways) are beginning to be in place, enabling distinct periods of rest instead of the almost continuous activity that occurs during the first trimester (Hofer, 1981). The repertoire of body movements remains the same as those seen in the first trimester, but what has changed is the frequency of the various movements (Nijhuis, 1995). There are now fewer startles, stretches, and general body movements. In the first trimester hiccups were one of the most frequently observed body movements, but now these occur much less often. However, breathing, another activity that also results in diaphragm movement, is becoming more frequent, increasing from an incidence of about 5 percent of the time to about 30 percent of the time (Visser, 1992). During these intervals breaths occur about once every second. Since breathing movements require a lot of energy, more breathing movements occur after a meal, since glucose levels are higher and more energy is available (Mulder, 1992). As described previously, although breathing movements do not result in any exchange of amniotic fluid, these prenatal movements are thought to be important for lung development. In addition to increased breathing, there is also an increase in the number of eye movements. Organized bursts of activity emerge followed by gradually lengthening periods of rest, with periods of total inactivity lasting up to 20 minutes.

The Auditory System

By the beginning of the sixth month, the auditory system ear is sufficiently developed to respond to sound. However, neither the ear nor the brain areas serving hearing are completely formed at this stage. One major immaturity can be seen within the sensors of the ear itself, i.e., the tiny hair cells within the cochlea, which vibrate when stimulated by sound and convert these vibrations into electrical messages that are then sent to the brain. Another immaturity is apparent within the nerve fibers which carry these messages. Consequently, the fetus's ability to hear different sounds is somewhat limited by these factors. However, almost all frequencies can be heard, although lower frequencies will be heard better than higher-pitched sounds (Abrams, Gerhardt, & Peters, 1995). The sounds that the fetus hears have to pass through various maternal tissues, which effectively cut out the higher frequencies; consequently, those sounds entering the fetus's ears are predominantly low-frequency ones. However, even though the auditory environment of the fetus is largely limited to lower-frequency sounds, it is quite varied. These include the background noises of mother's pulsing heartbeat, which changes constantly as both mother and fetus move and when maternal pulse and blood pressure change. Borborygmi are the gastrointestinal sounds associated with digestion, and these are part of the fetal sound experience. Mother's voice is by far the most frequently heard and loudest sound (Fifer & Moon, 1995). However, there is no unambiguous way of determining exactly what the fetus is hearing, since the mother is listening to sound traveling through air, whereas the fetus is listening to sound that has traveled through the amniotic fluid with no air spaces on either side of the eardrum. Furthermore, the rest of the auditory system is still immature, and so we do not know how well these sounds are converted into electrical signals by the sensors in the ear, or what the fetus's brain makes of these messages. However, we can learn something about what the fetus is hearing by looking at her response to sound (Hepper, 1992).

At this age, fetus's hearts beat faster in response to most sounds. Very loud sounds will result in a very fast heart rate. As the fetus gets older, her response will change based on the sound intensity, how deeply she is sleeping, and how familiar she is with the sounds (Lecanuet, Granier-Deferre, & Busnel, 1995). The fetus will also respond to some sounds by moving her limbs, or sometimes by stopping her movement in the middle of a high-activity period. One study has shown that fetuses will actually startle and empty their bladders following the loudest of sounds (Zimmer, Chao, Guy, Marks, & Fifer, 1993). Changes in brain electrical activity during sound stimulation have been measured

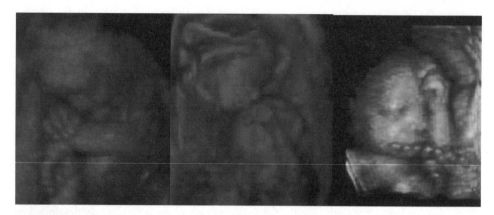

Figure 18.3   From left to right, photos are images of second trimester fetuses captured by noninvasive 3D ultrasound. Photo 1 is a 27-week-old fetus with limbs intertwined, photo 2 is 23-week-old twins, and photo 3 is a 23-week-old fetus showing face, arm, and umbilical cord. (Photos courtesy of (1) Dr. Armin Breinl, Austria; (2) Dr. Armand Vergnaud, France; (3) Dr. Juan Carlos Pons, Venezuela)

in prematurely born infants by 27 weeks gestational age. Sounds are thought to cause permanent changes in the developing auditory system which are probably required for normal brain maturation. Permanent changes are also reflected in newborn perceptual capacities and sound preferences as a newborn. Areas of the brain devoted to processing and remembering "multimodal" stimulation are probably also affected, since during some sound experiences several senses are activated at once. For example, when a mother speaks, her diaphragm moves, resulting in movement of the fetus; consequently those pathways that sense pressure, touch, and balance are also stimulated along with the auditory system.

The Third Trimester

The Visual System

By the seventh month of the pregnancy, the fetus's eyelids are no longer fused closed. The fetus will spend some time with her eyes open and will now be making blinking movements. Externally, the fetus's eyes will look fully formed. There are some still some minor immaturities in their gross structures, but the major source of immaturity in the fetus's visual system is within the neural structures of the eye, the retina, and the pathways to the brain. Nonetheless, if the fetus were born now, she would have some vision, even at this early age. Babies of this age can easily distinguish between light and dark (Taylor, Menzies, MacMillan, & Whyte, 1987) and have the ability to discriminate form to some extent (Dubowitz, Mushin, Morante, & Placzek, 1983). Certainly by 30 weeks of age, the premature newborn is able to see patterns of fairly large size provided that they are of sufficiently high contrast (e.g., black stripes on a white background) and fairly close to the baby's eyes (Grose & Harding, 1990). The fetus does have the basic "equipment" to be able to see, even though this ability is really not in use until birth. The lighting within the uterus is very poor. Only the very brightest of lights might provide a reddish glow but would not be sufficient even for an adult visual system to distinguish shapes clearly. The part of the brain associated with vision has a fairly protracted development, not surprising given the level of sophistication of the mature visual system. At this stage in development, the basic layered structure of the primary visual cortex is complete. The cells from the thalamus connect predominantly to the fourth layer of the visual cortex. The next important stage in visual development, the formation of many connections between the neurons in the visual cortex, is just beginning this month. These connections continue to develop post-natally, until the child is about 8 months of age (Huttenlocher & DeCourten, 1987). The most rapid period of connective development occurs after birth when the fetus's visual system is being stimulated by the external world. At this point in time the baby is proba-bly relatively near-sighted. However, by the time she is due to be born, the relative growth of the cornea and eyeball will compensate for this (Weale, 1982). Even though the curva-ture of the cornea and the length of the eye are coordinated by the time the baby is born, immaturities within the lens or perhaps the muscles working the lens will result in the baby having a relatively short range of focus. This is perfect for the task in hand, looking at the faces of the people that are holding her. The ability to focus on objects across the room will soon develop in the first months of life.

Physical Growth

Up until the beginning of the third trimester, much of the energy provided by the mother's diet has been used in forming the fetus's body and internal organs. Pigmented fatty tissue, brown fat, is now laid down on the fetus's muscles and under the skin, and as time goes on, so the size of the cells in the fatty tissue increases, leading to a thickening of this layer. Although the fetus is currently protected in the warm environment of the amniotic fluid and has no need to regulate her own temperature, this layer of insulating fat is impor-tant since it will help the fetus to maintain a constant body temperature once outside the womb. In addition to preventing heat loss by providing a layer of insulation, brown fat cells are actually capable of producing heat themselves. By the time the fetus is full-term there will be large stores of these concentrated in her back and neck. Ensuring an ade-quate maternal diet and a healthy lifestyle will enhance this important "fattening up" of the fetus's body. This is a time during which the fetus's size increases rapidly, and in the final month of the pregnancy the fetus will be gaining as much as 1 oz per day. Adequate maternal nutrition has been shown to be important in the formation of adequate fat deposits, and fasting during the last three months of pregnancy can dramatically alter this process (Lumey, Stein, & Ravelli, 1995). A daily caloric intake of approximately 2700 calories is thought to be necessary to maintain a healthy pregnancy. Prenatal exposure to tobacco and alcohol have also been shown to have an inhibitory effect on fat deposition in fetuses. A failure to acquire adequate fat deposits will also contribute to lower birth weights in these babies (Haste, Brooke, Anderson, & Bland, 1991). Low-birthweight chil-dren are not just poor at temperature regulation; these infants are at greater risk for many developmental problems, as will be described below in more depth.

Behavioral Organization

The fetus's behavior is becoming progressively more organized as she approaches term. She is no longer the continually moving creature of five months ago; instead she has distinct patterns of rest and activity. In fact, two dominant patterns of behavior have now emerged. The fetus will spend most of her time either in active sleep or quiet sleep. By this stage, the fetus will only be spending about 20 to 30 percent of her time in a deep sleep state, where she will remain motionless, her heartbeat steady, and her breathing movements when they occur are rhythmic. Not surprisingly, this state is known as quiet sleep. For most of the rest of the time the fetus will not be awake but in a state similar to neonatal active sleep. The fetus initiates many different body movements in this sleep state and the eyes move rapidly back and forth and open periodically. Heart rate and breathing patterns will tend to be irregular and the fetus will be responsive to the sensory stimuli that she is naturally exposed to in her uterine environment. During periods of active sleep the fetus may be more reactive to sounds and touch. Consequently most of the time, the fetus's brain is "buzzing" with electrical activity as messages about her environment are constantly being sent from her sense organs to the brain, and other signals generated by the brain itself are sent all over her body. In this way, many muscles and organs are all being stimulated or "exercised." It is thought that this level of activity is probably necessary for adequate development and further maturation of the vital organs and the nervous system. This is borne out by studies of mothers who took certain types of medication (chiefly for hypertension and depression) during pregnancy. These drugs were shown to reduce the amount of active sleep their babies experienced and as a result these babies were shown to have smaller heads, brains, brain cells, and fewer brain connections (Mirmiran & Swaab, 1992). The putative advantage of being able to carry out all this activity in a state of active sleep rather than wakefulness is to conserve energy.

The fetus is making fewer general body movements now – these movements probably only occur about 15 percent of the time. The fetus is also making breathing movements fairly frequently (about 30 percent of the time) and there is a barely perceivable slowing in the rate at which she breathes in comparison to one month ago (still about once every second). It is also likely that the fetus will be making more breathing movements approximately one hour after the mother has eaten. This is thought to be because more energy is available and breathing movements are very energy-consuming (Visser, 1992). These breathing movements are important for lung development, which is undergoing a vital period of maturation at this time in readiness for birth.

In contrast to one month ago, the 9-month-old fetus no longer spends quite as much time in a state of active sleep. In active sleep, the fetus makes general body movements, some breathing movements, and her heart rate tends to be irregular, often with large accelerations. Her eyes will move rapidly back and forth and probably even open and close from time to time. However, since the fetus's brain has matured in the last month, more inhibitory pathways have now developed, thus reducing the amount of movement the fetus performs. Consequently, the fetus will have longer periods when she is resting quietly in a deep sleep. In fact, she will now spend about half the time in this state. During quiet sleep, the fetus is quiet and not moving and her heart rate is steady. The fetus may or may not be making breathing movements, but when she does, these tend to be rhythmic and steady in nature (Nijhuis, 1992). On the whole, the fetus's activity and rest periods alternate cyclically throughout the day. Already the length of one entire activity–rest cycle has lengthened from that seen one month ago, and now probably lasts about 80 to 100 minutes (Visser, 1992). However, superimposed on this cyclical rhythm are maternal physiological factors such as hormone levels, breathing, heart rate, and uterine activity (Mirmiran & Swaab, 1992). Variations in some or all of these factors are thought to influence the fetus's behavior over the course of the day. In general there is a peak in activity occurring when the mother is asleep, in the late evening, and a relative lull in activity in the early hours of the morning (Patrick, Campbell, Carmichael, Natale, R., & Richardson, 1982).

The reflex behaviors that the baby will demonstrate after she is born, notably, breathing, rooting, sucking, and swallowing, are in place now. Another protective reflex that the baby will demonstrate is an eye blink in response to a rapidly approaching object or bright lights. Like the breathing reflex, this remains in place throughout life. Other reflexes that have less obvious functional significance include the toe-curling reflex, the finger-grasping reflex, and the startle reflex. These reflexes all disappear within the first year of life. Another reflexive behavior that has received a good deal of attention is the stepping reflex. If resistance is provided to her feet the fetus will make stepping movements, placing one foot in front of the other. This reflex usually disappears in the first two months after birth. There is some argument as to whether this activity is a kicking motion (Thelen, 1986) or whether it is the precursor of early walking (Zelazo, 1983). It has also been suggested that this reflex may help in the birthing process itself (Kitzinger, 1990).

Sensory Development

Some senses, such as touch, begin development early in pregnancy and this sense is probably the most highly developed at this stage in the fetus's life. When the fetus moves around she will be touching the uterine wall, the umbilical cord, and also herself. The fetus will touch her own face more frequently than any other body part. So the fetus is provided with a wide breadth of physical sensations which probably help to promote further development of the physical sensation of touch. Although initially the fetus would have moved her head and neck away from the source of touch, now she moves toward it with her mouth open. This is the precursor of the "rooting reflex," which helps the baby to find the nipple for nursing. Now if the palm of the fetus's hand is stroked her fingers will close for a moment and the toes will curl if the sole of the foot is touched (Hepper, 1992).

As was noted previously, it is difficult to separate the sense of taste and smell when the fetus is in the womb. However, we do know that the flavors and odors from foods that the mother eats are transmitted into the placental blood and the amniotic fluid. The taste buds within the tongue and mouth are probably present and being stimulated. The mechanism underlying the sense of smell is perhaps less clear. It is not known whether most stimulation of the "smell receptors" occurs when the amniotic fluid washes in and out of the nose, or when a more concentrated source of odor – the bloodstream full of nutrients (and odors) from the placenta – passes very close to these receptors (Schaal et al., 1995). The fetus is capable of hearing now, as is evidenced by changes in heart rate and/or movement in response to externally presented sounds (Lecanuet & Schaal, 1996) and by electrophysiological studies of preterm infants. During the final trimester the fetus is exposed to a wide variety of sounds, particularly the sound of her mother's voice, heartbeat, and stomach sounds, but also to external noises (Abrams et al., 1995; Fifer & Moon, 1995; Lecanuet & Schaal, 1996). As already noted, although the fetus's eyelids are now open and the child can see in a rudimentary way, there is very little stimulation of the visual sense while in the womb. This is probably the least developed of all the senses at birth. The maturation of the sense of vision is very dependent upon adequate stimulation (Blakemore & Cooper, 1970), which can only occur once the child emerges from the dark environment of the womb. However, a premature infant as young as 28 weeks can distinguish light from dark (Taylor et al., 1987), coarse patterns of high contrast (Grose & Harding, 1990), and track a highly colored object (Dubowitz, Dubowitz, Morante, & Verbhote, 1980). At this stage of development the infant's acuity is poor and is therefore unable to resolve fine detail (Dubowitz et al., 1983).

Learning and Memory

The fetus does exhibit some very basic early memory at this point in time. It is not really known how long these memories last, but many examples of uterine learning are present at birth. The uterine environment provides a rich array of sensory stimuli, from touch, smell, taste, and sounds, and it has been conclusively demonstrated that newborn babies recognize and show a preference for many types of stimuli that they were exposed to in the womb. Probably the most striking example of this is the preference that newborn babies show for their own mother's voice. Studies have shown a neonatal ability to discriminate sounds heard *in utero*, either the mother's voice or the language heard *in utero* (Mehler et al., 1988; Ockleford, Vince, Layton, & Reader, 1988). Contingent sucking procedures have been used to detect preferences for mothers' versus strangers' voices, native versus non-native language phrases, and recordings of mothers' voices filtered to simulate intrauterine speech (reviewed in Moon & Fifer, 2000). Other studies have looked at how a newborn baby is able to recognize the smell of his or her own mother's breast milk (Makin & Porter, 1989), and this is thought to be attributable to some familiarization with the odors and tastes from the mother's diet while in the womb. In fact, it has been shown that babies of women who change their diets dramatically after their baby is born, typically to a less spicy one, are more likely to experience feeding difficulties (Hepper, 1992). Other research has concentrated on demonstrating how a baby in the womb actually modifies his or her behavior over time in response to a particular type of stimulation. Researchers have shown that babies will move in response to a loud sound occurring only a few feet from the womb. However, if this sound occurs repetitively, the fetus is capable of demonstrating an early learning and memory capability, habituation and dishabituation to novel sounds (Hepper, 1995; Leader, 1995; Lecanuet et al., 1995; van Heteren, Boekkooi, Jongsma, & Nijhuis, 2000).

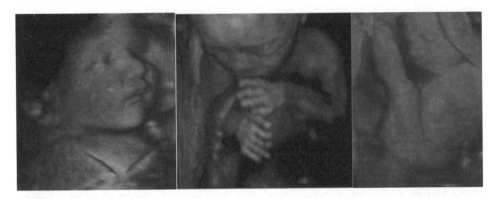

Figure 18.4   From left to right, photos are images of third trimester fetuses captured by noninvasive 3D ultrasound. Photo 1 is a 37-week-old fetus in quiet sleep, photo 2 is a fetus sucking, and photo 3 is of a 30-week-old fetus with limbs extended. (Photos courtesy of (1) Dr. Armin Breinl, Austria; (2) Obgyn.net; (3) Dr. Saied Tohamy, Egypt)

Labor will provide the final context for environmental input to shape or elicit adaptive behavior, or in some cases, to convey risk. The sensory perceptual experience of the fetus during contractions may stimulate independent respiration (Ronca & Alberts, 1995). Stimulation of catecholamine release may aid in the transition to postnatal life by, for example, protecting against birth asphyxia and promoting neurologic adaptation (Lagercrantz & Slotkin, 1986; Otamiri, Berg, Ledin, Leijon, & Lagercrantz, 1991). Thus, the normal fetus should emerge after nine months with a full complement of skills required to meet the next challenge, i.e., adaptation to environment of the infant. However, there is a wide range of individual differences in the capacity to respond to the postnatal environment, and some infants will be more vulnerable than others to atypical or at-risk developmental trajectories.

Risks to Fetal Development

Perinatal complications can have their origins in parental preconception conditions as well as emerge from gene–environment interactions throughout embryogenesis and gestation. Atypical developmental trajectories range from congenital malformations to subtle variations with apparent minor clinical significance (Ashmead & Reed, 1997; Sweeney, 1998). Two to 3 percent of newborns are diagnosed with frank congenital abnormalities and another 2 to 3 percent of children are identified as having them before age 2. Although numbers vary somewhat, it is estimated that for 50 percent of the congenital abnormalities, the cause remains unknown. Genetic factors are thought to account for roughly 10–15 percent of congenital defects, while environmental agents acting alone – such as alcohol, excess quantities of vitamin A, and radiation – are thought to cause another 10 percent of them. The rest of the congenital anomalies are believed to be the result of multifactoral causation, that is, the result of genes and environment interacting together (Ashmead & Reed, 1997; Milunsky & Milunsky, 1998). Some sources estimate that research will eventually show that multifactoral causation actually may account for up to 75 percent of these anomalies (Ashmead & Reed, 1997). Abnormal developmental trajectories – ranging from subtle to significant – also can be associated with intrapartum risks such as those resulting from labor complications, for example, hypoxia during delivery, or those resulting from multiple births, which can result in an increased incidence of low birth weight and preterm delivery (Tough, Greene, Svenson, & Belik, 2000).

In this section of the chapter, we cover some of the common abnormal infant phenotypes with well-mapped-out genetic etiologies (e.g., Down's syndrome). We next discuss some of the environmental risks for fetal development, traditionally known as teratogens (from the Greek word for monster, *teratos*). However, our focus here is on research exploring the mechanisms by which even subtle alterations in the intrauterine environment can influence fetal neurobehavioral development and have an impact on the child's long-term health. The effects of alcohol and smoking on fetal development are discussed, in addition to the influence of minimal alcohol use and environmental smoke exposure. Well-established aspects of prenatal nutrition are covered, such as folic acid, as well as new research linking weight gain during pregnancy and protein intake to the child's risk for heart disease. Finally, new data are discussed indicating that women's mood during pregnancy, specifically stress and anxiety, may affect fetal development.

Chromosomal Disorders

The DNA forming the human genetic code is stored in the cell nucleus in structures called chromosomes. Human chromosomes consist of 22 pairs called autosomes and two sex chromosomes (XX, for females; or XY, for males). In chromosomal defects, whole chromosomes are missing or duplicated, or parts of them are missing or duplicated. The most common abnormalities are monosomies, in which there is only one copy of chromosome pair, or trisomy, in which there are three representatives of a chromosome pair. Most monosomies are not viable, except for Turner's syndrome, in which the individual has an X chromosome and no second sex chromosome. A person with Turner's syndrome is phenotypically female but sterile. Overall, chromosomal abnormalities are seen in 1/200 live births and in 50–70 percent of first trimester miscarriages (Ashmead & Reed, 1997; Robinson, Linden, & Bender, 1998).

There are three major trisomies of the sex chromosomes, all of which survive. In Klinefelter's syndrome, individuals have XXY trisomy and are phenotypically male, but infertile. Individuals with XYY trisomy also are phenotypically male and often exhibit impulsive and aggressive behavior. XXX individuals have a female phenotype and are often retarded (Robinson et al., 1998).

There are three major autosomal trisomies. The most common is Down's syndrome, with three copies of chromosome 21. Down's syndrome is characterized by varying degrees of mental retardation, anomalous facial features, and, for approximately a third of the cases, serious heart defects. Extra copies of chromosomes 13 (Patau syndrome) and 18

(Edward's syndrome) result in severe defects of the central nervous system and morpho-logical malformations such as cleft lip (Ashmead & Reed, 1997).

Finally, some chromosomal abnormalities are the result of the translocation or rearrangement of chromosomal segments. Some affected individuals have no abnormal-ities, however they are at greater risk for producing gametes with chromosomal alterations in structure and/or number. New techniques have recently enabled researchers to iden-tify chromosomal microdeletions, which only span a few contiguous genes (Sweeney, 1998; Wilson, 1992).

Abnormal numbers of chromosomes are usually caused by an error in the separation of chromosomes into appropriate daughter cells during meiotic division. For reasons still only partially understood, there is a dramatic increase in the risk of chromosomal anom-alies with advancing maternal age. For example, risk of Down's syndrome at age 20 is 1/2000; at age 30 it is 1/1000; by age 37 it is 1/200 (Davidson & Zeesman, 1994; Hsu, 1998).

Single Gene Disorders

Disorders can result from a single gene abnormality or allele, dominant or recessive, on either an autosome or a sex chromosome. An allele is an alternative form of a particular gene. An autosomal recessive (AR) disorder will be expressed in a child when each parent (who is heterozygous) has one allele with the mutation, giving the child two of these alleles, one from each parent (making them homozygous). There is a 25 percent chance of heterozygous parents having an affected (homozygous) child. The risk of an affected individual having a child with the disorder depends on his or her partner's status with respect to the genetic mutation, and, therefore, on how rare the disease is. Research sug-gests that every individual is heterozygous for approximately 8–10 AR genes linked to disease. Examples of autosomal recessive genetic disorders are: sickle cell disease, cystic fibrosis, and Tay–Sachs disease. An autosomal dominant (AD) disorder will be expressed with just one abnormal allele present. A parent affected with an AD disorder has a 50 percent chance of passing this disease onto his or her child. Huntington's disease, Marfan syndrome, and polycystic kidney disease are examples of autosomal dominant disorders (Ashmead & Reed, 1997).

Sex-linked diseases or functional disorders are known as X-linked characteristics because in most cases there are no corresponding alleles on the Y chromosome. In X-linked inheritance, all daughters of an affected male are carriers and there is no male to male transmission. X-linked disorders can be recessive or dominant. Because males only have one X chromosome, an abnormal gene on an X chromosome results in disease in all affected males. For females to be affected by an X-linked disorder, they need either to be homozygous or to have most of their normal X chromosomes inactivated (called Lyonization). X-linked recessive disorders are: Duchenne muscular dystrophy and hemophilia.

X-linked dominant traits are expressed in females but most often lethal in males. Females survive the X-linked dominant disorders because of random inactivation of the abnormal X chromosome in half of females' cells, allowing for expression of the normal gene by the other normal X chromosome. Examples of X-linked dominant disorders include hypophosphatemic (vitamin D-resistant) rickets and Kennedy disease (spinal and bulbar muscular atrophy) (Ashmead & Reed, 1997). Certain ethnic groups are at greater risk for specific genetic disorders than others. For example, in Ashkenazi Jews (Jews of Eastern European descent), 1 in 30 is a carrier of Tay–Sachs disease, while approximately 8 in 100 African Americans from North America are carriers of the sickle cell gene (Davidson & Zeesman, 1994).

Environmental Influences

Alcohol

Heavy maternal alcohol consumption profoundly influences fetal and child development. The most severe effects are found in offspring of women alcoholics, who consume, on average, six standard drinks per day (one standard drink = 12 oz beer = 5 oz of wine = 1.5 oz of liquor or 15 g of absolute alcohol). For the children who survive, the effects include mild to severe physical anomalies and cognitive and behavioral impairments. However, other adverse fetal outcomes include increased risk for spontaneous abortion, stillbirth, premature placental separation, intrauterine growth restriction, and, some studies suggest, preterm birth – itself a risk factor for future health problems, poor development, and newborn mortality (Smigaj, 1997).

Children of women who abuse alcohol and who meet criteria for Fetal Alcohol Syndrome (FAS; approximately 1.97 per 1000 live births in the United States) have craniofacial dysmorphology, including smaller head circumference and a flattening of the nose area, other congenital anomalies, and long-term attention deficits as well as mental retardation. However, a subset of children do not meet the criteria for FAS but nonetheless show significant impairment related to their mothers' alcohol use during pregnancy. These children exhibit some of the behavioral and cognitive deficits associated with FAS and are referred to as having either prenatal exposure to alcohol (PEA), Fetal Alcohol Exposure (FAE), alcohol-related birth defects (ARBD), and alcohol-related neurodevelopmental disorders (ARND). The rates of babies born with these partial FAS syndromes are believed to be much higher than for frank FAS (Mattson & Riley, 1998; Roebuck, Mattson, & Riley, 1999). There are several possible pathways by which maternal alcohol use affects the developing fetus. Alcohol, which freely crosses the placenta, affects fetal cell activity. Specifically, alcohol increases cellular peroxidase activity, decreases DNA synthesis, disrupts protein synthesis, and impairs cell growth, differentiation, and neural cell migration. Alcohol also impedes placental transfer of amino acids and glucose, adversely affecting fetal growth, and alters the chemical makeup of maternal blood, causing maternal vasoconstriction and chronic fetal hypoxia (Hanningan, Saunders, & Treas, 1999; Smigaj, 1997).

The developmental timing and frequency of drinking episodes during pregnancy (e.g., maternal abstinence after the first trimester versus binge-drinking throughout pregnancy) can greatly alter the impact that maternal drinking will have on the fetus. In general, drinking during the first trimester results in craniofacial abnormalities, while exposure during the second and third trimesters coincides with the period of rapid brain development, influencing fetal central nervous system development. In particular, new research with animal models suggests that there may be an enhanced period of vulnerability to cerebellar cell loss in humans during the 24–32 weeks of pregnancy, when Purkinje cell dendritic growth is occurring (Goodlett & Johnson, 1999).

Recent studies based on autopsy reports and tools of modern neuroscience such as magnetic resonance imaging (MRI) have identified neuroanatomical variations in the brains of children with FAS. Autopsy reports indicate that the brains of FAS children are microencephalic (abnormally small). The MRI studies generally show reductions in the volumes of both the cerebral and cerebellar brain regions in FAS children. Follow-up reports of behavior and cognitive development indicate that significant *in utero* exposure to alcohol is associated with attentional deficits, mental retardation, and poor academic performance. Data from recent neuropsychological studies comparing FAS and PEA children to controls matched for age, gender, and ethnicity indicated that FAS and PEA children have lower overall IQ scores as well as lower scores on most subtests. Similar studies from the same laboratory suggest that FAS children perform less well on verbal measures of comprehension and naming ability, and have inferior fine-motor speed and coordination (Roebuck et al., 1999). These findings of cerebral cortex/cerebellum anomalies as well as cognitive and motor weaknesses in FAS/PEA children are consistent with current neuroscience research indicating the interrelatedness of cognitive and motor development (Diamond, 2000). It is clear that high levels of prenatal alcohol exposure have a dramatic and long-term impact on development, even when the strict criteria for FAS is not met. Because there is no known level of safe alcohol consumption during pregnancy and because the effects of lowered intake, although present, are likely to be subtle and hard to detect, complete abstinence during pregnancy is recommended (Smigaj, 1997).

Smoking

Despite major efforts to warn pregnant women of the dangers cigarette smoking poses for their fetus, smoking is still one of the most preventable risk factors for an unsuccessful pregnancy outcome (Bulletin, 1997). The adverse consequences of prenatal exposure to maternal smoking are well known; some of the newest research focuses on the effects of passive smoking or environmental tobacco smoke (ETS) during pregnancy on birth outcomes.

On average, babies born to smokers weigh 100–200 g less than those of nonsmokers and have twice the risk for fetal growth restriction (Horta, Victora, Menezes, Halpern, & Barros, 1997; Walsh, 1994). Furthermore, independent of the risks for lower birth weight, smoking is associated with risk for prematurity and perinatal complications, such as premature detachment of the placenta (Andres, 1996; Kyrklund-Blomberg & Cnattingius, 1998). Cigarette smoking also is associated with a two- to threefold increase for Sudden Infant Death Syndrome (SIDS) (Golding, 1997). Finally, more subtle effects of fetal exposure to maternal smoke have been found during childhood. Behavioral problems and cognitive weaknesses, including problems with attention and visuoperceptual processing, have been associated with smoking during pregnancy (Fried & Watkinson, 2000; Fried, Watkinson, & Gary, 1992; Wakschlag et al., 1997).

Maternal cigarette smoking adversely affects fetal development – often with long-term consequences for child health – by causing a chronic reduction in nutrient and oxygen delivery to the fetus as well as acute hypoxic injuries (Lambers & Clark, 1996). Nicotine and carbon monoxide are the two main agents of these effects. Nicotine induces vaso-constriction in the placental and fetal vascular beds, reducing oxygen and nutrient input to the fetus. Carbon monoxide, which binds to hemoglobin to form carboxyhemoglo-bin, reduces the oxygen-carrying capacity of blood. It also increases the affinity of hemo-globin for oxygen so that oxygen release to tissues is inhibited (Walsh, 1994). Because the fetus gains weight at a rapid rate during the third trimester, studies indicate that mater-nal smoking during this period has the greatest impact on fetal growth (Lieberman, Gremy, Lang, & Cohen, 1994). Smoking-induced reductions in oxygenation throughout pregnancy have far-reaching effects on cellular and tissue development in the fetus, influ-encing the development of the central nervous system and cardiorespiratory functioning, to name a few.

The strong effects that active smoking exerts on pregnancy outcomes has led researchers to investigate whether maternal exposure to environmental tobacco smoke (ETS) also has an influence on fetal development. New data indicate that even ETS poses risks for the fetus. Studies suggest that exposure to passive smoking during pregnancy is associated with reductions in fetal weight ranging from 25–40 g (Spitzer et al., 1990; Windham, Eaton, & Hopkins, 1999) as well as greater likelihood of a low-birthweight baby (Mainous & Hueston, 1994).

Nutrition

As described previously, in order to support the developing fetus, women must increase their caloric intake to reach between 2700–3000 calories per day. In addition, specific nutritional requirements must be met for healthy fetal development. For example, adequate amounts of calcium are needed for fetal bone, muscle, and transmitter pro-duction; sufficient supplies of iron are necessary for fetal red blood cell and tissue production (Judge, 1997). Recently, the central importance of folic acid to fetal devel-opment has emerged. Specifically, in the last ten years, research has shown that inade-quate amounts of folic acid are linked to serious congenital abnormalities known as Neural Tube Defects (NTD). Consisting primarily of anencephaly ("brain absence") and meningomyelocele (a protrusion of the brain), these NTDs are induced in the first 28 days of pregnancy when the early foundation of the spinal cord, the neural tube, is forming (Sweeney, 1998). Folic acid plays roles in nucleic acid and protein synthesis as well as in neural and red cell development, all of which are underlying processes in neural tube development (Judge, 1997). Because the impact of folic acid deficiency on fetal development cannot be reversed, it is recommended that women increase their folic acid intake prior to conception. On the other hand, because more than half of the pregnan-cies in North America are unplanned and because women living in poverty intake below optimal levels of folic acid, primary prevention of NTD has yet to be accomplished (Koren, 1994).

Recent research from epidemiological and animal studies indicates that independent of gross congenital anomalies, women's food intake and/or weight gain during pregnancy may subtly affect fetal development in ways that have implications for the child's future medical and mental health. For example, in several large samples, low birth weight has been linked to increased risks for future cardiovascular disease (CVD), and for factors, such as high blood pressure, associated with CVD (Clark et al., 1998; Law et al., 1993; Moore, Cockington, Ryan, & Robinson, 1999; Rich-Edwards et al., 1997). To account for this association, researchers hypothesize that aspects of the fetus's cardiovascular functioning are "programmed" *in utero* by maternal nutritional and/or hormonal factors (Barker, 1995). One line of investigation suggests that reductions in maternal protein intake decreases the activity of a placental enzyme that protects the fetus from maternal stress hormones, thereby exposing the fetus to elevated levels of these stress hormones, which is associated with lower birth weight and higher blood pressure in the offspring. Although the emerging data with human pregnancy are not entirely consistent with this hypothesis, animal studies support this line of thinking (Langley-Evans, 2000; Langley-Evans, Welham, Sherman, & Jackson, 1996). Other possible mechanisms that might account for the association between maternal protein intake, low fetal weight, and increased risk for CVD include the possibility that low protein intake reduces the size of the pancreas and glucose tolerance, leading to low birth weight and alterations in metabolism (Charif, Ahn, Hoet, & Remacle, in press).

New research also indicates that women's nutrition during pregnancy and baby's birth weight also might be markers for physiological processes that place the infant at risk for future breast cancer (Michels, Trichopoulos, Adami, Hsieh, & Lan, 1996; I. Morgan, Damber, Tavelin, & Hogberg, 1999) and psychiatric illness (Susser, Brown, & Matte, 1999). Specifically, epidemiological studies suggest that higher birth weight is associated with an increased risk for breast cancer (I. Morgan et al., 1999). Other studies based on the offspring of Dutch women pregnant during the Nazi food embargo ("the Dutch Hunger Winter") suggest that extreme undernutrition (less than 1000 calories a day) during first and second trimesters (and thus occurring during rapid brain reorganization) is associated with the risk of becoming schizophrenic or having antisocial personality disorder (Neugebauer, Hoek, & Susser, 1999; Susser et al., 1999). Although the mechanisms underlying these associations are not yet known, it is likely that future research will clarify the impact of variations in maternal nutrition and newborn weight on the child's physical and mental health.

Psychosocial Stress

Psychosocial stress during pregnancy has long been linked to negative birth outcomes such as low birth weight and prematurity (Istvan, 1986; Lobel, 1994; Lobel, Dunkel-Schetter, & Scrimshaw, 1992; Stott & Latchford, 1976). Current findings are largely consistent in pointing to stress-induced maternal vasoconstriction as contributing to diminished fetal oxygen and nutrient intake, and consequently, reduced birth weight and stress-elicited surges in stress hormones as precipitating labor and, consequently, early delivery (Lobel, 1994; Lobel et al., 1992; Wadhwa, Dunkel-Schetter, Chicz-DeMet, Porto, & Sandman, 1996; Wadhwa, Porto, Garite, Chiez-DeMet, & Sandman, 1998). However, it is only relatively recently that animal studies and research on fetal development have discovered the influence of maternal stress on fetal neurobehavioral development.

In animal models, offspring whose mothers are exposed to acute stress during pregnancy (e.g., electric shock) versus controls exhibit long-term changes in behavior and the regulation of stress hormones. Prenatally stressed animals show inhibited, anxious, fearful behavior throughout the life span, hypothesized to result from their excessive level of endogenous arousal. Specifically, prenatally stressed rats suppress ultrasonic vocalization to separation from their mother (K. Morgan, Thayer, & Frye, 1999; Takahashi, Baker, & Kalin, 1990) and try more often to escape from novelty (Vallee et al., 1997). In tests with primates, prenatal stress is associated with poorer neuromotor maturity and distractibility (Schneider, 1992; Schneider & Coe, 1993; Schneider, Roughton, Koehler, & Lubach, 1999). The offspring of rats exposed to an acute stressor compared to controls also have elevated ACTH stress hormone responses as preweanlings (Takahashi & Kalin, 1991; Takahashi, Kalin, Barksdale, & Vanden Burtgt, 1988) and increased stress-induced corticosterone secretion as adults (Vallee et al., 1997). Because prenatally stressed animals are compared to genetically similar controls, the evidence from these studies suggests that physiological processes associated with stress during pregnancy may have an impact on developmental processes. Researchers now hypothesize that over the course of pregnancy, the frequency and magnitude of maternal stress may have a cumulative effect, shaping fetal and child central and peripheral nervous system development. There are two primary systems that likely mediate the possible influence of maternal psychiatric symptoms on the fetus: the maternal autonomic nervous system and the hypothalamic–pituitary–adrenocortical (HPA) axis.

Increased sympathetic activation

Stress is associated with elevated and/or chronic sympathetic activation and with the release of catecholamines and vasoconstriction. Vasoconstriction is believed to alter uteroplacental blood flow, causing subsequent oxygen and calorie reduction to the fetus and thereby affecting fetal growth (Copper et al., 1996; McCubbin et al., 1996) and possibly influencing fetal central nervous system (CNS) development (Teixeira, Fisk, & Glover, 1999). Increased catecholamine levels may affect the fetus by sustaining maternal vasoconstriction and increased blood pressure (McCubbin et al., 1996; Shnider, Wright, & Levinson, 1979).

The HPA axis

The hypothalamic–pituitary–adrenocortical (HPA) system plays a major role in stress responses. Briefly, cortisol, a glucocorticoid stress hormone, is the primary by-product of the HPA axis in humans. Cortisol is regulated by the hypothalamus in the brain via its secretion of corticotrophin-releasing hormone (CRH) to the pituitary, signaling for it to secrete ACTH, which, in turn, causes cortisol to be secreted from the adrenal cortex. In response to experiences of threat or challenge, the hypothalamus, largely through contact with other brain centers, initiates a cortisol response. In turn, as part of a negative feedback loop, increasing levels of circulating ACTH and cortisol inhibit further release of CRH. Although there is controversy as to how much biologically active maternal cortisol crosses the placenta (Gitau, Cameron, Fisk, & Glover, 1998; Glover, Teixeira, Gitau, & Fisk, 1999), there is consensus that CRH and ACTH are synthesized by the placenta (Sandman, Wadhwa, Chicz-DeMet, Porto, & Garite, 1999). Some evidence suggests that in pregnancy, increased HPA-axis functioning is associated with elevated levels of psychosocial stress (Wadhwa et al., 1996). Although still exploratory, the data indicate that increases in maternal sympathetic and HPA-axis activity associated with stress may affect the fetus and are consistent with animal models that highlight the potential impact of altered maternal physiology on offspring development, particularly on the developing glucocorticoid system in the fetal brain.

Psychosocial stress during pregnancy has been associated with alterations in neurobehavioral development in the fetus as well. In a comprehensive examination of fetal ontogeny, DiPietro, Hodgson, Costigan, and Johnson (1996) assessed fetal variables in relation to maternal variables. Fetuses of pregnant women who reported greater life stress had reduced parasympathetic and/or increased sympathetic activation as measured by reduced fetal heart rate variability (HRV). Moreover, fetuses of mothers who reported greater stress and had faster baseline heart rate (HR) showed a delay in the maturation of the coupling of fetal HR and movement, hypothesized to be an index of impeded central nervous system development (DiPietro et al., 1996). Low socioeconomic status – often associated with increased social stress – is associated with higher and less variable fetal HR throughout the second and third trimesters (Pressman, DiPietro, Costigan, Shupe, & Johnson, 1998).

Anxiety during pregnancy also has been linked to alterations in pregnant women's physiology and fetal behavior. Pregnant women who have high concentrations of CRH, which is associated with increased anxiety and life stress, have fetuses with a diminished capacity to dishabituate, that is, to respond significantly to the presence of a novel stimulus after having habituated to a repeated series of stimuli (Sandman et al., 1999), indicative of an alteration in CNS development.

In a recent study from our laboratory examining the effects of acute maternal stress and anxiety on fetal development (Monk et al., 2000), pregnant women's anxiety was associated with differences in fetal HR activity. During a cognitive challenge to mothers in the final month of pregnancy, fetuses of women describing themselves as more anxious showed significant HR increases and the fetuses of less anxious women exhibited nonsignificant decreases during the mental stressor. The data indicate that over the course of gestation, maternal psychological variables such as stress and anxiety acting via alterations in maternal physiology may influence fetal neurobehavioral development.

Significantly, in children and adults, differences in cardiac functioning, such as increased HR and reduced HRV, are associated with mood disorders (e.g., Monk et al., in preparation; Sloan et al., 1994) and are believed to indicate weaknesses in an individual's competency to modulate emotional reactivity (Porges, Doussard-Roosevelt, & Maiti, 1994). Furthermore, although the research in this area is just emerging, studies indicate that there is continuity between fetal and infant development. For example, work from the Kagan laboratory indicates that low resting HR during the prenatal period predicts lower levels of crying and motoric responses to novelty at 4 months old (Snidman, Kagan, Riordan, & Shannon, 1995). Using sonographic visualization, Groome found that fetuses who move at certain rates during active sleep move at the same relative rate at 2 and 4 weeks postpartum (Groome et al., 1999). Other exploratory research suggests that a relatively greater number of weak body movements, as opposed to strong, full-body ones, was positively associated with the amount of crying during the first three months of life (St. James-Roberts & Menon-Johansson, 1999). The authors speculate that an inability to inhibit responsiveness is the common underlying characteristic linking increased fetal body movements and greater crying. In the most extensive study of fetal to newborn continuities, DiPietro et al. (1996) found that indices of fetal neurobehavior accounted for as much as 60 percent of the variance of infant temperament. In general, higher fetal activity resulted in increased fussiness and inconsistent behavior, while greater periodicity resulted in lower scores on these variables. Taken together, these findings indicate that the development of fetal phenotypes – vulnerable to mother's psychosocial stress – have implications for the child's future development.

Emerging Questions and the Future of Fetal Research

In this chapter, we have summarized normal stages of fetal development as well as recent approaches to the study of risks for abnormal outcomes. A key implication of this work is that what takes place prior to postnatal life is of central importance to the child's development. Hence, it is only a slight exaggeration to assert that the future success of developmental research rests, in part, on the attainment of an even better understanding of the prenatal period.

Two overarching hypotheses will guide the majority of future fetal research: (1) the premise that there is continuity between fetal and infant development; (2) the premise that the *in utero* environment – from maternal nutrition to maternal stress hormones – is significant to development just as the postnatal environment is. Furthermore, both of these research premises are consistent with the contemporary approach to developmental studies known as dynamic systems (DS) (Karmiloff-Smith, 1998; Lewis, 2000; see also chapter 3 in this volume). Briefly, DS theory emphasizes the dynamic, recursive interactions inherent in developmental processes such that prior interactions continually shape subsequent ones and new structures or properties of the organism come into existence (emerge) through ongoing processes intrinsic to the organism–environment system. Such an approach allows for the centrally directed, unfolding aspect of fetal development, in which the progress of fetal development is largely protected from the vagaries of environmental input, to the reality of immensely diverse outcomes resulting from the unique cascades of interacting genes and subtly different environments. With its emphasis on the inherently dynamic quality of development, DS theory provides an organizing perspective for studies characterizing how developmental processes – and future trajectories – are initiated long before birth.

As knowledge accumulates about the timing and mechanisms involved in the *in utero* construction of the brain and central nervous system, particularly during the second and third trimesters, future research endeavors will likely focus on the use of new technology to investigate fetal and infant neurobehavioral continuities as well as on measuring differences in babies exposed to alterations in the prenatal environment. Specific topics will likely include:

- Characterization of fetal CNS development and its relation to infant brain–behavior relationships as assessed by infant EEG and behavioral measures.
- Epidemiological, animal, and clinical investigations of how risk for adult diseases, such as hypertension, may be "programmed" *in utero* by inadequate nutrition.
- Advances in genetic research detailing the mechanisms of cell proliferation, migration, death, and connectivity during the fetal period, what factors influence these processes, and the resulting neurobiological alterations to development.
- The influence of exposure to high levels of ambient air pollution during pregnancy on fetal and newborn development using DNA and behavioral assays.
- The role of maternal stress as well as psychiatric conditions in the development of child neurobehavioral problems.
- The possibility that fetuses experience pain.

The roots of infant development are being uncovered by paying closer attention to the nature and timing of prenatal gene–environment interactions. The identification of fetal phenotypes, and the underlying brain–behavior relationships, are the sine qua non for these investigations into the origins of normal and abnormal developmental trajectories. Development begins before birth; increasingly, we are learning how to study it that way.

Further Reading

England, M. A. (1996). *Life before birth* (2nd ed.). London: Mosby-Wolfe.

Hannigan, J. N., Spear, L. P., Spear, N. E., & Goodlett, C. R. (Eds.). (1999). *Alcohol and alcoholism: Effects on brains and development.* Mahwah, NJ: Erlbaum.

LeCanuet, J.-P., Fifer, W., Krasnegor, N., & Smotherman, W. (Eds.). (1995). *Fetal development: A psychobiological perspective.* Hillsdale, NJ: Erlbaum.

Nathanielsz, P. W. (1992). *Life before birth: The challenges of fetal development.* New York: W. H. Freeman.

References

Abrams, R., Gerhardt, K., & Peters, A. (1995). Transmission of sound and vibration to the fetus. In J.-P. LeCanuet, W. Fifer, N. Krasnegor, & W. Smotherman (Eds.), *Fetal development: A psychobiological perspective* (pp. 315–330). Hillsdale, NJ: Erlbaum.

Adlerete, E., Eskenazi, B., & Sholtz, R. (1995). Effect of cigarette smoking and coffee drinking on time to conception. *Epidemiology, 6*(4), 403–408.

Andres, R. L. (1996). The association of cigarette smoking with placenta previa and abruptio placentae. *Seminars in Perinatology, 20*, 154–159.

Ashmead, G. G., & Reed, G. B. (Eds.). (1997). *Essentials of maternal and fetal medicine.* New York: Chapman & Hall.

Barker, D. J. (1995). Fetal origins of coronary heart disease. *British Medical Journal, 311*, 171–174.

Blakemore, C., & Cooper, G. F. (1970). Development of the brain depends on visual environment. *Nature, 228*, 477–478.

Bradley, F., & Mistretta, C. (1975). Fetal sensory receptions. *Physiological Review, 55*, 352–382.

Bulletin, A. E. (1997). Smoking and women's health. *American College of Obstetricians and Gynecologists.*

Charif, H. R. B., Ahn, M. T., Hoet, J. J., & Remacle, C. (1998). Effects of taurine on the insulin secretion of rat fetal islets from dams fed a low protein diet. *Journal of Endocrinology, 159*(2), 341–348.

Clapp, J. I., & Rizk, K. (1992). Effect of recreational exercise on mid-trimester placental growth. *American Journal of Obstetrics and Gynecology, 167*(6), 1518–1521.

Clark, P. M., Atton, C., Law, C. M., Shiell, A., Godfrey, K., & Barker, D. J. (1998). Weight gain in pregnancy, tricept skinfold thickness, and blood pressure in offspring. *Obstetrics and Gynecology, 91*, 103–107.

Copper, R. L., Goldenberg, R. L., Das, A., Elder, N., Swain, M., Norman, G., Ramsey, R., Cotroneo, P., Collins, B. A., Johnson, F., Jones, P., & Meier, A. (1996). The preterm prediction study: Maternal stress is associated with spontaneous preterm birth at less than thirty-five weeks' gestation. *American Journal of Obstetrics and Gynecology, 175*, 1286–1292.

Cowan, W. (1979). The development of the brain. *Scientific American, 241*, 113–133.

Davidson, R. G., & Zeesman, S. (1994). Genetic aspects. In G. Koren (Ed.), *Maternal–fetal toxicology* (pp. 575–600). New York: Marcel Dekker.

DeCasper, A. J., & Fifer, W. P. (1980). Of human bonding: Newborns prefer their mother's voices. *Science, 208*, 1174–1176.

DeVries, J. (1992). The first trimester. In J. Nijhuis (Ed.), *Fetal behavior: Developmental and perinatal aspects* (pp. 3–16). New York: Oxford University Press.

Diamond, A. (2000). Close interrelation of motor development and cognitive development and of the cerebellum and prefrontal cortex. *Child Development, 71*, 44–56.

DiPietro, J. A., Costigan, K. A., Hilton, S. C., & Pressman, E. K. (1999). Effects of socioeconomic status and psychosocial stress on the development of the fetus. *Annals of the New York Academy of Sciences*, 356–358.

DiPietro, J. A., Hodgson, K. A., Costigan, S. C., & Johnson, T. R. B. (1996). Development of fetal movement: Fetal heart rate coupling from 20 weeks through term. *Early Human Development, 44*, 139–151.

Dubowitz, L. M. S., Dubowitz, V., Morante, A., & Verbhote, M. (1980). Visual function in the pre-term and full-term newborn infant. *Developmental Medicine and Child Neurology, 22*, 465–475.

Dubowitz, L. M. S., Mushin, J., Morante, A., & Placzek, M. (1983). The maturation of visual acuity in neurologically normal and abnormal newborn infants. *Behavioural Brain Research, 10*, 39–45.

Duenholter, J., & Pritchard, J. (1976). Fetal respiration: Quantitative measurements of amniotic fluid inspired near term by human and rhesus fetuses. *American Journal of Obstetrics and Gynecology, 125*, 306–309.

Fifer, W., & Moon, C. (1989). Psychobiology of newborn auditory preferences. *Seminars in Perinatology, 13*(5), 430–433.

Fifer, W., & Moon, C. (1995). The effects of fetal experience with sound. In J.-P. LeCanuet, W. Fifer, N. Krasnegor, & W. Smotherman (Eds.), *Fetal development: A psychobiological perspective* (pp. 351–366). Hillsdale, NJ: Erlbaum.

Flower, M. (1985). Neuromaturation of the human fetus. *Journal of Medicine and Philosophy, 10,* 237–251.

Fraga, C. G., Motchnik, P. A., Wyrobek, A. J., Rempel, D. M., & Ames, B. N. (1996). Smoking and low oxidant levels increase oxidative damage to sperm DNA. *Mutation Research, 351,* 199.

Fried, P. A., & Watkinson, B. (2000). Visuoperceptual functioning differs in 9–12-year olds prenatally exposed to cigarettes and marihuana. *Neurotoxicology and Teratology, 22,* 11–29.

Fried, P. A., Watkinson, B., & Gary, R. (1992). A follow-up study of attentional behavior in 6-year-old children exposed prenatally to marihuana, cigarettes, and alcohol. *Neurotoxicology and Teratology, 14,* 299–311.

Gebrane-Younes, J., Hoang, N., & Orcel, L. (1986). Ultrastructure of the human umbilical vessels: A possible role in amniotic fluid formation. *Placenta, 7,* 173–185.

Genbacev, O., Bass, K. E., Joslin, R. J., & Fisher, S. J. (1995). Maternal smoking inhibits early cytotrophoblast differentiation. *Reproductive Toxicology, 9*(3), 245–255.

Gitau, R., Cameron, A., Fisk, N. M., & Glover, V. (1998). Fetal exposure to maternal cortisol. *Lancet, 352,* 707–708.

Glover, V. (1999). Fetal pain: Implications for research and practice. *British Journal of Obstetrics and Gynaecology, 106,* 881–886.

Glover, V., Teixeira, J., Gitau, R., & Fisk, N. M. (1999). Mechanisms by which maternal mood in pregnancy may affect the fetus. *Contemporary Reviews in Obstetrics and Gynecology,* 155–160.

Godrey, K., & Baker, D. (1995). Maternal nutrition in relation to fetal and placental growth. *European Journal of Obstetrics, Gynecology and Reproductive Biology, 61,* 15–22.

Goland, R. S., Tropper, P. J., Warren, W. B., Stark, R. I., Jozak, S. M., & Conwell, I. M. (1995). Concentrations of corticotrophin-releasing hormone in the umbilical-cord blood of pregnancies complicated by pre-eclampsia. *Reproduction Fertility Development, 7,* 1227–1230.

Golding, J. (1997). Sudden infant death syndrome and parental smoking – a literature review. *Paediatrics and Perinatal Epidemiology, 11,* 67–77.

Goodlett, C. R., & Johnson, T. B. (1999). Temporal windows of vulnerability within the third trimester equivalent: Why "knowing when" matters. In J. N. Hannigan, L. P. Spear, N. E. Spear, & C. R. Goodlett (Eds.), *Alcohol and alcoholism: Effects on brains and development* (pp. 59–91). Mahwah, NJ: Erlbaum.

Grodstein, F., Goldman, M., & Cramer, D. (1994). Infertility in women and moderate alcohol use. *American Journal of Public Health, 84*(9), 1429–1432.

Groome, L. J., Swiber, M. J., Holland, S. B., Bentz, L. S., Atterbury, J. L., & Trimm, III, R. F. (1999). Spontaneous motor activity in the perinatal infant before and after birth: Stability in individual differences. *Developmental Psychobiology, 35,* 15–24.

Grose, J., & Harding, G. (1990). The development of refractive error and pattern reversal VEPs in pre-term infants. *Clinical Vision Sciences, 5,* 375–382.

Hanningan, J. H., Saunders, D. E., & Treas, L. M. (1999). Modification of alcohol-related neurodevelopmental disorders: In vitro and in vivo studies of neuroplasticity. In J. N. Hannigan, L. P. Spear, N. E. Spear, & C. R. Goodlett (Eds.), *Alcohol and alcoholism: Effects on brains and development* (pp. 39–58). Mahwah, NJ: Erlbaum.

Hasegawa, M., Houdou, S., Mito, T., Takashima, S., Asanuma, K., & Ohno, T. (1992). Development of myelination in the human fetal and infant cerebrum: A myelin basic protein immunohistochemical study. *Brain Development, 14*(1), 1–6.

Haste, F. M., Brooke, O. G., Anderson, H. R., & Bland, J. M. (1991). The effect of nutritional intake on outcome of pregnancy in smokers and non-smokers. *British Journal of Nutrition, 65*(3), 347–354.

Hepper, P. (1988). Adaptive fetal behavior: Prenatal exposure affects postnatal preferences. *Animal Behaviour, 36*, 935–936.

Hepper, P. (1992). Fetal psychology: An embryonic science. In J. Nijhuis (Ed.), *Fetal behavior: Developmental and perinatal aspects* (pp. 129–156). New York: Oxford University Press.

Hepper, P. (1995). The behavior of the fetus as an indicator of neural functioning. In J.-P. LeCanuet, W. Fifer, N. Krasnegor, & W. Smotherman (Eds.), *Fetal development: A psychobiological perspective* (pp. 405–418). Hillsdale, NJ: Erlbaum.

Hofer, M. (1981). *The roots of human behavior.* San Francisco: W. H. Freeman.

Hooker, D. (1952). *The prenatal origin of behavior.* Kansas: University of Kansas Press.

Hooper, S., & Harding, R. (1995). Fetal lung liquid: A major determinant of the growth and functional development of the lung. *Clinical and Experimental Pharmacology and Physiology, 22*, 235–247.

Horta, B. L., Victora, C. G., Menezes, A. M., Halpern, R., & Barros, F. C. (1997). Low birthweight, preterm births and intrauterine growth retardation in relation to maternal smoking. *Paediatrics and Perinatal Epidemiology, 11*, 140–151.

Hsu, L. Y. F. (1998). Prenatal diagnosis of chromosomal abnormalities through amniocentesis. In A. Milunsky (Ed.), *Genetic disorders and the fetus: Diagnosis, prevention, and treatment* (pp. 179–248). Baltimore: Johns Hopkins University Press.

Huttenlocher, P., & DeCourten, C. (1987). The development of synapses in striate cortex of man. *Human Neurobiology, 6*, 1–91.

Istvan, J. (1986). Stress, anxiety and birth outcomes: A critical review of the evidence. *Psychological Bulletin, 100*(3), 331–348.

Jackson, M., Mayhew, T., & Boyd, P. (1992). Quantitative description of and elaboration and maturation of villi from 10 weeks gestation to term. *Placenta, 13*, 357–370.

Judge, N. E. (1997). The physiology of pregnancy. In G. G. Ashmead (Ed.), *Essentials of maternal fetal medicine* (pp. 26–40). New York: Chapman & Hall.

Kandel, E. R., Schwartz, J. H., & Jessell, T. M. (2000). *Principles of neural science.* New York: McGraw-Hill.

Karmiloff-Smith, A. (1998). Development itself is the key to understanding developmental disorders. *Trends in Cognitive Sciences, 2*, 389–398.

Kitzinger, S. (1990). *The complete book of pregnancy and childbirth.* New York: Alfred A. Knopf.

Kolb, B., & Wishaw, I. (1985). *Fundamentals of human neuropsychology.* New York: W. H. Freeman.

Koren, G. (1994). Periconceptional folate and neural tube defects. In G. Koren (Ed.), *Maternal–fetal toxicology* (pp. 129–132). New York: Marcel Dekker.

Korner, A., Schneider, P., & Forrest, T. (1983). Effects of vestibular-proprioceptive stimulation on the neurobehavioral development of preterm infants: A pilot study. *Neuropediatrics, 14*, 170–175.

Kyrklund-Blomberg, N. B., & Cnattingius, S. (1998). Preterm birth and maternal smoking: Risks related to gestational age and onset of delivery. *American Journal of Obstetrics and Gynecology, 179*, 1051–1055.

Lagercrantz, H., & Slotkin, T. A. (1986). The "stress" of being born. *Scientific American, 254*, 100–107.

Lambers, D. S., & Clark, K. E. (1996). The maternal and fetal physiologic effects of nicotine. *Seminars in Perinatology, 20*(2), 115–126.

Lampert, R., & Schochet, S. (1968). Demyelination and remyelination in lead neuropathy. *Journal of Neuropathology and Experimental Neurology, 66,* 1007–1028.

Langley-Evans, S. C. (2000). Critical differences between two low protein diet protocols in the programming of hypertension in the rat. *International Journal of Food Science Nutrition, 51,* 11–17.

Langley-Evans, S. C., Welham, S. J. M., Sherman, R. C., & Jackson, A. A. (1996). Weanling rats exposed to maternal low-protein diets during discrete periods of gestation exhibit differing severity of hypertension. *Clinical Science, 91,* 607–615.

Law, C. M., de Swiet, M., Osmond, C., Fayers, P. M., Barker, D. J. P., Cruddas, A. M., & Fall, C. H. D. (1993). Initiation of hypertension in utero and its amplification throughout life. *British Medical Journal, 306,* 24–27.

Leader, L. R. (1995). The potential value of habituation in the prenate. In J.-P. LeCanuet, W. Fifer, N. Krasnegor, & W. Smotherman (Eds.), *Fetal development: A psychobiological perspective* (pp. 383–404). Hillsdale, NJ: Erlbaum.

Lecanuet, J.-P., Granier-Deferre, C., & Busnel, M.-C. (1995). Human fetal auditory perception. In J.-P. LeCanuet, W. Fifer, N. Krasnegor, & W. Smotherman (Eds.), *Fetal development: A psychobiological perspective* (pp. 421–429). Hillsdale, NJ: Erlbaum.

Lecanuet, J.-P., Schaal, B. (1996). Fetal sensory competencies. *European Journal of Obstetrics, Gynecology, and Reproductive Biology, 68,* 1–23.

Lewis, M. (2000). The promise of dynamic systems approaches for an integrated account of human development. *Child Development, 71,* 36–43.

Lieberman, E., Gremy, I., Lang, J. M., & Cohen, A. P. (1994). Low birthweight at term and the timing of fetal exposure to maternal smoking. *American Journal of Public Health, 84,* 1127–1131.

Lobel, M. (1994). Conceptualizations, measurement, and effects of prenatal maternal stress on birth outcomes. *Journal of Behavioural Medicine, 17*(3), 225–272.

Lobel, M., Dunkel-Schetter, C., & Scrimshaw, S. C. (1992). Prenatal maternal stress and prematurity: A prospective study of socioeconomically disadvantaged women. *Health Psychology, 11*(1), 32–40.

Lou, H. (1982). *Developmental neurology.* New York: Raven Press.

Lumey, L. H., Stein, A. D., & Ravelli, A. C. (1995). Timing of prenatal starvation in women and birth weight in their first and second born offspring: The Dutch Famine Birth Cohort study. *European Journal of Obstetrics, Gynecology, and Reproductive Biology, 61*(1), 23–30.

Lund, R. (1978). *Developmental plasticity of the brain.* New York: Oxford University Press.

Magoon, E., & Robb, R. (1981). Development of myelin in human optic nerve and tract: A light and electron microscopic study. *Archives of Ophthalmology, 99,* 655–659.

Mainous, A. G., & Hueston, W. J. (1994). Passive smoke and low birth weight. Evidence of a threshold effect. *Archives of Family Medicine, 3,* 875–878.

Makin, J., & Porter, R. (1989). Attractiveness of lactating females' breast odors to neonates. *Child Development, 60,* 803–810.

Masi, W. (1979). Supplemental stimulation of the premature infant. In T. M. Field (Ed.), *Infants born at risk* (pp. 367–388). New York: Scientific Publications.

Mattson, S. N., & Riley, E. P. (1998). A review of the neurobehavioral deficits in children with fetal alcohol syndrome or prenatal exposure to alcohol. *Alcoholism: Clinical and Experimental Research, 22,* 279–294.

McCubbin, J. A., Lawson, E. J., Cox, S., Sherman, J. J., Norton, J. A., & Read, J. A. (1996). Prenatal maternal blood pressure response to stress predicts birth weight and gestational age: A preliminary study. *American Journal of Obstetrics and Gynecology, 175,* 706–712.

Mehler, J., Jusczyk, P., Lambertz, G., Halsted, N., Bertoncini, J., & Amiel-Tison, C. (1988). A precursor of language acquisition in young infants. *Cognition, 29,* 143–178.

Michels, K. B., Trichopoulos, D., Adami, H. O., Hsieh, C., & Lan, S. J. (1996). Birthweight as a risk factor for breast cancer. *Lancet, 348*, 1542–1546.

Milner, A. D., Marsh, M. J., Ingram, D. M., Fox, G. F., & Susiva, C. (1999). Effects of smoking in pregnancy on neonatal lung function. *Archives of Disease in Childhood, Fetal Neonatal Edition, 80*(1), F8–14.

Milunsky, A., & Milunsky, J. (1998). Genetic counseling: Preconception, prenatal, and perinatal. In A. Milunsky (Ed.), *Genetic disorders and the fetus: Diagnosis, prevention, and treatment* (pp. 1–52). Baltimore: Johns Hopkins University Press.

Mirmiran, M., & Swaab, D. (1992). Effects of perinatal medicine on brain development. In J. Nijhuis (Ed.), *Fetal behavior: Developmental and perinatal aspects* (pp. 112–128). New York: Oxford University Press.

Molina, J., Chotro, M., & Dominguez, H. (1995). Fetal alcohol learning resulting from contamination of the prenatal environment. In J.-P. LeCanuet, W. Fifer, N. Krasnegor, & W. Smotherman (Eds.), *Fetal development: A psychobiological perspective* (pp. 419–438). Hillsdale, NJ: Erlbaum.

Monk, C., Fifer, W. P., Sloan, R. P., Myers, M. M., Trien, L., & Hurtado, A. (2000). Maternal stress responses and anxiety during pregnancy: Effects on fetal heart rate. *Developmental Psychobiology, 36*.

Monk, C., Kovelenku, P., Ellman, L. M., Sloan, R. P., Bagiella, E., Gorman, J. M., & Pine, D. S. (in preparation). Reduced cardiovascular autonomic control in pediatric anxiety disorders.

Moon, C., Cooper, R. P., & Fifer, W. P. (1993). Two-day-olds prefer their native language. *Infant Behavior and Development, 16*(4), 495–500.

Moon, C., & Fifer, W. P. (2000). Evidence of transnatal auditory learning. *Journal of Perinatology, 20*(8S), S37–S44.

Moore, V. M., Cockington, R. A., Ryan, P., & Robinson, J. S. (1999). The relationship between birth weight and blood pressure amplifies from childhood to adulthood. *Journal of Hypertension, 17*, 883–888.

Morgan, I., Damber, L., Tavelin, B., & Hogberg, U. (1999). Characteristics of pregnancy and birth and malignancy in the offspring. *Cancer Causes Control, 10*, 85–94.

Morgan, K. N., Thayer, J. E., & Frye, C. A. (1999). Prenatal stress suppresses rat pup ultrasonic vocalization and myoclonic twitching in response to separation. *Developmental Psychobiology, 34*, 205–215.

Mulder, E. (1992). Diabetic pregnancy. In J. Nijhuis (Ed.), *Fetal behavior: Developmental and perinatal aspects* (pp. 193–208). New York: Oxford University Press.

Mulvihill, S., Stone, M., et al. (1985). The role of amniotic fluid in fetal nutrition. *Journal of Pediatric Surgery, 20*, 668–672.

Negro-Vilar, A. (1993). Stress and other environmental factors affecting fertility in men and women: Overview. *Environmental Health Perspectives, 101*(Supp. 2), 59–64.

Neugebauer, R., Hoek, H. W., & Susser, E. (1999). Prenatal exposure to wartime famine and development of antisocial personality disorder in early adulthood. *Journal of American Medical Association, 282*, 455–462.

Nijhuis, J. (1992). The third trimester. In J. Nijhuis (Ed.), *Fetal behavior: Developmental and perinatal aspects* (pp. 26–40). New York: Oxford University Press.

Nijhuis, J. G. (1995). Physiological and clinical consequences in relation to the development of fetal behavior and fetal behavioral states. In J.-P. LeCanuet,, W. Fifer, N. Krasnegor, & W. Smotherman (Eds.), *Fetal development: A psychobiological perspective* (pp. 67–82). Hillsdale, NJ: Erlbaum.

Ockleford, E. M., Vince, M. A., Layton, C., & Reader, M. R. (1988). Responses of neonates to parents' and others' voices. *Early Human Development, 18*, 27–36.

Otamiri, R. G., Berg, G., Ledin, T., Leijon, I., & Lagercrantz, H. (1991). Delayed neurological adaptation in infants delivered by elective cesarean section and the relation to catecholamine levels. *Early Human Development, 26*, 51–60.

Patrick, J., Campbell, K., Carmichael, L., Natale, R., & Richardson, B. (1982). Patterns of gross fetal body movements over 24 observation intervals in the last 10 weeks of pregnancy. *American Journal of Obstetrics and Gynecology, 136*, 471–477.

Perera, F. P., Jedrychowski, W., Rauh, V., & Whyatt, R. M. (1999). Molecular epidemiologic research on the effects of environmental pollutants on the fetus. *Environmental Health Perspective, 107*, 451–460.

Pittman, R., & Oppenheim, R. (1979). Cell death of motor neurons in the chick embryo spinal cord: IV. Evidence that a functional neuromuscular interaction is involved in the regulation of naturally occurring cell death and the stabilization of synapses. *Journal of Comparative Neurology, 187*, 425–446.

Porges, S. W., Doussard-Roosevelt, J. A., & Maiti, A. J. (1994). Vagal tone and the physiological regulation of emotion. In N. A. Fox (Ed.), *The development of emotion regulation* (pp. 167–186). Chicago: University of Chicago Press.

Prechtl, H. F. R. (1984). Continuity and change in early neural development. In H. F. R. Prechtl (Ed.), *Continuity of neural functions from prenatal to postnatal life* (pp. 1–15). London: SIMP.

Pressman, E. K., DiPietro, J. A., Costigan, K. A., Shupe, A. K., & Johnson, T. R. B. (1998). Fetal neurobehavioral development: Associations with socioeconomic class and fetal sex. *Developmental Psychobiology, 33*, 79–91.

Purpura, D. (1975). Morphogenesis of visual cortex in the preterm infant. In M. Brazier (Ed.), *Growth and development of the brain* (pp. 33–49). New York: Raven.

Rakic, P., Stensas, L. J., Sayre, E., & Sidman, R. L. (1974). Computer-aided 3 dimensional reconstruction and quantitative analysis of cells from serial electron microscopic montages of fetal monkey brain. *Nature, 250*, 31–34.

Rich-Edwards, J. W., Stampfer, M. J., Manson, J. E., Rosner, B., Hankinson, S. E., Colditz, G. A., Willett, W. C., & Hennekens, C. H. (1997). Birthweight and the risk of cardiovascular disease in adult women. *British Medical Journal, 315*, 396–400.

Robinson, A., Linden, M. G., & Bender, B. G. (1998). Prenatal diagnosis of sex chromosome abnormalities. In A. Milunsky (Ed.), *Genetic disorders of the fetus* (pp. 249–285). Baltimore: Johns Hopkins University Press.

Robinson, J., Chidzanja, S., Kind, K., Lok, F., Owens, P., & Owens, J. (1995). Placental control of fetal growth. *Reproduction, Fertility and Development, 7*, 333–344.

Roebuck, T. M., Mattson, S. N., & Riley, E. P. (1999). Prenatal exposure to alcohol: Effects on brain structure and neuropsychological functioning. In J. N. Hannigan, L. P. Spear, N. E. Spear, & C. R. Goodlett (Eds.), *Alcohol and alcoholism: Effects on brains and development* (pp. 1–16). Mahwah, NJ: Erlbaum.

Ronca, A. E., & Alberts, J. R. (1995). Maternal contributions to fetal experience and the transition from prenatal to postnatal life. In J.-P. LeCanuet, W. Fifer, N. Krasnegor, & W. Smotherman (Eds.), *Fetal development: A psychobiological perspective* (pp. 331–350). Hillsdale, NJ: Erlbaum.

Roth, I., Corry, D. B., Locksley, R. M., Abrams, J. S., Litton, M. J., & Fisher, S. J. (1996). Human placental cytotrophoblasts produce the immunosuppressive cytokine interleukin 10. *Journal of Experimental Medicine, 184*, 539–548.

Sandman, C. A., Wadhwa, P. D., Chicz-DeMet, A., Porto, M., Garite, T. J. (1999). Maternal corticotrophin-releasing hormone and habituation in the human fetus. *Developmental Psychobiology, 34*, 163–173.

Schaal, B., Orgeur, P., & Rognon, C. (1995). Odor sensing in the human fetus: Anatomical, functional and chemoecological bases. In J.-P. LeCanuet, W. Fifer, N. Krasnegor, & W. Smotherman (Eds.), *Fetal development: A psychobiological perspective* (pp. 205–238). Hillsdale, NJ: Erlbaum.

Schneider, M. L. (1992). The effect of mild stress during pregnancy on birthweight and neuromotor maturation in rhesus monkey infants (*Macaca mulatta*). *Infant Behavior and Development, 15,* 389–403.

Schneider, M. L., & Coe, C. L. (1993). Repeated social stress during pregnancy impairs neuromotor of the primate infant. *Journal of Developmental Behavioral Pediatrics, 14,* 81–87.

Schneider, M. L., Roughton, E. C., Koehler, A. J., & Lubach, G. R. (1999). Growth and development following prenatal stress exposure in primates: An examination of ontogenetic vulnerability. *Child Development, 70,* 263–274.

Seeds, A. (1980). Current concepts of amniotic fluid dynamics. *American Journal of Obstetrics, 138,* 575–586.

Shnider, S. M., Wright, R. G., Levinson, G. (1979). Uterine blood flow and plasma norepinephrine changes during maternal stress in the pregnant ewe. *Anesthesiology, 50,* 524–527.

Sidman, R., & Rakic, P. (1973). Neuronal migration, with special reference to developing human brain. *Brain Research, 62,* 1–35.

Sloan, R. P., Shapiro, P. A., Bigger, J. T., Bagiella, E., Steinman, R. C., & Gorman, J. M. (1994). Cardiac autonomic control and hostility in healthy subjects. *American Journal of Cardiology, 74,* 298–300.

Smigaj, D. (1997). Drug abuse in pregnancy. In G. G. Ashmead (Ed.), *Essentials of maternal fetal medicine* (pp. 185–201). New York: Chapman & Hall.

Snidman, N., Kagan, J., Riordan, L., & Shannon, D. C. (1995). Cardiac function and behavioral reactivity during infancy. *Psychophysiology, 32,* 199–207.

Spitzer, W. O., Lawrence, V., Dales, R., Hill, G., Archer, M. C., Clark, P., Abenhaim, L., Hardy, J., Sampalis, J., Pinfold, S. P., et al. (1990). Links between passive smoking and disease: A best-evidence synthesis. A report of the Working Group on Passive Smoking. *Clinical and Investigative Medicine, 13,* 17–42.

St. James-Roberts, I., & Menon-Johansson, P. (1999). Predicting infant crying from fetal movement data: An exploratory study. *Early Human Development, 54*(1), 55–62.

Stansbury, K., & Gunnar, M. (1994). Adrenocortical activity and emotion regulation. In N. Fox (Ed.), *The development of emotion regulation* (pp. 108–134). Chicago: Society for Research in Child Development.

Stark, R., & Myers, M. (1995). Breathing and hiccups in the fetal baboon. In J.-P. LeCanuet, W. Fifer, N. Krasnegor, & W. Smotherman (Eds.), *Fetal development: A psychobiological perspective* (pp. 51–66). Hillsdale, NJ: Erlbaum.

Stott, D. H., & Latchford, B. A. (1976). Prenatal antecedents of child health, development, and behavior. *Journal of American Academic Child Psychiatry, 15*(1), 161–191.

Susser, E. B., Brown, A., & Matte, T. D. (1999). Prenatal factors and adult mental and physical health. *Canadian Journal of Psychiatry, 44,* 326–334.

Sweeney, L. J. (1998). *Basic concepts in embryology: A student's survival guide.* New York: McGraw-Hill Companies Health Professions Division.

Takahashi, L. K., Baker, E. W., & Kalin, N. H. (1990). Ontogeny of behavioral and hormonal responses to stress in prenatally stressed male rat pups. *Physiology and Behavior, 47,* 357–364.

Takahashi, L. K., & Kalin, N. H. (1991). Early developmental and temporal characteristics of stress-induced secretion of pituitary-adrenal hormones in prenatally stressed rat pups. *Brain Research, 558*, 75–78.

Takahashi, L. K., Kalin, N. H., Barksdale, C. M., & Vanden Burtgt, J. A. (1988). Stressor controllability during pregnancy influences pituitary-adrenal hormone concentrations and analgesic responsiveness in offspring. *Physiology and Behavior, 42*, 323–329.

Taylor, M. J., Menzies, R., MacMillan, L. J., & Whyte, H. E. (1987). VEPs in normal full-term and premature neonates longitudinal versus cross-sectional data. *Electroencephalography and Clinical Neurophysiology, 68*, 20–27.

Teixeira, J. M. A., Fisk, N. M., & Glover, V. (1999). Association between maternal anxiety in pregnancy and increased uterine artery resistance index: Cohort based study. *British Medical Journal, 318*, 153–157.

Thelen, E. (1986). Treadmill-elicited stepping in seven-month-old infants. *Child Development, 57*, 1498–1506.

Torday, J. (1990). Androgens delay fetal lung maturation in vitro. *Endocrinology, 126*, 3240–3244.

Tough, S. C., Greene, C. A., Svenson, L. W., & Belik, J. (2000). Effects of in vitro fertilization on low birth weight, preterm delivery, and multiple birth. *Journal of Pediatrics, 136*, 618–622.

Vallee, M., Mayo, W., Dellu, F., Le Moal, M., Simon, H., & Maccari, S. (1997). Prenatal stress induces high anxiety and postnatal handling induces low anxiety in adult offspring: Correlation with stress-induced corticosterone secretion. *Journal of Neuroscience, 17*(7), 2626–2636.

Van Heteren, C. F., Boekkooi, P. F., Jongsma, H. W., & Nijhuis, J. G. (2000). Fetal learning and memory. *Lancet, 30*; 356(9236), 1169–1170.

Van Woerden, E., & van Geijn, H. (1992). Heart-rate patterns and fetal movements. In J. Nijhuis (Ed.), *Fetal behavior: Developmental and perinatal aspects* (pp. 41–56). New York: Oxford University Press.

Visser, G. (1992). The second trimester. In J. Nijhuis (Ed.), *Fetal behavior: Developmental and perinatal aspects* (pp. 17–25). New York: Oxford University Press.

Wadhwa, P. D., Dunkel-Schetter, C., Chicz-DeMet, A., Porto, M., & Sandman, C. A. (1996). Prenatal psychosocial factors and the neuroendocrine axis in human pregnancy. *Psychosomatic Medicine, 58*, 432–446.

Wadhwa, P. D., Porto, M., Garite, T. J., Chiez-DeMet, A., Sandman, C. A. (1998). Maternal corticotrophin-releasing hormone levels in the early third trimester predict length of gestation in human pregnancy. *American Journal of Obstetrics and Gynecology, 179*, 1079–1085.

Wakschlag, L. S., Lahey, B. B., Loeber, R., Green, S. M., Gordon, R. A., & Leventhal, B. L. (1997). Maternal smoking during pregnancy and the risk of conduct disorder in boys. *Archives of General Psychiatry, 54*, 670–676.

Walsh, R. A. (1994). Effects of maternal smoking on adverse pregnancy outcomes: Examination of the criteria of causation. *Human Biology, 66*, 1059–1092.

Weale, R. (1982). Ocular anatomy and refraction. *Documenta Ophthalmogica, 55*, 361–374.

Wheeler, T., Sollero, C., Alderman, S., Landen, J., Anthony, F., & Osmond, C. (1994). Relation between maternal haemoglobin and placental hormone concentrations in early pregnancy. *Lancet, 343*(8896), 511–513.

Wilson, G. N. (1992). Genomics of human dysmorphogenesis. *American Journal of Medical Genetics, 42*, 187–196.

Windham, G. C., Eaton, A., & Hopkins, B. (1999). Evidence for an association between environmental tobacco smoke exposure and birthweight: A meta-analysis and new data. *Paediatrics and Perinatal Epidemiology, 13*, 35–57.

Wynn, M., & Wynn, R. (1994). Slimming and fertility. *Modern Midwife, 4*(6), 17–20.

Zelazo, P. (1983). The development of walking: New findings and old assumptions. *Journal of motor behavior, 15*, 99–137.

Zimmer, E. Z., Chao, C. R., Guy, G. P., Marks, F., & Fifer, W. P. (1993). Vibroacoustic stimulation evokes fetal micturition. *Obstetrics and Gynecology, 81*, 178–180.

Chapter Nineteen

Early Intervention and Risk

Douglas R. Powell

Introduction

Early intervention programs for infants at risk of developmental delay due to family environment conditions or economic disadvantage have grown rapidly in the past four decades. The expansion has been driven by widespread concern about the deleterious and long-term effects of poverty on young children, stunning statistics about the incidence of child abuse and neglect, images of families as increasingly less capable of providing optimal childrearing environments for very young children, and by the "earlier is better" assumption that prevention efforts at the beginning points of life are a prudent investment in the development of social capital.

Intervention efforts have grown in sophistication over time in response to advances in our understanding of how environmental factors interact with infant development. Research results from well-designed longitudinal studies of early intervention programs now offer promising points of departure for new initiatives. Studies of the long-term consequences of children's early experiences in families also emphasize the magnitude of the intervention task that lies before us (Hart & Risley, 1995). At the same time, early intervention policies and practices of the past four decades have been characterized by periodic hopes of huge benefits from minimalist efforts, such as expecting lasting intellectual gains from listening to the music of Mozart in infancy.

Beginning in the mid-1990s, interest in early intervention from birth or the prenatal period also has been fueled by widespread attention to brain development in the first three years of life. A public awareness effort highlighting research on brain growth in the early years was launched with the help of Hollywood celebrity Rob Reiner, a national "I Am Your Child" campaign that included extensive news media attention, a 1997 White House Conference on Early Childhood Development and Learning, and a widely disseminated report on the results of brain research (Shore, 1997).

The case for intervention in the earliest years of life was made in an influential policy report issued by the prestigious Carnegie Corporation of New York, titled *Starting Points*. The report poignantly summarized alarming numbers about infant mortality rates, proportion of lower-birthweight babies, proportion of babies immunized against childhood diseases, rates of babies born to adolescent mothers, and percentage of victims of physical abuse who are under the age of 1 year in the United States. The report also cited research on brain development and the effects of early environments, noting that the quality of young children's environment and social experience has a decisive, long-term impact on their well-being and ability to learn. The Carnegie report called for programs and policies that promote responsible parenthood, quality childcare choices, good health and protection, community-level supports for young children and their families (Carnegie Task Force on Meeting the Needs of Young Children, 1994). While critics have argued that findings of brain development research have been overstated and misunderstood (e.g., Bruer, 1999), programs for at-risk infants such as Early Head Start continue to expand and scientific knowledge about infants' intellectual development continues to be sought by an eager lay public (e.g., Gopnik, Meltzoff, & Kuhl, 1999).

The 1960s are an appropriate starting point for a review of early intervention programs, although parenting education (Schlossman, 1976) and child care for infants (Clarke-Stewart & Fein, 1973) have long histories. Scholarly work such as Hunt's (1961) seminal volume on environmental influences and the ambitious early childhood efforts of the United States federal government's War on Poverty initiative ushered in a new era of attention to needs of young children living in economically disadvantaged circumstances. Early programmatic approaches to infant education focused primarily on the mother–infant dyad. By the early 1970s, growing concern about multiple stresses facing families led to a broader early intervention focus on families and their environments. Especially influential was Bronfenbrenner's (1974) report on the effectiveness of early intervention that called for ecological intervention in the form of family support systems. Equally influential was theoretical and empirical work on the concept of risk. Specifically, the transactional model of development set forth by Sameroff and Chandler (1975) contributed significantly to the field's view of developmental outcomes as a complex interplay of child and his or her experience rather than a function of the individual alone or the context alone. Also, research results strengthened practitioners' ability to identify risk indices associated with child abuse and neglect (Gray, Cutler, Dean, & Kempe, 1979).

The employability skills of low-income adults became a prominent United States domestic issue in the 1990s, prompting welfare reform policies that emphasize job skills and work. Parents of very young children are not immune from society's welfare-to-work goals, and in the 1990s early intervention strategies were incorporated into programs also aimed at improving low-income parents' job-related skills. The programs attempt to integrate two historically separate interventions: (1) self-sufficiency services designed to improve parents' educational levels, vocational skills, and employability, and (2) child development services that may include preventive health care, parenting education, and high-quality child care or early childhood education (Smith & Zaslow, 1995). These are often called two-generation programs.

This chapter reviews the nature and effectiveness of early intervention programs aimed at infants of low-income families and families at risk of child maltreatment. Important differences exist across early intervention programs in terms of content, methods, and theoretically based assumptions about the direction of influence in parent–child interaction (Cowan, Powell, & Cowan, 1998). Accordingly, this chapter attempts to summarize the distinguishing features of an intervention so as to avoid perpetuating the notion that all home visiting is alike, for instance. Program descriptions and research are organized into two major approaches to early intervention: programs that work primarily with parents, and programs that provide services directly to child and to parent. Program differences within each set are noted. The chapter ends with an identification of key issues facing early intervention targeted at infants and their families.

Focus on Parents

Most early intervention programs aimed at infants work with parents (almost exclusively mothers) in an attempt to have influence on the child's home environment. Home visiting is especially common. Among its benefits are the program worker's opportunity to secure first-hand information about the home and family circumstances in which the child is being reared, including the opportunity to tailor program content to family preferences and conditions. The interventions described in this section work primarily with parents, although their goals encompass child outcomes. The programs are organized into three subcategories based on a program's primary emphasis regarding the content or substance of the intervention and the desired outcomes. It is now common for early intervention programs to embrace a range of outcomes, and the categorization of programs offered herein represents a program's degree of emphasis on an area rather than the entirety of its approach.

Parenting Education with Emphasis on School-Related Outcomes

The need to improve economically disadvantaged children's intellectual skills, especially as preparation for school success, has been a central concern of society during the four decades covered by this chapter. Three home-visiting programs developed during the 1960s contributed in major ways to our early understanding of whether parent-focused work is an effective way to support child development in lower-income families. They are the Mother–Child Home Program (Levenstein, 1972), the Florida Parent Education Infant and Toddler Program (Gordon, Guinagh, & Jester, 1972), and the Ypsilanti-Carnegie Infant Education Project (Lambie, Bond, & Weikart, 1974). The Mother–Child Home Program remains active today through training and technical assistance services offered through the National Center for Mother–Child Home Program in Wantagh, New York.

These early programs were pioneers in the application of child development theory and research to the design of program strategies for enhancing parents' support of infant and toddler development. Piaget's description of the sensorimotor stage of development was a significant, although not sole, basis of information and activities offered to parents in the Ypsilanti-Carnegie Infant Education Project and the Florida Parent Education Infant and Toddler Program. Language development theory and research was the starting point for Mother–Child Home Program's emphasis on verbal interactions. While conceptual and pedagogical differences clearly existed across these programs, they had a common focus on activity-based parent–child interaction. In the Florida program, for example, a paraprofessional parent educator taught the mother an activity she was expected to do during the week with her infant. In the Mother–Child Home Program, "toy demonstrators" conducted home play sessions with mother and toddler together around gifts of toys and books. Although parent–child activities were the focus of home visits in these programs, visitors were not uninterested in the range of issues faced by the lower-income families they served. For example, in the Ypsilanti-Carnegie program, home visitors reportedly acknowledged and listened to parents' problems and concerns, made referrals to community services when appropriate, and recognized that a child-focused parenting education program cannot be all things to all people (e.g., Lambie et al., 1974).

The early programs also were among the first to systematically examine the effects of parent-focused interventions in the very early years of children's development. The Florida Parent Education Program and the Mother–Child Home Program were among the 14 projects in the Consortium for Longitudinal Studies (1983) organized in 1975 to answer the question of whether early education programs had measurable long-term effects on the performance of children from low-income families. Studies were generally based on quasi-experimental designs yielding short- and long-term program effects on child outcomes that were promising but not robust.

The Mother–Child Home Program (MCHP), which begins when children are 2 years of age, has been subjected to more evaluation than other interventions in this early group of programs. A quasi-experimental design study of the MCHP found mean Stanford–Binet differences of 13 points between MCHP and control groups one year postprogram (Madden, Levenstein, & Levenstein, 1976). A subsequent experimental evaluation of the MCHP found small effects on preschool children's intellectual achievements and mothers' behaviors and no effects in preschool. Interestingly, a variation of the program in which toys and books were supplied without home visits was as effective as the full program on children's IQ but not on maternal behavior (Madden, O'Hara, & Levenstein, 1984). Levenstein and colleagues report that, in a recent exploratory follow-up study, young adults who had participated in the MCHP as toddlers were significantly less likely than randomized controls to drop out of school (15.7 percent vs. 40 percent) and more likely to have graduated (84.1 percent vs. 53.9 percent) (Levenstein, Levenstein, Shiminski, & Stolzberg, 1998). Scarr and McCartney (1988) examined effects of the MCHP in Bermuda using random assignment with a socioeconomically diverse sample and a broad range of cognitive, social, and emotional outcome measures. Results indicated that the program had few demonstrable effects on any segment of the sample, including the socioeconomically disadvantaged. Scarr and McCartney speculate that one reason for the lack of effects is that nearly all children in Bermuda were in group child care due to maternal employment, and thus they had preschool experiences that are comparable to those provided by the intervention.

Parents as Teachers (PAT) is a widely used program that endeavors to improve children's school readiness through parent education and support in the early years. Established as a pilot program in Missouri in 1981, the program has now served more than 500,000 families in more than 2000 sites in 49 states and six foreign countries. The program's premise is that "babies are born learning" and "parents are their first and most influential teachers" (Winter, 1999). The program seeks to increase parents' knowledge of child development and appropriate ways to foster their child's growth and learning. Specific outcomes focus on school success, prevention of child abuse and neglect, and home–school–community partnerships. Personal visits usually carried out in the home are a core program service. There is a detailed curriculum that sets forth parent–child activities and information for each visit. Visits are to be one hour in length and are scheduled at a frequency that accommodates local budgets and presumably family needs (weekly, biweekly, or monthly). The program design also calls for periodic group meetings which provide opportunities for parents to share insights and to build informal support networks. Further, parents and home visitors are to monitor children's progress to detect and address any developmental problems, and families are to be linked with needed community services. The home visitors, known as parent educators in the PAT program, are given one week of preservice training in delivering the PAT model by trainers certified by the Parents as Teachers National Center.

Like most research on home visiting, evaluations of PAT generally have entailed quasi-experimental designs with working- or middle-class white families and/or populations living in nonurban areas. Summaries of some ten studies of PAT (Winter, 1999) generally point to positive child outcomes, especially intellectual competence (e.g., Pfannenstiel & Seltzer, 1989). These studies leave unanswered the question of whether PAT is an effective intervention with low-income, minority, and at-risk families.

Recently an evaluation was conducted of PAT's effectiveness with a largely low-income Latino population in Salinas Valley in northern California (Wagner & Clayton, 1999). The program began as a pilot in 1990 and randomized trial was begun in 1992. There was a "graduation" of participating families in 1996 when children reached their third birthdays. Salinas Valley is primarily an agricultural area with a predominantly Latino population and high demand for seasonal farm labor. Unemployment was the highest in the state at the time of the PAT demonstration. Families with children no older than 6 months were recruited to the program through programs such as local Women, Infants, and Children (WIC) office. Evaluators randomly assigned 497 families to participant and control groups, with a 60 percent probability of assignment to the participant group ($n = 298$) and a 40 percent probability of assignment to the control group ($n = 199$).

Monthly home visits were offered to the PAT group for as long as families chose to remain in the program, up to the child's third birthday. PAT program participants received an average of 20 visits over three years, ranging in length from 28 to 50 minutes. Less than 15 percent of participant group families attended any group meetings. Attrition from the program was high: 43 percent left the program over three years.

However, family tracking procedures and incentives enabled researchers to secure assessments for almost 73 percent of the original sample at the time of the children's third birthdays.

Overall, there were no PAT effects on parenting knowledge, attitudes, or behaviors, but there were small to modest positive effects on other aspects of child development, including self-help, social, and cognitive development. An analysis of differential effectiveness pointed to program benefits for Latino families but not for non-Latino families served by the Salinas Valley PAT program. Specifically, Latinas scored higher on a measure of parenting sense of competence than non-Latinas, and the children of Latina mothers received greater program benefits (i.e., better scores in assessments of self-help, social, and cognitive development) than children of non-Latina mothers. Children of Spanish-speaking Latina mothers appeared to benefit the most within this population comparison; effects were marginally larger for children of Spanish-speaking Latina mothers. Based on divorce and separation rates in the sample, Wagner and Clayton (1999) speculate that the poor outcomes for non-Latina mothers and their children may have been a function of significantly higher rates of marital instability during the Salinas Valley PAT program. Overall, greater exposure to the Salinas Valley PAT program (which may be a proxy for other family variables) was not associated with greater parenting effects, but remaining in PAT through the children's third birthdays was significantly related to higher scores in cognitive, social, and self-help domains of children's development.

It is not surprising to find modest results from what arguably can be seen as a minimalist intervention with a population that is difficult to serve. Even among those families that persisted with the Salinas Valley PAT to the child's third birthday, there was an average of 28 home visits in three years and more than 40 percent had gaps of four months or more in their home visits, mostly because families returned to Mexico for extended periods each winter. It appears that PAT worked best in Salinas Valley for children of Latina families with limited English proficiency who were able to remain in PAT through three years.

Home Visiting from an Ecological Perspective

As noted in the introduction to this chapter, in the 1970s early intervention programs shifted from an almost exclusive focus on the mother–child dyad to concern for the family and community contexts of the parent–child relationship. Bronfenbrenner's (1974) conclusion that early intervention should provide family support systems led to an ecological approach to a number of early interventions. Several types of strategies are described below.

Parenting Education and Family Case Management

Case management is a common approach to helping families make connections with social, educational, and health services in a community. Often a goal of the case manager is to foster an integration of services that are tailored to a family's needs. Case management was a core element of the federal Comprehensive Child Development Center Program (CCDP), one of the country's largest and most visible two-generation interventions. CCDP sought to enhance the physical, social, emotional, and intellectual development of children in low-income families from birth to age 5; provide support to their parents and other family members; and assist families in becoming economically self-sufficient. Eligible families included those with incomes below the federal poverty line, and with unborn children or children under 1 year of age (focus child). Families were to agree to participate in the program for five years. The program was launched in 1989 and 1990 in 24 sites in 22 states. Close monitoring was carried out in an effort to minimize local variations and thus enable a strong test of a single, coherent model (St. Pierre & Layzer, 1999).

The CCDP used home visiting to provide case management and early childhood education. Visits were to begin during each focus child's first year of life and continue until the child entered school. Visits were conducted two to four times per month, varying from 30 to 90 minutes in length. For children from birth through 3 years of age, the early childhood education services were delivered through home visits focused on parenting education. At least one-half of the CCDP children had enrolled in a center-based program by age 4 or 5 years. In many projects, the case management staff person also provided the early childhood education component during a single home visit. In other projects, the case manager and another staff person with early childhood training (but no case management responsibilities) visited the home on alternating weeks.

Case managers were to assess the goals and service needs of individual family members and the family as a whole, develop a service plan, refer the family to services in the community, monitor the family's receipt of services, and provide counseling and support to family members, especially mothers. A formal family needs assessment was conducted within three months of enrollment and every six months thereafter. It was to be updated every three months and, importantly, to serve as the basis for a service delivery plan. Commonly specified goals of families included better housing, improved parenting skills, access to child care and health care, better transportation, and increased income. In response, programs attempted to provide access to a range of services for parents (e.g., job training, housing referrals) and for children (e.g., developmental screening and assessment, health care). Initially in the program, case managers were paraprofessionals (see subsequent section on Issues).

Each program had an early childhood coordinator who selected or developed a curriculum for the early childhood component of the home visits. This person also trained the home visitors to deliver the services. The focus was on educating parents in infant and child development and in parenting skills rather than working with children directly. A typical session would look like this: the home visitor would suggest an activity to the parent, the parent would engage the child in the activity, and the home visitor would comment or maybe suggest alternative approaches and other activities. For parents who seemed hesitant, the home visitor might demonstrate the activity with the child. The biweekly sessions lasted about 30 minutes. Thus, a parent who was present for every session received a maximum of 13 hours of parenting education a year from CCDP (St. Pierre & Layzer, 1999).

An experimental evaluation of CCDP's effects was conducted in 21 of the original 24 program sites. The total sample consisted of 4410 families (2213 assigned to CCDP and 2197 assigned to the control group). Data were collected annually for a five-year period beginning in 1990. Overall, the study sample was racially/ethnically diverse (43 percent African American, 26 percent Hispanic, 26 percent white), low income, and poorly educated (51 percent of mothers had not graduated from high school at the point of entering CCDP). More than one-third of the mothers were under 18 years of age when they gave birth to the focus child.

The results are easily summarized: CCDP did not produce any important positive effects on participating parents or children when compared with control group families. Specifically, CCDP had no statistically significant effects on participating mothers' economic self-sufficiency or parenting skills. There were no program effects on focus children's cognitive or social-emotional development or health. Also, there were no differential effects on subgroups of participants (e.g., teen parents). Further, the length of time a family was enrolled in CCDP was not associated with statistically significant difference in outcomes achieved; on average, families were enrolled for 3.3 years. Positive changes that occurred in the lives of CCDP families (e.g., increases in vocabulary and achievement scores, mothers in the labor force) also occurred in control group families. One of the 21 sites (Brattleboro, Vermont) had statistically significant and moderately large positive effects on children's cognitive development; families' employment, income and use of federal benefits; and parenting attitudes. Researchers speculate that a unique mix of factors in this site (e.g., relatively high level of state services to low-income families, experienced and stable senior staff, clear project focus on children and their education) may have combined to contribute to positive program effects (St. Pierre & Layzer, 1999).

The aforementioned Parents as Teachers (PAT) program was combined with comprehensive case management services for adolescent parents in a demonstration program launched in 1991 in four California communities (Wagner & Clayton, 1999). The intent was to produce positive life changes for both parents and children. Both a case manager and a PAT parent educator served each family. Case management services focused on achieving such positive outcomes as improved education and postponed repeat child-bearing for the young mother. The demonstration included a combined intervention of PAT and case management as well as stand-alone PAT and case management intervention groups. Teens were eligible for the program if they were less than 19 years of age and either were pregnant or had babies who were less than 6 months of age. Evaluators randomly assigned the adolescents into one of four groups: (1) PAT alone, (2) case management alone, (3) PAT plus case management, and (4) an untreated control group. The total sample of 704 families was diverse in terms of ethnic and socioeconomic characteristics. About one-half of the mothers were Latina, about one-quarter were African American, and the remainder were Caucasian. Mothers were between 15 and 18 years of age at time of enrollment, and the majority were enrolled in or had completed high school. Few mothers were married.

The PAT and combined intervention groups were offered monthly home visits and PAT group meetings through the children's second birthdays. Participants received an average of ten visits during the two-year period. Participant attendance at group meetings was low, similar to the case for the Salinas Valley PAT program described earlier. The comprehensive case management services, modeled after California's Adolescent Family Life Program, entailed face-to-face contacts provided as often as teens needed but at least quarterly. Case managers provided referrals or arranged for services to address issues such as psychological functioning, health status, nutrition, and education and vocational goals. In the combined intervention group, case management contacts were separate from the PAT program visits. On average, participants in the case management and combined intervention groups received ten case management contacts in two years. Thus, a teen mother in the combined intervention group received an average of 20 in-person contacts from both PAT and case management staff during the program. There were additional telephone contacts (an average of six for the PAT group, eight for the case management group, and 17 for the combined intervention group). There was a significant level of attrition: at the program's two-year end, data were collected for only 52 percent of the original families (51 percent of each intervention group and 54 percent of control group teens). In other words, 57 percent of teens in the three intervention groups left the Teen PAT program before their children's second birthdays (Wagner & Clayton, 1999).

The Teen PAT program had little or no benefit on most outcome measures for either parents or children from PAT services, either alone or in combination with case management services. Specifically, the Teen PAT program had no effects on parenting knowledge, but there was a positive impact on a subscale measuring acceptance of children's behavior among teens in the combined intervention. Children in the combined intervention experienced significant gains of one or more months over the control group in cognitive development, and there were significantly fewer opened cases of child abuse or neglect. There was a significantly higher rate of full immunization in the case management only intervention. Greater exposure to program services was not related to greater parenting impacts, similar to the Salinas Valley PAT finding, and only cognitive development was influenced positively when teens received the intended level of exposure of case management contacts (four per year) in the case management group only. The Teen PAT program used the general PAT curriculum, and the Parents as Teachers National Center subsequently developed a new curriculum and training program for parent educators who work with teen parents (Wagner & Clayton, 1999).

Case management may be a flawed way to organize support for a family. The CCDP and Teen PAT evaluations provide no evidence for the effectiveness of this approach through home visits with families with very young children. Bickman (1996) also found that an integrated continuum of mental health and substance abuse services for children and adolescents did not produce better clinical outcomes than those at a comparison site. The CCDP program evaluators suggest that social programs may be more effective if services are provided directly rather than through an organization of existing services (St. Pierre & Layzer, 1999).

Adult-focused interventions often give little or no attention to children. Inattention to children is common for adolescent pregnancy and parenthood interventions, for instance; programs assume that improved functioning of the teenager in turn will contribute to improved child outcomes (Coley & Chase-Lansdale, 1998). In contrast, the

CCDP and PAT programs were clearly interested in child outcomes, yet indirect means to these ends – through a modest amount of parenting education work in the home – were employed. The biweekly, 30-minute in-home parenting education work offered through the CCDP, for example, is a minimalist intervention in a family system that most likely already has a well-entrenched set of childrearing beliefs and practices (St. Pierre & Layzer, 1999).

Home Visiting with Emphasis on Health-related Outcomes

It is informative to compare results of the CCDP and Teen PAT case management strategies to results of two well-known home-visiting programs, the Nurse Home Visitation Program (Olds et al., 1999) and Hawaii's Healthy Start Program (Duggan et al., 1999). Neither program uses the "case management" term in a dominant way to describe the assistance given to parents, yet the home visitors in each of these two programs seek to help families make productive connections with existing resources in the community. Importantly, both programs give major, although not exclusive, attention to improving the health-related outcomes of mothers and their young children. One of the significant differences between these two programs is the use of professional nurses versus trained paraprofessionals.

The Nurse Home Visiting Program (NHVP) was established in 1977 in Elmira, New York as a research demonstration program, and as of July 1998 was operating in 70 communities in ten states, serving approximately 2500 families. Nurses visit first-time, low-income mothers and their families in their homes during pregnancy and the first two years of the child's life. There are three goals: (1) to improve pregnancy outcomes by helping women alter their health-related behaviors (e.g., reduce use of cigarettes, alcohol); (2) to improve child health and development by helping parents provide more responsible and competent care for their child(ren); and (3) to improve families' economic self-sufficiency by helping parents engage in future planning, including future pregnancies, further education, and work. The plan is to conduct home visits every week to two weeks, but the frequency of home visits varies by stage of pregnancy, child age, and the mother's needs.

Nurses follow a detailed protocol for each visit. For example, during pregnancy, the nurses help women complete 24-hour diet histories on a regular basis and plot weight gains at every visit. They also teach women to identify the signs and symptoms of pregnancy complications. After delivery, the nurses help mothers and other caregivers observe the signs of illness and to take temperatures, for instance, and promote parent–child interaction by helping parents understand their infants' and toddlers' communicative signals. In addition to helping promote behaviors that affect pregnancy outcomes and the health and development of children, the nurses help women build supportive relationships with family members and friends, and link women and their family members with needed health and human services. The visits last between 75 and 90 minutes each (Olds et al., 1999).

A randomized trial of the NHVP was conducted in Elmira with more than 400 women, 85 percent of whom were either unmarried, adolescent, or poor. Women who participated in the program experienced greater informal and formal social support, smoked fewer cigarettes, had better diets, exhibited fewer kidney infections by the end of pregnancy and, among those identified as smokers, were less likely to have a premature baby (Olds, Henderson, Tatelbaum, & Chamberlin, 1986). The program was helpful in reducing abuse and neglect among poor unmarried mothers, and in reducing emergency room visits for injuries among all children, irrespective of risk (Olds, Henderson, Chamberlin, & Tatelbaum, 1986). Four years after the delivery of their first children, participants in the program who were low-income and unmarried at the time of program entry were found to have had fewer subsequent pregnancies and greater participation in the workforce (Olds, Henderson, Tatelbaum, & Chamberlin, 1988). A 15-year follow-up of the Elmira sample found no differences on maternal life-course indices such as subsequent pregnancies or subsequent births for the full sample. However, there were differences for program participants who were poor and unmarried at the time of program entry in a number of maternal life-course areas, including fewer subsequent births, longer time between the births of their first and second children, fewer months on welfare, and fewer months receiving food stamps. Also in the 15-year follow-up, the adolescent children of poor unmarried program participants reported fewer instances of running away, fewer arrests, fewer convictions and violations of probation, fewer lifetime sex partners, fewer cigarettes smoked per day, and fewer days having consumed alcohol in the past six months (Olds, Henderson, Cole, et al., 1998). A vast majority of the Elmira sample was white. Recently Olds and colleagues have replicated the Elmira intervention with a randomized trial in Memphis, Tennessee with a largely African American population. Short-term findings are similar to those found in higher-risk Elmira groups (Kitzman, Olds, Henderson, et al., 1997; see also Olds et al., 1999).

In contrast with the use of nurses in the NHVP, paraprofessional lay home visitors were used in seven programs represented in the Child Survival/Fair Start initiative launched in the early 1980s (Larner, Halpern, & Harkavy, 1992). The intent of the community helpers was to assist disadvantaged, low-income mothers with infants in accessing available health, nutrition, and childrearing supports in order to improve their capacity for self-care. Quasi-experimental designs were used to study each program. Among the six programs with evaluation components, populations included barrio families in Texas, young African American mothers in rural Alabama, isolated families in Appalachia, migrant Mexican American farmworkers in south Florida, recent Haitian immigrants, and adolescent parents in several cities. Results across the programs point to "mixed, conditional" effects (Larner, 1992, p. 242) on a range of outcome areas. Five of the six programs had significant effects on at least three major outcomes, some in the prenatal period and others following birth (e.g., increased use of well-child checkups).

Hawaii's Healthy Start Program (HSP) evolved from a home-visiting program established in the mid-1970s and based on Kempe's lay therapy model (Gray et al., 1979). The program is designed to prevent child abuse and neglect and to promote child health and development in newborns of families at risk for poor child outcomes. There are two main program components: (1) early identification of families with newborns at risk of child abuse and neglect, and (2) home visiting by trained paraprofessionals.

Early identification involves review of a mother's medical record at the obstetrical unit. Family risk for abuse is measured in 15 areas, including parents not married, unemployed partner, inadequate income, unstable housing, less than high school education, marital or family problems, history of depression, and inadequate prenatal care, among other items. When a mother's record suggests risk or provides insufficient information, Kempe's (1976) Family Stress Checklist is used to secure a more precise understanding of risk. In the home-visiting component offered to families at risk of child abuse or neglect, para-professionals seek to establish a trusting relationship with parents and actively assist in addressing existing crises, role model problem-solving skills, and help link families with needed services such as housing, income, nutritional assistance, and child care. Home visitors also provide parenting education by modeling effective parent–child interaction and ensuring that each child has a continuing source of pediatric care (a "medical home"). The HSP model calls for three to five years of home visiting of decreasing intensity as families achieve milestones. It is anticipated that families will receive weekly home visits for the first year of program participation. Individualized service plans are to be developed at least every six months, with a focus on achievable goals such as getting infant immunizations (Duggan et al., 1999).

The most recent study of HSP is an attempt to determine the success of expanding HSP to six sites serving geographically defined communities on Oahu. Random assignment has been used to form an intervention group (373 families), a main control group (270 families), and a testing control group (41 families) that is evaluated only at three years to assess whether the study's intensive data collection has influenced outcomes.

The findings tell of difficulties of working with high-risk populations. Not unlike the Teen PAT program described earlier, HSP program workers found it challenging to engage and retain the participation of some families. For instance, home visitors were unable to make direct contact with 3 percent of referred mothers and never visited another 9 percent. For the 88 percent with at least one visit, the time from birth to the first visit was 23 days on average. In terms of attrition, 10 percent of referred families were considered inactive by their program sites by the time the child was 3 months of age, 30 percent by 6 months, 44 percent by 9 months, and 51 percent by 12 months. For all referred families, there was an average of 13 home visits in the infant's first year. For families still active at one year, there was an average of 22 visits, with nearly half visited at least every two weeks. Outcome results indicate that, after two years of service provision, HSP was successful in linking families with pediatric medical care, improving maternal parenting efficacy, decreasing maternal parenting stress, promoting the use of nonviolence discipline, and decreasing injuries resulting from partner violence in the home. However, there was no overall positive program on the adequacy of well-child health care, maternal life skills, mental health, social support, or substance use, child development, the child's home learning environment, parent–child interaction, pediatric health-care use for illness or injury, or child maltreatment (Duggan et al., 1999). Important differences were found across agencies in terms of implementation of the program, and these results are discussed in the final section of this chapter.

The Healthy Families America (HFA) program launched in 1992 by the National Committee to Prevent Child Abuse (now known as Prevent Child Abuse America) was initially guided by Hawaii's HSP and other family support initiatives. HFA seeks to promote positive parenting and to prevent child abuse and neglect. HFA services have been implemented in more than 300 communities in 40 states, the District of Columbia, and Canada. A network of researchers examining the HFA program in diverse sites has been established and preliminary findings, mostly from quasi-experimental designs, suggest that HFA programs may have the most success at improving parent–child interactions (Daro & Harding, 1999).

Interventions with Emphasis on Reworking Parents' Past Experiences

In the past two decades there has been expansion of a unique set of intervention programs aimed at helping the mother rework existing understandings (or "working models") of intimate relationships. Attachment theory typically provides a framework for these interventions (van IJzendoorn, Juffer, & Duyvesteyn, 1995). Interventionists focus directly with the parent–infant relationship, and the relationship between mother and interventionist is viewed as a key element of the change process (e.g., Booth, Mitchell, Barnard, & Spieker, 1989). For instance, the initial session in the Infant–Parent Psychotherapy Program is used to address a mother's negative expectations about the therapist or the program (Lieberman & Pawl, 1993; Lieberman, Weston, & Pawl, 1991). Trust-building experiences are key, and may involve instrumental support such as driving the mother to an appointment. Infant mental health intervention programs often assume that parents have had past negative experiences in intimate relationships, such as rejection or abandonment, that need to be reworked through the intervention program.

The Steps Toward Effective, Enjoyable Parenting (STEEP) program (Erickson & Egeland, 1999) illustrates the use of attachment theory in early intervention. Established in 1987, the STEEP program is designed to promote healthy parent–child relationships and to prevent social and emotional problems among children born to first-time parents characterized by such risk factors as poverty, youth, limited education, social isolation, and stressful life circumstances. Participants are recruited through obstetric clinics during the second trimester of their pregnancy. The program consists of a mix of biweekly group sessions and biweekly home visits. In keeping with the relationship-based nature of the program, the home visitor is also the same person who conducts the group sessions for a cohort of eight to ten families. Home visits begin at time of enrollment and continue until the child's second birthday, if not longer. Participation in the group sessions begins shortly after the babies are born. The program is designed to enhance parents' understanding of child development, strengthen parents' use of social support, and help parents reflect on what they learned in their own early relationships and how that influences the way they respond to their own children. In this latter area, STEEP program facilitators help parents "examine their own working models, confront sometimes painful memories, and identify positive experiences they wish to pass on to their children" (Erickson & Egeland, 1999, p. 13). If there are missed appointments, the STEEP program facilitator continues to show up for as many visits as have been agreed upon, in an effort to demonstrate that the worker will not reject or abandon the parent.

The group sessions begin with parent–child interaction time, with developmentally focused planned activities that may be altered if the facilitator wishes to pursue a spontaneous teachable moment in the session. This interaction time is followed by a casual meal and then "mom-talk" time while babies remain with caregivers who provide developmentally appropriate activities. "Mom-talk" time is for informal support and semi-structured activities that address the parents' own issues (e.g., balancing child and adult needs).

The STEEP program uses videotaped parent–infant interaction to heighten parents' sensitivity and responsiveness to their child's needs. Parent and infant are videotaped in a routine task (e.g., feeding) or unstructured play interaction. The STEEP facilitator uses a process of open-ended questions to encourage parents to focus on "what their baby is telling them and to recognize their own skills in adapting to their baby's needs" (Erickson & Egeland, 1999, p. 12). It is a tool for stimulating discussion of child development and helping parents see through their child's eyes. Among other benefits such as providing a permanent record for monitoring the family's progress over time, the videotape reportedly becomes a treasured keepsake for the family.

An evaluation of the STEEP program with 154 pregnant women (92 percent single), one-half assigned to the intervention and one-half to a control group, found positive program effects on mothers' understanding of child development, life management skills, depressive symptoms, repeat pregnancies (within two years of the birth of the baby), and sensitivity to their child's cues and signals. However, there were no differences between the intervention and control group mothers in quality of attachment when babies were 13 and 19 months of age (Erickson & Egeland, 1999; Egeland & Erickson, 1993).

Research on the Infant–Parent Psychotherapy Program, which used clinically trained professionals, indicates that intervention mothers had higher scores than control mothers in empathy and interactiveness with their children, and their toddlers had higher scores than controls on quality of partnership with their mothers. At 24 month of age, toddlers who had earlier shown avoidance, resistance, and anger when their mothers returned after a short absence now showed increased signs of secure attachment after their mothers received one year of intervention. There was no improvement over the same period for control toddlers who entered the study with anxious attachment (Lieberman & Pawl, 1993).

Focus on Children and Parents

Interventions that provide services directly to child and to parent are the focus of this section. Obviously the programs described in the preceding section had child outcomes as a primary goal, but services for children were provided indirectly by the intervention program via parent-mediated resources or linkages with social, health, and educational agencies in the community. In contrast, the interventions described below included an educational component provided directly to the target child and they also include direct work with the parent. The interventions are presented chronologically in terms of start date, so as to highlight changes over time in the early intervention research and program development knowledge base.

Head Start's Parent–Child Center program was among the first parent–infant programs to be offered on a relatively widespread basis nationally. Launched as a pilot effort in 1968 as part of the War on Poverty effort, the program initially was located in 36 communities across the United States. The centers offered programs for children, programs and activities for parents and other family members, health and nutrition services, and social services (Lazar et al., 1970).

The early experiences of the Parent–Child Center are a reminder of the limitations of available expert knowledge about how to work with infants and toddlers from economically disadvantaged families in center-based programs in the late 1960s. Program evaluators found that program staff were better qualified to deal with parents than with infants; in most centers, staff had a limited repertoire of activities to engage the infants and a limited knowledge of characteristics of infant and toddler development. As a result, program services for children were the weakest components of the Parent–Child Centers. Evaluators found, for instance, that some staff interactions with babies were well intentioned but developmentally inappropriate, and that equipment and activities designed for 4- and 5-year-old children often were introduced to 2- and 3-year-old children; typically the toys, trikes, chairs, tables, sinks, and puzzles were too big and too complicated for children under 3 years of age (Lazar et al., 1970).

The early experiences of the Parent–Child Centers also illustrate the challenge of maintaining a program focus on infant education in the context of overwhelming family problems. Programs learned that "it is extremely difficult to launch a baby-oriented program when the basic desperate needs of parents are not met" (Lazar et al., 1970, p. 409). As a result, early implementation of the program offered relatively little for the child; more program time and money were devoted to adults than directly to infants. Other center-based programs for low-income parents of infants and toddlers encountered a similar press among parents to address the daily obstacles of living in poverty. A content analysis of open-ended conversations among mothers of children under 3 years of age who participated in long-term parent discussion groups while their young children attended an educational children's program found that topics related to basic family needs dominated discussions for at least the first three months of a group's existence. Conversations squarely focused on children's development eventually occupied an increasing amount of group discussion time over a one-year period (Powell & Eistenstadt, 1988).

Probably the most sophisticated program development and research effort regarding comprehensive programs in the late 1960s and early 1970s was the Parent–Child Development Center (PCDC) initiative. Programs were to be developed, stabilized, evaluated, and then replicated and evaluated again in different sites (Dokecki, Hargrove, & Sandler, 1983). Three original PCDC sites were established in New Orleans, Houston, and Birmingham, Alabama. Each offered comprehensive services to low-income families with young children. The curriculum for mothers included information on child development and childrearing practices, home management, nutrition and health, and personal development, and the use of community resources. There was a simultaneous program for children and an array of medical and social services for participating families. Mothers were to remain in the program until their baby was 36 months of age. This general model had variations across the three sites, including the entry ages of children (ranged from 2 to

12 months), staging and mix of home- versus center-based services, and approaches to teaching and learning (Andrews et al., 1982).

Experimental evaluations of the PCDC program found that children in each of the three sites achieved superior Stanford–Binet scores at the time of program graduation (when children were 36 months of age), and program mothers scored significantly higher than control group mothers on dimensions of positive maternal behavior. Significant differences between program and control group mothers emerged on several maternal dimensions after 24 months of participation. The PCDC children maintained their IQ gains one year after leaving the program (Andrews et al., 1982) but not beyond (Bridgeman, Blumenthal, & Andrews, 1981). A 1- to 4-year follow-up study of the effects of the Houston PCDC found that boys whose mothers did not participate in the program exhibited more negative behavior than boys whose mothers did participate (Johnson & Breckenridge, 1982).

Two other research-based comprehensive programs developed during this early period also are important to note. Both were based in one site only and used quasi-experimental designs to study program effects.

The Yale Child Welfare Project was a small but intensive family support program provided to 17 impoverished inner-city families who delivered a healthy firstborn child in 1968–1970. The program began during the mother's pregnancy and continued to 30 months postpartum. Each family received pediatric care, social work, child care, and psychological services provided in an individualized manner by a four-person team of pediatrician, home visitor, primary child care worker, and developmental examiner (Provence, Naylor, & Patterson, 1977). A ten-year follow-up study of 18 children from 17 families and a control sample of 18 children from 18 families found positive program effects on intervention children's school attendance and boys' use of special school services, but no program effects on children's IQ scores. Program mothers were more likely to be self-supportive, have more formal education, and have smaller family sizes than mothers who had not been in the program (Seitz, Rosenbaum, & Apfel, 1985). A later follow-up study found benefits for the intervention children's siblings (or program "diffusion effects"). Intervention program siblings had better school attendance than did control group siblings, were less likely to need supportive or remedial services, and were more likely to be making normal school program (Seitz & Apfel, 1994).

The Syracuse Family Development Research program provided high-quality child care beginning at 6 months of age at Syracuse University's Children's Center plus weekly home visits by a paraprofessional "child development trainer," who served as a "knowledgeable friend" to the parent and taught families Piagetian sensorimotor games to play with their infant, offered nutrition information, and provided liaison help with community services as well as general social and material support for the parenting role. Program services were provided for five years. A ten-year follow-up study of 65 program families and 54 control families found positive program effects on the incidence and severity of juvenile delinquency, child and parental attitudes toward self and the environment (i.e., problem-solving orientation), and school performance (grades, attendance, teacher ratings) of program girls but not boys in junior high school (Lally, Mangione, & Honig, 1988).

More recently, the Carolina Abecedarian Project has demonstrated long-term effects of sustained participation in a high-quality early childhood program beginning in infancy.

The Abecedarian Project was targeted at children at risk for developmental retardation and school failure, based on sociodemographic factors which were weighted and combined into a risk index with a prespecified cut point. The families were low-income and 98 percent were African American due to the confound of poverty and race in the United States and the limited number of economically disadvantaged white families in the university town where the project took place (Campbell & Ramey, 1994). Infants entered the childcare program at a mean age of 4.4 months. The center operated eight hours a day, five days a week for 50 weeks per year. The infant curriculum focused on cognitive, language, perceptual-motor, and social development. Parents served on the center's advisory board and were offered a series of voluntary educational programs on topics such as family nutrition, legal matters, and toy making. Families facing problems with housing, food, transportation and the like were offered supportive social services. There also were periodic family social events held at the center.

A total of 111 infants from 109 qualifying families were randomly assigned to the early childhood program or a control group. Within each of these groups, a second random assignment occurred prior to kindergarten entry, enabling one-half of each preschool-age group to receive a school-age intervention program. This design enabled the researchers to examine the relative effectiveness of the following: five years of preschool intervention only, three years of school-age intervention only, eight years of both preschool and school-age intervention, and no intervention. The school-age intervention consisted of a home/school resource teacher for each child and the child's family. Positive effects of the preschool program on intellectual development and academic achievement were maintained through age 12. In the first two years of school, children who received preschool only had higher academic achievement test scores than children who received no preschool intervention. Children who received the preschool intervention plus continued help in the early grades received higher academic achievement scores in kindergarten and first grade than children who received preschool only or no intervention. The school-age treatment alone was less effective (Campbell & Ramey, 1994; Ramey & Campbell, 1987). Recent results of a follow-up study of the children at age 21 years indicate those who attended the program beginning in infancy were more likely to attend college or hold high-skill jobs, and the adolescent mothers of infants in the Abecedarian program were far more likely to have completed high school after their infant received the intervention (Ramey, 1999).

Lessons and Questions

Definitive early intervention policies and practices should be based on a convergence of program research findings from multiple settings and studies. To this end, the existing database is promising in some areas but inadequate in others. High-quality educational child care for the infant combined with supportive services tailored to the parent and family appear to be an effective way to support the healthy development of very young children living in high-risk circumstances. In contrast, there is little empirical evidence to indicate that parenting education alone is a useful way to have impact on significant child outcomes in families characterized by high-risk circumstances such as adolescent parenthood. There also is no evidence to support the case management strategy of working with parents of young children.

Whether interventions are more effective with professional versus trained paraprofessionals as staff persons remains unanswered. Strong arguments can be made for the use of lay home visitors yet the supervision needs can be expensive (Larner et al., 1992). Preliminary results from a comparison of nurses versus trained paraprofessionals in the Nurse Home Visitation Program in Denver suggest there are cost-sensitive benefits in using nurses (Olds et al., 1999).

Best practices in enabling parents to better understand and relate to their young children also need to be discerned. Simply modeling a desired adult–child interaction or encouraging a parent to act in a certain way may be insufficient teaching strategies with high-risk populations. The use of videotape as a self-reflection tool in the STEEP program is promising in this regard. Concrete feedback to parents in the form of supportive coaching also may be helpful (Neuman & Gallagher, 1994). The pedagogical quality of parenting education provided in the home visits described above is unclear.

In this regard, research on program implementation is essential for improved understanding of how programs actually function and what conditions are necessary for programs to be effective. Multisite studies of interventions typically uncover meaningful differences in how different agencies carry out a given program model. Outcome data are best understood in the context of program processes.

One cannot ignore the community context in which families and programs attempt to function. Poor and high-risk families generally reside in poor and high-risk neighborhoods. Hints of this general pattern are noted repeatedly in this chapter's references to attrition and the overwhelming challenges faced by programs in engaging families. Existing intervention programs generally work outward, from the infant and family to the community. Yet inadequate health, educational, and social services, unsafe neighborhoods, and dysfunctional patterns of social life are impossible referral sources for intervention programs that attempt to link families to stable and positive sources of help. An equally important starting point for interventions is to move inward, from a community's formal and informal resources to families and infants.

Further Reading

Cowan, P. A., Powell, D., & Cowan, C. P. (1998). Parenting interventions: A family systems perspective. In W. Damon (Series Ed.) & I. E. Sigel & K. A. Renninger (Vol. Eds.), *Handbook of child psychology: Vol. 4. Child psychology in practice* (pp. 3–72). New York: Wiley. This chapter provides a comprehensive review of parenting interventions, many of which pertain to infancy. It offers a state of the field and sets forth a framework for working with parents within a family systems perspective.

Erickson, M. F., & Kurz-Rimer, K. (1999). *Infants, toddlers and families: A framework for support and intervention.* New York: Guilford Press. This volume draws on the professional experiences of infant/toddler intervention work at the University of Minnesota and pertinent research to set forth principles and exemplary practices in early intervention with high-risk families. Attention is given to building on family strengths, enhancing parental knowledge, and strengthening family support networks. There is an extensive annotated professional resource bibliography.

Hart, B., & Risley, T. (1995). *Meaningful differences in the everyday experiences of young American children.* Baltimore: Brookes. Results of a longitudinal study of verbal interactions in families of varying socioeconomic status are reported in an accessible manner. Especially informative are the comparisons across welfare, working-class, and professional families, and the predictive power of early language experiences in the home. There are interesting extrapolations about the intensity of needed early intervention.

The Future of Children. This journal, published by the David and Lucile Packard Foundation, is a source of research and policy analysis on children's issues. Recent issues have focused on home visiting, children in poverty, child abuse and neglect, and child health issues, for instance.

Zero to Three. This professional journal is published by the Zero to Three organization and typically includes thoughtful articles written by professionals who carry out relationship-based early intervention programs. Consistent attention is given to staff supervision and development issues.

References

Andrews, S. R., Blumenthal, J. B., Johnson, D. L., Kahn, A. J., Ferguson, C. J., Lasater, R. M., Malone, P. E., & Wallace, D. B. (1982). The skills of mothering: A study of Parent–Child Center Centers. *Monographs of the Society for Research in Child Development, 47* (6, Serial No. 198).

Bickman, L. (1996). A continuum of care: More is not always better. *American Psychologist, 51,* 689–701.

Booth, C. L., Mitchell, S. K., Barnard, K. E., & Spieker, S. J. (1989). Development of maternal social skills in multiproblem families: Effects on the mother–child relationship. *Developmental Psychology, 25,* 403–412.

Bridgeman, B., Blumenthal, J., & Andrews, S. (1981). *Parent–Child Development Center: Final evaluation report.* Submitted to the US Department of Health and Human Services. Princeton, NJ: Educational Testing Service.

Bronfenbrenner, U. (1974). *Is early intervention effective? A report on longitudinal evaluations of preschool programs* (Vol. 2). Washington, DC: Office of Child Development, Department of Health, Education, and Welfare.

Bruer, J. T. (1999). *The myth of the first three years: A new understanding of early brain development and lifelong learning.* New York: Free Press.

Campbell, F. A., & Ramey, C. T. (1994). Effects of early intervention on intellectual and academic achievement: A follow-up study of children from low-income families. *Child Development, 65,* 684–698.

Carnegie Task Force on Meeting the Needs of Young Children (1994). *Starting points: Meeting the needs of our youngest children.* New York: Carnegie Corporation of New York.

Clarke-Stewart, K. A., & Fein, G. G. (1973). *Day care in context.* New York: Wiley.

Coley, R. L., & Chase-Lansdale, P. L. (1998). Adolescent pregnancy and parenthood: Recent evidence and future directions. *American Psychologist, 53,* 152–166.

Consortium for Longitudinal Studies (1983). *As the twig is bent . . . Lasting effects of preschool programs.* Hillsdale, NJ: Lawrence Erlbaum Associates.

Cowan, P. A., Powell, D., & Cowan, C. P. (1998). Parenting interventions: A family systems perspective. In W. Damon (Series Ed.) & I. E. Sigel & K. A. Renninger (Vol. Eds.), *Handbook of child psychology: Vol. 4. Child psychology in practice* (pp. 3–72). New York: Wiley.

Daro, D. A., & Harding, K. A. (1999). Healthy Families America: Using research to enhance practice. *The Future of Children, 9,* 152–176.

Dokecki, P., Hargrove, E., & Sandler, H. (1983). An overview of the Parent Child Development Center social experiment. In R. Haskins & D. Adams (Eds.), *Parent education and public policy* (pp. 80–111). Norwood, NJ: Ablex.

Duggan, A. K., McCaflane, E. C., Windham, A. M., Rohde, C. A., Salkever, D. S., Fuddy, L., Rosenberg, L. A., Buchbinder, S. B., & Sia, C. C. J. (1999). Evaluation of Hawaii's Healthy Start Program. *The Future of Children, 9,* 66–90.

Egeland, B., & Erickson, M. F. (1993). Attachment theory and findings: Implications for prevention and intervention. In S. Kramer & H. Parens (Eds.), *Prevention in mental health: Now, tomorrow, ever?* (pp. 21–50). Northvale, NJ: Jason Aronson.

Erickson, M. F., & Egeland, B. (1999). The STEEP program: Linking theory and research to practice. *Zero to Three, 20,* 11–16.

Gopnik, A., Meltzoff, A. N., & Kuhl, P. K. (1999). *The scientist in the crib: Minds, brains, and how children learn.* New York: William Morrow.

Gordon, I. J., Guinagh, B. J., & Jester, R. E. (1972). The Florida Parent Education Infant and Toddler Program. In M. C. Day & R. K. Parker (Eds.), *The preschool in action* (pp. 95–127). Boston: Allyn & Bacon.

Gray, J. E., Cutler, C. A., Dean, J. G., & Kempe, C. H. (1979). Prediction and prevention of child abuse and neglect. *Journal of Social Issues, 35,* 127–139.

Hart, B., & Risley, T. (1995). *Meaningful differences in the everyday experiences of young American children.* Baltimore: Brookes.

Hunt, J. M. (1961). *Intelligence and experience.* New York: Ronald Press.

Johnson, D. L., & Breckenridge, J. N. (1982). The Houston Parent–Child Development Center and the primary prevention of behavior problems in young children. *American Journal of Community Psychology, 10,* 305–316.

Kempe, H. (1976). *Child abuse and neglect: The family and the community.* Cambridge, MA: Ballinger.

Kitzman, H., Olds, D. L., Henderson, C. R., Jr., et al. (1997). Effect of prenatal and infancy home visitation by nurses on pregnancy outcomes, childhood injuries, and repeated childbearing: A randomized controlled trial. *Journal of the American Medical Association, 278,* 644–652.

Lally, J. R., Mangione, P. L., & Honig, A. S. (1988). The Syracuse University Family Development Research Program: Long-range impact of an early intervention with low-income children and their families. In D. R. Powell (Ed.), *Parent education as early childhood intervention* (pp. 79–104). Norwood, NJ: Ablex.

Lambie, D. Z., Bond, J. T., & Weikart, D. P. (1974). *Home teaching with mothers and infants.* Ypsilanti, MI: High/Scope Educational Research Foundation.

Larner, M. B. (1992). Realistic expectations: Review of evaluation findings. In M. B. Larner, R. Halpern, & O. Harkavy (Eds.), *Fair start for children: Lessons learned from seven demonstration projects* (pp. 218–245). New Haven, CT: Yale University Press.

Larner, M. B., Halpern, R., & Harkavy, O. (Eds.). (1992). *Fair start for children: Lessons learned from seven demonstration projects.* New Haven, CT: Yale University Press.

Lazar, I., Anchel, G., Beckman, L., Gethard, E., Lazar, J., & Sale, J. (1970). *A national survey of the Parent–Child Center Program.* Prepared for Project Head Start, Office of Child Development, Department of Health, Education, and Welfare. Washington, DC: Kirchner Associates.

Levenstein, P. (1972). The Mother–Child Home Program. In M. C. Day & R. K. Parker (Eds.), *The preschool in action* (pp. 27–49). Boston: Allyn & Bacon.

Levenstein, P., Levenstein, S., Shiminski, J. A., & Stolzberg, J. E. (1998). Long-term impact of a verbal interaction program for at-risk toddlers: An exploratory study of high school outcomes in a replication of the Mother–Child Home Program. *Journal of Applied Developmental Psychology, 19*, 267–285.

Lieberman, A. F., & Pawl, J. H. (1993). Infant–parent psychotherapy. In C. H. Zeanah (Ed.), *Handbook of infant mental health* (pp. 427–442). New York: Guilford Press.

Lieberman, A. F., Weston, D. R., & Pawl, J. H. (1991). Preventive intervention and outcome with anxiously attached dyads. *Child Development, 62*, 199–209.

Madden, J., Levenstein, P., & Levenstein, S. (1976). Longitudinal IQ outcomes of the Mother–Child Home Program. *Child Development, 47*, 1015–1025.

Madden, J., O'Hara, J., & Levenstein, P. (1984). Home again: Effects of the Mother–Child Home Program on mother and child. *Child Development, 55*, 636–647.

Neuman, S. B., & Gallagher, P. (1994). Joining together in literacy learning: Teenage mothers and children. *Reading Research Quarterly, 29*, 383–401.

Olds, D. L., Henderson, C. R., Jr., Chamberlin, R., & Tatelbaum, R. (1986). Preventing child abuse and neglect: A randomized trial of nurse home visitation. *Pediatrics, 78*, 65–78.

Olds, D. L., Henderson, C. R., Jr., Cole, R., et al. (1998). Long-term effects of nurse home visitation on children's criminal and antisocial behavior: Fifteen-year follow-up of a randomized trial. *Journal of the American Medical Association, 280*, 1238–1244.

Olds, D. L., Henderson, C. R., Jr., Kitzman, H. J., Eckenrode, J. J., Cole, R. E., & Tatelbaum, R. C. (1999). Prenatal and infancy home visitation by nurses: Recent findings. *The Future of Children, 9*, 44–65.

Olds, D. L., Henderson, C. R., Jr., Tatelbaum, R., & Chamberlin, R. (1986). Improving the delivery of prenatal care and outcomes of pregnancy: A randomized trial of nurse home visitation. *Pediatrics, 77*, 16–28.

Olds, D. L., Henderson, C. R., Jr., Tatelbaum, R., & Chamberlin, R. (1988). Improving the lifecourse development of socially disadvantaged mothers: A randomized trial of nurse home visitation. *American Journal of Public Health, 78*, 1436–1445.

Pfannenstiel, J. C., & Seltzer, D. A. (1989). New Parents as Teachers: Evaluation of an early parent education program. *Early Childhood Research Quarterly, 4*, 1–18.

Powell, D. R., & Eistenstadt, J. E. (1988). Informal and formal conversations in parent discussion groups: An observational study. *Family Relations, 37*, 166–170.

Provence, S., Naylor, A., & Patterson, J. (1977). *The challenge of daycare.* New Haven, CT: Yale University Press.

Ramey, C. T. (1999). *Presentation on long-term effects of Carolina Abecedarian Project.* Washington, DC: US Department of Education.

Ramey, C. T., & Campbell, F. A. (1987). The Carolina Abecedarian Project: An educational experiment concerning human malleability. In J. J. Gallagher & C. T. Ramey (Eds.), *The malleability of children* (pp. 127–139). Baltimore: Brookes.

Sameroff, A. J., & Chandler, M. J. (1975). Reproductive risk and the continuum of caretaking casualty. In F. D. Horowitz, M. Hetherington, S. Scarr-Salaptek, & G. Siegel (Eds.), *Review of child development research* (Vol. 4, pp. 187–244). Chicago: University of Chicago Press.

Scarr, S., & McCartney, K. (1988). Far from home: An experimental evaluation of the Mother–Child Home Program in Bermuda. *Child Development, 59*, 531–543.

Schlossman, S. (1976). Before Home Start: Notes toward a history of parent education in America, 1897–1929. *Harvard Educational Review, 46*, 436–467.

Seitz, V., & Apfel, N. H. (1994). Parent-focused intervention: Diffusion effects on siblings. *Child Development, 65*, 677–683.

Seitz, V., Rosenbaum, L. K., & Apfel, N. H. (1985). Effects of family support intervention: A ten-year follow-up. *Child Development, 56,* 376–391.

Shore, R. (1997). *Rethinking the brain: New insights into early development.* New York: Families and Work Institute.

Smith, S., & Zaslow, M. (1995). Rationale and policy context for two-generation interventions. In S. Smith (Ed.), *Two generation programs for families in poverty: A new intervention strategy. Advances in applied developmental psychology* (Vol. 9, pp. 1–35). Norwood, NJ: Ablex.

St. Pierre, R. G., & Layzer, J. I. (1999). Using home visits for multiple purposes: The Comprehensive Child Development Program. *The Future of Children, 9,* 134–151.

Van IJzendoorn, M. H., Juffer, F., & Duyvesteyn, M. G. C. (1995). Breaking the intergenerational cycle of insecure attachment: A review of the effects of attachment-based interventions on maternal sensitivity and infant security. *Journal of Child Psychology and Psychiatry, 36,* 225–248.

Wagner, M. M., & Clayton, S. L. (1999). The Parents as Teachers program: Results from two demonstrations. *The Future of Children, 9,* 91–115.

Winter, M. (1999). Parents as Teachers (Appendix B). *Young Children, 9,* 179–189.

Chapter Twenty

Early Social Development in Young Children with Autism: Theoretical and Clinical Implications

Sally Ozonoff and Mikle South

Theoretical Overview

Autism is a lifelong developmental disorder typified by social difficulties, communicative limitations, and a restricted range of interests and behaviors. Onset of the disorder is before 36 months of age, although it is not always recognized at this time. Boys are more often affected than girls, with gender ratio estimates ranging from two to four males for every female with the disorder (Lord & Schopler, 1987). While once considered a rare condition, recent prevalence estimates suggest that autism occurs in approximately 1 in 1000 individuals (Bryson, Clark, & Smith, 1988). Higher prevalence estimates probably do not indicate an increase in the occurrence of autism, but rather, better detection of the disorder, particularly in its milder forms (Gillberg, Steffenburg, & Schaumann, 1991).

The most commonly used diagnostic system in the United States is the *Diagnostic and Statistical Manual of Mental Disorders*, 4th edition (DSM-IV; American Psychiatric Association, 1994). As specified in the DSM-IV, all individuals with autism demonstrate evidence of difficulties with social relatedness and verbal and nonverbal communication, as well as limited or idiosyncratic interests and behaviors. In the social domain, the symptoms listed in the DSM-IV include impaired use of nonverbal behaviors (e.g., eye contact, facial expression, gestures) to regulate social interaction, failure to develop age-appropriate peer relationships, little spontaneous seeking to share enjoyment or interests with other people, and limited social-emotional reciprocity. DSM-IV symptoms of communicative dysfunction include delay in or absence of spoken language, difficulty initiating or sustaining a conversation, idiosyncratic or repetitive language, and imitation and pretend play deficits. In the behaviors and interests domain, there is often an encompassing preoccupation or unusual interest that is abnormal in intensity, inflexible adherence to nonfunctional routines, stereotyped body movements, and preoccupation with parts or sensory qualities of objects (APA, 1994). In order to meet criteria for a diagnosis of Autistic Disorder (as it is called in the DSM-IV), an individual must demonstrate at least six of the 12 symptoms listed above, with at least two coming from the social domain and one each from the communication and restricted behaviors/interests categories. Additionally, at least one of the symptoms must have been present before 36 months of age (APA, 1994).

What has become increasingly apparent in the last decade is that the symptoms of autism vary widely in severity and span a continuum from easily recognized deviant behaviors to much milder difficulties (Wing, 1988). The classically autistic individual is socially remote, has little communication ability, and is absorbed in stereotypic behavior. What has been less well recognized is that an individual who is socially outgoing, talkative, and has no stereotyped mannerisms can also meet DSM-IV diagnostic criteria for Autistic Disorder. What does an aloof, mute individual share with an engaging, talkative person that makes them both autistic? A core difficulty in autistic people of all functioning levels is reciprocity. Even mildly affected individuals with autism who are quite interested in others have difficulty with social reciprocity. Their relationships tend to be one-sided and do not involve the same level of mutuality, shared interests, and intimacy observed in their nonautistic peers. They often talk in monologues without giving others a chance to contribute, have difficulty building and developing on comments made by others, and engage in less chatting for purely social purposes. Their interests tend to be idiosyncratic and difficult for others to share, revolving around unusual themes such as vacuum cleaners, automobile hubcap emblems, or venomous snakes.

Thus, there is an emphasis on the social symptomatology of autism; even in the symptom domains of communication and repetitive interests, it is the abnormal social quality of the behaviors that distinguishes them from typical development. This chapter examines several domains of social development, highlighting their distinctive course in autism. While autism is by no means a disorder only of infancy, it first becomes apparent during this period and is characterized by deviations in a number of early developmental domains. In this chapter, we review the theoretical and clinical implications of the research conducted on attachment, joint attention, imitation, play, and theory of mind abilities in both autism and typical development.

Review of Developments in the First Years

Attachment

Autism was first conceptualized as a disorder of attachment. Early theories, such as those espoused by Kanner (1943) and Bettelheim (1967), suggested that the social withdrawal of autism was a reaction to a severe disruption in the parent–child bond, caused by parental (usually maternal) unavailability, emotional distance, and rejection of the child. These theories have been resoundingly defeated, yet the notion that autism involves deviant attachment remains in the minds of many. Clearly, the social and communicative behavior of those with autism is disrupted; in fact, these symptoms must, by definition, be present to fulfill diagnostic criteria for the disorder. Yet empirical studies of the specific caregiver-oriented and relationship behaviors that are part of the constellation that we call "attachment behaviors" (e.g., differentiation of caregivers from others, proximity seeking, response to separation and reunion) consistently demonstrate that attachment is one of the *least* disrupted social domains in autism. In the research we are about to review, minor deviations in the attachment behavior of young children with autism emerge, but appear due to factors other than poor attachment *per se.*

Most empirical investigations of attachment in autism, as in typical development, have used Ainsworth's Strange Situation paradigm (Ainsworth, Blehar, Waters, & Wall, 1978). This research task measures the security of the attachment relationship by observing infants' responses to separation from and reunion with primary caregivers. Evidence of secure attachment is provided by some distress or concern at separation (although not all securely attached infants will demonstrate negative emotion) and relatively prompt soothing and comforting upon the caregiver's return. Insecurely attached infants, on the other hand, demonstrate behaviors at either of two extremes, displaying great emotional distress at separation that is not resolved upon reunion or very little response to separation or reunion (Ainsworth et al., 1978). In typical samples, approximately two-thirds of normally developing infants are securely attached, while about a third display evidence of insecure attachment (Ainsworth et al., 1978). Adaptations to the implementation and scoring of the Strange Situation paradigm were made in most investigations of autism because the children studied tend to be of higher chronological age than that for which the paradigm was originally developed.

The first investigation of attachment in autism was carried out by Sigman and Ungerer (1984a). Proximity-seeking social behaviors, such as touching, standing, or sitting close to the caregiver or experimenter, were coded, as were more distal social behaviors, including smiling at or vocalizing to either adult. Young children with autism (mean age of 52 months) demonstrated several signs of attachment. First, they displayed significantly more proximity-seeking and distal social behavior upon reunion with their mothers than upon reunion with the experimenter. Second, proximity seeking to mother significantly increased from free play before separation to reunion, suggesting a specific reaction to separation. This was the very first investigation to demonstrate even rudimentary attachment capacity in individuals with autism, a group for whom such abilities had long been assumed to be absent. For this reason, it was a landmark study. Its contributions to understanding the differences in attachment that are also present in autism was important as well. Sigman and Ungerer found that children with autism, unlike those who are developing typically, displayed very little distress during separation. Additionally, both symbolic play skills and mental age were positively correlated with attachment behavior in the autistic sample, but negatively correlated with it in the normally developing sample. Thus, although these young children with autism were, as a group, displaying proximity-seeking and other attachment behaviors, they were also clearly demonstrating both delays and deviations from the normal developmental trajectory of attachment.

In a follow-up to this study, Sigman and Mundy (1989) compared preschool children with autism (mean chronological age 52 months) to preschool children with non-autistic developmental delays (DD) matched on both chronological and mental age and normally developing young children matched on mental age. They found that reunion behavior of the autistic and DD groups was very similar, but differed from that of the typically developing children in including less distress at separation and less proximity seeking at reunion. They suggested that these differences may have been a function of chronological age and consequent exposure to separation. The lack of differences between the autistic and DD groups suggests that differences in attachment behavior in autism are largely due to mental handicap, rather than a primary consequence of autism. All but one of 14 children with autism demonstrated evidence of attachment, such as preferential direction of social behaviors toward the mother over the examiner, proximity seeking at reunion, or distress at separation, a rate higher than in the Sigman and Ungerer (1984a) study.

Using a slight modification of Ainsworth's Strange Situation, Shapiro and colleagues examined attachment classifications (e.g., secure vs. insecure), comparing young children with autism or pervasive developmental disorder not otherwise specified (PDD; a milder or atypical version of autism) to those with mental retardation or developmental language disorder alone (Shapiro, Sherman, Calamari, & Koch, 1987). They demonstrated that 52 percent of the autism/PDD group demonstrated a secure (B) attachment to their mothers, while only 33 percent of the mentally retarded and 12.5 percent of the language-disordered group did so. Shapiro et al. found no relationship between autism severity (total symptom score) and attachment security. These findings were replicated by Rogers and colleagues, who found no differences in proximity seeking, contact maintenance, or attachment security between an autistic and matched developmentally delayed group, as well as no correlation between security ratings and autism severity (Rogers, Ozonoff, & Maslin-Cole, 1991). This same group, in a 1993 study, found no children with autism who were unattached and 50 percent who demonstrated a secure (B) attachment classification (Rogers, Ozonoff, & Maslin-Cole, 1993). In this later study, autism severity was again not related to attachment security; the best predictor of attachment was developmental level.

More recent investigations have replicated these basic findings, as well as extended them. Capps, Sigman, and Mundy (1994) explored differences in social behavior between securely and insecurely attached children with autism, finding that the former were more responsive to parental bids for joint attention, made requests more frequently, and had better receptive language abilities than the latter. Dissanayake and Crossley (1996) examined several social behaviors directed toward parents and found that attachment behaviors were much better preserved in autism than other caregiver-oriented behaviors, such as showing and giving objects and participating in mutual play. Proximity-seeking behaviors did not discriminate the autism and Down's syndrome groups studied in this investigation, while joint attention behaviors did (see below).

In conclusion, it appears that the notion of the unattached autistic child can be put to rest. Almost all children with autism, across several studies, display attachment-related behaviors that are different with caregivers than with unfamiliar adults. The quality of the attachment in the majority of children with autism is secure. However, there appear to be both delays and deviances in the attachment behavior of the autistic child. Several studies have demonstrated correlations between mental age and attachment behavior and quality. This suggests the hypothesis that children with autism may move from insecure to secure attachments with age and development, a situation clearly different from typical children. Their proximity-seeking behaviors sometimes include idiosyncratic behavioral displays, such as hand flapping to indicate excitement or positive affect, that are not seen in children without autism, requiring some modifications to existing coding systems.

Autistic children appear to experience, or at least display, less distress upon separation than typically developing children. This may reflect the higher chronological age of the subjects in studies of autism, but again may necessitate modifications to attachment classification systems when used with children with autism. In summary, the disturbances in the attachment behavior of those with autism are much less than previously suspected and appear secondary to developmental handicap rather than primary to autism. So what social difficulties do appear primary to autism?

Joint Attention

Difficulty coordinating attention between people and objects is thought to be one of the earliest-appearing deficits in children later diagnosed with autism. In contrast to attachment behaviors, joint attention behaviors have been demonstrated to be deficient in young children with autism in every study in which they have been examined. In typically developing infants, the ability to use gestural communication to orient other people and modify their behavior begins emerging before the first birthday. The pointing gesture is used in two ways: first, it is used to modify the environment and, later in development, to modify other people's attentional states (Bates, Camaioni, & Volterra, 1975). In the first emerging behavioral sequence, imperative communication, the infant uses pointing to obtain an object. In the second, declarative communication, the infant uses pointing to obtain a person's attention. Both are person–object sequences, with similar means but quite different ends. In typically developing children, imperative pointing emerges, on the average, approximately three months before declarative pointing (Camaioni, Perucchini, Muratori, & Milone, 1997). It is declarative pointing that is central to joint attention. Joint attention behaviors include declarative pointing, coordinated eye gaze, gaze monitoring, and shared affect (Bakeman & Adamson, 1984). They are epitomized by the following scenario: an infant sees an object/event of interest, looks to the parent, points, looks back at the object, and possibly vocalizes in a manner conveying excitement. The intent of this communication is simply to share awareness of the object or event: that is, to say "Do you see what I see and isn't it wonderful?" Such sequences occur many times a day during the second year of life of a typically developing toddler. What of the young child with autism?

Several studies have demonstrated that imperative pointing, or gestural communication for requesting functions, is generally intact in autism (Baron-Cohen, 1989a; Camaioni et al., 1997; Curcio, 1978; Wetherby & Prutting, 1984). In contrast, joint attention and its subcomponent, declarative pointing, are much more disordered. Both Curcio (1978) and Wetherby and Prutting (1984) reported that all of their participants with autism were able to use gestures to request, but none used them purely to orient others' attention to objects or events. Mundy and colleagues demonstrated a slightly different dissociation (Mundy, Sigman, Ungerer, & Sherman, 1986). The preschool children with autism in their study engaged in as much simple social interactional behavior, such as reaching for others, physical play, and eye contact after a tickle, as normal and mentally handicapped controls. However, they exhibited significantly less joint attention, including alternating attention between a toy and an adult, showing a toy to an adult, and pointing for declarative purposes. This same research team demonstrated that joint attention impairments are accompanied by deficits in sharing emotions with others (e.g., directing smiles toward the person with whom the infant is sharing attention; Kasari, Sigman, Mundy, & Yirmiya, 1990). Loveland and Landry (1986) found that children with autism used significantly less advanced forms of joint attention than non-retarded children with language handicaps, calling others' attention to external objects or events through touching or taking adults by the hand, rather than through pointing. The autistic participants in this study also demonstrated significantly more difficulty comprehending joint attention behavior (e.g., following the gaze shift or point of another person) than the language-delayed group.

These early studies of joint attention have since been replicated many times (DiLavore, Lord, & Rutter, 1995; McArthur & Adamson, 1996; Swettenham et al., 1998). Later investigations have revealed some variability in the degree of joint attention behavior displayed by young children with autism, however. The impairment is relative, rather than absolute, and some autistic children do develop joint attention skills, albeit much later than normal (Camaioni et al., 1997). Individual differences in joint attention are significantly more predictive of later language development than either initial language level or IQ (Mundy, Sigman, & Kasari, 1990), supporting the developmental theory that early gestural communication and coordination of attention are important precursors of more advanced language development (e.g., Bates, 1979). Individual differences in joint attention behaviors appear to be a function of developmental level, with higher-functioning children (e.g., higher mental age and/or IQ) demonstrating deficits only in the pointing component of joint attention, while lower-functioning children also display impairments in the eye-contact and gaze-monitoring aspects of joint attention (Mundy, Sigman, & Kasari, 1994). Joint attention deficits are more highly correlated with other social symptoms of autism than with the severity of specific autistic behaviors, such as stereotyped body movements, perseverative object use, or unusual sensory responses (Mundy et al., 1994).

In summary, joint attention disturbance appears to be a specific characteristic of young autistic children that distinguishes them from young children with typical development and non-autistic developmental delays. Impairments in both comprehension and production of joint attention have been documented. Since joint attention emerges very early in normal development, its absence or delay may be observable before disturbances in other domains are evident. Some have argued, in fact, that joint attention behaviors are precursors to the development of more advanced social behavior, such as pretend play and theory of mind skills (Baron-Cohen, 1991a; Charman, 1997). As discussed below, these research findings have had substantial clinical impact, effectively pushing back the earliest possible age at which a diagnosis of autism can be made.

Imitation

It has been argued that the ability of very young children to imitate others is an essential component of cognitive, communicative, and social development (Bruner, 1972; Meltzoff, 1985). Research with autistic children has consistently demonstrated deficits in imitative competence, relative to their performance on other sensorimotor tasks (Curcio, 1978; Sigman & Ungerer, 1984b) and to various control groups (Rogers & Pennington, 1991; Stone, Ousley, & Littleford, 1997). The meaning and specificity of these findings remain unclear (Smith & Bryson, 1994), though recent research focusing on the basic mechanisms of deviant imitation in autism (e.g., Rogers, Bennetto, McEvoy, & Pennington, 1996; Stone et al., 1997) promises new understanding of its role in both normal and atypical development. This section briefly summarizes imitation research in autism from within the perspective of major theories of imitation in normal development.

Piaget (1962) proposed six stages in the normal acquisition of imitative ability, culminating between 18 to 24 months with the appearance of, first, deferred imitation and then mental representation of objects and events beyond the self. Piaget theorized that the infant, essentially born without psychological processes, gradually *learns* imitation through positive reinforcement of reflex actions (e.g., a caregiver smiling in response to the infant's smile). The development of mental representation and ability to use and manipulate symbols is vital to the development of imitation in Piaget's account. Meltzoff (1985) offers an alternative argument, based on extensive research data, that newborns are in fact already endowed with a powerful, supramodal representational ability. His data suggest that infants are capable of imitating simple facial gestures within 72 hours of birth and of deferred imitation by 14 months. Meltzoff contends that these abilities are initially innate rather than learned, though experience is subsequently important for the refinement and functional use of imitation. Both Piaget's and Meltzoff's theories underscore the importance of imitation for later cognitive and social maturation.

The first major study of imitation in autism (DeMyer et al., 1972) used tasks from standard developmental batteries involving actions upon objects, as well as movements of the hands and fingers. Young children with autism-like disorders (mean age of 5 years 6 months) performed more poorly overall than mentally retarded controls; within the autism group, body imitation was more impaired than imitation with objects. DeMyer et al. suggested that autistic children show a sort of apraxia, that is, imitation deficits are a function of an inability to actually perform the actions, rather than a lack of understanding of the meaning of the action. They theorized the presence of a visual memory impairment, so that without the visual cues offered by the presence of the object, the organization of movements is more difficult. Though the idea of a visual memory impairment has since been discounted (Jones & Prior, 1985; Rogers et al., 1996), the search for the underlying mechanisms that sustain imitation continues. One more recent hypothesis attributes the imitation deficits of autism to a fundamental neurological impairment (e.g., Rogers & Pennington, 1991; Smith & Bryson, 1994), mirroring Meltzoff's theory of imitation in normal development, while another hypothesis, built on Piaget's theories, attributes the imitation deficits in autism to a cognitive deficit in symbolic ability (Baron-Cohen, 1988; Curcio, 1978).

The general symbolic deficit explanation of the imitation deficits in autism has generally not been supported by existing empirical evidence. One key prediction of this theory is that abstract, symbolic gestures should be more difficult to imitate than meaningless, arbitrary movements. Jones and Prior (1985) found that older autistic children (mean age of 8 years 7 months) were less able than age- and mental ability-matched controls to reproduce meaningless arm and hand movements. Rogers and Pennington (1991) proposed a theoretical framework for autism in which motor imitation is seen as a principal social deficit of the disorder. Working from a paradigm similar to Meltzoff's (Meltzoff & Gopnik, 1993), they theorized that a biological deficit in early motor imitation deprives the autistic child of the ability to process interpersonal affective information, with a cascading effect on social and communicative development, including the ability to form a theory of mind. In a study of high-functioning autism-spectrum adolescents and young adults, Rogers et al. (1996) reported that the experimental group (mean age = 15.5 years; mean Full-Scale IQ = 89) demonstrated impairments, relative to a mixed-diagnosis comparison group, on tasks measuring hand imitation, face imitation, and pantomiming use of familiar objects. Imitating meaningless actions (e.g., arbitrary hand or finger movements) was more difficult for those with autism than imitating meaningful movements (e.g., pretending to take off a baseball cap); this same pattern was seen in the non-autistic control group. The authors felt that this imitative profile argued strongly against a symbolic explanation for the imitation deficits of autism. This conclusion was further supported by two recent studies, one finding that autistic children were able to imitate symbolic play as well as or better than Down's syndrome and normal children matched on verbal mental age (Libby, Powell, Messer, & Jordan, 1997), and the other reporting that very young children with autism (mean age = 31 months) had more difficulty imitating nonmeaningful than meaningful actions (Stone et al., 1997). Smith and Bryson (1994), in their review of imitation in autism, conclude that the available empirical evidence implies a core handicap in the ability to represent and organize actions at a basic neurological level, rather than at the symbolic level.

Rogers and Pennington (1991) have emphasized the importance of considering imitation as a multidimensional construct. For example, the copying of distinct phrases and tones referred to as echolalia is a common diagnostic feature of autism. Rogers and Pennington contend that this dissociation between often good verbal and usually poor motor imitation suggests that their respective neural pathways develop differentially. Similarly, studies generally find that body imitation is significantly harder for young children with autism than imitation of actions upon objects, suggesting that these represent independent dimensions of behavior (DeMyer et al., 1972; Stone et al., 1997).

Stone et al. found that the *pattern* of acquisition of different imitation skills (e.g., actions on objects, actions on the self, etc.) was the same across autistic and non-autistic groups, suggesting that the imitation impairment of autism represents a *delay* rather than a *deviance*. This is a likely explanation for results from two studies (Charman & Baron-Cohen, 1994; Morgan, Cutrer, Coplin, & Rodrigue, 1989) which did not find group differences in imitation between autistic and control samples: both studies used simple infant imitation tasks with older children, all of whom performed at or near ceiling level on the measures.

In summary, autistic children do acquire some imitative capacity, but at a much slower rate than other children. This delay may have profound consequences for other early-developing social and communicative behaviors. Imitation is not a unitary construct and should be viewed at the very least in terms of separate mechanisms governing imitation of body movements (e.g., motor imitation), imitation with objects (e.g., symbolic imitation), and vocal imitation. Motor imitation deficits in particular have been repeatedly demonstrated across all ages, both relative to comparison groups and to other imitation skills, within autism samples. As studies with better control groups 'emerge (e.g., Rogers et al., 1996; Stone et al., 1997), the autism-specific nature of at least some imitation impairment is becoming more apparent. Whether abnormalities of imitation in autism are primary neurological deficits (present perhaps from birth) or the product of a failure of metarepresentational capacity remains controversial, though evidence is growing in favor of the former interpretation. Such distinctions have important implications for research on the etiology of autism.

Play

Impaired play is a well-documented feature of autism and is central to its diagnosis in all classification systems (APA, 1994; Schopler, Reichler, & Renner, 1986; Wing, Gould, Yeates, & Brierley, 1977). Play behaviors emerge in a typical sequence in the course of normal development (Belsky & Most, 1981; Nicolich, 1977; Ungerer, Zelazo, Kearsley, & O'Leary, 1981). The first form to emerge, during the first year of life, is sensorimotor play, which consists primarily of simple object manipulation (e.g., mouthing, holding, dropping objects). Around the first birthday, infants begin to combine objects in relational play (e.g., banging, stacking, placing objects inside each other). Pretend play emerges toward the end of the second year of life and encompasses two subcategories, functional and symbolic play. Functional play appears first and includes self-, other-, and object-directed acts that involve using toys in the conventional manner intended (e.g., feeding a doll, putting a toy car in a garage). Symbolic play emerges from approximately 20 months on. Its hallmark is the use of objects in an "as if" manner: animating a toy figure, transforming an object, assigning a nonliteral role to the self or a play partner, or enacting behaviors in a context different from those with which they were conventionally associated. The vast majority of autism research has focused on symbolic play and its abnormalities. Most studies find that sensorimotor and relational play are relatively intact in young children with autism (Baron-Cohen, 1987; Libby, Powell, Messer, & Jordan, 1998). The extent of impairment in functional play is less clear. Two studies failed to find significant differences between children with autism and matched controls (Baron-Cohen, 1987; Libby et al., 1998), but others have documented group differences even in functional play (Jarrold, Boucher, & Smith, 1996; Lewis & Boucher, 1988; Stone, Lemanek, Fischel, Fernandez, & Altemeier, 1990). What is relatively clear, however, is that symbolic play skills are most seriously affected in individuals with autism.

An early study using maternal reports of play behavior found that children with autism tended to fixate on one or two objects and use them "ritualistically," rather than in a symbolic manner (DeMyer, Mann, Tilton, & Loew, 1967). None of the autistic children in a large sample studied by Lorna Wing and colleagues (1977) exhibited symbolic play; one-third demonstrated stereotyped play involving simple repetitive manipulations of objects. In contrast, 87 percent of the mentally retarded group in this study displayed symbolic play and only 11 percent displayed stereotypic play. These data and later studies (e.g., Baron-Cohen, 1987) suggest that the symbolic play deficits seen in young children with autism are not simply a function of mental handicap or delayed development, but are relatively specific features of the autistic syndrome.

Leslie (1987) outlined three types of symbolic play: object substitution, in which an object is used as if it is something else (e.g., using a banana as a telephone), attribution of false properties, in which properties are attributed to an object that do not in reality exist (e.g., pretending a doll is ill), and reference to an absent object (e.g., driving a car along an imaginary road). Libby et al. (1998) examined the relative frequency of these three types of symbolic play in a longitudinal study of autism. They found that most examples of symbolic play were of the object substitution type and that no references to absent objects were made. This pattern distinguished the autism group from two comparison samples matched on verbal mental age, one with Down's syndrome, the other typically developing.

Different theories of the origin of the pretend play deficit in autism have been proposed. An early and very influential theory was Leslie's (1987) metarepresentational account. Leslie attributed pretend play impairments to broader symbolic deficits that are an inherent and primary part, he hypothesized, of the autistic syndrome. Leslie distinguished between primary representations of the world ("This is a banana") and metarepresentations ("*I think* this is a banana" or "This banana is *a telephone*"). According to Leslie, metarepresentation permits the transgression of reality, the decoupling of an object's "true" properties from other possible properties that is required for symbolic play. He proposed that similar metarepresentational mechanisms underlie the propositions involved in the development of a theory of mind and thus linked these two areas of impairment functionally. Another hypothesis about the mechanism underlying symbolic play impairments in autism was proposed by Harris (1993), who suggested that executive function deficits (specifically, cognitive inflexibility) prevented children with autism from disengaging from the schema normally elicited by objects, thus limiting nonliteral transformations (i.e., pretend play schema).

More recently, the importance of setting conditions and task structure to the production of symbolic play has become apparent. While relatively few symbolic acts are produced spontaneously by children with autism in free-play situations, they increase significantly under more structured play conditions (Charman & Baron-Cohen, 1997; Gould, 1986; Jarrold et al., 1996; Lewis & Boucher, 1988, 1995; McDonough, Stahmer, Schreibman, & Thompson, 1997; Ungerer & Sigman, 1981). The level of support varies across studies, from simple encouragement or elicitation (e.g., "Show me what you can do with these") to explicit instruction (e.g., "Feed the doll") to modeling of symbolic acts by the experimenter. In every study, significant increases in the frequency, duration, and complexity of symbolic play acts occurred in the scaffolded condition; in some studies, this support eliminated previously existing group differences in symbolic play (Lewis & Boucher, 1988; Jarrold et al., 1996). This robust finding has led to the speculation that low levels of pretend play are secondary not to the cognitive, general symbolic, or social impairments of autism, as originally hypothesized (e.g., Harris, 1993; Leslie, 1987), but to low motivation or inability to generate play acts without prompting (Jarrold et al., 1996; Lewis & Boucher, 1988, 1995; Roeyers & van Berckelaer-Onnes, 1994). This view sees the problem not as lack of possession of an ability, but as failure to apply or use available skills. This is a common dissociation seen in autism, whereby the mechanics to perform a skill are possessed but not actively employed when appropriate. This pattern has been documented, for example, in the theory of mind literature, with autistic individuals passing paper-and-pencil tests of higher-order mentalizing in controlled laboratory situations but giving no evidence of using these skills in their everyday interpersonal interactions (Bowler, 1992; Ozonoff & Miller, 1995). Similarly, a clear dissociation between spontaneous recall and elicited or prompted recall has been demonstrated in the memory literature on autism (Boucher & Warrington, 1976; Tager-Flusberg, 1991). Whether a similar dissociation explains the symbolic play deficits of autism warrants attention in the future.

Emerging Questions, Paradigms, and Issues

In the first years of studying autism, research focused on delays and deviances in specific domains of development, such as joint attention and imitation. In recent years, there has been increased emphasis on developmental continuities and discontinuities in these impairments, how they evolve over the course of development, and how they are related to symptoms in the older child with autism. Current research has also striven to apply early research findings to practical issues, such as improving the accuracy and timeliness of diagnosis. The next section covers these recent developments in the autism literature.

Theory of Mind

Developmental psychologists have long recognized that the human capacity to attribute mental states to the self and to others is an essential skill, one which underlies most social interaction (Povinelli, 1993; Zelazo, Burack, Benedetto, & Frye, 1996). Premack and Woodruff (1978) coined the term "theory of mind" to describe the ability to (1) appreciate beliefs, intentions, knowledge, pretense, and perception in the self and in others; and (2) to understand the link between mental states and action. This competence allows a person to infer what others are thinking and then predict or manipulate others' behavior. A theory of mind (ToM) is thought to develop gradually, in stage-like manner, in typical children, with the most important elements, including the ability to take the perspective of other people, appearing around age 4 (Frye, Zelazo, & Palfai, 1995; Roth & Leslie, 1998).

In 1985, Baron-Cohen, Leslie, and Frith published a seminal study which reported that autistic children demonstrated profound impairment, relative to Down's syndrome and normally developing controls, on a task intended to measure theory of mind ability. Subjects were presented with a scenario in which two dolls, Sally and Anne, sat in front of an empty basket and a covered box. Sally placed a marble in the basket and then left the scene. Anne moved the marble to the box, in full view of the child, and Sally then returned, unaware of the change. The child was asked the critical question, "Where will Sally look for the marble?" While 85 percent of the Down's syndrome group and 86 percent of the normal group answered this question correctly ("in the basket"), only 20 percent of the autism group did so. Two control questions, regarding the location of the marble at the beginning of the story and its latest location, were correctly answered by all subjects. The essential deficit in the autism group was hypothesized to be an inability to appreciate that the doll, Sally, possessed a different knowledge than the child.

This research group went on to suggest that the ToM deficit is the unique, modular cognitive deficiency which underlies the pattern of social and communicative symptoms specific to autism (e.g., Baron-Cohen, 1989b; Frith, 1989). This claim, with its hope of providing a relatively simple explanation for most aspects of a complex disorder, caused extraordinary excitement among autism researchers (Bailey, Phillips, & Rutter, 1996). The process of examining this claim has generated a tremendous amount of knowledge regarding ToM processes in both normal and clinical populations (see Yirmiya, Erel, Shaked, & Solomonica-Levi, 1998, for a review), as well as useful theories regarding the implications of ToM for both typical and autistic cognitive and social development. This section reviews a few highlights from these 15 years of inquiry.

In order for theory of mind to be considered a primary deficit in autism, it should meet three criteria, as outlined by Ozonoff, Pennington, and Rogers (1991; see also Zelazo et al., 1996): (1) it should be relatively universal among autistic individuals; (2) it should be specific to autism, that is, not apparent in other disorders; and (3) its causal precedence in development should be firmly established. Each of these criteria will be considered separately. The first concern, regarding the universality of ToM handicap in autism, was questionable from the start: while 80 percent of the children studied by Baron-Cohen et al. (1985) failed the Sally–Anne false-belief paradigm, 20 percent did pass the test. Research from other groups (reviewed in Yirmiya et al., 1998) has shown pass rates for autism-spectrum samples of as high as 60 percent on ToM tasks. Ozonoff, Rogers, and Pennington (1991) divided high-functioning autism-spectrum children (mean age of approximately 12 years) into a high-functioning autism (HFA) group and an Asperger's syndrome (AS) group (essentially, autism with high verbal abilities) and found significant performance differences on a variety of ToM tasks, with the AS group achieving better scores on each component. Performance between the AS group and matched normal controls was not significantly different: the AS group was equal to the controls on simple first-order ToM tasks as described above, though somewhat worse on a more difficult, second-order task which requires another level of understanding, a "he thinks she thinks" paradigm.

ToM advocates (Baron-Cohen, 1991b; Baron-Cohen, Jolliffe, Mortimore, & Robertson, 1997; Happe, 1995) have responded with revised models which hypothesize that ToM may simultaneously represent a *deviance* and a *delay* in autism, in that individuals with autism may eventually develop ToM capacity, but never at a normal level. They proposed that high pass rates in many older, high-functioning autism-spectrum samples were because the tasks were too simple for the higher developmental level. Baron-Cohen et al. (1997) created a task intended to measure "adult" ToM, which involved inferring the cognitive states of faces that were cut out of magazines from above the middle of the nose. The autistic-spectrum group of adults performed significantly more poorly than a Tourette's syndrome control group, though uncertainties about the suitability of matching left important questions regarding alternative explanations. While such evidence lends support to claims that some ToM impairment seems pervasive in autism, it does not fully rescue the notion of ToM as a universal deficit in autism.

Ozonoff, Pennington, et al. (1991) noted that the specificity criterion is the least essential to establishing the primacy of the ToM deficit, if one accepts that there may be a *pattern* of multiple primary deficits which work together to cause the range of impairments seen in autism. The hypothesis that ToM by itself is the core, unique handicap in autism has proven untenable, however. While Baron-Cohen et al. (1985) found Down's syndrome patients to be unimpaired on the Sally–Anne false-belief task, Zelazo and colleagues (1996) reported that their Down's syndrome sample performed significantly worse than controls matched on verbal mental age. A meta-analysis by Yirmiya et al. (1998) found that, across all relevant studies, individuals with autism performed less well than individuals with mental retardation of undifferentiated etiology, who performed less well than mentally retarded individuals with Down's syndrome, who performed less well than individuals developing normally. Thus there is a clear gradient of ToM capacity, which while probably more severe in autism than in most groups, is not exclusive to that disorder.

The search for ToM deficits has recently been extended to prelingually deaf children. One research team found that 65 percent of their subjects failed standard first-order false-belief tasks (Peterson & Siegal, 1995). They suggest that ToM capacity requires practice conversing about mental states, to which deaf children are rarely exposed in their homes; most families who do sign converse primarily about concrete topics (Peterson & Siegal, 1995). Russell et al. (1998) replicated this finding, reporting that 83 percent of their youngest group of deaf children (age 4–9 to 7–11) failed ToM tests; at age 13–17, 40 percent of their group still failed the tests. These authors echoed Peterson and Siegal's claim that prelingually deaf children learn ToM gradually, only after many years in school of conversing about mental states with peers who are fluent in sign language. A number of researchers (Happe, 1995; Ozonoff, Rogers, et al., 1991; Prior et al., 1998; Sparrevohn & Howie, 1995; Zelazo et al., 1996) have reported evidence that ToM development is strongly associated with factors not specific to autism, including verbal mental age, intelligence, chronological age, and other cognitive constructs such as executive functioning. These authors dispute that ToM is a specific, modular cognitive unit as hypothesized by Baron-Cohen and colleagues. Many studies which have failed to find such correlations have been hampered by inadequate or inappropriate controls, especially with regard to verbal ability (Yirmiya et al, 1998; Zelazo et al., 1996).

The third criterion for primacy states that ToM must be plausible as a developmentally causal mechanism. One of the most intriguing aspects of the ToM hypothesis has been its ability to explain a broad range of social and communicative symptoms commonly seen in autism (though notably, it offers little explanation for the restricted, stereotyped behaviors that are also hallmark characteristics). Nonetheless, the causal hypothesis of ToM has been criticized because of its late development. Whereas ToM appears around age 4 in normal children, symptoms of autism are typically noted before age 2 (Bailey et al., 1996) and, by definition, by age 3 (APA, 1994). Evidence for very early deficits in autism (see below) has prompted the question of how ToM handicap can be a primary etiological factor if it does not emerge until after most other symptoms are present. Some have argued that several early impairments, such as joint attention (see above), are developmental precursors to ToM (e.g., see Baron-Cohen, 1991a). According to this model, understanding *beliefs* is preceded by understanding *attention*. Baron-Cohen argues, for example, that while the normally developing infant comes to understand at around 9 months that an adult who points at an object is expressing a selective interest in that object, the autistic infant does not make the connection between the gesture and the mental state (e.g., attention or interest). The same logic applies to the *production* of joint attention. The normally developing toddler uses integrated pointing and gaze to influence the attention of adults; the autistic toddler, on the other hand, does not try to influence the mental state of the adult. In sum, Baron-Cohen (1991a; see also Leslie & Happe, 1989) claims that precursors to metarepresentational ability are present within the first year of life, providing a developmental link between infancy and theory of mind research with older children. The relevance of this hypothesis to early diagnosis and intervention is discussed below.

Several groups have implicated other cognitive constructs as equal to, or even preceding, ToM in the etiology of autism. Indeed, Alan Leslie, one of the original proponents of the ToM hypothesis, has recently argued (Roth & Leslie, 1998) that normally developing ToM explicitly requires an executive function component, a "selection processor (SP)." On the standard false-belief task, for example, this SP serves to "inhibit a default and normally correct assumption, in this case, that the content belief is true." While Leslie maintains that it is the modular ToM, and not executive functioning, which is primarily impaired in autism, Frye and colleagues (Frye et al., 1995) have theorized that the difficulties with ToM tasks in autism stem from an impairment in rule-based reasoning. They constructed non-mentalizing tasks with demands similar to those used to measure ToM, such as the necessity to acknowledge two perspectives simultaneously and choose between opposing judgments. Normally developing 3-year-olds were unable to complete either the ToM or the non-mentalizing tasks, 4-year-olds were able to complete some of each, and 5-year-olds were proficient at both types of tasks. The similarity of developmental course between mental-state and non-mental-state abilities suggested that children may apply a similar form of reasoning to both. The perseveration of both 3- and 4-year-olds reported for Frye et al.'s (1995) non-mentalizing card-sort task is consistent with the suggestion of Ozonoff, Pennington, et al. (1991) that ToM deficits in autism may reflect more of a perseverative tendency (e.g., getting stuck on the fact that the ball is in the box in the Sally–Anne task) than an inability to appreciate mental states. Other researchers (e.g., Frye et al., 1995; Povinelli, 1993) have also argued that both normal and autistic children may pass ToM tasks through mechanisms much different than the hypothesized strategy of understanding mental states. Methodological and psychometric concerns associated with common ToM tests (Charman & Campbell, 1997; Mayes, Klin, Tercyak, Cicchetti, & Cohen, 1996; Yirmiya et al., 1998) raise additional questions regarding the construct validity of ToM.

Isolating the neurobiology of ToM may illuminate some of autism's most fundamental features. The prefrontal regions have long been implicated in both social and cognitive deficits in autism (Damasio & Maurer, 1978; Ozonoff, Rogers, et al., 1991). A group at the MRC Cognitive Development Unit in London (Fletcher et al., 1995; Happe et al., 1996) have used functional magnetic resonance imaging (f-MRI) techniques to study brain activation during verbal mentalizing tasks (reading stories and answering questions silently) in both normally developing volunteers and a group of five patients with a diagnosis of Asperger's syndrome (AS; a variant of high-functioning autism characterized by relatively well-developed language and an early history of normal language acquisition). A comparison of the two groups implicated differences in the medial prefrontal cortex (Brodmann's area 8/9), which was activated during the task in the normal group but not in the AS patients; the AS group showed activation instead in a bordering region (corresponding to Brodmann's area 9/10). This discrepancy led the MRC researchers to hypothesize "that the Asperger subjects' mentalizing performance was subserved by a brain system in which one key component is missing." Baron-Cohen and colleagues have argued for the involvement of the orbito-frontal cortex in ToM reasoning, based on evidence from imaging studies and from studies of orbito-frontal lesion patients (Stone, Baron-Cohen, & Knight, 1998). Winner and colleagues (Winner, Brownell, Happe, Blum, & Pincus, 1998) tested patients with known right-hemisphere damage and found that they performed more poorly than controls on second-order ToM tasks, such as distinguishing jokes from lies. They conclude that some right-hemisphere structures are necessary for an intact theory of mind. While research in this area is still sparse, increased attention to the topic and rapidly improving imaging techniques offer great potential for bringing new understanding regarding ToM development.

In sum, the initial excitement generated by theory of mind research has been tempered somewhat by the realization that ToM, by itself, cannot explain all aspects of autism. Empirical investigations have demonstrated that ToM is not universally deficient in all people with autism, is not specific to autism, and is preceded temporally by other, more fundamental social abnormalities. Nonetheless, ToM research in typical, autistic, and other clinical samples continues to offer important insights into human development. Recent studies employing methods of increasing technological sophistication promise to be especially rewarding.

Early Identification and Diagnosis of Autism

Research on the early social development of individuals with autism has considerably advanced the ability to identify young children at a much earlier age than was previously possible. The research reviewed in this chapter has turned out to have very important clinical implications, as indicated in this final section. The onset of autism occurs, by definition (APA, 1994), before 3 years of age. In reality, parents first become concerned about their child's development much earlier, usually well before the second birthday (Siegel, Pliner, Eschler, & Elliott, 1988; Smith, Chung, & Vostanis, 1994). Accurate diagnosis is typically delayed for several years, however, with intervening incorrect or partial diagnoses common (Siegel et al., 1988). Delays in diagnosis are particularly unfortunate given the recent development of several highly effective early intervention programs for autism (Lovaas, 1987; Rogers & Lewis, 1989; Schopler, Mesibov, Shigley & Bashford, 1984). Such specialized interventions are neither intended for nor offered to non-autistic children, so timely diagnosis and accurate differentiation of autism from non-autistic developmental disorders are essential. Identification of early-appearing features of autism also has important research and theoretical implications. As reviewed above, precedence in development and the ability to explain later-developing symptoms of the disorder are critical criteria that any psychological deficit of autism must fulfill to be considered "primary" or of causal significance in the disorder (Rapin, 1987). Failure to satisfy these particular criteria was one part of the eventual downfall of the theory of mind hypothesis for explaining autism, for example. Thus, the search for developmental precursors of autistic symptoms is important in many ways.

As indicated in the sections above, research on the early social abilities of young children with autism sheds some light on what the early symptoms of autism are, particularly investigations that compared children with autism to chronological- and/or mental-age-matched comparison subjects. This body of work suggests that early joint attention, imitation, and symbolic play abilities discriminate young children with autism from those with non-autistic developmental delays; thus, they are good candidates for early identifiers of autism. Even more powerful in the search for early discriminators are research designs that examine behavioral signs and their developmental timing in very young children *before* diagnosis. Early investigations employed retrospective designs, asking parents to recall their earliest concerns about their now-diagnosed child with autism. These studies found that the most common initial symptom recognized by parents was delayed or abnormal speech development; however, in most cases social symptoms appeared to predate the language abnormalities in parents' retrospective reports (Dahlgren & Gillberg, 1989; DeMyer, 1979; Klin, Volkmar, & Sparrow, 1992; Rogers & DiLalla, 1990). The difficulties with retrospective designs are many, however, including problems of memory and interpretation, as well as lack of parental expertise in recognizing early symptoms of autism.

More recently, two types of prospective designs have predominated in the search for very early indicators of autism. One involves coding videotapes of infants and young children who are later diagnosed with autism; the other involves longitudinal follow-up of young children referred for developmental delay. Both approaches complement the retrospective strategy, as well as the research examined earlier in this chapter, in highlighting the importance of early social behavior in identifying autism. Osterling and Dawson (1994) compared first birthday party videotapes of children later diagnosed with autism to those of typically developing children. They found four behaviors that discriminated the groups at 1 year of age, including eye contact, showing objects, pointing, and orienting to name. These four signs together classified 91 percent of cases correctly. A second videotape study of 12–30-month-old children prediagnosis confirmed the power of joint attention behaviors, such as pointing, looking at faces, alternating gaze, and showing objects, in discriminating autism from typical development (Mars, Mauk, & Dowrick, 1998); other behaviors in this study that differentiated the groups were following verbal directions, using single words, and imitating verbalizations. All of the autistic participants and 96 percent of the typically developing participants were accurately identified with this group of variables. This study did not, however, standardize the situations in which the children were videotaped, nor the ages at which they were coded, as the Osterling and Dawson study (1994) did. Both investigations used coders blind to later developmental status of the children. Neither, however, used a mentally handicapped or developmentally delayed comparison sample. Thus, these studies cannot address whether the joint attention and other social-communicative discriminating behaviors are identifying *autism* or the mental handicap that is highly comorbid with it.

Longitudinal prospective investigations have been better able to address this issue. In a very important study, Lord (1995) examined 30 young children referred to a developmental disabilities clinic, first at age 2 and then again at age 3. Slightly over half the sample was eventually diagnosed with autism at age 3, while the others were diagnosed with nonspecific developmental delays. The behaviors that best discriminated the groups at age 2 and predicted eventual diagnosis at age 3 were directing attention (e.g., showing objects) and attending to human voice. The correct classification rate at age 2 using this algorithm was 83 percent. At age 3, pointing and attention to voice continued to discriminate the groups, with two additional behaviors adding to diagnostic accuracy (which now reached 100 percent), use of other's hand as a tool and hand or finger mannerisms (e.g., flapping, flicking, posturing). Gillberg and colleagues (1990) conducted a similar study, but without developmentally delayed comparison subjects, that examined 28 very young children suspected of having autism (range = 8 to 35 months, with 20 percent of the sample under 1 year of age). The most common early symptoms reported by parents, prediagnosis, were abnormalities of gaze, orienting to voice, and play.

Based on their earlier empirical work on joint attention, pointing, and theory of mind, Baron-Cohen and colleagues developed a measure for general medical practitioners or pediatricians to use at well-baby 18-month examinations, the Checklist for Autism in Toddlers or CHAT (Baron-Cohen, Allen, & Gillberg, 1992). Five key behaviors were identified: pointing to express interest or direct attention, pretend play (both functional and symbolic), showing objects, interest in other children, and social play (e.g., peek-a-boo-type face-to-face interactional games). A large group of 18-month-olds was screened with the measure, approximately half of whom were at higher-than-average genetic risk for autism by virtue of having a sibling with the disorder. Four children (all from the high-risk group) were later diagnosed with autism at 30 months of age. What distinguished them at 18 months from the larger sample was a pattern of failure on at least two of the five key indicators. No child failing zero or one items was later diagnosed with autism and no child failing two or more items did not have autism. In a later epidemiological study of 16,000 randomly selected British 18-month-olds, this research team, again employing the CHAT, identified ten cases who, upon longitudinal follow-up, were later diagnosed with autism (Baron-Cohen et al., 1996). All ten children failed to point to express interest, monitor another person's gaze (e.g., turn to look in the same direction as an adult was looking), and demonstrate pretend play. Two additional children failed all three items at 18 months, but were later diagnosed with non-autistic developmental delays, providing an 83.3 percent specificity (true positive) rate for the CHAT. Since the CHAT was designed as a screening measure used to refer children for specialist evaluations, rather than as a diagnostic tool in and of itself, the rate of false positives is relatively unimportant as long as it is not excessively high.

The clear conclusion we can draw from this literature is the significance of early social behavior in diagnosing autism. No so-called "positive symptoms" of autism (e.g., atypical behaviors that are present), such as hand mannerisms, ritualistic and perseverative behavior, sensory abnormalities, or obsessional interests, identified cases of autism before age 3. When present, these were clearly later-developing features of the syndrome (Lord, 1995). "Negative symptoms," or typical behaviors expected in normal development that are absent, are what predict autism. Specifically, it is largely social limitations, rather than communicative deficits, that discriminate those with autism from those with other developmental problems.[1] Language delay is a typical feature of both nonspecific developmental delay and specific mental retardation syndromes, as well as, of course, the central symptom of speech-language disorders; thus, it is clearly far from specific to autism. Dozens of social milestones are passed before an infant would even be expected to utter a first word, further emphasizing the importance of early social behavior in the earliest possible diagnosis of autism. Despite this, there is often a misguided emphasis on communication, particularly verbal, deficits. Many a clinician and parent has suppressed or dismissed concerns about social development until their suspicions are later confirmed by the absence or delay in expressive language. Two recent studies suggest that early motor abnormalities may also be present in infants and young children with autism (Baranek, 1999; Teitelbaum, Teitelbaum, Nye, Fryman, & Maurer, 1998), but these studies advocate using motor deficits to *augment*, rather than replace, measures of social responsiveness in the early diagnosis of autism.

Conclusion

This chapter reviewed five areas of social development, attachment, joint attention, imitation, play, and theory of mind, and their relationship to autism. Evidence was summarized suggesting that all but attachment are impaired in children with autism and distinguish them from both typically developing and mentally handicapped but non-autistic comparison subjects. This research, originally embarked upon for purely empirical reasons, has turned out to have very important practical implications. These same behaviors are the most important means of identifying autism in very young children, something that is essential to the best outcome of the disorder. It is critical for primary care providers and parents to appreciate the central importance of early social behaviors in evaluating the developmental "health" of their children. This research may also stimulate new therapeutic techniques for autism focusing on teaching social behavior that typically unfolds naturally. For example, programs to teach joint attention and its components (e.g., gaze monitoring, pointing) may be developed in the future and may lead to even better outcomes for young children with autism. Finally, the centrality of early social behaviors to early diagnosis of autism suggests that the domain of social behavior may provide some of the most fruitful leads in the search for primary causal deficits of the condition.

Note

1 Some early autistic deficits, such as limited joint attention, can be alternately categorized as either social or communicative in nature. Either way, they are *preverbal* impairments, further emphasizing the centrality of behaviors other than expressive language in first diagnosing autism.

Further Reading

Bailey, A., Phillips, W., & Rutter, M. (1996). Autism: Towards an integration of clinical, genetic, neuropsychological, and neurobiological perspectives. *Journal of Child Psychology and Psychiatry, 37,* 89–126. This paper reviews current theories and empirical research on the etiology of autism and its symptoms.

Baron-Cohen, S., Tager-Flusberg, H., & Cohen, D. J. (Eds.). (1993). *Understanding other minds: Perspectives from autism.* New York: Oxford University Press. This book reviews both supportive and critical evidence of the "theory of mind" hypothesis of autism.

Sigman, M. (1998). Change and continuity in the development of children with autism. *Journal of Child Psychology and Psychiatry, 39,* 817–827. This review article summarizes the deviances and delays in social-communicative development seen in autism and examines continuities and discontinuities in them across the life span.

Yirmiya, N., Erel, O., Shaked, M., & Solomonica-Levi, D. (1998). Meta-analyses comparing theory of mind abilities of individuals with autism, individuals with mental retardation, and normally developing individuals. *Psychological Bulletin, 124,* 283–307. This article provides a critical review and meta-analysis of the very large theory of mind literature in autism.

References

Ainsworth, M. D. S., Blehar, M. C., Waters, E., & Wall, S. (1978). *Patterns of attachment.* Hillsdale, NJ: Lawrence Erlbaum.

American Psychiatric Association. (1994). *Diagnostic and statistical manual of mental disorders* (4th ed.). Washington, DC: Author.

Bailey, A., Phillips, W., & Rutter, M. (1996). Autism: Towards an integration of clinical, genetic, neuropsychological, and neurobiological perspectives. *Journal of Child Psychology and Psychiatry, 37,* 89–126.

Bakeman, R., & Adamson, L. B. (1984). Coordinating attention to people and objects in mother–infant and peer–infant interactions. *Child Development, 55,* 1278–1289.

Baranek, G. T. (1999). Autism during infancy: A retrospective video analysis of sensory-motor and social behaviors at 9–12 months of age. *Journal of Autism and Developmental Disorders, 29,* 213–224.

Baron-Cohen, S. (1987). Autism and symbolic play. *British Journal of Developmental Psychology, 5,* 139–148.

Baron-Cohen, S. (1988). Social and pragmatic deficits in autism: Cognitive or affective? *Journal of Autism and Developmental Disorders, 18,* 379–402.

Baron-Cohen, S. (1989a). Perceptual role taking and protodeclarative pointing in autism. *British Journal of Developmental Psychology, 7,* 113–127.

Baron-Cohen, S. (1989b). The autistic child's theory of mind: A case of specific developmental delay. *Journal of Child Psychology and Psychiatry, 30,* 285–297.

Baron-Cohen, S. (1991a). Precursors to a theory of mind: Understanding attention in others. In A. Whiten (Ed.), *Natural theories of mind: The evolution, development and simulation of everyday mindreading* (pp. 233–251). Oxford: Blackwell.

Baron-Cohen, S. (1991b). The development of a theory of mind in autism: Deviance and delay? *Psychiatric Clinics of North America, 14,* 33–51.

Baron-Cohen, S., Allen, J., & Gillberg, C. (1992). Can autism be detected at 18 months? The needle, the haystack, and the CHAT. *British Journal of Psychiatry, 161,* 839–843.

Baron-Cohen, S., Cox, A., Baird, G., Swettenham, J., Nightingale, N., Morgan, K., Drew, A., & Charman, T. (1996). Psychological markers in the detection of autism in infancy in a large population. *British Journal of Psychiatry, 168,* 158–163.

Baron-Cohen, S., Jolliffe, T., Mortimore, C., & Robertson, M. (1997). Another advanced test of theory of mind: Evidence from very high functioning adults with autism or Asperger syndrome. *Journal of Child Psychology and Psychiatry, 38,* 813–822.

Baron-Cohen, S., Leslie, A. M., & Frith, U. (1985). Does the autistic child have a theory of mind? *Cognition, 21*, 37–46.

Bates, E. (1979). *The emergence of symbols: Cognition and communication in infancy.* New York: Academic Press.

Bates, E., Camaioni, L., & Volterra, V. (1975). The acquisition of performatives prior to speech. *Merrill-Palmer Quarterly, 21*, 205–226.

Belsky, J., & Most, R. K. (1981). From exploration to play: A cross-sectional study of infant free play behavior. *Developmental Psychology, 17*, 630–639.

Bettelheim, B. (1967). *The empty fortress.* New York: Free Press.

Boucher, J., & Warrington, E. K. (1976). Memory deficits in early infantile autism: Some similarities to the amnesic syndrome. *British Journal of Psychology, 67*, 73–87.

Bowler, D. M. (1992). "Theory of mind" in Asperger's syndrome. *Journal of Child Psychology and Psychiatry, 33*, 877–893.

Bruner, J. (1972). Nature and uses of immaturity. *American Psychologist, 27*, 687–708.

Bryson, S. E., Clark, B. S., & Smith, I. M. (1988). First report of a Canadian epidemiological study of autistic syndromes. *Journal of Child Psychology and Psychiatry, 29*, 433–445.

Camaioni, L., Perucchini, P., Muratori, F., & Milone, A. (1997). A longitudinal examination of the communicative gestures deficit in young children with autism. *Journal of Autism and Developmental Disorders, 27*, 715–725.

Capps, L., Sigman, M., & Mundy, P. (1994). Attachment security in children with autism. *Development and Psychopathology, 6*, 249–261.

Charman, T. (1997). The relationship between joint attention and pretend play in autism. *Development and Psychopathology, 9*, 1–16.

Charman, T., & Baron-Cohen, S. (1994). Another look at imitation in autism. *Development and Psychopathology, 6*, 403–413.

Charman, T., & Baron-Cohen, S. (1997). Prompted pretend play in autism. *Journal of Autism and Developmental Disorders, 27*, 325–332.

Charman, T., & Campbell, A. (1997). Reliability of theory of mind task performance by individuals with a learning disability. *Journal of Child Psychology and Psychiatry, 38*, 725–730.

Curcio, F. (1978). Sensorimotor functioning and communication in mute autistic children. *Journal of Autism and Child Schizophrenia, 8*, 282–292.

Dahlgren, S. O., & Gillberg, C. (1989). Symptoms in the first two years of life: A preliminary population study of infantile autism. *European Archives of Psychiatric and Neurological Science, 283*, 169–174.

Damasio, A. R., & Maurer, R. G. (1978). A neurological model for childhood autism. *Archives of Neurology, 35*, 777–786.

DeMyer, M. K. (1979). *Parents and children in autism.* Washington, DC: Victor Winston and Sons.

DeMyer, M. K., Alpern, G. D., Barton, S., DeMyer, W. E., Churchill, D. W., Hingtgen, J. N., Bryson, C. Q., Pontius, W., & Kimberlin, C. (1972). Imitation in autistic, early schizophrenic, and non-psychotic subnormal children. *Journal of Autism and Childhood Schizophrenia, 2*, 264–287.

DeMyer, M. K., Mann, M. A., Tilton, J. R., & Loew, L. H. (1967). Toy play behavior and use of body by autistic and normal children as reported by mothers. *Psychological Reports, 21*, 973–981.

DiLavore, P. C., Lord, C., & Rutter, M. (1995). The pre-linguistic autism diagnostic observation schedule. *Journal of Autism and Developmental Disorders, 25*, 355–379.

Dissanayake, C., & Crossley, S. A. (1996). Proximity and social behaviours in autism: Evidence for attachment. *Journal of Child Psychology and Psychiatry, 37*, 149–156.

Fletcher, P. C., Happe, F., Frith, U., Baker, S. C., Dolan, R. J., Frackowiak, R. S. J., & Frith, C. D. (1995). Other minds in the brain: A functional imaging study of "theory of mind" in story comprehension. *Cognition, 57*, 109–128.

Frith, U. (1989). A new look at language and communication in autism. *British Journal of Disorders of Communication, 24*, 123–150.

Frye, D., Zelazo, P. D., & Palfai, T. (1995). Theory of mind and rule-based reasoning. *Cognitive Development, 10*, 483–527.

Gillberg, C., Ehlers, S., Schaumann, H., Jakobsson, G., Dahlgren, S. O., Lindblom, R., Bagenbolm, A., Tjuus, T., & Blidner, E. (1990). Autism under age 3 years: A clinical study of 28 cases referred for autistic symptoms in infancy. *Journal of Child Psychology and Psychiatry, 31*, 921–934.

Gillberg, C., Steffenburg, S., & Schaumann, H. (1991). Is autism more common now than ten years ago? *British Journal of Psychiatry, 158*, 403–409.

Gould, J. (1986). The Lowe and Costello play test in socially impaired children. *Journal of Autism and Developmental Disorders, 16*, 199–213.

Happe, F. G. E. (1995). The role of age and verbal ability in the theory of mind task performance of subjects with autism. *Child Development, 66*, 843–855.

Happe, F., Ehlers, S., Fletcher, P., Frith, U., Johansson, M., Gillberg, C., Dolan, R., Frackowiak, R., & Frith, C. (1996). "Theory of mind" in the brain: Evidence from a PET scan study of Asperger syndrome. *NeuroReport, 8*, 197–201.

Harris, P. (1993). Pretending and planning. In S. Baron-Cohen, H. Tager-Flusberg, & D. J. Cohen (Eds.), *Understanding other minds: Perspectives from autism* (pp. 228–246). New York: Oxford University Press.

Jarrold, C., Boucher, J., & Smith, P. K. (1996). Generativity deficits in pretend play in autism. *British Journal of Developmental Psychology, 14*, 275–300.

Jones, V., & Prior, M. (1985). Motor imitation abilities and neurological signs in autistic children. *Journal of Autism and Developmental Disabilities, 15*, 37–46.

Kanner, L. (1943). Autistic disturbances of affective content. *Nervous Child, 2*, 217–250.

Kasari, C., Sigman, M., Mundy, P., & Yirmiya, N. (1990). Affective sharing in the context of joint attention in interactions of normal, autistic, and mentally retarded children. *Journal of Autism and Developmental Disorders, 20*, 87–100.

Klin, A., Volkmar, F. R., & Sparrow, S. S. (1992). Autistic social dysfunction: Some limitations of the theory of mind hypothesis. *Journal of Child Psychology and Psychiatry, 33*, 861–876.

Leslie, A. M. (1987). Pretense and representation: The origins of "theory of mind." *Psychological Review, 94*, 412–426.

Leslie, A. M., & Happe, F. (1989). Autism and ostensive communication: The relevance of metarepresentation. *Development and Psychopathology, 7*, 205–212.

Lewis, V., & Boucher, J. (1988). Spontaneous, instructed and elicited play in relatively able autistic children. *British Journal of Developmental Psychology, 6*, 325–339.

Lewis, V., & Boucher, J. (1995). Generativity in the play of young people with autism. *Journal of Autism and Developmental Disorders, 25*, 105–121.

Libby, S., Powell, S., Messer, D., & Jordan, R. (1997). Imitation of pretend play acts by children with autism and Down syndrome. *Journal of Autism and Developmental Disorders, 27*, 365–383.

Libby, S., Powell, S., Messer, D., & Jordan, R. (1998). Spontaneous play in children with autism: A reappraisal. *Journal of Autism and Developmental Disorders, 28*, 487–497.

Lord, C. (1995). Follow-up of two-year-olds referred for possible autism. *Journal of Child Psychology and Psychiatry, 36*, 1365–1382.

Lord, C., & Schopler, E. (1987). Neurobiological implications of sex differences in autism. In E. Schopler & G. B. Mesibov (Eds.), *Neurobiological issues in autism* (pp. 191–211). New York: Plenum Press.

Lovaas, O. I. (1987). Behavioral treatment and normal educational and intellectual functioning in young autistic children. *Journal of Consulting and Clinical Psychology, 55,* 3–9.

Loveland, K. A., & Landry, S. H. (1986). Joint attention and language in autism and developmental language delay. *Journal of Autism and Developmental Disorders, 16,* 335–349.

Mars, A. E., Mauk, J. E., & Dowrick, P. W. (1998). Symptoms of pervasive developmental disorders as observed in prediagnostic home videos of infants and toddlers. *Journal of Pediatrics, 132,* 500–504.

Mayes, L. C., Klin, A., Tercyak, K. P., Cicchetti, D. V., & Cohen, D. J. (1996). Test-retest reliability for false-belief tasks. *Journal of Child Psychology and Psychiatry, 37,* 313–319.

McArthur, D., & Adamson, L. B. (1996). Joint attention in preverbal children: Autism and developmental language disorder. *Journal of Autism and Developmental Disorders, 26,* 481–496.

McDonough, L., Stahmer, A., Schreibman, L., & Thompson, S. J. (1997). Deficits, delays, and distractions: An evaluation of symbolic play and memory in children with autism. *Development and Psychopathology, 9,* 17–41.

Meltzoff, A. N. (1985). The roots of social and cognitive development: Models of man's original nature. In T. M. Field & N. A. Fox (Eds.), *Social perception in infants* (pp. 1–30). Norwood, NJ: Ablex.

Meltzoff, A. N., & Gopnik, A. (1993). The role of imitation in understanding persons and developing a theory of mind. In S. Baron-Cohen, H. Tager-Flusberg, & D. J. Cohen (Eds.), *Understanding other minds: Perspectives from autism* (pp. 335–366). New York: Oxford University Press.

Morgan, S., Cutrer, P., Coplin, J., & Rodrigue, J. (1989). Do autistic children differ from retarded and normal children in Piagetian sensorimotor functioning? *Journal of Child Psychology and Psychiatry, 30,* 857–864.

Mundy, P., Sigman, M., & Kasari, C. (1990). A longitudinal study of joint attention and language development in autistic children. *Journal of Autism and Developmental Disorders, 20,* 115–128.

Mundy, P., Sigman, M., & Kasari, C. (1994). Joint attention, developmental level, and symptom presentation in autism. *Development and Psychopathology, 6,* 389–401.

Mundy, P., Sigman, M., Ungerer, J. A., & Sherman, T. (1986). Defining the social deficits in autism: The contribution of non-verbal communication measures. *Journal of Child Psychology and Psychiatry, 27,* 657–669.

Nicolich, L. M. (1977). Beyond sensorimotor intelligence: Assessment of symbolic maturity through analysis of pretend play. *Merrill-Palmer Quarterly, 23,* 89–100.

Osterling, J., & Dawson, G. (1994). Early recognition of children with autism: A study of first birthday home video tapes. *Journal of Autism and Developmental Disorders, 24,* 247–259.

Ozonoff, S., & Miller, J. N. (1995). Teaching theory of mind: A new approach to social skills training for individuals with autism. *Journal of Autism and Developmental Disorders, 25,* 415–433.

Ozonoff, S., Pennington, B. F., & Rogers, S. J. (1991). Executive function deficits in high-functioning autistic individuals: Relationship to theory of mind. *Journal of Child Psychology and Psychiatry, 32,* 1081–1106.

Ozonoff, S., Rogers, S. J., & Pennington, B. F. (1991). Asperger's syndrome: Evidence of an empirical distinction from high-functioning autism. *Journal of Child Psychology and Psychiatry, 32,* 1107–1122.

Peterson, C. C., & Siegal, M. (1995). Deafness, conversation and theory of mind. *Journal of Child Psychology and Psychiatry, 36,* 459–474.

Piaget, J. (1962). *Play, dreams, and imitation in childhood.* New York: Norton.

Povinelli, D. J. (1993). Reconstructing the evolution of mind. *American Psychologist, 48,* 493–509.

Premack, D., & Woodruff, G. (1978). Does the chimpanzee have a "theory of mind"? *Behavior and Brain Sciences, 4,* 515–526.

Prior, M., Eisenmajer, R., Leekam, S., Wing, L., Gould, J., Ong, B., & Dowe, D. (1998). Are there subgroups within the autistic spectrum? A cluster analysis of a group of children with autistic spectrum disorders. *Journal of Child Psychology and Psychiatry, 39,* 893–902.

Rapin, I. (1987). Searching for the cause of autism: A neurologic perspective. In D. J. Cohen & A. M. Donnellan (Eds.), *Handbook of autism and pervasive developmental disorders* (pp. 710–717). New York: Wiley.

Roeyers, H., & van Berckelaer-Onnes, I. A. (1994). Play in autistic children. *Communication and Cognition, 27,* 349–360.

Rogers, S. J., Bennetto, L., McEvoy, R., & Pennington, B. F. (1996). Imitation and pantomime in high functioning adolescents with autism spectrum disorders. *Child Development, 67,* 2060–2073.

Rogers, S. J., & DiLalla, D. L. (1990). Age of symptom onset in young children with pervasive developmental disorders. *Journal of the American Academy of Child and Adolescent Psychiatry, 29,* 863–872.

Rogers, S. J., & Lewis, H. (1989). An effective day treatment model for young children with pervasive developmental disorders. *Journal of the American Academy of Child and Adolescent Psychiatry, 28,* 207–214.

Rogers, S. J., Ozonoff, S., & Maslin-Cole, C. (1991). A comparative study of attachment behavior in young children with autism or other psychiatric disorders. *Journal of the American Academy of Child and Adolescent Psychiatry, 30,* 483–488.

Rogers, S. J., Ozonoff, S., & Maslin-Cole, C. (1993). Developmental aspects of attachment behavior in young children with pervasive developmental disorders. *Journal of the American Academy of Child and Adolescent Psychiatry, 32*(6), 1274–1282.

Rogers, S. J., & Pennington, B. F. (1991). A theoretical approach to the deficits in infantile autism. *Development and Psychopathology, 3,* 137–162.

Roth, D., & Leslie, A. M. (1998). Solving belief problems: Toward a task analysis. *Cognition, 66,* 1–31.

Russell, P. A., Hosie, J. A., Gray, C. D., Scott, C., Hunter, N., Banks, J. S., & Macaulay, M. C. (1998). The development of theory of mind in deaf children. *Journal of Child Psychology and Psychiatry, 39,* 903–910.

Schopler, E., Mesibov, G. B., Shigley, R. H., & Bashford, A. (1984). Helping autistic children through their parents: The TEACCH model. In E. Schopler & G. B. Mesibov (Eds.), *The effects of autism on the family* (pp. 65–81). New York: Plenum Press.

Schopler, E., Reichler, R. J., & Renner, B. R. (1986). *The childhood autism rating scale (CARS) for diagnostic screening and classification of autism.* New York: Irvington.

Shapiro, T., Sherman, M., Calamari, G., & Koch, D. (1987). Attachment in autism and other developmental disorders. *Journal of the American Academy of Child and Adolescent Psychiatry, 26,* 480–484.

Siegel, B., Pliner, C., Eschler, J., & Elliott, G. R. (1988). How children with autism are diagnosed: Difficulties in identification of children with multiple developmental delays. *Developmental and Behavioral Pediatrics, 9,* 199–204.

Sigman, M., & Mundy, P. (1989). Social attachments in autistic children. *Journal of the American Academy of Child and Adolescent Psychiatry, 28,* 74–81.

Sigman, M., & Ungerer, J. A. (1984a). Attachment behaviors in autistic children. *Journal of Autism and Developmental Disorders, 14,* 231–244.

Sigman., M., & Ungerer, J. (1984b). Cognitive and language skills in autistic, mentally retarded, and normal children. *Developmental Psychology, 20,* 293–302.

Smith, B., Chung, M. C., & Vostanis, P. (1994). The path to care in autism: Is it better now? *Journal of Autism and Developmental Disorders, 24,* 551–563.

Smith, I. M., & Bryson, S. E. (1994). Imitation and action in autism: A critical review. *Psychological Bulletin, 116,* 259–273.

Sparrevohn, R., & Howie, P. M. (1995). Theory of mind in children with autistic disorder: Evidence of developmental progression and the role of verbal ability. *Journal of Child Psychology and Psychiatry, 36,* 249–263.

Stone, V. E., Baron-Cohen, S., & Knight, R. T. (1998). Frontal lobe contributions to theory of mind. *Journal of Cognitive Neuroscience, 10,* 640–656.

Stone, W. L., Lemanek, K. L., Fischel, P. T., Fernandez, M. C., & Altemeier, W. A. (1990). Play and imitation skills in the diagnoses of autism in young children. *Pediatrics, 86,* 267–272.

Stone, W. L., Ousley, O. Y., & Littleford, C. D. (1997). Motor imitation in young children with autism: What's the object? *Journal of Abnormal Child Psychology, 25,* 475–485.

Swettenham, J., Baron-Cohen, S., Charman, T., Cox, A., Baird, G., Drew, A., Rees, L., & Wheelwright, S. (1998). The frequency and distribution of spontaneous attention shifts between social and nonsocial stimuli in autistic, typically developing, and nonautistic developmentally delayed infants. *Journal of Child Psychology and Psychiatry, 39,* 747–753.

Tager-Flusberg, H. (1991). Semantic processing in the free recall of autistic children: Further evidence for a cognitive deficit. *British Journal of Developmental Psychology, 9,* 417–430.

Teitelbaum, P., Teitelbaum, O., Nye, J., Fryman, J., & Maurer, R. G. (1998). Movement analysis in infancy may be useful for early diagnosis of autism. *Proceedings of the National Academy of Sciences, 95,* 13982–13987.

Ungerer, J. A., & Sigman, M. (1981). Symbolic play and language comprehension in autistic children. *Journal of the American Academy of Child Psychiatry, 20,* 318–377.

Ungerer, J. A., Zelazo, P. R., Kearsley, R. D., & O'Leary, K. (1981). Developmental changes in the representation of objects in symbolic play from 18 to 34 months of age. *Child Development, 52,* 186–195.

Wetherby, A. M., & Prutting, C. (1984). Profiles of communicative and cognitive-social abilities in autistic children. *Journal of Speech and Hearing Research, 27,* 364–377.

Wing, L. (1988). The continuum of autistic characteristics. In E. Schopler & G. B. Mesibov (Eds.), *Diagnosis and assessment in autism* (pp. 91–110). New York: Plenum Press.

Wing, L., Gould, J., Yeates, S. R., & Brierley, L. M. (1977). Symbolic play in severely mentally retarded and in autistic children. *Journal of Child Psychology and Psychiatry and Allied Disciplines, 18,* 167–178.

Winner, E., Brownell, H., Happe, F., Blum, A., & Pincus, D. (1998). Distinguishing lies from jokes: Theory of mind deficits and discourse interpretation in right hemisphere brain-damaged patients. *Brain and Language, 62,* 89–106.

Yirmiya, N., Erel, O., Shaked, M., & Solomonica-Levi, D. (1998). Meta-analyses comparing theory of mind abilities of individuals with autism, individuals with mental retardation, and normally developing individuals. *Psychological Bulletin, 124,* 283–307.

Zelazo, P. D., Burack, J. A., Benedetto, E., & Frye, D. (1996). Theory of mind and rule use in individuals with Down's syndrome: A test of the uniqueness and specificity claims. *Journal of Child Psychology and Psychiatry, 37,* 479–484.

Chapter Twenty-one

Infant Mental Health in a Changing Society

Donna M. Gelfand

Introduction

Assessment of another person's mental health poses great challenges. Many of the emotional and cognitive manifestations of mental disorders are subtle, largely covert, or completely hidden. Only distinctive disturbances of overt behavior are apparent to others, and even then the unusual behavior's significance or purpose may be obscure. As the following discussion indicates, it is especially difficult to identify and interpret disordered behavior in infants. The observer may puzzle over highly unusual infant behavior and wonder why a baby persistently ignores her caretakers, strikes out at them wildly, cries inconsolably, doesn't learn to speak, or clings desperately to her mother. Such atypical behavior patterns could be considered either temporary aberrations or signs of mental disorder.

Older clients' mental states are often diagnosed from self-descriptions of their thoughts and feelings and their reports of the particular contexts in which difficulties arise. Indeed, the sufferer's reports are virtually essential for making a diagnosis for some internalizing disorders such as depression and anxiety. Yet self-report requires a sense of self, which may be largely unformed in young children. It is not until the age of 2 years, when the neural circuits that unite the brain's limbic structures with the frontal lobe are sufficiently developed, that an awareness of feelings and attitudes about self emerges (Kagan, 1998). Lacking the ability to distinguish between self and others and to identify emotional states of the self, infants are unlikely to be capable of self-report, even if they possessed the necessary expressive language skills to do so.

How then can clinicians identify mental health and disorder in preverbal infants? It is only within recent decades that tools such as operant learning techniques, rigorous, objective ratings of the infant's performance on standardized behavioral tasks, and sensitive physiological measures have been developed to provide windows on infant perceptual and cognitive processes. In consequence, our beliefs about babies' mental abilities have been nearly reversed from the former, uninformed opinion that infants' senses are dull or generally undeveloped to an increasing appreciation for the cleverness and adaptability of young children. Today's predominant school of thought is based on a large body of research and selectively ascribes acute observational and reasoning abilities to young babies. Nevertheless, caution is in order, and some authorities warn against uncritically crediting infants with advanced perceptual and reasoning abilities that surpass those that can be discerned in 3-year-olds (Haith, 1998). Careful and critical analyses of infants' abilities are under way in research laboratories throughout the world.

Historical Views of the Infant as a Person

Humans can be categorized as mentally healthy or mentally ill, but members of other species are not similarly described. (Except by doting pet owners, who believe that their animals are incredibly sensitive and intelligent.) Are human infants sufficiently like adults to be capable of experiencing varying states of mental health or illness? Recognition of infant capacities differs across cultures and historical eras. If only humans can become mentally ill, are infants included in this group?

There is at least one affirmative answer to this question. The US government now officially recognizes that even newborns may suffer from emotional disturbances. According to the Center for Mental Health Services (1993), the federal definition of childhood serious emotional disturbances states: "Children with a serious emotional disturbance are persons, from birth up to age 18, who currently or at any time during the past year have had a diagnosable mental, behavioral, or emotional disorder." There has been an historical progression from doubting infants' full humanity to recognizing that they share adults' human characteristics to the extent that they can have mental or emotional disturbances. It is instructive to trace how the latter, modern view arose.

The concept that the infant is a person is a relatively recent historical development. In medieval times, infants were viewed primarily as being unformed possessions of their families. The European Enlightenment in the eighteenth century brought the vision that children were appealing and interesting in their own right. Since then scholarly and popular perceptions of children increasingly recognized their human qualities. However, the idea that infants are not yet quite human has proved remarkably persistent even into modern times.

In his widely influential writings on parenting, the early twentieth-century American behaviorist John Watson advised parents to avoid contact with their infants except for meeting their basic physical needs. Watson advocated leaving babies alone as much as possible so they could grow healthy without the adverse influences of maternal smothering and spoiling.

Infants were not even accorded a gender in scientific writings. As recently as several decades ago textbooks referred to the infant as a gender-neutral "it," rather than as he or she. Even now, many science authors refer to infants as "it" and question babies' full humanity. In his best-selling book on the natural history of life on earth, Richard Fortey (1997) wrote: "The new toddler knows that it has done something important when it is able to totter three steps from a chair leg to its mother's outstretched arms. . . . The baby's delight coincides with the moment that it becomes human" (p. 296). What a revealing comment! Is an "it" human in all senses of the term, and how does walking or talking convey humanity on the infant? This passage reveals a profound hesitation to accord full species characteristics to very young children.

The question about infants' capacity to experience adult-like feelings arises as a practical issue in the field of medicine. Long into the twentieth century surgeons maintained that infants could not perceive pain, and consequently performed painful procedures on them without anesthetic. Ironically, this was at a time when veterinary medicine routinely employed anesthetics during surgery on animals.

In the psychological sphere, young children are not popularly thought to long remember or suffer from separation from their primary caretakers. The quality of infants' attachments to their primary caretakers and their obvious preferences and other expressions of affection were not, and still are not, considered as compelling evidence in child custody cases. Courts commonly supposed that young children can be manipulated by the provision of treats or privileges to show that they prefer one parent over the other and that their preferences are often unwise. Moreover, it is supposed (in the absence of research evidence) that their custody preferences are not only ill-founded, but also easily altered. However, the courts' failure to use mental health experts' opinions in custody and treatment cases may also stem from the lack of clear and convincing research evidence that early childhood experiences have a permanent effect on the child's later adjustment outcomes (Horner & Guyer, 1993). Lacking such evidence of an enduring effect on adjustment, judges and child welfare officers rely on other factors such as the custom that the mother is the preferred custodian of the children.

In short, adults have long ignored the feelings and preferences of infants, considering them mentally limited and something less than fully human. However, modern research methods have spread the view that infants are sufficiently intelligent and perceptive to experience states of psychological health or mental disorder. The next logical question is how psychological disorders might arise in the course of infant development. The next section presents an overview of some of the major theoretical approaches to the study of infant adjustment.

Theories of Infant Mental Health

Theories play a prominent role in the understanding and treatment of infant psychological disorders. The theoretical assumptions made about the nature and sources of health and illness determine the ways in which disorders are described, diagnosed, and prevented or remediated. There is no overriding, generally accepted explanation of infant disorders, in part because there is a range of types of disorders and in part because scientists differ in their theoretical preferences. The major theories of infant psychopathology can be variously traced to roots in psychoanalytic theory, ethological evolutionary theory, physiology, or environmental explanations including learning theories. Some accounts stem from more than one conceptual base (attachment theory draws on both psychoanalytic thought and the science of ethology). It is impossible to do justice to these complex theories in just a few paragraphs, so the following descriptions are overviews only, describing some of the basic assumptions of each approach to the study of infant psychopathology.

Ethological and Psychodynamic Theories

In the 1980s and 1990s, ethologically oriented attachment theory (Ainsworth, Blehar, Waters, & Wall, 1978; Bowlby, 1969–1980) emerged as a dominant paradigm in the study of infant mental health. This approach was based on psychoanalytic tenets about the importance of very early experiences with the mother in the formation of personality. Attachment theory also arose from ethological observations of strong attachments of infants of many species, ranging from birds to primates, to their parents or parent substitutes. Human babies were also observed to form strong, primary attachments to their mothers, treating the mothers as a source of emotional regulation and a secure base from which the baby could begin to explore and master the world. A healthy or secure attachment and an internalized mental representation of the appropriately nurturant behavior of a sensitive, warm mother give the infant a good start in life. Insecure attachments may set the stage for future adjustment problems.

Attachment studies with humans originally focused on the quality of the infant's emotional attachment to a primary caretaker, usually the mother. Subsequent research expanded to embrace infants' attachments to others, such as fathers, other caretakers, and siblings. Research has investigated the long-term effects of early attachment quality on the child's social adjustment in preschool, elementary school, and later years. Possible intergenerational attachment influences are being studied to trace the effects of parental attachment styles on their offspring. These developments in attachment theory and research illustrate the integration of infant studies with the fields of child development and even adult adjustment. Infancy is no longer a separate and isolated area for investigation, but often contributes as one element in a life-span perspective on human development.

Learning and Conditioning

From the 1920s to 1960s, many psychologists believed that learning mechanisms accounted for much of infant behavior, including psychopathology. B. F. Skinner (1953) offered an influential description of behavior as controlled by its immediate consequences. Skinner demonstrated the operant conditioning of a wide range of voluntary acts through the provision of reinforcing consequences immediately following the behavior. Through operant learning procedures, babies were taught the elements of verbal expression, motor skills, and even developmentally advanced skills such as reading through shaping or reinforcing successive approximations to the final performance. Acquired involuntary responses, such as specific fears, were attributed to classical conditioning through pairing with inherently frightening stimuli, such as loud sounds, lightning strikes, or loss of support. Other stimuli were shown to acquire reinforcing properties through pairing them with established reinforcers in a classical conditioning procedure. Conditioning was presumed to account for a wide range of infant skills and problems, including eating and sleeping disturbances, fears and anxiety, failure to develop normal motor and social skills, and others. The investigator's attention was on skill acquisition by the infant through training the caretakers in precise instructional techniques which they used to teach their children. Thus the scientist's focus was on the individual infant, although reciprocal influences of infant and parent or teacher on the other were recognized. The learning approach emphasized precision, tight environmental control, and attention to the accumulation of separate, identifiable skills in the study of human development.

Organismic and Dynamic Systems Models

The field of child psychopathology next progressed to observations of the overall quality of the mother–infant relationship and parenting practices. The rise of the previously described ethological models of attachment (Bowlby, 1969–1980) began in the 1980s, along with a growing recognition of the *transactional* nature of caretaker–infant interactions (Sameroff, Seifer, & Barocas, 1983). In the transactional view, babies are considered essential *contributors* to the relationship and to the caretakers' behavior as well as being recipients of adults' actions. Family members, including the infant, bring their own contributions to family interactions and the behavior of each person is continually influenced in the interchange (Parke & Tinsley, 1987). Today the infant no longer is seen as a separate entity, and studied independently from the family and community contexts. The *organismic* approach, which considers the whole infant rather than separate mechanisms and abilities, dominates in the current study of infant psychological development (Parke, 1992). Researchers who pursue the organismic approach concentrate on the study of growth as a function of infants' relationships with parents and other regularly encountered caretakers and family members.

Most lately theorists have developed approaches such as *dynamic systems models* featuring the emergent nature of the self as arising through the process of self-organization occurring in relationships from the dynamic properties of social interactions (Fogel, 1993; Fogel & Thelen, 1987). That is, the infant's sense of self is generated within interchanges and relationships with caretakers. Pathological relationships limit the infant's social development. We have a sense of self in relation to others and as part of that relationship, but not independently. In the dynamic systems view, humans are truly and essentially social beings.

Genetic and Physiological Influences

Genetic contributions to developmental deviations have been hypothesized for many years. At first, simple genetic models were investigated, but single-gene anomalies proved more applicable to a limited number of severe developmental-delay disorders than to the more common disorders of social and emotional behavior and regulation. Disorders involving multiple genes and chromosome sites are now generally preferred as possibly underlying disorders such as anxiety, depression, and schizophrenia. Although false leads abound, it is probable that at least some of these disorders will prove to have genetic contributors.

The recent emergence of computer-based, noninvasive methods for studying infants' physiological functioning and the availability of improved measures of infant temperament have stimulated new theories linking individual differences in inborn temperament type with autonomic activity. In one such approach (Porges, 1996), records of infants' heart-rate patterns provide measures of vagal tone that are linked to physiological arousal and stress hormones (cortisol level). These recordings provide a means of monitoring the physiological functions supporting an individual's ability to cope with social interactions and stress. Babies with higher vagal tone are more alert and easier to soothe (Huffman et al., 1998). Older children with higher vagal tone show better performance on cognitive tasks (Porges, 1997). Although questions remain about measurement and interpretation (Berntson et al., 1997), the study of vagal tone provides new light on early infant self-regulation and socioemotional adjustment. Advances in genetics and neurobiology show great promise of revealing the biological foundations of some aspects of psychological functioning and the development of disorders.

The most prevalent approach to infant psychosocial development incorporates both genes and environment. Growth is governed by genetically based abilities emerging in a predetermined sequence as well as by social and physical environmental factors. The study of infant mental health has become truly developmental, emphasizing the many interacting person and environmental factors that govern growth throughout the life span.

The next section reviews some recent research that has led to greater appreciation of infants' abilities. Disruptions in the development of key skills might result in some of the recognized mental disorders of infancy.

Research on Infants' Abilities

There are many unresolved questions concerning infants' abilities. What do babies know and at what age do they know it? For example, how early in life can babies recognize their mother's face and voice? Are there fewer separate and distinct types of mental disorders during infancy than later in life? Are there sensitive periods for the establishment of stable aspects of psychological functioning, such as attachment to caretakers or gender identity, or is development a more temporally flexible process?

The preceding list of questions does not necessarily mean that we know little and there are few answers about infant psychopathology. In fact, infant psychological functioning is a very active topic for research, and each year brings new evidence of previously undocumented early sensitivities, capabilities, and psychological disorders.

Observers who believe that babies are largely unaware of their physical and social worlds will be surprised at how wrong they are. Just a few examples of infant abilities reveal young infants' sensitivity to emotional cues and their remarkable ability to relate to others. Humans seem to be predisposed to form relationships with their parents (or other primary caretakers). In the first few days after birth, infants can recognize their mother's face, based on features such as the outer contour of the mother's head and the separation line between her face and hair (Karmiloff-Smith, 1995). They can also distinguish their mother's odor and voice from those of other women (Hepper, Scott, & Shahidullah, 1993; Karmiloff-Smith, 1995). During the second half of the first year of life, infants engage in social referencing in which they seek cues to interpret novel, potentially threatening situations from observing the behavior of others. They attend closely to others' affective expressions, particularly their mothers', for guidance in how to respond when encountering stimuli such as loss of physical support or the approach of a self-propelled mechanical toy monster complete with flashing lights and novel sounds. If the mother expresses fear or avoidance when the monster approaches, the infant becomes wary, but is apparently reassured by the presence of a calm, confident mother (Campos & Stenberg, 1981). These early perceptual and cognitive skills seem to reveal a close, positive relationship between infant and mother and to promote future healthy social development.

At the age of 2 years, the average baby has established a basic sense of self, as previously noted, and clear and accurate perceptions of others. For example, well before the age of 1 year, babies can distinguish male and female faces. Moreover, they can label others as either girls or boys correctly before they reach age 3 (Fagot & Leinbach, 1995). At this same age, aggression rates drop sharply in girls (Fagot, 1977, 1985). Thus, establishment of sex-role behavior begins in infancy, and presumably could also be disrupted during this age period, perhaps with lasting consequences.

Enduring individual differences in language skills and cognitive performance can also begin in infancy. Two-year-olds display individual differences in language and cognitive skills that can prove surprisingly stable over time. Groups of infants who have larger vocabularies at 2 years of age have higher than average IQ scores as 4-year-olds, particularly on verbal measures (Bornstein & Haynes, 1998). This suggests that the roots of accelerated or delayed verbal abilities may trace back to infancy.

Not only do infants understand words and speech patterns, but they also have some understanding of others' intentions. In one study, when 18-month-olds were shown a model initiating but failing to complete a set of simple acts, such as putting a ball into a bucket, they reenacted the unfinished but intended acts. However, they reenacted the behaviors only when they were performed by an actual person, but not when demonstrated by a machine (Meltzoff, 1995). Like adults, infants apparently think in terms of goals as connected to people, but not to inanimate objects.

By the end of the first year of life, children who have succeeded at a task or explored a novel stimulus look at their companions brightly and share smiles. This affective referencing and sharing occurs early and provides a sensitive indicator of social adjustment (Osofsky & Eberhart-Wright, 1992). Affective referencing and sharing is notably absent in infants with autistic disorder. Sometimes these social behaviors are suppressed because the infant experiences abuse or severe neglect. It is hardly surprising that high-quality care (which emphasizes sharing and social stimulation) is associated with good infant and child adjustment (NICHD Early Child Care Research Network, 1998; Scarr & Eisenberg, 1993). The corollary is that neglect or abuse and extended separation from the primary caretaker can produce agitation, self-regulation problems, and depressed affect in infants and toddlers (Field, 1996).

The research evidence shows that infants are attuned to their physical and social worlds. They seem predisposed to form enduring relationships with their parents, whom they can recognize as individuals surprisingly early in development. The parent serves as the source of care, protection, and information about the world, and is the baby's first teacher. Early experiences, individual differences in health status, and the quality of the early rearing environment can all have profound consequences on the child's development. In some disorders, such as autism, the baby seems not to become attached to parents in the ordinary way, and may even shun social contact generally. In other disorders, early gains in motor and social-emotional development may be lost and profound retardation sets in. Many early disorders are recognized through general developmental delays or the infant's failure to attain a normal pace of development of a variety of abilities.

Classification of Infant Developmental Disorders

The list of clinical disorders recognized in infancy is shorter and the disorders included tend to be more severe than many of those listed in diagnostic classifications for older individuals. This paucity of infant disorder categories reflects the difficulty in identifying and diagnosing disorders in preverbal infants. It is sometimes easy to recognize that a baby is severely delayed, but difficult to determine the specific identity of the disorder. Also, infant behavior is notoriously changeable and is closely tied to states of physical health and illness. Thus, psychological problems are difficult to detect unless they are so severe as to be unmistakable, as in profound mental retardation, neurological abnormalities, or severe developmental delay.

Uncertainty about the nature and prognosis of many infant disturbances also makes clinicians cautious about pronouncing that a particular infant has some type of developmental disorder. If the prognosis is uncertain, the problem may well decrease or disappear over time, so there is no need to worry already concerned parents about something that may not represent a persisting problem. Pediatricians are highly reluctant to suggest that a baby may have adjustment problems because of the difficulties inherent in early diagnosis and the possibility that the parents could overreact. Consequently, pediatricians often reassure worried parents that their infant's problems are likely to spontaneously remit over time.

This optimistic view is frequently justified, since the most prevalent parentally reported problems of infants are transitory ones such as excessive fussy or colicky behavior, dysregulation of physiological functioning including feeding and sleeping problems, and failure to thrive (AACAP, 1997). Many of the preceding problems abate or completely disappear over time, especially if they are never so severe as to qualify as clinical disorders. In the second year of life, parents begin to report problems in children's social functioning, including aggression, overactivity, defiance, and impulsivity. In a minority of cases, these are the precursors of more serious, clinical disorders such as oppositional disorder, conduct disorder, or attention deficit hyperactive disorder (ADHD). The range of disorders increases during childhood and adolescence, and less severely disruptive problems can be more readily detected both within the family and at school. Throughout childhood, developmental delays in sensorimotor and cognitive functioning and lack of social sensitivity and responsivity to others constitute major sources of concern.

The mental health community has recognized a limited number of disorders of infancy and early childhood. These disorders are included in the official diagnostic manual of the American Psychiatric Association (1994), the *Diagnostic and Statistical Manual of Mental Disorders*, 4th edition (DSM-IV). Many of the same disorders appear in the diagnostic classifications of the World Health Organization (1992), called the *International Classification of Diseases* (ICD-10). The ICD-10 was designed to coordinate and share subcategory code numbers with the DSM-IV and to provide a standardized diagnostic system for international use. A group of North American infancy psychiatrists associated with the National Center for Clinical Infant Programs (NCCIP; 1994) is developing and testing additional categories to complement those in the DSM-IV. The general categories of disorders applicable to infancy that these three schemes have in common are:

1   childhood autism or autistic disorder;
2   atypical pervasive developmental disorder variably termed pervasive developmental disorder not otherwise specified (DSM-IV), atypical autism (ICD-10), or atypical pervasive developmental disorder (NCCIP);
3   reactive attachment disorder of infancy, early childhood, or childhood (deprivation syndrome in NCCIP);
4   anxiety disorders, which are termed separation anxiety disorder in the DSM-IV and ICD-10 nosologies.

In addition, some eating or feeding disorders such as rumination and pica are included in nosologies of infant mental disorders.

The NCCIP classification scheme includes more categories of disorder in infancy than the other two. The greater number of categories in NCCIP could be because it was developed specifically and exclusively for infants, by infant mental health specialists rather than by a group dominated by adult specialists with less acquaintance with young children's problems (Emde, Bingham, & Harmon, 1993). For example, the NCCIP lists a number of types of regulatory disorders, including hypersensitivity, underreactivity, active-aggressive, mixed regulatory disorders, and sleep and eating disorders. As noted previously, these are the types of problems for which infants are most often referred to pediatricians.

In the next sections, each of the major categories of infant disorders will be described in more detail. The DSM-IV, which is perhaps the most widely accepted and used diagnostic system, will serve as the primary source of the categories of disorder discussed in this chapter.

Major Categories of Infant Adjustment Disorders

Pervasive Developmental Disorder

An individual infant's rate of progress can be assessed through the appearance of various skills or developmental milestones at predictable or average ages. Developmental milestones include the appearance of the social smile, the progression of motor skills beginning with moving the trunk, pulling oneself upright, and culminating in unassisted walking, expressing and understanding speech, and forming an emotional attachment to the major caretaker(s). When a baby's development falls behind and clearly and persistently fails to meet norms for several of these developmental milestones, a pervasive development disorder may be diagnosed. For example, a baby of 1 year of age who has a pervasive development disorder may fail to recognize her own name, utter no words, and make little progress toward walking. Pervasive developmental disorders typically appear within the first 30 months of life and are characterized by severe distortions and limitations in an infant's social, cognitive, emotional, and language development. Many different areas of functioning are adversely affected. In older individuals, these performance failures would lead to a diagnosis of mental retardation. This category of pervasive developmental delay clearly does not apply to an otherwise normal baby who is slow to acquire a specific skill such as talking or walking. To qualify as a pervasive development delay, the problems must be severe and multiple, affecting many aspects of the infant's functioning. Autistic disorder is one example of a condition that falls within the general classification of pervasive development delay.

The DSM-IV classification schema distinguishes between *autistic disorder* and other disorders that are also pervasive but do not meet the criteria for autistic disorder. These latter syndromes are termed *pervasive developmental disorder not otherwise specified* (or atypical pervasive developmental disorder). *Rett's disorder*, *Asperger's disorder*, and *childhood disintegrative disorder* are also identified in DSM-IV as disorders that may appear in the first three years of life. These disturbances are often accompanied by mental retardation, ranging from profound to mild. Various physical problems may also be present, including chromosomal abnormalities, CNS structural abnormalities, and a history of infections.

Autistic disorder

Autism is a widely recognized though rare disorder that occurs in 2 to 5 among 10,000 individuals, or less than 1 in 1000 (American Psychiatric Association, 1994; Fombonne & du Mazaubrun, 1992). Less stringent diagnostic criteria can increase the rate to the 10–14 cases per 10,000 reported in one Japanese study (Ohtaki, Kawano, Urabe, & Komori, 1992). The onset is before the age of 3 years, and parents typically report that their child shows abnormal aloofness and failure to develop normal communication within the first year of life. Normal patterns of attachment to caretakers and the ability to relate to others socially are greatly disturbed.

DSM-IV criteria for autism include: (1) *impaired quality of social interaction*, such as lack of normal eye contact and social give-and-take, flat facial expression, odd body postures, and failure to use either speech or gestures to engage others in social interaction; (2) *impaired communication*, including absent or delayed spoken language, sometimes accompanied by stereotyped, repetitive, or idiosyncratic language, or echolalia (simply repeating what the other person has just said rather than replying). Although physically capable of language, some autistic children are mute. Make-believe play is deficient or absent (i.e., imaginary play such as holding a tea party for dolls or pretending that a block is a vehicle); and (3) *unusual, highly selective, repetitive and stereotyped behavior*, such as fascination with looking at lights or spinning objects. The infants may also hysterically insist on particular nonfunctional rituals and preferences, such as eating only white food, only liquids, or playing with a mop, but not with toys. Infants with autism often protest loudly and for prolonged periods if their stereotyped routines are interrupted, the environment is changed, new caretakers are introduced, or the furniture is repositioned. This "insistence on sameness" may help the child with mental retardation and severe attentional and other processing problems to function in an otherwise baffling or overwhelming environment (Gelfand, Jenson, & Drew, 1997; Kauffmann, 1993).

Although some children with autism improve with age, many do not, particularly if they also suffer from mental retardation. In fact, 75 percent of children with autism have IQ scores below 70 (Kauffmann, 1993; Sue & Sue, 1990). Children who fail to develop communicative speech and also display mental retardation are particularly likely to continue to suffer from pervasive disabilities in later life. Moreover, those who are markedly below average in intelligence are more likely to develop harmful self-stimulation routines, such as head banging, hair pulling, scratching, and biting themselves. The source and function of self-injury is not well understood, but sometimes removing reinforcing attention and other valued activities contingent on self-injurious behavior reduces its rate (Kauffmann, 1993). Overall, autism strikes two to four times as many males as females, but the females with autism are more likely to be severely afflicted (Volkmar, Szatmari, & Sparrow, 1993).

The treatment of children with autistic disorder has received great public and professional attention. Several decades of parental lobbying for more research on autism have stimulated development of effective therapies. Behavioral techniques have been developed to teach highly dysfunctional children specific skills such as attending to the therapist, imitating others, compliance with requests, uttering words and sentences and holding simple conversations, and controlling self-injurious behavior. Although such programs aid in the management of developmentally delayed children, neither behavioral programs nor pharmacological therapies produce lasting improvements once the therapy is discontinued. For most children with autism, the disorder is a lifelong disability. Those with the greatest developmental delays and IQ scores below 50 in early childhood rarely recover to live normal lives (Lockyer & Rutter, 1969).

Even the "high-functioning" autistic children with functional speech and formal schooling appear odd and unresponsive socially, have few if any friends, and remain dependent on their families as adults (American Psychiatric Association, 1994). A few display islets of mental ability, often combined with some unusual, idiosyncratic interest, so they can memorize music and some give skilled musical performances, recite the details of complex rail or subway systems or name the day of the week from calendars over periods of decades. Despite these apparent gifts, in other areas of cognitive and social ability, the same individuals may appear sadly deficient.

The highly atypical mental, social, and emotional functioning of children with autistic disorder and the condition's resistance to treatment of any type lead most authorities to conclude that it has a largely organic basis. Many promising research leads about etiology have resisted replication. As yet it is unclear whether autistic disorder will ultimately be traced to genetic, infectious, or other causes.

Other pervasive developmental disorders

This diagnostic category constitutes several disorders, including atypical autism, Rett's disorder, childhood disintegrative disorder, and Asperger's disorder. Some features of these disorders resemble autism, but others are different. All are grave conditions from which relatively few individuals recover to live normally independent adult lives. As with other disorders, children with milder cases have better prognoses.

DSM-IV lists a category of pervasive developmental disorder not otherwise specified, which includes *atypical autism*. This condition resembles autistic disorder but differs in some respects, whether because of lesser severity, absence or difference in form of the usual autistic symptoms, or later age of onset. This is a so-called garbage-can category for diagnostic use when a child is less severely affected or is seriously and pervasively impaired mentally and emotionally but does not meet criteria for autistic disorder, another pervasive developmental disorder, or any other mental disorder (American Psychiatric Association, 1994).

Both *Rett's disorder* and *childhood disintegrative disorder* are marked by a serious regression in many areas of functioning following at least two years of apparently normal development. Rett's disorder apparently only afflicts females. In Rett's disorder, head growth begins normally but falls behind normal between the ages of 5 and 48 months. The infant loses previously developed hand skills and develops stereotyped movements that resemble wringing or washing of the hands along with severe retardation in motor skill development, including poorly coordinated walking. Affected infants also display severely impaired language skills and loss of interest in social interactions.

Childhood disintegrative disorder is even less prevalent than autistic disorder and usually occurs together with severe mental retardation, which limits learning of all types. Many different areas of functioning are severely disrupted. The onset can be sudden or insidious and most often occurs after three to four years of seemingly normal development. Boys are more commonly affected than girls.

Asperger's disorder differs from the other pervasive disorders in that the child may show no marked general delay in language development, cognitive development, or the appearance of adaptive and self-help skills. However, there is a severe distortion and deficit in social interests and interaction skills. Autistic-like restricted repetitive and stereotyped interests and behavior patterns form a portion of Asperger's syndrome.

Reactive Attachment Disorder and Insecure Attachment

In the United States, nearly 1 child in 200 is physically abused and almost 1 in 100 is so badly treated as to meet the legal criteria for physical neglect (Cappelleri, Eckenrode, & Powers, 1993). Infants are particularly likely to be mistreated because they are immature and unable to defend themselves. Early and very severe maltreatment can lead to reactive attachment disorder, particularly if no adequate alternative caretaker, such as a grand-parent, is available to counteract the effects of seriously deficient parenting. Even in the absence of traumatic abuse and neglect, less obvious forms of maltreatment can heighten the child's risks of later psychopathology (Carlson, 1998; Cicchetti, Toth, & Lynch, 1995). An infant's attachment security can be threatened if the primary caregiver (usually the mother) provides very inadequate care.

Main and Hesse (1990) identified a type of insecure attachment they characterized as *disorganized/disoriented*, because the infant shows no coherent pattern of attach-ment behavior. Upon reuniting with the caretaker after a brief separation, the infant displays very unusual behavior. The typical child reunites happily with the caretaker (secure attachment) or consistently resists or avoids her (coercive or avoidant types of insecure attachment). In contrast, the infants with a disorganized/disoriented attachment strategy may appear dazed, frozen in place, or become apprehensive upon seeing the caretaker. Some may first strongly avoid her but immediately afterward insistently cling to her, so their behaviors do not follow a typical or logical sequence. Unlike most other children, these chil-dren display no organized coping strategy in tests of attachment, which is why their behav-ior is termed disorganized (Main, Kaplan, & Cassidy, 1985). Such disorganized attachment is thought to stem from having a frightening or frightened caretaker who provides the baby with conflicting cues about how to behave (Carlson, 1998).

The disorganized/disoriented attachment type is associated with deviant rearing con-ditions such as: (1) severe and chronic maternal depression during the child's infancy (Teti, Gelfand, Messinger, & Isabella, 1995), (2) early maltreatment (Carlson, Cicchetti, Barnett, & Braunwald, 1989), (3) prenatal alcohol or drug exposure (O'Connor, Sigman, & Brill, 1987; Rodning, Beckwith, & Howard, 1991), or (4) hostile, intrusive, and insen-sitive caregiving (Lyons-Ruth, Repacholi, McLeod, & Silva, 1991). Note that several of the preceding conditions are likely to co-occur in high-risk families. However, not all chil-dren who develop the disorganized/disoriented attachment relationship or other insecure attachment relationships also develop psychopathology. Rather, as a group, they are more likely than others to form poor peer relationships and experience multiple problem behav-iors during childhood.

Reactive attachment disorder

In some instances of markedly disturbed care, such as the child's prolonged hospitalization or extreme deprivation or physical abuse, children under 5 years old may develop reactive attachment disorder of infancy or early childhood. This disorder consists of markedly dis-turbed and developmentally inappropriate social relatedness in most contexts and with most individuals. The disturbed behavior may be either inhibited or disinhibited. In the inhibited type, the child displays a mixture of approach and avoidance or frozen watchfulness and will neither initiate interactions nor respond appropriately to most social overtures. This behavior pattern resembles the reaction of the infant with disorganized/disoriented attachment to the mother, but in the reactive attachment disorder syndrome, the infant responds in similar fashion to everyone. In the disinhibited type, the child is indiscriminately sociable, lacks selective attachments to primary caregivers and familiar persons and shows excessive familiarity with strangers. To qualify as creating one of the subtypes of reactive attachment disorder, the child's care must be demonstrably pathogenic. Either the child's basic physical needs go unmet, emotional needs are persistently disregarded, or repeated changes of primary caregivers preclude formation of stable attachments. These diagnostic categories are limited to severe conditions and little is known about them, even regarding their prevalence. They are thought to be very rare.

Anxiety Disorders

In DSM-IV, the latest edition of the American Psychiatric Association's diagnostic manual (American Psychiatric Association, 1994), the number of childhood anxiety disorders was reduced from several to only one: separation anxiety disorder, which is classified under the broader category of other disorders of childhood and adolescence. The previous edition of the DSM included a broad category of anxiety disorders of childhood and adolescence and the additional specific categories of avoidant disorder and overanxious disorder as well as separation anxiety disorder.

Separation anxiety disorder

A child who absolutely insists on being near a parent or other close caregiver for most of the time, vigorously resists separation, even to go to bed, and shows excessive distress when not at home with parents may have separation anxiety disorder. According to DSM-IV criteria, the disorder must be intense, present continuously for at least four weeks, and inappropriate for the child's age. The onset may be as early as the preschool years, but many symptoms are detected only through the child's verbal reports, such as fear of attending school, worries about getting lost or kidnapped, or nightmares about separation. Consequently, separation anxiety disorder is more likely to be diagnosed in older children who can voice their concerns. There are virtually no definitive studies of its prevalence in the first few years of life.

Young children who develop separation anxiety disorder are more likely than others to have mothers with panic disorder or first-degree biological relatives with separation anxiety disorder (American Psychiatric Association, 1994). Thus, both genetic predisposition to anxiety and environmental family influences may contribute to development of separation anxiety. Research by Kagan and his colleagues (Hirshfeld et al., 1992; Kagan, Reznick, & Snidman, 1987) indicates that some 10–15 percent of white infants are temperamentally inclined to *behavioral inhibition*. This condition is thought to be inborn and consists of a pattern of anxious and withdrawn behavior including clinging or dependence on parents, fearfulness and withdrawal from new situations, and physiological arousal in unfamiliar settings. These anxious and avoidant behaviors appear during infancy and resemble separation anxiety disorder. Behavioral inhibition may be a risk factor for later anxiety disorder during childhood (Biederman et al., 1993), but only a minority of children with behavioral inhibition develop anxiety disorders. Other factors, such as the family environment, may also play important roles in the outcome for the behaviorally inhibited infant (Silverman & Ginsburg, 1998).

Eating and Feeding Disorders

If physical disorders such as gastrointestinal and general medical conditions or illnesses can be ruled out, certain disruptions in eating and elimination are diagnosed as mental disorders in DSM-IV. Feeding disorder of infancy or early childhood most often begins within the first year of life and results in significant growth delay over a period of at least one month. Sometimes conditions such as parental ignorance about babies' nutritional needs, abuse, or neglect are associated with this condition.

In rumination disorder, the infant repeatedly regurgitates and rechews food. This condition occurs repeatedly after a period of normal eating and over at least a one-month time span. The resulting malnutrition can result in significant weight loss and even death. In pica, the infant persistently eats nonnutritive substances over a period of at least one month. A variety of unsavory and sometimes dangerous substances are consumed, including paint (especially dangerous if the paint is lead-based), plaster, dirt, hair, or cloth (American Psychiatric Association, 1994). Enuresis and encopresis are not diagnosed before the child reaches the age of 4 or 5 years, so they are not typically considered disorders of infancy.

This brief overview of some of the most widely recognized psychological disorders of infants indicates that relatively little is known about the classification and accuracy of diagnosis of these conditions, except for eating and feeding disorders. In the case of the rare disorders, such as the pervasive developmental disorders, solid information is lacking on their prevalence, gender distribution, etiology, prognosis, and treatment. Because these conditions are so rare, the accuracy with which they can be diagnosed is not established, handicapping both research and treatment. The exception is autistic disorder, which can now be diagnosed with increasing accuracy because it has been better studied than other early disorders.

It is not enough to produce descriptions of infant disorders, since the descriptions may prove to be inaccurate or unusable in clinical practice. The next issue to be addressed is whether the disorders described in DSM-IV and other classifications can be reliably applied by clinicians. A variety of tests, observations, and rating scales have been devised to assist in the diagnosis of infants.

Infant Assessment

Among the numerous impediments to accurate assessment and diagnosis of infant psychological disorders is a strong bias among physicians, mental health workers, and the public in general to consider infants' adjustment difficulties as transitory and readily out-grown. Many pediatricians are reluctant to diagnose emotional disorders in infants and young children lest the diagnoses worry parents needlessly about a condition that will turn out to be transitory. However, pacifying the parents does not help them deal with an infant who suffers from a serious psychological disorder. Accurate assessment is as essential for infants as for adults, if not more so.

Psychological assessments of infants differ from assessments of older groups in three major ways: (1) *nonverbal* or performance tests and behavioral observations are more often used with infants; (2) relatively few reliable, standardized measures have been developed for use with infants, compared to the many tests for adults; and (3) infants are more often studied in the context of their relationships with family members than individually.

There are clear age-related differences in reliance on language in assessment. Infants' very limited expressive and receptive language precludes the use of verbal self-reports in assessment and diagnosis. Imagine how similar communication limitations would affect assessment of older age groups. The most frequently used diagnostic tools would be unavailable for use with adults who lacked receptive and expressive language. There would be no verbal IQ tests and no self-reports of emotional states or personality attributes, such as the often-used Beck Depression Inventory, the standardized tests of general intelligence, the MMPI (Minnesota Multiphasic Personality Inventory), and many others in common use with adults. Also, there would be no conversational diagnostic interview, which is the basis of most psychiatric assessment. It is much more difficult to pinpoint the difficulties of young children than those of adult clients.

Because of the relative imprecision of classification of early childhood disorders, it is more difficult to assess whether or not an infant meets diagnostic criteria for a particular disorder (AACAP, 1997). Further, there is considerable overlap in the symptoms of different disorders. For example, significant delays or regression in the development of language characterizes many disorders, including autistic disorder, pervasive developmental disorder (not otherwise specified), childhood disintegrative disorder, psychic trauma disorders, mental retardation, and some affective or mood disorders. When the same problems are used to indicate different disorders, reliability of diagnosis drops dramatically (Gelfand et al., 1997, chap. 12). Assessment of young children is severely impeded because clinicians cannot use diagnostic tests and procedures that rely largely or totally on verbal communication. Overall, low reliability in diagnosis, disagreements about the classification of disorders, and inadequate testing and observation methods all severely limit clinical work with infants.

Further, because babies interact so closely and continually with their caretakers and are so dependent on their parents and families to ensure their health and well-being, their whole social context must be assessed. Many researchers and clinicians have concluded that the basic unit of study is not the baby, but rather the baby in interaction with the mother or other major caregivers. The transactional view that infant and caregiver must be viewed as a unit, with each influencing the other, is widely accepted in contemporary clinical practice. Thus, both parents' reports of infant behavior and actual observations of their interactions are important aspects of the assessment process.

Standardized Tests and Observations

A limited number of psychological tests and rating scales have gained acceptance as measures of emotional adjustment and cognitive development, particularly reasoning, memory, and language abilities. Most of these tests compare the individual infant's abilities against the norms for age-mates, giving higher scores for more developmentally advanced performances. More standardized tests assess infants' cognitive abilities and daily living skills than test emotional and social adjustment. Examples of scales measuring early cognitive development include: (1) the Bayley Scales of Infant Development for infants from 2 to 30 months old (Bayley, 1969), (2) the Vineland Adaptive Behavior Scale, offering forms for diverse ages, from infants to adults with mental disabilities (Sparrow, Balla, & Cicchetti, 1984), and (3) the McCarthy Scales of Children's Abilities (McCarthy, 1972), designed for use with older infants through 8-year-olds. Standardized tests of language performance include Lee's Developmental Sentence Analysis (1971), the Peabody Picture Vocabulary Test (Dunn & Dunn, 1981), and the Reynell Developmental Language Scales, Revised (Reynell, 1977, 1991).

Many clinicians prefer to assess language development of very young children informally during the general testing and interview process (Minde & Minde, 1986). Sole reliance on clinical impressions to assess infants without recourse to age norms or standards makes for serious unreliability of judgment from one clinician to another.

Quality of the home environment and adequacy of the child's care can be assessed using Caldwell's (Bradley & Caldwell, 1984) Home Observations for Measurement of the Environment (HOME ratings). A trained home visitor interviews the parent and rates aspects of the home and family environment, including the mother's sensitivity to and involvement with the child, acceptance of the child's behavior, and provision of developmentally appropriate play materials. The organization or disorganization and variety of the infant's schedule and physical environment are also rated, giving an overall picture of the setting in which the child is being reared. HOME scores are positively related to impoverished children's cognitive performance and are lower in families with mothers diagnosed with depression (George, Jameson, Gelfand, Altman, & Teti, 1996; Goodman, 1992).

The quality of an infant's emotional attachment to the mother or other primary caretaker can be measured by highly trained observers during a standardized sequence of brief separations and reunions of mother and infant in a laboratory setting. The Strange Situation Test developed by Ainsworth tests the security of the infant's *attachment* to the caretaker (Ainsworth et al., 1978). Alternative attachment security tests consist of lengthy home observations and expert observers' ratings in addition to parent self-reports (attachment Q-sorts), or mother-reports alone. As previously described, the resulting classification of the infant as securely or insecurely attached (with several types of insecure attachment rated) is useful in detecting early adjustment problems that may forecast future adjustment problems.

Assessment of *parents' attitudes and behavior* may be a portion of the assessment of the infant's status. Abidin's Parenting Stress Index (Abidin, 1986) is a standardized self-report instrument for parents designed to identify family stress, dysfunctional parenting, parent–child relationships, and the child's risk for deviant development.

Other parent-report questionnaires are available to assess child temperament, attachment status, and other aspects of early functioning that could be related to mental health. At least one problem behavior noted in some 2-year-olds, aggressive behavior, correlates moderately and significantly ($r = .55$) with the same children's aggressive behavior at age 9 years, despite age-related differences in the particular form of the aggression displayed (Achenbach, 1992). Thus parent reports of at least some infant problem behaviors such as attachment and aggression can be clinically important.

Because the parent–infant relationship is so important to the child's development, it is highly desirable to evaluate the quality of their dyadic relationship. Most clinicians provide brief verbal descriptions of their observations regarding the quality of the parent–infant relationship. However, the NCCIP manual provides a Global Assessment Scale (GAS) that rates the relationship on a 90-point scale, ranging from dangerous and indicating imminent danger to the infant on the low end to an unusually well-adapted dyad on the top. The GAS provides users with a common vocabulary to facilitate communication within the mental health community. Unfortunately, there is little information to suggest that the Global Assessment Scale can be used reliably by clinicians in everyday practice, nor is it clear how relationship quality relates to the development of infants' problems (Emde et al., 1993). Until these issues are addressed in research, this scale offers little advantage over simple narrative or having clinicians characterize the adult–infant relationship in verbal terms.

The field of infant mental health is itself in its infancy. Good information is lacking on the prevalence, gender distribution, etiology, prognosis, and treatment of the rarer infant disorders, such as several of the pervasive developmental disorders. The accuracy with which these disorders can be diagnosed is not established, handicapping both research and treatment, since no one can be sure that the conditions of the same name that are studied at various times and places are actually identical.

Early Intervention and Treatment

Early interventions typically focus either on the child or the parent(s). Some programs for parents include other family members who have regular contact with the child, such as grandparents, as well as non-related but regular care providers. Infant- and parent-oriented interventions are not mutually exclusive, and each may include elements of the other. For example, when the infant is given special stimulation programs, the caretakers are often trained to administer the procedure at home. However, the interventions can be usefully grouped according to the relative attention given to teaching specific skills to the child or to supporting the parents and promoting overall family functioning.

Infant-focused Interventions

Sensory stimulation programs are frequently prescribed for infants with developmental delays. Many different modes of stimulation are used, including visual and auditory enrichment of the baby's environment and rocking and massage, delivered either manually or by machine. Field (1999) has found that brief daily massage sessions benefit premature infants and autistic children, among other special-needs groups. In one study, preterm infants who received 15-minute massages three times a day for ten days gained weight more quickly and could be dismissed from the hospital earlier than untreated infants. The normal developmental increase in norepinephrine and epinephrine (catecholamine) levels during infancy was also facilitated by the massage (Kuhn et al., 1991).

In a recent study, full-term infants of adolescent mothers responded well to massage, made greater weight gains, became more responsive, relaxed, sociable, and easy to soothe (Field, Grizzle, Scafidi, & Schanberg, 1996). This simple intervention promises to have many benefits. There is new interest in massage therapy among mental health professionals, although massage itself has long been used informally by parents and medical personnel. Relatively little well-controlled research has yet addressed the psychological and physical effects of massage therapy on infants, although the early results are promising.

Skills Training for Infants

Infants who lag far behind age-mates in social and cognitive development may require individualized stimulation and training. Most programs are behaviorally based, and all interventions begin with the establishment of a warm, sensitive, responsive relationship between therapist and infant. Frequently the therapist teaches the parents to administer at least some portion of the training sessions to their child. Couples learn efficient teaching methods that benefit their babies and become more self-confident parents. Parenting self-efficacy expectations grow when parents successfully train their own children and become less dependent on professionals.

The specific behavioral methods used may begin with training infants to attend to and imitate the trainer, follow simple instructions, utter specific sounds and words, and hold the head upright. Training may then progress to teaching the infant to crawl, rise from a sitting position, walk, feed him or herself, use a toilet, and other developmental achievements. Ideally, infants acquire these skills in the normal course of living and with little or no professional intervention. However, when they cannot do so, individualized behavioral programs are invaluable. Often, however, effective intervention requires much more than acquisition of a set of specific skills. Most programs for severely disordered infants are multifaceted and aim to improve many aspects of the infant's and family's life.

Improving Home Environments

Infant care has progressed far from the early twentieth-century view that babies need only a nutritious diet and adequate sanitation in order to thrive. Contemporary professional and public opinion recognizes the vital importance of an additional component, warm and loving care by emotionally available regular caretakers. A wealth of empirical research has revealed the importance of high-quality care and stimulating surroundings in facilitating children's psychological development (NICHD Early Child Care Research Network, 1998). Any family condition that creates a climate of neglect, violence, abuse, despair, and insecurity for young children is likely to exacerbate their problems or create new ones. It is very difficult to help children without addressing the needs of their parents and siblings as well. Impoverished, ill-educated, or psychologically disturbed mothers who find childrearing particularly challenging may need prolonged and multifaceted professional help.

Early childhood intervention programs that provide additional physical and psychosocial stimulation have been found to promote the cognitive development of infants at risk because of psychological disorders, family poverty, low socioeconomic status, and other risk factors (Bradley, Caldwell, & Rock, 1988). The quality of the infant's living environment during infancy predicts later cognitive and language competence through age 5 (Bradley et al., 1988). This consistent research finding suggests that programs aimed to increase infants' quality of care and variety of daily stimulation will enhance their cognitive development.

Head Start, the national US effort at early education for young children from impoverished families, is a successful example of early intervention aimed at improving many aspects of children's lives. Serving primarily low-income preschool children ages 3 to 5, Head Start programs offer early childhood education, health screening and referral, mental health services, nutrition education, hot meals, family social services, and programs of parent employment, training, and involvement with children. The Head Start program benefits children's school adjustment and social competence, both during preschool and afterward (Zigler & Muenchow, 1992). A similar program beginning in infancy or during the mother's pregnancy could benefit many American families.

Comprehensive Parent-training Programs

Parent-training programs aim to improve parenting practices and family relationships on the assumption that improved family functioning will promote child development (Gelfand et al., 1997, chap. 4). Parents of infants with pervasive developmental delay are taught various relationship-building and direct stimulation procedures to build their child's basic emotional, social, and cognitive skills. Such programs are very ambitious and attend as much to parent and child motivation as to child management. One of the most impressive such programs was developed by Webster-Stratton and Herbert (1994). These authors advocate that therapists be very approachable, adopting a collaborative style with parents rather than acting as remote experts on childrearing. Although this model teaches participants specific skills, it also seeks to accomplish a more ambitious goal. The Webster-Stratton and Herbert intervention respects the parents' values and childrearing philosophy, builds their knowledge about child development, and helps them to acquire the necessary behavioral and social instructional techniques to help their infants. This approach acquaints parents with developmental norms by which to judge their child's progress and set realistic expectations. The intervention is complex and consists of immersion in a program of individual and group discussions, readings, viewing videotapes of appropriate management of delayed infants, homework assignments, self-observation, and recording of parent and child behavior. Therapists respect the parents' values, autonomy, and responsibility for developing solutions that are best for their particular family (Herbert, 1998). This builds parents' self-confidence (parenting self-efficacy feelings) that will lead them to persist in the face of difficulties that inevitably arise and sometimes defeat treatment efforts (Bandura, 1989). This intervention draws upon a large body of research on treatment effectiveness, incorporates many behavioral techniques of demonstrated utility, and thus has great promise.

A major limitation is the daunting amount of time and effort required of both parents and professionals, which makes the comprehensive parent-training approach prohibitively expensive and time-consuming for some families. However, neglecting to treat a severely delayed child may ultimately be more expensive yet if the untreated child continues to need mental health services, special education, and never becomes a self-supporting adult.

Requirements for Effective Early Intervention

Many early intervention programs have been developed and tested during the past several decades (Pumariega & Glover, 1998). Most of these programs have aimed to prevent developmental delays in children who are born into extreme poverty or whose parents are incapacitated in some way (e.g., by dependence on drugs or alcohol or by mental disorders such as depression or schizophrenia). Other groups who have received early intervention include extremely premature, low-birthweight babies, abused or neglected children, and those with congenital disabilities.

Effective early interventions for these various groups of children share certain features. Disorders are usually associated with many risk factors, so interventions must be complex and include many different features (Coie et al., 1993). Prevention programs often focus on children who are at risk for one or more problems and live in high-risk environments, for example, developmentally delayed or physically abused infants living in impoverished families. The range of intervention techniques is fairly limited at present. In many instances, sensory stimulation sessions are introduced, including holding or rocking the infant, the massage therapy described previously, or provision of visually complex pictures, mobiles, and developmentally appropriate play materials, which are believed to be cognitively stimulating. Caretakers are trained to provide warm, sensitive, stimulating care on a daily basis. A common prescription for at-risk infants is parental instruction in appropriate parenting practices and the development of loving relationships. Families may also require more general help in the form of instruction in problem-solving skills, improved health practices, communication, and mutual support skills (Winett, 1998). Parents who are economically dependent on welfare and charity programs may also be given educational and work opportunities and help in adapting to the workplace.

In their review of early intervention efforts, Craig and Sharon Ramey (1998) concluded that some fragmented and minimal programs are not sufficiently powerful to benefit children. For example, introduction of weekly home visits for a few months or enrolling the young child in a therapeutic nursery school for a few hours each day may both fail to produce noteworthy improvement, whereas a more ambitious, intense, and sustained effort over a period of several years can succeed. Thus comprehensive and prolonged interventions which provide health, training, support, and perhaps parental job-training services have larger effects than interventions that are less extensive (Ramey & Ramey, 1998). If they are to profit from mental health services, many families require a broad spectrum of individualized services, even including help with housing, income, employment, medical care, and social and emotional support (Schorr & Schorr, 1988). Not all of these measures are customarily considered to be mental health interventions, but they may be necessary adjuncts to the more usual mental health services for families with many needs.

In addition, the more effective interventions began as early as possible in the child's life, preferably in infancy or as early as their heightened risk status can be identified (Ramey & Ramey, 1998). Further, the more effective interventions contacted the families many times a week for extended periods of months or years and treated the child directly, perhaps with specific skill training, and not just indirectly through training caretakers. Finally, long-term benefits are sustained when the environment is managed so it supports and maintains the children's gains. For example, a child who had improved but was subsequently given insufficient verbal stimulation from a psychologically disturbed mother may lose newly acquired speech skills. Adverse environmental factors such as inadequate or dangerous parenting practices, deficient health care, poor schooling, and anti-social peer groups must be vigorously counteracted if the child is to become *and remain* psychologically and physically healthy. The family's childrearing practices may slide into inadequacy and the child's newly acquired gains may be rapidly lost if parents resume their previous problematic drug or alcohol consumption, if one or both parents are arrested for criminal activities, or if a mother's depression recurs. In a pathogenic environment, developmental advances will diminish and new problems will arise. The challenge for mental health workers is not limited to producing temporary improvements in children's development, but must extend to sustaining those gains through the children's formative years.

Summary

With the recognition that infants possess many adult-like characteristics came the belief that infants too can be mentally ill or healthy. Contemporary diagnostic classification systems or taxonomies agree in recognizing certain infant mental disorders: (1) reactive attachment disorder of infancy, (2) anxiety disorders (sometimes limited to separation anxiety disorder), and (3) pervasive developmental disorders including childhood autistic disorder and atypical pervasive developmental disorder. Regulatory disorders of eating, sleeping, and elimination also are diagnosed during infancy.

Little is known about the nature, prevalence, and etiology of the rarer infancy disorders (e.g., Rett's disorder, childhood disintegrative disorder, and Asperger's disorder). In contrast, the more prevalent autistic disorder has been extensively studied and can be better diagnosed and treated.

Standardized infant assessment techniques are few and limited mainly to examiner-administered scales of infant development and parents' self-ratings and ratings of their children's problem behaviors. Trained observers can report on infants' attachment security and on the quality of the home environment, although these latter two types of ratings are more likely to be used in research than in clinical services. Much remains to be done to develop more accurate diagnostic procedures and more effective early intervention tactics.

Research experience indicates that the task of assisting developmentally delayed and disturbed infants and their families is far from accomplished. Babies are extremely sensitive to their surroundings, so family poverty, poor education, hopelessness, ill health, or abuse and neglect inevitably adversely affect the young. Such factors are most likely to hurt infants who are vulnerable because of ill health or developmental delay. The most effective interventions provide a wide variety of individualized services to troubled families. This comprehensive approach has proved effective for preschool children enrolled in Head Start school-based programs and suggests that similar programs beginning earlier in the child's life could help millions.

Further Reading

Fogel, A. (1993). *Developing through relationships: Origins of communication, self, and culture.* Chicago: University of Chicago Press. An innovative view of how we become social beings by a developmental psychologist trained in physics. A challenging but rewarding read.

Kephart, B. (1998). *A slant of sun: One child's courage.* New York: W. W. Norton. A parent's encouraging account of her infant son's descent into pervasive developmental disorder not otherwise specified, and his emergence as "a successful second grader" through the efforts of parents, professionals, and ordinary people in his life.

Ollendick, T. H., & Hersen, M. (Eds.). (1998). *Handbook of child psychopathology* (3rd ed.). New York: Plenum Press. This edited volume presents recent reviews of virtually all aspects of child psychopathology, from basic issues to prevention and treatment. An excellent resource for students, clinicians, and researchers.

Ollendick, T. H., & Prinz, R. J. (Eds.). (1998). *Advances in clinical child psychology* (Vol. 20). New York: Plenum Press. The last in a series of clear and informative reviews of issues in child psychopathology. Includes everything from early feeding problems to research on services delivery to families.

Zero to Three. National Center for Clinical Infant Programs, 2000 14th Street North, Suite 380, Arlington, VA 22201-2500. Six issues per year describe the latest developments in areas of infant care, such as parenting in violent environments, special needs babies, and children of disturbed or disabled parents.

References

AACAP (American Academy of Child and Adolescent Psychiatry). (1997). Practice parameters for the psychiatric assessment of infants and toddlers (0–36 months). *Journal of the American Academy of Child and Adolescent Psychiatry, 36* (10 Supplement), 215–365.

Abidin, R. R. (1986). *Parenting Stress Index* (2nd ed.). Charlottesville, VA: Pediatric Psychology Press.

Achenbach, T. M. (1992). *Manual for the Child Behavior Checklist/2–3 and 1992 Profile.* Burlington: University of Vermont Department of Psychiatry.

Ainsworth, M. D. S., Blehar, M., Waters, E., & Wall, S. (1978). *Patterns of attachment: A psychological study of the Strange Situation.* Hillsdale, NJ: Erlbaum.

American Psychiatric Association. (1994). *Diagnostic and statistical manual of mental disorders* (4th ed., rev.). Washington, DC: Author.

Bandura, A. (1989). Regulation of cognitive processes through perceived self-efficacy. *Developmental Psychology, 25,* 729–735.

Bayley, N. (1969). *Bayley Scales of Infant Development: Birth to two years.* New York: Psychological Corporation.

Berntson, G. G., Bigger, J. T., Eckberg, D. L., Grossman, P., Kaufman, P. G., Malik, M., Nagaraja, H. N., Porges, S. W., Saul, J. P., Stone, P. H., & van der Molen, M. W. (1997). Heart rate variability: Origins, methods, and interpretive caveats. *Psychophysiology, 34,* 623–648.

Biederman, J., Orsenbaum, J. F., Bolduc-Murphy, E. A., Faraone, S. V., Chaloff, J., Hirshfeld, D. R., & Kagan, J. (1993). Behavioral inhibition as a temperamental risk factor for anxiety disorders. *Child and Adolescent Psychiatric Clinics of North America, 2,* 667–684.

Bornstein, M. H., & Haynes, O. M. (1998). Vocabulary competence in early childhood: Measurement, latent construct, and predictive validity. *Child Development, 69,* 654–671.

Bowlby, J. (1969–1980). *Attachment and loss* (Vols. 1–3). London: Hogarth Press.

Bradley, R. H., & Caldwell, B. M. (1984). The HOME Inventory and family demographics. *Developmental Psychology, 20,* 114–130.

Bradley, R. H., Caldwell, B. M., & Rock, S. L. (1988). Home environment and school performance: A ten-year follow-up and examination of three models of environmental action. *Child Development, 59,* 852–867.

Campos, J. J., & Stenberg, C. R. (1981). Perception, appraisal and emotion: The onset of social referencing. In M. E. Lamb & L. R. Sherrod (Eds.), *Infant social cognition: Empirical and theoretical considerations* (pp. 783–816). Hillsdale, NJ: Erlbaum.

Cappelleri, J. C., Eckenrode, J., & Powers, J. L. (1993). The epidemiology of child abuse: Findings from the Second National Incidence and Prevalence Study of Child Abuse and Neglect. *American Journal of Public Health, 83,* 1622–1624.

Carlson, E. A. (1998). A prospective longitudinal study of attachment disorganization/disorientation. *Child Development, 69,* 1107–1128.

Carlson, V., Cicchetti, D., Barnett, D., & Braunwald, K. (1989). Disorganized/disoriented attachment relationships in maltreated infants. *Developmental Psychology, 25,* 525–531.

Center for Mental Health Services (1993). Federal definition of childhood serious emotional disturbance. *Federal Register, 58,* 29422–29425.

Cicchetti, D., Toth, S. L., & Lynch, M. (1995). Bowlby's dream comes full circle: The application of attachment theory to risk and psychopathology. In T. H. Ollendick & R. J. Prinz (Eds.), *Advances in clinical child psychology* (Vol. 17, pp. 1–75). New York: Plenum Press.

Coie, J. D., Watt, N. F., West, S. G., Hawkins, J. D., Asarnow, J. R., Markman, H. J., Ramey, S. L., Shure, M. B., & Long, B. (1993). The science of prevention: A conceptual framework and some directions for a national research program. *American Psychologist, 48,* 1013–1022.

Dunn, L. M., & Dunn, P. P. (1981). *Peabody Picture Vocabulary Test – Revised.* Circle Pines, MN: American Guidance Service.

Emde, R. N., Bingham, R. D., & Harmon, R. J. (1993). Classification and the diagnostic process in infancy. In C. H. Zeanah, Jr. (Ed.), *Handbook of infant mental health* (pp. 225–235). New York: Guilford Press.

Fagot, B. I. (1977). Consequences of moderate crossgender behavior in preschool children. *Child Development, 48,* 902–907.

Fagot, B. I. (1985). Changes in thinking about early sex role development. *Developmental Review, 5,* 83–98.

Fagot, B. I., & Leinbach, M. D. (1995). Gender knowledge in egalitarian and traditional families. *Sex Roles, 32,* 513–526.

Field, T. (1996). Attachment and separation in young children. *Annual Review of Psychology, 47,* 541–561.

Field, T. M. (1999). Massage therapy effects. *American Psychologist, 53,* 1270–1281.

Field, T., Grizzle, N., Scafidi, F., & Schanberg, S. (1996). Massage and relaxation therapies' effects on depressed adolescent mothers. *Adolescence, 31,* 903–911.

Fogel, A. (1993). *Developing through relationships: Origins of communication, self, and culture.* Chicago: University of Chicago Press.

Fogel, A., & Thelen, E. (1987). Development of early expressive and communicative action: Reinterpreting the evidence from a dynamic systems perspective. *Developmental Psychology, 23,* 747–761.

Fombonne, E., & du Mazaubrun, C. (1992). Prevalence of infantile autism in four French regions. *Social Psychiatry and Psychiatric Epidemiology, 27,* 203–210.

Fortey, R. (1997). *Life: A natural history of the first four billion years of life on earth.* New York: Alfred A. Knopf.

Gelfand, D. M., Jenson, W. R., & Drew, C. J. (1997). *Understanding child behavior disorders* (3rd ed.). Fort Worth, TX: Harcourt Brace.

George, T. M., Jameson, P., Gelfand, D. M., Altman, I. A., & Teti, D. M. (1996, June). *Home environments of depressed and nondepressed mothers.* Poster presented at the Conference of the Environmental Design and Research Association, Salt Lake City, UT.

Goodman, S. H. (1992). Understanding the effects of depressed mothers on their children. In E. F. Walker, R. H. Dwordin, & B. A. Cornblatt (Eds.), *Progress in experimental personality and psychopathology research* (pp. 47–109). New York: Springer.

Haith, M. (1998). Who put the cog in infant cognition? Is rich interpretation too costly? *Infant Behavior and Development, 21,* 167–179.

Hepper, P. G., Scott, D., & Shahidullah, S. (1993). Newborn and fetal response to maternal voice. *Journal of Reproductive and Infant Psychology, 11,* 147–153.

Herbert, M. (1998). Family treatment. In T. H. Ollendick & M. Hersen (Eds.), *Handbook of child psychopathology* (3rd ed., pp. 557–580). New York: Plenum Press.

Hirshfeld, D. R., Rosenbaum, J. F., Biederman, J., Bolduc, E. A., Faraone, S. V., Snidman, N., Reznick, J. S., & Kagan, J. (1992). Stable behavioral inhibition and its association with anxiety disorder. *Journal of the American Academy of Child and Adolescent Psychiatry, 31,* 103–111.

Horner, T. M., & Guyer, M. J. (1993). Infant placement and custody. In C. H. Zeanah, Jr. (Ed.), *Handbook of infant mental health* (pp. 462–479). New York: Guilford Press.

Horowitz, F. D. (1992). The challenge facing infant research in the next decade. In G. J. Suci & S. S. Robertson (Eds.), *Future directions in infant development research* (pp. 89–104). New York: Springer Verlag.

Huffman, L. C., Bryan, Y. E., del Carmen, R., Petersen, F. A., Doussard-Roosevelt, J. A., & Porges, S. W. (1998). Infant temperament and cardiac vagal tone: Assessments at twelve weeks of age. *Child Development, 69*, 624–635.

Kagan, J. (1998). Is there a self in infancy? In M. Ferrari & R. J. Sternberg (Eds.), *Self-awareness: Its nature and development* (pp. 137–147). New York: Guilford Press.

Kagan, J., Reznick, J. S., & Snidman, N. (1987). The physiology and psychology of behavioral inhibition. *Child Development, 58*, 1458–1473.

Karmiloff-Smith, A. (1995). Annotation: The extraordinary cognitive journey from foetus through infancy. *Journal of Child Psychology and Psychiatry, 36*, 1293–1313.

Kauffmann, J. M. (1993). *Characteristics of emotional and behavioral disorders of children and youth* (5th ed.). New York: Macmillan.

Kuhn, C., Schanberg, S., Field, T., Symanski, R., Zimmerman, E., Scafidi, F., & Roberts, J. (1991). Tactile kinesthetic stimulation effects on sympathetic and adrenocortical function in preterm infants. *Journal of Pediatrics, 119*, 434–440.

Lee, L. L. (1971). *The Northwestern Syntax Screening Test.* Evanston, IL: Northwestern University Press.

Lockyer, L., & Rutter, M. (1969). A 5- to 15-year follow-up study of infantile psychosis III. Psychological aspects. *British Journal of Psychiatry, 115*, 865–882.

Lyons-Ruth, K., Repacholi, B., McLeod, S., & Silva, E. (1991). Disorganized attachment behavior in infancy: Short-term stability, maternal and infant correlates and risk-related subtypes. *Development and Psychopathology, 3*, 377–396.

Main, M., & Hesse, E. (1990). Parents' unresolved traumatic experiences are related to infant disorganized attachment status: Is frightened and/or frightening parental behavior the linking mechanism? In M. T. Greenberg, D. Cicchetti, & E. M. Cummings (Eds.), *Attachment in the preschool years* (pp. 161–182). Chicago: University of Chicago Press.

Main, M., Kaplan, N., & Cassidy, J. C. (1985). Security in infancy, childhood and adulthood: A move to the level of representation. *Monographs of the Society for Research in Child Development, 50* (1–2, Serial No. 209).

McCarthy, D. (1972). *McCarthy Scales of Children's Abilities.* New York: Psychological Corporation.

Meltzoff, A. N. (1995). Understanding the intentions of others: Re-enactment of intended acts by 18-month-old children. *Developmental Psychology, 31*, 838–850.

Minde, K., & Minde, R. (1986). *Infant psychiatry: An introductory textbook.* Beverly Hills, CA: Sage.

NICHD Early Child Care Research Network. (1998). Early child care and self-control, compliance, and problem behavior at twenty-four and thirty-six months. *Child Development, 69*, 1145–1170.

O'Connor, M. J., Sigman, M., & Brill, N. (1987). Disorganization of attachment in relation to maternal alcohol consumption. *Journal of Consulting and Clinical Psychology, 55U*, 831–836.

Ohtaki, E., Kawano, Y., Urabe, F., & Komori, H. (1992). The prevalence of Rett syndrome and infantile autism in Chikugo district, the southwestern area of Fukuoka prefecture, Japan. *Journal of Autism and Developmental Disorders, 22*, 452–454.

Osofsky, J. D., & Eberhart-Wright, A. (1992). Risk and protective factors for parents and infants. In G. J. Suci & S. S. Robertson (Eds.), *Future directions in infant development research* (pp. 25–42). New York: Springer Verlag.

Parke, R. D. (1992). Social development in infancy: Looking backward, looking forward. In G. J. Suci & S. S. Robertson (Eds.), *Future directions in infant development research* (pp. 1–24). New York: Springer Verlag.

Parke, R. D., & Tinsley, B. J. (1987). Family interaction in infancy. In J. Osofsky (Ed.), *Handbook of infant development* (2nd ed., pp. 579–641). New York: Wiley.

Porges, S. W. (1996). Physiological regulation in high-risk infants: A model for assessment and potential intervention. *Development and Psychopathology, 8,* 29–42.

Porges, S. W. (1997). The integrative neurobiology of affiliation. *Annals of the New York Academy of Sciences, 807,* 62–77.

Portales, A. L., Porges, S. W., Doussard-Roosevelt, J. A., Abedin, M., Lopez, R., Young, M. A., Beeram, M. R., & Baker, M. (1997). Vagal regulation during bottle feeding in low birth weight neonates: Support for the gustatory-vagal hypothesis. *Developmental Psychobiology, 30,* 225–233.

Porter, F. L., Porges, S. W., & Marshall, R. E. (1988). Newborn pain cries and vagal tone: Parallel changes in response to circumcision. *Child Development, 59,* 495–505.

Pumariega, A. J., & Glover, S. (1998). New developments in services delivery research for children, adolescents, and their families. In T. H. Ollendick & R. J. Prinz (Eds.), *Advances in clinical child psychology* (Vol. 20, pp. 303–343). New York: Plenum Press.

Ramey, C. T., & Ramey, S. L. (1998). Early intervention and early experience. *American Psychologist, 53,* 109–120.

Reynell, J. (1977). *Reynell Developmental Language Scales (RDLS) Manual* (Rev. ed.). Windsor, England: NFER.

Reynell, J. (1991). *Reynell Developmental Language Scale* (US ed.). Los Angeles: Western Psychological Service.

Ritvo, E. R., Freeman, B. J., Pingree, C., Mason-Brothers, A., Jorde, L., Jenson, W. R., McMahon, W. M., Petersen, P. B., Mo, A., & Ritvo, A. (1989). The UCLA-University of Utah Epidemiologic Survey of Autism: Prevalence. *American Journal of Psychiatry, 146,* 194–199.

Rodning, C., Beckwith, L., & Howard, J. (1991). Quality of attachment and home environments in children prenatally exposed to PCP and cocaine. *Development and Psychopathology, 3,* 351–366.

Sameroff, A. J., & Emde, R. (Eds.). (1989). *Relationship disturbances in early childhood: A developmental approach.* New York: Basic Books.

Sameroff, A. J., Seifer, R., & Barocas, R. (1983). Impact of parental psychopathology: Diagnosis, severity or social status effects. *Infant Mental Health Journal, 4,* 236–249.

Scarr, S., & Eisenberg, M. (1993). Child care research: Issues, perspectives, and results. *Annual Review of Psychology, 44,* 613–644.

Schorr, L. B., & Schorr, D. (1988). *Within our reach: Breaking the cycle of disadvantage.* New York: Anchor Press.

Silverman, W. K., & Ginsburg, G. S. (1998). Anxiety disorders. In T. H. Ollendick & M. Hersen (Eds.), *Handbook of child psychopathology* (3rd ed., pp. 239–268). New York: Plenum Press.

Skinner, B. F. (1953). *Science and human behavior.* New York: Macmillan.

Sparrow, S. S., Balla, D. A., & Cicchetti, D. V. (1984). *Vineland Adaptive Behavior Scales: A revision of the Vineland Social Maturity Scale by Edgar A. Doll.* Circle Pines, MN: American Guidance Service.

Sue, D., & Sue, S. (1990). *Understanding abnormal behavior* (3rd ed.). Boston: Houghton Mifflin.

Teti, D. M., Gelfand, D. M., Messinger, D. W., & Isabella, R. (1995). Maternal depression and the quality of early attachment: An examination of infants, preschoolers, and their mothers. *Developmental Psychology, 31,* 364–376.

Volkmar, F. R., Szatmari, P., & Sparrow, S. S. (1993). Sex differences in pervasive developmental disorders. *Journal of Autism and Developmental Disorders, 23,* 579–591.

Webster-Stratton, C., & Herbert, M. (1994). *Troubled families: Problem children.* Chichester: Wiley.

Winett, R. A. (1998). Prevention: A proactive-developmental-ecological perspective. In T. H. Ollendick & M. Hersen (Eds.), *Handbook of child psychopathology* (3rd ed., pp. 637–671). New York: Plenum Press.

World Health Organization (1992). *The ICD-10 classification of mental and behavioural disorders: Clinical descriptions and diagnostic guidelines.* Geneva: Author.

Zigler, E., & Muenchow, S. (1992). *Head Start: The inside story of America's most successful educational experiment.* New York: Basic Books.

Chapter Twenty-two

Sensory Deficits

Gunilla Preisler

Introduction

Questions concerning the consequences of deafness and blindness and even deaf-blindness on a person's mind have fascinated philosophers and scientists for centuries. Deafness has for a long time been associated or even equated with being dumb. In the English language the term "deaf and dumb" was, and sometimes still is, used for people who are deaf or profoundly hearing impaired. Blindness has often been thought of as associated with wisdom. The prophet Tiresias was blind, as were many other sages in ancient and medieval times. But what is it really like to grow up as deaf or blind? What are the implications for development if the child lacks one of these important senses, or even both of them? Can a deaf child develop language without access to hearing? Can a blind child participate in the world outside without being able to perceive it visually? Can a deaf-blind child develop any competencies without access to either hearing or vision? Can studies of these children give us any new insights into normal infant and child development? These are questions that will be discussed in this chapter. First, however, it is necessary to set this work in the context of current infant research.

The Competent Infant

It was not many decades ago that pediatricians maintained that newborns and young infants experienced a totally confusing perceptual world in which they perceived nothing or almost nothing at all. During the last 25–30 years experimental as well as observational studies of early mother–infant interaction, with improved methods of studying the interplay between the two, have given us new insights not only on the perceptual capacities of the infant, but also about their emotional, communicative, social, and cognitive abilities. This in turn has meant that we have a new view of the potentialities of the growing child. We now talk about the competent child, and even the competent infant. Development is regarded as a process involving caregiver and child, where both play an active role in the interaction (Stern, 1995).

Important Milestones in Early Development

There are some important milestones in normal development in infancy that will be used when describing the development of deaf, blind, and deaf-blind children. These occur roughly at birth, 1.5, 3, 9, and 18 months of age (Trevarthen, 1988). From birth, infants enter into an exchange of feelings and communicative acts with the mother or the father. Eye contact is sought and movements of eyes and mouth, hand gestures, and vocalizations can be imitated by the infant (Meltzoff, 1986). These observations have resulted in a new view of the infant as a competent partner in social interaction. When the infant is between 1 and 2 months old, the infant and the caregiver start to communicate by means of cooing, vocalizations, eye contact, smiles, and body movements in dialogue-like exchanges. The caregiver starts to sing and even to engage the infant in different body games. Two to three months later, this interest in social interaction gradually turns into an interest in the environment. Infants now start to explore the characteristics of objects and can also show intentions by pointing with eyes and hands. For a period of time infants' interest in social interaction seems to diminish, but returns later at the age of 8 to 9 months, when they show a desire to share their new-won experiences about the world with another.

During the first months of life caregivers and infants mutually create sequences of reciprocal behaviors, so-called social dialogues. In these dialogues parents are responding to their infants in the same modality as the infant is using – a smile from the infant is met by a smile from the parent. At approximately 9 months, according to Stern (1985), caregivers start to add a new dimension to their imitation-like behaviors and expand their way of communicating into a new category of behavior that Stern calls affect attunement: the smile is not only met by a smile but also with an exaggerated facial expression, and always with vocalizations. There are, according to Stern (1985), three general features of behaviors that form the basis of attunement. These are intensity, timing, and shape: the loudness of a caregiver's vocalization can match the force of the infant's arm movement; the temporal beat of the movement of the caregiver can match the behavior of the infant; and finally, the form of the infant's movement can be abstracted and rendered in a different act by the caregiver. This way of sharing affect is one of the most important features of intersubjective relatedness.

After this period of presymbolic communication, the infant, at the age of 18 months, can enter into a world of symbols and starts using a language code in communication. Intersubjectivity, a synchronized attention to and understanding of events and others' emotions, is viewed as essential to other developing competencies such as language and social cognition (Studdert-Kennedy, 1991). Intersubjective experiences begin in the first year of life and continue to be refined as children and their relationships mature and become more complex. In normally developing infants, intersubjective experience is viewed as a spontaneous development, evolving out of natural contexts of child–caregiver interactions. It is both the infant's perceptual, motor, socioemotional, and cognitive competencies and the caregiver's sensitivity and responsiveness that are the basic ingredients to the experience of intersubjectivity. The sharing of meaning in joyful interactions and early mutual play with turn-taking qualities are crucial prerequisites for language development. The most significant things that the infant needs to learn about language are written on the face, the body, the gestures, and the voice of those who talk (Locke, 1995). Preverbal abilities in children, including the use of conventional gestures such as pointing and showing, symbolic play, imitation, and the use of tools, have proven to be important predictors of later language development (Bates, Benigni, Bretherton, Camaioni, & Volterra, 1979; Greenspan, 1997).

One important research finding with special relevance to the development of children with sensory functional disabilities is the notion of amodal perception, through which infants appear to experience a world of unity in which information received in one sensory modality can be translated or encoded into another sensory modality (Meltzoff, 1986; Stern, 1985). Due to this intersensory equivalence severe visual impairment is seldom detected before the age of 2–3 months of age, deafness seldom before the age of 6–12 months, and usually at an even later age, because parent–infant interaction is so similar to that of a normal parent–infant interaction. This early intersensory coordination declines at the age of 4–5 months (Stern, 1985).

It is obvious that both vision and hearing are the primary senses for input of information about the surrounding world. However, studies of deaf infants as well as of blind infants, and even of deaf-blind infants and children, now show that the plasticity of the brain seems immense and that there are also potentialities in communication for children lacking these senses. As the traditional way of conducting studies of children with functional disabilities has been to compare them with children without disabilities, they have always appeared less able and less competent than the latter group. Today many researchers have changed focus from the study of what children cannot do to what they can do, from a deficit model to a competence model, resulting in a quite different view of these children's abilities. A competence model will be the emphasis adopted in this chapter.

Being Born Deaf

As deafness has often been considered a severe obstacle in interpersonal communication and language development, this section starts by describing the findings of studies of deaf infants over the last decades with respect to the development of communication and language.

Being deaf means having severe difficulties or no abilities at all to perceive speech, even using a hearing aid. In Western countries approximately one child out of every 1000 newborns has a severe sensorineural hearing loss. Two to three children per 1000 are born with a congenital hearing impairment over 40 dB, which for most individuals means having difficulties in perceiving normal speech. Then there are children who have a progressive or an acquired hearing impairment identified at a later age. Thus, the older the population of children, the more incidents of hearing impairment will emerge. In most cases, approximately one-third of the population of deaf infants, the etiology is "unknown" but is probably due to genetic factors. About 25 percent of the cases have hereditary causes. Other causal factors in hearing loss can be congenital defects or early damage to the auditory system resulting from meningitis, prematurity, or viral infections.

Communication with a Deaf Child

As more than 90 percent of deaf children have hearing parents (Schein, 1996), a most important issue for parents and educators concerns how to communicate with a child who is unable or has severe difficulties in perceiving and producing spoken language. In addition to the trauma of adjusting to the diagnosis and the challenges of planning for both present and future, the parents must also make decisions about mode of communication (Meadow-Orlans & Sass-Lehrer, 1995). The situation is even harder for parents because opinions differ on whether to use a manual–gestural–visual language code, i.e., a sign language, or to make the deaf child lipread and to learn a language based on oral/aural skills. The argument behind using sign language is that this is the natural language of deaf people. It is based on a code of communication which is appropriate for a person who cannot perceive speech sounds. On the other hand, the majority of the deaf children's parents are hearing, and in most cases with no earlier experience of sign language. Therefore they have to learn an entirely new language in order to be able to share a common language code with their child. Another reason why there has been, and in many parts of the world still is, a negative attitude to sign language is the belief that a proper language can only be a spoken language and that language (i.e., speech) is a prerequisite for thinking. However, intensive linguistic studies of signed languages have shown that sign language has all the characteristics of a proper language, although the rules differ (Stokoe, 1972). On the other hand, sign language is used by a minority group in almost all societies, and therefore in many countries parents are recommended to use speech and hearing in communication with their deaf child.

The Development of Communication in Deaf Infants

Suspicion of deafness or a profound hearing impairment is seldom made before the age of 6–12 months. When parents try to recall the time prior to suspicion and diagnosis many of them report that they noticed that their child did not seem to react to noises or very loud sounds. But when they started to cuddle and play and talk to their infants, they cooed and smiled and answered them, in much the same way a hearing infant would do.

During the first year of life, when vision plays a most important role in normal mother–infant communication, studies of mother–deaf infant interaction have shown that infants are able to share in the communication with their hearing others much to the same extent as the hearing infant (Jamieson & Pedersen, 1993; Robinshaw & Evans,

1995). They also take part in body games, give-and-take, and peek-a-boo games with their parents. They explore toys, they imitate their mother's actions, and they start to take part in early pretend play. They show their intentions and wants and they take active part in protoconversations (Preisler, 1995). The hearing impairment is seldom a serious obstacle to communication until the age when hearing children normally begin to talk. If habilitation of the deaf child becomes focused on the use of communicative signals that are suited to auditory perception and extremely difficult to interpret visually, mutual understanding is often impeded, and breakdowns in communication become the rule rather than the exception. Studies of toddlers or preschoolers have shown that hearing parents using an oral/aural approach in communication use more directives and different control techniques in interaction with their deaf child (Meadow-Orlans, 1987; Schlesinger & Meadow, 1972). Deaf children were more passive, less attentive than hearing children, and they tended to withdraw from social interaction.

Communicative expressions used by parents and by deaf infants

There is a common belief that deaf infants are silent because they cannot hear their own voice. But studies have shown that this is not the case. Maestas y Moores (1980) found that deaf infants vocalized frequently at the age of 3 months. There was no difference in number of vocalizations in a study of 9- to 18-month-old deaf and hearing infants (Koester, 1995). Deaf infants have been observed to vocalize when they are solving problems, or when they are involved in joyful social interactions (Preisler, 1995). But in deaf infant–deaf signing parent interaction infants have been observed to engage in manual babbling (Pettito & Marentette, 1991).

Deaf infants seem to be aware very early that they must watch the faces and the expressions of their caregivers. The most extensive studies of the early communication between deaf infants and their parents have been conducted by researchers associated with Gallaudet College, Washington, DC. Among the topics studied has been the visual attention of deaf infants (Erting, Prezioso, & O'Grady Hynes, 1990). Deaf infants appeared to watch their mothers' faces and hands more intensively compared to the hearing infants, who in a similar setting attended more closely to the environment. By 3 months of age, deaf infants seemed to have learned that they must engage the mother visually if the communication in progress was to continue. Hearing infants with deaf mothers were also more likely to focus primarily on their mothers' faces during normal interaction at the age of 6 months. At this age, they had probably learnt that in order to get their mothers' attention they had to have other means than auditory communication.

One often raised question is whether it is possible to replace the emotional information that is expressed in suprasegmental features of caregiver speech with visual, kinesthetic, or tactile cues. Erting et al. (1990) showed that modifications in caregivers' sign language communication were very consistent with modifications made by caregivers who used spoken language. The way hearing adults talk to their hearing infants, with special temporal patterns, prolonged vocalizations, rhythmic repetitions and pitch contours, can be expressed equally well with facial expressions, movements of eyebrows, gestures, signs, and tactile means. This was also found in a longitudinal study of deaf infants with deaf parents from the age of 6 months and onwards (Preisler, 1993, 1995).

The sensitivity of caregivers

One important determinant of the later quality of the infant–caregiver relationship is how sensitive the caregiver is to the infant's communicative attempts (Ainsworth, Blehar, Waters, & Wall, 1978). Research on mother–infant interaction has shown that there is an association between infants' social and cognitive competence and their mothers' sensitivity to their infants' needs (Bornstein, 1989). In the first months of life infants have expectations of particular patterns of behavior from their caregivers (Stern, 1985, 1995). However, if the caregiver behaves in a way that is unusual to the infant, the infant reacts very quickly. The first response is usually that infants try to modify their way of communicating, testing different means to attract caregivers' attention and affection. If infants do not succeed in attracting the attention and care of their caregivers, they may become withdrawn. There is now a growing number of early neonatal screening programs which aim to identify, as early as two days after birth, whether the child has a hearing loss or not. One important question to be discussed in this context is whether an early diagnosis will affect caregivers' sensitivity to their infants' way of communicating during a period of natural bonding, when even mothers of normally developing babies are at risk for depression. Caregivers of newly identified disabled infants are also at risk for depression when two life events occur closely in time; a new baby in the family as well as the identification that the very same baby has a disability. Both events, independently of each other, are significantly associated with psychiatric disorder in the postpartum year (Copper & Stein, 1989). Studies of infant disability and of maternal depression have identified both these factors as powerful indications of depression in the year following childbirth (Murray, Kempton, Woolgar, & Hooper, 1993). There is a risk that if the infant has a functional disability, like a hearing impairment, the parents' intuitive parenting skills might be less appropriate. In combination with the infant's special needs, the parents may feel inadequate as caregivers. This in turn might result in a self-fulfilling prophesy of unsatisfactory interaction (Meadow-Orlans & Spencer, 1996). In addition to stress created by the very diagnosis of deafness, stress for hearing parents may emanate from a sense that their usual (vocal/spoken) way of communicating is inadequate for the needs of a child who is deaf. It has been proposed that stress related to the diagnosis of deafness is one reason for repeated research findings showing that hearing mothers with deaf infants are less sensitive than mothers with hearing children (Greenberg, 1980; Schlesinger & Meadow, 1972). But recent studies have shown that hearing parents of deaf infants are able to communicate with their baby in a way that is highly appropriate for the infant's needs in early dyadic communication. The problem may arise later, in the preschool years, when language is more vital in communication (Spencer & Lederberg, 1997). Hearing parents have been found to provide more visual experience to deaf than to hearing infants during early face-to-face interactions, but also during play with toys or objects (Koester, 1994). But as infants grow older visual gaze also involves joint attention to objects. Hearing parents have then been found to have some difficulties in coordinating their visual responses with their deaf child. In a study by MacTurk, Meadow-Orlans, Koester, and Spencer (1993) it was found that when hearing mothers incorporated visual or tactile stimulation with their 9-month-old infants the interaction at 18 months was more positive compared to interactions where these means of communication were not used. This finding confirms the importance of using response modalities which are matched with the sensory capabilities of the infant (Koester, 1994).

Meadow-Orlans and Spencer (1996) hypothesized that both deaf and hearing mothers might have difficulties in responding to infants whose hearing status is different from their own. Therefore they compared data on 80 mothers' sensitivity and their infants' attention defined as their ability to coordinate attention to mothers and objects. The mothers were hearing with hearing infants, hearing with deaf infants, deaf with hearing infants, and deaf with deaf infants. The dyads were observed at 9, 12, and 18 months of age. The results showed that mothers whose infants' hearing status matched their own were rated equally sensitive to their infants. Hearing mothers of deaf infants were rated less sensitive, and even less sensitive were deaf mothers of hearing infants. The authors discussed these results in terms of intuitive parenting. Parents with infants who are not at risk or who have no specially identified needs interact in a way that most parents do. This means that they use their intuitive parenting skills and that is "good enough" for the needs of their baby. But a hearing mother with a newly diagnosed deaf baby has no intuitive or experiential basis for interacting with a deaf child. It does not yet seem to come naturally for them to provide their infants with optimal visual input.

Interactional styles of parents of five deaf and five hearing infants were studied by Robinshaw and Evans (1995) by means of video and audio recordings. A measure was used that was elaborated by Kaye and his colleagues (1981) called "turnabout," defined as a gestural and/or vocal contribution which both responds to the previous turn by the partner and attempts to elicit a response from the partner. It is thus an extension of a "turn," which refers to only one of these aspects. The analyses showed that there was a clear pattern of behavior for each of the caregivers interacting with their normally hearing infants. When the recordings started, the children were 9 months old. At this age the parents acknowledged and responded to approximately half of the infants' contributions as if they were communicative. Then there was a sudden growth of intentional communication and symbolic vocalizations up to the age of 15 months. The caregivers' sensitivity also increased. The sensitivity of caregivers of deaf infants did not follow the same pattern as for hearing children. In the hearing mother–deaf infant dyads, the pattern of interaction was more complex. Some parents were sensitive to their infants, while others were not. The authors discussed the result in light of family factors, habilitation, service given, and so on. In the first months following identification, each of the families with a deaf infant described their mode of communication as predominantly oral/aural. None of the parents had at this stage started to use British Sign Language (BSL). This decision reflects to some extent the language used in the family, which was English, but also other factors such as expectation that early amplification and habilitation would benefit the infant's linguistic development, and the parents' readiness to accept or to challenge the advice given by professionals. Furthermore, there was a dramatic change in the caregivers' use of turnabouts, i.e., in the sensitivity to the child's way of communicating, when they started using signs as a regular way of communicating instead of symbolic gestures or signs as occasional support to spoken words.

Early Language Development in Deaf Children

In deaf children exposed to sign language, the first stages of conventional and referential communication are more easily established than in deaf children exposed to oral/aural communication. Objects are directly in view and each partner can signal his or her intentions visually to the other. But deaf children learning sign language must divide their attention between the mother's signs and the objects or activities to which these relate if they are to note the analogous correspondences between signs and familiar routines. Several studies of early interaction between deaf parents and their deaf infants have shown how deaf parents use touch in various ways to reinforce interaction and to help the infants to attend visually (Erting et al., 1990; Maestas y Moores, 1980; Preisler, 1993, 1995). Mothers have been observed to sign on the infant's body or to form the infant's hand into the shape of signs. The mothers' signing seems more simplified and they emphasize the key signs in utterances (Harris, Clibbens, Tibbitts, & Chasin, 1987). Mothers have been observed to pay careful attention to their infants' faces and eye direction, ensuring that their children could see most of their signed utterances. They also signed in such a way that the child could observe the sign while still attending to the context to which the sign related. The mothers most frequently signed within the child's preexisting focus of attention (Harris et al., 1987). This was also shown in a longitudinal study by Preisler (1993), from which the following example is taken of a deaf infant called Anton, at 9 months of age, and his deaf mother:

> The mother holds a doll in front of Anton.
> Anton crawls towards the doll, takes it and starts to explore it, with hands and eyes.
> Anton looks at his mother.
> The mother looks at Anton; signs "DOLL" and points at the doll.
> Anton looks at the doll.
> The mother fetches a small toy animal, that moves backwards and forwards when touched.
> Anton looks at it. He seems interested in the toy.
> The mother touches his cheek gently.
> She gets Anton's visual attention and signs: "EYE" (the sign is expressed by pointing at one's own eye), then points at the animal's eye.
> Anton follows her pointing with his eyes.
> The mother points at Anton's eyes.

Deaf parents who are native signers of American Sign Language (ASL) or Swedish Sign Language (SSL) report that their children start to produce signs as early as 6 months of age (Folven & Bonvillian, 1991; Preisler, 1995). One suggestion is that the 6-month-old's signs are comparable with manual babbling. These manual forms can be conventional if the parents respond to them in a systematic way. One common measure of language development is to note when children produce up to ten words. The signing children in Folven and Bonvillian's study attained a vocabulary of ten different signs at an average age of 13.5 months (range = 11.0–16.5 months), a mean age significantly earlier than the 15.1 months reported by Nelson for hearing children (1973). The content of the initial ten-item vocabularies was highly similar; each child's first sign production occurred within a nonreferential context as an imitation or as a request for action. The children did not use

signs referentially on average until they were 12.6 months of age. This age of onset therefore does not appear to differ from the typical age of 13 months reported for first referential spoken word usage (Bates, O'Connel, & Shore, 1987). Early nonreferential signing
typically antedates initial speech by several months, providing support for the view that
motoric constraints largely determine the onset of speech.

Cochlear Implants in Deaf Children

The most common question that parents of deaf infants ask their doctors at the time of
diagnosis is whether their infant's hearing loss can be medically or surgically treated. Until
recently, the answer was no. There was no method to "cure" deafness. In the 1970s,
however, a new technique was developed, first on adults and later tested on young children, called cochlear implant. It can briefly be described as a hearing aid surgically placed
in the cochlea. In most countries the lower age limit for receiving an implant has been 2
years of age, but even younger children have received implants. The rationale for an early
implant is to give the child auditory experiences as early as possible in order to stimulate
his or her speech perception and later speech production. Comparative studies have been
made between children using an implant and children using different conventional
hearing aids. The criteria for being a potential recipient are in most countries that the
child must be cognitively and emotionally stable and able to endure intensive hearing
training after implantation. Mental retardation or other cognitive or psychiatric disorders
are seen as contraindicative for an implant. The motivation of both parents and children
is seen as important in post-implant habilitation. It is therefore a selected sample of deaf
children who have received an implant. Research results have shown that a cochlear
implant can be more effective than ordinary hearing aids for the development of children's perception and production of speech. The children studied have mainly been
engaged in different oral programs and the aim is to be able to integrate them into
preschools and schools for the hearing. Most of the studies comprise children older than
2 or 3 years of age. The results show that the children can perceive sounds in their surrounding, that they can perceive single spoken words and even sentences, and also
produce a limited set of words and sentences in laboratory conditions or in well-known
contexts with one partner (see, e.g., Osberger, Maso, & Sam, 1993; Walzman et al., 1994).
In a longitudinal study of 22 deaf children, it was found that after three years' experience
of wearing a cochlear implant, most of the children could produce three- to five-word
sentences and could take part in oral dialogues if the content was about the here-and-
now and if the context was well defined, but they had severe difficulties in taking part in
spoken conversations in natural interactional settings with parents, siblings, peers, and
teachers (Preisler, Tvingstedt, & Ahlström, 1997, 1999). Thus they were still considered
to be socially deaf.

Summary

Studies of early patterns of communication in deaf children have shown that these children can communicate and interact with their parents in much the same way as hearing

children if they are given opportunities to use their intact senses for communication and learning. The development of communication and language shows a very similar pattern compared to that for hearing children. Vision can obviously compensate for the hearing loss in early dialogue-like exchanges and in various forms of social play. A logical question is, therefore, how do blind children, who have to rely mainly on the auditory sense, communicate with their parents and how do parents manage to stimulate their blind infant?

Being Born Blind

Blindness – defined as the total absence of sight – is fairly infrequent in Western countries, whereas it is still more common in countries in the Third World due to malnutrition or lack of medical facilities. The incidence among Western countries can be estimated as fewer than 15 per 100,000 children born. There are many different causes of visual defects. In most cases of severe visual impairment something is wrong with the eyes. In the most severe case, anophthalmia, the eyes are actually missing. In retinoblastoma, a malignant tumor develops early in the retina. If treatment, which involves removal of one eye (or, in very rare cases, both eyes) and/or radiation therapy of the tumor, are not begun immediately, the tumor can spread along the optic nerve to the brain and cause visual impairment. Brain damage can cause blindness, although in such cases the eyes are usually normally developed. Prematurely born babies have been and still are at risk of being blind. Children with blindness due to retinopathy of prematurity (ROP) are also at risk of having cerebral damage. A strong association between ROP and autistic disorder has been found. This association is most probably mediated by brain damage and is largely independent of the blindness *per se* (Ek, Fernell, Jacobson, & Gillberg, 1998). A common cause of blindness is congenital cataract, in which the lens of the eye is cloudy. Congenital glaucoma is a further condition that is usually inherited.

Development of Communication in Blind Infants

Diagnosis of blindness is seldom made before the age of 4–5 months, and therefore studies of early patterns of interaction between parents and blind infants are rare. Exceptions are if the child has a defect, such as being born without eyes (anophthalmia) or if there is a congenitally hereditary illness in the family. But there are some studies which can give an idea of this early mother–infant communication. Als, Tronick, and Brazelton (1980) regularly observed a child, born without eyes, from soon after birth up to the age of 15.5 months in interaction with her mother and father in the home setting. They carefully describe how the mother interacted with her baby and how she addressed her in an intimate manner, in a way that also occurs in the interaction of sighted infants and their parents. Through continuous tactile and vocal input, the mother stimulated the infant to take part in communication. At 3 weeks of age the infant was able to modulate her state when in face-to-face situations with her parents. She could become very attentive:

"her face softening and brightening with raised cheeks and open mouth, her arms relaxing, either opening to the side of her body or resting on her chest" (p. 27). This infant's development in general was characterized by step-like spurts of new organization and periods of consolidation. There were also at times periods of disorganization and seeming regression before the next level of organization was reached. Als et al. (1980) commented on how specific adults' expectations are about the signals and displays coming from an infant, even if the infant is blind, but also that it takes a great deal of skill and patience on the part of the parent to read and understand the infant's expressions.

In one of the most extensive longitudinal studies of blind children's development, Selma Fraiberg (1977) particularly focused on the infants' different communicative expressions. She studied the development of ten congenitally blind children for a period of three years, starting from the age of 1 month. She observed the children in interaction with their mothers by means of filming as well as by direct observation. Analyses of these filmed interactions showed that blind infants exhibited a restricted repertoire of facial expressions. Only two different types could be registered – a happy and an unhappy face. The social smile was found to occur irregularly in the blind infants as a reaction to their mother's voice. Fraiberg found that the mothers of the blind infants had difficulties in reading their infant's nonvisual expressions. Only two out of ten mothers could interpret their infant's actions and reactions without special support. These mothers were considered "extraordinary" mothers, with great experience of children. The remaining eight mothers had severe difficulties in reading and interpreting their infant's intentions and wants. Other researchers have also found that blind infants exhibit a more limited repertoire of facial expressions, show less responsiveness, and initiate contact with their mothers less frequently compared to sighted infants (Tröster & Brambring, 1992). But lack of behaviors that require visual information processing cannot be interpreted as an indicator of a delay in social-emotional development. The blind infant's level of social-emotional development is in many cases expressed in reactions that differ from those in, for example, sighted infants (Tröster & Brambring, 1992). But blindness can also cause difficulties for infants in reading and understanding their caregivers' emotional expressions as well as knowing whether their actions and reactions have an effect on others (Bigelow, 1995). Again, the skill of the caregiver is of utmost importance for the formation of a relationship between caregiver and child.

Communicative Expressions Used by Parents and by Blind Infants

In order to study which communicative behaviors blind children use in interaction with their parents as well as which means of communication parents use, seven blind infants were observed from 5 months of age up to early school age (Preisler, 1995, 1997). Analyses of the interactions showed that, when first observed between the age of 5–6 months, the blind children reacted to and elicited contact initiatives from their parents. They took active part in protoconversations by means of smiles and cooing, with articulation-like lip movements as though they were imitating their mothers' speech sounds. They used body movements and even eyebrows to signal turns in conversations. Expectancy awareness in rhythmic body-touching songs was also observed in these infants. When the mothers initiated contact with their babies, they primarily used their voices but also tactile communicative means. Observations showed that at this age children preferred being with another person rather than manipulating objects or toys. With few exceptions, mothers were responsive to their infants' facial expressions, body movements, and vocalizations, interpreting them as meaningful parts or as turns in dialogue-like exchanges. They made comments on the infants' emotional states or they referred to their relationship. The way these mothers behaved when the children were 5–6 months old did not differ in any significant way from the way mothers of sighted babies communicate with their children.

From approximately 6–7 months of age, blind children's interest in exploring the environment increased. They manipulated toys with fingers and mouth and they started to explore the characteristics of objects. At this age, mothers and their infants started to share affects, and the mothers, just like mothers of sighted infants, gradually started to use affect-attunement behaviors. This has also been described in a study of two blind infants observed from the age of 7 months of age (Urwin, 1983). Urwin observed how the mothers mock-imitated their babies' fusses, coughs, splutters, and sneezes and in this way "dramatized" their babies' actions.

Blind children do not use gestures like pointing, either with their eyes or their hands, and they do not use hand gestures like showing or giving. In some instances, pointing with the head or upper part of the body can be observed when the infant becomes attentive to sounds. But these means of communication are not always registered or even understood by their parents and are therefore not very effective means of communication, as can be illustrated in the following example of a 12-month-old blind boy, Fred, and his mother. The example is taken from Preisler (1993). In this interaction Fred's mother is trying to engage Fred in a give-and-take-game with a ball. There is a bell inside the ball in order to facilitate the blind baby's ability to pay attention to the toy.

> The mother and Fred are sitting opposite one another and they are rolling the ball between one another a couple of times. Fred is grasping the ball when it comes near him, and upon request, he lets it fall down on the floor, and the mother catches it.
> The mother makes verbal comments on what they are doing.
> After a short while, Fred becomes very still and he looks puzzled.
> He turns his head to the side and vocalizes: "Ehh?"
> "Ah, ah" the mother replies. "Don't you want to play with mummy any more?"
> Fred turns his head towards her and utters very softly: "Mmmm."
> He stretches out his hands for the ball.
> He sits very still. He turns his head to the side.
> "Can mummy have the ball?" the mother asks.

They proceed playing with the ball for a short while. The mother tries to verbally encourage Fred to take part in the give-and-take game, but Fred looks puzzled. Finally – and luckily for the interaction – the sound of a truck in the street outside can be heard. The mother confirms Fred's experience by uttering:

> "It is the truck, the truck with the snow-plough."

Initially the mother misinterpreted Fred's expressions. She thought that he was uninterested in the play, while in fact he was concentrated and listening to an unfamiliar sound in the environment, and even asking what it was by turning his head to the side and vocalizing with a question-like tone of voice: "Ehh?"

The absence of coordination of eye pointing with finger and hand pointing reduces the natural opportunities to refer to external events. It also makes it more difficult for caregivers to read the preference and interest of the child (Landau & Gleitman, 1985; Preisler, 1993, 1995; Rowland, 1983; Urwin, 1983). The blind child cannot see the caregiver's world of referents and cannot easily determine when the caregiver is trying to establish joint reference. This apparent lack of attention toward the outside world by the blind child might in turn discourage caregivers from initiating activities involving external referents. Perhaps for this reason early communication between blind children and their parents seems to consist primarily of physical games and routines in which the referent is the interaction itself (e.g., repetitious games of bouncy-bouncy in which the child learns to anticipate the parent's physical position at different points in time). The merger between conventionality and external reference can be delayed (Bates et al., 1979). In her study of two blind infants, Urwin (1983) found that prior to the emergence of speech both babies' blindness posed constraints on establishing communication about objects and events located outside their own immediate sphere of action. Urwin found that the two mothers' way of communicating with their child differed somewhat, particularly their use of techniques in order to establish a smooth interaction. The mothers responded to their infants' facial expressions and body movements and made comments on their babies' actions, intentions, and experiences. The mothers acted in different ways, but the rules of interpersonal communication between mother and infant were similar up to the age of 1 year. After this age, there was a change. In one case the mother was very eager to use toys in interaction. This child had some residual vision in one eye, which could explain a greater interest in the surrounding world than if the child had been totally blind. The toys were used in give-and-take games as well as in pretend play. The mother made the toys the content of the interaction and in this way mother and child could establish joint attention and joint reference. In the other case, the interaction was mainly without toys, as the mother did not find that the child showed any interest in them. This child's world of experience was very restricted. When he started to talk, his speech was repetitive and imitative. It referred mostly to his own body and to phrases. Many investigators have identified this as characteristic of blind children's speech. Urwin's interpretation was that the form of social interaction will have consequences on the child's language acquisition.

Early Language Development in Blind Children

Observations of blind infants' play show that they seldom engage in pretend play until toward the second half of the second year (Fraiberg, 1977; Preisler, 1995; Urwin, 1983). This is also the time when blind children start to use language in communication.

Some studies of blind children's early language development suggest that the onset of speech is relatively late (Warren, 1984). In an extensive study of 86 neurologically intact blind children's early language development, Norris, Spaulding, and Brodei (1957) showed that more than 25 percent of these children produced two words when they were 15 months old, more than 50 percent achieved this vocabulary in the period from 18 to 21 months, and more than 75 percent by 24 months. This is roughly eight months later than sighted full-term normal infants usually reach the same language level (Lenneberg, 1967). But 85 percent of the subjects in Norris et al.'s (1957) study were premature births (with ROP), which might explain some of the delay. However, in other studies the same difference between blind and sighted children's early speech development has not been found. Bigelow (1990) asked mothers to record their blind children's words from before they had recognizable words to the acquisition of a 50-word vocabulary, which is approximately the time children start combining words into two-word sentences. Bigelow found no differences between blind and sighted children' early language development. The blind children acquired their 50-word vocabularies between the age of 16 to 21 months. Sighted children generally acquire their 50-word vocabularies between the age of 15 to 20 months, which suggests a delay of 1 month (Nelson, 1973).

McConnachie and Moore (1994) found a delay of several months in the acquisition of the first ten words used by a sample of 16 severely visually impaired children. Mulford (1988) collected data from 16 individual case studies and found no major delay in these children's language development. However, Moore and McConnachie (1994) suggest that the children in the case studies were an unusually successful group, which could explain this difference. Even if there is no consensus about whether there is a delay in blind children's early language development, there is a common view among researchers that there is a relationship between mothers' speech to their infants and the nonverbal context in which it occurs. This relationship is difficult to establish if the child is blind, as the relationship is most naturally established by mothers making comments on activities and objects on which their children are focusing their visual attention. It has been suggested that the rate of children's early language development can be influenced by the extent to which adult speech provides opportunities to relate linguistic input to a familiar nonverbal context. This provides the infant with an opportunity to note correspondences between familiar routines and accompanying linguistic descriptions. For sighted mothers of blind children, it is a difficult task to attain this correspondence between linguistic input and nonverbal context as they can have difficulties in reading what their children are paying attention to.

Caregivers' Communicative Style

There are some studies focusing on the communicative styles or language input of blind children's parents in relation to their language development. Blind children have to rely even more on the linguistic input of their parents than sighted children to get information and to gain understanding of the surrounding world. Kekelis and Andersen (1984) compared the language directed to visually impaired children as well as to sighted children. Their results indicated that the parents of visually impaired children used more imperatives and fewer declaratives than the parents of sighted children. They thereby provided their children with less information about the functions and the attributes of objects. There was also a tendency for these parents to ask their blind child to repeat labels or to request labeling of objects from the child.

Thorén (1994) analyzed the verbal input of the parents of seven blind children participating in the longitudinal study mentioned earlier (Preisler, 1993, 1995), categorizing a vast number of mothers' verbal utterances when their children were between 18 and 36 months old. One finding was that the parents of those children who later were found to have developed normally in a socioemotional-communicative sense used more confirmations than directives in their verbal communication to the child during the observation period. These parents' communicative patterns also showed a high degree of regularity and stability, independent of time or situation. In those cases where the child's socioemotional and communicative development later was found to be less optimal, the parent's early communication showed an opposite pattern. Their utterances consisted of more directives than affirmatives, or were in some cases equally distributed between the two. These parents' communication also showed a more varied and unstable pattern, with frequent changes depending on the context. Thus, it was probably more difficult for these children to anticipate their parents' reactions and responses, resulting in confusion and uncertainty in the children.

The First Words

Blind children's first words usually refer to food and to items they act upon, such as puppy, doll, key, and so on. This is also what many sighted children refer to in their first words. But blind children often choose to label objects that can be characterized as having the properties of perceptual change. They name items that produce auditory change or give tactual sensation. Compared to sighted children, blind children have more labels that refer to specific referents rather than classes of objects. Because of their more restricted sensory experience compared to sighted children, their word usage is more tied to the original referents of their words (Bigelow, 1990). Self-action and perceptual change are salient variables for young blind children, as they are for young sighted children. The major difference is that perceptual change for blind children comes from other modalities than vision (see also Dunlea, 1989; Mulford, 1988).

Summary

Studies of early patterns of communication between blind infants and their parents show that the absence of visual information about the world, and therefore the dependency on auditory and haptic stimulation, diminishes the blind infant's opportunities to learn and to understand interpersonal rules in communication, the relation between objects and symbols, as well as knowledge about the environment. The auditory sense does not seem to compensate for the lack of vision in the same way as vision can compensate for the lack of auditory input in early child development.

Being Born Deaf-Blind

How can children who lack both vision and hearing communicate with their parents about their feelings and experiences as well as about the physical world around them? Deafness *per se* does not have to be a serious obstacle to early caregiver–infant communication if children are allowed to use their intact senses, while blindness poses more constraints on the interaction. Helen Keller, who was both deaf and blind, describes in her book, *The Story of My Life*, her awakening awareness of the world when her young teacher started to spell words in her hand. Gradually she understood that everything had a name. This happened over a century ago. How is the situation for deaf-blind children different today?

There are few cases reported where the child is both totally blind and deaf (Andrew, 1989), the group as a whole being most heterogeneous. Within the population of young children diagnosed as deaf-blind, there are children with a varying degree of hearing and visual impairment, with or without additional disabilities, but also children with cortical visual and or central auditory disabilities (Michael & Paul, 1991). Approximately 94 percent of these children have some residual vision and hearing (Fredericks & Baldwin, 1987).

Infants who are deaf-blind are generally reported to be less responsive and less active than non-disabled infants of comparable age. The parents must work to elicit responses from them, even though studies have shown that a caregiver can develop social interaction through movements and by haptic means. But as the infant cannot hear the voice of the mother or see her face, not only the physical but also the social world is severely restricted for the child. Further complications for parents are the difficulty of reading and interpreting the infant's signals. This in turn can result in a feeling of failure or helplessness. In addition, these children often have severe medical problems, which makes the situation even more difficult to cope with for their parents. One of the main problems for parents in the early interaction is responding to the infant's actions and reactions. This is a serious matter, because it is through the responsiveness of the caregiver that the infant can gradually begin to anticipate that his or her actions will cause a change. Experiences of contingency in social interaction are difficult to achieve in interplay with deaf-blind children as they cannot hear the voice or see the facial expressions of their parents.

Development of Communication in Deaf-Blind Children

Six children and their parents participated in a longitudinal study of the development of communication between deaf-blind children and their parents (Preisler, 1996). The children were between 6 months and 3.9 years old when first video-observed in natural interactional settings with their parents. Common to the children was the fact that they were blind or severely visually impaired as well as severely hearing impaired. Four had additional functional disabilities, such as mental retardation and/or cerebral palsy. Detailed transcriptions of the video-recorded interactions showed that the children could communicate with their parents and the parents with their child. Even if the expressions varied and sometimes were difficult to interpret, the analyses showed that the development of communication followed the same path as that for "normal" children; from interest in social interaction and social plays with the caregiver, to interest in the physical environment and an intent to share their experiences with somebody else. Some of the children already used symbols in communication at the commencement of the study, while others did so toward the end of the observed period. The social plays most frequently observed were different turn-taking and body-movement games. Movements, sounds, and touch were important communicative expressions in these playful activities. Thereafter the children started to show an interest in and attention to the environment. They started to touch, taste, smell, or in other ways investigate and test characteristics and functions of objects and toys. After an intensive period of exploration, their interest in social interaction returned, but now on a somewhat more advanced level as they wanted to share their interest in something with somebody else. The children's expressions varied as well as the content of the communication, but the aim was the same: to establish and maintain a meaningful and joyful interaction. But every single achievement took a long time to acquire for these children. It was also difficult for the parents to observe and discover that their child had made progress, and also to understand how these achievements could fit into a normal chain of child development. The parents of the deaf-blind children faced further difficulties in translating a spoken language into a tactile sign language. But even if the number of signs or the variation of the signs used were limited, it could be registered how important the hands were as a channel of communication – the children's own hands, as well as the caregivers'. Initially parents grasped the children's hands and formed them into a sign. But in these instances there was a risk of hindering children's free use of their hands. When the parents instead started to offer their own hands to their children, the dialogue became more extended. When their communicative style became more child-centered and affirmative and less directive, communication became more functional and smooth.

A Model for Support of Infant–Caregiver Interaction

Chen and Haney (1995) have developed a model for promoting learning through active interaction (PLAI) in order to support deaf-blind infant–caregiver interaction. They maintain that much of the stimulation given to deaf-blind children is of a far too passive character, with the focus often on stimulating the infant's residual vision and/or hearing. Chen and Haney question the meaningfulness of this approach from the infant's perspective. Their model instead is aimed at creating an environment for learning and for mutually satisfying exchanges through intervention strategies focusing on developing contingent responsiveness in caregivers. By first observing parent–infant interaction by means of video-recording and then identifying what is typical for each pair, parents are given feedback on their own as well as on their babies' communicative behaviors. The most important part of the model is to concentrate on the caregivers' ability to give immediate responses to their infants' expressions. In the feedback sessions with parents, those instances where there is a reciprocal and joyful interaction between infant and caregiver are focused on in order to promote and strengthen parents' capacity for responding and interpreting their child's expressions.

Conclusion

Communication between blind, deaf, and deaf-blind children and their parents shows a similar pattern of early interaction as that of non-disabled children. Even if development proceeds very slowly for children with severe and multiple sensory disabilities, it follows the same path as those for a normal child: from person–person communication to person–object to person–person–object communication. The results of detailed analyses further show that the potential for a child with sensory disabilities to engage in meaningful interaction is to a great extent dependent on the ability of the caregiver to adapt to the infant's capabilities and to give space for the child to take an active part in the interaction – to follow rather than direct the child. Joyful interaction seems to be of special importance for the child's psychological well-being, not to mention that of the parents.

Research on normal mother–infant interaction has led to a gradual change in our perspective on the child's development. A sensitive caregiver who responds to the infant's initiatives and who develops them further can have a positive effect on development. In those families where a baby is born with sensory functional disabilities, the situation is somewhat or even radically different. Most of these parents have never met an adult who is deaf or blind, let alone a child, and almost certainly not one who is both deaf and blind. Traditionally, support services for families with children with sensory disabilities have focused on the children's performance and skills, or rather, their lack of performance and skills. This is also the type of support that is requested by many parents, as they notice that their child's development is delayed compared to non-disabled children of comparable age. The problem with such an approach is that there is a risk that the focus will be on the disability, not on the child. Another approach is to strengthen the relationship between parents and child. Video-recordings of the caregiver and the infant interacting have become a frequently used means for giving feedback to parents as well as making them – and often also researchers – aware of what the child in fact can do, achieve, and communicate. Such data indicate also that most parents are sensitive and responsive to their deaf, blind, or deaf-blind child's communicative expressions. This in turn can have positive effects on the parent's feeling of being a good-enough parent. And this is perhaps the best starting point for positive development in the child.

Research on different aspects of psychosocial development in children with sensory disabilities has primarily focused on the first two to three years of life. This is probably due to the fact that these years are considered the most important for later development. But as children grow up, other children become important actors in the psychosocial arena. In order to learn social rules and practices children need to interact with peers. But many children with sensory impairments like deafness and blindness have difficulty finding peers to interact with. Deaf children exposed to sign language attending a sign language school program have no problems communicating with other deaf signing children. But many deaf children are mainstreamed in the ordinary school system with hearing children. What are the consequences on their socioemotional development if they cannot communicate in a smooth and fluent way with peers? Growing up as a blind child means having very different experiences of the world compared to a sighted child. Blind children experience the physical and social world primarily by auditory and haptic means, which is reflected in their play and verbalizations. How is it possible to share in a meaningful way this auditory and haptic world with a sighted child? These are some of the issues that need to be explored further in order to promote positive socioemotional development in such children.

References

Ainsworth, M. D. S., Blehar, M. C., Waters, E., & Wall, S. (1978). *Patterns of attachment: A psychological study of the Strange Situation*. Hillsdale, NJ: Erlbaum.

Als, H., Tronick, E., & Brazelton, B. (1980). Affective reciprocity and the development of autonomy. *American Academy of Child Psychiatry, 19*, 22–40.

Andrew, A. K. (1989). Meeting the needs of young deaf-blind children and their parents: Part II. *Child: Care, Health and Development, 15*(4), 251–267.

Bates, E., Benigni, L., Bretherton, I., Camaioni, L., & Volterra, V. (1979). Cognition and communication. From nine to thirteen months. In E. Bates (Ed.), *The emergence of symbols: Cognition and communication in infancy* (pp. 69–140). New York: Academic Press.

Bates, E., O'Connel, B., & Shore, C. (1987). Language and communication in infancy. In J. D. Osofsky (Ed.), *Handbook of infant development* (pp. 149–203). New York: Wiley.

Bigelow, A. (1990). Relationship between the development of language and thought in young blind children. *Journal of Visual Impairment and Blindness, 84*(8), 414–419.

Bigelow, A. E. (1995). The effect of blindness on the early development of the self. In P. Rochat (Ed.), *The self in infancy: Theory and research* (pp. 327–347). Elsevier.

Bornstein, M. (1989). Between caretakers and their young: Two modes of interaction and their consequences for cognitive growth. In M. Bornstein & J. Bruner (Eds.), *Interaction in human development* (pp. 197–214). Hillsdale, NJ: Erlbaum.

Chen, D., & Haney, M. (1995). An early intervention model for infants who are deaf-blind. *Journal of Visual Impairment and Blindness, 89*(3), 213–221.

Copper, P. J., & Stein, A. (1989). Life events and postnatal depression: The Oxford Study. In J. Cox & E. S. Paykel (Eds.), *Life events and postpartum psychiatric disorder*. Southampton: Southampton University Press.

Dunlea, A. (1989). *Vision and the emergence of meaning: Blind and sighted children's early language*. Cambridge: Cambridge University Press.

Ek, U., Fernell, E., Jacobson, L., & Gillberg, C. (1998). Relation between blindness due to retinopathy of prematurity and autistic spectrum disorders: A population-based study. *Developmental Medicine and Child Neurology, 40*, 297–301.

Erting, C., Prezioso, C., & O'Grady Hynes, M. (1990). The interactional context of deaf mother–infant communication. In V. Volterra & C. Erting (Eds.), *From gesture to language in hearing and deaf children* (pp. 97–106). New York: Springer Verlag.

Folven, R. J., & Bonvillian, J. D. (1991). The transition from nonreferential to referential language in children acquiring American sign language. *Developmental Psychology, 27*(5), 806–816.

Fraiberg, S. (1977). *Insights from the blind*. New York: Basic Books.

Fredericks, H., & Baldwin, V. (1987). Individuals with sensory impairments: Who are they? In L. Goetz, D. Guess, & K. Stremel-Campbell (Eds.), *Innovative program design for individuals with dual sensory impairments* (pp. 3–15). Baltimore: Paul H. Brookes.

Greenberg, M. (1980). Social interaction between deaf preschoolers and their mothers. The effect of communication method and communicative competence. *Developmental Psychology, 16,* 465–474.

Greenspan, S. I. (1997). *The growth of the mind and the endangered origins of intelligence.* Reading, MA: Addison-Wesley.

Harris, M., Clibbens, J., Tibbitts, R., & Chasin, J. (1987). *Communication between deaf mothers and their deaf infants.* Paper presented at the 1987 Child Language Seminar, University of York, UK.

Jamieson, J. R., & Pedersen, E. D. (1993). Deafness and mother–child interaction. Scaffolded instruction and the learning of problem-solving skills. *Early Child Development and Parenting, 2,* 229–242.

Kaye, K., & Charney, R. (1981). How mothers maintain "dialogue" with two-year-olds. In D. Olson (Ed.), *The social foundation of language and thought.* New York: Norton.

Kekelis, L., & Andersen, E. (1984). Family communication styles and language development. *Journal of Visual Impairment and Blindness, 78,* 54–64.

Koester, L. S. (1994). Early interactions and the socioemotional development of deaf infants. *Early Development and Parenting, 3*(1), 51–60.

Koester, L. S. (1995). Face-to-face interactions between hearing mothers and their deaf or hearing infants. *Infant Behavior and Development, 18,* 145–153.

Landau, B., & Gleitman, L. (1985). *Language and experience.* Cambridge, MA: Harvard University Press.

Lenneberg, E. H. (1967). *Biological foundations of language.* New York: Wiley.

Locke, J. (1995). Development of the capacity for spoken language. In P. Fletcher & B. MacWhinney (Eds.), *The handbook of child language* (pp. 278–302). Oxford: Blackwell.

MacTurk, R., Meadow-Orlans, K. P., Koester, L. S., & Spencer, P. E. (1993). Social support, motivation, language and interaction. *American Annals of the Deaf, 138*(1), 19–25.

Maestas y Moores, J. (1980). Early linguistic environment: Interactions of deaf parents with their infants. *Sign Language Studies, 26,* 1–13.

McConnachie, H. R., & Moore, V. (1994). Early expressive language of severely visually impaired children. *Developmental Medicine and Child Neurology, 36,* 230–240.

Meadow-Orlans, K. (1987). *Deaf and hearing mothers of deaf and hearing infants: Interaction during the first year.* Paper presented at the World Conference for the Deaf, Helsinki, Finland.

Meadow-Orlans, K. P., & Sass-Lehrer, M. (1995). Support services for families with children who are deaf: Challenges for professionals. *Topics in Early Childhood Special Education, 15*(3), 314–334.

Meadow-Orlans, K. P., & Spencer, P. (1996). Maternal sensitivity and the visual attentiveness of children who are deaf. *Maternal Development and Parenting, 5*(4), 213–223.

Meltzoff, A. N. (1986). Imitation, intermodal representation and the origins of the mind. In I. B. Lindblom & R. Zetterström (Eds.), Precursors of early speech (pp. 245–265). *Wennergren International Symposium Series, 44.*

Michael, M. G., & Paul, P. V. (1991). Early intervention for infants with deaf-blindness. *Exceptional Children, 57*(3), 200–210.

Moore, V., & McConnachie, H. R. (1994). Communication between blind and severely visually impaired children and their parents. *British Journal of Developmental Psychology, 12,* 491–502.

Mulford, R. (1988). First words of the blind child. In M. Smith & J. Locke (Eds.), *The emergent lexicon* (pp. 293–338). London: Academic Press.

Murray, L., Kempton, C., Woolgar, M., & Hooper, R. (1993). Depressed mothers' speech to their infants and its relation to infant gender and cognitive development. *Journal of Child Psychology and Psychiatry, 34,* 1083–1101.

Nelson, K. (1973). Structure and strategy in learning to talk. *Monographs of the Society for Research in Child Development, 38.*

Norris, M., Spaulding, P. J., & Brodei, F. H. (1957). *Blindness in children.* Chicago: University of Chicago Press.

Osberger, M. J., Maso, M., & Sam, L. K. (1993). Speech intelligibility of children with cochlear implants, tactile aids or hearing aids. *Journal of Speech and Hearing Research, 36,* 186–203.

Pettito, L. A., & Marentette, P. F. (1991). Babbling in the manual mode: Evidence for the ontogeny of language. *Science, 251,* 1493–1496.

Preisler, G. (1993). Developing communication with blind and with deaf infants. Stockholm University, Department of Psychology. *Reports* (No. 761).

Preisler, G. (1995). The development of communication in blind and in deaf infants: Similarities and differences. *Child: Care, Health and Development, 21*(2), 79–110.

Preisler, G. (1996). Patterns of interaction between deaf-blind children and their parents. In A. M. Vonen, K. Arnesen, R. T. Enerstvedt, & A. V. Nafstad (Eds.), Bilingualism and literacy concerning deafness and deaf-blindness (pp. 223–227). *Skådalen Publication Series, 1.*

Preisler, G. (1997). Social and emotional development. Blindness and psychosocial development 0–10 years. In V. Lewis, & G. Collis (Eds.), *Blindness and psychological development in young children* (pp. 69–85). Leicester: British Psychological Society (BPS) Books.

Preisler, G., Tvingstedt., A.-L., & Ahlström, M. (1997). The development of communication and language in deaf preschool children with cochlear implants. *International Journal of Pediatric Otorhinolaryngology, 41,* 263–272.

Preisler, G., Tvingstedt., A.-L., & Ahlström, M. (1999). Cochlea implantat på döva barn: En psykosocial uppföljningsstudie (Cochlear implants in deaf children: A psychosocial follow-up study). *Socialmedicinsk Tidskrift, 1*(1), 53–61.

Robinshaw, H. M., & Evans, R. (1995). Caregivers' sensitivity to the communicative and linguistic needs of their deaf infants. *Early Child Development and Care, 109,* 23–41.

Rowland, C. (1983). Patterns of interaction between three blind infants and their mothers. In A. Wills (Ed.), *Language acquisition in the blind child* (pp. 114–132). Beckenham: Croom Helm.

Schein, J. (1996). The demography of deafness. In P. C. Higgins & J. E. Nash. *Understanding deafness socially* (2nd ed., pp. 21–43). Springfield, IL: Thomas.

Schlesinger, H. S., & Meadow, K. (1972). *Sound and sign: Childhood deafness and mental health.* Berkeley, CA: University of California Press.

Spencer, P. E., & Lederberg, A. R. (1997). Different modes, different models. Communication and language of young deaf children and their mothers. In L. B. Adamson & M. A. Romski (Eds.), *Communication and language acquisition: Discoveries from atypical development* (pp. 203–230). Baltimore: Paul H. Brookes.

Stern, D. (1985). *The interpersonal world of the infant.* New York: Basic Books.

Stern, D. (1995). *The motherhood constellation.* New York: Basic Books.

Stokoe, W. (1972). *Semiotics and human sign languages.* The Hague: Mouton.

Studdert-Kennedy, M. (1991). Language development from an evolutionary perspective. In N. Krasnegor, D. Rumbaugh, R. Schiefelbusch, & M. Studdert-Kennedy (Eds.), *Language acquisition: Biological and behavioral determinants* (pp. 5–28). Hillsdale, NJ: Lawrence Erlbaum Associates.

Thorén, A. (1994). *Språk och samspel mellan blinda barn och deras föräldrar* (Language and interaction between blind children and their parents). Unpublished thesis, Stockholm University, Department of Psychology.

Trevarthen, C. (1988). Infants trying to talk. In I. R. Söderbergh (Ed.), *Children's creative communication* (pp. 9–31). Lund: Lund University Press.

Tröster, H., & Brambring, M. (1992). Early social-emotional development in blind infants. *Child: Care, Health and Development, 18*, 207–227.

Urwin, C. (1983). Dialogue and cognitive functioning in the early language development in blind children. In A. Wills (Ed.), *Language acquisition in the blind child* (pp. 142–161). Beckenham: Croom Helm.

Warren, D. (1984). *Blindness and early childhood development.* New York: American Foundation for the Blind.

Walzman, S., Cohen, N., Gomolin, R. H., Shapiro, W. H., Shelly, R. O., & Hoffman, R. A. (1994). Long-term results of early cochlear implantation in congenitally and prelingually deafened children. *Journal of Otology, 15*(Suppl. 2), 9–13.

Part IV

Contexts and Policy Issues

Introduction

Part IV reviews risk factors not discussed in the previous section – such as prematurity, safety, and nutrition – and, in addition, sets these and other concerns into a wider context of public policy. The chapter by Barratt covers a wide range of risk and policy issues. These include poverty, day care, infant mortality, abuse, and neglect. A variety of intervention programs – such as Head Start, welfare, health care, and nutritional supplementation – are reviewed to assist families in finding medical care, nutritional support, income support, developmental assessment, child care, and family resources such as parental leave and home-visiting programs. Barratt argues that to address the major problems of infants at risk, a response from society as a whole is needed. In particular, Barratt argues that universities need to be more directly engaged in both research and public policy to help infants at risk.

Friedman, Randolph, and Kochanoff review the history of research on the effects of nonparental child care on infant development. Much of this research suffers from a variety of theoretical and methodological problems that make the findings inconclusive. A major portion of this chapter is devoted to reviewing the findings of a study of the effects of day care that used a broad-based national sample across a variety of childcare contexts, such as family day care and center day care. The results strongly suggest that when the quality of care is good and there is a supportive family environment, day care has no harmful effects and may even contribute to social and cognitive development of infants.

Karns presents an extensive review of the health, nutrition, and safety factors affecting infants. Each of these areas has direct implications for parents and for public policy. She addresses issues related to diseases in infancy, environmental risks to infant health, hospitalization of infants, and immunization policies. The section on nutrition has a detailed discussion on the differences between breast- and bottle feeding and the advantages of human milk to infant growth. Minimum daily nutritional requirements are given and there is a section on consumer protection and car safety. Much progress has been made in providing for the health and safety of infants, but more needs to be done, especially for low-income families.

The final chapter by Fogel takes a historical perspective on beliefs and policies about infants and their care. The chapter traces the roots of infant care in prehistoric hunter–gatherer societies, where close physical contact between mothers and infants developed in concert with nearly continuous breastfeeding of infants. In these societies, as judged by studies of modern-day hunter–gatherers, infants are loved and indulged. Beginning with the recorded history in Western cultures (Greece, Rome, and Judeo-Christian cultures), there is increased documentation of the use of a balance of love and control, indulgence and training for infants. In some societies and at some historical periods, more of an emphasis is placed on training and control, while in other cases more is placed on indulgence. This dialectical process has continued up through the twentieth and twenty-first centuries, which have brought an unprecedented interest in and documentation of infant development. The chapter concludes with some speculations about the future of infancy and infant care, a period in which we may see the complete elimination of birth defects and risk factors and the knowledge that may make it possible to optimize development for every infant.

Chapter Twenty-three

Infancy Research, Policy, and Practice

Marguerite Barratt

Introduction

If we are to create an "engaged university" (Kellogg Commission on the Future of State and Land-Grant Universities, 1999), it is imperative that we take the vast knowledge about infants that resides on campuses, and is summarized so well in this volume, and see its application to the everyday lives of infants. The "scholarship of engagement" (Boyer, 1996) has the potential to forge a direct path between what we know broadly about infants and its application for each infant in the context of his or her own family, community, state, and nation. At the moment, that path is very meandering.

Infancy researchers, such as the ones writing in this volume, clearly care very deeply about the well-being of infants and each one can delineate the implications of his or her work for infants and their families. But the link between knowledge and action based on that knowledge could be much stronger. Policies are in place to implement some of what we know is important for infants, a number of which will be reviewed in this chapter. Further, some communities have created their own programs to address the needs of infants, and some of these efforts will also be reviewed. But it will become clear that we know so much more than is being implemented in the everyday lives of infants. To address this, a number of mechanisms for pulling together research, policy, and practice will be presented.

Theoretical Framework

Bronfenbrenner's (1979) conceptualization of the multiple influences on children provides a useful framework for this examination of the application of infancy research to the lives of infants. At the level of the microsystem, infants are influenced by mothers, fathers, childcare providers, and others who come into direct contact with them. At the level of the exosystem, infants and their caregivers are influenced by the organizations and systems in which they participate. Examples include (1) childcare programs that organize the care infants receive; (2) employers who set constraints on parents of infants; (3) community programs that support families; and (4) local, state, and national policies that affect infants. As public policies and community programs are reviewed, these influences will be touched on.

Researchers are often unfamiliar with the lived experiences of infants in families who are different from their own. From the ivory tower of the university it is easy to forget that the poorest families in the United States are young families with infants, and that one-third of infants are born to single mothers (Federal Interagency Forum on Child and Family Statistics, 1998). From the ivory tower of the university it is also easy to lose contact with the policy context of early development. However, the ecological perspective being adopted in this chapter makes it essential to consider infant development in the context of families, communities, states, and nations.

Policy and Practice

The United States will be used as a case example in considering the policy context of infancy. The United States is geographically large and encompasses cultural, ethnic, and racial diversity. In the United States there is an income spread that is larger than many other countries such that we have significant numbers of infants in extremely poor families and significant numbers of infants in very rich families. In the United States, almost 4 million infants are born each year, 15 percent African American, 18 percent Hispanic, and 25 percent are born into poverty (National Center for Health Statistics, 2000).

As policies affecting the lives of infants in the United States are described, it is worth keeping in mind that the United States is precisely that, a collection of states. Increasingly, federal legislation provides Block Grant funding to states and provides some broad guidelines within which that money can be spent. States then are free to make individual choices about exactly how to implement federal policies, and states can even request waivers of the federal statutory limitations.

As a further development, states are undergoing a devolutionary process of delegating decision making to local levels. For example, in Michigan, each of the 83 counties has established a Multi-Purpose Collaborative Body to bring together the human service funding organizations for regular meetings and decision making. These collaboratives usually include social services, health, education, and public health, and they are asked to work together to make community-level decisions about implementation of policy.

This means that, in the United States, policies affecting infants are often made at the federal level, adjusted at the state level, and implemented at the community level. Accordingly, it is complex to describe infancy policy. It will be apparent in the descriptions below that the federal legislation allows, for example, states to cover costs of some services to poor families whose incomes exceed the minimums. The following review includes policies in the United States affecting medical care, nutrition, income support, developmental assessment and support, child care, safety, and supports for parents. Included is some of the research base for the policies and descriptions of the policies themselves.

Medical Care

Prenatal care

It is clear that prenatal care contributes significantly to the well-being of infants. Research shows that infants are less likely to be born preterm when mothers receive prenatal care, and comprehensive prenatal care for low-income women has been shown to reduce infant complications (Lowry & Beikirch, 1998). Prenatal care beginning in the first trimester is one of the Healthy People 2000 and Healthy People 2010 goals in the United States (US Department of Health and Human Services [DHHS], 1991, 2000). The 1987 baseline data indicated that 76 percent of mothers giving birth had prenatal care during the first trimester; for 1997 it was 83 percent; the goal for 2010 is 90 percent. As part of the federal Medicaid program for low-income families, states provide programs that cover the costs of prenatal care for low-income pregnant women whose incomes are at or below 133 percent of the federal poverty level. Individual states may choose to cover women at a higher percentage of the poverty level (up to 185 percent). In the United States 38 percent of the births are covered by Medicaid (Annie E. Casey Foundation, 1999). In many states, there is a presumptive eligibility for this coverage such that pregnant women are provided with temporary coverage immediately on the basis of an application completed at many clinics (including public health departments and family planning clinics). That process facilitates early and immediate access to prenatal care. To assure continuity of care, once eligibility is established, Medicaid coverage continues until 60 days after the end of the pregnancy.

Health care for infants

Although it is clear that health care for infants contributes to well-being, infants in the United States are not all receiving routine well-child care and are not all receiving timely treatment of acute and chronic medical problems. For example, in 1997 only 78 percent of 2-year-olds were fully immunized (Annie E. Casey Foundation, 1999). Healthy People 2010 includes as a goal having 80 percent of 6-year-olds fully immunized (DHHS, 2000). In the United States, Medicaid is administered by each state to provide coverage of medical expenses for children in poor families where the family income is at or below 133 percent of the federal poverty level. In addition, under the federal legislation "Children's Health Insurance Program" (CHIP), many states have created low-cost state insurance programs for families who are not quite poor enough to qualify for Medicaid. About 25 percent of children are covered by Medicaid or other public health insurance (Annie E. Casey Foundation, 1999). The medical expenses of middle-income and well-off families are usually covered by private insurance provided or subsidized by employers. In between the group of poor children whose insurance is covered by public funds and the better-off children whose insurance is covered by employers, 14 percent of young children are not covered by medical insurance (Annie E. Casey Foundation, 1999). Healthy People 2010 targets 100 percent health-care coverage for children (DHHS, 2000). Beyond the financial barriers, other significant barriers to medical care include scheduling difficulties, transportation difficulties, attitudinal barriers, dissatisfaction with services, and lack of information about financial supports (Omar, Schiffman, & Bauer, 1998; Riportella-Muller et al., 1996).

Health care for parents

A significant body of research (e.g., Field, 1995) indicates that maternal depression – particularly chronic depression – and other forms of mental illness interfere with the development of relationships between mothers and infants. Healthy People 2010 (DHHS, 2000) includes a goal of having at least half of those suffering from depression receiving treatment; currently less than one-quarter receive treatment. Specifically reducing postpartum depression is also a current national goal. Some of the deficits in the children of substance-abusing mothers are attributable to the chaotic environments these mothers provide for their infants (e.g., Mayes, 1995), and health care could include substance abuse treatment. These lines of evidence suggest the importance of healthy parents for infants' well-being, yet the United States has not invested broadly in the health of parents. Medicaid insures poor children, but usually not their parents.

Nutrition

Prenatal nutrition

In the United States, the federal Special Supplemental Nutrition Program for Women, Infants and Children (WIC) provides food vouchers to pregnant women who are poor and at nutritional risk. WIC eligibility includes family incomes at or below 185 percent of the federal poverty level. Nutritional risk includes such risk as anemia, underweight, and poor eating patterns. Through WIC, women also receive education about healthy eating during pregnancy and screening for anemia. The WIC program serves approximately 45 percent of pregnant women and newborn infants in the United States, and nearly all eligible pregnant women participate. Women enrolled in the WIC program have been shown to be less likely to deliver infants who are small for gestational age (Ahluwalia, Hogan, Grummer-Strawn, Colville, & Peterson, 1998) and less likely to die in the first year (Moss & Carver, 1998).

Breastfeeding

Breastfed infants have fewer ear infections, allergies, and respiratory infections, are less likely to die of SIDS (Sudden Infant Death Syndrome), and even may grow into children with higher IQ scores (Stuart-Macadam & Dettwyler, 1995). Mothers who breastfeed their infants return more quickly to their prepregnancy weight and are less likely to develop breast cancer premenopausally. Healthy People 2000 and Healthy People 2010 both aim for 75 percent breastfeeding in the newborn period and 50 percent breast-feeding at 6 months (DHHS, 1991, 2000). In addition, Healthy People 2010 has a goal of 25 percent breastfeeding at 1 year; even though that is the recommendation of the American Academy of Pediatrics (1997), the current level is only 16 percent. Income-eligible women (at or below 185 percent poverty) who are breastfeeding their infants receive vouchers for healthy foods from WIC to provide the extra nourishment that their bodies need during lactation. Increased breastfeeding in low-income women served by WIC can result in significant cost savings (Heinig, 1998). Some communities, clinics, and hospitals employ lactation consultants to provide access to information and individual consultation to breastfeeding women. Some communities have developed peer support programs through which women volunteers support new mothers who are breast-feeding, although the research evidence on the effectiveness of these peer support programs is equivocal (e.g., Arlotti, Cottrell, Lee, & Curtin, 1998; Caulfield et al., 1998; Morrow et. al., 1999).

Nutrition for infants

Years of evidence suggest the importance of nutrition during the first years (see chapter 25 in this volume), yet in the case of poverty in the United States, there may not be enough food for children. WIC provides vouchers for healthy food for income-eligible children up to 5 years old, as well as education for their parents. The Child and Adult Care Food Program is a federal program that is a downward extension of the school lunch program; this subsidizes the cost of snacks and meals served to children in childcare programs. Children whose families have incomes at or below 130 percent of the federal poverty level receive these foods free; between 130 percent and 185 percent of the poverty level, the price is reduced. The Child and Adult Care Food Program also provides oversight for menus and education for childcare providers. Another federal program that helps with nutrition for families with infants is the Food Stamp Program, which provides income-eligible parents with vouchers that stretch their food dollars. Parent education about nutrition, food safety, purchase of food and food preparation is the focus of the Expanded Food and Nutrition Education Program (EFNEP) offered nationwide by the Extension branch of each state's Land-Grant University. As a longstanding outreach effort of the Land-Grant University in each state, Extension provided this education to small groups and in homes.

Food pantries and food banks

State and community initiatives to address infant nutrition issues include the development of local food pantries that provide food for families in need. Food distributed by food pantries is made available through volunteer donations (local food drives) as well as food banks that accept large donations of food and organize their distribution through local food pantries. Food pantries are also a source of formula and diapers for infants, and so particularly serve families with young children. Local food pantries each create their own guidelines, and many have barriers that limit the food that infants and their families actually make use of (Tableman, 1999). For example, families may be limited to receiving food once a month or to accepting only bags with specific items.

Income Support

Welfare

In the United States, the federal income support program, Aid to Families with Dependent Children (AFDC), was replaced in 1996 by Temporary Assistance to Needy Families (TANF) in an effort to move families off the welfare rolls and into the world of work (Zaslow, Tout, Smith, & Moore, 1998). This program provides some financial support for the 25 percent of children under 3 years old who live in poverty (National Center for Children in Poverty, 1997), although with TANF families now have lifetime limits on receiving support such that only 60 months of support may be received and work requirements are part of the program. Families who exceed the number of months and families who do not meet work requirements are "sanctioned" and often may not receive federal support, although states are given some flexibility in this. Effects of these significant changes in federal and state income support on infants and young children are uncertain, although research is under way (Zaslow et al., 1998). The decline in participation in income support programs has been accompanied by declines in participation in other programs, including Food Stamps, Medicaid and state health insurance programs, even though families may remain eligible (Ellwood, 1999).

Child support

In the United States today, almost one-third of infants are born to single mothers (Federal Interagency Forum on Child and Family Statistics, 1998), and non-custodial parents, usually father, are often obligated to provide financial support for their minor children. The collection of child support has been facilitated by procedures that make it easier to establish paternity. Hospitals are now required to make available official forms that fathers can complete to establish their paternity, and mothers are given the opportunity to provide information to help track down putative fathers and determine paternity. When paternity is established, courts order non-custodial parents to provide child support, and procedures have been established to make it relatively straightforward to collect child support. For example, wages are garnished at the point when child support is ordered, and income tax refunds and lottery winnings are intercepted when child support is owed. These procedures, some of which derive from the Personal Responsibility and Work Opportunity Reconciliation Act of 1996, go part of the distance toward providing financial resources for the support of infants (Zaslow et al., 1998).

Earned income tax credit

This federal program provided refundable credits for low-income families in the United States. The money can be provided monthly or in an annual lump sum. As an income support program for working parents, this has been particularly effective in lifting families out of poverty (Scholz, 2000). Some states also have a state Earned Income Tax Credit.

Developmental Assessment and Support

The United States does not have a public health system through which each infant passes for regular checks. This is in contrast to, for example, Japan, where all infants receive developmental and physical checkups at 3 or 4 months of age. For poor children who are served by Medicaid, each child in the United States should receive Early and Periodic Screening, Diagnosis, and Treatment (EPSDT) services that include review of medical history, measurements, sensory screening, developmental assessment, and other checking. With the assignment of Medicaid patients to Health Maintenance Organizations (HMOs) for medical care, this has become the responsibility of medical care providers. For children not served by Medicaid, each state has developed Child Find programs, including media campaigns, to help find children with developmental delays and sensory impairments who would be eligible for services under the Individuals with Disabilities Act (Part C). Where delays or impairments are detected, each state has a lead agency responsible for providing supportive services to children between birth and 3 years old who have handicapping conditions. The specific services that are needed are developed jointly by families and professionals and documented in an Individualized Family Service Plan.

Child Care

Chapter 24 in this volume provides some information on child care during infancy. In the United States, over half of the mothers of 12-month-old infants work outside the home. A few of these infants accompany their mothers to work, some are cared for by their fathers while the mothers work, others are cared for by relatives, and the remainder are cared for by paid providers in the infants' homes, in family childcare settings, or in childcare centers.

What does a good childcare program look like? There is an emerging consensus that by paying attention to three structural aspects of child care, the overall care provided to infants and toddlers in childcare programs can be enhanced. Childcare programs that have one adult taking care of no more than three infants, that keep infants in groups of six or fewer, and that have trained childcare providers provide the most supportive care (e.g., American Public Health Association and American Academy of Pediatrics, 1992). For example, in those programs providers are most likely to be nurturing (NICHD Early Child Care Research Network, 1996). However, the NICHD Study of Early Child Care (1999) indicates that 20 percent of infants from ten communities across the United States are in childcare programs that meet *none* of these standards. This is important because the quality of child care in infancy has been linked to socioemotional development (NICHD Early Child Care Research Network, 1998).

In the context of welfare reform and the Personal Responsibility and Work Opportunity Reconciliation Act of 1996, considerable public money from the TANF program has been put into paying for child care for infants whose mothers are returning to work (Zaslow et al., 1998). Each state has developed its own procedures for determining reimbursement rates and procedures. For example, Wisconsin has a tiered reimbursement system that provides a higher level of reimbursement for care provided in high-quality programs. In many states, that care is largely provided by friends and relatives who are exempt from state regulations (Capizzano, Adams, & Sonenstein, 2000). Federal money also subsidizes the costs of child care with a federal tax credit of up to $400 per child toward families' childcare costs.

Infant Safety

In the United States, policies related to the safety of infants have largely been the responsibility of state departments of public health or community health, and their efforts include media campaigns, booklets, and policy changes. The federal agency, Center for Disease Control (CDC), provides support for these efforts and tracks their impacts. Messages about car-seat safety, placing children on their backs to prevent SIDS, crib safety, and safe walkers are part of these efforts. For example, Healthy People 2010 aims to increase the number of infants who are placed on their backs to sleep from 35 percent to 70 percent (DHHS, 2000). Some safety topics are more specialized, such as the importance of testing rural well water that infants will drink for nitrates from fertilizer runoff, and some topics are very general, such as the safe food-handling procedures that are described on grocery bags. (See chapter 25 in this volume for more information about feeding.) Because of the aging housing stock in the United States, screening for lead poisoning is an important part of the safety of young children. One-quarter of American children receive injuries needing medical attention each year (US Bureau of the Census, 1996), and unintentional injuries are the leading cause of death in children 1 to 4 years old (DHHS, 2000).

Infant mortality

The rate of infant mortality in the United States is approximately 7.3 per 1000 births (Annie E. Casey Foundation, 1999). This places the United States below many other industrialized countries, and the infant mortality rate in some American cities is higher than the rate in some third world countries. Infant mortality in the United States is particularly linked with lack of early prenatal care, preterm birth, and extreme disadvantage. Healthy People 2010 aims to cut infant mortality to 4.5 percent (DHHS, 2000).

Abuse and neglect

Each state has created a system of child welfare services for addressing issues of abuse and neglect. About 26 percent of the abuse and neglect cases referred for investigation are for children 3 years or younger (US Department of Health and Human Services, 1995). Where a report of neglect or abuse is substantiated, states use some combination of case-work, criminal prosecution, mandatory parenting education, and foster care as tertiary preventions to protect children from future maltreatment. Infants and toddlers make up a disproportionate number of the children who are removed from their home and placed in foster care for abuse and neglect. In addition to formal foster-care systems run by public, secular, and nonprofit agencies, many infants are in informal care with relatives (kin care) as a result of abuse and neglect or suspicions of abuse and neglect.

Supporting Parents

Family Resource Centers

In the 1980s Family Resource Centers were developed as a strategy to support parents. The idea was that communities could better support the development of infants and children if they would centralize parents' access to information and support (Little, 1998). Family Resource Centers have offered parent education classes, parent support groups, respite care for children in stressed families, and other programs. Support from state governments, as well as from the Children's Trust Fund in each state, has been instrumental in this development.

Home-visiting programs

Beginning in the 1990s and continuing today, many communities and professionals in the United States have created home-visiting programs to welcome new infants and to educate and support infants' parents. Programs use nurse home visitors, social workers, paraprofessionals, and volunteers to optimize the development of infants, particularly high-risk infants. It is estimated that more than half a million pregnant women, infants, and their families in the United States are being served by home-visiting programs (Gomby, Culross, & Behrman, 1999). In spite of the wide proliferation of these programs, evaluations of current home-visiting models suggest that they have limited ongoing effectiveness. Only the Nursing Home Visitation Program has been documented to have long-run impact, and for that program, benefits seem to particularly accrue to high-risk families (Karoly et al., 1998; Olds et al., 1999).

Early Head Start

As a downward extension of the widespread federally funded Head Start program for 3- and 4-year-olds, Early Head Start (http://www.ehsnrc.org/) began in 1994 to serve pregnant women and families with children under 3 years old who are income-eligible. Currently over 500 sites nationally offer flexible services designed around each child, each family, and each community. With a focus on promoting children's development, pregnant women, infants, and young children are served with a combination of home visits and group activities. A national evaluation of effectiveness is under way.

Parental leave

In the United States, federal law guarantees that parents who take up to 12 weeks' leave to take care of their newborn infants can return to their same job or a similar job; however, this only applies to parents who work for employers with over 50 employees. This leave does not need to be paid leave, though some employers allow parents to use accumulated sick leave and vacation time toward the 12 weeks. A few states have parental leave policies that are slightly different from the federal law. Policies in the United States are in stark contrast to other countries, which offer periods of paid leave that range up to part-time pay over a period of three years (e.g., Sweden, Finland). Recent federal proposals may lead to allowing states to use unemployment funds to cover some paid parental leave. Research suggests that maternity leave of less than six weeks is a risk factor for depression (Hyde, Essex, Clark, & Klein, 1996) and that shorter leave periods are associated with less optimal mother–infant interaction (Clark, Hyde, Essex, & Klein, 1997).

Policy Summary

For a moment, to make this policy information more concrete, imagine a poor single American mother's negotiation through the policy maze. Welfare support from Temporary Assistance to Needy Families will pay a monthly stipend for a time, although there may be work requirements. The amount of support for a single mother and her infant is small, for example about $350 per month in Michigan. The case worker who enrolls the mother and infant may or may not also be empowered to enroll the family for food stamps, Medicaid, or state-funded child health insurance, and even if empowered to enroll for these programs, may not be knowledgeable about the intricacies of eligibility. Food stamps might provide about an additional $150 toward food costs for this mother and infant. Enrollment for WIC supplemental food is probably a separate stop, with questions about financial and nutritional need; WIC provides coupons that can be redeemed for specific nutritious food at most stores. Eligibility for home-visiting and socialization experiences from Early Head Start or a locally organized home-visiting program is probably a separate stop in communities that offer these services. In many states there is now public support of help finding a job and finding child care, but considerable leg work is involved, perhaps with the infant in tow. In other words, although policies provide numerous supports for needy families with infants, most communities have not made access to supports a convenient process.

This review of policies in the United States has presented descriptions of how programs *should* work and described who *should* be able to participate. And indeed, some of the information that researchers know is reflected in those policies. However, many families do not make use of the programs for which they are eligible. Some families are unaware of their eligibility, others do not want to participate in stigmatized programs. Some families run up against barriers of transportation, red tape, or waiting lists. Other families only receive partial services. For example, a record review in North Carolina indicated that only portions of the Early and Periodic Screening, Diagnosis, and Treatment (EPSDT) protocols were being administered (Richardson, Selby-Harrington, Krowchuk, Cross, & Williams, 1994). Clearly policies do not reflect much of what we know about infants, and what has been enacted into policy is not necessarily being implemented and having impact.

At the same time that we have accumulated huge amounts of knowledge about infants in the academy, the public is clamoring for help in solving many social problems that begin in infancy. Rob Reiner's "I Am Your Child" video has seen broad national distribution as an effort to focus public attention on the importance of the early years. Legislatures across the United States are considering and enacting initiatives that address the early years. For example, North Carolina has its Smart Start and Michigan has a Ready to Succeed initiative for supporting infants, young children, and their families. A national initiative, "Fight Crime, Invest in Kids" (http://www.fightcrime.org), is focusing increasing attention on early childhood.

The public appetite for information about infants has been fed, for example, by coverage such as *Newsweek*'s "Your Child's Brain" (Begley, 1996). Charismatic public speakers who are practitioners and consultants are riding the conference circuit. Free-standing organizations that are not part of universities such as Families and Work Institute (http://www.familiesandwork.org), Child Trends (http://www.childtrends.org), Zero to Three (http://www.zerotothree.org), and Children's Defense Fund (http://www.childrensdefense.org) are providing the print and Web materials and are providing leadership. The *New York Times* reviews books such as *Ghosts from the Nursery* (Karr-Morse & Wiley, 1997) and *The Myth of the First Three Years* (Bruer, 1999) that provide popular audiences with accessible information about infancy.

Engaged University

Where is the academy in this dialogue? Infancy researchers need to share what they know so that families, communities, states, and nations can put that knowledge into action. Policy makers, practitioners, and citizens need to be welcome when they make inquiries of the academy and need to find a willingness to enter into two-way dialogue. Infancy researchers can also play an important role in helping the public interpret what it is hearing. Researchers can help differentiate among (1) what we know solidly, (2) what is suggested by research, (3) what we are pretty sure is not true, and (4) what we know is not true.

Institute for Children, Youth, and Families

The Institute for Children, Youth, and Families at Michigan State University (http://www.icyf.msu.edu) is making specific efforts to use research to inform policy and practice for infants. The Institute is sited within the university as a multidisciplinary unit with an infrastructure in support of research, policy engagement, and scholarly outreach. It works to facilitate collaborations among faculty across campus and between on- and off-campus partners. The Institute has a focus on six topic areas, including the youngest, child well-being, youth development, parent and family development, diversity, and community capacity building. Among these areas, the current primary focus is on the youngest – infants and toddlers.

Four examples will be described from the Institute for Children, Youth, and Families at Michigan State University of our efforts to become an engaged university in the infancy arena. The first effort is directed toward state-level policy makers, the second effort is directed to local-level policy makers, the third is focused on students, and the fourth includes on- and off-campus partners.

The Institute for Children, Youth, and Families has created Michigan Family Impact Seminars as a model for bringing scholarly knowledge to policy makers. Following the format of seminars that have been held at the federal level and in Wisconsin (Bogenschneider, 1995), and with technical assistance from the National Policy Institute for Family Impact Seminars (http://sohe.wisc.edu/fampolicy/), we assembled a bipartisan, bicameral Legislative Advisory Committee to select topics of particular legislative interest. For Spring 2000 Child Care and Education was selected as the first topic, and Children and Divorce as the second. For each topic we brought three national experts with a history of scholarly publication to participate in the seminar and in a luncheon with legislators. These were educational events designed to provide research-based information; they did not advocate or lobby for specific policies or legislation. As a companion to the seminar, we prepared an attractive easy-to-read briefing report summarizing the research and the three talks – 500 copies of the Child Care and Education briefing report have been distributed to date (and it is available on our website, www.icyf.msu.edu).

As indicated earlier, many policy decisions that formerly took place at the federal level are now delegated to states which, in turn, delegate to communities. Accordingly, the Institute for Children, Youth, and Families is explicitly working in the area of community capacity building by providing technical assistance to some of the local Multi-Purpose Collaborative Bodies and their subcommittees that focus on the youngest children. This on-the-ground work is supported by a campus work group that is reviewing scholarly literature on multiple stakeholder collaborations. Thus we are able to offer research-based knowledge about infant development, about best practices, and about the collaborations that will lead to change.

The third effort of the Institute for Children, Youth, and Families at Michigan State University is to offer the Interdepartmental Graduate Specialization in Infant Studies (IGSIS). This specialization is completed concurrently with a master's degree or doctoral degree in any of a dozen participating departments on campus: Anthropology; Audiology and Speech Sciences; Counseling, Educational Psychology, and Special Education;

Family and Child Ecology; Food Science and Human Nutrition; Kinesiology; Nursing; Pediatrics and Human Development; Psychiatry; Psychology; Social Work and Sociology. This program provides students the opportunity to obtain a comprehensive academic experience based on current research and theoretical understandings of the field of human infancy and to have a practical internship placement working with infants in the community. Thus the next generation of infancy scholars is being trained in the application of infancy knowledge to policy and practice.

The Institute for Children, Youth, and Families has developed work groups as one model for engaging Michigan State University with off-campus partners to address infancy issues. The Michigan Applied Research on Child Abuse and Neglect work group was initiated jointly with the Michigan Children's Trust Fund and Michigan State University. This prevention-focused work group now includes partners from several disciplines from five Michigan universities and community partners from several parts of state government, community-based service providers, business people, and nonprofit umbrella organizations. The Michigan Breast Feeding Research Network includes partners from the WIC program, state government, practitioners, and faculty from several disciplines at three Michigan campuses. These work groups provide forums for discussion of research, policy, and practice. Each work group explicitly includes partners from on- and off-campus as well as faculty participation from several disciplines.

These four examples from the Institute for Children, Youth, and Families at Michigan State University give models for seeing that the knowledge of infancy that is summarized in this volume sees application in the lives of infants. Michigan State University is particularly committed to this scholarly engagement, partly because of leadership at the level of the University President and the University Provost (Simon, 1999). Michigan State University is also a Land-Grant University with an explicit mission to reach out to citizens. In the United States each state has at least one Land-Grant University with an Extension unit explicitly responsible for this mission. Through local Extension offices in most counties and Extension faculty on campus, the application of research-based knowledge becomes a priority. Thus working with Extension may be one key to the application of knowledge about infants.

Engaged University Guidelines

As we move toward becoming an "engaged university," and as we implement projects such as those described above, we are guided by the Kellogg Commission's (1999) report to the National Association of State Universities and Land-Grant Colleges (*Returning to Our Roots: The Engaged Institution*). Their report can facilitate our efforts to effect the application of infancy research to the lives of infants.

An engaged university is responsive and respectful (Kellogg Commission on the Future of State and Land-Grant Universities, 1999, p. x). The academy has to do more than provide expert answers to the questions that it thinks communities and practitioners should be asking about infants. Instead, the academy needs to participate in a two-way dialogue where we learn about the knowledge that is emerging in practice and about the questions that are important to families, practitioners, and policy makers. It is this dialogue that will lead to changes on and off campus.

An engaged university holds to academic neutrality. In other words, when we become involved in contentious issues, can we "maintain the university in the role of neutral facilitator and source of information" (Kellogg Commission on the Future of State and Land-Grant Universities, 1999, p. x)? Communities, policy makers, and citizens ask: "Does the new brain science indicate that windows of opportunity close at the end of the first three years?" "Can we prevent child abuse in our community with home visiting?" "Does breast-feeding make children smarter?" "At what age should parents begin reading to their children?" "Can appropriate care of infants raise IQ 40 points?" "What about Mozart for babies?" The academy treads a fine line in sticking to what we know and providing useful information in answer to questions like these.

The engaged university will need to work hard at coordination if it is to be useful (Kellogg Commission on the Future of State and Land-Grant Universities, 1999). Can we work together across traditional disciplinary boundaries, across unit boundaries on campuses, and across campuses? If the academy can coordinate across these boundaries, it will also enhance accessibility to communities, policy makers, and citizens. When the academy coordinates its efforts to address relevant questions, we will know who else is doing the infancy research on our campus and on neighboring campuses. Then it will not matter who is the point of access because we can make useful referrals within our networked academy.

If universities commit to becoming engaged universities, they will integrate this engagement across the research, teaching, and service missions of the university (Kellogg Commission on the Future of State and Land-Grant Universities, 1999). For example, as described above, the Interdepartmental Graduate Specialization in Infant Studies at Michigan State University is a multidisciplinary effort involving a dozen departments, and it provides students with coursework, seminars, and an internship experience that prepares them to work with infants in a number of fields.

Universities who make a commitment to engagement also commit resources to these efforts. "The most successful engagement efforts appear to be those associated with strong and healthy relationships with partners in government, business, and the nonprofit world" (Kellogg Commission on the Future of State and Land-Grant Universities, 1999, p. x). Our professional organizations recognize these needs. The American Psychological Association offers an annual award for "Distinguished Contribution to Psychology in the Public Interest" (e.g., American Psychological Association, 1999), and the work of the 1995 awardee, Dr. David Riley, included infancy work (American Psychological Association, 1996). The Society for Research in Child Development now publishes applied and policy studies in its journal, *Child Development* (Zigler, 1998), and for some time it has regularly published the Social Policy Report. Of particular interest is the Social Policy Report, "Beyond 'Giving Science Away': How University–Community Partnerships Inform Youth Programs, Research and Policy" (Denner, Cooper, Lopez, & Dunbar, 1999).

The new research agendas for infancy will be multidisciplinary action research agendas shaped jointly by families, service providers, government, business, and scholars. With this collaboration between the academy and the off-campus world, what the academy knows – about perception and cognition; about social, emotional, and communicative development; about risk factors; and about the contexts of early development – will be put to use by families, the practitioners who serve them, policy makers, and communities to optimize the development of infants.

Further Reading

Annie E. Casey Foundation. (1999). *KIDS COUNT data book: State profiles of child well-being.* Available from the Annie E. Casey Foundation, 701 St. Paul Street, Baltimore, MD 21202, or the Internet at www.aecf.org. The Annie E. Casey Foundation has provided ongoing support for surveillance of the statistics on children's well-being in each state. The annual report provides charts for each state that describes the circumstances of their children. County-level statistics are also available in state publications.

Boyer, E. L. (1996). The scholarship of engagement. *Journal of Public Service and Outreach, 1,* 11–20. From his perspective as the President of the Carnegie Foundation for the Advancement of Teaching, Boyer argues for the strengthening of connections between American society and universities.

Denner, J., Cooper, C. R., Lopez, E. M., & Dunbar, N. (1999). Beyond "giving science away": How university–community partnerships inform youth programs, research, and policy. *Social Policy Report* (Vol. 13, No. 1). Ann Arbor, MI: Society for Research in Child Development. Using examples from recent research with two youth programs, this report proposes that university–community partnerships afford the exchange of existing knowledge and generation of new knowledge that can bridge the gaps between research, practice, and policy for youth.

Kellogg Commission on the Future of State and Land-Grant Universities. (1999, February). *Returning to our roots: The engaged institution.* Washington, DC: National Association of State Universities and Land-Grant Colleges. This 1999 report of the Kellogg Commission on the Future of State and Land-Grant Universities lays out examples and principles as universities struggle with escaping their ivory-tower reputation and becoming more relevant. Ideas from this report are equally relevant for private colleges and universities.

Lerner, R. M., & Simon, L. A. K. (Eds.). (1998). *University–community collaborations for the twenty-first century: Outreach scholarship for youth and families.* New York: Garland. This edited volume provides specific examples from many American colleges and universities of connections that have been forged between universities and communities in the area of youth development.

Zaslow, M., Tout, K., Smith, S., & Moore, K. (1998). Implications of the 1996 welfare legislation for children: A research perspective. *Social Policy Report* (Vol. 12, No. 3). Ann Arbor, MI: Society for Research in Child Development. This report uses results from evaluations of welfare-to-work programs and findings of basic research on children and families to anticipate the implications for children of the 1996 federal welfare legislation.

Zigler, E. (1998). A place of value for applied and policy studies. *Child Development, 69,* 532–542. Zigler describes and celebrates the decision by the Society for Research in Child Development to include applied and policy studies in their journal, *Child Development.* This opens for the academy the possibility of conducting relevant work on infants and having that work published in one of the top journals in the field.

Web resources

Web resources include:

- The Families and Work Institute (http://www.familiesandwork.org/), a nonprofit organization committed to finding research-based strategies that foster mutually supportive connections among workplaces, families, and communities.
- Child Trends (http://www.childtrends.org), a nonprofit, nonpartisan research organization that studies children, youth, and families through research, data collection, and data analysis.
- Zero to Three (http://www.zerotothree.org/), the National Center for Infants, Toddlers and Families, dedicated to the healthy development of infants and toddlers.
- The Children's Defense Fund (http://www.childrensdefense.org/), which aims to ensure for every child "a Healthy Start, a Head Start, a Safe Start, and a Moral Start in life and successful passage to adulthood with the help of caring families and communities."
- The National Center for Children in Poverty (http://cpmcnet.columbia.edu/dept/nccp/cpf.html) at Columbia University, which is identifying and promoting strategies that reduce the number of young children living in poverty in the United States, and that improve the life chances of the millions of children under age 6 who are growing up poor.
- The Urban Institute (http://www.urban.org), a nonprofit policy research organization whose objectives are to sharpen thinking about society's problems and efforts to solve them, improve government decisions and their implementation, and increase citizens' awareness about important public choices.
- The Healthy People website (http://www.health.gov/healthypeople/) offers a wealth of information about this national health promotion and disease prevention initiative, as well as on-line access to the *Healthy People 2010* document.
- The Early Head Start program (http://www.ehsnrc.org/) supports the healthy development of infants, toddlers, and their families.

References

Ahluwalia, I. B., Hogan, V. K., Grummer-Strawn, L., Colville, W. R., & Peterson, A. (1998). The effect of WIC participation on small-for-gestational-age births: Michigan, 1992. *American Journal of Public Health, 88*, 1374–1376.

American Academy of Pediatrics Work Group on Breastfeeding. (1997). Breastfeeding and the use of human milk. *Pediatrics, 100*, 1035–1039.

American Psychological Association. (1996). Award for Distinguished Contribution to Psychology in the Public Interest: David A. Riley. *American Psychologist, 51*, 336–341.

American Psychological Association. (1999). Award for Distinguished Contribution to Psychology in the Public Interest: Bonnie Strickland. *American Psychologist, 54*, 246.

American Public Health Association and American Academy of Pediatrics Collaborative Project. (1992). *Caring for our children – national health and safety performance standards: Guidelines for out-of-home child care programs.* Washington, DC: American Public Health Association.

Annie E. Casey Foundation. (1999). *KIDS COUNT data book: State profiles of child well-being.* Available from the Annie E. Casey Foundation, 701 St. Paul Street, Baltimore, MD 21202, or the Internet at www.aecf.org.

Arlotti, J. P., Cottrell, B. H., Lee, S. H., & Curtin, J. J. (1998). Breastfeeding among low-income women with and without peer support. *Journal of Community Health Nursing, 15*, 163–178.

Begley, S. (1996, February 19). The Cover: Your child's brain. *Newsweek, 127*, 54.

Bogenschneider, K. (1995, January). Roles for professionals in building family policy: A case study of state family impact seminars. *Family Relations, 44*(1), 5–12.

Boyer, E. L. (1996). The scholarship of engagement. *Journal of Public Service and Outreach, 1,* 11–20.

Bronfenbrenner, U. (1979). *The ecology of human development: Experiments by nature and design.* Cambridge, MA: Harvard University Press.

Bruer, J. T. (1999). *The myth of the first three years: A new understanding of early brain development and lifelong learning.* New York: Free Press.

Capizzano, J., Adams, G., & Sonenstein, F. (2000). *Child care arrangements for children under five: Variation across states* (Series B, No. B-7). Washington, DC: The Urban Institute.

Caulfield, L. E., Gross, S. M., Bentley, M. E., Bronner, Y., Kessler, L., Jenson, J., Weathers, B., & Paige, D. M. (1998). WIC-based interventions to promote breastfeeding among African-American women in Baltimore: Effects of breastfeeding initiation and continuation. *Journal of Human Lactation, 14,* 15–22.

Clark, R., Hyde, J. S., Essex, M. J., & Klein, M. H. (1997). Length of maternity leave and quality of mother–infant interactions. *Child Development, 68,* 364–383.

Denner, J., Cooper, C. R., Lopez, E. M., & Dunbar, N. (1999). Beyond "giving science away": How university–community partnerships inform youth programs, research, and policy. *Social Policy Report* (Vol. 13, No. 1). Ann Arbor, MI: Society for Research in Child Development.

Ellwood, M. (1999, December). *The Medicaid eligibility maze: Coverage expands, but enrollment problems persist, findings from a five-state study.* Available: http://newfederalism.urban.org/html/occa30.html.

Federal Interagency Forum on Child and Family Statistics. (1998). *America's children: Key national indicators of well-being.* Washington, DC: US Government Printing Office.

Field, T. (1995). Psychologically depressed parents. In M. H. Bornstein (Ed.), *Handbook of parenting: Vol. 4. Applied and practical parenting* (pp. 85–99). Mahwah, NJ: Erlbaum.

Gomby, D. S., Culross, P. L, & Behrman, R. E. (1999, Spring/Summer). Home visiting: Recent program evaluations – analysis and recommendations. *The Future of Children, 9,* 4–26.

Heinig, M. J., (1998). Breastfeeding and the bottom line: Why are the cost savings of breastfeeding such a hard sell? *Journal of Human Lactation, 14,* 87–88.

Hyde, J. S., Essex, M. J., Clark, R., & Klein, M. H. (1996). Parental leave: Policy and research. *Journal of Social Issues, 52,* 91–109.

Karoly, L. A., Greenwood, P. W., Everingham, S. M. S., Hoube, J., Kilburn, M. R., Rydell, C. P., Sanders, M. R., & Chiesa, J. R. (1998). *Investing in our children: What we know and don't know about the costs and benefits of early childhood interventions* (Doc. No. MR-898-TCWF). Santa Monica, CA: RAND Corporation.

Karr-Morse, R., & Wiley, M. S. (1997). *Ghosts from the nursery: Tracing the roots of violence.* New York: Atlantic Monthly Press.

Kellogg Commission on the Future of State and Land-Grant Universities. (1999, February). *Returning to our roots: The engaged institution.* Washington, DC: National Association of State Universities and Land-Grant Colleges.

Lerner, R. M., & Simon, L. A. K. (Eds.). (1998). *University–community collaborations for the twenty-first century: Outreach scholarship for youth and families.* New York: Garland.

Little, P. M. D. (1998, October). Family Resource Centers: Where school readiness happens. *Early Childhood Digest.* Available from US Department of Education, National Institute on Early Childhood Development and Education (tel. 202-219-1672) or on-line at http://www.ed.gov/offices/OERI/ECI/digests/98october.htm.

Lowry, L. W., & Beikirch, P. (1998). Effect of comprehensive care on pregnancy outcomes. *Applied Nursing Research, 11,* 55–61.

Mayes, L. C. (1995). Substance abuse and parenting. In M. H. Bornstein (Ed.), *Handbook of parenting: Vol. 4. Applied and practical parenting* (pp. 101–125). Mahwah, NJ: Erlbaum.

Morrow, A. L., Guerrero, M. L., Shults, J., Calva, J. J., Lutter, C., Bravo, J., Ruiz-Palacios, G., Morrow, R. C., & Butterfoss, F. D. (1999). Efficacy of home-based peer counseling to promote exclusive breastfeeding: A randomized controlled trial. *Lancet, 353,* 1226–1231.

Moss, N. E., & Carver, K. (1998). The effect of WIC and Medicaid on infant mortality in the United States. *American Journal of Public Health, 1998,* 1354–1361.

National Center for Children in Poverty. (1997). *Early childhood poverty: A statistical profile* [On-line]. Available: http://cpmcnet.columbia.edu/dept/nccp/cpf.html.

National Center for Health Statistics. (2000). *Vital statistics of the United States, 1997, Part I, Natality – First release of files.* Available: http://www.cdc.gov/nchs/datawh/statab/ unpubd/natality/natab97.htm.

NICHD Early Child Care Research Network. (1996). Characteristics of infant child care: Factors contributing to positive caregiving. *Early Childhood Research Quarterly, 11,* 269–306.

NICHD Early Child Care Research Network. (1998). Early child care and self-control, compliance, and problem behavior at twenty-four and thirty-six months. *Child Development, 69,* 1145–1170.

NICHD Early Child Care Research Network. (1999). Child outcomes when child care center classes meet recommended standards for quality. *American Journal of Public Health, 89,* 1072–1077.

Olds, D. L., Henderson, C. R., Jr., Kitzman, H. J., Eckenrode, J. J., Cole, R. E., & Tatelbaum, R. C. (1999, Spring/Summer). Prenatal and infancy home visitation by nurses: Recent findings. *The Future of Children, 9,* 44–65.

Omar, M. A., Schiffman, R. F., & Bauer, P. (1998). Recipient and provider perspectives of barriers to rural prenatal care. *Journal of Community Health Nursing, 15,* 237–249.

Richardson, L. A., Selby-Harrington, M. L., Krowchuk, H. V., Cross, A. W., & Williams, D. (1994). Comprehensiveness of well child checkups for children receiving Medicaid: A pilot study. *Journal of Pediatric Health Care, 8,* 212–220.

Riportella-Muller, R., Selby-Harrington, M. L., Richardson, L. A., Donat, P. L. N., Luchok, K. J., & Quade, D. (1996, January/February). Barriers to the use of preventive health care services for children. *Public Health Reports, 111,* 72–77.

Scholz, J. K. (2000). Not perfect, but still pretty good: The Earned Income Tax Credit and other policies to support low-income working families. In *Helping poor kids succeed: Welfare, tax, and early intervention policies* (Wisconsin Family Impact Seminars Briefing Report). Madison: University of Wisconsin, School of Human Ecology.

Simon, L. A. (1999). Constructive and complex tensions in the art of engagement. *Journal of Public Service and Outreach, 4*(2), 2–6.

Stuart-Macadam, P., & Dettwyler, K. A. (Eds.). (1995). *Breastfeeding: Biocultural perspectives.* New York: Aldine de Gruyter.

Tableman, B. (Ed.). (1999). *Overcoming hunger in the United States* (Best Practice Briefs No. 8, 1998–99). East Lansing: Michigan State University, Outreach Partnerships.

Task Force on Infrastructure. (1999, May). *Infants, families and communities: Strengthening supports for healthy development* (Report to the David and Lucile Packard Foundation). Washington, DC: Zero to Three, National Center for Infants, Toddlers, and Families.

US Bureau of the Census. (1996). *Statistical abstract of the United States, 1996* (116th ed.). Washington, DC: US Department of Commerce.

US Department of Health and Human Services. (2000, January). *Healthy People 2010* (Conference Edition, 2 vols.). Available: http://www.health.gov/healthypeople/.

US Department of Health and Human Services, National Clearinghouse on Child Abuse and Neglect Information. (1995). *Child maltreatment: Reports from the states to the National Center on Child Abuse and Neglect* (No. HE 23.1018). Washington, DC: Author.

US Department of Health and Human Services, Public Health Service. (1991). *Healthy People 2000: National health promotion and disease prevention objectives* (DHHS Publication No. PHS 91-50212). Washington, DC: US Government Printing Office.

Zaslow, M., Tout, K., Smith, S., & Moore, K. (1998). Implications of the 1996 welfare legislation for children: A research perspective. *Social Policy Report* (Vol. 12, No. 3). Ann Arbor, MI: Society for Research in Child Development.

Zigler, E. (1998). A place of value for applied and policy studies. *Child Development, 69*, 532–542.

Chapter Twenty-four

Childcare Research at the Dawn of a New Millennium: Taking Stock of What We Know

Sarah L. Friedman, Suzanne Randolph, and Anita Kochanoff

Introduction

Research on child care is multifaceted and its actual and potential contributions are wide ranging. It provides a window into demographic and economic changes, societal values and resources that have shaped childrearing practices in the industrial world in the second half of the 1900s. Research on the links between child care and child development provides society with the data that can inform decisions about child care as a childrearing environment. Research on the links between child care and the family or the workplace can shed light on the contribution of child care to the well-being of the society at large. The primary goal of this chapter is to review what the scientific literature has taught us to date about child care, especially during infancy, and about the developmental outcomes of children who were placed in child care when they were infants. A second goal is to chart out areas for future research, as we currently understand them. Before embarking on the review of the scientific literature, we briefly spell out some of the major reasons that child care has been a focus of intense research activity by behavioral and social scientists. We also describe the different ways that child care has been conceptualized and assessed.

Why Is Child Care an Issue?

Child care has been perceived to be a societal public health issue and has attracted the interest of demographers, sociologists, and psychologists (Hofferth, 1996; Lamb, 1997; Tietze & Cryer, 1999). This perception of child care is a result of a conflict between the practice of using child care and cultural beliefs about the optimal conditions for the rearing of children (e.g., Brazelton, 1986). While the use of child care has increased, the belief that infants' healthy development is dependent on having the mother care for her child on a full-time basis has persisted. This belief has been supported by scholarly writings about the essential conditions for the rearing of well-adjusted children (e.g., Bowlby, 1973).

Historical changes in the economy of the United States and of other industrialized and developing nations (e.g., Swadener & Bloch, 1997), as well as changes of women's concepts of their roles in society and in the family, have together led to the increased participation of women in the workforce. These changes have also led to a substantive change in the rearing of infants and children.

The above changes have occurred in a society where the normative family structure is that of a nuclear family, increasingly consisting of a single parent and her or his children (Cherlin, 1999). When relatives are close by, they are likely to be in the workforce and unable to provide care for children when their mothers are working. Consequently, many employed mothers have come to rely on paid child care by non-relatives. While initially it seemed that there was a major shortage of childcare slots in the United States, a report suggests that currently there is a good match between supply and demand of child care (Hofferth, 1992). However, in the case of child care for children in poverty or for children with special needs, availability and affordability are still issues of concern (United States General Accounting Office, 1999). The child care that parents obtain for their children is not necessarily of high quality, because there are no market pressures or regulations that require providers to meet standards of high quality. Parents are frequently unaware of what would be considered markers of quality (Honig, 1995). They are interested primarily in safety, convenience, and in the cost of care. Licensing standards represent the floor of quality. The cost of child care in general, and of infant care in particular, is very high. It can reach up to 25 percent of the family income in the case of poor families (Hofferth, 1992).

The issues pertaining to child care become even more complex for children at biological, psychological, and/or social risk. Most of the public and scientific debate about child care has focused on child care for middle-class children, whereas the policy debate has focused both on child care for middle-class children as well as poor children. Still, very little attention has gone to children with physical or psychological limitations (Booth & Kelly, 1998, 1999a,b).

So, even though the use of child care for infants and older children is pervasive, the concerns about child care are still on the mind of parents, policy makers, and scientists who study child development. In this chapter we will present the historical changes in maternal employment and childcare use and the challenges to cultural beliefs and scientific theory that have stimulated research on child care and its links to child development. We will then focus on the conceptualization and the assessment of child care, the history of research on child care, and on the current state of knowledge about the links between child care and child development. We then move on to present new directions for research on child care which is motivated primarily by the sociocultural and economic factors that continue to keep the scholarly and public interest in child care.

Historical Changes in Maternal Employment and in Nonmaternal Care

The industrial world and developing countries have witnessed recent increases in the labor force participation of women and in childcare usage. In the 1980s, maternal employment rates in countries of the European Union increased on the average by 1.8 percent per year (Maruani, 1992). For example, in Sweden rates of maternal employment have changed from 59 percent in 1975, 74 percent in 1980, to 85 percent in 1985 (Gustafsson & Stafford, 1995). In 1966, 35 percent of all Australian women over the age of 15 were in the workforce. In 1988 the figure rose to 40.6 percent. As in other countries, this increase pertains to mostly married women and particularly to married women with children (Bryson, 1989). In Latin America, a growing number of the workforce is female, although that share is only 26.7 percent, as compared to 40 percent and 41 percent in Canada and the United States, respectively (Anonymous, 1995). While most industrial countries have experienced dramatic increases in labor force participation in the last two decades, the percentage of women holding jobs or seeking jobs has remained around 50 percent in Japan (Takahashi, 1998). In the United States, women's labor force participation increased dramatically in the four decades between 1950 and 1990, increasing from nearly one-third in 1948 to two-thirds in 1990 (Coleman & Pencavel, 1993; Fullerton, 1999). The labor force participation of women was accompanied by a dramatic increase in the proportion of mothers in the labor force. From 1968 to 1988, the proportion of young children with mothers in the labor force increased from 39 percent to 60 percent (Hofferth, Brayfield, Deich, & Holcomb, 1991) and in 1994, 55 percent of mothers of infants were in the workforce (Bachu, 1995). The above pertains to the US population as a whole and conceals the fact that the rate of employment and the historical changes were not the same in all segments of the population. For example, rates of employment among African American mothers have historically been high compared to rates of employment among European American mothers (Beckett, 1982; McLoyd, 1993).

The increase in working mothers led to an increase in the childcare market and to an increase in the proportion of young children in child care. For instance, in the United States, the proportion of children in kindergarten or preschool rose from 21 percent in 1978 to 39 percent in 1985 (Hofferth et al., 1991). According to 1988 US census data, by age 5, 87 percent of American children were spending some time in school or a preschool (Hofferth et al., 1991). Confirming such census data, several national studies indicate that *early* child care (i.e., for children under 3) has also become an increasingly normative experience. The rate of early child care for infants/toddlers was 63 percent in the National Child Care Survey, 1990 (Hofferth et al., 1991), 71 percent in the 1994 Survey of Income and Program Participation (SIPP; Casper, Hawkins, & O'Connell, 1994), and 76 percent in the 1996 SIPP. (Casper, 1996). These and other studies also indicate that parents place infants and toddlers in a variety of childcare settings and use multiple arrangements for the same child at the same time during infancy or toddlerhood (Hofferth, 1996). In addition, there is evidence that African Americans have traditionally had disproportionate rates of single-mother families (Hunter, Pearson, Ialongo, & Kellam, 1998; Randolph, 1995), suggesting a longer history of reliance on nonparental care.

The most recent historical changes in childcare usage in the United States are associated with state welfare policies. In 1988 the Family Support Act was passed in the US Congress. According to this law, parents whose youngest child was 3 years of age were required to work or prepare for work as a condition for getting financial support. In 1996 the Personal Responsibility and Work Opportunities Reconciliation Act (PL 104–193; PRWORA) was passed, requiring mothers of infants older than 6 weeks, who would have previously been eligible for government support (welfare) during their child's first three years of life, to enter the workforce. The law does not guarantee provisions for child care for these families, thereby stressing the capacity of available childcare arrangements to absorb more children and making the ground fertile for growth in the number of low-quality childcare settings.

The historical forces are similar around the world. Swadener and Bloch (1997) report that in many of the newly independent states (NIS) of the former Soviet Union and the former communist countries of East and Central Europe, governments have been pressured to cut back on social benefits that provided universal, though limited, support to families with young children. They offer the example of Russia, where many childcare programs for infants and toddlers have been closed down, and where kindergarten or day-care programs for 3- to 6-year-olds have decreased from nearly 80 percent coverage to 60 percent (or lower) coverage in the past few years (Bloch, 1996; Smirnova, in progress).

In other countries around the world, the need to compete globally has led governments to scale down the support for welfare policies. Such policies previously supported health care, provided mothers of children between the ages of 0 and 3 with support for staying home with their children, and supported programs for children in their first six years of life (Swadener & Bloch, 1997). In countries of the European Union, where there is a long history of organized early care and education for children (primarily Western Europe), there is a shortage in programs to meet the needs of children under 3 years of age. In Sweden, the economic pressures are forcing cutbacks in one of the world's most generous family support systems (Kallos & Tallberg Broman, 1997). In the five-year period between 1988 and 1993, however, several countries increased their coverage rates for younger children. The highest coverage rates are currently found in Denmark and eastern Germany (Tietze & Cryer, 1999).

This historical review, although brief and incomplete, makes it clear that the world-wide increase in maternal employment is associated with a decrease in government support for the nonmaternal care of the young children of employed women. Next we review the paradox between the reality of increases in the employment of mothers of young children and cultural beliefs about the unique role of mother as the central childrearing figure.

Child Care as a Challenge to Cultural Beliefs and to Scientific Theories

The placement of infants in child care challenges deeply held beliefs and scientific theories that stress the importance of early exclusive maternal care. A deeply held cultural belief in the United States is that families have primary, if not sole, responsibility for the rearing of their young (Steiner, 1981). By placing an infant or toddler in child care, the family is relinquishing some of its central responsibilities. This is the case even if it is the family that selects the childcare provider and requires that certain standards of quality care be met. The same line of thinking suggests that to the extent that child care is regulated or subsidized by the State, the family is handing over central family responsibilities to the State authorities whose childrearing values and goals may not match those of the family.

According to scientific theories, a mother needs to get to know her infant, and learn to understand her infant's nonverbal and verbal cues so that she can respond to the child sensitively. Likewise, through interaction with their mothers, infants come to know their mothers and to trust them as a source of emotional security and knowledge about the world. The sensitivity and responsiveness of the mother and the sense of trust of the child are at the heart of emotional security and the acquisition of social and cognitive skills (Bowlby, 1973; Brazelton, 1986; Klein & Feurestein, 1985). These theories do not specify the amount of time that is critical for the formation of healthy mother–child relationships, nor do they consider the possibility that infants and toddlers may develop normally and successfully when cared for by childcare providers who are caring and qualified. Empirical evidence from cross-cultural research challenges such theories given that children in nonindustrial societies are reared by multiple caregivers (Morelli & Tronick, 1991; Tronick, Morelli, & Ivey, 1992; Tronick, Morelli, & Winn, 1987). Likewise, historical analyses suggest that the unique childrearing role that mothers have in industrial societies is a very recent phenomenon (Cherlin, 1999; Popenoe, 1993). Based on these examples from other societies and historical times, it is possible to argue that quality child care and early childhood education programs may not be detrimental to the well-being of children in their care. Moreover, it has been argued that quality child care should offset the potentially harmful effects of inadequate or neglectful parenting, or the effects of being reared in disadvantaged environments, regardless of whether mothers are employed (Barnett, 1995; Caughy, DiPietro, & Strobino, 1994; Frede, 1995; Yoshikwa, 1995).

While much information has been collected, the results about the effects of child care have not been sufficiently consistent to resolve the concerns about the hypothesized harmful effects of child care on the development of children. Cultural beliefs are very well entrenched and are not easily dislodged even in the face of scientific evidence. At the same time, these beliefs and the concerns associated with them lead to a thirst for new information. This is evidenced by the enormous policy and media interest for scientific information about the effects of child care on children's development and about the role of families in the lives of children who are in child care.

Conceptualizing Child Care

The term child care refers to an arrangement for the routine care of children when their mothers are occupied away from their children. The arrangement is a result of an agreement reached between mothers of young children and others who are willing to provide care for children. The arrangement is frequently based on the exchange of fee for service. Most mothers enter such a routine arrangement to make it possible for them to hold a job, run a business, or go to school. Some enter such an arrangement in order to allow them to do volunteer work, carry out social obligations, or be engaged in other activities that cannot be done at the same time as taking care of a young child.

Some define child care as nonparental care (Lamb, 1997) and have turned the research lens on child care provided by individuals other than the parents. The assumption underlying this definition is that the nuclear family has the primary responsibility for childrearing. So, as far as childrearing goes, the parents are interchangeable and if the father is the primary care provider when the mother works, there is no need to evaluate the possible links between father care and children's developmental outcomes. Others define child care as nonmaternal care (NICHD Early Child Care Research Network, 1996, 2000a), thereby including care by the child's father when the mother works as a type of child care.

Child care is not a unitary concept. Childcare settings are different along many dimensions. Friedman and Amadeo (1999) have described childcare settings in terms of who provides care, where care is provided, how care is provided, and the children's experience in child care. For example, child care can be described in terms of the identity of the provider, his or her characteristics (education level; experience as childcare provider) or relation to the child (grandparent; non-relative). Child care can be provided in the child's home or some place else. Children may receive care at a relative's home, a childcare home, or a childcare center. The recipients of care may be an individual child or several children. The children may be of the same or different ages, of the same gender or ethnicity, or of different gender or ethnicity. The care that is being provided can be highly professional, with well-planned daily routines for providing experiences that promote child development, or it can be custodial. Children may experience the childcare setting as a place with loving adults, with friends to spend time with and to play with. They may experience it as a place with interesting things to do. At the other extreme are children who experience child care as a place where adults are harsh, the noise level is high, and where there is little to do or enjoy. Children vary in terms of the amounts of child care they experience. Some children are in child care for a few hours per week and others are in full-time child care, for more than 30 hours per week. Some children experience stability in child care. Others are going to different settings in any given week or their parents move them from one childcare setting to another to accommodate family finances and transient residential patterns.

Others have conceptualized child care in terms of aspects of the environment that are directly experienced by the child and in terms of aspects that influence the child indirectly. This conceptualization is based on Bronfenbrenner's ecological model of the physical and social environment (Bronfenbrenner, 1988, 1999). The physical and social aspects of the environment that can be experienced directly by the child are the proximal aspects, whereas those aspects that influence children indirectly are the distal aspects. For example, children in child care directly experience the way they are talked to and responded to, the presence of peers and the availability of toys, books, decorations, and television. They indirectly experience the education level of the childcare provider. This is the case since providers with higher educational attainment provide higher-quality environment (Burchinal, Roberts, Nabors, & Bryant, 1996; Clarke-Stewart, 1987; Dunn, 1993; NICHD Early Child Care Research Network, 1999a). Children in child care also indirectly experience the salary their providers receive. Providers with low income levels tend to leave their jobs for better jobs, thereby leading to instability in the experience of children in their care. Provider turnover is considered a negative experience for children and is associated with poorer developmental outcomes (Whitebook, Howes, & Phillips, 1990). The above ways of characterizing child care have guided the development of assessments of the childcare environment.

The Assessment of Child Care

Assessments of the childcare environment need to be tailored to the goals of the assessment. Existing measures of child care are associated with three practical assessment goals and the conceptualizations associated with these. Friedman and Amadeo (1999) classified the methods for assessing child care in three ways (1) assessments for state licensing; (2) assessments for accreditation; and (3) research assessments to scientifically evaluate the effects of child care on the psychological development of children.

States regulate the care of children in childcare homes (also known as family day care) and in childcare centers. They require that these settings will meet minimal standards of health, safety, and quality of care (Kontos, 1991; Phillips, Lande, & Goldberg, 1990). More specifically, these minimal standards pertain to group size, adult : child ratios, space requirements, equipment that is easily accessible to children; inaccessibility of cleaning materials to children; periodic health appraisal of staff; and activities that promote development of children's skills, self-esteem, positive self-identity, and choice of activities (Fiene & Nixon, 1985).

In contrast to licensing, standards for professional accreditation of individual childcare providers are very high and those who meet them provide physical, social, and educational environments that educators and developmental scientists consider of high quality. In addition to the accreditation of individual providers, childcare centers meeting very high criteria of quality may be accredited too (Caldwell et al., 1990; National Association for the Education of Young Children [NAEYC], 1991). The accreditation system evaluates many aspects of child care in great depth (Bredekamp, 1986). Accredited programs are efficient and carried out with attention to the needs and desires of children, parents, and staff. The staff must understand children's development and respond appropriately to children's needs. They are required to demonstrate positive, courteous, and flexible manner. The interactions between provider and child in accredited programs are characterized by warmth, personal respect, individuality, positive support, and responsiveness. In addition, accredited programs facilitate interactions among children to provide opportunities for the development of self-esteem, social competence, and intellectual growth.

Researchers have used different methods for evaluating the childcare environment (Phillips & Howes, 1987; Zaslow, 1991). In a review of such methods, Friedman and Amadeo (1999) have classified the methods used by researchers into three types:

1   Descriptive, easy to measure or verify aspects of the environment. These include space available, group size, provider : child ratio, equipment, cost, and administrative aspects such as auspices.

2   Global or summary measures of the quality of the childcare environment. The summary measures are based on instruments that evaluate many aspects of the environment. For example, the Early Childhood Environment Rating Scale (ECERS; Harms & Clifford, 1980) evaluates personal care routines, furnishing, language, motor activities, creative activities, social development, and adult needs. Another example is the Infant/Toddler Environment Rating Scale (ITERS; Harms, Cryer, & Clifford, 1990), which is an adaptation of the ECERS for observation of child care for younger children. The global summary measures are designed specifically for a particular type of care. Some are designed for evaluating center care and others are designed for childcare homes (Family Day Care Rating Scale [FDCRS], Harms & Clifford, 1984). These instruments have not been used for evaluating care in the child's own home or in the home of a relative or a neighbor who does not operate a childcare home.

3   Experiential measures. These include measures of the age of entry into care, the extent and stability of care received by the child, the provider's interaction with the child, and of the child's interactions with peers. The Observation Rating of the Caregiving Environment (ORCE; NICHD Early Child Care Research Network, 1996, 2000a) is the most comprehensive instrument designed to measure the proximal interactive experiences of children in child care. The frequency of behaviors indicating sensitivity, responsiveness, positive or negative affect, and the cognitive stimulation the child is receiving are recorded. The quality of the caregiving environment is also rated. The data collectors who record the frequency of the behavioral indicators of quality also rate the childcare environment using the ORCE rating scales. The ORCE can be used in different childcare settings, including center care, childcare homes, and care in the child's home or in the caregiver's home.

In general, the assessment of the quality of care is guided by what researchers consider quality of care based on their value judgments and theoretical orientation. Quality care is care that leads to outcomes that are valued in our society. In the United States, our society values children who are curious and imaginative, who use language effectively for communication, and children who are considerate of peers and adults. We value assertiveness but not aggression. We value skill in problem solving, creativity, and academic achievement. So we look in child care for predictors of such outcomes. These predictors include sensitivity and responsiveness to children's positive and negative affect, treating of children with respect, talking to children and answering their questions. The childcare predictors also include the extent to which childcare environments facilitate learning and positive interaction among peers. The more distal measures of quality include adult : child ratio, group size, provider educational level, and the provider's training in child development. These distal aspects of the childcare environment are childcare characteristics that set the conditions for higher-quality proximal care (Phillips & Howes, 1987). For a summary of the relations among the different measures of the childcare environment, see Friedman and Amadeo (1999).

The History of Research on Child Care and its Links to Child Development

When we encounter new people or visit new places our attention is drawn to their most striking features. We notice if the new individual is male or female, young or old, African American or European American. We judge new places in terms of their size, beauty, and similarity to places we know. As we get more familiar with people or environments, we pay attention to finer and finer details, many of which cannot be immediately apparent. The same is true about scientific research. Investigators start with simple questions and later move to ask more complex ones. Even though some primary questions may continue to guide research for prolonged periods of time, the research methods that are used to answer the questions may change in the direction of increasing sophistication, leading to new findings and new questions. In this vein, one can think about the research enterprise in the area of child care as consisting of waves that rise and recede. The waves bring changes in investigators' conceptualization of critical questions, in the sophistication of research methodology, and in the historical reality pertaining to maternal employment and to the supply and demand for child care. We have borrowed the metaphor of "waves" and the parsing of the flow of the history of research in the area of child care from others who wrote before us (Belsky, 1984; Hayes, Palmer, & Zaslow, 1990).

The First Wave of Research

The research concerning the effects of child care was first guided by a general fear about the detrimental effects of separating children from their mothers. There was concern that the development of children in child care may be compromised similarly to the development of children separated from their mothers for weeks or for years, as was shown by the literature on institutionalized and hospitalized children. Children who experience long-term separations were believed to experience acute distress syndrome, conduct disorders, problems in forming relationships, and intellectual deficits (Bowlby, 1973; Freud & Burlingham, 1944, 1973; Goldfarb, 1943; Provence & Lipton, 1962; Ribble, 1965; Robertson & Robertson, 1971; Spitz, 1945; Wolkind, 1974). Although psychologists came to learn that the lack of human relationships and intellectual stimulation characteristic of institutions was very different from the experiences characteristic of childcare environments, questions about the effects of child care remained. Therefore, the scientists contributing to the early wave of research wanted to find out if the development of children experiencing nonparental care was different from the development of children who were not placed in child care. Did child care have different effects on children depending on their family background? Were childcare effects different in different developmental outcome domains (cognition, language, peer relations, relations with mother)? In response to these questions, the first wave of research provided the valuable information that childcare participation was not predominantly harmful to children's development, and in some cases was even beneficial (e.g., Barnett, 1995; Caughy et al., 1994; Frede, 1995; Hayes et al., 1990; Yoshikwa, 1995).

The first wave of research was based on comparisons between children in child care and children reared at home by their mother. These first-wave studies, however, had methodological limitations. For example, the children in nonmaternal care were drawn primarily from high-quality, often university-based childcare centers, which represent only one of several types of nonmaternal care. These studies rarely examined individual differences among children (such as the age, sex, race, temperament, or health status of the children; the number of hours children spent in care; or the age at which the children entered care). Furthermore, variations in the family background of the children or the impact of the family environment on the development of the children were not taken into consideration. Variations in family characteristics and childrearing practices may be responsible for both the choice of child care and for the developmental outcomes for children in child care. In fact, family research showed that variations in family characteristics are associated in a predictable way with variations in children's developmental outcomes (e.g., Belsky, 1990; Bradley, Caldwell, & Rock, 1988; Hart & Risley, 1995). Moreover, research in later waves shows that the circumstances and characteristics of a family are strong determinants of age of entry into child care, as well as the type and quality of child care that families choose for their children (e.g., Kontos, Howes, Shinn, & Galinsky, 1997; NICHD Early Child Care Research Network, 1997a; Singer, Fuller, Keiley, & Wolf, 1998). Consequently, it is possible that the results found in the first wave of studies could be attributed, at least partly, to variations in family circumstances and characteristics rather than to childcare participation.

Although the first wave of research focused on center-care programs, most infants and young children had not been enrolled in center-based care. Between 1965 and 1993 there has been a continuous increase in the percentage of children enrolled in center care during the first, second, and third year of their life (Hofferth, 1996). In 1995 7 percent of children were enrolled in childcare centers before they were 1 year of age, 11 percent of 1-year-olds, 19 percent of 2-year-olds, and 41 percent of 3-year-olds were enrolled in center care (National Center for Education Statistics [NCES], 1996). With these figures in mind, the extent to which one can generalize from the first wave of studies is not known. It would probably be unwise to use findings from these studies as a base for statements about the link between childcare homes, care by a relative, or care in the child's home by a non-relative and children's development. In addition, while these early studies were based on presumably model programs of high quality, the investigators did not actually examine the quality of the care that children received (e.g., Field, 1991, 1994). Yet, knowing the quality of the childcare setting is important. Childcare settings, like families, vary in terms of the quality of the environment and the care that they provide (Helburn, 1995; NICHD Early Child Care Research Network, in press). In the same way that the quality of the home environment has been shown to impact children's development, it is reasonable to expect that variations in the quality of the childcare environment will have an independent impact on the developmental outcomes of children. This idea propelled the second wave of studies regarding the effects of child care.

The Second Wave of Research

The second wave of research included key demographic variables in analyses and sampled from ethnically and economically diverse populations. It focused the scientific inquiry on the link between variations in the quality of childcare settings and the development of children. Quality was frequently assessed with composite measures that evaluated the optimal use of space, materials, and experience to enhance the daily schedules, supervision, and development of the children. The second wave of studies shows that higher quality of care is associated with better developmental outcomes both in the cognitive and the social domains. Most of the findings were from studies in which the quality of care data and the developmental outcome data were collected at the same time. For example, McCartney (1984) found that center quality, measured in terms of adult utterances to children, predicted children's concurrent scores on the Adaptive Language Inventory as well as their free speech samples. Howes and Olenick (1986) found that children in low-quality child care were less compliant and more resistant than those in higher-quality child care. But similar results were found in longitudinal studies, where quality of care affected developmental outcomes measured years later (Howes, 1988; Vandell, Henderson, & Wilson, 1988).

While the results of the second wave of research show that quality is an important predictor of developmental outcomes, they did not provide information about the relation between specific aspects of quality and specific developmental outcomes. Neither did they assess the magnitude of improvement of children's development that is associated with the quality of child care. These very encouraging findings from wave two about the positive effects of the global quality of child care have served as an invitation for further investigation of the features of quality of care, when, why, and for whom they influence developmental outcomes.

The Third Wave of Research

The third wave of childcare research focused on the linkages between family and childcare environments. The results were mixed. Some studies showed no relations between family demographic characteristics and quality of child care (e.g., Howes, 1983; Howes & Olenick, 1986; McCartney, Scarr, Phillips, Grajek, & Schwarz, 1982). Other studies showed that parental education, occupational status, income, values, and behaviors were associated with the quality of child care most children experienced (Anderson, Nagle, Roberts, & Smith, 1981; Goelman & Pence, 1987; Kontos & Fiene, 1987; NICHD Early Child Care Research Network, 1999c, 2000b). More favorable family circumstances and more child-oriented values and behaviors were associated with higher quality of care in childcare settings. Low-income families with access to subsidized child care were the exception, since their children, who frequently experienced stressful and otherwise compromised family circumstances, were placed in high-quality child care (Ruopp, Travers, Glantz, & Coelen, 1979; NICHD Early Child Care Research Network, 1997a). The ways in which both the characteristics of the family and the features of child care influence children's development were also addressed by investigators of third-wave studies (e.g., Clarke-Stewart, Gruber, & Fitzgerald, 1994). Another focus of the third wave of research was on the link between the age of entry into care and the children's developmental outcomes. Howes (1990) found that initiation of low-quality full-time care in the first year of life was associated with the most detrimental developmental outcomes. Lamb, Sternberg, and Prodromidis (1992) found that insecure attachments were more common among children who were enrolled in child care between the ages of 12 and 17 months rather than at earlier ages.

The Fourth Wave of Research

It was becoming clear to developmental psychologists, especially those influenced by Bronfenbrenner (e.g., Bronfenbrenner & Crouter, 1983) who emphasized the importance of studying the details of contexts of development, that child care is only one of the environments in which children spend time. Thus, its effects cannot be understood without an understanding of how childcare characteristics interact with other factors that shape children's development. There are many features within any one setting, all of which should be examined separately, yet in context, in order to understand how these features work to influence children's development. Investigators have generally agreed that studies of child care and of the effects of child care would need to include childcare settings that vary in quality and type (center, childcare homes, relative care, in-home care by non-relative). Such studies would need to focus on the development of children from all walks of life – children who vary in terms of their economic background, their ethnicity, and family structure. Also, both healthy children and those who have developmental disabilities would need to be included. The children's rearing environments (family and child care) would need to be studied at similar levels of detail. Different facets of the children's development would need to be examined over time. The follow-up study of the same children and the contexts of their development would allow conclusions to be drawn about changes over time in the care children receive at home and away from home. It would also provide the opportunity to learn how characteristics of the children's environments, as these unfold over time, influence the development of the children as they mature.

Yet, the best that could be done toward the goal of surmounting the limitations of small studies was to aggregate information from such studies. This was done through reviews of the scientific literature and through meta-analyses. Reviews of the literature or meta-analyses (Belsky, 1988, 1990; Clarke-Stewart, 1989; Lamb, 1997; Lamb et al., 1992) are based on published reports, each of which has its methodological limitations. Also, reviews of the scientific literature and meta-analyses are of necessity unrepresentative of the phenomena that they describe. This is the case because scientific literature, by definition, includes only studies in which statistically significant results have been found. Research that has not led to statistically significant results is not likely to have been published, even though the lack of statistically significant findings may reflect the fact that no effects exist – not only in the study, but perhaps also in the larger universe of events that the study samples or represents (Mann, 1990; Roggman, Langlois, Hubbs-Tait, &

Rieser-Danner, 1994). Given the limitations of reviews of small studies and of meta-analyses, scientists need to use designs that overcome the limitations of previous research. Prospective and comprehensive large-scale studies of diverse samples, or of nationally representative samples, could provide a balanced picture of the care that children receive, and how characteristics of such care influence child development, but such studies were not yet available.

In the absence of large and comprehensive prospective studies that could provide some of the information described above, investigators turned to the National Longitudinal Survey of Youth – Child Supplement (NLSY). This is an ongoing study with the purpose of collecting child development information on children born to female respondents of the 1979 cohort of the National Longitudinal Survey of Youth. By 1994 NLSY included data on the more than 10,000 children ever born to the female respondents from the 1979 cohort (West, Hauser, & Scanlan, 1998). The NLSY79 includes an overrepresentation of black, Hispanic and (through 1990) economically disadvantaged European American respondents. The wealth of information about the mothers, their children and families is in the public domain and available to interested individuals at low cost. Information regarding the 1979 cohort can be accessed at http://stats.bls.gov:80/nlsy79.htm and regarding the child and young adult data at http://www.chrr.ohio-state.edu/NLSY79-ChildYA/. The data afford analyses regarding the effects of parental characteristics and experiences on the well-being and the development of their children. Retrospective data about child care allow analyses about the effects of child care on the development of the children (Baydar & Brooks-Gunn, 1991; Belsky & Eggebeen, 1991; Mott, 1989). Likewise, the data set has been useful for answering questions about the relations between maternal employment and child care, policy issues and child care, and family choices about child care and childcare availability. (For publications based on the study, access http://www.chrr.ohio-state.edu/nls-bib).

Another example of a large data set that is amenable for analyses pertaining to the development of children of employed mothers is the British National Child Development Study (NCDS), which is described in the National Research Council report on longitudinal surveys of children (West et al., 1998). The sample size is approximately 16,500 and includes all persons born in England during the week of March 3–9, 1958. In 1991, a random sample of children of a third of the respondents was added. A recent report based on 1700 families from this data set addresses the links between maternal employment and children's reading, math, and behavioral adjustment in the second generation of NCDS (Joshi & Verropoulou, 1999; hj@cls.ioe.ac.uk).

Since it became apparent that answering the many important questions about child care and its effects would require large-scale prospective research, in 1989 the National Institute of Child Health and Human Development (NICHD) initiated the NICHD Study of Early Child Care (NICHD Early Child Care Research Network, 1998b, in press). Soon afterwards NICHD supported a parallel investigator-initiated study of children with developmental disabilities (Booth & Kelly, 1998, 1999a,b; Kelly & Booth, 1999). The NICHD Study of Early Child Care is the most comprehensive longitudinal study conducted to date to determine the conditions under which family and out-of-home experience enhance and/or undermine children's psychological and physical health over time. Toward this end, a large team of researchers, including psychologists and physicians from NICHD and from universities across the United States, have collaborated to study more than 1300 children born in 1991 in hospitals located in the vicinity of ten research sites. What is especially noteworthy about this work is its focus upon diverse families, diverse out-of-home experiences, and diverse scientific methods to measure experiences in the family, in child care, preschool, kindergarten, school, and after-school care. Diverse scientific methods were also applied to the study of the children's psychological and health development. Results to date pertain to quality of child care, the choices families make when selecting child care, and to the effects of family characteristics and childcare characteristics on the cognitive, social, and health development of children in the first three years of life. (For details see the next section.) Analyses are in progress regarding child development through first grade and new data collection pertaining to the middle childhood years is in progress. The data set with data from the children's first three years of life is now available for interested investigators. (For details about the study, access www.nichd.nih.gov/crmc/secc or contact friedmas@exchange.nih.gov.)

In light of the above discussion about the limitations of small studies, it is not surprising that the NICHD Study of Early Child Care published papers with results that indirectly question the validity of findings of smaller-scale studies. For example, the NICHD Study found that age of entry into child care, the number of hours children spend in child care, childcare quality, or the number of childcare settings children attended during the first 15 months of their life did not affect their security of attachment to their mothers. However, children of mothers who were at the low end of the continuum in terms of their sensitivity and responsiveness were at risk for insecure attachment when they were in more than minimal amounts of child care, more than one care arrangement, or in poor-quality care (NICHD Early Child Care Research Network, 1997b). Other examples are to be found in the next section.

While the NICHD Study of Early Child Care has a relatively large and diverse sample, it is not a nationally representative study. The Early Childhood Longitudinal Study Birth Cohort 2000 (ECLS2000) will provide information about a nationally representative sample of about 15,000 children born during the calendar year 2000. The sample will consist of children from various racial, ethnic, and socioeconomic backgrounds. ECLS2000 will provide national data about (1) the development of children from birth through first grade; (2) the transition to nonparental care, to early education programs, and to school; and (3) children's progress during preschool, kindergarten, and first grade. Like the NICHD Study of Early Child Care, the design of the ECLS2000 is guided by the ecological model, according to which children's development depends on the interaction between the child, family, care and education programs, and the community. Preliminary data are promised for the year 2002. (For further information, the e-mail contact is jerry_west@ed.gov.)

Another large study of child care was initiated in September, 1995 by the Administration on Children, Youth, and Families (ACYF). Approximately 3000 children under 12 months of age and their families were randomly assigned to the Early Head Start Program or a comparison group at 17 different sites in the United States. The families met Head Start eligibility guidelines and included approximately 10 percent infants and toddlers with disabilities. The Early Head Start Research and Evaluation Project has five components, one of which is an impact evaluation to study in depth the effects of the programs on children, parents, and families, using an experimental design descriptive study. The data set was released in the year 2000. (Further information can be obtained from jlove@mathematica-mpr.com.)

The fourth wave of research also includes randomized field trials designed to test various welfare and employment policies that include measures of parental psychological status, family functioning, parenting, nonparental care, and child outcomes. Examples include the New Chance Demonstration, the National Evaluation of Welfare to Work Strategies (formerly the JOBS Evaluation), the Self-Sufficiency Project, the New Hope Demonstration, and the Connecticut's Work-First Program. (The details regarding these and other similar studies are available on a website maintained by the Research Forum on Children, Families, and the New Federalism; http://www.researchforum.org.) For example, New Chance, a voluntary program available to young mothers on welfare in 16 sites across the United States, offered its participants education, training, free child care, and other services. A link between child care and mother-reported behavior problems was found (Bos & Granger, 1999). On examining the role of possible mediators in producing this finding, Bos and Granger found that instability in childcare arrangement might have caused the effect. In addition, the analyses suggested that center-based child care may benefit children, especially boys, as it increases their performance on a school readiness test.

The research methodology pertaining to child care and its links to child development has evolved over the years. It started with small studies of samples of convenience with no consideration to variations among children in terms of their family background and experiences. Child care was conceptualized as nonparental care or nonmaternal care, but variations in the childcare experience in terms of age of entry, hours of care, or quality of care were not considered in the early studies. Over the years researchers focused their attention on more and more aspects of the childcare setting and on the children's experiences in child care. Likewise, the idea that optimal conditions of child care may vary with the child's age influenced the assessments used for the evaluation of the childcare environment. The need to statistically control for family characteristics became more obvious and the assessments of family control variables became more differentiated with time. Questions about the specificity of quality and of the links between aspects of childcare quality and children's developmental outcomes came to dominate the research agenda. In parallel, researchers came to realize that child care and its links to developmental outcomes may vary for children from different family backgrounds or with different developmental limitations or needs. The increasing domination of the ecological theoretical model as a framework for studying human development on the one hand, and the increased interest in studying nationally representative samples on the other hand, have led to the most recent wave of large-scale longitudinal studies that collect data about child care as a tool that families use in rearing their children. Following is a brief description of the state of scientific knowledge about (1) the links between child care and children's development, and (2) the relations between family characteristics and the development of children who experienced child care in infancy.

The State of Knowledge about Child Care and Child Development

Most of the scientific literature regarding child care and developmental outcomes does not allow us to draw conclusions about the influence (causal effects) of child care on the development of children. The same literature can, however, tell us about the links or associations between child care and children's performance in different domains, such as the social, emotional, and cognitive areas of development. This is the case because in most of the studies that were conducted the researchers did not randomly assign children to the childcare group or to the exclusive maternal care group. Instead, children were studied in the settings that their parents selected for them; and, therefore, the findings may be due not to child care but rather to family characteristics that determine both the selection of child care and the developmental outcomes of children. It is known that the decisions of parents as to whether or not to place their children in child care are determined by family circumstances. Likewise, the decisions about the age at which the child is placed in child care, the number of hours the child spends in child care, and the quality of care that the child experiences are all determined by family characteristics such as family income, ethnicity, maternal attitudes, and the quality of mothering (NICHD Early Child Care Research Network, 1997a). These same family characteristics are also known to predict children's developmental outcomes (e.g., Baumrind, 1989; Bornstein & Tamis-LeMonda, 1989; Friedman & Cocking, 1986). In order to increase the likelihood that the links that are found between child care and children's outcomes are due to child care, recent studies have statistically controlled for the association between family variables and children's developmental outcomes. Yet, the study designs (natural history rather than experimental designs) and the analytical methods used limit our findings to ones pertaining to associations among variables and, consequently, interpretations of cause and effect are not warranted.

Child Care and the Development of Children Who Experienced Child Care in Infancy

Child care and security of attachment

One focus of intense investigation by researchers of child care was the relation between child care and the child's sense of trust in the mother (security of attachment). Building on Bowlby's theory of attachment (Bowlby, 1973), there was reason to be concerned about the possibility that routine daily separations from the mother would be associated with less opportunity for the infant and his or her mother to form close and warm relationships that are characterized by maternal sensitivity to the needs of the infant and the infant's trust in the mother as a source of security (Barglow, Vaughn, & Molitor, 1987; Jaeger & Weinraub, 1990; Owen & Cox, 1988). The studies that ensued indirectly validated the theoretically driven concern as shown by several analyses based on clusters of small studies (Belsky & Rovine, 1988; Clarke-Stewart, 1989; Lamb et al., 1992). For example, in the analysis by Belsky and Rovine (1988), 43 percent of the infants in early and extensive care were classified as insecurely attached to their mother, while only 26 percent of the infants with more limited childcare exposure were insecurely attached. The hypothesis that routine daily separations from the mother interfered with the cultivation of maternal sensitivity and the building of the child's trust in the mother was not directly validated, however. The studies did not evaluate maternal sensitivity and the findings could still be attributed to the childcare experience in itself. Relevant evidence comes from studies of mother–child interaction where the mother's sensitivity and responsiveness are evaluated. The majority of such studies did not find statistically significant links between the amount of child care and mothers' behaviors toward their young children (e.g., Burchinal, Bryant, Lee, & Ramey, 1992; Egeland & Heister, 1995). However, the NICHD Early Child Care Research Network (1999c) found that the more hours the child spent in child care, the less responsive the mother and the less engaged the child. Similar results are reported by Belsky (1999) and by investigators who focused on the first six months of life (Campbell, Cohn, & Meyers, 1995; Stifter, Coulehan, & Fish, 1993).

More recently, two studies (NICHD Early Child Care Research Network, 1997b; Roggman et al., 1994) failed to replicate the attachment findings from earlier studies. This lack of replication may be due to differences in the characteristics of the mothers participating in the early as compared to the more recent studies. There were more mothers in the workforce at the time the latter studies were conducted. In addition, there was greater cultural awareness about issues pertaining to child care and to the negotiation of women's dual roles as mothers and employees. These conditions may have allowed the mothers in the latter studies to be more confident about their employment and more sensitive to the needs of their children.

Child care, social competence, and behavior problems

Investigators of the association between child care and children's development were concerned about the possibility that children in child care may be less socially competent and have more behavior problems. Since families have an important role in socializing their children, it was argued that the role of the family might be diminished when children are in child care, thereby leading to less favorable outcomes among children in child care. Studies of the effects of maternal employment or of child care on the social adjustment of children found statistically significant associations between child care or maternal employment status and social adjustment, so that children in child care were at higher risk for poor social adjustment. The findings emerged in studies that controlled for family variables as well as in studies that did not have this methodological advantage (Baydar & Brooks-Gunn, 1991; Belsky, 1988, 1990; Crockenberg & Litman, 1991; Egeland & Heister, 1995). However, the NICHD Study of Early Child Care found little evidence that early, extensive, and continuous nonmaternal care was related to problematic child behavior (NICHD Early Child Care Research Network, 1998a). Finally, it found that among the childcare predictors, childcare quality was the most consistent predictor of child's social functioning, with better quality associated with better outcomes and lesser quality associated with poorer outcomes (NICHD Early Child Research Network, in press).

Child care and cognitive and language development

Not only were researchers concerned about the effects of child care on the socioemotional development of children, they were also concerned about the effects of child care on cognitive and language development. Socioemotional and cognitive/linguistic development are believed to be interdependent (e.g., Kopp, 1997; Lazarus, 1991; Lewis & Michalson, 1983). Therefore, the assumed disruption of the parent–child relationship due to extensive child care could lead to negative effects on cognitive development (e.g., van IJzendoorn, Dijkstra, & Bus, 1995). The evidence about the effects of *the amount of child care* on cognitive and language development has been mixed (e.g., Hayes et al., 1990; Lamb, 1997). Some studies reported a positive relation between the amount of infant care to school performance in middle childhood (Andersson, 1992; Broberg, Wessels, Lamb, & Hwang, 1997; Field, 1991). Some reported that early positive effects dissipated over time (Chin-Quee & Scarr, 1994). Others reported poorer later performance for children who received extensive child care when they were infants (Baydar & Brooks-Gunn, 1991; Joshi & Verropoulou, 1999; Vandell & Corasaniti, 1990). In the NICHD Study of Early Child Care, the relation between amount of child care in the first three years of life and the cognitive and linguistic performance of the children was not statistically significant (NICHD Early Child Care Research Network, 2000b). The picture emerging from studies of the relations between the *quality of child care* experienced during infancy and children's cognitive and language development is more consistent. Higher quality of care is associated with better performance (Burchinal et al., 1996; Galinsky, Howes, Kontos, & Shinn, 1994; Howes & Smith, 1995; Howes, Smith, & Galinsky, 1995; NICHD Early Child Care Research Network, 2000b; Phillips, McCartney, & Scarr, 1987). Moreover, children in child care were not found to perform less well than children in exclusive maternal care on assessments of cognitive and language development (NICHD Early Child Care Research Network, 2000b).

Summary

The scientific literature about the association between child care and child development is rather mixed and difficult to summarize. The mixed findings are partly due to the fact that most of the studies were based on small and homogeneous samples of children. Perhaps the only thread that runs through the various studies is that the quality of the childcare environment makes a difference. That is, high-quality care is associated with better developmental outcomes.

Relations between Family Characteristics and the Development of Children Who Experienced Child Care in Infancy

Family circumstances, as well as specific maternal attributes, attitudes, and behaviors, have been found to influence the development of children who are in child care (e.g., Clarke-Stewart et al., 1994; NICHD Early Child Care Research Network, 1998b, 1999c, 2000b). More privileged environments, with more economic resources, higher maternal educational level, higher-quality homes, more sensitive and cognitively stimulating mothers were associated with better psychological outcomes for children who were in child care during their infancy. These results are similar to findings pertaining to children who are not in child care (e.g., Baumrind, 1989; Bornstein & Tamis-LeMonda, 1989; Friedman & Cocking, 1986). Evidence from a number of studies (Barglow et al., 1987; Jaeger & Weinraub, 1990; Owen & Cox, 1988) suggested that nonparental care experience in the early years might attenuate the influence of families on the development of their children. Howes (1990) found that parental involvement and persistence in managing children's behaviors were consistently stronger predictors of social and cognitive developmental outcomes of preschool and kindergarten children who were not placed in child care in infancy than they were for children who experienced infant child care. Dunham and Dunham (1992) found that maternal verbal behavior when the children were 13 months of age was predictive of children's vocabulary for children who were not in child care but not for children in extensive child care. However, findings from the NICHD Study of Early Child Care suggest that family characteristics predict to the development of all children (NICHD Early Child Care Research Network, 1998b). The NICHD study compared matrices of correlations between family predictors and developmental outcomes for children in extensive child care (>30 hours per week) and for children in exclusive maternal care (<10 hours of child care per week). No differences between the matrices were found. In other words, family demographic, personality/attitudinal and mothering/relationship variables predicted social and cognitive developmental outcomes similarly, regardless of the amount of time in care.

Directions for Future Research

Despite the growing body of research on child care and its links to maternal employment and to children's development, gaps still remain in our knowledge base. The focus of current research needs to be expanded to include more infants and toddlers, more economically disadvantaged children, more ethnic minority children (in the United States these include African American, Asian American/Pacific Islander, Native American/American Indian, and Hispanic/Latino children), and more children with developmental disabilities. Since child care ought to help families rear their children, there is a need to better understand the families of children in child care, their expectations from child care, and the influence that child care has on these families. There is also a need for conceptual work and scientific research about the features of quality of child care for children of different cultural backgrounds. The ecological perspective (Bronfenbrenner & Crouter, 1983) indicates that the effects of child care are not independent of sociocultural and sociopolitical contexts such as the family, social and public policies, culture, belief systems, and societal values (Swadener & Bloch, 1997). In the following section, we offer suggestions to (1) expand the research focus on child care to include a broader ecological perspective and (2) sharpen the research focus on childcare quality.

Expanding the Research Focus to Include a More Diverse Group of Children

While some societies are quite homogeneous in their populations (e.g., Japan and Denmark), other societies are characterized by diversity, due either to a long history or to recent migrations (e.g., the United States and the European Union). Racial and ethnic diversity are associated with differences in childrearing values and goals which have their origins in historical and cultural differences. Yet, the scholarly literature about child care in countries characterized by diversity has not addressed the question as to whether or not parents should seek to share the responsibility of transmitting their cultural values with the people who help them rear their children while the parents are at work.

Consider the case of the United States, where historically the social fabric has been ethnically and culturally diverse. The history of maternal employment and of child care for the different segments of American society has not been the same. African American women were more dependent than other women on income that they could generate themselves and entered the workforce before European American women (J. McAdoo, 1993). Consequently, the experience of African American families with nonmaternal care has a longer and more extensive history than the experience of families from other groups. That experience is not well documented and has not guided research about the expectations of families, the quality of care children have been receiving, and the links between child care for African Americans and the development of African American children. At present, in the United States children of color, particularly immigrant children, constitute the fastest-growing segment of the US population (H. McAdoo, 1993; The Urban Institute, 1999). Yet, these children and their families are underrepresented in the current scientific literature on child care and child development. The cultural values associated with childrearing among African Americans, Asian Americans, Native Americans, and Hispanic/Latinos are overlapping with but not identical to those among European Americans (for review, see Parke, 1997). These cultural differences as well as differences in the language the child hears and uses at home have implications for the expectations that parents may have for child care (Buriel & Hurtado, 1998). Likewise, they may have important implications for the promoting or inhibiting nature of the childcare environment into which children must fit (Garcia Coll et al., 1996). While there has been some public debate about the extent to which schools should foster the language and cultural heritage of Hispanic/Latino and African American children, the discussion about culturally related practices has only recently emerged in relation to child care and has not been investigated scientifically. Having reviewed the literature about child care, Johnson, Jaeger, Randolph, Cauce, and the NICHD Early Child Care Research Network (working paper) have concluded that research on child care for racial/ethnic minorities deserves special scrutiny.

There is also an increasing need for research about the role of infant child care in the development of children from diverse economic backgrounds. In particular, an expanded focus is needed for two groups of children: those whose families are on welfare and children in working poor families who do not take up (or are ineligible for) public assistance. Recent changes in maternal employment and childcare rates in the United States are associated with a law enacting welfare reform – the Personal Responsibility and Work Opportunity Reconciliation Act of 1996 (PRWORA). As already described earlier in this chapter, the law requires that persons who enroll in the welfare program, even single mothers of infants and toddlers, must enter the workforce, and to do so, must attend school or job training, beginning in some cases as early as six weeks after the child's birth. Moreover, there is now a lifetime limit on the number of years that an individual/family may be on the welfare rolls, although some exemptions apply. Prior to the 1996 PRWORA, welfare parents with infants and toddlers could stay at home with their children, or if they desired to work or seek job training they were guaranteed childcare assistance. The impact of welfare reform on the childcare market has been an increasing demand for slots, particularly for infants and toddlers. Some of this demand is met through subsidies to existing centers and family day-care homes that are licensed or regulated. However, it is expected that a large part of the demand is being (and will continue to be) met by placing children in unregulated settings of unknown quality. Research is sorely needed to examine the impact of child care on these children's development.

Although in the United States one-sixth of all poor children live in families who rely solely on public assistance for income (National Center for Children in Poverty, 1999), many young children live in working poor families. Children in working poor families are defined as those whose parents are working at least 35 hours (combined for two parents) in two-parent families, or in the case of a single-parent family, the parent is working at least 20 hours a week; and the family income is below the poverty line ($16,036 for a family of four in 1996; Child Trends, 1999). Recent research shows that family income is linked to age of entry of children into care, number of hours children spend in care, type of care (e.g., center, family day-care home, etc.), and to quality of care (Kontos et al., 1997; NICHD Early Child Care Research Network, 1997a; Phillips, 1995). Additional research is needed to examine the independent and combined contributions of poverty/low income status and various childcare features on very young children's development (NICHD Early Child Care Research Network, 1999a,b; Phillips, 1995).

Children with developmental disabilities have received very limited attention from childcare researchers (see Booth & Kelly, 1998, 1999a,b). Infants with disabilities include those with developmental delays of unknown origins, infants with Down's syndrome, and those with delays due to causes such as severe respiratory distress syndrome, abnormal neurological signs, severe chronic illness, neonatal seizures, and failure to thrive. Infants with disabilities start child care at later ages than other children, they are in care for fewer hours, they are more frequently cared for by a relative than by a non-relative or are in more formal care arrangements (Booth & Kelly, 1998). One of the most important problems reported by parents of children with disabilities pertains to child care (Axtell, Garwick, Patterson, Bennet & Blum, 1995; Bailey, Blasco, & Simeonsson, 1992; Freedman, Litchfield & Warfield, 1995; Herman & Thompson, 1995; Horner, Rawlins & Giles, 1987; Palfrey, Walker, Butler, & Singer, 1989). The issue of childcare availability is particularly acute since childcare providers are not always able or willing to accept children with special needs into their care arrangements (e.g., Berk & Berk, 1982; Chang & Teramoto, 1987). Parents are also faced with logistical problems such as distance from home or transportation between programs, or with caregivers who are not well trained to provide optimal care for their children (Klein & Sheehan, 1987). The number of problems that families face increases with the severity of their children's disability. Thus, while families of children with special needs account for a small percentage of the population, they are in need of child care and there needs to be a scientifically based understanding of the conditions under which these children thrive.

Expanding Research on the Families of Children Who Are in Child Care, on Care Providers, and Employers

When childcare researchers started to take into account differences among the families of the children in child care, they first focused on the socioeconomic status of the family but ignored family structure and sociocultural factors and their links to child care and child outcomes. The merit of including family structure variables is based on results from demographic research. Hofferth et al. (1991) found that mother-only families use childcare centers at higher rates than two-parent families (38 percent vs. 26 percent for children under 5), and have lower rates of parental care (1 percent vs. 31 percent). Further, mothers in mother-only families worked more hours per week than mothers in two-parent families (40 hours vs. 33 hours). Race/ethnicity was found to be related to family structure and maternal hours of employment. African American and Hispanic/Latino families were more likely than European American families to be extended (i.e., include intergenerational members; Hofferth et al., 1991). African American mothers worked more time than other mothers did, probably because they are more likely to be in mother-only families. Therefore, the interplay of these family structural and sociocultural factors as linked to childcare decisions and childcare consequences may lead to a deeper understanding of the links between families, child care, and child development.

In addition to focusing on the family socioeconomic status, investigators of child care have recently focused on the role of the mother in relation to child care and the development of children who are in child care. That focus led to the examination of maternal attributes, attitudes, and behaviors. We recommend that the role and influence of other family members also be considered in this research arena.

Family decisions about child care are frequently thought about as mothers' decisions. The extent to which this is true needs to be investigated. For example, Parke (1997) reports on the prominent role that African American grandmothers and husband-father figures have in making childrearing decisions. So, both parents and other kin may be important in shaping family decisions about when to start care, for how many hours, what type of care to select, and what quality of care to look for. It is also worth studying the extent to which being cared for by people with whom the mother and her children will continue to be in touch in contexts other than child care is the same as being cared for by people who interact with the child and his or her parents only over the business of child care.

We also believe that research needs to include a focus on family characteristics that have been neglected before. Here we refer to family cohesion, family strengths (e.g., routines, rituals, social support), family conflict, household and family composition, parents' mental health, parents' race/ethnicity, country of origin, assimilation and acculturation.

This is particularly important in the United States, where it is projected that from the year 2000, the majority of children will be of ethnic minority descent (primarily Hispanic/Latino, African American, and Asian American; Fisher, Jackson, & Villarruel, 1998). The growing number of immigrant children who come primarily from poorer and frequently wartorn countries will further contribute to the growing need for considering the above characteristics of families in research about the role of families and of child care in the development of children.

The scientific literature has focused primarily on the effects of child care on the development of children who are in child care. But one may want to consider the relation between child care and (1) the mother's well-being, (2) the childcare provider for whom child care is a place of employment, and (3) the mother's employer who is concerned about the continuity and stability of the work environment. For example, it has been hypothesized that childcare availability and affordability affect the well-being of mothers and fathers (Mason & Duberstein, 1992). Another hypothesis pertaining to child care and maternal well-being is that when children are in poor-quality child care, mothers are more stressed and less sensitive to the needs of their children (Jaeger & Weinraub, 1990). (Alternative ideas about the topic of child care and parents' well-being can be found in Galinsky, 1992; Phillips, 1992; Presser, 1992.) Providers are probably less stressed when they are well paid and their working environment is supportive of their professional needs (Phillips, Howes, & Whitebook, 1991). Perhaps employers would be more satisfied when children are in child care because mothers would be more focused on their job and less frequently absent from the job (Wolcott, 1990). So, the quality of child care should be evaluated not only in terms of its ability to enhance the developmental outcomes of children, but also in terms of the extent to which it serves as a stabilizing force in families and at the workplace.

Expanding Research on Quality of Child Care

If one assumes that quality features of child care are those features that are known or expected to lead to desired developmental outcomes, then our knowledge about features of quality of care is large yet limited. The outcomes that psychologists and educators identified pertain to the infant attachment to his or her mother and to the childcare provider; they pertain to the sensitivity of the mother to her child during mother–child interaction, to peer relations, to social competence, compliance, problem behavior, cognitive and language development. Pediatricians have focused on freedom from minor childhood illness as an important outcome for children in child care. So, the psychological scientific literature has information about the extent to which adult:child ratio, group size, provider education, provider attitudes and behaviors are linked to the outcomes that European and European American psychologists have been interested in. The pediatric scientific literature focuses on hygiene as a predictor of health in child care. Parents who are interested in learning about the effects of child care on the moral development of their children, or on the extent to which their children will have knowledge about and pride in their family cultural traditions, will not find scientific literature on these topics. Yet, the transmission of moral values and of the traditions of the culture are at the heart of childrearing.

The definition of quality is particularly difficult in a diverse society when different segments of the society have different childrearing practices and goals. In the United States, an important socialization goal of ethnic minority parents is fostering a sense of ethnic pride in children (Harrison, Wilson, Pine, Chan, & Buriel, 1990). Inculcating such pride may be difficult if the childcare environment celebrates the mainstream culture and ignores the children's ethnic culture. In the United States, childcare settings are expected to be authoritative, that is, democratic such that limits are negotiated in cooperation by the adult and the child (Baumrind, 1989), and to discipline children verbally. But African American parents favor physical punishment that is not coupled with the withdrawal of affection (Parke, 1997). Chinese American parents believe in strict discipline in the context of deep caring and teaching right from wrong (Parke, 1997). Consequently, their teaching and discipline style appear more controlling than that of European American parents. Given their childrearing values, African American and Chinese American parents may be less than fully satisfied with authoritative childcare settings. Latino families value social skills as much as or more than they value cognitive skills. They discourage competitive behavior that sets the child apart from the group (Parke, 1997). Their emphasis on cooperation and social sensitivity may differ, at least to some extent, from the emphasis that mainstream American culture places on the same values. The disparity in emphasis or in values may, in turn, lead to dissatisfaction with childcare settings adopting the mainstream culture. The implications of being reared in a family and a childcare setting that inculcate somewhat different values are unknown at this time.

The costs of high-quality care are high and are more so the younger the children. The costs of high-quality care are high (Willer, 1990) because quality is determined by the ratio of adults to children, the size of the group of children being cared for, the education of the childcare provider, and the training of the provider in child development (National Association for the Education of Young Children, 1991). From a societal point of view, the investment required in providing high-quality child care seems prohibitive (Haskins, 1992). So, some policy makers in the United States are looking for guidelines that will tell them what is the minimum of quality that will not harm children. If one goes on the assumption that childcare quality at a minimum ought to provide children with the benefits that exclusive maternal care would, then the quality of care would vary from one child to another. This is the case because families vary in the quality of mothering they provide. Clearly it is unrealistic to wish to provide children with quality of care that is tailored to match or exceed the quality of care provided by their own mothers. Rather, one would want to provide policy makers with (1) tools for evaluating the developmental benefits of different levels of compliance with childcare quality standards (NICHD Early Child Care Research Network, 1999a) and with (2) the dollar investments required for the implementation of such standards.

Expanding Research about Parents' Knowledge and Decision Making Regarding Child Care

In societies characterized by cultural diversity, there is clearly a need to have scientifically gathered information about what parents from different segments of our society consider to be goals of quality child care. Likewise, there is a need to obtain information regarding what parents know about the childcare characteristics that promote these goals. At present, few parents are aware of knowledge generated by scientists regarding child care, and many families are unaware of the importance of their selection of child care with specific characteristics for the child's later personal development and for his or her later contribution to society (Honig, 1995). Those interested in applied research could develop and evaluate programs designed to convey the lessons learned from the scientific research on quality child care to parents and other consumers.

Conclusion

Child care as a social institution is a product of economic realities and social changes that have led to a steady increase over the last 30 years in the participation of women in the workforce. It has come into being to help families with their childrearing responsibilities. Child care, like family, is not one and the same for all. It reflects the societal and personal values and the resources of the people that create it and participate in it. Like family, it is a human creation, which, in turn, shapes the life of its creators. Because child care is both a societal product and a childrearing tool, its characteristics and its influences will need to be continuously reinvented and evaluated. This chapter is aimed at summarizing what we know to date and what we think we need to learn in the future in order to maximize the usefulness of child care to the society it serves.

References

Anderson, C. W., Nagle, R. J., Roberts, W. A., & Smith, J. W. (1981). Attachment to substitute caregivers as a function of center quality and caregiver involvement. *Child Development, 52,* 53–61.

Andersson, B. E. (1992). Effects of day-care on cognitive and socioemotional competence of thirteen-year-old Swedish school children. *Child Development, 63,* 20–36.

Anonymous. (1995). Twelve trends carry Latin America through the 1990s: Part V. *Market Latin America, 3,* 11.

Axtell, S. A. M., Garwick, A. W., Patterson, J., Bennett, F. C., & Blum, R. W. (1995). Unmet service needs of families of young children with chronic illnesses and disabilities. *Journal of Family and Economic Issues, 16,* 395–411.

Bachu, A. (1995). *Fertility of American women: June 1994* (US Bureau of Census Current Population Report P20-482). Washington, DC: US Government Printing Office.

Bailey, D. B., Blasco, P. M., & Simeonsson, R. J. (1992). Needs expressed by mothers and fathers of young children with disabilities. *American Journal on Mental Retardation, 97,* 1–10.

Barglow, P., Vaughn, B. E., & Molitor, N. (1987). Effects of maternal absence due to employment on the quality of infant–mother attachment in a low-risk sample. *Child Development, 58,* 945–954.

Barnett, W. S. (1995). Long-term effects of early childhood programs on cognitive and school outcomes. *The Future of Children, 5,* 25–50.

Baumrind, D. (1989). Rearing competent children. In W. Damon (Ed.), *Child development today and tomorrow* (pp. 349–378). San Francisco: Jossey-Bass.

Baydar, N., & Brooks-Gunn, J. (1991). Effects of maternal employment and child-care arrangements on preschoolers' cognitive and behavioral outcomes: Evidence from the children of the National Longitudinal Survey of Youth. *Developmental Psychology, 27*, 932–945.

Beckett, J. O. (1982). Working women: A historical review of racial differences. *The Black Sociologist, 9*, 5–27.

Belsky, J. (1984). Two waves of day care research: Developmental effects and conditions of quality. In R. C. Ainsle (Ed.), *The child and the day care setting: Qualitative variations and development* (pp. 1–34). New York: Praeger.

Belsky, J. (1988). Infant day care and socioemotional development: The United States. *Journal of Child Psychology and Psychiatry and Allied Disciplines, 29*, 397–406.

Belsky, J. (1990). Parental and nonparental child care and children's socioemotional development: A decade in review. *Journal of Marriage and the Family, 52*, 885–904.

Belsky, J. (1999). Quantity of nonmaternal care and boys' problem behavior/adjustment at ages 3 and 5: Exploring the mediating role of parenting. *Psychiatry, 62*, 1–20.

Belsky, J., & Eggebeen, D. (1991). Early and extensive maternal employment and young children's socioemotional development: Children of the National Longitudinal Survey of Youth. *Journal of Marriage and the Family, 53*, 1083–1098. [Reprinted in D. DelCampo & R. DelCampo (Eds.), *Taking sides: Clashing views on controversial issues in childhood and society.* New York: Dushkin/McGraw-Hill, 1997.]

Belsky, J., & Rovine, M. J. (1988). Nonmaternal care in the first year of life and the security of infant–parent attachment. *Child Development, 59*, 157–167.

Berk, H. J., & Berk, M. L. (1982). A survey of day care centers and their services for handicapped children. *Child Care Quarterly, 11*, 211–214.

Bloch, M. N. (1996, October). *Age, stage, and grade: Transitions in development and schooling in Russian early schooling.* Paper presented at the International Conference on Vygotsky and Education, Moscow, Russia.

Booth, C. L., & Kelly, J. F. (1998). Child care characteristics of infants with and without special needs: Comparisons and concerns. *Early Childhood Research Quarterly, 13*, 603–621.

Booth, C. L., & Kelly, J. F. (1999a). Child care and employment in relation to infants' disabilities and risk factors. *American Journal on Mental Retardation, 104*(2), 117–130.

Booth, C. L., & Kelly, J. F. (1999b, April). *Child care for children at risk and with disabilities: Links with development at 30 months.* Poster presentation at the Society for Research in Child Development Biannual Conference, Albuquerque, NM.

Bornstein, M. H., & Tamis-LeMonda, C. S. (1989). Maternal responsiveness and cognitive development in children. In M. H. Bornstein (Ed.), *Maternal responsiveness: Characteristics and consequences. New directions for child development, 43* (pp. 49–61). San Francisco: Jossey-Bass.

Bos, J. M., & Granger, R. C. (1999, April). *Estimating effects of day care use on child outcomes: Evidence from the New Chance Demonstration.* Paper presented for the Biennial Meeting of the Society for Research in Child Development, Albuquerque, NM.

Bowlby, J. (1973). *Attachment and loss: Vol. 2. Separation.* New York: Basic Books.

Bradley, R. H., Caldwell, B. M., & Rock, S. L. (1988). Home environment and school performance: A ten-year follow-up and examination of three models of environmental action. *Child Development, 59*, 852–867.

Brazelton, T. B. (1986). Issues for working parents. *American Journal of Orthopsychiatry, 56*, 14–25.

Bredekamp, S. (1986). The reliability and validity of the Early Childhood Observation Scale for accrediting early childhood programs. *Early Childhood Research Quarterly, 1*, 103–118.

Broberg, A. G., Wessels, H., Lamb, M. E., & Hwang, C. P. (1997). Effects of day care on the development of cognitive abilities in 8-year-olds: A longitudinal study. *Developmental Psychology, 33,* 62–69.

Bronfenbrenner, U. (1988). Interacting systems in human development. *Persons in context: Developmental processes* (pp. 25–49). New York: Cambridge University Press.

Bronfenbrenner, U. (1999). Environments in developmental perspective: Theoretical and operational models. In S. L. Friedman & T. D. Wachs (Eds.), *Measuring environment across the life span: Emerging methods and concepts* (pp. 3–28). Washington, DC: American Psychological Association.

Bronfenbrenner, U., & Crouter, A. C. (1983). The evolution of environmental models in developmental research. In W. Kessen (Series Ed.) & P. H. Mussen (Vol. Ed.), *Handbook of child psychology: Vol. 1. History, theory, and methods* (4th ed., pp. 357–414). New York: Wiley.

Bryson, L. (1989). The proletarianization of women: Gender justice in Australia? *Social Justice, 16,* 87–102.

Burchinal, M. R., Bryant, D. M., Lee, M. W., & Ramey, C. T. (1992). Early day care, infant–mother attachment, and maternal responsiveness in the infant's first year. *Early Childhood Research Quarterly, 7,* 383–396.

Burchinal, M. R., Roberts, J. E., Nabors, L. A., & Bryant, D. M. (1996). Quality of center child care and infant cognitive and language development. *Child Development, 67,* 606–620.

Buriel, R., & Hurtado, M. (1998). *Child care in the Latino community: Needs, preferences, and access.* Claremont, CA: Tomás Rivera Policy Institute.

Caldwell, B. M., Sartorius, N., Orley, J., Banaag, C. J., Hardeman, W. J., Jegede, R. O., & Tsiantis, J. (1990). *WHO Child Care Facility Schedule.* Unpublished manuscript, University of Arkansas at Little Rock.

Campbell, S. B., Cohn, J. F., & Meyers, T. (1995). Depression in first-time mothers: Mother–infant interaction and depression chronicity. *Developmental Psychology, 31,* 349–357.

Casper, L. M. (1996). Who is minding our preschoolers? *Current Population Reports* (Series 70, No. 53). Washington, DC: US Bureau of the Census.

Casper, L. M., Hawkins, M., & O'Connell, M. (1994). *Who's minding the kids? Child care arrangements, Fall 1991.* Washington, DC: Bureau of the Census.

Caughy, M. O., DiPietro, J., & Strobino, D. M. (1994). Day care participation as a protective factor in the cognitive development of low income children. *Child Development, 65,* 457–471.

Chang, A., & Teramoto, R. (1987). Children with special needs in private day care centers. *Child and Youth Care Quarterly, 16,* 60–67.

Cherlin, A. J. (1999). *Public and private families.* Boston, MA: McGraw-Hill.

Child Trends. (1999). *Working poor families with children: A statistical portrait.* Washington, DC: Child Trends Research Brief.

Chin-Quee, D. S., & Scarr, S. (1994). Lack of early child care effects on school-age children's social competence and academic achievement. *Early Development and Parenting, 3,* 58.1–58.10.

Clarke-Stewart, K. A. (1987). Predicting child development from child care forms and features: The Chicago study. In D. A. Phillips (Ed.), *Quality in child care: What does research tell us?* (pp. 21–42). Washington, DC: National Association for the Education of Young Children.

Clarke-Stewart, K. A. (1989). Infant day care: Maligned or malignant? *American Psychologist, 44,* 266–273.

Clarke-Stewart, K. A., Gruber, C. P., & Fitzgerald, L. M. (1994). *Children at home and in day care.* Hillsdale, NJ: Erlbaum.

Coleman, M. T., & Pencavel, J. (1993). Trends in market work behavior of women since 1940. *Industrial and Labor Relations Review, 46,* 653–676.

Crockenberg, S., & Litman, C. (1991). Effects of maternal employment on maternal and 2-year-old child behavior. *Child Development, 62,* 930–953.

Dunham, P., & Dunham, F. (1992). Lexical development during middle infancy: A mutually driven infant–caregiver process. *Developmental Psychology, 28,* 414–420.

Dunn, L. (1993). Proximal and distal features of day care quality and children's development. *Early Childhood Research Quarterly, 8,* 167–192.

Egeland, B., & Heister, M. (1995). The long-term consequences of infant day-care and mother–infant attachment. *Child Development, 66,* 474–485.

Field, T. (1991). Quality infant day care and grade school behavior and performance. *Child Development, 62,* 863–870.

Field, T. M. (1994). Infant day care facilitates later social behavior and school performance. In H. Goelman, E. Jacob, et al. (Eds.), *Children's play in child care settings: SUNY series children's play in society* (pp. 69–84). Albany, NY: State University of New York.

Fiene, R., & Nixon, M. (1985). The instrument based program monitoring information system and the indicator checklist for child care. *Child Care Quarterly, 14,* 198–214.

Fisher, C. B., Jackson, J. F., & Villarruel, F. A. (1998). The study of African American and Latin American children and youth. In W. Damon & R. M. Lerner (Eds.), *Handbook of child psychology: Vol. 1. Theoretical models of human development* (5th ed., pp. 1145–1207). New York: Wiley.

Frede, E. C. (1995). The role of program quality in producing early childhood program benefits. *The Future of Children, 5,* 115–132.

Freedman, R., Litchfield, L., & Warfield, M. E. (1995). Balancing work and family responsibilities: Perspectives of parents of children with developmental disabilities. *Families in Society: The Journal of Contemporary Human Services, 76,* 507–514.

Freud, A., & Burlingham, D. T. (1944). *Infants without families: The case for and against residential nurseries.* New York: International Universities Press.

Freud, A., & Burlingham, D. T. (1973). *Infants without families: Reports on the Hampstead Nurseries, 1939–1945.* New York: International Universities Press.

Friedman, S. L., & Amadeo, J. (1999). The child care environment: Conceptualizations, assessments, and issues. In S. L. Friedman & T. D. Wachs (Eds.), *Measuring environment across the life span: Emerging methods and concepts* (pp. 127–165). Washington, DC: American Psychological Association.

Friedman, S. L., & Cocking, R. R. (1986). Instructional influences on cognition and on the brain. In S. L. Friedman, K. A. Klivington, & R. W. Peterson (Eds.), *The brain, cognition, and education* (pp. 319–346). Orlando, FL: Academic Press.

Fullerton, H. N. (1999). Labor force participation: 75 years of change, 1950–98 and 1998–2025. *Monthly Labor Review Online, 122*(12); http://stats.bls.gov/opub/mlr/1999/12/art.labs.htm.

Galinsky, E. (1992). The impact of child care on parents. In A. Booth (Ed.), *Child care in the 1990's: Trends and consequences* (pp. 159–171). Hillsdale, NJ: Erlbaum.

Galinsky, E., Howes, C., Kontos, S., & Shinn, M. (1994). *The study of children in family child care and relative care: Highlights of findings.* New York: Families and Work Institute.

Garcia Coll, C., Crnic, K., Lamberty, G., Wasik, B. H., Jenkins, R., Garcia, H. V., & McAdoo, H. P. (1996). An integrative model for the study of developmental competencies in minority children. *Child Development, 67,* 1891–1914.

Goelman, H., & Pence, A. (1987). Effects of child care, family, and individual characteristics on children's language development: The Victoria Day Care Research Project. In D. A. Phillips (Ed.), *Quality in child care: What does research tell us?* (pp. 89–104). Washington, DC: National Association for the Education of Young Children.

Goldfarb, W. (1943). The effects of early institutional care on adolescent personality. *Journal of Experimental Education, 12,* 106–129.

Gustafsson, S. S., & Stafford, F. P. (1995). Links between early childhood programs and maternal employment in three countries. *The Future of Children, 5,* 161–174.

Harms, T., & Clifford, R. (1980). *Early childhood environmental rating scale.* New York: Teachers College Press, Columbia University.

Harms, T., & Clifford, R. (1984). *The family day care rating scale.* New York: Teachers College Press, Columbia University.

Harms, T., Cryer, D., & Clifford, R. (1990). *The infant/toddler environment rating scale.* New York: Teachers College Press, Columbia University.

Harrison, A. O., Wilson, M. N., Pine, C. J., Chan, S. Q., & Buriel, R. (1990). Family ecologies of ethnic minority children. *Child Development, 61,* 347–362.

Hart, B., & Risley, T. (1995). *Meaningful differences in the everyday experience of young American children.* Baltimore: Brookes.

Haskins, R. (1992). Is anything more important than day-care quality? In A. Booth (Ed.), *Child care in the 1990's: Trends and consequences* (pp. 101–115). Hillsdale, NJ: Erlbaum.

Hayes, C. D., Palmer, J. L., & Zaslow, M. J. (1990). *Who cares for America's children?* Washington, DC: National Academy Press.

Helburn, S. W. (Ed.). (1995). *Cost, quality and child outcomes in child care centers* (Tech. Rep.). Denver: University of Colorado at Denver, Center for Research in Economic and Social Policy, Department of Economics.

Herman, S. E., & Thompson, L. (1995). Families' perceptions of their resources for caring for children with developmental disabilities. *Mental Retardation, 33,* 73–83.

Hofferth, S. L. (1992). The demand for and supply of child care in the 1990s. In A. Booth (Ed.), *Child care in the 1990's: Trends and consequences* (pp. 3–26). Hillsdale, NJ: Erlbaum.

Hofferth, S. L. (1996). Child care in the United States today. *The Future of Children, 6,* 41–61.

Hofferth, S. L., Brayfield, A., Deich, S., & Holcomb, P. (1991). *National Child Care Survey, 1990.* Washington, DC: The Urban Institute.

Honig, A. S. (1995). Choosing child care for young children. M. H. Bornstein (Ed.), *Handbook of parenting: Vol. 4. Applied and practical parenting* (pp. 411–435). Mahwah, NJ: Lawrence Erlbaum Associates.

Horner, M., Rawlins, P., & Giles, K. (1987). How parents of children with chronic conditions perceive their own needs. *American Journal of Maternal Child Nursing, 12,* 40–43.

Howes, C. (1983). Caregiver behavior in center and family day care. *Journal of Applied Developmental Psychology, 4,* 99–107.

Howes, C. (1988). Relations between early child care and schooling. *Developmental Psychology, 24,* 53–57.

Howes, C. (1990). Can the age of entry into child care and the quality of child care predict adjustment in kindergarten? *Developmental Psychology, 26,* 292–303.

Howes, C., & Olenick, M. (1986). Family and child care influences on toddlers' compliance. *Child Development, 57,* 202–216.

Howes, C., & Smith, E. W. (1995). Relations among child care quality, teacher behavior, children's play activities, emotional security, and cognitive activity in child care. *Early Childhood Research Quarterly, 10,* 381–404.

Howes, C., Smith, E., & Galinsky, E. (1995). *The Florida Child Care Quality Improvement Study.* New York: Families and Work Institute.

Hunter, A. G., Pearson, J. L., Ialongo, N. S., & Kellam, S. G. (1998). Parenting alone to multiple caregivers: Child care and parenting arrangements in Black and White urban families. *Family Relations: Interdisciplinary Journal of Applied Family Studies, 47,* 343–353.

Jaeger, E., & Weinraub, M. (1990). Early nonmaternal care and infant attachment: In search of process. *New Directions for Child Development, 49,* 71–90.

Joshi, H., & Verropoulou, G. (1999, October 13). *Maternal employment and child outcomes: Analyses of the NCDS (1958 Birth Cohort) second generation.* Presented at the Equality Action Seminar, 11 Downing Street, London, England.

Kallos, D., & Tallberg Broman, I. (1997) Swedish child care and early education. *Early Education and Development, 8,* 265–284.

Kelly, J. F., & Booth, C. I. (1999). Child care for infants with special needs: Issues and applications. *Infants and Young Children, 12,* 26–33.

Klein, P. S., & Feurestein, R. (1985). Environmental variables and cognitive development: Identification of the potent factors in adult–child interaction. In S. H. Harel & N. J. Anastasiow (Eds.), *The at-risk infant.* Baltimore: Paul Brookes.

Klein, N., & Sheehan, R. (1987). Staff development: A key issue in meeting the needs of young handicapped children in day care settings. *Topics in Early Childhood Special Education, 7,* 13–27.

Kontos, S. J. (1991). Child care quality, family background, and children's development. *Early Childhood Research Quarterly, 6,* 249–262.

Kontos, S. J., & Fiene, R. J. (1987). Child care quality, compliance with regulations, and children's development: The Pennsylvania Study. In D. A. Phillips (Ed.), *Quality of child care: What does research tell us?* (pp. 57–80). Washington, DC: National Association for the Education of Young Children.

Kontos, S., Howes, C., Shinn, M., & Galinsky, E. (1997). Children's experiences in family child care and relative care as a function of family income and ethnicity. *Merrill-Palmer Quarterly, 43,* 386–403.

Kopp, C. B. (1997). Young children: Emotion management, instrumental control, and plans. In S. L. Friedman & E. K. Scholnick (Eds.), *Why, how and when do we plan? The developmental psychology of planning* (pp. 103–124). Hillsdale, NJ: Lawrence Erlbaum Associates.

Lamb, M. E. (1997). Nonparental child care: Context, quality, correlates, and consequences. In W. Damon (Series Ed.) & I. E. Sigel & K. A. Renninger (Vol. Eds.), *Handbook of child psychology: Child psychology in practice* (4th ed., pp. 783–915). New York: Wiley.

Lamb, M. E, Sternberg, K. J, & Prodromidis, M. (1992). Nonmaternal care and the security of infant–mother attachment: A reanalysis of the data. *Infant Behavior and Development, 15,* 71–83.

Lazarus, R. S. (1991). *Emotion and adaptation.* New York: Oxford University Press.

Lewis, M., & Michalson, L. (1983). *Children's emotions and moods.* New York: Plenum Press.

Mann, C. (1990). Meta-analysis in the breech. *Science, 249,* 476–480.

Maruani, M. (1992). *The position of women in the labor market.* Women's Information Services (Report No. 36). Brussels: European Communities.

Mason, K. O., & Duberstein, L. (1992). Consequences of child care for parents' well-being. In A. Booth (Ed.), *Child care in the 1990's: Trends and consequences* (pp. 127–158). Hillsdale, NJ: Erlbaum.

McAdoo, H. P. (1993). Ethnic families: Strengths that are found in diversity. In H. P. McAdoo (Ed.), *Ethnic families: Strength in diversity* (pp. 3–14). Newbury Park, CA: Sage.

McAdoo, J. L. (1993). The roles of African-American fathers: An ecological perspective. *Families in Society: The Journal of Contemporary Human Services, 74,* 28–34.

McCartney, K. (1984). Effect of quality of day care environment on children's language development. *Developmental Psychology, 20,* 244–260.

McCartney, K., Scarr, S., Phillips, D., Grajek, S., & Schwarz, C. (1982). Environmental differences among day care centers and their effects on children's development. In E. G. Zigler & E. W. Gordon (Eds.), *Day care: Scientific and social policy issues* (pp. 126–151). Boston: Auburn House.

McLoyd, V. C. (1993). Employment among African American mothers in dual-career families: Antecedents and consequences for family life and child development. In J. Frankel (Ed.), *The employed mother and family context* (pp. 180–226). New York: Springer.

Morelli, G. A., & Tronick, E. Z. (1991). Efe multiple caretaking and attachment. In J. L. Gewirtz & W. M. Kurtines (Eds.), *Intersections with attachment* (pp. 41–51). Hillsdale, NJ: Lawrence Erlbaum Associates.

Mott, F. L. (1989). *Child care use during the first year of life: Linkages with early child development.* Working paper. Columbus, OH: Ohio State University, Center for Human Resource Research.

National Association for the Education of Young Children (NAEYC). (1991). *Accreditation criteria and procedures.* Washington, DC: Author.

National Center for Children in Poverty (NCCP). (1999). *Young children in poverty.* YCP fact, 7/20/99.

National Center for Education Statistics (NCES). (October, 1996). Statistics in brief: Child care and early education program participation of infants, toddlers, and preschoolers. (NCES 95-824).

NICHD Early Child Care Research Network. (1996). Characteristics of infant child care: Factors contributing to positive caregiving. *Early Childhood Research Quarterly, 11,* 269–306.

NICHD Early Child Care Research Network. (1997a). Familial factors associated with the characteristics of nonmaternal care for infants. *Journal of Marriage and the Family, 59,* 389–408.

NICHD Early Child Care Research Network. (1997b). The effects of infant child care on infant–mother attachment security: Results of the NICHD Study of Early Child Care. *Child Development, 68,* 860–879.

NICHD Early Child Care Research Network. (1998a). Early child care and self-control, compliance and problem behavior at twenty-four and thirty-six months. *Child Development, 69,* 1145–1170.

NICHD Early Child Care Research Network (1998b). Relations between family predictors and child outcomes: Are they weaker for children in child care? *Developmental Psychology, 34,* 1119–1128.

NICHD Early Child Care Research Network. (1999a). Child outcomes when child care center classes meet recommended standards for quality. *American Journal of Public Health, 89,* 1072–1077.

NICHD Early Child Care Research Network. (1999b, April). *The roles of work and poverty in the lives of families with young children.* Paper presented at the Biennial Meeting of the Society for Research in Child Development, Albuquerque, NM.

NICHD Early Child Care Research Network. (1999c). Child care and mother–child interaction in the first three years of life. *Developmental Psychology, 35*(6), 1399–1413.

NICHD Early Child Care Research Network. (2000a). Characteristics and quality of child care for toddlers and preschoolers. *Journal of Applied Developmental Science, 4*(3), 116–135.

NICHD Early Child Care Research Network. (2000b). The relation of child care to cognitive and language development. *Child Development, 71*(4), 960–980.

NICHD Early Child Care Research Network. (in press). Nonmaternal care and family factors in early development: An overview of the NICHD Study of Early Child Care. *Journal of Applied Developmental Psychology.*

NICHD Early Child Care Research Network. (working paper). Studying the effects of early child care experiences on the development of children of color in the US: Towards a more inclusive research agenda. *Developmental Review* (under review).

Owen, M. T., & Cox, M. (1988). Maternal employment and the transition to parenthood. In A. E. Gottfried & A. W. Gottfried (Eds.), *Maternal employment and children's development: Longitudinal research* (pp. 85–119). New York: Plenum Press.

Palfrey, J. S., Walker, D. K., Butler, J. A., & Singer, J. D. (1989). Patterns of response in families of chronically disabled children: An assessment in five metropolitan school districts. *American Journal of Orthopsychiatry, 59,* 94–104.

Parke, R. (1997). Socialization in the family: Ethnic and ecological perspectives. In W. Damon (Series Ed.) & N. Eisenberg (Vol. Ed.), *Handbook of child psychology: Vol. 3. Social, emotional, and personality development* (5th ed., pp. 463–552). New York: Wiley.

Phillips, D. A. (1992). Child care and parental well-being: Bringing quality of care into the picture. In A. Booth (Ed.), *Child care in the 1990's: Trends and consequences* (pp. 172–179). Hillsdale, NJ: Erlbaum.

Phillips, D. A. (Ed.). (1995). *Child care for low-income families.* Washington, DC: National Academy Press.

Phillips, D. A., & Howes, C. (1987). Indicators of quality in child care: Review of research. In D. A. Phillips (Ed.), *Quality in child care: What does the research show us?* (pp. 1–19). Washington, DC: National Association for the Education of Young Children.

Phillips, D. A., Howes, C., & Whitebook, M. (1991). Child care as an adult work environment. *Journal of Social Issues, 47,* 49–70.

Phillips, D. A., Lande, J., & Goldberg, M. (1990). The state of child care regulation: A comparative analysis. *Early Childhood Research Quarterly, 5,* 151–179.

Phillips, D. A, McCartney, K., & Scarr, S. (1987). Child-care quality and children's social development. *Development Psychology, 23,* 537–543.

Popenoe, D. (1993). American family decline, 1960–1990: A review and appraisal. *Journal of Marriage and the Family, 55,* 527–555.

Presser, H. B. (1992). Child care and parental well-being: A needed focus on gender and trade-offs. In A. Booth (Ed.), *Child care in the 1990's: Trends and consequences* (pp. 180–185). Hillsdale, NJ: Erlbaum.

Provence, S., & Lipton, R. C. (1962). *Infants in institutions: A comparison of their development with family-reared infants during the first year of life.* New York: International Universities Press.

Randolph, S. M. (1995). African-American single mothers. In B. Dickerson (Ed.), *African-American single women: Understanding their lives and families* (pp. 117–145). Thousand Oaks, CA: Sage.

Ribble, M. A. (1965). *The rights of infants: Early psychological needs and their satisfaction* (2nd ed.). New York: Columbia University.

Robertson, J., & Robertson, J. (1971). Young children in brief separations: A fresh look. *Psychoanalytic Study of the Child, 26,* 264–315.

Roggman, L. A., Langlois, J. H., Hubbs-Tait, L., & Rieser-Danner, L. A. (1994). Infant daycare attachment, and the "file drawer problem." *Child Development, 65,* 1429–1443.

Ruopp, R., Travers, J., Glantz, F., & Coelen, C. (1979). *Children at the center: Final results of the National Day Care Study.* Cambridge, MA: Abt Associates.

Singer, J. D., Fuller, B., Keiley, M. K., & Wolf, A. (1998). Early child-care selection: Variation by geographic location, maternal characteristics, and family structure. *Developmental Psychology, 34,* 1129–1144.

Smirnova, E. (in progress). The changing context of daycare for young children in Russia. In M. N. Bloch, A. Margolis, V. Rubtsov, & G. G. Price (Eds.). *Vygotskian education and educational reform in Russia in the preschool and primary school.* Book manuscript in preparation.

Spitz, R. A. (1945). Hospitalism: An inquiry into the genesis of psychiatric conditions in early childhood. *Psychoanalytic Study of the Child, 1,* 53–74.

Steiner, B. (1981). *The futility of family policy.* Washington, DC: Brookings Institution.

Stifter, C. A., Coulehan, C. M., & Fish, M. (1993). Linking employment to attachment: The mediating effects of maternal separation anxiety and interactive behavior. *Child Development, 64,* 1451–1460.

Swadener, E. B., & Bloch, M. N. (1997). *Early education and development, 8,* 207–218.

Takahashi, H. (1998). Working women in Japan: A look at historical trends and legal reform. *Japan Economic Institute Report, 42,* Newsletter.

Tietze, W., & Cryer, D. (1999). Current trends in European early child care and education. *Annals of the American Academy of Political and Social Science, 563,* 175–193.

Tronick, E. Z., Morelli, G. A., & Ivey, P. K. (1992). The Efe forager infant and toddler's pattern of social relationships: Multiple and simultaneous. *Developmental Psychology, 28,* 568–577.

Tronick, E. Z., Morelli, G. A., & Winn, S. (1987). Multiple caretaking of Efe (Pygmy) infants. *American Anthropologist, 89,* 96–106.

United States General Accounting Office. (1999, November 15). *Education and care: Early childhood programs and services for low-income families.* Report to Congressional Requesters from the Health, Education, and Human Services Division. (GAO/HEHS-00–11).

The Urban Institute. (1999). Welfare reform and children of immigrants. *National Council on Family Relations Report, 44,* 16.

Van IJzendoorn, M. H., Dijkstra, J., & Bus, A. G. (1995). Attachment, intelligence and language: A meta-analysis. *Social Development, 4,* 115–128.

Vandell, D., & Corasaniti, M. (1990). Child care and the family: Complex contributors to child development. *New Directions for Child Development, 49,* 23–37.

Vandell, D. L., Henderson, V. K., & Wilson, K. S. (1988). A longitudinal study of children with day-care experiences of varying quality. *Child Development, 59,* 1286–1292.

West, K. K., Hauser, R. M., & Scanlan, T. M. (Eds.). (1998). *Longitudinal surveys of children.* National Research Council, Committee on National Statistics, Board on Children, Youth, and Families. Washington, DC: National Academy Press.

Whitebook, M., Howes, C., & Phillips, D. (1990). *Who cares? Child care teachers and the quality of care in America (Final report).* National Child Care Staffing Study. Oakland, CA: Child Care Employee Project.

Willer, B. (1990). Estimating the full cost of quality. In B. Willer (Ed.), *Reaching the full cost of quality in early childhood programs* (pp. 55–86). Washington, DC: National Association for the Education of Young Children.

Wolcott, I. (1990). The structure of work and the work of families: Towards a merger in the 1990s. *Family Matters, 26,* 32–38.

Wolkind, S. (1974). The components of "affectionless psychopathy" in institutional children. *Journal of Child Psychology and Psychiatry, 15,* 215–220.

Yoshikwa, H. (1995). Long-term effects of early childhood programs on social outcomes and delinquency. *The Future of Children, 5,* 51–75.

Zaslow, M. J. (1991). Variation in child care quality and its implications for children. *Journal of Social Issues, 47,* 125–138.

Chapter Twenty-five

Health, Nutrition, and Safety

Jeanne Thibo Karns

Introduction

Health, nutrition, and safety of infants are topics of concern in all cultures and across the recorded history of all past civilizations. Concerns such as the quality of human breast milk and the protection of infants from environmental dangers are universal. However, solutions to issues such as how to wean the infant from breast milk to alternate substances reveals great cultural diversity.

The mother's role in society as the primary nurturer of the infant through all types of caretaking is emphasized. The challenges to and support of this role can be seen in the influences of the father's social support for breastfeeding, employment expectations for the mother, and community norms.

Nationally and internationally, efforts to provide for the welfare of infants are evident in immunization, nutrition, and product safety regulations. The impact of these regulations is reflected in the basic interactions within the home and the community.

Health: Prevention and Risks

The clinical practice guidelines of the American Academy of Pediatrics emphasize the importance of preventive care to keep infants well and to treat medical and developmental problems at the earliest possible stage. Unfortunately, many infants in both developing and developed countries often do not receive even the minimum of standard care. Poverty influences infant health not only in increased risk factors but also in decreased access to health care (American Academy of Pediatrics, 1997; Kibel & Wagstaff, 1995).

Perinatal Morbidity and Mortality

In developed countries, fewer than 1 percent of infants die in the perinatal period, the weeks just before and after birth. The improved viability has primarily occurred as a result of technological achievements in sanitation, immunization, antibiotics, nutrition, blood replacements and intensive medical treatment of at-risk newborns.

Many European countries have the lowest global rates of perinatal infant mortality, while the United States ranks number 20 among developed nations. In 1996, neonatal deaths in the United States were 3.9 per 1000 live births for whites and 9.2 for African Americans. This is an economic cause, not a racial factor. The high rate of perinatal deaths reflects the discrepancy in health care received by the poor and the nonpoor.

The primary causes of illness and death of the infant in the weeks before and after birth are largely preventable in developed countries. Low birth weight (LBW) and prematurity can be best treated by good prenatal care and nutrition for the mother. When infants are born premature and small, advances in medicine can achieve successful treatment in many cases. In the United States, perinatal and neonatal mortality rates are now lower for prematurity than for birth defects (McGanity, Dawson, & van Hook, 1999). In 1995, 22 percent of infant deaths under 1 year of age were due to congenital anomalies and 13 percent were due to disorders related to prematurity. Infants less than 24 weeks gestational age and less than 700 grams are most at risk for mortality, with 80 percent estimated mortality rate. Infants at 2000 grams and 34 weeks gestation have only a 1.5 percent risk of perinatal mortality.

Immunization

Immunization has become a triumphal success in reducing morbidity and mortality during the last 50 years. The administration of vaccines during infancy has saved lives and improved quality of life by preventing diseases and their complications. The post-World War II baby boomers were the last generation in developed countries to routinely become infected with "childhood diseases" such as measles and mumps. With the introduction of a vaccine for chicken pox (varicella) during the 1990s, children may now grow up without contracting any of the infectious diseases that caused permanent defects and impeded growth and development for previous generations.

Throughout the globe, immunizations are the most cost-effective medical treatment available. Immunization has been so effective in eliminating smallpox from the world that children no longer need to be given smallpox vaccine. Polio was targeted for global eradication in the year 2000 by the World Health Organization. North America is on the verge of eliminating measles. Immunizations for ten diseases are routinely recommended in developed nations. (See Table 25.1 for immunization timetable.) Although many vaccines require repeated doses, new combination vaccines allow more than one disease vaccine to be given in the same injection, thereby decreasing the number of injections needed and increasing the possibility of immunization of more children (American Academy of Pediatrics, 1999b,c,d). Infants living in or traveling to developing countries may need additional immunizations for locally specific problems, such as yellow fever, hepatitis A, and Bacillus Calmette Guerin vaccine (BCG) for tuberculosis. Additional immunizations may also be needed because of disruption of technological environmental safeguards, such as water purification systems, following natural disasters. These immunizations include vaccines for typhoid fever and cholera (Kibel & Wagstaff, 1995). All immunizations have the risk of side effects, the majority of which are very mild and are outweighed by the potential consequences of the diseases (Wong et al., 1999). In the United States, only about two-thirds of children by 2 years of age have received all appropriate immunizations (American Academy of Pediatrics, 1995b).

Infant Circumcision

Circumcision of newborn infants is a common practice in many cultures. Circumcision of males is the most prevalent. The foreskin of the penis is surgically removed. This procedure can be performed in a medical setting or as a religious ceremony. In the Jewish faith, the ceremony is called a breith or brit and is performed by a mohel, a person trained in the performance of the ceremony. As a medical procedure, male circumcision is more common in the United States than in other developed and developing countries (American Academy of Pediatrics, 1999a; Wong et al., 1999).

Until the late 1990s, medical circumcision was performed without anesthesia, a practice still current in many hospitals. Topical, oral, and/or injected anesthetics are now recommended for pain control during this surgical procedure (American Academy of Pediatrics, 1999a; Rabinowitz & Hulbert, 1995; Wellington & Rieder, 1993).

The medical communities of the Western nations have issued position statements advising against male circumcision. The lack of strong verifiable medical benefits places the decision to circumcise on cultural and religious grounds (American Academy of Pediatrics, 1999a; Australian Medical Association, 1997; British Medical Association, 1996; General Medical Council, 1997). Should parents request circumcision of newborn males, the physician should explain the potential risks and benefits of the procedure and of not performing the procedure to insure that the parents understand that male circumcision is elective and not required by governmental law.

In contrast to male circumcision, female circumcision is found exclusively among the cultures of Africa, the Middle East, and Asia or among immigrants and their descendents from these areas. Cultures vary in prescribing how much tissue is removed, including the clitoris, and part or all of the labia minora. In the most severe form of female circumcision the labia majora is also cut and sewn together to form a tight band covering the urethra and vaginal openings. The procedure may also include piercing, stretching, cauterization, or scraping of genital structures or insertion of caustic substances into the vagina. Complications are numerous (Armstrong, 1991; Institute for Development Training, 1986; McCleary, 1994; World Health Organization, 1997).

Also known as female genital mutilation, female circumcision is performed on infant girls in some cultures; however, the practice is more common for older girls and adolescents. Annually, an estimated 4 to 5 million procedures are performed (Kouba & Muasher, 1985; Ntiri, 1993). Female circumcision is based on cultural beliefs that the procedure

Table 25.1 Recommended childhood immunization schedule, United States

Vaccines are listed under the routinely recommended ages. Lines indicate range of acceptable ages for immunizations.

Age Vaccine	Birth	1 month	2 months	4 months	6 months	12 months	15 months	18 months	4-6 years	11-12 years	14-16 years
Hepatitis B	Hep B1 --------	Hep B2 --------			Hep B3 --------						
Diphtheria, Tetanus, Pertussis			DTaP or DTP	DTaP or DTP	DtaP or DTP		DTaP -------- or DTP		DtaP or DTP	TD --------	
H. influenzae Type b			Hib	Hib	Hib	Hib --------					
Polio			Polio	Polio		-------- Polio --------			Polio		
Measles, Mumps, Rubella							-------- MMR ---		MMR		
Varicella							-------- Var --------				

Approved by the Advisory Committee on Immunization Practices (ACIP), the American Academy of Pediatrics (AAP), and the American Academy of Family Physicians (AAFP)
Source: American Academy of Pediatrics

will preserve group identity, prevent promiscuity by removing structures associated with sexual arousal, preserve virginity, and increase sexual pleasure for men (International Association for Maternal and Neonatal Health, 1991). The practice has been condemned by the World Health Organization and is considered child abuse, and therefore illegal in most developed countries (American Academy of Pediatrics, 1998).

Environmental Toxins

The infant is the most vulnerable member of society. Environmental toxins can attack immature organ systems, resulting in illness, delayed development, and permanent impairment. The effects on cognition and behavior are only beginning to be studied.

Passive tobacco smoke has been found to have a harmful effect on the health of infants and toddlers. Infants living with a smoker are more likely to be admitted to a hospital for treatment of bronchitis and pneumonia. Passive smoke and illness have a dose-related response. An increase of just five cigarettes a day smoked by the mother was shown to result in a linear increase of 2.5 to 3.5 incidents of lower respiratory (bronchial and lung) illness per 100 children at risk. Infants with both parents smoking experienced pneumonia and bronchitis at twice the rate of infants of nonsmokers. Passive smoking is also associated with a fourfold risk of hospitalization for serious infectious illness of all types. Numerous studies have shown dose-related responses between passive smoke and middle ear infections and complications, including the need for tympanostomy tube placement surgery.

The relationship between passive smoke and Sudden Infant Death Syndrome (SIDS) statistically appears to be independent of both birth weight and gestational age, indicating that the passive smoke is a main effect, not just a contributor to the risk of SIDS. A more detailed discussion of SIDS is presented later in this chapter. Overall, exposure to passive smoke leads to increased risk of illness and possibly death for infants and young children (American Academy of Pediatrics, 1997).

Lead in the environment can cause developmental delay, illness, and death in infants. Biologically, lead binds into sites reserved for calcium, thereby adversely affecting cellular processes that depend upon calcium. Additionally, lead has a devastating effect on the central nervous system. Lead interferes with the brain activity associated with visual-motor abilities, including the ability to recognize and copy shapes, visualize objects in space, and form nonverbal concepts. In US studies of both low-income and middle-income families, a dose-related response was found for amount of lead levels of children and intelligence test scores. Children with higher levels of lead exposure had lower scores on intelligence tests. Additionally, exposed children may have learning and behavioral problems as well as physical symptoms of listlessness, uncoordination, altered consciousness, seizures, coma, and death. Laws in the United States banning lead solder on food cans, lead in gasoline, and lead in paint have eliminated the most frequent sources of lead poisoning. These toxins are still threats in developing countries, however. The primary source of lead poisoning in developed countries is deterioration of lead paint on older structures. The lead dust can be inhaled from the air. Teething infants can chew on painted surfaces, directly ingesting the lead. As with other health and safety hazards of infancy, the children living in poverty are the most at risk (Farley, 1998; Knestrick & Milstead, 1998).

Sudden Infant Death Syndrome (SIDS)

Sudden Infant Death Syndrome is the term used to describe the unexpected death of an infant, often while sleeping, without other known cause. SIDS is not one disease or environmental risk. It is thought to have multiple causes and influences. In developed countries, SIDS is the number one cause of death for infants between 1 week and 1 year of age. In Canada, SIDS claims 1 out of every 1000 live-born infants (Canadian Foundation for the Study of Infant Deaths, 1999; SIDS Alliance, 1998). A study in Cape Town, South Africa found an incidence of SIDS of 1.06 per 1000 live births for whites and 3.41 per 1000 for colored (mixed-racial, low-SES African) infants (Sinclair-Smith & Kibel, 1986).

Four primary factors have been isolated as related with SIDS. The first is suffocation. Infants placed on their stomachs to sleep, or who roll onto their stomachs during sleep, have a much higher incidence of SIDS. Soft bedding is thought to create an air pocket around the infant's face, allowing the infant to breathe lower and lower levels of oxygen or perhaps to rebreathe expelled carbon dioxide. Water beds, bean bag chairs, sheepskins, and pillows are not recommended for infant use. Co-sleeping of infants in parents' beds may present a hazard not because of over-rolling of the adult onto the infant but because of the softness of adult bedding for a prone infant. A 15 percent to 20 percent decrease has been shown for the rate of SIDS since the 1992 recommendation of the American Academy of Pediatrics that infants should be placed to sleep on their backs rather than prone (American Academy of Pediatrics, 1996c).

The second factor is second-hand tobacco smoke. The presence of tobacco smoke in the infant's environment is highly correlated with SIDS. The immature lungs of the infant may not be able to withstand the stress of inhaled smoke. A third factor is overheating. Infants should not be allowed to become too hot, especially with blankets or comforters on or around the infant's head. Finally, the low occurrence of SIDS is correlated with breastfeeding. At least some cases of SIDS may be related to infection, especially colds and other upper respiratory infections. Breast milk imparts immunity to infants during the first year of life, particularly during the first six months, the most dangerous period for SIDS (American Academy of Pediatrics, 1996c; Canadian Foundation for the Study of Infant Deaths, 1999; Scheers, Dayton, & Kemp, 1998; SIDS Alliance, 1998).

Medical Treatment and Hospitalization of Infants

Newborn intensive care units in hospitals are often the first homes for many infants. Medical pharmacological and technological advances have dramatically increased the survival rate of infants with illness, birth defects, and trauma. Many infants who would have died just one decade ago now survive at the cost of enduring medically invasive and stressful procedures, ranging from venipunctures to major surgery. During hospitalization, touch by adults often becomes associated with painful stimuli. Bright lights and monitor alarms interfere with normal sleep cycles. A variety of caregivers over weeks, and at times months, disrupts attachment formation.

Research on nociception, the perception by the nerves of injurious influences or painful stimuli, now supports the position that the fetus, newborn, and older infant do feel the sensation of pain (Anand & Hickey, 1987; Fitzgerald, 1995). A variety of pain assessment scales use physiological and behavioral activity to rate the infant's pain; however, the variability in infant reaction to pain makes pain assessment difficult (Attia et al., 1987; Bozzette, 1993; Cote, Morse, & James, 1991; Franck, 1987; Grunau & Craig, 1987; Grunau, Johnston, & Craig, 1990; Johnston & Strada, 1986; Krechel & Bildner, 1995; Shapiro, 1989). Wong et al. (1999) state that "When in doubt about pain in infants, base your decision on the following rule: Whatever is painful to an adult or child is painful to an infant unless proved otherwise" (p. 412).

Many studies have shown adverse effects of untreated pain in infants on short-term and long-term physiological, social, and cognitive levels. Examples include recoil and withdrawal when touched, changes in blood chemistry, gaze aversion, poor sleep patterns, attention deficits, learning disorders, and poor adaptive behaviors (Anand & Carr, 1989; Anand & Hickey, 1987; Anand, Grunau, & Oberlander, 1997; Barba, 1991; Fitzgerald, 1995; Fitzgerald, Millard, & McIntosh, 1989; Penticuff, 1987; Wong, 1992).

Infants are at the greatest risk of any age child for suffering psychosocial stress caused by separation during hospitalization and medical treatment. Infants are forming attachments that can be disrupted by long separations. Unlike older children, infants are unable to understand the events of hospitalization, and to use coping strategies to deal with the stress of hospitalization. The practice of parental rooming-in during infant hospitalization has been advocated as part of family-centered care (Child Life Council, 1994; Shelton & Stepanek, 1994; Wong et al., 1999). In addition to preventing anxiety caused by separation, rooming-in also allows the mother to continue to breastfeed the ill infant and to be present to comfort the infant during and after medical procedures.

Nutrition

Human milk has always been recognized as the appropriate first food of infants. Yet throughout history, many cultures have devised alternate methods for feeding infants. Milk from other mammals, including goats, sheep, and cows, has been modified to serve as alternatives for human milk, as well as grain product milk substitutes from rice and soy beans.

The wetnurse is a lactating woman who suckles another infant in addition to her own. A wetnurse may be used because of illness of the mother, maternal preference, economical factors, or cultural norms. The tradition of the wetnurse is found in many cultures today. In Western cultures, the technological equivalent of the wetnurse can be found in human milk banks. Lactating women pump their milk and donate it for use by premature infants, ill infants, and infants with allergies to formula. Standards for the collection and distribution of human milk have been established by the Human Milk Banking Association of North America (Human Milk Banking Association of North America, 1993; Powers, Naylor, & Wester, 1994).

The World Health Organization recommends feeding human milk exclusively to infants until 6 months of age. The American Academy of Pediatrics, the Canadian Paediatric Society, and the American Dietetic Association recommend the exclusive use of human milk until 6 months, with continued breastfeeding supplemented by other foods until past the infant's first birthday.

Composition of Human Milk and Formula

Biological and chemical research has led to a greater understanding of the complexities of human breast milk. Colostrum is the milk produced by the mother's breasts during the first few days after birth. Compared to the later mature milk, colostrum is higher in protein and lower in sugar and fat. Colostrum is yellow and sticky, while mature milk is thinner with a bluish or creamy color (Lawrence, 1999).

The bioactive composition of human milk includes living cells and many nutrients not yet identified and therefore unavailable in formula substitutes. The primary known nutrients in human milk are shown in Table 25.2.

Infectious illness is one of the primary causes of delayed growth and development in the young infant. In numerous studies, human milk has been found to have a protective effect by imparting the mother's current immunity to the infant when the infant is exclusively breastfed. The immunological components of human milk protect the infant from contagious diseases during the early months, particularly those diseases including diarrhea that can quickly dehydrate infants, causing electrolyte imbalances and death.

The whey protein of human milk is more easily digested than bovine milk and promotes more rapid gastric emptying. Human milk whey proteins line the gastrointestinal tract and become the first defense against illness. Infants fed only human milk have fewer and less severe gastrointestinal illness during the first 13 weeks of life and are less likely to need hospitalization. Human milk also carries protection against Haemophiulus influenzae type b infection (Kleinman & Committee on Nutrition, American Academy of Pediatrics, 1998).

Colostrum of preterm mothers contains an even greater amount of antimicrobial properties than does the colostrum of full-term mothers, thereby imparting a greater protective factor to the more vulnerable preterm neonate (Lawrence, 1999).

Otitis media (OM, ear infection) occurs half as often in exclusively breastfed infants as in formula-fed infants. Additionally, these infants have half as many recurrent OM infections. Severe and prolonged OM can lead to delayed speech development. Infants with cleft palate may have almost continuous OM due to the altered physical structure. A study by Paradise, Elster, and Tan (1994), however, found these same protective benefits of human milk to extend to the cleft palate infants.

The antibodies of each mother are unique to her, depending on her exposure to antigens and genetics. Beginning evidence is now available suggesting that breastfeeding may impart lifelong immunity to some types of infections (American Academy of Pediatrics, 1995a; Newburg & Street, 1997).

Table 25.2 Composition per liter of mature human milk

		Units	Amount
Energy		kcal	680
Lactose		g	72
Protein		g	10.5
	Whey/casein	%	72/28
Fat		g	39
	Medium chain	%	2
	Long chain triglycerides	%	98
Carbohydrate		g	72
	Lactose	%	100
Minerals			
	Calcium	mg	280
	Phosphorus	mg	140
	Magnesium	mg	35
	Sodium	mg	180
	Potassium	mg	525
	Iron	mg	0.3
	Chloride	mg	420
	Zinc	mg	1.2
	Copper	mg	0.25
	Iodine	μg	110
	Selenium	μg	20
	Manganese	μg	6
	Fluoride	μg	16
	Chromium	μg	50
Vitamins			
	A	RE	670
	E	mg	2.3
	D	μg	0.55
	K	μg	2.1
	C	mg	40
	Thiamin (B)	mg	0.21
	Riboflavin (B)	mg	0.35
	Niacin	mg	1.5
	Pyridoxine (B)	mg	93
	Panthothenic acid	mg	1.8
	Folate	μg	85
	B	μg	0.97
	Biotin	μg	4
	Folic acid	μg	24
	Ascorbic acid	mg	40

Values are given for one liter of mature human milk. Infants vary in volume consumed per day.
Source: Adapted from Institute of Medicine (1991). Nutrition during lactations-milk composition. Washington, DC: National Academy Press, 116; Shils, Olson, Shike, & Ross (1999); Kleinman & Committee on Nutrition, American Academy of Pediatrics (1998)

The flavor of human milk is sweet and includes the flavors of the foods, spices, and beverages consumed by the mother. Amniotic fluid also contains the taste of the mother's foods. Since the fetus swallows amniotic fluid, conditioning to the predominant taste preferences of a culture may begin prior to birth (Mennella, 1997). This may explain why toddlers in Mexico will eat a salsa of chilli peppers, tomatoes, and garlic that is considered too spicy hot by adults of other cultures. Conversely, some infants may refuse to feed or may ingest less human milk when the mother has eaten garlic or spicy foods. Infants' preferences for the taste of salt are related to their dietary experience. At 6 months of age, infants who were primarily fed human milk, a low-sodium food, showed less preference for salt than infants fed a wider variety of foods (Harris, Thomas, & Booth, 1990).

Formulas used as substitutes for human milk have successfully been used for decades, with the strongest surge of acceptance in the baby boom generation following World War II. Cow's milk is the primary component of formula. Goat milk and vegetable soy formulas are also available for infants who are allergic to cow's milk. Soy and rice formulas may also be acceptable to vegetarians if they do not breastfeed.

Characteristics of human milk and formula may result in different feeding schedules. The easier digestibility of human milk causes the stomach to empty more rapidly than with formula. Throughout the day and night, human milk varies in nutritional density. These factors combine to create a more varied feeding schedule for breastfed infants. Prior to growth spurts, infants suck longer and more frequently on the breast, resulting in an increased production of milk. A demand feeding schedule responds to the infant's behaviors indicating hunger, such as crying and increased sucking. Scheduled feeding is more commonly associated with formula feeding. Infants fed formula tend to ingest more even volumes throughout the day and night. The longer digestion period for formula results in more evenly spaced and predictable feeding times.

The nutritional needs for infants and toddlers fed by formula and nonmilk foods are shown in Table 25.3. Formulas vary in composition, including the sources of proteins, carbohydrates, and fats. Protein usually is a composite of bovine milk and whey, soy, or hydrolyzed protein. Fats may include oil from coconut, soy, palmolein, sunflower, corn, and safflower. Carbohydrates may include lactose (milk sugar), corn syrup, sucrose, cornstarch, dextrose, or tapioca. Commercial formulas vary in the amount of proteins, fats, carbohydrates, electrolytes, minerals, and vitamins included, although all formula sold in the United States meet Recommended Daily Allowances (RDA) as established by the National Research Council Food and Nutrition Board. Because cow's milk is low in iron, it should not be substituted for formula between 6 and 12 months of age. Even though formulas cannot duplicate the unique composition of human milk, they are acceptable substitutes for human milk for women living in developed countries with the economical resources needed to purchase them and sanitation resources needed to prepare them (Kleinman, 1998; Shils, Olsen, Shike, & Ross, 1999).

Much higher levels of essential nutrients are required in formula than naturally occur in human milk because of differences in bioavailability. Absorption of nutrients from formulas by infants is much lower than absorption rates from human milk. United States RDA nutrient levels are based on the absorption of nutrients by infants fed formula. An exclusively breastfed infant will have a calcium intake of 250–330 mg with an absorption rate of 55 percent to 60 percent, yielding a retention of 150–200 mg of calcium. Formula

Table 25.3 Recommended daily allowances of nutrients for normal infants fed formula and solid foods

Nutrient	Unit	Recommended intake per day		
		0–6 Months	*6–12 Months*	*1–3 Years*
		Weight = 6 kg	*Weight = 9 kg*	*Weight = 13 kg*
Energy	kcal	650	850	1300
Fat	g			
Carbohydrate				
Protein	g	13	14	16
Electrolytes and minerals				
Calcium	mg	400	600	800
Phosphorus	mg	300	500	800
Magnesium	mg	40	60	80
Sodium	(mg)[a]	120	200	13
Chloride	(mg)[a]	180	300	13
Potassium	(mg)[a]	500	700	26
Iron	mg	6	10	10
Zinc	mg	5	5	10
Copper	(mg)[b]	0.4–0.6	0.6–0.7	0.7–1.0
Iodine	μg	40	50	70
Selenium	μg	10	15	20
Manganese	(μg)	0.3–0.6	0.6–1.0	1.0–1.5
Fluoride	(mg)[b]	0.1–1.0	0.2–1.0	0.5–1.5
Chromium	(μg)	10.0–40.0	20.0–60.0	20.0–80.0
Molybdenum	μg	15.0–30.0	20.0–40.0	25.0–50.0
Vitamins				
A	μg RE	375	375	400
D	μg	7.5	10	0.1
E	μg[a] TE	3	4	6
K	μg	5	10	15
C	mg	0.3	0.4	40
Thiamin	mg	0.3	0.4	0.7
Riboflavin	mg	0.4	0.5	0.8
Niacin	mg NE	5	6	9
B	μg	0.3	0.6	1
Folate	μg	25	35	50
B	μg	0.3	0.5	0.7
Biotin	(μg)	10	15	20
Pantothenic acid	(mg)[b]	2	3	3

RDA shown for formula- and solid food-fed infants. RDA values are higher than nutrients shown for human milk (Table 25.2) due to the lower bioavailability of nutrients from these foods

[a] Minimum requirements (mg/day) rather than recommended

[b] Estimated safe and adequate daily intake

Source: Data from Food and Nutrition Board. National Research Council (1989). *Recommended dietary allowances* (10th ed.). Washington, DC: National Academy Press; Shils, Olson, Shike, & Ross (1999)

has a calcium absorption rate of 40 percent, therefore requiring as much as 500–660 mg of formula calcium intake to match the retention rate of human milk. The discrepancy of absorption rates for iron is even greater. Only 10 percent of iron from cow milk base formula and 4 percent of the added iron from iron-fortified formula is absorbed. With human milk, infants absorb 50 percent of the iron intake.

Diverse formulas are available for infants with special needs. Soy formulas are available for infants with allergies. Lactose-free formulas have been devised for infants with lactase deficiency. Formulas low in minerals and electrolytes that provide a low renal solute load are available for infants with renal or cardiovascular diseases (Kleinman, 1998).

In developing countries, formulas continue to present problems of appeal to women. These women cannot afford adequate amounts of formula to nourish their infants and may dilute the formula with additional water. In areas with poor sanitation the water used to prepare the formula and clean the bottles may introduce infectious organisms into the infant's system. For these mothers, breastfeeding still remains the best method for early feeding. The World Health Organization enacted the Code of Marketing for Breast Milk Substitutes in 1981 in an effort to halt the Westernization appeal of formulas in developing countries where families have neither the economic nor sanitation resources needed for successful formula feeding. This code prohibits the mass direct advertising of formula to mothers, free commercial gifts of formula for newborns, inducements to retailers and health professionals, and the use of medical facilities to promote formulas. Additionally, formula labels are required to state that breast milk is superior to the formulas.

Recent studies still show strong appeal of Western attitudes and behaviors. In Sri Lanka, 32 percent of formula-fed infants were more likely to be fed expensive formulas from multinational companies even though cheaper, nutritionally comparable state-subsidized formulas were available (Wijekoon, Thattil, & Schensul, 1995). Vietnamese immigrants in London were found to have begun breastfeeding while in Vietnam but to have switched to formula after immigration (Sharma, Lynch, & Irvine, 1994).

Xenobiotics

Just as the fetus is vulnerable to substances passed through the placenta from the mother, the nursing infant ingests the products present in the mother's body. Xenobiotics include the study of the transference of infectious and toxic agents through breast milk.

Numerous studies have well established that all drugs are excreted into breast milk (Kleinman, 1998). Many commonly consumed drugs have been found to have harmful effects when transmitted to infants through human milk. The chemical components of alcohol and tobacco are readily transmitted through breast milk. Contrary to folklore, infants ingest less human milk when mothers have consumed an alcoholic beverage compared with a nonalcoholic beverage (Mennella, 1997). The infant repeatedly exposed to small amounts of alcohol in breast milk may have long-term effects on motor development similar to those detected for Fetal Alcohol Syndrome (FAS) (Mennella & Beauchamp, 1992). The infant of a smoker has similar biochemical reactions as the mother to the nicotine of tobacco.

Examples of drugs that are contraindicated during breastfeeding include bromocriptine, cocaine, cyclophosphamide, cyclosporine, doxorubicin, ergotamine, lithium, methotrexate, phencyclidine (PCP), phenindione, amphetamine, heroin, and marijuana. All have been found to result in reduction of lactation, biochemical changes in the infant, depression of respiratory and circulatory systems of the infant, or to produce behavioral changes in the infant, including irritability, lethargy, and altered sleep states. The *Pediatric Nutrition Handbook*, 4th edition, of the American Academy of Pediatrics includes extensive lists of maternal drugs and radioactive compounds that are contraindicated during breastfeeding, maternal drugs with unknown effects on breastfed infants, and maternal drugs that are thought to be compatible with breastfeeding. Factors that influence the passage of medication into human milk include drug factors of molecular weight, lipid solubility, water solubility, protein binding, drug ionization, drug pH, half-life of the drug, dose, and route of administration (American Academy of Pediatrics, 1997; Banta-Wright, 1997).

Numerous case studies have been reported for breastfeeding mothers medicated for depression, anxiety, and schizophrenia. This is an important issue because of the severity of postpartum and/or long-term depression for some women, as well as the prevalence of chronic psychotic problems present in the general population.

Past research has well documented the negative impact on parenting behaviors if depression or other mental health problems are not treated (Campbell, Cohn, & Meyers, 1995; Field, 1987; Field, Morrow, & Adelstein, 1993; Fleming, Ruble, Flett, & Shaul, 1988; Fox & Gelfand, 1994; Gelfand & Teti, 1990; Gelfand, Teti, & Fox, 1992; Simmons, Lorenz, Wu, & Conger, 1993). The social interaction behaviors of infants can be influenced by the altered depressed-mother/infant interactions. These infants may be withdrawn, engage in less physical action and have more negative facial expressions and fussiness even when interacting with someone other than the depressed mother (Cohn, Campbell, Matias, & Hobkins, 1990; Cohn, Matias, Tronick, Lyons-Ruth, & Connell, 1986; Field et al., 1988; Field, Healy, & LeBlanc, 1989; Field et al., 1985; Pickens & Field, 1995). (See chapter 23 for a complete discussion.)

Psychotropic drugs studied include antidepressants, anti-anxiety and tranquilizers, antipsychotic agents and anticonvulsants. Concentrations in breast milk, infant urine, and infant plasma varied from trace to adult dosage levels. Influential variables include fore (beginning feeding) and hind (end feeding) milk variations, elapsed time since dosage, and the natural variation of fat and protein in human milk. The vast majority of studies showed no detectable short-term or delayed psychomotor, neurological, or behavioral changes in the infants, although limited case studies have reported increased crying, or decreased sleep. No developmental changes were detected in short-term or long-term studies, including one study that followed the infants until 1 year of age with periodic administrations of the Bayley Scales of Infant Development.

Accumulation effects may pose unknown risks because of the lower capacity of infants for drug elimination. No study to date successfully addresses this issue. Conflicting recommendations are made concerning use of these psychotropic drugs during breastfeeding. The benefits to mother and infant for breastfeeding are generally viewed to outweigh any currently unknown risks (Brent & Wisner, 1998; Breyer-Pfaff, Nill, Entenmann, & Gaertner, 1995; Spigset & Haegg, 1998; Stowe et al., 1997; Wisner & Perel, 1998;

Wisner, Perel, Findling & Hinnes, 1997; Yoshida & Kumar, 1996; Yoshida, Smith, Craggs, & Kumar, 1997, 1998a,b).

In only a few circumstances does the potential harm to the infant from contaminated human milk surpass the benefits gained by breastfeeding. Contraindications for breast-feeding include maternal addiction to abused substances and chronic uncontrolled infections. Hepatitis B and C, rubella, cytomegalovirus, and many bacteria, bacterial toxins, and viruses may be transmitted by human milk. The infant may acquire herpes simplex type I when lesions are located on the breast. Tuberculosis and many other infections are not contraindications unless the increased physical demand of milk production would strain the mother's well-being.

The risk of transmission of HIV infection from mother to infant *in utero*, during birth, or while breastfeeding is estimated in ranges from 15 percent to 50 percent. The risk of transmission of HIV from mother to infant from breastfeeding alone is estimated at 3 percent to 12 percent in various African populations (American Academy of Pediatrics, 1995a). If a mother is HIV-positive and the infant is not, either because the infant was not infected prior to birth or because the mother became infected after the pregnancy, breastfeeding may not be recommended if a viable alternative is available. Human milk does carry the virus; however, the transmission rate does not appear at this time to be as strong as transmission by sexual activity and IV drug use. For HIV-positive women in developed nations, use of commercial formulas is readily available and often subsidized by the government. Formula use is the recommended course of action for these families.

Among the HIV-infected population of many developing countries, a difficult dilemma exists. The mother is HIV-positive and the infant tests negative, indicating either that the infant was not infected during gestation and birth or that the virus is in the incubation stage and is not detected by current tests. Due to economics and poor sanitation standards, formula feeding is not a realistic alternative for many of these women (Bobat, Moodley, Coutsoudis, & Coovadia, 1997; Cutting, 1994; Hoover, Doherty, Vlahov, & Miotti, 1996; Mofenson, 1995; Rustein, Conlon, & Batshaw, 1997). The World Health Organization has stated that "in settings where the principle causes of death in children are malnutrition and infectious diseases, the recommendation of WHO is that breast-feeding be encouraged. In these settings the advantage of breast-feeding, even for a baby whose mother is HIV-positive, may outweigh the risks of bottle-feeding" (Kibel & Wagstaff, 1995, p. 245).

Social and Cultural Components of Infant Feeding

Infant feeding has been shown to be a potentially positive experience for both parents and infants. Dignam (1995) describes the successful breastfeeding interaction as characterized by intimacy, including reciprocity, mutual joy, harmony, concern for others, trust, and closeness. These same qualities can be shared during formula feeding.

Because breastfeeding takes significantly longer than bottle feeding, mothers and their breastfed infants have more opportunities for intimate social contact. Breastfeeding mothers report enjoying breastfeeding because it requires them to stop other activities and interact with their infants in an intimate manner (Epstein, 1993; Morse & Bottorff, 1992; Paul, Jaroslava, & Hanus, 1996).

The decisions to breastfeed and to maintain breastfeeding once begun are strongly influenced by the social support the mother receives and expectations concerning her competing activities. Van Esterik (1989) states that "infant feeding choices relate to the position and condition of women, ideologically and economically, in different societies" (p. 18). Factors discouraging breastfeeding include embarrassment, issues of convenience, lack of maternal confidence, and partner attitude. A study by Littman, Medendorp, and Goldfarb (1994) found that fathers indifferent to feeding method had partners with low breastfeeding behavior, at 26.9 percent, while the partners of fathers with strong approval of breastfeeding used breastfeeding 98.1 percent. In a Texas study of breastfeeding intentions, fathers had more negative attitudes toward breastfeeding and more misconceptions than mothers (Freed, Fraley, & Schanler, 1993).

Women who begin breastfeeding at birth may wean their infants to formula for a variety of reasons. Continued breastfeeding has been associated with strong support from the husband, no employment or maternal return to employment with flexible hours, breastfeeding advocacy by the medical community, and positive peer support for the mother.

Educational programs to encourage breastfeeding have been the most successful when they incorporate cultural norms and beliefs, breastfeeding skills, and are individualized to the needs of the mother. Examples of successful programs can be found in China, among the Vietnamese immigrants in Australia, and the Navajo living on reservations in Arizona (Jingheng, Yindi, Yongxin, & Jie, 1994; Rossiter, 1994; Wright, Naylor, Wester, Bauer, & Sutcliffe, 1997).

Studies on the influence of maternal employment on breastfeeding have found great variability. When a mother returns to employment after maternity leave, she is likely to switch to formula. A study of Italian first-time mothers found that longer maternity leaves were associated with longer breastfeeding, but also found that employed mothers were more likely to breastfeed than mothers remaining at home. A different study found breastfeeding is more likely among part-time employed mothers. In a study in Nigeria, the majority of mothers studied gave milk supplements to infants within the first weeks after birth. All mothers were employed, with professions ranging from high-status jobs in education and nursing to unskilled cleaners (Awoyinka, 1992). Mothers in low occupational grades in Spain were less likely to breastfeed than mothers in high-status employment, yet in the study in Nigeria, cleaners breastfed exclusively or longer than educators. Rural Muslim women in Israeli villages were found to initiate breastfeeding at a rate of 96 percent; however, only 57 percent continued beyond the sixth month (Azaiza & Palti, 1997). These differences may be attributable to the availability of breastfeeding education programs, the population segment targeted by these programs, and the differing cultural expectations of women with primary emphasis focusing on either family or high-status employment and education.

Some corporations employing a high percentage of women of childbearing age have begun lactation programs to assist mothers in maintaining breastfeeding while employed. Components include the provision of efficient electric breast pumps, refrigerated storage for pumped milk, and lactation consultants (Awoyinka, 1992; Cohen & Mrtek, 1994;

Escriba, Colomer, Mas, & Grifol, 1994; Lindberg, 1996; Romito & Saurel-Cubizolles, 1996; Thompson & Bell, 1997).

Cognitive Development and Human Milk

A relatively recent area of study has been the association between human milk, neuropsychological infant development, and later cognitive development. The majority of the studies show statistically significant though small effects supporting breastfeeding. Morley and Lucas (1994) followed preterm infants from infancy to 7.5 and 8 years. Infants who received human milk had higher developmental scores at 18 months and as older children than the formula-fed infants. In a study of 850 children by Rogan and Gladen (1993), the positive advantage of breastfeeding was detected throughout infancy (6, 12, 18, and 24 months) for children tested with the Bayley Scales of Infant Development, early childhood (3, 4, and 5 years of age) for children tested with the McCarthy Scales of Children's Abilities, and on English grades on report cards at grade 3. A dose-related response was noted, with increases in cognition of older children related to duration of breastfeeding in infancy. A similar study with 375 Australian children tested on the Bayley Mental Developmental Index at age 2 years, the McCarthy General Cognitive Index at age 4, and the Wechsler Full-Scale IQ at ages 7 and 11 to 13 years found small statistically nonsignificant benefits for breastfed children over formula-fed children (Wigg et al., 1998). Other studies in the United States, Britain, New Zealand, and India have found advantages for breastfed infants on pictorial language tests, intelligence tests, and visual acuity measures (Amanda & Singh, 1992; Golding, Rogers, & Emmett, 1997; Horwood & Fergusson, 1998; Johnson, Swank, Howie, & Baldwin, 1996; Pollock, 1994).

In contrast, a British study titled the National Survey of Health and Development did not find cognitive advantages for breastfed infants when other family factors were controlled in data from 511 first-born 8-year-olds (Richards et al., 1998). Similar neutral results for breastfeeding were found in a United States study of 342 subjects, age 10, when maternal and paternal education and annual income were considered (Malloy & Berendes, 1998).

Studies finding a cognitive advantage for breastfed children include studies with full-term and premature/low-birthweight infants. Several studies have been large population studies with hundreds of subjects, and in one study, 11,765 subjects. Other studies have had relatively few subjects and thereby low statistical power.

The mixed results of the cognition and breastfeeding studies are excellent examples of the difficulties encountered in many longitudinal studies. Much of the work has been retrospective, relying on archival records. Broad measures, such as school grades and IQ scores, may not be sensitive enough to discern any real effects on specific areas of cognition. Newer techniques looking at actual brain development are years away from practical use in studies with large numbers of subjects. Confounding factors, including family composition, birth order, parents' education and income, may have as much influence on development as any supposed effects of breastfeeding. Finally, the self-selection factor of which mothers choose to breastfeed and which do not also becomes tangled within issues of style of parent/infant interaction, amount of time spent in cuddling and play, physical contact, and dozens of other potentially intervening factors occurring from infancy to middle childhood.

Weaning, Introduction of Solid Foods

Weaning may be culturally viewed as a gradual process of accustoming children to the foods eaten by adults or as a cutting off of the infant's access to human milk. The process can be gradual with continued breastfeeding for years. In other cultures, weaning may happen quickly with change from breast or bottle made over a period of a few weeks. Breastfeeding well into the second and third years is a common practice in many developing nations of quite diverse cultures. The Quechua Indians of Peru, the Turkana nomads of Kenya, and the Gainj of Papua New Guinea share the behaviors of on-demand breastfeeding through the second year. In many cultures, a new pregnancy is the only reason used by mothers to halt breastfeeding prior to a duration of two years (Bohler & Bergstroem, 1995; Gray, 1994). In the United States and other Western nations, breastfeeding is more often halted during the second month.

Solid food introduction begins in most cultures with a basic staple, usually a grain, tuber, root, or fruit, cooked and softened with milk or liquid from cooking. Prechewing of food for young infants by an adult is an accepted practice in many cultures (Fildes, 1986). In Egypt, yogurt and bread soaked in liquids may be begun when the infant is 40 days old. A grain and fruit pap is fed to infants in Zaire in the first few weeks due to a belief that human milk is not sufficiently nutritious. Cassava, rice, beans, meat, and fish are diet staples by 5 months (Mennella, 1997). East Bhutan mothers introduce semisolid food at a median age of 3 months (Bohler & Bergstroem, 1995).

In the United States, parents are advised to begin supplemental foods at 6 months. To aid in detecting allergies or food intolerances, only one food at a time should be introduced. Weekly intervals should separate the introduction of each new food. Because they provide additional energy and iron, cereals are recommended to be the first foods introduced. Since cow's milk should not be used during the first year, dry cereals should be mixed with breast milk or formula. Rice cereal is the most easily tolerated cereal by most infants. Pureed vegetables, fruits, and meats can be begun after cereal feeding is well established. Combination foods should not be used until tolerance for all individual components has been established. Juices can be introduced when cup feedings are begun. Juices provide carbohydrates and vitamin C but should be limited to no more than 8 ounces per day so they do not replace breast milk or formula (Kleinman, 1998).

The developmental characteristics of the 6–9-month-old infant associated with readiness for solid foods include the fading of the extrusion reflex (tongue thrust upward and forward when object is placed in the mouth), the beginning of hand–eye coordination, the ability to sit, recognition of a spoon, biting and chewing, grasping with the hand, refusing food by keeping lips closed, and tooth appearance. Internally, the infant digestive system gains the ability to digest and absorb a variety of proteins, fats, and carbohydrates and renal maturity needed to excrete osmolar loads without excessive water loss (Kleinman, 1998; Wong et al., 1999).

Table 25.4   Feeding guide for children (age 2 to 3)

Food	Portion size	Servings	Comments
Milk and dairy products	$\frac{1}{2}$ cup (4 oz)	4.0–5.0	The following may be substituted for $\frac{1}{2}$ cup liquid milk: $\frac{1}{2}$–$\frac{3}{4}$ oz cheese, $\frac{1}{2}$ yogurt, $2\frac{1}{2}$ T nonfat dry milk
Meat, fish, poultry, or equivalent	1.0–2.0 oz	2	The following may be substituted for 1 oz meat, fish, or poultry: 1 egg, 2 T peanut butter, 4–5 T cooked legumes
Vegetable and fruits	4.0–5.0 oz		Include one green leafy or yellow vegetable for Vitamin A, such as carrots, spinach, broccoli, or winter squash
Vegetables raw**	Few pieces		
Vegetables cooked	2.0–3.0 T		
Fruit			Include one vitamin C-rich fruit, vegetable, or juice,
Raw	$\frac{1}{2}$–1 small		such as citrus juices, orange,
Canned	2.0–4.0 T		grapefruit, strawberries, melon, tomato, or broccoli
Juice	3.0–4.0 oz		
Bread and grain products	3.0–4.0 oz		The following may be substituted for 1 slice wholegrain or enriched $\frac{1}{2}$–1 slice of bread: $\frac{1}{2}$ cup spaghetti, macaroni, noodles, or rice; 5 saltines; $\frac{1}{2}$ English muffin or bagel; 1 tortilla
Cooked cereal	$\frac{1}{4}$–$\frac{1}{2}$ cup		
Dry cereal	$\frac{1}{2}$–1 cup		

** Do not give to children until they can chew well
Source: Adapted from M. E. Lowenberg (1993). Development of food patterns in young children. In P. L. Pipes & C. M. Trahms (Eds.), *Nutrition in infancy and childhood* (5th ed., pp. 168–169). St. Louis, MO: Mosby-Year Book; Kleinman & Committee on Nutrition, American Academy of Pediatrics (1998)

Nutritional Guidelines for Older Infants and Toddlers

As the growth slows during the second year, the calorie energy intake of infants also slows. Feeding guidelines for children between the ages of 2 and 3 years are shown in Table 25.4.

Eating becomes more of a social and fine motor interactive event than strictly a nutritional event. Food play is an expected and important part of toddler development. Increased finger control allows for experimentation with the physical properties of food. Social interaction at the family table may take precedence over consumption of prescribed quantities of food. Parents should not let these changes lead to negative interactions where the parent attempts to encourage the child to eat more while at the same time be less messy.

Until the age of 4, children should not be given foods that are hard, round, or that do not readily dissolve in saliva. Death by asphyxiation can result from choking. Foods that are most likely to cause choking include hot dogs, grapes, raw vegetables, popcorn, nuts, and hard candy (Kleinman, 1998).

Soy and rice milk formulas are available for infants of vegetarian families. Other milk substitutes such as kokkoh, a mixture of brown rice, sesame seeds, sweet brown rice, aduki beans, soybeans, wheat, and oats, have high-quality protein but cannot be ingested in sufficient volume to provide protein and energy needs. Infants given these milk substitutes may have inadequate weight gain and have specific nutritional problems, such as rickets, iron deficiency, and vitamin B12 deficiency.

Toddlers can be successfully weaned to a vegetarian diet with some precautions. Because vegetarian diets tend to be high in bulk, toddlers may be vulnerable to energy and nutrient deficiencies. Calorically dense foods, such as nuts, olives, dates, and avocados, should be encouraged. Additionally, toddlers should be encouraged to eat as wide a variety of foods as possible. The limited foods included in a macrobiotic diet may put toddlers at the greatest nutritional risk. Children given lacto-vegetarian (milk included) and lacto-ovo vegetarian (milk and eggs included) diets have been shown to have normal growth and development and are of less nutritional concern than pure vegetarian (vegan) diets (Kleinman, 1998).

Nutritional guidelines call for the infant to double the birth weight by 4 to 5 months and to triple the birth weight by 12 months. This rough guide gives a more accurate indication of diet adequacy than standardized tables that are normed on only one particular race and social-economic status. More clinical measures of adequate nutrition can be made with a weight-for-height table (Heird, 1999).

When macronutrient intake is inadequate, starvation results. Most human starvation results from protein and energy deficiency from lack of quantity of food, not from a lack of selected nutrients. The term semistarvation is also used to describe the condition of insufficient energy and protein provision. When the lean tissue loss reaches below 50 percent of body weight, death is probable. Death may result from the starvation itself or from infection, diarrhea with dehydration, starvation-induced immunodeficiency, hypothermia, anemia, or many other opportunistic conditions (Hoffer, 1999).

Kwashiorkor is the condition of insufficient protein intake. Marasmus is the condition of energy deficiency intake. Inadequate food intake leads to body wasting, growth retardation, and emaciation. The Ga tribe of the former Gold Coast (now Ghana) called kwashiorkor "the sickness the older child gets when the next baby is born." The most notable feature of this event is the lack of protein in the child's diet when weaned from milk (Torun & Chew, 1999, p. 964).

Marginal malnutrition may not limit energy and therefore may easily be overlooked. In a study of nutrition in a rural Egyptian village, many micronutrients were found to be suboptimal. In toddlers, cognitive and behavioral outcomes were significantly predicted by dietary quality (Kirkesy, 1994). Kibel and Wagstaff (1995) state that the weaning diet of third world children can be greatly improved by adding small amounts of animal protein or vegetable proteins with the basic weaning cereal. Energy can be improved by the addition of fat (margarine, oil, or peanut butter) or sugar.

Torun and Chew (1999) state:

> Protein-energy malnutrition is the most important nutritional disease in developing countries because of its high prevalence and its relationship with child mortality rates, impaired physical growth, and inadequate social and economical development. An epidemiological analysis from 53 developing countries indicates that 56 percent of deaths in children 6 to 59 months old were due to malnutrition's potentiating effects in infectious diseases and that mild and moderate malnutrition was involved in 83 percent of those deaths. (p. 964)

Malnutrition has a deleterious effect on mental growth and cognition. Malnourished children will have shorter periods of play and physical action and more rest time. The effects of malnutrition at an early age may include decreased brain growth, nerve myelination, neurotransmitter production, and velocity of nervous conduction.

Malnutrition occurs within a complex system of human social interaction. Poverty is the primary social/economic condition associated with malnourishment in both developed and developing countries. Many factors may influence the eventual developmental outcome of an infant or toddler experiencing malnutrition. These include the severity, timing, and duration of nutritional deprivation, the quality of nutritional rehabilitation and psychosocial support, and the degree of family stimulation. Even with treatment, many children will never be able to fully recover from infant/toddler malnutrition. Weight but not height can be restored, resulting in a stunted small adult body size. These children also appear to have later problems with cognition, creativity, and social interactions that may result from the complex dynamic environmental system within which malnutrition can occur (Torun & Chew, 1999).

Safety

Infant safety is influenced by a combination of a society's recognition of risk, the perceived cost/benefit ratio of enacting safety regulations, and the individual parent's motivation and ability to make changes in the immediate environment. In developing countries, the accidental death of infants is a major issue but tends to get overlooked because of the greater problems of infections, diseases, and malnutrition (Kibel & Wagstaff, 1995). In developed nations, infant safety issues become increasingly complex as a wider variety of available products introduce a comparable variety of new hazards.

Each major developmental milestone increases the variety of safety hazards for the infant. Rolling over, sitting up, grasping objects, crawling, walking, and climbing each widen the environment available for exploration and also injury.

Morbidity and Mortality

The strongest predictor of infant safety within the home is socioeconomic status (SES), a measure of the families' income, education, and social class. Education of parents is positively related to proactive home safety behaviors and fire-related safety behaviors. Additionally, higher family income removes the infant from the dangers found in poor housing, such as lead paint, pest infestation, and unprotected fall opportunities from windows, doors, and stairways. For example, children in poor families are more likely to live in apartment buildings than in single family homes. Children living in apartment buildings are five times more likely to fall from windows than are children living in single family dwellings. Most children experiencing window falls are males under the age of 3, playing unsupervised and living in large urban areas, low-income neighborhoods, and in deteriorating and overcrowded housing (National Safe Kids Campaign, 1996). Deteriorating housing is less likely to have safety features, such as window guards, even if required by zoning regulations.

The effect of SES on accident mortality is strongly evident in a study of burn mortality of South African children. The death rate for young children is seven times greater for economically disadvantaged colored (multiracial, low-SES African) children than for white children, whose lower death rate by burns compares favorably with that of developed nations.

The most frequent types of unintentional injuries in the United States for boys under the age of 1, in order of mortality, are mechanical suffocation, motor vehicle accidents, fires and burns, ingestion of food/object (choking), and drowning. For infant girls, the causes are mechanical suffocation, motor vehicle accidents, fires and burns, drowning, and ingestion of food/object (choking). These injuries account for 2.6 percent of all male infant (under age 1) deaths and 2.7 percent of all female infant deaths. These percentages jump to 38 percent and 34 percent, respectively, of all childhood deaths between the ages of 1 and 4, making injury the leading cause of death for children in this age group. Over the age of 1, more deaths and disabilities are caused by unintentional injuries than by all combined causes of diseases (Wong et al., 1999).

A study of mechanical suffocation deaths of 2178 infants between 1980 and 1997 found a relationship between the level of development of the infant and the mechanism of suffocation death. Wedging, especially between a mattress and crib side or room wall, is the primary source of mechanical suffocation death for infants between 3 to 6 months of age. Oronasal obstruction by objects, particularly plastic bags, is the second leading cause of suffocation in this study. Particularly vulnerable to this type of death are infants in the 0 to <3-month-old group and the 3- to <7-month-old group. The younger infants would be unable to grasp and move an obstruction away from their faces when accidentally encountered. The older infants' development has entered the exploratory level, with the ability to reach for and grasp objects. Plastic bags are a particular problem because the plastic adheres to the face through a combination of inhaling and static electricity. Additionally, plastic bags are strong, therefore they cannot be torn open by a struggling infant. Entrapments by suspension, hanging, and entanglement occur primarily with infants 7 months and older, and are associated with crawling and climbing infants encountering structural integrity problems of cribs and other infant furniture (Drago & Dannenberg, 1999). The data from the Drago and Dannenberg study came from death certificate reports. Their findings of significant danger of overlying for infants younger than 3 months of age must be viewed with caution in light of more recent findings concerning SIDS deaths associated with soft bedding. Death codes from earlier years reflect the knowledge base and judgment at the time of cause of death.

The most common source of suffocation for young children in the United States is latex balloons. These deaths could be prevented by not introducing latex balloons into the young child's environment. This includes not giving latex balloons to older siblings and not using latex balloons for decorations. Mylar and paper balloons are recommended instead (Baker & Halperin, 1995; Holida, 1993).

A major cause of infant mortality and morbidity occurs from drowning or near-drowning injury. Drowning is a fatal suffocation with death occurring within 24 hours of submersion in water. Near-drowning victims survive the first 24 hours but may later die. One-third of near-drowning victims who are initially comatose yet survive have significant neurologic impairment. Buckets, bathtubs, and toilets are the drowning sites most often found for infants under 1 year of age. Infants left alone in bathtubs, with or without support seats attached to the tub by suction cups, may fall over and not be able to turn themselves face up in the water nor sit up in the slippery tub. Toddlers and young children most often drown in unattended swimming pools. Infant swimming programs, while fun for parents and children, do not enable infants to be "water safe" and may foster in parents a false sense of security if they believe their infants can "swim" a few strokes (American Academy of Pediatrics, 1996a; Consumer Product Safety Commission, #5084). In Southern Africa, toddlers of economically privileged families are more likely to drown in pools than are infants from poor families. Economically middle- and upper-class families have more swimming pools, a luxury and a danger not available to the poorer families (Kibel & Wagstaff, 1995).

Less frequent but no less serious safety hazards include falls, poisonings, and strangulations. Many of these injuries and deaths occur in the presence of parents, who are either distracted or do not anticipate the increased dangers that accompany increased infant development.

Baby walkers have been called infant skateboards. Used primarily with infants between 5 and 15 months, the walkers enable infants to achieve surprising speeds. They also give infants access to hazardous areas, resulting in falls, burns, and poisonings. The primary cause of baby-walker injuries and deaths is falls down stairs (American Academy of Pediatrics, 1995c; Walker, Breau, McNeill, Rogers, & Sweet, 1996). Infants in walkers may receive more severe injuries when falling down stairs than do infants falling without walkers because of the increased kinetic energy due to the larger mass and higher initial speed (Lang-Runtz, 1983; Partington, Swanson, & Meyer, 1991). In the United States, an estimated 90 percent of infants use a walker before the age of 12 months and 50 percent sustain a walker-related injury. Stationary activity-center seats are recommended over walkers (Consumer Product Safety Commission, #5086; National Safe Kids Campaign, 1996).

A Swedish study found that most poisonings occur between 11 a.m. and noon and during the hour before the evening meal, when toddlers and young children are most hungry and parents are most busy and less vigilant (McKay, 1991). In Canadian and US studies of shopping-cart falls, the major predictors of shopping-cart injuries were children riding in the cart instead of in the seat, riding in the seat unsecured, and shopping trips that exceeded 23 minutes. Most children fall head first, with 66 percent needing treatment for head injuries, including 54 percent with severe injuries such as concussions and fractures. Shopping-cart falls are on the increase with over 16,000 young children injured in the United States in 1996 (Consumer Product Safety Commission, *Shopping cart injuries*; Harrell, 1994).

Ninety-three percent of window-cord strangulations in the United States occur to children under the age of 3. As with drownings, these are silent deaths because the victim cannot call for help. Infants left alone in their cribs are most likely to strangle on looped cords while playing or sleeping. Toddlers are more apt to get tangled in cords when climbing on furniture to look out windows. In the majority of window-cord strangulations (85 percent), parents are home at the time of the death (Rauchschwalbe & Mann, 1997).

Significant predictors of home-safety practices and fire-related safety behaviors by mothers include self-efficacy, more vigilant maternal supervisory style, knowledge concerning safety hazards, perception of possible risk of injury, maternal social support, and previous injury experience of the mother (Glik, Greaves, Kronenfeld, & Jackson, 1993; Greaves, Glik, Kronenfeld, & Jackson, 1994; Kronenfeld, Glik, & Jackson, 1991; Russell & Champion, 1996). The results of a Norway study show that parents of infants do take action to increase household safety when educated about possible dangers (Thuen, 1992). Even so, more can be done. An Australian study found between 8 and 12 safety hazards in 75 percent of the homes of young children. Encouragingly, an education intervention program was found to be significantly successful in reducing home hazards (Paul, Sanson-Fisher, Redman, & Carter, 1994). Safety education cannot be viewed as a one-time effort. As each generation reaches adult age and begins childbearing, they need to be made aware of hazards. As infants and toddlers develop, parents' attention needs to be directed to the increasingly complex possibilities for injury.

Consumer Protection for Infant Care Products and Furniture

The Consumer Affairs Bureau of Australia, the United States Consumer Product Safety Commission, the South African Bureau of Standards, and the Consumer Policy, Consumer Health Protection division of the European Commission and the United States Food and Drug Administration are examples of governmental agencies with the power to prevent the retail sale of dangerous items and to remove from retail sales any item found to present a danger. The widespread regulations of these agencies range from control of contaminants in baby food, the polymer composition of bottle and pacifier nipples, the size and construction of toys sold for use by children under the age of 3, fabric and design of infant clothing, and the construction and size specifications on infant furniture. The US Consumer Product Safety Commission has been fundamental in the regulation of crib mattress size and crib slat width to prevent accidental strangulation deaths of infants. Within the United States, the greatest danger from infant furniture comes from outdated models that escaped recall by manufacturers and are continually passed from family to family through the resale market.

The American Academy of Pediatrics has made the statement that most injuries are predictable and therefore preventable. Study of the causes of injuries have led to regulations on car safety seats, smoke detectors, child-resistant lighters, child-resistant lids on medication and household cleaner containers, and window guards on higher-story windows (American Academy of Pediatrics, 1996b).

Car Safety

Safety for infants during transportation in cars has been greatly increased by the development of infant safety seats. Even minor accidents can result in major head trauma and death for unrestrained infants. A study in Israel found that, of parents owning cars, 49.2 percent admitted to traveling with children held on their laps (Gofin & Palti, 1991).

Current infant safety seats are designed to enclose the infant in a protective shell attached to the car with adult seatbelts. Survival of infants in demolished vehicles where other passengers have been killed has become common testimony to the effectiveness of these safety seats. All states have laws requiring the use of safety seats for infants and children under 5 years.

Car safety seats sold in the United States since 1981 must pass a dynamic crash test. Pre-1981 seats are still available on the aftermarket, being sold at second-hand stores or passed from family to family. A bigger problem with used seats is missing pieces, missing instructions for correct use of the seat, seats recalled by the manufacturer for safety problems, and damage to the seat from previous crashes (American Academy of Pediatrics, 1996d; Cunningham, 1997). Airbags are being modified to better protect infants in safety seats (Air Bag Safety Campaign, 1998).

Results of studies on parents' behaviors in using infant car safety seats are discouraging. Few infants and toddlers are correctly belted into correctly installed seats (Air Bag Safety Campaign, 1998; Consumers' Research, 1996; Decina, 1997). Regulations from the year 2000 require car manufacturers to standardize infant car safety seat installation and belting mechanisms across all brands and models of cars. This change is expected to increase correct usage of infant car safety seats.

Conclusion and Future Trends

Western cultural influences on infant care practices in developing nations have both positive and negative impacts. Immunization efforts have eliminated or greatly controlled many of the contagious diseases that killed many infants in the past. Conversely, Western products, such as commercial formula, are sought by parents in many countries where the average family does not have the economic ability to afford these products. The desire is created, breaking down the traditional cultural support for breastfeeding, placing infants in danger.

As more middle-class women in developed countries have breastfed their infants, longitudinal studies are now taking place on the long-term benefits of human milk. These studies were not possible in the post-World War II era when the majority of middle-class mothers chose formula. Low-SES mothers who did breastfeed also presented too many potential confounding factors to successfully study the main effect of breastfeeding on later childhood development. Current research studies are finding possible correlations with later intellectual development and academic skills.

SIDS is now understood to be a variety of somewhat related factors that somehow contribute to the death of young infants. The campaign to place infants on their backs for sleep has resulted in a marked decrease in SIDS deaths. The contributions of other risk factors remain to be understood.

Finally, the complex ecological system related to optimal infant health and safety has yet to be understood. Cultural values change over time, as illustrated by the swing in popular feeding methods in the United States during the past century, from breastfeeding for the first 50 years to bottle feeding following World War II, then back to breastfeeding in the last decades of the twentieth century. The gap in health care between the poor and nonpoor is increasingly wide in all parts of the world. Immunizations can effectively prevent many devastating diseases yet are unused or unavailable to a sizeable percentage of the world's infants. The strong body of research on infant development has aided leaders in many countries in understanding the importance of early quality care of infants and the benefits of early intervention programs for infants at risk for developmental delays due to birth defects, disease, or environmental factors. Early intervention programs have been developed on the community, state, and national levels to identify those infants who would benefit from extra nutritional support, medical care, and developmentally appropriate therapy. Despite this understanding of the importance of optimal early care of infants for later development, routine care for infants of employed parents is often left to the least trained and most poorly paid members of industrialized societies. Advances in engineering create safer products, leading to fewer injuries and deaths. Conversely, most young adults become parents with no formal instruction in maintaining the health and safety of their infants.

Reductions in infant mortality and morbidity in developed countries during the last century testify that we have the ability to keep infants safe, healthy, and well nourished. The challenge of the twenty-first century will be to extend that opportunity to all infants throughout the world.

Further Reading

Batshaw, M. L. (1997). *Children with disabilities.* Baltimore: Brookes.

Beckman, P. J. (1996). *Strategies for working with families of young children with disabilities.* Baltimore: Brookes.

Kibel, M. A., & Wagstaff, L. A. (1995). *Child health for all: A manual for Southern Africa* (2nd ed.). Cape Town: Oxford University Press.

Kleinman, R. E., & Committee on Nutrition, American Academy of Pediatrics. (1998). *Pediatric nutrition handbook* (4th ed.). Elk Grove Village, IL: American Academy of Pediatrics.

Shils, M. E., Olsen, J. A., Shike, M., & Ross, C. A. (Eds.). (1999). *Modern nutrition in health and disease* (9th ed.). Hagerstown, MD: Lippincott, Williams, & Wilkins.

Widerstrom, A. H., Mowder, B. A., & Sandall, S. R. (1997). *Infant development and risk* (2nd ed.). Baltimore: Brookes.

Wong, D. L., Hockenberry-Eaton, M., Wilson, D., Winkelstein, M. L., Ahmann, E., & DiVito-Thomas, P. A. (1999). *Whaley & Wong's nursing care of infants and children* (6th ed.). St. Louis: Mosby.

References

Air Bag Safety Campaign. (1998). *New survey reveals infants continue to be placed in harm's way despite universal awareness of risks air bags pose to children* [On-line]. Kid Source: www.kidsource.com/kidsource/content4/air.bags.infant.html.

Amanda, M., & Singh, R. P. (1992). A study of intelligence of children in relation to infant-feeding practices and nutrition. *Indian Journal of Psychometry and Education, 23*(1), 23–28.

American Academy of Pediatrics. (1985, reaffirmed 1990). Infant swimming programs RE5045. *Pediatrics, 75*(4), www.aap.org/policy/362.html.

American Academy of Pediatrics. (1995a). Human milk, breastfeeding, and transmission of human immunodeficiency virus in the United States RE9542. *Pediatrics, 96*(5), 977–979.

American Academy of Pediatrics. (1995b). Implementation of the immunization policy (S94–26) RE9531. *Pediatrics, 96*(2), 360–361.

American Academy of Pediatrics. (1995c). Injuries associated with infant walkers RE9520. *Pediatrics, 95*(5), 778–780.

American Academy of Pediatrics. (1996a). Drowning in infants, children and adolescents RE9319. *Pediatrics, 92*(2), 292–294.

American Academy of Pediatrics. (1996b). Efforts to reduce the toll of injuries in childhood require expanded research RE9619. *Pediatrics, 97*(5), 765–768.

American Academy of Pediatrics. (1996c). Positioning and Sudden Infant Death Syndrome (SIDS): Update RE9647. *Pediatrics, 98*(6), 1216–1218.

American Academy of Pediatrics. (1996d). Selecting and using the most appropriate car safety seats for growing children: Guidelines for counseling parents RE9618. *Pediatrics, 97*(5), 761–762.

American Academy of Pediatrics. (1997). Environmental tobacco smoke: A hazard to children RE9716. *Pediatrics, 99*(4), 639–642.

American Academy of Pediatrics. (1998). Female genital mutilation RE9749. *Pediatrics, 102*(1), 153–156.

American Academy of Pediatrics. (1999a). Circumcision policy statement RE9850. *Pediatrics, 103*(3), 686–693.

American Academy of Pediatrics. (1999b). Combination vaccines for childhood immunization: Recommendations of the Advisory Committee on Immunization Practices (ACIP), the American Academy of Pediatrics (AAP), and the American Academy of Family Physicians (AAFP) RE9909. *Pediatrics, 103*(5), 1064–1077.

American Academy of Pediatrics. (1999c). Poliomyelitis prevention: revised recommendations for use of inactivated and live oral poliovirus vaccines RE9853. *Pediatrics, 103*(1), 171–172.

American Academy of Pediatrics. (1999d). Recommended childhood immunization schedule-United States, January-December 1999 RE9901. *Pediatrics, 103*(1), 182–185.

Anand, K. J., & Carr, D. B. (1989). The neuroanatomy, neurophysiology, and neurochemistry of pain, stress, and analgesia in newborns and children. *Pediatric Clinic North America, 36*(4), 795–822.

Anand, K. J., & Hickey, P. (1987). Pain and its effects in the human neonate and fetus. *New England Journal of Medicine, 317*, 1321–1329.

Anand, K. S., Grunau, R. E., & Oberlander, T. F. (1997). Developmental character and long-term consequences of pain in infants and children. *Child and Adolescent Psychiatric Clinic North America, 6*(4), 703–724.

Armstrong, S. (1991). Female circumcision: Fighting a cruel tradition. *New Scientist, 129,* 42–48.

Attia, J., et al. (1987). Measurement of postoperative pain and narcotic administration in infants using a new clinical scoring system. *Anesthesiology, 67*(3A).

Australian College of Paediatrics. (1996). *Position statement: Routine circumcision of normal male infants and boys* [On-line]. Parkville, Victoria: www.cirp.org/library/statements/acp1996/.

Australian Medical Association. (1997). Circumcision deterred. *Australian Medicine, 6–20,* 5.

Awoyinka, A. (1992). Nutritional knowledge and child feeding practices of mothers in Ile-Ife. *Early Child Development and Care, 80,* 43–52.

Azaiza, F., & Palti, H. (1997). Determinants of breastfeeding among rural Moslem women in Israel. *Family Systems Medicine, 15*(2), 203–211.

Baker, S. P., & Halperin, K. (1995). Designing the death out of balloons. *Journal of the American Medical Association, 274*(22), 1805.

Banta-Wright, S. A. (1997). Minimizing infant exposure to risks from medications while breastfeeding. *Journal of Perinatal and Neonatal Nursing, 11*(2), 71–84.

Barba, B. (1991). Pain memory in full-term newborns. *Journal of Pain Symptom Management, 6,* 206.

Bobat, R., Moodley, D., Coutsoudis, A., & Coovadia, H. (1997). Breast feeding by HIV-1-infected women and outcome in their infants: A cohort study from Durban, South Africa. *AIDS, 11*(13), 1627–1633.

Bohler, E., & Bergstroem, S. (1995). Premature weaning in East Bhutan: Only if mother is pregnant again. *Journal of Biosocial Science, 27*(3), 253–265.

Bozzette, M. (1993). Observation of pain behavior in the NICU: An exploratory study. *Journal of Perinatal and Neonatal Nursing, 7*(1), 76–87.

Brent, N. B., & Wisner, K. L. (1998). Fluexetine and carbamazepine concentrations in a nursing mother/infant pair. *Clinical Pediatrics, 37*(1), 41–44.

Breyer-Pfaff, U., Nill, K., Entenmann, A., & Gaertner, H. J. (1995). Secretion of amitriptyline and metabolites into breast milk. *American Journal of Psychiatry, 152*(5), 812–813.

British Medical Association. (1996). *Circumcision of male infants* [On-line]. www.cirp.org/library/statements/bma/.

Campbell, S. B., Cohn, J. G., & Meyers, T. (1995). Depression in first-time mothers: Mother–infant interaction and depression chronicity. *Developmental Psychology, 31,* 349–357.

Canadian Foundation for the Study of Infant Deaths. (1999). *What is SIDS?* [On-line]. http://www.sidscanada.org/sids.html.

Child Life Council. (1994). *Official documents of the Child Life Council* (2nd ed.). Rockville, MD: Child Life Council.

Cohen, R., & Mrtek, M. B. (1994). The impact of two corporate lactation programs on the incidence and duration of breast-feeding by employed mothers. *American Journal of Health Promotion, 8*(6), 436–441.

Cohn, J. F., Campbell, S. B., Matias, R., & Hobkins, J. (1990). Face-to-face interactions of postpartum depressed and nondepressed mother–infant pairs at 2 months. *Developmental Psychology, 26*(1), 15–23.

Cohn, J. F., Matias, R., Tronick, E. Z., Lyons-Ruth, K., & Connell, D. (1986). Face-to-face interactions, spontaneous and structured, of mothers with depressive symptoms. In T. Field & E. Z.
Tronick (Eds.), *Maternal depression and child development: New directions for child development*
(pp. 31–46). San Francisco: Jossey-Bass.

Consumer Product Safety Commission. (n.d.). *CPSC gets new, safer baby walkers on the market.*
CPSC Document # 5086 [On-line]. www.cpsc.gov/cpscpub/5086.html.

Consumer Product Safety Commission. (n.d.). *Shopping cart injuries: Victims 5 years old and
younger* [On-line]. www.cpsc.gov/library/shopcart.html.

Consumer Product Safety Commission. (n.d.). *CPSC warns of drowning hazard with baby
"supporting ring" devices: Safety alert.* CPSC Document #5084 [On-line].
www.cpsc.gov:70/00/CPSC_chdrown/5084.txt.

Consumers' Research. (1996, May). Safety standard revisions considered: Towards fewer serious
air bag injuries. *Consumers' Research*, 28–31 [On-line]. www.researcher.sirs.com/cgi-bin/
res-article-display?6TR029A.

Cote, J. J., Morse, J. M., & James, S. G. (1991). The pain *response* of the postoperative newborn.
Journal of Advances in Nursing, 16, 378–387.

Cunningham, C. (1997). *Be smart about air bags* [On-line]. Loma Linda University:
www.llu.edu/lluch/carseat.html.

Cutting, W. A. (1994). Breast feeding and HIV: A balance of risks. *Journal of Tropical Pediatrics,
40,* 6–11.

Decina, L. E. (1997). Child safety seat misuse patterns in four states. *Accident Analysis and
Prevention, 29*(1), 125–132.

Dignam, D. M. (1995). Understanding intimacy as experienced by breastfeeding women. *Health
Care for Women International, 16*(5), 477–485.

Drago, A. A., & Dannenberg, A. L. (1999). Infant mechanical suffocation deaths in the United
States, 1980–1997. *Pediatrics, 103*(5), E59.

Epstein, K. (1993). The interactions between breastfeeding mothers and their babies during the
breastfeeding session. *Early Child Development and Care, 87,* 93–104.

Escriba, V., Colomer, C., Mas, R., & Grifol, R. (1994). Working conditions and the decision to
breastfeed in Spain. *Health Promotion International, 9*(4), 251–258.

Farley, D. (1998). Dangers of lead still linger. *FDA Consumer, 32*(1), 16.

Field, T. (1987). Affective and interactive disturbances in infants. In J. D. Osofsky (Ed.), *Handbook of infant development* (2nd ed., pp. 972–1005). New York: Wiley.

Field, T., Healy, B., Goldstein, S., Perry, S., Bendell, D., Schanberg, S., Zimmerman, E. A., &
Kuhn, C. (1988). Infants of depressed mothers show "depressed" behavior even with non-
depressed adults. *Child Development, 59,* 1569–1579.

Field, T., Healy, B., & LeBlanc, W. G. (1989). Sharing and synchrony of behavior states and heart
rate in nondepressed versus depressed mother–infant interactions. *Infant Behavior and Development, 12,* 357–376.

Field, T., Morrow, C., & Adelstein, D. (1993). Depressed mothers' perceptions of infant
behavior. *Infant Behavior and Development, 16,* 99–108.

Field, T., Sandberg, D., Garcia, R., Vega-Lahr, N., Goldstein, S., & Guy, L. (1985). Pregnancy
problems, postpartum depression and early mother–infant interactions. *Developmental Psychology, 21*(6), 1152–1156.

Fildes, V. (1986). *Breasts, bottles and babies: A history of infant feeding.* Edinburgh: Edinburgh
University Press.

Fitzgerald, M. (1995). Pain in infancy: Some unanswered questions. *Pain Reviews, 2,* 77–
91.

Fitzgerald, M., Millard, C., & McIntosh, N. (1989). Cutaneous hypersensitivity following periph-eral tissue damage in newborn infants and its reversal with topical anesthesia. *Pain, 39*, 31–36.

Fleming, A. S., Ruble, D. N., Flett, G. L., & Shaul, D. L. (1988). Postpartum adjustment in first-time mothers: Relations between mood, maternal attitudes, and mother–infant interactions. *Developmental Psychology, 24*, 71–81.

Fox, C. R., & Gelfand, D. M. (1994). Maternal depressed mood and stress as related to vigilance, self-efficacy and mother–child interactions. *Early Development and Parenting, 3*, 233–343.

Franck, L. S. (1987). A national survey of the assessment and treatment of pain and agitation in the neonatal intensive care unit. *JOGNN, 16*(6), 387–393.

Freed, G. L., Fraley, J. K., & Schanler, R. (1993). Accuracy of expectant mothers' predictions of fathers' attitudes regarding breast-feeding. *Journal of Family Practice, 37*(2), 148–152.

Gelfand, D. M., & Teti, D. M. (1990). The effects of maternal depression on children. *Clinical Psychology Review, 10*, 329–353.

Gelfand, D. M., Teti, D. M., & Fox, C. E. R. (1992). Sources of parenting stress for depressed and nondepressed mothers of infants. *Journal of Clinical Child Psychology, 21*, 262–272.

General Medical Council. (1997). *Guidance for doctors who are asked to perform male circumcision* [On-line]. www.cirp.org/library/statements/gmc/.

Glik, D., Greaves, P. E., Kronenfeld, J. J., & Jackson, K. L. (1993). Safety hazards in households with young children. *Journal of Pediatric Psychology, 18*(1), 115–131.

Gofin, R., & Palti, H. (1991). Injury prevention practices of mothers of 0 to 2 year olds: A devel-opmental approach. *Early Child Development and Care, 71*, 117–126.

Golding, J., Rogers, I. S., & Emmett, P. M. (1997). Association between breast feeding, child development and behavior. *Early Human Development, 49*(Suppl.), S175–S184.

Gray, S. J. (1994). Comparison of effects of breast-feeding practices on birth-spacing in three soci-eties: Nomadic Turkana, Gainj, and Quechua. *Journal of Biosocial Science, 26*(1), 69–90.

Greaves, P., Glik, D. C., Kronenfeld, J. J., & Jackson, K. (1994). Determinants of controllable in-home child safety hazards. *Health Education Research, 9*(3), 307–315.

Grunau, R. V., & Craig, K. D. (1987). Pain expression in neonates: Facial action and cry. *Pain, 28*, 395–410.

Grunau, R. V., Johnston, C. C., & Craig, K. D. (1990). Neonatal facial and cry responses to inva-sive and noninvasive procedures. *Pain, 42*(3), 295–305.

Harrell, W. A. (1994). The impact of shopping cart restraints and adult supervision on near injuries to children in grocery stores. *Accident Analysis and Prevention, 26*(4), 493–500.

Harris, G., Thomas, A., & Booth, D. A. (1990). Development of salt taste in infancy. *Develop-mental Psychology, 26*(4), 534–538.

Heird, W. C. (1999). Nutritional requirements during infancy. In M. E. Shils, J. A. Olsen, M. Shike, & C. A. Ross (Eds.), *Modern nutrition in health and disease* (9th ed., pp. 839–856). Baltimore: Williams & Wilkins.

Hoffer, L. J. (1999). Metabolic consequences of starvation. In M. E. Shils, J. A. Olsen, M. Shike, & C. A. Ross (Eds.), *Modern nutrition in health and disease* (9th ed., pp. 645–666). Baltimore: Williams & Wilkins.

Holida, D. L. (1993). Latex balloons: They can take your breath away. *Pediatric Nursing, 19*(1), 39–43.

Hoover, D. R., Doherty, M. C., Vlahov, D., & Miotti, P. (1996). Incidence and risk factors for HIV-1 infection: A summary of what is known and the psychiatric relevance. *International Review of Psychiatry, 8*(2–3), 137–148.

Horwood, L. J., & Fergusson, D. M. (1998). Breastfeeding and later cognitive and academic outcomes. *Pediatrics, 101*(1), E9.

Human Milk Banking Association of North America. (1993). *Recommendations for collection, storage, and handling of a mother's milk for her own infant in the hospital setting.* West Hartford, CT: Human Milk Banking Association of North America.

Institute for Development Training. (1986). *Female genital mutilation: Proposals for change.* Chapel Hill, NC: Institute for Development Training.

International Association for Maternal and Neonatal Health. (1991). Female circumcision. *Mother and Child International Newsletter, 17,* 4–5.

Jingheng, H., Yindi, X., Yongxin, J., & Jie, X. (1994). Evaluation of a health education programme in China to increase breast-feeding rates. *Health Promotion International, 9*(2), 95–98.

Johnson, D. L., Swank, P. R., Howie, V. M., & Baldwin, C. D. (1996). Breast feeding and children's intelligence. *Source Psychological Reports, 79*(3, Pt. 2), 1179–1185.

Johnston, C. C., & Strada, M. E. (1986). Acute pain response in infants: A multidimensional description. *Pain, 24,* 373–382.

Kibel, M. A., & Wagstaff, L. A. (1995). *Child health for all: A manual for Southern Africa* (2nd ed.). Cape Town: Oxford University Press.

Kirkesy, A. (1994). Moderate malnutrition in an Egyptian village: Association with pregnancy outcome and infant development. *Nutrition Today, 29,* 30–38.

Kleinman, R. E., & Committee on Nutrition, American Academy of Pediatrics. (1998). *Pediatric nutrition handbook* (4th ed.). Elk Grove Village, IL: American Academy of Pediatrics.

Knestrick, J., & Milstead, J. A. (1998). Public policy and child lead poisoning: Implementation of Title X. *Pediatric Nursing, 24*(1), 37.

Kouba, L. J., & Muasher, J. (1985). Female circumcision in Africa: An overview. *African Studies Review, 28,* 95–110.

Krechel, S. W., & Bildner, J. (1995). CRIES – A new neonatal postoperative pain measurement score: Initial testing of validity and reliability. *Paediatric Anaesthesia, 5,* 53–61.

Kronenfeld, J. J., Glik, D., & Jackson, K. (1991). Home fire safety and related behaviors among parents of preschoolers. *Children's Environments Quarterly, 8*(3–4), 31–40.

Lang-Runtz, H. (1983). Preventing accidents in the home. *Canadian Medical Association Journal, 129,* 482–485.

Lawrence, R. A. (1999). *Breastfeeding: A guide for the medical profession* (5th ed.). St. Louis: Mosby.

Lindberg, L. D. (1996). Women's decisions about breastfeeding and maternal employment. *Journal of Marriage and the Family, 58*(1), 239–251.

Littman, H., Medendorp, S. V., & Goldfarb, J. (1994). The decision to breastfeed: The importance of fathers' approval. *Clinical Pediatrics, 33*(4), 214–219.

Malloy, M. H., & Berendes, H. (1998). Does breast-feeding influence intelligence quotients at 9 and 10 years of age? *Early Human Development, 50*(2), 209–217.

McCleary, P. H. (1994). Female genital mutilation and childbirth: A case report. *Birth, 21*(4), 221–223.

McGanity, W. J., Dawson, E. B., & van Hook, J. M. (1999). Maternal nutrition. In M. E. Shils, J. A. Olsen, M. Shike, & C. A. Ross (Eds.), *Modern nutrition in health and disease* (9th ed., pp. 811–838). Baltimore: Williams & Wilkins.

McKay, S. E. (1991, March 7). Take a crawl around to get toddler's view when home-proofing. *Toronto Star,* N12.

Mennella, J. A. (1997). A cross-cultural perspective. *Nutrition Today, 32*(4), 144–151.

Mennella, J. A., & Beauchamp, G. K. (1992). Alcohol in mother's milk: Reply. *New England Journal of Medicine, 326*(11), 767.

Mofenson, L. (1995). A critical review of studies evaluating the relationship of mode of delivery to perinatal transmission of human immunodeficiency virus. *Pediatrics Infectious Disease Control, 14,* 169–177.

Morley, R., & Lucas, A. (1994). Influence of early diet on outcome in preterm infants. *Acta Paediatrica Supplement, 405,* 123–126.

Morse, J. M., & Bottorff, J. L. (1992). The emotional experience of breast expression. In J. Morse et al. (Eds.), *Qualitative health research* (pp. 319–332). Newbury Park, CA: Sage.

National Safe Kids Campaign. (1996). *Falls* [On-line]. www.safekids.org/fact96/fall.html.

Newberg, D. S., & Street, J. M. (1997). Bioactive materials in human milk: Milk sugars sweeten the argument for breast-feeding. *Nutrition Today, 32*(5), 191–200.

Ntiri, D. W. (1993). Circumcision and health among rural women of southern Somalia as part of a family life survey. *Health Care Women International, 14,* 215–226.

Paradise, J. L., Elster, B. A., & Tan, L. (1994). Evidence in infants with cleft palate that breast milk protects against otitis media. *Pediatrics, 94,* 853–860.

Partington, M. D., Swanson, J. A., & Meyer, F. B. (1991). Head injury and the use of baby walkers: A continuing problem. *Annals of Emergency Medicine, 20,* 652–654.

Paul, C. L., Sanson-Fisher, R. W., Redman, S., & Carter, S. (1994). Preventing accidental injury to young children in the home using volunteers. *Health Promotion International, 9*(4), 241–249.

Paul, K., Jaroslava, D., & Hanus, P. (1996). Infant feeding behavior: Development in patterns and motivation. *Developmental Psychobiology, 29*(7), 563–576.

Penticuff, J. (1987). Neonatal nursing ethics: Toward a consensus. *Neonatal Network, 5,* 7–16.

Pickens, J. N., & Field, T. (1995). Facial expressions and vagal tone of infants of depressed and non-depressed mothers. *Early Development and Parenting, 4,* 83–89.

Pollock, J. J. (1994). Long-term associations with infant feeding in a clinically advantaged population of babies. *Developmental Medicine and Child Neurology, 36*(5), 429–440.

Powers, N. G., Naylor, A. J., & Wester, R. A. (1994). Hospital policies: Crucial to breastfeeding success. *Seminars in Perinatology, 18,* 517–524.

Rabinowitz, R., & Hulbert, W. C. (1995). Newborn circumcision should not be performed without anesthesia. *Birth, 22*(1), 45–46.

Rauchschwalbe, R., & Mann, C. (1997). Pediatric window-cord strangulations in the United States, 1981–1995. *Journal of the American Medical Association, 277,* 1696–1698.

Richards, M., Wadsworth, M., Rahimi-Foroushani, A., Hardy, R., Huh, D., & Paul, A. (1998). Infant nutrition and cognitive development in the first offspring of a national UK birth cohort. *Development Medical Child Neurology, 40*(3), 163–167.

Rogan, W. J., & Gladen, B. C. (1993). Breast-feeding and cognitive development. *Early Human Development, 31*(3), 181–193.

Romito, P., & Saurel-Cubizolles, M. J. (1996). Working women and breast feeding: The experience of first-time mothers in an Italian town. *Journal of Reproductive and Infant Psychology, 14*(2), 145–156.

Rossiter, J. C. (1994). The effect of a culture-specific education program to promote breastfeeding among Vietnamese women in Sydney. *International Journal of Nursing Studies, 31*(4), 369–379.

Russell, K. M., & Champion, V. L. (1996). Health beliefs and social influence in home safety practices of mothers with preschool children. *Image: The Journal of Nursing Scholarship, 28*(1), 59–64.

Rustein, R. M., Conlon, C. J., & Batshaw, M. L. (1997). HIV and AIDS from mother to child. In M. L. Batshaw (Ed.), *Children with disabilities* (4th ed., pp. 163–181). Baltimore: Brookes.

Scheers, N. J., Dayton, M., & Kemp, J. S. (1998). Sudden infant death with external airways covered: Case-comparison study of 206 deaths in the United States. *Archives of Pediatrics and Adolescent Medicine, 122*(6), 540–547.

Shapiro, C. R. (1989). Pain in the neonate: Assessment and intervention. *Neonatal Network 8*(1), 7–21.

Sharma, A., Lynch, M. A., & Irvine, M. L. (1994). The availability of advice regarding infant feeding to immigrants of Vietnamese origin: A survey of families and health visitors. *Child: Care, Health and Development, 20*(5), 349–354.

Shelton, T., & Stepanek, J. S. (1994). *Family-centered care for children needing specialized health and developmental services.* Bethesda, MD: Association for the Care of Children's Health.

Shils, M. E., Olsen, J. A., Shike, M., & Ross, C. A. (Eds.). (1999). *Modern nutrition in health and disease* (9th ed.). Hagerstown, MD: Lippincott, Williams, & Wilkins.

SIDS Alliance. (1998). *Facts about sudden infant death syndrome* [On-line]. http://www.sidsalliance.org/facts/main.asp.

Simmons, R. L., Lorenz, F. O., Wu, C. K., & Conger, R. D. (1993). Social network and marital support as mediators and moderators of the impact of stress and depression on parental behavior. *Developmental Psychology, 29*, 368–381.

Sinclair-Smith, C. C., & Kibel, M. A. (1986). Sudden infant death. *South African Journal of Continuing Medical Education, 4*(13), 7.

Spigset, O., & Haegg, S. (1998). Excretion of psychotropic drugs into breast milk: Pharmacokinetic overview and therapeutic implications. *CNS Drugs, 9*(2), 111–124.

Stowe, Z. N., Owens, M. J., Landry, J. C., Kilts, C. D., Ely, T., Llewellyn, A., & Nemeroff, C. B. (1997). Setraline and desmethylsertraline in human breast milk and nursing infants. *American Journal of Psychiatry, 154*(9), 1255–1260.

Taddio, A., Katz, J., Ilersich, A. L., & Koren, G. (1997). Effect of neonatal circumcision on pain response during newborn circumcision. *Pediatrics, 349*, 599–603.

Thompson, P., & Bell, P. (1997). Breast-feeding in the workplace: How to succeed. *Issues in Comprehensive Pediatric Nursing, 20*(1), 1–9.

Thuen, F. (1992). Preventing childhood accidents in the home: Parental behavior to reduce household hazards. *Scandinavian Journal of Psychology, 33*(4), 370–377.

Torun, B., & Chew, F. (1999). Protein-energy malnutrition. In M. E. Shils, J. A. Olsen, M. Shike, & C. A. Ross (Eds.), *Modern nutrition in health and disease* (9th ed., pp. 963–988). Baltimore: Williams & Wilkins.

United States Bureau of the Census. (1998). *Statistical abstracts of the United States* (118th ed.). Washington, DC: Author.

Van Esterik, P. (1989). *Beyond the breast–bottle controversy.* New Brunswick, NJ: Rutgers University Press.

Walker, J. M., Breau, L., McNeill, D., Rogers, B., & Sweet, K. (1996). Hazardous baby walkers: A survey of use. *Pediatric Physical Therapy, 8*(1), 25–30.

Wellington, N., & Rieder, M. J. (1993). Attitudes and practices regarding analgesia for newborn circumcision. *New England Journal of Medicine, 336*(17), 1197–1201.

Wigg, N. R., Tong, S., McMichael, A. J., Baghurst, P. A., Vimpani, G., & Roberts, R. (1998). Does breastfeeding at six months predict cognitive development? *Australian and New Zealand Journal of Public Health, 22*(2), 232–236.

Wijekoon, A. S., Thattil, R. O., & Schensul, S. (1995). First trimester feeding in a rural Sri Lankan population. *Social Science and Medicine, 40*(4), 443–449.

Wisner, K. L., & Perel, J. M. (1998). Serum levels of valproate and carbamazepine in breastfeeding mother–infant pairs. *Journal of Clinical Psychopharmacology, 18*(2), 167–169.

Wisner, K. L., Perel, J. M., Findling, R. L., & Hinnes, R. L. (1997). Nortriptyline and its hydroxy-metabolites in breastfeeding mothers and newborns. *Psychopharmacology Bulletin, 33*(2), 249–251.

Wong, D. L. (1992). *Physiological responses, facial expressions, and cry of infants during immunization in relation to their pain history.* University Microfilm (Order No. 9321617).

Wong, D. L., Hockenberry-Eaton, M., Wilson, D., Winkelstein, M. L., Ahmann, E., & DiVito-Thomas, P. A. (1999). *Whaley & Wong's nursing care of infants and children* (6th ed.). St. Louis: Mosby.

World Health Organization. (1997). *Female genital mutilation.* Geneva: Author.

Wright, A. L., Naylor, A., Wester, R., Bauer, M., & Sutcliffe, E. (1997). Using cultural knowledge in health promotion: Breastfeeding among the Navajo. *Health Education and Behavior, 24*(5), 625–639.

Yoshida, K., & Kumar, R. (1996). Breast feeding and psychotropic drugs. *International Review of Psychiatry, 8*(1), 117–124.

Yoshida, K., Smith, B., Craggs, M., & Kumar, R. C. (1997). Investigation of pharmacokinetics and of possible adverse effects in infants exposed to tricyclic antidepressants in breast milk. *Journal of Affective Disorders, 43*(3), 225–237.

Yoshida, K., Smith, B., Craggs, M., & Kumar, R. C. (1998a). Fluoxetine in breast milk and developmental outcome of breast fed infants. *British Journal of Psychiatry, 172*, 175–179.

Yoshida, K., Smith, B., Craggs, M., & Kumar, R. C. (1998b). Neuroleptic drugs in breast milk: A study of pharmacokinetics and of possible adverse effects in breast fed infants. *Psychological Medicine, 28*(1), 81–91.

Chapter Twenty-six

The History (and Future) of Infancy

Alan Fogel

Introduction

What is best for babies? Cuddling and indulgence? Early training for independent self-care? It seems as if there should be one right answer. Babies in every human society and ethnic group have similar needs and abilities. In practice, the answer depends upon the beliefs that people have about babies. Beliefs about infants and their care differ between cultures and they have changed dramatically over historical time within cultures.

The contemporary technology of infant care in Western society, for example, first appears in the eighteenth and nineteenth centuries, with an increase in pediatric medical care, advice books for parents, parental devotion to the individuality of each child, books written especially for young children, and other infant care products and resources. Some of the present-day beliefs about infants and their care, however, have their roots in prehistory.

Why is it important to understand the historical origins and historical pathways of beliefs about infants and their care? Cultural history is vast in its domain, encompassing beliefs and values about human rights, morality, marriage and family, war and peace, love and death. Beliefs about infants are important because to raise a baby is to plant a seed in the garden of culture. We bring babies up in ways that are consistent with responsible childhood and adult citizenship. Beliefs about babies are miniature facets of the cultural cosmos. No culture can survive without providing folkways to guide parental treatment of babies, and babies would wither outside the shelter of culture.

This chapter on the history and future of beliefs about infancy is based on research from secondary sources. These include the work of historians and anthropologists who have studied the primary sources of historical evidence, as well as translations into English of original historical documents. For prehistorical data, I rely on evidence from observers of modern hunter–gatherer societies as well as anthropological data. For the historical period, the focus will be on the work of historians and translators of original documents of Western culture (Judeo-Christian, Greek and Roman, and later European and American societies). This research approach may bias my interpretations in favor of the historian or translator who worked with the original documents and artifacts. A different point of view may arise from the work of a scholar who is competent to examine the evidence more directly.

This chapter traces the outlines of prehistorical and historical changes in beliefs about infancy by highlighting one major theme that was salient to me in collecting these materials, the historical continuity of a dialogue between *empirical* and *romantic* beliefs about infants. *On the empirical side are beliefs related to the early education, training, and disciplining of infants to create desired adult characteristics and to control the exploration, shape, and uses of the body. Romantic beliefs favor the pleasures of babies and adults. Romantic ideas advocate indulgence in mutual love and physical affection in relationships, they show a respect for the body and its senses and desires, and the freedom of expression of all of the above.* Although the terms empiricism and romanticism do not come into the English language until the eighteenth century, the earliest historical records reveal a dialogue between belief systems that will later come to be labeled as empirical or romantic. The continuous presence of these two themes across prehistorical and historical time suggests that they are both essential ingredients in adult relationships with infants. Sometimes romantic beliefs are predominant, sometimes empirical, and sometimes they are in balance with each other.

I focus on the dialectic between empiricism and romanticism because it is one way to link the historical changes in beliefs about infants, changes that might otherwise seem unrelated. The distinction between the empirical and the romantic is also useful because, as will be seen in the section on the twentieth century, scientific approaches to infancy have fluctuated between research devoted to the early training and education of infants on the empirical side, and research on the normal development and unfolding of the movements, senses, and feelings of the body. The chapter is divided into the following sections: The prehistory of infancy (1.6 million to 10,000 years ago), early civilizations (8000 BCE to 300 ACE),[1] the Middle Ages and Renaissance (third to sixteenth centuries), the Enlightenment (seventeenth to nineteenth centuries), and the recent past (twentieth century). The chapter concludes with a speculative section on the possible future of beliefs and practices about babies.

Prehistory of Infancy: 1.6 Million to 10,000 Years Ago

It is currently thought that all humans are descended from a small population of hunter–gatherers who first appeared in Africa during the Pleistocene epoch. The Pleistocene lasted between 1.6 million years ago and 10,000 years ago. Beginning about 10,000 years ago and continuing until the present time, humans gradually abandoned nomadic patterns and began to occupy permanent settlements and to develop agriculture. *Homo sapien* hunter–gatherer societies first appeared about 100,000 years ago and were descended from a long line of other human species that arose at the beginning of the Pleistocene.

By about 35,000 years ago, *Homo sapien sapien* hunter–gatherer groups existed in most locations in the old world, in Australia, and in the Americas. Societies of this period were composed of small bands of about 25 humans who sustained themselves by hunting game and gathering wild roots and plants to eat. They would roam typically less than 20 miles (30 kilometers) and it was rare to encounter another group. Generations lived their lives within this small sphere of people and place. Hunter–gatherer societies are believed to have been the only form of human society during the entire Pleistocene epoch. They did not leave artifacts or other documentation of their infant care practices (Wenke, 1990). Relatively few such societies survive today. While there is some controversy about whether surviving hunter–gatherers are similar to prehistorical hunter–gatherers, these contemporary groups are considered to be reasonable approximations to prehistorical lifestyles (Hrdy, 1999; Wenke, 1990).

The human ecology during the Pleistocene is considered to be the *environment of evolutionary adaptedness*, a term devised by John Bowlby, the founder of attachment theory (Bowlby, 1969). This is the African Pleistocene environment in which the mother–infant bond evolved for over a million years, an environment with large populations of predators who could easily kill and eat a baby. In order to protect the infant from this and other dangers, the infant was carried in a sling or pouch at all times, never left alone, and the caregiver responded immediately to fussiness in order not to attract the attention of predators. As a consequence, humans evolved a mother–infant relationship with continuous skin-to-skin contact and frequent breastfeeding (Barr, 1990).

The present day !Kung bushmen, a hunter–gatherer group living in the Kalahari desert in Africa, have been observed extensively. !Kung women carry their infants in a sling next to their bodies at all times. They breastfeed on demand, as much as 60 times in a 24-hour period. The infant sets the pace and time of breastfeeding.

> Nursing often occurs simultaneously with active play with the free breast, languid extension–flexion movements in the arms and legs, mutual vocalization, face-to-face interaction (the breasts are quite long and flexible), and various forms of self-touching, including occasional masturbation. (Konner, 1982, p. 303)

Infants also receive considerable attention from siblings and other children who are at eye-level with the infant while in the sling.

> When not in the sling, infants are passed from hand to hand around a fire for similar interaction with one adult or child after another. They are kissed on their faces, bellies, genitals, are sung to, bounced, entertained, encouraged, and addressed at length in conversational tones long before they can understand words. (Konner, 1982, p. 302)

The high rate of nursing prevents infant crying and has a natural contraceptive effect to prevent the birth of another child while the younger one still requires mother's milk. Births are spaced every four or five years (Konner, 1982; Wenke, 1990). The Elauma of Nigeria are also hunter–gatherers (Whiten & Milner, 1986). Three-month-old Elauma infants spend almost all their time, whether awake or asleep, in physical contact with an

Figure 26.1   Infants in hunter–gatherer societies are in nearly constant skin-to-skin contact with people, as shown with this woman holding a baby in Huli village, Papua New Guinea. (Photo © Amos Nachoum/Corbis)

adult or within 3 ft of the adult. Elauma mothers carry their babies with them while the mothers go about their daily chores.

A similar account is offered from observations of the Fore people of New Guinea, a rainforest hunter–gatherer group who remained isolated from the outside world until the 1960s. This group displays a "*socio-sensual human organization* which began in infancy during a period of almost continuous, unusually rich tactile interaction" (Sorenson, 1979, p. 289; italics are not in the original). Play with infants includes "considerable caressing, kissing, and hugging" (p. 297).

> Not only did this constant "language" of contact seem readily to facilitate the satisfaction of the infant's needs and desires but it also seemed to make the harsher devices of rule and regimen unnecessary. Infant frustration and "acting out," traits common in Western culture, were rarely seen. (Sorenson, 1979, p. 297)

Because of this indulgence of the senses and a relative lack of overt discipline, hunter–gatherer societies exemplify a primarily romantic culture. Observations of weaning both in the !Kung and the Fore, however, suggest that the training of infants – empirical beliefs and practices – is also important. Although !Kung adults report memories of the difficulty of losing their close contact with mother during weaning, they also report that these feelings were alleviated by the presence of other adults, siblings, and peers. Weaning occurs when the mother becomes pregnant with the next child. Adults believe that with the onset of pregnancy, the mother's milk will harm the nursing child and must be reserved for the unborn child. In the words of Nisa, a !Kung woman who spoke about her life,

> When mother was pregnant with Kumsa, I was always crying, wasn't I? One day I said, "Mommy, won't you let me have just a little milk? Please, let me nurse." She cried, "Mother! My breasts are things of shit! Shit! Yes, the milk is like vomit and smells terrible. You can't drink it. If you do, you'll go 'Whaagh . . . whaagh . . . ' and throw up." I said, "No, I won't throw up, I'll just nurse." But she refused and said, "Tomorrow, Daddy will trap a springhare, just for you to eat." When I heard that, my heart was happy again. (Shostak, 1983, p. 53)

Even here, in the most romantic of human lifestyles, in which the body and its senses are indulged and in which children receive very little discipline or restrictions, empirical beliefs are present in some form. The discourse between the romantic and the empirical may be a law of nature, derived from the simple truth that elders require of children some sacrifice if they are to grow into full co-participation. If the sacrifice is done in the flow of a balanced dialogue, it will soon be followed by a new and surprising indulgence. The springhare helps Nisa to let go of her tragic loss and gives her a feeling of sharing in the more adult-like ritual of hunting. There is also evidence that hunter–gatherer groups occasionally used infanticide – the deliberate killing of unwanted infants and an extreme form of empiricist practice – for infants who were sick or deformed, those who could not have survived under the rigors of the harsh environment.

For most of human evolution people lived close to the earth, either on open ground, in and near trees, in caves and other natural shelters. They were directly attuned to the earth, its climate, and its cycles. The basic elements of earth, air, fire, and water had enormous practical and spiritual significance. So far as we know, people did not distinguish themselves as separate from their ecology but as part of it, no different or more valuable than the basic elements, the plants, and animals (Shepard, 1998).

For people of the Pleistocene, the environment was not an objective collection of rocks and creatures; it was a form of consciousness in which there was an unquestioned and nonjudgmental sense of connection to all things. This has been called a *partnership consciousness* as opposed to the *dominator consciousness* that appeared later (8000–3000 BCE) with the formation of towns, social hierarchies, power structures, and warfare (Eisler, 1987).

Beginning about 35,000 years ago, humans developed what has been called *mythic culture*, which saw the origins of symbols, representations, language, and storytelling that served as a way of making sense of the universe. Myths worldwide express the belief that the world, and all its creatures including humans, is sacred. In mythic culture, the universe cannot be changed or shaped. Myths served to integrate and explain the various facets of life and death that were accepted as they were and never questioned (Donald, 1991).

At this time, the first representational art and artifacts began to appear, in the form of cave and rock paintings and small figurines (Wenke, 1990). The paintings depicted animal and human forms, possibly spiritual or mythic figures. The figurines were typically about

Figure 26.2   The Willendorf "Venus" (ca. 20,000 BCE) is one example of palm-sized statuettes that appeared to celebrate female fecundity. It is not clear whether these figures were used as talismans to promote fertility, as representations of a female goddess, or for some other purpose. These statuettes were common in central Europe 20,000 to 30,000 years ago. (Photo AKG London/ Erich Lessing)

palm size and represented women with prominent breasts, hips, and vaginas. They were believed by many to represent fertility, while others suggest that they represented a goddess-type deity and a matriarchal social order. These figurines may have conferred fertility on individuals and at the same time celebrated the mysterious life-giving power of the female.

It is probably during this phase of human prehistory that rituals for birth and death, along with mythical interpretations of their meaning, first appeared. Although there is relatively little archeological evidence, we can learn a great deal about birthing rituals and practices from studies of living tribal societies. In many tribal societies today, for example, birth occurs in the company of women, close female relatives and older "medicine" women, shamans who are expert in the practice of childbirth. Plant and animal extracts are used for the pains of pregnancy and childbirth. In some matriarchal societies, husbands are asked to change their behavior when their wives are pregnant, a practice called *couvade*. Fathers in the Ifugao tribe of the Philippines are not permitted to cut wood during their wives' pregnancy (Whiting, 1974).

Healing practices and prayer rituals were created in prehistory to foster healthy fetal development and childbirth. One common practice, used by the Laotians, the Navajo of North America, and the Cuna of Panama, among others, is the use of music during labor. Among the Comanche and Tewa, North American Indian tribes, heat is applied to the abdomen. The Taureg of the Sahara believe that the laboring mother should walk up and down small hills to allow the infant to become properly placed to facilitate delivery. Taureg women of North Africa deliver their babies from a kneeling position (Mead & Newton, 1967). Many of these practices are ancient in origin, having been passed down between generations of women, perhaps from prehistorical times. The effectiveness of some of these practices is being rediscovered and applied by birthing centers and midwives in Western cultures today. The past ten years has seen the emergence of professional *doulas*, women who are trained to provide advice, assistance, and emotional support to pregnant and laboring mothers.

There is a great deal of archeological evidence supporting the emergence of funeral rites during this period. Early burial sites contain vagina-shaped cowrie shells placed around the dead person, who is also painted with red ocher for the life-giving power of blood. Mythic humans made connections between death and life, and represented life in terms of female fecundity. Female goddess figures continued to appear in various manifestations, culminating with the goddesses of early agricultural (10,000–3000 BCE) and later urban cultures (2000 BCE until the present), including Aphrodite, Athena, and the Virgin Mary (Eisler, 1987).

Related to the belief system in which all things in the universe are connected and have equal status, hunter–gatherers have an egalitarian social structure with respect to age and gender differences and have little political hierarchy. An instructive comparative study was done between a hunter–gatherer group (the Aka) and a neighboring agricultural group (the Ngandu) in Central Africa. Both groups live in nearly identical ecologies and have subsistence economies. The Ngandu are sedentary farmers with political hierarchies and inequalities in age and gender roles. The Ngandu use more infant care devices compared to the Aka. Infant care devices – such as cradles, carriers, and toys – are not needed in the Aka due to the constant contact between infants and adults. The Ngandu infants wear more clothing, are more often physically separated from their mothers, and mothers are more likely to let their infants fuss or cry compared to the Aka. Like mothers in the urban cultures, the Ngandu mothers use more objects when playing with their babies (Hewlett, Lamb, Shannon, Leyendecker, & Scholmerich, 1998).

The comparison between the Aka and the Ngandu suggests that there may have been a diversity of early human habits and belief systems related to infancy, even during the Pleistocene. While virtually all humans 100,000 years ago lived in desert and grassland environments, migration patterns eventually led to adaptations for living in less arid climates such as coastal and mountain terrain. In the desert, infants must nurse frequently to prevent dehydration while this is not the case when the climate is more humid. Desert hunter–gatherers may have had to move frequently, requiring constant physical contact with the infant for safety. Coastal or riverbank hunter–gatherers may have had abundant resources close at hand, which would not have required extensive nomadic activity.

For these reasons, it is unwarranted to use the culture of desert-living hunter–gatherers as the sole basis for making inferences about species-normative patterns of the mother–infant relationship. The desert-living ancestral populations would have had mothers who did full-time infant care at the same time they did full-time work. Infants from other hunter–gatherer cultures may not have needed such constant protection and nursing from the mothers, allowing her to work while the infant was in substitute care (Hrdy, 1999).

In summary, infancy in prehistory was a very sensual and sensory experience. Infants developed an awareness of other human bodies from which they obtained nourishment, constant touch, affection, warmth, and support. They had the benefit of an extended family of group members. Once they began crawling and walking, infants became familiar with the feel and smell of raw earth and of plants. Living primarily outdoors and in earthen shelters, they became sensitized to changes in light and temperature, to the cycles and rhythms of the earth and its climate. To people living in urban societies today, this ancient way of life may seem primitive and dirty. On the other hand, it would be a primitive form of reasoning to reject the evidence of prehistory and what it has to tell us about human infants and their families.

For 1.6 million years, humans evolved to derive benefit from close touch and connection to other people's bodies, to the naked earth, to heat and cold, and to the smells, sounds, and tastes of the natural world. Humans of all ages perceived no distinctions between self and world, in the same way that young children today view others as extensions of themselves. They saw the world as animated with spirit and with the same kind of partnership consciousness as their own (Abram, 1997; Shepard, 1998).

The past 10,000 years is only 0.62 percent of human evolutionary history. If human evolution began at noon on an imaginary clock, villages and settled life would first appear at 4 minutes before midnight. Civilization, with urban centers and technologies, would arise about 2 minutes before midnight. The cradle of human consciousness is not a cradle at all. It is the belly of a parent, the loving hands of a brother or grandmother, the taste of milk rising from a teat, the smell of bodies, and a blanket of stars on a summer night. Every baby born today still has the opportunity to experience this romantic inheritance.

Early Civilizations: 8000 BCE–300 ACE

There is relatively little documentation about infancy and infant care in the art, artifacts, and writings of ancient civilizations. I came to my own interpretation about infancy in these civilizations based primarily on evidence related to beliefs about the family and about education.

The biblical Old Testament gives lengthy accounts of family genealogy of the Hebrew peoples. *Childbearing and childbirth were viewed as sacred acts, acts in which God was an active partner* (Frymer-Kensky, 1995). When Eve, the mythical original mother, first saw her son Cain, she said, "I have created a man with God" (Genesis 4:2).

There are many stories in the Old Testament about divine intervention in matters of fertility. Hannah, for example, prayed extensively and made vows to God to grant her the ability to conceive and give birth to Samuel. The Bible also gives detailed laws regarding women's behavior during menstruation, pregnancy, and childbirth. Although there are no direct descriptions of infancy in the Bible, it is clear from many of the stories that infants should receive loving care, appropriate blessings for a good and holy life, and that male infants should be circumcised. Parental devotion was also evident in stories about the suffering of parents who were asked to sacrifice their infants. When two mothers claimed to be the parent of the same child, Solomon's threat to kill the child revealed the true mother, whose pain was unmistakable. The Hebrew slave revolt in Egypt, which led to the Exodus and return to the promised land, was precipitated by a Pharaonic edict to kill Hebrew first-born sons. The story of Moses, sent floating down the Nile by his heart-broken family and adopted into love by Egyptian royal women, places the concept of human freedom in direct metaphorical alignment with the act of saving a single infant from death (Frymer-Kensky, 1995).

The Bible reminds parents not only to love but to educate their children, a combination of romantic and empiricist views. The importance of teaching children about culture was written in commandments to Abraham to "instruct" his children (Genesis 18:19). Regarding the important facets of Hebrew culture, parents were asked to "teach them intently to your children . . . when you sit in your home" (Deuteronomy 6:7). Child-rearing among the ancient Hebrews involved discipline accompanied by respect for the child, as the following passages illustrate: "Train a child in his own way, and even when he is old, he will not depart from it" (Proverbs 22:6); "Foolishness is bound in the heart of the child but the rod of correction shall drive it from him" (Proverbs 22:15); and "Chasten your son for there is hope, but set not your heart on his destruction" (Proverbs 19:18). While some have interpreted these statements as grounds for justifying corporal punishment, the Old Testament does not specify the type of punishment but makes clear the need for discipline in the context of love. Other Bible stories reveal the undesirable outcomes when discipline is too harsh or nonexistent or when parents fail to educate their children into the stories, rituals, ideals, and history of the culture.

History and literature from ancient Greece and Rome (500 BCE–300 ACE) also reveal a mixture of romantic and empiricist sentiments toward infants. On the one hand, writers advocated a strict upbringing for the purpose of creating a worthy citizen. Babies were thought to be soft and formless at birth and consequently needed to be hardened and molded. Various devices were used to keep infants' hands open, their legs held straight, and their arms strapped against the body. The right hand was loosened at 2 months to ensure that the child grew up right-handed. Swaddling bands were used to mold the infant's head and body shape. Infants were bathed in cold water to prevent them from remaining too soft. Nurses used bath times to further mold the child's skull into a round shape, while attempting to shape other body parts by pulling and stretching (Dupont, 1989). The binding and manipulating of infants was not uncommon in ancient times, as seen in the foot binding of girls in ancient China (which made their feet small but deformed) and head binding in the ancient Maya (Mexico). Head binding of infants can also be found in eighteenth-century Europe to give the head an oblong shape (Johnson, 1992).

Roman parents viewed these practices as an expression of their love, so children would grow up strong, their bodies well proportioned and held in appropriate postures. The recognition of the importance of the body for the developing person is salient in Greco-Roman heritage. Exercises for the body were thought to contribute to a strong moral character, a belief that was revived in the eighteenth and nineteenth centuries, following centuries of Christian doctrine that deemphasized the pleasures of the body. People from the educated classes in the Greek and Roman world were expected to hold their bodies in postures appropriate for each occasion and to speak in a dignified way. Gestures were stylized and specific to gender. The nude body was celebrated in real life – clothing was scant and sheer for both genders – and in nude sculptures of both males and females.

Parental devotion to children, especially among the wealthy, is well documented in Roman literature. Fathers and mothers were equally involved in the care of infants. Although infants were denied affection, older children whose character had begun to form were lavished with hugging and kissing (Dupont, 1989; Gies & Gies, 1987). Toys and games for young children and the values of love and protection for them have been found in artifacts and documents from ancient Egypt (2000–100 BCE) and Greece (800–200 BCE) (Greenleaf, 1978).

As in the Hebrew culture of the Middle East, Greeks and Romans invoked their own deities for assistance in supporting the baby's health and growth. Prayers and offerings were made for successful childbirth and at each stage of the infant's life. The belief that infants' birth and development was a collaboration with gods or goddesses seems to follow from the partnership consciousness of the Pleistocene. Infants in these ancient cultures were not seen as belonging to the parents or as brought into the world by human choice. Rather, they were seen as part of a divine plan, as one manifestation of the way the universe works either to the favor or disfavor of humans.

Following prehistorical societies, many early civilizations, such as ancient Rome, practiced infanticide. The male head of a Roman family had the duty to decide if a newborn should live or die. This practice eliminated infants who were malformed or sickly. Malformation was thought to be due to an animal nature. Many healthy babies were also left to die because the family was too poor or the child unwanted (Dupont, 1989). Infanticide continued in Europe throughout the Middle Ages, until Christian beliefs diminished the regular use of the practice.

Hebrews did not routinely use infanticide. The story of Moses and the Exodus from Egypt shows that the concept of killing infants was appalling to the Hebrews. Since the Middle Ages, the narrow passage through the Red Sea and to eventual freedom is a central metaphor in Jewish prayers for successful childbirth through the birth canal (Frymer-Kensky, 1995). These ancient Hebrew ideas about the sanctity of childbirth and the creation of new life were later incorporated into Christian beliefs.

In summary, we can never know about the details and diversity of actual infant care practices during ancient historical times. Documents written by educated leaders may contain more prescriptive and idealistic visions of parenting, visions that the ordinary family may or may not have put into practice. It seems clear, however, that both romantic and empirical beliefs about infants can be found in the earliest written documents of Western cultures. Roman writings tended to weigh the empirical side more heavily, while the Hebrews showed more of a balance between love and discipline. Following the traditions of mythic culture, these ancient historical societies believed that infants were conceived in partnership with a deity that was beyond themselves. Education was required in order to create an adult who was best attuned to the will of the gods or goddesses who were responsible for the mythical foundations of the cultural practices: to cultivate the body and its senses in order to be more in touch with divinity in the human and non-human world.

Middle Ages and Renaissance: Third to Sixteenth Centuries

The early Middle Ages in Europe (300–1100 ACE) began with the fall of the Roman empire and the gradual spread of Christianity. Primarily rural populations began to settle in cities and towns. Political boundaries changed during a series of conflicts for power and control over territory. These factors contributed to the growth of an educated urban population living next to a class of urban poor who subsisted in more unhealthy conditions than the poor living in the countryside. Because of disease, malnutrition, urban pollution, and ignorance, infants of the urban poor were more likely to die or to suffer birth defects than those from rural areas. Because disease claimed the lives of both infants and of mothers in childbirth, many destitute or orphaned children walked the streets as beggars, thieves, and prostitutes. The prognosis for children growing up in urban poverty is not much different today.

After 400 ACE, the Christian church began having an impact on the beliefs and practices of European childrearing. Christians, following ancient Jewish practices, advocated parental love and worked to protect children from infanticide, abortion, and maltreatment. Gravestones for infants began to appear at this time, as well as special penances if a parent had done some wrong to a child (Gies & Gies, 1987).

One of the first written accounts that focuses specifically on infant development and infant care beliefs can be found in the *Confessions* of St. Augustine (354–430). Augustine was from North Africa. He studied in Rome and Milan and later became a priest in Alexandria. His autobiographical account in the *Confessions* (1991) begins with a remarkably detailed and developmentally appropriate reporting of his own infancy. He describes his birth and goes on at length about how he sucked from the breast and his patterns of quieting and crying. He reports that his first smiles occurred during sleep, which can be observed in infants today.

Augustine considers it important to establish the source of his data in the following way. "This at least is what I was told, and I believed it since that is what we see other infants doing. I do not actually remember what I then did." And he goes on, "Little by little, I began to be aware where I was and wanted to manifest my wishes to those who could fulfill them as I could not. For my desires were internal; adults were external to me and had no means of entering into my soul" (Augustine, 1991, p. 8).

Augustine struggled, as he did throughout the *Confessions*, with the moral implications of his "childish" acts. Many of these infantile actions, especially those regarding the pleasures of the body, would have been immoral from his adult Christian perspective. He concluded that what would be wrong for an adult was natural for babies. Since babies could not voluntarily control their behavior, he decided that they were expressing God's will and should therefore be tolerated for the indiscretions of their youth. "Was it wrong that in tears I greedily opened my mouth wide to suck the breasts?" (Augustine, 1991, p. 9). He decided that it was indeed acceptable only because it will pass away with age. These writings express one of the clearest and earliest statements in the romantic tradition, that the natural tendencies of infants are to be accepted, tolerated, and loved.

Evidence of romantic views and Christian love for infants can be seen in the writings of Gregory of Tours (sixth century), who describes an epidemic of dysentery that killed many infants: "and so we lost our little ones, who were so dear to us and sweet, whom we had cherished in our bosoms and dandled in our arms, whom we had fed and nurtured with such loving care" (Gies & Gies, 1987, p. 60). Around the same time, the church developed forms of penance for killing infants: three years for abortion and ten years for infanticide. Other writers of the time report parental mourning of infant death.

We know a great deal about the emotional life of people in the Middle Ages. Events such as the death of an infant would have been marked by deep mourning, benedictions, and ceremonies. One historian of the Middle Ages describes everyday life this way:

> All experience had yet to the minds of men the directness and absoluteness of the pleasure and pain of child-life . . . Calamities and indigence were more afflicting than at present; it was more difficult to guard against them, and to find solace. Illness and health presented more striking contrast; the cold and darkness of winter were more real evils . . . All things presenting themselves to the mind in violent contrasts and impressive forms, lent a tone of excitement and of passion to everyday life and tended to produce that perpetual oscillation between despair and distracted joy, between cruelty and pious tenderness which characterize life in the Middle Ages. (Huizinga, 1954, pp. 9–10)

We can infer from Christian art and theology that these heightened emotions occurred at times of both birth and death. In the early Middle Ages, representations of Christ depicted him as an adult engaged in acts of kindness and love. By the late Middle Ages (1100–1300 ACE), images of Christ focused either on his death and the deep mourning of his companions, or on his infancy and the joy of the mother–child bond. The paintings of the infant Christ held by Mary continued to evolve during this period. When Christ first appears in painting as an infant, the posture and body proportions are more adult-like. By the later Middle Ages, Christ looks more like an actual infant. The infant Christ is typically shown in stylized clothing and with adult-like facial features and mannerisms. One painting depicted Christ as an infant making the Catholic gesture

Figure 26.3   Cimabue, *Madonna of the Angels*, 1270. In this late medieval painting, Christ is represented in stylized form with adult-like gestures. (Louvre, Paris/Photo Hervé Lewandowski, RMN)

of benediction to a group of people kneeling before him. In Renaissance art (after 1400 ACE), by contrast, infants and children began to look and behave differently from adults. Children were sometimes shown playing with toys (Koops, 1996). Not only does the infant Christ begin to look more like a real baby, but we also see the emergence of secular paintings of everyday family life and portraits of individual children.

Also appearing in the later Middle Ages were several written medical texts giving advice for childbirth and early infant care. Trotola, a female physician in twelfth-century Italy, advised rubbing the newborn's palate with honey, protecting it from bright lights and loud noises, and stimulating the newborn's senses with cloths of various colors and textures, and with "songs and gentle voices" (Gies & Gies, 1987). In England at the same period, birth often occurred in a warm chamber with plenty of bath water, accom-

Figure 26.4 Raphael, *The Virgin and Child with St. John the Baptist*, 1507. By the time of the Renaissance, Christ was depicted more like a real baby, with an appearance distinctly different from adults. Around this time, secular paintings of children begin to appear, showing an increasing interest in the individual. (Louvre, Paris/Photo J. G. Berizzi, RMN)

panied by the scent of olives, herbs, and roses. It was attended by a female midwife and female friends bringing good fortune and joy (Hanawalt, 1993). During the Middle Ages as in ancient times, the body was viewed as part of God, the earth, the family, and the community. Birth took place in public, attended by female relatives, neighbors, and midwives.

In both Jewish and Christian beliefs of this time, the mother and infant's shared embodied experience were as sacred and important as that shared between husband and wife in the act of love and conception. The great romantic tales of the Middle Ages created the concept of courtship, honor, love, and sacrifice in couple relationships. Trotola's prescriptions for birth – with colorful textiles and captivating aromas – would also have been found on the bodies and in the bedrooms of courting and newly married couples. The romantic view of love and the sacred body did not extend to other sexual or pleasurable acts outside of those reserved human relationships that were deemed by Christians and Jews to be part of the expression of God's love. Because of these beliefs, there was a gradual historical decline in the importance of the pleasures of the body, its movements and senses.

Christian baptisms – like weddings – were a public ritual welcoming, taking place in the church where ancestors were buried. The biography of Bishop Hugh of Lincoln (1140–1200) describes details of infant action during one baptism led by the Bishop. The infant "bent and stretched out its little arms, as if it were trying to fly, and moved its head to and fro. The tiny mouth and face relaxed in continuous chuckles" (Gies & Gies, 1987, p. 203). Apparently, Bishop Hugh took great pleasure in the baby, who was wrapped in the spiritual significance of the ceremony.

Following the ancient Roman empiricist traditions, infants in the Middle Ages were seen by upper-class families as pliable and soft, needing swaddling and straightening. Wetnurses began to be used extensively for the wealthy. A wetnurse was a woman who was paid to nurse the child with her own milk in order to spare wealthy women from the task of nursing the baby themselves. Selection of wetnurses was important because they were believed to transmit character to the child. Writers, mostly from the church, condemned the practice of giving children to wetnurses from the poorer classes because the child could pick up the habits and diseases of the nurse. The Renaissance artist, Michelangelo, half-jokingly claimed that his skill in sculpture was derived from his wetnurse, the wife of a stonecutter (Gies & Gies, 1987).

Infanticide, however, was still practiced in the late Middle Ages. Although parents had to suffer penances, it was not a crime equivalent to homicide as it is today. By the thirteenth century, some cities in Europe created church-run hospices to adopt orphaned children as an alternative to infanticide, since a child who died unbaptized was barred from heaven for all eternity (Le Goff, 1987). In some countries today, with urban stress and poverty, infants are left in parks and in trash bins. Some cities in the United States and Northern Europe have begun programs that allow mothers to drop unwanted infants at local hospitals without prosecution. Social service agencies then help to find foster homes for these children. Times may have changed, but some of the problems still remain.

The European Renaissance (1450–1650) began in Florence, Italy where wealthy patrons funded the development of art and science on a scale not seen since ancient times. This flowering of culture gave rise to the emergence of a philosophy of *humanism*. Figures such as Galileo Galilei, Leonardo da Vinci, and Michelangelo revived an interest in the fullest development of the person that was found during the classical period in ancient Greece and Rome. Paintings of nude figures, of secular themes, and of ordinary people rather than religious figures heralded a reawakening of the values of empiricism and romanticism that were part of classical traditions. As a consequence, the rearing of children took on more importance.

Responsibility for oneself and for one's children was shifted toward the individual. God was still present but people were beginning to feel empowered to make more decisions for them-

selves and their children. At this time, we begin to see the emergence of written philosophies of childrearing in Western cultures. One example comes from Michel de Montaigne (1533–1592), of France. He condemned violence in education, favored training for honor and freedom, and condemned wetnursing.

> A true and well-regulated affection should be born and then increase, as children enable us to get to know them; if they show they deserve it, we should cherish them with a truly fatherly love . . . we feel ourselves more moved by the skippings and jumpings of babyish tricks of our children than by their activities when they are fully formed, as though we loved them not as human beings but only as playthings. Since in sober truth things are so ordered that children can only have their being and live their lives at the expense of our being and of our lives, we ought not to undertake to be fathers if that frightens us. (Screech, 1991, p. 435)

As a result of the spread of Renaissance humanism throughout Europe, by the eighteenth century a profound shift in Western cultural consciousness coalesces, one that emphasizes the importance of individuals in their own right. Up through the seventeenth century, the ancient belief persists that all people, including infants, are part of a larger cosmos of God in partnership with the family. Before the eighteenth century, children were typically given the names of family members, often that of an older sibling who had died, in order to emphasize the historical and sacred connection of one person to another. One sign of the shift toward individuality in the early eighteenth century is that children begin to be given unique names showing their special status as human beings (Stone, 1979). This focus on individuality led gradually to the emergence of private homes, arguments for the freedom of children and of people of all ages, and separate rooms in the house for children. At the same time, we begin to see an increasing distance from nature and from a direct connection with the earth and with God (Gelis, 1989).

In summary, this period in Western culture has two phases. The first was a gradual change in classical ideas about the importance of the body and its senses. Christian empirical beliefs favored innocence, chastity, and denial of the senses as a pathway to God. In contrast, the classical empirical traditions acted to the favor of the gods by shaping the body into a form to be enjoyed and displayed. Augustine could forgive the infant's hungers only until a proper Christian education could begin. This showed that Christians were more romantic in their views about infancy than the Romans, for example, who advocated relatively early and severe discipline of the mind and body. One could say that the Christians were more romantic about babies while the Romans were more romantic about older children and adults.

The second phase of the period from the third to the sixteenth centuries is the emergence of humanism during the Renaissance. This period is a reprise of the classical themes about the body and its senses set against the historical background of 800 years of Christian domination of Western culture. Galileo and other leading Renaissance figures were made famous as much by their important discoveries as by their conflicts with church authority and belief. These struggles, begun in the palaces of the most wealthy secular and religious leaders, led eventually to a broader cultural shift in the importance of the individual as distinct from God, family, and society.

The Enlightenment: Seventeenth to Nineteenth Centuries

During the eighteenth century, new ideas about the value of human life, dignity, and freedom began to emerge, a shift of cultural consciousness that is called the "Enlightenment." On the one hand, there is a revival of classical romantic beliefs as exemplified in the writings of Jean-Jacques Rousseau (1712–1778). Rousseau, who lived during the period of the French revolution from the monarchy, argued that childhood was a time of special privilege, that children bring goodness into the world, and that education should be sensitive to the needs and inclinations of the infant and young child. Rousseau initiated a social movement that, for the first time, acquires the name *romanticism*. Many of Rousseau's ideas, however, had their origins during earlier historical periods. What is new here is the emphasis on the romantic individual, the importance of the child as a person in his or her own right.

Included in this movement are the great English Romantic poets, such as William Wordsworth (1770–1850), who wrote of childhood in a way that would have been recognized by members of a hunter–gatherer community.

> Behold the Child among his new-born blisses,
> A six years' darling of pygmy size!
> See, where 'mid work of his own hand he lies,
> Fretted by sallies of his mother's kisses,
> With light upon him from his father's eyes!
> (From "Imitations of Immortality from Recollections of Early Childhood,"
> in Williams, 1952, p. 263)

Other authors, such as William Blake (1757–1827) and Charles Dickens (1812–1870), also wrote about the life and fate of individual children, but they had a less than romantic view about them. In *Oliver Twist* and other famous stories, Dickens courageously exposed the effects of disease, poverty, child abuse, and child labor for all to see. Thus, while the value of the individual was on the rise, people disagreed about what was "natural" compared to what needed to be provided for the child's healthy development. John Locke (1632–1704) believed that children needed more guidance and discipline than the romantics advocated. Locke argued that education should provide the skills to make rational choices. The philosophical movement to which he belonged was for the first time given the name *empiricism*. The origins of Locke's ideas can be found in ancient sources such as the Old and New Testaments and Roman ideas about education.

Locke's books could be found right beside the Bible on family bookshelves in eighteenth-century Europe and the American colonies. Not only did he believe in rational education but he echoed the contemporary cultural ideals about the importance of the individual. He wrote, "the little and almost insensible expressions on our tender infancies have very important and long-lasting consequences" (as quoted in Clarke-Stewart, 1998, p. 104).

Reversing centuries of Christian doctrine that elevated the spirit above the body, Rousseau and Locke revived the ancient Greek and Roman ideals about the importance of the body in healthy moral development. Locke gave us the now well-known expression, "A sound mind in a sound body, is a short but full description of a happy state in this world." Rousseau suggested that children should "run, jump and shout to their heart's content." Their ideas became used by nineteenth-century reformers of educational practice in Europe and North America, who advocated that school curricula contain art, music, and physical education (Friedrich-Cofer, 1986).

Swaddling was abandoned during the eighteenth century because Locke complained that it restricted the infant's freedom of movement and prevented the mother or wetnurse from hugging and caressing the baby. Parents were advised that infants should exercise early and use their legs. Within a few years, swaddling was being condemned in England as an assault on human liberty.

The eighteenth century, and its rising concern for the individual, also saw a proliferation of advice books for parents. Between 1750 and 1814, 2400 different child-rearing advice books were published. By 1800 an entirely new concept entered society: books published exclusively for young children. A large range of inexpensive children's books appeared as quickly as the spread of computer games in the late twentieth century. Around the same time there was an increase in the number of family portraits for the middle and upper classes. The invention of photography and film a century later, and digital recording media after another century, continued to expand this tendency to document individual and family lives. The introduction of the Kodak Brownie camera in the early part of the twentieth century brought family documentation even to the poor. The Brownie was easy to use, inexpensive, and users did not have to develop the film themselves.

The rise of the importance of the individual corresponded with an increase in the importance of the nuclear family. There was a shift away from the use of wetnurses and a move toward the maintenance of a private family home. These two changes had the effect of lessening the duration of breastfeeding. Prior to the eighteenth century, infants were breastfed at least 18 months. Because the value of the individual applied not only to infants but to their mothers and fathers, a conflict began to appear between the rights of parents and the rights of infants. Mothers wanted their own personal time and began to see breastfeeding as their responsibility and their burden. The result was that infants were weaned earlier. Husbands wanted their wives to remain sexually available and attractive and became jealous of the infant's monopoly of the breast, which was a factor contributing to the relative increase in the importance of the conjugal bond in relation to the mother–child bond. These historical changes in the family were not seen in all cultures but became the norm for Western families.

The family, rather than the church or educational system, became the main location for instilling beliefs and values. This was especially true for families moving to the American colonies. The families that took the risky step of crossing the ocean to the New World had the goal to protect their children from the corrupting ideas of the Old World and to raise children according to their own beliefs. Colonists believed in the value of education and that families should be autonomous from government control (Clarke-Stewart, 1998).

During the nineteenth century, the child became an integral part of the definition of the family. What has been called the "discovery" of the child was due to a number of historical currents that flowed through urban Europe and North America. The first current

Figure 26.5   During the nineteenth century, infants and children became accepted as unique individuals. They received given names that were different from names of other family members, had the benefit of pediatric care, and the opportunity for educational enrichment. Note how this Berlin family (ca. 1896) dressed each of their children, including the infant, with unique and well-tailored clothing. (Photo AKG London)

was the segregation of the family from the workplace and the decline of child labor (thanks in part to Dickens). Second, society began to define the mother's role as major supervisor of the home. It may surprise many people that the full-time mother and housewife is a relatively recent historical invention. The final current established love or sentiment (rather than religion, family inheritance, or economic well-being) to be the bond holding the family together (Hareven, 1985). This latter current was also coupled with a rise in the significance of the love bond between spouses. As a result, parents became more loving, permissive, and egalitarian with children (Clarke-Stewart, 1998).

The development of this segregated nuclear family and its full-time mother was at first confined to the white middle class. Families from other classes and ethnic and racial groups continued to live in extended families in which love, work, and education all took place within the home and child care was shared by all family members. Women in these families continued to work in the fields and in the home in the company of their babies, a practice that had been going on for most of human history (Hareven, 1985). The late twentieth and early twenty-first centuries, on the other hand, have seen a decline of the nuclear family and the reemergence of extended families, communal living, and the rise of single-parent families.

Welfare and medical institutions devoted exclusively to children did not appear in Europe and North America until the 1850s. Around the same time, we see the development of immunization against childhood diseases and the pasteurization of milk. Maternal deaths during childbirth also declined due to the invention of anesthesia and procedures for sterilizing medical instruments (Greenleaf, 1978). These medical advances further solidified the family by reducing infant mortality. On the other hand, they led to a growing trend to move childbirth out of the home and the company of female friends and relatives and into hospitals surrounded by unfamiliar medical (mostly male) and nursing staff.

Educators in the nineteenth century, following Locke and Rousseau, viewed the child's body as essential to the development of the whole individual. If a child was obese, physically awkward, or handicapped, he or she could expect to receive guidance from the school. In American schools today, that mandate only extends to the "special needs" or handicapped child, primarily because of laws that emphasize the value of each individual and not because of a belief in the importance of a sound body. Curricula in the nineteenth century left plenty of time for free expression and creativity for the body, such as gymnastics and dance. Team sports and other exercise programs were not viewed in economic and competitive terms as in North American schools today. Rather, exercise for children was supposed to create a foundation for the continuation of physical exercise through adulthood. These programs grew out of the Greco-Roman and Enlightenment emphasis on the importance of the body as well as the mind (Friedrich-Cofer, 1986).

Empiricist views could be seen in the rise of education for infancy. Infant schools in the nineteenth century were meant for poor children, for early prevention of childhood disorders, for combating urban crime, teaching reading, or to give poor children proper middle-class values and supports (Clarke-Stewart, 1998). Infant schools later became available to middle-class families. In 1840, in Massachusetts, half of all 3-year-olds were enrolled in infant schools. Later in the nineteenth century, however, the practice of sending infants to school was condemned because it put too much pressure on children. The romantic view reemerged in the belief that children should develop naturally instead of being "pushed." Similar ebbs and flows of the value of infant education (schools, musical training, reading, etc.) can be seen throughout the twentieth and early twenty-first centuries.

The nineteenth century was also a period in which science became a new voice of authority, gradually supplanting religion as the sole source of knowledge and guidance. Observations of infants were first recorded by educated European and North American parents during the eighteenth and nineteenth centuries. Their diaries, known as "baby biographies," were partly meant to document the individual child and his or her development and partly meant as observations in the scientific tradition of natural history. One has to put the baby biographies into the prior historical context to understand their significance. Never before had people devoted time and energy to the documentation of the life of a single, individual baby.

Biographers were aware of the distinction between a more empirical approach and a more romantic approach to their recordings. Charles Darwin, for example, recorded the development of his son, William. When William was only a few months old, Darwin was trying to be an objective observer. Darwin added more references to himself as his affections for William grew and as William became more expressive. Darwin thought these references to himself were unscientific, so they were deleted in the versions of his diary that he published (Conrad, 1998).

Female diarists were more romantic. Elizabeth Gaskell (1810–1865), a well-known English novelist of the time, wrote a brief biography of her oldest daughter, Marianne, the first of her seven children. Gaskell focuses mostly on moral development, in comparison to the male diarists who recorded primarily sensorimotor and expressive development (Wallace, Franklin, & Keegan, 1994). Gaskell recognized her stance as participant observer in the following passage describing Marianne at 6 months.

> I should call her remarkably good-tempered; though at times she gives way to little bursts of passion or perhaps impatience . . . she is also very firm . . . what I suppose is obstinacy really, only that is so hard a word to apply to one so dear. But in general she is so good that I feel as if I could hardly be sufficiently thankful, that the materials put into my hands are so excellent and beautiful. And yet it seems to increase the responsibility. If I should misguide from carelessness or negligence! (Gaskell, 1996, p. 5)

This passage is enlightening because it gives us a view of the infant–mother relationship and not just of the infant. Diaries were later dismissed by more empirical (i.e., less romantic) scientists in the twentieth century, in part because they could not be verified.

In summary, the most radical historical change in beliefs about infancy began to unfold during the period between the seventeenth and nineteenth centuries. The rise in the importance of the individual had its roots in earlier Judeo-Christian beliefs about the value of human life and the importance of cultural education. The Renaissance saw a decline in religious art and the emergence of secular themes, texts, and paintings about ordinary people rather than religious or mythical figures. *Although these historical roots are unmistakable, the rapid advances in technology, in science, and in education during the Enlightenment created the conditions for a major historical change in cultural consciousness – the emergence of the "individual" – a change that affects every aspect of life in Western societies today.* The codification and consolidation of human rights, liberties, and self-enhancement was propelled by people who had unique names, whose identity was founded upon personal accomplishments, and who grew up in a family that respected them as growing individuals. Baby biographies, and the belief in the importance of individual infants, opened a path into a historically unprecedented documentation of infancy during the twentieth century.

The Recent Past: The Twentieth Century

Changes in beliefs about infancy seem to have accelerated during the twentieth century, in part because of mass communication about infancy and infant care and because of an increase in scientific studies of infancy. It may be that beliefs and practices related to infancy changed every few years in all historical periods. Because these beliefs and their fluctuations were not documented, however, we have no way of knowing. The history of infancy during the twentieth century is characterized by continual debates between romantic and empirical sentiments, as well as shifts every five to ten years between infant care practices favoring one view or the other. It also becomes increasingly difficult to separate the history of infancy research from the history of infants in the family. Infancy research has impacted every facet of infant care. At the same time, scientists as people living during these times were impacted in their own life histories with the beliefs of the larger culture, and those beliefs permeated the methods and values of their science.

Earlier debates over romanticism versus empiricism were replaced in part by discussions about the contributions to development of *nature* (genes) versus *nurture* (environments). Arnold Lucius Gesell (1880–1961), following in the romantic tradition, claimed that the orderly developmental changes seen in early development were specified by the genes; developmental stages were "natural." Gesell made careful measurements of developmental changes in size, motor skill, and behavior in infants and young children, the first scientist to use a one-way mirror for unobtrusive observation and the first to use film to record behavior. John B. Watson (1878–1958), an empiricist by contrast to Gesell, believed that, given the right kind of "nurture," infants were entirely malleable. He taught small children to be afraid of cuddly animals by making loud noises whenever they touched the animals, research that would be considered unethical today. Watson was successful, however, in convincing people that even the most basic and innocent of infant behaviors could be shaped by outside forces.

Watson's childrearing advice harkened back to the ancient Romans. Parents were told not to hug and kiss their children, except on the forehead before going to bed, or a pat on the head if they performed well on a task. Mother love was a "dangerous instrument. An instrument which may inflict a never healing wound, a wound which may make infancy unhappy, adolescence a nightmare, an instrument which may wreck your adult son or daughter's vocational future and their chances for marital happiness" (Watson, 1928, *The Psychological Care of the Infant and Child*, as quoted in Konner, 1982, p. 311). Watson was especially appealing to immigrants coming to North America, people who believed that they could make a new life for themselves and their children. Anyone could succeed, regardless of past history or genetic heritage.

Given the ancient historical dialectic between empirical and romantic beliefs, Watson's extremism was begging for a romantic counterargument. It appeared in the work of William James, Karl Jung, John Dewey, and Sigmund Freud, all of whom emphasized the emotional and creative aspects of the child, highlighting love, indulgence of the infant's needs, and the freedom of the individual. Freud (1856–1939), for example, recognized that all infants experienced emotional highs and lows and that even infants felt the need for love and possessed powerful desires. Freud recognized the importance of the body – the oral, anal, and genital regions – as powerful organizers of the developing psyche. The vicissitudes of infant care led to a more or less repressed adult, one who accepted and enjoyed the body or felt repression about the body and its desires.

Freud's daughter, Anna, taught parents to hold and cuddle their babies, to indulge their senses and respect their emotions. She counseled parents to be patient in order to allow their babies the time to manage their own desires in appropriate ways (A. Freud, 1965). On the other hand, Freud's ideas blamed parents who could not meet their children's needs. Parents were considered to be the main cause of neurosis and repression in their children. At the same time, during the 1930s and 1940s, there was an increased demand for infant education in nursery schools. This was meant to counter an overdependence on parents, prevent neurosis, and to give group training (Clarke-Stewart, 1998). It was also a response to the shortage of male workers during World War II and the need for women to join the workforce.

Following the war, the 1950s became a period of the redomestication of women in the United States. Mothers were expected to be the main infant care providers and fathers were meant to be the wage earners (Lamb, Sternberg, & Ketterlinus, 1992). During this decade, there was revival of a more romantic view of relationships. This was the era of Abraham Maslow, Carl Rogers, Fritz Perls, and Willem Reich, each of whom created psychotherapies of caring, warmth, mutuality, responsibility, and affectivity. Reich in particular, a disciple of Freud, emphasized the importance of the body and its full expression of desires, senses, and pleasures as a key to psychological health.

This is the period in which John Bowlby, mentioned earlier, began to publish his classic studies of mother–infant attachment. Bowlby believed in the importance of a close and affectionate mother–infant bond, a bond he believed to be primarily and exclusively with the infant's biological mother. He based his conclusions in part on observations done on hunter–gatherer societies and in part on the evolution of humans during prehistory. A similar approach was taken by reformers of hospital childbirth procedures, who advocated a reduction in maternal anesthesia and a return to more natural and traditional approaches such as controlled breathing, upright postures, and home births. These reformers favored breastfeeding over bottle feeding, and looked to Pleistocene practices in order to make childbirth a more satisfying and pleasurable experience for mother and infant. Few mothers and few hospitals of this era, however, adopted these practices.

The dialectic began to swing toward empiricism again in the 1960s and 1970s in the rapid growth of scientific approaches to psychology inspired in part by the Cold War, when Western leaders decided that the education and training of their citizens was the best way to combat the technological threats of advanced weapon systems. Research on infancy turned away from studies of emotion and focused more on infant learning and cognitive development. *The Competent Infant* (Stone, Smith, & Murphy, 1973) reflected a desire by scientists to discover early signs of intelligence in infants. Many parents placed their infants into highly structured programs to teach reading, word learning, music, and mathematics before the age of 3 years.

The rise of the women's liberation movement during this period conspired also to create increased demand for infant day care and nursery schools. Betty Freidan's publication of *The Feminine Mystique* in 1963 led to an increase of women who sought individual fulfillment in their lives through employment and schooling. A final trend leading to increased demand for infant care during this period was the rise of single mothers who needed to be employed in order to support their children (Lamb et al., 1992).

The work of Jean Piaget from Switzerland and Lev Vygotsky of Russia began to inspire scientific understanding of infant cognitive development and how the infancy period served as a foundation for later intellectual functioning. Both Piaget (1952) and Vygotsky (1978) can also be read as primarily romantic thinkers since they viewed child development as a profoundly creative action, arising in the "natural" discourse between young children and their environments, including the cultural environment. In their view, the environment was not shaping the child but providing what the child needed at the time and place in which learning was most likely to occur. Paradoxically, however, their work was read and applied – in infancy research and in early childhood education – primarily for its empiricist connotations; absorbed into the cultural search to make babies smarter.

This empiricist trend continued in the 1980s by an interest in helping and educating infants who were at risk for developmental difficulties, such as infants who were premature, handicapped, or victims of abuse. This focus on risk was associated with the empiricist idea that all humans can excel, given the right kind of childrearing (Clarke-Stewart, 1998). The same philosophy also brought the ideal of a "supermom" who could be employed, be a great mother, and wonderful and loving wife. The 1980s also saw an increase in the amount of time fathers spent with their babies.

The romantic view returns in the 1990s with a rise in studies of parent–child relationships, emotional development and attachment, and communication and language (Schneider, 1998), while the more empirical approaches to infant development continued to grow in such fields as cognitive neuroscience and behavior genetics. The trends of the 1970s and 1980s, which focused on babies growing up and getting smart as quickly as possible, are currently being replaced by ideas about slowing down and appreciating each phase of a baby's life. Research today has expanded to encompass diversity in parenting and culture: families at risk, substance abusers, handicapped infants, different ethnic groups, gay-lesbian families, fathers, preterm infants, and infantile autism. Meeting an infant's socioemotional needs is seen as important as cognitive and academic growth. There is also a focus on threats to safety such as accidents, abuse, crime, and the origins of psychopathology.

The recent return to romanticism has led to the growth of the holistic health and medicine movement with a focus on body awareness, yoga, massage, meditation, and the healing potential of relationships (Schneider, 1998). These ideas have their origins in ancient non-Western cultural beliefs, such as Chinese, Japanese, Indian, and Native American approaches. In this chapter on Western culture, there is no opportunity to review the history of beliefs about infants in these other cultures. A notable characteristic of these cultures is that, even in the twentieth and early twenty-first centuries, the individual has not become salient in the cultural consciousness. These cultures, like ancient Western culture, were founded upon a mythical culture in which humans were connected to all things. Their traditions focus on understanding and utilizing relationships between people, relationships between the various systems of mind and body, and between people and their social and physical environments. These cultures tend to be more romantic than empirical, accepting infant behavior in its "natural" form and rejecting early discipline and training of infants (cf. Kojima, 1986).

There is also a recent trend in Western cultures toward using knowledge about infancy to contribute to the healing of children and adults. Current psychoanalytic traditions advocate a therapist–client relationship that is modeled after what is believed to be the most healthy form of the mother–infant relationship: a balance between love and playfulness on the one hand, and encouragement for independence and self-awareness on the other (Ehrenberg, 1992; Stern, 1985; Winnicott, 1971). There has been a partnership between therapists for adults and scientists who observe the mother–infant relationship. Somatic awareness therapeutic approaches to adult healing are based on the re-creation of observed patterns of infant learning through movement and touch. All of these methods are founded upon the view that there is something rejuvenating that occurs when adults reexperience their bodies and their interpersonal relationships in a way similar to being a baby.

Watsu, for example, is an aquatic somatic awareness method that explicitly attempts to re-create an optimal infant experience. During a Watsu session, clients are moved freely in warm water, stretched gently, and cradled in the practitioner's arms. "By being moved so freely through the water, by being stretched and repeatedly returned to a fetal position, the adult has the opportunity to heal in himself whatever pain or loss he may still carry from that time" (Dull, 1995, p. 65).

In the Rosen Method, clients lie on a padded table while the practitioner's open hands make gentle contact with areas of the body that appear to hold muscular tension and restrict free breathing. Rosen practitioners believe that the body tells its own story shaped by early life experiences, many of them forgotten and unconscious. As a result of either ordinary or traumatic events, people shape themselves through muscular tension in whatever way that helps them to survive. Through the gentle touch of the Rosen Method, people deeply relax and breathe easier and begin to remember the experiences in which they learned to unconsciously contain their tension. Through that knowledge, the individual can regain fuller movement, ease, and a sense of well-being (Wooten, 1995).

Moshe Feldenkrais invented a system of body movement education that reawakens, develops, and organizes capacities for kinesthetic (sensorimotor) learning. Whereas children before the age of 3 learn movements by relying on their sensorimotor experience, older children and adults in technological cultures often behave according to social expectations, distancing themselves from their bodily feelings. Because the Feldenkrais method involves the emulation of how young children learn, its therapeutic value hinges on releasing capacities for learning that had been left behind in childhood (Reese, 1985).

In summary, as in past centuries, the twentieth century continues the historical ebb and flow and romantic and empirical beliefs about babies. Individuality, human rights, and personal freedoms have become such a major component of Western cultures that it is easy to forget the "individual" was a cultural invention that became elaborated during the eighteenth, nineteenth, and twentieth centuries. Yet, from the perspective of the vast time scale of human existence on this planet, the individual is an aberrant form of consciousness. It was invented only a few seconds before midnight on the imaginary clock of human evolution that began at noon. It does not generalize to other cultures from whom we have recently borrowed expertise in the healing arts: the Native American and the Chinese, for example.

The pleasure derived from exploration of the body – like the pleasure of sexual activity – was probably one evolutionary means for making sure that people developed the body in order to use it as a pathway to the fullest forms of connections with others and with the environment. The individual arose out of the historical and prehistorical romantic traditions respecting the value of the body and its senses. While the romantic view has lasted for as long as humans can remember, it is less clear – since the individual is a relative newcomer to human consciousness – whether the concept of the individual will survive and enhance human life or whether it will die out like many other cultural inventions.

Whatever the ultimate significance of the individual for human growth and development, it is uniquely Western in its origin and application. The constitutional governments of most Western nations are founded on the value of the individual. Virtually every law enacted for and about infants and the family in the United States during the twentieth century, for example, is based on the notion of rights. *The concept of the individual has spawned new forms of infancy beliefs such as the importance of independence training, a sense of entitlement that pervades early parent–infant discourses about the self, and a sense of fairness and rights that underlie Western conceptions of morality and ethics.*

Beyond the continued development of the concept of the individual infant, it is difficult to summarize the changes in infancy during the twentieth century. For further reference, I have written a book about what is known and understood about infants (Fogel, 2001). Partly, the difficulty of encapsulating the recent history of infancy is due to the complexity of change and partly to the historically unprecedented extent of documentary evidence. In addition to what has been mentioned, there are currently dozens of scientific journals devoted to prenatal and infant development, many magazines and books for parents, and thousands of Internet sites about infancy, ranging from scientific reports, to advocacy organizations, to infant care advice, and to family photos and videos. At least twice each week there is a story in my local newspaper about pregnancy, childbirth, or infancy, about life and death of babies in families, about technological and genetic innovations, or about legal and ethical issues such as harvesting stem cells from aborted fetuses. We are on the threshold of a future in which infancy may change in unknown ways.

The Future

The specifics of the future cannot be foreseen. The general pattern, the empirical–romantic dialogue, will continue. As in the past, each of these poles will affect the other. Just as Watson's ideas were challenged by Freud and Freud's by proponents of early intellectual development, opposing views will arise as counterbalances to each other, changing each other and the concept of infancy in the process. In order to create a reasonable and scientifically based account of the future, I will limit this section to extrapolations of current innovations that are already changing the nature of infancy.

The empirical trends of the future will be related to finding new ways to control repro-duction, fetal, and infant development: the increasing application of engineering and biotech-nology to the end of shaping the infant's body and mind to conform to a cultural ideal. People in the future will not use a Roman mechanical device for giving an infant's head or body a particular shape. Instead, they will regulate the development of body form using a fine-tuning between genetic and environmental processes involved in pre- and postnatal development.

The romantic trends of the future will involve the continued discovery of the rejuvenating aspects of re-creating infancy for adults and the revival and preservation of some of the pat-terns of the Pleistocene parent–infant relationship. Future humans may not all have access to the outdoors but these environmental conditions may be created by virtual means. The pleasures of close contact and sensory indulgence between parents and infants will become universally recognized as essential ingredients for the healthy development of the indi-vidual and society.

Speculation about empirical trends in the future comes from current genetic research. Scientists have already shown that replacing, selecting, or cloning genetic material is only part of the developmental story. The environment – its structure and timing – is also crucial to the developmental process. We will know the precise environmental conditions under which certain genes will be expressed while others are suppressed. Part of the envi-ronmental control of the genes could come from within the organism. Scientists are already envisioning transplants of organic computers into the fetus or infant, transplants that will combine developmentally with inherited or altered genetic material to harness the body's power for releasing its own enzymes and transmitters that help regulate gene action for healthy development.

In this manner, all developmental disorders will be eliminated. Since close to 90 percent of human dysfunction and disease originates in the prenatal and perinatal periods, this will mean the elimination of handicaps, sensory impairments, psychological disor-ders, and most of the major diseases from which people currently suffer. And, since vir-tually all disorders – including aging – are developmental disorders (they grow over time), accidents and injuries, made very rare by the same kind of engineering that now produces automobile seat belts and air bags, will be the only cause of death. Organic computers that selectively regulate gene action could also be used to treat the few adult injuries and ailments that do not have their origins in the prenatal and infancy periods.

In the short run, this achievement will come at a huge expense: genetic experiments designed to eliminate an undesirable trait will have the unpredictable consequence of altering the more adaptive traits with which such genes are typically associated. Bipolar disorder, for example, is correlated with creativity. How can one be eliminated without inhibiting the other? Since genetic experimentation on humans will be considered un-ethical, genetically engineered plant and animal species will alter the biosphere in ways that threaten human survival. Humans will be challenged to save themselves as a species.

A new wave of empiricism will lead the way toward the solutions to these problems. In the not-too-distant future, the world will witness the birth of a new generation of genetically altered humans. Their parents, the children of survivors of the ecosystem breakdown, will have begun the return to romanticism. Freedom from disease and deformity will lead to an era of peace and creativity. This idyllic period will later fade as humans face some new threat that requires us to revive empiricism and restrict personal freedoms for the sake of disciplined adaptation.

These generations of genetically engineered people will have a different patterning of development stages. Some developmental periods will be speeded up, others slowed down. We already know that individuals age faster when they are under stress. The environmental stress has the effect of speeding up the developmental process, making a child more adult-like and giving an adult the appearance of premature aging. It is already the case that children in industrialized nations – with the best health care, education, parental love and support, and easy access to the world via the Internet – are speeding up their early phases of development. They begin adolescence earlier than when I was a teenager in the 1950s. They also end adolescence later, with continued financial and emotional reliance on the family into their twenties and thirties. In the future, these processes will have been understood and our genes will have been modified to better fine-tune our developmental rate of change with regard to the vicissitudes of life. New stages may emerge in the life course, stages that cannot even be imagined today.

It is easier to contemplate a historical change in the duration and meaning of adolescence, since it is already happening. Could infancy also be shortened or extended? Infancy, in the sense of helplessness, could be curtailed if infants could control their environments at earlier ages than is typical today. Research has already shown that very young babies can be taught to control environmental consequences by sucking faster or slower on an automated nipple. Perhaps babies will be able to use their sucking to activate their own email address and favorite websites in the crib-side media center. They could communicate with parents on-line. If parents were unavailable, the baby could select virtual images of parents that interact – perhaps even with tactile contact – in the most satisfying ways, day or night. Those human-looking robots in science fiction don't just have to fly space ships, kill aliens, and be romantic partners. What about robotic wetnurses to deliver contact and milk, sing lullabies, and play games, just when the baby needs them?

These devices will do more than just spoil babies. They will deliver culturally acceptable educational programs, provide culturally appropriate discipline and limit setting, all tailored to the requirements of the parent's values and the needs of the individual child. Parents will be able to adjust the inputs for their child but only within the limits dictated by the culture and by the ranges of genetic tolerance for stimulation and change. These will come preset by the manufacturer.

Do these empirical achievements necessarily foster an uncomfortably sterile, regimented, totalitarian society such as that depicted in many science fiction accounts of the future? Does bioengineering mean the loss of human diversity, a reduction of the indeterminism and creativity that gives human life, as we've known it, its mystery, playfulness, and surprises? Will there be romanticism in the future?

The more humans learn about how to predict and control behavior and development, the more we will realize *the limits of control*. The most comprehensive theory that exists today, which explains the growth and development of physical, biological, and psychological systems – the theory of dynamic systems – has already firmly established that at the heart of all forms of order is disorder. *Chaos* is a mathematical concept that expresses the property of complex systems to have some general structure that repeats over time but never in exactly the same way. Dynamic systems theory allows for the possibility of indeterminism, the idea that not everything a person does, and not every turn in that person's development, can be predicted from known laws or principles. *Indeterminism suggests that even if we could measure all the relevant variables, regulate all the genes and environment in a system, we still could not completely predict its future behavior* (Fogel, Lyra, & Valsiner, 1997; Prigogine & Stengers, 1984).

Because of this, mystery and self-discovery will be recognized as central to the development of healthy human beings. Education will become a lifelong practice of enrichment and self-development. Since developmental pathology will have been eliminated, the healing professions of today will be transformed into forms of educational enrichment. Moshe Feldenkrais, for example, was insistent that his method was not healing or therapeutic but rather educational. Feldenkrais movement exercises are called lessons and professionals are called teachers or practitioners. Schools will become community centers in which people will have a great deal of free time to directly interact with each other and to devote to creativity and the improvement of self, family, and society. Life and work will blend together in the setting of the extended family and community. The indulgent self-discovery that is the essence of infancy and early childhood today will be extended throughout the life course. The infancy period will thus be elongated in the form of continued playfulness, openness to new experiences, and a lifelong commitment to getting up after falling down.

Humans will become nomads in the land of self-discovery. Small groups will journey together to explore different parts of this and other worlds, different parts of themselves, and different parts of each other. In the land of self-discovery, there will be no fences, no personal property, an endless supply of nourishment for growth. A sense of the possibility for a connection to all things will permeate every person's life.

A balance between body, mind, and spirit will be the goal of development at all ages. Humans will discover that the appropriate environments to enhance our genetic potential involve the cultivation of all the senses: taste, touch, hearing, sight, and smell. Music, dancing, and all forms of artistic and athletic expression will be part of every person's upbringing. Body awareness, meditation, touching and being touched, and spiritual practice will be daily events. Contact with nature will be available to everyone: no home will be without a real or virtual garden and parks will dominate urban landscapes. Entertainment media will bring realistic adventures, losses, journeys, and romance into people's lives, so – like people in medieval times – they can experience all of their emotions on a daily basis.

Because of the intrinsic value of indeterminism and the evolutionary significance of diversity, humans will find ways to create and cultivate healthy differences between each other. As disease, poverty, deprivation, and disability are eliminated, other differences between people will be enhanced. The palate of skin colors, cultures, talents, body shapes and sizes will become more differentiated. All humans will accept and celebrate their differences as part of what is "natural" for the species in order to enhance our ability to adapt to unforeseen changes. Every baby will be an important addition to society, welcomed into a network of love and touch. Because the ecosystem and the geopolitical system will have regained its balance, no one will be unwanted, no one will be poor or hungry, no one will lack services and supports. Every newborn will be entitled to love, security, shelter, nutrition, self-enhancement, and an extended family.

In my romantic vision, we will indeed preserve our humanity. In fact, we will enhance what it means to have a human body that needs touch, love, and adventure. What we hunt and gather will be different but we will not cease wanting to participate in those endeavors.

Another future can be imagined: one that denigrates needs as frailties and that succeeds to eradicate them from the gene pool. Our bodies will no longer be susceptible to heat and cold, hunger and pain. Sensation will become extinct. What would a baby in this future be like? Hard and withdrawn? Sucking power from a global energy grid with wide, vacant eyes? A disembodied mind?

Since the romantic pleasures are our million-year inheritance and since they continue to be revived even after centuries of repression, I don't believe that humans could long endure this type of future. Enlightened romanticism requires training in how to use the body, how to develop one's skills at self-discovery and self-expression, how to remain connected with others and the world around us. Without romanticism, empiricism becomes harsh and intolerable. Endurance and indulgence, self and other, separateness and connection, mind and body: these are birthrights.

Note

1   The abbreviations BCE (before the common era) and ACE (after the common era) will be used to mark dates. These are equivalent to the Christian markings of BC and AD.

References

Abram, D. (1997). *The spell of the sensuous.* New York: Vintage Books.

Barr, R. G. (1990). The early crying paradox: A modest proposal. *Human Nature, 1,* 355–389.

Bowlby, J. (1969). *Attachment and loss: Vol. 1. Attachment.* New York: Basic Books.

Clarke-Stewart, K. A. (1998). Historical shifts and underlying themes in ideas and rearing young children in the United States: Where have we been? Where are we going? *Early Development and Parenting, 7,* 101–117.

Conrad, R. (1998). Darwin's baby and baby's Darwin: Mutual recognition in observational research. *Human Development, 41*(1), 47–64.

Donald, M. (1991). *Origins of the modern mind: Three stages in the evolution of culture and cognition.* Cambridge, MA: Harvard University Press.

Dull, H. (1995). *Watsu: Freeing the body in water* (2nd ed.). Harbin, CA: Harbin Springs.

Dupont, F. (1989). *Daily life in ancient Rome* (Trans. C. Woodall). Oxford: Blackwell.

Ehrenberg, D. (1992). *The intimate edge: Extending the reach of psychoanalytic interaction.* New York: W. W. Norton.

Eisler, R. (1987). *The chalice and the blade: Our history, our future.* San Francisco: HarperCollins.

Fogel, A. (2001). *Infancy: Infant, family and society* (4th ed.). Belmont, CA: Wadsworth.

Fogel, A., Lyra, M. C., & Valsiner, J. (Eds.). (1997). *Dynamics and indeterminism in developmental and social processes.* Hillsdale, NJ: Erlbaum.

Freud, A. (1965). *Normality and pathology in childhood.* New York: International Universities Press.

Friedrich-Cofer, L. K. (1986). Body, mind, and morals in the framing of social policy. In L. K. Friedrich-Cofer (Ed.), *Human nature of public policy: Scientific views of women, children and families* (pp. 97–173). New York: Praeger.

Frymer-Kensky, T. (1995). *Motherprayer: The pregnant woman's spiritual companion.* New York: Riverhead Books.

Gaskell, E. (1996). Elizabeth Gaskell's diary. In J. A. Chapple & A. Wilson (Eds.), *Private voices: The diaries of Elizabeth Gaskell and Sophia Holland* (pp. 11–71). New York: St. Martin's Press.

Gelis, J. (1989). The child: From anonymity to individuality. In P. Aries & G. Duby (Eds.), *A history of private life* (pp. 309–325). Cambridge, MA: Harvard University Press.

Gies, F., & Gies, J. (1987). *Marriage and the family in the Middle Ages.* New York: Harper & Row.

Greenleaf, P. (1978). *Children throughout the ages: A history of childhood.* New York: Barnes & Noble.

Hanawalt, B. A. (1993). *Growing up in medieval London: The experience of childhood in history.* New York: Oxford University Press.

Hareven, T. K. (1985). Historical changes in the family and the life course: Implications for child development. *Monographs of the Society for Research in Child Development, 50* (Serial No. 211), 8–23.

Hewlett, B. S., Lamb, M. E., Shannon, D., Leyendecker, B., & Scholmerich, A. (1998). Culture and early infancy among central African foragers and farmers. *Developmental Psychology, 34*(4), 653–661.

Hrdy, S. B. (1999). *Mother nature: A history of mothers, infants, and natural selection.* New York: Pantheon.

Huizinga, J. (1954). *The waning of the Middle Ages.* New York: Anchor Books.

Johnson, D. H. (1992). Body: Recovering our sensual wisdom. In D. Johnson & I. Grand (Eds.), *The body in psychotherapy: Inquiries into somatic psychology* (pp. 1–16). Berkeley, CA: North Atlantic.

Kojima, H. (1986). The history of child development in Japan. In H. Azuma & H. Stevenson (Eds.), *Child development and education in Japan* (pp. 39–54). New York: Academic Press.

Konner, M. (1982). *The tangled wing: Biological constraints on the human spirit.* New York: Holt, Rinehart, & Winston.

Koops, W. (1996). Historical developmental psychology: The sample case of paintings. *International Journal of Behavioral Development, 19*(2), 393–413.

Lamb, M. E., Sternberg, K. J., & Ketterlinus, R. D. (1992). Child care in the United States: The modern era. In M. E. Lamb, K. J. Sternberg, C. Hwang, & A. Broberg (Eds.), *Childcare in context: Cross-cultural perspectives* (pp. 207–222). Hillsdale, NJ: Erlbaum.

Le Goff, J. (1987). *The medieval world* (Trans. L. G. Cochrane). London: Collins & Brown.

Mead, M., & Newton, N. (1967). Cultural patterning of perinatal behavior. In S. Richardson & A. Guttmacher (Eds.), *Childbearing: Its social and psychological aspects* (pp. 142–244). Baltimore: Williams & Wilkins.

Piaget, J. (1952). *The origins of intelligence in children.* New York: International Universities Press.

Prigogine, I., & Stengers, I. (Eds.). (1984). *Order out of chaos: Man's new dialogue with nature.* New York: Bantam Books.

Reese, M. (1985). Moshe Feldenkrais's work with movement: A parallel approach to Milton Erickson's hypnotherapy. In J. K. Zeig (Ed.), *Ericksonian psychotherapy: Vol. 1. Structures* (pp. 410–427). New York: Brunner/Mazel.

Saint Augustine. (1991). *Confessions* (Trans. Henry Chadwick). New York: Oxford University Press.

Schneider, K. J. (1998). Toward a science of the heart: Romanticism and the revival of psychology. *American Psychologist, 53*(3), 277–289.

Screech, M. A. (Ed. & Trans.). (1991). *Michel de Montaigne: The complete essays*. Harmondsworth: Penguin.

Shepard, P. (1998). *Coming home to Pleistocene*. Covelo, CA: Island Press.

Shostak, M. (1983). *Nisa: The life and words of a !Kung woman*. New York: Vintage Books.

Sorenson, E. R. (1979). Early tactile communication and the patterning of human organization: A New Guinea case study. In M. Bullowa (Ed.), *Before speech* (pp. 289–305). New York: Cambridge University Press.

Stern, D. (1985). *The interpersonal world of the infant*. New York: Basic Books.

Stone, L. (1979). *The family, sex and marriage in England 1500–1800*. New York: Harper & Row.

Stone, L. J., Smith, H., & Murphy, L. (1973). *The competent infant*. New York: Basic Books.

Vygotsky, L. S. (1978). *Mind in society*. Cambridge, MA: Harvard University Press.

Wallace, D. B., Franklin, M. B., & Keegan, R. T. (1994). The observing eye: A century of baby diaries. *Human Development, 37*, 1–29.

Wenke, R. J. (1990). *Patterns in prehistory: Humankind's first three million years*. New York: Oxford University Press.

Whiten, A., & Milner, P. (1986). The educational experiences of Nigerian infants. In H. V. Curran (Ed.), *Nigerian children: Developmental perspectives* (pp. 34–73). London: Routledge & Kegan Paul.

Whiting, B. (1974). Folk wisdom and child-rearing. *Merrill-Palmer Quarterly, 20*, 9–19.

Williams, O. (1952). *Immortal poems of the English language*. New York: Washington Square Press.

Winnicott, D. W. (1971). *Playing and reality*. New York: Basic Books.

Wooten, S. (1995). *Touching the body, reaching the soul: How touch influences the nature of human beings*. Santa Fe, NM: Rosen Method Center Southwest.

Subject Index

Author Index